D1527013

From Protest to Challenge

VOLUME 5

From Protest to Challenge

A DOCUMENTARY HISTORY OF
AFRICAN POLITICS IN
SOUTH AFRICA,
1882-1990

VOLUME 5

NADIR AND RESURGENCE, 1964–1979

Thomas G. Karis and Gail M. Gerhart

INDIANA UNIVERSITY PRESS   BLOOMINGTON & INDIANAPOLIS

© 1997 by Thomas G. Karis and Gail M. Gerhart

The paper used in this publication meets the minimum requirements of American National Standard for Information Sciences—Permanence of Paper for Printed Library Materials, ANSI Z39.48–1984.

Manufactured in the United States of America

Cataloging information for this series is available from the Library of Congress.

ISBN for this volume 0-253-33231-1 (cloth : alk. paper)
LCCN for the series 72-152423

To all
who died
for freedom and equality
in South Africa

Contents

PART ONE: ESSAYS

PART TWO: DOCUMENTS

3. Above-Ground Multiracial Opposition

4. The Black Consciousness Movement: The Formative Years, 1967–1971   458

5. The Black Consciousness Movement: Confronting the State, 1972–1976   497

6. The 1976 Soweto Uprising

8. The Politics of the System   628

9. Buthelezi and Inkatha   669

10. The Liberation Movements, 1975–1979   690

11. Crackdown and Resistance after Soweto

MAPS

NELSON MANDELA

Karis and Gerhart's fifth volume is an invaluable addition to their earlier documentary history of the national liberation struggle in South Africa and includes a priceless collection of new primary historical sources. It ignites vivid flashes of memory, for example, of the innumerable briefings we received on Robben Island from younger comrades who were sentenced to varying terms of imprisonment in so many political trials after Rivonia.

The analysis and the documentary evidence demonstrate that the characterization by some historians of the period after the proscription of the African National Congress and the Pan Africanist Congress as a decade of silence is mistaken. Resistance to the brutality of the apartheid state, though stifled by extreme repression and violence on the home front, was never killed. It took on new forms. The terrain was Robben Island, the neighboring African states, and the growing number of anti-apartheid platforms internationally. Internally, it was displayed through the ever-increasing confidence of the oppressed, which was positively regenerated through the Black Consciousness Movement, the militant workers' strikes, the student revolts, and the growing capacity of Umkhonto we Sizwe—all building up to a mood of open defiance.

This book, therefore, enables the student of history to reconceptualize the decade after Rivonia as an essential preparatory phase for the popular mass democratic upsurges in the post-1976 era, eventually resulting in the historic negotiated settlement.

The volume is an impressive overview of liberation politics from 1964 to 1979 in South Africa, emphasizing aspects of the struggle which until recently have largely been hidden from both public and scholarly eyes because of the nature of exile and prison life and the surreptitiousness of clandestine political and military work, as well as by the deliberate distortions of apartheid propaganda. The book stands out as poignant testimony to the will and determination of our people and their leaders—irrespective of the cost in human terms—to win freedom.

This then is the book's real value. It opens pathways for critical reflection and further avenues for historical reinterpretation and understanding. I was pleasantly reminded that so many of the historical actors in the volume are serving in parliament and in other capacities within the new democratic government today. Equally, the painful memory of those who never lived to see this day lingers on.

Writing about contemporary South African political history in a comprehensive, informed, and balanced way is not always easy. In this volume Karis and Gerhart display a commendable mastery of the historian's craft, laying before us a rich collection that will most certainly stand future generations in good stead.

Nelson Mandela

President of the Republic of South Africa

PREFACE

This volume, the fifth in the *From Protest to Challenge* series, examines and documents the liberation struggle in South Africa from its nadir in 1964 to its resurgence by 1979. Four earlier volumes traced the long history of resistance against white domination and the pursuit of racial equality during the period 1882-1964. These years ended with the outlawing of the African National Congress and the Pan Africanist Congress in 1960, the decision of these movements to turn to violence, and the sentencing of Nelson Mandela and other ANC leaders in 1964 to life imprisonment for committing sabotage and preparing for guerrilla war.

At that stage, hard questions faced the decimated opposition. How could blacks regroup and resist a white regime that was intransigent, powerfully armed, and bolstered by the major western powers? Could the liberation movements from exile effect major change through a strategy of guerrilla warfare, or would change depend principally on internal political resistance? What part could be played by non-Africans in pressing for an end to the apartheid system? This volume examines how the answers to these and other questions evolved in the 16 transitional years that preceded the tumultuous decade of the 1980s and the revolutionary change of the 1990s, when a conflict widely perceived as intractable was resolved through negotiation.

As in previous volumes, we have reproduced a selection of primary documents that includes some of landmark significance and others that vividly illustrate the passions and thinking of the time. The introductory chapters place each document in its immediate historical context. We have written with both beginning students and specialized readers in mind. By providing copious notes and references to an immense archive of documents and interviews available on microfilm, we hope that this volume will be a point of departure for serious researchers at every level. At the same time, we have tried to write background essays that offer knowledge and insight to the general reader.

The project of a documentary history was originally conceived in 1962 by Thomas Karis and Gwendolen Carter as a slim book of selected documents from the record of the treason trial of 1956-1961. The project grew, resulting in successively larger volumes subtitled *Protest and Hope, 1882-1934; Hope and Challenge, 1935-1952;* and *Challenge and Violence, 1953-1964.* A fourth volume, *Political Profiles, 1882-1964,* consists of biographies of politically prominent Africans, Indians and Coloureds, as well as whites involved in black politics. These four volumes were published by the Hoover Institution Press during 1972-1977. A supplementary volume, *South African Political Materials: A Catalogue of the Carter-Karis Collection,* is an inventory of the documentary archive, available on 71 reels of microfilm, upon which the four volumes were based.

On the completion of this work in 1977, we had no expectation of continuing the project, although each of us continued to interview resistance activists and to collect political documents. Our hope was that the project might become a stepping stone for a new generation of scholars. More original material was becoming available, much valuable oral history remained to be recorded, and interest in the reconsideration of South African history was growing. We looked forward to more historical studies of black politics by South Africans themselves. Today, with the publication of volume 5, these expectations are as pertinent as they were almost two decades ago.

During the repressive years after 1963, with the rise of black consciousness and African labor protest, the Soweto uprising of 1976 and the regime's brutal reaction to it, the times called for the ablest South Africans to make history, not write it. Nevertheless, the 1970s and 1980s yielded a proliferation of original research and critical reinterpretations of South Africa's past, much of it by South African academics in exile, both black and white. Yet by the mid-1980s, no scholars appeared to be systematically collecting primary materials with an eye to assembling a post-1964 documentary history. Only in 1985 did we begin considering the feasibility of producing an update of the earlier volumes. Karis had just taken early retirement from the City University of New York, where he was the executive officer of the doctoral program in political science, and Gerhart, who had participated in the writing of volumes 3 and 4, had returned to New York after working in Africa for almost two decades and was teaching at Columbia University.

With the encouragement of many South Africans we became committed to the project. Karis held discussions with movement exiles in Zambia and Tanzania in late 1985. There were further opportunities for discussion in Lusaka and Maputo in 1986 when we travelled to southern Africa as part of a fact-finding tour led by the Reverend Jesse Jackson. Meanwhile, a grant from the Rockefeller Foundation enabled us to conduct interviews in New York while bringing together exiled South Africans and South African visitors to the United States. Planning became more concrete during discussions in 1986 with David Lewis, a South African then in residence at Columbia

University. Besides offering us his expertise on the trade union movement, Lewis was able to relieve our perennial concern about visa denials by offering to supervise the collection in South Africa of the relevant documents for the chapter on trade unions in this volume. In 1987 we began work with a year's grant from the Ford Foundation and the following year received three-year grants from the National Endowment for the Humanities, an independent federal agency, and the Ford Foundation. One projected volume grew to three—*Nadir and Resurgence, 1964-1979; Challenge and Victory, 1980-1990;* and *Political Profiles, 1964-1990*—and our original timetable for a three-year project grew increasingly elastic as we confronted the need to collect and digest the ever-growing mass of documentary and trial material being generated by the deepening conflict in South Africa.

In this volume, Gerhart has written the opening chapter and the chapters dealing with the above-ground multiracial opposition, the black conscious-ness movement, the Soweto uprising, and black politics after Soweto. Karis has written the chapters on the politics of "the system," Buthelezi and Inkatha, and the liberation movements, and Lewis has written the chapter on black workers and trade unions. We are content for readers to infer what they believe can be inferred about our politics and biases from what we have written. While it should be clear that we are deeply sympathetic to the broad movement for justice and equality in South Africa, we hope that readers will find that we have also aimed to be nonpartisan and fair to all segments of opinion.

We have once again been aware in the preparation of this volume that the study of history from primary documents has both advantages and draw-backs. Primary sources can liberate students and teachers from the tyranny of received opinion and open up opportunities for original insight and interpretation. This is as true for the formal records of organizations— constitutions, minutes of meetings, reports, policy statements, speeches—as it is for more ephemeral materials such as flyers, pamphlets, diaries, letters, poetry and songs. Trial testimony presents the special problem of filtering out truth from the discourse and tactics of legal defense. A disadvantage of trying to reconstruct history from documents is the inevitably incomplete, fragmentary and distorted nature of the record. Interviews, therefore, have been indispensable in filling out and giving life to the written record and, incidentally, involving us vicariously in the lives of extraordinary and often heroic people.

Although much oral and written political communication in South Africa has been in languages other than English, almost all the documents selected for reproduction here are in English in order to insure accessibility to a broad readership. Also, many important forms and expressions of political dissent are not recorded in writing. We have sought to take popular culture into account, but we recognize that we have not done justice to its importance. Another issue in documentary research—the sensitive or controversial nature of some organizational records—poses a special challenge to the historian and sometimes requires the patience to wait out long embargoes.

In our case, for example, despite obtaining initial approval at the highest level, it took more than four years of persistent effort to obtain a copy of the ANC's little known "Green Book," reproduced in chapter 10.

Access to sources was often a problem under the police state conditions pertaining in South Africa after 1963. Even the act of applying to enter South Africa raised questions of conscience for some academics. Compared to the repression and hardships suffered by political activists, our travails were minor; yet for researchers they are worth recalling. The annoyances and frustrations included visa delays and denials, obvious surveillance, the assumption that all telephone calls were tapped and mail opened, restriction on entry to certain areas, questioning by the police, and the theft or confiscation of documents. Beginning in 1969, Karis was denied visas for a decade and visited surrounding countries instead, doing so in 1977, for example, by making five overnight stays in the international transit area of the Johannesburg airport. After admission to the country in 1979, 1980, 1983, and 1985, it was disconcerting to be refused a visa in March 1989 only to be readmitted in November.

These challenges have only made more rewarding the task of helping to record, interpret and make available the history of the South African liberation struggle. We again affirm the sentiments expressed in volume 3: the enduring satisfaction of being able to present evidence of the patient and courageous efforts of South Africans of all races through their own words, and our gratitude for the warm friendship and cooperation extended to us by people across the political spectrum. In the pre-1990 era, we hoped that *From Protest to Challenge* would contribute not only to a deeper understanding of South African history but also to the movement against apartheid. In particular, we hoped that it would add evidence to the debate about who were "authentic" leaders. Today there are new challenges, and we hope that these volumes and the archive of documentary and interview materials on which they are based (available on microfilm) may contribute in some way to the reform of history curricula in South Africa and, through the use of primary sources, to the improvement of teaching and learning methods. At a time when South Africa's identity as a nation is being rapidly and dramatically recast, its students and scholars have an important role to play in reconceptualizing the meaning of their country's troubled history. It is with anticipation that we look forward to their work.

Thomas G. Karis

Gail M. Gerhart

ACKNOWLEDGMENTS

We have incurred many debts in the preparation of this book, few of which can adequately be repaid. We wish particularly to express our appreciation to the South Africans who have given us their time in interviews and conversations, some on many occasions over the years. Their names appear in footnotes in this volume, and are listed in the Sources. We are also deeply indebted to a number of fellow scholars and researchers who have shared their extensive collections of primary material with us, especially Howard Barrell, Victoria Butler, Tom Lodge, and E. S. Reddy.

Among those who have generously shared other research material, interview records, or privately acquired documents with us are Geoff Budlender, Fran Buntman, Jim Cason, Rob Clarke, Helena Dolny, Andries Du Toit, Stephen Ellis, Anriette Esterhuysen, Liesl Fichardt, Julie Frederikse, Nigel Gibson, Paul Goller, Magnus Gunther, Baruch Hirson, Pierre Hugo, Henry Isaacs, the late Helen Joseph, Ahmed Kathrada, Greg Lanning, Ismail Mahomed, Gilbert Marcus, Johann Maree, Cedric Mayson, Govan Mbeki, David Mesenbring, Smangaliso Mkhatshwa, Marti Mueller, Prexy Nesbitt, Pascal Ngakane, Quraish Patel, Ina Perlman, Benjamin Pogrund, Rory Riordan, David Russell, Aracelly Santana, and Ben Turok.

Amanda Armstrong, Arthur Chaskalson, David Dison, Priscilla Jana, Denis Kuny, David Soggot, and Raymond Tucker have given us access to invaluable trial materials. Many years ago, Strini Moodley provided materials from the South African Students' Organisation. We are also indebted to Benjamin Pogrund for the documents he has collected and preserved over many years. Important historical memoranda, drawing on personal political experiences, were written for us by John Daniel, Bennie Khoapa, Mpho Mashinini, Joe Matthews, Smangaliso Mkhatshwa and the late Jabulani Nxumalo ("Mzala"). Valuable comments on parts of the draft manuscript were made by Roley Arenstein, Mary Benson, George Bizos, Fran Buntman, Colin Bundy, Craig Charney, William Foltz, Ahmed Kathrada, Gerry Maré, Fatima Meer, Malusi Mpumlwana, M. J. Naidoo, Beyers Naude, Vladimir Shubin, Jack and Ray Simons, Tim Smith, Ben Turok and Cap Zungu. Gavin Andersson, Peter Brown, Baruch Hirson, Josiah Jele, Ahmed Kathrada, the late Marion Lacey, Govan Mbeki, Annica Van Gylswyk and Randolph Vigne took time to respond to inquiries for information.

Archivists and librarians at more than a dozen institutions have enormously facilitated our work. We are especially grateful to Moore Crossey of the Yale University Library for his unstinting help. The late Betsy Widenmann of Columbia University likewise gave us constant support. We also wish to express our thanks to the staffs of the African Studies Library and the Manuscripts and Archives section of the University of Cape Town Library, the Archives division of UNISA, the Cooperative Africana Microform Project, the Cory Library at Rhodes University, the Historical Papers section of the Cullen Library of the University of the Witwatersrand, the Institute for Commonwealth Studies of the University of London, the International Defence and Aid Fund, the National University of Lesotho, the Inkatha Institute, the Popular History Trust/South African History Archive, SACHED, the UN Center Against Apartheid, and York University Library (UK).

On May 3 and June 23, 1989, workshops were held in Cambridge, Massachusetts, and New York to elicit suggestions and criticisms from South African scholars and activists in the United States. We wish to thank the following participants for their useful contributions to the early shaping of this book: Saths Cooper, Andre Du Toit, Fred Dube, Henry Isaacs, Clement Keto, Tom Lodge, Andrew Lukele, Bernard Magubane, Vincent Maphai, Anthony Marx, Moeletsi Mbeki, Aggrey Mbere, Peter 'Molotsi, Moses Nkondo, E. S. Reddy, John Samuel, Mala Singh, Prem Singh, Joe Thloloe, and Sonny Venkatrathnam.

The research assistants who have participated in the assembling of this volume of *From Protest to Challenge* are legion. We have valued their many contributions, great and small. We are especially grateful for the unique work done by Senti Thobejane, as well as for the prodigious labors of Milissa Day, Paul Gready, Moira Lubbock, Scott Meserve, Goolam Vahed, Sonny Venkatrathnam, Mary Ann Vincent, Jennifer Squires, Johannes Modibedi, Pierre Louis, Lee Feldshon and Msokoli Qotole. Others who have left their mark on this book are Terri Barnes, Amy Bayer, Doris Carter, Sara Chaganti, Sarah Dailey, Julia Dengel, Roger Falcon, Leslie Gerhart, Nathaniel Gerhart, Betsy Guzman, Omar Hopkins, Omar Jadwat, James Karis, Lisa Kavanaugh, Claire Keeton, Lindi Khanyile, Sipho Mahamba, Oupa Makhalemele, Xolani Malawana, Sebastian McKay, Kehla Mdluli, Phumlani Mkhize, David Mogorosi, Oupa Mokuena, Niza Motola, Nhlanhla Ndebele, Lizzie Ngugi, Erica Porter, Timothy Porter, Janet Roitman, Shoki Sekele, Themba Shabangu, Heidi Siegell, Patrick Tandy, Jeffrey Udell, Benjamin Wauchope, Jacqueline Williams, and Hleziphi Zita. Leo Manne, Helet Merkling, Phumla Mdontswa, Peter 'Molotsi, and Meebisi Ndletyana helped with translations.

The Graduate Center of the City University of New York and its Ralph Bunche Institute on the United Nations gave us much needed assistance and facilities. In particular, we thank Benjamin Rivlin, the Institute's director, Nancy Okada and Michael Speer, as well as Annette Phillips and Alanda Bozeman who helped with the typing of documents.

This project would not have been possible without the financial support of the National Endowment for the Humanities and the Ford Foundation. We are especially grateful to William Carmichael and David Bonbright of Ford for their initial encouragement and their confidence that the project would eventually come to fruition. We also extend thanks to John Stremlau and the Rockefeller Foundation. Most recently, we have been fortunate to have in John Gallman of Indiana University Press a publisher who is an enthusiastic supporter of scholarship on South Africa.

Last and most of all, we want to express our warmest appreciation to our spouses, Mary Karis and John Gerhart, for their constant support and forbearance during the time that we have been wedded to this project.

We thank the following for granting us permission to reprint the following documents: Doc. 2: "It's Difficult to Decide My Identity," column by Nat Nakasa, *Rand Daily Mail,* June 20, 1964, reprinted in *The World of Nat Nakasa* (Johannesburg: Ravan, 1975), used by permission of Ravan Press. Doc. 3: "This Kid Is No Goat," poem by Oswald Mtshali, about 1969, from *Sounds of a Cowhide Drum* (Johannesburg: Renoster Books, 1971), reprinted by permission of Mbuyiseni Oswald Mtshali and Ad. Donker, Johannesburg. Doc. 4: Excerpt from "The Sportsman's Choice," by Dennis Brutus, 1971, in Alex La Gums, ed., *Apartheid: A Collection of Writings on South African Racism by South Africans* (London: Lawrence & Wishart, 1972), reprinted by permission of Dennis Brutus. Doc. 41: Speech by Steve Biko, "White Racism and Black Consciousness," in H. W. van der Merwe and D. Welsh, eds., *Student Perspectives on South Africa* (Cape Town: David Philip, 1972), reprinted by permission of David Philip Publishers. Doc. 94: Excerpt from M. B. Naidoo, "The South African Indian Council: An Assessment from Within," in Surendra Bhana and B. Pachai, eds., *A Documentary History of Indian South Africa* (Cape Town: David Philip, 1984), reprinted by permission of David Philip Publishers.

ACRONYMS

AICA	African Independent Churches Association
ALC	African Liberation Committee
ANC	African National Congress
APDUSA	African People's Democratic Union of South Africa
APLA	Azanian People's Liberation Army
ARM	African Resistance Movement
ASA	African Students' Association
ASSECA	Association for the Educational and Cultural Advancement of the African People
ASUSA	African Students' Union of South Africa
AZAPO	Azanian People's Organisation
BAWU	Black Allied Workers' Union
BCP	Black Community Programmes
BPA	Black Parents Association
BPC	Black People's Convention
CI	Christian Institute
COSAS	Congress of South African Students
CPRC	Coloured Persons' Representative Council
CRC	Coloured Representative Council
CUSA	Council of Unions of South Africa
FOSATU	Federation of South African Trade Unions
FRELIMO	Frente de Libertação de Moçambique
GSC	General Students' Council
IDAMASA	Interdenominational African Ministers' Association of South Africa
MK	Umkhonto we Sizwe
MPLA	Movimento Popular de Libertação de Angola

NAFCOC	National African Federated Chamber of Commerce
NAYO	National Youth Organisation
NCL	National Committee for Liberation
NEC	National Executive Committee
NGK	Nederduitse Gereformeerde Kerk (Dutch Reformed Church)
NIC	Natal Indian Congress
NUSAS	National Union of South African Students
OAU	Organisation of African Unity
PAC	Pan Africanist Congress
PEBCO	Port Elizabeth Black Civic Organisation
RC	Revolutionary Council
SABC	South African Broadcasting Corporation
SACC	South African Council of Churches
SACP	South African Communist Party
SACTU	South African Congress of Trade Unions
SASM	South African Students' Movement
SASO	South African Students' Organisation
SCA	Soweto Civic Association
SOMAFCO	Solomon Mahlangu Freedom College
SPRO-CAS	Study Project on Christianity in Apartheid Society
SRC	Students' Representative Council
SSRC	Soweto Students' Representative Council
TUACC	Trade Union Advisory and Coordinating Council
TUCSA	Trade Union Council of South Africa
UBC	Urban Bantu Council
UCM	University Christian Movement
UCT	University of Cape Town
UNB	University of Natal (Black)
UNISA	University of South Africa
UNITA	União Nacional para a Independência Total de Angola
UNNE	University of Natal (Non-European)
UWC	University of the Western Cape
WRAB	West Rand Administration Board
YMCA	Young Men's Christian Association
ZAPU	Zimbabwe African People's Union

Part One

Essays

1. Setting the Stage

Between 1964 and 1979, the South African system of white minority rule known as apartheid was perpetuated and strengthened despite growing resistance from the country's black majority. That resistance is the subject of this book. To enable readers to contextualize the political events and documentary record presented here, this introduction examines in broad outline the historical setting of black resistance, focusing on three aspects: the international factors shaping South Africa's racial struggle, the economic and social forces conditioning black politics, and the attempts by South Africa's ruling National Party to keep a tight lid on the cauldron of black dissent through a combination of police-state repression and cautious reform.[1]

What obstacles did the opponents of apartheid face in the period after Rivonia? It has often been observed that people make their own history, though not under conditions of their own choosing. To understand the long struggle against apartheid, one must take into account not only the ways in which people organized, persevered and sacrificed to bring about its defeat, but also what obstacles—physical, psychological, political—they overcame in doing so. For both the defenders of the status quo and for its challengers, the interaction of ends, means, and obstacles was seldom simple. Obstacles shaped the means used to pursue goals; those means in turn often generated new reactions that further frustrated or advanced the achievement of the goal. In the 1960s and 1970s, South Africa's dominant minority pursued its goal—the perpetuation of its own dominance—in the face of obstacles that were serious but appeared in the short run to be surmountable. In the longer run, however, many measures adopted to secure continued white supremacy (the ethnic segregation of African universities and the creation of

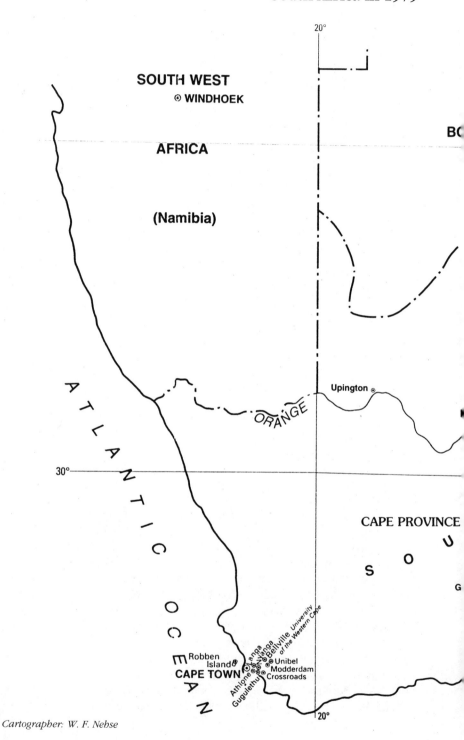

South Africa in 1979

Cartographer: W. F. Nebse

RHODESIA
(Zimbabwe)

MOZAMBIQUE

Limpopo

Limpopo

IA

◉ Sibasa

Makgatho Farms ◉

Pietersburg ◉   ◉ Turfloop/
University of the North

GABORONE ◉

TRANSVAAL

Babelegi
◉

Lobatse ◉   Mabopane ◉   ◉ Hammanskraal
Winterveld ◉   ◉ Mamelodi
Atteridgeville ◉ ◉PRETORIA   MAPUTO
Mafikeng ◉   JOHANNESBURG◉◉Witbank   (Lourenço Marques)
Krugersdorp ◉◉Rivonia
Kagiso ◉ ◉ ◉Tembisa
Roodepoort ◉ ◉ ◉Benoni   MBABANE
Sebokeng ◉   ◉Springs   SWAZILAND
Sharpeville ◉◉ ◉ ◉ Kwa Thema
Vereeniging◉   Soweto   Kempton Park

Vaal

◉ Kroonstad   ◉ Madadeni   ◉ Nongoma
Newcastle ◉   ◉ Osizweni

ORANGE   Ulundi ◉

FREE   Ladysmith NATAL   Richard's Bay
BLOEMFONTEIN   ◉   Ngoye◉
◉   *University of Zululand*

STATE   ◉ MASERU   PIETERMARITZBURG
LESOTHO   Edendale ◉   Botha's Hill ◉
Hammarsdale ◉   ◉ ◉KwaMashu
Mariannhill   ◉ ◉DURBAN
Umlazi   ——— 30°

Y ◉

Orange

H

Lady Frere   Umtata
◉

Healdtown   Stutterheim
Fort Beaufort ◉   ◉ ◉King William's Town
Alice   ◉ Zwelitsha
Fort Hare University   ◉EAST LONDON
Grahamstown ◉

Kei   *Lovedale*   *Dimbaza*   *Ginsberg*   *Mdantsane*

◉ Uitenhage
Zwide ◉◉
◉New Brighton   0   100   200   300
PORT ELIZABETH
Miles

30°

collaborationist black local authorities, for example), had unintended consequences, opening opportunities for opponents of the system to seize the
initiative and gain new advantages.

Faced with a morass of adverse conditions not of their own making, the
liberation forces endeavored to mobilize the resources and adopt the
strategies and tactics most likely to advance their cause. In the short run, their
options were often limited and fraught with risks. For example, once in exile
and committed to waging guerrilla war (the only course likely to satisfy its
political base at home), the African National Congress had few options at the
height of the Cold War but to seek military assistance from the Eastern bloc,
despite the knowledge that this would hand a powerful propaganda weapon
to Pretoria in its pursuit of Western support. All such choices had consequences, some that were foreseen and others that became clear only with
hindsight. But political actors could not be clairvoyants. They acted within
landscapes of obstacles and possibilities, instincts for survival and tolerance
levels for pain. The more we remain mindful of these landscapes, the better
we are likely to understand how South Africa's people became the architects
of their own history.

International Forces

Nineteen sixty four, a year that was the best of times for much of newly
independent East and West Africa, was the worst of times in the southern
areas of the continent where the tides of empire had not yet receded. Anti-
colonial wars were gathering momentum in the Portuguese colonies of
Angola and Mozambique and soon would spread to Britain's rebel colony of
Rhodesia where the dominant white settler minority made a unilateral
declaration of independence from Britain in 1965. Zambia and Malawi
became independent in 1964, but were to live in the shadow of war for more
than a generation. The independence of the British territories of Botswana,
Lesotho and Swaziland was pending but clouded by an ongoing economic
dependence on South Africa—a dependence even more constraining in
South West Africa where South Africa itself was the de facto colonial power.
White-ruled South Africa, the economic colossus of the continent, with its
military strength and its geographical buffer of dependent and friendly
territories, seemed invincible in the face of all pressures for political change.

Geopolitical conditions in 1964 were not promising for the African
National Congress and its offshoot, the Pan Africanist Congress, the two
South African liberation movements that had gone into exile after being
declared illegal in 1960. Their intention was to mount a guerrilla war; but
guerrilla armies require supply lines, infiltration routes, rear bases and
reception structures. All routes lay through hostile territory, and until
Zambia's independence in late 1964, the nearest state willing to serve as a
rear base was Tanzania, more than 1500 miles from South Africa's northern
border. Once independent, Zambia, though vulnerable, became a headquarters for exiles; but access to South Africa's borders was still blocked by white-

ruled Rhodesia, where Ian Smith's government was capable of cutting off Zambia's southern and eastern rail links to the sea. In the late 1960s, with Chinese aid, Zambia and Tanzania began the construction of a costly new rail line to give Zambia a northern outlet to the sea through Dar es Salaam.

Landlocked Botswana, which also lies between Zambia and South Africa, became independent in 1966 under a government strongly sympathetic to the anti-apartheid cause but constrained by its extreme vulnerability to economic reprisals from South Africa and Rhodesia. Rhodesians owned Botswana's only rail line, its principal link to ports in South Africa. Most other major enterprises in Botswana were South African owned or dependent on South African finance and technical know-how. South African refugees crossing over Botswana's long and unpatrolled border were given asylum; but Botswana offered no facilities to the liberation movements, who were required to move their recruits out as soon as possible to points farther north. At its northern extreme, Botswana's border meets Zambia's at a single point west of Victoria Falls on the Zambezi River, where a small ferry plies between the two banks. Here South African refugees were allowed to transit north out of Botswana, but not to enter the country going south with any military purpose in mind. Lesotho, completely surrounded by South Africa and similarly cautious because of its economic vulnerability, was also prepared to offer asylum to refugees but not to permit its territory to be used for the launching of attacks on its powerful neighbor.

In an attempt to free South West Africa from Pretoria's grip, two founding members of the League of Nations, Liberia and Ethiopia, brought suit against South Africa in the World Court, challenging its right to continue to rule the territory under the terms of the original League mandate. In July 1966, the Court ruled in South Africa's favor on a legal technicality, dashing the hope that a portion of South Africa's defensive buffer might be rapidly removed. A further setback soon followed in 1967. Responding to the frustrations of its men, and hoping to demonstrate the capabilities of Umkhonto we Sizwe, its untested but highly motivated guerrilla force, the ANC, in cooperation with the Zimbabwe African People's Union, sent several groups of guerrillas into Rhodesia en route to South Africa to establish bases. The action ended in failure. Some were killed and others were captured and imprisoned. When the Soweto uprising erupted nine years later, Umkhonto had still not fired a single shot inside South Africa's borders.

Notwithstanding the solidarity with the liberation movements demonstrated by Ethiopia, Liberia and other African countries in international forums like the Organization of African Unity (OAU) and the United Nations, independent Africa had few material resources to invest in the anti-apartheid cause. No African government could challenge South Africa militarily, and many (including Zambia) for solely economic reasons needed or wanted to trade with her. Under Prime Minister John Vorster in the late 1960s, South Africa began an effort to promote friendly relations with independent black states—variously called "dialogue," "detente," or the "outward policy." Until the violent uprising of 1976 accentuated South Africa's pariah status internationally, the policy enjoyed some success, raising the prospect that trade boycotts would be undermined and South Africa's diplomatic isolation might diminish.[2] The liberation movements failed to exercise much leverage in this situation, and appear to have been caught off guard altogether when a high level meeting of independent African states in Lusaka in 1969 adopted a policy statement urging a negotiated solution in South Africa—a stand endorsed by the OAU but rejected by the movements, who perceived that any negotiated solution at that time would be overwhelmingly on Pretoria's terms. Only in the area of international sporting contacts did African countries step forward with virtual unanimity to support the exclusion of South Africa, first from participation in the 1968 Olympics in Mexico and later from membership in the International Olympic Committee (*Document 4*).

The sports boycott was psychologically wounding to white South Africans but did not detract from their fundamental sense of physical security. That sense was dramatically jarred, however, when the Portuguese army, weary of fighting unending colonial wars, toppled the government of Marcello Caetano in Lisbon in April 1974. African guerrilla movements had liberated not only their own people from a right-wing dictatorship, but also the people of Portugal. In Angola, competing nationalist groups continued to fight for control of the country. The African National Congress was offered training facilities and Cuban assistance in areas of the country under the rule of the Soviet-backed MPLA government in Luanda, while Pretoria, with encouragement from the American Central Intelligence Agency, entered the civil war on the side of the southern-based UNITA movement. Mozambique became a sovereign state in June 1975 under a radical socialist government. Now the ANC had its first rear base contiguous to South Africa, with Swaziland as a convenient transit area.[3] Time would reveal how able and willing Pretoria was to punish the governments and people of the former Portuguese colonies for their audacity in opposing minority rule. Angola was devastated by 20 more years of war, and much of Mozambique was reduced to rubble. Had Mozambique in 1975 adopted the prudent stand of Botswana, it would not have remained one of the world's poorest countries two decades later; but neither would the ANC have been able to mount and sustain the hundreds of guerrilla actions of the late 1970s and 1980s that, despite their minor direct effect on the security of the South African state, served as a constant inspiration to black militants and a source of worry and demoralization to white civilians.

Of all the external obstacles confronting the liberation movements in the 1960s and 1970s, the most insuperable was the strong economic and political linkage between the Pretoria regime and the governments of the major Western powers. Although publicly critical of apartheid, the governments of Britain, the United States, France and West Germany took a consistently hostile stand toward proposals for economic sanctions. Corporate investment, particularly from Britain, and loans from Western banks, flowed freely to South Africa, where rates of profit were high and the country's status as a major mineral producer lent long-term stability to the business climate.

Opposition to US investment by anti-apartheid activists and by black Americans—12 percent of the US population—had little effect on American policy. The years 1964–65 saw the culmination of the long struggle of black Americans for racial equality under the law, but marked only the beginning of their mobilization for the achievement of some measure of political and economic power. Only toward the end of the 1970s did black American political leaders begin to swing any noticeable weight in the formation of US policies in Africa.

Cold War competition was a decisive factor in Western tolerance for Pretoria. To offset its much condemned racial policies, the South African government stressed its fierce opposition to communism and its willingness to serve as a Western ally in the global effort to contain Soviet expansion. This line played well in conservative business and political circles, and constrained the Western powers from putting teeth into their anti-apartheid rhetoric. That the ANC, the PAC, the South West African People's Organisation, Mozambique's FRELIMO and Angola's MPLA, and both major Rhodesian nationalist movements were all deeply beholden to the Eastern bloc for military supplies and training—delivered under the auspices of the OAU—and that they all espoused variants of Marxist-Leninist ideology, further served to tilt Western opinion toward Pretoria and to leave African liberation movements out in the cold.

Faced everywhere in the West (except the Netherlands and Scandinavia) with official attitudes that ranged from cool to openly hostile, South Africa's exiled political movements strove to win support from liberal and anti-establishment groups and individuals. To a limited extent they succeeded in obtaining scholarships for their members, as well as publicity and public exposure for their leaders. In time these efforts helped to foster wider knowledge and a firmer moral consensus against Pretoria in Western countries. These trends were further strengthened in the early 1970s by the decision of the Geneva-based World Council of Churches to commit funds annually to the ANC and PAC for humanitarian uses, and to campaign against foreign investment in South Africa. Within the UN's General Assembly and specialized agencies, sympathy for the anti-apartheid cause was intense. Only in the Security Council, where the enforcement powers of the world body are centered and the US, Britain and France wield a veto, was it virtually impossible to turn the UN into a pressure point for Pretoria's isolation.

The South African government's ability to shrug off the criticisms of the world remained relatively strong until the Soweto uprising of 1976–77. As long as international markets for South African minerals remained buoyant, inflows of foreign capital and new technology held steady, and white voters continued to return the National Party to power by wide margins, excuses could be found for the ignorance and malevolence of other countries. The Soweto revolt gave rise to doubts that were new and unexpected, however. Foreign investors now had reason to question the country's long-term prospects for stability. South Africa's propaganda image of itself as a successfully evolving "multinational" society was exploded by media images of white police killing black school-children in ghetto streets. The Transkeian homeland, granted "independence" at the height of the uprising, failed to win international recognition, sinking Pretoria's hopes that territorial partition could win legitimacy for continued minority control in "white" South Africa. Pressures intensified from anti-apartheid groups and religious bodies worldwide, forcing some multinational companies to pledge adherence to codes of corporate conduct that sat ill with South African "traditions" in the workplace. The death in police custody of black leader Steve Biko in September 1977, and the crackdown on dissident black organizations a month later, further exposed the South African government to the world's condemnation, forcing many whites to conclude, some publicly and many privately, that sweeping reforms were essential if the country's future was to be insured against turmoil and ultimately against radical revolution. In September 1978 John Vorster was replaced as prime minister by P. W. Botha when the English-language press revealed that huge sums of public money had been spent by Vorster's Department of Information on secret propaganda projects to boost the country's international image.

Life under Apartheid

During the 1960s the South African economy expanded at an average rate of 6.1 percent per year, with manufacturing emerging as the fastest growing sector.[4] In the industrial workforce, the number of Africans—68 percent of South Africa's population in 1964—grew accordingly. Since there were not enough whites to fill all new skilled and semi-skilled jobs, some Indian, Coloured and African workers gradually moved into positions that required higher levels of training. Although wage scales continued to be racially discriminatory in nearly all industries, the trend toward higher skill levels among African workers created the potential for greater economic bargaining power to develop with time. As industrial employment expanded, the number of Africans living in large towns and cities also rose, enhancing the possibilities for political communication and mobilization. Communication was the easiest in cities where a single African language group predominated, for example Zulus in Durban, or Xhosas in Cape Town, Port Elizabeth and East London. In the multilingual industrial heartland of the Witwatersrand, running east and west from Johannesburg and extending north toward Pretoria and south toward Vereeniging, rapid communication was more complicated, but because city and factory life brought daily interaction between Africans from many groups, commonalties of interest were strong. Many marriages took place across tribal lines, and city children grew up speaking multiple languages (sometimes within the compass of a single sentence).

The accelerating urbanization and detribalization of Africans, as well as their nascent bargaining power as workers, all seemed to point to the inevitability of their incorporation as full citizens of a modern industrial state.[5] This was an outcome that the country's ruling Afrikaner minority was dedicated at all costs to preventing, and the story of apartheid in the 1964–1979 period is the story of the battery of obstacles erected by the South African state to forestall precisely these "inevitable" trends. Central to the design of apartheid was the plan, first formulated by Prime Minister Hendrik Verwoerd in the late 1950s, to partition South Africa into white and black "national states." By creating nine (later ten) separate ethnic "homelands" (or "bantustans") for Africans, government policy aimed to reinforce divisive tribal identities and make them the basis for a system of patronage that Pretoria could manipulate to shunt politically ambitious individuals onto innocuous dead-end tracks. Eventually each homeland was to become an "independent" country, as if it had been the ward of a white South African colonial metropole. This, the ruling National Party hoped, would invest apartheid with the legitimacy of the decolonization process then in progress elsewhere on the continent.

The dilemma of African urbanization would thereby be resolved. As foreigners in "white" South Africa, Africans would have no political rights there and would be entitled to work only on terms laid down by the South African state, just as citizens of Turkey or Portugal became guest workers in Germany or France. Africans would work in "white" South Africa only as migrant workers whose wives and children remained behind in their own "nations." Until such time as "independence" ushered in the use of passports, the long-standing—and bitterly resented—pass laws for Africans were to remain in force. These multipurpose laws enabled state authorities to inhibit the movement of Africans to cities, and to limit workers' ability to sell their labor in a free market—a well established method of depressing wages. In 1967, a typical year, 479,114 Africans, or 1,313 people a day on average, were prosecuted for pass-related offenses.[6] Since African workers were deemed in apartheid ideology to be "unready" for collective bargaining, African trade unions remained unrecognized, and strikes by African workers continued to be illegal. This obstacle to African economic empowerment was not overcome until the end of the 1970s.

Three serious problems confronted the apartheid planners when they contemplated the viability of the Verwoerdian blueprint. One was the absence of any way to legitimize the continuing exclusion of Indians and Coloureds from common citizenship, given that no potentially "independent" ancestral homelands could be demarcated for them. The second problem was the lack of enthusiasm among Africans for the entire homelands concept. Pretoria could easily co-opt most officially designated Bantu Authorities ("traditional" leaders who were to head the administrative apparatuses of the homelands), but it was hard to disguise the opposition of articulate Africans, both in the cities and in the homelands themselves, to the forfeiting of their common identity and citizenship. African opinion could be officially dismissed by state authorities as immature or uninformed, but there was no evading the reality that a policy so unpopular was going to be difficult to implement without severe coercion.

Most vexing of all, however, was the third problem: what to do with the million-odd Africans who by 1964 were already permanently urbanized, and whose numbers would grow rapidly by natural increase even if no further rights to permanent residence ("section 10 rights") were granted.[7] Official doctrine dictated that these urbanites should eventually "return" to their ancestral homelands, whether or not they had any de facto ties there. In reality, this goal was clearly unachievable. Although hundreds of thousands of rural Africans in "white" South Africa were forcibly removed from their homes and shunted to the homelands without much organized resistance or world scrutiny between 1964 and 1979, large-scale removals of permanent urban populations would have undermined economic growth, and would have been politically too risky, given the likelihood that Sharpeville-type confrontations would occur. This left a compromise solution, still highly unpopular with Africans, but seemingly feasible from the state's point of view: the construction of a local government system that would link all urban Africans with their designated homelands, and would be manned by a compliant corps of collaborationist "councillors." In time, however, this solution also proved counterproductive to the purposes of the state because councillors increasingly became the targets of popular anger.

Despite the growth of the African working class in size and sophistication during the 1964–1979 period, the obstacles to its political mobilization were still formidable. Both migrant and non-migrant workers faced the constant insecurity created by the pass laws and by the ability of employers to fire or retrench workers at will. Economic growth slowed in the 1970s, unemployment rose, and inflation ate into the real incomes of all but the relatively skilled. In spite of the real income gains of some workers and a slight narrowing of wage gaps between blacks and whites in some industries, the majority of African working-class families struggled constantly to make ends meet and the rural families of migrant workers suffered a steady erosion of their already dismal standards of living. In 1970 the per capita income of Africans was estimated to be $105, lower than the similar measure for Senegal, Ghana, Liberia and Zambia.[8] Under these circumstances, the great majority of Africans lacked the margin of economic and personal security that could have enabled them financially to support the building of political or labor organizations. This scarcity of resources posed a major obstacle that began to be overcome in the 1970s only with the entrance of small but significant numbers of radical white, Coloured and Indian organizers into the labor movement to supplement the pioneering work of African unionists. To those Africans who were wary that members of other racial groups might try to set political agendas different from their own, the question of interracial cooperation posed an ongoing dilemma: to go it alone with meager resources, or to accept that cooperation might mean reaching some accommodation with non-African viewpoints.

Beneath the surface of township life a continuing transformation of social and cultural attitudes was in progress. Beginning in the early part of the century with the establishment of the first sizable African urban communities, and accelerating rapidly in the high-growth years after World War II, this process of change saw rural customs and perspectives gradually displaced by the habits and outlooks of city life. In the eyes of social conservatives, the image of the city was one of decadent materialism, outlandish fads, violent crime, and the breakdown of religious piety and parental discipline. To those already swept into the maelstrom of urban transformation, these images were not the whole picture. City life was brutal and frustrating, but it was also exciting, and for those with ambition, quick wits and a bit of luck, it held out the possibility of wealth and self-advancement.

Rising literacy levels from the 1950s onward, and the attainment of secondary and university education by hundreds and eventually thousands, created a growing African middle class within which there was a nascent intellectual elite attuned to ideas and norms in the wider world. Mass newspaper readership rose steadily, and despite censorship of foreign publications deemed undesirable by the state, black intellectuals were able to follow political trends in Europe, America and the emerging post-colonial world through books and magazines that filtered into the country through travelers and progressive bookstores. In cosmopolitan Johannesburg and to lesser degrees in other urban centers, African tastes in music, dress and entertainment became increasingly eclectic, merging new influences with old patterns in a kaleidoscopic cultural melange. By the 1950s these influences had produced a distinctive South African literary genre typified in the popular writings of Can Themba, Todd Matshikiza, Casey Motsisi, Lewis Nkosi, and Nat Nakasa. *Document 2,* a 1964 column by Nakasa in the Johannesburg *Rand Daily Mail,* captures the bumptious yet subtle expression of this evolving city culture as it came up against the doctrinaire racism of apartheid.[9]

Discouraged by the repression of the early 1960s, the cream of African writers, musicians and artists left South Africa for exile.[10] The political lull in the latter part of the decade became mirrored in black intellectual life, where there remained an ideological and spiritual vacuum that could only partially and fleetingly be filled by ideas imported from outside South Africa. "Where have all the angry young men gone?" asked township poet Oswald Mtshali (*Document 3*). His answer was that some were still around, but that their world was one of alienation, aimlessness and despair—hardly an auspicious environment for political renewal.

Constructing a Police State

On June 12, 1964, in an event that would thereafter be recalled as the darkest moment in the history of the anti-apartheid struggle, a judge of the Pretoria Supreme Court passed sentence in the Rivonia trial, condemning Nelson Mandela and seven other members of Umkhonto we Sizwe to life imprisonment for committing sabotage and preparing for guerrilla war.[11] All organized efforts by the ANC to pressure Pretoria to make reforms were relentlessly crushed. In other political trials in the early and mid-1960s, the state packed many hundreds of its opponents off to prison for the broadly defined crimes of sabotage, "communist activity" and attempting to further the aims of the banned ANC and PAC. Save for remnant groups of activists who had been able to flee into exile, the ANC and its ally the South African Communist Party were decimated, along with the breakaway Pan Africanist Congress, its violent offshoot known as Poqo, and a number of other small dissident organizations.

At the time of the Rivonia trial, the National Party government, representing the country's aspiring white Afrikaans-speaking minority, had fully entrenched itself in power following its initial election victory in 1948. Its members were reaping the economic fruits of political power and the psychological satisfaction of belonging to an uncompromising white supremacist party dedicated to defending their privileged status. The smaller English-speaking parliamentary opposition parties had lost any real hope of regaining power through the ballot box. By 1963 the Nationalists felt strong enough to try to break all organized extraparliamentary opposition to their policies, even if this meant abrogating certain fundamental rights of individuals to due process of law. Justifying their actions on the grounds that South Africa faced a threat of communist subversion, the Nationalists in 1963 passed a law permitting the police to detain anyone for questioning for up to 90 days without charge. In 1965 this was extended to 180 days, and later to an indefinite period.

Unrestrained by the rules of habeas corpus—a prisoner's right to be charged with a specific crime or released—the security police after 1963 were thus free to use any means they wished, including torture, to extract confessions from suspects or to force detainees to appear as witnesses for the state in political trials. In September 1963, the first 90-day detainee, Solwandle Looksmart Ngudle, a member of the ANC underground, died in police custody in what was officially described as a suicide. Despite the adverse publicity generated by dozens of subsequent deaths in detention, plus ample evidence of the use of torture by the security police, the National Party clung unrelentingly to its power to use detention without charge. Being determined wherever possible to dispose "legally" of its opponents by the use of judicial proceedings, it freely engaged in subverting the very norms of justice and "civilization" it claimed to be defending. From detention without charge it was only a small step to the carrying out of dozens of political assassinations in the 1970s and 1980s, the organization of kidnappings, vigilante violence, "contra" warfare by the Zulu Inkatha movement in the 1980s, and the secret campaign of "dirty tricks" waged over three decades against apartheid's critics inside and outside South Africa.

While cruder forms of physical brutality were usually reserved for blacks, subtler methods were used against white anti-apartheid organizations and individuals. In 1968, multiracial political parties were proscribed, forcing the Liberal Party to disband. In 1972, the Schlebusch Commission, a parliamentary body, was set up to investigate white liberal organizations to determine if any were engaged in subversive activities. Two were found to be "affected organizations" and were prohibited from receiving funds raised outside South Africa. The passage of a later law imposed further curbs on the access of dissident groups to foreign funding. Censorship laws, and threats of more of them, sufficed to prevent critical journalists in the English-language press (other than those responsible for the 1978 Information Department scandal) from becoming anything more than an occasional political nuisance.[12]

When restrictive laws aimed at groups proved insufficient to silence dissent, ways were also available to deal with troublesome individuals. Under the 1950 Suppression of Communism Act, the Nationalists had already given themselves the power to ban individuals from public life without subjecting them to judicial proceedings. If the Minister of Justice, for reasons he was not required to disclose, believed that a person's activities furthered the aims of communism, he could issue that person a banning order, prohibiting him or her from attending gatherings (defined as meetings of more than two people), leaving a specified magisterial district, giving public speeches, publishing anything or being publicly quoted by anyone, or communicating with any other banned person. At the minister's discretion, a banned person could also be house arrested for 12 or 24 hours a day, be prohibited from entering the premises of any school, newspaper or trade union organization, and be required to resign from any organization. A banned person could also be banished to a remote town or rural area. In late 1964 there were 303 people living under banning orders. In 1971, after many banned people had chosen to leave the country, there were 274. In late 1976 the number stood at 128, and by 1979 it had risen again to 152.[13]

All these measures and others, including the arbitrary seizure of passports, the deployment of spies and informers, and the prohibition of outdoor meetings and demonstrations, were designed to prevent the National Party's opponents from organizing effective resistance to its continued rule. The Nationalists were convinced that if all signs of instability or dissent could be eliminated or dismissed as communist-inspired, they could successfully install cooperative black leaders in positions of intermediate authority over the country's black population. With this veneer of democratic legitimacy achieved, they believed, domestic critics would be mollified and South Africa would become fully restored to the good graces of the Western powers. Each time there was a setback to the unfolding of this fundamental vision (the most notable one during the 1964–1979 period being the Soweto uprising), new refinements in the basic program ("reforms") would be announced, and the timetable for the program's implementation would be accelerated. Tensions inside the National Party would rise and recede, but the reliability—and ruthlessness—of the security forces would remain undiminished.

1964: The Nadir of Resistance

The year 1964 marked the nadir of black resistance to the apartheid system. Opposing the power and the political program of the apartheid government, let alone constructing viable alternatives to them, were chimerical goals by any objective measure. The forces represented by the National Party were united, determined, well armed, and impervious to all moral appeals that clashed with their own ideological precepts. Forces opposed to the National Party and its policies were divided, uncertain, unarmed and unorganized for the task of mobilizing either popular resistance or international action.

The choices facing African nationalists emerged with clarity and poignancy in a speech by Professor Z. K. Matthews, South Africa's preeminent black intellectual of the time and a former leader of the ANC in the Cape Province (*Document 1*). Addressing a church conference in Zambia (then still Northern Rhodesia) in May 1964, Matthews reviewed African political approaches to white domination historically and assessed the contemporary conflict. How did Africans define their political goals? Some, he said, now saw South Africa as no different from the rest of the continent where "Africa for the Africans" was a legitimate objective. This type of nationalism (identified with the PAC and Poqo) ignored South Africa's demographic realities and was bent on "pointless" violence. A different definition of African nationalist goals emphasized the legitimate demand that all South Africans be accorded rights as full and equal citizens in a democratic, nonracial nation. This had been the goal of the ANC since its founding and remained its goal in 1964. What methods had been used in pursuit of this goal? The patient tactics of petitions, litigation, deputations and participation in government-created advisory bodies had all proved futile, Matthews noted. Strikes and passive resistance had been met with repression, until eventually all opposition by Africans had been outlawed and driven underground. As Nelson Mandela had explained in his statement from the dock at the Rivonia trial only a few weeks earlier, the ANC had thus turned to violence, not with the objective of killing whites or driving them from the country, but as a protest against the denial of African rights, and as a means of insuring that popular anger, rather than deteriorating into counterproductive terrorism, would be guided by responsible leaders.[14]

Matthews' implicit defense of the decision to create Umkhonto we Sizwe avoided any direct speculation on Umkhonto's probable efficacy. Politically, the decision to turn to violence had undoubtedly won support for the ANC among Africans, and helped it regain some of the ground lost to the PAC at the time of the 1960 Sharpeville emergency. That Umkhonto would win any concessions from Pretoria was extremely improbable, however, given the government's huge military advantage. By 1964 the underground structures of the ANC had collapsed and its members were being imprisoned or driven into exile. Externally the ANC found itself in a situation of frustrating impotence. Meanwhile harsher security laws were being enacted at home, and white public opinion was shifting to the right. When the Umkhonto fighters who were captured in Rhodesia in 1967 arrived on Robben Island, ANC prisoners gave them a hearty welcome and soon took to singing a new version of the calypso "Banana Boat Song": "Take-o, take-o / Take the country the Castro way."[15] Good for morale but steeped in wishful thinking, such scenarios of military triumph could not have been further removed from political reality.

Taking a more detached view of the vulnerabilities of the apartheid state and the potential strength of African numbers, an objective assessment in 1964 might have pointed to political agitation and organization among the country's urban population as the surest way forward. The material interests and the personal dignity of ordinary township dwellers were being violated daily by the apartheid system, and there was no secret about this elementary fact of African life. Yet here too, the obstacles were formidable and the safe political toeholds few. As the security forces rounded up hundreds of activists and anyone suspected of being associated with them, fear increasingly gripped ordinary Africans. Discussing politics, even among close friends, became a high-risk activity. Informers were everywhere. Parents warned their children to avoid trouble with the police, and censored family conversations to shield the younger generation from knowledge of the turbulent history of the 1950s. Opinion surveys by a leading social researcher in the late 1960s indicated that most Africans felt "an overwhelming sense of the inevitability of white power," and that among many of the less educated, "despite their envy and even hatred of whites . . . the ethos of a conquered people" prevailed.[16]

Under such conditions of apathy and fear there were no prospects for mass mobilization, even had an experienced cadre of skillful organizers been present and prepared to assume the risks—a precondition that in any case was absent. But somewhere in the gathering gloom of the police state of Hendrik Verwoerd and John Vorster (Verwoerd's Minister of Justice and later his successor as prime minister), there were gaps and spaces where the iron control of the security establishment had yet to penetrate. Somehow these political spaces had to be found and utilized to begin to resuscitate popular resistance and link it where possible to the external forces. Somewhere in the society there had to be people willing to assume the responsibility for these dangerous tasks. And somehow the pall of fear and resignation had to be lifted so that Africans in their vast numbers could be rallied to the liberation cause, ready to stay the course and to pay the human cost, whatever it might be.

Notes

1. In South Africa "black" is sometimes used to denote only Africans, and sometimes to include Africans, Indians and Coloureds, which is the usage adopted in this book.

2. Vorster made secret diplomatic visits to the Ivory Coast in September 1974 and Liberia in February 1975. See Sam Nolutshungu, *South Africa in Africa* (Manchester: Manchester University Press, 1975), and Deon Geldenhuys, *The Diplomacy of Isolation: South African Foreign Policy-Making* (New York: St. Martin's Press, 1984).

3. The ANC was required by the government of Mozambique to transit through Swaziland rather than crossing Mozambican-South African borders directly.

4. Simon Brand, "A Critical Issue: South Africa's Economic Development Prospects," *Development Southern Africa*, 3rd issue, 1977, p. 8.

5. Whether this outcome was "inevitable" within a capitalist economic system or would require a socialist revolution was a subject of heated debate among academics and intellectuals in the 1970s and 1980s. See, for example, Lawrence Schlemmer and Eddie Webster, eds., *Change, Reform and Economic Growth in South Africa* (Johannesburg: Ravan Press, 1978); Stanley B. Greenberg, *Race and State in Capitalist Development: Comparative Perspectives* (New Haven: Yale University Press, 1980); and Merle Lipton, *Capitalism and Apartheid: South Africa, 1910–1986* (Aldershot, Hants: Wildwood House Ltd., 1986).

6. *Survey of Race Relations 1967* (Johannesburg: South African Institute of Race Relations), p. 173. In 1964 South Africa's population, projecting from 1960 census data (*Survey of Race Relations 1964,* p. 135), was

Whites	3,335,000
Coloureds	1,703,000
Indians	520,000
Africans	11,915,000
	17,473,000

In 1979, the estimated total population including the Transkei and Bophuthatswana was 27,400,000. *Survey of Race Relations 1979,* p. 70.

7. Under the pass laws, no African could remain in an urban area for more than 72 hours unless he or she had a valid labor contract there, or else qualified for "section 10" rights under the 1945 Bantu (Urban Areas) Consolidation Act as amended in 1952. This Act conferred rights of permanent residence in an urban area only on those Africans who (a) had resided continuously in that area since birth; or (b) had worked continuously in that area for the same employer for ten years; or (c) had lawfully resided continuously in that area for at least 15 years; or (d) was the wife, ummarried daughter, or minor son of a male falling under (a), (b), or (c).

8. *Southern Africa,* February 1972, p. 20. In the same year the ratio of white to African per capita income was estimated to be 14.9:1. See Stephen R. Lewis, *The Economics of Apartheid* (New York: Council on Foreign Relations Press, 1990), p. 39.

9. Nakasa, a Johannesburg journalist, won a Nieman fellowship to attend Harvard University in 1964–65. Refused a passport, he left South Africa on an exit permit that denied him the right to return. He committed suicide in New York City on July 14, 1965.

10. See Mbulelo Mzamane, "The Impact of Black Consciousness on Culture," in N. Barney Pityana et al., eds., *Bounds of Possibility: The Legacy of Steve Biko and Black Consciousness* (London: Zed Books; Cape Town: David Philip, 1991), pp. 179–80. Census data shows a remarkable brain drain: between 1960 and 1970 the number of Africans with bachelor's degrees in South Africa fell from 2,009 to 1,400, and the number with M.A. and Ph.D. degrees fell by 80%. Unpublished manuscript by Craig Charney.

11. Those given life sentences were Nelson Mandela, Walter Sisulu, Govan Mbeki, Raymond Mhlaba, Ahmed Kathrada, Andrew Mlangeni, Elias Motsoaledi, and Dennis Goldberg. See volume 3 of *From Protest to Challenge* for an account of the Rivonia trial.

12. Until Afrikaner opinion began to fracture in the aftermath of the 1976 uprising, the Afrikaans press proposed no alternatives to government policies, nor did the state-run South African Broadcasting Corporation, notorious for its slavish pro-Nationalist bias.

13. Figures are from the South African Institute of Race Relations *Surveys.*

14. For Mandela's Rivonia trial speech, see *From Protest to Challenge,* volume 3, pp. 771–96.

15. Indres Naidoo, *Prisoner 885/63, Island in Chains: as told by Indres Naidoo to Albie Sachs* (Harmondsworth, Middlesex: Penguin Books, 1982), p. 215.

16. Lawrence Schlemmer, quoted in Muriel Horrell, *Action, Reaction and Counter-Action* (Johannesburg: South African Institute of Race Relations, 1971), pp. 132–33.

2. The Liberation Movements, 1964–1975

Prospects for the outlawed opposition were bleak during the decade between the end of the Rivonia trial and the independence of Mozambique. With the unearthing of Umkhonto's headquarters at Rivonia on the outskirts of Johannesburg in 1963 and the virtual elimination of its underground network within the next two years, the ANC's center of gravity shifted to the leadership in exile. Oliver Tambo, the ANC deputy president, had left the country to rally international support just before the ANC was banned during the Sharpeville emergency of 1960. At the time of the Rivonia raid, several senior leaders of the ANC and a few from the Communist Party (SACP) were abroad or were quickly able to leave the country. With the exception of Robert Sobukwe, most PAC leaders had been released from prison by 1964, and many had also fled into exile.

Exiles had to undergo a transformation from being activists in protest politics to living as revolutionaries planning campaigns of sabotage and guerrilla action for which they had little temperament and virtually no experience. They faced new and complex problems for which there were no easy answers: no direct access to the Republic because of a cordon sanitaire of white-ruled territories, uncertain relations with often sensitive newly independent African governments, meager funds, attenuated lines of supply, and the knowledge that structures of support at home had been smashed. "The lot of the exile who works for a return to his country is a bitter one," wrote Brian Bunting, a veteran Communist, in 1975. "He has to function in an alien environment, struggling in the face of every discouragement to maintain not only his own morale but that of his colleagues who are working and fighting with him." Bunting noted many setbacks and desertions and the problem of maintaining discipline. "Men who are trained and ready to go

Southern Africa in 1979

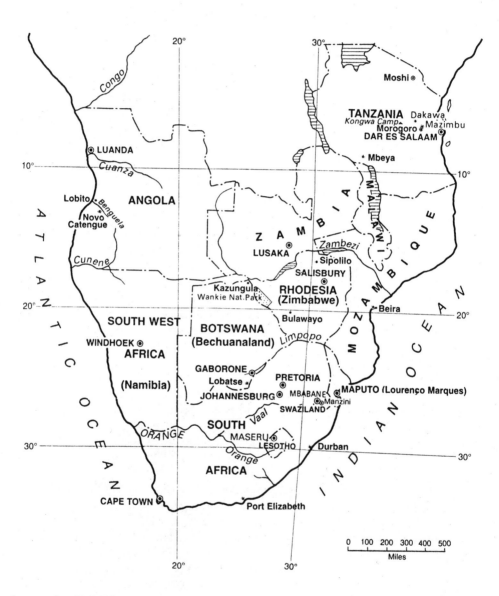

Cartographer: W. F. Nehse

into action are frustrated by delay, grow fractious and sometimes kick over the traces."[1]

Meanwhile, developments at home and in the region promised a revival of resistance. The black consciousness movement was well underway by 1970. The spontaneous mass strikes of early 1973 marked the beginning of a new period of labor militancy. Two years later the liberation of Mozambique and Angola from colonial rule heightened the morale and expectations of all radical opponents of the South African government. Although some activists drifted out of political life and a few even accepted positions in government-sponsored bodies, hundreds and eventually many thousands retained their commitment to resistance despite torture, prison, bannings and exile. They demonstrated a capacity not only to respond to the regime but also to take their own initiatives and to rekindle long-held popular aspirations. However, very little progress was made in building underground structures before the Soweto uprising. Meanwhile, the younger black consciousness generation pursued its own independent course; but as it met repression and developed links with the older leadership, it moved to close ranks. By the end of the 1970s, the majority of its members were to gravitate to the better-organized ANC, although the PAC was also able to recruit new talent and manpower.

The African Resistance Movement

On June 12, 1964, the day Mandela and his comrades were sentenced to life imprisonment at the Rivonia trial, the African Resistance Movement (ARM) announced its existence. Its leaflets saluted "other revolutionary freedom movements in South Africa" and in particular "the men of Rivonia," who had "our deepest respect for their courage and efforts" (*Document 6*). The announcement was timed to coincide with the sabotage of power pylons near Cape Town and on the Witwatersrand as part of a strategy to "strike where it hurts most" but also to "avoid taking life for as long as possible." That avoidance ended on July 24 when a white member of ARM, John Harris, acting on his own, placed a suitcase filled with dynamite in the "whites-only" concourse of the Johannesburg railway station. Harris, a teacher and an activist in the sports boycott campaign, had been a member of the Liberal Party until forced to resign by a ban. He telephoned the police to clear the area, but when the bomb exploded, it seriously injured over 20 people, including an elderly woman who later died. The editor of the *Rand Daily Mail* compared the station explosion to Sharpeville in its emotional impact on whites.[2]

ARM was a mainly white organization with perhaps 50 to 60 members whose history throws light on the recurrent efforts of small numbers of fervently anti-apartheid white South Africans to identify themselves with black liberation. Despite the illegal status of the SACP in the 1950s and 1960s, for example, white communists continued to be deeply involved in opposition politics. The Liberal Party, formed in 1953, attracted whites who hoped to use parliamentary politics to promote their views. By the early 1960s, African members were in the majority and dominated the party's National Committee although most senior office holders were white. A few were shifting to extraparliamentary activity. Solidarity among Liberals, the white left, and the ANC was complicated by anti-communist sentiment among most Liberals. In personal relations with blacks, many Communists developed a closeness and sometimes intimacy that few Liberals experienced. A few whites who were former Communists joined ARM, but most of the members came from the Liberal Party. About 16 remained formal members of the party as a cover while working underground.

The ARM was the successor to a group called the National Committee for Liberation (NCL). The NCL had first emerged during the 1960 emergency and was made up of shadowy sub-groups centered around Monty Berman (an expelled member of the SACP), John Lang (a Liberal Party leader in the Transvaal), former ANC Youth League activists who claimed over 100 members in Soweto for a group called the African Freedom Movement (AFM), plus other independent groups in Durban. A key link among these groups was Baruch Hirson, a member of the Trotskyist Socialist League of Africa. Although whites in the NCL saw the participation of Africans as crucial, little interracial contact developed within the movement, leaving the public perception that NCL/ARM was an all-white group even though Africans carried out several sabotage attacks and were among the state witnesses who later testified at the trials of ARM members.

After Berman's release from prison, he tried to initiate cooperation with the ANC and his former comrades in the Communist Party, but his approaches were rejected. His group began its sabotage campaign with an arson attack in September 1961 and the toppling of a power pylon in October before Umkhonto we Sizwe (Spear or Assegai of the Nation, in Zulu) began its campaign on December 16, 1961. Umkhonto announced its existence in a flyer that stated that it was not connected in any way with the NCL.[3] Four days later, an NCL flyer announced that it had destroyed some power lines in Johannesburg and stated: "The NCL welcomes the appearance of the 'Assegai of the Nation.' Both the 'Assegai of the Nation' and the NCL support the Liberatory Movement. However, no one group has the responsibility for fighting for the freedom of its country."[4]

In May 1962 a dozen people met in Johannesburg, including Berman, Hirson, two members of the AFM, and Liberals from Durban and Cape Town (notably Randolph Vigne and Eddie Daniels, the latter classified as Coloured). The meeting agreed to form a national coordinating body and to retain the NCL name. The NCL was organized in cells, with members using coded names, clustered in Johannesburg and Cape Town, with a small group in Durban and a committee in London to raise funds. NCL thinking is illustrated by a memorandum, probably drafted by Berman and his wife, sent from London to South Africa after the Rivonia arrests in mid-1963 (*Document 5*). It described the NCL as "a small elite group, distinguished by its technical competence and secure organization." In reviewing the status of other resistance groups, it displayed high confidence in the central role that it could play in the achievement of a joint command with a cooperative ANC and a marginalized and diminishing SACP.

The documents of the NCL (which renamed itself the African Resistance Movement in June 1964) were remarkably lacking in a coherent rationale for sabotage or in long-range policies. There was general agreement on socialist aims, differing degrees of distrust or antagonism toward the Communist Party, and a recognition that the ANC and the PAC potentially had mass appeal. Various motives were advanced to justify sabotage: to boost mass morale, to encourage other groups to form and plan attacks, to attract support away from the Communists, to win support for a working-class movement, to help in bringing about a general insurrection, and—a characteristically liberal motivation—to bring benighted whites to their senses. Perhaps encouraged by the NCL's technical superiority to Umkhonto, an NCL document said to be drafted mainly by Randolph Vigne painted an optimistic picture of the group's potential role in a joint command. The NCL should strengthen itself, it said, so that when "the revived military bodies of the ANC and PAC" came together, the NCL would be prepared "to recruit, train, and jointly lead" the National Freedom Army.[5]

Membership grew after mid-1963. The most notable addition was Adrian Leftwich, a member of the Liberal Party who had been president of the National Union of South African Students. Between August 1962 and June 1964, the ARM carried out 16 acts of sabotage, mainly disabling power pylons and signal cables, but its attacks were overshadowed by Umkhonto's activity. Given the growing sophistication of Pretoria's repressive tactics and the anger of whites in reaction to sabotage, doubts about the continuing usefulness of the technique were growing within the ARM when on July 4, 1964, a crackdown on the movement netted Leftwich and found suspicious papers in his possession. Some members who were warned in time managed to leave the country. Within two weeks, ARM was effectively crushed. A few days later, John Harris left his bomb in the Johannesburg station. He was quickly apprehended. The furious security police physically assaulted white detainees for the first time—Harris's jaw was broken; and more arrests were made on suspicion of ARM activity. Leftwich, fearing that he would receive a much longer sentence than others, quickly crumbled, turned state witness, and broke down in a dramatic display of contrition on the witness stand. Ten of those charged were sentenced to prison terms. Harris was hanged, the only white person to be executed for a politically inspired act of violence between 1960 and 1990.

Looking back in later years, some whites in the extraparliamentary opposition have regarded the young intellectuals of ARM as naive. It is difficult to identify their concrete achievements. There was no question about their courage or commitment, yet they had no roots in a mass movement and built no links to the major African organizations. As with Bram Fischer, the white Communist who a few years later was to sacrifice a prestigious career for the sake of demonstrating solidarity with the black struggle, what began with a commitment to effective action ended instead in an expression of dissent that was almost purely symbolic. Meanwhile, if any presumption existed that blacks would follow white leadership, that presumption was soon to be swept aside by the rising tide of the black consciousness movement.

The ANC: Rivonia to Wankie, 1964–1968

Formidable as were the challenges of exile, the increasingly sophisticated machinery of repression at home proved even more daunting. Joe Slovo, a Johannesburg advocate and a leader of the underground SACP who was to emerge as the key Umkhonto strategist, wrote later about the misassessment of the situation in 1963:

> We were still working on the approach that the enemy security apparatus was what we knew in the fifties. . . . However firm the old type of policemen like [head of the Witwatersrand security police, Major A. T.] Spengler [was], they were not torturers. Not only did they create a new force but they also began to legislate for new techniques. In a sense up to about 1960/61 the underground struggle was fought on a gentlemanly terrain. There was still a rule of law. You had a fair trial in their courts. Nobody could be kept in isolation. Up to 1963 I know of no incident of any political prisoner being tortured. The whole legal structure which existed lulled us into feeling that we could do much more than we eventually discovered we could. We underestimated the potential for the growth in viciousness of the enemy security apparatus and the fact that the counter revolution learns from the revolution.[6]

Police intelligence improved and, backed up by ever more sweeping security legislation, police methods became increasingly brutal. After his retirement as head of intelligence for the security police, General Herman Stadler praised the training of ANC fighters who infiltrated into South Africa during the exiled years but claimed that the police knew the "whole history" of people who began leaving the country in the 1960s. The police accumulated more than 6,000 photographs of such people, including more than 4,000 who were known to have undergone military training, he said. In addition, police kept dossiers on the families of trained guerrillas, because "as soon as they come in, funny enough, they make contact with these people." Furthermore, nearly every prisoner released from Robben Island— the country's main prison for political offenders—was constantly monitored so that "as soon as they [started] talking to people, then we [were] bound to know about it." Understandably, people became wary of contact with former prisoners—some of whom nevertheless became key operatives in the ANC and PAC undergrounds.

Stadler disingenuously denied that torture was practiced, except for "the odd instances" but conceded that the perception among detainees that "they are going to be assaulted and tortured" aided interrogation. Therefore, some guerrillas quickly volunteered to cooperate, defected, or were "turned." Stadler's prize exhibit was Leonard Nkosi, who was among the ANC guerrillas who entered Rhodesia in 1967 en route to South Africa. Nkosi made his way to South Africa, was captured, used his "fantastic memory" to tell the police everything they wanted to know, gave evidence in trials, joined the police, and was then "the first to be killed by the ANC."[7]

There is convincing evidence in numerous affidavits, in court testimony, and in inquests that after the Rivonia arrests the police increasingly used torture in questioning suspects—prolonged solitary confinement in threatening conditions, brutality in the form of beatings, electric shock, days and nights of standing deprived of sleep, and violent assaults leading to death. Torture "of the most sadistic and obscene nature" was experienced by Mac Maharaj, prior to his trial for subversion in 1964.[8] From September 1963 to September 1969 at least 18 political detainees died in highly suspicious circumstances while in detention. In September 1969 Abdullah Haron, a 45-year-old Muslim religious leader in Cape Town, was tortured and died after being detained for 123 days. The security police claimed that he had fallen down a flight of stairs.[9]

As part of a country-wide effort to mop up remnants of resistance, over 1,000 persons were detained without charge over the 18 months following the passage of the 90-day detention law in 1963. This measure was succeeded in 1965 by the 180-day detention law and in 1967 by the Terrorism Act, allowing for indefinite detention without trial. Hundreds of those detained in the early 1960s were eventually charged and brought to trial in remote towns in the Eastern Cape. Defendants were frequently sentenced to five to six years imprisonment for relatively harmless actions deemed to be furthering the aims of the ANC or PAC. Under the Sabotage Act of 1962, however, which provided for heavy penalties including death for loosely defined offenses, long sentences were given to people convicted of membership in Umkhonto, Poqo (a genuinely terrorist offshoot of the PAC), the ARM, and the banned Yu Chi Chan Club, primarily a discussion group with a Trotskyist orientation in the western Cape.

The power of the security police under the Terrorism Act was illustrated in a celebrated case at the end of the 1960s, the "trial of the 22," which was concerned with efforts to revive the ANC. Former ANC activists and sympathizers, 17 men and five women, were detained in May and June 1969. The most prominent was Winnie Mandela, the wife of Nelson Mandela. Under the Terrorism Act, anyone suspected of having information about subversive activity could be held incommunicado for interrogation in solitary confinement for an indefinite period without access to anyone and with judicial review expressly excluded. The numerous charges, many of which were speculative and not clearly supported by evidence, opened the doors wide for police to try to obtain forced confessions. The 22 were accused of engaging in discussions and correspondence with the ANC, possessing ANC publications, encouraging recruitment or listening to radio broadcasts from Tanzania, organizing pro-ANC groups and meetings, visiting prisoners in order to obtain instructions, arranging funerals where speeches were made, searching for targets for sabotage and devising means for obtaining explosives (but not selecting sites or making or possessing explosive materials), and encouraging feelings of racial hostility.

When the trial finally began in December, the relatively liberal judge allowed the defense to cross-examine state witnesses about their treatment, and they testified to being tortured.[10] Joel Carlson, the defense attorney, had the accused prepare statements describing their interrogation. These revealed that most had been brutally assaulted and forced to stand around the clock while being questioned. Two had been suspended from ropes for refusing to talk, and one had been lifted by her hair. Because of a heart condition, Winnie Mandela had been allowed to remain seated during five continuous days and nights of interrogation.[11] Two-months later, the embarrassed prosecution withdrew the charges without explanation, and all the accused were acquitted.

The state had been foiled by its own courts, but this did not prevent the government from having the accused immediately redetained (except for three who had become state witnesses) and recharged with essentially the same offenses. This flouting of the principle of double jeopardy sparked protest by white critics in South Africa and internationally. Leaders of the National Union of South African Students, engaged in political soul-searching at the time, were particularly shaken. Women of the Black Sash began a series of all-day demonstrations in Johannesburg. *Document 15* is a proclamation they produced. The new trial did not get underway until August 1970, this time under the Terrorism Act which provided for the death penalty. (The Suppression of Communism Act, at issue in the first trial and deemed more palatable to Western opinion, carried a maximum sentence of only ten years.) The accused, except for a captured Umkhonto guerrilla who had been added to their number, were again acquitted, after 17 months of confinement. Shortly afterwards, Winnie Mandela was placed under house arrest, and all of the other accused were banned.

In 1970 the ANC still lacked underground structures and Umkhonto had not fired a single shot on South African soil. Preparations for armed action had been slow and makeshift through the 1960s. After Tambo left South Africa, he had to establish communication with other ANC leaders and leaders of allied organizations who were abroad. A few had preceded him. Tennyson Makiwane, an ANC Youth League activist, had left in 1959 and was working with the nascent international sanctions movement in London. Moses Mabhida, a leader of the ANC in Natal and chairman of the South African Congress of Trade Unions (SACTU), left in 1960 to work with the international trade union movement. Also in 1960, Dr. Yusuf Dadoo of the South African Indian Congress left for London, and Joe Matthews for Basutoland. All these men except Tambo were also members of the SACP. They and Tambo were among 50 or more representatives who met in Lobatse, Bechuanaland, in October 1962 at the first ANC conference since 1959. It was an emotional reunion, presided over by Govan Mbeki of the

ANC and the SACP, who was to be one of the Rivonia men sentenced to prison for life two years later.

By 1964, a core of political veterans had left South Africa and were living scattered throughout Africa and Europe. Moses Kotane, secretary general of the SACP and a leading member of the ANC, left in January 1963 with Duma Nokwe, the ANC's secretary general. Their mission, in part, was to open ANC offices in sympathetic countries. Kotane became treasurer-general of the ANC in exile with responsibility for procuring funds and supplies and arranging for guerrilla training and welfare.[12] Other prominent ANC leaders soon joined Tambo: the nationalist Robert Resha; J. B. Marks (elected chairman of the SACP in 1962); Alfred Nzo, who succeeded Nokwe as secretary-general in 1969; and Thomas Nkobi, who became treasurer-general in 1973. Also in exile was Patrick Molaoa, who had been elected national president of the ANC Youth League in 1959 and who was to be killed in Rhodesia at the age of 43.

Members of the Communist Party were so dispersed that not until 1966 was the Party able to assemble the remnants of its Central Committee for a meeting.[13] Joe Slovo was declared a prohibited immigrant in Tanzania and went to London to join his wife, Ruth First. Other members of the SACP who were in exile by 1964 included Dan Tloome, Themba Mqota [Alfred Kgokong], Brian and Sonia Bunting, Jack and Rica Hodgson, Lionel and Hilda Bernstein, and Michael Harmel. Jack Simons, banned from teaching at the University of Cape Town, left for Lusaka in 1965 with his wife, Ray Alexander, the veteran trade unionist. Among others who had left South Africa by 1964 were leaders of organizations allied to the ANC: Leslie Masina, the first general secretary of SACTU, and Mark Shope, a later SACTU secretary-general (both were prominent in the ANC); M. P. Naicker, former vice-president of the Natal Indian Congress and a member of the SACP's Central Committee, who became the ANC's London publicity and information director; Moosa Moolla, a leader of the Transvaal Indian Youth Congress who had escaped from a police station in the heart of Johannesburg; George Peake, first national chairman of the South African Coloured People's Organization; and Reginald September, secretary-general of SACPO's successor, the South African Coloured People's Congress. Most, if not all, of these allies were also members of the Communist Party.

Critical problems faced the ANC in the years leading to its next major conference which was held in 1969 in Morogoro, Tanzania. It was necessary to create an effective leadership, develop the strategy and tactics of armed struggle, provide guerrilla training for the would-be fighters who were trickling out of the Republic, plan routes of infiltration back into South Africa, create support structures for returning guerrillas inside the country, deal with the impatience and grievances of men in military training, and integrate non-African members of allied organizations into the ANC. Once enough senior leaders were present abroad, Tambo was able to tackle these issues with a reconstituted National Executive Committee (NEC) that slowly became enlarged through co-optation.

In May 1965 and again in November 1966, enlarged meetings of the NEC were held in Dar es Salaam, Tanzania, the site of the ANC's first headquarters in exile.[14] For purposes of consultation, the meetings included not only senior members of Umkhonto but also representatives of the SACP, the Indian Congress, the Coloured Congress, and SACTU. ANC leaders had been accustomed since the 1950s to close and informal relations with leaders of allied groups. In an understanding with the ANC, none of these groups established separate offices abroad. Exceptions were the direct contact that SACTU maintained internationally with trade unions, and the SACP's relations with other Communist parties. The ANC had its own direct relations with the governments of socialist countries.

By 1965 the government of Julius Nyerere had become concerned about the growing number of southern African liberation movements and their military wings headquartered in Tanzania's capital city. At the end of the year, the ANC, except for its diplomatic representatives, was required to move to Morogoro, about 150 miles west of Dar es Salaam. Construction of the Kongwa training camp also began on empty land another 130 miles west of Morogoro.[15] A small number of Umkhonto cadres had received advanced military training since 1961 when a group went to China, and others had trained in the Soviet Union and elsewhere. Yet the leadership in general knew little about guerrilla warfare. By 1967, when and how guerrillas could return to South Africa was preoccupying Tambo, Joe Matthews and other ANC strategists. Recruits finished their basic military training in a year at most. As Matthews has recalled, with some understatement:

> The boredom of spirited men soon sprouted a series of grievances at the [Kongwa] camp. The leadership of the camp left much to be desired. There was a great deal of heavy drinking of intoxicating liquor. The camp commander, Ambrose Makiwane, was crude in the treatment of the men and introduced practices that left much resentment. As always in such situations, the solidarity of the men began to crumble, and groupings began to form based on places of origin, tribe, and ideology. But at the root of the problem was the perceived delay in any plan to get back home to fight apartheid with the new weapons they had been trained to use.[16]

The major obstacle to returning home was the absence of underground structures in South Africa to receive and support guerrillas who succeeded in entering the country, but the compelling argument was made that military initiatives were necessary "to stimulate the process of regeneration" of such structures.[17] There were also other pressures on the leadership to act. Not only did the ANC have "to mollify a restless guerrilla force that had already been tied down to Kongwa camp too long," according to Matthews, but the African Liberation Committee of the Organization of African Unity was demanding action, and the Tanzanian and Zambian governments were anxious to know "when organizations were going to get down to real fighting."

In 1967 the ANC entered into an alliance with the Zimbabwe African

People's Union, and a decision was made to send ZAPU and ANC guerrillas from Zambia into Rhodesia. The ANC group was named "the Lutuli detachment" in honor of Chief Albert Lutuli, the ANC president-general, who died in July 1967.[18] According to Chris Hani, its leader:

> [T]here was a strong feeling amongst soldiers that we needed to acquire experience, combat experience, and consolidate our position in Zimbabwe, so that even an unliberated Zimbabwe should serve as a rear base for Umkhonto we Sizwe. We felt that once we had a foothold in Zimbabwe, it would be easy to push through both men and supplies into the northern part of South Africa and ultimately deep inside. That was the thinking but it never really worked.[19]

Hani recalled later that Tambo became "totally involved" in military preparations, slept with the men in the open bush near the Zambezi River, and "was there up to the last moment of crossing" in July.[20] A group of about 80 crossed the river and headed for the Wankie game reserve. The group then split, with a small number moving east to establish a base. The mission of the main body of 50 men under Hani, however, was to move into South Africa to establish Umkhonto units.[21]

On August 19, 1967, Tambo and J. R. D. Chikerema, the ZAPU vice-president, issued a joint statement, saying in part:

> Furious fighting has been and is taking place in various parts of Southern Rhodesia. From the thirteenth of this month, the area of Wankie has been the scene of the most daring battles ever fought between Freedom Fighters and the white oppressors' Army in Rhodesia. Only last night the Rhodesian Regime admitted having been engaged in a six-hour battle yesterday. In fact, the fighting in this area has been going on continuously for a full six days. Both the Rhodesian and the South African regimes have admitted that South African Freedom Fighters belonging to the African National Congress have been involved in these courageous battles, fighting their way to strike at the Boers themselves in South Africa.[22]

The Wankie campaign was the first direct (although unintended) confrontation between large groups of South African guerrillas and enemy soldiers. The bravery of Umkhonto's guerrillas became the stuff of heroic legend. Major-General Ron Reid-Daly, who was to form the Rhodesian Selous Scouts, a brutally effective special force, has described the "several nasty reverses" of early ambushes by Umkhonto and prolonged fighting. At one point, he wrote, the encounters "began to assume the proportions of a military disaster." The Rhodesian troops became "thoroughly demoralized, retreated in panic, leaving weapons and equipment behind them."[23] South African police and helicopters, on request, quickly joined the Rhodesian forces. "For the first time since 1906, the time of Bambatha in Natal," an Umkhonto strategist later observed, "the colonial forces of South Africa were met with fire-power from the oppressed community."[24]

Ultimately, however, the Wankie campaign—"a heroic failure" in Slovo's words—was misconceived and poorly planned, as Hani made clear in a later commentary on the campaign (*Document 10*).[25] The campaign failed to accomplish its objectives and resulted in the death or capture of the guerrillas or their retreat—including Hani's own—into independent Botswana, where they were imprisoned.[26] "After much haggling and furious criticism by the OAU," according to Matthews, Botswana sent the ANC-ZAPU guerrillas back to Zambia after about a year and a half. Those captured in Rhodesia remained in prison until Zimbabwe's independence in 1980. A few did reach South Africa and were captured, including one—celebrated by General Stadler—who joined the South African security police.

Robben Island: The Early Years

Separated from Cape Town harbor by eight miles of the choppy south Atlantic, Robben Island was used as a penal colony by successive South African governments and in the 1960s became the country's principal prison for black political offenders. It was there that the PAC's Robert Sobukwe was sent as a "special" prisoner for six years after the expiration of his three-year sentence in 1963, there that the leaders of the banned Congress movement were incarcerated with life sentences following the 1964 Rivonia trial, and there that many hundreds more joined them over the following decades. Rather than scattering prisoners among many prisons and keeping leaders as far apart from each other and from their followers as possible, the government chose to concentrate almost all male political offenders in one top-security facility. There it sought to isolate and demoralize its enemies, cut them off from news, demean them by brutal and arbitrary treatment, and make them invisible. Within the prison, efforts were made to separate leaders from the rank and file, to limit internal communication, and to make political communication with the outside world impossible. Political and ideological opponents were grouped together, perhaps in the expectation that any unity among them would be fractured and divisions would sharpen.

Life and work were miserable during the early years, especially during the bitterly cold and wet winters. Even in winter, after a day's hard labor, prisoners had to strip naked outside and wash with cold sea water, drying themselves with towels the size of a large napkin.[27] Accounts by prisoners have told of mass assaults, sadistic treatment by warders, and the many indignities of prison life, including differentiations made in the diet and clothing provided to prisoners of different races. Mandela and a few other high profile prisoners were never physically assaulted although most were punished by occasional periods of solitary confinement. Raymond Mhlaba endured six months in isolation, a punishment imposed with no formal charge or hearing. Mandela's study privileges were suspended for four years after he illegally wrote and buried an autobiographical manuscript.[28] For educated men, arbitrary limitations on correspondence courses and the use of books were hard to endure. Restrictions on visits, the withholding and censorship of mail, and the prohibition on newspapers and radios produced frustration. Not until 1978 was censored news broadcast by radio, and only in 1980 were prisoners allowed to buy censored newspapers.

Prisoners were held mainly in communal cells. The Rivonia group were placed in a section of single cells, section "B," and this came to be widely perceived as the "leadership section." However, some rank-and-file prisoners were in that section, and leaders such as Harry Gwala (during his first sentence) and George Mbele were not. Numbers in the single-cell section varied as new prisoners arrived and others were released. The single-cell section represented a wide range of political outlooks, but a majority were members of the ANC or the Communist Party or both. Among the most prominent in the early years, in addition to Mandela, Mhlaba, Walter Sisulu, and Govan Mbeki (all former members of the ANC national executive) were Ahmed Kathrada, Mac Maharaj, and Joe Gqabi. PAC leaders included, at different times, Zeph Mothopeng, Clarence Makwetu, John Pokela, and Selby Ngendane. Eddie Daniels was the only representative of the ARM. Convicted of revolutionary conspiracy in 1964 were former members of the Trotskyist Non-European Unity Movement who had formed the Yu Chi Chan Club (YCCC) or National Liberation Front, notably Neville Alexander, its intellectual leader, and Fikile Bam, a University of Cape Town law student. In 1972 Kader Hassim, Sonny Venkatrathnam and others from the African People's Democratic Union of South Africa (APDUSA), an affiliate of the Unity Movement, arrived.

As prisoners who were highly conscious of their political role and optimistic about eventual victory, the leaders of the various groups faced immediate problems of organization and risky, difficult communication within their own section and between sections.[29] Organization was necessary for maintaining solidarity, discipline, and morale and for making demands to the authorities. Somehow ways had to be found to protect individual dignity, improve conditions, and strengthen readiness for the day when prisoners would rejoin their organizations outside prison. To organize and to act collectively were evidence of political continuity and gave grounds for optimism. What emerged over the years was a complex and changing array of groups and committees. The development of sporting and cultural activities in the 1970s was marked by the writing of constitutions, rules, and minutes. Formal organization in the future would find elaborate antecedents on Robben Island.

The ANC's leadership on the island was both more cohesive and more contentious than that of other political groups. Disciplinary committees organized for various sections provided a training ground for leadership and for clandestine work. When the Rivonia leaders arrived, Mhlaba recalls that one person was assigned to draw up a structure for the single-cell section. The ANC membership in that section approved a proposal for the establishment of a "High Organ" to be concerned with ANC activity in the prison. It was composed of the four men who had been members of the national executive. When possible, it convened a general members meeting although this was "extremely dangerous and thus infrequent."[30] Mandela and Mhlaba acted as the High Organ's "secretariat." Whenever the High Organ wanted to exchange documents with another section, the secretariat would direct the communications committee to accomplish this.[31]

In dealing with the prison authorities in the mid-1960s, the High Organ acted as the representative of all prisoners in the single-cell section. After Neville Alexander complained that the High Organ was not truly representative or democratic, a new committee named "Ulundi" was organized, composed of representatives from all parties. It acted as a disciplinary committee but according to Mandela was purely consultative.[32] While never directly challenging Mandela's status as a leader, members of the Trotskyist groupings were critical of what they perceived as his willingness to seek negotiated accommodations with the prison authorities, and some resented what they perceived mistakenly as privileged treatment accorded him by the warders. When APDUSA members arrived in the single-cell section in 1972, ANC, PAC, and YCCC each had two members in Ulundi, and ARM and the South West African People's Organisation each had one. For a time, Fikile Bam headed Ulundi with the support of the ANC.[33]

The High Organ, headed by Mandela, continued to function as the top ANC body but occasioned some controversy because all of its four original members were Xhosa-speakers. This disturbed Mandela "because it seemed to reinforce the mistaken perception that we were a Xhosa organisation." He had always found such criticism "vexing and based on both ignorance of ANC history and maliciousness." The solution adopted was to co-opt a fifth, rotating member—Kathrada or Laloo Chiba.[34] All ANC members agreed on the need for unity, but this did not foreclose intense and prolonged debate on strategy and tactics. The proper mix of defiance and accommodation with prison officials was often a contentious issue. Another long debate concerned the Communist Party, which was not organized as a separate entity on the island. Govan Mbeki and Harry Gwala, both SACP members and men whom Mandela recognized as "very senior ANC colleagues," argued that the Communist Party and the ANC were one and the same. Mandela disagreed, the debate "grew progressively acrimonious," and a lengthy secret document was prepared and smuggled out to the ANC in Lusaka. The separateness of the ANC and the Party was confirmed by Lusaka, Mandela has said, and "the argument eventually withered away."[35]

Whether or not government-sponsored political bodies ought to be boycotted or dealt with pragmatically was another long-standing debate on the island. This issue had embroiled the ANC periodically since the early 1940s. As Govan Mbeki later recalled, "sharp differences" on this issue between Mandela and Sisulu, on the one hand, and himself and Mhlaba, on the other hand, were initially sparked by the question of whether to support the contesting of elections in the Transkei by the party in opposition to Chief Kaiser Matanzima. Mandela and Sisulu strongly favored doing so, while Mbeki and Mhlaba were opposed.[36] *Document 21* is a memorandum on the 1969–1975 period by one or more anonymous authors that was smuggled out of the island and is extraordinary for the severity of its criticism of the four leaders. It describes a recomposition of the High Organ in 1973 and

1974, power struggles, challenges to the status of Mandela as leader, and a resolution of the conflict that reinstated the original members of the High Organ and reaffirmed Mandela's leadership. If essentially accurate, the memorandum reveals that senior ANC leaders, although serving life sentences, were as deeply involved in the ongoing politics and debates of the movement as those outside prison walls.[37]

Meanwhile, immediate grievances on the island needed to be confronted. Prisoners in all sections debated the tactics that might be used. ANC men argued for any action that might improve conditions so long as it was not demeaning or undignified, for example, calling a warden *baas* (boss).[38] Efforts to improve conditions and end degrading behavior by warders took several forms over time: petitions, deputations, appeals to political or judicial authorities, and mass protests through hunger strikes or "go-slows." Supporters in South Africa or abroad were occasionally galvanized by smuggled messages or contact with former prisoners, and meetings with family members and lawyers sometimes led to pressures from outside. The most appreciated visitor was Helen Suzman, the Progressive Party member of Parliament, who came in 1967. Each year thereafter she applied to return but had to wait seven years before being allowed to do so.[39] Nevertheless, her voice contributed to the improvement of conditions. Enforcement of regulations became more relaxed, and opportunities for discussion and for mixing at sporting and cultural activities opened up. Concessions and improvements fluctuated but in time were substantial.

For prisoners serving long sentences, the sense of years wasted could be mitigated by the pursuit of education, both formal and informal. In the early years a concentrated effort was made to eliminate illiteracy. Dikgang Moseneke of the PAC, sentenced at the age of 15 to ten years in 1963, has recalled that within a few years everyone in his section could read and write at least in his mother tongue. Each learner was issued "little wonderful certificates" headed "The University of Robben Island" for each step passed.[40] Many also learned English for the first time, and some English-speakers learned Afrikaans. Once permission was obtained for prisoners to take correspondence courses through commercial schools or the University of South Africa, some earned two or even three degrees. Before that time prisoners organized their own classes, conducted whenever and wherever they could come together. Bam has recalled that "just about anybody who had a degree or any form of education was allocated a subject to teach." The teachers would convene hurriedly each morning and set the program for the day. "Then Les [van der Heyden] would arrange that his English class would be . . . working around him," wielding picks and shovels at the lime quarry. "At about 8:30 a.m., Wilfred Brutus, his junior history class . . . . Pascal Ngakane, who was a doctor, would discuss his biology class. So there was always movement when you got to the work place, little groups assembling in different places, and you knew that there were classes in progress."[41]

Academic study aside, the experiences of prisoners on the island were a political education unparalleled anywhere outside prison walls. Here in an intimate microcosm of "the system," men from all age groups, regions, language groups, and stations in life—lawyers, doctors, students, journalists, unschooled laborers, Africans, Coloureds and Indians, nationalists, Marxists and liberals—rubbed shoulders and shared the grim severity of long-term incarceration. Thrown together by the prison authorities as part of a strategy of control, they developed, collectively over many years, a culture of comradeship, cooperation and learning, of fierce debate coupled with a political tolerance necessitated by their circumstances. These mechanisms, evolved to ensure their own integrity and survival, later became an important part of the intangible legacy left by the apartheid era to the culture of post-apartheid politics.

The 1969 Morogoro Conference

The failure of the Wankie incursion generated bitter complaints and recriminations against the leadership of Umkhonto we Sizwe. The festering sense of grievance came to a head after Hani's return to Lusaka when he wrote a critical memorandum about the campaign signed by six others. "The memo began with a fierce criticism of the lack of attention to the guerrillas when they returned," Joe Matthews later recalled. It attacked Duma Nokwe and Joe Modise and contrasted the harsh conditions of men in the military camps with those in the political wing. Moses Kotane, the treasurer-general, was criticized for giving priority to exile over "home." Tambo treated the memorandum as a challenge so serious that he called a meeting attended by all guerrillas and members of the ANC who were in Zambia. In an emotional speech, he expressed anger at the attack on Kotane, who had suffered a stroke and was in a Moscow hospital. Remarkably, however, according to Matthews, there was no official discussion of Hani's memo by the ANC leadership.[42] Instead, Tambo proposed to the National Executive Committee that a "consultative conference" be held. A full-fledged national conference as prescribed by the ANC constitution could not be held in exile. The last one had met in 1959, and no election of the NEC had been held since 1958.

The consultative conference which met at Morogoro in the last week of April 1969 to address the ANC's serious organizational and strategic problems also confronted further uncertainties introduced by the Lusaka Manifesto. The Manifesto was adopted on April 16, 1969 in the Zambian capital at a conference of 14 heads of independent states in East and Central Africa.[43] The manifesto, signed by all but Malawi, was conciliatory toward Pretoria in tone. It had been drafted by Tanzanian and Zambian leaders without consulting the ANC or PAC, and its implications appeared ominous. Members of the Organisation of African Unity had promised in 1963 to boycott South African and Portuguese goods, to contribute one percent of their budgets to an OAU fund for liberation, and even to provide volunteer freedom fighters. Only Tanzania, Zambia, and Congo (Kinshasa) had given consistent support to the OAU Liberation Committee or the liberation movements. Now even the continued support by Tanzania and Zambia and, in general, the solidarity of African states with the liberation struggle appeared shaky.

The Manifesto, which was endorsed by the OAU and later adopted by the United Nations General Assembly, was a statement laying out the diplomatic position of independent African states toward the wars wracking southern Africa. It emphasized the desirability of a negotiated end to apartheid, and offered "some compromise on the timing of change" so long as South Africa accepted "the principles of human equality and dignity." The Manifesto did not treat the liberation movements as major players and appeared ready to "urge" them to "desist from their armed struggle" if certain conditions were met. The signatories were not disposed to support armed struggle and had reason to worry about becoming targets of South African reprisals. Meanwhile, the South African government welcomed dialogue and insisted that "separate development" was based upon the Manifesto's principles of equality and dignity. Moreover, the Republic was prepared to offer economic assistance to African states to win their cooperation. Would independent Africa sell out the liberation movements? The failure to consult the ANC or PAC was a humiliating exposure of their diplomatic weakness. None of the liberation movements in southern Africa, given their dependence, publicly criticized the Manifesto. Their hopes lay in its bottom line: if no other choice existed, it said, Africa would "support the struggle for the people's freedom by whatever means are open."

The Morogoro conference of April 25–May 1, 1969 represented a serious though not notably effective effort by the ANC to pull itself out of the doldrums of exile and to formulate strategies and methods that could further its revolutionary objectives. Discussions were held among units of the ANC and its allies in South Africa, Tanzania, Zambia, Algeria, Egypt, Great Britain, East Germany, the Soviet Union, and India. Memoranda of grievances and comments from members of the ANC, Umkhonto, and allied organizations in exile were also widely solicited. Matthews, who helped coordinate the elaborate conference preparations, recalls "a veritable torrent" of replies, many of them dealing with the personal conduct of members of the NEC, Umkhonto officers, and representatives in offices abroad. Ben Turok, a white member of the SACP then living in Dar es Salaam, submitted a blistering memorandum, to which Matthews responded in detail. Taken together, these two statements (*Document 13*) convey the complex interplay of material, diplomatic, political and psychological problems facing the ANC at the end of its first decade in exile.

Delegates have described the lengthy discussions as frank, high-spirited and heated. The main conference documents, except for organizational and military plans, were circulated in advance for discussion. The most important was an analysis of "Strategy and Tactics," drafted by Slovo with some amendments by Matthews and Duma Nokwe (*Document 14*).[44] Over 70 delegates representing regions and training camps were present, including 11 invited representatives from allied organizations—five Indians, three whites, and three Coloureds. Although the conference was merely "consultative," decisions were made on issues of membership and leadership that had been festering for several years. The agreement among members of the old Congress alliance that only the ANC would maintain offices abroad had left allied Indian, Coloured and white exiles in organizational limbo. (At home, the Indian and Coloured congresses were virtually defunct but not banned, unlike the white Congress of Democrats.) In practice, the issue was academic since membership of Umkhonto was nonracial and non-Africans were invited to meetings of the ANC's National Executive Committee or to represent the ANC at international conferences. Opposition to admission of non-African members was voiced not only by some "Africanists" but also from within the Communist Party where there was sensitivity about any diminution of the ANC's African image. In the end the conference decided to open ANC membership to all members of the Congress movement in exile, although Africans alone would remain eligible for election or co-optation to the NEC.[45] Whether membership of the NEC might be opened to non-Africans was deferred for future consideration. (Such a decision was made in 1985 by a consultative conference in Zambia.)

Electing a new NEC was made easier by the resignation of all members of the old executive before the conference began. Tambo was re-elected as acting president by acclamation.[46] The NEC was streamlined by reducing its size from 23 to nine. In addition to Tambo, the other elected members were Alfred Nzo (who replaced Nokwe as secretary-general), J. B. Marks, Moses Mabhida, Moses Kotane, Joe Matthews, Thomas Nkobi, Flag Boshielo ["W. Mokgomane"], and Mzwai Piliso. Answering directly to the NEC was a new body created at the conference, the Revolutionary Council, headed by Tambo with Matthews as secretary. Its responsibility was to integrate political and military strategy for the struggle within South Africa. Unlike the NEC, the Revolutionary Council included Indian, white, and Coloured members: respectively, Yusuf Dadoo, who was vice-chairman, Slovo, and Reginald September. The changes in membership and leadership were to be at the center of continuing controversies regarding the role of Communists and non-Africans in the ANC.

The "Strategy and Tactics" document was the most important attempt since the formation of the ANC in 1912 to formulate a comprehensive analysis of the ANC's role. It rejected the thesis that military action alone could generate mass resistance and emphasized "the primacy of the political leadership" and the political mobilization that had to accompany military activities for the eventual "conquest of power." Throughout the 1970s, however, as Howard Barrell has argued, "ANC strategy continued as if armed activity was the primary politicising agent."[47] In setting forth a "scientific" strategy for achieving "the success of the national democratic revolution," "Strategy and Tactics" essentially reiterated the analysis of the SACP's program of 1962, that the South African system was "colonialism of a special type." These words did not appear in the ANC document; but in virtually identical language, "Strategy and Tactics" declared that "the main content of the present stage of the South African revolution is the national liberation of . . . the African people." It did not, however, go on to define a subsequent stage foreseen in the 1962 Party program: "the advance of our country along non-capitalist lines to a communist and socialist future," building on the "indispensable basis" created by the achievement of the non-socialist aims of the Freedom Charter.[48] Another feature of the ANC's newly proclaimed radicalism was the "special role" assigned to South Africa's "working class whose class consciousness complements national consciousness." In 1969, national consciousness was still pre-eminent. Given the reality of white solidarity ("strengthened by world imperialism"), the ANC faced "confrontation on the lines of colour—at least in the early stages of the conflict." Thus the ANC's strategy demanded "the maximum mobilisation of the African people as a dispossessed and racially oppressed nation, . . . a stimulation and a deepening of national confidence, national pride and national assertiveness."

The Communist Party and the ANC

"The Party Triumphant." Was this the significance of the Morogoro conference? Was the cornerstone of the Communist Party's policy "the effective takeover of the ANC" and the maintenance of domination and control?[49] Did the SACP hijack the ANC at Morogoro, bringing it "under the complete domination of a small clique loyal to the white-led South African Communist Party" as was later alleged by the ANC's dissident "Makiwane eight" faction?[50] The documents adopted at Morogoro testify to the intellectual predominance of their Communist drafters, but by 1969 the relationship between leaders of the SACP and of the ANC had become so symbiotic that "triumph" and "control" do not convey its complex reciprocal nature and commonness of purpose.

Although in exile most SACP members were not openly known, African Communists were also members of the ANC, and this became true of non-African SACP members after 1969. A majority of the members of the ANC's new (and still all-African) executive were members of the SACP, as were the Indian, white, and Coloured members of the Revolutionary Council: Dadoo, Slovo, and September. Furthermore, as Slovo has said, after Morogoro "no significant differences existed between the two organizations on the immediate content, strategy and tactics of the South African revolution."[51] These facts may be regarded as a triumph for the SACP, but such a judgment connotes triumph over opposition or by covert subversion. More difficult to ascertain, given the practice of seeking consensus, are the particular role of Communists in decision-making and the circumstances in which Communists and non-Communists differed significantly. Nevertheless, there is no doubt that key figures in the Communist Party were of critical importance, ideologically and operationally. They were among the ANC's most able, dedicated, and courageous members. Although a minority, they constituted the most cohesive group within the ANC and were best positioned to influence the ANC's direction. For a full description of the dynamics of the relationship, one must await historical evidence that is not now available.

The SACP, having been outlawed in 1950, reconstituted itself underground in 1953 and announced its existence during the 1960 state of emergency. In 1961 ANC and SACP leaders and other members of the Congress alliance managed to meet secretly for several days and nights of clandestine discussions with Chief Lutuli in the Durban area. Agreement was reached that Umkhonto we Sizwe should be launched as an organization ostensibly independent of the ANC (to protect former ordinary members of the ANC from the danger of being associated with violence), but that it should in fact be jointly led by the ANC and the SACP.[52] Thereafter, members of the ANC and the SACP were united in Umkhonto. Meanwhile, at the SACP's 1962 conference, which elected a predominantly African Central Committee, the party adopted a document, "The Road to South African Freedom," which was to be its major policy statement until 1989. Combining Marxist-Leninist class analysis and African nationalism, it envisaged a "national democratic revolution" as the first stage toward the higher stage of socialism. Historians Shula Marks and Stanley Trapido have suggested that "contrary to much received opinion," the theory of the 1962 document "was shaped at least as much by the demands and strengths of African national-ism, especially in the Transvaal, as it was by the ideology of the SACP."[53]

After the Rivonia raid, SACP leaders were scattered, and it was difficult to assemble the Central Committee. In 1967 Kotane, who was in East Africa, knew of plans for the Wankie incursion, but some other members of the SACP Central Committee did not. Slovo, living in London, learned of it from the press. Immediately after the Morogoro conference, the ANC and the SACP met jointly, the first formal meeting of its kind. According to Slovo, it was an "official meeting between representatives of the NEC of the ANC and representatives of the Central Committee of the SACP to discuss our common contribution to the struggle and our closer collaboration from then on."[54] During the years of exile, Marks and Trapido have suggested, "the SACP was even more influenced by the ANC than the ANC was influenced by it. The SACP may well have come close to losing its identity and raison d'etre as a 'working-class party' in the process."[55] Kotane at times even suggested that the SACP be liquidated.[56] It appears, however, that most members held to the perception of the SACP as a vanguard workers' party.

By 1969, the SACP had been clandestine for nearly two decades. Its membership was almost entirely secret because of justified fears that openness would subject members to targeted attack and assassination. Secrecy was also needed because communists were not welcome in many African countries. Within the ANC, however, there appears to have been little preoccupation with the identification of SACP members. In any event, although the SACP claimed to be tightly controlled and disciplined, differ-ences of opinion arose often, and membership could lapse. The SACP's influence among the ANC's nationalists was heightened not only by its reputation for loyalty but also by the ability and dedication of most, if not all, of its members. The SACP recruited those whom it considered to be the best and the brightest. At the same time, the elitist nature of a self-professed vanguard party could make for tension in relations with non-Communists. The SACP's sensitivity to any perception that its members were arrogant was evident in *Document 9,* a confidential creed issued by the Central Committee defining "the duty of a Communist."

The contributions made by Communists to the liberation movement spanned many types of work. Moses Kotane and J. B. Marks, whose lives ended in exile, were highly respected ANC leaders. At the direction of the SACP a few months before Umkhonto announced its existence, six pioneer military recruits secretly left South Africa for about ten months to receive training in China. Raymond Mhlaba was the leader of the group, composed of Wilton Mkwayi, Andrew Mlangeni, Joe Gqabi, Steve Naidoo, and Patrick Mthembu. Mhlaba succeeded Mandela as commander of Umkhonto; and, after visiting military training camps in Algeria, Morocco, and Egypt and failing to receive messages warning him not to return, returned to Rivonia just a week before the fateful raid.[57] A different role was assumed by writer Ruth First. Tambo, in particular, and other high officials relied on her, often on short notice, to write substantial and incisive memoranda and speeches. Other Communists helped to ensure that the ANC's principal news and propaganda organs, *Sechaba* and *Spotlight on South Africa* (later called *ANC News Briefing*) appeared regularly from the mid-1960s onwards. SACP members underground in South Africa, beginning in the late 1960s, pioneered the production of propaganda "leaflet bombs."

A unique place in South Africa's history is occupied by Bram Fischer, who was leader of the SACP underground after Rivonia. An Afrikaner advocate much admired for his integrity, personal warmth, and legal skill, he was the grandson of a prime minister of the Orange River Colony and the son of a judge-president of the Supreme Court in the Orange Free State. As a Rhodes scholar at Oxford in the early 1930s, he traveled in Europe, witnessing the rise of Hitler and the revolutionary social experiments of the Soviet Union. He became a Marxist and some time after the outbreak of World War II joined the Communist Party. In 1964 he was one of 14 whites charged with membership of the illegal SACP. Nevertheless, he was allowed to go to London to make a legal appeal to the Privy Council in a commercial case. He had promised to return and did, but soon afterwards went into hiding. Although it can be said that Fischer while underground accomplished little in material or organizational terms, his identification with the black cause during its bleakest hours had an enormous symbolic impact. When captured, he was tried on more serious charges, including conspiracy to recruit persons for military training. He was convicted and sentenced to life imprisonment. Of all personal explanations of belief by opponents of apartheid, his speech from the dock on March 28, 1966, is one of the most eloquent (*Document 7*).[58]

The importance of individual Communists may have been even greater than was apparent because, ironically, the SACP refrained from seeking full credit for its work in order to avoid the appearance of control or manipulation, especially since non-Africans were among its leaders. In one respect, however, the SACP had an unavoidable prominence: its identification with the Soviet Union. This posed a problem for ANC members who were concerned about the ANC's reputation for independence when it sought support from countries outside the Soviet bloc. The ANC sought to avoid entanglement in the tensions between the Soviet Union and China. When the Pan Africanist Congress and other movements issued a pro-Peking statement in 1966, the ANC and its allies condemned "the dangerous turn" that had been taken. "We contend that the main task facing our people is not to delve in ideological disputes that beset the world communist movement but to seek support for our national liberation democratic revolutions." There was no time, it said, "to debate who is correct and who is not in the interpretation of Marxism-Leninism."[59]

Nevertheless, statements by SACP members frequently conveyed the impression that the ANC was aligned with the Soviet Union. Duma Nokwe, the ANC's secretary-general until 1969, issued a statement supporting the Soviet invasion of Czechoslovakia in August 1968.[60] Matthews has emphasized that through attendance at international meetings of Communist parties and allied organizations, the ANC and the SACP were able conveniently to inform the socialist world of ANC policy and needs; yet when SACP speakers addressed such meetings, the price was involvement of the ANC in Soviet disputes. For example, at a meeting of Communist parties in Moscow in June 1969, J. B. Marks, after declaring that he would not "engage in polemics with the rather puerile 'ideological' propositions advanced by the Maoist group," attacked the activities of the Chinese government as "aiding and abetting the enemy." Speaking as chairman of the SACP, Marks also extended greetings "from all revolutionaries of our country" and "our non-Communist comrades."[61] Chinese leaders considered the speech a statement of ANC policy.

Communist members of the ANC were undoubtedly a major asset. "Scientific socialism" gave them a confident world view; yet, as rigidly ideological Marxist-Leninists who were consistently pro-Moscow, they carried much intellectual and historical baggage. Among non-Communists in the ANC, the image of the organization as Communist-controlled was troublesome, and by the mid-1970s two notable efforts to correct this image and to reduce or offset Communist influence were undertaken, both with unsuccessful results.

Okhela and Breytenbach

The first centered on Breyten Breytenbach, who was widely regarded as the foremost living Afrikaans poet and was personally admired by a tiny minority of dissident Afrikaner intellectuals. Breytenbach was living in Paris in 1972 when Johnny Makatini, the ANC's representative in Algiers, encouraged him, presumably with the approval of Tambo, to join with a few other non-Communist white exiles to form a secret support group.[62] The group, which called itself Okhela (Zulu for "to ignite"), was given assistance and some training in undercover work by Dutch and French anti-apartheid activists. Things began to go wrong in August 1975, when the South African police, apparently alerted by an informer in Europe, observed the arrival at Johannesburg's Jan Smuts airport of the 36-year-old Breytenbach, traveling in disguise on a false passport and carrying the draft of an Okhela manifesto.[63] After following him for 19 days and observing his many contacts, the police arrested him. Many of the people he had contacted were detained, but none was actively implicated in Okhela or charged. During his highly publicized trial, Breytenbach groveled before the judge and begged forgiveness but was sentenced to nine years in prison. Embarrassed by Breytenbach's behavior during his trial and by publicity about his ties with the ANC, the ANC denied involvement with Okhela, which soon disintegrated.[64]

Okhela prompted much sensational press speculation about dramatic splits in the ANC between communists and non-communists. One journalist concluded that Okhela was competing with the SACP "for the leadership of South Africa's white radicals" and thus threatened "to split the ANC wide open" and to become a "highly dangerous adversary for the Republic's security forces."[65] More realistically, Okhela, like the African Resistance Movement, was an attempt by a white organization to cooperate with the ANC while maintaining independence from the Communist Party and whites sympathetic to it. The ideological tensions and suspicions which characterized such relations were often exacerbated in exile, especially among feuding anti-apartheid and ultra-left groups. Okhela was affected by such tensions, but its stance was neither clear-cut nor coherent. Persons sympathetic to it included doctrinaire anti-Stalinists as well as pragmatists, perhaps influenced by black consciousness, who were critical of whites who joined the ANC as individuals and presumed to act as leaders. "White consciousness," they said, called for a recognition that whites could not escape being part of the oppressors' class and should seek liberation by directing their efforts at fellow whites and preparing them for the day when they would follow African leadership.[66]

Okhela never became established as a functioning organization and never had more than a few members. It had no strong leader with a thought-out strategy and no background of credibility with the ANC. Any effort by Makatini and Tambo to encourage the founding of Okhela was understandable as part of the ANC's traditional policy of reaching out to all whites, not only radicals. They could not have expected, however, that such a makeshift effort could undermine the ANC-SACP alliance or dislodge members of the SACP from key positions.

Challenge and Expulsion: The Makiwane Eight

The second attempt to challenge the influence of the SACP within the exiled ANC took shape among a dissident ANC faction centered around Tennyson Makiwane. In July 1975, at the unveiling of the tombstone of the veteran ANC leader Robert Resha in London, Ambrose Makiwane, Tennyson's cousin, delivered the program's main tribute. Resha, he said, had "fought tooth and nail against. . . treachery" at the "disastrous" Morogoro conference of 1969, "which opened membership to non-Africans." "A small clique" had "hijacked" the ANC. Only near the end of his tribute was Makiwane explicit about the object of his attack. "The Africans," he said, "hate the domination of the Communist Party of South Africa" (*Document 18*). Nokwe, who was in the audience, reacted with fury, especially because foreign diplomats were present, and declared to a colleague that he would bring about the expulsion of Makiwane and his allies.[67] In September, the National Executive Committee expelled the two Makiwanes and six other "traitors" (*Document 19*). In a statement of grievances directed mainly at the "white-led" SACP, the eight rejected "with utter contempt the illegal and unconstitutional expulsions . . . by a clique of desperate men and traitors" (*Document 20*). In response, the SACP compared the eight to "the PAC clique before them" and quoted Tambo's warning at the Morogoro conference against "provocateurs and enemy agents" (*Document 22*).

The eight presented the only troublesome challenge to the ANC's leadership in its 30 years of exile.[68] Most in the group had played substantial roles, and at least four were themselves long-standing members of the SACP. Personal grievances about position and power played a part, especially for those adversely affected by the 1969 streamlining of the NEC. Ideological grievances also weighed heavily; the group produced lengthy explanations of their philosophy of African nationalism and African unity. Their criticisms were essentially replays of the Africanist criticism within the ANC in the 1950s that led to the formation of the Pan Africanist Congress. Statements of the eight varied in the emphasis given to their opposition to Communists and whites, but it appears that animus against white Communists was aroused more by whiteness than Communism. Thus they inveighed against "White middle-class liberals, headed by the Slovos, who masquerade as Marxists [and] will stop at nothing to maintain their privileged position in the national liberation struggle of the African people."[69]

The conflict had been brewing since the late-1960s when tensions became apparent between ANC nationalists and non-African allies in Britain. It continued into the mid-1970s, when those who had been expelled set up "the ANC (African Nationalists)." There had been little overt organization among the dissenters in the years before the expulsion, but they met periodically, mainly in Britain. In December 1966 matters began to come to a head, according to Themba Mqota, when an NEC-sponsored meeting in Dar es Salaam raised the problem of non-African pressures for a revival of the Congress alliance in exile. Mqota, Jonas Matlou, and Resha were present as well as Tambo and perhaps a dozen people who were members both of the ANC and the Communist Party. Reviving the alliance, Mqota believed, would revive an unfair "racial parity." According to him, the non-Africans at the meeting did not accept the argument of Kotane (the Communist leader most sensitive to nationalism) that every revolutionary should "subordinate himself to the will of the African people without demanding membership" of the ANC.[70] The matter continued to fester until the Morogoro conference.

Despite Communist sensitivity about any appearance of minority domination, the ANC assigned Reginald September, a Coloured, to head its London
office after Morogoro. "Every external mission," the SACP defensively
pointed out later (in *Document 22*), "is (with the exception of New Delhi and
London) headed by an African." Tambo made several efforts to conciliate the
African nationalists, who continued to argue that the Morogoro decision was
unconstitutional because the conference was merely a "consultative" one.
On one occasion, Tambo called a secret two-day meeting in London with
only African members present and appeared sympathetic (some believed) to
the demand that membership policy be reviewed.[71] In January 1975, the
critics convened a meeting of African ANC members in London—said to
have been attended by 50 to 60—which resolved to improve "internal
democracy," to appeal to the NEC for a review of the open membership
decision, and to review relations between the ANC and the Communist Party
because the latter appeared "to exercise undue influence."[72]

Nokwe's angry reaction to Ambrose Makiwane's July graveside speech
appears to have been the catalyst for the NEC decision to expel the
dissidents. Not until a September 1975 meeting of the NEC, however, did
Tambo confront the question of expulsion. Although statements by the eight
had been vituperative in their language about Tambo, he continued to
believe that reconciliation was possible. According to customary procedure,
the accused should have received a letter explaining the charges and setting
a date when they would be heard. The weakness of Tambo's leadership at
the time was revealed by the committee's refusal to postpone the issue or
defer to his concern about procedure. After Nokwe's "very strong" argument,
a vote was taken to expel, with Tambo dissenting. Afterwards, the eight
wrote to Tambo, and he replied; but since the matter had been decided, he
"assumed the position of the executive."[73] Mac Maharaj, commenting later on
the range of problems Tambo had to deal with in exile, observed that after
this crisis he finally began to find his feet. Instead of just maintaining a
political balancing act among groupings within the ANC, Tambo "in a very
quiet, gentle way" became more assertive in moving things his own way.[74]
The alternative would have been to accept the status of a figurehead while
the ANC's aggressive left wing increasingly determined policy.

Following their expulsion, the Makiwane eight entered a political wilderness but bravely sought to launch a "reformed" ANC: the ANC (African
Nationalists). It could not match the structure and resources of the Tambo-
led ANC, nor did it have any hope of recognition by Nelson Mandela, whom
it spoke of as the true leader, or by the Organization of African Unity. It held
discussions with the PAC, the Unity Movement, and other exile groups, and
at a press conference in Dar es Salaam called for "a common front," but in
vain.[75] Meanwhile, the eight set up a provisional National Executive Committee in December 1975, circulated literature, and launched a propaganda
journal. At a conference in London in August 1978, characterized by its
organizers as an authentic conference of the ANC, Jonas Matlou, acting as
chairman, called on Africans to demand of their leaders in the "several South

African liberation movements" that they join the ANC (AN) "to build a Black Revolutionary United Front." In the course of his speech, however, he referred with explicit embarrassment to "internal disagreements" in the leadership and action taken against dissident members.[76]

The episode of the Makiwane eight was a reminder of the undertone of racially inspired nationalism—chauvinism to its detractors—always flowing beneath the surface of the ANC's consistent adherence to multiracial cooperation. Tambo was surely concerned about the resurfacing of Africanist ideology; but reflecting on the episode many years later, he observed that "open membership . . . was not really the thing. They just wanted to be leaders—that is all. It was a power struggle."[77] Members of both the ANC and the SACP have speculated about the importance of personal resentment and ambition in explaining the actions of the eight, but ideology was also an important concern. Throughout the episode, the group never had any realistic prospect of displacing the ANC's established leadership, nor did it persevere or gather strength. As it fragmented in 1978, Thami Bonga, one of the eight, writing from London under a pseudonym to Tennyson Makiwane in Swaziland and another colleague in Lesotho, declared that the ANC was "the only viable political organization . . . our political home" and argued that they should return.[78] Despite the angry rhetoric that had colored the relationship, most of the eight returned to the ANC fold in the 1980s.

Tennyson Makiwane's personal fate was a tragic postscript. In February 1979 he joined Kaiser Matanzima's Transkeian government, becoming the first and only senior ANC leader in exile to defect to "the system." Makiwane acted as a consultant and roving Transkeian ambassador and was believed in the ANC to be revealing confidential information. In July 1980 he was shot dead in Umtata by an unknown gunman. Tambo denied in a press conference that the ANC was responsible. Rumors about responsibility were rife, but it seems highly probable that Makiwane was killed by an ANC assassin.

Revival of the Natal Indian Congress

Indian political organization, usually dated from the founding of the Natal Indian Congress by Mohandas Gandhi in 1894, focused initially on protest against discriminatory restrictions. By the 1950s, the South African Indian Congress, with a following in the Transvaal and Cape as well as Natal, came under radical leadership and entered an alliance with the ANC, joining with it in Gandhian tactics of civil disobedience in the 1952 Campaign for the Defiance of Unjust Laws. Able to assist with money, dedicated organizers, and contact with foreign supporters, the NIC was a valued member of the ANC-led Congress alliance in the turbulent decade leading up to Rivonia. It became defunct and was never banned although many of its members were banned, imprisoned, or left the country to become activists in exile.

In October 1971 at a meeting in Phoenix, Natal, a number of former activists revived the Natal Indian Congress.[79] They did so after abortive efforts had been made earlier in the year by Indians and liberal-minded whites to revive the ANC's multiracial tradition through a campaign for clemency for political prisoners. In November 1970, after the expiration of a five-year banning order, the ebullient Mewa Ramgobin, who was in his late thirties, had consulted with sympathetic white friends about organizing such a campaign. The government was expected to extend clemency to many prisoners on May 31, 1971, the tenth anniversary of South Africa's becoming a republic. The formation of a Committee for Clemency in February 1971 had the earmarks of pre-1960s campaigns.[80] It proposed to make moral appeals by the use of petitions, prayer meetings, and deputations. Plans to circulate biographies of prisoners were intended to revive memories of the Congress alliance by featuring its heroes, in particular, Mandela, Sisulu, Ahmed Kathrada, and Billy Nair. On the day before a "mass prayer meeting" in Pietermaritzburg on May 16, the Minister of Prisons announced that during the Republican festivities tens of thousands of prisoners would be given special remission of sentences but that this would not extend to any prisoner who had been sentenced for endangering the safety of the state.[81] Soon afterwards, Ramgobin was not only banned again but also placed under house arrest for five years. Instead of retreating, however, Ramgobin's colleagues pressed forward.

In seeking to rebuild the Natal Indian Congress as an ethnic component of a multiracial opposition, Indian activists of the older generation faced the problem of relating to a younger generation of highly politicized Indians who opposed ethnically separate organizations and alliances with liberal whites. In July 1971 over 400 people attended a meeting called by an ad hoc committee to provide a mandate for a renewed Congress. Black consciousness advocates who were Indian urged that "Indian" be replaced by "people's," meaning "black." Although some veteran supporters of the NIC did use "black" to refer to all who were disenfranchised, the terminological issue was a fundamental one for those who identified with the liberal traditions of the multiracial Congress alliance of the 1950s, which included whites. In commenting on the July meeting, the *SASO Newsletter* of September 1971 injected some confusion with a dual message. It insisted that the mandate of the meeting was to act immediately for a people's congress and at the same time to "work toward the consolidation of the Indian people . . . who are self-reliant and proud of their culture, heritage, and their colour." However, no basic shift in the NIC's orientation ever occurred.[82] Tensions in relationships with the black consciousness militants largely came to an end as most of the members of the NIC's Durban Central Branch moved from the NIC to the newly-formed Black People's Convention in mid-1972.[83]

Ramlall Ramesar, a 53-year-old stalwart of the old Congress, who was acting secretary of the NIC, had accused the South African Students' Organisation of propagating racist policies; but in November 1973 he appealed for cooperation with SASO and "all organisations striving for a nonracial democracy." No progress was made, however, in achieving his goal of "a common blueprint for joint action" (*Document 17*). In the same month, M. J. Naidoo, an attorney, succeeded George Sewpersadh as president after Sewpersadh had been placed under ban. Naidoo also attended the Bulugha conference discussed in Chapter 8, where he called for the release of the leaders on Robben Island. His recurrent concern was about "our freedom fighters rotting in Robben Island, or living in exile or silenced under banning restrictions."[84] A modest man, Naidoo stepped aside in November 1978 when Sewpersadh was again elected president after the expiration of his ban.

The clout of the Natal Indian Congress in opposition politics was minimal; its primary importance during the 1970s may have been its role in holding aloft the importance of demonstrating that Indians identified themselves with the aspirations of Africans. Subject to bannings of persons and meetings, lacking a treasury and a voice in the press, seeking to engage people who were fearful of the regime's retaliation, the NIC did not achieve mass membership nor was it able to implement any ambitious program of action. It claimed to have 28 branches in 1972 and just under 7,000 members, but afterwards its strength declined. By April 1977, the number of branches was down to 14 or 15.[85] Although the 1973 secretarial report (*Document 17*) reviewed a variety of activities, the reports that followed described bans on efforts to organize mass meetings and a program of activity that was meager. Ramesar in 1978 declared: "It cannot be too strongly emphasized that the spreading of certain ideas is an important part of the freedom struggle," including the idea "that the more affluent classes cannot separate themselves from the rest of the Black people."[86]

The PAC in Exile

The Pan Africanist Congress, which broke away from the ANC in 1959 over the issue of accommodating the interests and views of whites, Indians and communists in the liberation struggle, had less than a year to build its organization before the Sharpeville massacre led to its banning in 1960. Robert Sobukwe and many other PAC leaders were jailed. When they came out—many after two or three years but Sobukwe not until 1969—they were restricted by bans; many of the national and regional leaders, however, managed to leave the country. Nana Mahomo, Peter 'Molotsi, and Peter Raboroko, members of the PAC National Executive Committee, had left in 1960 and were based abroad. A fourth, Z. B. Molete, remained underground and acted as president. In 1964 'Molotsi and Raboroko were joined in Dar es Salaam by two other members of the NEC, A. B. Ngcobo and J. D. Nyaose. Meanwhile, Potlako Leballo, the secretary-general, had fled to Basutoland in 1963 after his release from prison. Skillful in drawing power to himself, he established a PAC headquarters in Maseru, assumed the position of acting president, and nominated a Presidential Council with himself as chairman. Although some PAC activists had political experience going back to the 1940s, the organization's strategic philosophy relied less on painstaking organization than on heroic leadership, which was expected to trigger spontaneous mass action. Only Sobukwe had genuine charisma, however.

The record of the PAC in exile was not illustrious. Its scattered and quarrelsome leaders failed to create stable structures or a continuity of respected leadership. Its years in exile are primarily of interest as a case study of the perils faced by a movement unprepared for revolutionary work, dependent on foreign goodwill, only indirectly in touch with developments at home, and lacking in leadership, organization, strategy, and ideological clarity.[87]

Shortly before the police raid on the ANC's underground headquarters at Rivonia in July 1963, the PAC suffered a self-inflicted wound from which it never fully recovered. In a press conference in March 1963 in Maseru, Leballo boasted that the PAC and Poqo, a genuinely terrorist network of small groups, were the same and were about to launch a revolutionary war throughout South Africa. A few days later, the South African police confiscated letters being carried across the border for mailing to PAC members in South Africa, and soon afterwards they obtained lists of more names found in raids in Maseru by the Basutoland police. A massive wave of arrests followed. Within three months, Pretoria was able to announce that of 3,246 suspected members of PAC and Poqo who had been arrested, 1,162 had already been convicted and sentenced.[88] PAC and Poqo cells were smashed although scattered shoot-outs and arrests in the late 1960s were cited by exiled leaders as evidence that an underground was still functioning. In reality, the PAC within the country before the Soweto uprising and, for that matter, during the remainder of the 1970s, was virtually moribund and unable to organize any highly visible guerrilla or propaganda activity. Some of its supporters, while avoiding public identification with the PAC, were to find political outlets in the black consciousness movement.

A man of brash courage and immense stamina, Leballo had a reputation as someone who could mobilize support and win the loyalty of young militants through flamboyant rhetoric. He alienated other founding members of the PAC, however, who regarded his press conference of March 1963 as a disaster and challenged his constitutional legitimacy as acting president and his claim to "absolute dictatorial powers."[89] At the center of leadership battles, Leballo was conspiratorial and unscrupulous in dealing with perceived enemies, taking actions that in some cases led to their imprisonment or even death. His critics matched him in vituperation, with the result that the exiled PAC came to be "cleaved by feuding, power struggles, expulsions, walk-outs, corruption and murder."[90]

The PAC gained a propaganda advantage in March 1966, but whether or not it added to the organization's strength seems doubtful. Exiled leaders of the South African Coloured People's Congress in London decided to dissolve the organization and, in effect, to merge with the PAC. In the late 1950s, the organization probably had only a few hundred members; their number in exile is not known. Barney Desai, its president, and Cardiff Marney, its chairman, signed a statement, *Document 8,* announcing that they were joining the PAC "as Africans and equals." They called on Coloureds and Indians to follow their example. The PAC regarded Coloureds as Africans whereas the ANC, despite being allied to the Coloured People's Congress before 1966, did not invite non-Africans to join as individual members until the open membership decision of 1969. Desai and Marney alluded to the racially separate components of the Congress alliance by condemning supporters of "sectional and racial activity as enemies and traitors." They also criticized the role of Communists. Leballo added Desai, Marney, and K. A. Jordaan to the PAC's executive committee.[91]

During 1967–1968, the conflict that had festered since 1962 between Leballo and most other senior members of the PAC's National Executive Committee went through several critical stages, concluding with victory for Leballo and his supporters. The complex series of events, public stances, and actions of mutual mistrust illustrated not only the internal struggle for power but also the organization's dependence on the recognition and resources of the Organization of African Unity's African Liberation Committee (ALC) and the governments of Tanzania and Zambia. Under pressure from the ALC and the Tanzanian government, a "re-organization" meeting of the PAC was held in Moshi, Tanzania in September 1967, the first meeting since 1962 of members of the NEC who were abroad.[92] Preparatory meetings were held under the auspices of the executive secretary of the Liberation Committee, George Magombe of Tanzania, and involved most of the men who were to be at the conference.

The conference itself brought together—from Lusaka and London as well as Dar es Salaam—Leballo, 11 other members of the NEC, and David Sibeko, the chief representative in Tanzania. Six, in addition to Leballo, had been in the founding leadership of the PAC in 1959: Molete, Raboroko, 'Molotsi, Mahomo, Nyaose, and A. B. Ngcobo, the treasurer-general. 'Molotsi, Mahomo, and Nyaose had been suspended from the NEC, but because of the "good-will" at the preparatory meetings, their suspensions were lifted. Others present were co-opted members of the NEC, the three former members of the Coloured People's Congress and Templeton M. Ntantala, a Leballo loyalist who was the PAC's military commander. In an opening speech, Magombe declared that all the members of the OAU wished for "a lasting solution to the problem of disunity within the leadership of the Pan Africanist Congress" and also for a common front with the ANC. Leballo delivered a "revolutionary message to the nation," and Tsepo Letlaka responded, declaring that Leballo's leadership was "unreservedly accepted by all." Letlaka also joined Leballo in repudiating proposals presented by Raboroko and Ngcobo in 1966 at a United Nations seminar in Brazil endorsing international intervention in South Africa. Letlaka agreed that the United Nations was dominated by Western capitalist imperialism. The conference "heavily censured" Raboroko for his advocacy of intervention, and Ngcobo was suspended from the NEC and from his post as treasurer-general for failing to present a financial report. He was also accused of heading a clique of counter-revolutionaries and promoting "factionalism, tale-bearing, parochialism and tribalism."[93] Relationships were further convoluted by the appointment of Raboroko to a commission of inquiry into Ngcobo's activities, headed by Nyaose and including Molete.

Shortly after the Moshi conference, Leballo issued a statement declaring that discussion had been "brutally frank" and machinery had been designed to bring back into the fold all who had been suspended or expelled. "We emerge from this meeting as a solid unit," Leballo concluded, "completely satisfied that we have attained the goals we had set ourselves."[94] Six months later Letlaka and Molete appeared to agree when they declared:

> Despite many grave difficulties, the Party emerged from the Moshi NEC meeting with firm decisions of rejuvenation, reconciliation, revitalization and unity. All the Leballo-inspired expulsions and suspensions were withdrawn and set aside and all Party members who were willing to join the Revolution and place themselves under democratic Party discipline were invited to return to the fold. Everybody believed that a fresh start could be made. . . . [95]

But Letlaka and Molete added: "this was obviously far from Leballo's intention." In June 1968, a self-styled "National Executive Committee" consisting of Molete, Raboroko, 'Molotsi, Nyaose, Ngcobo, and Letlaka met in Dar es Salaam and voted to expel Leballo from the PAC.[96] Leballo responded with press statements declaring that the "splittist" meeting was "totally unconstitutional" and that he had decided, after wide consultation, to exercise his emergency powers. He quoted the 1959 Disciplinary Code: "Where normal processes of free discussion fail to curb factional tendencies, then firm iron discipline should come into play, and factional elements, no matter how important, should be chopped off without ceremony." Thereupon, after noting that Ngcobo had already been suspended at the Moshi conference, he suspended the others from the NEC until they met five conditions, including a pledge of loyalty to the acting president, himself.[97]

What followed was a fiasco for the seven, a group that might be called the PAC establishment. Both sides faced a critical meeting of the ALC in Algiers in July 1968. To prepare for the meeting, Molete and Raboroko left Dar to meet Letlaka, Nyaose, and Ngcobo in Lusaka while 'Molotsi and Mahomo went separately to the United States and London to consult with PAC members. All were to come together in Algiers. Meanwhile, in early July, the five in Lusaka, contravening Zambian regulations, traveled to a remote PAC camp to inform some 20 guerrilla recruits of what had happened in Dar. What followed was later described in detail, with "shock" and "utter chagrin," by Molete in a memorandum entitled "The Grand Epilogue": detention and abuse by Leballo's men, intervention by Zambian officials who informed the five that the OAU was suspending material and financial aid until the PAC settled its internal disputes, imprisonment of the five in Lusaka, consultation with the Zambian authorities by the five and by Leballo, who had arrived in Lusaka, the banning of the PAC in Zambia, the arrest of every male member of the PAC, including Leballo—41 in all—and their deportation to Tanzania.

There it became evident that the Tanzanian government continued to recognize Leballo. His office remained open, and he continued to receive financial aid from the People's Republic of China. *Document 12*, a confidential memorandum of November 1968 by Leballo, concluded that "the remnants of this dissident clique must be wiped out." Defeated and resettled as a refugee in Kenya, Molete wrote to the ALC almost two years later (*Document 16*) urging that his group, "the popularly elected leaders of the PAC and the African people of South Africa," be recognized as the true National Executive Committee. His statement criticized Leballo for becoming enmeshed as a spy for the Nyerere government in a coup plot by Tanzanian dissidents. The judge in the case described Leballo as a police agent and referred to the "somewhat exalted view he has of his own importance."[98] Nevertheless, Leballo's service as an informant and the chief witness for the prosecution won President Nyerere's gratitude and helps to explain Leballo's longevity as the recognized PAC leader in Tanzania.

The ANC before the Independence of Mozambique

During the first half of the 1970s, the seeds of the ANC's renewal were germinating in the rise of black consciousness and labor militancy. These seeds were being nourished by independent strategic assessments made by members of the new generation and also by their contacts with underground and exiled members of the banned movements. But accurately reading the signs and signals from inside South Africa was often difficult for ANC strategists in exile, whose instincts strongly inclined them toward conceptualizing the problem of liberation primarily in terms of externally-based military operations. From the vantage point of the time, this was hardly surprising. Twentieth century revolutions in Russia, China, Cuba and Algeria had succeeded through armed struggle. Guerrilla warfare was slowly defeating even a military behemoth like the United States in Vietnam. In sub-Saharan Africa, although most former colonies had achieved independence by relatively peaceful means, the governments of Portugal and white-ruled Rhodesia had held out against majority rule, giving rise to armed movements that by the early 1970s were fighting wars of national liberation in Angola, Mozambique, Portuguese Guinea, and Rhodesia. South West Africans were adopting armed resistance to throw off South African rule. There seemed to be no other option, not only to those in exile who were cut off from day to day political currents at home, but also to many young militants inside South Africa for whom military action held a strong appeal.

Political action of several types was seen as essential in facilitating the success of revolutionary warfare. International diplomatic and propaganda activity was needed to isolate and weaken the South African government and to raise funds and material support for the armed struggle and the maintenance of the ANC's external offices and personnel. Political propaganda inside South Africa was regarded as essential to keep alive the ANC's name and reputation, to attract guerrilla recruits, and to sway the black civilian population to lend active support to guerrilla fighters. Lower priority appears to have been given to political action unassociated with military strategy: the organization of protest and agitation around popular grievances, the infiltration of above-ground organizations by ANC partisans, or the systematic targeting of system collaborators for ridicule and repudiation.

Until Pretoria's ring of buffer states was broken by the independence of Mozambique in 1975, the difficulty of communicating with supporters at home and building underground structures proved extremely frustrating to the ANC. Despite the setbacks of the Wankie campaign, scenario-building exercises continued to revolve around military thinking. In 1970—a year when a draft ANC strategy proposal pronounced the organization within the country "almost dead"[99]—a large ANC delegation went to the Soviet Union, where it held lengthy meetings with experts in "irregular warfare." During the meetings, according to Matthews, a Soviet major-general of wide experience

> repeated over and over again, that without a proper and secure machinery which could receive and sustain guerrillas at home, any plan was doomed to failure no matter how just the cause. He was questioned about Cuba. The major-general virtually considered the success of the Cuban revolution as a fluke, a failure of intelligence on the part of opponents of Castro. Most of those who landed on the coast were wiped out. A handful including Castro survived to carry on. But the project as such had not been a success and should not be repeated.

Notwithstanding this advice, elaborate and expensive plans, known as "Operation J," were made over several years, culminating in 1971, to land guerrillas on the Transkeian coast. An old yacht, the *Aventura,* was purchased, and a crew of Greek Communists recruited. A radical Australian, Alex Moumbaris, and others reconnoitered and filmed the Indian Ocean coastline; 27 possible landing sites were reduced to six. Because the Suez Canal was closed, the yacht sailed around the Cape to Somalia to pick up some 50 guerrillas who were trained in sea landing and were expected to carry arms, explosives, and communications equipment. But the ship broke down and had to be abandoned.[100] Moumbaris and five others who were waiting inside the country were caught and received severe sentences.

In spite of the difficulty of getting guerrilla operations underway, channels nevertheless existed through which the ANC could make propaganda and inform the South African public about its continued existence. Beginning in the late 1960s and more reliably from about 1973, South Africans began receiving the ANC's "Radio Freedom" on short wave from Zambia and Tanzania (*Document 11*).[101] Inside the country, funerals offered an occasion for ANC supporters to publicize heroes of the past. Albert Lutuli's funeral in August 1967, for example, is said to have attracted a crowd of over 7,000 people. At the unveiling of Lutuli's tombstone five years later, Chief Buthelezi, Alan Paton, and others spoke publicly about the legal days of the ANC. The crowd shouted slogans, sang political songs, and men and women in ANC uniforms marched—all recorded by security police cameras.[102] Other meetings commemorated deaths in detention or called for the release of political prisoners.

ANC propaganda made its most dramatic impact when leaflets were scattered by explosive devices suspended from high buildings or set off in crowded areas simultaneously in major cities. Newspapers reported these actions on their front-pages and sometimes, despite official threats, reproduced the propaganda. The organization and training of propagandists was initiated in 1966 in London by a committee of the SACP which included Dadoo, Slovo, Jack Hodgson and Ronnie Kasrils. Its aim was to train recruits and to distribute material, obtain intelligence, and establish cells in South Africa. Beginning with a 1966 leaflet commemorating the 45th anniversary of the founding of the Communist Party, material was posted to South Africa or arrived in false-bottomed suitcases. By 1975 at least 25 couriers and agents had been trained, according to Kasrils, although many later became inactive. A few were Africans and Indians, but most were white.[103] Material written outside was smuggled into South Africa for reproduction, and some was written by members inside. Communication was often in invisible ink. Some leaflets and pamphlets were distributed by mail, innocently as "Season's Greetings" or in the form of comic books or Marxist classics, including a Xhosa translation of Lenin inside false covers.

In October 1971, the police disrupted a cell network of possibly 25 people in Johannesburg when they stopped a car carrying hundreds of leaflets and a Communist publication, *Inkululeko*. While being interrogated the following day, and giving no one away, the car's young driver, Ahmed Timol, allegedly committed suicide by jumping from a tenth floor window at security police headquarters. The network survived, according to Kasrils. Among other underground operatives who were apprehended during the 1970s were several young white members of the SACP. Raymond Suttner, a law lecturer at Natal University, was convicted in late 1975, after operating underground for two years. At the end of his trial, the crowd in the courtroom returned his clenched fist salute and burst forth with the African national anthem, *Nkosi Sikelel' iAfrika*.[104] Suttner had been trained in underground work in London as had two whites from Cape Town, Jeremy Cronin, a University of Cape Town lecturer, and David Rabkin, a journalist. After some stressful years, they and another operative, Anthony Holiday, also a journalist, were arrested during the Soweto uprising. Tim Jenkin and Steve Lee, members of another underground cell, exploded their first leaflet bomb before June 1976, and were not caught until 1978. All served prison sentences ranging from seven to 12 years.

The capture, trial and imprisonment of underground activists in these years was evidence of failure, but also evidence that the liberation movements existed. With the suppression of Poqo and the ANC, the number of political trials fell off in the late 1960s but then began to increase again in the mid-1970s. Whereas many cases had gone unreported in the press in the 1960s, media attention increased in the 1970s, making political trials a propaganda vehicle for both the government and the liberation movements.

In the doldrum period following the Morogoro conference, a handful of trials inside South Africa highlighted the ongoing efforts of the ANC to build internal networks. The two trials of Winnie Mandela and others in 1969–70, which ended in acquittal for all but one accused, revealed the amateur nature of political activity among many of those involved.[105] By contrast, the 1971 trial of James April, a young Coloured Umkhonto fighter, showed both the dedication and professional potential of the ANC's military personnel. A former student at the University of Cape Town, April had undergone military training in Czechoslovakia, taken part in the Wankie campaign, and returned to South Africa with forged papers to train other guerrillas and to establish communication with leaders outside. He was sentenced to 15 years imprisonment. In another 1971 trial, the state sought to eliminate a white sympathizer of the banned opposition—the Anglican Dean of Johannesburg, Gonville ffrench-Beytagh—through the provocations of a police spy. Ffrench-Beytagh was charged not only with giving money from the London-based Defence and Aid Fund to dependents of banned individuals but also with participating in terroristic activities of the ANC and SACP, distributing revolutionary pamphlets, and inciting the Black Sash, an organization of eminently respectable middle- and upper-class white women, to prepare for violence. He faced the death penalty but received the minimum sentence of five years, which was overturned on appeal.[106]

A major trial that ended in 1972 revealed the political and military ineffectualness of the ultra-left Unity Movement of South Africa, a federated body of African, Indian, and Coloured organizations, and the African People's Democratic Union of South Africa (APDUSA), its individual membership body. From its inception in the 1940s, the Unity Movement attacked ANC mass campaigns as unprincipled, reformist and collaborationist. It had itself been moribund since the early 1960s, when I. B. Tabata, APDUSA's president, and other prominent members left the country. A small number of members continued to function within South Africa, primarily as study groups. Factions differed regarding the emphasis that should be given to African predominance, class, and armed struggle. Some members at home also accused the exiles of abandoning the political struggle and thus losing their standing as leaders. In contrast, the legitimacy of ANC leaders abroad was never challenged by followers at home.

Tabata and his associates in Lusaka decided in 1970 to try to revive APDUSA.[107] He hoped for recognition and assistance from the OAU, which recognized only the ANC and the PAC. Allegedly, Tabata planned to have four men infiltrate South Africa to recruit at least 200 men for military training, possibly in Egypt. In early 1971 the police detained and severely beat or tortured scattered followers of APDUSA in the rural Transkei and urban centers. Thirteen men—Africans, Coloureds, and Indians—were brought to trial. Among them was Kader Hassim, a prominent attorney in Pietermaritzburg who himself had sought to revive APDUSA but did not recognize the authority of the exiles and opposed recruitment for military training. The Lusaka recruiters had come to his house, thus compromising him. The trial lasted nine months and heard about 100 state witnesses and testimony from an embittered Hassim, who explained his opposition to violence.[108] The accused had done little but faced many charges. All were convicted, receiving prison sentences ranging from five to eight years.

Although police often tried to fabricate incriminating evidence in political trials, court records provide much confirmation of the ANC's focus on building its military capability. Defendants charged under the Terrorism Act were typically accused of trying "to distribute propaganda material in support of a movement to overthrow the Government of South Africa by violent means; to recruit persons to join or support such movements; to train, or cause people to be trained in the art of waging war and subversion; to secretly take people outside of South Africa for such training; to secretly return people to South Africa who had received military training, and to smuggle arms, explosives and ammunition into South Africa; to establish arsenals and hide-outs; to commit acts of sabotage; to infiltrate associations; to establish and extend an underground organisation in South Africa by the creation of secret groups and cells; and to arrange finance to further the above-mentioned objects."[109]

Frequently the state was able to apprehend underground operatives before they had gone much beyond the stage of intending to commit such deeds; sometimes the work was further advanced. Substantial underground activity was unearthed in Natal beginning late in 1975 when police carried out swoops against a suspected ANC network. About 50 people were arrested, many of whom reportedly were tortured. Two of those arrested had been kidnapped from Swaziland; another, Joseph Mdluli, died from police beatings within 24 hours of his arrest. In early 1976 ten of the arrested men were brought to trial, including Harry Gwala, a former SACTU trade unionist who had completed an eight-year sentence on Robben Island in 1973. In proceedings that lasted over a year, the accused were charged with communicating with the external ANC and recruiting fighters for military training abroad. All but one were convicted; Gwala and four others received life sentences.

By 1974 the ANC was trying to move beyond its military preoccupation in order to take advantage of the resurgence of political and labor activity inside South Africa. The Gwala trial revealed that efforts had been made to bring activists out of the country to be trained as trade union organizers who could return to revive SACTU. Serious attempts to gain a foothold for the ANC inside the black consciousness movement had also begun. Tension in Botswana between the ANC and independent-minded refugees from black consciousness organizations had raised the threat that black consciousness might establish itself as a "third force" in exile politics, even to the point of launching its own competing military wing. As a movement drawn from the youth generation inside South Africa, black consciousness could legitimately claim to be more in touch with "home" than the older exiles, putting its leaders in a position to challenge the claims of the ANC and PAC to speak for black South Africans internationally. After several years of only mixed success in co-opting black consciousness exiles in Botswana, the ANC adopted more aggressive tactics in trying to infiltrate black consciousness organizations inside the country.

To outward appearances, however, despite minor advances, the liberation struggle seemed stagnant and on the defensive. Internally, any timetable of revolutionary challenge seemed fanciful. Externally, military initiative was stalled. Then on April 25, 1974, with the startling unpredictability that so often characterizes great historical moments, the Portuguese government was removed from power by its disaffected military commanders, ushering in a new era in the politics of southern Africa. As Mozambique and Angola moved rapidly toward independence, new prospects for guerrilla warfare opened up and hopes revived that armed struggle, coupled with internal political renewal, might soon tip the balance of power against Pretoria.

Notes

1. Brian Bunting, *Moses Kotane: South African Revolutionary, A Political Biography* (London: Inkululeko Publications, 1975), p. 280.

2. H. Lever, "The Johannesburg Station Explosion and Ethnic Attitudes," *Public Opinion Quarterly,* Summer 1969, p. 181.

3. *From Protest to Challenge,* volume 3, pp. 716–17.

4. Leaflet by the National Committee for Liberation announcing its activities after an act of sabotage on December 20, 1961.

5. "The National Committee for Liberation—background and aims," memorandum written after September 1963.

6. Joe Slovo, "The Sabotage Campaign," *Dawn: Journal of Umkhonto we Sizwe,* Souvenir Issue, 1986, p. 25.

7. Interview of Howard Barrell with Herman Stadler (October 1990). Vladimir Shubin, a Russian specialist in intelligence, argues that Stadler's claims are exaggerated. Letter from Shubin to Karis, September 1995.

8. Hilda Bernstein, *The Terrorism of Torture* (London: Christian Action Publications, 1972), p. 43. Also see *Apartheid and the Treatment of Prisoners in South Africa* (New York: United Nations, 1967), and Allen Cook, *South Africa: The Imprisoned Society* (London: International Defence and Aid Fund, 1974).

9. Barney Desai and Cardiff Marney, *The Killing of the Imam* (London: Quartet Books, 1978), and Bernstein, pp. 33–34.

10. Conversation with George Bizos, a member of the defense team (October 1989).

11. *South Africa: Trial By Torture—The Case of the 22* (London: International Defence and Aid Fund, May 1970). Severe treatment was also inflicted upon two women, Shanthie Naidoo and Nomwe Mamkhala, who were detained as witnesses but refused to testify. Naidoo was sentenced to two months and then redetained for 369 days. Joyce Sikakane, *A Window on Soweto* (London: International Defense and Aid Fund, 1977), pp. 66ff.

12. Bunting, pp. 276 and 280.

13. Conversation with Joe Slovo (October 1990). Shubin remembers a meeting of the Central Committee in 1964.

14. Oliver Tambo, "Directive on the Nature of the Forthcoming Conference," March 1969.

15. Stephen Ellis and Tsepo Sechaba, *Comrades against Apartheid: The ANC and the South African Communist Party in Exile* (London: James Currey, 1992), p. 47, states without giving a source that in 1964 Joe Modise, the ANC's top military commander, "commanded up to two thousand South African exiles based in camps in Tanzania, at Kongwa, Mbeya, Bagamoyo and Morogoro." According to a PAC source, in 1964 the ANC had two camps between the city and

the Dar es Salaam airport, Camp Lutuli and Camp Mandela, with 100 to 150 men in each, awaiting departure for military training. Conversation with Patrick Duncan (February 1964).

16. Joe Matthews, unpublished manuscript, 1990. Other quotations attributed to Matthews below are from this manuscript.

17. Joe Slovo, "The Second Stage: Attempts to Get Back," *Dawn,* Souvenir Issue, 1986, p. 33.

18. Lutuli, aged and with poor hearing and sight, was killed by a train on a railway bridge near his home in Stanger, Natal. Although lacking evidence, the ANC suggested foul play and spoke in a press release of the circumstances being "shrouded in mystery." *Spotlight on South Africa,* vol. 5, no. 29, July 21, 1967. Tambo, in a 1973 memorandum to Karis, said of Lutuli's death, "His widow does not accept the Government story that he was struck by a train. Neither do we."

19. Chris Hani, interviewed by Rory Riordan, *Monitor: The Journal of the Human Rights Trust,* Port Elizabeth, December 1990, p. 10.

20. Chris Hani interviewed by Luli Callinicos, *New Nation,* April 30–May 6, 1993.

21. Both Matthews and Major-General Reid-Daly of the Rhodesian forces use the figure 80. Ron Reid-Daly, "War in Rhodesia—Cross-Border Operations," in Al J. Venter, ed., *Challenge: Southern Africa Within the African Revolutionary Context: An Overview* (Gibraltar: Ashanti Publishing Limited, 1989), p. 152. The Wankie campaign was also referred to as "the Wankie-Sipolilo campaign," the latter name referring to an area infiltrated by ANC guerrillas in the northeastern part of Rhodesia, where incursions occurred until well into 1968.

22. "ANC-ZAPU Military Alliance," *South African Studies 1: Guerrilla Warfare* (London: The Publicity and Information Bureau, African National Congress, 1970), pp. 3–4.

23. Reid-Daly, pp. 153–54.

24. Mzala [Jabulani Nxumalo], "Development of the ANC's Military Strategy," unpublished manuscript, 1991, p. 6.

25. Conversation with Slovo. Also see criticism and commentary on the campaign in the ultra-left journal, *The Black Dwarf* (London), November 26, 1969, under the title "South Africa Betrayed." The Youth and Students section of the ANC in London issued a reply on December 3, 1969, much of which was reproduced in the Christmas 1969 issue of *The Black Dwarf.*

26. It is impossible to arrive at definitive statistics on the numbers of dead, wounded, and captured. Reid-Daly states that 30 "terrorists" were killed and 20 captured, and the rest escaping to Botswana. Matthews recalls that 12 men, including Hani, were imprisoned in Botswana. In 1971 the ANC published an incomplete list, naming 13 who died, seven who were serving life imprisonment in Rhodesia, and five serving long sentences in South Africa. *Sechaba,* December 1971–January 1972, pp. 15–17.

27. Conversation with Ahmed Kathrada (September 1993).

28. Nelson Mandela, *Long Walk to Freedom* (New York: Little, Brown and Co., 1994), pp. 415–18. Mac Maharaj smuggled out another copy of the manuscript when he was released.

29. Harry Gwala was never able to talk directly with anyone in the single-cell section during the eight years of his first confinement on the island but communicated by smuggled notes. Conversation with Harry Gwala (December 1989). Kathrada, Sibusiso Ndebele and a third person were the librarians for their separate sections and were able to talk while prolonging the time spent to organize books (conversation with Kathrada). Probably the most ingenious method of communication in the early days was devised by Maharaj. It involved writing messages in very small print, wrapping them in cellophane, and inserting them in packed feces in grooves inside a toilet. Interview of Victoria Butler with Mac Maharaj (February 1988).

30. Mandela, p. 385.

31. Conversation with Raymond Mhlaba (December 1989).

32. Mandela, pp. 377–78, 385–86.

33. But see conversation with Sonny Venkatrathnam (October 1993).

34. Mandela, p. 386. Document 21 states that M. D. [Naidoo] joined the High Organ in 1967.

35. Mandela, pp. 374–75.

36. Letter from Govan Mbeki to Karis, September 4, 1995.

37. Fuller accounts of leadership conflicts and personal relationships on Robben Island must await the writing of future memoirs and the inquiries of future historians. Meanwhile, although

Document 22 purports to present "an accurate summary" of events, it is not an "official" document and contains "several vital inaccuracies," according to Ahmed Kathrada and others with whom he has consulted. (Letter from Kathrada to Karis, September 2, 1995). Mbeki adds that the memorandum misrepresents the situation by characterizing the disputes as a power struggle. "From the onset," he says, "the decision was taken by the High Organ that Nelson would be our spokesman and that position continued until we parted in 1982 when he and four others were transferred from Robben Island to Pollsmoor [prison]." Mbeki describes as hazy his recollection that Joe Gqabi, Wilton Mkwayi, and Michael Dingake may have been among those who constituted the later High Organs. (Letter from Mbeki to Karis, September 4, 1995).

38. Letter from Kathrada to Karis, April 6, 1996. See Neville Alexander, *Robben Island Dossier 1964–1974* (Cape Town: University of Cape Town Press, 1994), pp. 15 and 27, and interview of Butler with Maharaj.

39. Helen Suzman, *In No Uncertain Terms: A South African Memoir* (New York: Alfred A. Knopf, 1993), pp. 149–65.

40. Quoted in the Robben Island research papers of Fran Buntman. Interviews with Dikgang Moseneke (August 1979) and Moseneke and George Mukalake (July 1980).

41. From transcript of "Robben Island: Our University," a film by Lindy Wilson, excerpted in Tom Lodge and Bill Nasson, *All, Here, and Now: Black Politics in South Africa in the 1980s* (New York: Ford Foundation and Foreign Policy Association, 1991), p. 301.

42. Matthews manuscript, 1990.

43. See Nathan Shamuyarira, "The Dangers of the Lusaka Manifesto," *The African Review* (Dar es Salaam), vol. 1, no. 1, March 1971. The Manifesto is reproduced in Martin Minoque and Judith Malloy, eds., *African Aims and Attitudes: Selected Documents* (London: Cambridge University Press, 1974), pp. 267–73.

44. Matthews drafted the NEC's report on the situation inside South Africa, the organizational plan, and an analysis amplifying the Freedom Charter. Nokwe drafted the international report. At a meeting of the coordinating committee, Tambo expressed "considerable misgivings," in Matthews' words, about the international report because "the language was so Marxist and sounded more like the report of a European rather than that of an African freedom fighter." But Tambo did not suggest altering the report, and it remained as drafted by Nokwe.

45. The ANC's constitution did not limit membership to Africans, but only a few non-Africans ever became members during the years of legality. Opening ANC membership to non-Africans in exile was cleared with the leaders on Robben Island. It was also approved in principle before Tambo left South Africa. Conversation with Oliver Tambo (March 1991).

46. Tambo was elected deputy president in 1958 and became acting president after the death of Lutuli. He rejected an NEC proposal that he assume Lutuli's title, believing that such an action was a policy decision that had to be agreed upon by the leaders on Robben Island. Conversation with Tambo. He accepted the title of president in 1977.

47. Howard Barrell, "The Turn to the Masses: the African National Congress' Strategic Review of 1978–79," *Journal of Southern African Studies*, vol. 18, no. 1, March 1992, p. 71.

48. "The Road to South African Freedom," in *South African Communists Speak: Documents from the History of the South African Communist Party, 1915–1980* (London: Inkululeko Publications, 1981), p. 314.

49. "The Party Triumphant" is the title of chapter 3, Ellis and Sechaba, which deals with the period 1969–1975. This pioneering book has the ring of authenticity; but in the absence of documentation, its detail is open to question. Although the book contains judgments about the party's "control" of the ANC, its discussion is often more subtle. The authors recognize that after 1960 the identity of the ANC, the SACP, and Umkhonto became "blurred" and that (p. 6) the three "effectively merged to the point that it became difficult to define the three separately." Yet they were still separate.

50. Document 20.

51. Sol Dubula [Joe Slovo], "The Two Pillars of Our Struggle: Reflections on the Relationship between the ANC and SACP," *The African Communist*, no. 87, fourth quarter, 1981, p. 30.

52. On the position of the NEC in June 1961 see *From Protest to Challenge*, volume 3, pp. 648–51, and conversation with Mhlaba.

53. Shula Marks and Stanley Trapido, "Introduction" to special issue on the social history of resistance in South Africa, *Journal of Southern African Studies,* vol. 18, no. 1, March 1992, p. 3.

54. Joe Slovo, extracts from a speech about J. B. Marks in March 1983, *The African Communist,* no. 95, fourth quarter, 1983, p. 89. See also Dubula, "The Two Pillars of Our Struggle," p. 31.

55. Marks and Trapido, p. 3. Their suggestion was elicited by the analysis of David Everatt, "Alliance Politics of a Special Type: the Roots of the ANC/SACP Alliance, 1950–1954," *Journal of Southern African Studies,* vol. 18, no. 1, March 1992.

56. Anonymous source.

57. Conversation with Mhlaba. Mthembu turned state witness in the Rivonia trial and was later assassinated. The first woman to receive military ("self defence") training in the Soviet Union was Ruth Mompati. Conversation with Mompati (March 1989).

58. After Fischer's death, Francis Wilson, a Christian liberal, wrote in *South African Outlook,* May 1975, pp. 67–68: "Everybody, right across the political spectrum from far left to far right, acknowledges (especially if they are sure that nobody is listening to them) that he was one of the most marvelous of men. His warmth, his integrity, his courtesy, his concern for any individual cast a spell on practically everybody who ever met him, however much they disagreed with his political views. . . . [T]he real tragedy is not that Bram Fischer was a communist, but that so many Christians in South Africa are Stalinists."

59. "Statement Issued as a Result of Statement Appearing in Hsinhuas of 21 & 22 June, 1966," signed by the ANC, Frelimo, the Idea Popular de la Guinea Ecuatorial, and ZAPU, Cairo, June 24, 1966. The statements released through Hsinhua News Agency of Beijing came from the Bechuanaland Peoples' Party, the Basutoland Congress Party, the PAC, the South West African National Union and the Swaziland Progressive Party.

60. "Statement by the ANC (SA) on the Situation in Czechoslovakia, 9/19/1968." In a conversation with Tambo in Lusaka in 1968, Karis recalls Tambo's response when asked about a pro-Soviet statement by the ANC. It was a wink and a smile and a statement that he had to remember the welfare of the men in the camps.

61. "Address by John Marks," *International Meeting of Communist and Workers' Parties,* Moscow, 1969 (Prague: Peace and Socialism Publishers, 1969), pp. 666–72.

62. Makatini assured Okhela members that they had the approval of top elements in the ANC but were not to mention the organization's existence to rank and file members. At one point, Tambo himself came to address them secretly. Lawrence Weschler, "An Afrikaner Dante," *The New Yorker,* November 8, 1993, p. 84.

63. Breyten Breytenbach, *The True Confessions of an Albino Terrorist* (New York: Farrar Straus Giroux, 1983), pp. 383–90, reproduces "Okhela Manifesto, Draft proposal submitted to militants for comment and/or amendment, Paris, June 1975," pp. 383–90.

64. Weschler, p. 92. Breytenbach was tried a second time in May 1977 while serving his first sentence. The second trial was a bizarre effort by the state to prosecute him for recruiting a young warder into Okhela, smuggling letters out of prison, and making terrorist plans. He was acquitted (except for smuggling letters) and fined R50. One of his lawyers in the second trial found him "a childlike character, brilliant and naive at the same time." Conversation with Ernie Wentzel (July 1980).

65. David Beresford, *Sunday Times,* April 10, 1977.

66. South African Liberation Support Committee (SALSCOM), *Towards an Understanding of the Role of Whites in the South African Struggle* (pamphlet, London, early 1978), and Horst Kleinschmidt, ed., *White Liberation: A Collection of Essays* (Johannesburg: Spro-cas 2, 1972). One of Okhela's members, Bill Anderson, provides an example of a non-doctrinaire white seeking a role in the liberation struggle. He deserted from the South African army, joined Okhela but became disillusioned with it and broke away to form SALSCOM, which was critical of the ANC and sought to build an alternative to it. But later Anderson changed course again and became active in ANC military intelligence. Interview of Howard Barrell with Bill Anderson (April 1990). See also Ronnie Kasrils, *"Armed and Dangerous": My Undercover Struggle against Apartheid* (Oxford: Heinemann, 1993), pp. 261–63, and conversation with David Sibeko (June 1979).

67. Conversation with Seretse Choabi (April 1989).

68. The only other expulsion of a dissident group involved the "Marxist Workers' Tendency within the ANC" (MWT), led by four South African whites in Britain—Rob Peterson, Paula Ensor, Martin Legassick, and David Hemson—whose background was either in academia or black trade union activity. Influenced by the thinking of Trotsky, they criticized the SACP's Stalinism, its two-stage theory, and guerrilla warfare. SACTU, they argued, should not be a recruiting agent for Umkhonto but should concentrate on building mass trade unions and arming the workers. In October 1979 the ANC in London suspended the group. They were expelled in 1985 but continued to regard the MWT as being within the ANC. See ANC "Resolutions Adopted by the Second National Consultative Conference," June 16–23, 1985, p. 51; "Conference Expels 'Left-wing' Deviationists," *Sechaba*, August 1985, pp. 18–24; and Martin Legassick, "The Past and Present Role of the Marxist Workers' Tendency of the ANC," in Ian Liebenberg, Fiona Lortan, Bobby Nel, and Gert van der Westhuizen, eds., *The Long March: The Story of the Struggle for Liberation in South Africa* (Pretoria: HAUM, 1994), pp. 173–86. The MWT had an intellectual influence but never won an organized popular following. Legassick (p. 173) claimed that from the MWT's emergence, "most of its supporters have been black."

69. *The African Nationalist,* December 1976, p. 30. Also see *Maluti: Official Journal of the African National Congress (African Nationalists)* vol. 2, nos. 2/3, 1978, p. 9. The opening editorial of this issue refers to "the power of certain White ethnic groups" [Jews?], p. 3.

70. Themba Mqota [Alfred Kgokong], "A Man of the People," part of "Invitation and Programme for the Unveiling of the Tombstone of the late Robert M. Resha," pp. 4–6.

71. Conversations with Pascal Ngakane (October 1977 and March 1989).

72. "Draft Resolutions of the Meeting of African Members of the A. N. C. resident in the U. K. held on January 4th, 1975 at the Co-op Hall, 129 Seven Sisters Road, London N.7."

73. Conversation with Tambo (March 1991).

74. Interview of Howard Barrell with Mac Maharaj (November 1990).

75. *The African Nationalist,* vol. 1, no. 1, November 1976, p. 21.

76. *Maluti,* vol. 2, nos. 2/3, 1978, p. 7.

77. Conversation with Tambo (March 1991).

78. Letter from "David Smith" [Thami Bonga] to "Richard Mnguni" [Tennyson Makiwane] and "Marcus du Preez" [Pascal Ngakane], September 21, 1978.

79. The report on the meeting in the ANC's official organ, *Sechaba,* February 1972, highlighted the appearance of Chief Lutuli's widow, who opened the convention. "This in itself was an act of defiance by the new leadership of the NIC."

80. Press Statement, Committee for Clemency (S. A.), signed by Mewa Ramgobin, February 25, 1971. Among the other members of the Committee, eight were white (six liberals and two on the political left, Richard Turner and David Hemson), five Indians, including Dr. M. B. Naidoo of the South African Indian Council, and an African lawyer. Conversation with Mewa Ramgobin (July 1989).

81. *The World,* May 5, 1971.

82. George Sewpersadh, president of the revived NIC, expressed the prevailing argument against making membership nonracial. Because government policy had separated the races for years, "it would be difficult and unwise, at this stage, to form an organisation representing all the races." Winning "massive support" would be unlikely, and even Indian support might be lost. "Natal Indian Congress—The Significance of Its revival," *Reality,* May 1972. Nevertheless, in 1974 "Indian" was dropped from the membership clause of the constitution but to little effect. The NIC operated within the Indian community, and only two or three non-Indians joined, including Archie Gumede, a pro-ANC leader. Conversation with M. J. Naidoo (December 1989).

83. Conversation with Saths Cooper (October 1972).

84. M. J. Naidoo, Presidential Address, March 26, 1976.

85. According to M. J. Naidoo and R. Ramesar, the NIC had no money, not even dues, and the leaders paid expenses out of their own pockets. Conversation (May 1977).

86. Secretarial Report by R. Ramesar to the Natal Indian Congress, November 18, 1978.

87. The PAC made an original contribution to political language, however: the use of

"Azania" as a new name for South Africa. Peter Raboroko, while in Ghana in 1961–1962, published an article using "Azania," a term with ancient etymological roots. When asked to edit a news bulletin in late 1965, he chose *Azania News* as the title and (Peter 'Molotsi has said) "no one took him to task." Conversations with Peter 'Molotsi (1977) and P. L. M. Gqobose (April 1990). By April 1966, the PAC began to refer to itself as the "PAC of Azania (South Africa)." "Viva Azania!" was heard during the Soweto uprising. Its appropriation by black consciousness organizations, which were eclectic in their borrowing of evocative terms, and its use by some supporters of the ANC, for example, Winnie Mandela, gave it such wide currency by the late 1970s that it was no longer necessarily identified with the PAC. The ANC argued that the name's historical connotations were anti-black (land of slaves rather than blackman's country) and that any new name should be popularly chosen after South Africa was free. See "The Real Meaning of 'Azania': Time for an end to the Myth," *Sechaba,* third quarter 1977, p. 64. Meanwhile, SASO's Barney Pityana observed that "Azania" had become an accepted term "and the ANC must get used to it." Conversation with Pityana (May 1979). See Motsoko Pheko, *Apartheid: The Story of a Dispossessed People* (London: Marram Books, revised ed., 1984), p. 107; David Dube, *The Rise of Azania: The Fall of South Africa* (Lusaka: Daystar Publications, 1983), pp. 43–45; and letter from 'Molotsi to Karis, October 29, 1977. Etymologies are discussed in Peter Dreyer, *Martyrs and Fanatics: South Africa and Human Destiny* (New York: Simon and Schuster, 1980), pp. 215–21.

88. Gail M. Gerhart, *Black Power in South Africa: The Evolution of an Ideology* (Berkeley: University of California Press, 1978), p. 253. Africans in the PAC argued that the difference between "PAC" and "Poqo" was only linguistic and that "Um-Afrika Poqo" meant "Pan Africanist Congress" in Xhosa. Conversation with T. T. Letlaka, Z. B. Molete, A. B. Ngcobo, and Peter Raboroko (September 1968).

89. According to the biographer of Patrick Duncan, the first white member of the PAC, "To his opponents, Leballo was simply an extremist, power-hungry, spendthrift, divisive in politics, a womanizer, disloyal to his subordinates; to those who, like Duncan, respected him, he was brave, intelligent, and a charismatic leader of ordinary people." C. Jonty Driver, *Patrick Duncan: South African and Pan-African* (London: Heinemann, 1980), p. 223. According to Leballo and John Pokela in "Background to official appointments and policy statement," June 20, 1964, Sobukwe appointed Molete acting president with effect from September 1960 and later appointed Leballo as acting president. The President, according to Leballo and Pokela, had "absolute dictatorial powers . . . during all [the] time the movement is banned and in revolution." Letlaka argued that Sobukwe had not delegated emergency powers to Leballo. "The Aftermath of the Moshi Conference within the Pan Africanist Congress," January 1968, pp. 7–11. For the PAC constitution, see *From Protest to Challenge,* volume 3, pp. 524–30.

90. Benjamin Pogrund, *How Can Man Die Better . . . Sobukwe and Apartheid* (New Brunswick: Rutgers University Press, and London: Peter Halban, 1991), p. 349.

91. Peter Raboroko, "Report on the South African Revolution, Part II, Forces of Subversion," November 2, 1968, p. 15.

92. "Pan Africanist Congress of Azania (S. A.), Report of National Executive Committee Meeting, Moshi, Tanzania, 19th to 22nd September, 1967," issued by the Department of Publicity and Information, Lusaka. The preparatory meetings and participants are described in a "Communique," pp. 1–2.

93. In "Report of the Treasurer-General to the Commission of Inquiry Set Up by Moshi Meeting (19–21 September, 1967) of the National Executive Committee of the Pan Africanist Congress of South Africa," September 27, 1967, Ngcobo detailed the whole "sordid" story of irregularities. "The total amount of monies that have not been accounted for staggers the imagination." A "piquant example" of expenditure without his knowledge was the order by Leballo of "some trousseau at Jan Mahomed's Outfitters, Independence Avenue, Dar es Salaam, comprising perfumes, perfume sprayers, brocade material, and ladies' undergarments."

94. Potlako Leballo, "P. A. C. Re-organisation Conference, Moshi—September 1967."

95. Z. B. Molete and T. T. Letlaka, "A Clarion Call to All Members of the National Executive Committee, Representatives, Functionaries, Cadres and General Members of the Pan Africanist Congress of Azania (S. A.) Abroad," April 2, 1968, p. 2.

96. Z. B. Molete, "The Grand Epilogue—A Sequel to Leballo's Expulsion," [after September 22, 1968].

97. Potlako Leballo, "Press Statement," June 11, 1968; Leballo, "Public Statement," June 20, 1968.

98. Extracts from the record of the Court of Appeal, July 23, 1971, are in "The Call for Unity and a United Front," issued by the ANC (1972?).

99. "Draft Proposal for a New Strategy of the African National Congress," November 1970.

100. Kasrils, pp. 112–13 and Kasrils, "The Adventure Episode," *Dawn,* Souvenir Issue, 1986, p. 43. A fuller account is in the interview of Howard Barrell with Ronnie Kasrils (October 1990). Two teams of three persons each were set to receive the guerrillas and to dig caches and transport the men elsewhere. Joe Slovo (from whom "Operation J" took its name) later recalled that the yacht was bought for £75,000. "It was towed eventually into Mombasa [and] bought by a Kenyan cabinet minister to transform it into a night club." Conversation with Slovo.

101. There is evidence that Radio Freedom influenced the thinking of many young people to become active in the underground and to leave for military training. Conversations with Sibusiso Ndebele (December 1989), Johnny Issel (December 1989) and Stone Sizane (May 1990).

102. "Last Journey to Groutville," *Sechaba,* December 1967; conversation with Nkosazana Dlamini Zuma (July 1988); Alan Paton, *Reality,* September 1972.

103. Information on underground propaganda has been drawn from the interview of Barrell with Kasrils; Kasrils, pp. 114–16; conversation with Jeremy Cronin (October 1993); Tim Jenkin, *Escape from Pretoria* (London: Kliptown Books, 1987); "Statement to defence counsel by Charles Anthony David Holiday," 1976; and *The African Communist,* no. 56, first quarter, 1974, pp. 15–16. *Sechaba* (the Nation) began publication as a monthly in January 1967, and *Amandla-Matla* (Power), an ANC newsletter, in 1972. The Communist Party's *Inkululeko* (Freedom) began in July 1971.

104. See Raymond Suttner, speech from the dock, *The African Communist,* no. 65, second quarter, 1976, pp. 83–89. Suttner's mother, Sheila Suttner, was active in the Human Rights Committee, a front for the ANC, formed by a multiracial group in September 1974, to call for the release of detainees and political prisoners. See *HRC Bulletin,* April 1975.

105. See Emma Gilbey, *The Lady: The Life and Times of Winnie Mandela* (London: Jonathan Cape, 1993), pp. 71ff.

106. See Gonville ffrench-Beytagh, *Encountering Darkness* (London: Collins, 1973), and *The State v. The Dean of Johannesburg* (Johannesburg: South African Institute of Race Relations, 1972).

107. See *State v. Kader Hassim,* 1971–1972, and conversation with Kader Hassim (December 1989).

108. Sonny Venkatrathnam, an ally of Hassim who served six years, said in his testimony (p. 5,603) that the Unity Movement "was a complete shambles by the end of 1964, beginning of 1965" whereas up to early 1964 "normal APDUSA activities" continued, for example, house meetings, the distribution and publication of literature, and boycotts. Kader Hassim and Karrim Essack, his brother, belonged to different factions within APDUSA. Hassim criticized his brother for "virtually preaching racialism by elevating the African sector over and above all other sectors." *State v. Kader Hassim,* p. 4,908. Essack left South Africa in the mid-1960s and wrote *The Armed Struggle* (Dar es Salaam: Thakers Ltd., 1976), which celebrated "revolutionary violence."

109. Indictment in *State v. Sexwale* ("the Pretoria 12"), discussed in Glenn Moss, *Political Trials: South Africa: 1976–1979* (Johannesburg: Development Studies Group Information Publication 2, University of the Witwatersrand, June 1979), p. 3.

3. Above-Ground Multiracial Opposition

South Africans involved in underground political activity faced formidable risks by the mid-1960s, yet people who sought to oppose government policies openly, using methods that were entirely legal, also faced obstacles that were often insurmountable. Every liberal or multiracial organization that was engaged in more than token opposition to National Party policies found itself the target of government harassment, and some groups and individuals endured almost constant obstruction and intimidation. With its majority in Parliament unassailable, the National Party was willing formally to tolerate the ineffectual parliamentary opposition parties, only one of which, the tiny Progressive Party, stood for any serious alternatives to official apartheid policies.[1] Outside the bounds of parliamentary politics, however, the Nationalists adopted an attitude of suspicion and belligerence toward all voices challenging the status quo, particularly if such voices had agitational overtones and in any way hinted at potential links between activist white dissent and mass black grievances.

The Onslaught on Dissent

Among the government's prominent but relatively moderate critics were the English language press, the liberal South African Institute of Race Relations, and the Black Sash, an organization of white women established in the 1950s to protest the National Party's disregard for the rule of law. The English press, which for the most part confined itself to the same conservative parameters of debate and definitions of patriotism that were observed in parliament, was a needling voice but rarely a genuinely threatening one. Its one success in exposing major government malfeasance—the Information Department scandal in 1978—shook the National Party briefly and accelerated the momentum of reforms already underway, but resulted in no lasting diminution of National Party power.[2] Disinclined to question fundamental assumptions of white supremacy, and restricted by loosely-defined laws from reporting on matters defined as vital to state security (including prison conditions, police conduct, and military matters), the English press in the 1960s and 1970s was largely self-policing. More questioning but less influential in relation to white public opinion, the liberal Institute of Race Relations and Black Sash were usually ignored by the government when carrying out their functions as welfare and research organizations, but subjected to harassment and intimidation whenever their members crossed the line between these pursuits and activities regarded as openly political. By the end of the 1970s, the Institute of Race Relations had fended off an effort by younger staff members to radicalize its elitist approach, and was maintaining its stolidly non-activist position.[3] The Black Sash welcomed input by younger members during the 1960s and 1970s and gradually broadened its field of operations beyond the running of legal advice centers for working-class Africans to include more aggressive public education campaigns on a range of human rights issues. For the most part, however, these three organized expressions of liberal dissent represented no immediate challenge to National Party power: none were openly supportive of the outlawed black liberation movements or of the foreign proponents of economic sanctions, and none were involved in building up an independent black political capacity for resistance.

What the National Party government under Prime Minister John Vorster (1966–1978) was determined to stamp out was any political activity by Africans directed at the goal of majority rule, and any organized effort by non-Africans to act in support of this goal. Where whites of such description were concerned, the government's objective after Rivonia was to silence all radical voices, and if possible to force vocal opponents to leave the country. Outspoken foreign church personnel were regularly expelled when their visas came up for renewal. Police harassed and tapped the phones of whites engaged in welfare work through the Defence and Aid Fund, an organization set up in the late 1950s to assist the families of political prisoners and trial defendants. By the time the Fund was declared illegal in March 1966, many of its activists had emigrated. Liberal-minded professionals were visited by security police who hinted darkly that any activities that assisted "communists" would be regarded by the state as criminal. In the early 1970s, a government panel, the Schlebusch (later Le Grange) Commission, was appointed to study the activities of prominent white liberal organizations with the aim of cutting off foreign funding to any that were discovered to be "subversive." After several years of contentious investigation, one organization (the Institute of Race Relations) was declared nonsubversive, one (the University Christian Movement) disbanded itself before the Commission's findings were announced, two (the National Union of South African Students and the Christian Institute of Southern Africa) were barred from receiving foreign funds, and later one, the Christian Institute, was banned.

Where Africans were concerned, the state's objective was to eliminate all hard-core resistance and thereby clear the political arena for a new type of pliant black leadership which would cooperate with the National Party's plan to partition South Africa geographically into white and black ethnic spheres. Although some Africans of activist disposition were willing to experiment with the "separate development" politics of tribally defined local advisory bodies and homelands, most rejected the Nationalists' proposed new deal. But where were the rejectionists to direct their political energies? Outside the collaborationist structures being created by government, opportunities for legal participation in politics were few. In the face of the state's campaign of intimidation, attempts by blacks to organize open oppositional activity came to a virtual standstill after Rivonia.

Some blacks found a political home in the Liberal and Progressive Parties, which enrolled members of all races even though whites alone could vote and stand as parliamentary candidates. The Liberal Party after 1960 stood for universal adult suffrage, while the Progressives favored a qualified franchise and enrolled black members in two different categories, depending on whether or not they met the proposed qualifications of income and education.[4] A few blacks were elected to national positions in the Liberal Party, but both the Liberals and Progressives were perceived by blacks as white-led parties with no serious prospect of becoming rallying points for black resistance. Liberals were increasingly restricted by individual banning orders and painted as subversive by the government after a dozen or so party members were implicated in the sabotage activities of the African Resistance Movement in 1964. When the Prohibition of Political Interference Act of 1968 made multiracial political parties illegal, the Liberals decided to disband rather than comply. The Progressives, who had never given up hope of becoming a force in parliamentary politics, chose to continue as an all-white party. From 1961 to 1974 they succeeded in returning only one member to parliament, Helen Suzman, who represented an affluent suburb of northern Johannesburg. She regularly voiced spirited objections to the discriminatory laws and administrative practices under which blacks suffered, and her efforts contributed to the lingering hope felt by some blacks that white South Africans, through debate among themselves, might eventually decide to abandon apartheid.

Outside the politics of parliamentary parties, a small number of younger Africans in the early 1960s made cautious attempts to keep alive the traditions of the banned liberation movements through student-based associations. In Durban in December 1961, university students inclined toward the ANC formed the African Students' Association (ASA). A comparable PAC-oriented grouping called the African Students' Union of South Africa (ASUSA) also emerged at about the same time. Efforts by both groups to attract high school students were only sporadic. Both groups lacked financial resources, a perennial handicap of African organizations. Neither ASA nor ASUSA enrolled more than a small formal membership, and their leaders suffered regular police harassment. Similarly lacking in funds and ineffectual as anything more than discussion groups were several small student organizations oriented towards the Trotskyist Non-European Unity Movement, including the Durban Students' Union, the Cape Peninsula Students' Union, and the Society of Young Africa (SOYA). By the time the underground liberation movements were decimated in the mid-1960s, these student groupings had gone the way of ASA and ASUSA and been effectively extinguished.

The sweeping powers of the security police and the bullying manner in which its officers arrested, detained, and interrogated scores of people, often on the flimsiest pretexts, induced widespread anger but also fear. Evidence emerged of the growing presence of police informers on university campuses, in welfare and religious organizations, and in township shebeens (illegal bars). Even in African homes, most parents treated politics and the history of the resistance movements as taboo subjects in the belief that this would protect their children from the risks of political involvement. As the average living standard of urban blacks inched upwards during the economic boom of the 1960s, it was possible to take refuge in vague hopes of gradual change. A sullen silence descended on black political life, broken only intermittently by the barely audible verbal protests emanating from liberal whites.

The National Union of South African Students

During the brief life span of ASA and ASUSA, students from the black universities also continued to take part in the activities of the multiracial National Union of South African Students (NUSAS).[5] The core constituency of NUSAS was in the white English-language universities, and most of its national leadership was drawn from the Students' Representative Councils of the Universities of the Witwatersrand, Cape Town and Natal, and Rhodes University in Grahamstown in the eastern Cape. The majority of students on these campuses were as apolitical or conservative as the rest of the country's white population, but the students who became leaders in NUSAS tended to be liberals strongly opposed to apartheid. As leaders, they welcomed the participation in NUSAS of students from African, Coloured and Indian centers of higher education, though these students were always a minority of the membership. Whites, who were 19 percent of South Africa's population in the mid-1960s, made up over 90 percent of those studying in post-secondary institutions.[6]

Because NUSAS became the seedbed in which a potent strain of black nationalism was to germinate in the late 1960s, a brief consideration of its historical development is useful. NUSAS was founded in 1924, and in its early years served as a forum for association between white students at the country's English and Afrikaans-language universities. From the mid-1930s, the Afrikaans campuses began to withdraw under the influence of Afrikaner nationalists who were intensifying the drive for a more exclusionary definition of Afrikaner identity. In the same period, radical English-speaking whites at the opposite end of the political spectrum pushed for admission of the black University College of Fort Hare to NUSAS, a proposal which accelerated the departure of the Afrikaner students. Each year, the national officers of NUSAS threaded their way along a middle path between the desire to maintain at least minimal fraternal relations with the Afrikaans campuses, and a growing belief that black students should be represented in the organization.

After the National Party's victory in the 1948 general election, the lingering hope of eventual reunification between English and Afrikaner students receded, and the central focus of debate in NUSAS shifted to tension on the English-language campuses between the liberal urge to involve NUSAS in the wider issues of national politics, and the conservative view that the organization should confine itself solely to student matters. By the end of the 1950s the liberals had prevailed, largely because of student reaction against the perversely-named Extension of Universities Act of 1959. This law barred further admission of blacks to the nominally nonracial ("open") English universities—where only a tiny but symbolically important number, academically integrated but socially segregated, had ever managed to enroll in any case. The Act instead provided for the establishment of segregated universities for Indians, Coloureds and Africans, with Africans in turn divided along linguistic lines.

NUSAS zealously petitioned and demonstrated against the threatened imposition of university apartheid, despite menacing denunciations from government ministers. The more stubbornly the state emphasized racial and ethnic differentiation, the more NUSAS policy came to reflect a liberal counter-ideology that insisted that racial differences were of no importance. Many Indian and Coloured students felt drawn to this common society liberalism. Admiration for the militancy of NUSAS also spread among African students, especially those looking for new forms of political expression after the banning of the ANC and PAC in April 1960. By the time the June 1964 Rivonia verdict brought African resistance to its historical nadir, NUSAS, with significant black support, had become the country's single most outspoken extraparliamentary group opposing apartheid policies.

Black students in NUSAS were few, but they exercised a strong pull on the opinions of the organization's white leaders, who felt altruistically drawn to the vision of liberation and equality which was of such compelling urgency to blacks. Most black students saw NUSAS as too moderate, despite the inclination of its leaders to take public positions well to the left of mainstream white opinion. Black skepticism acted as a further goad to white NUSAS leaders to demonstrate their commitment in action as well as words. As NUSAS became more vocal in criticizing government measures like 90-day detention, the organization also moved quietly to initiate action projects such as assistance to political prisoners and their families. Students graduating out of activist roles in NUSAS looked for new ways to express their rejection of government policies: some emigrated, some became active in liberal organizations, and a handful—including a former NUSAS president, Adrian Leftwich—secretly joined the African Resistance Movement (ARM).

The dilemmas of white student radicalism and its romantic dreams of an alliance with black militancy were reflected in a crisis that seized NUSAS early in 1964 while the Rivonia trial was still in progress. At a student conference in Dar es Salaam, Tanganyika, the NUSAS delegate, Martin Legassick, was confronted by the passage of a resolution condemning NUSAS for being unrepresentative of South Africa's black majority. Shaken by this rejection, Legassick wrote at length to NUSAS president Jonty Driver, proposing ways of cutting NUSAS free from its conservative moorings on white campuses and restructuring it as an arm of the banned liberation movements. Debate over the organization's future intensified in NUSAS leadership circles as black students, including Mewa Ramgobin, an Indian member of the NUSAS executive committee, pressed for a more radical stance. In April 1964 at a NUSAS leadership training seminar at Botha's Hill in Natal, Driver delivered a discussion paper reviewing the debate (*Document 23*).

Driver embraced the radical position in principle, but rejected the specific reorganization proposals put forward by the radicals on the grounds that these would fatally weaken the organization. He agreed that the political work of NUSAS was much more important than its purely student-based activities such as discount schemes and student loans. Ideally, he argued, NUSAS should be lead by Africans, or at least guided by their views; practically speaking, however, this could not come about democratically because African university students were vastly outnumbered by whites.

Driver rejected the proposal that NUSAS drop the system of "center affiliation" under which campuses voted whether to affiliate to NUSAS, then dues were automatically charged to every student at affiliated campuses, giving the organization a strong financial base. The alternative to center affiliation was a system of voluntary individual membership that pertained on unaffiliated campuses. The latter produced a membership which was much more politically committed, but also much smaller and less able to generate substantial funds. Legassick and other radicals advocated a switch to individual membership on all campuses, in part because blacks might become a majority within the smaller organization that would result. A NUSAS thus transformed could assume the role of intellectual vanguard in the liberation struggle; it could be freer to recruit politically dedicated white activists, to work in close liaison with the underground ANC, and if necessary even shift its operational base abroad. Driver disagreed with these proposals on the grounds that any attempt to implement them would bring about the certain collapse of the organization. When the issues were put to the participants at the Botha's Hill seminar, the radical position was rejected.

The matter did not end there, however. Driver's speech was leaked to the National Party press, which reported Legassick's ideas and some of Driver's comments as if they were official NUSAS policy. Pamphlets by conservative students were circulated on white campuses alleging that NUSAS had declared itself a wing of the liberation movement and was preparing to go underground. White student opinion reacted with a sharp turn to the right.

Disaffiliation movements gathered momentum on several campuses until July when the reaction subsided after the annual NUSAS congress voted by a large majority to censure Driver for the recklessness of his Botha's Hill speech. For the next few years the organization swung back toward its customary centrist position while still maintaining a strong rhetorical opposition to government encroachments on academic freedom and civil liberties.

Where the average white student drew back from radicalism, many African students were increasingly attracted by the reputation of NUSAS when this was reinforced by the Botha's Hill episode and by the July 1964 arrests of ARM members, some of whom were former NUSAS activists. Vitriolic attacks on NUSAS by John Vorster, Verwoerd's minister of justice and later his successor as prime minister, also added to its positive image among blacks. The Nationalists, who were always looking for opportunities to paint their critics as communist-inspired or moved by violent intent, exploited the white reaction against Driver's speech to the full, labeling NUSAS a "camouflaged Communist Party."[7] New laws to curb NUSAS activities were promised, and its office bearers were punished with a stepped up barrage of detentions, bans, passport withdrawals, and where technicalities presented an opportunity, deportations. To discourage liberal ideas from spreading to black campuses, the student bodies at Turfloop, Fort Hare and the University of Zululand at Ngoye were forbidden to affiliate to NUSAS, a prohibition which naturally only enhanced the appeal of participation. Clandestine branches were formed on an individual membership basis, and protests periodically occurred against the ban on center affiliation by the black universities. By the late 1960s, African involvement in NUSAS had risen from the token levels of the 1950s to a point where as much as a quarter to a third of the delegates at annual conferences were black.

While there was no practical prospect of NUSAS itself becoming African-led, the organization's methods of operation nevertheless became an important contributing factor in the emergence of a new approach to leadership among Africans. NUSAS differed from the normal voluntary organization in that its membership was constantly changing. The average student in the South African university system obtained a bachelor's degree in three or four years and moved on. As a consequence, the leadership of NUSAS was passed down annually to a new crop of students, with members of the national executive only occasionally serving for more than one year. This rapid turnover necessitated an efficient leadership recruitment and training system, and one was well established by the time the significant influx of black students into NUSAS began in the 1960s.

Each winter vacation, which falls in July in the southern hemisphere, NUSAS held its annual student congress at which delegations from all campuses and branches came together for a week of speeches, policy discussions, and social get-togethers. Election of national officers would take place for the upcoming academic year (running from January to December), usually with the candidates from the largest campuses, Cape Town and the

University of the Witwatersrand in Johannesburg, predominating. An inter-mingling of older and younger students would occur in which the leadership soon to graduate would scout out prospective talent for Students' Represen-tative Councils (SRCs), campus newspapers, and various NUSAS committees. The scouting would continue among the freshmen entering in January, and during the next short vacation in April or May, NUSAS would hold its national training seminar, to which new activists in campus local committees would be selectively invited, sometimes after first participating in local or regional seminars. By the late 1960s, when the dues-paying membership of NUSAS was about 20,000 and there were local campus committees at over 20 colleges and universities, the national training seminars drew 60 to 100 recruits who met together with the older leadership for several days of intense discussions, debate, and instruction in organizational skills. By the convening of the next July congress, the formation was well underway of a new cohort of national NUSAS leaders, linked by contacts between cam-puses, and cultivated through bonds of friendship with more experienced older students.

This pattern, in which each set of student leaders almost immediately began to reproduce itself and induct its successors into the procedures of organizing and policy-making, was suited to the needs of an organization with a constantly changing membership. The pattern was also ideally suited to the needs of an organization under attack from a government with the power to incapacitate individual leaders through bans and deportations. In the short run, an understudy could be prepared to replace every office-holder; in the longer run, the ability of the organization to spread its influence throughout the society was enormously enhanced by the rapid graduation of large numbers of activists through the skills-training and political socialization process that characterized the NUSAS leadership cycle. In the early 1970s, the black consciousness movement was to adopt and utilize this process to great advantage, and Steve Biko and Barney Pityana, the movement's principal founders, owed to it a measure of their own successful leadership styles.

In other respects, NUSAS exposed African students to experiences which had a much more ambiguous impact. Being in a minority meant accepting the reality of white control and the inevitability that the NUSAS national agenda would predominantly reflect white student concerns. Even where black students could exert persuasive pressure on national NUSAS leaders behind the scenes, the leadership was ultimately obliged to work out compromises that would leave the moderate student base of its support intact. Only one African successfully ran for election to a high national office—Thami Mhlambiso, who served as NUSAS vice president in 1961–62. Sometimes black students who took part in representing NUSAS found themselves used as tokens of white liberal enlightenment more than as spokesmen in their own right for the country's black majority.

At the psychological level, the dynamics of black-white interaction were complicated, as the writings of Biko were later to attest. Many white students who were drawn into participation in NUSAS harbored strong guilt feelings toward blacks and were anxious to prove that they were not racists. This emotional baggage traveled with them into their social contact with black students, causing much of their behavior to take the form of moral and political posturing. NUSAS opened to them, as well as to black students, a world that was otherwise almost unknown in South Africa at the time, in which white and black could meet as social equals to hold parties, debates, and freewheeling discussions about anything from popular culture to esoteric philosophy. White students usually dominated these discussions, which revolved as a result around topics central to their own middle-class lives. Consciously or otherwise, their tendency was to proceed from the paternalistic feeling, common to liberal and conservative whites alike, that what blacks needed or wanted was to assimilate whatever values, attitudes, and knowledge were presumed to account for the supposedly more "advanced" culture of whites. Invariably, as Biko later recalled, it was the blacks who did almost all the listening, often coming away with a reinforced sense of their own inferiority, but drawing comfort from the experience of being treated ostensibly as equals by the whites.

Not all whites in NUSAS uncritically embraced the liberal orthodoxy that racial and cultural differences were inconsequential. Driver in his Botha's Hill speech, for example, presciently urged NUSAS to move toward a new definition of nonracialism where the different values and needs of groups were acknowledged, and privileged whites agreed to accept leadership by the oppressed majority. In the emotionally beleaguered world of the white liberal student of the 1960s, however, this was wisdom not easily grasped. Thus when black students walked out of NUSAS to form their own blacks-only organization in 1969, the typical white student reaction was one of angry disbelief and wounded pride, particularly since the new South African Students' Organisation (SASO) seemed bent on identifying white liberals as a prime target for criticism. Where was the white activist to turn if rejected by the very people who ultimately stood to benefit most by NUSAS activism?

Several years of agonized soul-searching went by while NUSAS leaders tried to impress on white students the necessity to see themselves not as instruments of change but as "instrumental to change generated elsewhere."[8] Intellectually inquiring students, influenced by New Left currents in Europe and the United States, began turning to neo-Marxist social theories and searching for the roots of liberalism's failings in the history of western capitalism. One particularly influential catalyst in this process was Richard Turner, a charismatic young political science lecturer at the University of Natal in Durban. As an undergraduate, Turner had observed the futility of actions taken by students in the ARM; he had later been a doctoral student at the Sorbonne just before the French student uprising of 1968. He had concluded that students could be potent political players, but that their activism had to be informed by theories of social change far more radical than those of the average South African liberal.

The rupture between NUSAS and SASO created a situation where the force of Turner's personality and opinions intersected with the need among white student activists to find a new political identity and role. Turner was frequently invited to speak on white campuses and at NUSAS seminars, where his lucid analyses contributed both to the legitimation of black consciousness ideas and to the spread of philosophical radicalism among white students (*Document 27*). At the University of Natal, he inspired a circle of activists to begin investigating the conditions of black workers, first on the campus and later in the Durban municipality. These explorations combined data-gathering with representations before government Wage Boards and eventually, for a few dozen hard-core white student activists, direct participation in trade union organization and the education of black workers. Several other campuses, coordinated through NUSAS, established similar student Wages Commissions starting in 1971. By the time the government issued banning orders to Turner and seven NUSAS activists at the height of the Durban strikes in February 1973, a small but promising link had been forged between the nascent independent trade union movement and a young generation of radical whites who were ready to lend their skills and energy to the task of building black worker organizations.[9]

NUSAS in the meantime continued to run scholarship schemes for needy students, but also worked quietly to finance the books and fees of political prisoners taking courses by correspondence. Awareness campaigns that aimed at educating students about the policies of the National Party government still remained a central activity. In protest against enforced racial segregation in sports, NUSAS successfully campaigned at the Universities of Cape Town and the Witwatersrand to end the holding of all-white intervarsity games. Celebrations of the tenth anniversary of the Republic were targeted for protest in 1971. Rather than seeing these campaigns only as a means of enlightening a wide audience of potential liberals, NUSAS leaders increasingly hoped to use such activities to attract a dedicated cadre of student recruits who could be politicized and nurtured to become social activists after completion of their degrees. In the early 1970s, NUSAS was already a training ground for future personnel of the Black Sash, the Institute of Race Relations, the liberal press and the reviving black trade union movement; by the end of the decade it had also become a seedbed for a small but growing number of progressive educational and community organizations, public interest legal groups, and the radical fledgling alternative press.

Defiant in the face of the February 1973 bannings and the government's threat (later implemented) to prohibit it from receiving foreign funds, NUSAS in 1974 proposed a campaign for the release of political prisoners. Most campuses perceived this as too risky, but at the University of the Witwatersrand, plans went forward, culminating in the last week of May 1974 with rallies, speakers, leafleting, and an illegal demonstration in the streets adjacent to the university campus in Johannesburg. One of the campaign leaflets, the rally speech of 1950s veteran Helen Joseph, and a post-mortem assessment by student leader Glenn Moss (*Documents 28, 29* and *30*) offer an illuminating view of the campaign's organization and impact. Two years later, the events of the campaign were used by state prosecutors to try to prove charges of subversion ("furthering the aims" of the banned ANC and Communist Party) against Moss, three other NUSAS leaders, and a university lecturer—an effort which proved unsuccessful in court but temporarily put the survival of NUSAS still further at risk.[10]

By the late 1970s, the government's assaults on NUSAS and the perception among many students that the organization had moved too far to the left had brought white student dissent to a low point. All but a few campuses had voted against center affiliation, cutting still further into the organization's weakened financial base, while the NUSAS trial of 1976 had revealed the ubiquitous activities of police informers on the English campuses. Turning inward to focus again on less confrontational issues of identity and role, NUSAS in 1977 took up the theme of "White Consciousness" (*Document 32*), stressing the need for white students to identify with Africa and for white universities to reform their curriculums to make them relevant to South Africa's requirements as an African country. Belittling this new-found "White Africanism" as "a package deal of slogans, cliches and images which might have at one stage interested black students, but now would be considered irrelevant," members of the small but growing white left urged student intellectuals to put aside abstract reformulations of racial identity, white as well as black, in favor of a class-based ideology more relevant to South Africa's historical and political realities.[11]

The University Christian Movement

Meanwhile, onto the crisscrossing thoroughfares of church and student life in the late 1960s had come the University Christian Movement (UCM), an organization with an unconventional approach that was to make it a midwife of radical black politics in the decade to come.[12] Denominational student societies were a long-standing fixture on university campuses, as was the interdenominational Student Christian Association. In the post-Sharpeville period these groupings came under new pressure to declare their orientation toward secular issues including apartheid, political violence, and the gathering threat of foreign economic sanctions against South Africa. Some of this pressure was generated by the needs of black students who were facing the eclipse of all overtly political black organizations. Some of the pressure came from affiliated church bodies abroad. The Student Christian Association, organized at both high school and university levels into separate sections for Africans, Coloureds, English-speaking and Afrikaans-speaking whites, responded defensively to calls by the World Student Christian Federation to repudiate segregation. In 1964, the Student Christian Association withdrew from the Federation, and in the following year split into four separate bodies along racial lines. In 1967, after discussions between members of the multiracial Anglican and Catholic student federations and liberal remnants from the old Student Christian Association, the University Christian Movement was launched with the intent to revive interracial and ecumenical links among university students.

The main impetus for the formation of UCM came from a handful of liberal white clergymen, most of whom had served as university chaplains or were in the theology faculties of the white English-language universities. Several had developed extensive contacts on black campuses. On one level, they were responding to the worldwide student ferment of the 1960s and the disillusionment of a younger generation with outmoded religious forms and traditions. "There is a growing group of intelligent young people who just will not be reached or retained by the church while it persists with a style of life, language, philosophy, ethics, and worship which reeks with the smell of the moth balls of previous centuries," wrote Basil Moore, a Methodist minister and Rhodes University theology lecturer who became UCM's first president.[13] Among Catholics, the wave of reforms generated by the second Vatican Council of 1962–65 lent increased legitimacy to ecumenical contacts and liturgical innovation. For the UCM, the use of experimental liturgies became a way to stake out the organization's new identity and to attract and unite students across denominational lines, even submerging barriers between Protestants and Catholics. The organization of multiracial vacation work camps under UCM's aegis offered students a time-tested way to experience their beliefs in action, while candid and emotional discussions in small groups gave students an opportunity to express their problems and concerns. Most importantly, UCM gave clear evidence that it intended to be a vehicle for students to address political and social issues from a standpoint critical of government policy (*Document 25*).

The UCM's founding conference took place in Grahamstown in July 1967 with official backing from the Methodist, Anglican, Catholic, Presbyterian and Congregational churches. About 90 students and clergymen were present, including many blacks, whose numbers were swelled by a group already in Grahamstown for the annual conference of the National Catholic Federation of Students. An executive committee of ten was elected which included Moore as president, Colin Collins (a Catholic priest who was chaplain to the National Catholic Federation of Students), Winifred Kgware (whose husband, William Kgware, was on the faculty at Turfloop), and several Indian, Coloured, and African students. Membership on an individual basis was adopted. The organization's popularity grew rapidly, and over the next two years 30 UCM branches were established on the campuses of universities, seminaries and training colleges. When the second national UCM conference convened in July 1968, 60 percent of the delegates were black.

Discussions at UCM meetings centered on social and political issues, and reflected the impatience felt by most students at the "platitudinous statements of the churches," Collins later recalled.[14] White students who had been brought up in churches that preached against apartheid were eager to become actively involved in opposing racial injustice. Black students, although more conservative than whites in their attitudes toward church tradition, nevertheless welcomed the UCM because at the time there was no other organization on the national scene through which they could meet to discuss their political concerns, given the overwhelmingly white membership of NUSAS. The new black universities set up after 1959 were taking shape in an climate of isolation and repression, and their students were trying to reach out to one another and develop lines of communication across the country. Denominational groups had thrived in the early 1960s, in part because they provided a vehicle for this communication; when the UCM was founded these groups provided a ready-made constituency which was preponderantly black. This in turn meant that from the beginning the atmosphere at national UCM conferences was qualitatively different from the NUSAS pattern. Being in a minority, white students pressed their opinions less volubly and did more listening. Perhaps as a result of the maturity of Moore, Collins and other older advisors, there was ready acknowledgment that black students had problems, beliefs and objectives distinctly different from those of whites.

Although the formation of UCM was prompted by circumstances rooted in South Africa, the organization cultivated international ties in Europe and the United States which became a valuable source of moral and material support. Trends toward ecumenism in the World Student Christian Federation had also led to the founding of a group called the University Christian Movement in the United States in 1966, with which the UCM in South Africa corresponded. In December 1967, Basil Moore and two black students attended the annual conference of the American UCM in Cleveland and were able to raise enough money to hire a full-time secretary, purchase a car, and cover some program costs. Other financial support was later forthcoming from the World Student Christian Federation, and by September 1969 UCM's executive committee noted that 87 percent of the organization's small budget was coming from overseas.[15]

Essential as money was to the viability of the organization, the effect of ideas coming from outside South Africa proved even more central to the UCM's impact in the longer run. "In theology and in social action South Africa is a geographic and cultural backwater of the world," Collins noted after attending a World Student Christian Federation conference in Finland in August 1968.[16] Traveling abroad, until late 1969 as director of the Education department of the Southern African Catholic Bishops Conference and thereafter as General Secretary of the UCM, Collins brought back to South Africa the latest literature, organizing techniques, and progressive ideas of the radical social reform groups he encountered. Moore did the same until his passport was withdrawn by the government in 1968, but he remained in contact with currents of new thought overseas, and by 1970 had begun to obtain and disseminate James Cone's writings on "black theology" then circulating in the United States. In July 1968, the annual UCM conference held at Stutterheim was attended by two representatives from the University Christian Movement of the United States.[17] Contact with foreign activists, media coverage of student revolts in France and the United States in 1968, and exposure to the limited amount of radical foreign literature finding its way into the country, all reinforced the conviction taking hold among South African student activists that their own discontents were legitimate and in tune with progressive thinking in the wider world.

One organizational technique of the 1960s imported and pioneered by the UCM was Paulo Freire's method of raising political consciousness through literacy teaching, an approach which excited much interest among black students. Another innovation was the use of "T-groups" (sometimes called "directed group dynamics courses"), in which participants were encouraged to sharpen intercultural sensitivities and develop leadership and organizational skills through small group interaction. UCM incorporated T-grouping into what they called "formation schools" (a term borrowed from the language of Catholic theological training), which brought together members in each region for leadership training through discussions, speakers, and interracial exchanges. NUSAS, with a membership that overlapped with UCM's, was experimenting with similar small-group techniques at the time. SASO would later borrow both the terminology of the "formation school" and some of its techniques in the training of its own leadership.

It did not take long for UCM to attract government suspicion. Members of the security police began to harass members. Two issues of *One for the Road,* the UCM magazine, were banned, and Collins, who had mailed a copy of one issue to William Kgware at Turfloop, was charged with distributing banned literature. Kgware was pressured to dissociate himself from UCM, and by late 1968 the organization had been barred from holding meetings on the campuses of Fort Hare, Ngoye, Turfloop and the (Coloured) University of the Western Cape. Vorster, in the threatening manner which had become his political trademark, announced his intention to investigate UCM, warning that "when I am finished it will not be my fault if steps are taken against this movement."[18] Moore's passport was withdrawn, while Collins, who had decided to leave the priesthood in 1970, received a military call-up in 1971, but instead went into exile. Moore followed him in early 1972, after being banned and house arrested. Black UCM leaders Justice Moloto and Stanley Ntwasa were banned and confined to Mafikeng and Kimberley respectively. By the time the Schlebusch Commission was appointed to investigate the activities of liberal organizations in mid-1972, government intimidation and the withdrawal of support by several sponsoring churches had induced UCM's executive committee to disband the organization and to transfer most of its material assets to the South African Students' Organisation.

The Churches and the Christian Institute

Under circumstances of forced political retreat in the mid-1960s, it might have been logical for blacks to look to their religious organizations as havens where they could rebuild their strength and confidence in preparation for a new round of resistance. Over two thirds of Africans and 90 percent of Coloureds were at least nominal Christians, and a large proportion were church members.[19] Black churchgoers far outnumbered white. Moreover, in the glare of world attention following Sharpeville, South Africa had become the object of unprecedented scrutiny by foreign and international church bodies, particularly the World Council of Churches and the Reformed churches of the Netherlands. The movement for racial equality in the United

States, largely led by black churchmen and powerfully articulated in a politico-religious idiom by Martin Luther King, was scoring widely publicized victories. Under the protective wing of the churches in South Africa, unfulfilled potential for putting pressure on the apartheid system clearly existed.

There were serious impediments to the realization of this potential, however. The Dutch Reformed churches, with the third highest number of black adherents in the country (one and a half million in 1970), were informally but tightly linked with the National Party government. The several thousand African independent churches that had been created by schisms beginning in the late nineteenth century drew their enormous following (more than two and a half million by 1970, nearly a quarter of all African Christians) almost entirely from very poor, semi-literate and socially marginal strata of the black population. Their leaders avoided confrontation with white authorities and preached syncretistic variants of Christianity which helped cushion the strains of social change and economic hardship for individual believers. Unsuited as a refuge or an organizational base for members of the educated African middle class, the independent churches remained impervious to politicization in a modern nationalist sense.[20]

Of more promise as vehicles for political change were the Roman Catholic and English-language Protestant churches, which in the 1960s claimed some 8 million black and 1.7 million white adherents. Yet these too were enmeshed in colonial patterns of thought and organization carried over from their missionary origins and constantly reinforced by the dominant racist norms of South African society. Verbal expressions of goodwill abounded, but discriminatory church practices were commonplace and went generally unquestioned by white clergy and laity. Congregations were separated by race, ministers' stipends and benefits reflected sharp racial differentiations, and vastly disproportionate amounts of church money was spent on facilities for whites. While black clergy were limited to pastoral responsibility for segregated congregations, whites maintained a paternalistic but unyielding grip on positions of denominational leadership. Few blacks dared to complain publicly about racism in their churches, but privately many condemned it and warned of the anger and disillusionment it was engendering in younger Africans.

In relation to government policies, Peter Walshe has observed, the English-language churches until the period of the 1960 emergency "adopted a complaining but essentially passive mode of relating to the established culture of white power," notwithstanding the occasional efforts of individual nonconformist churchmen to stem the tide of complacency.[21] Even on those occasions when the unchristian behavior of whites or the moral contradictions of apartheid theories were indicted by white church leaders, their criticisms nearly always betrayed an unconscious assumption that whites alone could be the agents of significant change: no improvement in race relations or changes in government policy could be expected until enough whites, through patient education and moral exhortation, could be persuaded to undergo a change in outlook. Thus in the perception of even the most conscience-stricken whites, South Africa's fate was at stake in a contest of good and evil where whites alone were the active protagonists. If blacks had any role to play, it was assumed to be that of silent spectators to a campaign being waged on their behalf by more powerful benefactors. Only very rarely did maverick white clerics—most notably the British-born Michael Scott in the 1940s and Trevor Huddleston in the 1950s—unabashedly identify and involve themselves with the political initiatives of Africans.

Jolted by the international reaction to Sharpeville, religious leaders came together in December 1960 at a major conference in Johannesburg which began tentatively to nudge the churches toward a bolder stance. This meeting, known as the Cottesloe Consultation, brought together 86 theologians and Protestant leaders, including 17 blacks and six representatives of the Geneva-based World Council of Churches. About a third of those attending were from the Dutch Reformed churches. Despite conflicting views about whether apartheid theory—construed as the ideal of separate-but-equal—could ultimately be reconciled with Christian doctrine, the delegates formulated a final conference statement that reached the cautious conclusion that much greater effort would be necessary to achieve a social and political reality in South Africa consistent with religious principles. Among the Dutch Reformed churchmen at Cottesloe who accepted the principle of separate-but-equal as morally sound, the problem still remained unsolved of how justly to implement apartheid in practice.

Cottesloe marked a guarded step forward from earlier institutional lassitude in the English-language denominations, but in the Dutch Reformed churches it precipitated a reactionary backlash. The very mild conference statement aroused a storm of objection in Afrikaner ruling circles, and led within a few months to moves by all branches of the Dutch Reformed church to repudiate Cottesloe and to withdraw from the World Council of Churches and the South African Christian Council. This deeply dismayed the handful of Dutch Reformed churchmen who had by this time privately concluded that apartheid was morally indefensible in either practice or theory. Coming together informally around the Reverend C. F. Beyers Naude, who at the time of Cottesloe was the second highest ranking official in the General Synod of the Nederduitse Gereformeerde Kerk (NGK), the largest of the Dutch Reformed denominations, a group of these Afrikaner dissidents in May 1962 began to publish a monthly magazine, *Pro Veritate,* through which they hoped to revive the ferment which had seized the Afrikaans churches at the time of Cottesloe. They failed to stem the reactionary tide, however, and Naude in particular found himself ostracized and vilified by his former NGK associates as they closed ranks to defend National Party policies. Wounded but undeterred, Naude—a one time member of the Broederbond and a son of one of its founders—in September 1963 accepted the directorship of the newly formed Christian Institute (CI), a pioneering ecumenical organization which aimed to work for racial justice and against the NGK's perversion of Christian doctrine to serve Afrikaner political goals.

Discouraged by his failure to make headway in the Afrikaans churches after several years of effort, Naude gradually shifted his focus, first to the problems of the Coloureds, who share the language and culture of the Afrikaners, and some years later to Africans, in what was to be one of the most unusual personal and political odysseys in modern South African history.[22] Little by little, the Christian Institute attracted a small but dedicated membership of clerical and lay activists from the Catholic and English Protestant churches as well as from among Dutch Reformed dissidents. Unlike NUSAS, whose leaders were constrained from assuming the role of a self-consciously radical vanguard because of their desire to coax along a more conservative mass membership, the CI was unhindered by any need to defer to the status quo instincts of the average white South African Christian. Through the pages of *Pro Veritate* and in local study groups, it gradually became, according to Walshe, "a thoroughly disturbing . . . voice; describing the full impact of apartheid on blacks, condemning the structures of injustice, assailing complacency, struggling to articulate an alternative vision for society and trying to discern appropriate methods to bring something of that vision into being."[23] As the black consciousness movement emerged with the spread of SASO, Naude's growing empathy with blacks and his intimate understanding of the Afrikaners' own ethnic nationalism caused him quickly to perceive the constructive potential of the movement and to place the resources of the CI behind the efforts of Biko and his lieutenants.

Throughout its decade and a half of existence, the CI played a vital energizing role for reform-minded church leaders in all denominations, particularly in the 1960s when the only other existing mechanism for regular contact across denominational lines was the rather moribund Christian Council. By the late 1960s the Christian Council had become better organized and more boldly led and, together with the CI, increasingly took the initiative in putting forward a theologically-based critique of government race policies. Inspired by the World Council of Churches' landmark Conference on Church and Society which Naude and Anglican Bishop Bill Burnett attended in Geneva in 1966, the CI and the Christian Council under Burnett's leadership organized a series of regional meetings in South Africa leading up to a national conference on Church and Society in Johannesburg in February 1968. Out of this meeting evolved a committee, drawn from both organizations, which by mid-1968 had drafted a document called "A Message to the People of South Africa" (*Document 24*). This statement was eventually signed by 600 ministers from the 27 member churches of the Christian Council (which in May 1968 changed its name to the South African Council of Churches). In August 1968, 7,000 copies of the text, produced in several languages, were circulated for discussion in all affiliated congregations and annual church assemblies. Eventually all the member denominations of the South African Council of Churches (SACC) but one, the Baptists, gave the document their full or conditional endorsement.

The "Message" was the strongest joint church pronouncement since Cottesloe. Though laden with heavy theological language, its meaning was unambiguous: apartheid, or "separate development," rested on a "false faith" that was in conflict with scriptural precepts; Christians thus had a duty to reject it as immoral, even if this brought them into conflict with the customs and laws of the country. The suggestion that churches might sanction the breaking of laws, as John de Gruchy has noted, was going for "the jugular vein in the body politic."[24] The reaction from National Party newspapers, pulpits and political platforms was swift and scathing. There were people out to subvert the government "under the cloak of religion," Prime Minister Vorster told a National Party meeting in Brakpan in September 1968. There were some clerics "playing with the idea . . . that they should do the kind of thing here in South Africa that Martin Luther King did in America. I want to say to them, cut it out; cut it out immediately for the cloth you are wearing will not protect you if you try to do this in South Africa."[25] Acerbic letters passed between Vorster and groups of angry clergy, and English and Afrikaans editorial writers exchanged volleys of verbal fire.

The "Message" marked a critical juncture in church-state tensions in at least two ways. Firstly, by implying that the churches had a responsibility to act as well as to pass moral judgments, the document opened the door for church-sponsored political protest and civil disobedience, a potentiality which Vorster's fulminations were obviously intended to discourage. In practice, however, almost no serious attempts to apply the tactics of the American civil rights movement were made over the next decade. Whites interested in experimenting with civil disobedience were too few, and blacks, who might have provided the numbers, tended to look back on the 1952 Defiance Campaign and conclude that such tactics had already been tried and found wanting. Thus, although there continued to be vague calls to action from both white and black church leaders now and again, and charitable activities such as aid to prisoners increased, no bold acts of political defiance were inspired by the "Message."

More significantly, the "Message" was the last major collective expression by the South African churches of the long unquestioned colonial style of leadership in which whites spoke over the heads of blacks to other whites in trying to find a formula for reform. Black reticence, and the availability of the escape route into religious separatism, had permitted the perpetuation of this pattern well into the 1960s. But now discontent among black clergy was deepening and being fed by persistent frustration over the discriminatory terms of employment in most multiracial churches. How could church leaders condemn discrimination in the wider society if the churches themselves practiced it in regard to ministers' stipends, wrote Reverend Simon Gqubule in a church magazine in April 1968, echoing a common grievance.[26] More challenging because of its broader implications for the future of white control was the daring argument put forward by a young priest, Smangaliso Mkhatshwa, in an article in a Catholic lay journal in early 1968. It was time to Africanize the church, he said, not only in its liturgy and theology, but also in its leadership. "Direction of church affairs is fully entrenched in 'white' hands . . . but now . . . the winds of change are blowing, not only outside the church but, equally, they are howling inside her as well," he wrote. White trusteeship would have to go, he implied, because Africans were growing tired of being treated as perpetual minors.[27] Two years later, a "Black Priests' Manifesto," authored by Mkhatshwa and four other rebels (*Document 26*) shocked the Catholic hierarchy with its outspoken criticisms of racism in the church.

A similarly assertive mood, articulated through the student-led black consciousness movement, was at that point sweeping the country's institutions of higher education, bringing with it in less than a decade a far-ranging transformation in the attitudes and behavior of South Africa's whites and blacks towards one another. The impact of the black consciousness movement on both seminary students and clergy in the multiracial churches was profoundly unsettling, and sometimes led to acrimonious confrontations. But by 1978, when Desmond Tutu became the first African appointed General Secretary of the SACC, the subordinate position of blacks within denominational hierarchies was becoming a thing of the past, although many vestiges of older authority patterns still remained. Along with the "blackening" of church leadership, a strong interest in the ideas of black theology, introduced into South Africa by the UCM in 1970, and later in liberation theology as developed in Latin America, helped by the end of the 1970s subtly to restructure the ideological underpinnings of Christian belief and practice, incrementally forcing churches to shift their focus away from narrow pietistic concerns and toward the grievances and social needs of the country's oppressed majority.

Once the pent up frustrations of black clergy had begun to surface, nowhere did they come forth more forcefully than in the Nederduitse Gereformeerde Kerk, the very institution most concerned with assuring South Africans that their government was guided by Christian principles. Segregated into white, African, Coloured, and Indian branches, the NGK was a conservative institution in which whites held all senior positions, managed all theological training, and controlled most funds well into the 1970s. Black clergy in the NGK "daughter" churches worked alongside white "missionaries" from the "mother" church, accepting differential status and remuneration as part of the price of job security and the relatively well endowed facilities provided to daughter churches. Although in the wider black community there was a stigma attached to being part of an "apartheid" church, there were compensations as well: black NGK members were often given preferential consideration by government officials. With the arrival of the "winds of change," however, long latent resentments emerged.[28] Ministers of the African NGK began openly to condemn government policies, and in 1975 they defied tradition at their annual general synod by electing an African moderator (head), voting to join the SACC (to which the "mother" church was blatantly hostile), and publicly calling for a merger of the four race-based branches of the NGK—a proposal that was rejected repeatedly by white NGK leaders as "impractical." By the late 1970s, the customarily silent Coloured NGK had likewise adopted a militant position, in part under the influence of the outspoken Reverend Allan Boesak (*Document 33*). Behind a thin veneer of theological debate, a tense political stand-off prevailed as the 1970s drew to a close. While the "mother" church fought to contain damage to its image and standing through manipulating its financial power over the rebellious but resource-poor "daughters," black NGK militants sought firmly and persistently to apply ideological pressure to one of the main props of the apartheid state.

In the following decade, the conflict within the NGK was to move onto a world stage with Boesak's election as head of the World Alliance of Reformed Churches in 1982. By then, however, the wider pressures of international church politics had already been impinging on events in South Africa for some time, largely as a result of a decision by the World Council of Churches (WCC) to offer support to the South African exiled liberation movements. Over the course of the 1970s this development, combined with the impact of black consciousness and the increasing weight of black leadership in the churches, gradually intensified the church-state confrontation and pushed the churches towards an increasingly explicit alliance with the forces of political change.

Following several years of discussion in the late 1960s, the WCC voted in 1970 to establish a Program to Combat Racism on a global scale. A special fund administered from Geneva began making annual financial contributions to 19 organizations around the world, including the banned ANC and PAC of South Africa. Although earmarked solely for humanitarian and educational purposes, the grants implied moral acceptance of the use of violent means to combat racism when other means had been exhausted—an application of the principle of a "just war." This WCC decision caught South Africa's churches unprepared, and their initial reactions in 1970 were instinctively conservative: violence might be a reality, but churches could never condone it, nor could they play their proper conciliatory role unless they remained neutral in situations of conflict. Only the UCM voiced a contrary position, pointing out that the churches had failed to demonstrate their "neutrality" by not condemning the government's high-cost military build-up.[29]

Growing Church-State Confrontation

After the first shock of the WCC decision had been absorbed, its enormous implications prompted a searching debate in denominational forums and within the South African Council of Churches. Endorsing international support for the ANC and PAC was impossible. But if South African churches could not approve of the WCC's methods of combating racism, what better methods could they propose?

Whereas denominational leaders sometimes felt a need to defer to the conservative views of their wealthiest parishioners, the SACC was less constrained by immediate pressures of accountability and needed only to work for a consensus among denominational representatives at its annual

National Conferences. Even less answerable to a conservative base, the Christian Institute by the early 1970s was raising most of its funds in Europe and North America where it had found strong backing for its activities in support of the African independent churches and the black consciousness movement. Occupying offices in the same building in Johannesburg as the SACC, the forward-thinking staff of the CI exerted a steady influence on the deliberations of the SACC leadership as they searched together for a theologically defensible response to the challenge of the WCC's initiatives. Little by little, steps were taken to focus attention on the responsibility of churches to root out discriminatory practices within their own ranks as well as to correct injustices in the wider society. The tendency of church bodies to make moral pronouncements but never to take concrete actions to challenge government policies was acknowledged as a weakness to be overcome. And lastly, where the underlying legitimacy of South Africa's government—as distinct from the morality of particular policies—had never previously been called into question in church pronouncements, new voices within church councils now began to advocate far more fundamental confrontations with the status quo.

When a WCC Central Committee meeting in Utrecht in 1972 decided that the world body would divest itself of shares in all companies doing business in minority ruled African countries, the CI publicly endorsed the decision but the SACC and the South African Catholic church approached this highly contentious subject more cautiously, calling only for foreign companies in South Africa to improve their employment practices. Security legislation made it illegal in South Africa to advocate economic sanctions. Had the majority of the SACC's member churches been willing to defy this law, calling for economic sanctions would have constituted a bold step over the line between mere verbal criticism of the government and concrete action to combat apartheid. The moral lines of argument on the issue were not ideally clear-cut, however; whites would be squeezed by economic sanctions, but blacks would inevitably suffer the most from a prolonged economic downturn. Opinion was divided, and in the end the churches chose to draw their battle lines elsewhere.

Leaving foreign churches and anti-apartheid groups to wrestle with the question of foreign investment, loans and trade, the South African churches turned their attention instead to the issues of violence and war first raised by the WCC in 1970. If the exiled liberation movements—referred to as "terrorists" in the South African media and by the government—were indeed fighting a "just war" against an immoral system, was it not immoral to fight in defense of that system? Perennial debates on the subject of violence and conscientious objection took on a new urgency after the fall of the Caetano government in Portugal in April 1974. Mozambique and Angola, once buffers for Pretoria against its enemies, now seemed likely to become launching pads for guerrilla attacks. Three weeks after the Lisbon coup, a meeting of the All African Conference of Churches convened in Lusaka. During the meeting, members of the South African delegation were able to meet with representatives of the ANC.[30]

This face to face encounter with liberation movement members made a deep impression on the delegation, according to John Rees, the SACC General Secretary, who was present. Reporting to the SACC's National Conference at the end of July, he admitted that it had come as a revelation that some members of the exiled movements were practicing Christians who believed that taking up arms against South Africa was fully consistent with their religious faith. A long discussion ensued at the SACC conference, during which it came out that several participants (39 of the 56 conference delegates were black) had sons who had left South Africa to join the exiled movements. "The conference under those circumstances had good reason to consider carefully how the SACC could respond to the expectations of the liberation movements" that the churches oppose apartheid, Wolfram Kistner of the SACC staff later wrote. The churches could not end migratory labor, influx control, or job reservation—but they could encourage their members to refuse to do military service, which is what they did in a strongly worded resolution (*Document 31*), passed by a wide majority, that gave frank recognition to the struggle of the liberation movements as a "just war" against an immoral and violent system. "The resolution [was] meant to make the members of the SACC aware of the confrontation between South African churches and the state . . . [and] to enhance the credibility of their concern for justice in the eyes of the liberation movements," according to Kistner.[31] With this 1974 resolution, in fact, the churches for the first time could be said to have clearly taken sides—or as many blacks saw it, to have changed sides, from tacitly condoning the status quo amidst verbal protestations, to actively "siding with the oppressed."[32] Even the Progressive Party felt compelled to repudiate the resolution, so unacceptable was it to white opinion. The English language press followed suit. Only NUSAS, and Archbishop Denis Hurley on behalf of the Catholic church, supported the SACC stand.

The state's response was predictably angry, but by mid-1974 its campaign to contain the challenge of the churches and the Christian Institute had long been underway. The National Party had risen to power partly through its skill in fashioning a civil religion that merged notions of political loyalty and divine will in the minds of Afrikaners who had suffered dispossession and humiliation.[33] The Nationalists fully appreciated the power of religion as a political weapon, and they were determined to stop the emergence of any alliance between nationalism and religion among their enemies. To this end, they were willing to use any judicial or extrajudicial means necessary. The Schlebusch Commission—a body unconstrained by formal judicial proce-dures—laid the groundwork for the Affected Organisations Act, passed through parliament in February 1974. The Act made it illegal for any South African organization to receive foreign funds for political purposes. Any organization deemed to have done so could be declared "affected" and forbidden to raise funds abroad. In September 1974, on the recommendation of the Commission, NUSAS was declared "affected," and in May 1975, a similar restriction was placed on the Christian Institute.

Silencing Naude was more difficult. Charged with an offense when he refused to testify to the Schlebusch Commission, he was uncowed by threats of court action, and in the end the government embarrassed itself by harassing him with punitive litigation. Banning him under the Suppression of Communism Act was an option, but it would have been unconvincing to label such a distinguished clergyman a communist. ("I do not say these people are communists, but they are playing into the hands of the leftists," declared Koot Vorster, Moderator of the NGK General Synod and brother of the prime minister, after Naude had played a leading role in proposing the SACC resolution on conscientious objection.)[34] CI publications detailing the use of torture and detention by the police were banned. In the early days of the Soweto uprising, Naude was issued a public warning by the Minister of Justice to desist from involving himself in the disturbances. The CI nevertheless continued to provide office space to the South African Students' Movement, and to help finance its running costs. When 18 opposition organizations were declared unlawful in the crackdown of October 19, 1977, the CI was one of them, and Naude was one of several churchmen banned for five years under the terms of the Internal Security Act, a new law superseding the Suppression of Communism Act that made it possible for the government to silence dissident individuals even in the absence of any alleged evidence linking them to communism.

If legal methods of silencing dissent came to naught, arbitrary or secret methods could be applied to prevent churches or their leaders from mounting effective opposition: a passport canceled, a period of detention for "questioning," a tire slashed during the night, or a family pet left dead on a doorstep. Propaganda attacks in the government controlled media were also standard fare. *Document 35* is a retort to the South African Broadcasting Corporation by Mandlenkhosi Zwane, the Catholic bishop of Manzini, following a distorted report of the Pope's remarks on liberation theology at a conference in Mexico in early 1979. The effect of the report, Zwane implied, was to do "untold harm to the image of the Catholic Church in South Africa." The government on its part, while determined to target church bodies whenever possible, recognized that much of the political challenge came not from churches as institutions but from "troublesome" religious leaders speaking and acting as individuals. Its response was to apply a range of tactics aimed at intimidating, compromising or corrupting individuals. Occasionally it scored successes; for example, Reverend Mzwandile Maqina and Bishop Isaac Mokoena, both associated with independent African churches, were turned from government critics to government allies in the 1980s. In other cases, such tactics backfired, helping to create martyrs and legitimize leaders in the ranks of the opposition.

One churchman who thrived on confrontation was Desmond Tutu, a feisty and articulate Anglican priest who relished preaching to the government about morality. Emerging as a leader in the mid-1970s with his appointment first as Dean of St. Mary's Cathedral in Johannesburg, then as Bishop of Lesotho, and in 1978 as General Secretary of the SACC, Tutu spoke with forthrightness about the grievances of Africans and the evils of government policies, always anchoring his comments in a religious framework shorn of abstruse theological language. Invited to sit on a government-appointed committee to advise on urban policy after the government had launched its post-Soweto efforts at reform, Tutu refused. Instead, he became increasingly outspoken in calling for the churches to defy unjust laws. When asked on Danish television in October 1979 for his views on Denmark's purchases of South African coal, Tutu expressed personal support for trade boycotts, provoking a furious reaction from the government. He replied to the attacks in a fighting tone that signaled a new willingness to put the church at the forefront of the political struggle, challenged the leaders of the National Party to join past tyrants who had persecuted Christians only to end up "the flotsam and jetsam of forgotten history" while the church endured (*Document 36*). Several months later, Tutu's passport was withdrawn, but the restriction of his movements did nothing to limit his influence, which was to grow even more troublesome to Pretoria in the 1980s.

The decade and a half following the 1964 Rivonia trial was a bruising period for multiracial opposition groups, but in another sense it was a time of rapid forward movement in which outmoded forms of action and thought gave way to new approaches better suited to challenging the apartheid system. While the National Party enjoyed some success in preventing the growth of effective alliances between its white and black opponents, it failed to circumscribe the political challenge posed from the churches. Nor did it prevent liberal and radical whites from helping to midwife the two most potent organizational innovations among blacks, the black consciousness movement and the independent trade unions. The two organizations most instrumental in supporting the black consciousness movement, the University Christian Movement and the Christian Institute, were destroyed and their leading activists silenced—but not before, like the chinook salmon in Robert Lowell's poem (quoted in *Document 25*), they had cleared the last step of roaring water, "alive enough to spawn and die." NUSAS, whose Wages Commissions had contributed substantially to the rebirth of African trade unionism, ended the period weakened, but nevertheless stood poised to return to national resistance politics as the racial polarization of the black consciousness movement began to recede.

More fundamental than the fate of particular organizations and individuals was the underlying change in the relationship between blacks and their white liberal supporters at the personal and psychological level. Under the impact of the black consciousness movement and fed by events in the outside world, most importantly the African victory over Portuguese colonialism in Angola and Mozambique, long-standing attitudes of paternalism among white liberals and of deference and dependence among blacks faded dramatically, opening up creative new possibilities for African initiative and leadership. Although few white liberals were ready to conceive of a future political order run fully on majoritarian principles, there was a new fluidity in thinking about alternatives to the status quo. Cautiously approaching the subject of political transformation at the end of the 1970s, white liberals in the Black Sash and the Institute of Race Relations held regular private discussions with black community leaders in a quiet effort to foster interracial dialogue and work towards a consensus at the level of liberal elites (*Document 34*). Blacks in such private forums felt much freer to speak their minds and challenge outdated liberal assumptions than they would have at the time of Rivonia. On both sides of the racial divide, despite the tightening net of repression, a new hope and a new realism prevailed, such that most participants in ongoing multiracial political efforts would have probably accepted the conclusions drawn by exiled intellectual Ruth First, assessing the situation of white liberals in the 1970s: "An articulate and courageous minority has continued through the years to protest," she wrote,

> sometimes on grounds of humanity and the abandonment of liberal rule of law traditions, sometimes because the logic and imperatives of the South African situation cry out for principled opposition to rescue the future of not only blacks but also whites. But the lessons of this protest phase [are] inescapably that while student mobilization, the church, the press, the women's Black Sash movement and liberal opinion in general can help to expose the government's worst excesses, can act to keep alive the norms of a more principled approach and, most importantly, can spread disarray in the White establishment, in the end any meaningful assault on this system must come from the blacks.[35]

Notes

1. The Progressive Party, formed in a breakaway from the United Party in 1959, changed its name to the Progressive Reform Party in 1975 and to the Progressive Federal Party (PFP) in 1977 after mergers with other former United Party groupings. In 1990 the PFP changed its name to the Democratic Party.

2. The scandal centered around disclosures that the Department of Information had spent huge sums on secret projects to improve South Africa's international image after the Soweto uprising, and had used public money to launch a pro-government English newspaper, *The Citizen*. The scandal forced Prime Minister John Vorster to resign and dashed the ambitions of Dr. Connie Mulder to succeed him.

3. See Paul B. Rich, *Hope and Despair: English-Speaking Intellectuals and South African Politics 1896–1976* (London: British Academic Press, 1993), chapter 4.

4. See *Survey of Race Relations 1961* (Johannesburg: South African Institute of Race Relations, 1962), p. 18. According to Peter Brown of the Liberal Party, the party had a paid-up African membership of over 5,000 in 1968, a number about five times the paid-up membership of whites, Indians and Coloureds combined. Letter from Peter Brown to Gerhart, August 21, 1991.

5. Information in this section has been drawn from NUSAS documents and from conversations with Steve Biko (October 1972), Mewa Ramgobin (July 1989), and Neville Curtis (June 1990).

6. See Martin Legassick and John Shingler, "South Africa," in Donald K. Emmerson, ed., *Students and Politics in Developing Countries* (New York: Praeger, 1968), p. 107, and Neville Curtis and Clive Keegan, "The Aspiration to a Just Society," in H. W. van der Merwe and D. Welsh, eds., *Student Perspectives on South Africa* (Cape Town: David Philip, 1972), p. 110.

7. Martin Legassick, *The National Union of South African Students: Ethnic Cleavage and*

Ethnic Integration in the Universities, Occasional Paper no. 4 (Los Angeles: African Studies Center, University of California, 1967), p. 47.

8. Curtis and Keegan, p. 27. Curtis was NUSAS president in 1970 and 1971.

9. See chapter 7. Banned with Turner in February 1973 were Neville Curtis, Paul Pretorius, Paula Ensor, Phillipe Le Roux, Sheila Lapinsky, Clive Keegan and Chris Wood. On the night of January 8, 1978, Turner was shot through the window of his home in Durban by an unidentified gunman and died in the arms of his 13-year-old daughter.

10. *State v. Moss* (the NUSAS trial), 1976. The other defendants were Cedric de Beer, Charles Nupen, Karel Tip, and Eddie Webster.

11. Anonymous, "The Poverty of Africanism," *Work in Progress,* no. 2, November 1977, p. 5.

12. Information in this section has been drawn from the archives of the UCM and from conversations with Biko and Justice Moloto (June 1989) and the interview of David Mesenbring with Moloto (November 1977).

13. Basil Moore, "Worship 'Happenings'," *Pro Veritate,* September 1968, p. 16.

14. Colin B. Collins, "How It Really Happened," unpublished manuscript, 1979?, p. 5.

15. "Minutes of the Meeting of the Executive Committee held at Wilgespruit on 13–14 September 1969," p. 6.

16. "UCM Happening '69," Annexure 6, August 2, 1969.

17. The two were Mary McAnally and Timothy Smith, the latter a student at Union Theological Seminary in New York who later became a key figure in the international sanctions movement.

18. *Sunday Times,* August 17, 1968.

19. *Survey of Race Relations 1964,* p. 18.

20. Statistics on religious affiliation are given in Ernie Regehr, *Perceptions of Apartheid: the Churches and Political Change in South Africa* (Scottsdale, Pennsylvania: Herald Press, 1979), p. 282.

21. Peter Walshe, *Church versus State in South Africa: the Case of the Christian Institute* (London: C. Hurst and Co.; Maryknoll, NY: Orbis Books, 1983), p. 6.

22. See Colleen Ryan, *Beyers Naude: Pilgrimage of Faith* (Cape Town: David Philip, 1990). The Broederbond was a secret society of Afrikaner nationalists intimately allied to the National Party.

23. Walshe, p. 42.

24. John de Gruchy, *The Church Struggle in South Africa* (Cape Town: David Philip; Grand Rapids: Eerdmans, 1979), p. 120.

25. *Survey of Race Relations 1968,* pp. 22–23.

26. S. Gqubule, "Discrimination in the Church," *South African Outlook,* April 1968, reproduced in Francis Wilson and D. Perrot, eds., *Outlook on a Century: South Africa 1870–1970* (Alice: Lovedale Press, 1973), pp. 681–82. For data on stipends of ministers by race and denomination, see Lesley Cawood, *The Churches and Race Relations in South Africa* (Johannesburg: South African Institute of Race Relations, 1964). Also see conversation with Mcebisi Xundu (March 1989).

27. M. P. [Smangaliso] Mkhatshwa, "Africanisation of the Church," *Challenge,* vol. 5, no. 1, January/February 1968. Also see conversation with Mkhatshwa (July 1989).

28. The phrase "winds of change" entered South African political rhetoric when British prime minister Harold Macmillan used it in a speech to the South African parliament in February 1960, referring to the advancing tide of black nationalism in Africa.

29. "UCM's Response to S. A. Church Leaders on the WCC Grant to 'Liberation Movements'," *SASO Newsletter,* September 1970, pp. 20–21.

30. On the events surrounding the 1974 SACC resolution on conscientious objection see Wolfram Kistner, "Response of the South African Council of Churches to the WCC Programme to Combat Racism (1969–1979): a Documentation," February 8, 1980, pp. 9–10. Kistner does not specify whether PAC representatives were also present, but at this time the PAC had been expelled from Zambia.

31. Kistner explains that although the churches had previously defended the rights of conscientious objectors (such as Jehovah's Witnesses), in 1974 for the first time they sought to

encourage South Africans to become objectors, a much bolder position in relation to the state. On this issue, see *War and Conscience in South Africa: the Churches and Conscientious Objection* (London: Catholic Institute for International Relations and Pax Christi, 1982).

32. Frank Chikane, who became SACC General Secretary in 1987, has identified the 1974 resolution on conscientious objection as the most decisive moment in the history of the SACC's effort to define its theological and political position on apartheid. See Frank Chikane, "A Critical Examination of the Theology and Praxis of the SACC, 1968–1988," M.A. thesis, University of Natal, 1992, passim.

33. This is the theme of Dunbar Moodie, *The Rise of Afrikanerdom: Power, Apartheid, and Afrikaner Civil Religion* (Berkeley: University of California Press, 1975).

34. Quoted in *War and Conscience,* p. 31.

35. Ruth First, "Protest and Politics in the Shadow of Apartheid," *New Middle East,* July 1972, p. 19.

4. The Black Consciousness Movement: The Formative Years, 1967–1971

Young Africans in the early 1970s began to overcome the apathy and fear that had crippled black politics in the immediate post-Rivonia years. Sloughing off the passivity that most whites had mistaken for contentment, urban African youth became infused with an aggressive spirit that helped sweep South Africa toward the cataclysm of 1976–77. At the same time that urbanization and the expansion of industry was bringing increasing numbers of adults face to face with the harsh conditions of working-class life, economic growth continued to generate a rapid expansion in schooling, drawing an ever larger proportion of young Africans under the malign influence of the state's system of Bantu education. These conditions created fertile ground for the mobilization of popular discontent, and in 1969–70 a political revival started to take shape.

The most important vehicle of this political renewal was the black consciousness movement. Deriving momentum from the humiliation of past defeat, like so many movements of ethnic mobilization including that of the Afrikaners half a century earlier, the black consciousness movement began with a period of intense introspection among young intellectuals and moved through phases in which enemy tactics were analyzed, symbols and strategies of resistance were formulated and elaborated, and political activity was set in motion with the aim of inspiring the most powerful possible awakening. Reactions by the state to this new challenge were initially confused. Eventually steps were taken to contain the movement's spread, but by the time the full repressive force of the security establishment was brought to bear, the Soweto uprising had already permanently altered South Africa's racial balance of power.

The nature and significance of the black consciousness movement are the subject of contradictory interpretation among scholars and political activists alike. The movement has been characterized both as an elite phenomenon and as the genesis of the broad youth insurrection of 1976–77; both as weakly organized and as the most successful attempt at popular mobilization seen up to that time in South Africa; both as a minor detour off the main historical path of ANC-centered resistance and as a major contributing factor in the ANC's revival. Some anti-government whites saw it as a healthy development, but most condemned it as the ugly step-child of apartheid's racism.[1] Liberals used its emergence as a stick to beat the National Party for creating revolutionary nationalism among blacks; Marxists dismissed black consciousness as hopelessly naive about how to further the revolutionary cause. After the movement's heyday, no firm consensus prevailed among its original partisans regarding the significance of its philosophy. A few maintained that it should remain the ideological centerpiece of the struggle for equality, while others believed its ideas had served their purpose and should be seen as mainly of historical importance. For as long as future circumstances in South Africa reinforce both the ideal of a color-blind society and the aspiration of Africans to play a leadership role commensurate with their numbers, the ongoing tension produced by this contradiction is likely to influence retrospective assessments of the black consciousness movement.

The "Bush" Universities

The environment that nourished African political revival in the late 1960s was neither rural poverty and powerlessness, nor the factory floor, where steady increases in the size and skill level of the African work force held out the possibility of power to come. Instead the campuses of the country's ethnically segregated black universities provided the constituency for nationalism. Here in the ranks of the nascent black intelligentsia the state was methodically but often clumsily pursuing its strategy for breeding a compliant future leadership class, programmed to play a cooperative role in maintaining the social order. The approach was scientific, but the chemistry went badly wrong.

University segregation was almost a decade old before it became apparent that it was producing hothouse conditions for the growth of a new spirit of resistance. In keeping with apartheid ideals, the misnamed Extension of University Education Act of 1959 had made it illegal for the country's white universities to enroll any black student without government approval. The only exceptions were the University of South Africa, where instruction was by correspondence, and the University of Natal, which was permitted to run a "Non-European" medical school. The Act mandated the creation of four new universities, one each for Coloureds (in Cape Town), Indians (in Durban), and Zulus (the University of Zululand at Ngoye), and one for Africans from the Sotho, Tswana, Venda, Pedi and Shangaan-speaking groups centered in the Transvaal and Orange Free State (the University of the

North at Turfloop). Fort Hare, a private university which since 1916 had drawn African students from every part of the country and as far north as Uganda, was taken over by the government and restricted to Xhosa-speakers.

Since ethnic self-segregation at university level had helped to foster a separate Afrikaner identity, educational planners in the National Party expected that tribally-based universities would provide similar psychological underpinnings for the future "independent" African homelands. Segregation of Indians and Coloureds would minimize tendencies for the subject races to identify with one another, and all nonwhite students would be rescued from the bad influences believed to be at work in the white English-medium universities.

An emphasis on control pervaded the thinking of Afrikaner administrators appointed to oversee the development of what blacks soon labeled the tribal or "bush" colleges. All three African universities were situated in rural districts far from major cities and from each other. Access to their campuses was tightly monitored to exclude unwanted influences, and careful screening sought to insure that curricula, library holdings, and campus cultural life were cleansed of corrupting intellectual material. Nearly all faculty members were white, with a heavy preponderance of Afrikaners, for whom creation of the tribal colleges had provided a new realm of sheltered employment. A decade after the founding of the "Coloured" University of the Western Cape, for example, whites still made up 90 percent of the faculty, and of these, more than 90 percent were Afrikaners.[2]

The customary race hierarchy of the wider society and its accompanying pattern of attitudes and behavior were replicated in campus life. Black faculty members were excluded from university policy-making councils, paid on lower salary scales, and promoted at a slower rate than whites. Failure to act deferentially toward white staff could mark black teachers or students as bad influences and create obstacles to their career advancement. Intellectual enlightenment ranked low among institutional priorities, and obedience high. Infractions of campus dress codes, such as neglecting to wear a tie in class, could result in reprimands or even suspension.[3] While such icons of western culture as neckties were being defended, officials paid lip-service to the importance of strengthening distinctive ethnic cultures, or at least those aspects of them which reinforced racial hierarchy. Kogila Moodley, who taught at the Indian university in the late 1960s, has written, for example, that special attention was given to "the concept of caste . . . in an attempt to show the supposed affinity between Indian and Afrikaner thought."[4]

Black students faced painful dilemmas in deciding how to react to these demeaning conditions. Qualifying for university entrance elevated them into a tiny elite among their peers, and held out to their often struggling parents the promise that they would become well-employed. Many held government or other scholarships which they stood to forfeit if they behaved in a cheeky manner or engaged in unapproved campus activities. Students who risked the nonconformity of protest also risked becoming martyrs to a seemingly hopeless cause. The available scope for organization and maneuver was extremely limited. On each campus, discontent among students could be rapidly communicated because the condescending approach of the authorities sensitized all students, even those who arrived at university with a low level of political awareness. But communication between campuses was much more problematic; telephone service was limited, and travel expensive. For the enterprising student with outside contacts, obtaining unapproved books and journals was difficult but not impossible. News about world events was accessible, although usually filtered through the slanted South African media. However, any move to organize student societies, activities, or outside speakers required approval from university authorities. Black lecturers were punished for giving talks on unauthorized subjects. Where administrative sanctions failed to quell political activities among students, university principals turned readily to the services of the security police who questioned and intimidated offending individuals.

One realm where protest could be registered with relative impunity was in student government. Wherever Student Representative Councils (SRCs) were elected, university principals tried to incorporate them into the apparatus of control by threatening members with disciplinary action unless they worked to keep other students in line. One result was that students at Fort Hare, the Coloured and Indian universities, and the Transvaal College of Education for Indians refused to elect SRCs in the 1960s and early 1970s, and students on other campuses boycotted the annual council elections in substantial numbers. But gains made through noncooperation were marginal and lay merely in depriving the authorities of whatever slight increase in legitimacy might be derived from channeling control through black intermediaries rather than exercising it directly. On the debit side, students lost the benefit of having a leadership structure of their own to coordinate whatever resistance was tactically possible. Reluctance to push collectively against the pressures of state domination mirrored the fear, demoralization, and lack of organization evident more widely in black society.

From time to time, however, students dared to protest against campus conditions. The late 1960s were years of worldwide student radicalism, and even South Africa's quarantined black campuses felt the fever. In August 1968, when French and American student revolts were fresh in the news and white students at the University of Cape Town were involved in a campus sit-in protesting the government's veto of the appointment of an African, Archie Mafeje, to the university's faculty, students at Fort Hare decided to boycott the installation ceremony of their new principal, J. M. de Wet. In the absence of an elected student leadership, the new principal selected students whom he alleged were ringleaders, and these were subjected to police questioning and room searches. Matters escalated until over 300 students were suspended in early September. All but 22 of those suspended were eventually permitted to return after signing pledges of good behavior. The 22, who included Barney Pityana, Justice Moloto, Chris Mokoditoa, and Kenneth Rachidi, all later prominent in the black consciousness movement, were expelled. Such ventures into the politics of protest bore meager fruit. Somewhere in the potential repertoire of resistance tactics there were ways to shift the balance in favor of blacks, but students had yet to discover them. Before imagining wider change, black students first needed to find ways of mobilizing the resources within their own ranks. This in turn required that older assumptions about protest, power, and ideology be reappraised in light of the black student experience.

Black Students and NUSAS

The radicalization of NUSAS during the post-Rivonia quiescence, the outspokenness of its leadership, and the vehement condemnation which this earned from the government, elevated the organization to a position of high esteem in the eyes of blacks. "Getting into NUSAS" became a goal of many students at the tribal colleges, where requests to allow campus affiliation were routinely rejected but semi-clandestine off-campus branches could be formed. One student strongly attracted to NUSAS was Steve Biko, who in 1966 entered his first year at the University of Natal Non-European medical school.[5] Biko, soon to emerge as one of the most gifted leaders in the history of South Africa, had grown up in Ginsberg location outside King William's Town in the eastern Cape, the third of four children in a close-knit township family. His father, a municipal policeman, died when he was four, and his mother raised the family with her earnings as a domestic worker. In 1963 when Biko was 16, his older brother Khaya was jailed for nine months for allegedly participating in the activities of Poqo at Lovedale Institution where both were attending school. The taint of his brother's arrest and of his own brief interrogation by the police was taken as sufficient grounds for Biko's expulsion from Lovedale, but the following year he was admitted to St. Francis College at Mariannhill in Natal, a liberal Catholic secondary school, where he graduated in 1965.

The University of Natal Non-European section (UNNE), where Biko began his medical training in 1966, was familiarly known as Wentworth after the area where African, Indian and Coloured students lived at considerable distance from the main university campus in Durban. There in a rare housing arrangement at the Alan Taylor Residence, students from the three subordinate racial groups lived, worked and socialized on an equal-status basis. Also important in shaping Biko's evolving political outlook was the university's Student Representative Council, which had a tradition of unhindered participation in NUSAS.

Biko had been a student at Mariannhill in 1964 when Jonty Driver's speech at Botha's Hill (*Document 23*) attracted press attention and, together with the arrests of former NUSAS members in the African Resistance Movement the same year, caused NUSAS to be widely perceived as a quasi-subversive organization. Like many black students at the time, Biko found the image and philosophy of NUSAS appealing. He disliked the paternalistic approach of his liberal white teachers at Mariannhill but had nevertheless emerged from high school a firm believer in what he termed "common society liberalism," of which NUSAS then stood as the most courageous public proponent. He became an eager participant in NUSAS activities, was invited to the NUSAS leadership training seminar of early 1966, and attended its July national congresses in 1966, 1967 and 1968, the first year as an observer and later as a UNNE delegate.

Biko's brilliance in conference debates and his appealing combination of affability, self confidence and intense commitment quickly identified him to national NUSAS officials as potential leadership material. As early as July 1966 there was talk of grooming him to be the first black NUSAS president.[6] Biko's experience in NUSAS, however, increasingly convinced him that blacks had to operate on their own. Participation in NUSAS might partially substitute for the type of black student politics crushed by the Verwoerd government in the early 1960s, but NUSAS itself, with its roots in the white middle class, could never lead the struggle for black emancipation that by this time was becoming the central preoccupation of Biko's life.

At the time Biko became active in NUSAS, about a quarter of the delegates at its annual congresses were African, Indian or Coloured, and the proportion was steadily growing with increasing enrollment at the black universities. Government pressure was meanwhile becoming more threatening. After John Vorster became prime minister in late 1966, he made no secret of his intention to curb NUSAS and to place every possible restriction on the ability of universities to promote or accommodate multiracial activity. Confident that they were morally superior to their racist and authoritarian critics, white students active in NUSAS increasingly settled into a stance of rhetorical self-righteousness coupled with extreme caution toward any form of radical action.

Open disagreements between whites and blacks at national conferences became more frequent. Sometimes these took shape around such trivial but symbolic issues as whether the national flag should be flown over the conference center. Sometimes the stakes were higher, as in the defeat of a black motion at the 1966 congress to cancel annual campus fund-raising festivals (known as "rags") unless these were racially integrated. Each controversy was a test of the willingness of the white NUSAS majority to bow to the pressure of black opinion represented by a minority of delegates—but a minority which felt itself to be speaking on behalf of a national majority. Invariably the black positions were rejected as impractical or imprudent, and some proportion of the black delegates joined the whites in voting them down.

At the July 1967 NUSAS congress held at Rhodes University in Grahamstown, delegates arrived to discover that the university was observing a government ruling forbidding the accommodation of nonwhites on the campus. Indian and Coloured delegates were to be accommodated in Grahamstown, and Africans would sleep at a church in the township. Meals on campus would be served to whites only. In the first hour of the conference Biko and the UNNE delegation brought a motion to adjourn until a nonracial venue could be found. The NUSAS executive proposed a motion merely censuring the university. After an intense late-night effort by the UNNE students to rally support, the delegates voted 42 to 9 against adjournment. For Biko, it was a decisive moment: whites in NUSAS spoke eloquently about justice, but when challenged to put principles into practice, they backed away. He later recalled realizing that for a long time he "had been holding onto this whole dogma of nonracialism almost like a religion, and feeling that it is sacrilegious to question it;" yet whites lacked similar commitment. "They had this problem . . . of superiority, and they tended to take us for granted, and they wanted us to accept things that were second class. They could not see why [we] could not consider staying in that church, and I began to feel therefore that our understanding of our own situation in this country was not quite coincidental with that of the whites."[7]

It now seemed to Biko that black interests could never be adequately defended or promoted by a white-oriented organization like NUSAS where the majority was satisfied with mere moral posturing. Some of his anti-NUSAS friends at Wentworth had always taken this view, but now he not only accepted their position but moved beyond it into an exploration of alternatives. He was convinced that black students needed their own organization in which they could speak for themselves instead of relying on liberal whites to articulate their goals and prescribe their modus operandi.

The Emergence of SASO

Two years elapsed between the Rhodes congress and the formal launching of the South African Students' Organisation (SASO) in July 1969. During this period, Biko corresponded and talked with black students around the country, arguing that a blacks-only organization was needed. From his base at the medical school he recruited a cluster of able fellow students committed to the risky undertaking: Goolam "Gees" Abram from Wentworth, Petrus Machaka and Harry Nengwekhulu from Turfloop, Barney Pityana from Fort Hare whom Biko had known as a classmate during his brief period at Lovedale, and others who moved in or out of active participation with the fluctuations of their academic and personal lives. In December 1968, a consultative meeting was held at Mariannhill at which a name and draft constitution were approved, and plans were laid for a formal launching conference at Turfloop in July 1969.

The odds against SASO's survival were heavy. Many students dismissed it as doomed from the start, knowing that any voice raised in political dissent would attract the attention of the omnipresent security police, not to mention their willing allies in the administrative apparatuses of the black universities. Moreover, running a national organization cost money, and how could black students hope to come up with adequate funds? Not least was the ideological problem posed by a blacks-only organization. Did this not imply an acceptance of the whole despised "separate development" framework? Around this core of rational and moral doubts swirled other arguments: some students still believed that NUSAS represented the best expression of their own anti-racist ideals; others, from the Africanist tradition of the PAC, objected to Biko's notion that SASO should ally Africans with Indians and Coloureds. By late 1970, however, SASO had overcome these doubts among a majority of its potential constituents and moved into a prominent position on most of the black campuses.

SASO's success in establishing and consolidating itself as a force in national life for more than eight years reversed a defeatist pattern of political expectations, and demonstrated that well planned initiatives by blacks could ultimately create changes powerful enough to undermine the prevailing political order. In SASO's case, there were three conditions that facilitated this success. First, SASO took root because of its capacity to seek out, recognize, and exploit every potential material and intangible resource that could be wrung out of its resource-poor political environment. Second, its early leadership was skillful in devising tactics that, at least for the first few critical years, were able to outwit the system of rigid controls that kept blacks politically immobilized. Most important was the ability of the early leadership to craft an ideological appeal capable of striking a responsive chord among large numbers of young blacks. These strengths did not flow from a plan worked out in advance, but emerged in stages as SASO's leadership confronted day to day political reality, drawing at each point on Biko's compelling leadership and his remarkable talent for inspiring the best efforts of those around him.

Ironically, the earliest allies to whom SASO's founders turned were the leaders of the existing liberal student organizations. Although the rank and file white members of NUSAS were antagonistic to SASO from the start, NUSAS leaders, including Duncan Innes and his successor as NUSAS president in 1970 and 1971, Neville Curtis, admired Biko, were sympathetic to his analysis of the shortcomings of liberalism, and worked closely with him to establish an organizational relationship that would minimize rancor and competition. During SASO's emergence as a full-fledged national movement, it borrowed heavily from the organizational model evolved by NUSAS, including the methods of leadership recruitment and training that were to account for the resilience of the black consciousness movement once the state's delayed reaction set in.

SASO's relationship with the nonracial University Christian Movement was even more instrumental in assuring its early survival. After determining who his potential allies were at the 1967 NUSAS congress at Rhodes, Biko remained to attend a UCM conference in Grahamstown. UCM, then less than a year old, had attracted a membership that was almost half black. Its 1967 conference enabled Biko to canvass support informally for the idea of a black organization, a process he continued at later UCM meetings.

While using UCM as a recruiting ground, Biko and Pityana also began building a close relationship with Colin Collins, Basil Moore and several other whites in the UCM leadership. Like their counterparts in NUSAS, UCM's leaders tended to be more radically disposed than their organization's white rank and file. Despite their personal commitment to interracial cooperation, Collins and Moore recognized that until blacks could organize and lead their own challenge to the apartheid system, any political efforts by liberal whites would be unavailing. When full-time UCM staff positions were later taken up by Justice Moloto, Chris Mokoditoa and Stanley Ntwasa, no barriers were imposed on their close association with SASO. Quietly but deliberately, the UCM became an inconspicuous but vital organizational backstop to SASO, providing financial and logistical support, contacts with potential overseas backers, and an expanded network through which political literature could be obtained and circulated among student activists.

Beating the system of state controls was a challenge for early SASO activists and called for innovative tactics. Up to a point, this meant simply taking advantage of the system's failure to construct a completely airtight political environment for African students. Book censorship was tight but never total, for example. Ethnic segregation was the norm but, as at Wentworth, there were gaps. Besides spaces left open by the system's imperfections, there were other opportunities evident to SASO's strategists. Biko saw, for example, that if effectively organized and led, Student Representative Councils could enlarge the space for student activism. Besides creating a platform for SASO, a national network of SRCs could enable campus leaders more effectively to stand up to university authorities in voicing student demands. When Pityana and 21 other students were expelled from Fort Hare in 1968, the Turfloop SRC had organized a sympathy strike. Such demonstrations of solidarity could incrementally shift the administration-student balance of power, even if they could not always prevent the victimization of individual students. Moreover, SRCs could obtain funds from university authorities to subsidize intervarsity sports tournaments and student social gatherings which could provide cover for SASO's organizing activities. SRCs could also command office space, duplicating machines, and telephones, essential resources that SASO on its own could not afford. Gradually, SASO's support for SRCs gained ground until by 1973 every black campus had an elected student council.[8]

Although adopted almost entirely for other reasons, SASO's policy of racial separatism also helped to create a zone of noninterference from the state within which the fledgling organization could mature unimpeded. When the movement's founders set out to build an organization from which whites would be excluded, they knew it was an approach that would temporarily confound the security establishment. Vorster, while promoting a benign view of separate development as a policy beneficial to blacks, had also put a high priority on destroying the handful of multiracial organizations that still existed. By taking a separatist approach, SASO could avoid falling within Vorster's priority-target area, and could buy time while "the system" tried to decide whether the organization was an asset or liability in the promotion of apartheid. As late as mid-1971, the pro-government Afrikaans press, on the rare occasions when it threw a glance in SASO's direction, still reflected the wishful idea that the new spirit afoot among blacks would soon find its proper outlet in the homelands. By the time this illusion had been dispelled, the organization was already firmly rooted and its ideological seeds widely sown.

On the ideological front, the development of SASO was carefully managed to create a united constituency. Biko believed that the organization should identify the interests of Indians and Coloureds with those of Africans, and that it should aggressively reject any involvement by white liberals so as to impress on blacks the need to take the initiative in their own struggle. He wanted to elevate "blackness" as an inclusive and positive concept of identity, and to discredit the demeaning terms "non-white" and "non-European." Within the unique interracial setting of Wentworth these ideas seemed plausible, but none of them found ready acceptance in the broader milieu of student politics, where the majority of Africans were still fixed on the goal of "getting into NUSAS." Outside Wentworth, notwithstanding the abstract appeal of common-society liberalism, Africans, Indians and Coloureds remained socially distant from one another, and even those Coloureds and Indians who sided politically with Africans felt uncomfortable referring to themselves as "black." Africans generally did not regard Indians and Coloureds as people whose oppression was on a par with their own. To bring a majority of students to accept the new "black" terminology and identity, Biko first had to build a consensus among his closest colleagues and then move slowly to increase SASO's membership while easing the position of the organization step by step toward his envisioned goal.

The communique drawn up at SASO's inaugural conference in July 1969 (*Document 38*) is evidence that forging a new ideology was an uphill effort. Too many Indian and Coloured students still rejected the term "black" for it to be used in place of "non-white." To appease NUSAS loyalists, the communique claimed that SASO was not being formed in opposition to NUSAS but merely as an organization through which better contact could be maintained among "non-white institutions of higher learning." Gradually, however, African students responded more and more favorably to the arguments for an all-black initiative, and a growing number of Coloureds and Indians also began to see merit in the idea. *Document 37,* which describes a student meeting at Wentworth in March 1969, vividly conveys the atmosphere of raw racial feeling which accompanied the emergence of what one white student called this "new black consciousness."

Inventing Black Consciousness

The emergence of SASO brought to the surface an outpouring of anger and frustration held in check during the preceding decade. Black students at tertiary institutions were the most caught up in the revolt against old habits of acquiescent behavior, but the fever slowly spread through urban communities into high schools, and eventually into some of the remoter rural corners of the country. By the late 1970s it was not unusual for someone driving through country districts to be greeted by children at the roadside making fist-up Black Power salutes. The message of the movement was simple and compelling. It was also flexible and ambiguous enough to accommodate a range of older black political attitudes, though as we shall see, not all of them.

At the core of the message was a call for black self-reliance and self-assertion. "Blacks are tired of standing at the touchlines to witness a game that they should be playing," Biko declared in February 1970. "They want to do things for themselves and all by themselves."[9] A deep sense of inferiority, inculcated through the system of Bantu Education and reinforced by white arrogance, had to be erased and replaced by pride in black values. Fear of whites and of the government had to be replaced by a new courage built on group solidarity. All victims of white oppression had to draw together, not to indulge in self-pity as victims, but to find strength in numbers and to work together to bring about fundamental changes. Just how the apartheid system might eventually fall could not be foreseen, nor could SASO discuss the subject openly without stepping over the line between legal and illegal activity. But no doubts existed about the ultimate objective—liberation through revolution—or about the urgent need for blacks to go on the offensive as a first step toward this end.

SASO's founders knew that self-defeating black attitudes could not be refashioned overnight. They were also acutely aware that premature confrontations with white authority could spell the end of the entire high-risk experiment. They thus decided to concentrate initially on projecting an image of SASO as an inward-looking movement concerned primarily with self-evaluation among blacks, and secondly, on destroying student attitudes of deference toward white liberals. By the time SASO marked the end of its first year with a General Students' Council (GSC) at Wentworth in July 1970, the organization had begun to sharpen its focus on what the preamble of its constitution called "psychological liberation." The GSC called for an elevation of student "consciousness" and officially moved to the use of "black" instead of "nonwhite." A resolution calling for derecognition of NUSAS as a "true National Union" was passed overwhelmingly." The SASO leadership was now ready to begin the drive for their second objective, and in August, the *SASO Newsletter* carried a scorching attack on white liberals by Biko under the title "Black Souls in White Skins?"

Whereas the National Party justified racial discrimination by reference to the hypocritical ideals of "separate development," the article asserted, white liberals disclaimed any responsibility for apartheid. Yet their approach was merely more subtle in its self-serving outcome. Liberals claimed to want racial equality, but in the artificially integrated circles which they created, real equality never existed because racially-based complexes of superiority and inferiority still prevailed. Whites did all the talking, and blacks the listening. Liberals relieved their guilt by expressing aversion to discrimination and by mixing with carefully selected blacks in these circles, knowing that they were also free at any time to extract whatever they wanted "from the exclusive pool of white privileges." Meanwhile, blacks were lulled into taking a back seat in their own struggle, and even into believing that the small, artificially integrated circles were somehow a step toward liberation. Black complexes of dependency and powerlessness—the product of "300 years of deliberate oppression, denigration and derision"—could only be erased by "a very strong grass-roots build-up of black consciousness," Biko argued, "such that blacks can learn to assert themselves and stake their rightful claim."[10]

The term "black consciousness," which entered SASO discourse during 1970, was not precisely defined at first, but beneath the protective abstractness of the term lay a clear resemblance to the fundamental message of racial nationalism: South Africa was a black country on a black continent where ultimately black values, interests, and leadership should be dominant. When the second General Students' Council met at Wentworth in July 1971, an explicit though somewhat guarded definition of "black consciousness" was set out for the first time in the SASO Policy Manifesto (*Document 44*):

(i) BLACK CONSCIOUSNESS is an attitude of mind, a way of life.
(ii) The basic tenet of Black Consciousness is that the Blackman must reject all value systems that seek to make him a foreigner in the country of his birth and reduce his basic human dignity.
(iii) The Blackman must build up his own value systems, see himself as self-defined and not as defined by others.

The long range goal was not to drive whites out of South Africa, but rather to transform the basis of black-white coexistence. "South Africa is a country in which both Black and White live and shall continue to live together," the Manifesto declared. The push for black awareness was merely a means by which blacks could begin to rid themselves of subservient status in their own country. The white man had come into the African house as a guest and had taken it over, Biko wrote in early 1971 (*Document 41*). Ultimately, blacks "wanted to remove him from our table, strip the table of all trappings put on it by him, decorate it in true African style, settle down and then ask him to join us on our own terms if he liked." The true integration of equals could then occur, instead of the artificial integration envisioned by white liberals in which blacks were expected to abandon their own way of doing things and assimilate into the system of values and codes of behavior established and perpetuated by whites.[11] Ideally, national culture would someday become a "fusion of the life-styles of the various groups," Biko wrote in "Black Souls" in one of his most explicit expressions of African nationalism; however, "one cannot escape the fact that the culture shared by the majority group in any given society must ultimately determine the broad direction taken by the joint culture of that society. This need not cramp the style of those who feel differently but on the whole, a country in Africa, in which the majority of the people are African must inevitably exhibit African values and be truly African in style."

SASO's campaign to assert the dignity of all things black struck a particularly resonant chord among university students, many of whom were struggling to find a satisfying identity within South Africa's rigidly stratified society. Between 1961 and 1970, enrollment at the five "bush" campuses rose from 811 to 4,601.[12] Growing enrollment—necessary to justify the construction of five separate ethnic universities—steadily increased the number of people affected by the problem. University students were positioned to enter the highest stratum accessible to members of the subordinate races. Government authorities urged them to see their role as the uplifting of their respective "groups," but many saw this merely as an invitation to become privileged instruments within the state's mechanisms of control. It was clear that once enough members of the black middle class had become co-opted by the government as teachers, clerks, and bantustan bureaucrats, the National Party was planning to set the machinery of domination on automatic and leave blacks to run it themselves.[13]

African students felt alienated no matter which direction they turned.[14] In the urban townships where most had grown up, less educated people, including their age peers, looked up to them with exaggerated awe as a social elite. Most had little in common with rural or small town blacks near the remote "bush" campuses. Whites living in these areas often regarded black students with hostility. After university, white employers in the private sector might hire them because of a shortage of skilled whites, but students were aware that educated blacks in white industry and commerce were usually treated with suspicion and not advanced if promotion meant placing them in authority over whites. They knew that little or no respect would be accorded to their degrees earned at the tribal universities. Their white student counterparts regarded the black colleges with condescension, as did older black graduates whose education had been completed before the introduction of university apartheid and the state-designed and controlled "Bantu Education" curriculum imposed on African schools by the Verwoerd government in the 1950s.

Cultural alienation further reinforced these obstacles to the development of a personal sense of purpose. Urban African culture was an evolving amalgam of many traditions, black and white. For African university students, however, as well as for Coloureds, there was strong pressure to meet the popular expectation that they should resemble whites whose social status they were approaching by virtue of their education. Commercial advertising exhorted them to dress, eat, and furnish their homes in styles preferred by whites. Skin lightening creams and hair straighteners aggressively marketed to black women reinforced a premise that black was not beautiful. Yet at the same time, it was pure fantasy to believe that adopting white cultural norms would result in the actual acceptance of blacks as social equals by whites. A generation earlier, before the advent of National Party rule, white liberals had held out the vague promise of eventual assimilation, but by 1970 it was impossible for anyone to cling to such a delusion.

Exclusion from the social company of whites was wounding enough to educated Africans, but more insulting were the National Party's persistent efforts to force a neotraditional "Bantu" identity on Africans in order to lend credibility to its plan for "independent" ethnic homelands. Black consciousness as "an attitude of mind, a way of life" provided a means of scoffing at imposed tribal identities, and of asserting the undivided community of interests not only of all Africans, but of all those excluded from power by the apartheid system.

To the government's myth that all Africans were tribal "Bantus," black consciousness posed its own counter-myth: the existence of a common "black" identity. Writing in the *SASO Newsletter* of September 1970, Biko made no claim that a single black culture existed, but merely that the presence of a common enemy made the creation of a broader base useful (*Document 40*). As momentum gathered to popularize black consciousness, some of its adherents insisted that a core of common cultural traits could be found among Africans, Indians, and Coloureds, but most agreed only that intergroup empathy could exist, based on the common experience of discrimination. "No muse inspires the TECON people," declared the program notes for a 1973 "Black Images" festival featuring a performance by the Theatre Council of Natal (TECON), an Indian drama group. "Black artists, writers, poets, actors . . . are all moved by the Black experience—that ugly-beautiful, pathetic-sublime, maelstrom of despair-hope-anger-pain-and finally, cold-hard resolve. You can only come out of this melting pot beautifully black—or DEAD."[15]

Many Indians and Coloureds regarded Africans as social inferiors, and indignantly rejected being called "black." It was one thing for black Americans to identify with a remote and glamorized vision of Africa, Coloured educator Richard van der Ross observed. They could even popularize "a very noticeable Papuan hairstyle" and call it "Afro."

> But in South Africa, the Africans with whom the Coloured people come into contact are not the idealised, romanticised possessors of an exotic culture all their own, but the urban African of the South African city and village. He is poor, ill-fed and ill-clad. His housing, schooling, occupation, indeed his entire lifestyle is inferior to that of the Coloured people generally. And because this lifestyle is not regarded as exotic or desirable, the African himself is not seen through the same rosy spectacles through which American blacks see him.

Differences of language and culture, as well as of class, inhibited political identification, he added, as did uncertainty among Coloureds about whether Africans would sincerely rally in the future to the cause of Coloured equality.[16]

For some Coloureds and Indians, however, the black consciousness movement held out a welcome opportunity to modify racial self-images which had become uncomfortable. For Indians, who comprise less than three percent of South Africa's population, black consciousness offered greater strength of numbers and also hope that anti-Indian feelings among Africans would not lead to the kind of racial persecution then taking place in Uganda under Idi Amin. Among Coloureds, especially young people trying to come to terms with the ambiguities of Coloured identity—indigenous but not African, Afrikaans-speaking but not white—black consciousness offered an appealing alternative: being black and proud of it. As one activist later put it, "were we a buffer group? were we part of the solution? were we part of the problem? All of those were fairly simply answered by black consciousness."[17]

At the University of the Western Cape (UWC), where student politics were conducted mainly in English because even Afrikaans-speaking Coloureds associated their home language with oppression, there was a shift toward more comfortable discourse in Afrikaans. According to Jakes Gerwel, then one of a handful of Coloured lecturers at UWC, "Coloured people started identifying themselves as black people in their own right; they weren't going to play whites, they weren't going to play [Africans] . . . So gradually you could be an Afrikaans-speaking black [and get] away from that schizophrenia around Afrikaans."[18] To discredit official attempts to persuade Coloureds to think of themselves as distinct from other blacks, black consciousness adherents began using the term "*so-called* Coloured," a label which gained wide currency by the late 1970s and served as a constant reminder that "black" was the politically preferred terminology. Many socially conservative Coloureds were never persuaded to see themselves as allies of the African majority. Nevertheless, enough pro-black sentiment had been generated among Coloured intellectuals by 1973 to make National Party *verligtes*—the party's "enlightened" wing—press for serious reforms aimed at counteracting Coloured disaffection.[19]

Intellectual Influences

In searching for a constructive sense of purpose, black students had no models of collective self-fulfillment to draw on in South African history, other than Afrikaner nationalism's own road to power through ethnic mobilization. Yet the Afrikaner model was very rarely evoked by black students. Far more appealing were examples of struggle and progress from elsewhere in Africa and from the ongoing movement toward racial equality in the United States. By the late 1960s, political literature from these countries was finding its way into South Africa, providing important intellectual stimulation, and helping to inspire an outpouring of political writings by blacks unprecedented in South Africa's history.[20]

To say that SASO's ideology was imported from elsewhere in the black world would be to assign much too little significance to the life experiences and political intuition of the movement's founders. Rather, foreign writings, critically sifted for their most relevant ideas, enriched the language and analytical content of black consciousness thinking, adding greatly to its broader impact. Never had black South African intellectuals made such a deliberate and thoroughgoing attempt to borrow and selectively adapt foreign ideas in order to influence mass thinking; and never had efforts to shape mass thinking met with such success in so short a period, partly because the same influences at work on the thinking of intellectuals had already been at work through the media, independently preparing the African urban population, and students in particular, for the spread of the new self-image.

Coming of age politically in the 1960s, SASO's founders had watched most of Africa pass rapidly through the transition to independence, including the neighboring territories of Botswana, Lesotho and Swaziland. By 1970, the Portuguese were fighting unwinnable colonial wars in Angola and Mozambique, and Ian Smith's rebel government in Rhodesia was under pressure from world sanctions. Ghana's and Nigeria's generation of state-founders had been toppled in army coups, but optimism regarding Africa's future continued to prevail among black intellectuals. In South Africa the literature of African anticolonialism was supplemented by collections of the post-independence speeches of Julius Nyerere of Tanzania on the theme of *ujamaa,* or African socialism. When SASO's founders began their active search for ideological ammunition, some turned naturally to such writings as a source of inspiration and authority. Nyerere's 1967 Arusha Declaration rang true, wrote Barney Pityana, when it said: "We have been oppressed a great deal; we have been exploited a great deal; and we have been disregarded a great deal. It is our weakness that has led to our being oppressed, exploited and disregarded, Now we want a revolution—a revolution which brings to an end our weakness, so that we are never again exploited, oppressed or humiliated." "The message," concluded Pityana for the readers of the *SASO Newsletter,* "is simple. BLACK MAN YOU ARE ON YOUR OWN. Like Nyerere we must minimize reliance on external aid. No one in a position of power and prosperity can offer such aid as would threaten his own security."[21]

Also influential were the writings of the Martinique-born psychiatrist, Frantz Fanon, some of which—in English translation and openly sold—had become available in South Africa by 1968. Fanon provided a potent intellectual antidote to the doubts harbored by many blacks about the moral legitimacy of a strategy that promoted racial polarization.[22] *The Wretched of the Earth (Les Damnes de la Terre),* Fanon's most widely read book, was a caustic analysis of settler colonialism in Africa and its psychological conse-quences for rulers and ruled. Puncturing the pretense of white claims to moral and cultural superiority, Fanon ridiculed colonialism's self-serving definitions of right and wrong, and described with approval the tendency of racial conflicts to assume a Manichaean quality of good-against-evil. Feelings of anger and hatred in the oppressed, he said, were not symptoms of moral weakness but healthy responses to the indignity of being treated as subhuman.

Fanon, Nyerere, and most African nationalist ideologues of the 1960s and 1970s coupled their anti-imperialism with a rejection of capitalism, which they held responsible for economic injustice in the third world. In SASO this view was taken as axiomatic, although explicit endorsements of socialism were avoided as too risky in the organization's formative period. (See, for example, the vague discussion of economic options in *Document 39*). Significantly, however, a superficial conviction that socialism was superior to capitalism did not carry over into a serious effort to explore Marxist analysis during SASO's early years. By the mid-1970s, interest in Marxism rose dramatically as confidence in the practical efficacy of race-based nationalism began to slacken. But in the years when black consciousness was being consolidated as a political credo, the classical writings of Marxism (banned but obtainable with effort) do not seem to have been in wide circulation among black students outside the small and highly intellectual circles of the Non-European Unity Movement. White academics in the English-medium universities and in exile, influenced by the radical New Left of Europe and the United States in the 1960s, were about to beget an influential school of neo-Marxist historiography that would further discredit the moral authority of South African liberalism and boost the intellectual appeal of class analysis. But in 1969–70 this new intellectual wave had not yet struck. Instead many of those in SASO who experienced interracial fraternization within NUSAS were put off by the superiority complex of radical whites who considered themselves Marxists. Their intellectualized embrace of class analysis, Biko believed, served them well by permitting them to identify with, and even presume to give leadership to, the oppressed, while helping them deny the guilt-laden reality of their membership in the oppressor group.

> [T]hough whites are our problem, it is still other whites who want to tell us how to deal with that problem. They do so by dragging all sorts of red herrings across our paths. They tell us that the situation is a class struggle rather than a racial one. Let them go to van Tonder in the Free State and tell him this. We believe we know what the problem is, and we will stick by our findings.[23]

SASO's strategy of racial solidarity and separatism was better served ideologically by the writings of black Americans. Through a combination of historical accident and the multiple spillover effects set in motion by the retreat of colonialism in Africa, black intellectuals in South Africa found themselves facing an acute crisis of identity and action just at a time when the struggle of American blacks was reaching a similar spiritual crossroads. Between the 1954 Supreme Court decision barring school segregation and the 1965 Voting Rights Act, legal barriers to racial integration in the United States were swept away by the militant campaigns of the civil rights movement. But disillusionment followed these victories as the continuing realities of racism and class disparities became more starkly apparent. Riots erupted in American ghettos, and the rhetoric of black populist politics grew increasingly radical, challenging traditional assimilationist aspirations and posing instead a range of separatist or pluralist visions.

The literature of black American separatism reached South Africa through bookstores and libraries, and some made its way directly into black student networks through white liberals sympathetic to the emerging spirit of black militancy. Most avidly consumed were *Soul on Ice* by Eldridge Cleaver, *Black Power: The Politics of Liberation in America* by Stokely Carmichael and Charles Hamilton, and the *Autobiography of Malcolm X*, which remained unbanned in South Africa until 1974. Tapes of speeches delivered by Malcolm X and Martin Luther King also circulated among students. American catchwords like "relevance" and "power structure" entered South African political discourse, along with the term "black consciousness" itself, and the aggressive visual symbol of the upraised fist. The advent of photocopying machines and cassette tape recorders facilitated the diffusion of newly acquired material, and new techniques for the mass production of printed T-shirts gave SASO a sartorial vehicle for popularization of the "Black Power" fist motif.[24] Afro hair styles and symbolic paraphernalia also spread, as did a preference for African rather than Christian or "European" first names. By the end of the decade, striking auto workers at the Ford factory in Port Elizabeth listed among their demands (*Document 84*) that the company must lift its ban on the wearing of medallions in the shape of Africa. That worker pressure for economic concessions could be juxtaposed in this way with an assertion of racial identity suggests that awakened nationalism was by no means confined to the educated middle class.

African-American literature contributed rhetorical trademarks to the message of black consciousness as well as lending new respectability to SASO's arguments for a blacks-only approach.[25] The exercise of drawing comparisons between the contrasting racial situations in South Africa and the United States also helped to sharpen the analytical thrust of black consciousness thinking. *Document 39*, for example, a report on two SASO leadership training seminars held in September 1970, notes that one seminar group had to analyze Carmichael and Hamilton's statement that "before entering the open society we must first close our ranks." For black Americans as a minority, the group concluded, the statement made sense and reflected the assessment that "if you can't beat them, join them, but join them from a position of strength;" whereas in South Africa the statement had meaning only within the context of a new kind of open society in which the pacesetters would be the black majority.

The topics discussed in *Document 39*—capitalism and socialism, integration and separation, the history of the black struggle and its future, tactics and strategies of change—point to the intense thirst for political enlightenment that the black consciousness movement inspired. Students were no longer willing to allow their schooling to stand in the way of their education. After a decade of silence, a new generation was finding its voice, not least because of the catalytic effect of ideas emanating from elsewhere in the black world. Writing about his exposure to SASO as a first-year student at Ngoye in 1970, Mosibudi Mangena recalls the excitement surrounding campus speeches by Biko, Pityana, Nengwekhulu and others.

They put their message across passionately, courageously, convincingly and eloquently. They epitomised self-confidence and commitment. I had never seen such confident young black men before. They quoted frequently from Fanon, Nkrumah, Malcolm X . . . . Except for Nkrumah I had not heard of these other names before. . . . One of the immediate consequences of our involvement with SASO was a scramble for political knowledge. Apart from a host of discussion groups and seminars, there was a hunt for relevant reading material, especially works by the Nkrumahs, Fanons, Du Bois's and so forth. The bush universities' libraries were of no help in this regard and personal enterprise was the only way out. Friends and liberal bookshops became the more likely sources of these precious "jewels." Within a short time, such material was as common on our book shelves as was Charles Dickens or Shakespeare.[26]

Inevitably, this "scramble for political knowledge" sparked an intense curiosity about South Africa's own history of racial struggles. Fear had caused this subject to assume taboo proportions in the 1960s, as parents and teachers tried to protect the younger generation from "dangerous" knowledge about past confrontations between blacks and the state. Barney Pityana and others who grew up in the eastern Cape, where the ANC had its strongest following in the 1950s, have recalled that adults did not speak about the Congress movement but referred obliquely to "the big thing" of the past. As a child in her home area near Pietermaritzburg, Nkosazana Zuma remembers hearing about young men who had left the country to train as guerrillas; but nobody would disclose "what this training was all about, or where they were. I just knew that so-and-so's big brother had gone . . . to learn how to use guns and fight."[27] The average school child in the early 1970s, according to one Soweto political figure at the time, had never heard of the ANC or the PAC, and could not identify the names of Lutuli, Mandela or Sobukwe.[28]

At the time of SASO's founding, the university students who knew most about the liberation organizations of the past were those whose older relatives had belonged to political movements or trade unions before the crackdown of the early 1960s, or who themselves had belonged to ASA or ASUSA before these were suppressed. Harry Nengwekhulu and Temba Sono, two early leaders in SASO, had been members of ASUSA, and Pityana had been involved in an ASA-initiated group at Lovedale. Some of Biko's relatives were PAC supporters.[29] Strini Moodley's father had been a trade unionist and a member of the Communist Party.[30] Aubrey Mokoape, a medical student active in SASO, as a 16-year-old at Orlando High School in Soweto had been arrested with Robert Sobukwe on the day of the Sharpeville massacre in March 1960 and had spent a year in prison.[31]

These connections as well as individual contacts between SASO members and political veterans of older generations gradually opened a window into the experience of past movements, providing substance for study and argument at late-night student discussions in SASO's formative years. Written sources supplemented oral ones. Clandestine copies of Edward Roux's *Time*

Longer Than Rope, Mary Benson's *South Africa: The Struggle for a Birthright,*
and Mandela's *No Easy Walk to Freedom* circulated among students, along
with a dog-eared miscellany of pamphlets and papers preserved in cup-
boards and files by Unity Movement intellectuals, former Communists,
members of the Civil Rights League in Cape Town, and other radicals. "I was
very attached to the SRC files" of the Natal medical school, Biko later
observed, because they were a cache of historical records: old political
debates, writings by student leaders quoting political sources and the like,
much of which was useful in helping SASO members draw out lessons from
the history of black resistance.[32]

Ultimately, it is notable that black consciousness intellectuals made no
systematic effort to rewrite black history or demolish the canons of colonial
historiography, although they made occasional reference to the need to do
so. The need to change the future proved too compelling, and the task of
changing the past was left to radical white academics. Nevertheless, in
probing the lessons of black history and making contact with resistance
survivors, SASO leaders mined the deposits of obscure but accessible
political knowledge and used what they found to refine their own strategic
approaches.

Examining with hindsight the early intellectual influences on SASO, it is
also noteworthy that one important component of New Left thinking—its
critique of gender discrimination—made no impact on the black consciousness movement. Focused entirely on the need to revolutionize the attitudes
and assumptions underlying black-white relationships, black consciousness
was oblivious to analogous forms of domination and oppression affecting
women. Women who became prominent activists in the movement, including Dr. Vuyelwa Mashalaba, Dr. Mamphela Ramphele, Deborah Matshoba,
Brigitte Mabandla, Thenjiwe Mtintso, Winnie Kgware, Dr. Nkosazana
Dlamini Zuma, and Sibongile Mthembu, injected no lasting feminist dimension into its theory or praxis, both of which remained marked by patriarchal
values and a sexist style and rhetoric.[33]

Black Theology

While SASO was pursuing the development of its blacks-only organization and philosophy, some rank and file members continued to participate
in the activities of the multiracial and theologically unconventional University Christian Movement. Taking into account the burgeoning black student
sentiment against "artificial integration" following the founding of SASO, the
UCM began concentrating on a few specific projects, two of which—the
promotion of literacy and the popularization of black theology—involved
blacks exclusively.[34] Black theology, which had emerged as a religious
theme in the United States in the late 1960s, might have remained a subject
of interest only among academic theologians in South Africa had it not been
widely aired by Basil Moore in 1970 in a provocative paper entitled "Towards
a Black Theology." So positive was the response among blacks that a Black

Theology Project was established within UCM, and a coordinator appointed—Stanley Ntwasa, a student at the Federal Theological Seminary at Alice in the eastern Cape. In 1971 seminars were organized to develop and promote the new perspective, and in 1972 a book of papers from these seminars, *Essays on Black Theology,* was published by UCM, and immediately banned by the government.[35]

Coming as an unplanned dividend alongside SASO's campaign to raise political awareness among blacks, black theology buttressed the appeal of black consciousness as a moral and political alternative to the ideology of liberalism. Though complex in its philosophical implications, black theology proceeded from two simple themes of Christian belief—that God favors the poor, and that Christ came to liberate the oppressed. These themes were projected as the core of a situational or contextual theology, one not necessarily appropriate to all Christians in all circumstances, merely one specifically suited to the religious needs of blacks in a racist society. Where white missionaries had imposed religious beliefs enmeshed with European cultural practices and values, black theology stood for the indigenization of church symbols, liturgies and ethical teachings. In place of an emphasis on the saving of individual souls through acts of faith, it proposed that the spiritual liberation of downtrodden peoples could be achieved through a reorientation of religion away from the particular beliefs, priorities and church personnel associated with oppression. White paternalism, whether of the crude kind embodied in the theology of the Dutch Reformed Church or the more benign variant of the mainline English churches, was identified as an obstacle to the realization of divine will. Since the overwhelming majority of Christians in South Africa are black, black theology emphasized that the time was long overdue for blacks to assume leadership of church institutions. The goal was a Christianity in which the equal humanity of blacks was recognized; but first the colonial religion of the mission churches had to be replaced by a religion that approached life and faith through the experience of the country's suffering majority. In time such a reformed Christianity would become the vehicle for the spiritual liberation of whites from their own hypocrisy, as well as a means to draw back into the church those blacks, particularly the young, whom white hypocrisy had driven away.

The excitement and debate surrounding the introduction of these ideas is conveyed in *Document 42,* a report by Ntwasa on a national UCM seminar on black theology held in March 1971. Meeting four months later at Wentworth for its annual General Students' Council, SASO passed a resolution on black theology formulated by a commission led by Ntwasa, this time in his capacity as a SASO member (*Document 43*). "Christianity as propagated by the white dominant churches," the resolution maintained, "has proved beyond doubt to be a support for the status quo, which to Black people means oppression." The task of black theology, declared the commission, was to "free Black people not only from estrangement to God but also from slave mentality, inferiority complex, distrust of themselves and continued dependence on others culminating in self-hate."

The initial enthusiasm generated by black theology gave rise to high hopes in SASO that the mood of awakening nationalism would spread rapidly into seminaries and from there into black churches with their powerful grassroots outreach. Eventually it became clear that these hopes were unrealistic given the conservative nature of church institutions, black as well as white. Most white clergymen perceived black theology as an attack on their leadership by blacks who were "unqualified" to hold responsible positions. To many English-speaking white Christians, black theology bore an alarming resemblance to the situational theology that Afrikaner nationalists had turned into a civil religion to justify their monopoly of political power. At seminaries where black ministers were trained, it was difficult to insert a bias for black theology or community activism into the syllabus as long as white staff continued heavily to outnumber black. The problem was scarcely eased as blacks over time were promoted to replace whites but proved almost as partial as their predecessors to the traditional academic curriculum.

Nevertheless, support for the basic tenets of black theology was readily forthcoming from a number of leading black clergymen, including Anglican Bishop Alphaeus Zulu, Manas Buthelezi, Desmond Tutu, and others who later became prominent, including Allan Boesak of the Coloured Dutch Reformed church who became student chaplain at the University of the Western Cape in 1976. Many seminary students who were touched by the debates of the early 1970s found their thinking influenced by black theology. But a large gap remained between preaching a theology of self-respect and actually reorienting black churches to become bases for social insurgency. Black ministers enjoyed a social prestige and security in their communities which could be put at risk by activities that aroused the ire of local white authorities or conservative church higher-ups. In the 1970s, discretion almost always proved the better part of valor for those in such positions, and this left black congregations without strong direction from men who under less repressive conditions might have been an important leadership element in their communities.[36]

Biko, Ntwasa, Pityana and others in SASO labored optimistically but with meager results to plant the gospel of radical politics in the cautious ranks of the Interdenominational African Ministers Association (IDAMASA). Working in close touch with Basil Moore, whom the Christian Institute hired in 1971 to prepare a theological training syllabus for the African Independent Churches Association (AICA), SASO also strove informally to draw ministers in the politically conservative separatist churches into the popularization of black theology. Setbacks were many, including the banning of Moore and Ntwasa in early 1972, and factional disputes within AICA were frequent. Over the longer run, black theology as a doctrine of political activism failed to take root in black churches, not because the plant itself lacked vigor but because the socio-political environment in which it was trying to root itself in the early 1970s was still stubbornly inhospitable to its growth.[37]

Evolving Political Strategies

In debating which principles should guide SASO strategy, it was natural that Biko, Pityana, Nengwekhulu and others who came and went from SASO's early inner circle were heavily influenced by what they took to be lessons from the history of the ANC and PAC. Since the older movements had no organized presence in the country at the time of SASO's emergence, these lessons could be considered with some detachment. "Unlike us," Biko said in 1972, "they are powerless. So that we feel it's not our duty to relate to them in the way that they would like; it is their duty to relate to us in the way that they would like."[38] In SASO's experience, the distinction between the ANC and PAC was extremely vague in the popular mind, and their exile organizations were regarded as inconsequential. Respect could therefore be expressed for political veterans of an earlier era and for the men imprisoned on Robben Island, but there was no sense in which early SASO leaders saw themselves as mere caretakers, temporarily manning the political helm until the return of a generation of older and more capable captains.

In fact, SASO's founders began with opinions about the historical liberation organizations which were rather critical, and which seem only to have been confirmed by further discussion and reading in the 1969–73 period. Except for Robert Sobukwe, who was admired and sometimes consulted by Biko and other SASO leaders, the past leadership of PAC was dismissed as inept.[39] PAC was credited with recognizing the importance of building a spirit of black self-reliance, but was faulted for appealing to Africans only. The Non-European Unity Movement had grasped the principle of building a broader black front, but its approach had been too intellectual. The ANC had also appreciated the importance of building alliances among the oppressed but, SASO leaders believed, it had made the mistake of including whites, with the result that blacks were deflected from developing the type of militant nationalism best suited to the task of political mobilization.

Given the lingering loyalties of older people toward the ANC, PAC, and Unity Movement, SASO leaders generally refrained from criticizing these organizations openly. Reverence for past resistance movements and for their heroes and martyrs was the main theme at annual commemoration days held by SASO on the anniversary of the Sharpeville massacre. On rare occasions Biko openly criticized the ANC's alliance policy, as he did in a speech at the Abe Bailey Institute in Cape Town in January 1971 (*Document 41*). As time went on, these critical comments earned him hostility from the exiled ANC leadership as well as from ANC and Natal Indian Congress partisans inside the country who feared that black consciousness was trying to position itself as a successor to the Congress movement. In Biko's view, conditioned as it no doubt was by the sense that SASO was operating in a political vacuum, organizational rivalries could only confuse and impede black progress; the healthiest outlook for young and old alike was "there's no more PAC, there's no more ANC, there's just the struggle."[40]

When SASO began designing its organizational strategy in 1968-69, it applied one clear lesson of the preceding political era by adopting an emphasis on the systematic recruitment and training of future leadership.[41] In the 1950s, the ANC had been hammered by banning orders restricting its office-holders and by the arrest of its top activists in the mammoth treason trial. The PAC, anticipating similar repressive moves against its high-profile leaders, attempted to recruit a second and even third layer of shadow leadership. Little progress toward this objective had been made when the PAC made its ill-fated decision to launch a confrontational anti-pass campaign in March 1960, but the intention had been sound and represented an advance over the ANC's tendency to neglect the building of organizational strength at lower levels.

The participation of Biko, Pityana, Abram and others in NUSAS in the late 1960s had enabled them to observe the annual cycle of leadership recruitment and training that had served NUSAS well as a student organization with an ever-changing membership. SASO initially adopted an almost identical system, electing a new team of national officers annually, then modified the pattern in 1971 by adding three administrative positions with longer terms (secretary-general, permanent organizer, and publications director). Each year's election tallies were used to appoint off-the-record shadow leaders ready to step in should there be a sudden vacancy in the executive committee.[42] Most significantly, SASO adopted the training procedures used by NUSAS and UCM to identify, inform, and orient potential new leadership. Using training seminars (called "formation schools"), SASO radiated its ideas, motivating energies, and organizing skills out through the ranks of university students, and later through the larger population of high school students and urban youth. In time, the catalytic process thus set in motion played a decisive part in infusing the wider society not only with a greatly enhanced sense of political possibilities, but also with an entire new generation of energetic leadership.

In the six years before the Soweto uprising, hundreds of young blacks passed through formation schools organized first by SASO and later by offshoots of the black consciousness movement. Dozens of training workshops were conducted, sometimes lasting three or four days, using the conference facilities of church organizations such as St. Ansgar's or Wilgespruit in Roodepoort west of Johannesburg, or the Edendale Lay Ecumenical Centre near Pietermaritzburg. Attendance at a typical session might range from a dozen to more than 60 participants.[43] Not since the Communist Party had developed worker night schools as a way to teach, recruit and motivate party cadres had such an effective method of organized politicization been applied among black South Africans.

The principal objective of the formation school was to "conscientize," that is, to transpose mere anger into a more informed political understanding and response to what SASO called "the system." "The system" was more than a damning epithet. The term suggested that apartheid had to be conceptualized as an interconnected web of relationships tying together the psychological and the physical, the economic and the political, the student realm and the perceptions and expectations taught to students regarding adult life. The more deeply one could comprehend the workings of this system, the more astutely one could begin to devise means for its destruction. Given the heightened vigilance of the state by the time of SASO's emergence, its organizers pursued their proselytization knowing that the amount of time available might be brief, and that the main measure of their success would be the ability of their recruits to spread and reproduce the conscienticization process.

In addition to providing political education and offering students the opportunity to engage in the kind of open questioning and discussion which rarely occurred in home, school, or church, formation schools were used to drive home the message of self-reliance. "In vocalising and popularising the idea of black consciousness your aim is to give people a faith in themselves and their struggle. That hope must be sustained as an active hope. It must compel them to do things for themselves," declared one training document. "We must never allow people to cultivate a passive hope that God will one day come down to solve problems. God is not in the habit of coming down to earth and solving people's problems."[44] Blacks with education had to shoulder responsibility for changing the future of all blacks, despite the inevitable material sacrifices this would entail, wrote Biko in another briefing document distributed at a formation school held at Edendale in December 1971. "To play our role as future leaders of the community we must inculcate in our minds the martyr mentality. We must cease to see ourselves as people affected by history but as people who will shape history" (*Document 45*).

These were heady sentiments that could not be embraced with equal zeal by everyone who heard them. Nevertheless their psychological impact was profound, especially when enhanced by Biko's powerful persuasiveness as a speaker. "He had an extraordinary magnetism," wrote his friend and confidant Aelred Stubbs. "His hold on his all-black audiences was almost frightening; it was as if they were listening to a new 'messiah'."[45] To underscore the message of non-dependency and to prevent SASO from becoming a personality cult, strong emphasis was placed on black consciousness philosophy and methods.[46] Biko himself preferred to exert leadership as much as possible from behind the scenes, encouraging those around him to exercise their own judgment and initiative once a policy position had been arrived at through debate. One result was a flowering of talent at the lieutenancy level in SASO; another was an incremental shift toward greater democratic participation and away from the more traditional leader-centered pattern of authority in black organizations.

Despite SASO's success in winning the allegiance of black university students, its founders gave little priority to the institutionalization of SASO itself as a long range goal. What seemed most important was the rapid dissemination of a strong set of operating principles, the instilling of solidarity and confidence, and the imparting of rudimentary skills which could later be applied in multiple spheres to build up and give leadership to black associational life. Students were taught how to conduct meetings, keep minutes, and observe basic rules of procedure. Open debate, critical analysis, workshop discussions, leadership accountability, fund-raising strategies, ways of dealing with the media—all these could be encouraged or taught in principle, and most could be demonstrated through simulation exercises within the context of the formation school. SASO then might pass from the scene, but black consciousness as a "way of life"—the nicely ambiguous phrase of the SASO Manifesto—could go on replicating itself within new organizations emerging in black society.

While accepting the inevitability of state retaliation, SASO's strategists hoped to keep their political ship afloat as long as possible. The confused response among university authorities to SASO's anti-liberal and separatist pronouncements was correctly anticipated, as was the general tendency of the state's security forces to underestimate the capabilities of an all-black organization. To take full advantage of the tactical opportunities created by this political space, and to not repeat errors made by the PAC, SASO from the outset avoided a confrontational political style. Patience and perseverance were stressed, self-defeating heroics discouraged. "Protest politics"—the staging of publicity-oriented demonstrations, boycotts, or other NUSAS-style "temper tantrums"[47]—were dismissed as both more risky and less effective in politicizing blacks than quiet one-on-one "conscientization."

In campus surroundings, SASO could build support by performing the basic functions of a student union, organizing vacation employment for students, throwing parties at intervarsity sports matches and holding fund-raising events. In relation to the larger political picture, however, major strategic questions soon loomed large. Rapid success in implanting the ideology of black consciousness propelled SASO's strategists onto new and uncertain ground. What were university students to do once they had persuaded everyone else in their immediate environment to embrace the SASO "way of life"? Obviously, they had to press outward beyond the confines of the campus to combat mass apathy and promote psychological liberation, "phase one" as it was sometimes called. But what strategies should be pursued to push forward what SASO had defined as the second phase—physical liberation?

Thoughts about "phase two" were murky and tended toward romantic fantasies about the inevitability of popular insurrection. "Black consciousness we believe is the preparatory stage of the people's revolution," declared one unusually candid SASO discussion paper.[48] Other writings made euphemistic references to a future time of rising tides, breaking chains, or a day when the struggle would "outgrow its traditional forms." Armed confrontation was imagined by almost everyone to be an inescapable part of the apocalyptic scenario of mass revolt, but cooler heads regarded political preparation as equally important, lest armed action fail for lack of broad popular support. It was here, they thought, that SASO would make its contribution—patiently and openly laying the foundation of a future for which specific planning was too dangerous in the short run. Preparing a complete strategy for liberation was, Biko confided to a foreign visitor in June 1971, "quite conceivable."

> But I think it is the kind of thing in this country which cannot be discussed and made public, even amongst the oppressed people themselves. So that what we are developing is a simple, above-board type of strategy, which is using the individual source of energy. The fact that one can on his own see himself as a man [means] you will not allow someone else to treat you as something less than a man. Hence your own preparedness as an individual to participate in an emancipation action is ensured. And what that emancipation action will be is a little bit beyond the scope of an organization like SASO. In other words, we get involved in step one. Who will be responsible for steps two and three, I don't know."[49]

Biko's traumatic experience during the Poqo scare of 1963 had made him wary of naive bravado. Late at night, student talk might revolve around revolutionary fantasies, but in the colder light of day action had to be cautious lest SASO meet a premature end. "Emancipation action" would take place over a faraway horizon, and before the intervening distance could be closed, more immediate practical goals had to be reached. Mass conscientization was one of these, and another was the psychological redirection of educated blacks away from a growing elitism and materialism and back toward an identification with the collective good of all blacks. If these practical objectives were to be pursued during the three brief years which most university students spent earning their degrees, SASO had to find ways to build meaningful links between students and the ordinary uneducated and semi-literate people who made up the majority of South Africa's black population. But how was this to be done?

It seemed realistic at the time of SASO's founding to start building these links by adopting the mode of vacation service projects familiar from NUSAS and UCM.[50] Students were accustomed to such projects, and it was an approach unlikely to arouse alarm among university authorities. The construction of rural schools and water systems, the staffing of clinics, and the teaching of literacy could go on as in the past, but attitudes toward such work would be shifted away from welfarism ("the privileged helping to improve the lot of the poor") to a community development approach—activating the poor to take control of their own lives. Such projects would narrow the social distance between the educated and uneducated, and create an entry point for students to bring the new gospel of black consciousness and political awareness to a grassroots constituency.

SASO's strategists drew heavily on the idealistic theories of Julius Nyerere and Paulo Freire regarding the potentialities for social mobilization among the poor. In Tanzania Nyerere was directing the early stages of an ambitious plan to collectivize agriculture, proceeding from the appealing theory that traditional peasant life in Africa was inherently communal. The ideas of

Paulo Freire, a Brazilian educationist, became popular in UCM and SASO in 1970–71 after Colin Collins began distributing copies of *The Pedagogy of the Oppressed*, Freire's prescription for the political awakening (*conscientização*) of the third world's poor through radical methods of literacy education.[51] The social diagnoses and cures incorporated in these theories strongly appealed to SASO's ideologues, who were searching for optimistic visions of how African society could be transformed. Augmented with progressive theories of community development culled from American texts, these perspectives armed SASO with an overly intellectualized approach to social activism, but one which at least offered a starting point for experimentation.

Not surprisingly, practical obstacles were seriously underestimated, and the results of many projects were disappointing. *Document 46*, which includes a frank report on community development projects for SASO's December 1971 formation school at Edendale, describes the problems encountered and lessons learned from these early experiments. Small communities rarely were cohesive. Local black authorities were obstructive. Students quickly became discouraged when projects went awry. For some, a patient back-to-the-grassroots strategy brought too little emotional satisfaction when set against the more virile vision of armed "action." To others, the exhortations of black consciousness about self-definition and self-direction seemed to have little relevance for the ordinary rural or township person, however appealing they might be to western educated elites experiencing powerlessness and frustration on the fringes of white society. To the extent that there was anger at the grassroots and not mere resignation, the focus was not on subjective matters like identity and racial nomenclature, but on the system's failure to provide for people's most pressing material needs— higher wages, housing, schools, health facilities, and land.

In 1972, however, the movement was still gaining momentum and consolidating the achievements of its first three years. The credo of solidarity and self-reliance had become the dominant outlook on black campuses, even making significant headway among politically cautious Coloured and Indian students. Far from merely riding a wave of anger generated by apartheid's indignities, the black consciousness movement was actively creating this wave through its campaign to persuade young blacks to adopt a new standard of moral condemnation toward the prevailing order. The movement was also starting to play a vital part in developing the political skills that would be the foundation of major black organizational advances in the 1980s. Focusing on the critical need to build black strength through networks of organization and communication, the movement had proved adept at seeking out weaknesses in the apartheid system, and was finding ways to use these political spaces to develop previously untapped resources in black society. The new talents, techniques and networks created in this process would continue to provide reservoirs of oppositional strength even when the movement itself began to lose ground to competitors who were able to appropriate the resources that black consciousness had first mobilized.

Notes

1. Helen Suzman used this phrase during a parliamentary debate on March 8, 1973, *House of Assembly Debates,* column 2264.

2. *Sunday Tribune,* June 17, 1973.

3. Charles Demas, a student suspended from the University of the Western Cape in 1970 for attending classes without a tie, was reinstated after students occupied the administration building in protest. *Sunday Tribune,* June 17, 1973.

4. Kogila Adam, "Dialectic of Higher Education for the Colonized: the Case of the Non-White Universities in South Africa," in Heribert Adam, ed., *South Africa: Sociological Perspectives* (London: Oxford University Press, 1971), p. 202. Also see Documents 52 and 53.

5. Information on Biko's views and life has been drawn from his own writings; his conversation with Gerhart in October 1972; his May 1976 testimony in the trial of *State v. Cooper,* reproduced in Millard Arnold, ed., *Steve Biko: Black Consciousness in South Africa* (New York: Random House, 1978); Lindy Wilson, "Bantu Stephen Biko: a Life," in N. Barney Pityana, et al., eds., *Bounds of Possibility: the Legacy of Steve Biko and Black Consciousness* (London: Zed Books; Cape Town: David Philip, 1991); and from conversations with his contemporaries including Barney Pityana (October 1972 and January 1988), Saths Cooper (October 1987), Harry Nengwekhulu (October 1972), Neville Curtis (June 1990), and Temba Sono (November 1973).

6. Conversation with Curtis. The matter is also referred to in M. Legassick and J. Shingler, "South Africa," in D. K. Emmerson, ed., *Students and Politics in Developing Countries* (New York: Praeger, 1968), p. 138, though Biko is not named.

7. Arnold, p. 8.

8. See Nkosinathi Gwala, "State Control, Student Politics and the Crisis in Black Universities," in William Cobbett and Robin Cohen, eds., *Popular Struggles in South Africa* (Trenton, NJ: African World Press, 1988), p. 182. Some SRCs remained unrecognized by university authorities, and some had to contend with anti-SRC factions, especially on campuses where the boycott tradition of the Unity Movement was strong, as at Fort Hare and the University of the Western Cape.

9. Letter to "SRC Presidents, National Student Organisations, Other Organisations, and Overseas Organisations, Re: South African Students' Organisation," February 1970.

10. Biko, "Black Souls in White Skins?" *SASO Newsletter,* August 1970.

11. Biko is said to have once driven this point home by switching from English to Xhosa in the middle of responding to a group of NUSAS whites who had argued that the organization was not an embodiment of a dominant culture.

12. Gwala, p. 175.

13. This metaphor was used by Malusi Mpumlwana in a conversation related in Joseph Lelyveld, *Move Your Shadow* (New York: Times Books, 1985), p. 297.

14. See Sipho Buthelezi, "The Emergence of Black Consciousness: an Historical Appraisal," in Pityana et al., p. 24.

15. "About 'Black Images'," program notes for Lamontville (Durban) performance of TECON and Dashiki, October 17, 1973.

16. Richard van der Ross, "Black Power," in Thoko Mbanjwa, ed., *Black Viewpoint 2: Detente* (Durban: Black Community Programmes, 1976?), pp. 37–38.

17. Interview of Julie Frederikse with Trevor Manuel (1985).

18. Conversation with Jakes Gerwel (April 1990).

19. See chapter 8 on the Theron Commission, appointed by Vorster in early 1973.

20. Information in this section has been drawn from SASO documents and from conversations with Biko, Nengwekhulu, Jerry Modisane (October 1972), David Thebehali (October 1972), Timothy Smith (August 1972), Sono, Diliza Mji (June 1987), Nkosazana Dlamini Zuma (June 1988), Peter Jones (July 1989), and Jackie Selebi (March 1989). Temba Sono in "South Africa: The Agony of Black Radical Rhetoric 1970–1974," an M.A. thesis for Duquesne University (1976?), argued that black consciousness was imported "lock, stock and barrel" from the United States, but he also acknowledged the influence of other external sources. Also see Temba Sono, *Reflections on the Origins of Black Consciousness in South Africa* (Pretoria: Human Sciences Research Council, 1993).

21. B. Pityana, "Priorities in Community Development," *SASO Newsletter,* September 1971, p. 14.

22. Robert Fatton in *Black Consciousness in South Africa* (Albany: State University of New York Press, 1986) has examined SASO's ideology explicitly in the light of Antonio Gramsci's argument that revolutions cannot occur until rulers' value systems and definitions of political morality have lost their legitimacy in the eyes of the ruled. Barrington Moore develops a similar theory in *Injustice: The Social Bases of Obedience and Revolt* (White Plains: M. E. Sharpe, 1978).

23. Biko, "Black Consciousness and the Quest for a True Humanity," in Steve Biko, *I Write What I Like* (London, Bowerdean Press, 1978; Oxford: Heinemann, 1978; San Francisco: Harper and Row, 1986), pp. 89–90.

24. We are indebted to Colin Bundy for pointing out that another technological innovation, the loud-speaker (or loud-hailer), was increasingly used by student activists in this period.

25. See Barney Pityana, "Afro-American Influences on the Black Consciousness Movement," a paper presented at Howard University, May 1979.

26. Mosibudi Mangena, *On Your Own* (Johannesburg: Skotaville, 1989), pp. 10–11.

27. Conversation with Zuma.

28. Conversations with Pityana (January 1988) and Thebehali; on the eastern Cape see Saki Macozoma, "Notes of a Native Son," *Monitor* (Port Elizabeth), 1988, p. 56.

29. Conversation with Biko.

30. Shelagh Gastrow, *Who's Who in South African Politics* (Johannesburg: Ravan Press, 1985), p. 195.

31. Shelagh Gastrow, *Who's Who in South African Politics,* Number 3 (Johannesburg: Ravan Press, 1990), p. 219. On the 1960 arrest of Sobukwe and others, see *From Protest to Challenge,* volume 3, p. 333.

32. Conversation with Biko.

33. The best analysis is Mamphela Ramphele, "The Dynamics of Gender Within Black Consciousness Organisations: a Personal View," in Pityana et al. Also see Zanele Dhlamini [Mbeki], "Women's Liberation: a Black South African Woman's View," *Sechaba,* September 1972. Ramphele notes that although a Black Women's Federation was formed in 1975 to mobilize women's support for political resistance, "there is no evidence to suggest that the BWF was concerned with . . . sexism." She argues that women who became leaders in the black consciousness movement did so as "honorary men," and lacked, at that stage of their lives, a distinctly feminist consciousness.

34. The UCM also had a Women's Liberation project, which drew interest almost exclusively from whites.

35. This book was reissued in expanded form, edited by Basil Moore, under the titles *Black Theology: the South African Voice* (London: C. Hurst and Co., 1973), and *The Challenge of Black Theology in South Africa* (Atlanta: John Knox Press, 1974).

36. Two well known exceptions among parish ministers in the 1970s were Frank Chikane and T. S. Farisani, both of whom have written about run-ins with security police in their autobiographies. Church conservatism in South Africa in this period presents an interesting contrast with black churches in the American south a decade earlier, which according to Aldon Morris, *The Origins of the Civil Rights Movement* (New York: Free Press, 1984), were important mobilizing centers for black protest.

37. Pityana and others expressed this view at a symposium on the history of black consciousness held in Harare in June 1990.

38. Conversation with Biko.

39. Sobukwe was released from Robben Island in May 1969, restricted to the town of Kimberley, and banned from attending gatherings.

40. Conversation with Biko. Also see Mamphela Ramphele, "Empowerment and Symbols of Hope: Black Consciousness and Community Development," in Pityana et al., pp. 163–64.

41. Conversations with Pityana (October 1972) and Modisane.

42. Conversations with Biko and Nengwekhulu. SASO's first four presidents were Biko (1969–70), Pityana (1970–71), Temba Sono (1971–72), and Jerry Modisane (1972–73). Biko became Publications Director in 1970, and was replaced in this position by Strini Moodley from 1971 to February 1973. In 1971, Pityana became Secretary General, and Nengwekhulu became Permanent Organizer.

43. Conversations with Kehla Mthembu (March 1989), Biko, and Zithulele Cindi (July 1989). In this period the youth department of the Methodist church, under the direction of the church's general secretary, Alex Boraine, also ran an energetic program of leadership training.

44. "Practical Application of the Ideology of Black Consciousness," 1970?, p. 2.

45. Aelred Stubbs, "Martyr of Hope," in Biko, *I Write What I Like,* p. 158. Stubbs, an Anglican priest who had assisted the Biko family at the time of Khaya's imprisonment in 1963, was on the faculty of the Federal Theological Seminary in Alice during the years of SASO's emergence when Biko and other SASO leaders were frequent visitors to the campus.

46. In his testimony in *State v. Cooper* Biko explained some of the steps taken by SASO to avoid a leadership cult, such as the publication of his regular column, "I Write What I Like," in the *SASO Newsletter* under a pseudonym ("Frank Talk"). Although the aversion to a personalistic leadership style was genuine, Biko's testimony underplays both his own informal influence on the organization and the disproportionate influence of the executive staff over the elected officers. See Arnold, pp. 126–30.

47. Editorial in *SASO Newsletter,* June 1970.

48. Anonymous, "The Repugnant Elements in the Western Culture," May 1974.

49. Interview of Greg Lanning with Biko (June 1971).

50. Information on community development is drawn from SASO documents and Ramphele, "Empowerment and Symbols of Hope." Also see Sam Nolutshungu, *Changing South Africa: Political Considerations* (New York: Africana Publishing Co., 1982), p. 191.

51. Biko mentioned Freire and offered a nonpolitical interpretation of his methods in his testimony in *State v. Cooper.* Arnold, pp. 233–35, presents the unedited transcript of the court stenographer, who recorded Biko speaking of "Paul Lafrere."

5. The Black Consciousness Movement: Confronting the State, 1972–1976

As soon as the South African Students' Organisation had built a strong following on black campuses, it began seeking ways to push its message outward into the larger society. It sought to attach itself to existing black organizations and cultural groups with the aim of re-orienting them in a black consciousness direction. As these efforts gathered momentum, rebellion erupted on black campuses in early 1972, testing the political commitment of thousands of students and plunging the black consciousness movement into a crisis of uncertainty over strategies of response. Students leaving universities sought outlets for their political energies, generating momentum for the founding of the Black People's Convention (BPC) in mid-1972. The state, alarmed by the growth of student militancy and jarred by sudden labor unrest in early 1973, abandoned its earlier indifference to the black consciousness movement, and in March 1973 issued banning orders to eight key SASO and BPC leaders. But just as SASO and its offshoots began to feel the strain of repression, guerrilla victories in Portugal's African colonies ignited new hope. Debate about "phase two"—the nature of the action to follow conscientization—intensified, and the banned liberation movements with their commitment to armed struggle gained rapidly in appeal. The problem of how to define its relationship to the African National Congress and Pan Africanist Congress assumed troublesome proportions for the black consciousness movement, and remained an unsolved question when the waves of youthful rebellion broke over the country in June 1976.

Building Organizational Resources

SASO's leaders ransacked their social surroundings for usable forms of organizational support with the same fervor they applied to the search for ideological reinforcement. Associational life was underdeveloped among blacks, but existing organizations, however weak, offered an arena where SASO could spread its influence and tap into networks of communication with grassroots opinion. Contact with two national organizations of black clergy—the African Independent Churches Association (AICA), and the Interdenominational African Ministers' Association (IDAMASA)—was given high priority. AICA, which had been created with the help of the Christian Institute, appeared to offer the greatest potential for grassroots linkages. Most of its active members were political conservatives, however, for whom AICA served less as a vehicle for the uplifting of their working-class congregants than as a channel of access to the financial assistance, training courses, and social recognition that flowed from the organization's relationship with the Christian Institute.[1] No amount of effort by SASO could transform the social reality which placed material security first in the minds of those who were most marginalized by the apartheid order. Although one AICA official, Reverend Mashwabada Mayatula, became active in the BPC, AICA as an organization proved resistant to conversion into a black consciousness vehicle.

IDAMASA, a long established group, confined itself to holding annual conferences, issuing occasional statements, and encouraging welfare work by its local branches. It responded more sympathetically to SASO's advances, and agreed to end a long-standing practice of inviting whites to sit on its executive committee. After SASO proposed the formation of a national nonstudent organization to promote black consciousness, IDAMASA was instrumental in bringing together a range of black organizations to explore the idea. When it became evident that the new body would be explicitly political, however, IDAMASA distanced itself from the plan.

SASO's attempts at infiltration also achieved mixed results with the Association for the Educational and Cultural Advancement of the African People (ASSECA), headed by M. T. Moerane, the editor of *The World*. ASSECA defined its purpose as opposition to Bantu education, but in practice it had no hope of affecting government policy and confined itself to organizing scholarships and donations to school improvement projects. It had several dozen local branches and regarded itself as a "mass" organization. In reality it was a body of middle-class notables whose harmless boosterism attracted financial support from several large corporations, making ASSECA one of the few black organizations with a steady bank balance. SASO saw ASSECA as a potential force for change if it could be re-oriented, and directed some of its activists to join ASSECA branches. But Moerane resisted radicalization, and although ASSECA, like IDAMASA, involved itself in the formative stages of the Black People's Convention, it too withdrew once BPC took shape as an overtly political body.

SASO also attempted unsuccessfully to build an alliance with the Natal Indian Congress (NIC), which reconstituted itself in late 1971 after almost a decade of dormancy. Critical of the NIC's decision to restrict membership to Indians, SASO agitated in vain at one of NIC's early meetings in July 1971 for its members to "think Black not Indian." Taking a different tack, two energetic young Indians committed to black consciousness—Strini Moodley and Saths Cooper—joined the NIC and took part in building up its Durban Central branch while urging other Indian activists to embrace a wider political identity. Although some sympathy for black consciousness existed among younger NIC members, the majority viewed SASO's ideas as threatening. "There is a genuine danger of black consciousness leading to black racism," wrote Farouk Meer in summarizing the outcome of NIC debates in early 1972.[2] Less publicly, many NIC members felt a strong loyalty to the traditions of the Congress alliance, in which Indians had maintained their separate organizational identity within a multiracial coalition that included whites. In proposing that blacks stigmatize all whites as enemies, SASO was rejecting these more liberal traditions of the 1950s that the NIC was hoping to resuscitate. Once the BPC was launched in mid-1972, Moodley and Cooper took most members of the NIC Durban Central branch with them into the new organization, and bad feeling between the NIC and the black consciousness movement continued.[3]

Ironically, SASO garnered far more material support through its handful of sympathetic white supporters than from the black organizations with which it tried to link itself. When skeptics accused the organization of hypocrisy for taking "white" money, their arguments were parried with rhetoric about how such money originated from the exploitation of blacks and thus could be "reclaimed." But the dilemma was a recurring one, and until blacks acting alone could muster sufficient funds to employ organizers, issue publications, and obtain and maintain telephones, offices, and vehicles, there would always be a strong case for ideologically accommodating white allies.[4] In the end, the anomaly of liberal support for black consciousness rested on the conviction of a few key whites that the time had come for blacks to assume leadership of their own cause. That SASO was able to attack white liberals and still attract their financial support was testimony in part to the quality of its early leaders, most of whom did not let their instrumentalist ideology of black-white relations interfere with their cordial relationships with supportive individual whites.

During SASO's dramatic growth between 1969 and 1971, student dues met only a fraction of the organization's costs, and the rest came almost entirely from contributions raised outside South Africa on SASO's behalf by Colin Collins and Basil Moore of the University Christian Movement. By 1971 SASO had established direct relations with two European funding groups (World University Service and the International University Exchange Fund), but still cooperated closely with the UCM. When the UCM disbanded in mid-1972, funds raised for its literacy and black theology projects were bequeathed to SASO, and its Johannesburg office passed to the newly launched BPC. BPC was "as poor as a church mouse," its National Organizer, Mosibudi Mangena later wrote, but by becoming "honorable squatters" in these premises it seemed to rise like a phoenix from the ashes of the dying UCM.[5]

Following its 1968 "Message to the People of South Africa," the South African Council of Churches in 1969–70 in collaboration with the Christian

Institute undertook a major research program called the Study Project on Christianity in Apartheid Society (Spro-cas). Spro-cas produced a series of informative publications critical of government policies, but by 1971 its overseas sponsors were pressing for an action program to follow up on the analytical exercise.[6] Spro-cas hired outgoing NUSAS president Neville Curtis in late 1971 to devise a program targeting white opinion, and Bennie Khoapa, a social worker with the YMCA, to design a program for blacks. In January 1972, with funds raised mainly by Beyers Naude from European churches, Spro-cas launched Black Community Programmes (BCP) with Khoapa as director, and a head office in Durban located in the same church building that housed SASO headquarters.

When neglect of his studies finally led to his departure from medical school in August 1972, Biko joined the paid staff of BCP with responsibility for youth activities. For the next three years, his activities were supported by BCP, first in Durban, and later in King William's Town after bans confined him there from March 1973. BCP eventually became associated in the public mind with black initiatives like the Zanempilo clinic outside King William's Town and a number of home industry projects. These were visible symbols of the self-reliance message of black consciousness, and they attracted substantial donations from South African as well as foreign sources, making BCP independent of the Christian Institute and Spro-cas by mid-1973. BCP's broader significance, however, lay in its more intangible, less publicized efforts to come to grips with the lack of organizational skills, communication networks, and political motivation among Africans.

BCP set specific objectives and began systematically to pursue them. Bokwe Mafuna, a journalist with trade union experience, was hired in September 1972 to plan for a national Black Workers' Council free of white control. Too ambitious, this goal was abandoned after Mafuna was banned in February 1973. More realistically, BCP conducted a countrywide survey of black organizations and in 1973 published a directory with information on about 70 of these, ranging from local burial societies and drama clubs to national groups like ASSECA and IDAMASA. BCP organized meetings to bring black churchmen, women's leaders and professionals of various kinds together, and to impress upon them their responsibility to exert leadership in black society. "Blacks have been made to depend on white energy, leadership, guidance and trusteeship," declared a 1972 BCP report, and thus have "allowed themselves to develop feelings of inadequacy and inferiority . . . [as well as an] exaggerated feeling of powerlessness which results in lack of creative initiatives. Added to this . . . is the desperate lack of skills arising out of an inadequacy of opportunities that characterize black life under white rule in South Africa."[7]

Compared to changing the orientations and attitudes of adults, shaping the outlook of the young proved far easier. Borrowing the model of the SASO formation school and enlisting Biko's experience and charisma, BCP worked with Harry Nengwekhulu, SASO's National Organizer, to organize leadership training seminars for local high school and youth groups starting in mid-

1972.[8] By the time Biko and Nengwekhulu were banned in March 1973, they had created a fledgling network of regional youth organizations and an umbrella body, the National Youth Organisation (NAYO), formed in May 1973. By 1974 the high school-based South African Students' Movement (SASM) in the Transvaal was making tentative efforts to link with Natal and eastern Cape student groups. The weakness of these early networks made them easy prey for state repression, and much of their budding leadership had disappeared into prison, exile, or local obscurity by the start of the June 1976 uprising. Nevertheless, their accumulated experiences became an important resource, both during the turbulent months of the uprising and afterwards when experimentation with organization-building resumed in the period of high-risk politics after the October 1977 crackdown.

Finally, in considering the mobilization techniques of the black consciousness movement, the importance of the written word should not be overlooked. The expansion of African education was steadily enlarging the audience for written political information by the time of SASO's rise.[9] As SASO saw it, the white-owned media gave journalists an undue influence in shaping the self-image of young blacks. *The World* and *Post,* white-owned Transvaal papers aimed at African readers, pursued a marketing strategy stressing sports, cheese-cake and crime stories. Radio programs reinforced negative stereotypes, constantly reminding the African of his "so-called superstitious background," complained one SASO activist, and playing "songs that far too frequently carry the only message the Black must hear— that he belongs to the bundus [boondocks]."[10] Government-controlled broadcasting was beyond reach, but the press was not, and SASO's 1970 conference called on students to write to *The World* and *Post* objecting to their "sensationalism that . . . undermines the morals of the people, underestimates their intelligence, and underrates their interest in current affairs."[11] As the black consciousness movement gained momentum, black journalists became some of its staunchest supporters. When lack of capital caused SASO to scuttle plans for a black-owned newspaper, black reporters from the Transvaal influenced by SASO formed the Union of Black Journalists (UBJ), thereafter a powerful influence in pushing political news and analysis to the fore for black readers. When the UBJ's Percy Qoboza succeeded Moerane as editor of *The World* in 1974, the paper assumed a tone increasingly challenging to government policy.

SASO initially avoided the press lest misleading coverage sow confusion on campuses where students had not yet affiliated.[12] But by 1971 reporters had become aware of SASO's news value and sporadically covered black consciousness events, playing on the theme that SASO was a "menace" worth watching. Frustrated over negative coverage by even the anti-government English press, delegates at SASO's July 1972 conference voted to expel the *Star* and *Rand Daily Mail,* citing their decision to send white instead of black reporters, and their refusal to replace the despised word "nonwhite" with "black." Duly chastened, the *Rand Daily Mail* became the first white paper to switch to "black," a shift also made in 1972 in the publications of the liberal Institute of Race Relations. By 1974 even the Afrikaans press and the National Party had abandoned "Bantu" in favor of "black," marking a milestone in SASO's battle to reshape popular perceptions, even though government usage pointedly stopped short of applying the new label to Coloureds and Indians.

SASO's leaders never expected to rely on the South African media to put over their message, and as soon as Pityana took over the presidency in mid-1970, Biko moved to be editor of the *SASO Newsletter.* At its zenith in 1972–73, the *Newsletter* printed 4,000 copies of each issue; and by the time these copies had been passed from hand to hand and taken home to younger brothers and sisters, the actual readership was several times this number. Pamphlets and booklets published by SASO also circulated widely.

The relatively securely financed BCP provided black consciousness with new outreach capabilities. In January 1973 the Christian Institute and Spro-cas launched Ravan Press in Johannesburg to bring out Spro-cas publications. Ravan helped BCP to produce its own publications series, which eventually included the BCP directory of black organizations, several booklets in a series titled *Black Viewpoints,* and the book-length annual *Black Review* published from 1972 to 1976. These well-produced materials sold briskly, enhancing the reputation of black consciousness ideas, and demonstrating the growing interest, especially among African readers, in serious "black"-oriented political and cultural commentary.[13] To what extent these publications achieved the goals set for them by the black consciousness movement—for example, that blacks should increasingly form their attitudes using other blacks as their point of reference instead of whites—it is impossible to say. It does seem indisputable, however, that taken together with the broad thrust of the movement, the popularization of black consciousness writings helped to edge aside the older "victim" stereotype of blacks frequently projected in influential liberal publications, replacing it with a new image of blacks as active agents creating their own future.

The 1972 University Crisis

With its base now strongly established at most black universities, teacher training colleges, and seminaries, SASO began the 1972 academic year with an aggressive recruitment drive aimed at entering freshmen. Four thousand SASO brochures and membership cards bearing the fist symbol were distributed to incoming students in February. At the University of the North at Turfloop, student diaries were printed containing the SASO Manifesto (*Document 44*) and a Declaration of Student Rights adopted at the July 1971 SASO General Students' Council. After the university authorities had seized the diaries and had the documents torn out, students burned the expurgated books in a campus bonfire.[14]

Turfloop's graduation ceremonies were held on April 29. Speaking for the graduates, the 1971 Students' Representative Council (SRC) president, O. R. Tiro, shocked the assembled dignitaries by attacking the segregated university system (*Document 47*). Even on its own terms, he said, the separate system of black universities was a failure because blacks were not in charge. Even where blacks were put in charge, as within the homelands framework, they became "the bolts of the same machine which is crushing us as a nation." But times were changing, he concluded, to loud student applause. "The magic story of human achievement gives irrefutable proof that as soon as nationalism is awakened among the intelligentsia it becomes the vanguard in the struggle against alien rule." Ultimately, no amount of coercion could halt the drive toward human freedom.

Tiro's speech stepped far over the boundaries of official tolerance, and on May 3, he was expelled from his post-graduate diploma course. Students began a lecture boycott and sit-in at the university's main hall in protest the next morning, police were brought onto the campus, the university was closed, and all 1,146 students were expelled. Rather than discouraging dissent, the expulsions sparked sympathy strikes on other campuses. When SASO held a formation school at the Federal Theological Seminary at Alice in the eastern Cape over the weekend of May 12, those present adopted a strike resolution that they named the "Alice Declaration" (*Document 48*). Noting that the situation could be "escalated into a major confrontation with the authorities," the Declaration resolved that students nationwide should close down black institutions of higher education through lecture boycotts.

High anxiety among parents fed the atmosphere of crisis, as did press criticism of the heavy-handed Turfloop administration. By June 1, when Turfloop was scheduled to reopen, every major black campus had endorsed strike action. Demands were framed that went beyond the issue of the Turfloop expulsions to reiterate long-standing student complaints about domination by white staff, biased curriculums, and demeaning campus conditions. At Turfloop, where those who signed pledges of good behavior were readmitted, students returned to find that 22 members of the SRC and SASO Local Committee, as well as Tiro, had been denied readmission. Upwards of 500—about half the student body—then left the campus vowing not to return. By the time protests had subsided elsewhere, more than 100 students had voluntarily abandoned their studies at Fort Hare and about 30 at the University of Zululand.[15] The following year there were new eruptions of protest against university authorities at Fort Hare and the University of the Western Cape, and several hundred more students temporarily or permanently dropped their pursuit of degrees.

SASO was not responsible for the initial confrontation at Turfloop, and if student anger had not boiled over, the organization might not have abandoned its disdain for "protest politics" just to demonstrate student rejection of apartheid education. Once the crisis erupted, however, SASO assumed leadership on most campuses, raising money for students who had lost their stipends, and drawing up ambitious plans—which remained largely unrealized—for a "Free University" that could enable students to study for foreign degrees by correspondence. In the end, trying permanently to shut down the bush universities—attractive as a rallying cry in the early stage of the protests—was not a goal that parents or most aspiring students could realistically support in the absence of viable alternatives.

On the face of things, little seemed to have been gained for the black cause out of the "June days" of 1972. SASO now faced open hostility from most university rectors, and was banned on several campuses. Many students paid a high price in lost opportunities, and paid it in a situation where little seemed to have been gained by their sacrifice. Frustrations were compounded both by the ambiguous outcome of the confrontation, and by the treatment of the protests in the English press. After covering the incidents surrounding Tiro's expulsion, reporters became distracted by the greater apparent news value of white protests in support of the Turfloop students. Liberal opinion was shocked when police viciously baton-charged a group of whites from the University of Cape Town demonstrating with placards outside St. George's Cathedral in downtown Cape Town on June 2. Police clashes with white students escalated, burying the story of the black anti-apartheid rebellion beneath an avalanche of liberal outrage over abrogations of free speech and the nakedness of Afrikaner hatred toward English student dissent.

The unsung heroism of the black student resistors was not lost on township communities, however. Individual parents no doubt regretted the defiance of their offspring, but black opinion generally was impressed with student resolve and became more receptive to radical student views. The stereotype of the African intellectual as nothing but a big talker lost currency because it was evident that many students put community goals and grievances above the promotion of their own careers.[16] Black consciousness might be the creation of an intellectual elite, but it was not a philosophy of elitism. It addressed all blacks unhappy with inferior education and white authoritarianism, and it challenged everyone to put political commitment above personal advancement. The unexpectedly positive response of Indian and Coloured students during the crisis also heightened political awareness in normally conservative minority communities in Natal and the Western Cape.

Secondary school students were particularly affected by the defiant mood of the universities conveyed by press accounts and by the return of boycotting and expelled students to their home communities. In the eyes of many younger students, the university rebels were heroes who had stood up to white domination.[17] The majority of Turfloop students were graduates of schools in Transvaal townships, and some who left university in mid-1972 managed to find jobs as teachers in their home areas. One student activist later estimated that over 30 university drop-outs found jobs in Soweto, where there was a serious shortage of teachers. In the belief that black communities should bear the responsibility of administering their own schools, the Bantu Education Department had unwittingly created a gaping political space by devolving hiring authority onto local headmasters and school boards—an authority later rescinded.[18]

Tiro was among those who found employment as a history teacher at

Morris Isaacson High School in Soweto. Aubrey Mokoena, the expelled 1972 SRC president at Turfloop, was hired by the Orlando North Junior Secondary School. Six months of pressure from the Bantu Education Department finally resulted in Tiro's dismissal, but not before the school had become thoroughly politicized and a strong core of its students had been organized into the South African Students' Movement, SASO's high school ally. Other university drop-outs joined the BCP's campaign to organize youth groups, and some, including Mthuli Shezi, who had been 1972 SRC president at the University of Zululand, focused on building up the new Black People's Convention. Jairus Kgokong, another veteran of the Turfloop walk-out, took an administrative job with AICA, a prime target of SASO's infiltration efforts.[19]

Challenge and Crisis in SASO

When SASO's third General Students' Council convened at St. Peter's Seminary at Hammanskraal near Pretoria in early July 1972, the organization was at the zenith of its influence. It had tasted battle with the enemy and emerged intact. Students involved in the walk-outs had created city-based SASO branches in Springs, Kroonstad, Pretoria and Kimberley, and swelled the numbers affiliated to Reeso, SASO's Reef branch run by Harry Nengwekhulu in Johannesburg.[20] As the minutes of the conference attest (*Document 49*), SASO's ambitions, though tempered by intense debates during the two month crisis, were still relatively unbounded by any sense of practical limits and included plans to organize younger students, workers, churches, the media, literacy campaigns, a "Free University," links with potentially supportive groups outside South Africa, and a host of other long-range projects. In the short term, however, the conference faced two serious crises.

On the opening day of the conference, Temba Sono, SASO's outgoing president, without warning to other executive members, delivered a lengthy and confusing speech advocating that SASO, in a spirit of "realism," should open a dialogue with whites, and drop its negative attitude toward bantustans. "His long and bombastic talk . . . left everyone stunned," Mosibudi Mangena later recalled.[21] In addition to the 70 delegates and alternate delegates, there were at least 100 observers present, including a dozen journalists. When Sono concluded, Biko, whom Mangena observed sitting with his head in his hands during the speech, immediately moved a motion of censure (Resolution 6/72 in *Document 49*) that passed unanimously, dissociating the conference from Sono's opinions and in some measure avoiding a public relations calamity.

SASO had long been wrestling with the tactical question of what to do about the homelands policy, and Sono's unexpected statements exposed the debate taking place behind the scenes. Everyone in SASO adamantly opposed partitioning South Africa into ethnic states. What many were uncertain about was whether ways might exist to exploit homelands politically. Many felt that homeland structures might open a route for radicals to insert themselves into positions of strategic contact with rural populations (*Document 39*); that in trying to teach people "the advantages of group action, [even] government-instituted bodies like UBCs [Urban Bantu Councils] and Bantustans" might have a positive role to play (*Document 45*); and that "tribal platforms" ought not to be dismissed out of hand if there were "well oriented" individuals in them "doing good work" (*Document 46*). Press reports carrying critical remarks by Sono about Gatsha Buthelezi in August 1971 had raised angry threats of disaffiliation at Ngoye making SASO leaders wary of attacking the handful of popular "system" figures like Buthelezi, Sonny Leon of the Coloured Labour Party and Collins Ramusi of Lebowa.[22]

Privately, however, SASO's strategists conceded by 1972 that the government was gaining ground in legitimizing homelands. It seemed clear that tactics of "fighting the system from within" had to be aggressively rejected, even if cordial relations with certain system politicians were still maintained with a view to wooing them away from the chimeras of "comfortable" politics.[23] At a minimum, SASO needed access to homeland areas where its community development projects were planned or in progress. To avoid confusion over the organization's attitude to homelands in principle, however, firm censure of Sono for his ill-considered speech was followed by resolutions further rebuking him, and calling on all homeland officials to resign.

A second crisis threatened to become public at the Hammanskraal conference but was successfully contained, again largely through the assertion of informal authority by Biko. This centered on the dilemma of "phase two:" should SASO go on indefinitely trying to raise political awareness, resolve, and capacity, or should it now move beyond the subjective preconditions for change toward more concrete preparations for revolution, including armed combat? Biko and most of the leadership were convinced that the organization must remain legal so that political mobilization could continue and spread. Time, they optimistically hoped, would reveal specific answers about "phase two." But for some, especially students involved in the campus walk-outs of May and June, counsels of patience were an inadequate response to questions about revolutionary strategy.

Behind the scenes a heated debate broke out, of which no trace was to appear in either the conference record or the press. Most vocal in pressing for SASO to develop a capacity to wage armed warfare was Keith Mokoape, Aubrey Mokoape's younger brother, who had walked out of the Natal medical school during the May-June protests. "Three options were open," he later wrote: "to continue with open mobilization inside South Africa in the hope that 'approaches' would be made by the underground structures of the established political organizations"; "to form a secret underground . . . to train and arm ourselves, and launch our own armed struggle from within the country"; or to go into exile and find a way of acquiring military training.[24]

Like the similar debates over tactics which erupted in NUSAS in 1964, the controversy in SASO might have become public as a divisive and damaging issue, ready-made for a government hoping to trap opposition groups engaging in illegal activity. But the danger was averted when Biko and Tiro confronted the militarists outside the formal sessions of the conference and told them "in robust language to leave SASO alone and to go and seek other grazing lands" if they wanted to engage in armed combat.[25] Although the debate was to intensify among students weighing their options as individuals, for Biko and most others in SASO's inner councils, open and above-ground consciousness-raising was where SASO's comparative advantage lay and where vast work remained to be done. The state was far more vulnerable politically than militarily. To jeopardize the future of SASO's legal activity by permitting a hot-headed element to drag the organization into high-risk heroics seemed the height of folly.

The Black People's Convention

Early in March 1971, a SASO delegation including Biko, Pityana, Aubrey Mokoape and Lindelwe Mabandla held separate meetings with a number of black organizations in Johannesburg, and won agreement that a joint consultation should be held. IDAMASA accepted the role of convenor. The result was a meeting in Bloemfontein in April that brought together representatives of SASO, IDAMASA, ASSECA, AICA, the YMCA, and the St. Peter's Old Boys' Association, a group of politically restive young Catholic priests who had trained at St. Peter's Seminary in Hammanskraal.[26] M. T. Moerane of ASSECA and Drake Koka, an energetic Catholic layman, then convened a follow-up meeting at Edendale near Pietermaritzburg in mid-August at which 26 African organizations were represented. The consensus was that a confederation of African organizations should be formed to promote "community development programs" and also represent African political opinion.[27] This confederation would work with "other black groups"—those of Indians and Coloureds, who had not been invited to Edendale—and would "keep contact with well-oriented blacks inside the system" while itself operating outside government-initiated bodies.

For SASO, this was not an ideal outcome, but since students could not be regarded as national leaders, older champions or at least figureheads initially had to be recruited. Fear was a serious obstacle among older Africans, who remembered how so many families and livelihoods had been blighted by arrests, prison, exile, and death in the early 1960s. To coax forward a leadership that was both socially respectable and politically courageous was not something SASO could accomplish overnight. Twenty-two years earlier, at the ANC's Bloemfontein conference of December 1949, leaders of the Congress Youth League had decided that Africans needed new national leadership, and in less than 24 hours they had recruited and installed a candidate of their own choosing, Dr. James Moroka, to head the ANC. By 1971, the expansion of education and the growth of urban society had made the pool of potential political players much larger; but in the meantime, opposition politics had become a much more dangerous game, shunned by all but the most dedicated and daring, which in practice meant preponderantly the young.

The Edendale gathering chose Koka to head an ad hoc committee to plan a follow-up conference, and Ben Khoapa, then still working for the YMCA, was commissioned with Biko to produce a draft constitution for the envisioned confederate body. Moerane remained involved, as did William Nkomo, a prominent Pretoria physician who like Moerane, had been active in the ANC Youth League in the 1940s. David Thebehali, a member of the Soweto Urban Bantu Council, who was regarded by some Africans as "well oriented," also participated, lending his support to the older majority who believed that the new body should subordinate politics to an emphasis on welfare goals. After a solid organization had been built up, Moerane and his supporters argued, a test of political strength might become possible. In the short run, however, this would only invite swift retaliation by the state.

Time would demonstrate the correctness of this assessment, but SASO, still in the full flush of its rapid success among students, was not in a mood for restraint. The next consultation met at the Orlando YMCA in Soweto in mid-December, 1971. Schools were on holiday, and SASO turned out in force, outnumbering the older supporters of the plan for a welfare-focused confederal body. Moerane as chairman was confronted by a vocal SASO bloc determined to scuttle what they termed the "nebulous" and "amorphous" confederal scheme in favor of forming an overtly political movement. By the time the three-day meeting ended, SASO had pushed through a motion to form a political body based on the philosophy of black consciousness, incorporating SASO's racially-inclusive definition of "black" (which Moerane had opposed), and working "completely outside the system-created platforms."[28]

The Black People's Convention was formally launched at Edendale in July 1972 with Reverend Mashwabada Mayatula as interim head, Koka as interim secretary-general, and other positions filled by SASO adherents. The first annual BPC congress met at Hammanskraal in mid-December, bringing together the interim executive with delegates from 25 newly founded branches. Winifred Kgware, a 54-year-old teacher who had helped sway the Orlando conference to support SASO's stand, was elected national president. Most of the organization's intellectual and organizational muscle continued to be drawn from SASO, despite efforts to attract older members. Mayatula, the pastor of a separatist church who had joined SASO as a theology student, was an older figure drafted into leadership in the hope that he would help attract a mass following. *Document 50* is his address to the Hammanskraal conference. Reflecting the messianic tradition of his church, the Bantu Bethlehem Christian Apostolic Church of Africa, the speech identified the BPC message of black liberation with the second coming of Christ—the Black Messiah. Freely mixing religious and political exhortation, Mayatula called for the BPC to achieve economic justice for blacks and (in a section of the speech that appears to have been drafted by a different author) he put forward the reasons why blacks should reject homelands. During its first two years, the BPC continued to sound these themes as well as to take policy positions on a range of international issues: against foreign investment and for international economic sanctions, against Pretoria's campaign to engage in dialogue with other African governments, and for the international boycott of white South African sports teams.

The BPC's leadership clung to high hopes in the face of daunting political odds. Since the outlawing of the ANC and PAC in 1960, blacks had been without credible national leaders who could present black views to the world from a platform inside South Africa. BPC wanted to fill this vacuum, and by addressing international issues it hoped to win media recognition, push itself forward as the voice of black opinion, and perhaps even attract the financial support of foreign solidarity groups. The organization publicly set its sights on the recruitment of one million members in three years.[29] The intense dedication of its youthful leadership and early enthusiasm for the BPC shown in diverse places, encouraged private speculation that BPC-led strikes and economic disruptions could ultimately destroy the system of white control—one scenario of "phase two" confrontation.[30] However, the actual mobilization of a mass membership ran headlong into the political realities of township life.

By December 1972, branches meeting the minimum number of 25 members for branch status had been formed in 25 areas. By December of 1973 there were only 34 branches, and the hope mirrored in Mayatula's 1972 speech remained unfulfilled that independent African churches, with their large working-class followings and intrinsic go-it-alone disposition, would prove a fertile recruiting ground. At the poorer end of the African social scale, apathy, fear, and psychological escapism ran too deep to be easily dispelled by conscientization strategies based on philosophical appeals.[31] Fear was also strong among the more educated and politically sophisticated, even when the goals of BPC were recognized as admirable. Too many people had been imprisoned on Robben Island for nothing more than having their names on the wrong list; moreover, past experience suggested that the judgment and credibility of political organizers should be assessed with skepticism. In the 1950s, workers who answered calls for politically inspired work stoppages had often been victimized by their employers, only to find that the political instigators could offer no material assistance. Parents who withdrew their children from schools after the introduction of Bantu Education had found that no alternatives were provided. Students in 1972 had walked out of tribal universities in protest—but would black conscious-ness support their aging parents or pay the school expenses of their younger brothers and sisters?

Leaders of the BPC were well aware that more than top-down political preaching was necessary to build a strong mass base and a cadre of middle level leadership. The July 1972 Edendale conference resolved "to stimulate formation of community groups . . . [and] to form residents vigilante committees for the protection of the interests of the community in their residential areas."[32] Other statements of intent echoed SASO's goals of promoting mass literacy and trade union organization, but lack of money and therefore of full-time organizers weakened the BPC even before the onset of government repression. Community-based projects remained the preserve of SASO and Black Community Programmes, while the BPC made only exploratory efforts to organize workers through the establishment in mid-1972 of the Black Allied Workers' Union (BAWU).

BAWU evolved out of the Sales and Allied Workers' Association, a union of salesmen and office workers begun by Drake Koka. With funds raised from abroad, BAWU set up offices as a general union in Johannesburg and Durban and later in the eastern Cape, enrolling members on an individual basis across industry and craft lines. Taking a strong black consciousness line initially, it criticized the paternalism of the white-led Trade Union Council of South Africa, and called on blacks to reject white leadership (*Document 80*). Although never strong enough to stage strikes or to win significant recognition from employers, BAWU contributed to the growing experience of Africans with trade unionism through the 1970s, and eventually gave birth to several breakaway unions, including the South African Allied Workers' Union which became a political force in the eastern Cape in the 1980s.

As an adjunct to the BPC, BAWU contributed little politically and under Koka's independent leadership it stood aloof from the separate efforts of Black Community Programmes and SASO to create a Black Workers' Council. When a wave of strikes swept Durban in early 1973, the black consciousness movement could not claim to have provoked or even anticipated the spontaneous action of the strikers. Whether the political revival inspired by black consciousness contributed to the truculent mood in Durban factories is impossible to say, but at least two flyers drafted by Saths Cooper, the BPC's public relations officer, were distributed among the strikers, one on January 9, the day the first strike erupted at Coronation Brick and Tile (*Document 51*), and the other in early February, urging Indian, Coloured and African workers to stand together. Cooper and four others were arrested and tried for inciting racial hostility, but the case ended in acquittal.[33]

Black Consciousness and Popular Culture

Black consciousness proved less successful in attracting mass support through organizational membership drives than through its subtler movement onto the terrain of popular culture. For the proponents of black consciousness, cultural expression was both a political goal in its own right and a means of politicization; and unlike more direct methods of political mobilization, it presented the state with quarry which was often too subtle and elusive to be snared. Cultural issues were at the heart of SASO's analysis of black political weakness. "Our culture, our history and indeed all aspects of the black man's life have been battered nearly out of shape in the great collision between the indigenous values and the Anglo-Boer culture," wrote Biko. Since blacks had been taught that all things black were inferior, they found themselves in the position of eternal pupils looking to the white man for guidance and approval. "Only he can tell us how good our performance is and instinctively each of us is at pains to please this powerful, all-knowing master," he observed. "This is what Black consciousness seeks to eradicate."[34]

The solution to white cultural hegemony, and to the alienation of the black man from himself, was not to fantasize about returning to pre-colonial Africa. Such a notion had no practical value for people who had already embraced modern life. Nor was it realistic to believe, like Nat Nakasa (*Document 2*) that somehow a composite nonracial South African identity had already emerged, in spite of whites' failure to acknowledge its existence. Before such a "fusion of the lifestyles of the various groups" could occur, Biko argued, blacks had to recognize, respect, and assert those distinctive qualities in their own culture which had survived despite the battering effects of racism, apartheid education and white-oriented Christianity. In contrast to the calculating and materialistic values that seemed to character-ize "Anglo-Boer" culture, black life was grounded in communal virtues like sharing, hospitality, and mutual respect. Borrowings from western culture could be accepted and appreciated, but never the attitude conveyed and too often internalized with them, that all things white were good and all things black were bad. Black consciousness, Biko wrote, sought to "show the black people the value of their own standards and outlook," and to "judge themselves according to these standards."[35]

Independence in drama, art, music and literature was a logical corollary to SASO's call for blacks to go it alone politically. Almost all black artists and performers functioned in the shadow of whites who stood as gatekeepers to the wider public. For an unknown African to approach an art gallery, a publisher, or a recording studio was virtually impossible. Commercial success depended on the patronage of white customers and thus on managerial skills and contacts of white agents. Not only did these agents press creative artists to shape their work in directions popular with white consumers, but artists were also exploited by agents who often acted more like employers than employees in relation to blacks whose work they promoted. These conditions bred a frustration among artists and performers which increased in the 1960s and 1970s as the white public's appetite for cultural expressions with an African flavor began to grow, fed by the appeal of musical productions such as *King Kong* and *uMabatha*.

The black consciousness movement, with its appeal for the independent and aggressive promotion of black culture, thus aroused an enthusiastic response from many people professionally engaged in cultural pursuits. Musicians who had looked down on music associated with rural and migrant life began to experiment with blending more traditional styles into the jazz and soul repertoires popular with urban audiences. The Theatre Council of Natal (TECON), a politically committed Indian drama group which had tried to cultivate white donors and audiences, decided in 1972 to devote itself exclusively to performing for blacks. Several members, including Strini Moodley and Saths Cooper, became leading activists in black consciousness organizations. In Johannesburg a confederation of black cultural groups called the Music, Dance, Art, Literature Institute or MDALI (Zulu for "creator"), was formed in 1972 with the aim of combating exploitation by white impresarios as well as "liberating the mental and creative processes" of black artists.[36] MDALI organized black arts festivals and worked with scanty financial resources to develop new artistic talent in Johannesburg and beyond. Dozens of new groups devoted to black music, drama, and poetry sprang up in townships across the country.

Poets, musicians, and theater groups were invited to perform at SASO conferences, and after its July 1972 symposium on "Creativity and Black Development," a booklet under the same title was published. Given that a prime objective of black consciousness was to encourage self-reliance and initiative, it would have been counterproductive for SASO to try to dictate the specific content of "black culture," but independence from white involvement or patronage was encouraged. Blacks who participated in multiracial drama groups were derided as "nonwhites," and criticism was directed at art which reflected a "victim mentality"—mere protest or lamentation—rather than an uplifting view which could motivate the search for solutions.

Ultimately, to merit the label "black" according to the canons of black consciousness, a performance, poem, or work of art had to convey a political message, either veiled or explicit. *Shanti,* a play by Mthuli Shezi performed in Natal and Transvaal townships in 1973, for example, told the improbable but politically instructive story of an Indian woman whose African lover fled South Africa to join the guerrilla army of Frelimo, Mozambique's liberation movement. The same troupe, the People's Experimental Theatre, staged an American play inspired by Malcolm X, *Requiem for Brother X.* Poetry readings, usually combined with performances by musical groups, stressed political themes and openly referred to revolutionary goals. *Document 56* engagingly describes a typical event of this kind in which black American influences were interwoven with South African themes of liberation.

The eyes and ears of the state were slow to detect the highly politicized cultural renaissance gathering momentum in the early 1970s. Concerts and theatrical productions were a long-standing feature of township life and aroused no automatic suspicion. Township administration was routinely overseen by paternalistic managers who had little reason to take notice of blacks who avoided conspicuous breaches of the law. African organizational activity was presumed to be innocent or ineffectual unless backed up by white or Indian skills and money. When government prosecutors began trying to build a court case against SASO and BPC under the Terrorism Act in late 1974, the political significance of black cultural activities seems finally to have became apparent to the security police, and censorship was increasingly applied, albeit inconsistently because several uncoordinated bureaucracies were involved.

From early 1975, the West Rand Administration Board (WRAB) required theater producers in Soweto to submit scripts for review before permits were issued for the use of township halls. Gibson Kente's musical *Too Late* was banned by the Publications Control Board, then unbanned after he revised the script, only to be prohibited again by WRAB officials. Nevertheless, three months later, Reverend Mzwandile Maqina's far more explicitly political *Give Us This Day* "took Soweto by storm," according to *The World,* playing to enthusiastic youth audiences.[37] By the time the Publications Control Board banned Maqina's polemical musical in May 1976, many performances of the show had been staged nationwide.[38]

Even after the security establishment took notice of the soaring popularity of politicized theater and music, it seemed at a loss to know what to do about it. The emotional and intellectual forces stirred up by artistic expression defied the range of simple solutions prescribed by doctrinaire apartheid. No laws were being flouted, and there was an elusiveness to the influences being set in motion. Black consciousness theater groups, for example, did not attract mass audiences, but they nevertheless created a taste for "relevant" entertainment which in time spilled over into the more polished and commercially-motivated work of Gibson Kente, the leading African impresario of light township theater. Catering to the shifting trends among students and young workers who made up a growing proportion of his market, Kente began with his 1973 production *How Long?* to intrude more political ("relevant") material into his plots and songs. When *How Long?* was a commercial success, he tried the formula again with *Too Late* in 1975, prompting the confused response from government authorities noted earlier.

The delayed and inconsistent reaction of government authorities to the politicization of township culture reflected the same ambivalence felt by university administrators faced with SASO's campaign to emphasize a more satisfying black identity. After all, apartheid doctrine as taught in Afrikaans universities and civil service training courses emphasized the importance of ethnic identity, especially "keeping the Bantu essentially Bantu" rather than having them adopt the inauthentic identity of pseudo-"Europeans." Seen thus, the development of "authentic" African culture could be regarded as a healthy trend in line with government policy. In an optimistic but doomed effort to capture control of Soweto's burgeoning cultural terrain, the West Rand Administration Board in 1975 established a "cultural section" headed by a would-be playwright named H. Pieterse. Besides assuming responsibility for cultural censorship, Pieterse organized WRAB's own black theater association to perform *Shaka,* a tribal-genre play authored by himself.[39] Local response was not enthusiastic. The government's problem, Pityana observed, was that it aimed to popularize "an arrested image of culture . . . a mere preservation of the species or specimen of the African past in the zoo of Afrikaner ideology."[40] As such it was worlds apart from what black consciousness was trying to project: not the backward-looking "authenticity" of ethnic customs, valuable though some might be, but a future-oriented "modern culture," in Biko's words, "a culture of defiance, self-assertion and group pride and solidarity. . . . Just as it now finds expression in our music and our dress, [so will it] spread to other aspects."[41]

Just Staying Up—or Going Forward?

We have seen how SASO's strategists at every stage emphasized organizational survival and the cultivation of new leadership talent in the country's constantly shifting student population. After the 1972 crisis, procedures were adopted for the national executive committee to replace members unexpectedly removed "through resignations forced or voluntary."[42] When the long anticipated interference finally came, SASO was temporarily stunned but soon regained most of its former momentum. BPC did not fare as well.

On February 26, 1973, the Minister of Justice signed banning orders restricting eight black consciousness leaders. Biko, Nengwekhulu and Bokwe Mafuna were on a national tour of youth organizations and were at Barney Pityana's house in Port Elizabeth's New Brighton township when the security police arrived. Also banned were Jerry Modisane and Strini Moodley (SASO's president and publications director), and two members of the BPC national executive, Drake Koka and Saths Cooper. The bans restricted the eight for five years to their home magisterial districts, and forbade them to attend gatherings (defined as meeting with more than one other person at a time). Nothing they said or wrote could be published or publicly quoted. Cooper and Moodley were also confined to their homes from 6 p.m. to 6 a.m. daily ("12-hour house arrest"), a bonus measure probably aimed at intimidating other Indians who might consider involving themselves in African politics.

The government gave no reasons for the restrictions; however, their imposition just after the Durban strikes of January and February 1973 raised speculation that the National Party was seeking scapegoats for the political embarrassment caused by the strikes.[43] Had the BPC and SASO in fact been making major progress in the labor field by February 1973, the bans on Koka and Mafuna—coupled with the death of Mthuli Shezi two months earlier—might have constituted a significant setback.[44] But in reality, SASO and BPC had made only exploratory beginnings in building lines of communication to workers, lagging far behind the advances made by the NUSAS Wages Commissions and the white-run Urban Training Project with their greater numbers and resources.[45] Ironically, the involvement of white students with African workers had been a byproduct of the SASO-NUSAS split, which had left white radicals without their traditional avenue for identification with the black cause.

Public and media reactions to the bannings were muted, but messages of solidarity and offers of help from foreign anti-apartheid groups buoyed morale as the targeted organizations struggled to reestablish their equilibrium. Henry Isaacs, a law student at the University of the Western Cape, became acting SASO president. Tiro took over as Permanent Organizer, and Ben Langa replaced Pityana as Secretary-General. Biko, who was not obliged by his ban to resign from Black Community Programmes, continued as BCP field officer but shifted his office to King William's Town where his restrictions required him to live. A decision by SASO to establish regional offices in 1972 had resulted in the appointment of Mapetla Mohapi, a former Turfloop student, as eastern Cape regional coordinator. Following Biko's banning, Mohapi centered his activities in King William's Town, and several other black consciousness veterans quietly moved there, formally to fill staff positions in Black Community Programmes, and unofficially to provide a support system for Biko as he tried to maintain contact with the movement in an ongoing advisory role.

The bannings of February 1973 aimed to suppress the black consciousness movement without outlawing its constituent organizations. Harassment intensified: offices were raided and burgled, leaders were shadowed by the security police, printers who produced black consciousness publications were threatened, and informers became more ubiquitous. Police picked up movement members in growing numbers and subjected them to intimidating interrogations. In a case that was a chilling sign of how rapidly the costs of activism were escalating, the BPC's national organizer, Mosibudi Mangena, was detained and convicted on a charge under the Terrorism Act, seemingly fabricated, that he had attempted to recruit two off-duty policemen for guerrilla training. By the end of 1973, a dozen more leaders had been banned, including every remaining member of the BPC's national executive committee except Winifred Kgware. Black Community Programmes director Ben Khoapa was banned in October and put under 24-hour house arrest in Durban's Umlazi township. Inevitably, BPC and SASO lost some of their capacity to attract new members, and funds became even harder to raise from South African sources. In 1974 not a single issue of the *SASO Newsletter* appeared. Nevertheless, earlier proselytization in high schools insured that freshmen continued to arrive at universities eager to become involved.

Black organizations, in Biko's metaphor from the sports field, were not showing much conspicuous forward movement; the most one could say was that they were still standing.[46] Yet there were new signs of life in areas of the country that had not previously been major centers of black consciousness sentiment. *Document 53,* a report to the July 1973 SASO annual conference, gives a sense of continuing work in the eastern Cape. Most dramatically, Coloured students at the University of the Western Cape in Cape Town, who had shown little interest in the movement earlier, erupted in mid-1973 in a defiant display of resistance.

Students at UWC experienced many of the frustrations common at the other ethnic universities, including authoritarian regulations, low academic standards, and the preponderance of white lecturers, including many poorly qualified Afrikaners. Most Coloured students came from apolitical homes where economically aspiring parents put emphasis on academic success. Others had been exposed to the dominant political tradition among Coloureds in the western Cape, the principled but essentially passive, rejectionist tradition of the Non-European Unity Movement. This tradition prescribed noncollaboration with all racially discriminatory institutions, but offered no solution to the reality that only one university—a racially segregated one—was open to Coloureds.

SASO's few early adherents at UWC were mainly students who had participated in NUSAS and UCM activities.[47] By 1972 they had succeeded in organizing a branch of SASO, as well as UWC's first Students' Representative Council (SRC). Enthusiasm for SASO picked up during the nationwide protests over the Tiro affair, and in September 1972 a new SASO-dominated

SRC was elected in a poll with a 61 percent student turnout—an astounding level of participation given the strength of "boycottist" attitudes. Friction between the administration and the SRC escalated as the authorities tried to contain the growing challenge from student critics of the university and of the apartheid system that it symbolized. The administration refused to recognize the SRC, tried to prevent national SASO leaders from visiting the campus, and colluded with security police who investigated student records or summoned individual students for questioning. On June 5, 1973, the SRC circulated an ultimatum—later dubbed *Die Geel Dokument* ("the yellow document")—calling on the administration to make reforms and listing ten student grievances (*Document 52*). When the rector made no response, students held a mass meeting on June 8 and demanded a reply. The next day police detained SRC leader Henry Isaacs, the acting SASO president. Protests resumed with new fervor, and after consultation with the Minister of Coloured Relations, the UWC administration closed the university and announced that all students would have to apply for readmission.

At this stage the government might have prevailed had students not immediately gone to work to regain the offensive. At a mass meeting on June 12 at St. John's Cathedral in Bellville, students voted by a large majority to reject the reapplication requirement and to call for the formation of parent-student committees, media mobilization to publicize complaints against the university, and a national tour by an Action Committee—which included low-profile members of SASO—to reinforce protests by the parent-student committees. The students' quick counter-attack and the well-focused nature of their demands generated a wave of support from Coloured parents, clergy, journalists, and UWC graduates nationwide. Local protest meetings culminated in a rally at Athlone Athletic Park in Cape Town on July 8 where a large crowd, estimated at ten to twelve thousand people, turned out. The roster of prominent speakers included Gatsha Buthelezi, Sonny Leon, Adam Small (who had supported the students by resigning his position as one of UWC's handful of senior Coloured faculty), and Fatima Meer, a prominent Indian academic whose forceful oratory raised cheers from the crowd when she gestured in the direction of Robben Island—visible on a clear day from high points in Cape Town—and declared "Power to our brothers way beyond Table Mountain."[48]

The Athlone rally was the largest black political demonstration staged in South Africa since the Sharpeville crisis of 1960. Two days later, university authorities announced that all students would be readmitted unconditionally. Student pressure for reforms resumed, tensions escalated again, and more suspensions occurred; but before the year was out, the administration was forced to appoint a commission of inquiry into student grievances and to replace the university's white rector with a Coloured.[49] The lessons were not lost on either blacks or whites: sustained, united and well-formulated challenges to white power—though not without cost to the challengers—could achieve measurable gains. Students who voiced their grievances could win support from the wider community. "The disturbing thing about the events at the University of the Western Cape," editorialized the Johannesburg *Sunday Times* a week after the Athlone rally, was that the authorities had "remembered all the old mistakes and repeated them with meticulous accuracy." The students, in contrast, returned to the fray "much more self-confident and militant. They have flexed their muscles, and found the exercise rewarding."[50]

In Search of "Phase Two"

A tactical retreat over the UWC expulsions did not incline the state toward a strategy of appeasement elsewhere. Harassment of SASO and BPC leaders continued, and Mangena's swift trial and conviction in October 1973 alerted activists to the ubiquitous danger of police surveillance. The BPC became temporarily quiescent as backstage moves went on to replace its banned leadership. Campus political activity cooled. But beneath the deceptively still surface, strong currents roiled around the foundations of the black consciousness movement. How useful was it to remain legal if the state could ban anyone without resorting to court action, or could rig a court conviction? How much more conscientization was necessary before the movement became serious about the specifics of "phase two"? Since many saw "phase two" as certain to involve armed struggle, was it not vital that the movement investigate links with the exiled ANC and PAC, who were known to be training guerrilla armies much like those fighting in Mozambique, Angola and Rhodesia?[51]

Open deliberation on these questions was impossible, and information on the exiled movements was hard to obtain. If acquired by a few people in one area, it could not be easily disseminated elsewhere. Mutual trust among blacks, which black consciousness had done much to promote, began to fray as rumors spread both hope and fear, fact and wishful fancy. By ones and twos and in small groups, venturesome young blacks followed the path of the first handful of SASO students who had disappeared into exile after the July 1972 conference at Hammanskraal. In September 1973, Mafuna and Nengwekhulu slipped over the border into Botswana. They were joined by Tiro, Tebogo Mafole of BCP, and Welile Nhlapo, and gradually by a trickle of others who had either been banned already or feared restriction or arrest. In Botswana, exploratory contacts began between the newcomers and older exiles linked to the liberation movements headquartered in Tanzania. Tentative assessments of the exiled organizations and their capabilities could now be made, and cautiously passed through trusted couriers to black consciousness networks inside South Africa.[52] The outlook for mounting a serious foreign-based guerrilla challenge seemed bleak. In February 1974 the dangerous nature of the search for "phase two" was made dramatically apparent when Tiro was murdered in Botswana by a parcel bomb.

As the number of young exiles grew and the inclination of many of them to remain aloof from the older movements became more manifest, friction mounted in Botswana. Would the black consciousness movement try to establish itself as a "third force" in exile politics, perhaps even try to build its own army? The ANC and PAC, frustrated by lack of progress after a decade in exile, had watched the emergence of black consciousness inside South Africa with a mixture of satisfaction and wary jealousy. Given that international support for the external organizations rested on their claim to represent South Africa's oppressed majority at home, SASO's autonomy was cause for worry. Its careful neutrality in the competition between the ANC and PAC had helped it attract support from people of all political backgrounds, uniting them behind a single new ideological formulation that defined South Africa as a "black" nation oppressed by an alien but potentially assimilable white minority. To avoid rivalry, SASO, and later BPC, had projected themselves as organizations trying to fill a vacuum, not to usurp the place of the ANC and PAC. After raising early objections to the formation of the BPC as "a betrayal of the older organizations," many former members of ANC and PAC had become active in local BPC structures, further blurring the lines of ideological differentiation between the old and new movements.[53]

In moments of optimism, black consciousness adherents hoped that SASO and BPC might become catalysts in a reunion of the historical movements into a single organization or united front. This seemed realistic as long as no organized presence of the competing senior organizations was evident inside South Africa. In exile, however, black consciousness refugees found the older movements implacably hostile to each other, as well as antagonistic to SASO, which they saw as a bumptious young rival to be cut down to size—"a baby organization of confused people," as one black consciousness activist observed.[54] Black consciousness organizations at home had learned to exploit the political resources in their environment with skill; outside, they found that the older movements jealously controlled almost all the resources available to exiles: access to host government officials and the inside information they could provide, as well as to opportunities for study and for onward transportation. Experience soon proved that the older organizations, as the only liberation groups recognized by the Organization of African Unity, also controlled all access to governments willing to provide military training and equipment, thus foreclosing any prospect that black consciousness exiles might establish their own independent army.

Beginning in late 1973 exploratory contacts triggered important new political calculations in all camps. The external PAC lacked the capacity to run anything more than a minimal recruiting effort inside South Africa, but for the ANC, such an effort now seemed both urgently necessary and at last feasible: feasible because the black consciousness movement had created an unprecedented level of political awareness; and necessary because the movement was resisting the ANC's welcoming overtures. ANC recruiting strategy accordingly began to focus on the penetration of black consciousness organizations within South Africa itself. From late 1974, the locus of effort shifted from Botswana to Swaziland where transit routes into South

Africa promised to open up once Frelimo assumed power in Mozambique. Inside South Africa, ANC veterans being released from Robben Island added new connecting points for the construction of an underground. On a student trip to Swaziland in 1975, several key SASO activists from the Natal medical school were recruited into the ANC. For these secret recruits, all of whom became members of the SASO national executive in 1975–77, "phase two" now assumed a clear new meaning and direction: the steering of the student movement toward identification with the aims, ideology, and leadership of the ANC.[55]

The 1974 "Viva Frelimo" Rallies

No forewarnings prepared South Africa for the army coup which toppled the government of Portuguese dictator Marcello Caetano on April 25, 1974. Lisbon's African colonies quickly embarked on a phased transition to independence, removing major portions of the geographical buffer zone that had separated South Africa from the hostile states of independent Africa. Equally momentous was the psychological impact: menacing uncertainties for whites, while the heady vision of white power overthrown by a guerrilla army assumed a palpable new reality to blacks, particularly as the collapse of Portuguese colonialism followed on the heels of the American retreat from Vietnam.

Hoping to inspire new energy in their battered ranks, SASO and BPC decided to stage "Viva Frelimo" demonstrations to celebrate Mozambique's coming independence. The possibility of holding demonstrations had been discussed in the doldrum period after the February 1973 bannings. The Athlone rally set an encouraging precedent. In the end, planning was rather haphazard. Some thought Mozambique's actual independence day would be a more fitting occasion; others, including Biko, held to SASO's long-standing view that public demonstrations belonged to an outmoded type of NUSAS-style "protest politics." But the Durban leadership decided to go ahead, and informed the press that a rally to be addressed by Frelimo representatives would be held at the Curries Fountain stadium in Durban on September 25. In other centers, the decision to hold demonstrations came too late to be implemented, except at Turfloop where a campus rally was planned.

On September 24, the Minister of Justice banned the rallies. Meanwhile, a SASO/BPC delegation dispatched to Lourenco Marques failed to persuade Frelimo to send speakers to address the demonstrations. In the early evening of the 25th, police using dogs and truncheons dispersed a crowd of several thousand assembled outside the Curries Fountain stadium in defiance of the ban. Arrests and raids at the Durban offices of SASO and BPC followed.

At Turfloop, handwritten placards bearing bellicose slogans were posted around the campus the morning of September 25: "The Dignity of the Black Man Has Been Restored in Mozambique and So Shall It Be Here," read one; others proclaimed "Frelimo Killed and Won. SA Blacks?," "Revolution!! Machel Will Help! Away with Vorster Ban! We are Not Afraid! Black Power!!!!"

and the like.[56] Police broke up a large indoor meeting, then baton-charged students as they dispersed. Several students were injured, and stones were thrown before intervention by the rector, the SRC, and members of the Black Academic Staff Association ended the melee and persuaded the police to withdraw. However, when several white staff members drove onto the campus later in the day, angry students blocked their way, broke a car window, punched a lecturer known for his racist attitudes, and roughed up several others. On September 27, with the question of disciplinary action still pending, the university closed for a scheduled two week break during which police carried out a series of arrests.

The abortive rallies might have caused little stir had they been allowed to proceed unobstructed. The Turfloop rector had decided not to stop the campus rally in spite of its uncertain legality. To the security police, however, the rallies presented a convenient pretext to step up repression of the black consciousness movement. By late 1974 at least 20 activists in SASO, BPC, BCP, BAWU and TECON had been restricted by banning orders, and police had decided that enough evidence of illegal activity could be marshaled to obtain court convictions against key figures in the movement.

A court case was a major undertaking, requiring time and careful preparation. But prevailing laws gave state prosecutors great latitude, and virtually all judges had a predisposition to favor the state in security cases. Nevertheless, for justice to be seen to be done in the eyes of the wider public—even within the contorted context of apartheid law and society— basic rules of evidence had to be observed. Before a case could be brought, the state had to identify individuals who could most convincingly be found guilty of legal violations, find witnesses to give credible testimony against them, and devise a legal strategy that could assure convictions.

The last of these tasks could be left to prosecuting lawyers, but the first two fell to the security police, who set about detaining and interrogating members of black consciousness groups. By mid-November at least 35 activists were being held under a variety of security laws that denied them contact with families or lawyers. In conditions where detainees could be held incommunicado for indefinite periods, police felt free to apply brutal forms of coercion to extract confessions or force detainees to become state witnesses (*Document 60*). In January 1975, 13 "Viva Frelimo" detainees were charged with offenses under the Terrorism Act.

The Black Renaissance Convention

Whether or not the trial of SASO and BPC leaders would finally deliver a knock-out blow to the black consciousness movement, the state's security establishment had good reason to believe that its most irksome opponents were on the ropes. The "Viva Frelimo" arrests had removed four of SASO's five national executive members from circulation—Muntu Myeza, Patrick Lekota, Pandelani Nefolovhodwe, and Rubin Hare—and similarly devastated the national leadership of the BPC. Yet just when black political organizations seemed near collapse, an unusual event, the Black Renaissance Convention, galvanized black opinion around a set of militant political principles. In December 1974 over 300 representatives of black organizations met for four days at Hammanskraal. The principal organizers were two dynamic clergymen, Maurice Ngakane, a staff member of the South African Council of Churches, and Smangaliso Mkhatshwa, who in 1970 had provoked controversy among Catholics with the "Black Priests' Manifesto" (*Document 26*). They saw the Convention as an opportunity for established leaders to come together in a spirit of solidarity and to assert leadership within the black community. Diligent planning and publicity ensured that the meeting would be broadly representative of black religious, educational, civic, labor, sport and welfare organizations. Attendance was restricted to Africans, Indians and Coloureds.

Ngakane and Mkhatshwa recruited a steering committee from among members of the donor organizations, but neglected to include representatives of SASO or BPC, although both were invited to send delegates to the Convention. This slight to groups that despite their relative youth regarded themselves as the "parent" bodies of black consciousness, meant that SASO and BPC members arrived in a belligerent and suspicious mood. As Mkhatshwa's report on the Convention (*Document 54*) indicates, the BPC feared that the organizers might intend to set up a rival political organization.[57] Even more vexing was the presence, by invitation, of a number of homeland and other "system" officials, one of whom—Collins Ramusi of Lebowa—had been invited to deliver the opening address.

More than two years had passed since SASO's decisive repudiation of all efforts to "work against the system from within," and the accommodating stance of the Convention's organizers toward people like Ramusi and the Labour Party's David Curry was more than the 20 or so SASO and BPC delegates could tolerate. As soon as the opening formalities were over, members of the SASO/BPC grouping began a barrage of objections, motions and points aimed at forcing the meeting to redefine its rather tepid aims and to exclude the "system" politicians from its deliberations. In the end, the Convention endorsed a declaration of principles of unprecedented militancy. Scrapping the bland language of culture and religion, its final Declaration and Resolutions not only condemned all manifestations of "separate development" and called for "a totally united and democratic South Africa . . . in which there is an equitable distribution of wealth," but also urged all blacks to agitate for the release of political prisoners, demanded that African trade unions be recognized, and urged the world to apply "cultural, educational, economic, manpower and military" sanctions against Pretoria.

Before the Black Renaissance Convention, outside the relatively small circles of SASO and BPC, there had been no such bold public articulation of black demands inside South Africa since the banning of the ANC and PAC at the time of Sharpeville. Years of African disorganization and silence had left the field open to the National Party to proceed with its plans for the construction of a pliant society where individuals would adjust to their assigned places in an ethnically fragmented and racially hierarchical system. The farcical Progressive Party-sponsored Bulugha conference held only a year earlier (see Chapter 8) was an indicator of how close the Nationalists were to neutralizing all criticism by whites of the blueprint for "grand apartheid." But contrary to design, blacks were now finding their own voices again. The militancy of the student movement had permeated the wider society and was no longer identified merely with youthful radicalism. Although many older blacks continued to disapprove of unconventional modes of speech and behavior among the young, the black consciousness organizations had achieved their aim of becoming opinion leaders far beyond student circles.

The black consciousness movement and its "revolution of identity" had also insured that when Africans again found their political voice, a substantial majority would choose to define themselves in terms of race and color rather than tribe, the identity the state was at such pains to promote. "Tribalism" had long been rejected in the political traditions of the educated stratum of African urban society as well as in movements of organized African labor, yet the success of Inkatha in building a tribally-based political force made clear the potential power of politicized ethnicity. Had SASO and BPC not rejected ethnic balkanization with uncompromising fervor in the 1970s, it is conceivable that the National Party's efforts to undermine the tradition of supra-tribal African nationalism might have prevailed. The success of the black consciousness movement in persuading many younger Coloureds and Indians to embrace a strategy of black solidarity was likewise a major accomplishment.

Black Consciousness in Court: The SASO Nine

The case of *State v. Cooper and eight others*—sometimes called "the SASO Nine"—opened in Pretoria in August 1975, and became the most publicized legal confrontation of the decade for black political organizations.[58] The state alleged that the accused had violated the Terrorism Act by conspiring to bring about revolutionary change and to foster feelings of racial hostility toward whites among blacks. The proceedings lasted for 16 months. Dozens of witnesses called by the state included three detained members of black consciousness organizations who were released in return for giving evidence against the accused. Stoffel van der Merwe, a political scientist at Rand Afrikaans University who was later appointed a cabinet minister by P. W. Botha, appeared as the state's main expert witness to explain the alleged revolutionary nature of SASO and its allied organizations.

For the defense, the task was twofold: to project the most legally benign view possible of the black consciousness movement, while at the same time making maximum use of the courtroom as a political forum. In respect to the first objective, Biko's belief that SASO and BPC would be most useful and long-lived as above-ground, nonconfrontational organizations seemed at least partially vindicated. Although evidence could be advanced by the state to show that revolutionary thoughts were common—inflammatory poems and the Turfloop posters, for example, or an unofficial letter by Mayatula urging Namibians to be ready to join a general strike—the prosecution failed to establish that SASO or its allied organizations actually planned to carry out violent acts. They were, the judge conceded, essentially protest organizations engaged in verbal agitation, not revolutionary groups plotting a violent overthrow of the government. Nevertheless, he concluded that their agitation and the type of change they sought—a radical political and economic redistribution of power and resources among South Africans—implied a revolutionary intent.[59] The defendants were found guilty under the Terrorism Act of "encouraging feelings of hostility" between the races, and of conspiring "with the intention of endangering the maintenance of law and order."[60] Six were given sentences of six years, and three of five years, terms that were relatively light given the state's major investment in the trial.

From the state's point of view, high-profile political trials like *Cooper* had the disadvantage of arousing unwelcome media attention. By the conclusion of the trial in December 1976, the accused had managed to attract considerable publicity for their cause, and through their behavior in court to convey a potent message of defiance toward white authority. The black consciousness movement, at a low ebb organizationally, eagerly seized the opportunity offered by the trial to place its mark on public thinking. At a preliminary court appearance in February 1975, the defendants emerged from the cells beneath the courtroom robustly singing a freedom song, *Unzima Lo Mthwalo* ("This Burden is Heavy") and making the raised fist salute.[61] On entering the dock they bellowed *Amandla!* ("power!") in unison at the startled spectators. At a subsequent appearance in March, when they repeated this display of insubordination, blacks in the packed public gallery stood and joined in loudly. At the end of the brief March proceedings, fighting erupted between the defendants and policemen guarding the dock as families and well-wishers surged forward to touch the accused and police struggled to push the prisoners down the stairway to the cells.

In the decade after Rivonia, the ever harsher security laws, long jail sentences, police torture, and the rising number of deaths among detainees had cast a dark pall of fear over popular attitudes toward political action, giving the state an increased psychological advantage. A central objective of the black consciousness movement had been to challenge this strategy of dominance-through-fear, and to condition blacks, especially the rising generation, both to respond aggressively and to adjust to the escalating personal sacrifices required. Leading by example, the *Cooper* defendants set out to make the most of the political theater of the courtroom. They maintained their combative stance throughout the trial, managing also to convert the courtroom into a forum for mature political instruction. In May 1976 when the defense subpoenaed Biko as a witness and he testified for five days with all his customary persuasiveness, the court and the public through the press were audience to an open seminar on the history, aims and principles of black consciousness, brilliantly tailored to suit the case for the defense, but uncompromising in its moral assertiveness.[62] Yet as only one skirmish in a widening psychological war, the trial and its impact on black opinion cannot be assessed in isolation from the widespread mood of anger gathering momentum more broadly. By the trial's end, the country was six months into the Soweto uprising and a new phase of confrontation had opened in liberation politics.

Ideological Tensions

It became evident at the Black Renaissance Convention that radical opinion was beginning to reflect left-wing influences that had not previously been an element in black consciousness thinking. When Sam Motsuenyane, the president of the National African Federated Chamber of Commerce, addressed the Convention, he was heckled with comments that suggested that "capitalists" were regarded as members of the enemy camp. Earlier the same day, "one delegate expressed his fears of the CIA and US imperialism" when an American telegram of greetings was read out (*Document 54*). Mafika Gwala, a black consciousness writer, whose closing speech was enthusiastically received, peppered his talk with attacks on the collaborationist tendencies of the black bourgeoisie and called on the Convention to recognize the fundamental need for an "economic interpretation of our struggle."[63]

The founders of SASO had specifically avoided Marxist rhetoric. The know-it-all manner of white leftists in NUSAS had antagonized them.[64] Organizational survival was SASO's top priority, and communism was the government's favorite bogey. SASO was looking for unifying themes and feared that an emphasis on class hostilities would be divisive and hinder efforts to mobilize financial support among the small number of well-to-do blacks. White America was not admired, but neither was the Soviet Union whose 1968 invasion had put an end to Czechoslovakia's democratic "Prague spring." In any case, Nengwekhulu informally observed in 1972, communists in South Africa preached "Russian communism," and no black person could ever trust Russians because Russians were whites.[65] Though shying away from such crude equations, Biko too believed that "a communist in South Africa . . . will be an instrument of Moscow," and thus an ally of what he considered Soviet imperialism.[66]

To criticize the South African Communist Party was not to reject all variants of socialism, however. The socialism most appealing to SASO in its early years was the African socialism of Julius Nyerere and Kenneth Kaunda, which stressed the equitable distribution of wealth and downplayed the concept of class antagonisms in favor of the values of unity and social harmony. If framed vaguely enough, this kind of socialism could even be seen as compatible with the pursuit of wealth by blacks through business activity, as long as such businesses were organized for "cooperative" rather than individual profit, and had as their goal some generalized notion of economic nationalism or strengthening of the whole "black community."[67] Since the open advocacy of socialism, no matter how unspecifically defined, seemed likely to excite unwelcome interest from the state, the term itself rarely appeared in early black consciousness writings, and eventually the equally unspecific term "black communalism" was adopted as a semantic stand-in.

By the mid-1970s, an interest in more orthodox Marxist formulations was increasingly evident in SASO. Left-wing literature from outside the country was becoming more accessible, and was also being produced inside South Africa by the anti-Soviet Unity Movement and its ally the African People's Democratic Union of South Africa (APDUSA).[68] Interest in class-based theories grew in proportion to impatience in SASO with the failure of black consciousness ideology to inspire more tangible political gains. Students who had participated in community development projects, or who had tried proselytizing for black consciousness among older township residents, had repeatedly come up against the gap between SASO's intellectual approach and the stark material preoccupations of the working poor.

The problems of politically mobilizing semiliterate or illiterate Africans were not new; they were simply more intractable than most students expected. Nor was class itself the problem in communication. SASO's members originated on average from a stratum of African working-class society somewhat higher than the median of the mass constituency they were attempting to mobilize, but language, culture and experience were common between the two groups despite their different levels of formal education.[69] The real cause of frustration was the inability of the black consciousness movement—owing to state repression and the movement's own lack of experience, creative imagination or both—to discover an effective method of bringing together its activists with their potential mass audience so that the former could activate the latent political energies of the latter. Leftist ideology and rhetoric increasingly became a substitute for the satisfaction of thwarted revolutionary impulses among SASO militants. Many of these themes are evident in *Document 55,* by an anonymous author in the *SASO Newsletter* of May-June 1975. "The frustration," the writer laments, "is that the Black intellectual is all the time aware that the 'message' should be taken to the man in the street. The 'HOW' is the problem."

A further influence pulling students to the left was their expanding contacts with the underground ANC and PAC. Although neither of the older movements had adopted Marxist ideology during their days as legal organizations, both took up the anti-imperialist rhetoric of their eastern bloc sponsors once in exile. Inside South Africa, SASO and BPC attracted many individuals with prior allegiance to one or another of the older movements, yet with only occasional lapses, the black consciousness movement had managed successfully to avoid involvement in ANC-PAC rivalry. By 1975, the problematic implications of this balancing act were becoming more evident.

On the Eve of Soweto

In 1975 the ANC and PAC were gradually assembling rudimentary underground networks made up of veteran members and prisoners released from Robben Island, and both movements were fishing for new recruits in the pool provided by the black consciousness movement. Many younger activists were attracted by the prospect of joining the armed struggle. Some regarded ideological fine points as a secondary consideration; others did not. SASO and BPC leaders were regularly approached by members seeking guidance on how to leave the country safely and what to do after leaving. The search for strategies and methods was at a crossroads.[70]

The pressure to work out a modus vivendi between black consciousness groups and the older liberation movements was acutely felt by Biko and his circle of lieutenants in King William's Town. As one means of building links, they established the Zimele Trust Fund to raise money for projects to employ released political prisoners, dozens of whom lived in dire poverty in the eastern Cape. Biko's authority in the affairs of the movement as a whole, however, was only an informal one. SASO, BPC, BCP and the plethora of black consciousness-oriented youth, high school and cultural organizations now functioned almost entirely independently of one other. Following the "Viva Frelimo" arrests in September 1974, Mapetla Mohapi and Malusi Mpumlwana were dispatched from King William's Town to Durban to keep SASO headquarters operating, but once a new leadership was in place, SASO returned to its autonomous course, which in practice meant the cultivation of ever closer relations with the ANC's underground in Natal.

Biko saw an urgent need for a unified movement of resistance in which minor differences over ideology and tactics would not detract from the pursuit of common goals. In a clandestine meeting with Robert Sobukwe in May 1975 he was able to obtain assurances of Sobukwe's full support for efforts to reunite the ANC and PAC.[71] Working mainly through Mpumlwana and Mohapi, Biko began an indirect dialogue involving Griffiths Mxenge and Harry Gwala, high ranking ANC underground leaders in Natal, Zeph Mothopeng and other PAC figures in Johannesburg, and an array of minor older leaders in the Cape and elsewhere. Plans to hold a secret unity meeting just after Christmas 1975 had to be aborted, but Biko's cautious efforts to broker dialogue and cooperation continued.

In mid-December 1975, the BPC staged its fourth national conference, attended by about 100 people, in King William's Town. Knowledge of the secret unity talks was limited to a handful of Biko's close confidants, but through this core group the BPC conference was steered toward discussion of major issues around which the unity negotiators hoped to build a consensus. A conference statement refining the definition of black consciousness aligned the movement with the ANC's multiracialism by stating that the aim of black consciousness was not "Black Power" but rather the creation of "a truly open plural society." In a gesture conciliatory to the PAC, the document used the name "Azania" for South Africa.[72] For purposes of the secret unity negotiations, however, the conference was principally directed toward fleshing out the ill-defined concept of "black communalism" so that both Marxists and non-Marxists could find it acceptable as a common vision of a future economic order. While those privy to the unity moves maintained silence regarding the hidden agenda, there were rumblings of dissent from some participants who believed the BPC was trying to stake out a "third force" position distinct from that of ANC or PAC. Following the conference, Biko and his confidants (who now included Kenneth Rachidi, the newly elected BPC president, and Mxolisi Mvovo, Biko's brother-in-law who had been elected vice president), drew up additional draft papers in preparation for a national symposium to produce a major policy document on black communalism.

This policy document, variously known as the "Mafikeng Manifesto" and the "30 Point Program" of the BPC (*Document 57*), was eventually debated at a symposium in Mafikeng in the northern Cape at the end of May 1976. Produced in draft form in King William's Town and amended at the Mafikeng meeting amidst heated discussion, the document proposed features for a mixed economy with a high degree of state ownership or control in virtually every economic sector, but a place also reserved for "private enterprise." The document called for more radical and specific changes than any economic blueprint ever proposed by a black political organization, or than any document of its kind produced up to the start of constitutional negotiations in the early 1990s. But it failed to have a unifying effect, to the disappoint- ment of its initiators, who seem to have proceeded from a mistaken belief that the disparate tendencies developing within the black consciousness movement actually revolved around differences of opinion about a future economic order.

In reality, even though economic debates generated convenient rhetorical litmus tests useful to partisans of one or another camp in identifying and stigmatizing their rivals, what really was at work in the growing mutual suspicions between the members of different tendencies was competition for political leadership in a struggle where all believed that victory was not only inevitable but might, as in Mozambique, occur much sooner than expected. Whatever ostensible reasons might be put forward for objecting to initiatives by the BPC, most ANC and PAC leaders felt threatened by those young and articulate leaders who did not formally subordinate themselves to the older organizations. Younger activists who pledged their loyalty to one or the other of the older groups soon came to share the view that unaffiliated black consciousness leaders must be intending to form a third liberation organization, a view lent some credence by the tentative attempts of some black consciousness exiles to do exactly that. From inside the black consciousness movement within South Africa, given its remarkably rapid and successful rise, it seemed to Biko and others that the older organizations were largely made up of ineffectual has-beens, people far away and out of touch with contemporary realities. Some might see armed struggle—and therefore the movements pursuing it—as the key to liberation, but Biko believed it was political struggle within South Africa that would eventually turn the tide. So why should the black consciousness generation join the older movements rather than the other way around?

To admit to personal rivalries would have been to lower the principled tone of political debate, and so discussions tended to focus around such questions as whether the ANC's Freedom Charter was out of date, and if so whether the Mafikeng Manifesto might be an appropriate update. On the face of it, the Manifesto was much more explicitly socialist than the Freedom Charter. But because it allowed a measure of legitimacy for private business, ANC partisans could stigmatize it as "capitalistic" and "unprogressive," thereby demonstrating their loyalty to the "scientific socialism" by then associated with the ANC-Communist Party alliance. To those aligned with PAC, appeals to the sanctity of the Freedom Charter or the use of epithets like "unprogressive" were enough to brand anyone in the black consciousness movement—and more specifically in SASO—as a "red." Lacking any experience of armed warfare but convinced of its necessity, frustrated with their powerlessness and grasping for the most convincing symbols of power and efficacy they could find, those who were moving into the orbits of the older movements felt a need to adopt the coded political language of their chosen camp as part of an ongoing process of shaping a new intellectual identity. In large part this was an adaptive process particular to the educated elite and not to the hundreds and later thousands of younger students and youths swept up in the revolt that was about to explode. For most people most of the time, disputes over socialism, black consciousness, the controversial clauses of the Freedom Charter, or the degree to which the ANC was beholden to the Soviet bloc, were not questions of any day-to-day consequence. Among many hard-core activists of the black consciousness movement, however, these ideological issues—both in their own right, and as weapons in the competition among would-be political leaders—loomed increasingly large as the dominance of the younger movement began to be challenged by the older liberation organizations. Several more years were to elapse before distinct lines would emerge to demarcate the variety of ideological tendencies ascendant in post-Soweto politics. But first, white and black South Africa alike had to face a fateful trial by fire.

Notes

1. On AICA see Peter Walshe, *Church Versus State in South Africa: the Case of the Christian Institute* (London: C. Hurst and Co., 1983), passim, and Colleen Ryan, *Beyers Naude: Pilgrimage of Faith* (Trenton, NJ: Africa World Press, 1990), pp. 124–27.

2. F. M. Meer, "The Natal Indian Congress, 1972," *Reality*, July 1972, p. 5. Meer refers to the NIC as a "black" organization, but then gives reasons why opinion at its April 1972 conference was opposed to black consciousness.

3. In December 1971 tensions flared when a NIC official, Ramlall Ramesar, publicly accused SASO of propagating the policies of the PAC. Since furthering the aims of a banned organization was illegal, SASO threatened to sue Ramesar for defamation, and a hostile stand-off followed. See letter from Pityana "to all SRC's and local committees re SASO vs. NIC controversy," March 3, 1972; Ben Khoapa, ed., *Black Review 1972*, pp. 6–8; the *SASO Newsletters* of January/February and March/April 1972; and conversation with Mewa Ramgobin (July 1989).

4. Later, when SASO's monopoly of the black political terrain disappeared with the growth of multiple groups of varying viewpoints, and as money became a major player in the high stakes politics of the 1980s, organizations with a strict "blacks only" philosophy found

themselves at an ever-increasing financial disadvantage. Even when white liberal organizations in the 1970s raised funds that subsidized radical black organizations, the relationships were often ambivalent. In Biko's view, for example, the Christian Institute was able to raise money abroad for AICA, and later for Black Community Programmes, because the black cause had become popular with progressive foreign donors. The Christian Institute was then able to finance itself by keeping a percentage of these funds to cover its own administrative costs— a not unreasonable arrangement, but one that to blacks gave the appearance of whites riding "on the black ticket." Besides funds, the Christian Institute provided office space to SASO and later to SASM in Johannesburg. Conversation with Biko (October 1972).

5. Mosibudi Mangena, *On Your Own* (Braamfontein: Skotaville, 1989), p. 36.

6. On Spro-cas see Peter Randall, *A Taste of Power* (Johannesburg: Ravan Press, 1973).

7. "Black Community Programmes Year Report, 1972," p. 1.

8. Students were usually differentiated from "youth," who were defined as young people not in school. While it is impossible to say precisely how many of these leadership seminars were conducted by BCP, Walshe (p. 155) states that ten were held in the Natal region in 1972, and others later in the Transvaal, Transkei, and eastern and western Cape. A typical one held at Edendale in August 1972, he says, involved 43 registrants.

9. Craig Charney has noted that "the number of literate urban Africans almost tripled between 1951 and 1970, when it reached 2.64 million, or two-thirds of adults in the cities. . . . Between 1962 and 1975, the number of Africans reading English-language dailies tripled to 1.1-million. . . . In 1975, more than 40% of urban African men read a newspaper every day. . . . [The percentage] was greatest in Soweto, where three out of four African men read a daily." Craig Charney, "Black Power, White Press: Literacy, Newspapers, and the Transformation of Township Political Culture, 1960–1976," unpublished paper, May 1992, p. 5.

10. Mafika Pascal Gwala, "Priorities in Culture for Creativity and Black Development," in Ben J. Langa, ed., *Creativity and Black Development* (Durban: South African Students' Organisation, 1973), p. 51.

11. "Resolutions adopted at the 1st SASO General Students' Council, July 4th–July 10th," 1970, p. 1.

12. Letters from Biko to Thami Mazwai, October 9, 1969, and to SRC Presidents and other organizations regarding SASO, February 1970.

13. According to Randall, about 3,300 copies of *Black Review 1972* and 4,250 of the first *Black Viewpoint* (September 1972) were printed. The latter sold out within a few weeks, according to the BCP annual report for 1972.

14. *Star,* March 16, 1972.

15. Widely varying statistics for student "walk offs" appeared in the press, SASO reports, the annual *Surveys* of the Institute of Race Relations, and personal accounts. Numbers given here are conservative estimates.

16. Conversation with Biko.

17. Conversation with Victor Sifora, headmaster of Ga-Rankuwa High School, Pretoria (October 1972).

18. Conversation with Kehla Mthembu (March 1989).

19. Testimony in *State v. Molokeng* (the NAYO trial), 1976, p. 223.

20. The Reef is the gold-bearing geological formation that runs west and south from Johannesburg and gives its name to the area.

21. Mangena, p. 28.

22. *The World* (Johannesburg), August 10, 1971, and conversations with David Thebehali (August 1972), Curnick Ndamse (October 1972), Temba Sono (November 1973), and Harry Nengwekhulu (September 1975).

23. Conversation with Biko.

24. Keith Mokoape, Thenjiwe Mtintso and Welile Nhlapo, "Towards the Armed Struggle," in N. Barney Pityana et al., eds., *Bounds of Possibility: the Legacy of Steve Biko and Black Consciousness* (London: Zed Press; Cape Town: David Philip, 1991), pp. 138–39.

25. Mangena, p. 30.

26. On the founding of the Black People's Convention see Sipho Buthelezi, "The Emergence

of Black Consciousness: an Historical Appraisal," in Pityana et al., pp. 124–26; "A Tea Party or a Political Party?," *Drum,* February 1972; and conversations with Ben Khoapa (June 1989), Biko, Saths Cooper (October 1972 and October 1987), Nengwekhulu (October 1972), Thebehali, and M. T. Moerane, Drake Koka, William Nkomo, Thebehali and Benjamin Pogrund with Gwendolen Carter (February 1972).

27. Khoapa, pp. 8–9.

28. "Minutes of the National Organisations Conference Held at the Orlando YMCA from 17 December to 19 December, 1971."

29. "Black People's Convention (B. P. C.) Historical Background . . ." [1974], p. 2.

30. This was suggested by Koka in a published interview, "Our priority is to break the spine of apartheid," *Intercontinental Press/Imprecor,* October 30, 1978. On December 19, 1973, Mayatula wrote to supporters in Namibia urging them to prepare to join in a "peaceful 'tools down' strike all over Southern Africa" which would occur once the BPC had "finished up [its] conscientazisation [*sic*] process;" meanwhile, he wrote, "tinned food must be stored away" in preparation for "the DAY OF RECKONING." A reference in "Black People's Convention (B. P. C.) Historical Background" to promoting "physical fitness" among youth may likewise suggest wishful thinking about less peaceful scenarios, as does the statement in a March 3, 1973, BPC press release that Vorster should "be warned that there will never be another Sharpeville but there could be another Vietnam." These documents featured prominently in the prosecution case during the trial of the SASO Nine (*State v. Cooper*) in 1975–76, though the defense dismissed them as reflecting idiosyncratic opinions of individual authors.

31. Mamphela Ramphele has recalled that for many students, participation in SASO's community development projects eventually "put paid to the romanticism we as students had about poverty and people's responses to it. We had not bargained for the 'bitter fruits of powerlessness' which pervade such poor environments. The majority of poor people we found in Winterveld [a homeland "resettlement" area near Pretoria] were enveloped in apathy and despair." M. Ramphele, "Empowerment and Symbols of Hope: Black Consciousness and Community Development," in Pityana et al., pp. 159–60.

32. Khoapa, pp. 12–13. Another term for "vigilante committees" in earlier years was "vigilance associations."

33. During the trial of the SASO Nine, Cooper was identified as the author of the first flyer, although it was signed by BPC president, Winifred Kgware. Judgment in *State v. Cooper,* December 15, 1976, p. 92.

34. Biko, "Black Consciousness and the Quest for a True Humanity," *Reality,* March 1972. See conversations with Lefifi Tladi (November 1976) and Cooper (October 1987).

35. Biko, "We Blacks," *SASO Newsletter,* September 1970.

36. Molefe Pheto, *And Night Fell* (London: Heinemann, 1983), p. 16.

37. *The World,* May 16, 1976.

38. In noting that persecution of a nontotalitarian type is often inconsistent, Barrington Moore's *Injustice: The Social Bases of Obedience and Revolt* (White Plains: M. E. Sharpe, 1978), p. 483, drawing on Gaetano Mosca, observes that frequently "the significant feature in accounting for the triumph of new social forms is not their capacity to resist fierce persecution, but the relatively lax and intermittent character of the persecution they faced." This laxness creates space within which enterprising political innovators can promote their causes.

39. See Robert Kavanagh, *Theatre and Cultural Struggle in South Africa* (London: Zed Press, 1985), p. 55; *The World,* May 30 and July 8, 1975; and *Drum,* July 1975, p. 17.

40. Barney Pityana, "The Black Consciousness Movement and Social Research," in John Rex, ed., *Apartheid and Social Research* (Geneva: UNESCO, 1981), p. 174.

41. Biko, "Some African Cultural Concepts," in Steve Biko, *I Write What I Like* (London, Bowerdean Press, 1978; Oxford: Heinemann, 1978; San Francisco: Harper and Row, 1986), p. 46.

42. Resolution 44/72 in Document 49.

43. Bans served several days earlier on eight whites connected with the NUSAS Wages Commissions seemed clearly linked to the strikes.

44. Shezi, who worked with Mafuna on SASO's Black Workers' Project, is remembered as the first black consciousness martyr. He died from injuries a few days after being pushed in front

of a train by a white railway worker at Germiston station in December 1972. On the efforts of SASO and BPC to link with workers, see Sam Nolutshungu, *Changing South Africa: Political Considerations* (New York: Africana Publishing Co., 1982), pp. 187–91.

45. See chapter 7.

46. Biko in Document 45 refers to the need for "that fine balance between staying up and going forward."

47. This account of the 1973 crisis at UWC is based on Henry Isaacs, *Reflections of a Black South African Exile* (unpublished manuscript, 1986); Mafika Pascal Gwala, ed., *Black Review 1973* (Durban: Black Community Programmes, 1974); a conversation with Edna van Harte (February 1992); and an interview of Julie Frederikse with Trevor Manuel (1985)

48. Isaacs, p. 164. Table Mountain lies between Athlone and Cape Town harbor.

49. Dr. Richard E. van der Ross was named the new UWC rector in October 1973, although his appointment did not take effect until the 1975 academic year.

50. "The Big Bungle," *Sunday Times,* July 15, 1973.

51. This section is based in part on conversations with Barney Pityana (January 1988), Nkosazana Dlamini Zuma (June 1988), Sibusiso Ndebele (December 1989), Diliza Mji (July 1989), Bokwe Mafuna (June 1990), Zithulele Cindi (July 1989), and Mthembu. Also see Mokoape, Mtintso and Nhlapo, "Towards the Armed Struggle."

52. *State v. Molobi* (1975) is a valuable record of this traffic in information. Eric Molobi, a friend of Tiro's who traveled several times between Johannesburg and Botswana in 1973 and 1974, was found by police in possession of evidence incriminating him in a scheme to organize underground cells in South Africa linked to an "external force" in Botswana. He claimed in his defence that the plan related to the legal organization of BAWU branches.

53. Isaacs, p. 67.

54. Molobi in *State v. Molobi,* p. 402. Friction developed around SASO's refusal to invite ANC leaders to speak at Tiro's funeral, as well as around the tendency of exiled ANC leaders to flaunt their patronage resources, especially opportunities for travel, study and military training.

55. The recruits included Diliza Mji and Norman Dubazana (medical students who were elected president and publications director of SASO respectively in July 1975), and Faith Matlaopane and Nkosazana Dlamini, also medical students, who became SASO president and vice president the following year.

56. From photographic exhibits in *State v. Cooper.*

57. On a fund-raising trip to Europe for the Southern African Catholic Bishops Conference earlier in 1974, Mkhatshwa consulted secretly with top exiled ANC leaders about plans for the convention, mainly to assure them that the organizers had no intention of establishing a new or rival organization. Conversation with Mkhatshwa (May 1995)

58. Charges were withdrawn against four of the original accused, leaving nine defendants: Saths Cooper, Strini Moodley, Pandelani Nefolovhodwe (1974–75 president of SASO), Muntu Myeza (SASO Secretary General), Zithulele Cindi (BPC Secretary General), Patrick Lekota (SASO Permanent Organizer), Dr. Aubrey Mokoape (SASO/BPC activist), Kaborane Sedibe (1974 Turfloop SRC president), and Nkwenkwe Nkomo (BPC National Organizer).

59. For legal analyses of the trial, see Barney Pityana, "Revolution Within the Law?" in Pityana et al., p. 205, and Michael Lobban "Black Consciousness on Trial: the BPC/SASO Trial, 1974–1976," unpublished paper, 1990. The judgment hinged ultimately neither on facts nor on law but on the subjective assumptions of the prosecutors and the judge that what the accused were advocating, were it to come to pass, would mean making changes in South Africa that were fundamentally unacceptable to whites.

60. Judgment by Justice W. G. Boshoff in *State v. Cooper,* 1976, pp. 242 and 256.

61. The Xhosa song, by James Calata, says: *"Asikhathali noba siyabotshwa sizimisel' inkululeko; Unzima lo mthwalo, ufuna sihlangane."* ("We don't care if we are arrested, we are determined to get freedom; This burden is heavy, it demands unity.")

62. Biko's testimony is reproduced in full in Millard Arnold, ed., *Steve Biko: Black Consciousness in South Africa* (New York: Random House, 1978).

63. Mafika Pascal Gwala, "Towards the Practical Manifestations of Black Consciousness," in T. Thoahlane, ed., *Black Renaissance: Papers from the Black Renaissance Convention* (Johannesburg: Ravan Press, 1975), p. 26.

64. Biko in 1972 remarked that white leftists adopted class analysis "primarily because they want to detach us from anything relating to race, in case it has a rebound effect on them because they are white, . . . as a defence mechanism. . . . And of course a number of them are terrible about it. They [pronounce judgments] again and again on this whole problem of black-white relationships in a court or a yard which is basically ours. They are terribly puritanical, dogmatic, and very, very arrogant." Conversation with Biko.

65. Conversation with Nengwekhulu (October 1972).

66. Biko to Bernard Zylstra in a July 1977 interview reproduced in closely paraphrased form in *The Reformed Journal,* December 1977, p. 14. On attitudes toward communism and socialism in SASO see conversations with Pityana (October 1972), Mafuna, Malusi Mpumlwana (June 1987), and the interview of Biko with Greg Lanning (June 1971). Also see Nolutshungu, pp. 157–62.

67. Biko attempted to explain this apparent anomaly during his testimony in the SASO Nine trial. See Arnold, p. 88.

68. For a Unity Movement response to the black consciousness movement, see Neville Alexander, "Black Consciousness: a Reactionary Tendency?" in Pityana et al., pp. 238–52.

69. Baruch Hirson in *Year of Fire, Year of Ash, The Soweto Revolt: Roots of a Revolution?* (London: Zed Press, 1979), and to a lesser extent Robert Fatton in *Black Consciousness in South Africa* (Albany: State University of New York Press, 1986), portray SASO as composed of a petty bourgeois elite divorced by class interests from the radical perspective of working class Africans. Nolutshungu argues that unless the actions of SASO demonstrably were biased toward the interests of the middle class (which he doubts), such a characterization is inaccurate.

70. Jairus Kgokong, a SASO leader giving testimony in 1976 in *State v. Molokeng* (the NAYO trial), p. 226, estimated that by the end of 1975 at least 200 adherents of the black consciousness movement had gone into exile.

71. Sobukwe was confined to Kimberley, but when his mother died in May 1975 in Umtata, he was granted special permission to transport her body to Graaff-Reinet for burial. The route took him through King William's Town where a secret meeting with Biko was arranged. Benjamin Pogrund, *How Can Man Die Better. . . Sobukwe and Apartheid* (New Brunswick: Rutgers University Press; London: Peter Halban, 1990), p. 351. On unity efforts before the Soweto uprising, see Wilson, pp. 54–55, and conversations with Pityana (October 1972), Mpumlwana (November 1987, August and December 1989), Patrick Cindi (October 1989), Jackie Selebi (March 1989), Johnny Issel (December 1989), Diliza Mji (June 1987), and Khoapa.

72. "Policy of Black Consciousness," December 16, 1975.

6. The 1976 Soweto Uprising

Like the rehearsal for revolution that shook Russia in 1905, the Soweto uprising took both rulers and ruled by surprise and, by the time its course was run, left both sides with as many unresolved political dilemmas as before. The uprising deepened existing disagreements in the National Party over how best to defend and legitimize Afrikaner power, and ultimately set the party on an uncertain course of reform which led to its eventual fall from power two decades later. Blacks were forced by the uprising to confront their failure to find a strategy for liberation, but they emerged from the confrontations of 1976–77 with a stronger sense of the vulnerability of white power, and a deeper appreciation of the need for thorough political organization. The revolt raised the awareness of millions of young South Africans who thereafter dated their political coming of age in relation to its events. To an unprecedented degree, South Africa's Coloured minority made common cause with the African majority in demonstrating its rejection of the apartheid system. For older generations of Africans, 1976 marked the transition from a period of conservative political culture in which the young played a distinctly subordinate role, to a new era of struggle energized by the participation and leadership of thousands of youthful activists for whom the student uprising had been a political baptism by fire.

The Emergence of Youth Politics

Almost as soon as university students in the South African Students' Organisation (SASO) began reinventing the ideology of black nationalism in 1970–71, the tough language and idealistic principles of SASO's new credo began to attract attention among African high school students.[1] SASO cultivated this attention, and resolved at its 1972 annual conference to build links with school age youth and to extend SASO's leadership training methods to include them. When the Tiro incident resulted in mass walk-outs by black university students in mid-1972, dozens of SASO activists found work as teachers in understaffed secondary schools, carrying the contagion of black consciousness out of one set of classrooms into another.

The defiant mood of black consciousness and its assertion of a positive black identity appealed strongly to many young Africans growing up in a time of unsettling cultural changes and dissonance in intergenerational relationships. In and around Johannesburg, where *The World* and the *Rand Daily Mail* carried reports on the university crisis and on statements made by black consciousness figures, high school students became avid consumers of news on their new idols. The East London *Daily Dispatch* fulfilled a similar informational function for students in the eastern Cape after Biko's restriction to King William's Town in March 1973 and his subsequent friendship with the liberal editor of the *Dispatch,* Donald Woods. The growing popularity of Afro dress, and of music, poetry, and township theater with a black consciousness message, further broadened SASO's appeal until "thinking black" had become an "in" thing among literate young Africans in the townships of the Witwatersrand and the eastern Cape. "We say it with all honesty," declared one student in a newsletter of the high school-based South African Students' Movement (SASM) in 1973. "We idolize Black consciousness. It is our only defence against a . . . system that corrodes one's spirit" (*Document 58*). A poem in the same newsletter hailed SASO's Bokwe Mafuna as a "deity of Africa" because of his defiant attitude in court when charged with a violation of his banning order.

SASO's aim in reaching out to a youth constituency was to lay the broadest possible foundation for future political organization. Emotional slogans and poems might capture the imagination of teenagers, but more important was the training of a cadre of committed and astute activists who, when the time was right, could guide future political action. High school students who might eventually be university students formed one pool of potential recruits; young school leavers, employed or unemployed, formed another. Chapter 5 describes how the creation of Black Community Programmes enabled Biko to take up full time employment as BCP's "youth coordinator" in mid-1972. Crisscrossing the country to meet with church and YMCA groups, youth clubs, student societies, and informal township social gatherings, Biko, Harry Nengwekhulu, Bennie Khoapa, Tebogo Mafole and other movement organizers pushed for the formation of regional youth federations which could draw existing groups together into larger umbrella bodies geared principally to school leavers.

In August 1972, the Natal Youth Organisation was launched at Edendale Lay Ecumenical Centre near Pietermaritzburg, followed in a matter of months by the formation of the Transvaal Youth Organisation (TRAYO), the eastern Cape Border Youth Union, and the Western Cape Youth Organisation. In early June 1973, representatives of these bodies met for four days in King William's Town and launched the National Youth Organisation (NAYO). All these organizations reflected the strong guiding influence of SASO's ideology and personnel as well as its programmatic focus on spreading political awareness through cultural activities, literacy projects, and propaganda against homeland and system collaborators.

By the time NAYO moved onto the political stage, however, this repertoire of low-risk tactics was steadily losing appeal. The authorities were banning high profile black consciousness leaders, and intimidating outspoken activists by rounding them up for questioning (and gratuitous beatings) at local police stations. The presence of informers was increasingly feared. Blacks who were suspected of spying at meetings faced being "workshopped"— roughed up until they confessed. One result of the ever harsher political climate was that NAYO and its constituent bodies tended to attract only those who were already highly politicized. One TRAYO leader testified in a 1976 trial that TRAYO at its height had only about a hundred members.[2] Most people who were bold enough to attend meetings and leadership seminars of groups like NAYO and TRAYO already considered themselves "conscientized," and had moved on to thinking about "phase two," the physical liberation that was to follow the stage of psychological preparation.

Preoccupation with "phase two" dimmed the enthusiasm of youthful recruits for the patient tactics designed a few years earlier to spread the philosophy of black consciousness. Planning for armed revolt now seemed much more urgent, especially after Mozambique's independence in June 1975 opened up new prospects for guerrilla infiltration across South Africa's northeastern border. Within a year of NAYO's founding, some of its members were organizing secret cells and trying to make contact with the older liberation movements in the hope of integrating themselves into what they imagined might be well-advanced underground plans for armed struggle. Some had left for exile or made forays to neighboring states to try to establish contact with the ANC or PAC, or with the Botswana-based representatives of the black consciousness movement. Others were cultivating friendships with ex-Robben Island prisoners, who in some cases were able by 1975 to facilitate links with the nascent but rudimentary ANC and PAC undergrounds.

Some participants in black consciousness youth organizations came from families with a background of involvement in the ANC, PAC, or the Unity Movement, but most had no knowledge of the older organizations and were eager to learn about them. In May 1974, a joint NAYO-TRAYO leadership seminar at Wilgespruit conference center in Roodepoort featured a speech by Zephania Mothopeng, a former national executive member of the banned PAC who at that moment was temporarily not under restriction orders. Despite the close affinity between the ideology of black consciousness and the PAC's variant of blacks-only nationalism, however, it was the nonracial ANC with its longer historical tradition and better organized networks that from 1975 onwards achieved the greatest success in attracting young new adherents.

NAYO in particular provided a fertile field for ANC recruitment. Between June and October 1975, police swooped on dozens of young people suspected of subversive activities under cover of NAYO and its affiliates, and seven of those arrested were tried for terrorism in what became known as the "NAYO trial" beginning in Johannesburg in late 1975. The trial provided many auguries of growing youth militancy. It showed that although very few young Africans were prepared to undertake high-risk political action, the number was appreciably growing. Events in Mozambique had imbued blacks with optimism and the white security forces with new ruthlessness. Brutal police interrogation methods were becoming a fact of life. This reality is addressed in *Document 63,* an article in the *SASO Newsletter* early in 1976. *Document 60,* by a young Coloured woman detained as a potential witness in the NAYO trial, describes police methods in grim detail.[3] Some of those detained were forced to sign false statements incriminating others; later, some detainees courageously recanted these statements in the witness box. At the NAYO trial the atmosphere among spectators became so charged that on March 18, 1976, a violent confrontation erupted between police and a large crowd gathered in the street outside the court building. *Document 62,* an eye-witness account of this incident by an unidentified friend of the defendants, offers striking evidence of the taut emotions ready to burst forth from beneath Johannesburg's surface calm.[4]

In reaching for the generation immediately junior to themselves, SASO's strategists particularly targeted senior secondary school students. Drop-out rates at every stage of the school system were high, with the result that Africans enrolled in the last two years of secondary school in the early 1970s comprised less than two percent of their age cohort.[5] These students, though predominantly working class in origin, formed an incipient intellectual and economic elite by virtue of their education. As potential university students, they were both SASO's constituency-to-be and the social group ultimately put most at risk politically by the state's long-term co-optive strategies. The physical concentration of high school students in institutional settings made them relatively easy to reach compared to working or unemployed youths, and their level of literacy made them recruitable through the written word as well as by verbal persuasion. The only barriers to their rapid politicization were the fears induced by parents, and the hostility of most government-employed teachers and school principals to anything exuding even the faintest whiff of politics. But even in boarding schools, the authorities were incapable of insulating their institutions against all black consciousness influences. Contacts with older siblings, the circulation of black consciousness publications, and the popularity of younger teachers infected with the SASO "virus," all ensured the fairly speedy dissemination of the new nationalism among secondary students. The bolder students in turn undertook to radicalize their more timid teachers, as *Document 58* attests.

Within two years of SASO's birth, secondary students had begun here and there to form small political clubs, often at the instigation of a teacher who was a closet radical. Organizing themselves as debating societies or community service clubs, these associations came and went as the friendship groups on which they were based formed or dissolved, or as school authorities interfered to restrain their activities. The principal of Inanda Girls Seminary near Durban shut down a political club which formed there in 1971, and in Cape Town a Coloured students' group called SABSA—the South African Black Scholars' Association—folded under pressure of police threats in 1973 after about two years of activity.[6] The most important of these high school groups was the Soweto-based African Students' Movement (ASM), which in January 1972 changed its name to the South African Students' Movement (SASM) as part of an ambitious plan, instigated by SASO, to convert itself into a national organization.

ASM took shape in the late 1960s around weekend and vacation study groups of Soweto students preparing for matriculation exams with the assistance of Tom Manthata, a young teacher at Sekano Ntoane High School who was also involved in the organization of church-based youth clubs. Manthata was a Catholic seminary drop-out who was disaffected with the church but drawn to the unconventional theology of the University Christian Movement in which his cousin, Justice Moloto, was a leading activist. Through Moloto and the UCM, Manthata became a friend of SASO's leaders and an adherent of its emerging philosophy. ASM fostered a handful of school debating societies that were nurtured by Manthata and several like-minded Soweto teachers, sometimes using the occasion of sports tournaments to arrange interschool debates on topics likely to stimulate political discussion. In July 1971 the organization made its first tentative foray into the public consciousness by staging a noisy demonstration to protest the excessive time students were required to spend practicing for choir competitions at the expense of their studies. The day after placard-waving ASM members had disrupted a national choir competition with 4,000 participants at Springs, the tabloid headlines of *The World* warned that children were "running wild."[7] ASM's message on this occasion was ostensibly nonpolitical, but the protest was an effort by the organization to put itself forward as a voice for student complaints. Peter Lenkoe, a student at Madibane High School and the president of ASM, reported to a SASO national executive committee meeting in Pietermaritzburg five months later that the organization was attracting between 700 and 800 participants to its meetings, though not all were dues-paying.[8]

When ASM reorganized itself as SASM in January 1972 it aimed to build a national movement of high school students, but found the task more formidable than anticipated. After about a year, branches were functioning at nine Johannesburg schools and a roughly equivalent number of schools scattered throughout the rest of the country, but progress was slow. Branches would be launched only to fall dormant within a semester or two. Traveling beyond the area of the Reef required money and mobility that SASM organizers in Johannesburg did not have. Getting access to a typewriter or telephone usually required that a Soweto student travel to the city center where such equipment could be borrowed at the offices of the

Christian Institute, the BPC, or REESO, SASO's Reef headquarters. Most students shied away from open participation in SASM meetings. Talk that was openly political provoked such stern reprimands from school authorities and parents that many students were fearful.[9] Inviting outside speakers to give lectures to school clubs was one relatively safe activity; university students prominent in SASO found themselves frequently invited to address high school debating societies. Cultural activities like concerts and plays were another way for SASM to draw an audience. The most interested students would then be invited to participate in weekend seminars at Wilgespruit or St. Ansgar's, church centers in Roodepoort which made their facilities available for student meetings. Here again the leaders of SASO usually made the principal input, organizing political discussions, simulation exercises, and workshops on techniques of organization, from how to raise funds, keep minutes, and run a meeting, to how to teach adult literacy using Paulo Freire's method of "conscientization" (see Chapter 4).

SASM, like NAYO, was set back by the March 1973 banning of SASO's top leadership, followed by the banning in September of Mathe Diseko, who was both president of NAYO and national secretary of SASM. SASM in Johannesburg went into eclipse until a new leadership was assembled in mid-1974 with the encouragement of SASO and the BPC. In the meantime, Biko and his coterie of lieutenants in King William's Town's Ginsberg location had stimulated the formation of SASM branches in several nearby high schools in the eastern Cape.

The rejuvenated SASM, coming on the scene after the Lisbon coup of April 1974, was increasingly driven by the new fever of interest in armed struggle. The ANC's Radio Freedom was now broadcasting regularly into South Africa on shortwave, and ANC leaflets and literature were circulating more widely than earlier. Some students drawn to SASM were determined to become guerrilla fighters and sought to leave South Africa by hazardous routes; some succeeded, some were caught, and more than a few turned back when discretion became the better part of valor. *Document 61,* a letter describing one student's escape route to Botswana, was presented as evidence for the prosecution in the trial of five SASM members from Healdtown high school in the eastern Cape who were caught while making departure plans in 1975. Bullets, wrote another Healdtown student with bravado, were "the only language that Vorster and his dogs understand. South Africa will be Africa's Vietnam."[10]

Intense debate and disagreement increasingly marred the relationship between older and younger activists as some who were impatient to join the exile armies took issue with others, usually older, who argued that guerrilla warfare would be fruitless until a stronger political foundation for revolution had been laid inside South Africa. At a conference for SASM leaders run by SASO and the staff of Black Community Programmes in King William's Town over Easter weekend in 1975, the emphasis was on building SASM as a body that would politicize high school students and make them agents for the organized radicalization of adult society in the future. *Document 59,* a paper prepared for the conference by Malusi Mpumlwana of the BCP, outlines behavioral do's and don't's appropriate for a growing cadre of political agitators working circumspectly "within the law but outside the system." It was still official policy in the senior black consciousness organizations to shun any identification with the illegal exiled movements, even if individual members chose to associate with them privately, and even though Biko through his lieutenants was engaged in protracted secret talks with underground representatives of the ANC and PAC in the hope of effecting a united front (see Chapter 5).

In SASM, would-be fighters outnumbered talkers, and counsels of caution from older activists often provoked resentment. "When we asked questions concerning the future programs of the people," Daniel Montsitsi, a militant SASM leader at Sekano Ntoane high school in Soweto, later recalled,

> we were told "We have to conscientise the black masses, as this will ensure understanding and support for us, then we shall be able to bargain from a position of strength." Unfortunately we were not in the mood to bargain or negotiate; we were impatient and militant, and rebellious of the black consciousness leadership. With puffed lips and closed eyes straight from [being beaten up by the police] . . . we did not feel like talking; we wanted to fight but did not know how. We made jokes about the leadership when our spirit was high, that they encourage us to conscientise the masses, until they reach a stage where they'll explode on their own.[11]

While abstract debates about the alternative merits of guerrilla warfare and mass insurrection continued unresolved, SASM through SASO received two donations from the International University Exchange Fund in Europe, one in late 1975 and the other in May 1976, totaling about $7,000. This made it possible to finance travel expenses and to employ a full-time SASM organizer, Zweli Sizani. Participation picked up in Soweto, and in early 1976 branches were in existence or in the process of forming in schools in Mamelodi, Mabopane and Atteridgeville in Pretoria, as well as in KwaThema (Springs), Kagiso (Krugersdorp), Tembisa (Kempton Park), Thaba 'Nchu in the Orange Free State, Kwa Mashu in Durban, and Athlone High School in Cape Town.[12] During the last weekend of May, the organization held a three day conference in Roodepoort where a range of topics related to student and national life was debated (*Document 65*). Three senior black consciousness figures addressed the meeting, along with SASM's outgoing president, Vusi Tshabalala, who called on his audience to brace for further harassment from the state. A new executive was elected, while Sizani continued as full-time organizing secretary. Although it may be an overstatement to claim, as Brooks and Brickhill do in their valuable history of the Soweto uprising, that by June 1976 "SASM was fully fledged as a national school student movement . . . [with] a well-organized structure, [and] a vigorous program of activities,"[13] it was true that the organization had survived through ups and downs and had established a measure of autonomy from adult influence.

Some of its activists had acquired substantial organizing experience and had a vision of SASM as a vehicle for the national mobilization of students, although even as late as May 1976 no one anticipated how such a mobilization might be triggered or what its outcome might be.

"This Burden Is Heavy . . ."

According to the minutes of SASM's May 1976 conference, the first subject debated was the government's highly unpopular imposition of Afrikaans as a medium of instruction in African schools on a 50–50 basis alongside English. Dual-medium instruction had officially been prescribed since the mid-1950s, but educationists had been critical of the policy, and their objections, plus a dearth of African teachers proficient in Afrikaans, had resulted in most African schools being granted annual exemptions from the formal requirement up through 1974. In that year policy shifted as Vorster and National Party pragmatists tried to appease party *verkramptes* (ultra-conservatives) who were unhappy about what they condemned as moves toward "liberalization," including the government's acceptance of racially mixed sports and its long delayed decision to introduce television—a step that white conservatives feared would strengthen the dominant position of English over Afrikaans in popular culture. Hence it was announced by the Bantu Education department that from 1975, African schools in the southern Transvaal region would be required to phase in Afrikaans-medium instruction in mathematics and social studies starting in Standard 5 (the seventh grade). African teachers and community school boards raised strong objections, but department officials were unbending. Students affected by the new policy showed poor exam results at the end of 1975. Fears of failure joined with political distaste for "the language of the oppressor" to fan student discontent as the next school year began.[14] Adding insult to injury just as the 1976 school year opened, Vorster announced in January that Dr. Andries Treurnicht, the hard-line leader of the *verkramptes,* would become the new deputy minister of Bantu Education.

Top to bottom, South Africa's school system under National Party rule was a showcase for institutionalized racial discrimination. African schools ranked lowest in state expenditure per pupil, numbers of trained teachers, and quality of school facilities. Schools for Indians and Coloureds fared somewhat better, while the system for whites consumed public resources out of all proportion to the number of students served.[15] These inequalities in no way reflected the level of demand for education in the respective racial communities. Educational achievement was one of the few paths out of poverty for Africans, and working-class parents often struggled over many years to meet the costs of the books, uniforms, and fees necessary to keep their children in school.[16] During the early 1970s, this thirst for education was assuaged to some extent by a rapid expansion in the number of secondary and university level places for Africans, effected by the state in response to demands from industry and commerce that something be done about the country's severe skills shortage. Between 1970 and 1975, the number of Africans pupils admitted to Form I, the first year of secondary school, rocketed from 49,504 to 149,251.[17] One result was that thousands of African teenagers began to reach levels of schooling far beyond those achieved by their parents, prompting growing intergenerational friction. At the same time, the unequal and inadequate commitment of resources to African schools meant that students struggled against deteriorating conditions in the classroom: double shifts, overcrowding, too few trained teachers, disappointing pass rates on all-important examinations—and a continuing perception of the unclosable gap between their own life chances and the opportunities enjoyed by young whites.

Township communities might have eased their way through this combustible mixture of hopes, frustrations, and generational tensions had South Africa's economy been in a phase of robust expansion. But the early 1970s were a period of retrenchment and slackening growth after South Africa's boom decade of the 1960s. Even before the country began to feel the effects of world recession and high inflation brought on by the soaring price of oil in 1973–74, its economy was beset by problems of technological change and the built-in biases of apartheid. Mining and agriculture—the original foundations of modern South Africa's growth and of its super-exploitation of unskilled black labor—now functioned alongside a large manufacturing sector increasingly constrained by the low productivity of labor and the meager buying power of African consumers. Persistent efforts by the Vorster government to expand South Africa's export markets in independent Africa through an aggressive diplomatic strategy of "detente" were achieving only limited success. The shortage of skilled labor had been addressed through the expansion of school enrollments, but no sooner had expansion accelerated than the economic downturn of the mid-1970s resulted in an ever higher number of school-leavers entering a job market which had all but ceased to grow. The economic malaise created by rising unemployment and rapid inflation was made worse by a precipitous decline in the gold price through most of 1975, depriving the country of the surplus of foreign exchange with which it customarily maintained its level of imports and eliminated its balance of payments deficit. By late 1975, South Africa was in a recession of crisis proportions.

Given their monopoly of decision-making in business and government, whites were in a position to determine whose belts would be tightened the most as economic conditions worsened. The construction of schools and houses in black urban areas came to a near standstill, and all efforts were abandoned to keep pace with the needs of expanding township populations for such services as garbage collection, sewer systems, and street lighting. Parsimony reached new extremes after 1973 when the government removed African urban areas from the control of adjacent white municipalities and placed them under 22 new Bantu Affairs Administration Boards directly answerable to the Minister of Bantu Administration. The boards laid off

African employees and replaced them with inexperienced whites whose salaries were paid out of board revenues from rents and township liquor sales, over which the government maintained a formal monopoly. Subsidies previously paid by white municipalities to maintain township services were discontinued, and instead a portion of township rent and beerhall revenues was redistributed to subsidize the administration of rural homelands. *Document 66*, a speech by Winnie Mandela, the wife of imprisoned ANC leader Nelson Mandela, given at the founding of the Soweto Parents Association shortly before the start of the uprising, conveys well the sense of popular anger at a situation which, in her words, had "deteriorated to the doldrums." In terms of both material living conditions and levels of public trust, township life was on a steady downward trajectory by the time violence erupted in June 1976.

The National Party's determination to impose the grand design of ethnic homelands further compounded the deteriorating quality of black urban life. Most troubling were new legal conditions accompanying the independence of the Transkei scheduled to take place in late 1976, with that of Bophuthatswana to follow soon after. In pursuit of its dream of creating a South Africa with no African citizens, the Vorster government stiffened the definition of homeland citizenship originally set out in the Transkei Constitution Act of 1963, eliminating dual citizenship and the option that urban Africans might choose to remain South African when "their" homeland attained independence. As the details of the Transkei's impending independence were increasingly aired in parliament and the press, it became evident that as many as 1.3 million urban Xhosa and their descendants were threatened with loss of their South African citizenship, together with what narrow but precious legal rights to urban residence this citizenship conferred.

As a concession to international and business pressures for South Africa to accord property rights to permanently urbanized Africans, renewable 30-year leasehold tenure on township plots had been introduced in 1975, raising the prospect that children would in future have a legal right to inherit houses built, bought, or improved by their parents. Under the new homeland citizenship provisions, however, the security of this new "right" was nullified.[18] Applications for leasehold (like applications for business licenses) were to be accepted only from those who had taken out homeland citizenship certificates. Moreover, children born after the independence date of their parents' designated homeland automatically became citizens of that homeland, forfeiting any legal right to live in "white" South Africa as adults, or to inherit any fixed property acquired there by their parents.

For people being forced to adjust to new levels of economic insecurity, the added uncertainty of the new homeland citizenship regulations deepened an already widespread sense of despair. "Do you want to make us really desperate?" asked Desmond Tutu, the Anglican Dean of Johannesburg, in a statement carried on the front page of the *Rand Daily Mail* on May 1,

1976. "Desperate people will be compelled to use desperate means" to achieve redress, he concluded. "I speak with words I hope I have chosen carefully—the issue of Transkeian citizenship is highly explosive."[19] A week later in an emotional letter to Vorster, Tutu again tried to warn that African patience was running out. "A people can take only so much and no more," he wrote (Document 64). "The history of your own people [the Afrikaners] . . . has demonstrated this, Vietnam has shown this, the struggle against Portugal has shown this. I am frightened . . . that we may soon reach a point of no return, when events will generate a momentum of their own, when nothing will stop their reaching a bloody denouement."[20]

Tutu's passing reference to the collapse of Portuguese colonialism only hinted at the powerful hopes and expectations that events in Mozambique and Angola had kindled among Africans. Not only had black guerrilla armies defeated Portugal, but South Africa's own invading army had been repulsed in its effort to prevent the Soviet and Cuban-backed Movimento Popular de Libertação de Angola (MPLA) from taking power in Luanda following Angolan independence in November 1975. "Winds of change" were blowing right on the country's borders, Gatsha Buthelezi told Sowetans packed into Jabulani Amphitheatre on March 14, 1976 (Document 101); South Africa had "burnt her fingers" trying to stop the inevitable. To all blacks, and especially to the young, one African student later recalled, the sudden and unexpected turn of events in Mozambique and Angola transformed the idea of liberation from something distant and abstract to "something *real,* something *possible.*"[21]

When the 1976 school year commenced in January, overcrowding in African schools reached new levels nationwide. To reduce the number of school years from 13 to 12, the Bantu Education department had decided in 1975 to abolish standard 6 (the eighth grade) from the following year, enabling students to proceed directly from standard 5 into the five years of secondary school leading to matriculation. Although this change promised eventually to relieve pressure on classroom space, it meant that in 1976, pupils finishing both standard 5 and standard 6 proceeded together into the first year of secondary school, creating an unwieldy bulge of numbers that meant yet more crowding and double shifts, more shortages of textbooks and qualified teachers. In the southern Transvaal, moreover, protests by teachers and a few African school boards had failed to roll back the ruling that Afrikaans instruction in half of all subjects be phased in starting at junior secondary level. The language ruling most immediately affected the very students caught in the effects of the bulge. For most African parents, mired in the desperate daily reality of survival, these hardships were just one more burden to be borne. But for school children in their teens—not yet faced with the full responsibilities of adulthood, but experienced enough to know how unfairly life's deck was stacked against them—the injustices of "gutter education" suddenly seemed unbearable. White arrogance, suffered for so long by their parents and teachers, seemed intolerable, as did the very meekness of the adult generation.

The Uprising Begins

Had authorities in the Bantu Education department been willing to bend on the Afrikaans ruling while the bulge of junior secondary pupils in the Transvaal endured a few semesters of intense overcrowding, South Africa might have been spared the cataclysm of violence and confrontation that swept black schools and townships starting on June 16, 1976. Instead, a demonstration against Afrikaans, planned as a one-day protest in Soweto, escalated into a nationwide uprising after police shot dead a number of student demonstrators, touching off a spiral of rioting and reprisal that rapidly spread to other areas. Fueled by the anger and determination of a radicalized youth generation, the uprising confronted whites with an unprecedented challenge to their dominance. Older blacks likewise experienced a loss of authority as parents, teachers, urban councillors and even respected senior political notables found themselves deferring to the high school students whose initiative, courage and energy were the driving force of the revolt.

Events on June 16 resulted from the intersection of student tensions over the Afrikaans issue with SASM's renewed efforts to build a national following. Through most of early 1976 the two developments ran parallel in Soweto secondary schools, where SASM concentrated its efforts on senior students while the language problem directly affected only students in Forms 1 and 2 (eighth and ninth grades). As mid-year exams approached, a class boycott over Afrikaans erupted among Form 1 and 2 students at Orlando West Junior Secondary School, spreading within a few weeks to seven other schools. Seeing an opportunity to take a leadership role in the aftermath of their May 28–30 conference, several members of SASM's national executive called a meeting at the Orlando YMCA in Soweto on the afternoon of Sunday, June 13, ostensibly to form a SASM regional branch. An unexpectedly large number of students turned up, and a regional executive committee was chosen, headed by Tsietsi Mashinini, a final-year student who was a leader in the SASM branch at Morris Isaacson High School in the Jabavu section of Soweto. After a heated discussion of the Afrikaans issue, Mashinini won unanimous approval for a proposal that students stage a mass demonstration on the following Wednesday. An Action Committee to organize the protest was formed by enlisting two representatives from each school under a leadership headed by Mashinini and Seth Mazibuko, a Form 2 student who had led the initial boycott at Orlando West Junior Secondary School.

By the time police tried to stop a singing column of children marching along Vilakazi Street toward Orlando stadium about 9 o'clock on the morning of Wednesday, June 16th, round-the-clock activity by the Action Committee had mobilized thousands of students to converge from every corner of Soweto, waving placards denouncing compulsory Afrikaans instruction. Police had made no preparations for the event, and their scattered early morning attempts to head off some of the demonstrators proved ineffective. Confronting the marchers on Vilakazi Street near the Orlando West school, a contingent of police fired tear gas canisters into the throng, but failed to dissuade the demonstrators, who responded by throwing stones. Rather than retreat, the police then shot into the crowd, killing 12-year-old Zolile Hector Pieterson and wounding several other children.[22] This ignited the fury of the marchers, who began to rampage through the township, smashing windows and using petrol to set fire to schools, vehicles of the West Rand Administration Board (WRAB), municipal beerhalls, and other government buildings. By evening Soweto was a battle zone as roaming mobs of youths sought more symbols of apartheid to put to the torch, and police tried to curb the destruction by shooting at anyone who appeared to be involved in the rioting. Violence continued in Soweto on June 17, and spread to Krugersdorp on the West Rand and to downtown Johannesburg where police and white thugs broke up a protest march by students from the University of the Witwatersrand. While the dead piled up at city mortuaries and hospitals strained to treat the wounded, newspapers around the world ran a photo of two crying teenagers carrying the limp body of Hector Pieterson. "Soweto" stood poised to join Sharpeville in the lexicon of the international anti-apartheid movement.

The uprising eventually affected more than 100 urban areas of South Africa and took nearly a year to run its course, passing through a series of stages as student leaders changed tactics in an effort to sustain the protests, draw in adult participants, and respond to government repression. The system of Bantu education and the government's regional Administration Boards remained targets throughout, along with black collaborators in the Urban Bantu Councils and homeland governments. Starting in August, a series of experiments with economic pressure was launched in which students tried to use stay-aways and consumer boycotts to weaken the state through blows directed at white business. Looking inward to the weaknesses of their own community, the students concentrated their reforming zeal on alcohol consumption, a problem afflicting many families and one for which a share of the blame could be laid on the system of municipal beerhalls. Pretoria's efforts to regain the initiative after June 16 were never wholly successful. A decision in early July to drop the Afrikaans requirement did little to diminish the momentum of the student crusade which by that time had begun to consolidate broad support because of the rising number of deaths and the government's callous displays of indifference towards the carnage. By the end of February 1977, unrest deaths stood officially at 575— 494 Africans, 75 Coloureds, two whites and one Indian.[23] As the "distur- bances" continued month after month, funerals of the victims became the occasion for new displays of student militancy, provoking yet more applica- tions of lethal force by the police. Attempts to quell the uprising by detaining supposed agitators merely caused the cycle of response and counter- response to escalate. The deaths of several detainees subjected to torture by the security police further fed the angry flames of revolt.

"To Be or Not to Be . . ."

Who were the young rebels of 1976, and what did they believe would be achieved by their sometimes suicidal defiance? Systematic surveys of participants were not made at the time, but impressionistic evidence supports the view that African and Coloured school pupils were joined in significant numbers by out-of-school youths, including *tsotsis* (young hoodlums) who were a perennial element in township society and used the anarchy of the opening days of the revolt in Soweto to loot liquor stores and rob township residents. Students at day schools were the prime movers, but upheavals also occurred at rural boarding institutions. University students staged protests at every black campus, and at the Universities of Zululand and the Western Cape, arsonists destroyed a number of campus buildings. Participants came from all social classes, ethnic groups, and ages. Children as young as ten were shot dead for raising a black power fist at the police, and hundreds of teenagers were held in police cells for extended periods, some for weeks at a time.[24]

Student thinking appears to have run the gamut from reformist to revolutionary, nonviolent to violent, and from naively emotional to tactically calculating. At the outset of the uprising, the conscious intent was simply to show whites how vehemently young blacks rejected the apartheid system of education, and also how frustrated they felt with the poverty and crowded conditions of township life. "If I die, that's one less person sleeping under the bed," a schoolgirl told a Soweto social worker who tried to persuade student demonstrators to go home on the morning of June 16.[25] During the rioting observers noted how common it was for groups of students to stop white motorists and force them to make the black power sign before allowing them to proceed, as if this fulfilled a deep desire to humble whites and make them show deference to black humanity. "As black parents," one Soweto resident observed, "we are forced to produce good sons and daughters who are passive, non-assertive, non-aggressive, good *Ja-baas* ("yes, boss") boys. If they are going to get anywhere they must not talk back. You may ask, why so much violence? One reason [is a] crying need to say 'Take notice of us—We are people.'"[26] Further nourishing the demand for respect and recognition was a sense of expectation that a successful revolution might soon occur in South Africa. "It happened at Angola—Why not here?" proclaimed a large banner hung in a classroom at Orlando West Junior Secondary School on June 16. The "revolutionary preparedness of the black masses" was evident, the radical diarist at the NAYO trial had concluded a few months earlier; all that was needed was "a powerful vanguard" prepared to "take up arms" (*Document 62*).

But in the absence of weapons that could be taken up, what were Soweto's would-be revolutionaries to do? One option was to concede the state's command of superior instruments of violence, and to try to sustain the insurrection through the use of nonviolent tactics. This still left open the question of what targets were to be singled out, and what strategic aims pursued. Another option was to wait and hope that the exiled liberation movements were at work organizing to return in force. Such expectations were encouraged from the early days of the revolt by the appearance of ANC leaflets in major urban centers urging people to "act," "protest" and "hit back" at the Vorster government (*Document 106*). While clutching at the straw of possible external intervention, however, student leaders faced the responsibility of trying to maintain the momentum of the uprising once the rioting of mid-June had subsided. Student courage during the days of violence had inspired an awed respect from black adults, but there were also critics who questioned whether the hundreds of dead and wounded was not too high a price for the meager achievement of a government climb-down on the Afrikaans issue.

It was not hard for the SASM students who constituted the core of the Soweto Action Committee to think back to the time before June 16 when the building of a constituency had been an uphill effort. Suddenly a constituency, even a potential national following, was standing ready; retreat would have been both ignoble and inconsistent with the precepts of the black consciousness movement, which had strongly impressed upon young people their responsibility to analyze, organize, and act as if the future of the country was in their own hands. In any case, under the circumstances prevailing in mid-1976, no group of older decision-makers was available to whom leadership could readily be passed. SASO and the BPC had been severely weakened by bans and repression, and by mid-July two of their remaining activists in Johannesburg, Tom Manthata and Ken Rachidi, had been detained. Nor did students look for guidance to the Soweto Parents Association, rechristened the Black Parents Association (BPA) a few days after June 16, a supportive group of Soweto professionals who had formed themselves into a welfare body to coordinate funeral arrangements and receive donations for the families of victims in the week following June 16. The BPA was willing to act as a mouthpiece for student demands, but it was not regarded by students as an ally in decision-making.[27] In the uncharted terrain of confrontation with the state, "black man, you are on your own" had become "black student, you are on your own."

The reopening of schools in the last week of July was marked by high absenteeism and outbreaks of arson at schools around the country. During the winter recess in July the Action Committee had realized that nothing could be organized until students returned to school. Burning schools was no solution. Political awareness was at fever pitch, but constructive action required the strengthening of communication networks that could only operate if students were congregating in schools on a daily basis. Moreover, the Action Committee itself needed to be expanded from its original complement of about a dozen students into a broader body with lines of contact into every Soweto secondary school, not just the ones that had been represented at the meeting of June 13. It was the consensus of the committee that after widening the base of organization, a protest should be organized around the demand that detained students be released. As a means of drawing in parents, students would call on all Soweto adults to stay at home for a three-day period to back up the student demand.

Soweto's Urban Bantu Councillors held a public meeting at Jabulani Ampitheatre on Sunday morning, August 1, to report on their consultations with the government regarding community grievances. There was a high turnout of students, who jeered the councillors' appeals for moderation and called for the release of detainees and a continued assault on Bantu education (*Document 67*). That afternoon at a smaller meeting of several hundred parents and students convened by the BPA at Regina Mundi church, further appeals were made for students to return to school. Tsietsi Mashinini addressed the meeting, endorsed the call for a return to schools, and announced that student leaders would meet the following morning at the Morris Isaacson High School.[28] When that meeting in turn convened on August 2, the Action Committee renamed itself the Soweto Students' Representative Council (SSRC), reconfirmed Mashinini as chairman, and arranged that each of Soweto's 40 junior and senior secondary schools be represented on the SSRC by two students. Murphy Morobe, another senior student at Morris Isaacson, became vice-chairman, replacing Seth Mazibuko who had been detained. It was agreed that a list of demands regarding Bantu education would be compiled and forwarded to the government through the BPA, and that on Wednesday, August 4, students would march to John Vorster Square security police headquarters in downtown Johannesburg to demonstrate for the release of detained students and other leaders. Parents were to be urged by their children to support student demands by not going to work between Wednesday and Friday.

Thus was launched a new confrontational phase of the revolt, centered on the stay-away. Like a black power fist thrust in the faces of white motorists, the 1976 stay-aways were primarily a demonstration of resolve and a vague threat that there could be worse to come if black demands were not met. Students imagined at the outset that prolonged work stoppages would cut into the profits of white business to such an extent that the economy might be faced with collapse. In due course it became evident that without strong labor unions, workers involved in stay-aways had no protection against victimization by employers, and thus worker commitment to political strikes was likely to be fragile and short-lived. Before pushing their newfound tactic beyond its limits, however, students in August and September organized three relatively successful stay-aways in Johannesburg, each of several days duration, plus one lasting two days in Cape Town, and another of two days in Tembisa (Kempton Park). Each of the stay-aways was preceded by leafletting, and in some areas, particularly in Soweto during the first stay-away, by intimidatory actions aimed by students at strike breakers.

Azikhwelwa! ("We don't ride," i.e. we don't travel to work), a slogan from the 1940s and 1950s that students had discovered in Edward Roux's banned but popular book *Time Longer Than Rope,* was adopted as the stay-away rallying cry.[29] Early on August 4, thousands of students converged on

Soweto's train stations and bus stops to prevent commuters leaving for the city. Eyewitnesses subsequently testified to the government-appointed Cillie Commission of inquiry that stone-throwing occurred at the stations, and that workers who managed to slip into the city were accosted by angry bands of students when they returned to the township that evening. Late on the morning of August 4, the student march on John Vorster Square, estimated by police at 15,000 strong, was thwarted by a blockade of police vehicles when it reached New Canada at the northeastern boundary of Soweto. After being dispersed with tear gas, the demonstrators retaliated with further arson attacks on buildings and vehicles, continuing the mayhem into the next two days amidst crude police efforts at riot control which left many new victims dead. The Minister of Police and Justice, James Kruger, vacillating between trying to cool the violence with conciliation or quell it by brute force, appears briefly to have entertained the idea of meeting with the BPA at the height of the destruction, but then reverted to basic National Party instincts by arresting the BPA members instead. By the third week of August, a surface calm had returned to Soweto, but violence had erupted elsewhere along the Reef and was spreading to the townships of the eastern and western Cape. In Johannesburg, Tsietsi Mashinini from hiding issued a blunt press statement condemning the heavy handed actions of the police (*Document 68*).

The second Soweto stay-away, called by the SSRC for August 23–25, was marked by lower levels of intimidation and a stronger public response than the one three weeks earlier. White shops, offices and industries reported 70–80% absenteeism by African workers. In a startling development on the afternoon of August 24, however, the burgeoning sense of student power was challenged when an enraged mob of Zulu workers from the huge Mzimhlope hostel in the Meadowlands area of Soweto stormed through adjacent sections of the township attacking houses and murdering and terrorizing their residents.[30] As families fled from the path of the armed marauders, men in the affected neighborhoods organized themselves for defense of their homes, and by nightfall and into the following week street battles took place pitting residents against hostel-dwellers, reportedly as police looked on or stayed clear of the trouble zones. Evidence soon emerged that this unforeseen backlash had in fact been incited by the police after a mysterious fire the morning of the 24th had damaged three blocks of the hostel.[31] It was probably not difficult for police to convince the hostel dwellers that young troublemakers needed to be taught a lesson. Students had made no attempt to explain or justify the stay-aways or the campaign against Bantu education to the largely migrant "bachelor" population of the Soweto hostels, nor had any apologies been made to them for the destruction of the municipal beerhalls which were a center of their social life. Even in the best of times, there were class tensions between the settled urban residents of South African townships and the less sophisticated semi-urbanized contract workers who made up the majority of inmates in the dreary barracks-like hostels of the Witwatersrand and Cape Town. Once confrontations had occurred between student strike enforcers and unsympathetic hostel-dwellers trying to go to work during the first stay-away, the events of August 24 were simply a case of tinder waiting for a spark.

The student leadership, braced for transition after a secret dash over the Botswana border by Mashinini on August 23, now also faced the urgent need to improve communications with Soweto's adult population. By shifting its venue from school to school, the SSRC was managing to convene a quorum approximately once a week and thus to keep its lines of contact open to students, and through them, by verbal means, to parents.[32] After the hostel clashes, however, leaflet communication assumed both a new importance and tone. *Document 69*, an SSRC flyer of September 7, is a straightforward appeal for unity and cooperation from all workers, including hostel dwellers. Through older allies in SASO and the BPC, indirect contact was made with representatives of Inkatha who at that stage also opposed the manipulation of Zulu migrants by the police.[33] Meetings in several Soweto hostels were convened, and the reasoning behind work stoppages explained. By September 13–15 when the SSRC staged a third well supported three day stay-away, most hostel dwellers joined in the strike, even taking it upon themselves in some cases to beat up their fellow hostel-dwellers who declined to participate.

Just when black students in Johannesburg began successfully drawing older generations into the uprising, unrest was also spreading spontaneously to new regions of the country. Diffused more by media coverage and word of mouth than by any coordinated effort on the part of students, news of the events of mid-June in Soweto had touched off sporadic demonstrations and arson attacks on schools and government buildings in townships scattered across all four provinces. The country remained largely calm through July, but by early August when schools reopened after the winter break, many students had resolved to add their voices to the Johannesburg protests, generally imitating the tactics of placard marches, targeted vandalism, and school boycotts to express rejection of Bantu Education. Secondary school students formed local Students' Representative Councils (SRCs) to lead the protests. On August 2, students at the University of the Western Cape launched a class boycott campaign which threw the campus into turmoil for several months and helped to ignite a spirit of revolt in Coloured secondary schools throughout the Cape peninsula.[34] African secondary students, who were far fewer than Coloureds in the Cape Town area, also began mobilizing, and on August 11 they staged marches in the townships of Langa, Nyanga and Gugulethu, the last of which ended in disorder and a police assault in which 16 demonstrators died. By late August, arson attacks, the stoning of buildings and vehicles, school disruptions and police shootings were occurring on an almost daily basis in both African and Coloured townships around Cape Town, as well as in towns scattered through the eastern and northern Cape, Transkei, the Orange Free State, and Transvaal. The only major region that remained relatively unaffected was Natal, where those protests and incidents that did occur were not met with the violent police responses which were the principal cause of bloodshed and escalating confrontation elsewhere.[35] In rural areas countrywide, police reported a rising incidence of unexplained fires on white farms and at sawmills, while a mysterious veld fire in mid-September touched off an explosion at a dynamite factory in Modderfontein.

Once militant protests gathered momentum in the western Cape in early August, schooling was disrupted and dozens of confrontations occurred between students and police. These incidents were confined to Coloured and African townships until September 1, when African students staged a peaceful placard march in downtown Cape Town. On the following two mornings, police were prepared when more students, this time both Coloureds and Africans, massed in the city's central business district. Tear-gas and baton charges dispersed the demonstrators on September 2, but on Friday, September 3, police fired both tear-gas and birdshot into startled crowds on Adderley Street as hundreds of fleeing protesters mingled into throngs of lunchtime onlookers. Offices and shops closed early, and gun shops sold out as panicky whites got their first close-up look at the uprising. As some units of the riot police quelled protests in the central city, other units fanned out to try to restore order in the townships. Reporting on one incident which by this time had become part of a familiar pattern, a correspondent for the *Rand Daily Mail* wrote that at about noon on September 3,

> the riot squad charged into the Alexander Sinton High School [in the Coloured township of Athlone] for the second time after cars had been stoned in the area. When pupils saw the police coming, they quickly locked themselves in classrooms. Police tried to kick down the doors but failed. They then broke windows in upper classrooms and tossed tear-gas canisters inside. Terrified children rushed out and were met with a hail of blows from police batons. Shotgun blasts reverberated through the quadrangle and screaming pupils ran in all directions. . . . Two schoolboys [were] hit by birdshot. . . . Girls were crying from the effects of tear-gas and some had fainted. Others were sobbing hysterically while teachers tried to comfort them. One schoolboy was rugby tackled by a policeman as he attempted to escape across the front lawn, and then kicked. The pupils dispersed soon afterwards, but within minutes cars in Thornton Road—which runs past the school—were [again] being stoned.[36]

Ten days later, Soweto students launched the third and most successful Johannesburg stay-away, calling on workers to strike for three days in support of the "student-worker alliance" for the "overthrowal of oppression" (*Document 70*). With absentee rates running as high as 80 percent in Johannesburg industry and commerce, Coloured and African workers in Cape Town joined in the work stoppage on September 15, sustaining their protest through the following day and making the combined September 13–16 stay-away, as Brooks and Brickhill have judged it, the high-water mark of the uprising and the most impressive political action ever to have been staged up to that point by black workers in South Africa.[37] Momentum was maintained the following week when Tembisa workers stayed home for two days, bringing production in the industrial complex of Isando northeast of Johannesburg to a halt. Two days later, inspired by the success of their counterparts in Cape Town and referring to themselves as revolutionaries who would rock the racist order (*Document 71*), Soweto students organized a brief but dramatic "invasion" of the central city on the morning of Thursday, September 23. Responding to what the white press described as central Johannesburg's "first taste of terror," camouflage-clad riot police arrested several hundred of the young invaders, sealing off downtown streets to traffic in order to better pursue their quarry.[38] A 16-year-old Soweto student arrested in the "invasion," Dumisani Mbatha, died in police custody two days later. At his funeral and those of several other student victims in October, thousands of mourners congregated singing freedom songs, only to be met by police determined to disperse what they saw as political demonstrations being held in defiance of a ban on outdoor meetings. What would otherwise have been emotional but nonviolent events turned into bloody confrontations as police fired on funeral crowds, provoking new outbursts of rioting. By the last week of October, the toll of those killed in the unrest since June 16 stood officially at 377.[39]

The Tide Ebbs

At the height of September's confrontations in Cape Town, police began using a strategy of mass arrests to break the momentum of the uprising. On a single day, September 10, police detained almost 200 people in the simmering African and Coloured townships of the eastern Cape, and four days later, a house-to-house sweep in Alexandra township in northern Johannesburg netted more than 800 alleged "agitators" and helped to break Alexandra's support for the stay-away of September 13–15. By October similar methods were being applied in Soweto as police sought to intimidate members of the SSRC and capture its leadership core. In a raid on Morris Isaacson High School the morning of October 22, police detained all the teachers and students present—a mere 78 people under the irregular conditions then prevailing in Soweto's schools—purportedly as suspects in connection with petrol bomb attacks on the houses of black policemen. The number of trials of students on charges of public violence rose steadily, while others who were suspected of being ringleaders or of having connections to political organizations were detained for interrogation under provisions of the newly enacted Internal Security Act. As the repression intensified, what in the early stages of the uprising had been a mere trickle of young people fleeing to sanctuary in neighboring countries by November had become a flood.

In Soweto, where Khotso Seatlholo, an 18-year-old final-year student at Naledi High School, had replaced Mashinini as head of the SSRC, October was a month of shifting tactics as three new national campaigns were promoted to mark a period of mourning for the dead. The squandering of money on liquor was the first new target; consumer spending during the Christmas holidays was the second. Shebeens—illegal township bars—were ordered to close or face student wrath, and adults were asked to forego holiday festivities and gift-giving as a sign of solidarity with those who had suffered death, detention, or victimization during the year (*Document 72*). Soweto shebeen proprietors tried bargaining with the SSRC for a compromise, but most fell into line. One establishment that refused to shut down was partially destroyed in a dynamite blast in late November. Cape Town shebeens proved less cooperative, and dozens were wrecked in early October by squads of youthful enforcers who smashed their merchandise in the streets. An SSRC call for a fourth stay-away on November 1–5 in Johannesburg (*Document 73*) was largely ignored by workers, but as Christmas approached the consumer boycott was widely observed, and even the National Professional Soccer League agreed to limit its schedule of games as a gesture of mourning.

In Cape Town, student determination to destroy beerhalls and shebeens had angered African migrant workers in the townships' huge single-sex hostel complexes, and in the holiday season, tensions boiled over as migrants, abetted by the police, attacked residents, leaving 26 dead over Christmas weekend. In a statement that was quickly banned, the Ministers' Fraternal of Langa, Gugulethu and Nyanga enumerated the injustices which had led to the confrontations in Cape Town, and invoked the subversive biblical injunction for Christians to "obey God rather than men" (*Document 74*).

The third national campaign initiated by the SSRC was a boycott of all end-of-year exams as a gesture of mourning and a symbol of the rejection of Bantu Education. Student opinion was far from unanimously in favor of a boycott, and in many parts of the country exams proceeded on schedule, despite scattered disruptions as some students used intimidation tactics to force others to comply with the protest. But in the core regions of organized student militancy—the Reef, Pretoria, Cape Town and the eastern Cape—the boycott was widely observed, leaving the heavily overburdened African school system with the prospect of record numbers of students having to repeat a year in 1977. When school officials proposed that those who had boycotted in November 1976 be allowed to sit make-up exams in February and March 1977, the SSRC was caught in the dilemma embodied in so many aspects of African life: to accept the hated "half loaf" dispensed by the apartheid system, or proudly starve. For each individual, the choice lay between sacrificing personal ambitions and disappointing the expectations of parents on the one hand, or living with the guilt of being declared a sell-out by one's peers on the other. After a confusing period of sending out conflicting signals, the SSRC left the decision to individuals, and retreated to a low-profile position for the early months of the new year. In January, Seatlholo fled to Botswana after being wounded by police gunfire in a car chase, and was succeeded as SSRC chairman by Daniel Montsitsi, who had been a final-year student at Sekano Ntoane High School.

The sense of defeat and division surrounding the exams boycott marked the low point of student prestige in a year which had otherwise witnessed an extraordinary inversion of past patterns of black leadership as parents deferred to their children for political guidance. Combined with the poor popular response to the November 1–5 stay-away, the exam debacle suggested a clear need for student leaders to revise their tactics and search for more achievable goals lest the momentum of the revolt continue to ebb. Student spirits were still high, and as a collective force, students remained potentially mobilizable countrywide since most had returned to school by early 1977 despite the lack of any substantive improvements. The government changed the name of the Bantu Education Department to the Department of Education and Training in 1977, and announced that textbooks would become free by 1979. In most immediate respects, however, school conditions had become worse because of the resignation of many teachers, the high number of students repeating, and the widespread damage to school buildings.

In Soweto and to varying degrees in other townships where SRCs had formed during 1976, student organization remained intact despite the removal or flight of many individual student leaders. In Soweto, a rudimentary structure of SSRC subcommittees functioned to deal with transport, "conscientising," the production of leaflets, and the forging of links with other regions. Dreams of quick revolutionary solutions had faded and been replaced with a working list of "major priorities" that included the scrapping of Bantu education, the release of students still in detention, the abolition of all government controlled "puppet bodies" such as Urban Bantu Councils and ethnic school boards, and the initiation of a national convention to negotiate South Africa's future.[40] This last aim, which had been proposed over many years by liberals but was regularly dismissed with contempt by the Vorster government, is poignantly discussed in *Document 75*.

Where collaborators were concerned, the SSRC had fought a long, low-intensity campaign of insult and criticism aimed at the ineffectual Soweto Urban Bantu Council, a body already held in low esteem by the public at the time the uprising began. Rioters had targeted the pretentious UBC office building from the first day of the revolt, and by September a number of UBC members were threatening to resign out of frustration at the council's unpopularity, which they attributed to the fact that its powers were purely advisory, and its advice was usually ignored. The SSRC took the view that the entire UBC should resign and be replaced by a legitimate representative body—one more like the BPA—chosen by Soweto residents. Disregarding the debates between the UBC and its critics, the West Rand Administration Board decided in April 1977 that from May 1, Soweto rents would go up, and that the rises would be unusually large due to WRAB's loss of revenues from the burnt-out municipal beerhalls. The decision came as a gift to the SSRC, which was looking for a way to breathe life into its campaign against collaborators. It soon became evident that the UBC members had known of the coming rent hikes and had done nothing to inform residents or mobilize them to fight the increases; the UBC could thus be blamed for the hikes, and given an ultimatum to resign. On April 27, what started as a peaceful and police-sanctioned march through Soweto by several thousand students protesting the rent increases, turned into a melee when marchers began stoning the UBC headquarters. The Administration Board nervously suspended the increases, and the SSRC scored a victory which restored its earlier prestige. Further demonstrating its power to muscle opponents aside, the SSRC through a combination of public shaming and anonymous threats, succeeded by the first week of June 1977 in forcing all leading members of the UBC to resign, leaving the government no choice but to officially suspend the already defunct body. Soweto's 26 ethnic school boards were targeted next, and plans laid for a campaign to force the resignation of black policemen.

But the flame of the revolt was sputtering out. The possibilities for mass action by unarmed crowds had become constrained by a combination of police controls and a growing realism among students about the costs and benefits of such tactics. As the emotional first anniversary of June 16 approached, police swoops netted Montsitsi and several dozen other Soweto student activists. Plans for the commemoration proceeded nationwide, and despite a spate of violent incidents, including two days of police-student confrontation in Uitenhage in the eastern Cape which left ten dead, most black communities held relatively peaceful memorial services, supported by a partial closure of schools, shops and offices. ANC underground pamphleteers exploded a leaflet bomb in downtown Johannesburg on the evening of June 15. Eight days later, the SSRC, now under the leadership of Trofomo Sono, an eleventh grader at Madibane High School, staged a second successful "invasion" of central Johannesburg, massing about 500 protesters at John Vorster Square security police headquarters to demand the release of student detainees. Police baton-charged the demonstrators and arrested 146. One youth was shot dead in simultaneous demonstrations in Soweto. On the same day, June 23, parliament put old wine in new bottles by approving legislation to replace Urban Bantu Councils with new-look Community Councils. The demise of the Soweto UBC—the uprising's last major shock to the apartheid system—had left the government undeterred in its resolve to operate through bureaucracies of black collaborators; there was simply no other practical method to administer the country's huge rightless majority. But the prospect that blacks would eventually come to accept this "indirect rule" arrangement was as dead as the uprising's martyred children.

Protest or Challenge?

It is not inconceivable that the uprising might have caused the entire edifice of apartheid to crumble had the white government been more deeply divided about what to do in the face of its deteriorating legitimacy, and had blacks been better organized to sustain pressure on the system. In the event, the balance of forces, though inching towards parity, still firmly favored the white state, buttressed as it was by a loyal and well financed military and police establishment, a supportive electorate, a conservative business class, and a bloc of international trading partners less concerned about South Africa's domestic politics than about its significance as a minor outpost in the Cold War.

Nevertheless, the uprising created the most acute political crisis faced by the government since the 1960 Sharpeville emergency. Realizing that the revolt posed no short run threat to its control of the state, the National Party adopted a hardline stance from the outset, never publicly conceding that the crisis might require any reconsideration of the fundamentals of its policy. There was in fact "no crisis" at all, Vorster declared in a widely quoted speech at Springs in late August 1976. Although occasional adjustments might be needed in the implementation of particular policies, he said, no South African should have any doubt about the moral or practical soundness of the course the government was pursuing. According to National Party cabinet ministers, members of parliament, and sundry pro-government experts who came forward to offer explanations to the Cillie Commission and elsewhere, the township disturbances were not the result of government policies, but were caused by agitators, *tsotsis,* unpatriotic elements in the English press who sought to incite discontent, and "confusion" regarding the school language issue caused by "poor communication." One Nationalist MP accused the parliamentary opposition of complicity in the revolt on the grounds that they claimed to have known that an explosion was imminent but did not make their information available. Vorster in a parliamentary address hinted darkly about a conspiracy of "certain organizations and persons, working together to achieve . . . obvious objectives."[41]

Behind the rhetorical facade of righteousness and unanimity, however, the uprising dramatically sharpened the festering conflicts within the National Party regarding the direction of "separate development." The party's right wing favored making no concessions to liberal or foreign opinion, regardless of the country's growing isolation from international trade, investment, and sport. Party realists, backed to varying degrees by the Afrikaner establishment in big business, the media, academia and the Broederbond, recognized that if the country's isolation were to persist and worsen, the economy would eventually collapse from the combined forces of population growth, unemployment, and a failure to attract new capital and technology. To prevent the further erosion of the country's international position, particularly after the calamitous publicity generated by the uprising, it was obvious to the realists that major repairs to South Africa's battered image would be necessary. Inevitably, reforms in the apartheid system would be required to achieve this as well as to cool black discontent. Coloured solidarity with Africans, however fleeting in its manifestations during the uprising, was worrisome and clearly required tactical concessions that would reinforce fragmentation along racial lines. The problem for the

National Party was how to garb reforms and concessions so that the conservative all-white electorate would see them as cost-free, *verkrampte* leaders in the party would accept them as consistent with past policy, and enough blacks would be seduced by them to enable South Africa to project a new international image of itself as ruled by a legitimate government standing for democratic principles and opportunity for all.

This was an impossible mission, but it was to take another decade of decline and another uprising—broader, more sustained, and more economically catastrophic—for its futility finally to be impressed on the inner core of the National Party leadership. In the meantime, despite the shedding of its right wing which broke away to form the Conservative Party in 1982, the party continued to cohere around the fundamentals of "grand apartheid" first conceived by Verwoerd: the creation of "independent" black ethnic mini-states, the eventual designation of all Africans as "foreign," the continued relegation of Coloureds and Indians to subordinate political status (despite their incorporation in 1984 into a tricameral parliament under a new constitution), and most importantly, the granite determination never to accede to the principle of one-person-one-vote in a unified South Africa. The uprising of 1976–1977 made no appreciable dent in the regime's pursuit of this basic blueprint. Instead, its response to the revolt was to intensify the search for new divide-and-rule tactics at home, and new maneuvers to improve its image abroad. The revolt, as John Kane-Berman observed at the time, was a turning point at which no turn was made—at least not by the government.[42]

It was among blacks that the revolt decisively altered both the pace and the direction of change in South Africa. In the decade preceding the uprising, Africans had registered enormous gains in potential power. Their economic leverage as consumers and skilled workers had grown tremendously, although it remained unrealized because of a lack of organization and the unrecognized status of African trade unions. In terms of international public opinion, the National Party government had already lost the moral high ground to the worldwide anti-apartheid movement, to the point where all that stood between Pretoria and the onset of a serious drive for economic sanctions in the West was a delicately nurtured public relations campaign, aimed at conservative opinion and designed to project an image of South Africa as a stable society earnestly seeking just solutions to its difficult problems. Politically, as we have seen, thousands of members of the youth and student generation had already been touched to one degree or another by the psychological and semantic transformations introduced by black consciousness. Among them was a small but very militant element who had distanced themselves totally from the fear and defeatism afflicting the adult generation, and were primed for action.

Though weak when measured against the task of ousting the National Party government, these youthful activists had acquired a level of self-confidence and organizational and leadership skill that put them a quantum leap beyond their parents' generation. Their ability to disseminate propaganda and to repeatedly bring large crowds of demonstrators into the streets was impressive; so was their physical courage in the face of brutal police methods. Yet their inexperience, and the superficiality of their knowledge about mass struggles of the past, meant that their ability to strategize was underdeveloped. They were a daring cadre of lieutenants without senior officers, a Red Guard without a Mao Zedong. Their energies could not be poured into any existing legal organizations where a more seasoned and strategically sophisticated leadership was already in place, because by 1976 the government's campaign of repression had insured that no such organizations were free to operate. For these young militants and the thousands of their peers who became highly politicized during the events of 1976–77, the uprising itself became a crash course in political reality, a harsh lesson in confrontation which, while failing to topple South Africa's rulers, vitally strengthened the forces challenging the established order.

Had the exiled liberation movements been far more advanced in the development of underground networks and military capabilities before 1976, they might have been able to ride the wave of student anger to create a level of chaos and bloodshed sufficient to prompt either foreign intervention or a move by whites toward negotiation. But their operations inside South Africa were still in an embryonic stage when the violence of June 16 erupted. A handful of white members of the ANC were producing the leaflets that began appearing in the late 1960s. A small number of older activists who had been released from Robben Island in the early 1970s were starting to organize underground ANC and PAC units. Both of the older movements tried to insert members from their fledgling undergrounds into the black consciousness movement, and to recruit people who were already active in its constituent organizations. By 1975, the leadership of NAYO and SASO had become ANC-oriented, while PAC had made inroads into the BPC. The steady exodus of young people crossing into the neighboring states with the goal of joining the movements outside continued, but the number of new recruits involved in underground activities within South Africa was small, probably numbering no more than 200 countrywide.[43] By June 1976, guerrilla attacks had not yet begun, nor had caches of weapons been accumulated.

The outbreak of violence in Soweto took the leaders of the underground liberation movements by surprise. Despite the restrictions under which they lived and their need to exercise extreme caution, leaders of the ANC in Johannesburg—Joe Gqabi, Martin Ramokgadi, and Elliot Shabangu—were able to establish contact with members of the Soweto student leadership fairly early in the uprising. Shabangu's nephew, Super Moloi, was one of a number of highly politicized students close to the nerve center of the SSRC. Once contact had been made, however, the material resources which the underground ANC could offer to the SSRC's would-be revolutionaries were disappointingly meager. The students were developing their own contacts for the printing and distribution of leaflets, the borrowing of automobiles, and the collection of funds; the Black Parents Association and later the South

African Council of Churches were taking charge of welfare functions for families affected by the violence. The ANC had little to contribute beyond a measure of logistical support for students wishing to leave the country. On a non-material level, it is difficult to determine the extent to which the SSRC leadership may have been influenced in its tactics, targets, or ideas by discussions with ANC veterans. The language of SSRC leaflets reflects no obvious effort to project the ANC's particular type of nonracial nationalism. Montsitsi in later years recalled being urged to target the UBC by Gqabi, Shabangu, and Winnie Mandela (who had been unbanned in 1975 and had established herself as a supporter of student activists, and of black consciousness, even before becoming a leader of the Black Parents Association in the week after June 16). It was unlikely that students needed urging in this direction, however, because they had already spontaneously demonstrated their rage against state-sponsored institutions from the first day of the June rioting. Perhaps more significant was Montsitsi's recollection that ANC veterans advised that once UBC members agreed to resign, the SSRC should be conciliatory toward them, rather than adopting a vindictive attitude.[44] Such tactical moves added to the SSRC's reputation for maturity and moderation.

There is no evidence, however, that the opinions of the ANC exerted any more influence on the SSRC leadership than the advice and assistance offered by other allies, including Drake Koka of BAWU (who assisted in producing the SSRC's stay-away leaflets) and Beyers Naude, Cedric Mayson and other whites in the Christian Institute and the South African Council of Churches (who assisted the SSRC financially). So large was the mass of Soweto's student population, and so coherent and effective its leadership by comparison with other organized black groups, it was only a matter of time before popular adulation led to the SSRC being spoken of as Soweto's "shadow government"—a self-image its leaders were not inclined to trade in for the status of junior partner in an alliance with any other group, particularly one whose capability to take on the enemy had turned out to be considerably less impressive than students had initially hoped or imagined.

Witnesses testified at the trial of Gqabi and Ramokgadi in 1977 that at a December 1976 meeting between Khotso Seatlholo and Naledi Tsiki, a member of the ANC who had been trained as a guerrilla in the Soviet Union, Tsiki invited the SSRC to form a working relationship with the ANC, but that Seatlholo refused on the grounds that the SSRC wanted to retain its autonomy.[45] It was agreed, however, that SSRC members were free to join the ANC as individuals, which indeed some by that time had already done. One grouping within the SSRC—the so-called "suicide squad—which initially specialized in petrol bomb attacks, late in 1976 converted itself into an ANC unit, carried out a number of acts of sabotage including the bombing of the defiant Soweto shebeen mentioned earlier, and was becoming involved in the recruitment of fighters to leave the country when its leader, Paul Langa, was arrested in January 1977.[46]

Post mortem analyses of the uprising, particularly from critics on the left, faulted the Soweto student leaders, and by implication other urban SRCs, for their inability to liaise collectively with black workers in any way other than through pamphleteering. Even in their stay-away leaflets, critics noted, students made little reference to concerns specifically affecting workers. If ANC or Communist Party veterans advised students to make contact with working-class leaders or place a more pointed emphasis on worker griev-ances, it appears to have made little or no impact on the SSRC's strategists. Reflecting on the uprising in later years, Morobe agreed that students had no notion of how to organize workers, but he also pointed out that given the conservatism of the Trade Union Council of South Africa to which almost all existing black unions were then affiliated, black workers themselves had no identifiable vanguard of politically progressive leaders with whom students could have established a working relationship.[47] It could perhaps be argued that the students' use of the stay-away as a tactic in 1976 was deficient because, unlike general strikes of indefinite duration, the stay-away serves a revolutionary purpose only if it is used as a device for the long term building of worker organization and worker consciousness—purposes not encompassed in the SSRC's thinking.[48] In the end, however, the political consciousness of black workers, like that of all blacks, sharpened signifi-cantly as a result of the drama and the traumas of the uprising, such that in its aftermath the pace of organization among workers accelerated rapidly.

Just as it is ahistorical to argue that students missed an available opportunity to forge a worker-student alliance in 1976, it is also inaccurate to characterize the uprising as merely focused around grievances relating to education, important as these were in initiating and fueling the rebellion.[49] Attacks, both planned and spontaneous, against government facilities and collaborators, demonstrations against the September 1976 visit of American Secretary of State Henry Kissinger, and the political language of most student leaflets and statements, all indicate that student leaders saw their activities as political and as directed toward fundamental and not merely reformist changes in the apartheid system, and that they hoped to direct the sometimes unfocused anger of their peers at political targets. The tactics they chose tended to be limited in imagination, and did not reflect any sophisticated revolutionary drive to build alternative institutions, create "liberated zones," or subvert the security forces—objectives which in any case would have required far more time and greater capability than students could muster acting alone in 1976. Nevertheless, there was a clear insurrectionary spirit to the revolt as it unfolded following the unplanned rioting of June, and this spirit fanned diffuse hopes and expectations of greater revolutionary action to come, attitudes which contributed to intense racial polarization in the aftermath of the uprising.[50]

In the short run, it was evident by mid-1977 that the government had come out on top in the township confrontations. The school system did not appreciably improve, and amelioration of township conditions occurred very slowly where it occurred at all.[51] Urban Bantu Councils were scrapped but replaced with similar bodies called Community Councils. Rent hikes were postponed in Soweto but eventually imposed. The term "separate development" was replaced in official discourse by "plural development" and the Department of Bantu Affairs changed its name to the Department of Plural Relations. Despite the obvious discomfort which the revolt had inspired in high places, day to day existence in the townships, with all its deprivations, controls and indignities, continued much as before.

At the subjective level, however, the uprising brought momentous developments in popular awareness. It created heroes, martyrs, and—most significantly—prison graduates for a new generation, and with them a new political consciousness and sophistication. Students in every major urban area and even in remote communities, and parents through their children, were affected by the revolt and drawn to reflect on the reasons for its ups and downs, the tactics of its leaders, and the responses of the authorities and of whites generally to the challenges it posed. Why did so many die? Why did the uprising fail to change the government's approach? What could have made it succeed? Could South Africa achieve change only through war like Mozambique, Angola, and Rhodesia, or could the system be brought down through unarmed action like the uprising but on a larger scale? For many activists the obvious solution was to take up arms; others put priority on political organization. Some in the former group held to a belief in quick and apocalyptic scenarios of revolution, but many who had become seasoned in the events of 1976–77 recognized the possibility that their political commitment might have to carry them through a long and taxing war of attrition fought on multiple fronts.

Notes

1. This section draws on the documentary records of the organizations mentioned, and on conversations with Biko (October 1972), Tebogo Mafole (March 1992), Tom Manthata (June 1990), Amos Masondo (July 1989), Daniel Montsitsi (July 1989), Murphy Morobe (May 1991 and September 1995), Kehla Mthembu (March 1989), Marti Mueller (November 1971), Gugile Nkwinti (July 1989), Jackie Selebi (March 1989), Victor Sifora (October 1972), Stone Sizani (July 1989 and May 1990), and interviews of Victoria Butler in February 1988 with Bheki Langa, Billy Masetlha, and "Lerumo Feta." Also see Ellen Hellmann, "Social Change Among Urban Africans" in Heribert Adam, ed., *South Africa: Sociological Perspectives* (London: Oxford University Press, 1971).

2. Joseph Molokeng in *State v. Molokeng* ("the NAYO trial"), reported in the *Rand Daily Mail,* May 6, 1976.

3. Following her release from detention, Belinda Martin came to the offices of the *Rand Daily Mail,* where journalist Clive Emdon recorded the statement that appears as Document 60. Emdon gave the statement to attorney Raymond Tucker, but instead of bringing a case against the police, Martin decided to leave South Africa. She later joined Umkhonto we Sizwe.

4. Document 62, handwritten in a small notebook or diary, was seized by police during 1976 or 1977 and presented as a trial exhibit for the prosecution in *State v. Twala* ("The Soweto 11") following the uprising.

5. This figure is derived from data in Sue Blignaut, *Statistics on Education in South Africa, 1968–79* (Johannesburg: South African Institute of Race Relations, 1981), and *Survey of Race Relations 1975* (Johannesburg: South African Institute of Race Relations, 1976), p. 220.

6. On the banning of the Junior African Students Council (JASC) at Inanda Seminary, see Document 49, resolution 43/72.

7. *Weekend World,* July 4, 1971.

8. "Report on SASO's Executive Council meeting, Edendale Lay Ecumenical Centre, 1–8 December, 1971."

9. Many young Africans shied away from politics not necessarily out of fear, but because their lives were focussed on other pursuits. In the April 1973 *SASM Newsletter,* for example, two SASM activists describe attending a "hippie gig" at Mofolo Hall in Soweto for the purpose of studying how the black hippie sub-culture of the time, in which peace, drugs, and love, including interracial sex, were central, might be infiltrated and politicized. The SASM students were outraged that some male hippies bartered their girlfriends to white university students in exchange for hard drugs, a practice SASM vowed to "exterminate." The hardcore hippies might be unreachable, the SASM researchers concluded, but their larger following of hangers-on were not beyond redemption because notwithstanding their "love" ethos, their dislike for whites was as great as the next person's. Nthanyane Maaga and Xola Nuse, "Report on a Hippie Fact-Finding Mission," *SASM Newsletter,* April 1973, pp. 5–8.

10. "Whites in South Africa as Oppressors," an essay by a student forced to testify for the state in the Healdtown trial, *State v. Ndukwana* (1976).

11. [Daniel] Sechaba Montsitsi, "Lessons From 1976," in *Beyond Reform: The Challenge of Change. Speeches presented at the NUSAS July Festival held at UCT, July 1983,* p. 40.

12. Alan Brooks and Jeremy Brickhill in *Whirlwind Before the Storm: the Origins and Development of the Uprising in Soweto and the Rest of South Africa from June to December 1976* (London: International Defence and Aid Fund, 1980), p. 88, and conversation with Morobe.

13. Brooks and Brickhill, p. 88. On SASM also see Nozipho J. Diseko, "The Origins and Development of the South African Students' Movement (SASM): 1968–1976," *Journal of Southern African Studies,* vol. 18, no. 1, March 1992.

14. Regarding the linguistic foundations of African nationalism in South Africa, the absence of a single unifying indigenous language is notable. Tsietsi Mashinini, one of the student leaders of 1976, is said to have whipped up audiences by reciting from Tennyson's "The Charge of the Light Brigade." *Commission of Inquiry Into the Riots at Soweto and Other Places in South Africa* (Cillie Commission, testimony, p. 4,962). The use of English as a lingua franca among politicized Africans helps explain the underdeveloped cultural dimension of African national-ism, as well as the tendency for African leadership to be disproportionately drawn from the most educated strata of society.

15. Average annual state expenditure per pupil in 1975–76 was R42 for Africans and R644 for whites. In 1972, African teachers earned "46 per cent of the salaries paid to whites in similar posts with similar qualifications." John Kane-Berman, *Soweto: Black Revolt, White Reaction* (Johannesburg: Ravan Press, 1978), p. 187.

16. In early 1976, one school uniform cost about 35 rand ($40) and a domestic servant's monthly wage in Johannesburg was about 30 rand ($34). *Rand Daily Mail,* February 14, 1976.

17. Baruch Hirson, *Year of Fire, Year of Ash, the Soweto Revolt: Roots of a Revolution?* (London: Zed Press, 1979), p. 98.

18. Thirty-year leasehold rights were not extended to Africans in the western Cape, where the National Party clung to the goal of arresting, even reversing, African urbanization.

19. Desmond Tutu, "Destroying a Birthright," *Rand Daily Mail,* May 1, 1976.

20. Tutu's letter, dated May 8, was reproduced in full in the English press on May 23 and in *EcuNews Bulletin,* a publication of the South African Council of Churches, on May 26, 1976.

21. Conversation with Nkosazana Dlamini Zuma (June 1988). Details of South Africa's military failure in Angola in 1975–76 did not emerge until early 1977, but enough had become public by March 1976 to confirm that the South African army had been repulsed by MPLA forces. The specter of advancing communist armies prompted wide debate among whites

about whether blacks would help defend South Africa in the event of a Soviet invasion. An informal poll taken by *The World* in March found black opinion running almost 5 to 1 for a "no" response, according to *Ecunews Bulletin,* March 17, 1976.

22. Eyewitnesses later gave conflicting testimony regarding the sequence of events at the Vilakazi Street encounter. The majority saw stones thrown after the teargas and before the shots; some claimed warning shots were fired in the air, while others denied this. (Testimony to the Cillie Commission, passim.) The Cillie Commission was appointed by the government in June 1976 to investigate the causes of the violence. It heard testimony in 1976 and 1977, but did not present its findings until 1980.

23. Estimate by the Cillie Commission. In May 1977, the Institute of Race Relations estimated that 618 had died up to that time. *Rand Daily Mail,* May 11, 1977.

24. The same May 1977 Institute of Race Relations report said that at least 16 children aged ten or under were among the dead.

25. Conversation with Deborah Mabiletsa (July 1980). A 1975 survey of the Diepkloof area adjacent to Soweto found "slightly more than one bed for every three people." Kane-Berman, p. 53.

26. Khuzine Ntshona?, "Soweto," undated and unsigned manuscript, mid-1970s, p. 28. The consistency of this mindset with the precepts of black consciousness is obvious. Though often characterized as "philosophical" or "ideological," black consciousness was fundamentally a simple matter of attitude. Its aim, as put by a young witness in a 1975 political trial, was to influence both its adherents and non-adherents "so that wherever they go they should accept their blackness. . . . And that if the white people have openly demonstrated a feeling of superiority, that they should be ready to reprimand them and tell them that they are also human beings." Xola Nuse testimony in *State v. Molobi,* pp. 98–99.

27. Of the detainees and awaiting-trial prisoners who, under one or another degree of duress, testified *in camera* before the Cillie Commission in early 1977, several made statements which implicated Winnie Mandela, a founding member of the BPA, in the planning of student actions. It was suggested, for example, that Tsietsi Mashinini sought her advice, and that she encouraged him to use violence against collaborators and the police. One witness testified that he had been tortured until he made a statement implicating Mrs. Mandela in the violence. From a legal standpoint, had the police been able to make a convincing case that she was the mastermind behind the revolt, all who participated in it might have been charged with the crime of "furthering the aims of a banned organization," the ANC.

28. Notes of West Rand police attending "Rockville Roman Catholic Church's Meeting," August 1, 1976.

29. Conversation with Morobe (May 1991).

30. Kane-Berman, p. 113, and Glenn Moss, in *Crisis and Conflict: Soweto 1976–1977,* M.A. thesis, University of the Witwatersrand, 1982, have questioned the press characterization of the attackers as "Zulu," since only about 15% of the roughly 10,000 inmates of Mzimhlope were Zulu-speakers in 1976. However, one eyewitness quoted in the *Rand Daily Mail* on August 25 estimated the size of the mob at 1,500, which could lend credence to the theory that the police who orchestrated the killing called for the formation of a specifically Zulu *impi* (fighting formation) to deal with the "upstart" youth of the township. Other African eyewitnesses including journalists corroborated the label, as did statements by the police referring to the just grievances of the "Zulus" against their victims. The weight of evidence thus seems to favor the view that most, if not all, of the attackers were Zulus. About 70 people died in the fighting. Kane-Berman, p. 113.

31. Gatsha Buthelezi made explicit accusations to this effect after visiting Mzimhlope hostel on August 27. Two black journalists, Peter Magubane and Gabu Tugwana, witnessed and overheard policemen interacting with the attackers.

32. Judgment of J. Van Dyk in the 1978–1979 trial of the SSRC leadership, *State v. Twala,* p. 95.

33. Conversation with Selebi, who noted that serious debates preceded these efforts to work with people who were regarded as part of the "system." Buthelezi addressed a mass meeting

of Soweto hostel dwellers on August 28 during which he accused police of inciting the attacks. See *Rand Daily Mail,* August 29, 1976.

34. An extended discussion of this period at UWC appears in an interview by George Fredrickson with Yvonne Muthien (May 1980).

35. Other factors contributing to the lower level of political activity in Natal may have included the absence of the compulsory Afrikaans ruling, the lesser impact of the homeland citizenship rules in a province where many homeland areas were in closer proximity to jobs in the large towns and cities, the slight improvement in wages following the 1973 Durban strikes, and the prominence of Chief Gatsha Buthelezi, who left no vacuum of adult leadership into which students could move. The role of Inkatha leaders in discouraging student militancy is discussed in testimony before the Cillie Commission by Leon Mellet, then a crime reporter for the *Natal Mercury,* and later revealed to be an undercover policeman (Cillie Commission testimony, pp. 4,199–4,207). Hirson's view that the 1976 uprising was principally inspired by the labor militancy of 1973 in Natal seems implausible in light of the relative quiescence of Natal in 1976.

36. *Rand Daily Mail,* September 4, 1976.

37. Brooks and Brickhill, p. 32.

38. Starkly contrasting impressions of the student marchers of September 23 were presented by the liberal *Rand Daily Mail* on September 24, which painted them as a mob of violent thugs using terror tactics, and by George Bizos, one of the lawyers who represented the 159 eventually charged with public violence, who described them as disciplined, mature and exemplary young people. Conversation with George Bizos (October 1989).

39. *New York Times,* October 24, 1976.

40. These are set forth in an undated SSRC document, "Major Priorities (and Other Projects)," drafted by Wilson Twala for chairman Daniel Montsitsi in early 1977. The subcommittees of the SSRC are listed in an undated SSRC document headed "Departments." Both documents were among the documentary exhibits presented in *State v. Twala.*

41. *House of Assembly Debates,* June 18, 1976, quoted by Brooks and Brickhill, p. 27. The MP who blamed the Progressive Party (H. J. van der Walt of Schweizer-Reinecke) was quoted in the *Sunday Tribune,* June 27, 1976. The English press was blamed by, inter alia, I. W. Ackermann, director of the Highveld Bantu Administration Board, in testimony to the Cillie Commission reported by the *Rand Daily Mail,* October 27, 1976. M. C. Botha, the Minister of Bantu Education, attributed the blow-up over Afrikaans to "confusion," presumably on the part of Africans.

42. Kane-Berman, p. 232.

43. Howard Barrell, *MK: the ANC's Armed Struggle* (London: Penguin Books, 1990), p. 32.

44. Conversation with Montsitsi. He also recalled being taught freedom songs from the 1950s by ANC veterans. Hirson states that "it was during the height of the Revolt that the clandestine ANC . . . was able to join the students in organising some of the most important activities of the Revolt," but he offers no substantiation for this except that one ANC leaflet supported the SSRC's August 23–25 stay-away call.

45. *Rand Daily Mail,* July 16, 1977, and record of *State v. Sexwale* ("The Pretoria 12"), 1977–1978. According to Morobe, the SSRC, or at least its inner core, had debated at length about whether to affiliate to the ANC or PAC, and had decided against it (workshop presentation, Albert Einstein Institution, May 4, 1991).

46. On the ANC's attitudes to the uprising, see chapter 10.

47. Conversation with Morobe (May 1991).

48. Glenn Moss has borrowed this argument from Rosa Luxemburg and developed it in his M.A. thesis. He does not address the problems created by the underdeveloped state of African trade unionism in 1976–77.

49. A June 16 anniversary feature in the *Star,* June 15, 1993, for example, reasserts the common but erroneous view that "the demands of the 'class of 1976' were largely confined to educational matters, mainly the scrapping of Afrikaans as a medium of instruction and free and compulsory education. But this approach changed significantly in the years following 1976,

largely because students realised that they had the capacity to force the Government to make social and political changes."

50. Attitude studies based on survey data in the post-1976 period are discussed in Lawrence Schlemmer, "Build-up to Revolution or Impasse?" in Heribert Adam, ed., *South Africa: the Limits of Reform Politics* (Leiden: E. J. Brill, 1983).

51. In contrast to the government's parsimony, big business took the view that Africans would be less susceptible to politicization if their material standards of living were rising and if those with middle class aspirations were able to satisfy their ambitions in some measure. The Urban Foundation, sponsored by business and embracing a philosophy of amelioration, was established in the aftermath of the uprising. By the late 1970s the National Party also came to accept this philosophy, which had formerly been identified with the "English" parliamentary opposition.

7. Black Workers and Trade Unions

David Lewis

The effort to build black trade unions moved through two phases during the decade and a half after 1964. The period before 1973 was characterized by official repression and comprehensive legal discrimination, employer hostility, weak organization, and by quiescence on the factory floor. The post-1973 period was characterized by the re-emergence of worker organization and sustained factory-floor militancy, the wresting of formal recognition from beleaguered employers, and the gradual establishment of legal toe-holds. The period culminated in the recommendations of the Wiehahn Commission, which finally conceded legal status to the independent union movement.[1] The crucial event dividing the periods was a wave of major strikes in Durban in 1973. Without apparent warning or premeditation, workers who had maintained a dissatisfied quiescence for more than a decade shut down dozens of factories in South Africa's second industrial city and by their action enshrined "1973" in the shorthand of South African resistance history.

It is the systemic character of the differences between pre-1973 and post-1973 South Africa that marks the Durban strikes as a watershed. They spawned dynamic organizations of resistance where none had existed during the previous decade. Industrial relations were forced onto the agenda of employers long used to ruling with the stick, occasionally tempered by a habitual paternalism. The government undertook a major reorientation of the legislative framework that for fifty years had regulated relations among African workers, employers and the state. These were not ephemeral shifts but major institutional changes marking off one era from another.

The 1973 watershed was not entirely unheralded. Major instances of labor unrest had occurred starting in the late 1960s in Cape Town, Johannesburg,

Durban itself, and in South West Africa. Although none of these actions was as momentous as the 1973 strikes, they help situate 1973 as part of a longer process rather than a bolt from the blue. Following the Durban strikes, the Soweto uprising brought further fundamental alterations in South Africa's political equation, as well as dramatic spillover effects in industrial relations. Nevertheless, there can be no doubt that in the period under consideration, the 1973 strikes stand as the definitive landmark in labor history, marking the start of a major working-class role in South Africa's political conflict and helping to define and shape the outcomes of that conflict. They remain, in short, the pivotal event around which black worker organization was constituted, a pivot created by black workers themselves.

Survival Years: 1964–1972

The trade union movement has been a persistent organizational expression of black resistance in South Africa in this century. Although often weak and divided and lacking in organizational resources and experience, African workers maintained a semblance of open union activity even during times when political forms of organization had faded nearly out of existence. It is thus a particularly powerful measure of the bleakness of the 1960s that in this period black union organization was all but snuffed out. The National Party governments of Hendrik Verwoerd and John Vorster worked systematically to restrict the unionization of Africans on the pretext that they had not yet reached the necessary stage of development to function as trade unionists and to withstand agitators.

South Africa's system of racially discriminatory industrial relations took shape well before the apartheid era. Fundamental policy was established in the Industrial Conciliation Act of 1924. It set forth the rights and obligations of trade unions and excluded all "pass-bearing natives" from the definition of "employee" and hence from the provisions of the act itself. African workers were therefore not represented in any of the official structures including unions that qualified for statutory registration. In short, African workers were prohibited from forming or joining registered unions and thus were denied access to official collective bargaining institutions as well as to general statutory protection. Unregistered African unions were not outlawed and, despite their considerable legal disadvantages, continued to flourish in the politically volatile climate of the 1950s. However, in the words of Ben Schoeman, the Minister of Labor after 1948, it was the National Party's intention to "bleed the unions to death." Where discriminatory industrial relations legislation failed to achieve this, the full force of security legislation could be deployed to try to accomplish the task.

The exclusion of "pass bearing natives" from the Industrial Conciliation Act's definition of "employee" gave rise to what were, even by apartheid's standards, some peculiar anomalies. The legislation was enacted before African women were forced to carry passes, which meant that for many years they were allowed to join registered unions. They constituted, however, an insignificant part of the industrial work force at that time. Of greater significance, the definition did not ensure that the unions were "pure" white, insofar as Coloured and Indian workers were not subject to the statutory definition that acted to exclude African workers. This then effectively permitted racially mixed registered unions, unions that excluded African workers but that nevertheless incorporated white, Coloured and Indian workers within their ranks.

Unions were free, however, to restrict their membership to workers of a particular racial group. Accordingly, there existed a phalanx of exclusively white unions with particularly strong representation in the public service and the mining industry. There were also unions restricted to either Coloured and Indian workers as well as a large core of racially "mixed" unions, although the latter were expressly discouraged by the National Party government that came to power in 1948. The 1956 Industrial Conciliation Act stipulated that no further mixed unions would be registered and that existing mixed unions would have to establish segregated branches holding segregated meetings and congresses. Moreover, only whites would be permitted to serve on the executive committees of mixed unions.

Narrow considerations of self-interest operated alongside racist attitudes and ideologies with varying results so that, for example, registered unions in the railways and the mines admitted white members only, while their counterparts in the engineering trades were generally mixed, and those in the garment and textile industries were frequently restricted to, or numerically dominated by, Coloured and Indian workers. This complex interaction of race, occupation and union membership powerfully conditioned relations within the union movement, accounting for its deep divisions.

In broad outline, where the union in question represented craftspeople and was intent upon protecting its monopoly of the craft in question, it was inclined toward a mixed membership, admitting Coloured and Indian artisans into its ranks. African workers were not permitted to become apprenticed; hence, craft or artisan status was denied them. Since they represented no direct threat to the craft monopoly enjoyed by the mixed unions, these unions saw no reason to incorporate Africans into their ranks.

Where a craft monopoly was not sufficient to guarantee privilege, or where, in other words, the job security and wages of white—and, to a smaller extent, Coloured and Indian—workers were threatened by low-paid African workers competing for the same jobs, apartheid used one of its most noxious weapons to featherbed its constituency. This was the notorious job reservation provision of the 1956 Industrial Conciliation Act, which permitted the Minister to reserve certain categories of work for particular racial groups. Section 77 of the Act was frequently invoked to protect semi-skilled white workers from competition from African, Coloured and Indian workers. It was also, on occasion, invoked to protect Coloured and Indian workers from their African counterparts. There was no particular incentive to organize across color lines when statute, rather than craft monopoly, forestalled competition. Moreover, as the manufacturing sector developed and the skill component of artisan work was increasingly diluted, the craft unions, no longer able to rely upon a monopoly of their skill for protection, also began to support the principle of job reservation.

African workers were not merely subjected to this organizational discrimination; there also existed all the normal provisions of apartheid, many of which were expressly directed at the more efficient exploitation and control of black workers. The list was endless: migrant labor, the central pillar of Verwoerdian economics, increasingly refined through the 1950s and 1960s; inferior education; the relentless application of residential segregation that acted to place black workers on the outskirts of the cities; inferior segregated factory amenities, and a growing wage gap between white and black workers.

Rocky ground, one might justifiably assume, for trade union organization. And yet no account of the period is complete without an understanding of the contribution of the union movement. Within this movement three broad strands were evident. First, and, for present purposes, foremost, were those unions in the frontline of the challenge to apartheid. While many of these were unregistered unions of African workers, they included important registered unions of Coloured and Indian workers that reluctantly accepted the formal strictures of apartheid in order to retain their registered status, but nonetheless worked closely with African workers and unions. The relationship between the African Food and Canning Workers' Union and the Food and Canning Workers' Union is probably the best example of this nominal division. Central to the vision of unions of this type was the notion that working-class interests could not be advanced by a narrow focus on the factory floor. The trade union struggle had, in this view, to be harnessed to the broader fight against political exclusion. From the mid-1950s these unions, representative of a persistent strand in South African working-class history, were grouped in the South African Congress of Trade Unions (SACTU), a member of the Congress Alliance.

The second strand of unionism in the pre-1973 period was represented by the Trade Union Council of South Africa (TUCSA). TUCSA and SACTU were formed in the 1950s (TUCSA, or as it was then named, the South African Trade Union Council in 1954, SACTU in 1955) from the ashes of the Trades and Labour Council, an organization that disintegrated in 1954 over the question of admitting African workers. Those who insisted upon admission of Africans formed SACTU. Those willing to compromise on the matter formed TUCSA. It is not surprising then that TUCSA's history, persistently reinforced on the one hand by the daily march of apartheid and on the other by the potential power of the African working class, ensured that this issue remained at the top of the organization's agenda.

TUCSA was a federation of registered unions, many of which had a racially mixed membership. It was politically dominated by craft unions desperately seeking the most effective way of protecting their privileged position relative to semi-skilled African workers. The tactical nature of this defense resulted in TUCSA's opportunistic vacillation between partial, intermittent, and highly conditional acceptance of unregistered African unions, counterposed with their outright exclusion as soon as white right-wing unions, some of whom were affiliated to TUCSA, threatened to disaffiliate or poach members away from TUCSA unions.

Finally, there were the all-white unions. They represented a conservative constituency whose narrow and short term interests account for some of apartheid's most notorious features, including job reservation. They were also an important factor in determining the limits of TUCSA's reluctant and expedient opposition to apartheid, a powerful counterweight to the few unions within TUCSA that supported a more resolute and liberal political stance from the federation. Any move to the left by TUCSA's leadership resulted in a move on the federation's right wing to decamp in support of the rigid racial differentiation favored by the all-white unions.

Although the nonracial character of SACTU was important—one of spirit as well as form—and SACTU itself often seemed seriously to consider the task of organizing white workers, this was never feasible. In a narrow material sense white workers were among the most highly rewarded beneficiaries of these "golden years" of apartheid. The likelihood that any of them, save the very rare individual sympathizer, would make common cause with black workers, was remote. In any case, the combination of crippling discrimination at the level of the industrial relations system, the deployment of wide-ranging security legislation, and the deep-seated, indeed intractable, divisions in the union movement, ensured that by the mid-1960s SACTU had all but ceased to exist.

A powerful reflection of the unrelenting police repression of the 1960s was the marked decline in strike action over the decade. Whereas between 1955 and 1960 there had been an average of 76 strikes a year, in 1962 and 1963 this dropped to 16 and 17 respectively. Although the numbers increased somewhat over the rest of the decade, they remained considerably below the average for the latter half of the 1950s.[2] At the opening of SACTU's 1964 annual conference, the ninth in its brief history, it was noted that the federation's general secretary was under 24 hour house arrest; the assistant general secretary was barred from union work and the person elected to replace her had already been deported; the president was being held under the 90 day detention law; an additional twenty-six SACTU leaders were barred from union work by banning orders, and 41 other unionists were in detention.[3] *Document 76*, a report presented to the 1963 annual conference of the African Food and Canning Workers' Union, bears witness to this relentless persecution, which was to be an unabating reality of union life throughout the period under review.[4]

TUCSA and African Workers

To the extent that TUCSA's avowedly apolitical stance inadvertently represented a political position, TUCSA was firmly in the center of the union movement. It was, moreover, the largest trade union body in existence and included a large number of Coloured and Indian workers in its ranks. In 1969, 23,560 workers belonged to its affiliated Coloured and Indian unions, and 129,830 belonged to racially mixed unions that included whites.[5] TUCSA enjoyed the statutory protection, respectability, and relative financial stability conferred by its registered status. On the other hand, its inability to accommodate the aspirations of SACTU's membership effectively confined TUCSA to a constituency that was a shrinking proportion of the country's work force.

Even though certain important TUCSA affiliates took advantage of racially based statutory protection, the attempts of the federation's leadership to remain in the political center, and their fear of losing the support of the federation's large Coloured and Indian affiliates, increasingly obliged TUCSA to offer at least token opposition to the growing manifestations of apartheid within the unions and on the factory floor. Thus, for example, TUCSA in 1965 called for the repeal of job reservation, but not on the grounds that it was inherently unjust. Rather, "the original need for job reservation had fallen away," the organization's president declared, because there were simply not enough whites "available to do the jobs which were reserved for them." Since blacks would inevitably be hired to fill the gaps, he said, the only way to protect the white workers' standard of living was to embrace the principle of equal pay for equal work.[6]

One might have expected more resolute opposition by TUCSA to government attacks on the status and internal operations of racially mixed unions, a matter of direct concern to the federation. There is, however, no evidence of such opposition. On the contrary, even those few TUCSA unions that enjoyed a reputation for genuine opposition to apartheid quickly surrendered in the face of legislative injunctions and right-wing poaching. For example, in 1966 the then racially mixed National Union of Distributive Workers (NUDW), the TUCSA affiliate most outspoken in its opposition to apartheid, divided itself into an all-white and an all-Coloured union. This decision was prompted by the formation of an all-white competing union clearly sponsored by the ultra-right (which never actually managed to get it off the ground), and by legislation compelling racial separation of the branches and executive structures of mixed unions. The threat of legislation which would have prevented mixed unions from utilizing check-off facilities for the collection of union dues seems further to have hastened NUDW's division.

Within TUCSA by this time, ritualistic tokens of opposition merely served as the backdrop to the far more important debate over whether or not to admit unions of African workers into TUCSA's ranks. The significance of this controversy lay partly in the clarity with which it revealed the contradictory character of TUCSA's centrist position, and the hypocrisy and opportunism needed to sustain it. But more significantly, the debate was clear evidence of the looming strength of African workers, even in their organizationally darkest period. Still effectively incapable of acting in its own name, the

African working class nevertheless was to preoccupy and ultimately destroy those unions not farseeing enough to realize that the privileges conferred by apartheid could not in the longer run substitute for the support of the African majority.

The debate within TUCSA over the admission (or, depending on the precise timing of the debate, the expulsion) of unregistered African unions was dominated by the most narrowly pragmatic considerations in combination with a deep-seated paternalism. In all likelihood, there were instances in which arguments that rested on questions of principle and ideology were presented in the bland language of pragmatism, the better to win support within TUCSA ranks. The arguments, both pragmatic and paternalistic, did not change much over time. The pragmatists stressed that the growing proportion of African to non-African workers rendered registered unions increasingly unrepresentative and hence vulnerable to undercutting. TUCSA unions had learned how ephemeral, in the face of changing economic and technological conditions, was the protection afforded by craft monopolies. Job reservation, designed to impose a statutory job monopoly, was viewed by TUCSA as too strongly counter to fundamental economic processes to afford much long term relief. Furthermore, the need to maintain international credibility required keeping the issue of African union affiliation alive and demanded at least a token opposition to job reservation.

If pragmatism dictated the necessity to bring African workers into the unions in the first place, then paternalism suggested that those unions which did recruit African workers operate under the tutelage of TUCSA lest they unwittingly fall prey to what the centrists viewed as insidious left-wing political influences searching for a foothold in the union movement. In 1967 TUCSA, in response to publicly expressed ministerial disapproval of the presence of a small number of weak African unions in its ranks, hastily convened a special conference to consider its position. The contribution of the General Secretary of the NUDW to this conference neatly encapsulates the ensemble of factors that appealed to the assembled TUCSA leaders: pragmatism ("we must recognise that the percentage of whites in industry is going to decrease every year"); international pressure ("we have achieved our greatest development . . . during the years that we have had our African unions associated with us. We have enjoyed enormous international prestige because of that fact."); paternalism ("We must lead and guide Africans who have not yet gained trade union experience . . ."). All this was adduced to counter a peculiarly South Africa blend of racism, fear of government, fear of right wing whites, and, above all, fear of the African majority (*Document 78*).

The reaction to both the pragmatic and paternalistic arguments serves as a reminder of the perils of life at a sanitized center in polarized South Africa. Whatever the merits of the pragmatic argument, white workers had, on the face of it, been well served by racial exclusiveness and were not eager to exchange this for an uncertain shared future, even one where the conditions of inclusion were as tightly drawn as those suggested by the TUCSA paternalists. The relative numbers of African workers portended too strongly the possibility that they would come to dominate the unions.

The South African government for its part viewed this pragmatism as the thin end of an integrationist wedge. Its views on African unions were plain: they were to "bleed to death," and the state was not prepared to countenance the possibility of a tourniquet being applied from within the ranks of the union establishment. Whenever the pragmatists won the day and succeeded in opening up TUCSA to African workers, the government would rattle its saber and several offended or intimidated TUCSA affiliates would resign or threaten resignation. Inevitably, the combination of highly elastic principles and powerful pragmatism would suggest reverting to the status quo, and African workers and their unions would then be expelled.

This fickle stance was not designed to win over the African working class, and neither was the highly attenuated character of the partnership offered by TUCSA. A baffling array of segregated subordinate ("parallel") unions, liaison committees, and other special structures were offered and withdrawn at regular intervals during the 1960s and 1970s. Meanwhile, the TUCSA bureaucracy drew up elaborate plans and prepared tortuous rationalizations designed to maintain itself at the center. Consequently, at no point was simple equality of status offered to African workers or their unions. It is little wonder then that these efforts on the part of TUCSA satisfied nobody: they offered nothing to the few African workers who participated in the TUCSA structures; they won no political credibility for TUCSA and, indeed, probably damaged it because of its offensive displays of paternalism; and they certainly did not succeed in incorporating African workers into subordinated pseudo-union structures. Nor did TUCSA ever come close to adopting a position that would have provided the basis of a closer relationship with unions affiliated to SACTU. For if TUCSA viewed the state and the right-wing unions as ideological opponents of its pragmatism, SACTU was so viewed in far greater measure.

But the anti-apartheid flame continued to flicker dimly among organized workers, particularly within the unions formerly affiliated to the now moribund SACTU. With the effective demise of SACTU by 1964 and the weakening of its major affiliates like the Food and Canning Workers' Union, the ineffectual and schizophrenic TUCSA represented the near totality of anti-apartheid opposition in the union movement. Some unions within TUCSA continued to demand a less vacillating stance from this body. The history of the pre-1973 period mirrors the 1950s in one sense: it is a tale of resisting police harassment, opposing blatant discrimination, and striving for unity in circumstances where historical conditions were anything but propitious. But in another sense the period stands in marked contrast to the 1950s. For while in the earlier period union organization had been an important part of heightened social conflict and organization, by the late 1960s the unions stood virtually alone in their exposure to the National Party juggernaut.

New Initiatives

The independent trade union movement was far weaker at the beginning of the 1970s than it had been a decade earlier, but there were glimmers of hope. Firstly, against all odds, some African unions had survived the onslaught of the 1960s and there were new organizations warily raising their heads above the parapets. Secondly, African workers themselves were demonstrating their dissatisfaction and resilience in sporadic outbursts of strike action. Thirdly, the debate in TUCSA continued. It was never to transform TUCSA into a democratic and nonracial trade union body, but it did persuade a small number of people in that organization that the future of the trade union movement belonged to African workers. This perception was to make a small, but vital, contribution to the momentous events on the union horizon. The combination of independent worker organization—islands of persistent opposition within the mainstream center of the union movement—and spontaneous worker action, was to come together in the 1970s and flower into a workers' movement of unprecedented vitality and strength. Its modest beginnings in the late 1960s and early 1970s warrant a fuller account.

The surviving affiliates of a now moribund and exiled SACTU were few by the end of the 1960s. Of the larger SACTU unions, only the Food and Canning Workers' Union and the nominally separate African Food and Canning Workers' Union made any real attempt to honor their oppositional past. Other important SACTU unions, notably the National Union of Clothing Workers headed by Lucy Mvubelo, and the Textile Workers Industrial Union, had long since disaffiliated from SACTU and become firmly ensconced in TUCSA.

Despite their desperate weakness, the food unions were still attempting to defend a small membership increasingly reduced to the Western Cape. They continued to pass conference resolutions commenting on the politics of the day, and constantly invoked the memories of past years, if not for their victories, then at least for the dignity and tenacity of the resistance that had characterized their history. The mere survival of a union like the Food and Canning Workers, in however reduced a form, constituted an important link with a radical past, as evidenced in *Document 77,* a report to the union's twentieth annual conference in 1967.

By the late 1960s the senior leadership of SACTU was almost all in exile, underground, or in prison, attempting against overwhelming odds to organize clandestine networks of communication among unionists and underground members of the ANC and the Communist party.[7] SACTU's radical tradition had left its mark on a leadership cadre that began to resurface in new organizations. If the union movement had been compelled to rely exclusively on these former SACTU affiliates, however, it would not have survived. At a crucial stage these remnants were bolstered by the emergence of other worker-centered organizations. The origins of these new organizations were diverse—the black consciousness movement, radical students on the white campuses, former SACTU organizers, and TUCSA dissidents—and for the most part entirely independent of, and often ignorant of, each other's activities.

The black consciousness movement, the leading element in the political resurgence of the early 1970s, was one of the new sources of energy feeding the revival of union organization. In July 1972 the third annual conference of the South African Students' Organisation resolved to start a Black Workers' Project with the avowed objective of establishing a national trade union council for blacks. (*Document 49*). While signaling a heightened awareness of the potential power of workers, this initiative by SASO ultimately bore little fruit. In the meantime, however, Drake Koka, the secretary of a newly founded union, the Sales and Allied Workers' Association, had become involved in founding the Black People's Convention, and under its auspices, converted his new organization into the Black Allied Workers Union (BAWU), a general union open to all black workers. The leadership of BAWU, and the black consciousness movement generally, observed TUCSA's twisting and turning around the question of admitting African workers, and took a very disparaging view of TUCSA's record (*Document 80*). At the same time, the black consciousness leanings of the BAWU leadership served to distance it from the SACTU tradition, which welcomed white involvement and even white leadership in unions comprised of blacks. Thus BAWU was isolated from all the older wings of the union movement, and had little means of drawing on their experience. Over the course of the 1970s it succeeded in establishing only a minor presence among workers, but through a number of splits and divisions in the late 1970s, it did give rise to the South African Allied Workers' Union (SAAWU) and the General and Allied Workers' Union (GAWU), both of which made a brief though significant impact on the union movement in the early 1980s.

The white student movement also threw its energies and resources into black worker organization. Isolated from the mainstream of resistance politics by the black consciousness orientation of the dominant black student and emerging community groupings, and inspired by the New Left student movements in Europe and America, radical students in the National Union of South African Students (NUSAS) turned their attention to trade unionism. White student involvement in black working-class issues was structured by the decision of the 1971 Congress of NUSAS to form Wages Commissions on each of its affiliated campuses. By 1972, under the energetic leadership of Jeanette Curtis, active groups existed on campuses in Cape Town, Durban, Pietermaritzburg, Grahamstown and Johannesburg.

The focus of the NUSAS Wages Commissions was intensely practical in nature. *Document 79,* a June 1973 report by the Wages Commission at the University of Cape Town, refers to many of their activities. The commissions concentrated on research into and exposures of wages and working conditions. Students made appearances before the government and employer dominated wage boards to argue for wage increases, and used student presses to print simple newspapers and pamphlets addressed to black workers. The Wages Commissions also established advice offices to provide legal assistance, where among other things they were able to focus on the legal right of African workers to form works committees, consultative structures designed as a substitute for unions. Although discredited as alternatives to union organization, works committees offered a halfway house to unorganized workers trying to draw themselves into closer forms of cooperation. Particularly when linked to centers which could provide continuing advice about legal rights, and which could provide contact with other committees offering what was often paternalistically referred to as "workers' education," these works committees expressed the commitment to take organization beyond the realm of mere advice and thus presaged the re-emergence of full-fledged trade unionism.

An important characteristic of these student initiatives of the early 1970s, and a significant aspect of their pragmatic character, was the wide range of political actors who were engaged in the task of effectively reestablishing trade union organization. Mention is made in *Document 79* of a good working relationship with the (Coloured) Labour Party, for example. In Durban, where a handful of white students from the University of Natal were active in union work, relations with the KwaZulu authorities were taken seriously, and KwaZulu's Chief Minister, Gatsha Buthelezi, was invited to lend his support by becoming the first president of the Institute for Industrial Education, a research and training organization established in 1973 which in time was to contribute to the resurgence of trade union activity.

However, the most enduring and significant relationships for purposes of union organization were those forged between TUCSA dissidents, white student activists, and former SACTU organizers, including Elijah Loza and Harold Nxasana. The contribution of SACTU activists is difficult to track because workers with past links to the political left tended to keep a low profile, but the responsiveness of former SACTU officials in each region to the re-emergence of union organization was undeniable. Significantly, their experience of SACTU's rise and fall frequently ensured a cautious approach to union organization and a respect for the pragmatic focus of the Wages Commission activists.

The TUCSA link is easier to identify. The issue of TUCSA's ambiguous relationship with African workers refused to die down. Following publicly expressed ministerial disapproval of TUCSA's 1962 Congress decision to admit "properly constituted African unions" to their ranks, a special congress of TUCSA held in December 1967 reversed the decision and expelled those of their affiliated African unions who had not been sufficiently cooperative to tender their resignations ahead of the special congress decision. This decision was overturned by the next ordinary congress held in April 1968 which voted in favor of TUCSA accepting affiliation from unions with African members. Following the decision of the 1968 Congress, 12 unions disaffiliated from TUCSA and given the new political balance in the federation, the 1969 Congress again voted to expel those affiliates with

African members. On this occasion the decision to refuse admission to African unions was entrenched in the constitution for a minimum two year period, subject to amendment by an 80 percent majority of the organization's members.

TUCSA's extraordinary vacillation exposed many of its least appealing attributes of opportunism, expediency, and racism. Yet this vacillation and the constant internal pressure to open the organization to African workers also revealed the existence of a small core of TUCSA officials and members who were deeply dissatisfied with the majority position in the organization and who were, often for diverse reasons, committed to the unionization of African workers.

Certain of these dissidents left TUCSA in order to promote the organization of Africans. Hence the director of TUCSA's African Affairs Bureau, Eric Tyacke, resigned from TUCSA after the unions for which his department had been responsible were expelled, and in 1971 helped establish the Urban Training Project (UTP), a Johannesburg-based workers' education and advice group. UTP became the forerunner and later educational arm of the Consultative Committee of Black Trade Unions, the precursor of the Council of Unions of South Africa (CUSA) formed in 1979. Many of the unions associated with the UTP had, like Tyacke himself, a past history with TUCSA, a background that helps explain their somewhat traditional and apolitical orientation toward trade union work—an approach reminiscent of TUCSA—combined with a powerful opposition to white leadership. Other TUCSA dissidents, especially those who held leadership positions in TUCSA affiliates or branches of affiliates, simply used their positions to carry on encouraging and facilitating the organization of African workers. These were chiefly based in Natal, a particularly strong site of labor related student activism and a relatively powerful SACTU tradition. Similarly, some TUCSA unionists in the Transvaal and Western Cape also supported, in varying degrees, the organization of Africans.

The combination of TUCSA dissidents, former SACTU organizers, and the local Wages Commission was extremely uneven, with the strength and commitment of each grouping varying from city to city. In addition, the interface with local and regional characteristics produced distinctive outcomes in each major center. The result was a kaleidoscopic array of organizations and policies. In Durban the General Factory Workers Benefit Fund was established in 1972 and was the initial form taken by black worker organization in that city. The Benefit Fund was quickly overtaken by the establishment of small unregistered unions which wasted little time in establishing in 1973 an umbrella body, the Trade Union Advisory and Co-ordinating Council (TUACC). The unions initially grouped in TUACC were the National Union of Textile Workers, the Chemical Workers' Industrial Union, the Metal and Allied Workers' Union, and, slightly later, the Transport and General Workers' Union. Several of these were initiated with the support of TUCSA affiliates, indeed, for a time, were formally "parallel unions," while others, like the Metal and Allied Workers' Union, were wholly independent from their inception.

In the Transvaal, the Urban Training Project serviced a group of unions several of which were former affiliates of TUCSA. In 1973 these unions also established a loose umbrella structure, the Consultative Committee of Black Trade Unions. In addition, the Natal based TUACC unions spread their influence to the Transvaal where an advice body, the Industrial Aid Society, assisted in forming small unions with yet another umbrella structure established to coordinate their activities, the Council of Industrial Workers of the Witwatersrand. The unions grouped in the latter structure were effectively the Transvaal branches of the Natal unions grouped in TUACC, representing an early attempt by this new breed of unions to organize nationally.

In the Western Cape, where the token support of some TUCSA unionists was outweighed by the implacable hostility of other more powerful affiliates—the (Coloured) Western Province Garment Workers' Union, for example—the local NUSAS Wages Commission, working together with ex-SACTU officials, in 1973 established a legal aid service (the Western Province Workers' Advice Bureau) and an educational arm, and assisted workers in the formation of works committees. *Document 81,* a memorandum from TUACC to TUCSA's national conference in September 1975, gives evidence of the frustrations and complexities of union development in this fluid period.

In Port Elizabeth, an important site of militant unionism in the 1980s, there was little organization of African workers before 1973, despite a substantial history of SACTU activity in the late 1950s. However, in 1967 a union for Coloured workers was formed in the automobile assembly industry, the city's major employer. This union, which was initially affiliated to TUCSA, later disaffiliated in 1976, largely in opposition to TUCSA's position with respect to African workers, and eventually drew close to the TUACC unions of Natal and the Transvaal.

These organizational stirrings were paralleled by important instances of industrial action. The most significant of these took place in South West Africa, still firmly colonized by South Africa, when in October 1971 some 13,000 Ovambo workers struck against low wages and poor working conditions. There were also some significant labor stoppages in major South African cities about this time. The Durban and Cape Town dockers took the lead in the country's two largest coastal cities, striking in 1971; and in Johannesburg, South Africa's industrial heartland, African bus drivers embarked on strike action in 1972 that was significant both because of its scale, but also because the actions of the drivers found organizational expression in the formation of the Transport and Allied Workers' Union, a union within the UTP fold.

There is no evidence that these actions were inspired, much less organized, by the fledgling unions and advice offices that were emerging in this period. Certainly the rudimentary support that these organizations were on occasion able to provide was valuable, and ranged from free legal advice to rides home after late night strategy meetings. More likely, it was the essentially spontaneous worker actions, inspired largely by economic hardship, that acted as a spur to organization rather than the oft-claimed converse. This pattern was confirmed by the momentous events looming on the horizon.

The Durban Strikes and Their Repercussions

Although the early 1970s saw a marked increase in the number of labor stoppages, nothing could have prepared the country for the massive escalation of strike action in 1973. On January 9, two thousand workers at Coronation Brick and Tile, a plant located in Durban, came out on strike in support of a demand for higher wages. Coronation Brick employed migrant workers with roots in rural Zululand. Some months previously their hostels had been visited by Goodwill Zwelithini, the Zulu king, who had apparently conveyed an undertaking by management to increase wages in the new year. When these promised increases were not forthcoming, the workers struck, and thus fired the first shot in what was to become a rolling strike wave that rapidly engulfed Durban and several other centers in Natal.

There were several remarkable features of the Durban strikes.[8] Firstly, the sheer magnitude of the strike action was noteworthy. In the period between the Coronation Brick strike in early January and the end of March, 146 establishments in the Durban area experienced strike action. These strikes involved 61,410 workers.[9] The strikes centered around, but were by no means confined to, the complex of large textile factories belonging to the British-owned Frame group of companies (*Document 86*). With the exception of the white miners strike of 1922 and the relatively short-lived action by 70,000 black miners in 1946, South Africa had never witnessed strike action on this scale. The number of different plants involved in the strike wave was unprecedented, as was the duration of some of the actions.

Secondly, the lack of visible leadership was remarkable. A strike involving over 60,000 workers at 146 plants would seem to demand active and visible coordination, and yet it proved impossible to identify the leadership. The reason was that the strikers were led from the factory floor, where grievances spontaneously ignited collective action. Despite later claims to the contrary, the Durban strikes were not the responsibility of underground political organizations, nor of the fledgling unions and advice offices. Persistent experience of employers and police singling out "agitators" or alleged ringleaders led to a refusal on the part of the workers to identify their leaders. The Institute for Industrial Education's account of the strikes vividly describes employer after employer pleading with thousands of striking workers to nominate representatives to conduct negotiations, only to be met with resounding refusals.[10] But possibly the most unusual feature of the Durban strikes was the relatively mild reaction from the authorities and the generally sympathetic response of the white public.[11] In most instances the striking workers won wage increases. A survey of whites in the Durban area indicated a remarkable degree of sympathy with the striking workers, who were generally perceived as underpaid; and the English language press was generally supportive of the strikers. In the public mind, the Frame group and in particular its hard-bitten founder and then chairman, Philip Frame, was widely held responsible for the strikes.

Most important, the state was uncharacteristically circumspect in its response. The police were unusually restrained, making few arrests and generally indicating that they did not wish to take a direct hand in what were perceived to be matters for resolution between the strikers and their employers. Even hard-line Prime Minister John Vorster, a former Minister of Police, was moved to acknowledge in parliament that "the events there contain a lesson for us all. . . . Employers, whoever they may be, should not only see in their workers a unit producing for them so many hours of service a day. They should also see them as human beings with souls."[12] In contrast, the Minister of Labor reaffirmed government policy and contented himself with swiping at "agitators" and citing the customary list of dark forces said to be threatening South Africa's "traditional way of life."[13]

These vigorous assertions notwithstanding, the Department of Labor took action that implicitly acknowledged that the strikers had legitimate grievances. The Minister of Labor ordered the Wage Board, a national statutory body that determined wages for many African workers, to launch an investigation into certain of the industries and work categories most strongly implicated in the strike wave. There had been persistent criticism from the press, opposition parliamentarians, and even some business people, of the long periods between investigations by the Wage Board, and of the length of time that it took to make its determinations.

In addition, the Department initiated new industrial relations legislation. The legislation fell far short of granting African workers the right to form and join registered unions, a reform that could have been accomplished by simply changing the definition of "employee" in the Industrial Conciliation Act. Instead the state opted in 1973, by way of an amendment to the Bantu Labour (Settlement of Disputes) Act, to establish yet another structure manifestly designed to substitute for full trade union rights. Since its original enactment in 1953, this statute had provided for a system of "works committees," essentially factory-based structures which were elected by the African workers and had limited rights of consultation with employers. Works committee members enjoyed formal protection from victimization, although because of the extreme difficulties of proving victimization and as a result of the onerous procedures of the Act, this protection was highly circumscribed.

The amended legislation introduced a new representative structure, the "liaison committee." This committee, comprising an equal number of employer and employee representatives, was, like the works committee, only accorded rights of consultation (not negotiation) and was generally perceived by workers as an even weaker structure of representation than the works committee. The result was that African workers were still not given the right to bargain or to organize collectively across units larger than the single factory or enterprise. The new legislation did, however, extend a right to strike, in practice so tightly circumscribed as to render legal strikes unrealistic.[14] Overall, the prospects for black union organization looked somewhat more favorable than they had for many years. Once again, international attention had been drawn to South Africa, in particular to the plight of workers under apartheid. Although the importance of this development was not immediately apparent, it was to have a major impact before long. Moreover, employers in both foreign and domestically owned companies were clearly unnerved by the Durban experience and manifested this in the granting of wage increases in the wake of the strikes, even in companies which had not experienced labor stoppages. The giant Anglo American Corporation, awash with profits from soaring gold prices, increased the wages of African mineworkers by 26 percent, a decision that in part seemed designed to preempt an extension of worker militancy to the mines.[15] Given the value placed by business on stability and predictability, influential employers began to question the long-term consequences of maintaining an industrial relations framework that effectively rested on the repression of union rights for African workers. The absence of an identifiable leadership with which to deal during the strikes had pressed this point home.

Above all, though, the strikes represented a revival after the dark years of the 1960s, a reawakening which imbued workers with a palpable new sense of confidence. The Institute for Industrial Education survey of workers involved in the strikes concluded:

> The workers struck because of low wages and the feeling that the employer would not do anything to remedy the wage levels unless drastic action was taken. They feel that the strikes were productive, but they remain very dissatisfied. Having discovered that the strike is an effective weapon, the majority are fully prepared to use it again. It may well be, therefore, that the most significant change wrought by the strikes is not in the workers' living standards, but in their sense of their own potential power.[16]

Unions Take the Offensive

This awakened sense of power was of particular significance when placed in the context of the re-emergence of worker organization. It is here that the rather motley collection of unions, advice offices, and workers' education projects took on an added importance. Prior to the Durban strikes these organizations represented little more than an idea; in their absence, however, the strikes may have only represented another brave but essentially limited chapter in the history of resistance to apartheid. In combination they constituted the first step along the road to the building of a trade union movement that was to play a pivotal role in the downfall of apartheid and much of what it represented in the sphere of labor relations. But in 1973 there was still a long road to travel. If the immediate prognosis seemed tentatively favorable, then the stern requirements of the medium term would demonstrate how important was this new "sense of their own potential power," as well as the fledgling organization and the international support all generated by the Durban strikes.

Once the strikes had subsided, it did not take long for all the familiar problems associated with union organization in South Africa to reassert themselves. In September 1973, police shot dead 11 black miners during a wage dispute at Western Deep Levels mine in Carletonville west of Johannesburg. The return to apparent normality elsewhere offered cover for routinely severe security operations to resume. In February 1974, four activists heavily involved in the Durban unions—Halton Cheadle, David Davis, David Hemson, and Jeanette Cunningham Brown—were banned. Leading African unionists including June-Rose Nala, Harold Nxasana and Obed Zuma were arrested and held under various security laws for lengthy periods. Some were severely tortured.

Police harassment was not confined to union offices or leaders. The police, apparently determined to prevent a repetition of the strikes, resumed a prominent role in industrial disputes. The Minister of Labour acknowledged on the floor of parliament that between January 1973 and June 1974, police intervened in 93 disputes, 44 stoppages, and 374 strikes. 905 workers were arrested in these interventions, of whom 646 were prosecuted.[17] While the distinction between "disputes," "stoppages" and "strikes" is not immediately apparent, the aggregate figures—almost certain to be understated—amount to a significant degree of police involvement in industrial relations matters. Where the police were formally constrained by the legal niceties and particular sensitivities that attached to industrial relations issues, they had at their disposal a legislative armory that allowed for the legal transformation of any act of opposition into a matter of state security. The Riotous Assemblies Act was frequently deployed against strikers, while security legislation in general was tightened up to accommodate the growing threat from the factory floor.

A 1976 dispute with members of the Metal and Allied Workers' Union at the Heinemann plant on the East Rand, described in *Document 82,* was one of the more prominent instances of labor action in the post-1973 period, and one which elicited a characteristically harsh reaction from the police. The Heinemann dispute also demonstrated another feature of post-1973 labor relations, namely intense employer reluctance to accept the re-emergence of African trade union organization. South African employers had consistently supported a limited extension of trade union rights to African workers in periods of intense shop floor activity, only to retreat to more familiar terrain as soon as the perceived threat receded. This was no less true of the 1970s than of the 1940s and 1950s. Hence, while prepared to make concessions in the teeth of the 1973 strikes, employers lost their enthusiasm for a reformist approach once police action had demonstrated the state's determination and ability to curtail the rebirth of the unions. This pattern was evident in the case of large companies as well as smaller, less sophisticated employers. Heinemann, for example, which was the site of a vicious battle for union recognition and where collaboration between management and the police was clearly evident, was a subsidiary of the Barlow Rand Group, South Africa's largest manufacturing conglomerate.

Yet there remained an important core of employers who recognized that independent union organization had been placed permanently on the agenda in South Africa, and who were accordingly beginning to canvass a less repressive approach to the emerging African unions. To the extent that it is possible to associate this view with any group of employers, it was probably most strongly represented among the multinational corporations with South Africa subsidiaries. There were a number of reasons for this. Multinationals tended to operate in industries that were most difficult to run in the absence of acceptable channels of employer/employee communication. Auto companies, for example, with their large-scale assembly line method of production, were particularly vulnerable to easy disruption. Multinationals also tended to have wider international experience in dealing with unions and were more sophisticated in their response to union pressures. How much weight to give to any one of these factors is not clear, however. The most important factor underlying the relatively greater willingness of certain of the large multinationals to accept the rise of the union movement was probably international pressure and the specific form that this began to take.

The general decline in anti-apartheid resistance in the late 1960s occurred on both the domestic and international fronts. International anti-apartheid work was essentially supportive of internal resistance, inevitably drawing its inspiration (or lack thereof) from the ebb and flow of struggle inside the country. The low level of articulated international interest in the plight of apartheid's victims in the late 1960s was accompanied by international capital's growing interest in South Africa's booming economy and the substantial returns that its sophisticated and highly protected domestic market offered to foreign investors. Furthermore, the expanding economies of the advanced industrial world ensured a ready market for South Africa's mineral resources. All in all, once the post-Sharpeville fallout had abated, economic relations in the form of both trade and investment opportunities in South Africa were highly lucrative, and constituted the substratum of relations between South Africa and the rest of the world.

After the Durban strikes this began to shift, with signs of renewed foreign concern centering on trade and investment, even before the Soweto uprising brought apartheid under fierce international scrutiny. Two developments illustrate well the new effectiveness of this international pressure. One was a series of articles by journalist Adam Raphael in *The Guardian,* the British daily, in March and April 1973 exposing the shockingly low wages paid to black workers by the South African subsidiaries of British companies. A second development was action by American dockworkers in Mobile, Alabama, who with support from the United Mineworkers Union of America refused in August 1974 to off-load South African coal. They argued that the coal contravened federal legislation regarding the importation of commodities produced by slave labor, and cited the South African Masters and Servants Acts as the legal basis of their claim. The Acts were hastily repealed.[18]

International pressure increasingly centered on calls for trade sanctions and disinvestment, or at least embodied the notion that the activities of foreign investors should be monitored to ensure that foreign companies were exemplary with respect to social responsibility as well as the wages and working condition of their black employees. Pressures also increased for employers to establish formal relations with the unions to which their workers belonged. These principles were eventually enshrined in two codes of conduct, the Code of the European Economic Community formulated in 1977, and the Sullivan Code, promoted as a standard for American multinationals starting in 1978.

This growing international attention was partly the cause and partly the effect of the increasingly important role played by the international union movement. European and North American unions, many quite conservative politically, might have balked at involvement in campaigns to alleviate political repression in other countries but viewed their contribution to anti-apartheid campaigns as an act of solidarity with fellow unionists. Disapproval of apartheid was becoming increasingly associated with the struggles of South African workers for recognition, an association which could only intensify the pressures for change.

The keen engagement of the black unions in bread-and-butter issues and the unions' apparently apolitical character made it easier for the international union movement to lend them support. SACTU had always experienced problems in its relations with European and North American unions, particularly with the cold war-oriented International Confederation of Free Trade Unions (ICFTU), to which most of the major western bloc unions belonged. SACTU was informally affiliated to the World Federation of Trade Unions (WFTU), the ICFTU's pro-communist rival in the international trade union world, and this plus its clear ties to the underground South African Communist Party made it unacceptable to the union establishment in the west.[19] When SACTU's political alliances were combined with an assertion that it had ignored bread-and-butter factory floor issues, or at least relegated them to a lower order of priority than political advocacy, its status as a bona fide union federation had been called into question.

This lesson had not been lost on those working to resuscitate African trade unionism in the early 1970s. While the unions of the early 1970s were certainly not apolitical, there were important distinctions between their political style and that of their predecessors in SACTU. For a variety of reasons, the unions of the 1970s maintained a far lower political profile than had been the case in the previous incarnation of union organization. Moreover, the black consciousness movement, which had emerged as the national political pacesetter in the early 1970s, was principally oriented toward black students and youth and, the Black Allied Workers' Union notwithstanding, failed to build any organizational base among black workers. The unions were thus operating in something of a political vacuum, and never felt called upon to demonstrate any clear political affiliation.

Above all, the unions' low political profile was dictated by a combination of prudence and strong desire for political autonomy, both of which were underlined by the SACTU experience. SACTU had been criticized from both the right and the left for its willingness to subordinate worker interests and requirements to those of the political movements with which it was associated. This, it was argued, led SACTU into imprudent and ill-prepared political campaigns that brought the full force of the state down upon its relatively undefended head. The leaders of the new crop of unions—some of whom were themselves former SACTU activists—were determined not to commit the same errors. Some leaders adhered strongly to the principle of independent working-class organization, viewing the subordination of a workers' organization to a multiclass political front as politically unacceptable. Others who did not oppose the association of unions with political groupings in principle, opposed them on pragmatic grounds, given the time needed to build up union strength in an environment of hostility from the state.

The unions of the immediate post-1973 period were extremely fragile and undefended. Although the membership of various worker-oriented organizations, particularly those based in Natal, increased rapidly in the immediate aftermath of the Durban strikes, it soon fell off again, leaving weak structures and an inexperienced leadership to cope with the rigors of union organization. Fledgling unions faced powerful state opposition as well as employers who had enjoyed a decade of unprecedented economic growth during which they had basked in the support of the international investor community. Although the authority of the state and employers had been disturbed by the events of 1973, their subsequent behavior demonstrated an intention to reassert traditional hard-line approaches to union organization. The mere existence of union organization was perceived as a threat. Union leaders facing these challenges put their organizations at risk if they took on an overt political orientation.

Caution called not only for a low political profile but also had an important effect on the organizational character of the emerging unions. Very close attention was paid to day-to-day factory floor issues and organization. Experience had taught that unions could survive in a hostile climate only by firmly rooting themselves among workers on the factory floor. Doing so would take time, and the sure way to achieve this was through close attention to bread-and-butter issues, such as health and safety standards, unfair dismissals, wages and working conditions.

This pragmatism was evident not only in the choice of issues but also in the manner in which unions entrenched themselves on the factory floor. Despite their deep-seated opposition to the works and liaison committee structures, the statutory bodies designed to substitute for trade unions, the unions did not hesitate to use the minimal legal protection that these committees offered in order to gain a foothold. Inevitably, when these committees were backed up by union organization, the unions would attempt to transform them into structures other than those envisaged by the law. They would take up distinctive issues and often coordinate their demands with those taken up in other organized factories. Above all, union-backed committees came to be distinguished generally by their attention to democratic procedures and the principle of accountability, including elections, mandates, and report backs, which in time became part of the distinctive modus operandi of the independent union movement.

The union world of the mid-1970s was characterized by intense debate over alternate tactics and strategies. The intensity of the debates sometimes even seemed to outstrip the actual weight and significance of the unions themselves, creating proverbial storms in a teacup. When involved in the discussions, some members of the underground ANC and Communist Party expressed concern that legal union organization might be achievable only at the expense of an overt political profile, thus compromising the ability of unions to contribute to the liberation struggle. The unions themselves debated the pros and cons of industrially-based unionism versus general unionism, and what precise approach should be taken to the works and liaison committees. Disagreements over the role of white union leaders also accentuated basic ideological divisions. These and a host of other issues contributed to the vibrant political life of the unions but also underscored the lack of unity in the union movement.

Nevertheless, the emphasis on careful shop floor organization slowly began to pay off. The unions were weak, divided, lacking in resources; their leadership was relatively inexperienced; yet they were beginning to post gains. Employers were beginning to deal with them; organization was beginning to stabilize; international support was strong; and some of the registered unions were clearly dissatisfied with the continued adherence of the established unions to the status quo. Most importantly, the unions were in place to take advantage of the storm that hit the country in the shape of the Soweto student uprising in 1976.

Workers and the Soweto Uprising

The Soweto uprising of 1976 fundamentally altered the political equation in South Africa, changing the context in which trade union development took place and interrelated with the re-emergence of popular political opposition. At least one commentator, Baruch Hirson, has claimed that the roots of the uprising lie in the 1973 strikes and the new assertiveness of working-class militancy and organization that these represented, but there is little evidence to support such a claim.[20] Although workers participated in the stay-aways that were an important feature of 1976, their role and that of unions was essentially a passive one. Contrary to Hirson's view, 1976 exercised a far more powerful impact upon the working class and its unions than did the latter upon the uprising.

The importance of the independent unions in the events of 1976 lies more in the fact of their existence than in any impact on events. When Soweto erupted, union membership was still small—only about 60,000 in 1975—but already surprisingly firmly entrenched.[21] The careful emphasis on building strong shop floor structures, concentration on key companies, notably multinationals, and shrewd manipulation of the scant cover provided by the law had paid off to the extent of securing for the union movement well organized pockets of membership in a range of factories. This consolidation of worker strength was given impetus by the adoption of increasingly complex technologies in manufacturing, forcing employers to rely on a more trained and stable factory workforce. By 1976, the presence of growing pockets of organized workers had begun to generate substantial divisions within employer ranks and between employers and the state over how best to deal with the nascent unions.

The Soweto uprising added fuel to these developments. It greatly spurred the growth of union organization although, as outlined below, it also gave impetus to the diverging tendencies within the movement. It added immeasurable urgency to the debates among employers and the state. Had growing union organization taken place in a political vacuum and during an economic boom, time might have existed for relatively languid reflection. However, in the context of renewed political confrontation and a slowing economy, the unions' mounting strength portended serious problems for the state and employers who urgently required a new strategy to deal with this threat.

The state's response to 1976 embodied a mix of repression and reform. The repressive response was predictably wide-ranging. Black student and community leaders were arrested in the thousands and mass resistance was met with the firepower at Pretoria's disposal. Union organizers were arrested and several died in detention. Others were banned in late 1976. But when eighteen organizations were outlawed in October 1977, the unions, including the black consciousness linked BAWU, were omitted from the list. This was not primarily a reflection of the unions' minor role at the time. Had the new unions not been perceived as threatening, the intense harassment of union leaders in the wake of the uprising would not have occurred. The government's option of banning the black unions outright was forestalled, in part, by the widespread international attention that they had attracted. The decision to intimidate leaders but permit union organization reflected a hesitant new reformism that began to characterize the approaches of the state and employers in the post-Soweto period.

Workers and the Wiehahn Reforms

The tentative reform strategy that emerged in the years following Soweto had powerful implications for the working class. The most significant concessions were not directed at the major grievances that emerged in 1976 or at the principal bearers of those grievances—the education system and the students. Rather, they were directed principally at the working class and were intended above all to insulate the economy from political conflict. The reform strategy had two legs. The first aimed to identify and extend privileges to particular classes and social strata among the black population, including elements of the working class. The Riekert Commission, appointed in August 1977, was in effect charged with designing this leg of the strategy. The second leg was an attempt to depoliticize the organized working class by incorporating it into a relatively privileged relationship with employers by means of the unions. In so doing, the state hoped to distance itself from the day-to-day relations between capital and labor which it believed would become the central preoccupation of black workers.

The blueprint for this reform of industrial relations was sketched out in the report of the Wiehahn Commission. This Commission, appointed in 1977, was charged with examining and recommending necessary changes to the industrial relations system. The underlying reasons for reexamination—and hence for appointing the Commission—were fairly clear. The unions had gained a toehold and were clearly not going to be made irrelevant by the various toothless committees embodied in the reforms that followed the 1973 strikes. Employers too were beginning to grapple with the permanent presence of the independent unions as a new fact of industrial life. Employers had already begun on their own to enter into collective bargaining agreements with them. The first such historic agreement had been signed in July 1974 by Smith and Nephew, a British multinational, and the National Union of Textile Workers, an unregistered union and an increasingly powerful rival of the TUCSA-affiliated Textile Workers Industrial Union.[22]

The state was thus faced with an intolerable situation in which a dual industrial relations framework was developing. One approach (works and liaison committees), being utilized principally by the independent unions, was firmly situated within the ambit of the law but lacked legitimacy in the eyes of workers; the other (de facto collective bargaining), was being pursued by the independent unions in a twilight world where it was neither illegal nor acceptable to those in power. The choice facing the state was either to ban the independent unions, or to bring them under the ambit of legislation that was highly restrictive but could generate a greater degree of consensus among employers, the international community, and black South African workers themselves. The fundamental change necessary to effect the latter approach was merely to broaden the definition of "employee" in the Industrial Conciliation Act to include Africans. This, it was hoped, would effectively deracialize industrial relations, subjecting African workers and their unions to the legislation already in force.

Just as successive white governments in South Africa had bought the political support or quiescence of white workers by offering them a legally privileged status, it was now the belief of optimists in the National Party that black workers could be similarly co-opted by incorporation into the industrial bargaining system. Full union rights, it was anticipated, would enable African workers to gradually negotiate improvements in their economic status, thus giving them a bigger stake in the stability and productivity of the industrial system. In time, their economically advantaged status would give rise to a conservative political outlook based on a desire to secure their position against challenges from the less advantaged. While waiting for the natural working out of this socioeconomic dynamic, the state could rely on its battery of security laws to contain any potential disruption.

Thus in practice the state opted for a two-track strategy of simultaneous reform and repression. Through the police, the courts, the prisons, and the use of banning orders, the Vorster government and the Botha government which replaced it in 1978 pursued the repressive path with undiminished vigor. Simultaneously the Wiehahn Commission, comprised of representatives of the state, employers, TUCSA, and ultra-right wing unions, carried out its two-year investigation of the industrial relations system. When the Commission reported in May 1979, it proposed that African workers be incorporated in the definition of "employee" and be permitted to form and join registered unions. The stated reason for the proposals was the necessity to control the growing union movement and, principally, to insulate the unions from the political world of the townships. An equally important principle underlying the recommendations was the need to insulate the state from industrial relations lest the state become a target of worker activism.

The Commission recommended that the former objective, the separation of factory and township, be achieved by incorporating the unions within the highly bureaucratic official industrial relations mechanism, backed up by specific prohibitions on political activity contained within industrial relations statutes as well as by general security legislation. The latter objective, the insulating of the state from industrial relations conflict, was expressed in the concept of "industrial self-governance," by which the Commission meant that responsibility for reform in the industrial relations field, ranging from desegregation of factory toilets to the removal of job reservation, was now to be worked out through negotiations between employers and the unions.

The state's initial response to these recommendations demonstrated the narrow limits of its reformism, the internal divisions within the ruling party over the wisdom of alternative courses of action, and the frequently ambivalent direction in which its tentative reform program was headed. It demonstrated the fear of many within the National Party leadership of treading the path of incorporation and co-optation, since this required the acceptance of relatively autonomous black organizations. What if they proved impossible to co-opt? Would they not be more difficult to shut out, having utilized the organizational breathing space that a strategy of incorporation presupposed?

Initially the Botha government responded to the Wiehahn recommendations by insisting that trade union rights be extended only to non-migrant workers, a scheme that would have excluded thousands of workers from neighboring states as well as those officially resident in the homelands. Secondly, the state strongly resisted the notion of nonracial unions, insisting that unions be racially defined if they were to be incorporated into the formal industrial relations structures. The prohibition on migrant workers generated such an angry response—even the black unions associated with TUCSA refused to accept this impractical stricture—that it was withdrawn immediately. The right to register nonracial unions, that is unions whose constitution contained no reference to race, was conceded only in 1981.

To Register or Not?

A debate quickly developed in the unions around the state's conditional acceptance of the Wiehahn Commission's recommendation that unions with African workers be permitted to apply for registration in terms of the industrial relations statutes.[23] Registration conferred certain legal rights; and, in the eyes of employers, it conferred a certain respectability on the unions in question. Ironically, it also imposed on them obligations to which unregistered unions were not subject, for example, it required financial accounting and membership reporting procedures.

Although unions were divided over whether or not to apply for registration, the debate did not center on issues of principle, but rather on tactical organizational questions. Both sides in the debate agreed that the offer of registration to African workers constituted a substantial victory after decades of union struggle. A consistent plank of union demands had been for a change in the definition of "employee" and at no stage did any of the major participants in the registration debate, including those that opposed registering, call for a boycott of the "system." On the other hand, none of the participants in the debate, including those who opted to apply for registration, declared themselves satisfied with the industrial relations system to which their members had now been given access. Those who opted for registration did so in the belief that entering the system would provide cover which could be used to the advantage of the unions; those who refused to apply for registration argued that the direct and indirect controls that characterized the industrial relations system would jeopardize the internal democracy that had become a valuable weapon for strengthening unions trying to organize in a hostile environment.

Principally the debate was conducted between the recently formed Federation of South African Trade Unions (FOSATU, described below), which decided to register, and, on the other hand, the General Workers Union and the Food and Canning Workers' Union, which decided not to. The lineage of the General Workers Union was similar to that of the FOSATU unions, but the character of the union differed from the characteristic FOSATU affiliate insofar as the GWU was structured as a general, rather than an industrial, union. (General unions bring together workers from more than one industry; industrial unions organize workers within a single type of industry.) Its activities were confined to one region, the Western Cape. The Food and Canning Workers' Union by the late 1970s was in the process of a marked organizational revival. It had been the strongest of the SACTU affiliates; and although its fortunes had declined somewhat, it had never, even in the period of retreat following SACTU's demise, entirely forsworn its militant foundations.

The underlying subtleties of the registration debate were later somewhat obscured by the increasing presence of unions that were established in the aftermath of 1976, including the South African Allied Workers' Union (SAAWU), the Motor Assemblers and Component Workers' Union (MACWUSA), and the General and Allied Workers' Union (GAWU), which shot to prominence in the early 1980s. These unions, established in the heady post-Soweto environment, were closely linked to community organizations, imbued with the politics of the time. In the registration debate, these politics translated into a strong "boycottist" position. That is, registration was opposed not because of tactical considerations but because of the ideological legitimacy that registration would confer upon the apartheid state.

Workers and Politics at the Grassroots

The "new labor dispensation" was one of the key reformist catch phrases of the late 1970s. The labor reforms obviously addressed themselves directly to the black working class. There was an overtly political content to the reforms insofar as they were designed to institutionalize the functioning of the unions and, more generally, to depoliticize—by desegregating or deracializing—the workplace. The more farsighted employers recognized a danger implicit in this process: institutionalizing and recognizing worker power on the factory floor in the specific absence of comparable measures elsewhere in civil society might have the effect of further politicizing rather than depoliticizing industrial relations. These fears were well founded. Although the changes in the industrial relations arena were significant, they were matched by important and less widely heralded developments in the townships.

The most distinctive political development in the years immediately after Soweto was the resurgence of open resistance to apartheid at the grassroots level. During 1977 the state unleashed its repressive might to restore "law and order," resulting in the killing in detention of Steve Biko and the banning in October of 18 organizations, mostly the leading black consciousness groupings. Yet no sooner had these organizations been outlawed than others appeared to take their place. The late 1970s were not marked by the formation of national political organizations—though AZAPO was formed in this period—nor by dramatic national confrontations. Rather, township politics in this period, drawing in part on the union model of elected worker representatives—shop stewards—was characterized by the mushrooming of localized grassroots community organization, persistently underpinned by ubiquitous youth organization, and the initiation of myriad local campaigns. It was likewise marked by a steady increase in union membership.

Local organizations varied throughout the country. In some areas they hardly existed. Elsewhere they thrived because they were deeply rooted but varied because of local conditions and idiosyncrasies. Nevertheless, some general observations can be made. Firstly, the escalation in both union membership and community organization were responses to the pressing economic conditions affecting all Africans at the time. That many of the community organizations and their major campaigns were forged around transport fare increases, rent hikes and the like was not evidence of activists in search of issues, but was rather a measure of the precarious economic circumstances of most township dwellers. This meant that they were also issues of primary concern to union members. It was therefore to be expected that the concerns and campaigns of the unions and community organizations would coincide at an early stage.

The growth of community organizations also reflected the attempt by students, unionists and other political activists to address the most serious shortcoming of the 1976 uprising, namely the failure to extend the uprising beyond the ranks of the students and to incorporate workers into the emerging new politics. The coexistence of factory and community organizations also created conditions that mutually facilitated the activities and interaction of each form of organization. It was far easier to recruit union members living in a township dominated by lively community organization than it was to organize, as the experience of the 1973-76 period showed, in an environment devoid of grassroots community activity. Similarly it was easier for community organizers to appeal to the organizational experience of seasoned union members than it was to organize afresh among workers untouched by factory organization. There were certainly instances, particularly in the Western and Eastern Cape, where unions and community organizations directly assisted each other, though, for the most part, the process of organizational cooperation was more indirect with one mode of organization creating a favorable climate for the activities of the other. Leadership skills developed in one context could also often be utilized in the other.

The relationship between unions and community organizations became a major political issue in the early 1980s when township organization began to mushroom. In the late 1970s, however, several highly successful instances of cooperation between the unions and community organizations had already occurred. The outstanding early examples were a 1979 pasta boycott called by the Food and Canning Workers' Union, referred to in *Document 83,* and a red meat boycott called in 1980 by the General Workers Union. These boycotts grew out of the refusal of employers to recognize African unions, and both generated considerable support in black communities. There were also other less successful instances of cooperation.

The process of union and community organization interaction was not always a smooth one. Memories of events in 1976 sometimes undermined more than facilitated cooperation between workers, particularly migrant workers, and community organizations. In both Cape Town and Soweto, the 1976 uprising involved major clashes between migrant workers and township residents. Although the press uncovered evidence that the police had a hand in these conflicts, they were rooted in antagonisms between impatient township youth with their distinctive urban culture and the more traditional rural migrants. Community and union activists made efforts to temper these antagonisms from 1976 onward, with some limited success.

Nevertheless, continuing tensions highlighted a problem that has dogged community organizations to the present, namely the tendency of these organizations to focus on permanent township residents often to the exclusion of the migrants living in the hostel complexes and those in the squatter camps. One effect of this was to exclude a large portion of the working class from township political organization and to increase some of the difficulties in forging links between the unions and community organizations.

The differing ideological and organizational emphases of the unions and community bodies became sharply evident in the conflict in Port Elizabeth in 1979 over the Ford Motor Company's dismissal of a community leader, Thozamile Botha. The conflict presaged heated debates that were to feature prominently in the union and community politics of the 1980s. Botha, who was not a union member, was employed as a draughtsman at Ford. He was dismissed because he was said to be spending an excessive amount of working time on community affairs. Botha and the Port Elizabeth Black Civic Organization (PEBCO) which he led saw the dismissal as victimization of a black political leader and appealed to the Ford workers for support. The union, the National Automobile and Allied Workers' Union (NAAWU), a relatively powerful affiliate of FOSATU, attempted to distance itself from the conflict, partly on the grounds that PEBCO was a middle-class organization and its problems were not a union matter. A large number of workers nonetheless struck in support of Botha and PEBCO, and opposed the union's unwillingness to engage in community affairs. *Document 84,* a summary of ongoing grievances during and after the strike, suggests that worker dissatisfaction extended far beyond the dismissal issue. The strike ultimately led to the formation of a splinter union, the Motor Assemblers and Component Workers' Unions of South Africa.[24] MACWUSA proclaimed that, in contrast with its established progenitor, it saw a legitimate role for unions in township politics. Workers' oppression did not end at the factory gate and the union had to be prepared to advance worker interests beyond the confines of the factory. Although NAAWU, the established union, had a somewhat checkered past, its union credentials were impressive. It had a relatively strong shop floor structures and a self confident worker leadership, with the result that Port Elizabeth motor workers were among the most militant in the country. The politics of NAAWU were inconsistent, and some in the union considered "politics" an illegitimate terrain for trade unions. The dominant faction of the union's leadership did not eschew politics, however, but rather stressed the primacy of working-class demands and leadership and, as in the case of PEBCO, were openly skeptical of organizations which incorporated non-working-class elements.

For the new unionism—represented in this instance by MACWUSA—militancy and political commitment were not to be measured by the nature and quality of union leadership or by militant industrial actions, but by a union's willingness to cooperate in broader community action. Questions of class leadership were easily resolved: workers were numerically dominant in the townships, and thus would tend to dominate community organization and leadership, particularly if the unions committed themselves to involvement and cooperation. By the early 1980s, "cooperation with the community" would become synonymous not only with a willingness to engage in politics generally, but also with a willingness to cooperate with the underground African National Congress. As the ranks of the exile ANC were filled with the Soweto generation of 1976 and as their influence began to percolate back into the townships, "politics" was increasingly raised not so much as an affiliation to a set of ideals and practices as to a specific organization. Thus it is not surprising that the issue should first have been raised in Port Elizabeth, historically a strong area of ANC activity and a city that had contributed its share of young activists to exile in the post-Soweto crackdown. If the ANC did not yet enjoy the heroic aura that it acquired in the 1980s, it was certainly already an emerging reality in the public's consciousness. The debate over the role of unions in political life was to occupy the ideological heights of resistance politics in the 1980s, permeating every aspect of trade union and political organization. The debate raised in the South African context many of the longstanding tactical and strategic questions that historically have concerned the labor movement elsewhere regarding the role of workers in struggles for political power.

Unity and Division: FOSATU and CUSA

The period following the Soweto uprising was marked by important instances of unity as well as division. The formation in 1979 and 1980 respectively of the Federation of South African Trade Unions (FOSATU) and the Council of Unions of South Africa (CUSA) reflected the strong pressures for unity while at the same time demonstrating the difficulty of drawing all bodies under a single umbrella organization. The rift between FOSATU and CUSA arose from a difference in outlooks, with CUSA placing high priority on black leadership while FOSATU held strongly to the view that unions and their leadership should be color-blind, or nonracial. *Document 85,* resolutions adopted at early FOSATU meetings, suggest the wide range of problems facing the new union federations in determining structures, procedures and policies.

At its formal founding in April 1979, FOSATU had approximately 45,000 members.[25] Its principal strength lay in Natal and the Eastern Cape, where its key affiliates were the Natal-based textile unions and the Eastern Cape auto workers. The Transvaal-based Metal and Allied Workers' Union was already exhibiting the characteristics that would ultimately make it the most robust and politically militant union in FOSATU. Presaging future developments, several affiliates and locals of the Consultative Committee (TUACC) and CUSA had by the early 1980s elected to join FOSATU. The Western Cape unions—the General Workers Union, the Food and Canning Workers' Union, and the Cape Town Municipal Workers Association—opted to remain unaffiliated.

CUSA's strength lay almost entirely in the Transvaal. Besides differing with FOSATU unions on the role of whites, geographical considerations were a factor in the rift. Some CUSA affiliates withdrew from the talks that resulted in the formation of FOSATU, alleging that TUACC unions were poaching on their Transvaal turf. CUSA's key affiliates were in the transport sector, where the Transport and Allied Workers' Union had been formed in the wake of the 1972 bus drivers' strike. Other key affiliates were in the food and chemical industries. CUSA's paid up membership at its formation totaled 30,000.[26]

Notwithstanding these efforts to build unifying structures, the post-Wiehahn period was characterized by growing division within the union movement. The differences were attributed, often somewhat sweepingly, to particular organizations. Hence, in spite of the deep differences between them, FOSATU and CUSA were popularly adjudged the most "pragmatic," while the General Workers Union, the African Food and Canning Workers' Union, and SAAWU, together with the other mushrooming "community unions," were thought to represent a more "principled" and militant current. In the early 1980s these divisions asserted themselves even more strongly, yet there were also powerful impulses toward unity. With hindsight, it is possible to see these abrasive differences as a jockeying for position within the broad unity toward which the trade unions were increasingly impelled.

Notes

1. The ascription "independent" has been used to refer to those unions whose primary thrust was the organization of African workers. This refers principally to their independence from the established trade union groupings. Other common but less precise ascriptions include "political unions," "emerging unions," "progressive unions," or "non-racial unions."

2. Philip Bonner, "Black Trade Unions in South Africa since World War II," in Robert M. Price and Carl Rosberg, eds., *The Apartheid Regime: Political Power and Racial Domination* (Berkeley: Institute of International Studies, University of California, 1980), p. 186.

3. Ken Luckhardt and Brenda Wall, *Organize or Starve! The History of the South African Congress of Trade Unions* (London: Lawrence and Wishart, 1980), p. 443.

4. The Food and Canning Workers' Union and the African Food and Canning Workers' Union, stalwarts of SACTU, were forced into a nominal separation by the legislation that prohibited African workers from belonging to registered trade unions, with the registered Food and Canning Workers' Union representing Coloured workers and the unregistered African Food and Canning Workers' Union representing Africans. Effectively, however, they continued to operate as a single union, working out of the same offices, and holding joint conferences and organizational campaigns while, for the purposes of complying with the statutory obligation to divide their activities, maintaining nominally separate minutes, books of account, elected office bearers, etc.

5. *Survey of Race Relations 1969* (Johannesburg: South African Institute of Race Relations, 1970), p. 115.

6. Trade Union Council of South Africa, "Report of Trade Union Council Conference, March 22–26, 1965."

7. In Document 77 the president of the African Food and Canning Workers' Union praised the union's former general secretary, Ray Alexander, and Elizabeth Mafeking, who had been forced to leave South Africa. "We know they are with us;" he said, "their ideas are with us." He understated the case. According to Alexander, in order to provide for continuity and to give

future advice, she visited every branch of the union to arrange for secret mail communication before she left South Africa in 1965. A code identified the Minister of Labour as "DRC," for example, and the secretary of the union as "Mother." Letters were sent by way of London. The exchange of correspondence occurred almost every week for a quarter of a century, until Alexander returned to the country in 1990. Conversation with Ray Alexander Simons (October 1993).

8. See Institute for Industrial Education, *The Durban Strikes, 1973* (Johannesburg: Ravan Press, 1974).

9. *Survey of Race Relations 1973,* p. 284.

10. Parenthetically, this style of leadership has an important consequence for a study such as this one: without offices, printing presses, bank accounts, and, frequently, the required degree of literacy, the key actors produced little documentation. See, however, Document 51 which is a strike flyer produced by the Black People's Convention.

11. See Document 17 on aid to the strikers by the Natal Indian Congress.

12. *House of Assembly Debates,* February 9, 1973, col 346. See Document 88 for Lucas Mangope's comments.

13. *Survey of Race Relations 1973,* p. 281ff. The schizophrenia of the government's approach to African unions was characteristic. While repressing them vigorously, the National Party was never willing to formally declare African unions illegal. Disputes confined solely to the factory floor posed no threat to the state, but it was difficult to impose on manufacturing workers the same kind of physical isolation from the wider society associated with mining. The government thus toyed with permitting African factory workers some form of expression, but vacillated in its view of the appropriate form.

14. For details, see *Survey of Race Relations 1973,* p. 286ff.

15. *The Economist* on July 7, 1973, reported that in 1972 "Anglo's pre-tax profits from gold-mining were more than five times its total black wage bill." Between 1911 and 1969, the real wages of African miners actually declined, according to Francis Wilson, *Labour in the South African Gold Mines 1911–1969* (Cambridge: Cambridge University Press, 1972), p. 46.

16. Institute of Industrial Education, p. 52.

17. *Survey of Race Relations 1974,* pp. 325–26.

18. *Survey of Race Relations 1974,* pp. 336–37.

19. SACTU decided in 1955 to affiliate to the WFTU, but never paid affiliation fees. Luckhardt and Wall, p. 378.

20. Baruch Hirson, *Year of Fire, Year of Ash: The Soweto Revolt: Roots of a Revolution?* (London: Zed Press, 1979).

21. *Survey of Race Relations 1975,* pp. 206–207.

22. "Recognition agreement between NUTW/TWIU and Smith and Nephew, July 19, 1974."

23. For the flavor of the debate, see *South African Labour Bulletin,* March 1980.

24. This conflict has been extensively documented. See, for example, *South African Labour Bulletin,* September 1980.

25. *Survey of Race Relations 1979,* p. 266.

26. *Survey of Race Relations 1980,* p. 166.

The Homelands in 1970

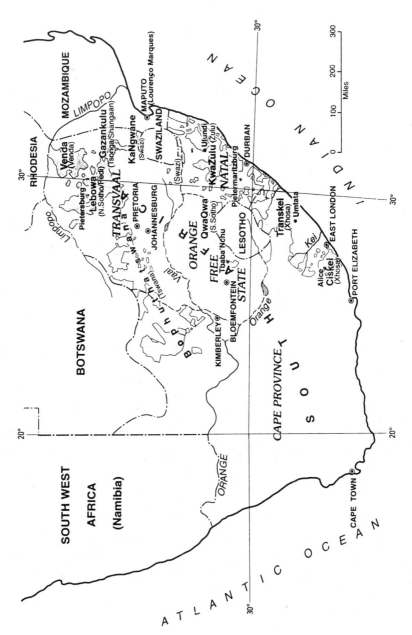

Cartographer: W. F. Nehse

8. The Politics of the System

Blacks in the years after Rivonia faced a perennial problem in acute form: whether or not to participate in political institutions sponsored by "the system." By doing so, one risked being co-opted and seen as a collaborator. By boycotting, one opened the way for opportunists who would help to legitimize Pretoria's divide-and-rule policies. In an earlier generation, members of the African National Congress had taken part in the Natives' Representative Council both to exploit it as a platform and to expose it as a "toy telephone" and thus undermine it from within. Their frustration helped to inspire the ANC's 1949 Programme of Action, which called for a policy of boycott. In practice, the ANC's policy was applied pragmatically or, according to opponents, opportunistically. The dilemma persisted, however, and during the 1960s, a new intensity characterized the arguments for and against participation in what many blacks dubbed the government's "dummy institutions."

To lend credibility to the argument that apartheid was a positive policy, the government of Prime Minister Hendrik Verwoerd (1958–1966) pressed forward with its plans to establish self-governing ethnic "homelands" or "bantustans," and to induce ambitious blacks to accept positions in their political and administrative structures. Even for African nationalists, who rejected ethnic balkanization in principle, it was possible to imagine that benefits could result from the government's scheme of "grand apartheid." Homelands, for example, could be used as a protected platform from which to make demands for more land for rural Africans and more rights in urban areas. By putting new financial and organizational resources into African hands, some believed, the government's policies might lead to unintended consequences that would eventually make the flawed institutions of homelands a stepping stone to genuine liberation.

The Homelands as Illusion, 1964–1973

In January 1962, Verwoerd announced with fanfare that the Transkei would rapidly move toward "self-government." The Transkei, the large "native reserve" to the north of the Kei River in the eastern Cape, was the obvious choice for the government's first experiment in political engineering. It had a nearly consolidated geographical area and almost all its people spoke a single language, Xhosa. Approximately 1,400,000 of the 2,400,000 persons thought in 1963 to be of Transkeian origin lived within the Transkei's borders. It also had experience with popular representation through local advisory bodies dating back to 1894, a political feature unique to the Transkei and the Ciskei, a Xhosa-speaking region south of the Kei. In 1955, the Transkei's central representative body, known as the Bunga, had accepted the Bantu Authorities system, designed by Pretoria to bolster the conservative position of government-paid chiefs.[1] Thereafter the Transkei became the prototype for the accelerated development of what were envisioned as ten nominally sovereign countries. In due course, all South Africa's Africans would become their citizens, no matter where they lived.

Apart from the question of whether homelands would ever become politically acceptable to their proposed citizens there lay another equally fundamental problem: the economic dependence of the homelands on Pretoria and their inability not only to attract Africans living in "white" South Africa but even to sustain their own people. Lacking an industrial base, the homelands were essentially rural reservoirs from which labor flowed to the central economy. They were composed of dozens of fragmented and scattered areas, comprising only about 13 percent of the country. Except for platinum deposits in Bophuthatswana, they had few natural resources. Most were eroded by overgrazing and subject to the inefficiencies of communal land tenure. Infrastructure was minimal. In these densely populated rural slums, most people lived at or below a level of bare subsistence, dependent upon cash remittances from relatives working as migrant laborers. Employment opportunities were scarce, and often involved long daily commutes to border industries located in "white" areas adjacent to homeland territories. As "surplus" Africans were "endorsed out" from cities through the application of the pass laws, and forcibly removed by law from farms and "black spots" (African freehold farming areas) in rural "white" South Africa, the homelands became dumping grounds in which population increase far exceeded meager rates of economic growth.

A virtual parody of a homeland was Qwaqwa, as described by a freelance writer in 1979:

> Qwaqwa homeland is just over twenty kilometres wide and covers 45,000 hectares of mountainous country on Lesotho's northern border. If you stand in one spot you can see all of Qwaqwa. Three million people are supposed to live there, on something the size of

four Karoo sheep farms. Ninety-eight percent of Qwaqwans live elsewhere—it is overcrowded by the 128,000 who do live there. They grow no crops, rear cattle and keep chickens. Workers commute out of Qwaqwa to Harrismith, Kestell and Bethlehem, where they spend their money too, as Qwaqwa has one or two stores but no real trading or industry.[2]

Given their inadequate revenue base, it was entirely predictable that the homelands would be overwhelmingly dependent on Pretoria for the financing of their budgets and would thus lack any political autonomy. With their leaders and bureaucrats in the pay of the central government, the homelands provided an opportunity for the National Party to construct the same pyramids of patronage power among Africans that it had already constructed among the large proportion of Afrikaners employed in the public sector. To give homeland "self-rule" more visibility and to provide a stake in the system to the new homeland elites, central government financing was gradually shifted from direct expenditure to subsidies administered by homeland chiefs and officials. These chiefs and officials in turn were in a position to dispense jobs, funds, contracts, licenses and favors to their own networks of clients, supporters and family members, building a structure of patronage that radiated outward to the remotest corners of the impoverished homelands and would, in the ultimate unfolding of "grand apartheid," it was supposed, also encompass the lives of urban Africans as they became full-fledged homeland citizens.

In what seemed to be the absence of political and economic alternatives for blacks—and National Party planners were determined to apply whatever repressive measures were needed to insure that alternatives remained inaccessible—this system appeared to offer the government potential and undisputed control over the evolution of African politics. Nevertheless, among the opponents of the system, both black and white, there was constant speculation about ways in which the homelands might become Trojan horses inside apartheid's gates, offering political space for opposition and resistance. By the early 1970s, homeland leaders were trying to boost their popularity through unity gestures that suggested the formation of a potential power bloc against the government. White liberals, suffering like Africans from the reality that their stocks of power and influence had never been lower, looked with hope on these efforts and tried to explore ways in which they could lend them support.

Two consecutive events in late 1973 fed the illusion that homelands might be the key to fundamental change in the apartheid system. At a meeting given much publicity by the English press, six homeland leaders came together for an unprecedented "summit" in Umtata, the Transkeian capital, on November 8 and expressed their support for the principle of federalism. Present were chief ministers Kaiser Matanzima of Transkei, Gatsha Buthelezi of KwaZulu, Lucas Mangope of Bophuthatswana, Hudson Ntsanwisi of Gazankulu, Lennox Sebe of Ciskei, and Collins Ramusi representing Cedric

Phatudi of Lebowa. Specific means by which a federation of homelands might exert pressure for change in South Africa were not mentioned in the resolutions taken at the meeting. Nor were any procedures for political coordination adopted, although George Matanzima, the Transkeian attorney general, had earlier made the surprising statement that he and Kaiser, his brother, were willing to "serve under whomsoever will be chosen by the people as the best man to lead them, whether he be a Zulu, Xhosa, Sotho or Tswana."[3] Resolutions were adopted calling for the consolidation of fragmented homeland territories and the abolition of laws restricting the free movement of Africans. Most important was an understanding to maintain a united front, to consult each other, and to refuse independence if the government failed to satisfy homeland demands for additional land.[4]

On the next day, five of the homeland leaders, not including Mangope, drove from Umtata to Bulugha, a white resort near East London, to take part in a three-day multiracial conference organized under the initiative of the Progressive Party with funding from an anonymous group of businessmen. In retrospect one can see that the Bulugha conference had no effect on the course of either white or black politics. Nevertheless, its verbatim record (*Document 90*) reveals much about the perceptions and hopes of liberal-minded or progressive whites and black "system" politicians in the mid-1970s and about the interactions between them. To the Progressive Party, looking for ways to add volume to its puny political voice, the idea of an alliance with homeland leaders was appealing. These leaders, said Donald Woods, editor of the East London *Daily Dispatch* and the conference convenor, were "the authentic voices of the voteless multitudes."[5] Representatives of all major South African newspapers, including *Die Transvaler* and *Die Burger,* were present; and there was also some international radio and television coverage. The Bulugha meeting, according to the introduction to the final conference report, "reflected the views of the leaders of four million Zulus, three million Xhosas, the people of Lebowa, Gazankulu, the Coloured and Indian communities of the nation and the liberal white South Africans most in sympathy with international concepts of democratic government." Only 12 of the 34 invited delegates were black, and of these only three—two members of the Natal Indian Congress, and an Indian businessman—were not part of "system" institutions. The 12 observers were all white. The final report claimed that the conference was "unprecedented" as South Africa's "first all-race assembly," although this overlooked a history of multiracial conferences going back to the 1920s, culminating in the multiracial conference of December 1957 at the University of the Witwatersrand, which was attended by a far larger, more diverse, and more representative group than the Bulugha conference.[6]

The focus of the conference was on "federation as a formula for a future South Africa." What was notable, however, were the subjects not discussed. Conspicuously absent was "how you actually persuade the ruling group to share power," in the words of one delegate. No one seemed to know how real change could be achieved, said Helen Suzman, the lone Progressive member of Parliament. In the absence of a "real change of climate" among whites, she believed that "in the end the key is probably going to be with the homeland leaders." Despite her usual realism, she wondered aloud "what would happen if one of the black homeland leaders or all of the homeland leaders, in fact, called the Government's bluff" and demanded genuine independence. They might, she suggested, obtain aid from foreign countries and raise loans abroad.

Since separate development was accepted as a political reality, there was no discussion of thwarting its progress to the stage of homeland independence. The problem of whether or not Africans outside the homelands would lose their South African citizenship was ignored. Since the early 1960s, the Progressives had advocated federalism as a system for decentralizing power. Now federalism was also praised as a system for overcoming fragmentation, restoring South African unity, and even expanding South Africa's embrace to bind the rest of southern Africa more tightly. The crucial question of the franchise in a federated South Africa was avoided, however. Political reality meant recognition of white fears. Accordingly, Colin Eglin, the leader of the Progressive Party, skirted around any discussion of his party's policy of constitutional restraints on majority rule through the use of a qualified franchise, or how this might mesh with the universal suffrage granted to homeland citizens.

Only toward the end did a submerged issue mar the meeting's self-congratulatory tone. It was evident, said M. J. Naidoo, the acting president of the Natal Indian Congress, that those leaders who were "banned or in exile or on Robben Island" were not present to take their "rightful place" at the conference. After saying that he "would not dare to suggest that Mr. Eglin or Chief Buthelezi is not a leader," Naidoo urged that the conference declaration call for the immediate release of Mandela and all other "silent leaders." Buthelezi, who had been treated by the white delegates as the star of the conference, reacted angrily.[7] Inferring that he had been denigrated as an inauthentic leader, a stooge, in the presence of "the world press," he heatedly recounted his own efforts to secure the release of political prisoners and the return of refugees. Nevertheless, no mention of the issue was made in the closing Declaration of Consensus, nor was a call made for the release of the "silent leaders." Instead, the declaration merely affirmed the need for "urgent change" and endorsed federalism and an entrenched bill of rights. The Bulugha declaration was adopted, said the Progressive Party newspaper, by "Black and White political leaders representing an overwhelming majority of South Africans" and was "a highpoint of political realism for South Africa."[8]

Had Lucas Mangope, chief minister of Bophuthatswana, been present at Bulugha, he would not have endorsed Buthelezi's sentiments on the release of political prisoners. "Moral support and sustenance for 'freedom fighters' are nothing more than complicity in murder of the innocent," he had asserted the year before.[9] Following the spontaneous strikes in the Durban area in early 1973, Mangope had made clear his identification with white political and business leaders, his assumption that no class conflict existed in relations between employers and labor, and his paternalistic avoidance of support for African trade unions (*Document 88*).

The meetings at Umtata and Bulugha were the climax not of political realism but of illusions among most homeland leaders and progressive whites about the potential power of a united homeland leadership. No matter how articulate or critical some homeland leaders might be, in reality they were firmly under the thumb of Pretoria, which had the power to cut off their support and disrupt their efforts to gain leverage through joint efforts. Their separate constituencies were not large or militant, nor were the leaders themselves disposed to mobilize a mass challenge to the regime's power. The withholding of migrant labor, sometimes mooted, was a totally unrealistic prospect. Chief Buthelezi in the mid-1970s began to talk of the eventual use of mass strikes and boycotts by workers and consumers, but in practice he discouraged all efforts to work toward this vision of mass action. Progressive Party leaders, lacking a constituency that could even remotely threaten National Party power, could do little more than make abstract rational arguments and moral appeals. Faced with the political reality of the government's homeland blueprint and the constraints of a police state, they, like the homeland leaders, sought to make the best of unpromising circumstances and in the process merely lent further credibility to the government's initiatives.

The Homelands as Sideshow, 1974–1979

Within a few months of lauding united action at the Umtata summit, Kaiser Matanzima shifted course. Ruthless and unpredictable, Matanzima was at heart a Xhosa nationalist whose parochial ambitions made him the ideal instrument for the realization of Pretoria's designs. Without consulting or even informing other homeland leaders, he led his Transkei National Independence Party to vote unanimously in March 1974 to begin negotiations for independence, even though there was no prospect that the Transkei's demands for additional land would be met. In late 1975 Mangope's ruling party in Bophuthatswana also made a surprise decision to move toward independence. On October 26, 1976, four months into the Soweto uprising—a development that was to diminish any political capital gleaned by the National Party from the homeland policy—the Transkei celebrated its independence. Bophuthatswana's followed in December 1977.

The decision by Matanzima and Mangope to opt for independence shattered any remaining illusion of homeland solidarity. Their defections damaged the credibility of the other homeland leaders who had vowed to reject independence and who claimed to be opposing the system from within. They believed that they had been treated shabbily by Matanzima and Mangope, and relations with them soured. Early in October 1976, before the Soweto uprising had subsided, they met with Prime Minister Vorster for seven hours. He refused to discuss the "unrest" in the country or the release of detained leaders on the pretext that such matters were under official review, and he rejected a national convention since he "saw no merit in the idea at all."[10]

Rather than concede their powerlessness in a game where Pretoria held all the aces, the homeland leaders—other than Matanzima and Mangope—continued to play their unity card, but to little avail. After their rebuff by Vorster, Buthelezi, Phatudi, and Ntsanwisi met at the Johannesburg airport Holiday Inn (a hotel with "international status," hence a racially open venue) and announced the formation of a Black United Front. The meeting was also attended by a group of prominent urban Africans—mainly middle class, middle-aged, and pro-Buthelezi—but was boycotted by black consciousness leaders. The initiative proved short-lived, partly because Phatudi and Ntsanwisi were wary of political efforts that might be dominated by Buthelezi.[11] Meanwhile, Buthelezi took a different tack by urging that regional "Inkathas" on the model of his own political party in KwaZulu be launched around the country, with a view to coming together later in a national association. When this proposal failed to take off, Buthelezi in early 1978 initiated a new coalition called the South African Black Alliance. It included representatives of Coloured and Indian groups, joined later by leaders of the small Swazi and Qwaqwa homelands. The Black United Front faded away, and the South African Black Alliance also came to little.

Their access to the top levels of government did not mean that homeland leaders could exercise any leverage over National Party policy through dialogue with high officials. *Document 91,* the "confidential" record of a nine-hour meeting in January 1975 between eight homeland leaders and Prime Minister Vorster in Cape Town, provides a rare view of the limited scope for give and take on such occasions. While appearing to be responsive to suggestions within the framework of official policy, Vorster was condescending, peremptory regarding issues not on his own agenda, and blunt in asserting his prerogative as the final arbiter of all disagreements. Illusions about the direction of government policy were no longer possible, yet the homeland rulers professed not to understand the distinction between "discrimination" and "differentiation" and the argument of Vorster, and Verwoerd before him, that as the policy of "separate development" unfolded, the former would give way to the latter. The discussion avoided the fundamental issue of political power and, by implication, a universal franchise and majority rule, since within the parameters of "system" politics the practical choice was not between majority rule and incremental change acceptable to the government but between perpetuation of the status quo and incremental change. Any serious challenge to white power required a radical if not revolutionary course of action, which homeland leaders had no inclination to pursue. The more articulate among them endorsed a vague vision of democracy in bland rhetoric suffused with wishful thinking, but stopped there.

Vorster dominated the discussion. No one responded when he challenged his listeners regarding the government's policy on "political power": "If this is not meaningful, then you must tell me because I do not want to waste my time." Nor did Buthelezi or Matanzima, past friends of Mandela, challenge

Vorster when he said he would not give Mandela amnesty because "he admitted in court that he was a Communist." (In fact, Mandela at the Rivonia trial had explicitly denied that he had ever been a member of the Communist Party.) Vorster lectured his listeners on black leadership, expressed his judgment that banning kept people out of trouble, and evoked "laughter" when he said that his wife's name was "Tini" like Tiny Nokwe, the wife of ANC leader Duma Nokwe.[12]

By 1975 the implications of Pretoria's plans for homeland development had been spelled out in some detail, and their devastating potential impact on the remaining rights of urban Africans had become more widely appreciated. For millions of Africans living permanently outside the Transkei or Bophuthatswana but ethnically linked to them, the consequences of "independence" were to be severe. People who had not been born in a homeland or ever visited one nevertheless stood, along with all their descendants, to lose their South African citizenship when "their" homeland became independent, contrary to earlier assurances by Matanzima and Mangope that they would have an option to retain it. At the January 1975 meeting with Vorster, Matanzima led off with a presentation that struck at a basic premise of government policy. As someone who endorsed separate development and believed in Xhosa nationalism, he nevertheless asserted that Africans were part of the "permanent population of the cities in which they live without allegiance to any homeland." His call for urban freehold land tenure rights for Africans was presented in the traditional language of South African liberalism: it would lead, he said, to "the building of a common society for all races." White governments had long recognized that such rights would justify demands for the franchise and political representation in the central government. Vorster therefore dismissed Matanzima's demand categorically, but said leasehold rights would be considered. Later he rejected an equally out-of-bounds and half-hearted suggestion by Buthelezi that Soweto be declared a homeland.

The homeland leaders' underlying concern, however, was less with the fate of urban dwellers than with the effects of urban policy on the foundations of their power in the homelands themselves. In discussing the language of instruction in urban schools, for example, they were animated in criticizing inadequate provision for vernacular instruction but oblivious to the complaints of urban students about the Afrikaans medium requirement in schools, complaints that were to spark off the Soweto uprising in June 1976. In any case, the ability of homeland leaders to speak for urban Africans was limited by the meager interest in homeland affairs among permanently urbanized Africans. Homeland elections did not attract much attention or participation despite the official theory that homeland citizens could be active in homeland politics wherever they lived. With the exception of Buthelezi, whose militant rhetoric drew substantial crowds in urban areas outside Natal, homeland leaders inspired little interest from city dwellers. When Matanzima spoke at Soweto's Jabulani amphitheater in November 1975 to make the case for Transkeian independence, he attracted a crowd of only about 400, many of them hecklers.[13]

Within most of the homelands themselves, organized opposition to rulers working with Pretoria was only minimally tolerated. In the Transkei, emergency regulations promulgated in November 1960 to deal with a short-lived peasant rebellion were retained throughout the 1970s and beyond. Their provisions included detention without trial, the prohibition of meetings held without official permission, arbitrary powers for chiefs and headmen, and punishment for statements considered critical of chiefly authority. Before nomination day for the last Transkeian pre-independence election in September 1976, Matanzima detained the entire executive of the opposition Democratic Party including its leader, Hector Ncokazi. In November 1979, the Transkei government banned 34 organizations, including not only the ANC and the PAC but also the South African Council of Churches and Buthelezi's Inkatha.[14] Dissenting voices were no more welcome in Bophuthatswana, Venda, Ciskei or KwaZulu, although nominal opposition parties existed for a time in the first three.

The facade of parliamentary institutions, the abolition of racial segregation, and the dropping of Bantu Education curriculums were all features that homeland governments hoped would lend weight to their quest for international recognition. When the Political Committee of the UN General Assembly recommended in late 1975 that the Transkei should be denied membership when it became independent, Matanzima tried to argue that it was a mere "accident of history" that the Transkei was negotiating with South Africa for its independence rather than with colonial rulers as had been the case with other African states. His comparison ignored a crucial difference, however: the price paid by some 1,500,000 so-called Transkeians born or living permanently outside the Transkei.

Even before Matanzima's surprise 1974 decision in favor of independence it was evident that hopes for international recognition were futile. While the international community smiled on decolonization, it frowned unambiguously on the partition of existing countries. South Africa's claim that its homeland policy was a case of decolonization was scarcely credible given the country's advanced state of economic integration and the fragmentation of the homeland territories. Partition as a matter of principle ran counter to the interests of every government in the world faced with an ethnic separatist movement. In Africa, such movements were numerous in the 1970s. Independent Africa's 1969 Lusaka Manifesto (see Chapter 2), endorsed by the UN General Assembly, rejected any alteration of boundaries in southern Africa. In early 1974, the Council of Ministers of the Organization of African Unity adopted a declaration that described homeland leaders as "puppets," reaffirmed "total rejection of . . . any so-called independent homelands within South Africa" and called for freeing Nelson Mandela, Robert Sobukwe, and all other nationalists who were in jail or restricted.[15] As long as independent Africa opposed recognizing the partition of South Africa, there was no likelihood of the rest of the world doing so. Participation by homeland leaders in Vorster's diplomacy of detente with black Africa brought no breakthroughs. Once the 1976 uprising pushed South Africa back into polecat status in the world community, the independent homelands managed to conclude minor agreements only with pariah countries like Taiwan and Israel in the 1980s but were never able to win formal international recognition.[16]

To the African National Congress on the eve of its resurgence in the late 1970s, the homelands were an irrelevant sideshow politically but in other ways a reality of concern. Their extensive systems of patronage as well as the strategic location of their territories presented the ANC with problems and opportunities. Looking back in 1985, the ANC's Commission on Strategy and Tactics produced an internal report that called attention to

> the reality of the bantustans, which, though puppet creations of the enemy, have spawned a vast bureaucratic apparatus and civil service and endowed a whole range of black professionals with the benefits of public office. Bantustanization has developed a momentum of its own, and significant number of government ministers, officials, civil servants and other hangers-on have acquired an economic and social stake in their survival. We must isolate the incorrigible collaborators and win over those whose job opportunities are not irreversibly dependent on the bantustan system. . . . [T]he creation of the bantustan armies opens up new opportunities for the winning over of black soldiers to our side and to capture or obtain weapons from them. . . . The changing social stratification of the bantustans also received our attention. The emergence of a working class within these areas was noted as was the dumping of the unemployed from the urban areas and the role that migrant labour must play in linking the bantustans with the urban areas and industry. . . . Urban [residential] areas that had been incorporated into bantustans such as Mdantsane [near East London] must become revolutionary springboards for mobilizing the people in the bantustans.[17]

The Commission raised once again the perennial problem of whether or not to become involved in "the system." It asked: should there be a pragmatic modification of the ANC's "correct policy of unconditionally rejecting the legitimacy of the bantustans?" Might a bantustan administration be overthrown and replaced by "a radical administration with sympathies for the liberation movement?" The answer was equivocal. Members of the Commission endorsed "flexibility" but did not believe that radical homeland administrations would have time to function. The Commission had "no doubt that Pretoria would intervene immediately to save its puppets," but by doing so it would destroy its bantustan policy, thus "leading to a transformation of its areas into bases for People's War."

The System in Urban Areas

The homelands were the centerpiece of the state's policy, but the urban areas, ostensibly adjuncts to the homelands, were the main centers of political resistance.[18] Most of the sophisticated African leaders, middle class and working class, were there. To keep these areas under control using the minimum of overt coercion required that the apartheid planners design a system of administration that would elicit the maximum voluntary compliance. By the 1960s, older forms of paternalistic domination could no longer be defended as legitimate, so Pretoria was faced with the problem of how to devolve increasing authority onto black surrogates who could enforce government policies while generating the least possible resistance.

Anyone responsible for the administration of African urban "locations" (townships) confronted the bedrock premise of successive white governments that Africans were to be regarded as "temporary sojourners" in "white" cities and not as permanent urban residents. The classic segregationist expression of the role of the African who entered an urban area had been expressed by the Stallard Commission in 1922: he should "minister to the needs of the white man and should depart therefrom when he had ceased so to minister."[19] "Redundant Natives," an earlier commission had warned, could become "professional agitators." The political implications were also starkly spelled out in 1922: "If the Native is to be regarded as a permanent element in municipal areas . . . there can be no justification for basing his exclusion from the franchise on the simple ground of colour." The rate of urban influx grew rapidly during World War II, and after the war the Fagan Commission of 1946–1948 recognized that there was "a settled permanent Native population" in the urban areas and that the process of integration could not be reversed.[20] This conclusion was endorsed by Prime Minister Jan Smuts on the eve of the 1948 election, but repudiated by the victorious incoming National Party, which reaffirmed Stallard, denied the existence of a permanently urbanized African population, and set out to reverse the process of integration. Once Verwoerd began painting his vision of development in the rural reserves in the 1960s, official policy envisaged that by approximately 1978 the demographic pattern of urbanization would be reversed as Africans were drawn back to their thriving "homelands."

After a decade of tightening the administration of "influx control" (pass laws), implementing residential segregation, and removing Indian traders from the more desirable urban commercial districts under the 1950 Group Areas Act, the National Party turned after Sharpeville to the "reform" of urban African administration. Older township Advisory Boards, created following the Stallard Commission, were gradually replaced with elected Urban Bantu Councils (UBCs) under African chairmen. Despite long-standing African calls for direct representation on white municipal councils, the Urban Bantu Councils Act of 1961 had as its object "the integration of the urban Bantu into the systems of government of their homelands."[21] Wherever African townships were multiethnic in composition, voting for UBCs took place on the basis of ethnically defined electoral wards. Until 1970 the councils also included representatives of homeland governments. In Johannesburg, home to roughly a fifth of all urban Africans, the Soweto Advisory Board was replaced by a UBC in 1968. Leonard Mosala, a prominent council member and an optimist about incremental change, reacted with shocked dismay when he heard the government's policy explained at the first council meeting. Blaar Coetzee, Deputy Minister of Bantu Administration, announced that Africans could not expect any political rights in "white" areas, that Soweto was not a municipality, and that in fact blacks who lived in urban areas were there only temporarily. Coetzee's speech, Mosala said years later, had "effectively aborted the UBC, which never recovered."[22]

Whereas homeland governments could move through stages of semi-autonomy and acquire the trappings of sovereign independence, nothing comparable was projected within the contours of official policy for the urban areas. Instead, each urban African was ultimately to become a citizen of a "foreign" country, living and working in "white" South Africa as a guest worker. Given their association with this and other unpopular state policies, African local government bodies, which gradually acquired substantial authority and patronage resources, had difficulty sustaining any real measure of popular legitimacy in urban townships. Yet they posed for African politicians and resistance groups the familiar question of strategy—to exploit or boycott—and they attracted not only opportunistic collaborators but also a small number of well-meaning and capable people, such as Mosala, who sought to soften the harshness of racial restrictions and the poverty of urban life.

Urban Bantu Councils focussed on issues such as housing, transport, crime control, sanitation, education, wages, and the administration of the pass laws. But implicit in specific grievances and demands were questions of finance and therefore of the franchise and political power. Rare was the council member, no matter how conservative, who did not give at least lip service to the consensus of politically conscious urban dwellers: rejection of the homelands policy in principle and endorsement of the aim of eventual equality in Parliament. The rhetoric of resistance swirled around the institutions of the system, and participants found themselves in a tense equilibrium as they responded alternately to critical constituents and to officialdom. Answerable at first to the officials of adjacent white municipalities who sometimes differed widely in outlook depending on which party controlled the municipal government, starting in the early 1970s UBCs were placed under the authority of Bantu Affairs Administration Boards, which were appointed by the Minister of Bantu Affairs and charged with uniformly applying the policies of his department.

To invest the system with greater credibility, and also to distance white officials from responsibility for unpopular policy decisions, it was the intention of the National Party gradually to devolve greater responsibility onto African township councils, just as homeland governments were to be given growing autonomy. The differences, however, were fundamental: while Pretoria was prepared to build up the homeland governments by subsidizing them despite their alleged sovereignty, it was increasingly unwilling to subsidize highly exploited African urban populations, insisting that they must meet the cost of services in their own segregated townships. This was virtually impossible given the extremely limited revenue base in these areas. Little commerce and no industries were located in African townships; moreover, because of the lack of freehold title, taxes ("rates") could not be charged on the value of land. A major source of revenue was the government monopoly on the sale of sorghum beer and, after 1961 when the sale of liquor to Africans was legalized, its monopoly on the sale of liquor in townships.

Until the 1970s, revenue from these sources, and also from municipalities, and indirectly from employers, had made housing subsidies possible since most Africans could not afford an economic rent. During the economic downturn of the mid-1970s, however, the Administration Boards became determined to reduce government expenditure on African areas, and to pass these costs as fully as possible to Africans themselves by requiring them to pay ever higher rents and service charges for water and electricity. As the unpopular task of extracting these revenues fell more and more to township councils in the 1970s, voter turnouts in council elections fell, even in smaller towns where councillors sometimes had a greater measure of public support. Increasing contempt was displayed toward councillors (those in the Orange Free State reported that they were called "castrated Boers," while UBCs elsewhere were dubbed "Useless Boys Clubs").[23] Use of their limited powers of patronage—to dispense trading licenses, sort out the problems of pensioners, or arrange the repair of street lights—could make little impact on the larger and more intractable realities of poverty and discrimination affecting the mass of township residents.

The nationwide upheavals of 1976 focussed rising public anger on the collaborative role of councillors. Members of the Soweto UBC, with the exception of Leonard Mosala, had failed to anticipate the events of June 16 and their aftermath; and they and other Soweto personalities whom white officials regarded as "leaders" also failed to appreciate the range and intensity of feeling among Soweto's youth.[24] The UBC offices were among the first targets of arson attacks when rioting swept Soweto on June 16–17. The Soweto council, like UBCs in most townships, was made up predominantly of middle aged small businessmen and traders who were conservative in outlook and out of sympathy with the militancy of the youth generation. Nevertheless, councillors in Soweto as elsewhere, within the limits of the impotent institutions which they manned, had repeatedly voiced fundamental African grievances and continued to do so with a combination of customary deference and new intensity as the government's inability to bring the 1976 unrest under control became more evident.

On June 18, a high official of the West Rand Administration Board called together some members of the UBC, teachers, churchmen, and other community representatives. From among them, there "surfaced" a Committee of 30.[25] Asked how the disturbances could be stopped, they replied that they as leaders should meet with the Minister. On the following day, M. C. Botha, Minister of Bantu Administration and Development and Bantu Education, met a delegation of 11 in Pretoria. T. J. Makaya, the UBC chairman, requested suspension of the Afrikaans requirement in schools. At the end, the Minister said he was "moved by the earnestness" of what he had heard. The most earnest was Lennox Mlonzi, a partisan of Matanzima. According to the minutes of the meeting, he said that "nobody could have foreseen the results of the action of the children and said that the leaders have now come with their caps in hand, pleading for mercy and the good judgment of the Minister."[26]

Some of the emotion masked by the obsequiousness displayed at the June 19 meeting apparently broke through on June 29 at a follow-up meeting of almost nine hours with administration officials. African participants warned of "hatred and ill-feeling toward the White people" and of violence that "could conceivably spread to White Johannesburg." *Document 92,* minutes of the meeting, conveys the flavor of these formal discussions as the uprising spread. The delegation included African councillors from Soweto, Alexandra, and other townships of the West Rand, a representative of the African Chamber of Commerce, and a trade unionist, Lucy Mvubelo. Also present was M. T. Moerane, once active in the ANC and a former editor of *The World.* *Document 93,* a memorandum to the Minister "by Soweto Black Community Leaders" (written by Moerane) warned of those who had learned from Mozambique that they should "fight it out" against the white conqueror. Although members of the delegation focussed more attention on the grievances of traders than of students and called for the more courteous administration of the pass laws rather than for their abolition, they also left no doubt that they saw the crux of African problems as political. Blacks permanently resident in urban areas, they said, "should be granted meaningful representation at all levels of government, from local authority to central government level." But they stopped short of an affirmation of the decades-long demand for one person one vote. What was wanted, said Moerane, was "sincere dialogue" and "participation in decision making."

Notwithstanding these earnest pleas, it became clear during the uprising that Pretoria was far more likely to respond with concessions when blacks initiated and sustained militant action than when they merely pleaded with the government to be reasonable. In 1977, a government commission under the chairmanship of Piet Riekert was appointed to study the status of urban Africans. When it reported in May 1979, it recommended that the government abandon the premise that all urban Africans were "temporary sojourners." Instead it urged recognition of the permanence of those with section 10 rights, and recommended encouraging the growth of a stable urban middle class.[27] To this end, it commended the granting of 99-year leasehold rights (but not ownership through freehold title) on township plots where Africans could build their own homes, a measure the government had already introduced in 1978. One government minister tried to demonstrate the continuity of this measure with previous government policies by asserting that the government wanted to make Africans less wary of acknowledging their links with the homelands by assuring them of their urban rights. Yet change, however convoluted, was taking place, even if it was accompanied by continued rhetorical commitment to the fundamentals of grand apartheid, as well as by complex and tightened controls over Africans "illegally" in towns. However, the pace of potential movement toward political rights was indicated by the paternalistic remark of Dr. George de V. Morrison, the Deputy Minister of Co-operation and Development, at the induction of the Gugulethu Community Council in Cape Town in September 1979: "People have to learn to crawl before they can walk."[28]

The Soweto uprising widely discredited collaborationist local government structures and led in Soweto itself to the collapse of the UBC in June 1977 after a campaign of intimidation by student militants forced the entire council to resign. By that time the government had already introduced legislation to replace UBCs with new-look structures called Community Councils. The new councils were not to be elected on an ethnic basis and were touted as a major step toward greater township autonomy since some of the former functions of the Bantu Affairs Administration Boards were now to be transferred to them. P. W. Botha, reputed to be less rigid than Vorster, became prime minister in September 1978 and soon selected Piet Koornhof, described widely in the press as flexible and forward-looking, to be Minister of Plural Relations (formerly Bantu Administration). Koornhof assured the chairmen of Administration Boards that they would continue to implement influx control and labor regulations. At the same time, in the new spirit of change, he declared: "Your task is to phase out your role as guardians since there has been a shift of emphasis from direct administration of Black people to a position where Blacks will manage and administer their own communities according to their own abilities." The process would be rapid, he said, because "this dispensation has been withheld from Blacks for so long."[29] Many blacks, however, remained unimpressed. Voter turnout in council elections failed to increase, and in the pivotal case of Soweto, dropped to a new low of 6 percent in 1978 from a high of 32 percent in 1968. David Thebehali, an ambitious former member of the UBC, won election with 97 votes in a 4.4 percent poll in his ward. Nevertheless, at the new Council's first meeting he was elected chairman and thus "mayor" of Soweto. In smaller cities and towns, voter turnout in community council elections averaged between 30 and 40 percent, but in the highly politicized townships of Port Elizabeth in 1978 the turnout was only 11 percent.[30]

The government's quest for credible African leadership with which it could deal encountered a perplexing new situation in 1977 in Johannesburg with the almost simultaneous collapse of the Soweto UBC and the emergence of a "Soweto Local Authority Interim Committee," popularly know as the "Committee of Ten."[31] The Committee of Ten, drawn from a more elite urban social stratum than the Community Council, was formed at an extraordinary meeting of 61 representatives of Soweto organizations held in late June at the offices of *The World*. Black consciousness militants were prominent in the meeting and represented on the Committee by Tom Manthata, Reverend Mashwabada Mayatula, and Thandisizwe Mazibuko of the Black People's Convention; but also on the Committee were ex-UBC member Leonard Mosala and several prominent businessmen who had not previously been politically active.[32] The Committee chose as chairman Dr. Nthato Motlana, a well-known physician and former member of the ANC who had been active in the Black Parents Association. According to John Kane-Berman, the new group was "the most broadly based body to emerge in Soweto in years," and Motlana was "Soweto's most popular civic and political leader."[33]

Going rapidly on the offensive, the Committee of Ten in July announced the broad outline of a plan for an autonomous and democratic Soweto. Motlana and some others favored direct representation on the Johannesburg city council but, seeing this as politically unrealistic, called for Soweto to be given full municipal status, not subject to the authority of the Minister of Plural Relations or the West Rand Administration Board. The Committee's notion of a self-governing, if heavily subsidized, city-state produced mixed reactions. Although the Committee decried any links with homelands, *Die Transvaler* and a number of Afrikaans academics were encouraged by the proposal, which they believed was moderate and reconcilable with National Party policy. The Committee planned a public meeting for July 31, 1977, when a ban on public meetings was due to expire, in order to introduce its blueprint.[34]

Rather than let a more popular body emerge as a rival to the discredited Soweto Community Council, the government decided to ban the meeting as well as a subsequent one called for the same purpose. Manie Mulder, chairman of the West Rand Administration Board, accused the Committee of Ten of looking for confrontation, and frivolously announced the formation of his own "Committee of 13," which later turned out to be nonexistent.[35] In the crackdown of October 1977, all the members of the Committee of Ten were detained and held for the better part of a year while Pretoria tried with little success to win public support for the community council system.

The replacement of Vorster by the reputedly more flexible P. W. Botha in September 1978 and the appointment of Piet Koornhof seemed to promise a new approach to urban policy. While the Riekert Commission continued with its deliberations, Koornhof formulated plans for six multiracial regional committees to advise a cabinet committee charged with reexamining the status of urban Africans. Recognizing that packing these committees with obvious collaborators from within the system would not endow the process with legitimacy, Koornhof decided to invite prominent critics to be among the members of his proposed regional committees. He confidently approached the task of winning their cooperation, believing that his personal sincerity could overcome their deep antipathy. During the planning stage of his maneuvers to co-opt credible leaders, he invited Motlana to Cape Town for a private meeting. "As soon as I walked in," Motlana recalled later, "we sat and stared into each other's eyes for five hours, no lunch, no nothing. . . . We disagreed on everything!"[36]

Koornhof forged ahead anyway, inviting Motlana and Percy Qoboza, the former editor of *The World* (who had also spent months in detention following the October 1977 crackdown), and Bishop Desmond Tutu, general secretary of the South African Council of Churches, to join his Pretoria-Witwatersrand-Vereeniging regional advisory committee. Koornhof assured them that participation would not mean endorsement of government policies and that the agenda would be open. Nevertheless, the three invitees were not tempted to lose their credibility by joining another "dummy institution" chaired by a white official, and they declined. Reverend Sam Buti, a popular civic leader in Alexandra township in Johannesburg and the moderator of the African branch of the Dutch Reformed Church, decided to accept Koornhof's invitation. He attended two of the four plenary sessions of the advisory committee, then decided in late 1979 under popular pressure to withdraw and join the boycott camp.[37] The time was passing when urban African opinion could accept the notion of "fighting the system from within" or "giving the system a try."[38] Instead, within a few months of declining Koornhof's invitation, Motlana with his colleagues in the Committee of Ten launched the Soweto Civic Association, taking an important initiative which was to be duplicated hundreds of times over in the early 1980s as black townships nationwide, bypassing the discredited community councils, formed grassroots residents' and civic organizations to express community grievances and press for the rights of full citizenship.

Coloureds, Indians, and the System

Coloureds and Indians faced questions about participation in the system similar to those faced by Africans; but whereas Africans calculated their political strategy in relation to its effects on white power, many Coloureds and Indians were more concerned with the consequences for their minority communities in the eventual outcome of the struggle between whites and Africans. All Coloured and Indian political activists endorsed, or at least gave lip service to, the goal of full citizenship rights for all. It did not follow, however, during the decade and a half after 1964, that the obvious strategy was to identify themselves politically with the African cause. How could this be done in the circumstances of a police state when experienced African leaders were in prison, banned, or in exile? In any event, most members of the older Coloured and Indian generations preferred to maintain their distance, both politically and socially, from the African majority. Predictably, opinion was divided about the utility of participating in state-initiated representational bodies. Using official platforms and the legal protection they afforded (if one did not go too far) had a pragmatic appeal and the qualified support of the ANC. That appeal was strengthened by the potential costs of adopting a boycott policy: the way would be open for opportunists—"quislings" in the lexicon of politicized Coloured intellectuals—to pose as champions of the people and to win credit for reformist carrots, thus gaining some popular support and creating confusion in opinion at home and internationally. On the other hand, boycott was endorsed by the black consciousness movement, which made a strong impact in the 1970s on Coloured and Indian students, who accepted inclusion with Africans as "blacks," the oppressed.

Although in similar predicaments, Coloureds and Indians differed in significant ways—historically, culturally, and in numbers—and these differences conditioned their relations with whites. The origins of the Coloured racial mixture, combining strains of Khoisan, white, Bantu, and Asian ancestry, were over three hundred years old. Descriptions of Coloureds as "bastards," as second-class citizens (lower than whites but higher than Africans), or as browns reflected the ambiguity of their status. Over four-fifths of about 2,600,000 Coloureds in 1980, heavily concentrated in the Western Cape, spoke Afrikaans as their home language. Many belonged to the Dutch Reformed Church. A Muslim minority, the descendants of Malay slaves, was predominantly urban, whereas a substantial portion of Coloureds of Christian background were farm workers. Coloureds, in short, did not have a single distinctive culture, yet participation in "Coloured" institutions meant acceptance of an imposed ethnic identity despite professions of South Africanism. The most politically sophisticated rejected the label of "Coloured" altogether.

Indian South Africans are the descendants of immigrants from both the south and the north of the Indian subcontinent. Many of their forebears were Hindu indentured laborers who came to Natal in the late nineteenth century. They also include a Muslim minority who have predominated in business and the professions. Indians are far fewer than Coloureds, 821,000 in 1980, or about three percent of the country's population, with over four-fifths living in Natal. Indians have been keenly aware of their vulnerability as a small and inward-looking minority, an awareness sharpened in the 1960s and 1970s by the biases shown against Indians in several independent African states. Indians who have succeeded in gaining an economic niche for themselves in retail trade have long suffered the resentment of others who felt excluded or exploited. Violent attacks by Zulus on Indians in Durban following a racial incident in 1949 long remained vivid in popular memory. Like the Indian majority, the Coloured majority has been relatively poor; but among the Coloureds there is no counterpart to the wealthy Indian merchant class, which has given a high priority to stability. In the 1960s and 1970s, the small Coloured middle class included professionals, small businessmen, government-paid teachers, trade union leaders, and skilled workers whose status improved during the economic growth of the 1960s, as did that of Indian skilled workers.[39]

For over a century, Coloured males who met a minimum educational and property qualification voted in the Cape Province on a common roll with whites, and even held the balance of power in some constituencies. After a prolonged constitutional crisis, the National Party removed Coloureds from the common voters' roll in 1956 and placed them on a separate roll. In 1968 Coloured representation in Parliament (by whites) was ended altogether and replaced by an advisory Coloured Persons' Representative Council, more commonly known as the Coloured Representative Council (CRC). This body attracted an up-and-coming new class of small businessmen and professionals steeped in the thinking of the National Party 'era.[40] The CRC was composed of 20 nominated members and 40 members elected nationally by universal adult suffrage among Coloureds. The first election was held in September 1969, and a subsequent one took place in 1975. Despite the fact that registration was compulsory under the law, registration for the two elections declined from about 76 percent of potential voters in 1969 to 53 percent in 1975, and the turnout from 37 percent of potential voters to 28 percent.[41]

The creation of the CRC as a national platform for Coloured political expression promoted the development of all-Coloured political parties, a wider politicization of Coloureds than in the past, and an unprecedented though modest degree of political electioneering. The most outspoken and popular party in Council politics was the Labour Party, founded in 1965. In its demands for a nonracial universal franchise and direct representation in Parliament, it shared the political aims of both the ANC and the Unity Movement. In maintaining that its participation in the Council was designed to expose the institution as a fraud and, through boycott of its functions, to destroy it, the Labour Party also followed ANC precedent. Its acerbic rhetoric sometimes almost matched that of the Unity Movement. Its leaders, however, were essentially moderates and pragmatists. Reviled as opportunists by opponents on their left, they courted confrontation by engaging occasionally in dramatic gestures of protest; but believing there was no alternative to acceptance of the realities of an all-powerful state, they avoided rupture in favor of pressure from within the system. Their frustrations, meanwhile, impelled them to identify with African leadership, and in particular with Chief Buthelezi, whose short-lived South African Black Alliance they joined in 1978.

The Labour Party's main rival was the Federal Coloured People's Party led by Tom Swartz, a real estate agent who had previously chaired a government-nominated advisory body called the Council for Coloured Affairs. Swartz—who was once described by a United Party member of Parliament as a "servile, bowing and scraping man,"[42]—talked of "a Coloured nation with an identity of its own" and promised to uplift the Coloured people and eventually show the whites "by our loyalty, our industry, our worthiness that we deserve equality."[43] Equally or even more conservative were three minor parties during the 1969 CRC campaign, all advocating policies that would insure a status for Coloureds superior to that of Africans.[44] Absent from the active political scene but operating from underground was a small remnant of activists from the South African Coloured People's Congress of the 1950s Congress alliance who in 1968 produced *Document 87,* a flyer denouncing collaborators and demanding the "right to sit in Parliament together with men like Nelson Mandela, Walter Sisulu, Bram Fischer or Dr. Dadoo."

Also overshadowed on the political scene in the late 1960s and 1970s were adherents of the ultra-left Unity Movement. Led mainly by Trotskyist Coloured intellectuals who categorically endorsed boycott, opposed mass protest as unprincipled, and were critical of the African National Congress for its alliance with the Stalinist-oriented South African Communist Party, the

Unity Movement had been more influential in the Western Cape in the 1950s than the ANC. The small but radical Teachers' League of South Africa kept alive the Unity Movement's heritage by condemning in vitriolic terms any participation in government bodies (*Document 95*).[45] Its pro-boycott position gained new vitality in the black consciousness movement, which denounced participation as emphatically as the Unity Movement but without its dogmatism.

When the Federal Party failed to win the 1969 CRC election, taking only 12 of the elected seats compared to 26 captured by the Labour Party, the government reacted by filling all 20 of the appointive seats with Federal Party members, including 13 who had failed to win seats in the election. On the grounds that his party had a majority in the Council, Swartz was appointed to the well-paid chairmanship of the executive committee, even though he had emerged in third place in his own constituency with only 1,667 votes as against the Labour candidate's 5,632.[46]

The Labour Party protested this brazenly undemocratic outcome by walking out of the Council, although its office holders continued to accept their salaries and perquisites. In many other ways the party's course was erratic and ambivalent. While posing as allies of the liberation struggle, party leaders found it necessary most of the time to put their first priority on the immediate bread-and-butter needs of their electorate and to de-emphasize long-run political change. More than politicians in any other organization operating within "the system," Labour Party leaders were disposed to bitterness and anger toward apartheid; but as prudent and ambitious men, they found it difficult to be intransigent while dealing with practical problems after they assumed control of the executive committee following the 1975 CRC election, or when meeting face-to-face with cordial white officials who sought to convince them of their good intentions. Meanwhile, wishful thinking was encouraged not only by officials who gave assurances that there would soon be a fully elected council but also by liberal Afrikaans intellectuals who drew much publicity in the 1970s by advocating the full political integration of Coloureds, whom they characterized as "brown Afrikaners."

Meanwhile, black consciousness and its ideal of a united black front posed an alternative set of tactics for the Labour Party. Only a minority of Coloureds were prepared to embrace the idea of a common identity with Africans, but the appeal of black consciousness to young Coloured militants became so great during the 1970s that Labour Party leaders had to reckon with it.[47] They incorporated the term "black" into their rhetoric, but used it inconsistently to signify both "African" and "nonwhite." Within black consciousness organizations, Coloureds displayed ambivalence toward "system" leaders like Sonny Leon of the Labour Party whose attacks on apartheid were popular and helped to fill the political vacuum of the early 1970s.

Leon had risen during World War II to the highest position open to a Coloured soldier, that of regimental sergeant major. He was later employed by the De Beers mining company and became a supporter of the United

Party. In assuming the leadership of the Labour Party in 1969 he replaced a leader who was accused of becoming too cozy with government officials. His outspoken opposition to the National Party gave him a reputation for militancy, and being denied a passport for several years in the mid-1970s contributed to his dissident image. By disposition, however, Leon was not a radical and felt little affinity with black militants outside the system, or with those who adhered to Marxist or revolutionary ideologies.[48]

By July 1974, three months after the Lisbon coup when even the Federal Party was taking a more critical line toward the government, Leon brought about a stalemate in the CRC when he introduced a motion declaring no confidence in the Council and demanding direct representation in Parliament as a prelude to universal enfranchisement. With Swartz himself abstaining, the motion was adopted. Departing from past practice, Prime Minister Vorster agreed to meet with a delegation selected by Leon. At a meeting on August 19, Vorster defended the government's policy of "parallel development" for Coloureds.[49] The Coloured people, Vorster's Minister of Bantu Affairs, Connie Mulder, had said, would never be represented in Parliament, either directly or indirectly, just as parallel lines would never meet even if they were "extended into infinity." In reality, Leon declared, the government and the Coloured people were on a collision course; the Labour Party would campaign for a mandate for parliamentary representation at the next Council election. Meanwhile, the party's immediate program stressed socioeconomic parity.[50]

The Labour Party was victorious in the March 1975 election for the CRC after a campaign during which an Anti-CRC Committee distributed thousands of "Don't Vote" leaflets and disrupted Labour Party meetings. Labour won 31 elective seats, a majority of the 60-member Council. It then surprised those who had believed its declarations that victory would be followed by a closing down of the Council. Arguing that the situation had changed because of legislation empowering the Minister of Coloured Relations to continue the Council's functions if the party carried out its threat, Leon accepted the chairmanship of the executive committee and also the appointment by the government of four party members to fill nominated seats. The party had done a political somersault.

Returning to its confrontational stance later in 1975, however, the Labour Party in November refused to approve the discriminatory Coloured administration budget, thus placing the government in the embarrassing position of having to act on its own if payments were to be made to some 25,000 Coloured officials and teachers and 150,000 pensioners. Leon was fired as chairman of the Council, and Labour Party members of the executive committee resigned. A nominated member from the Federal Party, Alathea Jansen, who was a government employee, was appointed as chairperson of the executive committee to sign the budget. From this point onward, the Labour Party succeeded in creating a ludicrous situation in the Council. "Year after year," wrote Richard van der Ross, one of the party's founders, "the Council would be summoned and would meet, the majority party (LP) would boycott the opening, brief debates would be held and there would be adjournment. The budget would be approved by Mrs. Jansen; and the Executive Committee, composed of Labour Party members (who had been re-elected to their positions by the Council after resigning), would continue during sessions and in the interim to administer their respective departments despite their opposition to the Budget."[51]

Meanwhile, differences within the Labour Party became more heated and confused. Party leaders were divided in their reactions to the 1976 uprising; some were shocked when Coloured youth joined the violent street protests in Cape Town between August and December. Consternation and frustration also followed the tabling of the report of the Theron Commission on June 18, 1976. This commission, appointed in 1973 to make recommendations regarding the future of the Coloured population, reported that "the vast and effective majority of Coloured people" strongly opposed the system of government-controlled representation and recommended that provision be made for unspecified but "satisfactory" forms of direct Coloured representation at all levels of the political system.[52] The Vorster government summarily rejected any notion that racial barriers between whites and Coloureds be dissolved and instead pressed forward with its own blueprint for a tricameral parliament in which Coloureds and Indians would be represented in segregated parliamentary chambers. To some in the Labour Party, Vorster's plan looked like a step forward; others took it as one more insulting rebuff to Coloured demands for full equality.

By mid-1978, despite the strongly rejectionist rhetoric of Labour Party statements on the new constitutional proposals, Leon publicly took the position that if the proposals were enacted, the Labour Party should enter a Coloured parliament, not only to prevent a take-over by conservatives but also "to wreck it in the same way that we have done with the Coloured Representative Council."[53] The ambivalence and ineffectualness of this position was not lost on the Labour Party's critics, or for that matter on the party's own leadership as it struggled to put an angry face on what had become an increasingly tame body. Reviled from the left by Unity Movement radicals who pointed to the "vast increase in the numbers of well-paid political collaborators" that the new constitutional dispensation would produce (*Document 95*), Leon and his colleagues also found their tactical alliance with Buthelezi doomed, since Inkatha could hardly endorse proposals that excluded Africans from parliamentary representation.

Compromised by his on-again-off-again brand of militancy, Leon was replaced as Labour Party leader by Reverend Allan Hendrickse in September 1978. Hendrickse returned the party to a more confrontational style in the CRC, refusing to give evidence to the government commission that was inquiring into the draft bill for the proposed constitution. P. W. Botha had meanwhile become prime minister. His frustration with the party's uncooperativeness reached a climax on November 9, 1979, when he met in a stormy session with Hendrickse and the CRC executive. In excerpts from the transcript of the meeting, published in the *Rand Daily Mail* on November

12 (*Document 96*), Botha said he did not believe the Labour Party spoke for "the responsible part" of the Coloured community and "finally" warned the group: "I say this now, again: one-man one-vote in this country is out. That is, never." The leaders who had met with Botha, Hendrickse said afterwards, had been "insulted, intimidated, and treated like children."[54] No doubt Botha would have preferred to perpetuate the life of the CRC until the promulgation of the new constitution; but the Labour majority had proved trying to his short temper, and he abolished the Council when its term expired in April 1980. "This is what we wanted," the Labour Party exulted in a retrospective rationalization of its tactics since 1965 (*Document 97*). "Only the Government could close the CRC. It could never have been done by boycotts or walkouts." The ANC's *Sechaba* congratulated the Labour Party for having paralyzed the Council "from within."[55]

Many thought Hendrickse had been radicalized when he was detained for two months in solitary confinement in August-October 1976. In January 1983, however, the Labour Party under Hendrickse's leadership decided to participate in the proposed Coloured parliament. Looking back over decades of political history, he said, "since 1910 the Coloured people have moved from the politics of protest to the politics of challenge," leading to the current "politics of negotiation" and "politics of persuasion," rather than defiance and confrontation.[56]

Among the Indians, unlike the Coloureds, participants in officially-sponsored bodies felt no pressure to win mass approval. The conservatism of many in the Indian upper and middle classes was grounded in their sense of the reality of white dominance and the advantages to be gained by accommodation to it. ANC activist Frene Ginwala, writing in exile in the 1970s, observed:

For a small section, drawn largely from the professionals, the entrepreneurs, the skilled technicians and wealthy businessmen, the economic boom [in the 1960s] coinciding with separate development has brought previously unimaginable wealth and opportunity. The less overt racism, the contact with white officials, the rare handshake from a Cabinet minister, the occasional consultation with Vorster, white political parties and businessmen create the illusion that they are in the center of power and influencing developments. South Africa's need to create a better international image, and the speeches about changes and eliminating racial discrimination add to the belief that change will come from within the system and if Blacks are patient and moderate all will turn out well.[57]

Working-class Indians, on the other hand, did not share in this optimism, wrote sociologist Fatima Meer.

The Indian in the street is painfully alive to his vulnerable position, which he sees as sandwiched between two nationalisms, African and Afrikaner, and is grateful for all he can get. He is aware of disparities, reacts with deep hurt when he is insulted for his color, but consoles himself when he looks at the rest of the world through South African eyes and believes that things could be worse. He has, too, the ability to withdraw into his group, his religion, his work, his family, and protected by the shell he thus forms, he can be happy, and in his happiness he preserves some dignity and passes something of it on to his children.[58]

Indian political organization dated from the founding of the Natal Indian Congress by Mohandas Gandhi in 1894 and focussed initially on protests against discriminatory restrictions. By the 1950s, the South African Indian Congress, with a following in the Transvaal and Cape as well as Natal, came under radical leadership and entered an alliance with the ANC, joining with it to experiment with Gandhian tactics of civil disobedience in the 1952 Defiance Campaign. Able to assist with money, dedicated organizers and contact with foreign supporters, the Indian Congress was a valued partner to the ANC in the turbulent decade leading up to Rivonia, and many of its members later left the country to become activists in exile.

With the crushing of the ANC and its allies inside the country, however, Indians became politically quiescent, leaving the government a free hand to introduce appointed bodies that purported to represent Indian opinion. At the end of the 1960s, Fatima Meer observed that the government had become unexpectedly successful not only in stifling all protest outside its own dummy bodies but also making Indians "dependent on the Department of Indian Affairs for a large range of everyday needs." Ordinary Indians found the Afrikaner bureaucrat more informed and approachable than English bureaucrats in earlier years, and those who were well-to-do responded appreciatively to the tactful and benevolent attitudes displayed by high officials toward members of the Indian social elite.[59] Yet the true extent of Indian support for Pretoria's overall political dispensation could only be tested through popular response to an elected Indian representative body.

In 1968, the government replaced an earlier advisory council with an appointed 25-member body called the South African Indian Council (SAIC). This body had no legislative powers, but its defenders argued that the patient and deferential approach of its members would achieve more in the long-run than intransigence of the kind shown by Indian leaders in earlier decades. "In the framework of the present political limitations, it becomes imperative to pay heed to the advice, 'stoop to conquer,'" wrote Dr. M. B. Naidoo, a member of the Council. "In the history of mankind races have survived not by confronting superior forces, which could have led to annihilation, but by wise and patient compromise that assured their survival" (*Document 94*). Council leaders, for example, A. M. Rajab (*Document 89*), were anxious not only to avoid antagonizing the state but also were alert to reassure the prickly Zulu Chief Buthelezi by dissociating themselves and the Indian community from the critical stance of the Natal Indian Congress (NIC), revived in 1971 by supporters of the old Congress alliance.

Wary of testing the depth of boycott sentiment, Pretoria moved at a cautious pace toward creating a fully elected council. In 1972 provision was made to add five members to the SAIC who would be elected by Indian local government committees. In 1974 the proportion of members thus elected in a council of 30 was increased to 15. The SAIC itself elected four members of an executive committee, but the committees' chairman was appointed by the Minister of Indian Affairs. J. N. Reddy, a banker who became chairman in 1973 at the height of the black consciousness movement, expressed concern about racial barriers facing the well-educated younger generation but asserted his belief that these barriers could only be overcome through "a change of heart on the part of the whites and in this regard dialogue and communication help to pave the way."[60]

When former activists revived the Natal Indian Congress in 1971, several important tactical questions required urgent answers. The NIC aimed to resuscitate the traditions of the Congress alliance and the Freedom Charter but had to find ways of doing this without exposing itself as an obvious surrogate for the ANC. It also needed to find ways of relating to the black consciousness movement without giving up its fundamental commitment to the protection of Indian group interests. Neither of these challenges was unproblematic, but most troublesome as time went on was the question of whether to try to use the SAIC as a forum to air the NIC's radical oppositional views. Opinion within the Congress was divided on the matter. Most members favored boycott, but some top leaders in the mid-1970s including M. J. Naidoo (who had unsuccessfully called for the Bulugha conference to demand the release of leaders on Robben Island) advocated participation on the grounds that all available platforms should be exploited and argued that the Coloured Labour Party had successfully built a mass support base by using participation tactics.[61] A few years later, after a trip abroad had enabled him to assess the opinions of exiles, Naidoo reversed his position and came out against the "participation with rejection" policy. Such a policy, he now argued, would confuse and embarrass the NIC's allies in exile and weaken their campaign to isolate South Africa and win the release of political prisoners. Of special concern to him was the effect upon radical African intellectuals within the country who might turn to "retribution . . . or a 1949 mentality" at what many would perceive as an Indian sell-out.[62] At the end of the 1970s, boycott remained the official position of the NIC, despite occasional attempts to reopen the debate, which continued into the 1980s.

Meanwhile the government, pleased with the influence it had acquired among Indian businessmen, moved gradually toward the establishment of a directly elected Council. Voter registration became compulsory for Indians in 1977. Finally in 1978 legislation was enacted for a Council of 40 elected members plus five who were to be nominated. After three more years of delay, an election was held in November 1981. Realizing Pretoria's worst fears, the average turnout in election districts was only about ten percent, the most effective national election boycott in South Africa's history. Sponsoring the boycott was a newly emergent Charter Movement, reminiscent of the Congress alliance of the 1950s, a multiracial coalition of more than 100 organizations that endorsed nonracialism and the ANC's Freedom Charter. Undeterred, the National Party pressed forward with its constitutional proposals to replace the failed Indian Council with an elected Indian house in a segregated tricameral parliament.

The end of the 1970s found the Botha government moving cautiously ahead with the implementation of its designs for a reformed political order. Despite rejectionist attitudes among the majority of Coloureds and Indians, plans were unfolding for the incorporation of these minorities as junior partners in national government. Where Africans were concerned, the National Party continued to adhere to the broad outlines of Verwoerd's blueprint for grand apartheid but was being forced in some respects to modify what had become an unworkable system of indirect rule. Three homelands had attained nominal independence (Transkei, Bophuthatswana and Venda), and a fourth, Ciskei, was on a path toward independence in 1981. Meanwhile, however, the outside world had declined to recognize South Africa's effort to "decolonize" its African population; the remaining homelands were resisting the notion of independence; and, most seriously, the great majority of urban Africans were opposed to the homeland citizenship being thrust upon them. Ever harsher enforcement of the pass laws had barely stemmed let alone brought about the reversal of the townward movement of Africans assumed in Verwoerd's original vision.

The permanent presence of Africans in "white" cities had reluctantly been conceded, but the unpopularity of state-imposed community councils was pushing urban Africans increasingly toward new organizational responses to "the system," including the formation of civic associations that in the 1980s would contest with the community councils for power and control. State-approved African "leaders," both in homelands and community councils, commanded substantial patronage resources as the 1970s drew to a close; they also could rely on backup from government security forces to protect them against political rivals. Herein, though, lay a fundamental dilemma for the state: whether to make still more concessions to African critics of the system in order to try to build a structure of control based on legitimacy and consent, or to resist demands for genuine democratic rights and rely ever more heavily on control through coercion.

Notes

1. On the political history of the Transkei, see Gwendolen M. Carter, Thomas Karis, and Newell Stultz, *South Africa's Transkei: The Politics of Domestic Colonialism* (Evanston: Northwestern University Press, 1967).

2. Jill Johnson, *Soweto Speaks* (Johannesburg: Ad. Donker, 1979), p. 47.

3. Patrick Laurence, *The Transkei: South Africa's Politics of Partition* (Johannesburg: Ravan Press, 1976), p. 99.

4. See Laurence, p. 101; Pascal Gwala, ed., *Black Review 1973* (Durban: Black Community Programmes, 1974), p. 29, and Thoko Mbanjwa, ed., *Black Review 1974/5* (Lovedale: Black Community Programmes, 1975), p. 19.

5. Woods had not yet met Steve Biko, who was to profoundly transform his perception of South African politics. See Donald Woods, *Asking for Trouble: Autobiography of a Banned Journalist* (London: Paddington Press, 1978; and New York: Atheneum, 1981).

6. See *From Protest to Challenge,* volume 3, pp. 299–302.

7. Alex Boraine was presiding. As he remembers the incident, Buthelezi rose in a fury, rushed up, and took over the microphone, saying that he had been attacked personally as a man who was not a leader. Boraine calmed him down with difficulty. Conversation with Boraine (June 1991). Naidoo remarked later that he and his colleague at the conference, Ramlall Ramesar, knew of Buthelezi's sensitivity to criticism and therefore, the night before, had carefully thought through what Naidoo would say. Nevertheless, Naidoo felt that his remarks had permanently alienated Buthelezi. Conversation with M. J. Naidoo and Ramlall Ramesar (May 1977).

8. *Progress: Newspaper of the Progressive Party of South Africa,* January 1974, p. 4.

9. Press statement by Chief Lucas Mangope, September 8, 1972.

10. *Survey of Race Relations 1976* (Johannesburg: South African Institute of Race Relations, 1977), pp. 27–28.

11. Conversation with Cedric Phatudi (August 1979). See Jill Wentzel, "Black United Front," *Reality,* July 1977, pp. 6–7. The meeting included a few Africans who were not participants in officially-sponsored institutions, for example, Lucy Mvubelo of the National Union of Clothing Workers, who opposed the ANC's advocacy of disinvestment, and Godfrey Pitje, a lawyer who had been president of the ANC Youth League. The steering committee of the Black United Front (sometimes referred to as the Black Unity Front) included, in addition to the three homeland leaders, Dr. Sipho Nyembezi as chairman, David Thebehali, and John Mavuso, all strong admirers of Buthelezi.

12. Although Vorster lectured his listeners on black leadership, his personal contacts with individual leaders—including his fellow advocate Duma Nokwe—were apparently almost nonexistent. The conversation with Nokwe recounted in Document 91 must have made a deep impression on him. It appears to be the same conversation with Nokwe in the 1950s recounted in his biography. In discussing Nokwe's motivation for becoming an advocate, Vorster suggested that he lacked an interest in helping his own people, and had told Vorster explicitly (and inexplicably): "No, I'm not interested in people. I'm interested only in governing this country—and we WILL govern this country one day." Quoted in John d'Oliveira, *Vorster—The Man* (Johannesburg: Ernest Stanton Ltd., 1977), pp. 260–61.

13. Laurence, p. 11. In March 1976, Lennox Mlonzi, a Xhosa member of the Soweto Urban Bantu Council, organized a meeting on Transkeian independence attended by an estimated 88 men. A police report of the meeting indicated that probing questions were asked about inadequate consultation, the consequences of independence for urban Africans, and why independence was being accepted prior to the release of Mandela and others from Robben Island. Police report of meeting on Transkeian independence, Soweto, March 28, 1976. Also see conversations with Lennox Mlonzi (June 1977 and October 1977).

14. Before banning the ANC and the PAC, Matanzima had invited them to set up offices in Umtata on condition that they abandon military means. He also sought to recruit individual Africans in exile. Tsepo T. Letlaka, a lawyer who had been the first president of the ANC Youth League in Cape Province and later a PAC leader, was one of the few who accepted Matanzima's invitation to return. In arguing for Transkeian independence, he used the language of national liberation with PAC overtones, indicating that "soil," in a mystical way, united the Transkei and the rest of South Africa. Talk by T. T. Letlaka, California Institute of Technology, December 1, 1975. Letlaka figured in a "bitter clash" in the Transkeian House of Assembly in March 1979 when a member attacked Sobukwe and Mandela. Then the Minister of Finance, Letlaka argued that Transkei should identify itself with the liberation struggle. *The Nation* (Johannesburg), March 1979. On Letlaka, see conversation with Reverend Mcebisi Xundu (October 1977).

15. Laurence, p. 119.

16. As independence approached in October 1976, the American State Department announced that it would not recognize the Transkei. Within hours after the celebration of independence, the United Nations General Assembly echoed this position in a 134–0 vote, with

one abstention, that of the United States. A public member of the US delegation has written that the US position "was based on minor legal quibbles, the sort of points we could have announced in explanation of a positive vote. . . . Once we were thought of as the world's conscience; now we seemed to be the world's lawyer." Stephen Hess, "Changing the UN: Irrelevant Forum," *The New Republic,* January 22, 1977, pp. 34–37.

17. African National Congress, "Commission on Strategy and Tactics," Second National Consultative Conference, June 1985, p. 17.

18. Some passages in this section have been taken from the chapter "Black Challenge" by Thomas Karis (without by-line) in *South Africa: Time Running Out* (New York: Ford Foundation and Foreign Policy Association, 1981).

19. Alf Stadler, *The Political Economy of Modern South Africa* (Cape Town: David Philip, 1987), p. 88.

20. David Welsh, "The Growth of Towns," in Monica Wilson and Leonard Thompson, eds., *The Oxford History of South Africa* (Oxford: Clarendon Press, 1971), volume 2, pp. 187, 190, 228.

21. Welsh, p. 230, quoting a member of Parliament.

22. Quoted in John Kane-Berman, *Soweto: Black Revolt, White Reaction* (Johannesburg: Ravan Press, 1978), p. 206. Mosala nevertheless continued to sit on the Council until its collapse after the Soweto uprising.

23. Members of township Advisory Boards in the period before 1964 had less authority than UBC members but were generally held in higher public regard. Members of the ANC served on Advisory Boards despite the pro-boycott decision of 1949, and leaders of the Congress of Advisory Boards joined ANC leaders in deputations to government officials. See *From Protest to Challenge,* volume 2, pp. 11 and 83, and volume 3, pp. 73 and 298. Advisory boards, especially before 1964 were sometimes headed by strong personalities who could point to successes. In 1976 the journalist Aggrey Klaaste recalled that "those gentlemen [of the old Advisory Boards] had a fighting spirit that has left its mark." *The World,* July 18, 1976.

24. Nor was the combustibility of the situation adequately appreciated by Percy Qoboza, the editor of *The World,* who was at dinner at the home of Helen Suzman on June 15. "We were academically speculating how much time we still had. . . . I specifically said, well, in three years we would be in serious trouble. Somebody said it might take ten years." Conversation with Qoboza (August 1979).

25. Conversation with David Thebehali (June 1977).

26. Minutes of meeting of government officials, Soweto Urban Bantu Councillors, and other leaders, Pretoria, June 19, 1976.

27. Section 10 rights are explained in chapter 1, note 7.

28. Quoted in *Work in Progress,* no. 15, October 1980, p. 5.

29. Quoted in Simon Bekker and Richard Humphries, *From Control to Confusion: The Changing Role of Administration Boards in South Africa: 1971–1983* (Pietermaritzburg: Shuter & Shooter, 1985), pp. 101–102.

30. *Survey of Race Relations 1978,* pp. 341, 349 and passim.

31. Discussion of the Committee of Ten is based in part on conversations with Chief Gatsha Buthelezi (August 1979), Ellen Kuzwayo (August 1979), Leonard Mosala (August 1979), Tom Manthata (August 1979), Percy Qoboza, Nthato Motlana (June 1987), and Curtis Nkondo (May 1989).

32. The original members of the Committee of Ten were Nthato Motlana (medical doctor), Vela Kraai (chairman of the Soweto African Traders' Association), Ellen Kuzwayo (a prominent social worker), Douglas Lolwane (National African Federated Chambers of Commerce), Tom Manthata (BPC activist employed by the South African Council of Churches), Lekgau Mathabathe (headmaster of the Morris Isaacson High School), Rev. M. V. "Castro" Mayatula (BPC activist employed by the Christian Institute), Thandisizwe Mazibuko (Black People's Convention), Leonard Mosala and Ramsey Ramokgopa (employees of the International Business Machines Corporation). Aggrey Klaaste (deputy editor of *Weekend World*) served as recording secretary. Percy Qoboza, editor of *The World,* was instrumental in convening the meeting but did not attend.

33. Kane-Berman, John, *Soweto: Black Revolt, White Reaction* (Johannesburg: Ravan Press, 1978), pp. 139 and 209.

34. Manifesto, "Soweto Local Authority," issued by the Committee of Ten, Soweto, July 1977.

35. Kane-Berman, p. 211.

36. Conversation with Motlana (June 1987).

37. Conversations with Dr. Stoffel van der Merwe (August 1979) and Motlana (June 1979).

38. In a mid-1979 attitude survey of 150 men in Soweto age 16 or older with at least a mid-high school education ("the most politicized groups of urban Africans"), a leading opinion pollster asked respondents: "Think of people like yourself in Soweto—people who live and work around you. Who would they see to be their real leaders?" The preferences were for (cumulatively) the Committee of Ten, former leaders of the banned Black Parents Association or of the banned Black People's Convention, 68%; African National Congress leaders in jail or exile, 21%; Chief Gatsha Buthelezi, 5%; other homeland leaders, 2%; PAC leaders, 1%; elected community councillors, 1%; and others, 3%. Lawrence Schlemmer, "Change in South Africa: Opportunities and Constraints," in Carl Rosberg and Robert Price, eds., *The Apartheid Regime* (Berkeley: University of California Press, 1980) pp. 276–77.

39. "A section of the brown middle-class, who constituted a political elite from the 1900s to the 1950s, and remain a social elite, withdrew from public political activity with the introduction of separate representative institutions. . . . Their place has been taken by the new middle class, who benefitted economically in the 1950s and 1960s from segregation, from protection of competition from White, African, and Indian traders and workers, from support of government policy and from the establishment of the Coloured Development Corporation. This new middle class, many of rural origin and mainly Afrikaans-speaking, are more represented in the Federal Party." Mary Simons, "Organised Coloured Political Movements," in Hendrik van der Merwe and C. J. Groenwald, eds., *Occupational and Social Change among Coloured People in South Africa* (Cape Town: Juta, 1976), p. 231.

40. Simons, p. 231.

41. S. T. van der Horst, ed., *The Theron Commission Report: A Summary of the Findings and Recommendations of the Commission of Enquiry into Matters Relating to the Coloured Population Group* (Johannesburg: South African Institute of Race Relations, 1976), p. 101. The source for potential voters is *Survey of Race Relations in South Africa 1975*, p. 14.

42. M. W. Holland, *House of Assembly Debates*, April 12, 1962, col. 3879.

43. *Rand Daily Mail*, February 20, 1969. Also see Tom Swartz, "Coloured Progress under Separate Development," in N. J. Rhoodie, ed., *South African Dialogue: Contrasts in South African Thinking on Basic Race Issues* (Johannesburg: McGraw Hill Book Co., 1972).

44. The leader of the Republican Coloured People's Party was prominent in the Griqua sub-group and advocated an extension of the Immorality Act to bar sexual relations between Coloureds and Africans. The leader of the Conservative Party was a Cape Town school principal who endorsed separate development for Africans and parallel development for Coloureds. The leader of the Transvaal Coloured National Party was a graduate of the University of Witwatersrand Medical School who saw the Coloureds as "a separate race" encroached upon by Indians and Africans. *Rand Daily Mail*, February 20, 1969.

45. "As an organisation, the League exists largely in name only and subscribers to the *Journal* are estimated in the low hundreds, whereas an organization like the Cape Teachers' Professional Association (CTPA), for example, has a membership of 8,500." Pierre Hugo, *Quislings or Realists? A Documentary study of "Coloured" politics in South Africa* (Johannesburg: Ravan Press, 1978), p. 3. See conversation with Franklin Sonn, who was the president of CTPA for many years (January 1978).

46. *Daily Dispatch* (East London), October 8, 1969.

47. Jakes Gerwel and Adam Small, the most senior Coloured lecturers at the University of the Western Cape at the beginning of the 1970s, were key people in the students' open identification as "blacks." Conversation with Gerwel (April 1990). Sipho Buthelezi, a BPC activist, was an observer at the Labour Party conference in 1973 and reported that it had adopted the entire black consciousness philosophy as "a political strategy." Conversation with Sipho Buthelezi (October 1977).

48. Leon was reported in 1973 as having privately expressed concern about young members in Durban who wanted the Labour Party to withdraw from the Council; they were being influenced by what he called "a strong Red element in Natal." *The Star,* April 21, 1973.

49. The transcript of the meeting is in Hugo, pp. 209–17.

50. For remarks by Mulder and Leon, see *Survey of Race Relations 1974,* pp. 13–18.

51. R. E. van der Ross, *The Rise and Decline of Apartheid: A Study of Political Movements among the Coloured People of South Africa, 1880–1985* (Cape Town: Tafelberg, 1979), p. 348.

52. See van der Horst, p. 118.

53. *Rand Daily Mail,* August 22, 1978. Also see *To the Point,* September 15, 1978 and *Work in Progress,* no. 23, June 1982, pp. 26–27.

54. *New York Times,* November 10, 1979.

55. *Sechaba,* May 1980.

56. Allan Hendrickse, "The leader of the Labour Party explains why he has decided to participate in government's planned new dispensation," *Leadership SA,* Winter 1983, p. 24. On his detention, see conversation with Hendrickse (May 1977) and Piet Coetzer, *Allan Hendrickse: Awaiting Trial* (Alberton: Librarius Felicitas, 1984).

57. Frene Ginwala, *Indian South Africans* (London: Minority Rights Group, 1977), p. 17.

58. Fatima Meer, "Indian People: Current Trends and Policies," in Peter Randall, ed., *South Africa's Minorities* (Johannesburg: Study Project on Christianity in Apartheid Society, 1971), p. 22.

59. Meer, p. 19.

60. J. N. Reddy, "South African Indian Council," in Thoko Mbanjwa, ed., *Apartheid: Hope or Despair for Blacks?* (Durban: Black Community Programmes, 1976), p. 26.

61. M. J. Naidoo, "SAIC—My Thoughts on the Subject," statement of March 9, 1976. Conversations with M. J. Naidoo and Ramlall Ramesar (May 1977).

62. M. J. Naidoo, "My Case Against SAIC Participation," statement of May 28, 1979. Conversation with M. J. Naidoo (December 1989). Naidoo was responding, in part, to the keen interest of younger people in reassessing the boycott strategy adopted toward the forthcoming SAIC election. See Glenn Moss, "SAIC—participation or boycott," *Work in Progress,* no. 10, November 1979. pp. 1–6.

9. Buthelezi and Inkatha

Chief Gatsha Buthelezi was unique among homeland leaders during the 1970s in his thrust for national prestige and power. With a limited but secure base as a hereditary chief connected to the Zulu royal family and political pre-eminence in KwaZulu, he also claimed national legitimacy as the above-ground exponent of the tradition and continuity of the African National Congress. Buthelezi was protean in the varieties of his appeal. He stoked the passions of Zulu ethnic nationalism. Throughout the decade he embraced the ANC and the ideals of its "founding fathers" while seeking to marginalize its leadership in exile. In the first few years of the black consciousness movement, he had a special standing among homeland leaders in the eyes of black university students. Steve Biko spoke of him as "a man who could easily have been my leader" if he had given up his homeland role.[1] Buthelezi's tone of radical urgency and his call for movement toward majority rule shortly before the start of the Soweto uprising in June 1976 appealed to anti-apartheid whites as well as blacks. But as popular pressures grew, his avoidance of protest initiated by others and his pragmatic conservatism became increasingly evident. He turned more and more to the whites who held political and economic power, representing himself as a black leader who could be relied upon to safeguard minority rights and capitalism.

Buthelezi sought to exploit his participation in the apartheid system for anti-apartheid ends, but by the end of the 1970s he had failed to win acceptance as part of the broad liberation movement. Instead, the system itself had exerted a co-optive influence upon him, and his popularity was in decline. Furthermore, Buthelezi had adopted the high-risk strategy of projecting himself and his following into a position of rivalry with the ANC.

Black consciousness leaders moved from ambivalence to rejection of Buthelezi as a source of confusion and division. His status as a political leader was reinforced with the launching in 1975 of Inkatha, a mass political movement that was linked with but independent of government structures. Although Zulu-based, it reached out nationally to other Africans and, through the South African Black Alliance, also to Coloureds and Indians in an ineffectual effort to supplant the ANC. Although Buthelezi's opposition to what he termed the "hideousness" of apartheid was almost entirely rhetorical and was pronounced from the relative safety of his government-paid position, by the time of the Soweto uprising he had become the most prominent black leader in the country. His position was enhanced by the English-language press and, in time, by a portion of the Afrikaans press, which featured his opposition to violence and economic sanctions.[2]

Buthelezi's ambitions for mass leadership were constrained by his sense of what was possible and by his and KwaZulu's financial dependence upon the central government. His power depended also upon his ability to cater to the special interests of KwaZulu's bureaucratic elite, its chiefs and small businessmen, and also, nationally, the white minority with its entrenched privileges. In Buthelezi's realistic calculation, protection for that minority was politically essential if there was to be any hope that power might be shared. Buthelezi appeared to welcome the rising militancy in the country—that of black labor from early 1973 and of young blacks during the Soweto uprising—and the success of revolutionaries who won independence for Mozambique and Angola in 1975. Yet his radical language was equivocal, and his threats of mass boycott and strike action by black consumers and workers were empty or left for implementation to the distant future. The major political developments of the decade responded to a revolutionary impulse not shared by Buthelezi, thus, from the standpoint of militants, leaving him behind the times.

After the Soweto uprising, some white liberals began to lose their earlier optimism that Buthelezi could become an effective national leader. Late in the 1970s, Buthelezi pulled back from advocacy of majority rule and spoke disparagingly of the liberation movement's "early cries for one man one vote." Critics who saw him as opportunistic and authoritarian became more strident, whereas sympathizers who accepted as bona fide his commitments to nonviolence and African liberation continued to look to his leadership. These different perspectives were complicated by reactions to Buthelezi's controversial personality. He was a man of warmth and charm but also of pride and ego. In private, his humor could approach self-mockery, but public criticism that Buthelezi saw as denigration could evoke fury and ugly threats.[3]

Nevertheless, major leaders of the ANC, at a time when its visibility was low, retained hope that Buthelezi could be a tacit ally and even speculated that he might be a more active ally in some future crisis. Their hope—or illusion—persisted until an Inkatha-ANC meeting in London at the end of October 1979. In going to London, Buthelezi talked ambitiously of arriving at a "united front" with the ANC. By this time, however, he was already seeing accommodation with the status quo as a surer road to power than casting his lot with the ANC. Early in 1980 he invited industrial and commercial entrepreneurs to enter "a three-way partnership": themselves, the National Party, and "black South Africa," whose organizational embodiment was Inkatha, "the only black group in the country which can be constructively involved in the future."[4] Meanwhile, leaders of the resurgent ANC came to see Buthelezi as an obstructive rival rather than as an ally; and in mid-1980, Oliver Tambo described him as having "emerged on the side of the enemy against the people."[5]

Buthelezi as Homeland Leader

To fulfill his ambition for national leadership, Buthelezi needed an independent power base. The government's homeland policy provided him an institutional framework but one subject to Pretoria's interests and financial control. KwaZulu was an impoverished homeland, fragmented in more than 44 pieces, whose people depended on migrants and commuting laborers for subsistence. Its government relied on the South African state for about three-quarters of its revenue. Because the hereditary nature of his chieftainship antedated the homeland offices he held, Buthelezi vehemently denied that his status as a chief was bestowed by the apartheid system. His official position, however, enabled him to predominate over the Zulu king and potential opponents among other chiefs. KwaZulu structures also had a symbiotic relationship with Inkatha.

Participation in the KwaZulu homeland structure offered Buthelezi the political opportunity to stand out as an opponent of Pretoria. That is, by staunchly opposing acceptance of formal independence, he was able to stake out a major claim to obstruction of apartheid policy. Yet his opposition to independence was ambiguous and in practice the distinction between formal independence and semi-autonomy was to become murky.

Buthelezi became acting chief of the 30,000 or so members of the Buthelezi clan in 1953 when he was 25 years old. Among hereditary Zulu chiefs, he was the only university graduate. In October 1955, he emerged as an effective public speaker in his first meeting with high officials. As one of those invited to address a conference of 300 tribal leaders in Natal called by Hendrik Verwoerd, then Minister of Native Affairs, he politely but firmly expressed common grievances and impressed his Zulu audience. He also incurred an irritated suspicion among white officials that was to earn him the distinction of police surveillance and was to dog him for years. The government did not confirm his chieftainship until two years later.

Buthelezi's official position inhibited his participation in political protest. When an ANC leaflet issued in the name of Chief Albert Lutuli urged a boycott of the inauguration of Zululand's first Bantu Regional Authority in October 1959, observers noted that Buthelezi stayed away. He explained that he had not been invited and that implementation of the Bantu

Authorities Act was understood to be voluntary.[6] In 1964 impatient officials declared that implementation was not voluntary, and Buthelezi publicly welcomed what he described as a clarification. Reacting after the Rivonia verdict of June 1964, he said he would comply, "for the only alternative would be revolution, which is something out of the question."[7] Buthelezi was installed later as chairman of a regional authority. In June 1970 chiefs elected him as Chief Executive Officer of the Zulu Territorial Authority. According to a leader of the South African Students' Organisation, Buthelezi had capitulated after having been long regarded as "the bastion of resistance to the institution of a territorial authority in Zululand."[8]

On the occasion of Buthelezi's election, the government's Department of Information expressed optimism about his ability to assist in implementing one of the key elements of the state's policy. "As one of the best educated and most articulate among the leaders of the [Zulu] nation," it said, Buthelezi could "enlist the support of the urbanised Zulu-speaking element outside the homelands who will have the status of citizens of the Zulu national unit." The press release concluded:

> Although at one time opposed to the establishment of the Bantu Authorities system in Natal, Chief Gatsha Buthelezi has gradually accepted the advantages of the Government's policy of separate development for his people. As indicated in his opening address at the inauguration of the Zulu Territorial Authority on 11 June, he wishes to see this policy implemented as rapidly as possible, with a view, ultimately, to gain full self-government, and to establish a Zulu state.[9]

In his address at the inauguration of the Authority on June 11, 1970, Buthelezi called for the government to assist in the development of "the whole Zulu nation" by providing for the representation of urban and rural Zulus who lived outside KwaZulu (*Document 98*). He proclaimed the loyalty of Zulus since 1910 "not only to the government of the day, but to white South Africa." The voluntary relinquishing of power in the future by "a metropolitan power such as South Africa . . . to a subject nation such as we are," he said, would be a historically unique event. As in many of his later speeches given under circumstances that highlighted his double-edged role, his rhetoric suggested obsequiousness but also included sly digs, tongue-in-cheek remarks, and occasional verbal rabbit punches, features that later became more common.

After becoming Chief Executive Officer, Buthelezi predicted, in a popular magazine sympathetic to the government, that KwaZulu would be given "full independence within a maximum of ten years."[10] In April 1972, the Zulu Legislative Assembly came into being, with 75 nominated and 55 elected members. In February 1977, KwaZulu moved from the status of a territorial authority to self-governance, with increased control over local affairs. Transkei had reached this status in 1963, 13 years before its nominal independence. In February 1978, KwaZulu's first general election took place and, in a low percentage poll of only 609,000 registered voters, members of

Inkatha defeated independent candidates for every one of the 55 elective seats. Only about 100 pro-Inkatha Zulus voted in Johannesburg.[11]

Movement toward KwaZulu independence then stalled. For Buthelezi, the goal of independence was rhetorical rather than actual since its premise was the grant of additional land and its consolidation. "We can dream our dreams" of a state once the boundaries are known, Buthelezi said when he predicted independence in ten years. In 1975, at the launching of Inkatha, he described independence as "a farce" so long as KwaZulu consisted of "separate pieces of inadequate territory for the largest ethnic group in South Africa."[12] Territorial consolidation was an unrealistic prospect, in part because it was at odds with the government's theory. The Commissioner-General of Zululand saw "Zulu Territorial Authority" in 1970 as

a misnomer. It should be called the Zululand People's Authority, because, you see, Zululand is split up into a patchwork of African areas separated by proclaimed white areas. This is the way it'll always remain—you can't expect the white sugar farmers to give up their areas and just move out. . . . [T]hey [the Zulus] must consolidate as a people— it can't be done territorially.[13]

Or, as expressed by Dr. L. I. Coertze, a National Party expert in constitutional law, "It makes no difference where a member of . . . [an] ethnic group finds himself. . . . It has nothing at all to do with borders . . . . He can be governed wherever he is."[14]

Buthelezi was too much the realist to expect the government to alter its policy in order to provide adequate land for a Zulu state. Even had it been willing to do so, the political dilemma inherent in the partition of South Africa would still have remained for Buthelezi: not only was he a Zulu leader who aspired to wear the mantle of Shaka as consolidator of the Zulus; he also aspired to wear the mantle of ANC leaders from Pixley ka Seme, his uncle and a founder of the ANC, to Lutuli, men who were committed to an undivided South Africa.

The ANC, Black Consciousness, and the PAC

In the 1970s Buthelezi regularly drew public attention to his membership in the ANC Youth League while he was a student at Fort Hare University College, the fact that Lutuli and others in the ANC had encouraged him to take up his hereditary role, and his contacts with ANC leaders before 1960 and afterwards in exile. His one exploit as a protester had occurred in 1950, his final college year, when he was one of several students accused of misbehavior during a student boycott of a visit by the Governor-General. He was expelled. In later years, Buthelezi made much of the fact that Seme had intervened to assist him. After being allowed to take his examinations in Durban, he received his degree. Although Buthelezi was a rank and file member of the Youth League, he appears not to have been an active member of the ANC after leaving Fort Hare.[15]

The ANC treated Buthelezi's participation in the homeland system as a tactical issue although in principle it was committed to the 1949 Program of Action, which called for the boycott of government-created bodies. Oliver Tambo defined the ANC's position in a speech in January 1980, when he asked: given the existence of the government's homeland program, how can it be stopped and then destroyed?

> We know that some of our people will have nothing to do with these institutions. We know that some are participating as irretrievable traitors or fortune seekers. We also know, however, that there are some who are participating in this enemy-imposed programme in pursuance of patriotic objectives, believing that such participation would weaken and facilitate destruction of these institutions from within.[16]

Patriots, he added, mobilized the people for struggle in preparation for "the seizure of power." He cited Paramount Chief Sabata Dalindyebo of Transkei, who had left South Africa and was present in Lusaka as he spoke.

Tambo's reluctance to make explicitly negative judgments about Buthelezi indicated the ambivalence that continued to exist within the ANC at the end of the 1970s. Speaking in 1985, Tambo reviewed the deterioration of the relationship and the blame due the ANC. He began by describing the expectation at the time of the Morogoro conference of 1969 that Buthelezi might become a key participant in the political mobilization of the homeland areas.[17]

> [W]e maintained regular contact with Chief Gatsha Buthelezi of the KwaZulu bantustan. We sought that this former member of the ANC Youth League who had taken up his position in the KwaZulu bantustan after consultation with our leadership, should use the legal opportunities provided by the bantustan programme to participate in the mass mobilisation of our people on the correct basis of the orientation of the masses to focus on the struggle for a united and non-racial South Africa. In the course of our discussions with him, we agreed that this would also necessitate the formation of a mass democratic organisation in the bantustan that he headed. Inkatha originated from this agreement.
>
> Unfortunately, we failed to mobilise our own people to take on the task of resurrecting Inkatha as the kind of organisation that we wanted, owing to the understandable antipathy of many of our comrades towards what they considered as working within the bantustan system. The task of reconstituting Inkatha therefore fell on Gatsha Buthelezi himself who then built Inkatha as a personal power base far removed from the kind of organisation we had visualised, as an instrument for the mobilisation of our people in the countryside into an active and conscious force for revolutionary change. In the first instance, Gatsha dressed Inkatha in the clothes of the ANC, exactly because he knew the masses to whom he was appealing were loyal to the ANC and had for six decades adhered to our movement as their

representative and their leader. Later, when he thought he had sufficient of a base, he also used coercive methods against the people to force them to support Inkatha.[18]

Before the rupture of 1979–80, the ANC displayed its fraternal attitude toward Buthelezi during his occasional encounters with ANC leaders abroad. Buthelezi tended to publicly exaggerate the significance of such contacts, implying that Tambo's public bear hugs connoted endorsement. Public expressions of ANC support for Buthelezi dated back to the early 1970s. In February 1971, the editor of *Sechaba,* the ANC's journal, published an article by P. V. T. Mbatha, an associate of Buthelezi, praising him as a "great leader of the people" who was "leading the Zulus against apartheid."[19] Ambivalence was evident two years later when *Sechaba,* after describing the bantustan policy as "a gigantic fraud," reprinted a talk by Buthelezi, delivered before the Scandinavian Institute for African Studies, "so that readers may see the dilemma in which some of those who are forced to serve on these institutions because of their position as chief of their people are placed."[20]

Tambo himself knew Buthelezi well and from time to time would discuss directly with him issues of importance to the ANC. In December 1973, Tambo spent a long night in Nairobi discussing statements that Buthelezi had made in the United States opposing sanctions and disinvestment. Tambo's persuasion was temporarily successful, as he has remembered it, since Buthelezi said "not a word" about these topics at an American-sponsored conference he attended immediately afterwards.[21] Despite Buthelezi's reiteration of his opposition to ANC policies in many later speeches, Tambo continued to believe until the London meeting that Buthelezi might yet yield to persuasion.

The "Makiwane eight," who were expelled from the ANC in 1975, accused Tambo of giving the impression that he supported Buthelezi's activities.[22] They saw as "duplicitous" Tambo's conciliatory personality and his readiness to smooth over differences. Buthelezi's public criticism of the Makiwane group served to identify him with the ANC, although after his break with the ANC in 1980, Buthelezi endorsed the expelled group's accusation that the Communist Party dominated the ANC. Buthelezi also identified himself with the ANC in criticizing black consciousness exiles who he alleged were pressing for the creation of a "third force" alongside the ANC and the Pan Africanist Congress. More nettlesome, however, were black consciousness critics within South Africa. Buthelezi hoped that he might discredit them if he could arrive at a "united front" with the ANC.

"From gaol I hear a message from Nelson Mandela and Walter Sisulu telling me to go on doing what I am doing on behalf of millions of black people," Buthelezi declared in a Soweto speech in October 1979.[23] The boldness of such public announcements, embracing the ANC, served to bolster Buthelezi's own credibility as a leader in the broad liberation movement. As his political machine and prominence grew, however, and as the ANC's own internal support burgeoned, he bridled at all suggestions that he was trying to ride on the popularity of the ANC. Between Buthelezi and his advisers, the conviction grew that the ANC as represented by those in exile really did not exist in South Africa and that "the true heir of the ANC" was Buthelezi himself.[24]

Many political and strategic considerations propelled the exiled ANC toward Buthelezi's embrace in the 1970s. His public statements were a propaganda windfall. As early as 1973 Buthelezi had called for "the release of Nelson Mandela and other black leaders on Robben Island" and the granting of immunity for Oliver Tambo to return home (*Document 100*).[25] On the other hand, ANC leaders were unhappy with Buthelezi's criticism of the campaign for disinvestment by foreign business during his travels abroad, his comments publicized in government propaganda, and the respectability he was giving to official policy by soliciting investment in KwaZulu. They understood that Buthelezi had to disavow violence, but his hobnobbing with conservative white political and business figures aroused the suspicion that he was following a political agenda quite different from, and in conflict with, their own.

Unlike Buthelezi's good relations with the ANC during the 1970s, his relations with the black consciousness movement were short-lived. For a time, cooperation had seemed possible. Buthelezi was among the speakers at a conference held in August 1971 to discuss the formation of the Black People's Convention. Although planners of the conference envisaged an organization that would reject homelands, they intended to maintain contact with sympathetic blacks operating inside the system. However, when the BPC was formally launched in July 1972 and appeared headed for confrontation, Buthelezi joined older and more cautious leaders in moving aside. He was not in 1972 or later disposed to be part of any movement that he could not control.

Meanwhile, debate continued within the South African Students' Organisation about the merits of "infiltration politics." In 1971 Temba Sono, president of SASO, visited the University of Zululand and spoke of the danger that homeland politics would lead to "warring nationalisms." Buthelezi was "a danger to black unity," he said. Sono has recalled that he was given

> the toughest experience during my presidency. Because these guys now started saying how can you attack Buthelezi when Buthelezi is in fact the best of them all? Virtually the whole student body took me to task to the extent they said now you resign. Otherwise we are disaffiliating from SASO.

He persuaded the students not to disaffiliate. Then at the University of the North, where the students were not Zulus, he again met criticism of SASO's policy. "I now had vivid evidence," he said later, that "Buthelezi's charisma and his standpoint [had] caught up the masses just like Sobukwe's" a decade earlier.[26]

Sono was affected by this experience and brought the debate within SASO into the open at its July 1972 General Students' Council by advocating some kind of cooperation with men like Buthelezi, whom he called a "force you cannot ignore." Sono pointed out, as Buthelezi himself frequently did, that black students made necessary compromises with "the system" by carrying passes and attending segregated universities. Biko, however, backed by others in the SASO leadership, described Sono's position as "very dangerous" and Buthelezi as the "one man who had led the entire world to believe in the Bantustan philosophy." Sono's position was voted down, and SASO's earlier ambivalence toward Buthelezi hardened into a strong rejectionist line. High school students in the newly formed South African Students' Movement translated Biko's considered criticism of Sono into spicy form in their newsletter in April 1973 (*Document 99*).

Had the black consciousness movement not taken a clear position of opposition to all blacks operating within government-created institutions, Buthelezi might have been able to pursue a strategic combination of verbal protest and pragmatic accommodation for many years. The more SASO and the Black People's Convention refused to exempt him from their attacks on system collaborators, the more relations between Buthelezi and black consciousness leaders became acrimonious, Although Inkatha maintained that it continued to "hold out the hand of friendship to all," Buthelezi's instinctive response to criticism was to launch fiery and vindictive verbal counterattacks. In 1973, the Black People's Convention attacked Buthelezi as a "reactionary" and "opportunist," and Buthelezi called its leaders a "clique of frustrated political nonentities."[27] The attitudes of students at the black universities hardened. For the proud and authoritarian Buthelezi, youthful opposition was galling. This was especially so in circumstances in which he was being honored. Thus after basking in the warmth of his reception by President Julius Nyerere in Dar es Salaam in December 1973, he was jeered by Tanzanian students who beat on the roof of his departing car.[28] In May 1976, another occasion for anger occurred when students stoned his car and shouted "sell-out! sell-out!" on his arrival to accept an honorary doctorate at the University of Zululand.[29]

Hostility directed at Buthelezi from radical blacks came to a head at the funeral of Robert Sobukwe, leader of the banned Pan Africanist Congress, at Graaff-Reinet in the eastern Cape in March 1978. When Buthelezi was observed at the open air ceremony, and in the presence of dozens of assembled dignitaries and an enormous crowd of mourners, "hordes of people rushed at him," recalls Benjamin Pogrund, Sobukwe's biographer, "upwards of 200 screaming and shouting people from a crowd of 5,000." Buthelezi was forced to run "a gauntlet of scuffles and kicks" by angry youths. "Some spat in his face. The jeers and screams cursed him as a 'stooge' and a 'sell-out.'"[30] A stone hit his leg, his secretary saved him from being stabbed, and his bodyguard fired shots that wounded three teenagers. Journalists saw him leave "in a shaking, crying rage of humiliation."[31]

Buthelezi later charged that a BPC-SASO "coterie of political thugs" in Soweto had planned to abuse him. He added that Desmond Tutu, general secretary of the South African Council of Churches, who had asked him to leave during the incident, revealed his "true motives" later when he described the youths at the funeral as "a new breed of blacks who have iron in their souls."[32] There continues to be controversy about the funeral incident. Clearly, black consciousness militants wanted to eliminate Buthelezi from the list of speakers. Buthelezi had claimed that "the PAC in London" had telephoned to ask him to attend. He cited two former leaders, A. B. Ngcobo and Nana Mahomo, who were in fact no longer active in the PAC.[33] Ngcobo was a member of a group of Zulus in London who were confidentially advising Buthelezi. Later Buthelezi claimed that he "actually went to the funeral because the ANC was banned," and "I was the ANC."[34] However, the actual invitation to Buthelezi to speak came neither from the PAC nor the ANC but from Ernest Sobukwe, a suffragan bishop of the Anglican Church who did not share his brother's political consciousness. He heard of Buthelezi's desire to attend and suggested that he speak.[35] To Buthelezi, the opportunity to associate himself with a popular hero like Sobukwe had come as a welcome political opening. His miscalculation arose in not foreseeing that he might encounter organizational rivals who embraced the same symbol of uncompromising nationalism.

Alan Paton, a former president of the defunct Liberal Party and an admirer of Buthelezi, attended the funeral. He described the incident as "an ominous historical occasion" and "a grave challenge to the future of our country."[36] The main significance of the episode, however, was the impact on Buthelezi himself, who became steadily more paranoid in his attitude toward his critics and more vitriolic in his verbal assaults on all detractors. Although Sobukwe had said before his death that Buthelezi had become co-opted by the state and was "more Zulu than nationalist,"[37] Buthelezi insisted that "the feelings of great warmth and affection between us never changed."[38] According to Pogrund, however, Buthelezi had failed to visit or phone Sobukwe during the years after his release from Robben Island in 1969.[39]

Sobukwe's death occurred at a time when the emphasis of black consciousness rhetoric was shifting from race to class. The Azanian People's Organisation, formed a month after Sobukwe's death, took up the new mode of analysis in targeting Inkatha. Buthelezi's strategy, AZAPO claimed, was "to place the leadership of the movement for national liberation firmly in the hands of the black petty bourgeoisie" and out of the hands of "the black working class." This strategy was supported by "the ruling class in all its various political forms, ranging from the National Party to the Progressive Reform Party."[40] Buthelezi was, indeed, making overtures to these groups, but he dismissed the criticism with contempt. Addressing officials of the Anglo American Corporation in early 1980, he said, "We here are all pragmatists. . . . I will, therefore, not hurl abuse at you for being white racists, nor will I define the South African situation as being inherently one of a class conflict."[41]

Inkatha and the National Arena

Buthelezi's aspirations for national leadership were evident as early as July 1971 in his first Soweto speech after the inauguration of the Zulu Territorial Authority. State repression had produced an empty national stage and an audience hungry for action. "Thousands Hail Chief Gatsha 'Hero of the Blacks'" was the banner headline in *The World*. In contrast to his tone on earlier occasions, Buthelezi declared that "White South Africa has never really governed us with our consent for the last 92 years ever since we were defeated by the British forces at Ulundi in the year 1879." He appealed to all Africans when, to cheers, he attacked ethnic grouping. "Whites are united by their colour," he said. "This is what we should do." Buthelezi used the word "radical," as he was often to do, to describe the change that was needed; but characteristically he also expressed hope for change through dialogue. Because of the willingness of the government to talk with leaders, he said, a new era might be in sight for South Africa.[42] Although appealing to Blacks at a time of repression, Buthelezi was also responding to signs of reform and positioning himself as a leader with whom a changing government could work.

From mid-1971 onward, Buthelezi aroused the hopes and expectations of a wide spectrum of South Africans and attracted international attention. In September 1971 he won a standing ovation from over 600 Afrikaans-speaking students at the University of Stellenbosch when he spoke of hope and dialogue.[43] In 1972 he addressed Indians in Lenasia. He expressed sympathy (but not support) for Africans on strike in Natal in early 1973 and called for the legal recognition of African trade unions.[44] (Barney Dladla, a KwaZulu executive councillor, went much farther in actively supporting the strikers, to the point where his popularity among them posed a potential threat to Buthelezi and led to his removal from the cabinet in 1974.)[45] The bannings and arrests of key black consciousness leaders in 1973 and 1974 left a vacuum for Buthelezi's outspoken leadership to fill. Traveling abroad, Buthelezi talked briefly with US President Richard Nixon at a public prayer breakfast in Washington and was received cordially by African leaders including Julius Nyerere and Kenneth Kaunda. He was able, he said, to facilitate Prime Minister John Vorster's efforts to attain detente in Africa. Buthelezi's quotable language was recognized in 1973 by the South African Society of Journalists when it gave him its first Newsmaker of the Year award. A Johannesburg *Sunday Times* poll reported on January 6, 1974 that he was the most popular leader in Soweto, ahead of Mandela and Sobukwe.

Buthelezi's charm and shrewdness, added to the evidence of his popular appeal, attracted many white admirers who believed that there could be no solution to the country's racial impasse until credible and legitimate African leaders could be found who were capable of building political bridges to the white population. Buthelezi recognized these white anxieties as a political resource which could be manipulated to build alliances in the business, liberal, and *verligte* Afrikaner communities. He formed a close association with Reverend Beyers Naude, director of the inter-racial and inter-denominational Christian Institute. In July 1972, *Pro Veritate*, its magazine, admiringly described Buthelezi as "the pace-setter for the bantustans—the embodiment of what the Pretoria government has always feared."[46]

In a move perhaps calculated to get out in front of rising popular anger in the midst of a sharp economic downturn, or to please the Christian Institute's church funders in West Germany, Scandinavia, and Holland, Buthelezi joined Naude in March 1976 in issuing a joint statement calling for "a radical redistribution of wealth, land and political power."[47] The statement generated large headlines and provoked Kaiser Matanzima, the Transkei's chief minister, to call the document "an immoderate left-wing manifesto verging on incitement to revolution and sedition."[48] The Naude-Buthelezi statement asserted that "foreign investment in the central economy is devoid of all morality," but preceded this conclusion with a long conditional "if" clause, and ended inconclusively by calling for a national convention in which blacks could speak for themselves on the issue of foreign investment. This was Buthelezi's first experiment with a threatening policy position at odds with the interests of the business community. Except for his reaction to the crackdown of October 1977, noted below, he soon returned firmly to the pro-investment fold.

Despite the radical tone of much of Buthelezi's rhetoric, his self-restraint regarding action and his readiness to compromise appealed to whites. Buthelezi stressed his belief in the need to decentralize state power. All white parties feared the prospect that blacks might some day dominate a unitary government under a winner-take-all system of majority rule. If and when a political compromise became unavoidable, white interests clearly lay in the decentralization of power through federal or confederal arrangements with constitutional guarantees of minority rights. Federalism also appealed to homeland leaders who opposed the partition that would result from full homeland independence. In January 1974 Buthelezi and Harry Schwarz of the United Party produced a joint "Declaration of Faith" in peaceful change leading to a federation of ethnic states. Alan Paton praised the declaration. Since he no longer believed that a unitary government based upon a universal franchise was a realistic goal in the immediate future, Paton saw federation as the only hope at that time for a common society and the United Party the only party powerful enough to implement it.[49]

Buthelezi made a detailed presentation of his ideas about a new constitution at the South African Institute of Race Relations in January 1974.[50] He envisaged a confederation consisting of three types of states: those in which the interest of an "African ethnic group" was paramount, those in which white interests were paramount, and those which were "multinational" in character. By allowing each state to decide on its own franchise and giving few powers to a federal parliament, Buthelezi suggested that the controversial issue of control of a central parliament "could at least be postponed for several generations." "The emphasis of his proposal, he said, was "on constituent independent states that should be established in terms of the Government's policy of Separate Development." Taken together with his support for detente and his tepid defense of workers' rights, these proposals placed him near the right end of the black political spectrum.

In 1975, the year in which African governments came to power in Mozambique and Angola, Buthelezi launched a "national cultural liberation movement": Inkatha yeNkululeko yeSizwe. A similar body had originally been formed in 1928 by King Dinizulu as a cultural organization named Inkatha ka Zulu.[51] Revived by Buthelezi in 1973, its new name when formally launched in June 1975 under a mandate from the KwaZulu legislature gave it a political cast. Its national scope was evident in the eligibility of non-Zulus to be members; but to avoid trouble with the government, leadership positions were limited to KwaZulu citizens. The Zulu King was Inkatha's patron, and Inkatha's constitution provided that the chief minister of KwaZulu was its president.[52] Although from time to time, opponents of Buthelezi, often with covert government support, sought to organize an opposition, they never made much headway in KwaZulu's de facto one-party state.

Once Inkatha was launched, the initiative was clearly with Buthelezi, who now had a new base on which to build a national constituency. The organization adopted the African anthem *Nkosi Sikelel' iAfrika* and the green, gold, and black colors of the ANC as its own. A paid-up membership of 100,000 was claimed by April 1976, of 150,000 in mid-1978, and over 250,000 in October 1979. Evidence for these claims is unavailable. Inkatha's rapid growth and its predominantly rural base, according to Lawrence Schlemmer, who was an occasional adviser to Buthelezi, were due "in large measure to the active cooperation of tribal chiefs, who established branches within their own constituencies."[53] Though its membership figures were swelled by rural dwellers, Inkatha came to represent a range of social and economic groups and included a substantial Youth Brigade and Women's Brigade. It had a special appeal to the KwaZulu bureaucratic elite who stood to gain the most from its patronage, those in the older generation who associated it with Zulu traditions, and to businessmen, teachers, and other middle-class Africans who placed a high value upon order and stability and saw Buthelezi as a strong and modern leader who shared these objectives.

Unlike any black political organization in South Africa before or since, Inkatha took on the attributes of a classic political machine, building support by dispensing patronage to friends and withdrawing it from foes. Inkatha's growth was accompanied by credible claims that membership was required for civil service positions and preference in KwaZulu—for example, for teaching posts and promotions or traders' licenses—allegations that Buthelezi branded as lies. A sympathetic analyst has written that the KwaZulu administration "imposed sanctions on teachers who [did] not mobilize Inkatha youth groups."[54] In rural KwaZulu the membership rolls of Inkatha were swelled by peasants and the families of absent migrant workers, many dependent for their livelihoods on local chiefs whose favor could be given or withdrawn at will in respect to land rights, pensions, permits for beer-brewing, wood-cutting, and many other needs. Chiefs who were appointed and paid by the KwaZulu government and who sat *ex officio* in the KwaZulu legislature, were left in no doubt that their tenure depended on their success in enrolling and mobilizing members to display Inkatha's political clout.[55]

Buthelezi's authoritarian style of leadership was well suited to the management of Inkatha's hierarchical networks of clientage. Policy decisions and favors descended from the top, and unquestioning loyalty was expected from those below. Training in organizational discipline and obedience began young with compulsory instruction in Inkatha principles in all KwaZulu schools. An Inkatha Women's Brigade was constituted in 1976, and its primary task was defined as the rearing of a rising generation loyal to the traditions of family, culture, and Inkatha.[56] Ethnic pride based on the warrior heritage of the Zulus was constantly evoked and linked to the person of Buthelezi as Zulu royalty. Many urban Zulus, especially well-educated professionals, found the anti-democratic character of Buthelezi's leadership unappealing and avoided identification with Inkatha, but others were attracted to the evocations of Zulu pride and past glory.[57]

Given the undisguised ethnic character of Inkatha, it is not surprising that Buthelezi's efforts to extend its reach beyond KwaZulu met with little success. Some officials in the late 1970s claimed that up to 40 per cent of the membership was non-Zulu, but this appeared to be highly exaggerated. Schlemmer estimated that during 1978/1979, over 95 per cent was Zulu-speaking although Buthelezi was emphasizing the membership's national scope. In his speech of March 14, 1976 in Soweto (*Document 101*) Buthelezi suggested that Africans throughout the country might organize their own Inkathas and that all Inkathas might later come together. When he saw no initiatives being taken, he called on non-Zulus to join his own movement. With the impending independence of Transkei in October 1976 and Bophuthatswana's independence in 1977, Buthelezi offered KwaZulu citizenship to anyone in danger of losing South African citizenship rights. The offer evoked little response.

The government looked with mixed feelings on Inkatha's growth. In the spreading turmoil that followed the events of June 1976 in Soweto, the Durban area remained comparatively calm, which the press attributed to Buthelezi's control over potentially disruptive elements. As a Zulu ethnic movement which appealed to conservative traditionalists and aroused fears of Zulu dominance among other African language groups, Inkatha fit snugly into the divide-and-rule strategy of separate development. However, as James Kruger, Vorster's Minister of Justice, warned Buthelezi in September 1977, any expansion of Inkatha beyond the Zulus would mean polarization of blacks against whites and could lead to a "life and death struggle" (*Document 102*).

Publicity to the effect that Buthelezi had a national rather than Zulu following reached its most dramatic level with the publication of an elaborate attitude study by West German researchers in June 1978. Its grand conclusion about black urban politics was that Buthelezi in 1977 was "*the* political figure of black South Africa."[58] The study found—in results which emitted a scientific glow since they were reported to the first decimal point—that Buthelezi was the political figure most admired by 43.8 per cent of urban Africans in Soweto, Durban, and Pretoria and that 40.3 per cent of his admirers were urban Africans who were not Zulus. The ratings of others were: ANC leaders, 21.7 percent (Nelson Mandela, in prison since 1962, was preferred by 18.6%); homeland leaders, 18.3%; PAC leaders, 7.4%; and black consciousness leaders, 5.6%.[59] The results regarding the ANC and Mandela were remarkable since they had been unable to act freely for over a decade and a half. Among the survey's shortcomings was its exclusion of the Xhosa-speaking areas of the western and eastern Cape, the latter being historically the most politicized and pro-ANC in the country. A different survey in 1979 asked men in Soweto who were 16 or older and whose education was standard eight (mid-high school) and above who they saw as their "real leaders." Buthelezi was ranked first by only 5%.[60]

On March 14, 1976, three months before the start of the Soweto uprising, Buthelezi appeared before a large crowd in Jabulani Amphitheatre in Soweto, to deliver what was probably the most impassioned and radical speech of his political life(*Document 101*). Asserting that Buthelezi's voice was "the authentic voice of blacks," the Christian Institute's magazine, *Pro Veritate,* published the text under the title "In this approaching hour of crisis." In the speech, Buthelezi declared that Africans "despised" separate development and that those who talked of dividing South Africa on the basis of ethnicity were "naive and dangerous." He dismissed the "federal formula" set forth in his lecture of January 1974 as a compromise "increasingly difficult to offer." The time had now come when "the country must move toward majority rule," he said. He did not define majority rule and, in equivocal fashion, also used the language of "power sharing." He warned of "this last hour" but declared that it was "not too late for a white change of heart." His prescriptions were vague: blacks should "act constructively," engage in "self help," and organize Inkathas, thus in time producing "a groundswell" which would bring about change.

Anti-apartheid whites gave the speech much favorable attention, but blacks were divided. Most black opinion leaders rejected Buthelezi, according to the South African Christian Council's *EcuNews Bulletin,* in a judgment different from *Pro Veritate's.* Two contrasting and anonymous reactions quoted were those of a former member of the ANC and a Black Consciousness spokesperson. The former accused Buthelezi of creating confusion about the difference between the ANC and Inkatha when he claimed the ANC's colors, slogans, and symbols as Inkatha's. The latter said that Buthelezi "would have been the undisputed leader of Black South Africa" if he had resigned after making the March speech.[61]

The Jabulani speech touched on the essence of Buthelezi's long-run strategy when he referred to a "groundswell" that would bring about change. Fundamentally, he argued that radical change could come nonviolently if organized grass-roots pressures—workers' power and consumers' power— were mobilized to force whites into a negotiating process that culminated in a national convention. Just when and how such power would be exercised was never specified. The prospect seemed to be one of confrontation although Buthelezi often disavowed this. While making tactical shifts,

Buthelezi never lost sight of the regime's repressive power and the limits to his initiatives. Meanwhile, the notion that someday the groundswell of numbers would overwhelm the oppressor gave a romantic dimension to Buthelezi's realism, justifying the postponement of action and bolstering popular faith in eventual victory.[62] The notion was reminiscent of the Sorelian myth, or vision, of the general strike, and it mirrored similar visions of a future mass insurrection held in virtually all extraparliamentary groups.[63]

The prospect of overwhelming confrontation buoyed the hopes of Buthelezi's more radical sympathizers. Among them were a small number of activist white ministers who staffed the Christian Institute in the mid-1970s. The Christian Institute also sought contact with the ANC during fund-raising trips abroad. Since Naude had his passport withdrawn in December 1974 and could not travel, he asked an enterprising and Zulu-speaking white business consultant, Walter Felgate, to represent him. Felgate also attached himself to Buthelezi and facilitated contacts among Buthelezi, the Christian Institute, and the ANC.[64]

When violence erupted in Soweto three months after Buthelezi's Jabulani speech, his reaction was typically cautious. About a week into the uprising, Cedric Mayson of the Christian Institute, piloting a private plane, brought Buthelezi to Johannesburg for a private meeting with a small group at Naude's home. The group discussed a proposal of Felgate that Buthelezi rally Zulus in support of student demonstrators and, traveling in Mayson's plane, that he put pressure on other homeland leaders to follow suit. Buthelezi refused. Buthelezi wanted "a big fire," Mayson later recalled, but felt that a general uprising could not be controlled. It seemed that what Buthelezi really meant was that he himself could not control such an outcome and that the ANC or other political competitors might be the main beneficiaries.[65] Two months later, however, Buthelezi flew to Johannesburg and won praise for appealing to migrant Zulu workers in Soweto to end their attacks on youthful demonstrators and residents.

In 1977, at the height of international reaction to Biko's death and of the government's dilemma over how to prevent a recurrence of mass unrest, top security officials decided to take Buthelezi's measure at a face-to-face meeting. On September 19, the Minister of Justice, James Kruger, a general from the security police, and an official from the Justice ministry met for over two hours with Buthelezi, C. J. Mtetwa, KwaZulu's Minister of Justice, and Inkatha's top official in Soweto, Gibson Thula. The Inkatha delegation taped the meeting and later released a transcript (*Document 102*). Kruger stated bluntly that the security of the Afrikaner state was his main concern. Inkatha had been "a force for good, up to now," said Kruger, but warned of retaliation if Inkatha expanded beyond the Zulus, as indeed it already was attempting to do. Buthelezi avoided making any commitment to accept independence for KwaZulu or to recruit only Zulus into Inkatha. (His central committee later confirmed that Inkatha would continue to be open to all Africans, and in July 1979 Inkatha's constitution was amended to remove all references to KwaZulu and to replace "Zulu" and "African" by "Black.")

Buthelezi's staunch African nationalist stand was apparent in the discussion, but so was his effort to distance himself from the exiled ANC and his failure to articulate effectively the democratic ideals of the liberation movement.[66] The meeting ended inconclusively but was followed a month later by Pretoria's crackdown of October 19, which cleared the black political arena of most of Inkatha's open competition.

That Inkatha could emerge strengthened after the crackdown raised the question of just what Pretoria hoped to gain by permitting Buthelezi to experiment with strategies for popular mobilization and control. One answer is that Buthelezi's tough talk in South Africa and on trips abroad lent credibility to the image of South Africa as an open society where critics had nothing to fear. In reality, by turning off the financial tap, or threatening to do so, Vorster could bring a recalcitrant KwaZulu government—Buthelezi and his large network of black clients—to heel at any time.

In his meeting with Kruger, Buthelezi indicated—perhaps with some bravado—that he believed he was operating near the outer limits of Pretoria's tolerance. The fact that the only restriction ever imposed on him was the withholding of his passport between 1963 and 1971 was undoubtedly a sensitive point; apparently to cast a cloud over others who were more severely treated, he would point out from time to time that "inconsequential" persons as well as heroes were banned or jailed. Nevertheless, the passport restriction had undoubtedly impressed Buthelezi with his own vulnerability, as did security police surveillance in the late 1960s and the banning of five issues of Inkatha's newspaper, *The Nation,* in 1979.[67] Apart from these minor exercises of control, Buthelezi in the late 1970s could reasonably consider himself free to maneuver for advantage against rival black leaders, so long as he posed no serious challenge to the state's security.

In the aftermath of the October 1977 crackdown, South African politics entered a new phase marked by political stock-taking among blacks and nervous apprehension among whites about the ability of the social order to survive future "Sowetos." Within the English and now sizable Afrikaner business communities, whose views carried heavy weight in white parliamentary parties, strong momentum gathered in favor of reforms which could reassure skittish foreign investors and lenders and defuse black economic grievances. In National Party inner circles, hard-liners lost ground to reform-minded *verligtes,* who appreciated that the party was sailing into treacherous waters and required a more skillful strategy of political survival. The Afrikaner working class still pulled the National Party in a conservative direction; among middle-class and well-to-do whites in all parties, however, a convergence of opinion in favor of reform was occurring.

Buthelezi was quick to grasp the political opportunities opened up by the search for a strategy of reform. Whites who were fearful of radical change now needed black allies as never before. A shrewd and self-confident black leader could take advantage of white fears and build a powerful base of support, both domestically and internationally, in preparation for an inevitable day of reckoning. This was a new kind of "constituency politics"—a favorite Buthelezi phrase—and now the constituents were not the system's victims but its most powerful guardians and beneficiaries. It was not unreasonable for him to envisage a future national crisis in which whites would seek salvation by turning to a capable black leader who had proven his capacity to work with them. In the meantime, Buthelezi had to build his image as a leader who could command broad popular support while also opposing foreign economic sanctions, condemning the ANC's pursuit of armed struggle, and committing himself to a political system that blocked majority rule and protected minority interests.

The October 1977 crackdown had an impact upon Black political activity that Buthelezi could not ignore. In reacting, he expressed stronger support for external pressure than ever before or after. "We all know that sanctions will hurt blacks more than whites," he said in the Johannesburg *Star* on November 3, 1977, echoing Albert Lutuli; "but we would rather accept this hardship than have bloodshed. I honestly believe that the only way to salvage what is left of a chance for peaceful change is through the international community applying sanctions." But "sanctions" was not defined. Buthelezi welcomed the United Nations Security Council's mandatory arms embargo of November 4, but the skepticism he had expressed about foreign investment in his joint statement with Beyers Naude soon gave way to denunciation of the advocates of disinvestment.

Although the crackdown once again left a vacuum for Buthelezi to fill, it also reinforced his sense of realism about the regime's repressive power. At the same time, the prospect of radical pressures for change needed to be held aloft. In seeking to forge black unity and support for a national convention, Buthelezi drew together a coalition called the South African Black Alliance (SABA) in January 1978 at Ulundi, the KwaZulu capital. A somewhat similar but abortive effort, a "Black United Front," had been formed on October 8, 1976.[68] It had made "no progress in forging black solidarity links," Buthelezi said in early 1978, "because of the crisis situation."[69] SABA was initially composed of Inkatha, the Labour Party, which had a majority in the Coloured Persons' Representative Council, and the Reform Party, a minority group within the South African Indian Council representative of middle-class Indians anxious about stability.[70] Leaders of the small Swazi and Qwaqwa homelands joined later. The alliance was an uneasy one—the Labour Party at the time agreed with black consciousness groups in supporting withdrawal of foreign business—and largely symbolic and given to rhetoric. At no time was it perceived by whites or the state as anything but moderate.

By the late 1970s Buthelezi had built a seemingly impregnable political base in KwaZulu. Potential or real political rivals within Inkatha had been removed from office, notably Barney Dladla in 1974 and in 1978 Sibusiso Bengu, secretary general since Inkatha's founding. Outspoken in his criticism of the exploitation of workers, Bengu's popularity with students and his clashes with Buthelezi reached a point that resulted in his expulsion from the central committee.[71] Free of internal challenges, Buthelezi was able to spend most of his time cultivating his political alliances. A critic, Reverend Mcebisi Xundu, alleged in October 1977 that during the previous six months in KwaZulu, Buthelezi never addressed a rural meeting. Instead, said Xundu, Buthelezi preferred to go abroad, meet dignitaries, and address white audiences, meanwhile enjoying the prestige of his position.[72] He met his second American president, Jimmy Carter, in March 1977. He already had close personal relations with leaders of the Progressive Reform Party (later the Progressive Federal Party), and in December 1976 had asked the party to enter into an informal alliance with Inkatha. Plans were made for regular contact. Most importantly, in 1978 Inkatha representatives began meeting with key members of the National Party, including Gerrit Viljoen, head of the secretive Broederbond, and Willem de Klerk, editor of *Die Transvaler.* By early 1980, a series of well-attended meetings had taken place, which were publicly reported but whose proceedings were confidential. Meanwhile, in September 1978, P. W. Botha, the candidate of the Nationalist Party *verligtes,* succeeded John Vorster as prime minister. Buthelezi contrasted Botha's flexibility with Vorster's rigidity. After a meeting of homeland leaders with Botha in January 1979, Buthelezi reported that there had been talk of a "new phase" and quoted Botha as having said to him, "You and I should form a front against Marxism."[73]

Most encouraging to Buthelezi was the appointment of Piet Koornhof as Minister of Plural Relations, "a man who recognizes," said Buthelezi, "that black people have a God-given dignity." In September 1979 in a private interview, Koornhof spoke of his "love" for Buthelezi, whom he considered a great man guided both by his role as a Zulu chief and by his sincerity as a Christian. While Buthelezi did have a record of activity as a Christian layman, some of his liberal white sympathizers—for example, Alan Paton, a devout Christian—were uncomfortable with Buthelezi's public piety and prayer breakfasts.[74]

Meetings with Botha and Koornhof gave Buthelezi new confidence in the possibilities of negotiation while reinforcing his conservative instinct that South Africa might have to "pass through phases" in order to "accommodate white fears, and other minority interests." These sentiments were expressed in a speech in August 1979 at a Christian conference in Sioux Center, Iowa in the United States (*Document 103*). Friends in American business had a role in the invitation. The tone and assumptions about the time available for political change were in marked contrast to the urgency of his "majority rule" speech of March 1976. Universal suffrage, which for over three decades had been a political rallying cry of African politics, was dealt with in a welter of words out of which emerged a dismissal of "our early cries for one man one vote" as unrealistic and power sharing based upon it as simplistic. Although noting that "democratic rule" (not "majority rule") was the goal, Buthelezi, expressed doubts about the interim role of "the impoverished peasant and the semi-literate black." Those who took up arms while other alternatives existed were engaged in "barbarism," Buthelezi told his American audience.

By the time of Buthelezi's departure for London two months later to meet with Oliver Tambo, his relations with the ANC had taken on a heightened importance, both for his popular credibility and his potential role as an interlocutor between radical Africans and conservative whites. In his annual rally in Soweto, in October 1979, Buthelezi reaffirmed once again that his goal was "majority rule." In contrast with the tone of his Iowa speech, he said that the struggle would be won with "peasant wisdom" and "black worker wisdom." But most indicative of the spirit in which he approached London was his claim that Inkatha and the South African Black Alliance were the pre-eminent political force in South Africa. The rally demonstrated "the hardest black political muscle in the country," he declared; Inkatha had "taken up the struggle where the ANC left it after it was forced into an exiled position." The point had now been reached, said Buthelezi, to form "our own informal government in the country." Without elaboration, he spoke of a strategy that resembled the ANC's later call to make South Africa ungovernable, that is, to have the South African Black Alliance emerge "as a de facto black power without whose cooperation civic administration becomes increasingly impossible."

Much of Buthelezi's strategic analysis of incremental change could be seen as politically sophisticated good sense, but characteristically the speech was redolent of Buthelezi's ego, his anger toward his perceived enemies, and warnings directed at black journalists and at Indians among others. A major part of his speech was a personal attack on Dr. Nthato Motlana, Chairman of the Soweto Committee of Ten, for challenging Buthelezi's earlier public claim that he was strengthening his links with the ANC. This could not be possible, Motlana had said, since the ANC would not "collaborate with traitors." Buthelezi, after reviewing his ANC pedigree and recent contacts with ANC leaders, called Motlana, with whom he had once had cordial relations, dangerous, opportunistic, delinquent, schizophrenic, hypocritical, greedy, stupid, ignorant, a skunk, and a baboon.[75]

The ANC's Break with Buthelezi

Inkatha's meeting with the ANC in London on October 30–31, 1979, was the climax of Buthelezi's effort to use his identification with the ANC against his political enemies and to win the ANC's public recognition of Inkatha's importance, if not pre-eminence, in the struggle at home. The effort failed. For a short time, however, Buthelezi was able to enhance his image and that of Inkatha by putting across his version of the meeting in the white-owned South African press. The atmosphere of the London meeting was cordial although disagreement on armed struggle and disinvestment was sharp. Afterwards, failing to hear from Tambo as promised, Buthelezi wrote a letter of warning to him in May 1980: "The seeds of black/black civil conflict are in fact being sown by anybody who refuses to give due and proper recognition to the people as they struggle and express themselves in the struggle through Inkatha."[76] The ANC broke publicly with Buthelezi a month later. Not until January 29, 1991, in Durban, did Buthelezi and his associates meet again with the ANC, now led by Nelson Mandela. The origins of the violence that was then raging in what Buthelezi called "the Inkatha/ANC conflict" originated at the "fateful meeting" in London in 1979, he said; and in attempting to publicly define the relationship between the two organizations, he was now "starting where we left off."[77]

Buthelezi headed a 17-member delegation to London that included most of the KwaZulu cabinet, all of whom were members of Inkatha's central committee, and leaders of the Inkatha Women's and Youth brigades. They met for two days with a smaller ANC team headed by Tambo and including Alfred Nzo, Thomas Nkobi, Johnny Makatini, Cap Zungu, and Thabo Mbeki. At Tambo's suggestion, much to Buthelezi's satisfaction, the presiding officer was the elderly Anglican bishop Alpheus Zulu, who had come with the Inkatha delegation. Tambo in his opening speech warmly welcomed the visitors. According to Oscar Dhlomo, Inkatha's secretary general, Tambo "praised Chief Buthelezi's role internally and clearly said that some leaders . . . would be regarded as puppets but certainly not Chief Buthelezi." Tambo then reviewed the history of the armed struggle. Discussion on contentious issues became quite heated at times but did not reach the point of acrimony or recriminations. The meeting "went off nicely," Tambo recalled years later, and "ended up nicely."[78]

The October 1979 meeting and the circumstances surrounding it revealed much about the perceptions, strategies and outlook of Inkatha and the ANC at the end of the 1970s. Their common sense of patriotism was expressed at the concluding dinner at the home of Oliver and Adelaide Tambo when all stood to sing *Nkosi Sikelel' iAfrika*. But Inkatha members stood stiffly at attention while ANC members held their closed fists high. Beneath the external symbols of their separate identities, the two groups were discovering how wide was the chasm of disagreement and competition that divided them politically. Despite its cordial social atmosphere, the meeting was of enormous significance for both sides. Playing down the importance of the hopes which the ANC had invested in its relationship with Inkatha, Tambo maintained in later years that the October 1979 consultation was just one of a series of discussions in keeping with the ANC's aim to reach out to potential friends and allies. The ANC recognized the desirability of developing links with a rural-based mass movement such as Inkatha and regarded Buthelezi as a friend. Even after October 1979, the ANC still hoped for his tacit complicity at a future time when Umkhonto we Sizwe was better able to infiltrate South Africa by way of independent Mozambique and Swaziland and when renewed efforts could be made to build underground structures within South Africa.

The stakes for Buthelezi were also high in London: the legitimation that ANC leaders could provide among blacks and foreign anti-apartheid activists (although Buthelezi vehemently denied that he needed it), acknowledgment of Inkatha's stature, and ANC support in defusing attacks by the black consciousness movement and pro-ANC groups. His relationship with the ANC could also be seen by fearful whites in South Africa as reassuring so long as Buthelezi continued to reject the ANC's violent actions and socialist proclivities.

In probing the ANC's position at the London meeting, Buthelezi asked the following, somewhat plaintive questions (quoted as he reiterated them when meeting with ANC leaders in January 1991):

1. Will ANC leadership in exile publicly acknowledge the fact that Inkatha is a vital force in the struggle?
2. Will ANC prepare a draft statement to anti-apartheid movements and discuss it with Inkatha?
3. Will ANC request donor agencies to support Inkatha projects on their merits and not reject them on political interests [sic] which distinguish Inkatha from ANC?
4. Will ANC publicly warn the Committee of Ten, WASA [Writers Association of South Africa] and COSAS [Congress of South African Students] and AZAPO [Azanian People's Organisation] that it is not in the interests of the struggle to attack Inkatha?
5. Will the ANC discuss with Inkatha stands the movement takes in international forums?
6. Will the ANC share with Inkatha information it gains from diplomatic connections?
7. Will the ANC advise relevant Government bodies and organisations that membership of Inkatha and the use of a South African passport does not disqualify applications for scholarships?
8. Will the ANC publicly endorse a decision by Inkatha to take over the political control of Soweto by, among other things, taking over Community Councils?
9. Will the ANC publicly endorse the SABA [South African Black Alliance] as a political move in the right direction?

Although Tambo later recalled that the meeting ended cordially, he also concluded that it "spoiled everything" as far as future cooperation between the ANC and Inkatha was concerned. While Tambo may have believed that a possibility of cooperation still existed in theory, what became clear during the discussions and subsequently was that Buthelezi was not an ally but a rival. An awkward lapse in communication followed the London meeting. According to Buthelezi, Tambo said that the Executive Committee would review in December the issues discussed and be in touch with him. No contact followed, however, adding to Buthelezi's sense of grievance. Reflecting candidly on what happened, Oscar Dhlomo observed years later:

> I think that the ANC might have been disappointed with the outcome of the meeting without showing it. . . . They might have thought that it would have been possible for Inkatha to act as some sort of internal surrogate for the ANC. . . . But they didn't tell us this was the case. I suspect when they analyzed the situation after the meeting, they found

that Chief Buthelezi and Inkatha could certainly not be that kind of an organization. . . . I think they felt that 'look, we misjudged the situation. Buthelezi and Inkatha are interested in total independence [from the ANC]. They are not going to support or facilitate our policies internally. Look how they argued about sanctions and the armed struggle at the meeting.' [On our part] we didn't regard the ANC as a superior organization to us.

The ANC's miscalculations regarding Buthelezi were evident in its expectation that both the fact of the meeting and its substance could be kept secret. The Executive Committee later claimed that the secrecy of the meeting and the confidentiality of the discussion were "an express and agreed upon condition."[79] Yet Buthelezi had arrived in London with a delegation of 17 people and after the meeting had gone public with the news that discussions had occurred. Buthelezi denied breaking any mutually agreed upon rules. The anger generated by the charges on both sides did little to mask the real issue: that the ANC's objectives could not be fulfilled without secrecy, nor Buthelezi's without publicity.

By 1979 Buthelezi had become skillful in media manipulation, a field of political combat in South Africa where the ANC enjoyed little opportunity to gain experience. The Inkatha delegation returned home to front-page headlines in the Johannesburg *Sunday Times*: "Gatsha's Secret Mission" and "Buthelezi plans a black front." The *Sunday Times'* London correspondent, Suzanne Vos, reported that the meeting was "a major breakthrough" for Buthelezi, thus setting the tone for much of the press commentary that followed. (Vos was later to be hired as an Inkatha publicist.) She quoted from conversations with Buthelezi and reproduced extracts from a memorandum he had submitted to officials in the British Foreign Office, stating that Inkatha and the ANC were destined to form a "united front" that would eliminate "third-force factors in the black consciousness movement." The *Sunday Times* also boosted Buthelezi's image by reporting (with a front-page picture) that he had met with Joshua Nkomo and Robert Mugabe, who were in London for Zimbabwe's independence negotiations at Lancaster House.[80] Speaking from Dar es Salaam, the Pan Africanist Congress issued a press statement asking "Who collaborates with whom?" It condemned the South African regime for sending Buthelezi "to go and attempt to seduce the fighters and leadership in exile" rather than itself going to Robben Island to talk with the leadership of the PAC and the ANC (*Document 104*).

By mid-June 1980, any hope that Buthelezi may have had for a "united front" was shattered, and the warmth of October had turned frigid. New criticism of Buthelezi's leadership had been sparked early in the year by his hard reaction to a rash of school boycotts that spread to KwaZulu and by his negative reaction to a petition campaign for the release of Mandela. The conspicuous resurgence of the ANC was underway in 1980, aided by the visibility of its sabotage attacks, or "armed propaganda," as ANC tacticians called them. On June 1, banner headlines reported that ANC guerrillas had sabotaged strategically crucial facilities, two SASOL oil-from-coal plants. Buthelezi had underestimated the ANC when he predicted in Iowa in August 1979 that "industrial sabotage" would not occur "in the foreseeable future." On May 20 Buthelezi sent a warning letter to Tambo—"brother and Comrade," concluding "with love and best wishes"—expressing "an ever-widening sense of disquiet" about the ANC's attitude toward Inkatha. The breakdown of communication since the London meeting signaled the end of the tacit alliance of the 1970s. A parting of the ways had come.

On the ANC's commemorative day of June 26, 1980, Secretary-General Alfred Nzo in London publicly condemned Buthelezi for the first time, using vitriolic terms that matched Buthelezi's own rhetoric against his enemies.[81] Probably more stinging to Buthelezi was a lower-keyed statement and press conference by Tambo himself in Lusaka on July 23. In rather unhappy personal remarks, Tambo said that the ANC had encouraged Buthelezi as it had encouraged others "to join the forces of the struggle . . . to oppose the independence of the bantustans." Since only occasionally did the ANC criticize individuals, he said, it had for a long time ignored the statements of the "hyper-sensitive" Buthelezi and would "turn a deaf ear" to them in the future. But now, he said, Buthelezi had "emerged on the side of the enemy against the people."[82]

In the circumstances of the early and mid-1970s, Buthelezi had shown promise as a national leader who publicly identified with banned liberation movements despite his role as a Zulu leader implementing official policy. From the perspective of 1980, his failure to fulfill his promise was not surprising. Popular pressures for action against the regime had grown after 1976. During the 1980s, constrained by his dependence on Pretoria, his need to maintain Inkatha's de facto alliance with white business, and his own accommodationist temperament, Buthelezi found it impossible to stay out in front of popular militancy or to destroy his political rivals by fiery rhetoric alone. He was to become an open enemy of the ANC and a spoiler in African politics.

Notes

1. Steve Biko, *I Write What I Like* (London: Bowerdean Press, 1978; Oxford: Heinemann, 1979; and San Francisco: Harper and Row, 1986), p. 86.

2. "In a remarkably short time the English-language press underwent a complete change in attitude toward homeland leaders. . . . The South African Institute of Race Relations reflected the new perspective" when it invited Buthelezi to deliver the annual Hoernle Memorial Lecture. Patrick Laurence, "Black Politics in Transition" in Ellen Hellmann and Henry Lever, eds., *Conflict and Progress: Fifty Years of Race Relations in South Africa* (Johannesburg: Macmillan, 1979), p. 67.

3. An effort to understand Buthelezi's personality may yield more insight about his behavior than an analysis of class interests. Shula Marks in 1986 criticized work in the field of South African political economy for its "heavy structuralism that has left little space for the role of the individual." *The Ambiguities of Dependence in South Africa: Class, Nationalism, and the State in Twentieth-Century Natal* (Johannesburg: Ravan Press, 1986), p. 71.

4. Buthelezi, "White Involvement in the Liberation Struggle in Southern Africa and the Free Enterprise System," speech of March 27, 1980, Johannesburg, pp. 3–4, 19, 23–24, 27–28.

5. Statement issued by President Oliver Tambo at a Press Conference held by the African National Congress on July 23, 1980. *Weekly News Briefings* (issued by the ANC in London), pp. 1–3.

6. Ben Temkin, *Gatsha Buthelezi: Zulu Statesman* (Cape Town: Purnell, 1976), p. 73.

7. Temkin, p. 96.

8. An unnamed SASO leader in the *SASO Newsletter,* reprinted in *Sechaba,* January 1973. Buthelezi relished descriptions of himself as the most subversive person in South Africa and was quick to say that he was prepared to resign when he had fully exposed the fact that sufficient land was not being added to KwaZulu. Conversation with Buthelezi (May 1971).

9. Department of Information press release, "Chief Gatsha Buthelezi—Chief Executive Officer of the Zulu Territorial Authority," June 1970.

10. *News/Check,* June 26–July 9, 1970.

11. *The Nation* (Johannesburg), March 1978, pp. 1, 4, 14. Mzala [Jabulani Nxumalo], *Gatsha Buthelezi: Chief with a Double Agenda* (London: Zed Books Ltd., 1988), p. 232.

12. Buthelezi, "General meeting convened for the purpose of launching the National Liberation Cultural Movement (Inkatha) at Umlazi," June 14, 1975.

13. *News/Check,* June 26–July, 9 1970.

14. Quoted in Gwendolen M. Carter, Thomas Karis, and Newell M. Stultz, *South Africa's Transkei: The Politics of Domestic Colonialism* (Evanston: Northwestern University Press, 1967), p. 63.

15. "He remained a member of the ANC until the movement was banned in 1960," claimed Oscar Dhlomo in a memorandum of February 26, 1981, "Buthelezi and Inkatha, Comment on the Document by Prof. Tom Karis," p. 5. According to Mzala, "there is no known record or substantial oral evidence that Chief Buthelezi was ever a member of the ANC [after leaving Fort Hare in 1950]," p. 229 and passim.

16. O. R. Tambo, speech of January 8, 1980, *Sechaba,* March 1980, p. 9.

17. Tambo did not allude, however, to an incident the year before Morogoro that had left a festering sore. Dorothy Nyembe, a one-time ANC leader in Natal, approached Buthelezi after a church service to ask if a guerrilla could come to his house. Buthelezi refused, saying that he was under surveillance. The security policy interrogated him, and later under subpoena he gave evidence for the state at the trial of Nyembe and 11 men. Buthelezi has said that he testified to what the police already knew and that ANC leaders were "appalled" that he had been approached by guerrillas and asked about a landing site for a submarine. Nyembe was sentenced to 15 years for harboring guerrillas. Differing accounts of Buthelezi's involvement with the Nyembe group are in Temkin, pp. 114–15, 119 and Jack S. Smith, *Buthelezi: The Biography* (Melville, South Africa: Hans Strydom, 1988), pp. 59–60. Buthelezi's later comments about the incident were reported in the *Rand Daily Mail,* April 17, 1984. The ANC secretary general in his condemnation of Buthelezi noted at the end of this chapter presumably referred to the Nyembe case when he said that for Buthelezi "to denounce this or that patriot as a member of the ANC" was to play "the vile role of a police agent."

18. "Political Report of the National Executive Committee, Presented by the President of the African National Congress," in *Documents of the Second National Consultative Conference of the African National Congress, Zambia, 16–23 June 1985,* pp. 20–21.

19. *Sechaba,* February 1971.

20. *Sechaba, March 1973.*

21. Conversation with Oliver Tambo (March 1991). But see Temkin, pp. 400–13.

22. Document 20. On ANC support for Buthelezi's efforts, see conversation with Inkatha leaders (July 1980).

23. Buthelezi, "A Black Perspective of Realism in the Black Struggle for Liberation," speech of October 21, 1979, Soweto.

24. Conversation with Buthelezi (January 1983). Jordan Ngubane, present at the conversation, endorsed Buthelezi's observation about the non-existence of the ANC in South Africa. On Buthelezi as "the true heir of the ANC," see private communication by Rowley Arenstein,

January 1981, 55 pages, evaluating a manuscript, "Buthelezi, Inkatha, and the ANC," by Karis.

25. In contrast to Document 100, Buthelezi in December 1991 was quoted as saying that the press had forgotten why Mandela "was put in jail in the first place. He was a convicted terrorist plotting the very bloody overthrow of the government." Quoted in *This Week in South Africa* (December 10–17, 1991), a publication of the South African Consulate General in New York.

26. Conversation with Temba Sono (November 1973).

27. "Statement Issued by the Black People's Convention," July 11, 1973.

28. *East African Standard,* Dar es Salaam, December 15, 1973.

29. *Sunday Express,* Johannesburg, May 9, 1976.

30. Benjamin Pogrund, *How Can Man Die Better: . . Sobukwe and Apartheid* (New Brunswick, NJ: Rutgers University Press, and London: Peter Halban, 1991), pp. 371–77.

31. Juby Mayet, *The Voice,* March 18–23, 1978.

32. Buthelezi's account of the funeral is in his speech, "Soweto After-Election Rally and Thanksgiving Prayer Meeting," in Soweto, April 9, 1978, *Inkatha,* vol. 1, no. 3, July 1978, pp. 13–14. Buthelezi said that "the whole ugly scene" was on television and "seen abroad." Bishop Tutu said afterwards that he did not "condone" the action of the youth. See Marjorie Hope and James Young, *The South African Churches in a Revolutionary Situation* (Maryknoll, NY: Orbis Books), p. 111 and, for Buthelezi's comments on Tutu, p. 208.

33. Buthelezi mentioned Ngcobo and Mahomo in an interview with Joe Thloloe, *Post* (Johannesburg), March 19, 1980. Also see *The Nation* (Johannesburg), April 1978, p. 2. Some years later, Oscar Dhlomo said that Ngcobo and Mahomo had asked Buthelezi "to go to the funeral to speak on behalf of black people." Memorandum of February 26, 1981, p. 4.

34. Conversation with Buthelezi (August 1979).

35. See Pogrund, p. 374. Conversation with Ernest Sobukwe (September 1977).

36. Alan Paton, *Sunday Tribune,* Durban, March 19, 1978, reprinted in *Save the Beloved Country* (Melville, South Africa: Hans Strydom Publishers, Second Edition, 1988), pp. 173–75.

37. The words quoted are Pogrund's, p. 331.

38. Buthelezi speech of April 9, 1978.

39. Pogrund, p. 346. On occasion, Buthelezi would refer to a smiling photograph of the two taken during a chance meeting in July 1973 and published in the *Rand Daily Mail.* When Sobukwe heard that Buthelezi had displayed this picture at a meeting with hostile students in Dar es Salaam and had boasted about "me and my friend Robert Sobukwe," Sobukwe reacted, according to Pogrund, with rare anger at being thus used. See Pogrund, pp. 345–47. Buthelezi later held up the picture before the KwaZulu legislature, saying, "It was an occasion of great jubilation for both of us because we had not met for almost 20 years." Temkin, p. 232. Buthelezi also referred to the picture in his speech of April 9, 1978, claiming that during the brief encounter, Sobukwe "encouraged me in the work I am doing and said to me in Zulu: "Uyabashaya mfundini . . . bashaye!" [You are giving it to them, my comrade, hit them!].

40. George Wauchope?, "The Role of the Workers," unsigned paper, 1980?, and conversation with Wauchope (July 1980).

41. Buthelezi speech of March 27, 1980. In May 18, 1980 at a "Kwa Mashu Prayer Meeting and Youth Rally," Buthelezi listed many groups engaged in a "total onslaught" against Inkatha, including "the academics of South Africa," especially those "long-haired intellectuals" engaged in Marxist analyses of Inkatha, "most of whom would be torn to shreds if they were to come here today. . . ."

42. *The World,* July 19, 1971.

43. *Pro Veritate,* July 1972, pp. 17–18.

44. He reassured employers that he believed in unions only as "machinery for negotiation," however, not as "instruments for organizing strikes." Temkin, pp. 200–205.

45. Mzala, pp. 168–74.

46. *Pro Veritate,* July 1972, p. 17.

47. *Pro Veritate,* March 1976, p. 15. According to Cedric Mayson, Buthelezi's advisor Walter Felgate originated the idea of the statement as a demonstration that blacks could mount credible threats to business interests if they wished. Conversation with Mayson (March 1991).

48. *Rand Daily Mail,* May 7, 1976. Buthelezi replied: "By saying this, Chief Matanzima is inciting the Central Government to take action against me." *Weekend World,* May 9, 1976.

49. *Sunday Tribune* (Durban), January 13, 1974.

50. M. G. Buthelezi, "White and Black Nationalism, Ethnicity, and the Future of the Homelands," the Alfred and Winifred Hoernle Memorial Lecture, Cape Town, January 16, 1974.

51. *"Inkatha"* is said to refer to the pad used by women to cushion loads they carry on their heads. For a more complex description of *Inkatha* as "a solemn symbol of unity in Zulu culture," see Mzala, pp. 116–17. For an analysis of ethnicity in Natal prior to 1949, see Shula Marks, "Patriotism, Patriarchy and Purity: Natal and the Politics of Zulu Ethnic Consciousness," in Leroy Vail, ed., *The Creation of Tribalism in Southern Africa* (London: James Currey, 1989).

52. "Inkatha is formally interlocked with the government of KwaZulu; ultimate decisions on policy both for Inkatha and (in certain respects) for the KwaZulu Legislative Assembly are formulated by the 'National Council.' This is the supreme body in KwaZulu, and it comprises the Central Committee of Inkatha, the Legislative Assembly of KwaZulu, and representatives of specialized functions within Inkatha." Lawrence Schlemmer, "The Stirring Giant: Observations on the Inkatha and Other Black Political Movements in South Africa," in Robert M. Price and Carl G. Rosberg, eds., *The Apartheid Regime: Political Power and Racial Domination* (Berkeley: Institute of International Studies, University of California, 1980), pp. 115–16.

53. Schlemmer, p. 116.

54. Schlemmer, pp. 118 and 123.

55. Mzala, pp. 128–33.

56. Shireen Hassim, "Reinforcing Conservatism: An Analysis of the Politics of the Inkatha Women's Brigade," *Agenda,* no. 2, 1988, pp. 3–16.

57. The sycophantic attitudes of some among the well educated are illustrated in a memorandum of meetings of four self-styled "intimate friends and advisers" of Buthelezi, all Zulu, on April 15 and 23, 1976 in London: E. Z. Sikakane, a Methodist minister based in Edendale, Natal, P. W. Mbatha, V. A. Shange, and A. B. Ngcobo, one-time treasurer of the Pan Africanist Congress. The memorandum was labeled "TOP SECRET—Strictly Confidential and Personal." For insistence that Inkatha was not a Zulu movement, see conversation with Rev. E. Z. Sikakane (August 1979).

58. Theodor Hanf, Heribert Weiland, and Gerda Vierdag, *South Africa: The Prospects of Peaceful Change* (London: Rex Collings, 1981), p. 354.

59. *Rand Daily Mail,* June 12, 1978. The decimal points were removed and the figures rounded out in the published volume.

60. A fuller account of the survey is in note 38 in chapter 8.

61. *EcuNews Bulletin,* March 17, 1976, pp. 6–7.

62. Jordan Ngubane, a veteran Zulu journalist who was prominent in the early ANC Youth League and later in the Liberal Party, returned to South Africa in 1980 to join Buthelezi after 17 years in exile. "Whenever I asked concerned Zulus what they would do with this [growing power], they almost invariably gave me a reply I had never heard before: 'We are waiting for Chief Buthelezi to tell us when and where to attack.'" Ngubane, "Why I Came Back," *Sunday Tribune* (Durban), July 6, 1980.

63. The persistence of romanticism about insurrection is criticized by Graeme Bloch in "Insurrection in South Africa," *Work in Progress,* May 1991, pp. 32–35.

64. As it became increasingly likely that the Christian Institute would be banned, Felgate pursued the idea of a black press that could survive the banning. Interested funders wanted ANC-Inkatha unity in support of it. During a meeting in London, Johnny Makatini of the ANC and representatives of the Christian Institute tried but failed to persuade Buthelezi. In Cedric Mayson's judgment, Buthelezi wanted to control the press himself. Conversation with Mayson.

65. Conversation with Mayson.

66. At the end of the meeting, Buthelezi expressed his "deep sorrow at the death of Steve Biko" but raised no question about the circumstances of his death. During Buthelezi's next speech in Soweto, January 29, 1978, he asked the audience to stand in memory of Biko. M. Gatsha Buthelezi, *Power Is Ours* (New York: Books in Focus), p. 153.

67. *The Nation* began publication in English and Zulu in Johannesburg in December 1976.

In 1979 it moved to Durban as a Zulu paper but suspended publication in 1980 because of problems of "money and management," according to Inkatha officials. For Buthelezi's "ownership" of *The Nation,* see Obed Kunene, "Newsroom Apartheid: A Black Editor's Account of Life with White Bosses," *More* (Columbia School of Journalism), December 1977.

68. On the Black United Front, see chapter 8.

69. Buthelezi, "Living from Crisis to Crisis," speech in Soweto, January 29, 1978.

70. Yellen Chinsamy, the Reform Party's leader, referred to Buthelezi as "our saviour." Conversation with Chinsamy (May 1978).

71. Bengu was alleged to have advocated mass action and support for the Black People's Convention. At the same meeting of the central committee that dropped Bengu, three members of the Youth League were expelled for urging mass action that Buthelezi rejected as likely to lead to senseless violence. *Survey of Race Relations 1978* (Johannesburg: South African Institute of Race Relations, 1979), p. 31. "Bengu seems to have been the last idealistic heretic in Inkatha's central committee and in some ways his dismissal signalled a growing intransigence in Inkatha's ideology and the muzzling of youthful dissent." Gerhard Mare and Georgina Hamilton, *An Appetite for Power: Buthelezi's Inkatha and South Africa* (Johannesburg: Ravan Press, 1987), p. 184 and passim.

72. Conversation with Reverend Mcebisi Xundu (October 1977).

73. *South African Digest,* January 26, 1979, p. 3.

74. Buthelezi's comment about Koornhof is in *The Star* (Johannesburg), air mail edition, December 2, 1978. For Koornhof's remarks, see conversation with him (September 1979. Buthelezi held multiracial prayer breakfasts in Durban to which over 100 people were invited once a year, according to an African minister who attended in 1977–1979 and found them "quite political." Alan Paton, despite his admiration for Buthelezi, read to Karis in 1979 his handwritten parody of a talk by Buthelezi at a prayer breakfast attended by whites, which included private thoughts in parentheses. It began: "Dear brothers and sisters in Christ (you shits)," and so on. Conversation with Paton (August 1979).

75. Buthelezi, speech of October 21, 1979.

76. Letter from Buthelezi to Oliver Tambo, May 20, 1980.

77. Remarks by Buthelezi at "Meeting of Inkatha Freedom Party and the African National Congress," Durban, Jan. 29, 1991.

78. All quotations attributed to Tambo and Dhlomo and not otherwise noted in this section are from conversations with Tambo (March 1991) and Dhlomo (December 1989). Description of the meeting also relies on a conversation with Cap Zungu (April 1991) and a memorandum of Zungu to Karis. There is no agreement on who first made the request for the meeting. Apparently representatives of both sides mutually arrived at a decision that the time had arrived when a meeting would be useful. The ambiguity of some comments is illustrated in Buthelezi's statement in 1985: "By 1978 negotiations had reached the point where I sent a formal delegation to meet with the ANC Mission in exile in Stockholm. . . . [W]hen my delegation reported back to me conveying the request from Oliver Tambo and his executive that we meet formally, I readily agreed." Address by Buthelezi, "King Shaka Day," September 28, 1985. According to Tambo, Buthelezi sent a representative to him to ask for a formal meeting. Tambo passed the message on to the Executive Committee, and it agreed to a meeting, the first formally planned consultation between the two movements.

79. "Political Report of the National Executive Committee, June 16–23, 1985 . . . ," p. 21.

80. *Sunday Times* (Johannesburg), November 4, 1979.

81. Alfred Nzo, "Statement to the June 26th Freedom Day Meeting," Camden Centre, London, *Sechaba,* September 1980, p. 6.

82. Statement issued by President Oliver Tambo, July 23, 1980," cited in note 5 above.

10. The Liberation Movements, 1975–1979

The gradual undoing of the apartheid state hinged at several critical historical junctures on developments external to South Africa. The most significant of these in the 1964–1979 period was the triumph of the anti-colonial revolutions in Angola and Mozambique in April 1974. In that month, the war-weary army of Portugal deposed the Lisbon regime of dictator Marcello Caetano, setting Portugal's African colonies on a path of rapid transition to independence. Unlike the cautious government of Botswana, the radical new pro-Soviet rulers of independent Mozambique and Angola were willing to offer their territories as staging areas for the ANC. By 1977, north and central Angola had become the site of several ANC military camps, even as the MPLA government in Luanda continued fighting to wrest large areas in the south of the country from the South African-backed rebel UNITA movement of Jonas Savimbi. In Mozambique, where the accession to power of Frelimo in June 1975 was uncontested, the ANC gained its first military infiltration route into South Africa from Mozambique through Swaziland.

The ANC: Soweto and After

After the independence of Mozambique, communication by the ANC with Natal and the Transvaal became easier, and it was possible for internal and external activists to meet in Swaziland where the regular border traffic of Swazis and South Africans provided cover for visitors and couriers on political missions. Several top activists in the South African Students' Organisation (SASO) who visited Swaziland to make contact with exiles were recruited into the ANC underground in late 1975. Meanwhile, ANC and PAC operatives released after serving prison terms made contact with black consciousness activists looking for ways to join the armed struggle. Using Lesotho as a base, Chris Hani worked from 1974 onward to organize cells within South Africa and to strengthen the ANC's underground recruiting network. During and after the 1976 uprising, he recruited the most promising youth from among those who fled to Lesotho. Siphiwe "Gebuza" Nyanda, who was based mainly in Swaziland and sometimes crossed into South Africa, headed Umkhonto's urban operations in the Transvaal beginning in 1977.[1]

Awaking late to the potentialities of student militancy, the ANC did not anticipate the uprising of 1976–1977. *Document 105* is a flyer drafted by the exiled ANC and sent to its internal cells with instructions that they reproduce and disperse it around March 21, 1976, the anniversary of the Sharpeville massacre. Appearing less than three months before the start of the uprising, the flyer contains no intimation that youthful anger in the country was near boiling point but seeks instead, for propaganda purposes, to highlight the retreat of the South African army in Angola. Looking back later on the Soweto uprising of 1976, Tambo praised the role—"however limited"—of ANC activists inside the country. It was true, he said, that in 1976–77 the ANC "had not recovered sufficiently to take full advantage of the situation that crystallised from the first events of June 16, 1976. Organisationally, in political and military terms, we were too weak. We had few active ANC units inside the country. We had no military presence to speak of. The communication links between ourselves outside the country and the masses of our people were still too slow and weak to meet the situation such as was posed by the Soweto Uprising."[2]

Nevertheless, once the revolt was underway, the ANC began trying to insert itself into student decision-making networks. ANC operatives in Mozambique began making contact with the Soweto Students' Representative Council (SSRC) through Elias "Roller" Masinga, one of the backroom strategists of the SSRC, whose father was an ANC loyalist. Elliot Shabangu, an ANC veteran in Soweto, established a link through his nephew, Super Moloi, another SSRC insider. Joe Gqabi, released in August 1975 after 12 years on Robben Island and absorbed soon thereafter into the ANC/SACP underground in the Transvaal, began efforts to recruit key members of the Soweto student leadership. It was his objective, Gqabi later stated in a memorandum to his lawyers following his arrest in December 1976, to influence the SSRC leadership to "normalize" the situation in the townships by persuading students to cease their dogged but undirected efforts to challenge the government through stay-aways, demonstrations and boycotts. "We said to the students that you can't call on the parents or workers to stay at home every week or every month and that it was not being realistic at all. We should try and normalize things and they should try and go back to school."[3]

Tactically, a reading of Lenin could have supported this position, since much of the activity of the uprising was spontaneous rather than carefully planned. At the same time, from the ANC's perspective, the unpredictable nature of the violence that was occurring nationwide by August and September 1976 posed a serious political threat: what if the uprising were to escalate into an uncontrollable crisis for the regime, leading to a Lisbon-like scenario of collapse? Would the ANC in its state of unpreparedness be able to gain control in the chaos, or might some other unforeseen leadership emerge to snatch victory in the name of the people?

Internationally, the violence of the uprising created an unprecedented opportunity for the exiled liberation movements to draw the world's attention to the anti-apartheid cause. Inside South Africa, however, the PAC lacked the capability to take any immediate advantage of the situation, and the ANC's propaganda response was cautious. *Document 106* is a leaflet produced by underground ANC supporters during the early weeks of the uprising. Subsequently, however, there is no documentary evidence that the ANC attempted to fan the revolt or to use it as an opportunity to generate written propaganda. Rather, by late 1976, it appears that the objectives of the external ANC had become defined as twofold: to cool the revolt, and to use the ranks of militant high school activists as a recruiting pool for Umkhonto.

Mosima "Tokyo" Sexwale and Naledi Tsiki, two young Umkhonto fighters recently returned from guerrilla training in the Soviet Union, were brought to secret meeting places in Soweto and Alexandra township in Johannesburg where they conducted weapons demonstrations for members of the SSRC in an attempt to recruit them to Umkhonto. Some were impressed and agreed to join. A Soweto shebeen bombing carried out in late 1976 by a group called the "suicide squad," led by a nonstudent, Paul Langa, but linked to the SSRC, may have involved some of these recruits. Other SSRC members, most notably Khotso Seatlholo, who replaced Tsietsi Mashinini as the council's chairman in August 1976, refused formally to subordinate the SSRC to the ANC's leadership, although by the time this decision was taken in late 1976 those in the inner circle of the SSRC must have known that a number of key individuals in the council's "braintrust"—Masinga, Moloi, Murphy Morobe and Billy Masetlha—had already been recruited. On New Year's Eve 1976, police arrested Joe Gqabi along with Moloi, Morobe and Masetlha. Masinga was netted later and was charged with Gqabi, Sexwale, Tsiki, and eight others under the Terrorism Act in the trial of "the Pretoria 12." *Document 107* is a portion of Sexwale's statement to the police following his arrest. Gqabi, who by mid-1976 was a member of the ANC's underground leadership in the Transvaal (called "the Main Machinery"), was acquitted along with Masinga and Petrus Nchabaleng, another senior man in the ANC underground, when Morobe, Masetlha and Moloi refused to become state witnesses.[4] Sexwale, Tsiki, Martin Ramokgadi, a 67-year-old member of the Main Machinery, and three others received long sentences.

Once the police began making systematic arrests nationwide in an attempt to break the revolt in late 1976, young blacks began fleeing South Africa for the safety of surrounding countries. Perhaps as many as 5,000 were eventually recruited into the ANC outside, vitally swelling the ranks of Umkhonto and providing the organization with new blood across the entire range of its political and diplomatic activities in exile. The two highest profile refugees from the uprising, however, refused to join either of the exiled movements. Tsietsi Mashinini, the charismatic first chairman of the SSRC, announced from abroad that, aside from any underground work in South Africa that students were not aware of, the ANC and PAC were "extinct internally" and "not doing anything."[5] Khotso Seatlholo, the second SSRC chairman, fled South Africa in January 1977 and went to Nigeria. Over the next five years, backed for awhile by the Nigerian government, and with some involvement by Mashinini and older black consciousness exiles, he attempted to launch an exile incarnation of the SSRC with its own military wing: the South African Youth Revolutionary Council (SAYRCO).[6] This initiative collapsed with Seatlholo's arrest in South Africa and imprisonment on charges of terrorism in 1982.

The Soweto uprising opened up new opportunities for popular mobilization, but the ANC was only gradually able to take advantage of them. The strategy and tactics adopted at Morogoro in 1969 had given priority to political leadership and emphasized that political mobilization should accompany armed struggle. In practice, however, the ANC's emphasis was on military activity—"armed propaganda"—as the primary agent for politicizing blacks and building the prestige of the ANC, a practice which continued throughout the 1970s. In the absence of secure organizational networks inside the country for receiving fighters and hiding weapons, most guerrilla attacks that occurred in the late 1970s were staged by Umkhonto members infiltrating through and backed up by support from Swaziland and Mozambique. Guerrillas were usually young, politically immature, and vulnerable to exposure by informers and other collaborators; thus, most survived for only a short time before being apprehended.

During 1977 bomb explosions and sabotage received much publicity. The unplanned but sensational "Goch Street incident" on June 13, 1977 occasioned much premature commentary about the start of urban guerrilla war and also yielded the ANC's first guerrilla-martyr to be executed, Solomon Mahlangu. He and two other young Umkhonto recruits who had left South Africa in late 1976 arrived in Johannesburg en route to Soweto for the first anniversary of the Soweto uprising. Acting in panic after being confronted by a private guard while they were walking down a Johannesburg street carrying their loaded weapons in a shopping bag, one of the men escaped. Mahlangu hid behind a bus, and the third ran into a passageway where he shot and killed two elderly whites having tea at the entrance to a warehouse. The killer was beaten so severely by police that he became brain-damaged and could not be prosecuted. Only Mahlangu, who had surrendered, was placed on trial. The judge acknowledged that he had not fired any shots but sentenced him to death. His fate became an international *cause célèbre*. President Jimmy Carter made a personal appeal for commutation, and the United Nations Security Council met on the eve of Mahlangu's hanging on April 6, 1979.[7] Later that year, the ANC named its new school at Mazimbu, Tanzania, the Solomon Mahlangu Freedom College.[8]

During 1977 the ANC was identified with half a dozen bomb explosions on railway lines, seven reported discoveries of arms and explosives in locations ranging from Mafikeng to Soweto and the Swaziland border, and several shootouts between police and guerrillas. The ANC also claimed the killing of an African detective who was an ex-ANC member and had given evidence in several trials. The ANC did not claim the destruction of a Pretoria restaurant or the shattering of shop windows in the Carleton Center in downtown Johannesburg (perhaps the work of a PAC follower), which caused many minor injuries.

Soon after the first anniversary of June 16, the ANC's National Executive Committee met in July 1977 to take stock. Its report is *Document 108*. The NEC coopted five men who had left South Africa after serving prison terms, and paid tribute to defendants recently sentenced in a terrorism trial in Pietermaritzburg: Harry Gwala and three others who received life sentences and four men whose sentences ranged from seven to 18 years. Only passing mention was made of the need to work through "legal organisations" and "to strengthen the combination of the illegal with the legal forms of confrontation." The bright spot was growing international solidarity. President Tambo had addressed the United Nations General Assembly, and the ANC was participating in meetings of leaders of the five "front line states." The report gave only slight attention to the task of infiltrating cadres into the country to do political work.

Such work was the special concern of the energetic Mac Maharaj, who was released from Robben Island in 1977 and in early 1978 became secretary of the only department under the Revolutionary Council concerned with political work, the Internal Reconstruction and Development Department. By late 1978, it "had begun to build on what remained of embryonic political structures which had been developed in Natal, the Transvaal, and eastern Cape in the mid-1970s but which had been largely destroyed in a series of political trials."[9] Its small number of underground units were concerned mainly with propaganda, creating reception networks, and developing links with popular organizations. According to Slovo, its units were to be completely separated from Umkhonto "combat groups," but were to be regarded as politically engaged when they used sabotage to attack "the ruling class, its property and personnel." Thus their priorities were "railway networks, though avoiding civilian casualties; oil, petrol and power installations; established informers; and police and other enemy personnel and installations . . . [and] actions against targets with special local or national significance, such as supporting mass political actions, hitting enemy personnel during any Soweto-type upsurge, or dealing with particularly hated officials."[10]

There were many signs of infiltration and preparation for guerrilla action during 1978. The press reported at least 12 discoveries of caches of weapons and explosives throughout the country, from Bophuthatswana to the suburbs of Durban. Among the items found were Czech machine guns and Soviet-made rifles and pistols. Police skirmishes and shootouts with guerrillas occurred mainly in the eastern Transvaal. In August the ANC claimed that an Umkhonto group, forced into combat in the Rustenburg area of the western Transvaal, had killed ten white soldiers in a four-hour battle and wounded many others but spared African members of the Bophuthatswana National Guard, who had been brought in as reinforcements. At least seven attacks on African detectives and witnesses for the state in ANC trials were reported; three were killed, including a senior detective who was a former member of Umkhonto and had been "brutal and vicious" (according to *Sechaba*) during the Soweto uprising. Bombs were exploded outside the Bantu Affairs offices in Port Elizabeth, and late in the year a bomb badly damaged the Community Council building in Soweto.

It is likely that official sources of information sought to minimize guerrilla activity and that not all incidents were reported in the press. On the other hand, the state had an interest in publicizing the bloodiest attacks and those that would excite white fears or win sympathy abroad. In September 1978 American viewers of a popular television program were treated to a harrowing statement by Brigadier C. F. Zietsman, chief of the security police, describing the ANC underground:

> They go all over the country, and they contact people in various places and get them to form cells and then to spread out all over the country.
> They are everywhere?
> They are everywhere. Our forces are one of the main targets. They have already murdered one of our black policemen; they have threatened me; they have kept us under observation in our houses of our black policemen; they have even kept observation of houses of white policemen in white areas.
> So no member of your force is safe?
> No member of the force, especially members of the security branch, is safe. The African National Congress has declared that they intend killing us all. They are everywhere.[11]

Police stations were popular targets as symbols of oppression. Bombs damaged three stations on the Witwatersrand in late 1977 and early 1978. ANC guerrillas made frontal attacks for the first time in May 1979 when they attacked the Moroka police station in Soweto with Soviet-made AK-47 automatic rifles and hand grenades. One African constable died, five others were injured, and hundreds of police dossiers were destroyed. Flyers left at the scene commemorated "June 1976" and described the attack as retaliation for the hanging of Mahlangu. Four ANC men made a similar attack on the Orlando police station in Soweto in November 1979, killing two Africans and wounding several others. Describing the difficulty of finding the attackers, a senior officer said, "In the bush you at least have a chance of tracking down your man, but in Soweto there are so many houses and places were a man can go to ground."[12]

The Minister of Police had warned earlier that "terrorists" were becoming better trained and had sophisticated arms. The unearthing of caches of arms suggested that many infiltrators entered unarmed. An exception was an armed group in a shoot-out near the Botswana border in January 1979. Each guerrilla, said the Minister, had a Makarov pistol, 39 blocks of TNT, 15 grenades, 300–350 rounds of ammunition, a transistor radio, and binoculars. Later in the year bombs were exploded in the Cape Town Supreme Court building, where a political trial was proceeding.

As the ANC's "armed propaganda" reached new levels of intensity, the courts became increasingly dramatic arenas of combat where the state and the ANC faced off before a media audience. When the judge decided that state witnesses would testify *in camera* at the trial of 12 Umkhonto guerrillas in Pietermaritzburg in late 1979, the accused issued a statement saying that although they had initially been prepared "to submit to the process of the court," they had now decided that "to exclude the public from such a trial is to exclude the very people who are affected by what the African National Congress is alleged to have done and seeks to achieve."[13] Seeing no point in participating in a closed trial, they dismissed their lawyers and instead attempted to disrupt the proceedings by shouting slogans—"Down with fascism!" "Down with capitalism!" "Long live Fidel Castro!"—giving clenched-fist salutes, singing freedom songs, smoking and lounging with their feet against the railing in their bullet-proof glass cage. Deploring the "blatantly provocative defiance" of the accused, an exasperated judge described one of the defendants whom he saw as the ringleader, the 24-year-old James Mange, as "a thoroughly repulsive and objectionable character."[14]

Mange was accused of guerrilla activities that were by now familiar: training in Zambia, the Soviet Union, and Angola, establishing caches of arms, reconnoitering sabotage targets, and recruiting. He was not, however, charged with any violent act to persons or property although he had planned to attack a police complex. In November 1979 the judge sentenced Mange to death and the 11 others, some of whom had been in armed clashes, to terms of imprisonment ranging from 14 to 19 years. During sentencing, the men held smuggled placards against the glass sides of the dock, one reading "Never on our knees." Like Solomon Mahlangu, Mange became a *cause célèbre*. On appeal his death sentence was commuted to 20 years.[15]

To most whites, the ANC's limited and scattered attacks were much more a low-intensity nuisance than a much-vaunted "armed struggle." Nevertheless, a long-term rise in guerrilla action posed special threats because of the vulnerability of South Africa's advanced economy, damage to the climate for foreign business, and the danger that sophisticated sabotage might be linked to political campaigns and accompanied by mass participation in simple forms of sabotage. Meanwhile, anxiety grew among isolated whites as an incident on January 4, 1980 illustrated. Three well-armed guerrillas attacked a police station in Soekmekaar, a town of less than 100 whites in the northern Transvaal, and escaped in a stolen car. They might return, the owner of the local garage told a reporter. "Anxiously, his eyes dart to the group of sullen-faced blacks working around the apron of the garage. 'They could even be here,' he says, and shudders visibly."[16] Not until Umkhonto executed its first major sabotage of strategically crucial facilities, the SASOL oil-from-coal plants, in June 1980 did the government express serious public concern, however. Contemplating the millions of rands damage done, the Minister of Minerals and Energy Affairs admitted to "shock . . . that terrorists could have been so successful."[17]

As South Africa crossed the threshold of a new decade of intensifying conflict, Pretoria's military supremacy remained unchallenged, but the ANC's "armed propaganda" was beginning to register important psychological gains. Despite its inability to turn the violence of 1976 directly to its advantage, the ANC had emerged as a major beneficiary of the uprising as young militants looking for "action" turned to it as the exile movement with the most to offer in resources for military training and scholarships for further education. AZAPO, formed in 1978 as a successor to the black consciousness organizations banned in October 1977, lacked the leadership or resources to compete for adherents nationally, although it rapidly adopted the Marxist rhetoric that had become the intellectual fashion of the period. Underground members and supporters of the ANC helped to form the Congress of South African Students and the Azanian Students' Organisation, and participated in the brief rise of the Port Elizabeth Black Civic Organisation. As community leaders across the country discussed and debated long-range strategies, what one later termed a "productive interaction" between underground and above-ground activists began to evolve.[18] With this evolution, popular perceptions of the ANC as the pre-eminent liberation movement spread as the organization moved into a period of rapid resurgence.

The PAC on Trial

The reputation for terrorism of Poqo, the PAC's armed wing, made the PAC a prime target for the police throughout the 1960s and 1970s. Although John Vorster, then Minister of Justice, had declared in 1963 that he had "broken the backbone of PAC and Poqo," he lamented two years later that Poqo kept "rearing its head like a snake."[19] Occasional and localized Poqo activity continued, apparently ending in 1968.[20] As student violence and disruptions erupted nationwide in 1976, police stepped up surveillance on Zephania Mothopeng, after Robert Sobukwe the PAC's most senior leader within the country. In August he was detained, and in 1977 other former PAC members were picked up in widespread raids. In December 1977 Mothopeng and 17 others were put on trial for terrorism. The case was heard in Bethal, a small town with a large prison in the eastern Transvaal. Mothopeng was alleged to have said at a meeting in May 1976 that plans were being made for riots in which school children would stone and burn government buildings, leading to a country-wide revolution. The speech, described by a state witness, was out of character and Mothopeng denied making it. When sentencing Mothopeng in June 1979, however, the judge found that he had helped to sow the seeds of revolution and had predicted and helped to organize the riots in Soweto and elsewhere in South Africa.[21]

The PAC activity specified in the indictment in the Bethal trial covered the period from 1963 to 1977 but amounted to little of consequence for the regime. Nevertheless, the detailed testimony of state witnesses, although unreliable by definition, suggested a pattern of revolutionary effort whose expansion and intensification could have disrupted white complacency. The theme of the indictment was the revival of the outlawed PAC. Although conspiracy was alleged by the prosecution, many of the accused met each other for the first time when they appeared in court.[22] They ranged from age 20 to Mothopeng's 64 at the time the trial began, and they came from Johannesburg, Pretoria, East London, Cape Town, Kimberley, and Krugersdorp. Five had already served sentences on Robben Island.

The state charged that individual defendants had been involved in re-activating the PAC on Robben Island through secret meetings and lectures intended to prepare prisoners for underground work after their release, re-activating the PAC elsewhere in the country by taking part in meetings and organizing cells, disseminating propaganda through talks and literature, operating two front organizations (the Urban Resources Centre and the Young African Christian Movement, later re-named the Young African Religious Movement—YACM/YARM), contacting the PAC in Botswana, Swaziland, and Tanzania, obtaining funds and literature through couriers, recruiting and arranging transport abroad for military training (John Ganya, an ex-Robben Islander, was alleged to have recruited a group of 15 African municipal policemen and some 70 others in 1975 and later), organizing a Coordinating Committee in Pretoria in March-April 1976, and stoning and burning buildings and vehicles in Krugersdorp after June 16, 1976. Only in the case of Jerome Kodisang was a recruit alleged to have actually received military training, in Libya. Kodisang was a former member of the South African Students' Organization who admitted to training in Libya but not to membership of the PAC.

As accused number one, Mothopeng played a central role in the trial. His seniority was well established. He had been a member of the ANC Youth League in the 1940s, was elected president of the Transvaal African Teachers' Association in 1950, chaired the inaugural conference of the PAC, and served on its national executive. After Sharpeville in 1960, he was sentenced to two years. Arrested again in March 1963, he was convicted over a year later and imprisoned for three years. The indictment in the Bethal trial charged that he had sought to revive the PAC by addressing meetings on Robben Island and meeting twice with Sobukwe in 1975, six years after Sobukwe had been released from prison and restricted to Kimberley. By serving as director of the Urban Resources Centre and involving himself with YACM/YARM, he was alleged to have furthered the aims of the PAC by projects of bulk buying, a literacy scheme, a sewing scheme, and "youth awareness." "In the said literacy project," the indictment said, "the Dialogue Awareness Method (also called the Code or Paulo Freire Method) was used in such a way as to arouse Blacks to their so-called state of oppression." During the trial, a PAC member who had turned state witness testified that in early 1975 Mothopeng received a message from Dar es Salaam that he should revive the PAC and start sending recruits to Swaziland.[23] The most serious charges alleged indirect contact with exiled PAC leaders, the establishment of a courier system, and the promotion of recruitment for military training abroad.[24]

Mothopeng admitted that he had met with Sobukwe but insisted that they had not discussed current political matters. He flatly denied that he had done anything to further the aims of the PAC. How could he, he explained disingenuously, since the PAC had been banned and no longer existed? In a conversation years later, he described PAC activities on Robben Island that he had denied in court, for example, secretly changing places with prisoners in other large cells so that he could lecture on the PAC.[25] Unlike many other political leaders on trial, therefore, he did not admit to revolutionary activity, perhaps out of anger against state witnesses but perhaps in the expectation of a reduced sentence. *Document 112*, extracts from Mothopeng's testimony, includes his testimony on April 6, 1979, when his remarks about the hanging that day of ANC guerrilla Solomon Mahlangu were anything but disingenuous.

The trial resembled other political trials but also had some distinctive features. As in some other cases, most of the accused complained of severe assaults. Mothopeng, for example, described the use of electric shocks.[26] The accused entered the dock each day singing freedom songs. "Five minutes before the court is due to start sitting," *The Times* of London correspondent wrote on June 20, 1978, "there is a clanking of metal doors from the cells below, the soft, rhythmic strain of an African song drifts up into the court. As the singing gains momentum, the accused stream into the court waving fists and stamping feet in time to the tune, 'where are the sons of Africa?' they sing. 'They must stand up and be counted.'"

Such reporting was infrequent, however. Despite the political value for the government of inflammatory news about the PAC threat, the trial was closed to the public and held in an isolated town, with reporters allowed only if they had the permission of the police. Even diplomatic observers were on one occasion turned away by the judge. To enable white and African members of the legal team for the defense to be together, a local motel was given temporary "international status." One of the three advocates was an African as was the instructing attorney, Griffiths Mxenge, himself a former ANC political prisoner. There were 86 unindicted co-conspirators, with Sobukwe as number one, and an unusual number—165—of mainly anonymous state witnesses. About 90 percent of these were held in custody to prevent intimidation, and some were held in solitary confinement for as long as the accused—a measure designed to "facilitate" their cooperation.[27]

Unlike Mandela, Sobukwe and others in political trials, Mothopeng was not allowed to make a political statement in court. At the start of the trial, he refused to plead, saying, "M'Lord, without being disparaging or being disrespectful of the Court. . ." He was then interrupted:

> *By the Court*: I want a plea . . . (accused No. 1 continues speaking). Mr. Orderly, will you please remove No. 1 accused imme-

diately. I will not have an address made, I want a plea . . . I will not have speeches made.

>   Accused nos. 1 to 4 refuse to plead.
>   The Court enters a plea of not guilty by accused 1 to 4.

The press, however, reported the rest of Mothopeng's statement omitted from the trial transcript: "I do not recognize the right of this court to charge me."[28]

In June 1979, Mothopeng received a 15 year sentence, and 15 others received sentences ranging from five years, the minimum under the Terrorism Act, to 15 years. Zolile Keke's five-year sentence was suspended for five years (in 1981 he left the country on orders of the PAC), and one of the accused was acquitted.[29] After Soweto, PAC spokesmen in exile cited the dearth of arrests and prosecutions as evidence that the PAC underground was successful but also pointed to the Bethal trial and a few lesser trials as evidence of the PAC's pervasiveness and activity. Years later, after his release from prison in 1989, Mothopeng described "a constant stream" of convictions for PAC activity, noting that he could not recollect a single year from 1960 onwards when nobody was convicted for PAC activities.[30] The PAC never died and its potential remained, but the Bethal convictions marked the end of the PAC in the 1970s as a visible challenge to the regime.

The PAC in Exile

The Soweto uprising intensified the pressures on the PAC to rebuild itself. Although it had been unable to involve itself significantly in the uprising, the movement into exile of thousands of young militants offered unprecedented opportunities for revitalization. Competition with the ANC grew as both organizations faced the prospect of winning the allegiance of members of the younger generation who had gone through the fire. Meanwhile, the qualitative change in the struggle within South Africa made other pressures on the PAC more urgent. Could it establish stability and demonstrate competence and initiative? The PAC's standing—even its existence as an exiled liberation movement—was at risk in many forums: in cooperative African states, the OAU, the Non-Aligned Movement, the United Nations, and among foreign donors.[31] Robert Sobukwe's international standing gave the PAC prestige, but this declined with his death in February 1978. The organization also paid a price—a vacuum in leadership—for its near-deification of Sobukwe. After his death, the PAC's reputation continued to spiral downwards as internal conflict and the struggle for power reached new levels of vituperation and even violence.

During the four years before the Soweto uprising, a few of the black consciousness activists who left the country joined the PAC in Botswana or Swaziland. During the flood of departures starting at the height of the uprising and extending into 1978, the head of the South African security police made a frequently quoted estimate: 4,000 of the youths who had fled were in guerrilla training camps outside the country, three-fourths of them with the ANC, and most of the rest with the PAC. Yet the PAC's formal guerrilla strength at the end of the 1970s was quite reliably estimated at less than 450 men and women under arms, located mainly in Tanzania and Libya.[32] Henry Isaacs, a former president of the South African Students' Organisation who joined the PAC, has described the pre-Soweto group of exiles as better educated and politically more mature than the post-Soweto group. Furthermore, the latter had defied their parents, teachers, and authority and could not easily be disciplined. They had little understanding of the problems of conducting a revolution from exile but "were not about to defer to the authority of their older compatriots whose 15 year sojourn in exile was contemptuously dismissed as cowardice."[33]

Isaacs had a unique perspective on the PAC. He regarded black consciousness as ideologically closer to the PAC but did not share PAC prejudices about the ANC. After studying law in New Zealand and traveling in southern Africa, he became the PAC's acting representative in Australasia, a member of the Central Committee, and later its representative at the United Nations; but in March 1982 he resigned. From the outset, hoping that he could make a difference by working within a recognized liberation movement, he compared the lassitude of PAC life with the atmosphere of "urgency, seriousness and exuberance" in the black consciousness movement at home.[34] Isaacs felt flattered that many PAC members met him when he first landed at the Dar es Salaam airport—a former SASO president was a catch—but he soon realized that going to the airport was simply something to do.[35] The general routine in 1976 was discouraging.

> Each morning, the chief representative and other assistants opened the office at 7.30. Senior PAC officials trooped in later to read incoming mail, scrutinise invitations to conferences and, if necessary, nominate (normally from among their own ranks) delegates to such conferences. Occasionally, they discussed problems or read the *Tanzania Daily News*. In the course of the day, PAC members filed into the office, individually or in some groups. By noon the sparsely furnished office resembled a pass office in South Africa, with inert humans everywhere, waiting. They waited for the PAC's director of finance to approve expenditure of 100 shillings for firewood at a PAC residence in Dar es Salaam; they waited for 30 shillings for dry cleaning, or for hospital fees. There was never a bustle of activity, or signs of serious business. At 2:30 p.m. everyone spilled out of the office, dispersed to the PAC residences in various parts of Dar es Salaam where Tanzanian domestic workers had lunch ready. Eating, like most activities, was communal. After the meal, almost everyone retired for an afternoon siesta.[36]

Most discouraging of all, however, were the circumstances of new recruits and potential guerrillas.

The new recruits spent many months—some as long as two years—living in overcrowded conditions in cheap hotels in Dar es Salaam or PAC residences because the organisation lacked contacts or facilities in friendly countries to which they could be sent for military training or to continue their studies. Those who were sent for military training could not be despatched into the country to carry out military operations because the PAC had no arms, ammunition, or facilities in neighboring countries. Consequently, the military cadres remained in the PAC's bush camp in [Chunya] Tanzania, but the camp was essentially a holding pen. Frustration, economic hardship and social deprivation fueled lower rank rebellion. There was a power struggle between two factions in the PAC leadership, led, respectively, by the Acting President, Potlako K. Leballo, and his deputy, Templeton M. Ntantala. Consequently, the new recruits were drawn into the struggle and found themselves on opposing sides in a dispute of whose origins and dimensions they were largely ignorant.[37]

The new recruits played a critical role in the power struggle. Leballo had been Ntantala's patron and was responsible for his rise to the deputy chairmanship of the Central Committee and the position of commander-in-chief of APLA, the Azanian People's Liberation Army. Later Leballo had come to distrust him as a rival. Ntantala saw Leballo as poisoning "the young, untrained minds" of Soweto recruits, in particular some 35 young men whom he had attempted to use to create a personal army to overthrow the military leadership. Leballo's greed for "absolute personal power," in Ntantala's words, came to a head in a November 1977 "coup d'etat." *Document 109* is the first section of a paper, "The Crisis in the PAC," issued by Ntantala in April 1978 describing the events of the "coup." A particular complaint was Leballo's unilateral conferring of PAC membership on recruits. According to Ntantala, new recruits had clearly been told at the time they were recruited into APLA that they would have to apply for PAC membership and undergo a period of probation.

A month later in a document entitled "The Profiles of Leballo's Gang," Ntantala widened his attack, warning "all governments, nations, international organisations, other national liberation movements and individual personages" about five members of the Central Committee in addition to Leballo. He described actions to undermine PAC members in Botswana and Swaziland who were critical of Leballo. In Swaziland, Ntantala charged, Leballo and David Sibeko had falsely persuaded the government that PAC members, many of lengthy residence, were supporting the opposition to the monarchy. Some fifty were detained or were deported at considerable hardship.[38]

Once again the OAU's African Liberation Committee and the Tanzanian government pressed for "unity and reconciliation." This was the theme of the PAC's second consultative conference, held during the last week of June

1978 in Arusha, Tanzania. It attracted PAC members from Europe and North America as well as Africa, two observers from South Africa's Black People's Convention, and two stars: Tsietsi Mashinini and Khotso Seatlholo, former heads of the Soweto Students' Representative Council. From the time of a Central Committee meeting shortly after the events of the November "coup" until the evening before the conference was scheduled to begin, the Ntantala faction was at odds with Leballo and bitterly accused him of bad faith. When Leballo proposed to the Central Committee that it should take over the leadership of the army, Ntantala and five others walked out; but negotiations continued in response to pressure from a Tanzanian government-sponsored Reconciliation Commission, which included a representative of the Liberation Committee. Leballo, however, controlled the funding provided by the OAU, which included travel by air to Arusha; and his insistence prevailed that anyone (or almost anyone) who claimed PAC membership could attend and vote. Ntantala argued that to ignore established procedures would allow participation by deserters, drop-outs, and persons who had been inactive for years and did not understand the crisis. Nor was the practice of decision by consensus followed. In a conference of about 100 persons that was packed by the Leballo faction, Ntantala's faction was decisively outvoted.[39]

The focus of debate following Leballo's political report was its indictment of "the failure of the past military leadership." His report also included a Program of Action, *Document 110,* adopted by the conference, which is remarkable mainly for its rhetorical definition of problems rather than for its explication of strategy and tactics. For Ntantala, the conference turned into an inquisition, with wild cheering whenever "an emotional but largely pointless speech" was made and enthusiastic applause whenever someone shouted "some demagogic, meaningless slogans of Black Power, or made an obviously racist point," one that an adherent of "Marxism-Leninism-Mao Tse-Tung Thought" would not make. In attempting to rebut the charges of military failure, Ntantala's description of "successes, however insufficient," of difficulties and setbacks, of contact outside South Africa with representatives of unidentified mass movements and the provision to them of "ideological lessons" made little impact. Five months after the Arusha conference, the reconstituted Central Committee publicly exuded new confidence. A press release issued in New York announced that the Central Committee "has ordered its forces inside the country to intensify revolutionary activities and called on the Azanian people's popular organizations to rally behind their vanguard liberation movement and deal the enemy deadly blows."[40]

The strife centering on Leballo and Ntantala culminated in the expulsion of Ntantala and six other members of the Central Committee.[41] Incompetence, not ideology, was the explanation for the expulsions, Sibeko said later.[42] A more comprehensive indictment was laid out by Isaacs, who moved the expulsion. The newly elected Central Committee consisted of 13 members. Headed by Leballo as "chairman" (not "president"), it included Isaacs and the six against whom Ntantala had warned the world. In addition to the expulsion of Ntantala and his associates, over 60 others were named as persons expelled until they accepted the authority of the Central Committee.

Azania News, the PAC's official organ, hailed "the very stern measures" that were taken at the Arusha conference "to restore discipline." Thus, the PAC had emerged "more vigorous and more determined."[43] Even the Maoist journal *Ikwezi,* sympathetic to the PAC but usually critical, saw in the Arusha conference "a new beginning" because "the leadership under P. K. Leballo responded positively" to "the new liberation forces that have emerged, especially among the youth of Azania."[44] Nine months after Arusha, on April 6, 1979, the PAC celebrated its twentieth anniversary. Divisiveness and indiscipline had worsened, however, and complaints about Leballo acting without consultation or accountability had spread. At an anniversary rally in Dar es Salaam, a group of cadres humiliated him with boos and jeers in the presence of prominent outsiders and insults were hurled at him when he drove away.[45]

The Central Committee announced in a press release in May 1979 that Leballo was immediately leaving for medical treatment, without explanation, and that a Presidential Council of three would act during his absence: Vusumzi Make, David Sibeko, and Elias Ntloedibe.[46] The sense of crisis in the Committee was revealed in two confidential documents. The first was a report prepared by Isaacs for the Administrative Committee of the Central Committee.[47] Since the beginning of the year, "there has been a drastic deterioration in the state of the Party so that there are at present two heavily-armed, warring factions," he wrote. "Rank indiscipline, factionalism, gangsterism and even terrorism have reared their ugly heads. In fact, there have emerged two separate wings, almost two parallel organisatons—a *political* and a *military* with the military regarding itself as an independent entity which is accountable only to itself and the Chairman of the Central Committee."

The PAC was "poised on the eve of open gang warfare," Vus Make said in a meeting of the Administrative Committee on April 30. *Document 113,* which was marked confidential, is an abridgment of the minutes of a two-day meeting of the Committee. Make, Sibeko, Ntloedibe and others among the former supporters of Leballo, met under his chairmanship and blamed him and his lack of consultation and accountability. The PAC was virtually de-recognized, said Sibeko, as a result of the Tanzanian government's decision to prohibit entry of any PAC cadres until all cadres in the country had been infiltrated into South Africa. Sibeko suggested that Leballo take a "respite" while a political directorate of three ran the PAC, rebuilt APLA, and implemented the Program of Action. Putting the best face on the situation, Leballo acquiesced and nominated Make, Sibeko, and Ntloedibe to serve on a Presidential Council.

Isaacs has described the events that followed.[48] The Tanzanian government was pleased; but those who expected denunciation and Leballo's expulsion were not mollified by a triumvirate made up of three men who were closely identified with his discredited leadership. More threatening was the reaction of Leballo loyalists in the military. They conspired to assassinate members of the Central Committee and to reinstate Leballo and at the same time began to torture and kill military cadres who they suspected of loyalty to the Central Committee. Tanzanian officials refused (until March 1980) to intervene. On June 11, Sibeko was assassinated by a group of PAC cadres. Six men were eventually convicted of manslaughter, and each received a sentence of ten years. Efforts of hit squads to assassinate other members of the Central Committee continued for several months. Meanwhile, Leballo was understood to be in Libya.

During the first week of October 1979 an "extraordinary plenary" of the Central Committee declared that Leballo had violated the decisions of the Arusha conference and the meeting establishing the Presidential Council. It denounced and expelled him for "reactionary and counter-revolutionary activities." Leballo, the press release said, had thrown the PAC "into a serious crisis which culminated in the murder of Comrade David M. Sibeko." Expulsion had been demanded, it was said, by representatives of "the PAC cells and regional branches in Azania," and their position was "endorsed by the internal leadership presently in prison or living under restriction."[49] Vus Make became chairman and served until January 1981, when the Central Committee elected John Pokela, recently released after 13 years on Robben Island.

The history of the PAC in exile revolved primarily around competition among personalities while ideology and its significance for strategy and tactics were of lesser importance. The organization's foundation documents of 1959 and Sobukwe's pronouncements took on the importance of holy writ. Meanwhile, socialist ideas and Marxism-Leninism with a Maoist gloss won growing acceptance, given the PAC's opposition to the Soviet-supported ANC-Communist Party alliance, and China's support for the PAC, especially during its early years in exile.[50] It was a weakness of the PAC that its ideological stance, expressed differently by various leaders, never became clear and coherent, and the differences between leaders and factions were often blurred or, as in the case of Leballo, confounding.[51] Well-wishers found confusing the differing political lines addressed to intellectuals and mass audiences.[52] Marxism-Leninism was in general endorsed; but unlike the ANC, the PAC lacked an intimate ally as energetic as the Communist Party in recruiting intellectually promising young people and promoting their study of Marxism.

Ntantala and his fellow expellees aspired to become such a party, and during "the anguish of the bitter period" after the November 1977 coup, they prepared for, and in late 1979 founded in England "a Party of the working class," the Azania People's Revolutionary Party (APRP). After he was expelled from the PAC, Ntantala declared that he and his 70 or so fellow expellees had been liberated from "simple nationalism" and would build a "vanguard proletarian party" according to "Marxism-Leninism-Mao Tse-Tung Thought." APRP was that party, and its aim was to provide "the national liberation movements, ANC, PAC, UMSA [Unity Movement of South Africa], BCM [Black Consciousness Movement]," with the kind of "guidance" that the Communist Party had failed to provide.[53] This ambitious aim came to an end when Pokela readmitted the Ntantala group into the PAC.

In 1979 there was no prospect that a Marxist-Leninist party like Ntantala's, which sang "The Internationale" at its founding rather than *Nkosi Sikelel' iAfrika,* could be built to provide effective guidance to a mass movement. It fell to *Ikwezi,* the journal "based on Marxism-Leninism-Mao Tse-Tung Thought," published in England, to promote the building of an "Azanian" Marxist-Leninist party allied to the PAC. Although the PAC's leadership over the years had been "politically bankrupt," *Ikwezi* said, the "miserable" history of the revisionist ANC-SACP and its support of Soviet "social imperialism" were far worse. Furthermore, the PAC had the advantage of the influx of youth after the Soweto uprising (only "a section of it was temporarily deceived by Leballo's rhetoric"). *Document 115, Ikwezi's* call for an "Azanian" Marxist-Leninist party, is remarkable for prescribing, in effect, that the role of such a party in relation to the PAC should be essentially the same as that of the Communist Party in relation to the ANC. An "Azanian" party could avoid degenerating into Trotskyism, *Ikwezi* argued, by empha-sizing nationalism over socialism in the first stage of the revolution.

Robben Island

As prisoners convicted in the early 1960s completed their sentences, Robben Island disgorged about half its population of "politicals" by the mid-1970s, bringing the number held on the island down to approximately 400, probably less than a quarter of the total a decade earlier.[54] Conditions remained spartan, but some of the crude brutality of the early years had eased, and prisoners were no longer required to perform hard labor in the island's lime quarry.

Organized sport had been officially allowed since 1967. Sport was important not only in releasing tension but also in muting partisanship and generating a common enthusiasm. Initially some PAC prisoners and others opposed the use of sports facilities, arguing that they were designed as a propaganda stunt and that sport could not be played on a half-empty stomach. But they soon joined in.[55] Indres Naidoo, who completed a ten-year sentence in 1973, has described the Makana Football Association as having four PAC teams and four teams of ANC and "other" members, governed by a committee with equal representation for PAC and ANC and one representative of others. Soon, however, the teams became politically integrated, with 26 "sides" in three divisions. Naidoo was critical of the PAC and believed that political unity between it and the ANC would never be possible. Since discussion about sports and cultural activities was encour-aged, however, "it was not an uncommon sight to find a group of ANC sitting with PAC, talking earnestly and cracking jokes about everything except politics."[56] By the end of the 1970s a culture of sport had developed, climaxing in annual summer games, or mini-Olympics, held over two weekends. One of the most prominent organizers was Steve Tshwete, president of the Robben Island Amateur Athletic Association, who completed a 15 year sentence in 1979.[57]

Probably the most remarkable aspect of the burgeoning, complex structure of sporting, recreational, and cultural activities were the formal records—detailed and meticulous constitutions, minutes, and correspondence—kept by prisoners in the administration of their groups. The range of activity was much wider than sport. According to Tshwete: "Apart from sport we also organised choral groups, musical combos, a film club, a reading society and ballroom dancing groups. The guys who were involved in ballroom dancing taught us the waltz, the fox trot, the quickstep and so on and there would be competitions in the cells."[58] In many of these activities, prisoners gained experience in organization, cooperation and self-empowerment at the same time that they were enlivening the dreary routines of prison life. An appreciation was expressed in August 1974 by Michael Kahla in his annual report as chairman of the Prisoners Record Club. He outlined the challenging responsibility of protecting and enlarging the collection of phonograph records and the difficult process of choosing records to play in the light of "a barrage of complaints, suggestions and requests." He concluded by expressing "my deepest gratitude to you all for having conferred this office upon me. You have given me a schooling in administration, patience and understanding that no formal school could have given."

Robben Island may have been a microcosm of the wider struggle, but it differed in bringing together, in intimate closeness, members of the ANC, the PAC, the black consciousness movement, and two organizations with a Unity Movement background, the Yu Chi Chan Club/National Liberation Front and the African People's Democratic Union of South Africa (APDUSA). (The lone former member of the African Resistance Movement, Eddie Daniels, was effectively in the ANC camp.) Many non-political friendships and many common, non-political interests developed. Although the political groups tended to differ on tactics to be used in prison, much unity was achieved in protest efforts. Even the ideological differences that had divided the groups inside the country and continued to do so were softened for the most part as partisans came to understand each other better. Yet major differences in temperament and emphasis remained, and ideological unity was never achieved.

APDUSA and the Yu Chi Chan Club were of marginal significance and manifested their presence in doctrinaire and discordant ways. On tactics, for example, some members of the Unity Movement (a term often used to refer to both groups), initially argued that by accepting study privileges one compromised one's integrity since studying should be a right and not a privilege. When the ANC held a memorial meeting for Moses Kotane, APDUSA refused to attend because an ex-Liberal, Daniels, would be present. Earlier, when a memorial service was held for Chief Lutuli, Neville Alexander, whose relations with Mandela were mutually friendly and respectful, introduced what Mandela called the "one sour note:" "he accused Lutuli of being a patsy of the white man, mainly on the grounds that the chief had accepted the Nobel Peace Prize."[59]

"From the moment I arrived," Mandela has written, "I saw Robben Island as an opportunity to patch up the long and often bitter differences between the PAC and the ANC," an achievement that he believed "could set a precedent for uniting them in the liberation struggle as a whole." PAC men had preceded the ANC on the island, and Stanley Mogoba (later a Presiding Bishop of the Methodist Church) has recalled that PAC men assisted the ANC in learning the ropes when they arrived. Mandela, on the other hand, has described relations as "more competitive than cooperative" from the beginning—PAC men were "unashamedly anti-Communist and anti-Indian." Nevertheless, he made progress in discussing unity with Selby Ngendane (who had "mellowed") and Clarence Makwetu ("balanced, sensible"). In 1967 Mandela and Ngendane wrote to their respective followers in the general section advocating the idea of unity. Their hopes, however, were never realized.[60]

Many ANC men have commented on good working relations with the PAC, yet efforts at unity foundered on ideological shoals. Harry Gwala, a veteran of both the ANC and the Communist Party, has commented on how "we respected one another, we played together; we did all sorts of things together," including organizing a hunger strike together; but "there was no way of reconciling [our] ideological differences."[61] Kwedi Mkalipi, a PAC secondary school graduate from the Western Cape who began a 20 year sentence at the age of 31, has described men like himself as young, inexperienced, and seeing issues only in terms of skin color. Being thrown together with the ANC for the first time was "a queer situation" because "we sincerely believed [the ANC] were all Marxists" and "fellow travellers" with whites.[62] Exasperated by PAC arguments, Gwala and others decided that "it was high time that we enlighten" the PAC. They organized a debate in the general section one evening in 1967, with three speakers on each side. Gwala, Stephen Dlamini, and Milner Ntsangani spoke for the ANC. Gwala's verdict was that the PAC was "badly bruised" and therefore never again entered a formal debate.[63]

Communists and the PAC shared a long-standing hostility toward each other. The SACP did not have an organized presence on the island, nor were all of its members known. Mhlaba has said of that period "it was difficult to say who was in the Party, and who was not." Indeed, he thought of himself as "first an African, then I am a communist."[64] After Mothopeng returned to the island following the Bethal trial, he became involved in discussions on unity with Mandela and Wilton Mkwayi that extended into the beginning of the 1980s. "I was one of those," he recalled later, "really believing that it might be a useful thing that we have some method of working together as organizations at all levels." The SACP should identify itself as an independent party, he believed, and an ANC-PAC-SACP alliance should meet as such on Robben Island and outside. In this way, the PAC could "restrain" the Party.

With regard to any alliance operations, "we wanted to commit them, we don't fear them. And expose them because they have no following." It was unrealistic for Mothopeng to demand independent participation by the Party. Insistence on it, according to Mothopeng, "made the whole thing crash."[65]

Organizational tensions grew with the influx of young militants after the beginning of the Soweto uprising in June 1976. The first black consciousness adherent, Mosibudi Mangena, had arrived on the island in late 1973, to be followed by almost a dozen others before the uprising. "Although some of us were young," Mangena has written, when the post-Soweto youths arrived, "we suddenly found ourselves looking very old and moderate." This was "a different breed of prisoner than we had ever seen before," Mandela has said, "brave, hostile, and aggressive; they would not take orders and shouted "*Amandla!* (power!) at every opportunity."[66] The new generation had been engaged in street battles, some had been shot, and some had seen their friends shot dead. Most were high school students. Some belonged to black consciousness organizations, but others, including what some called "lumpen elements" or *tsotsis* (hoodlums) had simply taken part in rioting during the uprising and been convicted for public violence. Some were hot-headed and prone to violence on the island, causing problems both for the authorities and for veteran ANC leaders.[67] "We would punch the warders. If warders touched us, we would quickly punch back. There were daily skirmishes," Mike Xego later recalled. "Gradually Madiba [Mandela] and the others were told to tame us. It was not the regime but the ANC that cracked us. One by one, the ANC underground on Robben Island worked on us—on individuals—talking with us and smuggling notes to us."[68]

The arrival of dozens and then hundreds of new prisoners created opportunities for the older movements on the island to recruit new adherents. Mandela has maintained that the ANC did not attempt to recruit or to proselytize, believing that this would alienate both potential recruits and other parties; but recruiting, however defined, became common and the source of much tension in the late 1970s.[69] In December 1976 sentences were handed down in the trial of "the SASO Nine," and the nine arrived on the island determined to maintain the same belligerent stance that had attracted publicity to their cause during the trial. Attempting to set a standard of disciplined defiance for the "Soweto generation" of prisoners, who soon began to outnumber the "old timers," the black consciousness leaders pushed for a policy of maximum non-cooperation with the prison authorities, an approach long ago discarded as counterproductive by the older prisoners. Tempers flared as intergenerational competition for leadership ensued.

When Patrick "Terror" Lekota, after a period of intense discussions with older prisoners, broke ranks with the SASO Nine and announced his new allegiance to the ANC camp, he was ostracized by his former companions. In a celebrated incident in early 1978, while defending his opposition to any ban on what was called "cross-camp" recruiting, Lekota was gashed in the head with a garden fork by one of his antagonists. Following the advice of Mandela, who wanted to demonstrate that the ANC was "a great tent," Lekota refused to testify against his attackers in a judicial proceeding begun by the authorities.[70] After this incident, Mandela later recalled, "the floodgates seemed to open and dozens of BC (black consciousness) men decided to join the ANC, including some of those who had planned the attack on Terror."[71]

The arrival of the post-Soweto generation posed a challenge to the older prisoners who found the younger men seriously lacking in knowledge of political history. The most elaborate effort at political education was probably the ANC's "Syllabus A," a history of the ANC and its historical roots prepared late in the 1970s under the direction of the High Organ.[72] It was estimated that an individual could take three years of reading and discussion to complete it. Another syllabus was prepared for what was "essentially a materialist history of the development of human society."[73] Techniques were developed to copy and circulate materials on very thin paper, including books borrowed as texts for correspondence courses.[74] For the most highly politicized, political education was a revolutionary obligation. "We saw ourselves as revolutionaries," Tokyo Sexwale has said. His task was "to translate ANC policies so that everyone could understand them." For Sexwale, revolutionaries "lived according to a strict code of conduct," in which even female "pin-up pictures were not acceptable."[75] Politics and the revolution were all.

Commitment to the cause prompted ANC leaders on the island to develop ingenious ways of making contact with the leadership in exile and under-ground. Conversations with family visitors, though monitored, could be coded. Every circumstance that could justify a visit by a lawyer was exploited. Lawyers were not searched but were careful to avoid carrying incriminating documents. Through key words written down during conversation (bugging was assumed), political messages could be communicated.[76] Released prisoners also were commonly used to transmit messages to leaders outside. With time and patience, it was possible for Lusaka to clear very important decisions with leaders on the island. Thus, when the National Executive Committee in exile wanted Tambo to assume the title of president following the death of Albert Lutuli in 1967, Tambo refused, arguing that this was a "policy decision" that had to be agreed to by the leaders on Robben Island. He became acting president and accepted the title of president only in 1977 after those leaders had concurred.

In other instances, Mandela took important policy decisions alone or in consultation only with other members of the High Organ. In 1976, the year of Transkeian independence, the government conveyed an offer to Mandela that if he were to recognize the legitimacy of the Transkei government and agree to take up residence there, his sentence might be "dramatically reduced." He turned down the invitation, which he said "only a turncoat could accept." James Kruger, the Minister of Justice, came in person to the prison to proffer the government's proposal. After being rebuffed, he returned a month later with the same offer and received the same answer.[77] Anxious to appear reform-minded in the aftermath of the Soweto uprising, Pretoria's security chiefs were ready to play high-stakes poker with the freedom of their most prestigious prisoner. Perhaps they perceived then, or perhaps only much later, how possible it was that such a prisoner, endowed with the patience of Job, might in the end be holding the winning hand.

Re-thinking the ANC's Strategy

Toward the end of the 1970s the ANC faced practical problems that were both old and new. The enormous flow of new recruits to Umkhonto starting in 1976 created difficulties that were logistical, diplomatic, ideological, and pedagogical. Existing camps in Tanzania and Zambia were inadequate to deal with the influx. Over 100 students went to study in Nigeria and others were sent to Cuba, Egypt, the Soviet Union, and East Germany.[78] Recruits were given the option of military, academic, or other training. In the ANC, more than 70 percent opted for military training.[79] Beginning in 1977 military recruits were sent to relatively primitive facilities at Novo Catengue, south of Luanda, and to other areas of Angola.[80] Graduates of the camps received a variety of assignments: work as political instructors or in service or defense posts in Angola, advanced military, academic, or professional training in East Germany, the Soviet Union, or elsewhere, or transfer to Lusaka, the "forward areas" (Botswana, Lesotho, Mozambique, Swaziland), or into South Africa.

Managing the training of new recruits was a complex task. *Document 111,* excerpts from the diary of Jack Simons, provides a revealing glimpse of life at Novo Catengue, where the first contingent of 560 young exiles from the 1976 uprising—christened the "June 16 detachment"—were trained.[81] Simons, an admired scholar and a non-dogmatic Marxist, was the ANC's senior planner and exemplar of political instruction. He lived and taught in Novo Catengue from August 1977 until early 1978 and returned on January 4, 1979 on the eve of his seventy-second birthday. His diary covers the latter period, when one of his tasks was to reorient to the South African scene some 20 graduates of the Lenin School in Moscow. The great majority in the "June 16 detachment," who were among Simons's students, were from the Witwatersrand. Only about ten percent had been regular wage earners. About five percent were Coloureds or Indians, predominantly the latter. Many had been politicized through black consciousness and were unaccustomed to the ANC's multiracialism. Their educational levels ranged from illiteracy to university-level training. Some expressed themselves more confidently in African languages than in English, and instructors used both. Adjusting to the change from urban township life to the isolated and spartan camp was traumatic for some. A few were as young as 14. Women—about 20 in the detachment—generally adjusted well. Their overall educational level was higher than the average, and a few served as platoon commanders or commissars (the latter were concerned with political orientation and conditions of life).[82] Older exiles who had left South Africa in the 1960s found the undisciplined life style of urban youth troublesome. The use of dagga (marijuana) or liquor or sexual involvement with women in the area was strictly prohibited. Potentially most serious, however, was the problem of enemy agents among the trainees.

Full security screening of new exiles was impossible since it required that their backgrounds be investigated at home. Conditions in the camps were far from ideal, and suspicions inevitably arose that those who complained might be provocateurs and spies. In September 1977 an episode of mass food poisoning at Novo Catengue was attributed to enemy agents.[83] As paranoia took hold, cadres who fell under suspicion were treated more and more harshly until by the early 1980s severe punishment and beatings became the norm, and there was evidence of torture resulting in death. The Angolan camps, according to a confidential report by a 1984 ANC commission of inquiry, had by that time become "a dumping ground for enemy agents, suspects, malcontents and undisciplined elements," some of whom had been confined there since 1977. One cause of "bitterness and hostility in the men" was identified as "the low level of political consciousness." However, according to the report, problems in the camps before 1979 were handled well "because of the presence of the leadership on the spot, the availability of tried and tested comrades, the attempts to solve the problems politically and timeously and the relationship between all levels of the leadership and the rank-and-file." Because "political training" had been given priority, the Novo Catengue camp had "symbolised a vision of the People's Army."[84]

Once guerrillas were trained, their deployment raised questions of revolutionary theory and strategy that were intensely disputed within the ANC after Soweto.[85] There continued to be broad agreement on the ultimate objective, the seizure of power, and the necessity for armed struggle or military action to achieve it. There was continuing disagreement, however, on the priorities to be given to action by trained soldiers and to political mass action. Was military action required to generate popular support or was popular support a precondition for effective military action? Strategists envisioned "people's war" that would be "protracted," and with the masses "armed," but the vision of ultimate victory was clouded. Would the eventual "seizure of power" be primarily military with popular support or political (perhaps the long-dreamed-of general strike) with military support? On the other hand, there was rhetorical consistency in the recognition that political leadership should provide the overall direction of military action.

An early operational dispute arose from an incident in October 1976 when a guerrilla unit headed by Naledi Tsiki entered South Africa, acting under instructions from Joe Modise and his deputy, Joe Slovo, the leading military figures in the Revolutionary Council. In South Africa, the unit made contact with the "Main Machinery" of Joe Gqabi and Martin Ramokgadi, who claimed that as the political leaders on the ground, they would tell the unit what to do, when and how. Tsiki agreed that the military had to obey political orders but argued that those orders were transmitted to them by their military superiors and, accordingly, the unit could decide for itself. The dispute was referred to the leadership outside (presumably the Revolution-ary Council), which decided that the unit should have accepted the command of Gqabi and Ramokgadi, apparently because of Gqabi's military record dating back to the 1960s. The decision was reached, however, after the arrest of Tsiki and Gqabi and others at the end of 1976. Wider questions of authority were left unsettled.

The central debate was over how to build a political base within South Africa. Lacking such a base, the ANC had been unable to exploit the rise of black consciousness, the reemergence of trade unions, or the turmoil of the Soweto uprising. A vigorous participant in the debate was Mac Maharaj, secretary of the Internal Reconstruction and Development department. He criticized the priority given to cross-border raids and accused Modise and Slovo of following a militarist bent and ignoring the use of political mobilization. The Strategy and Tactics document of 1969 had established the assumption that "people's war" would be protracted and would develop primarily in rural areas. Critics argued that the 1976 uprising had shown the potential for urban insurrection. To guide such an insurrection, the ANC would require a political structure on the ground.

All these issues came to a head in a major review of strategy and tactics that coincided with a visit to Vietnam in 1978 to study the Vietnamese revolutionary experience. From Umkhonto's inception, its leaders had been influenced by the history of revolutions in Algeria, China, and particularly Cuba. They had carefully read Che Guevara's *Guerrilla Warfare* with its emphasis on the "detonator" approach, which held that armed action could be catalytic in bringing a political base into existence. Re-examination of this assumption became the principal outcome of the Vietnam visit, during which a delegation led by Tambo toured all parts of the recently reunited country and met with General Vo Nguyen Giap and representatives of "the Vietnamese Workers Party (now called the Communist Party of Vietnam)" over the period October 11–26. The delegation included Joe Modise (the commander of "Central Operations Headquarters," which fell under the Revolutionary Council), Joe Slovo (his deputy), Moses Mabhida (secretary of the Revolutionary Council), Cassius Make (the assistant secretary), and Thabo Mbeki, a rising star in the National Executive Committee. During the visit, Slovo is said to have undergone a conversion to the perspective previously championed by Maharaj. Calling for a reopening of the debate on how to construct a political base, he conceded that the ANC had not paid sufficient attention to combining legal and illegal actions nor given "proper weight to the significance of the many mass organizations which had recently arisen."[86]

The NEC and the Revolutionary Council met together in Luanda from December 27, 1978, to January 1 and considered the delegation's report.[87] In discussing the report, the joint meeting concluded that "the Vietnamese experience reveals certain shortcomings on our part and draws attention to areas of crucial importance which we tended to neglect." The joint committee's statement found "a golden thread of the strategic thinking of the

VWP (CPV) [Vietnamese Workers Party, later called the Communist Party of Vietnam] . . . consisting of many strands," and listed the following:

(a) the struggle was for the victory of a national democratic revolution which would proceed uninterruptedly to the construction of a Socialist Vietnam.
(b) throughout the struggle, while keeping under review the correlation of national and class forces with a view to drawing them into the struggle, the VWP (CPV) understood that the workers and peasants constituted the core of the revolutionary forces.
(c) The vanguard VWP would, while maintaining its independence, work with other patriotic forces.
(d) The VWP would continuously strive to create the broadest national front around a minimum program to unite all classes and strata; at all times to create legal and semi-legal organisations, work within and influence existing ones, leading all these forces on the basis of correct policies.
(e) the revolution could only succeed through the united strength of the masses expressing itself in organised political activity.
(f) revolutionary armed struggle itself can only succeed if it grows out of the mass political base.
(g) the political struggle is primary in all the phases of the revolution. Revolutionary violence is necessary for the victory of the revolution, but this violence must itself be constantly assessed and controlled to maintain the correct relationship with the political struggle.
(h) the Vietnamese struggle was part of the world revolutionary process, influencing and being influenced by it.

The joint meeting in Luanda selected a six-member Politico-Military Strategy Commission to examine strategic options and make recommendations in the light of the Vietnamese experience. In its statement, the meeting identified 12 "significant conclusions or proposals." The first five were the most important:

(a) elaboration of an overall strategy based on mass mobilisation.
(b) creation of the broadest possible national front for liberation.
(c) strengthening the underground machinery by drawing into it activists thrown up in mass struggle.
(d) development of operations out of political activity, guided by the needs and level of political mobilisation and organisation.
(e) creation of a central organ to plan, coordinate and direct all activities inside the country.

The Commission was composed of the members of the delegation to Vietnam except for Make, who was replaced by Joe Gqabi. Maharaj was not a member; apparently he preferred to devote himself to the work of the Internal Reconstruction and Development Department, traveling between forward areas to meet with home-based activists. After some eight months of consultation and discussion, the Commission produced a final report, drafted by Slovo, known as "the Green Book" because of its green cover.[88] Years later Slovo looked back upon this document as "the most thorough investigation, from every angle, of what was wrong with the organisation.[89] Part One of the report described the Commission's work schedule and its requests for assistance. One request was sent "by special emissaries" to "the Island" (ANC usage for Lesotho).[90] The final report praised the memorandum received in return (by Chris Hani) for "creating an organisational structure which, from top to bottom, is designed to plan and coordinate *all aspects of internal work* under the immediate direction of a single political collective, serviced by specialist departments." *Document 114* consists of Part One ("Introduction") and Part Two ("Our Strategic Line") of the report and two of its 14 annexures ("Summarized Themes of Our Strategic Line" and Memorandum from Lesotho).

"Our Strategic Line," presumably written by Slovo, declared that "at the present moment we are at the stage when the *main task* is to concentrate on political mobilisation and organisation so as to build up political revolutionary bases throughout the country." The armed struggle was "secondary." On the question of whether or not "the ANC, as a national movement, should tie itself to the ideology of Marxism-Leninism and publicly commit itself to the socialist option," the report stated that "No member of the Commission had any doubts about the ultimate need to continue our revolution towards a socialist order." (Since "Strategy and Tactics" in 1969 had linked "liberation and socialism," this statement was not surprising, but it is extremely doubtful that Tambo believed that the ANC "should tie itself to the ideology of Marxism-Leninism.") It was important to advocate this perspective or "to risk dominance within our revolution by purely nationalist forces which see themselves as replacing the white exploiters," the Commission declared. Nevertheless, it warned, such policies should be expressed "with a degree of tactical caution."

In discussing structure, the report stated that "in the forward areas the separation of political and military planning has, by and large, become almost total." What was needed was "a total organisational integration of political and military direction based on an overall plan for the whole country." The central organ envisaged by the NEC and the Revolutionary Council, said the report, should be the NEC's chief instrument for implementing its internal policy; and its members should be chosen from amongst "the most experienced, talented and leading cadres."[91] The future of the Revolutionary Council was left open. Furthermore, the work of the central organ should be duplicated by sub-organs in the forward areas. Would the existence of the proposed central organ pose "a danger for the NEC as the unquestioned leading decision-making body on every aspect of our strategy and tactics"? The Commission reported that it spent considerable time discussing this question and concluded that there was no such danger.

The National Executive Committee approved the Commission's report in

August 1979 in Dar es Salaam with one major exception described by Barrell as "disastrous."[92] The NEC rejected the proposal to create a new central operational organ, mainly because of fear among some NEC members, including Thomas Nkobi, the treasurer-general, that it might develop into a rival locus of power. The outcome in 1980, therefore, was the creation of "senior organs" in the forward areas (Mozambique, Botswana, and Lesotho but not Zimbabwe) with combined military and political functions but responsible to the parallel authorities of a Central Operations Headquarters and the Internal Reconstruction and Development Department, both falling under the Revolutionary Council, whose meetings had been irregular and poorly attended. A special operations unit for spectacular armed actions, something long-desired by Slovo, was also established and placed under his control. The unit was an anomalous development since it did not fall under the Revolutionary Council but was answerable directly to Tambo.

As the ANC entered the 1980s, it did so with a revitalized sense of the importance of above-ground mass mobilization as a prerequisite for "people's war." The ANC's strategic review of 1978–1979, proposing guidelines for the 1980s, was seminal although the "parallelism" of political and military approaches, criticized by the Green Book, did not come to an end. Despite the new priority on political rather than military action, the highlight of ANC activity in 1980 was the "armed propaganda" of spectacular sabotage. Displaying a new level of sophistication in targeting strategically crucial facilities, ANC guerrillas on the first night of June cut through security fences and attacked three SASOL oil-from-coal plants. People in Johannesburg saw a glow in the sky 50 miles away and read in the *Rand Daily Mail* the next morning the somewhat exaggerated pronouncement that South Africa had entered "a state of revolutionary war."[93] Potentially more significant, however, was the increasing involvement of ANC partisans—some independently and some in coordination with underground networks—in nascent political organization. Drawing energy from the highly politicized post-Soweto youth generation and enlisting the organizational skills and experience of the young adult generation schooled by the black consciousness upsurge of the early 1970s, these efforts were initially local and decentralized. Only in the early 1980s would they begin to cohere into the mass coalition, envisioned in the Green Book, that was to become the United Democratic Front.

Notes

1. Howard Barrell, *Conscripts to Their Age: African National Congress Operational Strategy, 1976–1986,* doctoral thesis, Oxford University, 1993, p. 26. Conversation with Oyama Mabandla (July 1992).

2. Oliver Tambo, "Political Report of the National Executive Committee to the National Consultative Conference," June 1985, p. 19.

3. "Statement by Joe Nzingo Gqabi, Accused No. 7," for the defense in *State v. Sexwale* (1978).

4. Morobe, Masetlha and Moloi served six-month sentences for their refusal.

5. Quoted in Alex Callinicos and John Rogers, *Southern Africa After Soweto* (London: Pluto Press, 1978), p. 163. Mashinini failed to find his feet politically in exile, falling initially under the influence of British Trotskyists and eventually living in political limbo in Guinea where he later died.

6. Memorandum by Mpho Mashinini on Tsietsi Donald Mashinini, 1991 and documents of SAYRCO.

7. The ANC called attention to the historic significance of April 6, the anniversary of Jan van Riebeeck's landing at the Cape of Good Hope in 1652. Nelson Mandela paid tribute to Mahlangu when he was reburied on April 6, 1993. *The Guardian* (Manchester), April 7, 1993. Statements by the ANC, members of the UN Security Council, and others are in *Solomon Mahlangu: Hero of South African Revolutionary Struggle* (Helsinki: World Peace Council in cooperation with the United Nations Centre against Apartheid, 1979).

8. "Second Council Meeting of the ANC Education Dept., Mazimbu—14–18 April Year of the Spear [1979]" and "SOMAFCO: Official Opening, 21–23 August 1985." The Solomon Mahlangu Freedom College (Somafco) was established in 1979 on land near Morogoro donated by the Tanzanian government. It developed four educational sectors (secondary, primary, nursery, adult education) and other services. In 1982 the Ruth First Orientation Centre was established at nearby Dakawa. See Pethu Serote, "Solomon Mahlangu Freedom College: A Unique South African Educational Experience in Tanzania," *Transformation,* no. 2, 1992, pp. 47–59.

9. Howard Barrell, "The Turn to the Masses: the African National Congress' Strategic Review of 1978–79," *Journal of Southern African Studies,* vol. 18, no. 1, March 1992, p. 79.

10. Interview of Howard Barrell with Joe Slovo (August 1989).

11. "CBS Reports with Bill Moyers—The Battle for South Africa," transcript, September 1978. Zietsman's statement resembles one made to Karis by a defense official, Brigadier Deysel, in January 1983. He said the problem posed by the ANC could be solved by killing every one of its members from Oliver Tambo on down.

12. *Sunday Express* (Johannesburg), November 4, 1979.

13. Quoted in a flyer, "Save James Mange," issued by the Southern African Information Programme of the International University Exchange Fund, n.d.

14. On the trial of James Mange and 11 others see "Trial of the Pietermaritzburg 12," *Africa,* February 1980; *Rand Daily Mail,* November 13–14, 1979; and "The Pietermaritzburg Twelve," *Dawn: Monthly Journal of Umkhonto we Sizwe,* December 1979.

15. Mange made one of the great comebacks in South African political history. Released from prison in the amnesties that followed the 1990 unbanning of the ANC, he became a reggae singer, founded his own political party and ran for president in the April 1994 election. He polled 10,575 votes, not enough to win a seat in parliament.

16. *Rand Daily Mail,* January 9, 1980 and *Sechaba,* April 1980, pp. 16–17.

17. *House of Assembly Debates,* June 3, 1980, col. 8,024.

18. Conversation with Frank Chikane (June 1995).

19. David Sibeko, *South Africa's Secret Trial: The PAC Bethal 18 Case* (Chicago: Liberator Press, December 1978), p. 8, and Gail Gerhart, *Black Power in South Africa* (Berkeley: University of California Press, 1978), p. 253.

20. Tom Lodge, "The Poqo Insurrection," in Lodge, ed., *Resistance and Ideology in Settler Societies* (Johannesburg: Ravan Press, 1986).

21. Press release, Mission to the UK and Continental Europe, Pan Africanist Congress of Azania, June 19, 1979.

22. Nicholas Ashford, *The Times* (London), June 21, 1978.

23. *State v. Mothopeng,* p. 272. Enoch Ngomezulu, a state witness, testified that in April 1976 Mothopeng gave instructions to be transmitted to PAC leaders abroad. Because PAC broadcasts on Radio Tanzania seemed to indicate a change in policy from national struggle to class struggle, Mothopeng believed that this was causing confusion and "ordered" (Ngomezulu's word) the leaders in exile to revert to the old policies. Another instruction was that the PAC abroad should repair its internal split. Soon afterwards, Ngomezulu testified, Mothopeng decided that as soon as he succeeded in reviving the PAC, he would leave the country because

he was not satisfied with Leballo's leadership and because Sobukwe did not wish to leave. *State v. Mothopeng,* pp. 277–79.

24. Control of funds in exile was a chronic cause of disaffection. Within South Africa, Mothopeng was sensitive about the handling of money. Ngomezulu testified that Mothopeng was told by a messenger that he should ask the PAC in Swaziland for money if needed. However, Mothopeng told Ngomezulu that he was "not keen to bring money into the country because this would cause problems amongst members as they would fight over money and this would lead to the whole thing being exposed to the police." Yet funds, especially for expenses to leave the country, were a continuing problem. Ngomezulu testified that John Ganya had complained after Soweto "that PAC people in Johannesburg were doing nothing to identify themselves with the plight of the students . . . [and] he alone was attending the funerals of the students who got killed in these riots and as a result of this he had a number of students who asked him to help them leave South Africa for military training." But he had no funds and sought them from Mothopeng. *State v. Mothopeng,* pp. 272 and 279.

25. Conversation with Zephania Mothopeng (December 1989).

26. *Azania News,* September–October 1979, and press coverage.

27. *State v. Mothopeng,* p. 118.

28. *Rand Daily Mail,* April 6, 1979.

29. Conversation with Zolile Keke (October 1981).

30. Conversation with Mothopeng.

31. For maintaining access to resources, recognition by the OAU was critical, not only in Africa but also in the United Nations. The OAU recognized both the ANC and the PAC, and in 1974 the UN General Assembly gave "observer status" to each. In 1979 and 1980 each organisation received $99,000 in UN funds annually. Conversation with Henry Isaacs (April 1981). Appeals from the OAU for a united front were met with ANC arguments that the PAC had "no roots" in South Africa and had "ceased to exist as a body." Letter from Duma Nokwe to the secretary general of the OAU, September 1967. To ANC claims that it was the only authentic representative of the South African people, the PAC replied in kind. The ANC's repeated calls for the OAU's de-recognition of the PAC were supported by pro-Soviet African states but failed in part because of the hostility of some African states to the Soviet Union.

32. Howard Barrell, "The Outlawed South African Liberation Movements," in Shaun Johnson, ed., *South Africa: No Turning Back* (London: Macmillan Press, 1988), p. 77, citing "PAC and Front Line State official sources." According to Henry Isaacs, when the Libyan government offered military training to the PAC, the PAC did not have enough recruits. Under an agreement with the Basutoland Congress Party, Lesotho nationals were sent to Libya under false pretenses. Isaacs, *Reflections of a Black South African Exile,* unpublished manuscript, 1986, p. 331, and T. M. Ntantala, "The Profiles of Leballo's Gang," May 5, 1978, pp. 5–8.

33. Isaacs, p. 361.

34. Leballo, on the other hand, at their first meeting "exuded energy. Pumping my hand vigorously, he said, 'Welcome, son of the soil!' after which he launched into a long, incoherent diatribe. At the end of ninety minutes, I had no idea at all of what he had said except that he was expelled from school because he removed a picture of the Queen of England." Isaacs, pp. 333–34.

35. Isaacs, pp. 325–26.

36. Isaacs, pp. 331–32.

37. Isaacs, pp. 360–61.

38. The five members of the Central Committee, who were named, were Victor Mayekiso, David Sibeko, Elias Ntloedibe, Vusumzi Make, and Jimmy Mokgoatsane. T. M. Ntantala, "The Profiles of Leballo's Gang," Dar es Salaam, May 5, 1978, and Isaacs, pp. 386–87.

39. Conference documents did not state the number in attendance. The number was 100 according to Reuters, July 5, 1978.

40. Press release, PAC Observer Mission to the United Nations, November 8, 1978. Writing in the mid-1980s, Isaacs, p. 428, said that "APLA has not been responsible for a single military operation and, in fact, its cadres have not fired a single shot since 1968."

41. The seven expelled were Ntantala, P. Gqobose, T. M. Bidi, P. Z. Mboko, N. Tshongoy,

K. Mokoena, and J. N. Jako. Discussion of the Arusha conference is based mainly on the "Political Report, Address to the P. A. C. Consultative Conference in Arusha, June 27–2nd July 1978, by Potlako K. Leballo, Acting President, P. A. C. of Azania," n.d.; "Salute the 2nd Consultative Conference of the Pan Africanist Congress of Azania!"; and "Report to the Pan Africanist Congress Consultative Conference in Arusha, June 27th–2nd July 1978 by Elias L. Ntloedibe, Administrative Secretary." Ntantala's unsigned review of the conference is in "The Pan Africanist Congress of Azania Consultative Conference Held in Arusha, United Republic of Tanzania on 27th June–2nd July 1978."

42. Ideology and talk of "rightists" (as he was labeled) versus "Marxists-Leninists" was unimportant. Conversation with David Sibeko (January 1979).

43. *Azania News,* November-December 1978, p. 1.

44. *Ikwezi* (Nottingham), December 1978, pp. 6–7.

45. Isaacs, pp. 400–401, and "Meeting of the Administrative Committee of the Central Committee of the PAC," April 30–May 1, 1979.

46. "Decisions of the Extra-ordinary Meeting of the Central Committee Held in Dar es Salaam from April 30 to May 1, 1979." Sibeko explained that Leballo's doctors had advised him to step down because of his high blood pressure and excessive work. Conversation with Sibeko (May 1979).

47. "Administrative Report Presented to the Administrative Committee of the Central Committee on April 30, 1979 by Henry Isaacs, Acting Administrative Secretary," Dar es Salaam.

48. Isaacs, pp. 403–404, 407–408.

49. "Press Release, Plenary Meeting of the Pan Africanist Congress of Azania Expels Potlako K. Leballo," Dar es Salaam, October 10, 1979.

50. Ntantala recounted that in 1965 he was in the first group of cadres to go to China for military training. Upon his return, he introduced classes in ideology, and by 1967, when a second group of cadres went to China, "the assimilation of the revolutionary ideas of Marx, Engels, Lenin, Stalin and Mao Tse-Tung was well underway." Ntantala's unsigned paper, "The Pan Africanist Congress of Azania Consultative Conference . . . 27th June–2nd July 1978."

51. In the late 1960s, according to Ntantala, Leballo was "greatly excited and enthusiastic" about Marxist revolutionary ideas, and "his own chosen speciality . . . was the Chinese military theory of people's war." "The Pan Africanist Congress of Azania Consultative Conference . . . 27th June–2nd July 1978." Yet later Leballo sought to ban a rigorously Marxist PAC treatise, "The New Road of Revolution" because, said Ntantala, he had not been "duly glorified" in it. He then talked of being anti-Communist. Ntantala, "The Crisis in the PAC," April 4, 1978.

52. Conversation with Barney Pityana (January 1988).

53. "Azania People's Revolutionary Party: Communique, Political Programme, Manifesto," n.d., p. 15. The founding convention took place in Britain during August 29–31 and September 3, 1979.

54. By the mid-1960s, over 1,000 PAC/Poqo prisoners were on Robben Island. An unpublished manuscript by Natoo Babenia in the Robben Island Archives of the Mayibuye Centre estimates that ANC prisoners on the island were well over 800 in late 1964.

55. Michael Dingake, *My Fight Against Apartheid* (London: Kliptown Books, 1987), p. 141.

56. Indres Naidoo, *Prisoner 885/63, Island in Chains: Ten Years on Robben Island as told by Indres Naidoo to Albie Sachs* (Penguin Books: Harmondsworth, Middlesex, 1982), pp. 219–23 and passim.

57. Tshwete later became Minister of Sport and Recreation in the first post-apartheid government.

58. Statement by Steve Tshwete in Jurgen Schadeberg, comp., *Voices from Robben Island* (Randburg: Ravan Press, 1994), p. 39. During a visit to the Transkeian home of P. S. Fadana, who served eight years on Robben Island, Karis saw a framed certificate on the dining room wall awarding Fadana and another prisoner first-prize in a ballroom dancing contest in 1967. Conversation with P. S. Fadana (October 1977).

59. Nelson Mandela, *Long Walk to Freedom* (New York: Little, Brown and Co., 1994), pp. 360 and 384, and conversation with Ahmed Kathrada (September 1993).

60. Mandela, pp. 384–85.

61. Conversation with Harry Gwala (December 1989). Ben Fihla of the ANC, who arrived on Robben Island in January 1964, has a harsher opinion of PAC prisoners in the earliest years. They ridiculed ANC's efforts to improve conditions, he has said, claiming that the ANC was engaged in a "pap [porridge] struggle." Conversation with Ben Fihla (October 1993).

62. Mkalipi quoted in Tom Lodge and Bill Nasson, *All, Here, and Now: Black Politics in South Africa in the 1980s* (New York: Ford Foundation and Foreign Policy Association, 1991), p. 298.

63. Conversation with Gwala.

64. Conversation with Raymond Mhlaba (December 1989).

65. Conversation with Mothopeng.

66. Mandela, p. 421.

67. Mosibudi Mangena, *On Your Own: Evolution of Black Consciousness in South Africa/ Azania* (Johannesburg: Skotaville Publishers, 1989), pp. 99–100.

68. Conversation with Mike Xego (October 1993).

69. Mandela, p. 423.

70. Mandela, pp. 423–24 and conversations with Mhlaba, Patrick Lekota (December 1989), Saths Cooper (October 1987), and Mothopeng.

71. Mandela, p. 424. Lekota acquired his nickname from his prowess on the soccer field.

72. On the High Organ see chapter 2.

73. Introduction by Colin Bundy in Govan Mbeki, *Learning From Robben Island: The Prison Writings of Govan Mbeki* (London: James Currey; Cape Town: David Philip; Athens, Ohio: Ohio University Press, 1991), pp. xxii–xxiii; Mandela, p. 407.

74. Even the first four volumes of *From Protest to Challenge* reached the island. According to Khehla Shubane, who was in the general section (conversation, March 1989), they were received by another prisoner on library loan from the University of South Africa. The loan was extended by paying repeated overdue fines. Meanwhile, the volumes were circulated and copied. Kathrada obtained a set while in Pollsmoor Prison. Early in the 1980s, a set was sent to "Commanding Officer, Robben Island Prison" at the suggestion of Neville Alexander, who was confident that prisoners would manage to see it.

75. Schadeberg, p. 35. The ANC also discouraged homosexual behavior, seeing it as likely to detract from discipline and dilute political commitment. See Fran Lisa Buntman, *From Hellhole to a Blessing in Disguise: A Study of Politics on Robben Island, 1963–1987*, B.A. honors thesis, University of the Witwatersrand, 1988, pp. 66–69.

76. Mandela, pp. 368, 351, 371, 404, and 412.

77. Mandela, pp. 418–20.

78. Conversation with Pioneer Mogale (November 1985), and Serote, pp. 47–59. According to Thabo Mbeki, the ANC in June 1980 had 100 students in Cuba, 15 in Nigeria, 8 in Cairo, 6 at the University of Zambia, and an undisclosed number in Britain, the Soviet Union, East Germany, West Germany, France, Bulgaria, Hungary, Rumania, Poland, India, Botswana, Mozambique, and the United States. *New York Times*, June 20, 1980. Stephen Davis, *Apartheid's Rebels: Inside South Africa's Hidden War* (New Haven: Yale University Press, 1987), p. 57, states that "the total estimated ANC population outside South Africa" in 1975 was 1,000 and in 1980, 9,000, but gives no source.

79. Chris Hani in *The Sowetan,* June 28, 1990.

80. Discussion of the Angolan camps is based largely on Jack Simons, *Political Sociology for Umkhonto Students,* unpublished manuscript, n.d., and Ronnie Kasrils, *"Armed and Dangerous": My Undercover Struggle Against Apartheid* (Oxford: Heinemann, 1993), chapters 10–12.

81. This paragraph is based on Simons, chapters 2 and 3 The manuscript covers the two periods when Simons lived and taught in Novo Catengue. It includes his personal diary of 1979, interviews with Simons himself, Chris Hani, Mzwai Piliso, Mark Shope and 13 other members of Umkhonto, and the texts of Simons' lectures. Simons had been a popular professor at the University of Cape Town and a member of the SACP's Central Committee. Despite bans beginning in 1952, he was allowed to teach until 1964 and later taught at the University of Zambia until 1975. Simons, a provocative teacher with a sardonic sense of humor, was critical of the Soviet Union. It was the ANC, not the SACP, that urged him to undertake his work at Novo Catengue.

82. At one point, an administrative decision was made that romantic affairs with the women were allowed only for general soldiers but not for instructors and administrators. Simons, chapter 2. The Stuart Commission, cited below, stated in March 1984 that in all camps there was "widespread complaint that people in administration use their positions to seduce women comrades," including married women, and that such women "are given special treatment and they tend to reject the authority of their immediate commanders." Regarding similar problems, Rica Hodgson commented later at Somafco on the loneliness and lack of social life there, the problem of providing adequate sex education, and the impossibility of obtaining legal abortions in Tanzania. In the event of pregnancy, both the woman and the man had to leave school, the man being responsible for finding work to help in supporting the child. Hodgson saw the ANC as rather puritanical. Conversation with Rica Hodgson (November 1985).

83. Chapter 2 of the Simons manuscript states that "Black September (1977) was a crisis period in the camp when an enemy agent attempted to poison the entire camp." Also see Kasrils, p. 175.

84. "Report: Commission of Inquiry into Recent Developments in the People's Republic of Angola [the Stuart Report]," Lusaka: March 14, 1984. The report was not released until 1993. An ANC recruit (Vusumuzi Buthelezi) who arrived in Angola in June 1978, described the treatment meted out to him for refusing to give up his "Zulu nationhood" in "African National Congress (EM) [external mission] Discriminates and Tortures," *Inhlabamkhosi (Clarion Call)* March 1984, an Inkatha publication. See Stephen Ellis, "Mbokodo: Security in ANC Camps, 1961–1990," *African Affairs*, vol. 93, 1994, which discusses four official ANC reports and other reports on human rights abuses during the ANC's years in exile.

85. This and the following paragraph are based on Barrell, *Conscripts,* chapters 3 and 4.

86. Barrell, *Conscripts,* pp. 188–89.

87. "Statement of a Joint Meeting of the NEC and the RC of the ANC (SA), held in Luanda on 27th December, to 1st January 1979." This statement is Annexure A of the Report of the Politico-Military Strategy Commission to the ANC [the Green Book], August 1979.

88. Conversation with Slovo (November 1993). Only a few copies were made and these were rarely seen outside the NEC except by key members of Umkhonto such as Jeff Radebe who were given it to study before going into South Africa.

89. Conversation with Slovo (October 1990).

90. We are indebted to Vladimir Shubin for identifying this usage.

91. Annexure E, "The Proposed Structure for Internal Work," described "a single centralised organ, headed by the President, which keeps the internal situation, in its totality, under continuous review, and broadly plans, coordinates and implements all internal political and military work," in other words, "a full-time collective concentrating exclusively on the internal struggle." The central organ would be serviced by specialized subordinate departments and could create new ones. Its responsibilities would include the implementation of political and military training programs in the camps and general administration of training programs provided by external allies.

92. See Barrell, *Conscripts,* chapter 5.

93. *Rand Daily Mail,* June 3, 1980.

11. Crackdown and Resistance after Soweto

It became possible with the perspective of later years to see how the Soweto uprising precipitated a fateful downturn in the fortunes of the apartheid system. At the time, however, the National Party's response to the uprising was merely to accelerate the implementation of plans that were already in place for the realization of Verwoerd's vision of "separate development." Once a few conciliatory gestures had been made to lower the temperature of township revolt in 1976–77, government strategists returned to their blueprints for the geographical partition of South Africa into a white heartland and ten independent African homelands. "If our policy is taken to its full logical conclusion as far as the black people are concerned," Connie Mulder announced on becoming Minister of Plural Relations in January 1978, "there will not be one black man with South African citizenship."[1] Such confident assertions masked the divisive policy debates inside the National Party on precisely how and at what pace to pursue the apartheid vision. There was little disagreement, however, about the necessity to deal ruthlessly with all black challenges wherever these arose. A build-up of the military proceeded as the collapse of the Smith regime in Rhodesia became more imminent. As the decade moved toward a close, the repression of internal dissent took an ever greater toll—at times with consequences quite unintended.

Biko's Death

Chapter 5 describes how rivalry and uncertainty about future directions had created divisions in the black consciousness movement by the time violence erupted in Soweto in June 1976. The national headquarters of the

South African Students' Organisation (SASO) in Durban had come increasingly under the influence of the ANC, while the Black People's Convention (BPC), weakened by bans and arrests, nominally operated out of Johannesburg but increasingly looked for leadership to Biko's inner circle in King William's Town in the eastern Cape. Working with Mapetla Mohapi and Malusi Mpumlwana, who were subject to relatively lighter restriction orders, Biko throughout the later part of 1975 patiently pursued contacts with the fledgling ANC and PAC undergrounds in the hope that a common liberation front could be forged. Disturbing reports from exiles in Botswana added impetus to this effort; dozens of adherents of black consciousness organizations were escaping across the border only to find themselves without an organizational home if they declined to join either of the two recognized exiled movements. The King William's Town leadership, frustrated by its inability to clinch a unity agreement under the difficult circumstances of secrecy inside South Africa, began looking for a way to smuggle someone out of the country to meet with senior ANC and PAC officials. When Biko's banning orders were relaxed to permit him to testify in the Pretoria trial of the "SASO Nine" in early May 1976, a risky plan to fly him to Botswana by private plane was considered but abandoned. The dangers inherent in underground work were painfully brought home when Mohapi was arrested and died at the hands of police interrogators at the Kei Road police station near King William's Town on August 5.[2]

As the violence of the ongoing Soweto uprising drew the world's attention to the possible impermanence of National Party rule, interest in Biko as the reputed founder of the black consciousness movement spread among journalists and representatives of businesses and foreign governments seeking contact with influential black dissidents. Donations increased to the projects of Black Community Programmes (run by Ben Khoapa from Durban and Biko and Mpumlwana from Ginsberg township in King William's Town), and in early 1977 Biko received an invitation from the American government to visit the United States—an impossible prospect under the terms of the banning order that confined him to the magisterial district of King William's Town, but one which he nevertheless formally declined lest the appearance of being pro-American compromise his ability to maintain a dialogue with SASO's growing left wing.[3] In addition to ideological frictions arising in SASO and the BPC over the controversial Mafikeng Manifesto (*Document 57*), there were also people in both groups who resented what they saw as control by "Ginsberg" over funds coming from abroad, and who believed that a portion of the money being received should be diverted into support for the ANC and PAC undergrounds. Biko and his lieutenants opposed any diversion.[4]

Amidst these unresolved tensions, the issue of unity among liberation groups loomed ever larger as the student revolt of 1976–77 spread and intensified, sending hundreds and eventually several thousand young people fleeing into neighboring countries. Harry Nengwekhulu, a founding member of SASO who had left the country in 1973, was authorized by the

BPC in early 1977 to establish an external office in Botswana to facilitate the reception of refugees, and to assist in the raising of funds and international support. This proved divisive because ANC and PAC leaders in exile took the move to mean that the black consciousness movement intended to set itself up as a new liberation group—a "third force." Their apprehensions in this regard were further fed by Biko's growing international reputation as a major political player. Despite these frictions, secret communication between Ginsberg and the internal ANC and PAC leadership continued because each stood to gain in some way by an alliance, the black consciousness movement by finding a modus operandi for cooperation without having to abdicate leadership to organizations whose capabilities it regarded as unproven, and the underground movements by linking with an internal "above ground" network of experienced political activists. Black consciousness adherents tended to be critical of the exile ANC's readiness in 1975 to seek an internal link with Inkatha, a view which found them ready allies among influential ANC operatives within the country who likewise opposed the link with Inkatha and hoped that the exiles' stance might be reversed.[5]

During the Soweto uprising if not earlier, the security police had become aware of efforts by the ANC and PAC to recruit followers in the black consciousness movement, and by early 1977 they had learned through Craig Williamson, a spy planted in the International University Exchange Fund in Geneva, of an agreement by Oliver Tambo and David Sibeko to meet with Biko if a way could be found for him to leave South Africa secretly.[6] Harassment of Ginsberg-based activists was stepped up. Mpumlwana was detained for five months in late 1976, and *Daily Dispatch* journalist Thenjiwe Mtintso, after a harsh period of detention, was banned and confined to her home area in Johannesburg. Mxolisi Mvovo, the acting president of the BPC, was banned in early 1977, and Dr. Mamphela Ramphele, director of the Black Community Programme's Zanempilo clinic outside King William's Town, was banished to Tzaneen in the northern Transvaal. In late March 1977 a legal charge was brought against Biko, who was accused of tampering with witnesses in a case of school arson that had occurred the previous year. Released on bail and eventually acquitted, he was then charged with breaking the banning orders which forbade him to communicate with other banned people, and was on bail awaiting trial on this charge at the time of his final arrest on August 18, 1977.

On August 17 Biko ignored his bans and drove to Cape Town with Peter Jones, a young Coloured accountant who had been sent to King William's Town by the BPC to assume some of the duties of Biko's four restricted colleagues. Several pressing items of business made the journey seem worth the risk. A serious rupture had occurred between left and right factions of the BPC in Cape Town, and Biko hoped to effect a reunification. In addition, he wanted to meet with Neville Alexander, a prominent figure in the left-wing Unity Movement whose ideas were gaining influence in black consciousness circles in the western Cape. When Alexander, who was also a banned person, refused to receive his visitors on the evening of the 17th, Biko waited briefly for him to reconsider, then set out with Jones on the long drive back to King William's Town. During the predawn hours of the 18th on the road between Grahamstown and King William's Town, they were stopped at a police roadblock. After their identities were determined, they were arrested and taken to police headquarters in Port Elizabeth. There Jones, who survived to recount his experiences, was interrogated, severely beaten and deprived of food, then held in detention without charge for 533 days.

Biko's death was reported to a stunned black public on the morning of September 13. During the subsequent judicial inquest, it was disclosed that he had sustained serious head injuries on or about September 7, and that on September 11 the chief district surgeon in Port Elizabeth had authorized that he be transferred for medical observation to Pretoria. He had then been driven the 740 miles to Pretoria, lying naked in the back of a police Land Rover, and had died in a cell at Pretoria Central Prison on the night of September 12. By September 14, the news that Biko was dead had made headlines around the world, and a storm of protest and outrage had begun to build both in South Africa and internationally.

Attempts by the government to deflect blame from the police rapidly proved counterproductive. Addressing a congress of the Transvaal National Party on September 14, James Kruger, the Minister of Justice, offered an official version of events: Biko had died from a hunger strike after refusing all food since September 5. Despite the implausibility of this explanation, a delegate, amidst laughter, rose to congratulate Kruger on being so democratic as to allow a prisoner his democratic right to starve himself to death. Asked how he felt about Biko's death, Kruger replied in a remark later quoted often: "I am not pleased, nor am I sorry. He leaves me cold."[7] Blacks were not left cold, however, nor were liberal whites who had worked with Biko and who had come, like blacks, to accord him a special preeminence among black leaders. His death was a portentous event, warned the Christian Institute; "From the ghettos of Ginsberg to the chancelleries of the West his death leads to a clear awareness that this ungodly and revolting society will be destroyed" (*Document 119*). Memorial services held countrywide culminated on September 25 with an emotion-charged funeral in King William's Town where speaker after speaker heaped blame on the government and warned that nothing could stop the desire of blacks to achieve equality and freedom (*Document 120*).[8]

Coming so soon after the countrywide uprising, Biko's death and Kruger's clumsy attempt to cover up its cause threw the National Party government into a defensive posture. Some Nationalists agreed privately with the parliamentary opposition that Kruger should resign; Kruger countered by promising that a thorough investigation would be made and that heads would roll if police bore any responsibility. Following a pattern that remained familiar over the next decade and a half, the "investigations" led nowhere. Two months after Biko's death, however, an official inquest (mandated by South African law in all cases of death from unnatural causes) opened in Pretoria before a full battery of the international press. Representing the Biko family, advocate Sydney Kentridge led testimony from the eight members of the security police and four doctors who had been in contact with Biko during his detention, meticulously laying bare the anomalies and contradictions in what he termed the state's conspiracy of silence to cover up the truth that Biko had died at the hands of his interrogators.[9] Ignoring the weight of the evidence, the presiding chief magistrate of Pretoria ruled in favor of the police, finding that Biko's death could not be shown to have been brought about "by any act or omission involving an offence by any person."[10]

The Biko inquest was not a trial in a formal sense, but it became a trial of the South African system in the court of world opinion. Biko was the twentieth detainee to die in police custody since March 1976, and the forty-second to die since the right of habeas corpus had been abrogated under security legislation passed in 1963.[11] Although released detainees gave accounts of torture and brutal beatings, the security police were routinely absolved of responsibility in detainee deaths, implying complicity by their superiors in the ministry of justice and sympathy if not outright collusion by magistrates in the judicial system. In addition to exposing the lengths to which the South Africa state had gone by 1977 in placing itself above the law, the Biko inquest also laid bare the extent to which other sectors of the white establishment had become cowed by the intimidating power of the state. Three doctors violated the ethics of their profession to lend credence to the explanation of Biko's injuries put forward by the police.[12] With a handful of notable exceptions, white journalists also chose conformity over courage. Bowing to threats by Vorster to pass stronger censorship laws if the press refused to "discipline" itself, the Press Council, a body established by newspaper owners, censured the liberal *Rand Daily Mail* for publishing a story on October 7 challenging Kruger's claims that Biko had died from a hunger strike. Barred by a pledge of confidentiality from disclosing his source—a pathologist who had attended the autopsy representing the Biko family and who was to appear as a witness at the inquest—the editor of the *Mail* was issued a reprimand which cast doubt on his own ethics. Subsequent revelations at the inquest brought no retraction from the timid Press Council.[13] As black anger festered, most whites succumbed to their fears about "black power," and when a snap election was called for November 30, 1977, the all-white electorate returned the National Party by an unprecedented margin.

The October 1977 Crackdown

In the run-up to November 30, the National Party staged a stronger than usual display of pre-election *kragdadigheid* (power) by summarily banning 18 opposition organizations and shutting down *The World* newspaper. Declared unlawful on October 19 along with *The World* were the Christian Institute and its journal *Pro Veritate,* the South African Students' Organisation (SASO), the Black People's Convention (BPC), Black Community

Programmes, the Soweto Students' Representative Council (SSRC), the South African Students' Movement, the National Youth Organisation, the Border Youth Union, the Eastern Province Youth Organisation, the Natal Youth Organisation, the Transvaal Youth Organisation, the Western Cape Youth Organisation, the Black Parents Association, the Zimele Trust Fund, the Black Women's Federation, the Union of Black Journalists (UBJ), the Medupe Writers Association, and the Association for the Educational and Cultural Advancement of the African People of South Africa. More than 50 leaders of the banned groups were detained, and individual banning orders were issued to Donald Woods, editor of the East London *Daily Dispatch,* Beyers Naude, the director of the Christian Institute, and more than a dozen other government critics.

Vorster anticipated that the crackdown would intensify the storm of international protest already generated by the Soweto uprising and Biko's death, but he also correctly calculated that white voters were tired of the world's condemnation and would rally to the National Party if it forcefully expressed their resentment of foreign critics.[14] He knew that with a strongly renewed electoral mandate, he would be able to consolidate support for an accelerated pace of reform, despite the objections of the party's powerful right wing. The progress of reform in turn would eventually placate world opinion, as well as winning tacit allies for the government among ordinary blacks whose first priority, he assumed, was an improved living standard, not the pursuit of a black nationalist political agenda. A precondition for the success of this strategy, however, was the thorough suppression of radical black opposition and its liberal white allies, whatever the short-term cost in adverse international publicity. Like the post-Sharpeville crackdown of 1960, the all-out repression of black opposition in 1977 was meant to buy time for the government to make adjustments in its survival strategy, and to take the steps seen as necessary for the strategy's implementation. The possibility that intensified repression might inspire stronger black opposition was an outcome the government's security experts tended to discount as they contemplated their preferred scenario: an expanding black middle class, politically moderate in temperament and linked to the structures of evolving ethnic homelands that in time—the plans were still imprecise—would be incorporated into some type of carefully designed federal or confederal constitutional order in which Afrikaners would be able to maintain their dominant position.

The South Africa of 1977 was far more politically polarized than the South Africa of 1960, however. The sidelining of a few hundred dissidents could not quell the truculent spirit of an entire generation of black youth radicalized by the confrontations of the uprising, nor could it easily convert them into docile followers of a collaborationist black elite after almost a decade of anti-system agitation by the black consciousness movement. A lull in black political activity was perhaps inevitable after the October crackdown; offices of the banned organizations were forcibly closed, and their equipment, supplies, and bank accounts impounded by the government.

Nevertheless, rebellion continued to smolder. Remnants of the SSRC issued a flier in late October, denouncing the bannings and defiantly warning Kruger to release detainees "or else!!!" (*Document 121*). Older township activists who had not been detained quietly discussed the possibilities for resistance that still remained open. Five days after the crackdown, a group of several dozen veterans from the banned organizations convened at the Chiawelo Lutheran Centre in Soweto and formed the Soweto Action Committee. Community Council elections were due to be held in three months, and police had detained all the members of the Soweto Committee of Ten—an informal group of popularly recognized community leaders which had formed after the collapse of the Urban Bantu Council in early June. In the absence of the Committee of Ten, the Chiawelo meeting resolved that a subcommittee of those present take up the campaign against collaborationist local government bodies. A second subcommittee was formed to take discreet soundings countrywide on the possible formation of a new national political body to replace the organizations banned on October 19.[15]

A deceptive quietude settled over township political life. Meanwhile, the locus of organizational resistance shifted temporarily to Modderbee prison in Benoni east of Johannesburg, where black leaders who had been rounded up in the crackdown were being held. The 50-odd detainees included most of the members of the Soweto Committee of Ten, and top office bearers of SASO, the BPC, the Soweto Teachers' Action Committee, and the Union of Black Journalists.[16] Since the immediate purpose of the crackdown was to prevent a resurgence of popular unrest before the November 30 general election—a six-week period which also coincided with the sitting of the controversial Biko inquest and the run-up to Bophuthatswana independence on December 6—the Modderbee detainees were held under the preventive detention clause (section 10) of the Internal Security Act, not under the harsher laws and conditions reserved for political prisoners who were to face trial or appear as state witnesses. Thus instead of being held in solitary confinement, the men detained at Modderbee—women were jailed elsewhere—were kept in four large communal cells and were permitted to intermingle.[17]

As days stretched into weeks then months filled with endless discussion, the Modderbee detainees became self-segregated into political camps centered around key strategic questions regarding the future. Should a new national political organization be launched, and if so, what should be its relationship to the established exiled liberation movements? In theorizing toward an effective ideology of revolution, should class join or even supersede race as a central mobilizing idea? And behind both these questions lay a more practical issue for each individual: whether or not to explicitly identify with, oppose, or remain neutral toward the African National Congress, the established movement which by late 1977 appeared to pose the most potentially credible armed challenge to the state. The detainees who had already joined the underground ANC, including former

SASO leaders like Diliza Mji, Mongezi Stofile, and Jackie Selebi, argued in favor of Marxist theory as the most time-tested expression of revolutionary truth. They christened their prison cell "Vietnam" and labeled the cells where less ideologically inclined BPC and Committee of Ten members predominated "America" and "Britain." While some in the BPC group favored forming a new national political body and welcomed the establishment of the Azanian People's Organisation (AZAPO) when news of it reached Modderbee in mid-1978, the "Vietnam" group was opposed to the new organization, seeing it as a potential rival to the ANC.

Leftward Moves

From its inception, the black consciousness movement had drawn partisans from both the ANC and PAC into its constituent organizations, and had maintained a neutral stance toward their long-standing rivalry. This created no problems as long as the exiled movements lacked any significant organizational presence inside South Africa. A prime objective of SASO, the BPC, and their various youth and student offshoots was to foster leadership skills and political commitment among as many potential activists as possible, leaving each individual to choose where and how to eventually apply the acquired skills and commitment. The spirit of black consciousness was aggressive, but its broad strategy was defensive: if political talent and motivation could be cultivated and continually reproduced widely enough among young blacks, no amount of repression by the state would be able to totally quell popular resistance. Blacks would then be able to move forward continually, seizing whatever organizational space was left open by the state in its own maneuverings. "In a population of about 30 million," the BPC declared in a training document in mid-1977, blacks had "a leadership potential of over half a million. And our population is indeed growing. By the time half a million Blacks are on the banning lists of the Ministry of Injustice, we have no doubt Blacks will be on the verge of freedom."[18]

Having cultivated a daring and dedicated generation of young leaders and a mass base ripe for action, however, the black consciousness movement found itself crossing the threshold of "phase 2" without any clear revolutionary plan of its own.[19] Chapters 5 and 6 describe how the movement's adherents by 1976 were increasingly gravitating toward the organizations which already had blueprints for "physical liberation," allying themselves with either the PAC or, more often, the better organized ANC. The Soweto uprising rapidly accelerated this process because as the practical limitations of unarmed mass insurrection became evident, the alternative of guerrilla warfare gained ground in the popular imagination. In practice, the black consciousness movement placed no barriers in the way of those who wished to align themselves with the underground guerrilla movements; this was consistent with the emphasis on individual initiative and choice. The choice between violent and nonviolent forms of resistance was regarded by most activists as a tactical, not a moral, matter. In the end, the only disjuncture between the black consciousness movement and the guerrilla organizations was an ideological one. Ideologically, a move to the PAC required little or no adjustment; but a shift to the ANC required a revised definition of the nature of the struggle and in particular of the enemy.

Speaking in July 1976 to SASO's eighth annual conference as the outgoing president, Diliza Mji, a student at the University of Natal medical school, had first expressed this shift in viewpoint by declaring that class interests rather than race should be the basic criterion in identifying the enemies of liberation (*Document 117*). The government, he pointed out, was busy in the cities and the homelands creating a black middle class to be its ally and agent in preserving the status quo. These blacks, through their cooperation with the apartheid order, were aligned with foreign investors who represented "imperialism, the highest form of capitalism," and it was capitalism which in the last analysis was the enemy against which all third world peoples and workers everywhere were pitted. If black consciousness was to survive as an articulation of mass aspirations, Mji concluded, it had to "start interpreting our situation from an economic class point of view."

Mji's speech reflected his own move into the ANC and toward the Marxist ideology embraced by many ANC intellectuals at the time. The appeal of Marxism to South African would-be revolutionaries was a powerful one in the mid-1970s: socialism was a doctrine of social leveling; the frontiers of the socialist world were expanding; Mozambique and Angola had defeated colonial governments by fighting under the banner of socialism and receiving assistance from the eastern bloc; the western powers were tacitly allied with Pretoria because of their common interest in opposing communist expansion and defending capitalism. Marxism provided a basis for sophisticated analyses and explanations of almost any political problem, and it offered a reassuring promise of the historical inevitability of victory. Moreover, for anyone who had moral or intellectual qualms about the racial exclusivity of the black consciousness approach—or who wanted to discredit its leaders politically—Marxism clearly pointed the way: race was an unscientific basis for explaining anything, and had to be superseded by an understanding of human history based on the central dynamic of class struggle.

Heated debates over Marxism had not been a feature of the black consciousness movement in the 1969–1975 period. Marxist literature was not easily accessible to black university students, nor had they been significantly touched by the radical analyses of South African history that a new generation of white neo-Marxist academics had begun to produce at British universities in the early 1970s.[20] During the immediate post-Soweto period, the spread of Marxist literature and ideas among black students helped to produce a fragmentation and blurring of viewpoints as individuals grouped and regrouped in their attempts to find a way forward. Among intellectuals, not everyone who was attracted to the ANC found Marxism completely persuasive, and not everyone who rejected capitalism or favored armed revolution felt drawn to the ANC. To many, capitalism seemed an evil system, but racism seemed worse and closer to the root of the problems faced by blacks. Posing a non-Marxist, social democratic vision of a future society, the leadership in Ginsberg produced a policy statement in early 1977 calling for a redistribution of wealth and an end to "unbridled capitalism" in a future "open society" guided by the Universal Declaration of Human Rights (*Document 118*). "Imperialist forces either of the old stock or the new" had to be resisted, the statement declared, so that South Africa in the future could take a non-aligned position in the East-West conflict. Blacks in the meantime, it said, had to oppose white strategies of building "a dangerous coalition between the white 'haves' and an upper crust of black 'haves,' against the interests and aspirations of a multitude of black 'have-nots' who form 95% of the black majority." There was no assumption in the statement of an ideology of class struggle as such, however; nor was there any attempt to reduce racism to a mere byproduct of economic interests. White racism and racists were still cast as the enemy, albeit not in the venomous tone so often present in earlier black consciousness writings.

A common thread running through the political analyses of both "scientific socialists" and black consciousness proponents was the fear that the common aspirations of blacks might be betrayed by their own elites. As the apartheid system came increasingly under siege internationally, the regime was stepping up its quest for legitimacy by wooing collaborators in the aspiring black middle class. By the time of Transkeian independence in October 1976, it was no secret that the National Party aimed to build up a class of African politicians, bureaucrats and businessmen with a stake in the existence of the homelands and state-sponsored urban councils. Like the business-oriented white United and Progressive Parties, which had long argued that South Africa would achieve political stability only if an African middle class was permitted to emerge and advance economically, the forward-looking strategists in the National Party by the mid-1970s had quietly accepted the logic of an incorporationist strategy—conditional upon the emerging African buffer class being firmly linked to the institutions of separate development. Without this mandatory link, nothing stood between a policy of gradual black advancement and the logic of eventual socioeconomic, and ultimately political, integration—an outcome utterly unacceptable to the National Party electorate. Hence would-be African leaders were to be allowed to achieve positions of political authority, but only within the institutions of separate development. Business licenses and long-term leases on township houses were available, but only to those with homeland citizenship certificates. Africans who were influential or wealthy enough to travel abroad could do so, but only on homeland passports. Coloured and Indian elites were also to receive National Party patronage while being similarly tethered to state-approved institutions and mechanisms. Inside ruling circles, *verligtes* ("enlightened" ones) differed with *verkramptes* ("narrow" ones) about the pace and mechanisms of reform, while party bosses formulated compromise positions which would hold together the fissiparous wings of Afrikanerdom. Spurred by the unexpected militancy of the Soweto revolt and the resulting threat of world sanctions, National Party reformers by late 1977 had moved their quest for new solutions into high gear.

It was natural for radical blacks to fear that government strategies of co-optation might succeed. At the same time, however, the restrictions of both grand and petty apartheid stood as a constant frustration and insult to all blacks, especially those able and enterprising enough to pursue careers in business or in middle-class professions. Even had there been no aggressive black consciousness movement in high schools and universities over the better part of a decade, few young blacks adults by 1977 would have been in any mood to readily accept the arbitrary limitations and hypocrisies of the apartheid system; it was common knowledge among too many people that the rest of Africa and the world had left behind such archaic forms of legalized discrimination. Many older black teachers, businessmen, journalists, clergymen, legal and medical professionals, social workers and office clerks nursed no less sense of grievance than their younger counterparts, even if experience had taught them to cover up their emotions more carefully. Indians and Coloureds often experienced as many career and workplace frustrations and insults as Africans. Whether middle-class blacks in large numbers would become active supporters of the prevailing social order was not really at issue; more pertinent was what degree of activism and commitment most would assume in opposing it, and what form their opposition would take.

Black traders ambitious to expand their business enterprises were the most directly hamstrung by petty government regulations that effectively prevented blacks from competing for the urban consumer market. Lacking any means to exert direct leverage over government policies, their only recourse was to complain as persistently and persuasively as possible, and hope that white business opinion and National Party *verligtes* would support their cause out of a sense of fairness. This approach brought paltry results most of the time. When Soweto erupted, however, black businessmen were among the first beneficiaries.[21] Several nettlesome restrictions on black traders were rapidly removed (including the requirement that homeland citizenship certificates be obtained before trading licenses could be granted), although many other limitations still remained, including the restricted access to credit which resulted from the prohibition on freehold land ownership by blacks in "white" cities. While black businessmen could hardly be expected to reject capitalism or to engage in overt forms of radical protest, their stake in the demise of National Party rule was substantial.

Outside the limiting terrain of the homelands, all black professionals faced barriers to their upward mobility imposed both by apartheid laws and regulations, and by the stubborn instinct of whites, including liberals, to cling to their positions of authority on the assumption that blacks were somehow not ready to be treated as professional equals. Power hierarchies in the church had become less racially rigid by the late 1970s, and salary differentials between some white and black medical professionals in the public service were slowly narrowing, but in every occupational field blacks struggled to get ahead in the face of myriad race-based obstacles.[22] As if to placate the National Party right wing, for example, African lawyers who had been occupying premises in downtown Pretoria and Durban were ordered in late 1977 to move their offices to adjacent townships. A protest from the Association of Law Societies succeeded in getting this order rescinded, but in its place a new regulation was imposed requiring African attorneys to apply in future for permits to establish offices in "white" areas.[23] Such frustrations, far from driving a wedge between the mass of ordinary blacks and an elite of relatively privileged professionals, stood as a constant reminder to the better educated that all blacks shared a common status as victims and subordinates in the apartheid order. Sentiments fostered by black consciousness helped to bolster an ethic of solidarity across emerging class lines, stigmatizing as sell-outs those blacks who pursued individual self-interest without also demonstrating commitment to group goals.

Among black professionals, journalists tended to feel most keenly the obligation to articulate group aspirations. When the UBJ was banned in the October 1977 crackdown, it re-emerged almost immediately as the Writers Association of South Africa (WASA).[24] Black reporters on white-owned newspapers were paid on lower scales than whites, were almost never promoted to positions of higher responsibility, and often had their stories toned down by white sub-editors before publication. Yet many black reporters and photographers had achieved prominence covering the student uprising when white reporters were afraid to enter the violent townships; their work had been a major factor in rising newspaper circulations, as well as in the growing politicization of thousands of blacks. Many black reporters had been assaulted by police and arrested in the line of duty, and some— including Joe Thloloe, Aggrey Klaaste, Percy Qoboza, Juby Mayet, Mike Mzileni, Thenjiwe Mtintso, and Enoch Duma—had suffered lengthy periods of detention. Thus when the UBJ reemerged as WASA, it was more militant than before. In the brief post-crackdown lull, its members acquired a reputation for black consciousness rhetoric and aggressive opposition to white control, both in the newsroom and more widely.

Caught up in the leftward movement of former SASO members and others gravitating toward socialism in the late 1970s, WASA began trying in its internal deliberations and publications to blend the language of race and class into a political discourse that could meld the traditions of the ANC, PAC, and black consciousness movement into a new amalgam. In a speech charged with the language of racial nationalism, the president of WASA, Zwelakhe Sisulu, told the organization's annual conference of September 1979 that the government was trying to divide blacks along class lines and drag some of them into its laager as a buffer against the rest; the response had to be a fighting spirit of black solidarity (*Document 125*). The growing social distance between middle-class and ordinary blacks was also targeted for criticism in an address to the congress by Winifred Kgware, a former president of the banned Black People's Convention. Taking a more explicitly ideological position, Durban journalist Quraish Patel told the conference that black workers needed to become class conscious as well as race conscious. "By virtue of the social arrangement of color" in South Africa, he said, "black consciousness is still necessary . . . as a foundation on which workers can come together and join hands as a class, recognizing themselves as black, exploited and powerful."[25] There was still no way that blacks and whites could work together in "non-racial" organizations, in the media industry or elsewhere, the conference resolved; whites had nothing to contribute to change (*Document 124*). Following Patel without explicitly condemning "capitalism" as the enemy, the delegates resolved that it was important to build class consciousness among black workers, starting from the "necessary base" of their race consciousness. In pursuit of this goal, the conference after heated debate decided to broaden WASA's own membership to encompass both writers and all other newspaper workers, thus forming the Media Workers Association of South Africa (MWASA), a full-fledged industrial union of the kind then emerging as a consequence of the Wiehahn reforms (see Chapter 7).

As time would prove, the government's decision to recognize African trade unions opened up promising possibilities for the mass mobilization of political resistance, but these potentialities still lay in the uncertain future in late 1979. Through its close and long-standing connections with former stalwarts of the South African Congress of Trade Unions, the ANC was relatively well positioned to take advantage of the new possibilities. Political and quasi-political groups coming out of the black consciousness movement were on less certain ground. Except for the limited efforts of the Black Allied Workers' Union, the black consciousness movement had established no organizational roots in the fledgling independent union movement. Nor had fleeting moments of success in mounting worker stay-aways during the Soweto uprising led to any lasting lines of communication between workers and students. Once the uprising had subsided, it was clear with hindsight that any serious insurrectionary attempt in the future would require worker participation that was far more organized. But how was this to be achieved?

This question was discussed at the initial launch of the Azanian People's Organisation (AZAPO), a year before the publication of the recommendations of the Wiehahn Commission. AZAPO was an offshoot of the Soweto Action Committee which had been formed at the Chiawelo meeting five days after the October 1977 crackdown. Organized by members of the banned groups who had escaped the arrests that landed so many activists in Modderbee, AZAPO aimed to demonstrate that blacks could not be intimidated, and that the government should not expect another period of quiescence like the one that had followed the post-Sharpeville crackdown of the early 1960s. It declared itself an overtly political organization from the start, and at its launching conference in Roodepoort in April 1978 it expressed the intention to forge a "student-worker alliance."[26] Striving to incorporate the new interest in class analysis without departing from the black consciousness framework, speakers at the launching conference asserted that white racism in South Africa relegated all blacks to the lowest social class; race was thus a "class determinant" and all blacks were workers regardless of their origins or occupations, while all whites belonged to the exploiting class.

The National Party government was in no mood to tolerate new agitational activities of the kind anticipated from AZAPO, and within a few weeks of the launch most of its national and branch office bearers had been detained. Charges were never brought, however, and within six months the leaders had been released and several had been issued banning orders. Regrouping, they returned to their original plans and at the end of September 1979, AZAPO was relaunched with a new executive committee headed by Curtis Nkondo, a former leader of the defunct Soweto Teachers' Action Committee. As the resolutions of the second launch indicate, AZAPO expected to carry on the black consciousness tradition of political proselytizing in black churches, and campaigning against collaborationist government bodies (*Document 126*). To these it now proposed to add a program of labor organization, beginning with research and training for its own members in a field that to most was unfamiliar terrain.

Monitoring the progress of AZAPO, first from reports filtering into Modderbee, and later from vantage points both inside and outside AZAPO itself, partisans of the ANC tended to regard this new political initiative with ambivalence. The ANC was facing open rivalry from a number of black consciousness leaders in exile who seemed bent on establishing themselves as a third recognized liberation movement.[27] It seemed possible that AZAPO was linked to this wider plan, since it was rumored to be receiving funds raised by the black consciousness movement outside. Open opposition to AZAPO by blacks inside the country would be regarded as divisive, however; moreover, the new organization might perform a useful function in drawing new activists into political work. Solidarity between black intellectuals and workers was also admirable, although if the common thread of solidarity was to be blacks-only nationalism, this had to be opposed in principle by the ANC and the Communist Party, a prospect almost certainly underestimated by AZAPO's founders. Their choice of Nkondo as president also reflected AZAPO's ambiguous ideological identity. Nkondo had never been strongly identified with the black consciousness viewpoint, and as a detainee in Modderbee after October 1977, he had opposed the establishment of any new overtly political body. Yet at 51, he was a popular older figure in Soweto, and it seemed possible that he might be able to bridge the ideological divisions emerging at leadership level. As events transpired, Nkondo's inclinations toward the ANC soon became apparent to his younger colleagues and this, coupled with an uncollegial leadership style, brought about his suspension as AZAPO head within a matter of months. With his demise went the last credible effort to patch together a unified front of black nationalist and multiracialist tendencies within the extraparliamentary opposition.[28]

The New Youth Politics

The winding down of the 1976–77 revolt resulted more from the decimation of student leadership through arrests and the flight of several thousand activists into exile than from any cooling of student anger. Many of the local student and youth organizations banned or disbanded in the October 1977 crackdown slowly revived, including the Soweto Students' Representative Council (SSRC), which renamed itself the Soweto Students' League. In the absence of most of the senior students who had taken the lead during the uprising, a less experienced generation of young people came forward who for the most part lacked any ties with the now-banned SASO and BPC. Interest in political analysis tended to be overshadowed by a thirst for meaningful action, but in the absence of analysis, action tended to be episodic and mainly centered on participation in symbolic occasions such as commemoration services, funerals, and meetings to pledge solidarity with the 11 SSRC leaders standing trial for terrorism and sedition in the Kempton Park Circuit Court near Johannesburg between September 1978 and May 1979.

Much student agitation, as before October 1977, continued to focus on the rejection of Bantu Education schools. The cruel dilemma of school boycotts persisted as young people searched for a way to drive home their demands. Boycott sentiment remained strong despite appeals by adults and by the Soweto Students' League for pupils to return to school while the campaign to scrap the inferior system continued. In late 1977 it was estimated that almost a quarter of a million pupils were boycotting schools nationwide; end-of-year examinations were again disrupted, and many teachers resigned in disgust during the year.[29] Vandalism during the uprising had in any case rendered many school buildings unusable, their windows and blackboards smashed, their walls and battered desks scarred by arson attacks.

Another ongoing focus of student protests was the rejection of black collaborators (dubbed "non-whites" by their detractors) who served in the police, acted as paid informers, or held office in government-established "dummy institutions." Here was an unambiguous target for youthful anger, and action against such people was often characterized by visceral hatred and a spirit of "desist . . . *or else!*" In a dramatic display of this aggressive mood in March 1978, several hundred student mourners who had been organized by the Soweto Action Committee to attend the funeral of PAC founder Robert Sobukwe, brought the proceedings to a raucous halt when Chief Gatsha Buthelezi appeared at the outdoor ceremony in Graaff-Reinet. Havoc reigned for half an hour until Buthelezi was persuaded to depart so that the funeral could continue. As the homeland leader made his way out through the crowd in humiliation, angry youths, spitting and shouting "stooge" and "sell-out," attempted to assault him, retreating only when a bodyguard fired a pistol at the attacking mob, wounding three people.[30]

While youth politics seemed in danger of drifting toward thuggery in

1978, the ANC in exile was still slowly adjusting to the unanticipated surge in its membership as young people continued to leave the country to join the armed struggle or seek opportunities for education outside the apartheid system. Before the eruption of township violence in June 1976, ANC strategists had assumed that insurrectionary activity would eventually occur first among workers.[31] They now recognized that students were both the most volatile and the most likely to offer themselves as military recruits, and their approach shifted accordingly. Working through underground members who had been close to the SSRC during the uprising (including Billy Masetlha, Super Moloi, and Roller Masinga in Johannesburg), Joe Gqabi, working from Botswana, began to funnel ANC funds into South Africa to start up a new student organization that would be secretly allied to the ANC.[32] After months of preparation, the Congress of South African Students (COSAS) was launched over the first weekend of June 1979 at the Wilgespruit Fellowship Centre in Roodepoort, pledging itself to fight against Bantu education while working to "normalize" relations between pupils, parents, and teachers. Calling itself an "anti-racial" organization willing to identify itself with any "progressive group" whose policy and principles were similar to its own (*Document 129*), COSAS signaled its intention to abandon the racial exclusiveness of black consciousness. By the time police began to target COSAS leaders for arrest in late 1979, the organization was already spreading rapidly, establishing local branches countrywide and moving the post-Soweto generation toward a new politics of community-based activism.

At the university level, the September 1979 relaunching of AZAPO helped to inspire the formation of a new organization, the Azanian Students' Organisation (AZASO), in which one of Curtis Nkondo's sons became the first organizing secretary. Although COSAS had originally appealed to students at all levels, it began to encourage tertiary level students to organize themselves in AZASO while it addressed itself to action-oriented high school aged recruits. By de-emphasizing ideology and appearing on common platforms with AZAPO and AZASO for the first year or so of its existence, COSAS leaders strove to mute their strong sympathies for the ANC while patiently working to popularize the multiracial ideals of the Freedom Charter among their members, most of whom were too young to have been steeped in the black consciousness ideology of the early 1970s. Meanwhile AZASO found its ranks increasingly divided between diehard adherents of black consciousness, some of whom had reduced a once positive philosophy of self-reliance to a dogmatic rejection of all whites, and "progressives" who acknowledged the positive side of black consciousness but argued that race should be seen primarily as a political factor which had been introduced in South Africa to facilitate economic and class exploitation.

Toward Grassroots Organization

During the strategic stock-taking of the late 1970s both inside and outside Modderbee, one recurring question was whether it might be possible to build grassroots groups that could somehow be "organizations without leaders." Pretoria's repertoire of repressive techniques was finite and had become predictably familiar during the decade of resistance that was now drawing to a close. Its central feature was the removal of high profile activists through banning orders, detention, and occasionally, accidentally or designedly, by death. Once banned, an organization could reconstitute itself under a new name, but organizations that depended on the leadership of a few key people could not so easily withstand the removal of these guiding individuals. An alternative was to leave national level organizing in abeyance while pursuing small-scale, decentralized organization that emphasized the bread and butter concerns of local communities. Ordinary citizens who feared high-risk political involvement were much less intimidated by participation in day to day community affairs. The security police would be hard pressed to find pretexts for removing all participants in public life at this level, and little by little, grassroots groups might be able to coalesce into larger bodies also characterized by a more anonymous style of leadership than in the past.[33]

Community-based organizations were not something new among black South Africans in the late 1970s.[34] Coloureds and Indians had a long tradition of voluntary associations, and many African townships had residents' committees, vigilance associations, *makgotla* (traditional courts), or ratepayers' associations, some of very long standing, that often were the creation of the community's small minority of petty traders, teachers or other professionals. Some of these local associations were inactive much of the time and came to life only in periods of high popular concern over crime, rising living costs, or calamities such as train or bus accidents. Some township organizations had a tradition of participation in advisory boards, councils, or management committees—the state-sponsored institutions of local government in nonwhite urban areas—while others opposed these bodies and tried to discredit them. An organization of the latter kind is illustrated in *Document 116,* the constitution of the Pimville/Klipspruit Residents' Committee, established in one section of Soweto in late 1975 in opposition to the ineffectual Urban Bantu Council. Many ordinary citizens who were nervous about engaging in "politics" readily involved themselves in the day to day civic activities of such organizations, concentrating on the demands of township dwellers for electrification, day care centers, improved health facilities and the like.

With an eye to these associational traditions, a commission organized at SASO's annual national conference in July 1973 to discuss urban strategies had suggested encouraging the formation of "residents' action committees which would work against the daily oppressive activities of the system . . . [and] make residents aware of the injustices of the system. To combat the fragmentation process," the commission had suggested "liaison between the action committees of the various black residential areas."[35] The July 1972 national conference of the Black People's Convention had endorsed a similar proposal. Opinion in the BPC and SASO was split, however, on the wisdom and viability of this approach. Some people had no patience with the incrementalism implied in such a process, especially in comparison with the quick results anticipated from military action. They argued that if blacks achieved the amelioration of township conditions through piecemeal local activity, the revolutionary ardor of the people as whole would be diluted. Others reasoned, conversely, that because the apartheid order inculcated attitudes of fatalism and dependency among blacks, substance therefore had to be given, through action, to the black consciousness principle of self-reliance: if blacks were to be the agents of their own liberation, every individual had to adopt an attitude of personal resistance to the daily injustices of the system, and personal responsibility for making change occur. In this view, victories scored on small issues would enhance popular confidence when the time came to attack larger targets, an axiom of collective action that in due course would be widely borne out in the growing independent trade union movement.[36]

The rising cost of living coupled with the deteriorating conditions of both urban and rural life under the apartheid system meant that popular grievances were unabated and needed no embellishment by resistance activists. The majority of urban African families struggled to survive on incomes near or below the poverty line, while migrant workers in township "bachelor" hostels lacked even the compensations of family life. In the underdeveloped homelands, where unemployment was rife, families left behind by migrant workers suffered severe deprivation. On white farms, African families living as labor tenants were being evicted, forced to sell their livestock and to resettle in the homelands, their menfolk then returning to the farms as migrant contract workers. Meanwhile the National Party's master plan for a South Africa without African citizens was being further implemented as the populations of dozens of remaining rural "black spots" and periurban squatter areas outside the homelands were forcibly removed and "relocated" within homeland borders—often on barren, remote, and unserviced sites.[37] These forced population removals, Orwellian in their conception and staggering in their scale, took place for the most part outside public view, and on terms and timetables wholly dictated by whites. Although homeland authorities sometimes went through the motions of objecting to the harsh conditions under which uprooted people were "dumped" in areas under their jurisdiction, they had neither the power to halt the process nor the resources to ameliorate its cruelties. Between 1960 and 1979, rural removals alone affected over a million Africans.[38] Hundreds of thousands more were forcibly moved to homelands from periurban squatter settlements and other areas deemed by whites to be "badly situated."

As the 1970s drew to a close, despite occasional dire predictions by white liberals that rural anger was explosive, it was the rural areas that offered the least potential for organized political resistance. Farm workers lived under the total control of their employers. Relocated communities in homeland "dumping grounds" struggled to adapt and survive in the stark conditions of their new surroundings. The ruthless manner in which many removals were effected left those removed with little means of resisting or of reversing the outcome. Remaining "black spot" communities (Africans with freehold title to farms located in white areas) faced removal under laws that gave white authorities an overwhelming advantage. Poverty, illiteracy, and geographical isolation meant that each threatened family and community stood alone against the power of white landowners and of the state. Cut off from information, publicity, and possible sources of support or legal advice, most of those faced with removal were helpless to resist.

Occasionally there was an exception to this bleak outcome. *Document 127* describes the destruction of the homes of the Makgato, a tribe of about 4,500 people living in a "black spot" 50 kilometers from Pietersburg in the northern Transvaal, who had been ordered to move to the homeland of Lebowa. About a quarter of the tribe agreed to move, but the rest resisted by fleeing with their movable possessions and seeking sanctuary with a larger neighboring tribe, the Batlokwa, who were also under threat of removal. The Batlokwa, who had long anticipated the removal attempt, put up spirited resistance, and were aided in their refusal to move by the government's fear of further adverse publicity of the type which had made the 1977 bulldozing of Modderdam and other squatter areas in the Western Cape an international symbol of apartheid's inhumanity. Removal of the Batlokwa (a community of over 70,000) was postponed, the Makgato rebuilt their demolished homes and schools, and in 1982 the government canceled the removal orders of both groups, making this one of the few successful cases of rural resistance to resettlement.[39]

Rarely could rural Africans look to black urban-based organizations to lend them material support in their travail. Even in the 1950s and earlier, when a large majority of Africans still lived on the land, organized African politics had almost always been town-centered, linking with rural protests only sporadically.[40] In the 1970s, black consciousness organizations militantly opposed the homelands policy in general, but focussed almost entirely on its political illegitimacy rather than on the heartless social engineering that was its central feature. The same conditions that prevented rural people from organizing themselves also hindered interventions from the outside. Although urban activists were in touch with rural areas through myriad personal and family connections, they were discouraged by the difficulties of organizing widely scattered and often illiterate and conservatively oriented communities. Of all the major political organizations of the 1970s, only Inkatha seriously sought to involve itself in rural areas, using its official status as a homeland party to build patronage networks of appointed chiefs and headmen throughout rural Zululand.

Somewhat more fertile ground for grassroots organization were the mushrooming periurban shanty settlements that adjoined South Africa's larger towns and cities by the late 1970s. These were largely the product of natural increase in urban populations over a period when government construction of housing for Africans, as a matter of policy, had come to a virtual halt. Government anti-urbanization policies notwithstanding, these squalid shanty towns were also home to thousands of "illegal" women and children whose breadwinners had found urban employment. Squeezed off white farms, removed from "black spots," and fleeing from the poverty and starvation of the homelands, women sought to provide for their children by moving to towns, either on their own or to join their migrant husbands. In times and places where the demand for African labor was steady or rising, many people were able to slip through the nets of the urban influx control system. In times of economic contraction, however, pass raids and the demolition of shanties became constant threats to these squatter communities, even to those individuals with section 10 rights of urban residence.[41]

The growth of urban squatter areas was occurring countrywide by the mid-1970s, but the phenomenon was most conspicuous in the Cape peninsula where employment opportunities had expanded rapidly in the years 1968–74.[42] By the end of that period, more than a dozen African and Coloured shanty settlements had sprung up around Cape Town, each with its own rudimentary residents' committees. As unemployment rose in the aftermath of the city's brief boom, the Cape Peninsula Bantu Affairs Administration Board (BAAB) stepped up efforts to expel "surplus" Africans, ordering employers to observe the Western Cape's policy of preferential hiring for Coloureds. But when city inspectors and police demolished African shanties in one place, their owners rebuilt them elsewhere, resisting all measures aimed at forcing men with employment to live in migrant hostels while deporting women and children to the homelands. *Document 122* describes how families pushed out of other areas of Cape Town built the Crossroads squatter settlement at the junction of Landsdowne and Klipfontein Roads east of Table Mountain starting in February 1975, initially with the informal permission of city officials. Caught in a legal and bureaucratic web of conflicting regulations and jurisdictions, the Crossroads families faced constant harassment, but managed to organize themselves as a community to police the settlement, construct two schools, and engage lawyers to defend residents from the constant threats of evictions and demolitions. A spirit of community solidarity, pride and self-help flourished. When authorities of the BAAB razed neighboring African shantytowns at Modderdam, Unibel and Werkgenot in 1977 and early 1978, Crossroads survived on a legal technicality and absorbed thousands of refugees from the demolished areas.

By mid-1978 the population of Crossroads was over 20,000 and still rising. Proximity to a major city and to two university centers of anti-apartheid activism (the Universities of Cape Town and the Western Cape) meant that the plight of the peninsula shanty dwellers attracted considerable attention from the media and from white and Coloured activists who became involved in relief efforts during the 1977 demolitions. The press highlighted the visit by a delegation of 200 Crossroads women to the BAAB offices in June to complain about pass raids. Liberals launched a "Save Crossroads Campaign" which drew worldwide attention through an international day of solidarity on July 30. *Document 123* is a sermon preached that day at a mass meeting in Crossroads by Reverend Sam Buti, a leading figure in the black Dutch Reformed Church. Over time, publicity reinforced the already defiant mood of the residents.

During a massive pass raid on September 14, 1978, there was a melee at Crossroads in which stones were thrown at police by angry residents. Dozens of people were injured and one resident was shot dead. At this stage, the risk of "another Soweto" and its potential costs to the South African economy became palpable enough to white business that the influential Urban Foundation (a post-Soweto reform initiative by major corporations) began actively to lobby for an anti-demolition policy.[43] The National Party leadership, weakened and divided by the Information Department corruption scandal which led to the resignation of Prime Minister John Vorster on September 20, was not persuaded, but was in a cautious enough mood to retreat temporarily while its own post-Soweto strategic rethink on urban policy was completed through the mechanism of the Riekert Commission. In May 1979, the Commission published its report proposing that greater security and mobility be allowed to Africans with section 10 rights, but that others be even more firmly excluded from any prospect of permanent urban residence. Just before the Commission published its findings, Piet Koornhof, the new Minister of Plural Relations (previously Bantu Administration), after several rounds of discussions with Crossroads representatives, announced that vacant areas east of Cape Town would be developed as new townships for Africans with urban residential rights, and that qualified individuals and their families living in Crossroads would be eligible for houses in the new areas once these were built. Although this was not the solution preferred by most residents, who wanted to be granted permission to remain at Crossroads and be assisted to upgrade the settlement with water, sanitation and other facilities, this reprieve was widely hailed as a victory for the squatters.

Such cases of successful resistance by individual black communities in the 1970s were few. Around Newcastle in Natal, where thousands of African families had been removed from "white" areas to the resettlement camps of Madadeni and Osizweni inside KwaZulu, a successful bus boycott was staged in late 1975 to protest against the rising cost of transport for people who found themselves living at greatly increased distances from their places of work. Similar bus boycotts erupted periodically during the decade. Township rent increases likewise provoked protests. Even where resistance was unsuccessful, or resulted only in postponing the measures being imposed, whether these were evictions or higher fares, rents or service charges, there were nevertheless important byproducts of the failed protests as well as of the successful ones: committees were formed, local leadership emerged, and communities gained experience with organization and mobilization around issues that were of vital daily concern to their members. Undergirding this growing organizational experience ran a continuing sense of moral outrage at the indignities of the apartheid system, now increasingly expressed in a language of rights. "You dare not accept a man's sweat and labor and at the same time reject him as a person," Buti told his Crossroads audience. "You dare not view him purely as a labor unit and dismiss or ignore him as a human being. If you accept him as a human being, then you must accept his normal basic needs, and make provision for such needs as: family life, housing, transportation, medical care, recreation and education."

By the end of the 1970s, the coalescing of community groups was taking place in some of the country's larger cities, where evictions, the scarcity of housing, and the rising cost of living were constant goads to action. In Johannesburg, Indians were unsuccessful in resisting eviction from the inner city neighborhood of Pageview in 1977, but at the same time other parts of the central city were gradually "greying" as working-class whites moved to the suburbs and cash-strapped landlords replaced them with Coloured and Indian tenants in defiance of the Group Areas Act. When police stepped up measures to expel these tenants, the tenants formed Actstop, an action committee to fight evictions. By late 1979, Actstop had recruited 48 Johannesburg lawyers willing voluntarily to defend "grey area" tenants charged under the Group Areas Act.[44] In Durban at about the same time, 20 existing community groups, brought together by the Natal Indian Congress, formed the Durban Housing Action Committee to agitate against rising rents and service charges, and to resist Group Areas evictions.[45] In Coloured areas of Cape Town, a similar process was underway, breathing new life into older community organizations, and fostering the growth of new ones.[46]

Unlike rural blacks who were handicapped by isolation, poverty, and illiteracy, urban dwellers could find a measure of safety and solidarity in numbers, and could draw on a larger pool of skills and financial resources in making collective responses to racial domination. Relatively weak communities, such as squatters facing removals, could usually do little to thwart the will of state authorities; their ranks could easily be split through inducements that persuaded some community members to accept government directives even if most complied only under duress. Established township residents, however, had greater potential leverage. When confronted with the imposition of stooge community councils and the burden of rising rents and levies, township residents could threaten not to recognize the unpopular authorities or to comply with their directives. If sufficiently organized, they could potentially make good on these threats by refusing to pay rents and levies. While not without a price in police harassment, arrests, court cases and fines, such resistance also imposed rising costs on the apartheid system—in lost revenue, adverse publicity, and the bureaucratic hassle involved in dealing with large-scale noncompliance.

Port Elizabeth at the end of the decade offered a foretaste of how much the political balance of forces might shift if the grievances of township residents and those of industrial workers on the shopfloor were to become linked and mutually reinforcing. In June 1979, an African trainee draughtsman at the Ford Motor Company, Thozamile Botha, was elected head of the residents' association of Zwide township. Four months later he was instrumental in bringing a number of other township associations together with Zwide's to form an umbrella body, the Port Elizabeth Black

Civic Organisation (PEBCO). With Botha at its head, PEBCO adopted a hostile stand toward Port Elizabeth's black community council and toward the high rents and new service fees levied by the council in an effort to implement government instructions that all African townships must become financially self-sufficient (*Document 128*). Opposition to the rents and fees was a popular cause among the city's black workers, and when Botha was fired at Ford for absenteeism, this touched off a two month wave of strikes and rallies in Port Elizabeth in which the demand for Botha's reinstatement, factory floor grievances (*Document 84*), protests against township conditions, and declarations of solidarity with exiled and imprisoned leaders of the ANC all became entwined.[47] The strikes were successful as an exhibition of growing worker strength, despite the nonparticipation of the National Automobile and Allied Workers' Union. As a demonstration of the ability of township-based civic organizations to frustrate the implementation of government policies, PEBCO's record in its first year was less clear. After a meteoric rise under Botha's powerful leadership, and a few moves that put white authorities on the defensive (the deputy minister of Cooperation and Development canceled a scheduled appearance in Port Elizabeth when PEBCO threatened to protest the visit with a city-wide stay-away), PEBCO's influence rapidly declined after Botha was detained and then banned in early 1980. Once again, a black organization had become overly dependent on high profile leadership that was vulnerable to government repression. Moreover, by openly articulating its goals as political, PEBCO had lost support among many cautious township residents who feared the personal risks of overt political involvement. Worker militancy on the shopfloor continued to rise, but several years went by before township-based organizing revived in Port Elizabeth.

In Johannesburg in the period immediately after the 1976 uprising and Biko's death, the state relied heavily on coercion to discourage blacks from resisting the implementation of state policies. Black consciousness organizations were banned, AZAPO was crushed by detentions when it first appeared, and all members of the Soweto Committee of Ten were detained in the October 19, 1977 crackdown. In the brief time between its formation in June 1977 and the incarceration of its members in October, the Committee of Ten had emerged as an authentic voice of the vast Soweto urban complex, articulating popular demands for improved services, property rights, and genuinely democratic local government for Soweto within the larger Johannesburg municipality. The Committee also reflected public opinion in rejecting the government's plan to replace the failed Urban Bantu Councils with similarly designed Community Councils. In place of this system, the Committee proposed an alternative plan for an elected Soweto local authority which would be independent of the West Rand Administration Board and free to raise revenues and rewrite regulations just like any other city government. Although *verligte* elements argued that the National Party should consider the Committee's proposals, hard-liners prevailed, and the entire Committee was jailed in the October 1977 crackdown.

As originally conceived at the time of the collapse of the Soweto UBC, the aim of the Committee of Ten was to provide progressive leadership for Soweto, drawing together the still-functioning remains of the Black Parents Association, the Soweto Students' Representative Council, the Black People's Convention, SASO and other black consciousness organizations in Johannesburg. The original Committee was elected by a group of 61 Soweto community leaders in late June 1977, and was chaired by Nthato Motlana, an incisive, tough-talking Soweto medical doctor with a background of ANC involvement in the 1950s. Despite being unrepresentative of Soweto's population in either a procedural or socioeconomic sense (being made up largely of middle-class professionals), the Committee enjoyed strong grassroots legitimacy because of the good reputations of its members, solid support from black journalists, and because of the endorsement of the SSRC, which could claim with some justification to be the voice of Soweto's 27,000 secondary school students, and even, by some accounts, "the de facto power in Soweto."[48] This intergenerational alliance was to be a distinctive feature of the post-Soweto period. While the 1976 uprising had clearly given many older Africans a new respect for the courage and dedication of youth, the crushing of the revolt had also brought home to younger people the necessity of forging cooperative relationships with older leaders who were capable of drawing vital adult constituencies—workers, parents, consumers—into united action. In this sense, the emergence of the Committee of Ten represented a return of authority, by mutual consent, to Soweto's parental generation.

Yet no mandate to speak for Soweto's residents, however clear, could automatically translate into grassroots strength capable of sustaining organizational activity in the absence of prominent leaders. The prolonged detention of the Committee of Ten in 1977–78 enhanced its prestige but brought its activities to a halt. Before the October 1977 crackdown, the Committee had spoken of transforming itself into a civic association with branches and a dues-paying mass membership, but little progress had been made toward this ambitious end. As long as it remained an elite group, the Committee could issue statements to the press, call public meetings when the government would allow this (which was rarely), and play a private advocacy role in meetings with sympathetic and influential whites; but its ability to actually thwart government policies by mobilizing mass noncompliance remained in doubt.

By the time the Committee's members had all been released from detention in late 1978, plans for establishing a mass base had been on hold for more than a year. In the intervening time, white liberals, big business and forward-looking elements in the National Party had become seized with a vision of reform in which steam would be released from South Africa's political pressure-cooker by measures to incorporate middle-class and permanently urbanized blacks into a new "insider" political status. Details still had to be debated and hammered out by the Riekert Commission, the Broederbond, and other centers of National Party strategic planning, but in the meantime Motlana and several other freshly released members of the Committee of Ten found themselves the object of what radical critics characterized as "a dizzy whirlwind courtship" as the Progressive Federal Party, the Urban Foundation, government ministers and leaders of the Broederbond all vied to solicit their opinions and test their susceptibility to co-optation.[49] Not until Motlana had rejected an invitation to serve on a government advisory committee on the future of urban Africans in May 1979 did it become clear that the Committee would adhere to its original intention of converting itself into a mass-based body pledged to oppose any compromise or collaboration with apartheid. At a two day conference in late September 1979, the Committee of Ten launched the Soweto Civic Association (SCA), constituting itself as an interim executive committee until branches could be formed and a full fledged executive elected. The Association's basic purposes, Motlana told the press, related only to civic upliftment in Soweto; neither he nor the new body aspired to any national political role.[50]

These disclaimers notwithstanding, the SCA immediately found itself under political fire from rival aspirants to leadership in Johannesburg, the country's largest city and political nerve-center. These rivals included David Thebehali, the chairman of the Soweto Community Council, who immediately launched a press campaign to denounce the SCA. More important was Gatsha Buthelezi, for whom Motlana's entrance onto the stage of mass politics posed a serious obstacle to his own ongoing bid for leadership preeminence in the Transvaal. Indeed, to Buthelezi's critics, this challenge was seen as one of the SCA's most notable achievements. In another sense, however, the SCA in its early years could make little more claim than Inkatha to be a genuinely democratic organization. Both were centrally directed by their chief executives, and accountability to ordinary members was only nominal. For the SCA, the building of branches, and ultimately zone, block, and street committees with the potential to be in daily communication with every citizen of Soweto, was a long and painstaking process that did not yield significant results until the mid-1980s when the majority of Sowetans decided to support a rent boycott that was already sweeping other townships across the country. By that time the post-Soweto youth generation had thrown the full force of its energies into community-level politics. Regardless of how popular the cause of resistance to government policies might be, effective and resilient political organizations could not spring up spontaneously, or from the mere exhortations of charismatic leaders. They had to be built and maintained by the work of many hands. At the end of the 1970s, this reality had come to be widely appreciated, but the real work and the patient building had yet to be seriously begun.[51]

The 1970s: A Decade of Transformation

Foreign visitors to South Africa in the late 1970s often commented that signs of change were everywhere: apartheid was being relaxed to such an extent that blacks could be seen strolling in parks, sitting on benches, and attending theaters previously reserved exclusively for whites. Interracial sports matches took place, and black traffic policemen directed white motorists at busy intersections. Much speculation revolved around the indeterminate social status of diplomatic representatives from Malawi, the only independent African country with an embassy in Pretoria. Did the opening of white private schools to the children of Malawian diplomats mean that separate racial school systems were on the way out? A few white Catholic schools began admitting small numbers of black students to test the waters after the Soweto uprising, and after some vacillation, Pretoria quietly acquiesced, reasoning, some speculated, that if a black urban elite was to become reconciled to separate development (now renamed "plural democracy"), an escape route from Bantu education would have to be opened up. Guided less by tactical choice than by economic necessity, the government by the 1970s was increasingly also turning a blind eye to the erosion of job reservation. As the demand for skilled workers steadily outstripped the supply of trained whites, black workers moved up, comprising an ever greater proportion of the industrial workforce and increasing their potential bargaining power correspondingly.

Perhaps most important in transforming South Africa in the 1970s, however, were changes not visible to the eye. These were the dramatic shifts in perception that altered the subjective reality of South Africans on both sides of the color line. Among whites, the Soweto uprising brought an erosion of the confidence that had underpinned nearly three decades of National Party rule, prompting an anxious search for reforms which could restore legitimacy to the familiar social order. Security concerns intensified as Mozambique, Angola, and Rhodesia threw off colonial rule, depriving South Africa of its buffer against guerrilla incursions. For Africans, the black consciousness movement had come, as one clergyman put it, like "a gushing wind."[52] It had transformed African nationalism from a widely held but bottled up ideology, publicly championed only by a persecuted vanguard, into the engine of a nationwide mass movement, driven by the aspirations of the youth generation and increasingly articulating explicit demands for radical change. "I am one of the youth of Soweto," a young activist told a Johannesburg court in November 1975. "What is called black consciousness is very much prevalent in Soweto. People talk about freedom, people talk about advancement, people talk about the desire to be allowed to enter into trade unions as members. And you will hear [it] in the trains, you will hear it in the buses, you will hear it everywhere. Even ministers have taken up their stand in preaching, in discussing, wishing that somehow everybody must be aware of the fact that we desire to be free."[53]

This transformation of black political culture was not so much a gradual adaptation to new circumstances as it was a dramatic rupture with longstanding habits of mass accommodation to inferior status. Catalyzed and spread through the writings and agitational activities of the South African Students' Organisation, the new culture of self-confidence, positive identity, and bold defiance shook the older generation of urban Africans out of its paralysis of fear, and awakened a thirst for political knowledge among the young. Attitudes of dependency and defeatism gave way to an aggressive new assertiveness and a repudiation of white allies as the trustees and interpreters of black interests. Blacks who had been selected as leaders through "the system" found themselves spurned and vilified, their followings confined to rural traditionalists or to such networks of political clientage as Pretoria's patronage enabled them to maintain. Into the organizational vacuum created by the repression of the 1960s had moved a new generation of black activists, much larger in number, more self-reliant, and better prepared with organizational and leadership skills than nationalists of any preceding era. This new generation had been tested in confrontations with the state, had learned the high cost of political commitment, and was steeled to press forward with its assault, "battle-ramming the status quo in all spheres," as an anonymous author in the *SASO Newsletter* expressed it with typical zest.[54]

Much of this assault could not be easily parried by the state because it came in unexpected and indirect forms, less as a battering ram than as a sneak attack. False or racist assumptions, laxity and miscalculation by the state all contributed to the creation of political space in which the new nationalism could take root and grow. Because apartheid ideology encouraged Africans to embrace ethnic identities, government security experts misread black consciousness when it first appeared, mistaking it for an end in itself rather than a mobilizing device. Racism caused most whites to underestimate the ability of an all-black movement to sabotage government designs. For example, the government planned for the rapidly expanding black universities to become feeder-institutions producing compliant ethnic-minded bureaucrats for the future independent homelands; instead, SASO converted the "bush colleges" into hothouses of anti-system protest. Most unexpectedly of all, the black consciousness movement was able to seize the opportunity afforded by the system's exclusion of Coloureds and Indians to fabricate a totally new composite social identity—"blackness"—defining all the country's dispossessed groups as a single oppositional front. By the time Pretoria had awakened to the need to cultivate Coloured and Indian support through co-optive reforms, the black consciousness movement had already established important political bridgeheads among Coloureds in the Western Cape and Indians both in Natal and the Transvaal.

A further assumption made by National Party planners was that Africans with secure urban employment could be seduced into support for the racially structured status quo and effectively separated from the mass of rural and migrant Africans based permanently in the homelands. The inducements of material advancement, the urban culture of individualism and conspicuous consumption, and the social snobbery that often followed from the acquisition of a university degree, all pointed to the plausibility of the assumption that Africans could be divided along class lines. All Africans with section 10 status were to be regarded as part of the insider class, which taken altogether would comprise perhaps 20 percent of the country's total African population.[55] Opposition to this plan from the excluded outsiders, it was assumed, would be weak and easily contained; opposition from dissident insider elements could be forcibly suppressed until such time as the benefits of insider status came to be generally accepted. The possibility that insider opposition would become uncontainable was not something the National Party could easily contemplate since it implied the ultimate prospect of white capitulation.

The 1980s would in fact see the collapse of the Nationalists' incorporationist strategy, but the foundations of its failure were already inherent in the transformations of the 1970s. The growing independent African trade unions saw no reason to differentiate between their migrant members living in hostels and their other members. The differentiation made no sense to employers either, and as a result, the government failed in its attempt to exclude migrants from registered unions in the aftermath of the 1979 Wiehahn Commission. On the broader political front, the effort to create a self-absorbed class of privileged urbanites ran head-on into the pervasive intellectual influence of the black consciousness movement, bolstered in the latter part of the decade by a surge of interest in socialism. Political activists from both the nationalist and socialist tendencies in the movement persistently preached solidarity across class lines and the rejection of elitist and "capitalist" attitudes and behavior. While no amount of mere agitation could completely discredit the private pursuit of wealth and status, this constant criticism did foster a defensive reflex among more well-to-do blacks, many of whom as a result felt compelled to demonstrate a more active commitment to resistance lest they be labeled tools of National Party policy.

It can be argued that these pressures for solidarity among blacks and against elitism were instrumental over the long term in fostering a democratic political culture among Africans. The rapid growth of grassroots politics and the recurring call for accountability by leaders were to be phenomena of the 1980s, but other features of an emerging democratic ethos were already discernible in the politics of the 1970s. Relative to earlier periods, the 1970s saw a rapid expansion of literacy and higher education among Africans, enabling many more people to participate in serious analysis and debate of political issues rather than uncritically following a course of action laid down by individual leaders or organizations. When SASO moved onto the empty stage of African politics at the start of the decade, it did so as an organization of university students who saw each other as peers and equals, unconstrained by any political orthodoxies or traditions other than the rules of procedure for meetings borrowed from NUSAS and the University Christian Movement. Leadership was collegial, and a high rate of turnover was assumed and welcomed, given that an important aim of SASO was to rapidly impart skills and experience so that students would be ready to make their contributions to organizational life wherever they later found themselves. Explicit attention was not always paid to democratic procedures, and the approach of Biko and his immediate lieutenants was sometimes manipulative. Nevertheless, apart from entrenched male dominance, there was a generally nonhierarchical, antiauthoritarian style inherent in university student politics that subsequently carried over into the high school, youth, and trade union movements as these evolved. In the articulation of political goals, "democracy" was strongly overshadowed by the demand for "freedom." "Freedom" was defined most often in terms of policies which would end discrimination and exploitation, and would enable blacks to participate in shaping and managing their own destinies. How these values or objectives ought to be translated into specific new institutions or systems of government was a matter left entirely to the future.

What role, if any, was left for white opponents of apartheid to play in black politics at the end of the 1970s? Blacks held a variety of conflicting views on this question, making the issue a divisive one that would continue to vex the resistance movement into the 1980s. AZAPO from its inception promoted an interpretation of black consciousness that excluded all white involvement. This position was popular with some in the youth and student generations, as well as among those black professionals who saw it as the correct antidote to the ongoing dominance of whites in every sphere. Others who had learned their politics in the early 1970s took a view closer to the pragmatic position of SASO and most of its affiliates in the heyday of the black consciousness movement: whites should not become leaders in black organizations, but their support in the form of money, logistical resources, and advice, was welcome as long as it came with no strings attached. According to this view, which had many adherents in the black consciousness wing of the growing independent trade union movement, blacks had demonstrated in the 1970s that it was possible to appropriate white resources without being forced to modify black agendas, to use whites without being used by them. This was a view which many student activists of the 1970s would take with them into the United Democratic Front in the 1980s, and into the exile or underground ANC, easing their transition into "nonracial" politics.

In addition to these two points of view, there was a third outlook that regarded any form of black exclusiveness as immoral or a sign of weakness. To this way of thinking, blacks who no longer had any complexes to overcome, or had never had any in the first place, had an obligation to relate to other people as individuals and not as members of particular groups, in politics as in all other aspects of life. For many blacks, as for South Africa's beleaguered minority of enlightened whites, this was the personal meaning of "liberation," and to believe it and live by it constituted the ultimate defiance of the apartheid system. By the end of the 1970s, this viewpoint appeared to be gaining ground, attracting "graduates" of the school of black consciousness, as well as whites for whom the experience of exclusion in the heyday of black consciousness had been a salutary lesson. If black consciousness was now largely dead and buried, this was all well and good, in the view of many. For others who marked its passing, it was a movement which had died of success, leaving a strong foundation on which to build for the struggles that lay ahead.

Notes

1. *House of Assembly Debates,* 2, 1978, cols. 578–579, quoted in John Kane-Berman, *Soweto: Black Revolt, White Reaction* (Johannesburg: Ravan Press, 1978), p. 239.

2. A government inquest found that no one could be held responsible for Mohapi's death, which the police attributed to suicide. Mohapi's family, in a successful suit, maintained that the alleged suicide note was a forgery. When Thenjiwe Mtintso, another member of Biko's inner circle, was interrogated by security police later in 1976, a wet towel was twisted tightly around her neck as a policeman said to her, "now you know how Mohapi died." *Star,* January 19, 1980.

3. Biko was detained two days after Mohapi's funeral, and held until December 1, 1976, when he was released to hold a meeting with visiting American Senator Dick Clark. In consultation with other detainees, Biko drafted and gave Clark a memorandum, highly critical of American policy toward South Africa, which is reproduced in S. Biko, *I Write What I Like* (London: Bowerdean Press, 1978; Oxford: Heinemann, 1979; San Francisco: Harper and Row, 1986).

4. Conversation with Jackie Selebi (March 1989). The camaraderie and sophistication of Biko's circle in Ginsberg drew the attention of many commentators. See Donald Woods, *Biko* (New York and London: Paddington Press Ltd., 1978); the memoir by Fr. Aelred Stubbs in the Bowerdean Press and Harper and Row editions of *I Write What I Like*; Cedric Mayson, *A Certain Sound: the Struggle for Liberation in South Africa* (Maryknoll, NY: Orbis Books, 1985); and Richard Attenborough's 1986 film *Cry Freedom*.

5. Conversations with Malusi Mpumlwana (August 1989) and Dikgang Moseneke (July 1980).

6. The IUEF was a scholarship fund financed mainly by the Scandinavian governments. Its involvement in the proposed summit meeting, at one stage planned for July 1977 in London, was alluded to by its director in an interview with the *Guardian* (UK), June 25, 1980.

7. *New York Times,* September 15, 1977.

8. Also see "Oh God, How Long Can We Go On?," Desmond Tutu's funeral eulogy, reproduced in his book *Hope and Suffering: Sermons and Speeches* (Grand Rapids: Eerdmans, 1984). *Isaziso* was a Transkeian paper edited by M. V. Mrwetyana.

9. "Counsel's Submissions on Behalf of the Biko Family," December 1, 1977, 77 pp. This document and the testimony of witnesses during the 14 day inquest are summarized in Hilda Bernstein, *No. 46—Steve Biko* (London: International Defence and Aid Fund, 1978), and in Woods, chapter 5. For a dramatization of the inquest see Jon Blair and Norman Fenton, *The Biko Inquest* (London: Rex Collings, 1978), from which a film was also made.

10. *Washington Post,* December 3, 1977. In 1979, without admitting culpability, the state in an out of court settlement agreed to pay $80,000 in damages to the Biko family.

11. Christian Institute, *South Africa—A Police State?,* pamphlet issued September 20, 1976, and *Star,* September 13, 1977.

12. Controversy over "the Biko doctors," which dramatically divided the South African medical profession, is recounted in Mary Rayner, *Turning a Blind Eye? Medical Accountability and the Prevention of Torture in South Africa* (Washington: American Association for the Advancement of Science, 1987), chapter 2. Also see Lawrence Baxter, "Doctors on Trial: Steve Biko, Medical Ethics and Courts," *South African Journal on Human Rights,* vol. 1, no. 2, August 1985; and N. B. Pityana, "Medical Ethics and South Africa's Security Laws: a Sequel to the Death of Steve Biko," in N. Barney Pityana et al., eds., *Bounds of Possibility: the Legacy of Steve Biko and Black Consciousness* (Cape Town and London: David Philip and Zed Press, 1991).

13. Allister Sparks, then editor of the *Rand Daily Mail,* discussed his dealings with the pathologist, Dr. Jonathan Gluckman, in "Unsung Hero of Biko Conspiracy," *The Observer* (UK), June 13, 1993.

14. American Vice President Walter Mondale had angered South African leaders by stating, in response to a reporter's question in Vienna in May 1977, that the American government favored a "one-man-one-vote" solution. After the October 19 crackdown, the US recalled its ambassador to South Africa for consultations, and dropped its earlier objection to an arms embargo favored by African members of the UN. Britain and France also reversed their past policy of vetoing all proposed sanctions against South Africa, and a resolution for a mandatory arms embargo unanimously passed the UN Security Council on November 4, 1977.

15. Conversations with Ishmael Mkhabela (July 1989) and Lybon Mabasa (April 1991).

16. Modderbee is the colloquial name of Modderfontein B prison. This section is based on conversations with Mongezi Stofile (June 1990), Selebi (March 1989), Diliza Mji (June 1987), Nthato Motlana (March 1979), Leonard Mosala (June 1979), Curtis Nkondo (May 1989), Beyers Naude (July 1980), and Gerhart's "Notes on Biko symposium, Harare, June 1990."

17. Potential state witnesses were usually held under section 6 of the 1967 Terrorism Act, and later under section 29 of the Internal Security Act. Ellen Kuzwayo, the only woman in the Committee of Ten, was arrested on October 19, and detained for five months at the Johannesburg Fort. She recounts the experiences of women detainees in her autobiography, *Call Me Woman* (London: The Women's Press, 1985).

18. "B. P. C. Leadership Training," July 1977?, 3 pp.

19. Sam Nolutshungu in *Changing South Africa: Political Considerations* (New York: Africana Publishing Co., 1982), pp. 182–83, drawing on information from exiled activist Welile Nhlapo, states that "a transition to armed conflict was being actively planned" by a committee that included Biko, a claim repeated by Les Switzer in *Power and Resistance in an African Society* (Madison: University of Wisconsin, 1993), p. 361. According to Malusi Mpumlwana, this "committee" was the group around Biko in King William's Town (originally including only himself and Mapetla Mohapi, but later a few others) whose principal aim was to reach an agreement with the underground ANC and PAC regarding cooperation and possible merger. This was seen as a means of preventing conflicts in Botswana where several separate black consciousness groupings were independently exploring how to acquire military capability and friction with the older movements was high. Biko believed that a unity agreement was an essential prerequisite for effective armed struggle, and that until such an agreement was in place (creating either a Patriotic Front as in Zimbabwe, or a single movement with internal and external wings as in Namibia), prospective fighters should be discouraged from leaving South Africa to seek military training. Whether this constituted an official "plan for armed struggle" by "the black consciousness movement" depended on whom you asked at the time, according to Mpumlwana. The black consciousness movement even at its zenith never had a central chain of command, and Biko's authority was always more informal than official, even after he was designated the "Honorary President" of the Black People's Convention in early 1977. Conversation with Mpumlwana (July 1994).

20. On the new South African historiography, see Harrison Wright, *The Burden of the Present: Liberal-Radical Controversy Over Southern African History* (Cape Town: David Philip, 1977).

21. See for example Sam Motsuenyane, "Effective Change in Commerce and Industry," speech to the South African Institute of Race Relations, January 1978.

22. Starting monthly salaries for nurses with equal qualifications in provincial hospitals in 1976 were R3,000 (whites), R2,340 (Coloureds and Indians), and R1,740 (Africans). *Survey of Race Relations 1977* (Johannesburg: South African Institute of Race Relations, 1978), p. 546. It was reported in 1975 that pay gaps were narrowing between white doctors and Coloured and Indian doctors in the Transvaal, but widening between whites and Africans. Earnings of African doctors in provincial hospitals as a percentage of the earnings of whites had fallen from 67.5–77.5% in 1973 to 64.7–72.9% in 1975. *The World,* February 14, 1975.

23. *Survey of Race Relations 1977,* pp. 397–98.

24. On black journalists in this period, see Andrew Silk, "Black Journalists in Johannesburg," *The Nation,* November 5, 1977; Denis Beckett, "The World in Microcosm," *South African Outlook,* November 1977; William A. Hachten, "Black Journalists Under Apartheid," *Index on Censorship,* May/June 1979; and Keyan Tomaselli and P. E. Louw, eds., *The Alternative Press in South Africa* (London: James Currey, 1991).

25. Winifred Kgware, transcription of address to the September 1979 WASA congress, and Quraish Patel, "In Search of Ideology."

26. "Minutes on the National Convention Convened by the Sub-Committee of the Soweto Action Committee (SAC)," Roodepoort, April 29–30, 1978.

27. By 1979 a loose exile grouping calling itself the Black Consciousness Movement of Azania (BCMA) had established offices in London and was in communication with other black consciousness adherents in the US, Europe and Africa. With participation from Barney Pityana, who had left South Africa in 1978, the BCMA tried to establish working relationships with the ANC and PAC in the continuing hope that a unification of liberation movements could be effected. The group found itself cold shouldered, however, and eventually dissolved. See "Report of the B. C. M. United Kingdom Region," July 1979, and "Black Consciousness Movement of Azania—'One Azania One Nation:' Our Urgent Tasks" 1980?

28. Information on AZAPO's formation is drawn from conversations with Ameen Akhalwaya (July 1980), Mabasa (April 1991), Mkhabela (January 1983 and July 1989), Nkondo (May 1989 and December 1989), Quraish Patel (July 1989 and December 1989), Dr. Joe Variava (October 1985), and George Wauchope (July 1980), and press reports, especially Ameen Akhalwaya, "Behind the Nkondo sacking," *Rand Daily Mail,* January 24, 1980.

29. Almost 500 Soweto teachers resigned during the uprising, of whom about 200 later asked to be reinstated. *International Herald Tribune,* March 11, 1978.

30. Conversations with Mabasa and Mkhabela (July 1989), then both of the Soweto Action Committee; *Rand Daily Mail,* March 13 and 21, 1978; and Benjamin Pogrund, *How Can Man Die Better . . . Sobukwe and Apartheid* (New Brunswick: Rutgers University Press; London: Peter Halban, 1990), pp. 371–77. Also see chapter 9.

31. Julie Frederikse quoting Jacob Zuma in *The Unbreakable Thread: Nonracialism in South Africa* (Bloomington: Indiana University Press; London: Zed Books, 1990), p. 124.

32. Information on COSAS is drawn from conversations with Mkhuseli Jack (July 1989), Mabasa, Khaya Matiso (July 1989), and Imrann Moosa (July 1989), the interview of Victoria Butler with Billy Masetlha (February 1988), and COSAS documents, especially "The Stormy Years of the Congress of South African Students: COSAS, 1979–1985," by Wantu Zenzile, 1989? Masetlha told Butler that it cost about R20,000 (then about $20,000) to get COSAS started.

33. Conversations with Mpumlwana (November 1987), Mewa Ramgobin (July 1989) and Cassim Saloojee (October 1987).

34. See Mizana Matiwana and Shirley Walters, *The Struggle for Democracy: A Study of Community Organisations in Greater Cape Town From the 1960's to 1985* (Cape Town: Centre for Adult and Continuing Education, University of the Western Cape, 1986), which notes (pp. 54–55) that the late 1970s saw a growing interest among social work students and practitioners in the radical writings of Saul Alinsky, Ivan Illich, and Paulo Freire. These writers stressed the importance of empowering poor people to organize and act on their own behalf. For a South African critique of standard "community development" principles in the 1970s, see "Community Organisation," *Work in Progress,* no. 11, February 1980, pp. 31–42.

35. July 1973 SASO General Students' Council, "Report: Commission on Urban and Rural. . . ."

36. According to Mpumlwana, this latter view was at the heart of the concept of black consciousness. The movement urged blacks to take charge of whatever situation they found themselves in, even in prison. ("If it's exercise time, tell the guard you want to do your laundry. If he bangs on your cell door, invite him to come in and share your meal; treat him as your guest and don't subordinate yourself.") Conversation with Mpumlwana (June 1987). While such principles of conduct may lend credence to a characterization of the black consciousness movement as "idealistic" in the sense of assuming that ideas will lead to action rather than the reverse, in fact the ideas offered practical guides to action in situations where personal and collective decisions about resistance and compliance had to be taken. Little has been written about the pre–1977 experiments of black consciousness organizations with community development activity, other than the valuable chapter by Mamphela Ramphele, "Empowerment and Symbols of Hope: Black Consciousness and Community Development," in Pityana et al. Connections between the black consciousness movement and the later growth of civic organizations are discussed by Matiwana and Walters, pp. 38–42.

37. See Cosmas Desmond, *The Discarded People: an Account of African Resettlement in South Africa* (Harmondsworth: Penguin Books, 1971), and Laurine Platzky and Cherryl Walker, *The Surplus People: Forced Removals in South Africa* (Johannesburg: Ravan Press, 1985).

38. See Charles Simkins, "The Economic Implications of African Resettlement," SALDRU Working Paper No. 43 (Cape Town, 1981), p. 3.

39. See Platzky and Walker, pp. 238–66.

40. See *From Protest to Challenge*, volumes 1–3, and Colin Bundy, "Land and liberation: popular rural protest and national liberation movements in South Africa, 1920–1960," in Shula Marks and Stanley Trapido, eds., *The Politics of Race, Class and Nationalism in Twentieth Century South Africa* (London: Longman, 1987).

41. On section 10 rights see note 7 in chapter 1.

42. See Josette Cole, *Crossroads: The Politics of Reform and Repression 1976–1986* (Johannesburg: Ravan Press, 1987); Andrew Silk, *A Shanty Town in South Africa: The Story of Modderdam* (Johannesburg: Ravan Press, 1981); and Keith Kiewit and Kim Weichel, *Inside Crossroads* (Johannesburg: McGraw-Hill, 1980).

43. See Robin Lee, "The Urban Foundation," in Hendrik van der Merwe et al., eds., *Toward an Open Society in South Africa: The Role of Voluntary Organisations* (Cape Town: David Philip, 1980), p. 105.

44. *Rand Daily Mail,* August 21, 1979, and conversation with Saloojee.

45. "A Brief History of the Durban Housing Action Committee (DHAC) and the Joint Rent Action Committee (JORAC)," n.d., and conversation with Ramgobin.

46. Conversation of Julie Frederikse with Trevor Manuel (1985), and Matiwane and Waters, passim.

47. See Carole Cooper and Linda Ensor, *PEBCO: A Black Mass Movement* (Johannesburg: South African Institute of Race Relations, 1981), and Michael Evans, "The Emergence and Decline of a Community Organisation: an Assessment of PEBCO," *South African Labour Bulletin,* vol. 6, nos. 2/3, September 1980.

48. Clive Smith, "Soweto and the Committee of Ten," *South African Outlook,* November 1977, p. 169. For a list of the original ten members of the committee see note 32, chapter 8.

49. "Committee of Ten," *Work in Progress,* no. 10, November 1979, pp. 7–10; conversation with Nthato Motlana (June 1987), and interview of Ina Perlman with Motlana (March 1979).

50. "How Motlana Sees the Future," an interview with Nthato Motlana in the *Rand Daily Mail,* September 24, 1979.

51. This assessment of the SCA draws on Khehla Shubane, "The Soweto Rent Boycott," B.A. Honors thesis, University of the Witwatersrand, 1987.

52. Conversation with Mcebisi Xundu (March 1989).

53. Testimony of Eric Molobi in *State v. Molobi,* November 16, 1975, p. 384.

54. *SASO Newsletter,* July/August 1975, p. 11.

55. The number of Africans with section 10 rights can only be crudely estimated since census data is approximate at best, and African population figures in 1979–80 were affected by the reclassification of de jure citizens of Transkei, Bophuthatswana and Venda as non-South Africans, as well as by the incorporation of large townships into homelands, e.g. Umlazi and Kwa Mashu (Durban) into KwaZulu, Mdantsane (East London) into Ciskei and Ga-Rankuwa (Pretoria) into Bophuthatswana.

Part Two

Documents

Documents have been reproduced using South African spellings. Obvious typographical errors have beeen corrected, and in some instances punctuation and spelling have been edited for the sake of clarity. Acronyms used in documents are explained by editorial insertions, or can be found in the acronyms list at the front of the book. In order to include a wide selection of materials, some documents have been abridged. Complete versions of these can be found in the Karis-Gerhart Collection.

1. Setting the Stage

Document 1. "The Road from Nonviolence to Violence." Speech by Z. K. Matthews at a conference sponsored by the World Council of Churches, Kitwe, Northern Rhodesia, May 1964

The history of relations between black and white ever since they met on the banks of the Fish River in the Cape in the eighteenth century has been one of conflict. For the best part of 100 years after their first contact, the struggle took the form of armed conflict. With every weapon they had at their disposal the blacks tried to defend their country against white encroachment or invasion. But in the end they lost the fight which went in favour of powder and shot as against spear and knobkerrie. One tribe after another was subdued. The last major clashes took place in the 1870s, in 1877 with the Xhosa, in 1878 with the Tswana and in 1879 with the Zulus. Since that time the only serious military uprising was that of the Zulus in 1906, the so-called Bambata's Rebellion which was really a protest against increased taxation.

For many years thereafter the Africans reluctantly accepted the rule of the white man but endeavored to fight for the amelioration of their lot and the removal of the disabilities under which they labour by the usual democratic methods of persuasion and discussion. Instead of continuing to fight the white man with the weapons of days gone by, they put aside their spears and sticks and decided to learn the white man's ways. Through church and school, through working for the white man in varying capacities, in urban and rural areas, they thought that they might eventually earn for themselves a respectable place in the new civilisation which the white man had brought to South Africa. They formed political, social and industrial organisations or associations of various kinds, and through them made representations to the powers-that-be for the redress of this or that grievance. They fondly believed that the disabilities under which they laboured were due to their backwardness in the arts of modern civilisation and that as they adapted themselves more and more successfully to the new ways of life, they would be accorded more and more recognition as fellow citizens of the white man. For that reason they co-operated with South African governments in various official bodies especially set up for the ventilation of their views on matters affecting their welfare (as substitutes for direct representation in the Councils of State). The Cape Africans were the only ones who enjoyed franchise rights, but even they always exercised their franchise rights in such a way that no exceptions could be taken to the manner in which they exercised them. With the aid of their franchise some of the best white parliamentarians were sent to the Cape legislature before Union and to the Union Parliament thereafter.

In other parts of the country where Africans did not enjoy franchise rights, they lived in hope that some day they would also be granted these rights, but in the meantime they co-operated with the governments concerned in other ways.

AFRICAN RESISTANCE: PARLIAMENTARY MEASURES

Thus, when the Union government established local or district councils in the areas set aside for Africans, they accepted these Councils, although they were not satisfied that through them they could achieve what they wanted to achieve, namely full citizenship rights. When the Native Conference was established under the Native Affairs Act of 1920 in terms of which the government periodically called together African leaders to consult them about proposed legislation affecting Africans, they co-operated with the government until the government itself ceased to convene those conferences. When the Advisory Boards were established in the urban areas in terms of the Natives Urban Areas Act, the Africans, although they did not believe that advisory bodies would achieve anything, nevertheless did what they could to show that they were prepared to give the system a trial. The same applied to the system of separate representation which was set up under the Representation of Natives Act of 1936. The Africans opposed that legislation most vigorously, but once it was placed on the statute book, they gave it a fair trial and thereby showed that it did not fit the bill.

Apart from co-operation with the government in official bodies specially set up to deal with African affairs, the Africans established their own non-official bodies through which they directed their requests to the government. Among the most important of these has been the African National Congress established in 1912. The history of the ANC since its inception has been marked by deputations and petitions and resolutions addressed to various Ministers of the Union government. ANC deputations have gone overseas to plead the cause of the African people. The first went to England in 1914 to protest against the passing by the Union Parliament of the Natives Land Act of 1913, a law which led to the eviction of hundreds of African families from European farms in different parts of the country.

The second overseas deputation of the ANC was the one which went to the Peace Conference in Paris in 1919. This deputation was inspired by President Wilson's Fourteen Points and in particular the idea that the war had been fought to bring about "Self-determination for small Nations." Among the small nations that needed self-determination, in the view of the ANC, were the African people of South Africa who had been deprived of their land and their citizenship rights by the white man in South Africa. Therefore they wanted the Peace Conference to look into their case.

The last big deputation to which reference might be made was that of 1942. This deputation, under the leadership of Dr. A. B. Xuma, then President-General of the ANC, interviewed Colonel Denys Reitz, the Minister of Native Affairs in Cape Town, and discussed with him a wide range of problems relating to the African position in South Africa. Among the points on which the Minister appeared to agree with the deputation was the necessity for the relaxation of the Pass Laws and the recognition of African trade unions. Since that time, far from the pass laws being relaxed, they have been consolidated, their enforcement tightened and they have been extended to African women. Instead of the recognition of African trade unions, a system was developed under which disputes between employers and African employees are settled by the intervention of government officials who are more concerned with the punitive measures they are empowered to employ than with the advancement of the cause of the African workers.

The ANC and other African organisations have of course not only made use of the weapon of the deputation and the conference resolution, they have also made use of the weapon of litigation. They have conducted or supported test cases in the law courts such as the famous case of Letanka in which the right of the Transvaal Provincial Administration to impose a poll tax on Africans was successfully contested in the Transvaal Supreme Court. But Africans found that the use of the law courts did not advance their cause to any appreciable extent. Not only is this method very costly financially, but the fact of the matter is that court victories in South Africa tend to be only temporary because when the government loses a case in court all it has to do is to amend the law suitably and the courts which must apply the law as they find it are rendered powerless to assist those adversely affected by the law.

Another weapon which has been used at different times by Africans is the strike weapon. This has been used mainly in the economic field. Here again the effectiveness of the strike weapon as far as Africans are concerned is nullified by the fact that for most types of African workers it has been made illegal for them to strike. So when a strike does take place the police intervene.

Finally, mention must be made of the fact that in recent years Africans have also resorted to the weapon of passive resistance. The biggest effort in that direction was the campaign known as the Campaign for the Defiance of Unjust Laws which was launched by the African National Congress in June 1952, and was directed solely against certain laws such as the Pass Laws which are based on racial discrimination. In launching this campaign, the

ANC invited all organisations and individuals, whatever their race or colour, to join with the Africans in the struggle to rid South Africa of racial discrimination. The Indians under the leadership of the South African Indian Congress, a few Coloureds under the leadership of the South African Coloured People's Organisation, and a few Europeans under the leadership of Patrick Duncan, the son of a former Governor-General of the Union, identified themselves with the campaign. During the campaign, more than 8,000 volunteers, including the top flight leaders of the movement, were arrested and sentenced to varying terms of imprisonment with hard labour, while some of the younger volunteers were punished by flogging. None of the men and women arrested offered any resistance to the treatment meted out to them, for when they volunteered, they took a pledge to observe the principles of non-violence and to suffer for the cause. All volunteers were expected to undergo a period of training and to observe a code of discipline based on moral and religious principles.

AFRICAN RESISTANCE: EXTRA-PARLIAMENTARY MEASURES
    This taking of the extra-parliamentary road has of course been forced upon the people. Year after year they have seen every session of Parliament piling one restriction upon another, one burden upon another, without any relief. How could they in the circumstances be expected to continue to look to Parliament as the source of their salvation? It has ben drummed into them by deeds as well as by words that Parliament has nothing in store for them and that their salvation, if any, must be sought outside the walls of this august body which wields supreme power in South Africa. This turning away from Parliament has been interpreted in some quarters as meaning that the non-whites want to work for the overthrow of Parliament and that therefore organisations like the ANC must be looked upon as subversive organisations out to undermine the independence and safety of the State. For that reason, since the Defiance Campaign there has been a great deal of loose talk about looking for evidence of treason by African individuals and organisations. The minister of Justice justified searches by Security Police of the homes and offices of individuals and organisations on the ground that they are searching for evidence of treason. This culminated in the Treason Trial of 1956–1961. The fact of the matter is that the African people are a highly loyal and law-abiding people. To attempt to persuade them to engage in activities directed against the independence and safety of the State would be no mean task for any group or individual that undertook it. When the African people say they are embarking upon extra-parliamentary methods, they do not mean thereby anti-parliamentary. For them extra-parliamentary means "outside Parliament to draw the attention of Parliament to our condition." For them it means "as we are precluded from influencing Parliament from within, let us see if we can influence the powers-that-be from without." Other South African citizens make use of press campaigns, protest demonstrations, processions, public meetings of protest, and the like, and nobody suggests that by these means they intend to overthrow the State but according to the

Union government, if this sort of thing is done by the non-white groups, especially by the Africans, then it amounts to subversion.

But the effect of Government attacks on African leaders and African political organisations is that they have been driven underground. As no public meetings among Africans are allowed except for weddings, funerals and religious services, private meetings are held and they conduct their business just the same. If the public opposition to Government measures is prohibited, private opposition which can be much more dangerous, must and will be organised. Until recently all the outstanding leaders of the Africans stood by the policy of non-violence in achieving their aims. But with the passage of time as this policy appears to the ordinary man not to yield any results, the leaders who stood for non-violence and for co-operation between black and white on the basis of equal opportunity, are being replaced by leaders who do not. The intransigence on the white side of the colour line is being met with similar intransigence on the black side of the colour line. Unable to get the ear of public authorities in their own countries, the non-whites have begun to look beyond their own borders for inspiration, guidance and direction. Already events in other parts of the continent of Africa are having a tremendous impact on the man-in-the-street in South Africa. Already he sees that people in other territories in Africa are on the march towards independence, some of them obtaining independence by peaceful methods, while others have had to fight to gain their freedom. It is not surprising that he begins to say to himself, "If we cannot achieve our freedom by peaceful means, we may have to resort to other methods." The question at the moment is not whether the latter methods will succeed, but whether they begin to appear to the African in South Africa as the only methods open to him.

GOVERNMENT POLICY: SEPARATE DEVELOPMENT

The government has for some time now decided that the only way in which to maintain contact with the African people is through the Native Commissioner, on the one hand, and the tribal chief on the other. Occasionally in addition to these personal contacts between individual chiefs and individual Native Commissioners, the Minister of Bantu Administration and Development has held meetings with groups of chiefs from certain defined areas—chiefs of Zululand, chiefs of the Northern Transvaal, chiefs of the Transkei, etc. These gatherings known as "Indabas" have given the minister the opportunity to expound at great length various aspects of the policy of apartheid and he has apparently been advised or has decided on his own that as long as he does that, he is keeping in touch with African opinion and need not worry himself about any other sections of African opinion. Unfortunately, these "Indabas" have not been the success that it was hoped they would be. They have not produced the peace and harmony which was hoped for in the Northern Transvaal from which indaba-ridden area more chiefs have been deported than from any other area. Chiefs supposed to be loyal to the government have not been able to produce the miracle of acting like Pied Pipers of Hamelin blindly followed by their people. The people have not hesistated to repudiate the chiefs where the latter have not adequately represented their views. This troubled state of affairs on the Reserves the government has attributed to the activities of the now banned ANC, thereby tacitly admitting that the ANC has a greater influence over the people in the Reserves than the so-called traditional leaders of the people. The fact of the matter is that the modern African "Chief" is not a chief "by the people" as he was hitherto, but a chief "by the government." The people do not regard him as their spokesman at all. They look upon him quite rightly as a government man—government appointed or government recognised. If he does not express "his Master's voice," he is liable to be deposed forthwith, and therefore, poor man, how can he be expected to express the views of the people, when he is not really a leader of his people but a servant of the government? It is this method of consultation which has resulted in the establishment of the Bantustan in the Transkei where a state of emergency still obtains.

The Nationalists believe that the peaceful way out is the way of separate development. This involves taking the Native Reserves as they are at present and converting them, however small their area, into a national home for the Africans in which they can, with state assistance, develop to their heart's content and enjoy all the rights in their own areas which the white man enjoys in his side of the country.

AFRICAN RESPONSE: FRUSTRATION AND DESPERATION

At the present moment thinking Africans look upon apartheid like a wolf in sheep's clothing, as something which must be recognised for what it really is and not for what it pretends to be. They look upon apartheid, whatever the form in which it appears, as a technique of domination, a system of maintaining the present *baasskap* (boss-ship) of the white man on a permanent basis. The white man is, of course, entitled to strive to maintain what he has gained for himself in the course of his stay in Africa, but what he really cannot expect is that the African should give his blessing to a state of affairs under which he always gets the worst of things. Being under the domination of another group is not exactly a pleasant thing for those who have to suffer it, and there is nothing else for the latter group to do but to continue to fight against domination until they overcome it.

South Africa has a European population of three million whites, many of whom have been established in Southern Africa for three centuries, and it can be taken for granted that they would be prepared to resort to violence in order to maintain their privileged position in the sub-continent. The non-white groups realise this and have hitherto always excluded the use of violence as a method of obtaining the redress of their grievances. They recognise that in any armed clash between black and white, the whites would be at a tremendous advantage, certainly at the outset, and that African loss of life would certainly be heavy. Responsible African leaders have always warned their people against any idea of resorting to arms in their struggle for liberation. But the question is whether they will always be prepared to listen to responsible leaders. There is more and more talk among the younger leaders about whether the method of non-violence will work in the South African context.

Some are beginning to suggest that the possibility of a resort to violence should not be ruled out altogether. They point out that in any case, as the struggle proceeds and is intensified, it will not be the African people but the government and its supporters who will resort to violence, and that it would be futile to expect the people assailed not to defend themselves in the best way possible. This is largely a counsel of desperation born out of the situation in South Africa in which the non-white groups are faced with a white population which is apparently impervious to the democratic processes of persuasion and discussion.

In view of the fact that there seems to be no possibility of the white man changing his outlook in this regard, all that remains is for him to be allowed to carry out his policy of separate development and for its impracticability to be established in the process. The doctrine of natural consequences seems to be the only one that can be followed with the white man who has decided to harden his heart against all appeals by the African for a reasonable approach to the problems of the country. Taking this road will undoubtedly bring much suffering upon many people and will delay the development of harmonious relations between the peoples of South Africa for decades, if not generations, but it seems that this futile attempt at turning back the clock of progress will have to take place before there can be a forward move in the national affairs of the country. Things will have to get worse before they can get better.

The trouble about this hardening of the heart against common sense and reason is that it evokes a similar response among those against whom it is directed. The African who believes that in the end reason will prevail is becoming a rarity. It is to be feared that by the time the white man is ready to adopt a reasonable attitude, he will find himself against a blank wall of black opposition. He will find that what he calls the "extremists" have taken over the leadership of the African group. Already the slogan—Africa for the Africans—which had been largely discredited when the Marcus Garvey movement was at its height in the twenties—is coming back into popularity in some African circles, and he would be a bold man who would dare to predict that it will not catch on this time. After all, the trend of events all over the African continent is that the time is more than overdue for Africans to be freed from old-style colonialism and imperialism, and that in most African territories means "Africa for the Africans." The undiscerning will not stop to ask themselves whether such a policy is appropriate for South Africa with its large population of settled Europeans. What they will content themselves with is that it would be intolerable for a pocket of colonialism and imperialism to be allowed to remain in South Africa when the rest of the continent is free from it.

Recent developments in South Africa have shown the extent to which

Africans have already travelled along the road to violence. Three distinct movements have emerged which show that significant sections of the non-white population, supported by some whites, have decided to abandon the way of non-violence. The first movement of which mention must be made is POQO. This seemed to include within its ranks a number of frustrated young men who decided to hit out wildly at anyone they believed belonged to the ranks of the oppressors, white or non-white. Their actions were classic examples of frustration and aggression in which the victims of their ill-will were chosen haphazardly without regard to any objective other than pointless destruction. Another movement is that of the YU CHI CHAN CLUB which apparently flourished in the Western Province, mainly among the coloured people. In the case against Dr. [Neville] Alexander and others who were alleged to have been members of this club, it appeared that their activities were in the stage of study and planning, but if the verdict of the court is to be accepted, the accused had decided to go the way of violence.

The movement about which the most authoritative statement has been made is UMKONTO WE SIZWE—The Spear of the Nation. Dealing with the origin of this movement Mandela, its chief spokesman, in a moving document, extracts from which have been widely published, has said: "At the beginning of 1961, after a long and anxious assessment of the South African situation, I and some colleagues came to the conclusion that as violence in this country was inevitable, it would be unrealistic and wrong for African leaders to continue preaching peace and non-violence when the government met our peaceful demands with force. Umkonto was formed in November 1961. Umkonto was to perform sabotage and strict instructions were given to its members right from the start that on no account were they to injure or kill people in planning or carrying out operations."

Dealing with the background of the movement Mandela states: "It is a fact that for a long time the people had been talking of violence—of the day when they would fight the white man and win back their country and we, the leaders of the ANC had nevertheless prevailed upon them to avoid violence and to pursue peaceful methods. When some of us met in May and June 1961, it could not be denied that our policy to achieve a non-racial state by non-violence had achieved nothing, and that our followers were beginning to lose confidence in this policy and were developing disturbing ideas of terrorism."

It is clear that Mandela and his colleagues were still inspired by the spirit of non-violence. They reluctantly recognised that violence was inevitable, but they were convinced that if it did come, it was their duty as responsible leaders of the people to take certain steps about it, namely to ensure (1) that such a movement should be under the guidance of responsible leaders like themselves imbued with the spirit of non-violence; (2) that it should be carried out without any loss of life, but should be directed against installations which did not involve danger to life.

There is no indication anywhere in the statement that it was the aim of Mandela and others to overthrow the state as such. Their movement remained a movement of protest against the disabilities under which their people laboured.

As he says: "Basically, we fight against two features which are the hallmarks of African life in South Africa and which are entrenched by legislation which we seek to have repealed. These features are poverty and lack of human dignity. South Africa is the richest country in Africa and could be one of the richest countries in the world. But it is a land of extremes and remarkable contrasts. The whites enjoy what may well be the highest standard of living in the world, while Africans live in poverty and misery. The lack of human dignity experienced is the direct result of the policy of white supremacy. White supremacy implies black inferiority. Legislation designed to preserve white supremacy entrenches this notion. Africans want to be paid a living wage. Africans want to perform work which they are capable of doing and not work which the government declares them to be capable of. Africans want to be allowed to live where they can obtain work and not to be endorsed out of an area because they were not born there. Africans want to be allowed to own land in places where they work and not to be obliged to live in rented houses which they can never call their own. Africans want to be part of the general population, and not confined to living in their own ghettos. Above all, we want equal political rights, because without them our disabilities will be permanent. I know that this sounds revolutionary to the whites in this country, because the majority of voters will be Africans. This makes the white man fear democracy. But this fear cannot be allowed to stand in the way of the only solution which will guarantee racial harmony and freedom for all. It is not true that the enfranchisement of all will result in racial domination. Political division based on colour is entirely artificial, and when it disappears so will the domination of one group by another."

Another matter to which Mandela draws attention is the commonly held assumption that when Africans fight for their rights they are inspired by Communism or directed by communists. As he states: "The ideological creed of the ANC is and has always been the creed of African nationalism. It is not the concept of African nationalism expressed in the cry "Drive the white man into the sea." The African nationalism for which the ANC stands is the concept of freedom and fulfillment for the African people in their own land. It is perhaps difficult for white South Africans with an ingrained prejudice against Communism to understand why experienced African politicians so readily accept Communists as their friends. But the reason to us is obvious. Theoretical differences amongst those fighting against oppression is a luxury we cannot afford at this stage. What is more, for many decades communists were the only political group in South Africa who were prepared to treat Africans as human beings and their equals; who were prepared to eat with us, talk with us, live with us and work with us. They were the only political group which was prepared to work with Africans for the attainment of political rights and a stake in society. Because of this, there are many Africans who, today, tend to equate freedom with Communism."

The many trials that are going on in South Africa and the thousands of

Africans who have been detained either under the 90 day "no trial" law or under Transkei Proclamation 400 of 1960, testify to the fact that a radical change is in process in the attitude of many Africans towards the possibility of bringing about political change by ordinary political processes. They also show the determination of the government representing the white population to crush with every means at its disposal, both legal and military, every movement among Africans for their liberation. The dilemma confronting African leaders as well as those who have their welfare at heart, is whether they should continue to urge their followers to stand by the methods of persuasion and discussion in the face of increasing and relentless force with which their attempts at the amelioration of their lot are met by the government. When the flower of African youth represented by men such as Mandela or Dr. Alexander are being sentenced to long terms of imprisonment during peace time, for fighting for their legitimate rights in what they believe to be the only ways open to them, can we say that the Christian thing to do is to advise them to acquiesce in their present situation and wait, Micawber-like, for something to turn up?

Document 2. "It's Difficult to Decide My Identity." Column by Nat Nakasa, *Rand Daily Mail,* June 20, 1964

A small audience in Germiston was told this week that the Afrikaans Press and Broadcast House had elevated "kaffirs" to "Mr." and "Mrs." instead of keeping "savages" in their place by traditional apartheid. This was said, according to the report, by Dr. L. E. Beyers, provisional Transvaal leader of the Nationaliste Bond.

There is one thing I like about Dr. Beyers and men who think like him. Such men are honest men. They have the courage of their convictions. It is unfortunate that there aren't many of them left in the 20th century. We have, to be sure, more than enough people who think like Dr. Beyers, but few of them have the courage to speak their mind.

As a journalist, I sincerely hope that men like Dr. Beyers will still be going strong when we get television in this country. I would encourage Dr. Beyers to say some of these things to a wide audience on television. I would volunteer to be used by the doctor as a sample of a young savage.

But then this country may not get TV for a long time. For the present, we have no choice but to allow such rare television material as Dr. Beyers to be wasted on small Bond audiences in Germiston.

Meanwhile, however, Dr. Beyers has set me thinking. In his talk this week Dr. Beyers was only contributing to a discussion which has been going to the Afrikaans Press debating whether it is a sin against apartheid to drink tea with Africans. Chief [Kaiser] Matanzima has just voiced the opinion that the people of the Transkei should be called Africans and not "Bantus" or "Natives," let alone "kaffirs" and "savages."

To my mind, the importance of this discussion is that all the questions asked relate to the question of my identity. Who am I? Where do I belong in the South African scheme of things? Who are my people?

Negroes in Harlem are asking themselves the same question. Some have tried to answer it by forming "Back-to-Africa" movements. Others have formed organisations like the Black Muslims.

I have the same problem on my hands. It often pains me to realise that even my speech cannot really be called me. This becomes worse, in my case, because I am more impressionable than most people I know. I am the sort that speaks like an American after meeting one or like an Englishman after interviewing a peer.

I am supposed to be a Pondo, but I don't even know the language of that tribe. I was brought up in a Zulu-speaking home, my mother being a Zulu. Yet I can no longer think in Zulu because that language cannot cope with the demands of our day. I could not, for instance, discuss negritude in Zulu. Even an article like this would not be possible in Zulu.

I have never owned an assegai [spear] or any of those magnificent Zulu shields. Neither do I propose to be in tribal wear when I go to the U. S. this year for my scholarship. I am just not a tribesman, whether I like it or not. I am, inescapably, a part of the city slums, the factory machines and our beloved shebeens [speak-easies].

I'm not even sure that I could claim to be African. For if I were, then I should surely share my identity with West Africans and other Africans in Kenya or Tanganyika. Yet it happens to be true that I am more at home with an Afrikaner than with a West African. Some of my friends who have been abroad say they got on best with Afrikaners they met in Europe instead of Englishmen or West Africans.

We saw some evidence of this when a number of Nigerian students passed through Johannesburg once. We took them to a party in Soweto where they were welcomed like long lost brothers. After marvelling at their flowing robes and talking some politics, we didn't know what to do with them.

Being Moslems—and millions of Nigerians are Moslems—they did not drink. We could not offer them meat because that also would have gone against their faith. They raised a laugh when they told us that some of their friends at home were polygamists. "We must explain," someone quipped, "that you chaps will have to make do with one girl each in this country. We can't fix you up with a lot in one shot."

Once we were through with this kind of talk, our visitors were abandoned in one corner of the room and nobody had much to say to them. They were perfect strangers, more so than the many South African Whites who spend some of their time in the townships. To speak of those Nigerians as "My people" would not make much sense, even though we all had flat noses.

I don't see that there is any justification in calling me a non-European either. That is as silly as this business of South African Whites who insist that they are Europeans. Some of them have never set foot in Europe. Nor did their grandfathers.

It is the insistence of the whites that they are "Europeans" which has, in part, inspired such silly slogans as "Africa for the Africans." The Africa of today is simply not the product of assegais and rain queens. Johannesburg was built by the White technical know-how and enterprise plus the indispensable co-operation of Black labour. To that extent, this city will never be Black or White. Black men cannot look at the tall buildings and say "this is ours" without being fraudulent. Nor can the Whites.

If I am right, therein lies my identity. I am a South African like Dr. L. E. Beyers. "My people" are South Africans. Mine is the history of the Great Trek. Gandhi's passive resistance in Johannesburg, the wars of Cetewayo and the dawn raids which gave us the treason trial in 1956. All these are South African things. They are a part of me. So is Dr. Beyers inescapably a part of me. And I refuse to think that part of Dr. Beyers is a "savage."

Document 3. "This Kid Is No Goat." Poem by Oswald Mtshali, about 1969

Where have
All the angry young men gone?
Gone to the Island of Lament for Sharpeville.
Gone overseas on scholarship,
Gone up North to milk and honeyed uhuru.
Gone to the dogs with the drink of despair.

Yesterday I met one in a bookstore:
he was foraging for food of thought
from James Baldwin, Le Roi Jones
Albert Camus, Jean-Paul Sartre.

He wore faded jeans and a heavy sweater,
he saluted me with a
"Hi! brother!"
He was educated in a country mission school
where he came out clutching a rosary
as an amulet against
"Slegs vir Blankes—For Whites Only"

He enrolled at Life University
whose lecture rooms were shebeens,
hospital wards and prison cells.

He graduated cum laude
with a thesis in philosophy:
"I can't be black and straight
in this crooked white world!
"If I tell the truth
I'm detestable.

"If I tell lies
I'm abominable.
"If I tell nothing
I'm unpredictable.
"If I smile to please
I'm nothing but an obsequious sambo.

"I have adopted jazz as my religion
with Duke Ellington, Count Basie,
Louis Armstrong as my High Priests.
"No more do I go to church
where the priest has left me in the lurch.
"His sermon is a withered leaf
falling from a decaying pulpit-tree
to be swept away
by violent gusts of doubt and scepticism.

"My wife and kids can worship there:
they want to go to heaven when they die.
"I don't want to go to heaven when I'm dead.
"I want my heaven now,
here on earth in Houghton and Parktown;
a mansion
two cars or more
and smiling servants.
Isn't that heaven?"

DOCUMENT 4. "The Sportsman's Choice." By Dennis Brutus, 1971 (abridged)

Apartheid South Africa is accepted by a large part of the world as one of the perennial problems of our time—widely and generally condemned, but without much expectation of change; and so the press treats it as a rather tedious subject, with little that is fresh, and the man in the street feels that little can be done about it.

But there is one aspect of the apartheid policy which frequently gets into the news, and where it seems, not only that things are happening, but they are actually bringing about some changes in a rather tiresome scene.

This is sport, which has regularly, for some years, been debated and disputed in various parts of the world, and for a time captured the headlines in Britain, in the course of a South African rugby tour and an aborted cricket tour. And there were other sports events, including South Africa's exclusion from the Olympic movement and suspension from world athletics, which attract international attention. . . .

For someone not familiar with the South African scene, it is not easy to grasp the extent to which sport dominates the thinking of most South

Africans. Perhaps the most graphic demonstration of this is the extent and the frequency of sports issues appearing in the headlines of most of the daily newspapers—disasters and international affairs elsewhere are mere trifles compared to a rugby victory or even anticipation of a victory!

Sport is, of course, woven into the fabric of the apartheid society—and is determined by it. It may well be that those in other countries who object to protests being directed at South African sportsmen are simply not aware of how completely all South African sport is directed by the apartheid policy. They tend to assume that it is sport pretty much as it is played elsewhere in the world. But in fact all sport is run on rigid racial lines, and it was because he understood how essential it was that apartheid should be preserved that the late [Prime Minister] Dr. [Hendrik] Verwoerd made his famous Loskop Dam speech. Speaking of the inclusion of the Maoris in the New Zealand rugby team to South Africa, he declared that if a single Maori was permitted to be a member of the team it would be sufficient to sabotage the entire structure of the South African society.

But things have changed in some measure since then. Under Mr. Vorster and in the face of the opposition from his rebels who formed their own party, he has since allowed a New Zealand touring team to play in South Africa which included Maoris—and a Samoan.

How has this change come about? It is in fact the direct result of persistent pressure, both from South Africans and the world, who have stood resolutely against the intrusion of racialism into an area to which it can have no pretence of belonging, that of sport. . . .

The beginnings: because the non-Whites were excluded from the national sports bodies, they tended to set up their own organisations—first regional and then national. They too tended at first to have racial divisions among themselves, mainly because they were separated and found themselves in pockets throughout the country. But they became increasingly aware of the requirements of the world bodies—that racialism was forbidden, and sought to eliminate racial clauses from the constitutions. At the same time they became conscious of the anomaly—the national bodies of their country were not only non-national, but they were also guilty of contravening the statutes which forbade racial discrimination. Perhaps the most important factor was the emergence of some sportsmen of very high standard—people who could have qualified for the national representative teams if it were not for their colour. From this came the determination to seek recognition for their sportsmen from the national bodies, and failing that, through appeal to the international bodies governing world sport for a particular code. . . .

It was [the] failure of the separate sports bodies to make headway which led to the realisation that it was necessary to co-ordinate their efforts. The first effort, the CCIRS (Co-ordinating Committee for International Recognition of Sport) failed for lack of support. Many sportsmen were timid and unsure of the powers of the police. But the later SASA (South African Sports Association) set up in 1958 prospered and gained increasing strength, particularly when it successfully led opposition to a tour by an all-Black cricket team—a ruse to protect the White cricket body from protest at the meetings of the International Cricket Conference. But SASA was unable to crack the solid opposition of the supreme body for sport in South Africa—the South African Olympic Committee—and so was forced into creating a direct challenge to the Olympic Committee, which did not conceal its support for racism in sport, by setting up a rival body—SAN-ROC—the South African Non-Racial Olympic Committee.

SAN-ROC had a relatively short run in South Africa. The President [Dennis Brutus] was banned from membership of any sports body, attending any sports meeting and sent to prison. The acting chairman [John Harris], who subsequently became involved in underground sabotage activities, was convicted of causing an explosion and hanged. The other members of the Committee were intimidated or hounded by the police so that some fled the country and others were forced to withdraw from activities.

But SAN-ROC had a considerable impact and to it must be credited the first major success—the exclusion of the country from the Olympics at Tokyo in 1964.

SAN-ROC took on a fresh lease of life in Britain in 1966 where some members of the Committee revived the body, were joined by the President, now exiled from South Africa, and generously assisted by Christian Action and the International Defence and Aid Fund of Canon John Collins, began to campaign vigorously.

Because only the White bodies from South Africa were recognised as members of the international sports bodies, SAN-ROC had no official standing at international congresses, but it was able to do a great deal by way of lobbying and preparation of memoranda and documents which were made available to delegates attending these congresses. . . .

It is often argued that the pressures exerted on apartheid are futile, and simply harden the position. But the facts demonstrate the reverse. While South African sports administration, often dictated to by the politicians, have declared their determination never to change and never to abandon their policy, they have in fact made considerable modifications in an attempt to avoid total isolation in international sport. The most numerous were offered at Teheran, in an effort to avoid exclusion from Mexico. These included the agreement that, for the first time, there would be non-Whites in the party who would be permitted to wear a South African uniform and march under the South African flag and who would be allowed to travel together. This was being offered for the first time in history. In tennis and golf there have also been concessions. It would appear that non-Whites from other countries (but *not* from South Africa) will be permitted to take part in international team events in future. (The refusal of a visa to Arthur Ashe, the Black US tennis champion, was based on two grounds: he was coming as an *individual* to take part in the championships and not as a member of a Davis Cup team, and secondly he was accused of having made political statements against apartheid.) But the biggest concession made thus far—since it touches rugby, the national game—is the one referred to earlier, namely, the total reversal by Mr. Vorster of the policy of Dr. Verwoerd, which excluded Maoris from the visiting All-Blacks (the name of the representative New Zealand rugby team—they had in fact always been all-White). Thus the team which toured South Africa in 1970 included two Maoris and one Samoan— admittedly they were very fair—and an Afrikaans paper, arguing for the inclusion of Maoris had pleaded that their skins were tea-coloured! But this was a major advance, and its consequences are as yet incalculable.

The tour evoked some interesting responses. It is fairly evident that non-Whites deliberately attended these matches to support the All-Blacks, and that they singled out the non-Whites in the side for special adulation—to the extreme irritation of White South Africa, and as a result non-Whites suffered ill-treatment at the hands of the police and of White spectators. Many non-Whites gloried in the successes of the All-Blacks and the discomfiture of the Whites; and some have gone on to ask the awkward question, why, if it is permissible for White South Africans to play against non-Whites from elsewhere, should it not be permissible for them to play against non-Whites of their own country?

A more interesting response has been that of the White South Africans who follow sports other than rugby, particularly the cricketers. They have seen their own tour of Britain cancelled as a result of massive protest in Britain in retaliation of their Government's refusal to allow a non-White on the British team to South Africa. ("The D'Oliviera affair": the MCC [Marylebone Cricket Club] cancelled their tour of South Africa after being told that they could not select a non-White who had come from South Africa.) For them the question was, why should the rules of apartheid be bent for the sake of the rugby fans, but not in the case of other sports, many of whom were already forced into isolation?

It is this pressure which holds some interesting implications for the future. . . .

2. The Liberation Movements, 1964–1975

Document 5. Memorandum of the National Committee for Liberation. London, mid-1963

The NCL still remains a small elite group, distinguished by its technical competence and secure organisation, rather than by its size or effectiveness. In the existing situation, having failed to establish itself as the means of coordinating and federating all revolutionary activity, it is unlikely to grow to the extent where it can displace The Spear [Umkhonto] or Poqo from their positions as being the revolutionary arms of the ANC and PAC. It has however an undoubted initiative over the other organisations in the degree of its technical competence. At the moment it seems better organised in the Cape than in the Transvaal where its level of activity is very low.

The need for unity. There is an overwhelming need for unity.

Outside South Africa. The parties here consist of the NCL's own committee. The ANC which seems to be in very good shape not only in Dar es Salaam but also in Algiers and London. It seems to have a certain amount of money. There seems to be a distinct difference in attitude to members of the NCL on the part of ANC members in Dar where several distinct suggestions of cooperation were made recently to your representative. In London there seems to be no such feeling. This may arise from the fact that all the White comrades seem to have congregated in London.

The PAC by contrast is broke and badly split abroad. Molotsi and [R]adebe seem to be following Leballo while Mahomo is trying to build himself a new empire in the Congo. The latest information from Mahomo suggests that the PAC in Maseru has fragmented and that Molefe and Leballo have fallen out.

Our impression is that the PAC has become frankly opportunist and has little organisation worth having.

Inside South Africa. Here by common consent is where unity of command must first be established. There seem to be three other possible parties apart from NCL. These are Spear, Poqo, and Apdusa. From events known here and at home it seems that we might well be nearest to Apdusa in that [they] seem to have been crippled by recent arrests and Tabata seemed keen to cooperate—indeed this is the line that he has been selling [Tanganyikan foreign minister, Oscar] Kambona. However, if we cooperate first with Apdusa, this might alienate the ANC and this is an important consideration. Also Apdusa is very sectarian. ANC abroad seems keen to cooperate. It is difficult to assess to what degree they have been destroyed by the Rivonia arrests. If accounts of sticker campaigns in Johannesburg, Pretoria and Cape Town are correct, they would still seem to have personnel but they seem to lack materials and training. In this regard it is worth noting that they have in excess of 150 persons waiting the end of [the Central African] Federation with a view to returning to South Africa. All these have been trained but not to the satisfaction of Makiwane in that they have had a standard military course. We cannot comment on the PAC at home. They seem to have received their quietus. If we are not in touch with ANC at home, then contact can be proceeded with in Dar. The pulling power of the ANC outside South Africa must be appreciated—especially in relation to the committee of 9 [African Liberation Committee]. This is far less true of PAC.

Proposal: The proposal that is made to each of these organisations should clearly be a joint command. Each organisation should be asked to do what it can do best. It is to be hoped that in due course a complete blend will be achieved and a full unity of effort and purpose. There has obviously been for a long time an unexpressed reluctance to getting involved with the Communist Party of SA. It should be recognised that whatever the facts of the situation, the Spear is a partnership between the ANC and CP and it is recognised as such by the ANC. Therefore unless it is suggested that an organisation should be created in opposition to Spear—which seems frankly impractical—NCL members should face the fact that the CP is to play a part. On analysis it seems that if unity is achieved this part will decrease with time. Our analysis in the early days of the movement included the assumption that most of the CP members with any ability would be knocked off by the government or exiled within a short while of sabotage commencing. This has proved to be true. Therefore while those fellows are still certainly part of the partnership abroad, they are not so at home—for obvious reasons— and they will soon be seen to have outlived their usefulness to the ANC here. In fact we are continually asked to do certain jobs for them here. This is curious in the light of the facts that there are folk like [Joe] Slovo and [Jack] Hodgson in London. We suggest therefore that now is the time to try and find unity with Spear at home and that the fear of an association with the CP should be diminished by the facts set out above. It should be the motto of the NCL "by our works ye shall know us" and deeds make friends quicker than words. Eric feels about the CP: They will continue their dominant position from overseas in same way as happened in Spain because they will be in position to control flow of money and supplies at later stage of struggle. Don't underestimate Joe and Co—even though they will be [weakened] in South Africa. Their dominant position abroad will be of *maximum* importance. This does not affect our possible working with Spear but our perspective must be clear on their future role.

Initially we suggest a liaison based on a practical project to be decided by you. We give as an e.g. 2 points 20 mile distant on a railway line. NCL and Spear to do one each at the same time. Only one member from each group to be in contact therefore maximum security. Ultimate joint command will have to flow from practical liaisons.

What can the NCL offer? We can offer a number of things that remain unsolved in spite of the fact that three years have gone by since Sharpeville. Looking at the strategic situation beyond South Africa for the moment it seems that the free world has provided for South Africa very few of the services it requires if the revolution is to proceed. Amongst these are proper training facilities, transport and supplies. The key to some of these problems might be provided by the independence of Zambia but not all will be solved or nearly as many believe.

Transport. This is linked of course to the availability of supply but it is doubtful whether the independence of Zambia will ease the problem. The link between Zambia and Bechuanaland is through the point at Kazungula. Here at best Zambia has fifty yards of the river bank which will probably be policed. At worst none. What seems abundantly clear is whatever this situation might be, while it may be possible to pass men through this gap back into Bechuanaland for transport to SA (and even this might be difficult if proper controls are placed on the crossing by Bechuanaland), it will be virtually impossible to use this route for materials. The question that is raised by these facts is whether, for the moment, materials can be transported into S. A. from the North. If money was available we suggest that the NCL should seriously consider the suggestion originally made that Torquil be used from the Cape to liaise with passing vessels, using Betty's Bay or a similar place for unloading. It is interesting to note that Torquil has aroused interest in Dar es Salaam quarters for this very reason.

Training. Northern Rhodesia is about to become the new training ground for SA. We should consider what part we can play in this. We have already translated certain works into Sotho. We have a lot of know-how. Will we want our own training place or can we in concert with others make a very material contribution to training facilities in Zambia.

Materials. In spite of much talk about the availability of materials it seems clear that there is not much likelihood of these being provided by nations in the quantities that will be required.

We suggest therefore that the NCL looks upon itself as a sort of specialist cadre, which will set up the sinews of the struggle. That is the procurement of materials, their transport and training. We must continue with direct operations. We must try to participate in the field to an increasing extent. Should we liaise with groups with manpower, however, we should concentrate on maximum exploitation of our specific abilities.

Document 6. Flyer of the African Resistance Movement announcing its formation, June 12, 1964

The African Resistance movement (ARM) announces its formation in the cause of South African Freedom. ARM states its dedication and commitment to achieving the overthrow of the whole system of apartheid and exploitation in South Africa. ARM aims to assist in establishing a democratic society in terms of the basic principles of socialism.

We salute other Revolutionary Freedom Movements in South Africa. In our activities this week we particularly salute the men of Rivonia and state our deepest respect for their courage and efforts. While ARM may differ from them and other groups in the freedom struggle, we believe in the unification of all forces fighting for the new order in our country. We have enough in common.

The time for talking is past. The present regime and its supporters, internal and foreign, have shown that they are not prepared to respond in any way to the peaceful demands of the people of South Africa for full participation in all aspects of the political, economic and social life of the country. Instead, oppression has increased.

ARM does not only talk. ARM acts. ARM has acted. ARM has declared and will declare itself through action. This is the only language our rulers understand. And ARM, with other freedom forces will harry and resist the oppressors until they are brought to their knees.

White South Africa has often been given the opportunity to align itself with progress. It has constantly refused to do so. It has sought only to build for itself on the backs of the people a comfortable bastion of profit, power and privilege.

ARM declares its fight not against the whites as such, but against the system they so jealously defend. ARM will avoid taking life for as long as possible. ARM would prefer to avoid bloodshed and terrorism. But let it be known that if we are forced to respond to personal violence—and we cannot forget decades of violence, torture, starvation and brutality against us—we shall do so.

For the present ARM will inconvenience and confuse. ARM will disrupt and destroy. ARM will strike where it hurts most. We will not cease until the present vicious system and rule by force is crushed. ARM does not wish to see one form of domination replaced by another. It works for a full political and social revolution.

To Verwoerd, Vorster and their men we say: you will NEVER stop the pulse of the new society which even now, beats in our factories and cities, our mines and farms—and YOU KNOW IT.

To the people of South Africa, we say:

ARM NOW FOR FREEDOM

Document 7. Speech from the dock by Bram Fischer, March 28, 1966 (abridged)

I am on trial for my political beliefs and for the conduct to which those beliefs drove me. Whatever labels may be attached to the fifteen charges brought against me, they all arise from my having been a member of the Communist Party and from my activities as a member. I engaged upon those activities because I believed that, in the dangerous circumstances which have been created in South Africa, it was my duty to do so. . . .

My first duty then is to explain to the Court that I hold and have for many years held the view that politics can only be properly understood and that our immediate political problems can only be satisfactorily solved by the application of that scientific system of political knowledge known as Marxism. . . .

When I consider what it was that moved me to join the Communist Party, I have to cast my mind back for more than a quarter of a century. . . . [T]here remain two clear reasons for my approach to the Communist Party. The one is the glaring injustice which exists and has existed for a long time in South African society, the other, a gradual realisation as I became more and more deeply involved with the Congress Movement of those years, that is, the movement for freedom and equal human rights for all, that it was always members of the Communist Party who seemed prepared, regardless of cost, to sacrifice most; to give of their best, to face the greatest dangers, in the struggle against poverty and discrimination. . . .

Though nearly forty years have passed, I can remember vividly the experience which brought home to me exactly what this "White" attitude is and also how artificial and unreal it is. Like many young Afrikaners I grew up on a farm. Between the ages of eight and twelve my daily companions were two young Africans of my own age. I can still remember their names. For four years we were, when I was not at school, always in each other's company. We roamed the farm together, we hunted and played together, we modelled clay oxen and swam. And never can I remember that the colour of our skins affected our fun, or our quarrels or our close friendship in any way.

Then my family moved to town and I moved back to the normal White South African mode of life where the only relationship with Africans was that of master to servant. I finished my schooling and went to university. There one of my first interests became a study of the theory of segregation, then beginning to blossom. This seemed to me to provide the solution to South

Africa's problems, and I became an earnest believer in it. A year later to help in a small way to put this theory into practice, because I do not believe that theory and practice can or should be separated, I joined the Bloemfontein Joint Council of Europeans and Africans, a body devoted largely to trying to induce various authorities to provide proper (and separate) amenities for Africans. I arrived for my first meeting with other newcomers. I found myself being introduced to leading members of the African community. I found I had to shake hands with them. This, I found, required an enormous effort of will on my part. Could I really, as a White adult, touch the hand of a black man in friendship?

That night I spent many hours in thought trying to account for my strange revulsion when I remembered I had never had any such feelings toward my boyhood friends. What became abundantly clear was that it was I and not the black man who had changed, that despite my growing interest in him, I had developed an antagonism for which I could find no rational basis whatsoever.

I cannot burden the Court with personal reminiscences. The result of all this was that in that and in succeeding years when some of us ran literacy classes in the old Waaihoek location at Bloemfontein, I came to understand that colour prejudice was a wholly irrational phenomenon and that true human friendship could extend across the colour bar once the initial prejudice was overcome. And that I think was lesson No. 1 on my way to the Communist Party, which has always refused to accept any colour bar and has always stood firm on the belief, itself two thousand years old, of the eventual brotherhood of all men.

. . . [the Communist Party's] White members were, save for a handful of courageous individuals, the only Whites who showed complete disregard for the hatred which this attitude attracted from their fellow White South Africans. These members, I found, were Whites who could have taken full advantage of all the privileges open to them and their families because of their colour, who could have obtained lucrative employment and social position, but who, instead, were prepared for the sake of their consciences to perform the most menial and unpopular work at little or sometimes no remuneration. These were a body of Whites who were not prepared to flourish on the deprivations suffered by others.

But apart from the example of the White members, it was always the communists of all races who were at all times prepared to give of their time and energy and such means as they had, to help those in need and those most deeply affected by discrimination. . . . The Court will bear in mind that at that stage, and for many years afterwards, the Communist Party was the only political party which stood for an extension of the franchise. . . .

But I have to tell this Court not only why I joined the Communist Party when it was a legal party—when at times it had representatives in Parliament, the Cape Provincial Council and the City Council of Johannesburg. I must also explain why I continued to be a member after it was declared illegal. . . .

[D]uring the past fifteen years or more . . . [compelling reasons have] led many thousands of South African citizens, including many of the country's kindliest and wisest and, in normal circumstances, most law-abiding citizens, to transgress against unjust laws.

My own case is but a single one which illustrates to what our laws have driven such widely different persons as: Chief Luthuli, Nelson Mandela, Robert Sobukwe, Dr. G. M. Naicker, Nana Sita, Hugh Lewin, Jean Middleton, Alan Brooks and thousands of others, young and old, men and women. . . .

The last subject I want to mention is personal. Therefore I hesitated before deciding to do so. But I shall not be giving evidence or making a statement in mitigation and perhaps I should acquaint the Court with one aspect of my background.

I was a Nationalist at the age of six, if not before. . . . I remained a Nationalist for over twenty years thereafter and became, in 1929, the first Nationalist Prime Minister of a student parliament.

I never doubted that the policy of segregation was the only solution to this country's problems until the Hitler theory of race superiority began to threaten the world with genocide and with the greatest disaster in all history. The Court will see that I did not shed my old ideas with ease.

It was when these doubts arose that one night, when I was driving an old ANC leader to his house far out to the west of Johannesburg that I propounded to him the well worn theory that if you separate races you diminish the points at which friction between them may occur and hence ensure good relations. His answer was the essence of simplicity. If you place the races of one country in two camps, said he, and cut off contact between them, those in each camp begin to forget that those in the other are ordinary human beings, that each lives and laughs in the same way, that each experiences joy or sorrow, pride or humiliation for the same reasons. Thereby each becomes suspicious of the other and each eventually fears the other, which is the basis of all racialism. . . .

All the conduct with which I have been charged has been directed towards maintaining contact and understanding between the races of this country. If one day it may help to establish a bridge across which White leaders and the real leaders of the non-Whites can meet to settle the destinies of all of us by negotiation and not by force of arms, I shall be able to bear with fortitude any sentence which this Court may impose on me. It will be a fortitude strengthened by this knowledge at least, that for twenty-five years I have taken no part, not even by passive acceptance, in that hideous system of discrimination which we have erected in this country and which has become a by-word in the civilised world today.

In prophetic words, in February 1881, one of the great Afrikaner leaders addressed the President and Volksraad of the Orange Free State.

His words are inscribed on the base of the statue of President Kruger in the square in front of this Court. After great agony and suffering after two wars they were eventually fulfilled without force or violence for my people.

President Kruger's words were:

Met vertrouwen leggen wij onze zaak open voor de geheele wereld. Het zif wij overwinnen, het zij wij sterven: de vrijheid zal in Afrika rijzen als de zon uit de morgenwolken. [With confidence we place our case before the entire world. Whether we are victorious or whether we die, freedom will arise in Africa like the sun from the morning clouds.]

In the meaning which those words bear today they are as truly prophetic as they were in 1881. My motive in all that I have done has been to prevent a repetition of that unnecessary and futile anguish which has already been suffered in one struggle for freedom.

Document 8. Statement of dissolution of the South African Coloured People's Congress, by Barney Desai and Cardiff Marney, London, March 1966 (abridged)

For 13 proud years of its existence on the South African political scene the Coloured People's Congress has struggled with uncompromising militancy and grim determination against white supremacy. Our Congress was established to develop the political consciousness of the 1.7 million people of so-called mixed race, to combat racialism amongst them and to link their struggle with the general movement for democracy of the oppressed as a whole. It has always been our belief that the destiny of the coloured Africans is indissolubly bound up with the oppressed black Africans and that there should finally be a unified organisation, cutting across race lines, representing all the enslaved masses of our country. . . .

It has previously been widely held that sectional organisations representing exclusive group interests of the different "races" were the best vehicles to weld all the oppressed masses into the national liberatory fold. Historical differences and administrative convenience or difficulties were the reasons advanced by those who wished to develop the race organisations as units of the broader movement. Joint struggles against white tyranny and imperialist exploitation, it was contended, would bring about unity at the lowest level and in turn generate moves towards a unified mass organisation. This was the aim of the Congress Alliance, which was a confederation of racial organisations: the African National Congress (a mass organisation of black Africans); the South African Indian Congress (the movement of Africans of Indian descent); the South African Coloured People's Congress (for coloured Africans); the Congress of Democrats (representing the white Africans) and the non-racial South African Congress of Trade Unions.

Noteworthy as this experiment was, it failed. It multiplied racialism and entrenched it in the sectional organisations. It led to a monumental betrayal of the best interests of the enslaved masses. Our Congress now feel duty bound to reveal to the people that when, in 1962, the CPC proposed to the African National Congress (as the major mass organisation in the Alliance) that it should open its doors for all the oppressed groups and that in return the Coloured People's Congress would dissolve, the proposal was flatly rejected and the ANC leadership unashamedly announced that it could no longer meet with the other Congresses for joint consultation as was the practice in the past.

Since that time ANC leadership have used the fiction of a Congress Alliance as a matter of political expediency. None the less, the CPC has over the past three years patiently reasoned with the ANC leadership, pointing out that their sectional stand presented a grave danger to the best interests of our struggle and helped to strengthen racialism. . . . Not only have we been rebuffed in our efforts but we have had to witness the external leadership of the ANC conduct a campaign of slander and disruption against the CPC leadership.

In a recent statement the ANC leadership made the remarkable assertion that they alone as black Africans, can take decisions on behalf of the African people. This is nothing less than inverted Verwoerdian reasoning. As if the Khoi-Khoi (Hottentots) and the Batwa ("Bushmen") tribes as the forebears of the Cape Coloured people were not Africans who were virtually exterminated in the first battles against the European invaders of South Africa 300 years ago. . . .

Months of careful and considered deliberations together with the accumulated experience of our past associations have convinced the Coloured People's Congress that a decisive break must be made with the past. We will nevertheless warmly cherish our comradeship with the rank and file of the African National Congress who, we are sure, will discover and deal with the treachery of their leadership who are now champions of multi-racialism and reformism. This is the time for boldness and foresight. Convinced that our actions represent a watershed in South African politics and that they must have the greatest influence on the future development of our common struggle, we therefore solemnly:

(1) Declare that the South African Coloured People's Congress is dissolved;

(2) Recognise the revolutionary character of the Pan Africanist Congress, and announce our acceptance of their comradely invitation to join the PAC as Africans and equals, dedicating ourselves to building up one nation and wage a single struggle against the common enemy of white supremacy and its foreign backers who have made our country their looting ground.

(3) Call on South African Coloureds and Indians numbering two and a half million enslaved people to follow our example by becoming members of the dynamic Pan Africanist Congress, and for all time bury their racial tags.

(4) Brand those who would continue sectional and racialist activity as enemies and traitors to the cause of our liberation; and

(5) Affirm our determination to uphold the noble ideal of a non-racial socialist democracy in our beloved country.

Issued on behalf of the South African Coloured People's Congress by: Barney Desai, President, S. A. Coloured Peoples Congress; Former Chairman, Transvaal Indian Youth Congress; Former Executive Member, Transvaal Indian Congress; Former Councillor of the City of Cape Town. Cardiff Marney, Chairman, S. A. Coloured People's Congress; Former Secretary, Cape Town Municipal Workers' Union.

DOCUMENT 9. "The Duty of a Communist in the National Liberation Army—Umkhonto we Sizwe." Internal memo by the SACP Central Committee, 1967

The Central Committee of the South African Communist Party warmly greets all Communists who are taking part in the armed struggle for the liberation of our country.

For decades it has been a cardinal principle of the South African Communist Party, the revolutionary party of the working class, to support the struggle for freedom and democracy. For this reason our party has given primary importance to the building of a united front of National liberation centred around the African National Congress. In all the struggles of the past forty years and more, Communists in common with their non-communist colleagues have fought numerous campaigns against national oppression, racialism and exploitation. Communists believe that ultimately the whole world including South Africa will become a communist society in which classes and exploitation have been abolished and all human beings enjoy complete equality in all spheres of life. But the task of building such a society cannot even begin until the people are free from national oppression and the system of white minority rule is smashed. The paramount duty of the South African Communist Party today is to participate in and support the struggle for freedom in our country whose main content is the freedom of the African people. This struggle has now entered the new phase of armed revolutionary war.

When Umkhonto was established, Communists readily joined the national army at the behest of the Party. Now fighting is raging in Zimbabwe and no doubt soon the masses in South Africa will be engaged in revolutionary armed struggle. In these circumstances it becomes necessary to spell out clearly the duty of all communists in the liberation army and in propaganda work among the masses.

1. It is the duty of Communists in Umkhonto we Sizwe to be an example of devotion and loyalty to the military command of Umkhonto we Sizwe and the political leadership of the African National Congress.

2. It is the duty of Communists to set an example of hard work and zeal in the performance of their duties in the army and always to be the first to volunteer for the most difficult tasks.

3. Communists must constantly raise the level of their political consciousness through study of the latest developments in South Africa and abroad. Such knowledge must be shared with all freedom fighters in a spirit of humility. On no account must Communists give the impression of "knowing everything." Communists must always be willing to learn from others as well as teach them.

4. Communists wherever they are represent the high ideals of Communism and the liberation of all mankind from the bonds of oppression. Therefore it is the duty of Communists strenuously to oppose all direct or indirect manifestations of racialism, tribalism or narrow nationalism. Communists will always defend the unity of the revolutionary forces both communist and non-communist and espouse the progressive nationalism of the African National Congress as enshrined in the Freedom Charter. Any person who puts forward tribalist, racialist or other ideas that produce confusion and division is not a Communist.

5. In the course of the struggle the best elements, that is, those that are most far-sighted, resolute and determined in the fight for liberation and social progress are always drawn to the Communist Party. Communists do not consider that leadership consists in competing for positions in the national movement, still less by engaging in intrigues. But by reason of their devotion to duty and work and also by their political understanding of the needs of the movement they gain the confidence of the nation. This process applies in the South African Revolution.

6. Revolutionary struggle is not an invitation to a picnic. All Communists must therefore make it part of their duty to instil the spirit of sacrifice wherever they are; to inspire the freedom fighters in the periods of difficulty; to constantly emphasize that the victory of the revolution is inevitable. Communists must vigorously combat any inferiority complex or spirit of despair or cynicism among freedom fighters.

7. Our party is a party of the oppressed worker and poor peasant. Our members must always set an example of devotion to the people and respect for their interests and traditions. In our political work and personal conduct we must always seek to win the masses by persuasion and example. There is no duty nobler than the fight for the liberation of the masses. This noble fight must not be sullied by arrogance and immoral behaviour such as theft of property; molesting of women or drunkenness which would lower the prestige of the movement and also endanger its security.

8. Communists fight for the unity of the revolutionary forces and liberation movements of Southern Africa and throughout our continent. We are internationalist and it is the duty of Communists always to spread knowledge and act in solidarity with the struggles of people in other parts of the world against imperialism for freedom and independence, for peace and socialism. The value and meaning of international solidarity must be constantly placed before the eyes of the freedom fighters and the masses of the people.

DOCUMENT 10. "The Wankie Campaign." Article by Chris Hani, *Dawn: Journal of Umkhonto we Sizwe*, Souvenir Issue, 1986 (abridged)

The Luthuli Detachment was one [of] those detachments that were well prepared and well trained. I'm saying this because I personally participated in the preparations. A lot of time was allocated for the detachment to be together in the bush to be able to train together in order to ensure that physically we were ready for the rigorous task that lay ahead. But in addition to the physical preparation there was also the political preparation, the need for us to forge an understanding between the forces of Umkhonto we Sizwe and the forces of ZAPU and to understand the historical necessity of the battles of Wankie. . . .

When we began the process of crossing, we were ready for anything, and the spirit of MK combatants was very high. The crossing point was not an easy one, it was a place which was quite rocky and the current of the Zambezi was strong. But these seeming obstacles and difficulties did not deter us at all. After crossing the river, there was a spirit of elation and joy, due to the fact that we had already crossed the first obstacle, mainly the river, and we were now all looking forward to participating in the long march deep into Zimbabwe and ultimately reaching our destination, South Africa.

The spirit of cohesion and unity between ourselves and ZAPU was magnificent. We were working together as one unit, consulting and discussing together. There was no friction whatsoever within this unit. . . .

From the very beginning we began to notice that we were not at all conversant with the terrain across the river. For instance, moving away from the Zambezi river we had expected to come across streams and rivulets with water, but as soon as we moved a few kilometres from the Zambezi river we realised that it was quite a dry area. There were no rivers, no streams, and people were getting water from boreholes. So this problem of no rivers necessitated an earlier contact with the people. . . .

Secondly, we were beginning to run low on food supplies. So again we had to contact the people. It is important in all military preparations, whatever military strategy is worked out, to emphasise the need to contact people. But it is dangerous to contact the people at random and that is what we were forced to do. . . .

But in all fairness when we established this contact we were met with enthusiasm by the people. We were given water and even fresh supplies of food. This was very useful and enabled us to continue for a few days marching towards the South of Zimbabwe. Within the game reserve of Wankie a decision had been taken by our H. Q. in Lusaka that the unit had to split into two. There was the unit that had to move towards the east, towards an area called Lupane, and there was also the main unit which had to march towards the South.

Within the unit moving towards the South was quite a substantial number of those comrades whose mission was eventually to reach South Africa and establish MK units within the country. In the unit moving towards the South with the eventual aim of getting to South Africa were comrades Lennox Lagu, myself, Peter Mfene, Douglas Wana, Mbijana, the late Victor Dlamini, Castro, Mashigo (the ANC Chief Representative to Lusaka), Paul Sithole, Desmond, Wilson Msweli, Shooter Makasi, Eric Nduna, Basil February and James April. Lennox was the most senior in our group. I was the group's commissar.

The unit marching towards the East was to base in Zimbabwe, the aim being to establish an MK presence in Zimbabwe which could be used in future to service MK combatants passing through Zimbabwe. In other words, the whole concept of the Wankie campaign was to build bridges, a Ho Chi Minh trail to South Africa. . . .

They made contact with the enemy quite early, about two weeks after we had parted. One of the battles they were engaged in will probably go down in the history of MK military operations as one of the most heroic. . . . So this caught them [the Pretoria regime] by surprise, and there was so much panic that immediately after this, the regime in Pretoria dispatched more troops to Zimbabwe to fight the Luthuli Detachment.

A big battle was now looming on Zimbabwean soil, not just between the settler forces of Ian Smith but the combined forces of Smith and the SADF [South African Defense Force]. We noticed after three to four weeks of our presence in Zimbabwe that there was a lot of aerial reconnaissance by the enemy. . . . We were sure that it was only a matter of days before we would have to engage the enemy.

But interestingly enough there was a spirit of looking forward to battle with the enemy. . . . We had undergone very serious training in the Soviet Union and other places and had always looked forward to this historical engagement between ourselves and the forces of the enemy. . . . [T]here is nothing [so] scintillating and stimulating to a soldier as to test his whole reactions in actual battle, your responses when you are under fire. . . .

There were reasons why we moved mostly at night. We discovered once again that the terrain was very bad. It was empty, with no cover except for shrubs, especially as we moved deeper into Zimbabwe towards Matebeleland. . . . During the day we took cover, dug foxholes and trenches in preparation for any possible engagement with the enemy and used the cover of darkness to cover as much ground as possible in our march towards the South. But again I want to point out that I as a Commissar found the spirit of the men quite magnificent. . . . We could only survive on game meat and that was also risky. Shooting and killing wild animals was a way of signalling to the enemy and his agents that we were around. Yet there were no alternatives. . . .

I think the biggest legacy of the Luthuli Detachment at Wankie was the sort of absolute commitment of our fighters to the revolution to an extent where to them things like hunger and thirst were not primary. . . .

Then came the days of our battles. The first battle we fought was in the afternoon. . . . we noticed that the enemy was not far from us. We had detected the motorised enemy earlier. The vehicles were visible from a distance. Since it was during the day we deliberately refrained from engaging the enemy at that particular point in time. But it was quite clear that the enemy also noticed that we were around. . . . In the afternoon the enemy moved into the offensive by firing at random at the sector where we had taken position.

We had decided earlier on that each and everyone ought to be very economic with the ammunition he had due to the fact that we did not have access to enough ammunition except what we were carrying. . . .

So the usual psychological war of the enemy of firing furiously at our sector continued coupled with shouting and calling on us to surrender. From the very beginning during the course of our preparations we had made it clear amongst ourselves that surrender was out of the question. We were not going to fire back unless we had a clear view of the enemy. The enemy got impatient. They stood up and began to ask "Where are the terrorists?" This was when there was a fusillade of furious fire from us. That fusillade, the furious nature of that reply, drove away the enemy. They simply ran for their dear lives leaving behind food, ammunition and communication equipment. In this first epic battle we lost three comrades: Charles Seshoba, Sparks Moloi and Baloi—one comrade Mhlonga was wounded. On the side of the enemy we must have killed between 12 to 15, including a lieutenant, a Sergeant-Major, a Warrant Officer and a number of other soldiers. The rest literally ran helter-skelter for their lives. One memorable thing about that encounter was the fact that this was the first time that we had what I can call a civilised meal, cheese, biltong, meat and other usual rations carried by the regular army. For us this represented a feast. So it was a good capture. We also captured a brand new LMG, some machine guns, uniforms and boots.

It was a memorable victory and to every soldier victory is very important. This was a virgin victory for us since we had never fought with modern weapons against the enemy. For us that day was a day of celebrations because with our own eyes we had seen the enemy run. We had seen the enemy frozen with fear. That lifted our spirits and transformed us into a fighting force. We had also seen and observed each other reacting to the enemy's attacks. A feeling of faith in one another and recognition of the courage of the unit developed.

This was important and we knew from then on there was no going back. . . . We moved on after having that fantastic feast. We proceeded because it could have been dangerous just to celebrate and wait there. We knew the enemy was going to organise re-inforcements. . . .

We were running short of food, there was no water and our uniforms were tattered. There was not even rivers where we could have a decent bath. But again this has to be taken in its proper perspective. Despite these difficulties basically our morale was not affected. There were days after that when the enemy was quite fanatic in its aerial reconnaissance.

A week after this battle there was another one. . . . the enemy had carried out furious bombardment not far from us using Buccaneers and helicopters. But fortunately for us the bombing and strafing was about two kilometers away. . . .

The commander of the joint MK-ZAPU Detachment took the decision that this was the time to raid the enemy. We organised units to go and raid the enemy. I was in that together with James April, Douglas Wana, the late Jack Simelane, Victor Dlamini and others. We crawled towards the enemy's position and first attacked their tents with grenades and then followed with our AKs [AK-47 guns] and LMGs. The enemy fought back furiously and after fifteen minutes we called for reinforcements from the rear, and within ten minutes we overran the enemy's position. In that battle we killed the enemy's colonel who was commanding. His name was Thomas, a huge chunk of a man wearing size 10 boots. We killed a few lieutenants and other soldiers.

The story was the same as in our previous battle. The enemy fled leaving behind supplies, weapons, grenades, uniforms and communication radios. Another victory for our detachment. I want to emphasise the question of victory because the Luthuli Detachment was never defeated in battle.

Our supplies became depleted and we were moving to a barren part of Zimbabwe. We decided that it would be futile to continue fighting because the enemy was bringing in more reinforcement. So we deliberately took a decision to retreat to Botswana. The aim of this decision is important to emphasise. This was no surrender to the paramilitary units of Botswana government. It was important for us to retreat to strategic parts of Botswana, refresh ourselves, heal those who were not well, acquire food supplies and proceed. We then crossed over to Botswana. But by this time the South African regime had pressurised the Botswana government to prevent us from getting into Botswana. We found a situation where the Rhodesian security forces joined by the South Africans were pursuing us, and within Botswana the para-military force had been mobilised to stop us from entering Botswana.

We had to discuss seriously what our response was going to be if the Botswana security forces confronted us. It was difficult to reach a decision, it was really a dilemma. Botswana is a member of the OAU, and in theory it is committed to the struggle for the liberation of South Africa. So Botswana does not constitute an enemy of the liberation movement, an enemy of ZAPU and the ANC. We came to the correct political decision that we were not going to fight them. When they came to meet us they played very conciliatory and friendly, saying that they had not come to harm us. They said their instructions were not to engage us and that all they wanted was that we surrender and our fate would be discussed amicably. They also promised that we would not be detained. We accepted the bonafides and surrendered, only to discover that they were actually being commanded by white officers from Britain and South Africa. This caused problems for us.

All of a sudden we were manacled, hand-cuffed and abused. Of course all this is history now. We were sentenced to long terms of imprisonment: 3, 5 to six years and ended up in the maximum security prison in Gaborone. . . .

Document 11. Transcription of ANC Radio Freedom broadcast, 1969?

VOICE: This is the African National Congress. This is the African National Congress. This is the Voice of Freedom. The ANC speaks to you! Afrika! Afrika! Mayibuye!

SINGING OF THE NATIONAL ANTHEM (NKOSI SIKELELE AFRIKA AND MORENA BOLOKA)

VOICE: The time has come. This Government of slavery, this Government of oppression, this Apartheid monster must be removed from power and crushed by the People! It must be removed by force! They will never stop the pass raids, the arrests, the beatings, the killings—they will continue to drive us out of our homes like dogs and send us to rot in the so-called Bantu homelands, they will continue to pay us miserable wages, and treat us as their beasts of burden until the day we beat them up and crush white rule! This land of ours was taken away by bloodshed, we will regain it by bloodshed. Sons and daughters of Afrika, you in your millions who have toiled to make this country rich, the ANC calls upon you: Never submit to white oppression; never give up the Freedom struggle; find ways of organising those around you—the African National Congress calls you to be ready—to be ready for war! You will soon learn how to make a petrol bomb. You will also learn how to shoot a gun. You must learn how to outwit the enemy, his spies and informers, and organise those around you. We are many, they are few. Our Coloured and Indian brothers must do the same. You must organise your people to fight the ghettoes and all the racial laws and in support of the armed struggle. We say to the enemy that we will not be bluffed by your toy parliaments like Matanzima's, like the Coloured Council and like the Indian Council. We want Freedom now! REAL FREE-DOM! But the whites will not give it to us. We have to take it. We have to take it by violence. We fight a guerrilla war. A guerrilla war is not a war of big armies. We have no big army. We organise ourselves into small groups. We attack the enemy suddenly when he is not expecting us. We kill them and take their guns and we disappear. Our brave young men have shown the way in their heroic battles in Rhodesia. Today they fight in Rhodesia, tomorrow they will fight in South Africa. All over the young men are showing the way. They are fighting the white racist armies in Angola, in Mozambique, in Rhodesia. The African National Congress calls upon you to prepare for the guerrilla war, the war of liberation. The ANC calls upon you to help our young men, our freedom fighters. We organise ourselves into small groups, we carry guns, suddenly we attack the enemy, we kill them and we take their weapons and we hide away—the forests, the mountains, the countryside, the People—hide the young men. Every one of you can help in this fight. Everyone can be a freedom fighter. In your factory, in your school, on the land, in your church, wherever you are amongst the People—you must find a way of organising those around you. If you work carefully you will be able to cheat the enemy and his spies and informers. You must be prepared. You must be ready to sacrifice. We refuse to live on our knees. We refuse to say "Ja Baas." We must prepare to rise against the white oppressor. Nelson Mandela said he was prepared to die for the freedom of our People. What do you say, my dear young brother, my dear young sister? Sons of Sekhukuni, Sons of Shaka, Sons of Hintsa, Sons of Moshoeshoe—the time

has come. Freedom lovers of South Africa, the time to fight has come. This is the message the African National Congress brings to you. You will soon learn how to make a petrol bomb. You will also learn how to shoot a gun. You must learn how to outwit the enemy and organise those around you. The enemy fears our organised might. We are many, the whites are few. We must find ways to organise our people. They pay us low wages because our skins are black, whilst the whites live in luxury. At work, in the factories, the mines, the docks, the offices, the kitchens, the fields, the railways, the roads, we demand equal pay for equal work NOW! They charge us high rents, high taxes, high fares on the trains and buses, we must organise in the townships, and in the streets and on the buses, we must demand a better life NOW! They give our children inferior education. We demand proper education that will enable our young people to be equal to other young people in the world. Our young people must be taught how to fly jet aeroplanes and how to fly the sputniks. In the schools, our young people must organise to resist Bantu Education. We demand free and equal education for all our children NOW! The whites have taken away the land of our people in the countryside, and have forced them to give up their cattle. We must resist the Matanzima stooges, we must resist the Bantu Authorities Act in the countryside. We want our land back. Our young men with guns will fight for it in the countryside. They will deal with the stooges and informers, the police and the white soldiers. Our people in the countryside must be told of their coming. They must hide and feed our freedom fighters, they must make their path easy and the enemy's path hard. The African National Congress calls upon our people to prepare for guerrilla warfare, the People's War of Liberation, NOW! Guerrilla war has brought victory to the people of Algeria, to the people of Cuba, to the people of Vietnam. Those people did not have big armies. They were like us. Guerrilla fighters organise themselves in small groups. Suddenly when the enemy is not expecting them, they attack. They kill and grab the guns and disappear. You sons and daughters of the soil, you must consider yourselves as soldiers in the guerrilla war. There are many ways to be a freedom fighter. You will soon learn how to make a petrol bomb. You will also learn how to shoot a gun. You must learn how to outwit the enemy and organise those around you. We are many, they are few. The African National Congress calls on all the oppressed people to organise and struggle and prepare to fight in the towns and countryside. Our brave men of Umkonto we Sizwe have shown the way. They fought heroically in Zimbabwe. They will fight in South Africa. You must start to find places where you can hide the weapons you might come across. You must have secret addresses of your reliable friends who will agree to hide you or your weapons or other freedom fighters. You must be ready to sacrifice. You must start now to find hiding places. The countryside, the bush, the forest, the mountain—these will also become your secret addresses. The time has come. The African National Congress calls upon you to organise and to prepare. Death to racialism! Mayibuy' Afrika! Amandla!
Ke Naka. Zemk' inkomo magwala ndini!

Ayi Hlome!

[Now is the time. The cattle are being stolen, you cowards! Be armed!]

SINGING OF FREEDOM SONGS.

DOCUMENT 12. "Report on Talks between the PAC and the OAU Liberation Committee Sub-committee" by Potlako K. Leballo, Dar es Salaam, November 20, 1968

At their 13th Ordinary session in Algiers, last July, the OAU Committee of Eleven adopted the following resolution regarding the Pan Africanist Congress:

"The Committee decided to suspend the assistance granted to the P. A. C. until such time that the Standing Committee on Information, Administration and General Policy *becomes fully satisfied that unity has been restored to the Movement*. (Their emphasis). In the meantime, Tanzania and Zambia, with the assistance of the Executive Secretary (ALC), were called upon to exert their influence to bring about unity in the Movement. The Standing Committee was requested to consider and report whether the suspension of assistance would be an effective means of exerting pressure on Liberation Movements to maintain unity within their ranks."

In terms of the above decisions the sub-Committee called a reconciliation meeting at the Headquarters of the African Liberation Committee, in Dar es Salaam, on November 12, 1968. At these talks the Party was represented by the Acting President, Mr. Potlako K. Leballo, and five other leading officials: Messrs. T. M. Ntantala, Member of the N. E. C. and Vice Chairman of the Revolutionary Command; David M. Sibeko, Elias L. Ntloedibe and Nimrod N. Sejake, of the Foreign Affairs and Information Secretariat and S. B. M. Mehlomakhulu, Chief Representative in Dar es Salaam.

The dissidents had [Tsepo] Letlaka, [Z. B.] Molete, [Peter] Raboroko and [A. B.] Ngcobo representing them. It was assumed that they also spoke on behalf of [Nana] Mahomo, [J. D.] Nyaose and [Peter] Molotsi, their partners in the abortive coup against the Party leadership, last June. Though Molotsi virtually denounced the coup before the ALC in Algiers, he has not maintained contact with the External Mission Headquarters since.

We are enclosing cuttings that cover the opening remarks by the Chairman of the sub-Committee whose speech was extempory. We must stress, however, that as from scratch he laid emphasis on the fact that the Committee was intent on emerging from the talks with concrete results. He made it clear that the OAU was prepared to support only those movements that operate effectively within their territories [words missing] and equally determined revolutionaries.

On November 13, the following day, the talks were continued behind closed doors at the TANU [Tanganyika African National Union] Parliament Buildings, which include the Speaker's Office (National Assembly), where the dissidents were given the first opportunity to present their case. They were in session from 10 a.m. to 2.30 p.m. and were recalled to another session which lasted from 5 p.m. to 8 p.m.

The following day the Acting President and his colleagues were called in and in one hour, acting as the Party's chief spokesman, the Acting President thoroughly exposed the counter-revolutionary role of the dissidents and made a satisfactory expose on home-front activity and co-ordination between National Headquarters, the underground cells and the External Mission. He also explained how the counter-revolutionary activities of the dissidents had hampered the Party's work.

Lies quashed

The Acting President's delivery was followed by close questioning from members of the Committee. It became apparent that the dissidents had concentrated their presentation on making scurrilous attacks on the person of the Acting President and attempted to use their personal hatred for him as a scapegoat for their anti-Party activities and non-participation in the revolution. The lies were quashed and further evidence was produced to prove their nefarious intentions. Their political bankruptcy was further exposed when they brought up their usual diatribe and putrid allegation, which was the cornerstone of their case, that I am not a South African; it turned them into a laughing-stock—particularly when we showed documentary evidence that Ngcobo himself was born outside the Republic.

At the end of our presentations the Committee expressed satisfaction with the manner in which we presented the Party's case and the co-operation we were ready to extend at all times.

The Committee then suggested a formula for joint talks between the renegades and the Party's official delegation and offered to submit proposals on how the renegades could possibly be rehabilitated and integrated into the Party. Since the formula did not in any way interfere with the status quo ante prior to the factionalist June meeting of the dissidents, the Party's delegation accepted it. It was agreed that our guideline would be the Moshi decisions, mainly: a) Acceptance of the leadership of the Acting President; b) Recognition of Maseru as the National Headquarters of the Party; c) and acceptance of the Revolutionary Command as the body charged with carrying out the day to day functions of the Organisation. Fortunately the Executive Secretary had participated in the Moshi meeting of the NEC and could testify that during that meeting the same dissidents had unanimously confirmed the above positions and that they had accepted without reservations the Party's general line on the waging of a people's war, as outlined in the Acting President's "Call to the Nation."

The dissidents rejected the proposals but after some persuasion by members of the Committee they made as if to agree. This was on November 14. The following day, however, they came back and threw the proposals out of the window; their arrogance roundly angered members of the Committee. Even at this stage it had become crystal clear as to whose interests the dissidents serve. At the end of the day the Party's delegation was called in and thanked very passionately for the co-operation it had shown throughout its appearances before the Committee. The Chairman reiterated that their mandate was to ensure that the revolution does not suffer and imparted it to us that the dissidents had been given the rest of the day during which to reconsider their stand and that the following day a joint and final session was being called at 10 a.m., back at the ALC headquarters.

Once more the dissidents confronted the Committee with a memorandum (we must point out that though the dissidents brought three loads of memorandums our side gave direct evidence, supplemented by a few documents for the purpose of substantiating the Party's case). In this new one they accused the Committee of "echoing Leballo's demand that they renounce the New Palace [Hotel] talks" and that for this reason they found it "impossible to accept the proposals."

Shall not shack [shirk] responsibilities

The new Minister of State for Foreign Affairs, Mr. Stephen Mhando, MP, had reinforced the Tanzanian delegation that morning. He made a passionate appeal to the dissidents to see the light and put the interests of the struggle before self. He assured the meeting that he would not shack [shirk] his responsibilities, if by that afternoon, sense had not prevailed and the dissidents remained adamant they were making [*sic*] on behalf of Africa and the Organisation of African Unity. The dissidents were unimpressed. The Committee had done more than it could and in his final address the Executive Secretary said it was a pity that all their efforts had not achieved the desired unity. He stressed, however, that the meeting had been quite a success because now they knew who the freedom fighters were; the meeting had helped them to identify freedom fighters and this would in future extend to all liberation movements. He promised that the Party's revolutionaries would not be let down and that as for those that had sabotaged the efforts of the Governments of Zambia and Tanzania and the OAU Liberation Committee, they left him with no alternative but to perform his duty, "in the interests of the African revolution . . . and I will act, no matter how unpalatable the action we take might be." The OAU was not interested in supporting international tourists, he concluded.

Dissidents detained.

The meeting rose, at 11.30 a.m. At about 1 p.m. Letlaka, Molete, Raboroko and Ngcobo were collected and put into detention. Their fate is now in the hands of the U. N. High Commissioner for Refugees; he must find a country that must accept them as refugees and not Freedom Fighters. The OAU will not allow them to use an inch of African territory for their anti-Party activities.

It has been disclosed that they have fat banking accounts, both in Zambia and this country. Letlaka is reported to have something in the region of £26,000 and Ngcobo £2,000 or so. During their stay here they kept very close contact with the U. S. Embassy and produced their memorandums there and at the USIS [US Information Service].

Nyaose is still in Nairobi where he occasionally issues a barrage against Tanzania and the African Liberation Committee for refusing to endorse their counter revolution; he too may get it in the neck soon.

Conclusion

The sub-Committee is to submit the report of its findings to the 14th ordinary session of the Committee of Eleven in Dakar, on January 15, next year. With the full support of External Offices and the National Headquarters we shall be able to emerge victorious even there. We expect that the ANC will make an all out bid to get us de-recognised on the flimsy excuse that the Party is split but they will have a hard time.

The remnants of this dissident clique must be wiped out so that the best of our efforts can be geared towards making revolution for the success of the armed struggle in the Fatherland. All comrades are expected to play their part with diligency and honesty of purpose. We must not let down our supporters who, now that the spoilers have been removed from our ranks, expect us to forge ahead without hindrance. New directives will come out as soon as the External Mission Headquarters, the Revolutionary Command and National Headquarters have consulted fully.

IZWE LETHU!!! [Our Land!!!]

POTLAKO K. LEBALLO
Acting President &
National Secretary

DOCUMENT 13. "What Is Wrong?" Memorandum by Ben Turok before the ANC's Morogoro Conference, April 1969, and "Reply" by Joe Matthews (abridged)

Memorandum by Ben Turok:

The present discussion will be based largely on experiences in Dar es Salaam and on information obtained from other comrades from time to time. . . .

WHAT IS WRONG? . . . No one in the movement can be content with the present situation; all must be aware of a deepgoing malaise such as we have never known before. . . .

Theoretical. . . . one must point to the absence of discussion documents of any kind for a long period, and to the utter failure of our leadership to introduce a political line in the movement which could orientate it to our main tasks: the struggle at home. . . .

Political. . . . In Dar es Salaam practically no efforts have been made over a very long time to keep the membership informed of the work of the leadership. There have been no reports back from conferences, no formal reports on the fighting in Zimbabwe, no discussion of the difficulties around us. Instead, we seem to have been faced by bureaucracy, heavily entrenched in office, hostile to questions and tightlipped in extreme. . . .

Style of work. . . . Our officials have come to adopt authoritarian attitudes towards comrades in lower positions. . . . Evidence of maladministration is massive. . . . There have been a number of cases of cash embezzlement which are known to many of us. . . .

Drunkenness was at one time a major feature of our office in Dar es Salaam—day and night. Some comrades were drunk for days on end, and those who should have set an example were sometimes no better. There has been an improvement recently, but the intention here is not to point a finger, it is to comment on a style of work wholly out of keeping with a serious movement. . . . [L]eading personnel who visit Dar es Salaam for short periods often stay in a hotel. . . . the sight of leaders spending evening after evening in a bar is not one of which can bring credit to our movement. . . .

Mobilisation of rank and file. . . . Perhaps the most deplorable aspect of the work of the movement in Dar es Salaam is the treatment meted out to our military comrades. A number of officials working at political posts have openly shown the most appalling contempt for the army men, failing to exercise common courtesy let alone according them the honour they deserve. Our men in Mandela camp live in squalor. They sleep on the floor on thin mats, their building is in disrepair and there is every evidence of gross neglect. . . . Our men are volunteers, they live a dull, monotonous existence of waiting. . . . The camp itself badly needs a face-lift. It needs some decoration, some facilities for amusement, a flat or two, a proper library with up to date magazines, in short, it must be turned into a home for the sick and the homeless. At present it is a slum.

WHY THINGS ARE GOING WRONG

. . . [T]here can be no doubt but that everyone in the movement is deeply concerned with our frustrations in going home. No one can be happy in exile. . . . THERE IS NO GOING BACK OUTLOOK. While we must pay the highest tribute to the action of our immortal heroes of Zimbabwe battles, it is obvious that those actions could only be regarded as one of the steps necessary. If the great majority of our personnel spent most of their time on concentrated activity oriented around the question of going home, little of the weaknesses mentioned in part 1 above would have emerged. What is required is a total approach to this problem with exploration at every level, with constant practical training in all related fields, for the numerous problems that the act of going home will bring out. How many of our leaders can read a compass proficiently? How many can move comfortably at night? How many are physically fit? How many know elementary first aid? Once we ask these questions it becomes immediately apparent that there are many who do not have the appearance of suitability for going home. . . . [T]oo many of our people are no longer concerned with the problems of the struggle but rather with those of adjustment to life in exile. And the temptations are often great for a life of comparative security and ease.

It is often said that for an organisation to be healthy, the discrepancies between the elders and the rank and file ought not to be too great. Obviously leaders need peace of mind, some comfort, and facilities for quiet work. However, it ought to be constantly borne in mind that these requirements ought not to be an excuse for the emergence of an elite. . . . [T]here has been little elective democracy in our movement for well over a decade. . . . democracy must be seen to operate—the power of recall is basic to discipline and mutual respect between leaders and led. . . .

PROPOSALS AND CONCLUSIONS

Immediate Tasks. Since an atmosphere of crisis prevails in our ranks at present it is necessary to take such concrete remedial action as will ease off the tension. The most helpful way this could be done is by a large scale planning operation centred around the problems of "going home". . . .

The most dynamic, imaginative and experienced personnel in the movement must be drawn into a special planning council to examine every aspect and every possibility. They will have to study all possible routes: land, sea and even perhaps air, in order that no possibility is missed. . . .

[W]hat is wanted is a vast network bearing vital information to the centre of operational planning and carrying instructions and suggestions for investigation outwards. . . .

Part of the work of this planning council should be the setting up of highly specialised training schools where our personnel are put through carefully prepared courses in the kind of activities they will be engaged in on return. . . .

Organisational. . . . In sum, it is suggested that comrades of all races be admitted to full membership of the ANC outside South Africa, on the condition that African comrades predominate and are seen to predominate on all committees and in the general work of the organisation.. . . .

Report Back. Regular report back conferences to check up on work planned ought to be held every few months. Leaders should give an account of their work and subject themselves to scrutiny. The replacement of tired leaders or those who have failed in their duties ought to be given attention regularly. Machinery for the election of replacements must be developed.

CONCLUSION

There is a great deal more to be said if our struggle is to rise to the heights of former days. We have a proud history of political struggle, and the heroes of Zimbabwe have blazed a new path of military action. It is up to those of us who are now lying relatively immobilised in exile to take up with new resolve the fight to free South Africa. There is no more noble task before mankind today.

Reply (unsigned) by Joe Matthews:

The Preparatory Committee has had an opportunity to study the document submitted by Comrade Turok which was found very interesting and illuminating. . . .

We note that the document begins by admitting a lack of information except such as has been gained in Dar es Salaam or from hearsay. It should be remarked that in the circumstances a great deal of caution would be required in drawing any general conclusions from such a limited experience.

Everyone in the movement is aware of the fact that the movement is in many ways going through a very difficult period. . . .

Much of the running around or "globe trotting" was devoted to arranging for training in various countries; collecting weapons; obtaining funds; persuading governments to allow camps in their countries which took years to achieve; to getting governments to agree to arms being brought into their countries and to allow them to be used for training; to go through the excruciatingly painful job of begging all kinds of governments and organisations for what appear to any revolutionary to be obvious and simple requests. . . .

It is highly doubtful if . . . [there is a] need to make a new theoretical analysis of the South African revolution and to raise the level of our ideological thinking. We are faced with actual, organisational and practical problems. How do you get well-armed men to designated bases in South Africa safely, so that they can carry out their tasks? How do you get trained underground workers into the country to do work and survive under those conditions? How do you set up efficient propaganda machinery inside the country? How do you get arms into the hands of the people in South Africa? . . .

The point made regarding accountability and the making of reports to inform the membership and so on is well made. . . . Though it should be borne in mind that the matters on which most people seek information and which have important political meaning are precisely those which are sensitive militarily and politically dangerous in countries that are not ours.

Being away from our mass base and without democracy in the form of meetings, conferences, elections and so on—quite clearly the danger of bureaucracy becomes sharp. . . . An examination of the experiences of the PAC and other movements will soon show that the utmost vigilance is required in any revolutionary movement against possibility of infiltration and disruption by enemy agents—this is especially so where the internal mass movement is not there to sift and vouch for people who come outside claiming to be members of the movement. . . .

The paragraph dealing with style of work seems to the Preparatory Committee to be too lurid, melodramatic and unjust. The statements are too general and sweeping and therefore cannot even be checked. . . .

"There have been a number of cases of embezzlement." This is a very serious charge. Our movement has severely punished some comrades found guilty of misusing funds. Fortunately this has not been a problem in our movement in contrast to some others. In fact, we have had the opposite accusation that our Treasury is too tight-fisted with money. . . .

It is regrettable that a few comrades in our movement are given to excessive drinking. But is the whole of our machinery to be castigated for this fault? If it is confined to some individuals, however prominent, should we not in fact say so and to use your words "point a finger"? . . .

As regards the problem of accommodation of "leading personnel who visit Dar es Salaam for short periods," they should stay at a hotel because they must be accommodated. The hotel they often go to is the worst in Dar es Salaam, precisely to save on costs. . . . There was a time when our headquarters were in Dar es Salaam and there were many comrades accommodated there. Then it was possible for comrades to stay at the residences of other comrades. . . . We do not know of leaders who spend "evening after evening in a bar". . . .

The paragraphs dealing with the need to involve our members more and those relating to the need to improve the conditions of MK men and also to intensify political work are high on the agenda of the conference. All proposals to this end are welcome. But here again, are some statements not too sweeping and generalised?

The suggestion that there has been an emergence of an "elite" is amazing. The conditions in which leading personnel are forced to work, certainly in Tanzania, can hardly be described as inducing the emergence of an elite. . . . The ANC leadership can hardly be described as living the life of an "elite" as compared with other members, including the MK, despite the remarks on Mandela camp. . . . The conditions under which our top leadership such as Tambo, Kotane, Marks and other leaders are living ought to fill members of the Congress movement with absolute shame if they had any conscience. . . .

The proposals in your document are all very welcome indeed and, in particular, the one for integration of all personnel in the ANC, we believe could be a tremendous step forward which could galvanise the whole movement. There is no doubt that something along these lines will emerge from our conference. . . .

We must stress that the aforegoing represents the view of the Preparatory Committee, which is responding to all contributions and will welcome further comments so as to ensure that we arrive at the conference completely united in our approach.

Some matters of an ideological and theoretical nature we have not dealt with because they will be with us for years during the revolution and are more long-term. The same applies to problems of strategy and tactics.

Document 14. "Strategy and Tactics." Statement adopted by the ANC at the Morogoro Conference, April–May 1969 (abridged)

The struggle of the oppressed people of South Africa is taking place within an international context of transition to the Socialist system, of the breakdown of the colonial system as a result of national liberation and socialist revolutions, and the fight for social and economic progress by the people of the whole world.

We in South Africa are part of the zone in which national liberation is the chief content of the struggle. On our continent sweeping advances have been registered which have resulted in the emergence to independent statehood of forty one states. Thus the first formal step of independence has been largely won in Africa and this fact exercises a big influence on the developments in our country.

The countries of Southern Africa have not as yet broken the chains of colonialism and racism which hold them in oppression. In Mozambique, Angola, South West Africa, Zimbabwe and South Africa, White racialist and fascist regimes maintain systems which go against the current trend of the African revolution and world development. This has been made possible by the tremendous economic and military power at the disposal of these regimes built with the help of imperialism.

The main pillar of the unholy alliance of Portugal, Rhodesia and South Africa is the Republic of South Africa. The strategy and tactics of our revolution require for their formulation and understanding a full appreciation of the inter-locking and interweaving of International, African and Southern African developments which play on our situation. . . .

The Relationship between the Political and Military

When we talk of revolutionary armed struggle, we are talking of political struggle by means which include the use of military force even though once force as a tactic is introduced it has the most far-reaching consequences on every aspect of our activities. It is important to emphasise this because our movement must reject all manifestations of militarism which separates armed people's struggle from its political context.

Reference has already been made to the danger of the thesis which regards the creation of military areas as the generator of mass resistance. But even more is involved in this concept. One of the vital problems connected with this bears on the important question of the relationship between the political and military. From the very beginning our Movement has brooked no ambiguity concerning this. The primacy of the political leadership is unchallenged and supreme and all revolutionary formations and levels (whether armed or not) are subordinate to this leadership. To say this is not just to invoke tradition. This approach is rooted in the very nature of this type of revolutionary struggle and is borne out by the experience of the overwhelming majority of revolutionary movements which have engaged in such struggle. Except in very rare instances, the people's armed challenge against a foe with formidable material strength does not achieve dramatic and swift success. The path is filled with obstacles and and we harbour no illusions on this score in the case of South Africa.

In the long run it can only succeed if it attracts the active support of the mass of the people. Without this lifeblood it is doomed. Even in our country with the historical background and traditions of armed resistance still within the memory of many people and the special developments of the immediate past, the involvement of the masses is unlikely to be the result of a sudden natural and automatic consequence of military clashes. It has to be won in all-round political mobilization which must accompany the military activities. This includes educational and agitational work throughout the country to cope with the sophisticated torrent of misleading propaganda and "information" of the enemy which will become more intense as the struggle sharpens. . . .

The White Group

. . . For the moment the reality is that apart from a small group of revolutionary Whites, who have an honoured place as comrades in the struggle, we face what is by and large a united and confident enemy which acts in alliance with, and is strengthened by, world imperialism. All significant sections of the White political movement are in broad agreement on the question of defeating our liberation struggle.

This confrontation on the lines of colour—at least in the early stages of the conflict—is not of our choosing; it is of the enemy's making. It will not be easy to eliminate some of its more tragic consequences. But it does not follow that this will be so for all time. It is not altogether impossible that in a different situation the White working class or a substantial section of it, may come to see that their true long-term interest coincides with that of the non-White workers. We must miss no opportunity either now or in the future to try and make them aware of this truth and to win over those who are ready to break with the policy of racial domination. Nor must we ever be slow to take advantage of differences and divisions which our successes will inevitably spark off to isolate the most vociferous, the most uncompromising and the most reactionary elements amongst the Whites. Our policy must continually stress in the future (as it has in the past) that there is room in South Africa for all who live in it but only on the basis of absolute democracy.

The African Masses—the Main Force for Liberation

So much for the enemy. What of the liberation forces? Here too we are called upon to examine the most fundamental features of our situation which serve to mould our revolutionary strategy and tactics. The main content of the present stage of the South African revolution is the national liberation of the largest and most oppressed group—the African people. This strategic aim must govern every aspect of the conduct of our struggle, whether it be the formulation of policy or the creation of structures. Amongst other things, it demands in the first place the maximum mobilisation of the African people as a dispossessed and racially oppressed nation. This is the mainspring and it must not be weakened. It involves a stimulation and deepening of national confidence, national pride and national assertiveness. Properly channelled and properly led, these qualities do not stand in conflict with the principles of internationalism. Indeed, they become the basis for more lasting and more meaningful co-operation; a co-operation which is self-imposed, equal and one which is neither based on dependence nor gives the appearance of being so.

The national character of the struggle must therefore dominate our approach. But it is a national struggle which is taking place in a different era and in a different context from those which characterised the early struggles against colonialism. It is happening in a new kind of world—a world which is no longer monopolised by the imperialist world system; a world in which the existence of the powerful socialist system and a significant sector of newly liberated areas has altered the balance of forces; a world in which the horizons liberated from foreign oppression extend beyond mere formal political control and encompass the element which makes such control meaningful—economic emancipation. It is also happening in a new kind of South Africa; a South Africa in which there is a large and well-developed working class whose class consciousness and [sic] in which the independent expressions of the working people—their political organs and trade unions—are very much part of the liberation front. Thus, our nationalism must not be confused with chauvinism or narrow nationalism of a previous epoch. It must not be confused with the classical drive by an elitist group among the oppressed people to gain ascendancy so that they can replace the oppressor in the exploitation of the mass.

But none of this detracts from the basically national context of our liberation drive. In the last resort it is only the success of the national democratic revolution which—by destroying the existing social and economic relationships—will bring with it a correction of the historical injustices perpetrated against the indigenous majority and thus lay the basis for a new—and deeper internationalist—approach. Until then, the national sense of grievance is the most potent revolutionary force which must be harnessed. To blunt it in the interests of abstract concepts of internationalism is, in the long run, doing neither a service to revolution nor to internationalism.

The Role of the Coloured and Indian People

The African, although subjected to the most intense racial oppression and exploitation, is not the only oppressed national group in South Africa. The two million strong Coloured Community and three-quarter million Indians suffer varying forms of national humiliation, discrimination and oppression. They are part of the non-White base upon which rests White privilege. As such they constitute an integral part of the social forces ranged against White supremacy. Despite deceptive, and, often, meaningless concessions they share a common fate with their brothers and their own liberation is inextricably bound up with the liberation of the African people.

A unity in action between all the oppressed groups is fundamental to the advance of our liberation struggle. Without such a unity the enemy easily multiplies and the attainment of a people's victory is delayed. Historically both communities have played a most important part in the stimulation and intensification of the struggle for freedom. It is a matter of proud record that amongst the first and most gallant martyrs in the armed combat against the enemy was a Coloured Comrade, Basil February. The jails in South Africa are a witness to the large scale participation by Indian and Coloured comrades at every level of our revolutionary struggle. From the very inception of Umkhonto they were more than well represented in the first contingents who took life in hand to help lay the basis for this new phase in our struggle. . . .

Our Fighting Alliance

Whatever instruments are created to give expression to the unity of the liberation drive, they must accommodate two fundamental propositions:

Firstly they must not be ambiguous on the question of the primary role of the most oppressed African mass and,

Secondly, those belonging to the other oppressed groups and those few White revolutionaries who show themselves ready to make common cause with our aspirations, must be fully integrated on the basis of individual equality. Approached in the right spirit these two propositions do not stand in conflict but reinforce one another. Equality of participation in our national front does not mean a mechanical parity between the various national groups. Not only would this practice amount to inequality (again at the expense of the majority), but it would lend flavour to the slander which our enemies are ever ready to spread of a multiracial alliance dominated by minority groups. This has never been so and will never be so. But the sluggish way in which the Movement inside the country responded to the new situation after 1960 in which cooperation between some organisations which were legal (e.g. SAIC, CPO, COD) [South African Indian Congress, Coloured People's Organisation, Congress of Democrats] and those that were illegal (e.g. ANC) sometimes led to the superficial impression that the legal organisations—because they could speak and operate more publicly and thus more noticeably—may have had more than their deserved place in the leadership of the Alliance.

Therefore, not only the substance but the form of our structural creations must in a way which the people can see—give expression to the main emphasis of the present stage of our struggle. This approach is not a pandering to chauvinism, to racialism or other such backward attitudes. We are revolutionaries not narrow nationalists. Committed revolutionaries are our brothers to whatever group they belong. There can be no second class participants in our Movement. It is for the enemy we reserve our assertiveness and our justified sense of grievance. . . .

The Working Class

Is there a special role for the working class in our national struggle? We have already referred to the special character of the South African social and economic structure. In our country—more than in any other part of the oppressed world—it is inconceivable for liberation to have meaning without a return of the wealth of the land to the people as a whole. It is therefore a fundamental feature of our strategy that victory must embrace more than formal political democracy. To allow the existing economic forces to retain their interests intact is to feed the root of racial supremacy and does not represent even the shadow of liberation.

Our drive towards national emancipation is therefore in a very real way bound up with economic emancipation. We have suffered more than just national humiliation. Our people are deprived of their due in the country's wealth; their skills have been suppressed and poverty and starvation has been their life experience. The correction of these centuries-old economic injustices lies at the very core of our national aspirations. We do not underestimate the complexities which will face a people's government during the transformation period nor the enormity of the problems of meeting economic needs of the mass of the oppressed people. But one thing is certain—in our land this cannot be effectively tackled unless the basic wealth and the basic resources are at the disposal of the people as a whole and are not manipulated by sections or individuals be they White or Black.

This perspective of a speedy progression from formal liberation to genuine and lasting emancipation is made more real by the existence in our country of a large and growing working class whose class consciousness complements national consciousness. Its political organisations—and the trade unions—have played a fundamental role in shaping and advancing our revolutionary cause. It is historically understandable that the doubly oppressed and doubly exploited working class constitutes a distinct and reinforcing layer of our liberation and Socialism [sic] and do not stand in conflict with the national interest. Its militancy and political consciousness as a revolutionary class will play no small part in our victory and in the construction of a real people's South Africa.

Beyond our borders in Zimbabwe, Angola, Mozambique, Namibia are our brothers and sisters who similarly are engaged in a fierce struggle against colonialist and fascist regimes. We fight an Unholy Alliance of Portugal, Rhodesia and South Africa with the latter as the main economic and military support. The historic ZAPU/ANC-Alliance is a unique form of cooperation between two liberation movements which unites the huge potential of the oppressed people in both South Africa and Zimbabwe. The extension of co-operation and coordination of all the people of Southern Africa as led by FRELIMO, ZAPU, SWAPO, MPLA and the ANC is a vital part of our strategy.

What then is the broad purpose of our military struggle? Simply put, in the first phase, it is the complete political and economic emancipation of all our people and the constitution of a society which accords with the basic provisions of our programme—the Freedom Charter. This, together with our general understanding of our revolutionary theory, provides us with the strategic framework for the concrete elaboration and implementation of policy in a continuously changing situation. It must be combined with a more intensive programme of research. examination and analysis of the conditions of the different strata of our people (in particular those on the land), their local grievances, hopes and aspirations, so that the flow from theory to application—when the situation makes application possible—will be unhampered.

DOCUMENT 15. "The 22." Statement by the Black Sash on the re-arrest of Winnie Mandela and 21 others, February 1970

In May and June 1969 large numbers of people were arrested and detained without trial specifically for interrogation. They were held in solidarity confinement incommunicado, i.e. without access to their families, friends, ministers of religion or lawyers.

22 of these people were formally charged in October 1969 and the trial proceeded in the Supreme Court until the 16th February, 1970. On that day the Attorney General appeared in Court and withdrew the charges.

The Judge formally acquitted all 22 accused. Normally, in such cases, acquitted persons are free to leave the Court.

These 22 people were then and there immediately redetained under the Terrorism Act and whisked away from the court to disappear from public sight and knowledge. The Terrorism Act gives the Security Police the power to hold detained persons incommunicado for an indefinite period, specifically for interrogation. They are entitled to see only their jailors and their interrogators.

"When circumstances permit they may see a magistrate once a month."

During the brief trial of the 22, State witnesses testified that they had been subjected to torture during their interrogation.

WHAT HAPPENS TO PEOPLE IN DETENTION?

What has been happening to these 17 men and 5 women since their redetention?

There is no way of finding out as no one has access to them.

HOW MANY OTHER PEOPLE ARE LOCKED AWAY WITHOUT TRIAL IN OUR PRISONS?

Figures are not available. It is "not in the interests of the State" to disclose this information.

During 1969, 9 people died in detention.

The laws of our country are circumventing the administration of justice. Some years ago the cry was "Charge or Release." This year 22 people were charged and were found not guilty of the charges against them.

THEY WERE NOT RELEASED.

These 22 people must not be forgotten.

NOR MUST ALL THE OTHER PEOPLE LOCKED UP WITHOUT TRIAL IN OUR JAILS BE FORGOTTEN.

We stand here today to record our total condemnation of a system which can remove people from their homes, take them to far away places, keep them in solitary confinement, interrogate them continuously, and detain them indefinitely before it is decided whether to charge them or not.

DOCUMENT 16. Statement by expelled members of the PAC to the OAU's African Liberation Committee, August 18, 1970

1. From the 4th to the 10th June, 1968, as a result of pressure from the Ministry for Presidential Affairs and the Government of the Republic of Zambia, and with the knowledge and approval of the Secretariat of the African Liberation Committee, the National Executive Committee of the Pan Africanist Congress of South Africa met in Dar es Salaam to "resolve its internal difficulties."

2. Amongst the decisions taken by the NEC of the PAC after days of deliberations, was to expel Potlako Leballo from the membership of the PAC.

3. This decision was communicated to Mr. George Magombe, Executive Secretary of the ALC, who stated that "this was an internal matter and they (ALC) could only advise." The decision was also communicated to the Zambian Government.

4. Two days later it transpired that this was a hoax and not acceptance because Mr. Magombe and the African Liberation Committee handed over the PAC office in Dar Es Salaam to Potlako Leballo and allowed him to hold a press conference under Tanzanian police protection, in which Leballo castigated the popularly elected leaders of the PAC and the African people of South Africa.

5. In August, 1968, the Zambian Government arrested the leaders and members of the PAC in Zambia, locked their offices and, after ten days of incarceration, whisked them to Tanzania, where they were sent to a remote wilderness, and to which they were restricted.

6. In November, 1968, the leaders of the PAC were summoned to Dar Es Salaam where for three days they held talks with representatives from the Governments of Tanzania and Zambia, assisted by the Executive Secretary of the ALC, Mr. Magombe.

7. Despite persuasions and threats, the leaders of the PAC and the African people of South Africa refused to yield an inch in their decision to expel Leballo from the organisation.

8. When, at the end of this meeting, the said representatives realised that the leaders of the PAC would not restore Leballo to membership of the PAC, they were bundled into one of the dungeons of the Tanzanian jails for ten days, and Leballo was allowed to operate in the name of the PAC and the African people of South Africa.

9. Leballo was expelled from membership of the PAC, inter alia, [for] being an *agent provocateur,* sabotaging the liberation struggle of the people of South Africa, and mismanagement of the funds intended for the said struggle.

10. With the intervention of the Christian Council of Tanzania and the UN High Commissioner's office for Refugees, the leaders of the PAC and the African people of South Africa were rescued from the Tanzanian jail and sought and were granted asylum in Nairobi, Kenya.

11. The men who heeded the call of the leaders of the PAC and who had been incarcerated with them after several attempts to join the leaders and several arrests and jailings by the Tanzanian Government, also ultimately found their way to Nairobi, Kenya.

12. Now therefore, the PAC dissociates itself entirely from the expelled Leballo's self-exposed role of international police informer and agent provocateur of the South African apartheid regime, which fact emerged spectacularly from the recent Tanzania Treason Trial. It does, however, note with satisfaction that this role is completely in character and conforms with the role for which the PAC expelled him, and is, as such, no matter of surprise to all loyal members of the PAC. This underscores the correctness of the PAC decision to expel him. By his own admission under oath, Leballo was recommended to "plotters" by Hilgard Muller, the fascist "Minister of External Affairs," and fascist Prime Minister Vorster's Secretary as being "their man."

13. By his own admission Leballo is not a South African citizen, nor is he a South African.

14. Leballo regards himself as "enemy number one of the South African Government."

15. In 1962, May, Leballo sought and was granted permission by the South African Government to be released from banishment in South Africa and repatriated to Lesotho, his homeland.

16. In December, 1962, Leballo sought and was granted permission to pass through South Africa to New York, where he addressed the General Assembly in the presence of Eric Louw, the then Foreign Minister of South Africa.

17. In January, 1963, Leballo sought and was granted permission by the South African Government to return to Lesotho, his homeland.

18. In April, 1963, Leballo called a press conference in Maseru in which he declared his intention to attack South Africa with his force of 150,000 trained men. As a result of this irresponsible utterance, the Maseru offices were searched, names of South African Freedom Fighters found and over 10,000 activists, all over South Africa, were arrested and sentenced to various terms of imprisonment from three to thirty-three years and to death.

19. In August, 1964, Leballo sought and was granted by the South African Government permission to fly through South Africa to visit African Independent States, Europe and other countries.

20. By his own admission under oath at the present Tanzanian Treason Trial, Leballo did not use "the Tanzanian Government's money" on his various visits to London and to Nairobi, while being used as a decoy to trap "plotters."

21. Leballo's two young sons have gone to England to study.

22. Leballo has been the sole recipient of monies into the PAC and the African people of South Africa to prosecute [sic].

23. By his own admission, from the month of March, 1968 to the present day, Leballo was solely engaged with his functions as a decoy in the present Tanzanian Treason Trial and not with anything to do with "liberation."

24. Mangaliso Sobukwe, leader of the Pan Africanist Congress of South Africa and of the people of South Africa, who a year ago was let out of prison, after nine years and is presently under guard and restriction in Kimberley, was recently refused an exit permit to leave South Africa. This is the first time South Africa has ever refused anybody an exit permit. We know who public enemy number one of the South African regime is. So does the South African Government.

25. In 1968, the Government of Zambia declared Leballo persona non grata, for "security reasons."

26. In 1970, the Government of Uganda, refused Leballo entry into their country. Your guess is as good as mine.

27. When the Leabua junta in Lesotho nullified the elections and declared a state of emergency in that country after it had become evident that the popular elections sought to give the reigns to the Pan Africanist BCP [Basutoland Congress Party] party, Leballo through the press urged Basotho people and "freedom fighters of the Pan Africanist Congress who have sought refuge in that country," to take arms and fight.

28. Thirty-five of our men are to be deported from Lesotho and five are already in Zambia.

NOW THEREFORE:

We pray that the ALC and the OAU restore the PAC to the National Executive Committee and recognise our June, 1968 decision.

We pray that all assistance be channeled through the proper officials of the PAC for the purpose for which it was intended.

We pray that the offices of the PAC, particularly in Zambia and Tanzania, through the offices of the ALC of the OAU be opened and handed over to the NEC of the PAC.

That the ALC and all other organs of the OAU hear the delegations of the NEC of the PAC at their place of choice and at their convenient time.

That the PAC be redeemed from the morass, confusion and wreckage into which Leballo has plunged it, in the interest of African Unity and the struggle for independence in South Africa.

We humbly pray,

Signed: Z. B. Molete
Secretary for Publicity &
Information for the NEC of the PAC
P.O. Box 1850, NAIROBI

DOCUMENT 17. Secretarial report by Ramlall Ramesar to the annual conference of the Natal Indian Congress, Durban, July 21, 1973 (abridged)

Events of the last year have brought home the fact that the tempo of the people is rising. There is a burning and spreading urge for freedom. This urge is being expressed in many ways.

The Workers, by their bold and decisive action, have highlighted the monstrous injustices flowing from a system rooted in the diabolical philosophy of Racialism. The wave of strikes that swept through Natal have made it clear that the Workers have no intention of allowing themselves to be exploited forever. . . .

The whole of democratic South Africa feels inspired by the united and courageous action of the black University students. To thousands of the oppressed people their action showed the way, like a torch in the dark. The message of their action is that fearless, massive and united action must bring results. Their action was a telling and decisive blow to the hideous concept of separate universities. . . .

It is one of the basic tasks of the Natal Indian Congress, together with all other liberatory organizations, to uproot and destroy all attempts to divide the people of South Africa.

Peace and harmony can only come from Universal Brotherhood.

The N. I. C. is cognisant of the fact that a greater political ferment has surfaced since its revival, and a variety of activities are sharpening the political awareness of the Black People. . . .

RELATIONSHIPS WITH OTHER ORGANIZATIONS

1. *LABOUR PARTY*
Speakers from the N. I. C. shared platforms at public meetings with members of the Coloured Labour Party on several occasions during the year. The two organisations co-operated in boycotting the Eartha Kitt Show in Pietermaritzburg and matches played at the National Football League.

2. *CITIZENS' ACTION COMMITTEE*
The N. I. C. in keeping with its policy to cooperate with all organisations interested in the upholding of civil liberties co-operated with this Committee during the course of the year.

3. *WORKERS*
The deplorably low wages earned by the mass of South African workers is of major concern to the N. I. C. It has worked in conjunction with the Labour Party and the Natal University [NUSAS] Wages Commission to create a united wages action to serve as a vigilante in protecting workers rights. It made recommendations to the Statutory Wage Board sittings to determine

the so-called minimum wages for workers on behalf of dock, cement and unskilled workers. It made representations during the year to the Minister of Labour for the institution of free and open trade unions for all workers, and for the abolition of job reservation. In Pietermaritzburg the N. I. C. works in very close liaison with the Textile Workers Union.

During the 1973 strikes, Congress expressed its solidarity with the workers through leaflets which were widely distributed in the Durban-Pinetown complex. Congress took the initiative in setting up a Relief Committee for the benefit of workers victimised as a result of the strikes. Legal aid, assistance to find new jobs for those dismissed, help in the way of groceries as temporary relief were provided by this Relief Committee.

4. BLACK PEOPLE'S CONVENTION AND S. A. S. O.

In pursuit of its stated policy of working with organisations sharing its goals the N. I. C. has attempted to work in harmony with both BPC and SASO. Congress officials gave all possible assistance to BPC members in February/March, 1973. It offered to organise protest meetings for SASO when its leaders were more recently banned. Congress believes that it is essential that all organisations striving for a non-racial democracy in South Africa must work out a common blueprint for joint action.

5. CIVIC AFFAIRS

The N. I. C. participated fully in voicing the Community's civic needs and in forestalling serious threats to further dwindling the Community's unsatisfactory services in residential areas.

CHATSWORTH

The decision of the Road Transportation Board to refuse to renew the certificates of Indian Bus Operators in Chatsworth caused great concern among the people. It was obvious that the stoppage of the buses would cause tremendous hardship to the people in Chatsworth.

The Natal Indian Congress took the lead in the mass action that was taken to prevent the stoppage of the buses. There were five members from Congress on the Bus Action Committee.

Congress played the main role in organising a Mass Meeting in Chatsworth on the 24th September, 1972 to protest against the stoppage of the buses. About 10,000 people attended the meeting. This meeting helped to demonstrate that the people wanted the buses to stay.

In November of last year a further meeting was held in Chatsworth by Congress; about 4,000 people attended this meeting. At this meeting the people supported the call by Congress to Walk to Work if the buses were stopped.

In January and February of 1973, Executive members of the Natal Indian Congress distributed 20,000 leaflets urging the people to protest if the buses were stopped. Congress made it clear that members of Congress would also walk with the people if the buses were stopped.

VICTORIA STREET MARKET

The N. I. C. was also prominent in its protest against the discontinuation of the Victoria Street Market following its destruction by fire. It arranged a public meeting and assisted in collecting signatures organised by the Woman's Cultural Group.

DURBAN HOUSING COMMITTEE

Congress was strongly represented at a Conference on Housing convened by the Durban Indian Child Welfare Society on the 14th April, 1973. A permanent Housing Committee was formed and N. I. C. officials are presently serving on this Committee.

6. *NEWSLETTER*

Congress published three Newsletters in the course of the year. These were widely distributed in the Durban and Pietermaritzburg areas.

7. *UNIVERSITY DURBAN WESTVILLE*

A Mass Meeting to coincide with the Official Opening of U. D. W. was organised as a protest against the injustices perpetrated at this institution. Speakers condemned the concept of separate tribal universities in general and the aims of the Government to use education as a means to foster its hated apartheid policy.

ARREST OF CONGRESS PRESIDENT:

Congress was represented at the Sharpeville Commemoration Meeting in Durban organised by the BPC. This participation resulted in the prosecution of the President of Congress on the charge of promoting racial hostility. The Judgement at his trial is an important one. The Magistrate Mr. Q. J. Van Rensburg stated:

"Many people are frustrated and embittered by the Country's Law. Newspapers publish such statements and attribute them to leading political figures. They have not been prosecuted for this."

This judgement clearly shows that it is not wrong and has never been wrong for anyone to criticize Government policies or actions.

CONCLUSION

. . . In carrying on with our struggle for a non-racial democracy we draw sustenance and inspiration from all those people whose dedication and sacrifices have set a solid foundation for the liberation struggle. Today we think of and pay our deep respects and tribute to all those people, those that are in jail, those that have been banned, the people that have been forced into exile, people who have been banished to remote areas and to everyone who has contributed to the freedom struggle, Black and White, and to whatever organisations they belonged. We also express our solidarity with all those in other organisations who are at present labouring for freedom.

DOCUMENT 18. Speech by Ambrose Makiwane at the unveiling of Robert Resha's tombstone, London, July 19, 1975 (abridged)

Our gathering here today is, according to custom, an act of bringing Robbie back to us. We talk about his inspiring deeds in order to arouse that deep sense of patriotism without which we cannot hope to be free in South Africa. . . .

Imagine the tears of the African women in South Africa when they think back and remember how they in agony and blood bore those who have fallen under the enemy's hand or those who are languishing on Robben Island, and greater is the wrath of these mothers, of every African, young and old when in spite of this the enemy is not properly identified and worse still, the ANC has been hijacked by non-Africans. Robbie fought tooth and nail against this treachery and like the warrior he was, died fighting.

The late Robbie was a former member of the National Executive Committee and former Deputy Volunteer-in-Chief. He was a foundation member of the ANC Youth League, having joined the ANC in 1939. Robbie was a staunch patriot and a man of action and remained true to the aims and objects of the ANC. The African National Congress was founded to build the unity of the African people and nationalism was to be the instrument used to achieve this objective.

Robbie threw himself in this task with all his heart. He understood well that the ANC was Africa orientated.

This is shown in the ANC anthem—God bless Africa. From the earliest times the African people of South Africa were viewing the South African situation in the broad context of colonised Africa. Their nationalism, their urge for freedom and unity was not limited to the narrow confines of their national boundaries. To them, their struggle was the struggle of the whole of Africa and all the African people abroad languishing under the yoke of colonialism. The ANC flag symbolises this and the fact that the anthem and the flag have been embraced by some African countries, is a farsightedness of the founding fathers of the ANC. Further, Africa and the world do realise that until South Africa is free, the Continent is not free. . . .

The trouble the African people have at present is that our strategy and tactics are in the hands and dominated by a small clique of non-Africans. This is the result of the disastrous Morogoro Consultative Conference of 1969, which opened membership of the ANC to non-Africans. At this conference Robbie opposed this on the grounds that, that was a violation of the policy of the ANC. All that was in vain. Robbie went to his grave having not submitted to the humiliation of the African by this small clique whose actions have brought a terrible set-back to our struggle. This small clique quickly consolidated itself, reorganised representation of external missions to suit its aims and carefully selected delegations to conference so that they acted robot-fashion. Nationalism is pooh-poohed. Those who espouse it are either isolated or branded as racist. The label of racist which the non-African clique uses against all Africans who oppose the control and the manipulation of the ANC by non-Africans is an anomalous one. It is anomalous because Africans suffer from the jack boot of white racism from the cradle to the grave, in their own country they are made aliens. Now this cruel form of white racism is extended, albeit covertly, to the Africans' own national organisation whereby opposition to non-African domination of the ANC carries heavy political penalties like isolation, character assassination and alienation.

Since 1969 the Executive Committee of the ANC has never functioned with full complement. Either some of its members are dead, sick or in full-time employment and the remainder are attending all international conferences, of course, under the aegis of this small clique or visiting certain countries whilst others are taboo. The resultant effect of this has been the estrangement of the ANC with many countries and many organisations and its dependence for support on few countries.

In 1971 an extended executive meeting of the ANC was convened in Zambia. Amongst other things, the meeting having observed that stagnation had set in in the ANC decided on the establishment of a national secretariat whose task would have been to revamp the organisation. Robbie was a member of this secretariat together with other leading members of the ANC. At the instance of the non-African clique, the secretariat was dissolved.

Robbie never accepted the dilution of African leadership of the ANC. This is the view of the African membership. He died championing and correctly reflecting the views of the African people. The realities of the South African situation reflect this. This is so because South Africa is an African country. The African is the most oppressed. He suffers the worst deprivation and exploitation. This is not being racialist, it is a fact, it is an objective reality.

If the African people are to achieve their independence, they have to unite. Robbie believed in unity. Robbie fought and died for unity—the unity of the African people. The manner in which we are to cherish the memory of so dedicated a leader of our people is to do the best we can to build this unity. The African people cannot be expected to wait indefinitely on the fringes of their organisation whilst non-Africans exercise the leadership function though unable to accept responsibility for the consequences of their actions. If nothing else, the radically changed situation in Southern Africa now favouring the struggling masses of South Africa calls for fundamental changes in the manner in which the ANC operates abroad. The ANC must be redirected to its true nationalist course. And the first step is for the members of the African National Congress to press relentlessly for a representative conference of the ANC with a view to putting its own house in order. Amongst the first [things] to be done in that conference is to cauterize this small non-African clique. If this small non-African clique claims to be non-racialist, it should from now on acknowledge that the essence of non-racialism lies in accepting the dignity of the African and the fight for liberation, for freedom from domination, from control from all sides both inside South Africa as well as outside South Africa. The Africans hate the domination of the Communist Party of South Africa.

Finally, I appeal to all people who want the overthrow of the system of Apartheid to support the African cause. Its triumph will make possible the triumph of democratic ideals—the ushering of an era of social advancement, peace, brotherhood and friendship among all the people of South Africa.

DOCUMENT 19. "Expulsion of a Conspiratorial Clique." Statement by the National Executive Committee of the ANC, Morogoro, December 11, 1975 (abridged)

A small discredited conspiratorial group of dissidents, some of them formerly active in the African National Congress, and other splinter movements, have recently intensified their campaign of lies, slander and malicious distortions intended to cause disruption within the ranks of the African National Congress and create confusion and demoralisation among the oppressed people of South Africa and the world public.

Determined, at all costs, to attract public attention to themselves, they deliberately conspired to use the name of the late Robert Resha and the solemn ceremonies connected with his death and the unveiling of his tombstone for an outright and unprecedented attack on the African National Congress of South Africa, its policies and its leadership. The attack was carried under cover of a booklet ostensibly published in memory of the late Robert Resha. This action was the culmination of a persistent and prolonged treacherous and subversive campaign by some of the ringleaders of this faction.

The overwhelming majority of the members of the African National Congress of South Africa, have for little less than a decade, been aware of the activities of some of the leaders of this faction, their arrogant defiance of decisions of the movement as well as their clandestine and futile attempts to discredit the organisation and its leadership.

Every effort was made to try and persuade these ringleaders to desist from their acts of subverting the struggle, but the tolerance and constructive approach of the movement was mistaken for weakness on its part and rewarded by these conspirators by an intensification on their part of attempts to sow division and confusion.

The mature silence of the organisation in public about the activities of the clique apparently made them shout their slanders louder and louder, and publish and distribute documents which challenge the very basis of the policies and decisions of our organisation. In fact, from their clandestine meetings, mainly confined in the U. K., they proceeded to create an organised clique with a constitution contrary to the principles and policies of the ANC of South Africa.

It was clear that what the faction tried to exploit as a London or U. K. problem arising from the decisions of the 1969 Morogoro Conference was a mere subterfuge for their activities against the ANC as a whole, its policies and its leadership of the revolution in South Africa against the fascists and their allies.

. . . [T]wo of the ring leaders of the faction, Ambrose Makiwane and Alfred Kgokong [Themba Mqota], were suspended from the National Executive Committee for 6 months in 1969 for their factional and disruptive activities and for defiance of the instructions of the organisation. They never abandoned their subversive campaign. The roots of this clique therefore existed before the Morogoro Conference in 1969. . . .

Let it be made abundantly clear that the policies of racialism and anti-communism have been and still are diametrically opposed to the policies, traditions and practices of the African National Congress. . . .

It now becomes clear why the behaviour and activities of the Mqota-Mbele group has received wide and thorough coverage in the South African and imperialist press. The enemy press and radio have blown the so-called 'divisions' in the ANC out of all imaginable proportions for their own propaganda end. . . .

It is not and can never be a revolutionary approach to seek to isolate ourselves from any actual or potential allies in the struggle for the liberation of our country. . . . For us, now, it remains a constant task to win over to our side all those whites who recognise the injustice of extreme national oppression in our country and are prepared to fight for its destruction, however primitive the level of that recognition and however timid that preparedness. . . .

Over the last 10 years, the National Executive Committee of the ANC has sought and obtained the guidance of the broad membership through conferences attended by delegates drawn from all levels of the organisation and reflecting different shades of opinion on issues affecting the struggle. Members of the Mqota-Makiwane clique have either participated in, or if they did not, voluntarily stayed away from these conferences. Invariably, however, these meetings were a great success and the resolutions were unanimously adopted. . . .

The ring leaders of the faction were each called upon to denounce the treacherous activities in which they participated or to face expulsion from the organisation. Alfred Kgokong Mqota, George Mbele, Ambrose Makiwane, Jonas Matlou, Tennyson Makiwane, O. K. Setlapelo, Pascal Ngakane, and Thami Bonga have categorically and arrogantly refused to denounce their counter-revolutionary activities and are now busy intensify-ing their anti-ANC activities. The National Executive Committee of the ANC hereby declares that these traitors stand expelled from the African National Congress of South Africa.

Document 20. Statement by eight expelled members of the ANC, London, December 27, 1975 (abridged)

By now it should be clear even to those who have a cursory acquaintance with the affairs of the African National Congress of South Africa that all is not well within that organisation. Chaotic conditions and anti-revolutionary tendencies have arisen within the external mission of the organisation. These have manifested themselves in various ways, namely:

* what is called the executive is, in fact, a self-appointed body which has steadily developed into a self-perpetuating bureaucracy which meets at its own sweet pleasure and exercises an unlimited tenure of office. It is accountable to no one and is a power unto itself;

* over the years, this executive has acted in an arbitrary manner in numerous matters involving long standing members of the ANC and its acts of omission, default, perjury, malice and vindictiveness have led to the isolation of many talented people who could be an asset to the organization;

* there has been conduct amounting to criminal neglect of dedicated cadres, who have received training. Some of these comrades fell into enemy hands in Zimbabwe and South Africa and they were forgotten the minute they were sentenced. . . .

* criticism of official ANC policy and practice has come to be regarded within the leadership circles as nothing less than treason. Democratic discussion and the constitutional process have been substituted by arbitrary punitive measures. There has been a series of expulsions;

* ANC policy is made in the interests of rank opportunism, military adventurism and political expediency such as:

(a) the arbitrary decisions on the 1967 Zimbabwe campaigns without prior discussion in the ANC national executive or authorisation by it. . . .

(d) the opening of ANC membership to whites, Indians and Coloureds at the 1969 Morogoro Consultative Conference of the ANC in complete disregard and violation of established ANC policy and constitutional procedure;

(e) the adoption by the said conference of a document entitled "Strategy and Tactics" which was never discussed in the conference itself at all. . . .

The latest madness has been the expulsion of eight leading members of the ANC without even laying charges against them and calling upon them to make a defense. Some of the expelled have made many sacrifices in the course of the struggle, stood trial and have even served long terms of imprisonment on the notorious Robben Island.

The manner of the expulsions itself is scandalous. Three of the expelled, first heard about them through the mass media and second hand sources. And five of them who reside in the United Kingdom heard of their expulsion at a multiracial meeting of South Africans and non-South Africans convened by the London ANC office on October 5, 1975. There they listened to an irresponsible tirade delivered by Duma Nokwe accusing them of being "imperialist agents," "anti-communists," "'racialists,'" and even "'tribalists'". . . .

First, we declare with utmost firmness, that not only do we reject with utter contempt, the illegal and unconstitutional expulsions but secondly, we pledge our determination to do all in our power to rescue the organisation from the morass into which it has been plunged by a clique of desperate men and traitors. . . .

A certain self-seeking and ambitious clique of non-Africans, rather than spend time organising their own people, has sought to impose its hegemony over the liberation struggle and to manipulate the ANC under the theme that the main forces in conflict in South Africa are the "progressives" on the one hand and the "reactionaries" on the other hand.

This formulation, in fact, is nothing more than a thinly disguised sectarian attempt to substitute a class approach for the national approach to our struggle. . . . [The ANC] has now fallen under the complete domination of a small clique loyal to the white-led South African Communist Party. . . .

We continue to appeal to them [the Indian and Coloured people] to fully identify themselves with the African cause. . . .

But the major anomaly of the SACP is the fact that it has no grass-root base— neither among the black workers nor the white workers. Its white leadership is drawn from middle class, South African White backgrounds, where the norm is to give instruction and patronising tutelage to the African—these people have found it impossible to divest themselves of this background even though they claim to be communists, hence their arrogant attempts to impose their hegemony on the national liberation movement in South Africa. . . .

In 1969, the SACP went further when it seized control of certain key departments in the ANC. This included the so-called Revolutionary Council, which includes Yusuf Dadoo, Joe Slovo and Reggie September. . . .

The Morogoro Conference also took place against the background of a crisis within the ANC cadre organisation. That crisis had surfaced in the form of a memorandum by seven militarily trained cadres articulating the mood of the men. The memo [written by Chris Hani] turned out to be a scathing criticism of the leadership and its conduct of the struggle. The majority of the leadership not only took unkindly to the criticism but was in a scape-goat seeking mood by the time the consultative conference was convened.

The conference itself was a multi-racial affair which was attended by Africans, Coloureds, Whites and Indians. But the SACP saw only one thing in the situation—the moment for the realization of its cherished goal of taking over the ANC.

True enough, the carefully worked out subterfuge passed as a call for "the integration of all revolutionaries". . . .

It is our considered view that Oliver Tambo has clearly betrayed the sacred trust and mandate given him by the ANC to head the external mission. He has betrayed the African wives and mothers who parted with their husbands and sons when they left to prepare for the liberation war. His conduct has been a betrayal of colleagues languishing in jail like Nelson Mandela, whose hopes of leaving Robben Island lie in the successful prosecution of the struggle.

No, the truth must be said as it is, that this man—that Oliver Tambo, is unfit to lead a revolutionary struggle.

THE WAY FORWARD

. . . [W]e solemnly pledge ourselves to work for the following:. . . .

(b) the forging of African unity as the fundamental base around which a broader coalition of all other democratic and revolutionary forces can be constructed.

This strategy has been the basis of our progress in the past. And even other recent international experiences like the Algerian and Vietnamese liberation wars proved beyond doubt that the formula to success lay in national unity, solidly based, not on wishy-washy platitudes and coined in an irrelevant context, but solidly on the concrete political forces at work in a particular situation.

Consequently, firm initiatives will be taken by us to bring this about;

(c) re-instatement of a foreign policy based on non-alignment;

(d) intensification of the struggle against White minority rule, racist oppression and exploitation and to fight for the triumph of the aims and objects of the ANC and for the victory of a national democracy in South Africa.

BROTHERS AND SISTERS—FROM THE BRINK OF DISASTER, FORWARD TO VICTORY

T. Bonga, A. M. Makiwane, J. D. Matlou, G. M. Mbele, A. K. Mqota, P. Ngakane, T. X. Makiwane, O. K. Setlhapelo

For information and Enquiries
Contact: T. Bonga,
61 Ashtead Road, London E.5.
Tel. 01-806-7486

Document 21. Memorandum on ANC "discord" smuggled out of Robben Island, 1975?

Introduction:

In 1969 some discord arose amongst the ranks of the Congress movement in the single cells section of the prison. The discussions lasted for over a period of six years (1969–1975). During its duration, it fluctuated in intensity at times reaching extreme tension and bitterness, at times abating in response to efforts to solve it.

Robben Island prison is divided into two main prisons—the ordinary criminal prison and the political prison, which in turn is subdivided into three subsections—the main section, D section (so called Terrorist Section), and the single cell section. The three sections are completely segregated and strict security measures are enforced by the jail authorities to see that no contact or communication of any sort exists between the sections. The Congress Movement, of course, runs its own efficient regular clandestine communications channels but [these] were never used to spread differences to the other sections and the dispute remained confined to the single cells section.

The population of the Congress Movement in the single cells section has never exceeded twenty-four, it oscillates with the number of discharged and new arrivals.

Since the beginning of the discord, quite a few members have been discharged from this section—all men who were naturally involved one way or the other—and could not have been impartial on the subject.

We don't think it far fetched that each independently might have reported on the dispute to the outside and in the process presented a biased interpretation of events. This report besides aiming at an accurate summary presentation of the major facts to correct individual distortions seeks to announce a happy resolution of the whole matter.

Background to the issues:

Our Executive Body in the Congress Movement is the High Organ. The original High Organ from 1965–1972 were: Madiba [Mandela], Xhamela [Sisulu], Govan [Mbeki], Ndobe [Mhlaba], joined in 1967 by M. D. [Naidoo] The only two sub-committees are syllabus and communications. Membership is organised into five units.

The dispute first erupted into the open when one unit proposed a discussion on the movement's attitude to separate development institutions (Coloured Labour Party, Bantu Homelands and Indian Council). Before then there was a simmering discontent among certain members because some of their fellow members were discussing these institutions informally with those of other organisations, and there was a rumour that Indian comrades who are not organised into a separate machinery had obtained permission from the High Organ to discuss the Indian Council and that they had done so and taken a decision which was not reported to the rest of the members of the Congress Movement. A split also existed in the communications committee on the issue of creating a machinery for communication with the external body. However, the bubble, as we say, was pricked by a suggestion for a formal discussion of the institutions of apartheid. After the High Organ had accepted and referred the matter for discussion to the units, one unit objected to such a discussion and suggested that the syllabus committee was the proper body to discuss the issue as a purely theoretical question. The High Organ then revoked their original decision and referred the topic to the syllabus committee. There was no mandate to the syllabus committee to give the topic any priority, and as the syllabus committee was already committed to its current programme the issue did not receive immediate attention, Meanwhile, there had developed a lot of suspicion and mistrust around this issue. There was a feeling among a section of the members that a move was afoot to undermine the Lobatse resolution [of the 1962 ANC conference in Bechuanaland] by those who seemed inclined to revise the boycott issue. There was also a related suspicion that either the initiators of the discussion or those who were alleged to favour a revising of the Lobatse resolution might take advantage of a consensus in their favour to send out directives to the organisation outside to operate according to their new tactics.

The delay in formal discussion of the issue did not help matters. It exacerbated the growing misunderstanding because discussion was driven to informal groupings which were built around like minded members. Such groups naturally degenerated into gossip cells and mud slinging camps with men from the High Organ spearheading whispering campaigns in opposite directions. The usual disciplinary code of confining differences within was broken when individual High Organ men vied with each other and broadcast their mutual recriminations to their own adherents in a vicious slander campaign.

Besides the issues referred to above, another thorny question which though not openly debated was an undercurrent as it will appear in the findings, was the question of Madiba's status.

The first attempt at solution:

Somewhere in 1970 the High Organ, suddenly alarmed by the tensions prevalent within the membership, discussed the differences and appealed to members to sink their differences and restore cordial relations. Govan initiated the attempt. Nothing concrete came out of this appeal.

The second attempt:

This was initiated by Govan in 1973, who felt that the situation had been deteriorating since the last appeal for unity. At this juncture the original High Organ had been succeeded by an entirely new one. In 1973 the original High Organ formulated a plan for a rotation system in the High Organ as a device to train other Congress Movement men in leadership and administration techniques. It was during the term of the second High Organ (1973–74) under this plan that Govan made his observation and suggested that the four original High Organ men as primary authors of the dissension should get together and explore ways and means of resolving the misunderstanding. The High Organ readily alleged causal blunders on which they did not even agree completely. The one remarkable statement in their report was that they had "no fundamental differences in principle."

The High Organ discussed the report, added some points of their own and submitted their report to the units, recommending that the report serve as a basis for settlement. One unit criticised the report severely, pointed out that the four original High Organ men had not applied the principle of self criticism in their deliberation as practised by revolutionaries in discussions of this nature and that a purely emotional appeal for unity was bound to flounder in the same manner as the previous one in the absence of a self critical background. This unit also recommended a commission of enquiry to investigate the whole dispute.

The High Organ which had not been convinced by the assertion of "no differences of principle" had also listed a series of questions revolving around the policies of the movement to be answered by the four original High Organ men to reassure themselves and the membership whether the dispute did not in reality centre after all around differences in interpretation of policy. The questionnaire and the criticism of the one unit were submitted to the four original High Organ for discussion. Unavoidable delays ensued, and it was not until 1975 that the four original High Organ met again to discuss the directives of the High Organ. By this time another High Organ had come in during 1974–1975.

This round of talks was a non-starter. It careered into a deadlock when the issue of self criticism was raised. Madiba withdrew from discussion alleging that Govan and Ndobe were not prepared to indulge in self criticism and that it was futile to pretend to solve the misunderstanding when they were not prepared to pay the price.

At this stage, the High Organ intervened and convened the four original High Organ men to jointly come together with the High Organ to review the discussions of the four original High Organ men and the whole dispute.

Personalities:

It is appropriate to indicate here that the four original High Organ men in the dispute have always been split. Madiba, Xhamela versus Govan and Ndobe on contentious issues, but the two who represented polar opposites in attitudes and opinions were Madiba and Govan. Their attitudes towards one another were not always supported or encouraged by the other two, namely Xhamela and Ndobe.

Discussion of the Nine:

In outlining the purpose of the joint meeting, the chairman of the High Organ expressed the concern of the High Organ on the downward course of healthy relations in the movement, reminded the four original High Organ men of their sacred role in the struggle [as senior?] members. He speculated that among other causes of the rift among the four original High Organ men a regionalism and different styles of work might be the main springs of disharmony.

It is not possible to report here in full on this discussion except to say it was long, frank and we think constructive and fruitful.

The central points were: the principle of self criticism, its theory and practise and its vital role in solving disputes; the struggle for power, its forms, its manifestations and its inherent dangers; individual and organisational mistakes in the whole dispute. The question of Madiba's status was raised by Ndobe who felt it created confusion in the minds of some and qualified as a decisive factor. He and Govan, however, questioned it on constitutional grounds and it was defended by Xhamela on the authority of Madiba's senior status before arrest and the practise of continuity of leadership status of individuals in jail situations and that it was not unconstitutional.

Among the five High Organ men, two sided with Govan and Ndobe and three with Xhamela. Because of the controversial nature of the issue it was referred to the general meeting together with other recommendations for final settlement.

Summary of findings:

The High Organ at the end of the discussions made the following findings:

1) The four original High Organ men were primarily responsible for disunity through maladministration and incorrect attitudes towards one another.
2) Immediate cause of misunderstanding was the proposal for discussion on separate development institutions.
3) Personal relations and clash of personalities between Madiba and Govan contributed to the discord.
4) Power struggle in jail was a factor in the dispute.
5) Questions of tactics were elevated to questions of principle in discussions.
6) Certain incidents which occurred before arrest and before arrival on Robben Island formed an undercurrent in the personal relations. In this regard the Zakele incident of 1958 can be cited as having constantly been referred to in criticism of some comrades with unfortunate results.
7) The principle of self criticism had not been applied to some degree by all of the four original High Organ men in previous discussions when attempts had been made to resolve the discord.
8) One allegation that had been made against some members that they were abandoning the armed struggle was found to have no substance, so was another that some members were fermenting racial discrimination.

Recommendations:

1. Organisational structure and administration.

The four original High Organ men were to be reinstated in the High Organ partly as a practical test of the effect of the unity discussion. Administrative efficiency was to be improved.

2. Discipline.

Promotion and enforcement of organizational discipline was to be given serious attention.

3. Political discussions:

Discussions on a variety of current political questions and events were to be undertaken.

4. Madiba's status to be finalised by the general membership.

A report back:

A summary report of the discussion was presented to a general membership meeting which though held under very difficult conditions achieved its purpose. After the report was given and by virtue of the difficult conditions for a meeting of this kind, the issue of Madiba's status was isolated for priority discussion. By an overwhelming majority the meeting reaffirmed Madiba's leadership of the Congress Movement on Robben Island prison.

Tight security precautions by the authorities subsequently precluded another general members meeting to consider the rest of the recommendations in the report.

The recommendations have been adopted by the membership through the units subject to amendments and recommendations that have not been discussed. The four original High Organ men are already working as recommended.

DOCUMENT 22. "The Enemy Hidden under the Same Colour." Statement by the Central Committee of the SACP on the "Group of Eight," 1976 (abridged)

South Africa's press has given a great deal of space to anti-Communist, anti-ANC and racist propaganda with which it has been fed by the group of eight who were recently expelled from the ANC for persistently betraying its political and organisational principles. . . . The slander that the ANC is run by the Communist Party is not something new; it has always been spread by the racists and those who act as their agents.

. . . [T]he ANC's Revolutionary Council is overwhelmingly African in composition including in its ranks only one Indian, one Coloured and one white, and with 100% African membership at its Headquarters. According to this group [of 8], this is enough to put the Revolutionary Council "under the hegemony" of the "clique of non-Africans." . . . Some of them have been Communists at some time and anti-Communists at others; some, racialists at times and multiracialists at others; tribalists and African nationalists; strongly pro-Soviet and equally strongly anti-Soviet and pro-China. . . .

On the surface their main complaint is against the Morogoro decision to integrate non-African revolutionaries into the ANC's External Mission. Yet all those in the group of 8 who were present at the Conference neither voted nor spoke against the decision. . . . Can it be that the group of 8 is saying that Indian and Coloured comrades on Robben Island and white comrades in Pretoria prison, some serving terms of life imprisonment for their part in both armed and unarmed struggle, should not have played a part, but should have restricted themselves to organising only among their own communities? Are they saying that non-African revolutionaries like Basil February, killed alongside Patrick Molaoa in Umkhonto's fighting ranks against racist troops, had no right to participate in the ANC's External Mission, or even to be a member of the ANC's Revolutionary Council?

. . . [W]hilst the racialist bogey cannot be used against African Communists (who constitute the overwhelming majority of our Party's leadership and membership) it becomes a convenient weapon of attack against national leaders like Dadoo and other non-African Communists. . . .

The decision to call the [Morogoro] Conference was taken unanimously by the NEC of the ANC, which at that stage included four members of the group of 8 and the late Robert Resha. . . .

The non-Africans who attended were in fact appointed as delegates by the ANC's executive (which at that stage included men like Makiwane, Resha and Matlou) to ensure the presence of at least a few comrades who had connections with the ANC's allied organisations—the SACP, SAIC [South

African Indian Congress], CPC [Coloured People's Congress], and SACTU. In any case, non-Africans formed a minute proportion of those who attended. Out of approximately 70 to 80 delegates there were only three coloureds, five Indians and three whites. The proceedings themselves were over-whelmingly dominated, both in numbers and contributions, by the rank-and-file delegates, particularly from Umkhonto. . . .

Morogoro did not dismiss the NEC of the ANC. The NEC in fact came to Morogoro with the announcement that it had resigned en bloc and that it had mandated the Acting President General with full powers (assisted by the late J. B. Marks and Moses Mabhida) to reconstitute the Executive. . . . During the proceedings the delegates from the camps did not hide their outrage about the personal misconduct of some of the officials and members of the NEC. Most of those belonging to the dissident clique who were members of the NEC were also targets for such criticisms.

. . . When the names of the new Executive were announced, all members of the previous Executive, such as Makiwane, Resha, Joe Matlou and others who were present at Morogoro, pledged their support to the new leadership and offered their services in any capacity. It should also be recorded that some of those who were not reappointed to the new Executive were S. A. Communist Party members who had also forfeited their right to serve on the leadership because of personal misconduct. . . .

It is now conveniently "forgotten" by those in the group of 8 who were present at Morogoro, that they did not speak or vote against the decision to integrate the non-African revolutionaries into the External Mission of the ANC. They in fact joined in the unanimous and tumultuous cheering which accompanied the adoption of the decision. . . . [The 8] dishonestly omit to mention that the decision explicitly referred ONLY TO THE EXTERNAL MISSION OF THE ANC. They also conveniently omit to mention that the decision EXPLICITLY EXCLUDED NON-AFRICANS FROM SERVING ON THE NEC OF THE ANC. . . .

Now, six years after the event, the group also, *for the first time,* dissociate themselves from the ANC Strategy and Tactics Document which they say "was never discussed in the Conference." Yet at the Conference itself they voted in favour of the document which like all others had been circulated for discussion long before the actual Conference took place. . . .

Every external mission is (with the exception of New Delhi and London) headed by an African. It therefore seems clear beyond any doubt that the continuous attack on the London office of the ANC because it is represented by a national leader like Reg September (who happens to be Coloured) is either crude Vorster-type racism or is cynically used as a cover for advancing corrupt political ambitions. . . .

It is for our Party that the group of 8 reserves its most poisonous distortions. In their hymn of hate against us, they falsify our history and deliberately distort the composition of the Party and the true nature of its relationship with the liberation movement. We say "deliberately" because in the case of at least two of the clique (Kgokong and Makiwane) they were both members of the SACP during the 50s. Both were subsequently expelled when, outside the country, they attempted to use the Party as a base for their tribalist and factionalist activity against the ANC. . . .

They [the 8] are part of the impure load which every revolution carries and when that load is thrown aside the journey to victory is always a swifter one.

3. Above-Ground Multiracial Opposition

DOCUMENT 23. "NUSAS." Paper by Jonty Driver, president, delivered at NUSAS National Seminar, April 1964 (abridged)

It is difficult to give this paper a title, because it concerns almost every aspect of NUSAS and, more particularly, the future of NUSAS, especially in the light of the Dar es Salaam Seminar [of East, Central and Southern African students in January 1964, which passed a resolution condemning NUSAS as unrepresentative of the South African majority. Two NUSAS leaders have prepared memoranda in response. . . .]

[First] are Martin Legassick's ideas, as a result of the Seminar and what happened there:

LEGASSICK ON THE ROLE OF NUSAS

" . . . There are three fundamentals for a student movement in South Africa. The first, and obvious, one is that it should represent the aspirations of the majority of people, and be a genuine wing of the liberation movement. The second is that it should be nonracial. Historically there is an evolution towards a satisfactory position, though there is need for further development on an ideological basis, and need for an attempt to regroup all forces with the same ideology. This is where I believe that the student movement in South Africa can play an important part—provided it works on the basis of an African majority membership [achievable through a shift to individual rather than institution-based membership]. . . . Our aim must be to regroup all students in South Africa, and South Africans studying outside who are with the liberation movement in all the basic aspects of its policy. We must act with genuine desire for the emergence of a representative student organisation, and not a desire to preserve NUSAS or ourselves. The base of the organisation may have to be shifted out of South Africa—though it is essential before this to be sure what sort of support the new organisation has at what University centres. Public cooperation in South Africa will have to be through "front groups" while the real work goes on underground. . . ."

Now a memo written by Magnus Gunther (a former International Vice President of NUSAS). . . . [Gunther defines the functions of NUSAS, considers the options of moving to individual enrolment, or a clandestine existence, and rejects them both.]

DRIVER ON THE ROLE OF NUSAS

. . . [The question which must be answered before we can decide on restructuring or not is: What are the Major Functions of NUSAS? Until we can answer that we cannot decide anything, because NUSAS is only as good as the things it does. For all the importance of having radical policy, policy is no use unless it is put into action.

There appear to be two major functions of NUSAS.

(1) *Leadership Training*—that is, the finding of potential leaders, black and white, and the training of these, not only in theory, but in practice—the teaching of political techniques, public speaking, Chairmanship, use of language and logic in politics, etc.

Obviously, this is one of the central functions of NUSAS, or else NUSAS would not be spending Rl,000 a year on this seminar. But it must be realised that this training is not only for NUSAS, but for other organisations as well. No one who is a NUSAS leader can stop being a leader when he leaves NUSAS. He must continue, working through other organisations towards the same ends that NUSAS works for. . . .

(2) *NUSAS as a radical organisation.* It is difficult to find a way of characterising this role, so it is called simply the "radical role;" that is, NUSAS as an active agent for change in South Africa. . . . The projects undertaken by NUSAS in an attempt to fill this radical role, are: (i) Loans (ii) Scholarships (iii) Sached [tutoring] (iv) Cadet [leadership training] (v) The literacy campaign (vi) The Political Freedom Fund (vii) The Prison Education scheme. Verbal details of these will be given.

The first two projects are public. The others are private, and the Executive and Assembly of NUSAS are under strict instructions not to mention them in public. Despite the temptation to do so, NUSAS cannot use them as publicity for itself; NUSAS wants to achieve something and does not want to jeopardise the projects by making political capital out of them. . . .

This brings me to the function of NUSAS which is often misunderstood: *the education of white students.* There are many who say that this is a waste of time since the time for bringing about political revolution in South Africa by changing the hearts and minds of whites is long past.

I personally agree that the political education of whites is not going to change the system in this country. But I do not think that is any reason at all for stopping the education of whites. When change comes to this country, and when there is, as there is bound to be, an African majority government, there is going to be a minority problem of a sort seen nowhere else in the world, *unless* there is political and social education of whites on a massive scale. Even if there were to be mass emigration of whites, at least 15% of the South African population is bound to remain white—and if the present attitudes of whites are not changed, that 15%–19% is going to be a real problem.

So the usual criticism that NUSAS wastes time with the education of white students cannot be accepted. NUSAS may not help a significant number of whites permanently out of the *laager* [circle of pioneer wagons], but at least some of the ideas of NUSAS must seep through to some whites, and one day they will adjust more easily to a changed system in this country.

In short, the function of NUSAS in educating whites is not to bring about change, but to make adjustment to change possible. . . .

It is now necessary to refer to Martin Legassick's theory of the role of NUSAS. . . . [S]uppose one accepts Legassick's conclusions, and turns NUSAS into an individual enrolment, voluntary organisation. There are some questions which must be answered.

Would NUSAS become an African majority organisation? [Given present enrolments in tertiary institutions, this is unlikely.]

How can NUSAS promote unity within the liberation movement? What practical steps can be undertaken—and it is clear that his argument for a new NUSAS depends solely on its fulfilling this function. *Is this a function of NUSAS or is it a function of a political party which could be formed?*

Factors not considered: There are other factors which Martin Legassick has not taken into account. . . . Minister [of Justice John] Vorster called on NUSAS to change from automatic enrolment to individual enrolment. In the event of NUSAS now converting to individual enrolment, it will be seen in both South Africa and overseas as a capitulation to Vorster.

[In any case, as things stand today] *the power movement in NUSAS is such that control over policy is passing more and more to Africans in NUSAS.*

On the basis of these comments, and the implied answers to the questions, a tentative conclusion can be drawn.

NUSAS HAS A VITAL ROLE TO PLAY IN THIS COUNTRY, SINCE IT IS ONE OF THE MOST ACTIVE AGENTS FOR CHANGE. WHILE THERE IS MUCH [THAT IS] EMOTIONALLY SATISFYING IN THE IDEA OF A SMALLER MORE COHERENT NUSAS, A RESTUCTURED NUSAS WOULD HAVE NO FUNCTION OF ANY PRACTICAL SORT. IT WOULD BE VERY SATISFYING FOR MANY RADICAL STUDENTS TO BE IN AN ORGANISATION OF THE SORT ENVISAGED BY MARTIN LEGASSICK, BUT NUSAS WOULD CEASE TO DO THE VERY VALUABLE WORK WHICH IT DOES NOW AND WHICH IT COULD DO. FURTHERMORE, TO CONVERT THE STRUCTURE OF NUSAS

ALONG THE LINES SUGGESTED BY MARTIN LEGASSICK WOULD SEEM TO BE A CAPITULATION TO MINISTER VORSTER AND HIS COLLEAGUES-IN-JUSTICE. FURTHERMORE, AN IMMEDIATE CHANGE IN STRUCTURE WOULD SIMPLY BE HASTENING A PROCESS WHICH IS AUTOMATICALLY RESULTING FROM THE SOUTH AFRICAN SITUATION.

QUALIFICATIONS

At the same time, there are many qualifications which must be added to the conclusion that NUSAS should continue as it is.

NUSAS MUST CONTINUE TO DEVELOP ITS PRIVATE ACTIVITIES, its practical projects, its unifying actions and its leadership training. If to do this it is necessary to cut down on public activities, such as student education, we must cut down ruthlessly. Our private functions are more important than our public functions. . . .

We must move towards a NEW DEFINITION OF NONRACIALISM. There are 2 attitudes towards nonracialism; one is the attitude which says "We must disregard a man's race and judge him on merit." The other is the attitude which says "The ideal situation is where one can disregard a man's race and judge him on merit alone. However, in the situation in the country, everything is determined by race—and those who are most oppressed must therefore lead the liberation movement." The attitude in NUSAS has always been the former. However, we must now adopt the latter attitude.

Arising from [the above], NUSAS MUST TURN ITS LEADERSHIP OVER TO AFRICANS. I do not mean by this that the white student must say to the black, "You must take over the leadership of NUSAS." But the whites must say to the blacks, "If you want to lead us, we shall follow you. . . ."

DOCUMENT 24. "A Message to the People of South Africa." Statement by the South African Council of Churches, September 1968 (AUTHORISED SUMMARY)

In the name of Jesus Christ.

We are under an obligation to confess anew our commitment to the universal faith of Christians, the eternal Gospel of salvation and security in Christ alone.

The Gospel of Jesus Christ is the good news that in Christ God has broken down the walls of division between God and man, and between man and man.

The Gospel of Jesus Christ declares that Christ is the truth who sets men free from all false hopes of freedom and security.

The Gospel of Jesus Christ declares that God has shown himself as the conqueror of all the forces that threaten to separate and isolate and destroy us.

The Gospel of Jesus Christ declares that God is reconciling us to himself and to each other; and that therefore such barriers as race and nationality have no rightful place in the inclusive brotherhood of Christian disciples.

The Gospel of Jesus Christ declares that God is the master of this world, and that it is to him alone that we owe our primary commitment.

The Gospel of Jesus Christ declares that the Kingdom of God is already present in Christ, demanding our obedience and our faith now.

This Gospel of Jesus Christ offers hope and security for the whole life of man, not just in man's spiritual and ecclesiastic relationships, but for human existence in its entirety. Consequently, we are called to witness to the meaning of the Gospel in the particular circumstances of time and place in which we find ourselves. In South Africa, at this time, we find ourselves in a situation where a policy of racial separation is being deliberately effected with increasing rigidity. The doctrine of racial separation is being seen by many not merely as a temporary political policy but as a necessary and permanent expression of the will of God, and as the genuine form of Christian obedience for this country. It is holding out to men a security built not on Christ but on the theory of separation and the preservation of racial identity; it is presenting the separate development of our race-groups as the way for the people of South Africa to save themselves. And this claim is being made to us in the name of Christianity.

We believe that this doctrine of separation is a false faith, a novel gospel; it inevitably is in conflict with the Gospel of Jesus Christ, which offers salvation, both individual and social, through faith in Christ alone. It is keeping people away from the real knowledge of Christ; therefore it is the Church's duty to enable our people to distinguish between the demands of the South African state and the demands of Christian discipleship.

The Christian Gospel requires us to assert the truth proclaimed by the first Christians, who discovered that God was creating a new community in which differences of race, language, nation, culture, and tradition no longer had power to separate man from man. The most important features of a man are not the details of his racial group, but the nature which he has in common with all men and also the gifts and abilities which are given to him as a unique individual by the grace of God; to insist that racial characteristics are more important than these is to reject what is most significant about our own humanity as well as the humanity of others.

But, in South Africa, everyone is expected to believe that a man's racial identity is the most important thing about him: only when it is clearly settled can any significant decisions be made about him. Those whose racial classification is in doubt are tragically insecure and helpless. Without racial identity, it seems, we can do nothing; he who has it, has life; he who has not racial identity has not life. This belief in the supreme importance of racial identity amounts to a denial of the central statements of the Christian Gospel. In practice, it severely restricts the ability of Christian brothers to serve and know each other, and even to give each other simple hospitality; it limits the ability of a person to obey Christ's command to love his neighbour as himself. For, according to the Christian Gospel, our brothers are not merely the members of our own race-group. Our brother is the person whom God gives to us. To dissociate from our brother on the grounds of natural distinction is to despise God's gift and to reject Christ.

Where different groups of people are hostile to each other, this is due to human sin, not to the plan of the Creator. The Scriptures do not require such groups to be kept separate from each other; on the contrary, the Gospel requires us to believe in and act on the reconciliation made for us in Christ. A policy of separation is a demonstration of unbelief in the power of the Gospel; any demonstration of the reality of reconciliation would endanger this policy. Therefore, the advocates of this policy inevitably find themselves opposed to the Church if it seeks to live according to the Gospel and to show that God's grace has overcome our hostilities. A thorough policy of racial separation must ultimately require that the Church should cease to be the Church.

The Gospel of Jesus Christ declares that God is love; separation is the opposite force of love. The Christian Gospel declares that separation is the supreme threat and danger, but that in Christ it has been overcome; it is in association with Christ and with each other that we find our true identity. But apartheid is a view of life and of man which insists that we find our identity in dissociation and distinction from each other; it rejects as undesirable the reconciliation which God is giving to us by his Son; it reinforces distinctions which the Holy Spirit is calling the people of God to overcome; it calls good evil. This policy is, therefore, a form of resistance to the Holy Spirit.

The Gospel of Jesus Christ declares that Christ is our master, and that to him all authority is given. Christians betray their calling if they give their highest loyalty, which is due to Christ alone, to one group or tradition, especially where that group is demanding self-expression at the expense of other groups. God judges us, not by our loyalty to a sectional group but by our willingness to be made new in the community of Christ. Christ is inevitably a threat to much that is called 'the South African way of life;' many features of our social order will have to pass away if the lordship of Christ is to be truly acknowledged and if the peace of Christ is to be revealed as the destroyer of our fear.

And Christ is master of the Church also. If the Church fails to witness to the true Gospel of Jesus Christ it will find itself witnessing to a false gospel. If we seek to reconcile Christianity with the so-called 'South African way of life' we shall find that we have allowed an idol to take the place of Christ. Where the Church abandons its obedience to Jesus Christ, it ceases to be the Church; it breaks the links between itself and the Kingdom of God. The task of the Church is to enable people to see the power of God at work, changing hostility into love of the brethren and to express God's reconciliation here and now. For we are not required to wait for a distant 'heaven' where all problems will have been solved. What Christ has done, he has done already. We can accept his work or reject it; we can hide from it or seek to live by it. But we cannot postpone it, for it is already achieved; and we cannot destroy it, for it is the work of the eternal God.

We believe that Christ is Lord, and that South Africa is part of his world. We believe that his Kingdom and its righteousness have power to cast out all that opposes his purposes and keeps men in darkness. We believe that the word of God is not bound, and that it will move with power in these days, whether men hear or whether they refuse to hear. And so, we wish to put to every Christian person in the country the question which we ourselves face each day; to whom, or to what, are you giving your first loyalty, your primary commitment? Is it to a subsection of mankind, an ethnic group, a human tradition, a political idea: or to Christ?

May God enable us to be faithful to the Gospel of Jesus Christ, and to be committed to Christ alone!

Document 25. Annual report of the Department of Social Concerns of the University Christian Movement, Johannesburg, 1969 (abridged)

Whew! What an exciting year! A year of great difficulties and some new discoveries. For the first 4–5 months since last Conference there was time for little else but holding the movement together as it reeled under the impact of attacks from the Prime Minister, the Special Branch [security police] and several executive resignations. All this was punctuated for good measure by the Mafeje affair and the Fort Hare problems. As a consequence our more creative work got off to a later start than anticipated. I would like to report on the major areas of interests.

I. RESEARCH

The initial emphasis in the department has been on research as the basis for relevant and effective action. It was difficult for some of us to face up to the inevitability of this need, but its necessity has become overwhelmingly clear. For this reason the first half of the year was spent on detailed research into the areas of literacy, minimum wage, work camps, church renewal, social change and the conflict between the Christian gospel and the ideology of apartheid. The findings are documented under the relevant motions of Event '68 [UCM's last annual conference].

II. MOTIONS OF EVENT '68

M14/68—*Minimum Wages*

After extensive consultation with sociologists, trade union leaders and economists it was decided to focus our concern in this area on [several] specifics:

1. The establishment of workers' committees:

The Native Labour and Settlement of Disputes Act allows for the establishment of such committees should the workers want them. If they request such a committee, management is legally bound to see that it is established and to consider its requests. Wages and conditions of employment can be discussed by the workers' committee. There are three phases to this project:

First, it is suggested that we press management to take the initiative and establish such committees in selected industries. We can do this through the personnel officers, etc.

Second, that we ask the National Development Foundation to run a leadership training school for officials of those workers' committees already established.

Third, that we request TUCSA to assist the workers' committees to set up a co-ordinating national committee at a later stage.

This is clearly a project of exciting potential, but can it be carried through by a part-time Director of Social Action? Our consultants suggest that this project be taken seriously but on a full-time basis if possible. They believe that this could be a more effective campaign than one aimed directly at raising minimum wages. . . . .

M17/68—*Social Change*

The question of "Christianity and Social Change in a non-violent context" was explored at a consultation organised in mid-January. It included several theologians, student leaders and the Director of the Christian Institute. The major recommendation produced by the consultation stressed the need for much more study and discussion on this basic Christian issue on each campus. It was suggested that each UCM branch should create one group studying the social implications of the gospel, methods of witness to these, etc. (The new Rhodes model for a local branch is most relevant).

A paper on the contribution of Gandhi's philosophy was prepared to coincide with 1969 as the Gandhi centenary year. It is being released next term for study, and UCM members are also urged to arrange a "Gandhi day" on campus during the first week of October (Gandhi's birthday).

M18/68—*Work and Study Projects*

Fifty circulars offering participating churches several work and study projects were sent to all the official journals of the churches for widening of the appeal and also to certain key clergymen, mission hospitals and church centres for their direct response. Publicity was given to this UCM appeal in *Race Relations News, The Vineyard, Seek, Concern, S. A. Outlook,* etc.

As a result of this appeal eleven offers were made. Four were accepted for the first half of the July vacation. . . .

The potential in this area is enormous and virtually untapped. A detailed memorandum outlining ten different projects of which building is only one has been submitted to interested persons in the Transkei and the response has been overwhelmingly positive and gratifying. I have great pleasure in announcing that service projects to the Transkeian people are "on"! It is now up to UCM students to get where the action is! The time has come to stop talking much of our liberal nonsense and nationalist rubbish, and do a job that makes a difference NOW! The time has come to get out amongst the "little people" of our society and help them to help themselves. A huge national Christian service department could develop around this, but we need a full-time staff appointment to get it off the ground. . . .

III. FURTHER ACTIVITIES AND ISSUES

• As Social Concerns Director I wrote a series of three articles for *One for the Road* on "Gospel or Ideology in South Africa." They were an attempt to identify the points of conflict between the gospel of Jesus and ideology of apartheid. The first article was also carried by *The Rand Daily Mail* and *The Daily Dispatch*. All three articles were also published by *Pro Veritate*. . . .

• I personally visited the Rector of Fort Hare University College, Prof. de Wet. He received me in a sincere and friendly way, and we had a most useful discussion about the banning of UCM on campus. We arranged to have another discussion in due course. . . .

CONCLUSION

I have three personal concerns for the movement. First, that we give priority to the question of deepening the level of each member's commitment to the man from Nazareth, to Truth and Love. Second, that we retain as much flexibility as is required to meet the challenges now confronting us. If we must change our shape to maintain our mission, let us be flexible enough to do so—as long as we never sacrifice our non-racial and ecumenical character. But we may have to change radically if we are not to become obsolete, or remain mutilated.

Third, that we become a community of hope—a community of men and women who radically anticipate the future by doing something positive about the present. This is the essence of our Christian commitment. We stand beyond the Exodus and the Resurrection as the community who live for the future in which new life, new institutions, new structures will be born. Of that we have no doubt. For as E. Bloch put it: "Man's basic stance when he is true to himself, is that of creative expectation, a hope that engenders action in the present to shape the future."

We could of course have anticipated that UCM would be persecuted precisely as it has been. It was sociologically entirely predictable. But neither that, nor our present situation is the norm for us. It is merely the threshold on which we reaffirm our joyous participation in the community of Christ— a community which always cuts right across all the pressure to socialise men for any ideology—a community which because of its commitment to Truth will meet its destiny. Or as the poet Robert Lowell stated it for each of us:

> O to break loose, like the chinook
> salmon jumping and falling back
> nosing up to the impossible
> stone and bone-crushing waterfall—
> raw-jawed, weak fleshed there, stopped by ten
> steps of the roaring ladder, and then

to clear the top on the last try,
alive enough to spawn and die.

Finally I would like to express my most sincere thanks to all who have worked with me over the past year. I am particularly indebted to the excellent co-operation of the executive, and especially to Colin Collins; also to the Rhodes Committee, the late Prof. D. Oosthuizen and several other nameless disciples whose assistance, fellowship and commitment made the job worthwhile and inspiring in a special sort of way. I cannot end without saying to them—thank you and Shalom!

James Polley
Director of Social Concerns

APPENDIX

FORMATION SCHOOL—EASTERN CAPE AREA, May 9–11, 1969

On Friday night about 48 of us arrived at Hogsback exhausted after a journey by bus and car. We had students attending from the Federal [Theological] Seminary (Alice), the Moravian Seminary (P. E.), Rhodes and Training College. Hot soup awaited us and was certainly very welcome after the dusty journey. After supper a short explicit talk by Colin Collins provided an introduction to the spread, life-style, orientation and international dimensions of UCM.

On the Saturday morning we divided into four groups, two of which discussed the life-style of the Movement, whilst the other two examined the spread and structure of UCM respectively. I personally found the discussions in my group very rewarding and stimulating. Racial and denominational barriers soon dissolved in favour of real friendship. It seems that this was a general experience for most of the participants I spoke to.

After morning tea the Rev. Desmond Tutu, a lecturer in theology at the Federal Seminary gave a very witty and most intelligent talk on "Theological Trends in the post-war era." He perceptively outlined the major changes that have taken place in man's thinking about God, Jesus Christ, and man himself. This was followed by further group discussions which focussed on the life-style of the contemporary Christian, with specific reference to those in UCM. On Saturday afternoon we moved into the next phase of our learning when three talks on "Human Dignity and the Christian in South Africa" were given. These were done by three students—an African, an Indian and a Coloured. It appears that this presentation was quite a revelation to several white students. A plenary discussion focussed on some very controversial but vitally important issues in this area and only ended when lamps were brought in and supper was announced. On Saturday night a brief discussion in groups was followed by a lively social.

On Sunday morning David Tucker, a lecturer in political philosophy at Rhodes read a paper on "Human Dignity and the Secular Man." This presentation reached the same high standard as the previous talks did, and opened our eyes to the considerable gap that exists between the norms of our South African society and the standards of the Christian ethic. A final discussion on practical issues in the Eastern Cape region was followed by a very moving common Eucharist in which we concluded our programme.

Having been asked to give my personal impressions, I would like to say that I felt this was a most important week-end and a very worth-while experience for all concerned. It challenged our objectives in UCM and motivated us to strive more determinedly after our ideals.

Varian Edwards
UCM Executive, Rhodes Branch

DOCUMENT 26. "Black Priests' Manifesto." January 23, 1970

OUR CHURCH HAS LET US DOWN

A group of African priests, gravely concerned about the role that Africans are allowed to play in the Roman Catholic Church in South Africa, met recently to discuss their grievances. In the belief that all other avenues are closed to them, they decided to publish their views in the manifesto that appears below. Those who signed are: Rev. Fr. P. M. Mkhatshwa, Rev. Fr. D. Moetapele, Fr. J. L. Louwfant, Fr. C. Mokoka, Rev. Dr. A. Mabona.

"INGANE engakhali ifela embelekweni." A Zulu proverb meaning that when someone fails to voice his grievances in time, he has only himself to blame if this results in a tragedy.

There was a time when most people believed that Africans had infinite patience. Their mental inertia and natural laziness were partly responsible for this.

Be that as it may, we want to state that the African is capable of an agonising "ENOUGH! ENOUGH!" In spite of our ordination to the priest-hood, we have been treated like glorified altar-boys.

We kept quiet even when it was our duty to speak up. We were afraid that our White colleagues would misunderstand our stand. Consequently the bad situation became worse.

After a long, prayerful self-examination we resolved to ventilate our grievances and take the public into our confidence. For one thing, Church politics are hidden from the rank and file; for another our fellow-men have the right to know the truth about their priests.

We are primarily concerned with the well-being of our Church. How long must we plead for its Africanisation in Southern Africa? No less an authority than the Supreme Pontiff has endorsed this urgent matter. Addressing the African Bishops on his recent visit in Uganda, the Pope said: "You can give the Church the precious and original contribution of negritude which she needs particularly."

At the same time Cardinal Zoungrana reminded his colleagues that before they could realise the Pope's ambition it was imperative to rediscover what he called "the African Soul."

The Black clergy have realised that aping Europe is not the answer to Africa's religious needs. Bishops and priests have expressed the need for Africanisation in Southern Africa.

Unfortunately the whole discussion has been treated as a big joke. African priests feel the frustration most, because the whole affair of indigenisation concerns them as spiritual leaders of their people.

The main objective of every missionary or pastoral activity is to serve the people of God, irrespective of colour, creed, place or sex. Therefore the White clergy must do this whenever a Black priest is not available. But alas! power corrupts. The Government's policy of restricting free entry of Whites into our townships has much to recommend it.

The Catholics pretend to condemn apartheid. And yet, in practice, they cherish it. The Church practised segregation in her seminaries, convents, hospitals, schools, monasteries, associations and churches long before the present Government legislated against social integration. The bishops, priests, and religious [personnel] are divided on the question of apartheid.

The statement of one late Metropolitan is still fresh in our minds. Bishop G. van Velsen made a public defence of apartheid when he was interviewed by the "Sunday Tribune" in March last year.

We know from reliable sources that a number of bishops and priests are sympathetic towards the policy. Quite rightly, of course, they condemn some aspects of its implementation, particularly those which bring suffering, and injustices.

If we understand the philosophers of separate development well, they argue that "as long as the Blacks are in our midst, their position will always be precarious and uncertain. Racial frictions will be inevitable. The Whites do not want to mix socially with Black people. They believe in preserving their identity as a White nation. So why encourage, let alone foist, integration on them? It won't work.

Let's be honest. The Whites would never accept a Black or multi-racial government. Whites in South Africa are not prepared to serve under Africans in any capacity. Socially, culturally and intellectually, the Whites consider themselves quite different from the Blacks. The obvious conclusion is that most Whites have opted out of the concept of integration.

Among other things, they feel that one can't break down traditions which are more than three centuries old, by the stroke of the pen.

As Christians we believe in a multiracial society. We feel this is the only way in which real Christianity can be practised. Unfortunately we haven't a free choice. Segregation, apartheid is imposed on us and living in a make-believe world won't help. So, if we have to have apartheid, we might as well insist on our own rights under it.

We suggest that our people should accept the situation and make the best of it. History is unpredictable. Perhaps one day things will change dramatically.

The African wants to rediscover his personality and identity. He wishes to develop all his faculties—mental, physical, aesthetic. We wonder whether he can achieve this in the midst of White people. Competition will always be in their favour.

Don't get us wrong. We are not preaching racialism, because we despise and loathe racists. What we are preaching is REALISM and common sense. Having set the scene, we want to enumerate a few grievances.

a) We deplore as well as condemn the *baasskap* [boss-ship] and *miesiesskap* [boss-ship by women] of the white clergy and religious over their African counterparts. You will destroy our morale, personality, and professional efficiency by the raw deal you give us.

b) We deplore your perpetuation of the false image of the African priest as a "glorified altar-boy" who happens to share in the White priesthood.

c) With tears in our eyes, we deplore the marooning and exiling of some African priests without redress. Even in a court of law, the accused is entitled to a fair, unbiased defence.

d) We humbly invite our Bishops to know their African parishes better. A fleeting, snap purple appearance on confirmation days leaves much to be desired.

e) We respectfully request the Hierarchy to open up new avenues for our priests, such as specialised apostolate, serving on the so-called national commissions, playing a meaningful role in the administration of dioceses and so on.

f) We ask the Hierarchy to expedite Africanisation. For instance, why can't Soweto have its own Black Bishop? Why should our townships be dominated by the White clergy and African priests be dumped in the bush, in non-viable parishes?

g) We loathe the unwarranted, self-appointed surveillance of the White priests over their Black colleagues.

h) We deplore the tripe that some missionaries write about Africans. We would like to add a few other suggestions.

The Bishops would do well to broaden their outlook on the apostolate of the Church. Individual bishops must be ready to "sacrifice" some of their priests to serve the interests of the Church even outside the diocese.

We suggest that a department of African affairs be created on a national level. Its main duty would be to look after the interests of the Black Catholics. It ought to be comprised of professionals, both lay and clerical, plus ordinary men with common sense.

We prefer to manage or mismanage ourselves, otherwise we shall for ever remain Black boys under the rectorship of the White boys. If the Catholic Church has hitherto failed to produce African pastors and rectors, then there must be something radically wrong with their training and apprenticeship. The Government is Africanizing its civil institutions. Why must the Church lag behind this progress?

Let our White colleagues cease to pretend to be impeccable angels at our expense.

By the way of conclusion, we would like to reassure readers that we are sincere men who wish to put things right in the Church. Please do not misunderstand us. We have in the past presented to the Hierarchy resolutions that were passed in July, 1966, but to no effect.

If anybody suspects us of mud-slinging, or defeatism for that matter, then our message has been misunderstood. We would be hypocrites if we pretended to be contented with the status quo. Our colleagues can rest assured that in any eventuality we shall be their best allies.

Should a fruitful dialogue emerge from this meditation so much the better for the CHURCH. We invite you to join us in reciting an act of loyalty:

"We the undersigned, profess and embrace the Catholic teaching in all its entirety. We firmly believe that Christ's Church is one, holy, catholic and apostolic. We hope to live, work and die as true sons of our beloved Brother and Saviour Christ."

DOCUMENT 27. "Black Consciousness and White Liberals." Article by Richard Turner, *Reality,* July 1972

The argument between "black consciousness" and "white liberalism" is heading towards greater confusion. Important problems of goals and tactics underlie the argument, but at the moment these issues are being obscured by misconceptions and by semantical confusions. In this article I want to look at one or two of these specific issues rather than to give an evaluation of the situation as a whole.

The major misperception is to see "black consciousness" as essentially an attack on "white liberalism," and nothing more. In fact, the attack is directed essentially against "white racist society" (SASO Manifesto Point 1), and the question of "white liberals" is considered to be of relatively minor importance. It has been given disproportionate significance in the way in which the white press has reported "black consciousness" meetings. For obvious ideological reasons there has been an attempt to distort "black consciousness" in an attempt to discredit both "black consciousness" and "white liberals" simultaneously.

To untangle the confusions it seems to me to be useful to distinguish between two different points which are being made about "white liberals." The first point is that, as a group, white opponents of apartheid are not a significant political force, and are certainly not going to be the chief agent in the overthrow of apartheid. It would therefore be wrong for blacks to orient their political activity towards an appeal to whites to help them. (There has always been a tendency for black political organisations to make appeals to the moral sensibility of the whites. It is this strategy that is being attacked by proponents of "black consciousness." And of course they are quite right to attack it. Blacks cannot leave their case to be argued by whites in the context of white political institutions.)

ASSUMPTIONS OF SUPREMACY
The second point that is being made is that the behaviour and beliefs of

"white liberals" often constitute a striking example of precisely how deep the assumptions of white supremacy run. It is in this sense that an analysis of the phenomenon of "white liberalism" is important to the case of "black consciousness".

However, it seems to me that their analysis is confused by a very loose use of the concept "liberal." To put it another way, the range of attitudes lumped together and described by the term "white liberalism" is uselessly broad. I shall first develop the critique of "white liberalism," and then attempt to present a more precise set of categories in which to embody the critique.

According to point six of the Saso manifesto: "Saso believes that all groups allegedly working for "Integration" in South Africa—and here we note in particular the Progressive Party and other Liberal institutions—are not working for the kind of integration that would be acceptable to the Black man. Their attempts are directed merely at relaxing certain oppressive legislations and to allow Blacks into a White-type society. That is, they are considering "an assimilation of Blacks into an already established set of norms drawn up and motivated by White society." (Point 5)

The point here is that this attitude remains arrogant, paternalistic and basically insulting. It involves the acceptance of the idea that to behave like whites is the ideal; it is to accept the concept of the "civilising mission" of the whites, the idea that, although blacks are not biologically inferior, they are culturally inferior. They may be educable, but they need whites to educate them.

For any group to treat another like this would be unpleasant, but for whites to make this sort of assumption about their cultural superiority is also laughable. It is arguable that the main "contribution" of western civilisation to human history was the development of a new and higher level of exploitation of person by person, and of a new and higher level of materialism. The theoretical Christian principles of Europe were contradicted by the factual concentration on the acquisition of material goods through the efficient exploitation of one's neighbours. Christian Europe was based on servile labour and, as it expanded, internally with the development of industrial capitalism, and externally through imperial conquest, it refined the mechanisms of exploitation. The working class at home, the "natives" abroad, were so much raw material for the accumulation of wealth. Naturally more efficient accumulation led to better science and technology, grander architecture, more sophisticated cultural leisure-time pursuits for the rich, and so to the illusion of superiority in "civilisation." But this superiority was based on an ethical void. Whites are where they are in the world essentially through having developed a great capacity to wield force ruthlessly in pursuit of their own ends. That is there is an integral relationship between the nature of the culture of the whites and the fact of their dominance in South Africa. The refusal of blacks to want to be "like whites" is not racism. It is good taste.

THREE CATEGORIES

In the light of the above, I would like to suggest that it would be useful to use three categories to classify the political attitudes of whites in South

Africa: racist, liberal and radical. Racists believe that blacks are biologically inferior or "different." Liberals believe that "western civilisation" is adequate, and superior to other forms, but also that blacks can, through education, attain the level of western civilisation. It is worth noting that many blacks have also accepted this position. Booker T. Washington in the United States, J. T. Jabavu, and the early leadership of the ANC, are examples. Radicals believe that "white" culture itself is at fault, and that both blacks and whites need to go beyond it and create a new culture.

It is important to notice that all three of these categories apply to blacks as well as to whites. There are black racists of all kinds, black liberals, and black radicals. Black consciousness is a form of radicalism. So far the argument has been formulated in terms of the categories "liberalism" and "racism," with resulting confusion on both sides. The introduction of the third category enables us to clear up these confusions, and to point to the real problem, which is the need for a new culture.

OBJECTIONS

Two objections are likely to be raised to this classification. Firstly, the term "liberal" has a long tradition. It is normally understood as referring to a set of beliefs about the limits of government, the importance of the rule of law, the rights of freedom of speech and assembly, and so on. Now obviously in this sense radicals, including proponents of black consciousness, can also be liberals. The problem here is whether we are to accept the traditional meaning of the word, or the meaning which has tended to become associated with the word in South Africa, particularly amongst blacks. Perhaps the only solution is to remember the ambiguity which the term has now acquired.

The second objection, from the direction of black consciousness, is in its strong form, that whites cannot be radical, and in its weak form that the existence of white radicals obscures the issues, prevents the development of self-consciousness amongst blacks, and so politically is no different from the existence of white liberals. The strong version is obviously untrue. To show that the weak version is also untrue, it is necessary to indicate what positive role there is for white radicals to play.

In an interview in 1969, Eldridge Cleaver was asked the following question: "Since the National Conference on New Politics, held two summers ago, what we have seen for the most part is not viable working coalitions, but whites acquiescing to the blacks, somewhat because of guilt feelings, rather than offering constructive criticism. What effect does this have on such a coalition?" Cleaver replied: "The guilt problem is part of the racial heritage of America. But such guilt feelings make many people non-functional from our point of view. This stance of acquiescence can be detrimental if a black is advocating a bad programme. Such a white cannot distinguish between what different blacks are saying; all he recognises is that a black is saying it. Motivation that is spurred by guilt doesn't make for reliable whites, and we have had many problems with people of this type." (*The Nation* Jan. 29, 1969)

PATERNALISM

The attitude that Cleaver is criticising is in fact the ultimate in white paternalism. "White" because it involves, on another level, the "They all look alike" mentality of racism; "paternalism" because it treats blacks as being incapable of listening to criticism and engaging in rational argument. Thus one must not confuse a) the fact that any political policy/strategy in South Africa must have as its unquestionable basis the objective of satisfying the needs of the black masses, irrespective of whether this clashes with white interests, with b) the idea that one must go along with the policy/strategy of any particular black leader just because he/she claims to be aiming at that goal. A political strategy has to be rooted in the needs of a particular group or groups, but it is also something which can be argued about in terms of objective criteria. Will the strategy work? Is it based upon an adequate analysis of the situation? In such discussions what is important is the validity of the argument, rather than the colour of the arguer. Even if there is to be, as is probably necessary, a tactical division of labour between white and black opponents of white supremacy, the results of their activities will be interrelated, and so will benefit from conscious co-ordination. In "private life" one has a right to demand to do one's own thing. But in politics the way I do my thing has implications for the way you do your thing.

Thus for whites, in the face of the phenomenon of "black consciousness," to believe that they must now simply shut up and leave it to the blacks would be a serious mistake. Nevertheless whites do need to re-evaluate themselves and their political roles, particularly in the light of two specific criticisms. For it is argued that in South Africa a black is likely to be much more politically effective than a white a) because there are no barriers between him/her and other blacks; and b) he/she is immediately, by the very fact of being black, pushed into political action. The white, on the other hand, is continually tempted by the possibility of a return to a life of privilege, and is in any event only working with blacks to work out his/her own personal psychological problems, in order to "find himself through contact with the Black man" (*SASO Newsletter* Vol.1, No. 3).

OVER-SIMPLIFICATION

However, although these points are important for whites to consider, it is also important for blacks to realise that they all involve over-simplification if they are absolutised. Even leaving aside the difficulties arising from divisions amongst black groups, there are two other problems here.

1) The idea that blacks can immediately communicate with blacks, and cannot meaningfully communicate at all with whites, involves an inadequate theory of communication. No two individuals have the same experience of the world. This means that they will always see things in more or less different ways. So communication between two people is always difficult. It is made more or less difficult by the size of the gap between the two sets of experience, and by the skill or otherwise of the two communicators in trying

to put themselves into one another's shoes. In South Africa a black and white will usually have had very different experiences, and this is likely to complicate communication. But it is not an absolute gap. Also, different blacks have different life experiences. They have in common the experience of being discriminated against, but each individual experiences this in terms of his/her own particular social situation and personality. There may also be areas of their lives where their experiences are entirely different—a wealthy, educated urban Indian man has a life experience different in many respects from that of a poor African peasant woman, and communication problems are likely to result.

2) The idea that blacks are automatically political, while whites only engage in politics for contingent personal reasons is a similar over-simplification. Whether or not individuals move out of the circle of their private concerns into the sphere of public co-operative action with their fellows is always a matter of choice. However bad an individual's situation is, he/she risks something in some ways worse by trying to change it—he/she risks being endorsed out, or losing the meagre salary he/she does have, or perhaps going to prison. Thus one has to make a choice, and that choice involves some sort of reflection on oneself and on one's own values. Some situations make this choice easier than do other situations. In particular, it is perhaps easier for a black to make this choice than it is for a white. But the difference is one of degree, not of kind.

Thus in both cases, the question of political action and the question of communication, there is difference of degree, rather than of kind, between black and white, and there are also factors to take into account besides colour. Even if colour is the main factor, and the difference of degree is very large, as is probably the case in South Africa today, it is nevertheless important to bear in mind the nature of the difference. For if black leaders believe that they have an intuitive understanding of the needs of the black people, and no need to motivate them to act politically, then they are not likely to be very effective leaders.

DIMENSION

To misperceive this difference of degrees as a difference of kind is also to ignore a further crucial dimension to the question of change in South Africa. Black consciousness is a rejection of the idea that the ideal for human kind is "to be like the whites." This should lead to the recognition that it is also bad for whites "to be like the whites." That is, the whites themselves are oppressed in South Africa. In an important sense both whites and blacks are oppressed, though in different ways, by a social system which perpetuates itself by creating white lords and black slaves, and no full human beings. Material privilege is bought at the cost of mental atrophy. The average white South African is scarcely one of the higher forms of life. For whites who have recognised this the desire to change South Africa is not merely the desire "to do something for the blacks." It is the urgent need for personal dignity and the air of freedom and love.

Having said all this, I would like to return to my earlier assertion that white critics of white supremacy are not a significant political force. This statement needs qualification in two ways. Firstly, although as a group white radicals are not a vital force, many of them have skills which make them useful as individuals in political activity.

Secondly, there is one major area of political work where they are perhaps best equipped to work. This is, as proponents of black consciousness have pointed out, in the area of changing white consciousness. It is vitally important to analyse the ways in which whites oppress themselves, and to devise ways of bringing home to them the extent to which the pursuit of material self-interest empties their lives of meaning.

LITTLE THOUGHT

Very little thought has been given to this problem. The characteristic "liberal" approach has been either to argue that the end of apartheid is really in the material interest of the whites, or else simply to appeal to abstract ethical principles, as against material self-interest, without making any attempt to show how the infringement of these principles vitiates the unique life of each individual. Whilst whites are wedded to materialism they will fight against change. In order to bring about this change as smoothly as possible there should be as many whites as possible who want to become full human beings and who recognise that to do so requires co-operation with all their fellows in changing South Africa.

At present, white consciousness is cabbage consciousness—a mindless absorption of material from the environment. The synthesis which both Steve Biko and Alan Paton were looking for, the synthesis of cabbage consciousness and its antithesis black consciousness, is human conscious-ness, and it is the possibilities and promises of human consciousness that we all need to explore.

I have tried to show in this article where the attacks by "black conscious-ness" on "white liberalism" are justified, and where they are too sweeping. Finally I would like to say that it seems to me that the time has come when both sides could fruitfully bury the argument. By now it should be clear to even the most insensitively paternalistic "white liberal" that he or she needs to examine his or her values very carefully indeed. For the proponents of black consciousness the best way to convince black people that salvation will not come from "white liberals" is by simply getting on with the work of community organisation.

Document 28. Flyer publicizing NUSAS campaign to release political prisoners, Johannesburg, May 27–30, 1974

Students in Johannesburg and Cape Town have called for the release of political prisoners. They have done so because many of them believe that men like Mandela are the true leaders of black people in South Africa.

If black men and women are to work for a new South Africa, where their children do not have to carry passes, and will be able to earn a living wage, then the leaders must be released.

If justice and humanity are to be found for black people, then those men who can help struggle for freedom must be let out of jail.

Chief Gatsha Buthelezi and Cedric Phatudi have joined the students in calling for the release of political prisoners. All the mighty nations of the world have called for freedom for black leaders in South Africa.

IF PASS RAIDS ARE TO END;
IF MEN ARE TO BE ABLE TO LIVE WITH THEIR WIVES AND CHILDREN;
IF COMFORT IS TO REPLACE POVERTY;
If these are to be so,
THEN MANDELA, SISULU, MBEKI AND MANY OTHER PEOPLE WHO ARE IN JAIL BECAUSE OF THEIR FIGHT AGAINST APARTHEID MUST BE RELEASED.

RELEASE ALL POLITICAL PRISONERS.

Issued by the Students' Representative Council,
        University of the Witwatersrand,
        1 Jan Smuts Avenue, JOHANNESBURG

Document 29. Speech by Helen Joseph at NUSAS rally, University of the Witwatersrand, May 28, 1974

Greetings to students, Fr. [Aelred] Stubbs, [NUSAS executive and SRC] Members.

Your slogan says—RELEASE ALL POLITICAL PRISONERS

I believe you are right and I stand wholeheartedly with you in this. But yesterday's meeting here and various press reports bring home to us that people don't speak with one mind even when supporting the campaign.

And this is obviously because of the word "ALL"—perhaps even with the words political and prisoner as well. But you and I apply the word prisoner to the banned and house arrested as well as to the prisoner in the gaol.

In fact, I'd go further and apply it to the majority of South Africa's white population who are imprisoned by their own fear of losing—of losing their wealth, their prosperity, their past and present status of the master group, their fear of losing their white prestige, and their fear of any means that might be used to take any of this away from them.

And to be a prisoner of that sort of fear is in many ways worse than to be a prisoner of conscience in a gaol.

But I am not here to talk about fear, only about releasing all political prisoners.

Just what do we mean by a political prisoner? According to the Prime

Minister, or was it the Minister of Justice? "There is no such person as a political prisoner in South African gaols."

But if that is so, then I find it difficult to understand why it's only the persons sentenced under the Suppression of Communism Act, or the Sabotage Act or the Terrorism Act and maybe a couple more of the same sort, why it's only these people who cannot earn remission of their sentences, but every other sort of prisoner can?

And by the others I mean what I would call the common law prisoners, who have been sentenced for real crimes against society, against their fellow men. And why is it only the men sentenced to life imprisonment under the Terrorism or the Sabotage Act, for whom the life sentence means the full term of their natural life? This doesn't apply to the murderer!

And I find it difficult also to understand why, if there are no political prisoners, why it is only persons sentenced under those special acts, who, on release from gaol, after they have served their full sentences, are subjected to further deprivations on their return to ordinary life—banning and restrictions orders of various kinds, and removal from their previous places of residence to such places as Mdantsane and Mabopane, where there is neither work, nor home, nor family? This doesn't happen to common law prisoners.

But why do I ask? It is all too clear, isn't it?

The political prisoner is the one who has sinned in the eyes of our laws— but I would say, not against society and his fellowman, but *for society and his fellowman.*

[He is] the man who has staked his own freedom to bring more liberty and justice for others. We may well not support the method, be it violence, or sabotage, but behind the method lies the motive—and that is to my mind what makes the political prisoner different from other prisoners. He has not acted for personal gain, but to gain rights for others.

What about our call for the release of ALL political prisoners?

Yesterday we heard Dr [Cedric] Phatudi, Chief Minister of Lebowa, draw his dividing line: on the right hand he would place "democratically oriented" persons, and on the other, (I suppose on the left hand!) the "declared communists"—a group which he has set apart from the other political prisoners, a group "with whom no chance can be taken."

But how can we, if [we] are to be fair, just accept such a distinction? Can we in fact allow of any distinction? Who is to decide, who is to be the judge? Can we really separate into sheep and goats? Do we want to?

Take the Rivonia trial just as an example. All eight were convicted under the Sabotage Act, yet not one was convicted as a communist. But Govan Mbeki himself declared himself to be one when he gave evidence.

So where does that get you? Release Mandela and Sisulu, but leave Govan Mbeki in gaol for life?

Or release Denis Goldberg, but leave Bram Fischer in gaol for life? I am speaking only of a few, but this division would cleave right through the political prisoners, wherever they are.

Perhaps others would draw some other distinction, the degree of violence planned, or its effectiveness? But surely such distinctions have been made already by the Courts in the passing of sentence.

What is common to all political prisoners is their desire to gain freedom and justice for their fellow men and the price they paid for that desire.

To me it would be immoral to embody any discrimination in our call for the release of political prisoners.

And what about the un-gaoled prisoners—the legion of the banned? We are all banned under the Suppression of Communism Act. Where would be the dividing line? I was never a communist by conviction or by knowledge either, or by membership, but I was banned under the Suppression of Communism Act, and now I am a sort of Technical Communist because the Minister declares me to be so—not [by] *my* declaration!

We are calling for the release of ALL political prisoners, gaoled or banned, and I maintain that there should be no divisions. Nor can I really accept [that] the call should be for only one or two leaders to be released. This is not a "Release Mandela and Sobukwe" campaign. Nor, I think, would they themselves want to be distinguished from their fellow political prisoners.

We condemn punishment without trial, we condemn these restrictive laws which turn men of conscience into prisoners of conscience—and our call must surely be for all.

And our call for release is made because S. A. needs these prisoners—these leaders of whatever rank. Needs them because she still hopes for a peaceful solution of her troubles [and] because that can only come about if there is—oh, this overused and much abused word—"dialogue."

But there can be no real and meaningful dialogue and acceptable dialogue unless those leaders now imprisoned or banned are included to represent their people alongside those who are free.

In Portugal, in Mozambique, right on our doorstep, this has happened. The political prisoners have been freed. Frelimo is accepted as vital to any meaningful discussion. Is it too much to ask for this to happen here? To ask for this to happen *now,* and not to wait until one day it may be forced upon us? Is it too much to ask that now this stain of political persecution by gaol, banning, exile, be washed away? Year after year the cry goes up, all over the world, "Release the political prisoners!" [Illegible], but we are concerned here and now with S. A. This outcry overseas grows louder year by year. And it is good to stand here today and to be able to join in it.

What about clemency, mercy? I know this is not the actual basis of our call, but I think it is to some extent basic to it. I don't see how you can exclude the personal element in our call.

Since the Rivonia trial ended in 1964, just ten years ago on June 12th, when the first life sentences were handed down for political offenses, the number of such sentences has grown over the years with succeeding trials. So let's take a brief look at the position now—it will be only a rough [outline], because it is difficult to arrive at the exact figures, and these I am sure will be only minimal figures.

There are said to be well over 200 political prisoners on Robben Island today. And of these, including the prisoners from S. W. Africa [South West Africa], there must be 19 serving life sentences. There are three or so who are serving more than 20 years, and a horrifying total of some 84 serving from 15 to 20 years, and still another 63 serving sentences of from 10 to 15 years, and then another [number] with smaller sentences.

Almost all of these sentences started somewhere along the line between 1964 and 1969. True, many of the original number have left the Island over the years, but these are the ones who remain and we are thinking about them. And the plain fact is that THEY HAVE BEEN THERE TOO LONG!

What of the 19 serving life—plus the 2 in Pretoria gaol? What of the group of over eighty who are serving between 15 and 20 years? Even if ten of these long long years have already passed, there are still from 5 to 10 years still to go. No, they HAVE BEEN THERE TOO LONG!

And the banned people, that vast legion of 1240 restricted since the first order in 1951? What of them? I don't know exactly how many there are now. I think the Minister admitted to 200 not so long ago—and there were anyway 80 or more banned last year, and to date, already eleven this year.

Of those 1240 more than one thousand were black, and for black people, a banning or a house arrest order is very much worse than for whites. And there have been more than a hundred placed under house arrest.

And the renewals? You'd think that 5 years would be long enough to satisfy even this government, but not at all. As the day of expiry draws near, you are torn between hope and dread—I know—you make plans, for a party, a holiday, you are human. But all too often comes a knock on the door, a few days before the ban is to expire, and somehow you know that there are two men on the outside. They will hand you some documents and you will close the door again on life for another five years.

Can we, as human beings, as people, tolerate this much longer? Are we not by our silence, condoning the cruelty? We must speak out, louder and clearer and join voices to the shouts from overseas "Release the political prisoners! All of them, gaoled, banned, exiled, wherever they be, let them go free!"

Some of these imprisoned men I have known personally. They were, and still are, my friends. We campaigned together in the exciting 1950's, we were side by side in the monumental folly of a treason trial. For nearly five years we travelled together backwards and forwards to Pretoria. We conducted our own defense during five months of detention—and you get to know each other very well in such times. I find that I remember them as they were then—time stopped ten years ago. My reason tells me that they are ten years older, as I am myself! But my mind is filled with them as I knew them then.

Mandela, Kathrada, Sisulu, Mbeki, Mkwayi—I wish I had the time or you the patience to listen, so that I could tell you about them as people.

They are my friends, but they are serving life sentences. True they turned to violent methods of struggle to bring about the change for their people and for our land, but only after long frustrating, disappointing years of nonviolent protest. I still remember how I listened to those hundreds of documents and speeches during the treason trial, and even then marvelled to myself: "how *could* they have been patient so long?" Was it any wonder that finally despair prevailed and nonviolence was abandoned as useless. (But let us not forget to ask ourselves, who made it useless? It certainly wasn't the Blacks.)

And there are many others there on the Island, and the few now left in Pretoria [Central Prison] and they HAVE *ALL* BEEN THERE TOO LONG!

If other countries can free their political prisoners, so can S. A. (She did so after the World War, anyway.) And in fact so *must* S. A.—if she genuinely wants peace. The leaders must be restored to the people who chose them.

And they must be restored to their families. I have not time to tell you of what the wives and mothers, the daughters and the sons have endured during these past ten years. And we shall never really know the full agony of those hundreds and hundreds of families, the tragedy of loss of the husband, the father, the son. The poverty, the responsibility of the children—and on what, with what? How? By asking for help from others. There was no other way.

And what of the deeply personal deprivation. The visits to the Island, so rare for so many in Natal and the Transvaal, because so far and so costly. And then the cruelly brief visit—half an hour, after travelling almost a thousand miles each way—and even then no privacy. And what of the children who cannot see their father again until they are sixteen? And then what do they see? A stranger's head and shoulders? And the agony of anxiety? So many of the prisoners are growing old now—well into their sixties—how long can their health be sustained? And the family knows nothing, except what can be gleaned during a visit. (Bram [Fischer's illness?]—his family did not know—they read it in the newspaper!)

Oh, they HAVE INDEED BEEN THERE TOO LONG!

Let us ask ourselves, can South Africa really go forward without these men? I believe not, they are indeed needed, needed by their own people, and needed by us too.

The change in Mozambique, in Angola, is dramatic, startling. Perhaps we cannot yet see exactly where that change is going to take us, but one thing I know, as surely as the night follows the day, this change is moving forward—forward to freedom.

Here our government still talks of peace in the land—but what an uneasy peace indeed. Political parties talk of peaceful evolution, gradual change but it is clear to me and to many, and indeed to some who see it but won't admit it, that there is ultimately only one real road ahead—and that is to majority rule. And the longer the whites put it off, or try to, the more we endanger ourselves, our future, our children.

And for this road ahead South Africa needs, *now,* men of stature, courage, conviction, integrity. Must they still be shut up in our gaols?

It seems that Robben Island has recently become precious. It has potentiality, it can become a plush holiday centre—for the very rich—whites, I presume?

ALL RIGHT MR VORSTER! *You* take Robben Island—the people don't want it. It would certainly turn my stomach to spend a holiday there. *You* take the Island—and GIVE US THE PRISONERS!

Document 30. Report by Glenn Moss, SRC President, University of the Witwatersrand, on NUSAS campaign for the release of political prisoners, May 27–30, 1974

The events and lessons of campaign '74—the call for the release of all political prisoners—have considerable importance for the future of Student Government at the University of the Witwatersrand. Many trends emerged which, if taken to their logical conclusions, necessitate many changes which must be implemented. Accordingly, this report deals both with the factual and the analytical.

1) THE IDEA OF A CAMPAIGN:
At December seminar last year, the following reasons for running a campaign were put forward:
(a) To recruit students for projects. One has to have students going through an educative process to ensure that new people are continually found to generate and continue leadership and projects.
(b) National campaigns can unify the National Union and the campus, and lead to discussions of ideology which are essential in terms of thought on long term goals.
(c) Running a campaign tends to create organisational skills amongst campaign leaders which is essential for the good running of Student Affairs.
(d) Campaigns can politicise and socialise people through united action. This can be most important in developing levels of consciousness.
(e) A well-planned, carefully chosen campaign can expose the facade of "peaceful, democratic South Africa."
(f) A campaign which is issue oriented can become a focus for groups studying South Africa and who operate overseas.
In addition to these, the following [should be considered?]
(1) The short-term, ostensible aim of a campaign is rarely achieved. This must be borne in mind, and must not lead to the disillusionment of students coupled with a feeling of futility.
(2) One must be very clear which groups, or combinations of groups the campaign is aimed at.
The success or otherwise of campaign '74 must be assessed against the above points.

2) IMPLEMENTATION:
Sunday 26th: Literally hundreds of posters, stickers and a large banner were put up on campus. The posters were varied, some advertising activities of the week, some being artistic calls for the release of all political prisoners.

Large stickers, printed in red, with the message "RELEASE ALL POLITICAL PRISONERS" were used to excellent advantage. Some 1,500 of these mini-posters went up at various times, and were generally most successful in terms of building up a "campaign atmosphere" on campus.

Monday 27th: Some 10 students arrived on campus at 7.00 a.m. to pamphlet students on the campaign. 10 students discover that most of the posters and stickers put up on Sunday night, together with the banner have been torn down. 10 students spend next two hours putting them all back, and adding a few more for good measure.

At that stage, some two thousand pamphlets announcing the campaign and the opening speech of the campaign, were distributed on campus. Lunchtime saw a packed Great Hall (over 1,300 students) ready to hear the first campaign speech, that of Cedric Phatudi, Chief Minister of Lebowa.

Then disaster struck. Phatudi refused to call [for] the release of ALL political prisoners, distinguishing between political prisoners who are "Communistically oriented," and those who are "democratically oriented." Phatudi was only prepared to call for the release of the second grouping.

A shocked and stunned Great Hall audience listened in silence to this refusal to demand the release of all political prisoners. Polite applause greeted the end of the speech, and most people immediately left the Great Hall.

Some students then picketed along Jan Smuts Avenue, but the pall hanging over campus after Phatudi's speech was heavy, and the picket broke up after about an hour.

All in all, the first day of campaign '74 had not been a success.

Tuesday 28th: 3,500 copies of the first WITS STUDENT special edition supporting the campaign were distributed. More posters etc. were put up on campus, and it was decided to hold the lunch-time meeting in the open air.

Helen Joseph and Father [Aelred] Stubbs spoke to about 1,000 people gathered on the Piazza, and they jointly did a lot to overcome the disillusionment caused by Phatudi's talk. By the end of the speeches, a far better atmosphere existed on campus, and a group of students went off to pamphlet black workers.

The group of people pamphleting were subjected to considerable harassments. After a uniformed policeman confiscated the pamphlets, numerous Security Branch and CID [Criminal Investigation Department] agents arrived, searched vehicles, took names and addresses of those pamphleting, confiscated five rolls of films and adopted a very threatening attitude.

With the police were about five squad cars, police dogs and the like. It was interesting to note excited black reaction both to the pamphlets, (very in favour of its contents) and to the police. Also interesting was the over-reaction of the police to an innocuous situation.

Wednesday 29th: During the morning, the "John Burger Show"—a slide and tape history of opposition movements in South Africa—was continually shown in the foyer of the Students Union. The atmosphere on campus was more explosive than the other two days, and considerable excitement was growing as to whether the planned protest march was to take place or not. (In fact, magisterial permission had been refused late the previous day, but I had had no opportunity to disclose this to the student body). Lunchtime saw the second open air meeting, addressed by Gerson Veii [of the South West African National Union] and myself. Veii's lines were good and hard, and the fact that he had served five years as a political prisoner, increased the impact of his talk. Despite the fact that he is not fluent in English, his talk was of considerable value. After Veii's talk, I spoke a little, announcing inter alia that permission for a march had been refused and that picketing and pamphleting would take place in the afternoon.

A large turn out on Jan Smuts Avenue was heartening, and suddenly people were lining up in the street, ready to march in defiance of the magistrate's prohibition.

A small group set off down Jan Smuts Avenue, marching under the banner "RELEASE POLITICAL PRISONERS." Having marched through Braamfontein it was then decided that the group was too small to risk confrontation, and the procession marched back to the picket lines. Exhilaration was high—students had got away with an illegal march.

At this stage, a group of students broke away, and left to go pamphleting in town—their exploits will be described below. Meanwhile, at the picket lines, the police began arriving—and as they arrived, so more students arrived. Suddenly, a police officer mumbled something inaudible into a megaphone, and seconds later the police charged, forcing students back onto campus, and arresting 11 students in the process.

For about another two and a half hours, police and students observed an uneasy truce but no other significant events occurred on the picket lines that day.

However, the group that went pamphleting encountered serious difficulties. While pamphleting, a large group of black workers gathered around to read the pamphlets. Police arrived, broke up the gathering with dogs, confiscated all the pamphlets, searched vehicles, detained a few people for questioning and took names and addresses.

Eventually, all those held were released, but the over-reaction of the police, and the attitude of black workers was again of considerable interest.

Wednesday was interesting, with far greater police action mirrored by increased student anger and activity.

Thursday 30th: The second special issue of WITS STUDENT was released, again with considerable impact. Lunchtime saw about 1,000 people on the Piazza, listening to a call for the release of political prisoners by Sonny Leon.

As his talk progressed, I became aware of a steady infiltrating of the crowd by security branch agents. The intention was to pamphlet on a mass base after the talk, and in terms of the past reaction of the police, trouble seemed inevitable. I had, however, kept the venues for pamphleting a complete secret, and I estimated that about 10,000 pamphlets could be distributed before the [words missing].

This, however, was not to be so. Immediately Sonny Leon's talk ended, a search warrant authorising confiscation was served, and all the pamphlets were confiscated. In addition to this, the [special] branch [the security police] made it clear that they intended raiding the SRC offices.

For once, however, our student body acted spontaneously. Down to the Students Union they rushed, barricaded the door and windows, pushed police away, allegedly assaulted certain police, threw them downstairs, until the team of police intent on raiding our office finally left—thwarted. They were indeed lucky not to have pierced the first wall of defence, because I saw a group of students manning the fire hoses at the top of the Union steps, and it was perfectly obvious what they intended doing to the first policeman who reached that area!

For the rest of the afternoon, students picketed along Jan Smuts Avenue, attacked various passing cars which threatened to run over the picket line, were pelted with eggs, et cetera.

That night, the showing of the movie "The Confession" closed down campaign '74.

So much for the facts. We must now examine, in retrospect, what campaign '74 achieved.

LESSONS OF THE CAMPAIGN:
The first major factor which emerged was that numbers of students CAN be got to meetings if one works hard on publicity. The woeful cry that student apathy is the cause of poor attendance merely masks the laziness or inefficiency of the wailers.

However, it emerges even more clearly that most students tend to miss or ignore the basic issues involved. During the campaign, the only mass action obtained apart from a passive attendance at meetings, was in response to police aggression.

In other words, the campaign tended towards an anti-police feeling, rather than positive action for a new political dispensation in South Africa. In terms of the experience of campaigns I have been involved in, I fear that this is a built-in limitation of mass student action in South Africa at present. It is too easy to identify "the police" as the problem, and get people excited about police action. This is, I think, a largely counter-productive situation which rarely leads to a raise in consciousness or educative process.

The next major factor to emerge related to choice of speakers. Firstly, I believe that we should steer clear of homeland leaders or leaders in the "apartheid institutions," when pushing emotive, mass based issues. Our experience during the campaign week was that these people tended to shirk this issue, throw a dampener on proceedings, and obscure the major thrust of the campaign. This is perhaps inevitable for leaders of the apartheid institutions, in that they invariably have to maintain the support of conservative groupings both in white and black South Africa.

The built-in contradiction, in this regard, is that we need "big name speakers" to attract students in a campaign and that these names, by virtue of their position in society, tend to be part of the white ruling elite, or the aspirant black bourgeoisie. Accordingly, their objective interests invariably differ radically from ours, and the lines they push at meetings tend to conflict with our original motivation for holding the talk.

The only way out of this inherent dilemma built into white student action seems to be to have a "name speaker" on a platform (to attract people, establish credibility etc) and have him followed up by a person with good lines and considerable oratorical ability.

It now becomes of importance to measure up the campaign against our original criteria for a campaign as listed in section 1 of this report. It is in these terms only that the success and viability of this campaign in particular, and mass student action in general, can be determined.

(a) The campaign in no way assisted recruitment for projects. This was because it was held too late in the year, and too close to mid-year examinations. If we are ever to follow up "campaign atmosphere," the actual campaign must be run at absolute latest in April.

(b) I think that the campaign had a reasonable effect in terms of unifying the "left" on campus. Certainly the fact that an illegal march was held—and the students got away with it—and student action prevented the police from carrying out a raid on our offices had an exhilarating and unifying effect on the people involved. A sense of efficacy and success is essential in any movement for change. However, I fear that the unity was not built on common beliefs or mutual perception of issues, but rather on an anti-police basis. I do not believe that this expanded the horizons and understanding of any students to a considerable degree.

(c) The running of the campaign certainly taught a few of us a lot in terms of organisation and tactics. This is an important aspect of any campaign work, but we never got enough people involved in the actual planning and implementation to claim this aspect as an unqualified success.

(d) Has been dealt with above.

(e) The exposure of the democratic facade of South Africa was, to a considerable degree, achieved. The whole thrust of the campaign related to the fact that South Africa's basic lack of freedom forced people into acts of illegality and violence. This point was made time and time again, and got through to a lot of people. In addition to this, the continual confiscation of pamphlets laid bare certain aspects of the society in full nakedness, and I believe that this was important in itself.

(f) The overseas interest and solidarity shown in the campaign was important and significant. I tend to wonder, however, exactly what this achieves in itself. Political prisoners as focus for overseas is important, but is certainly not the basic dynamic of South African society.

Most important to assess however, is how we got across to those groups we were aiming at. In the main, we were aiming at white students, and black workers. I have already dealt with the successes and failures we have had in relation to white students. Thus, all I want to do is mention very briefly that I believe the effect we had on the black community in Johannesburg was considerable. The response to our pamphlet was most exciting, and the letters I received from blacks about the campaign were numerous and congratulatory.

The point to make is that if we choose an issue obviously close to the black worker, produce publications (and publicity) on the matter, and distribute those publications, we will be doing important work. Even if campaign energy is used for nothing other than distributing tens of thousands of pamphlets, something significant will be coming out of the campaign.

We did not perceive this fully during our campaign. If we had, considerably more effort could have been employed to evade police confiscation of pamphlets; many distribution points could have been used, etc.

Accordingly, I must conclude that campaign '74 was a qualified success only. If we utilise the knowledge gained from mistakes and miscalculations made, gains will have been made. If a campaign is ever to be run again, we must build on the experience of the "release all political prisoners" campaign. I hope that this report in some way assists in that aim.

Document 31. Resolution of the South African Council of Churches on conscientious objection, August 2, 1974

The National Conference of the SACC acknowledges as the one and only God Him who mightily delivered the people of Israel from bondage in Egypt and who in Jesus Christ still proclaims that He will "set at liberty those who are oppressed" (Luke 4:18). He alone is supreme Lord and Saviour and to Him alone we owe ultimate obedience. Therefore "we must obey God rather than men" in those areas where the Government fails to fulfil its calling to be "God's servant for good" rather than for evil and for oppression (Acts 5:29; Romans 13:4).

In the light of this the Conference:
1. Maintains that Christians are called to strive for justice and the true peace which can be founded only on justice;
2. does not accept that it is automatically the duty of those who follow Christ, the Prince of Peace, to engage in violence and war, or to prepare to engage in violence and war, whenever the State demands it;
3. reminds its member Churches that both Catholic and Reformation theology has regarded the taking up of arms as justifiable, if at all, only in order to fight a "just war."
4. points out that the theological definition of a "just war" excludes war in defence of a basically unjust and discriminatory society;
5. points out that the Republic of South Africa is at present a fundamentally unjust and discriminatory society and that this injustice and discrimination constitutes the primary, institutionalised violence which has provoked the counter-violence of the terrorists or freedom fighters;
6. points out that the military forces of our country are being prepared to

defend this unjust and discriminatory society and that the threat of military force is in fact already used to defend the status quo against moves for radical change from outside the white electorate;

7. maintains that it is hypocritical to deplore the violence of terrorists or freedom fighters while we ourselves prepare to defend our society with its primary, institutionalised violence by means of yet more violence;

8. points out further that the injustice and oppression under which the black people of South Africa labour is far worse than that against which Afrikaners waged their First and Second Wars of Independence and that if we have justified the Afrikaners' resort to violence (or the violence of the imperialism of the English) or claimed that God was on their side, it is hypocritical to deny that the same applies to the black people in their struggle today;

9. questions the basis upon which chaplains are seconded to the military forces lest their presence indicate moral support for the defence of our unjust and discriminatory society.

The Conference therefore:

1. deplores violence as a means to solve problems;

2. calls on its member churches to challenge all their members to consider in view of the above whether Christ's call to take up the Cross and follow Him in identifying with the oppressed does not, in our situation, involve becoming conscientious objectors;

3. calls on those of its member churches who have chaplains in the military forces to reconsider the basis on which they are appointed and to investigate the state of pastoral care available to the communicants at present in exile or under arms beyond our borders and to seek ways and means of ensuring that such pastoral care may be properly exercised;

4. commends the courage and witness of those who have been willing to go to jail in protest against unjust laws and policies in our land, and who challenge all of us by their example;

5. requests the SACC's task force on Violence and Non-violence to study methods of non-violent action for change which can be recommended to its member churches;

6. prays for the Government and people of our land and urgently calls on them to make rapid strides towards radical and peaceful change in our society so that the violence and war to which our social, economic and political policies are leading us may be avoided.

DOCUMENT 32. "White Consciousness" and "White Liberation." Discussion documents for annual NUSAS congress, Johannesburg, November 29–December 2, 1976

White Consciousness

It is impossible for us as English speaking campuses to continue to pay lip service to the ideology which we have inherited. For too long we have attempted to disseminate a worldview imported from Europe and irrelevant to our present context both geographical (Africa), temporal (1976) and socio-economic (Third World).

We have eschewed searching for an identity because we considered ourselves to be members of a great international community. (The 'free world').

We have eschewed Nationalism and patriotism because we associated it with the unpatriotic repressive activities of the white elite.

We eschewed commitment because we were cosmopolitan and supercool.

We believed in everybody's right to an opinion so consequently believed ourselves in nothing at all. We were much too open-minded and "free" to accept any ideology.

We extended a hand of friendship to our black brothers oppressed by apartheid whilst we ourselves entered the commercial sector.

We thus lost all the words that could have helped us fight: "patriotism," "identity," "commitment," "ideology," "liberation." We gave them away with hardly a murmur. We were rightly branded colonialists by our African compatriots and told to keep out of the native policy. We confined ourselves to charity and welfare. The time has come to take back these words we have lost.

We must become patriots—proud of our country and our people.

We must become committed—to a free and united South Africa/Azania.

We must develop an ideology—suited to our present situation and capable of changing to meet the changing needs of history.

White English campuses must find out that they are also African campuses and so wake up to an African dawn.

Thus let us look now to our own humanity. We will be driven not by pity nor guilt, but by the desire to stand ourselves, fully human, in a human society.

Thus let us not think of "giving," of redistribution, but look towards creating a society where redistribution will prove unnecessary.

Let us now think of helping ourselves towards freedom and humanity and so be moved towards creating a free and human society.

But we must talk closer now and think of action. We must be early if we are not to be late already. History is on the march.

Men and women of Azania! Unite!

By Patrick Fitzgerald

White Liberation

I remember a chic radical pronouncement that was once popular on this campus: that white English-speaking students are irrelevant to social change, that we can only wait and see what happens, and hope that the victorious party will graciously permit us to contribute to their victory. I accept that the black man's struggle for freedom is not mine but I do not accept my irrelevance: I need a means of establishing my relevance and possible roles, not simply to contribute to someone else's future but to attempt to form my own.

The need to know and understand this society and our place in it has been long recognised. However, to see oneself as a legitimate part of Africa with as much right to participate and to derive benefits, to influence society towards one's own ideals instead of supinely accepting those of whoever rules, now or in the future, is for me a new dimension to being a white English-speaking student. This is what has led me into white consciousness (white Africanism).

The purpose of white consciousness is to establish my identity, not as an English-speaking pseudopod of Europe, but as an African who is white. I cannot become a black African, cannot adopt his culture and Weltanschauung. Thus I must forge an identity for myself that incorporates my European roots but at the same time cuts the umbilical cord of expatriate europeanism: an identity that is independent, localised in southern Africa and nationalistic in the noblest sense of that word.

At the same time, this new identity must be [a] liberating force and not another social cage. The idea of white Liberation is the most important aspect of the kind of white consciousness I hope to evolve. I do not believe that we are free: I believe that the privileged position we occupy in this society is actually a state of captivity, and that we are pampered and nurtured and protected for the same reasons that a herd of cattle is well cared for: we are valuable, and we have become so enamoured of our golden chains that we fear to lose them; we are frightened of Rousseau's call to revolution.

For these reasons I don't think that it is wise to fight for someone else's liberation in the hopes that he will be so kind as to free us once he is free. I see this as painfully naive and dangerously gullible.

What exactly this white consciousness will be is a question I cannot now answer: It must still be formulated. What I am sure of is that the need to formulate it has become an imperative we cannot ignore. We are southern African: I cannot and do not want to leave. For better or worse, this is my future. I intend to do as much as I can to make it for the better.

I close with a quote from a poem that appeared on campus during the Soweto unrest (may the gods forgive me if I quote it incorrectly).

> Freedom comes to those who take it
> Liberation comes to those who make it,
> and those who wait are waiting for
> a change of masters, nothing more.

By Rai Turton

Document 33. "The Sins of the Church Are the Sins of the Whites." Article by Reverend Allan Boesak, *Sunday Times*, April 23, 1978

To understand the role of the churches in South African society has always been important, for without this understanding one cannot really grasp the political realities of this country.

This is especially true of the Dutch Reformed Churches (NGK).

To understand the situation within the Dutch Reformed Churches, however, one would have to look at it from the underside, the viewpoint of the black Dutch Reformed person.

The NGK family consists of four churches, divided along ethnic and racial lines: The white NGK, the "coloured" Sendingkerk (mission church), the "Indian" Reformed Church in Africa and the African Dutch Reformed Church in Africa (NGKA).

Although these churches share the same confessional basis and dogma, they are completely separate, with separate structures, separate synods and separate training facilities.

Yet this does not make them fully independent churches. Each year the white NGK provides a staggering sum for "mission work," and this dependency on white funds is one of the strongest ties that binds the black "daughter churches" to the white "mother church."

Also the white church provides ministers who serve in the black churches, who get paid through white funds, who are, in fact, "lent" by the white NGK for any length time.

Most of these ministers, incongruously, still call themselves "missionaries" and most of them remain members of the white NGK even while becoming members of the black churches.

This does not mean that there are non-racial congregations in these churches. White and Black church members rarely meet, and then only on special occasions (with, as we saw in the Press, the gracious permission of the Minister for Plural Relations if this meeting is to be held in a white area).

PLATFORM

Structurally, the common platform of these churches is the Federal Council of the Dutch Reformed Churches which meets once every four years, has a purely advisory function and can take no binding decision for the churches represented there.

For many years now the financial situation, the dominant position of the whites within the black churches (for they have always occupied the positions of power in these churches) and the low level of political consciousness in the black NGKs have assured the white church of at least silent acquiescence and sometimes open support.

And why not? The white "missionaries" were, and most of them still are Nationalists who believed in their Government, who believed in Afrikaner Nationalism as God's gift to darkest Africa and, finally, who believed in the theology of the "volk" as expounded by the white NGK.

And once again, why not? This is how they were brought up, this is the theology they were taught in their white seminaries and, most of all, who in the black churches challenged them?

The few who did could be easily ignored, written off as lone voices agitating on the fringe, or threatened into silence. Knowing the role religion and the church play in the lives of millions of black people, the black NGKs became important for the success of Government plans.

Because apartheid has always been more than mere political philosophy—it is also a religious conviction—it needed a moral base, provided by the church.

It needed the assurance of God's approval, again provided by the church. It also needed to believe that the blacks (for whose sake this policy was devised) accepted the policy.

The silence of the black NGK was sufficient to supply the illusion to fit the need. We have reason to believe that this strong point has now become an Achilles heel for the Government and, consequently, for the white NGK.

The last few years have made it clear that the black churches have come into their own. As never before, they are now articulating their people's hurt and suffering, their fears and aspirations and the deep anger at a policy that dehumanises and humiliates them.

CHALLENGE

Unhesitatingly black spokesmen for the black churches are challenging the white NGK on:

• Its support and uncritical acceptance of Government policy and actions.

• The fact that the white church is essentially a "volkskerk" [people's church] whose loyalty is primarily to the cause of the Afrikaner and the National Party.

• Its theology, which not only accommodates but justifies Government policy as God-given and in accord with Scripture and the reformed tradition.

Moreover, what about its link with the secret Afrikaner Broederbond, of which no less than 10 percent of white NGK dominees [ministers] are members?

What about the fact that the church, together with the teaching profession, is the strongest force in the Broederbond, a sinister, secret organisation that cannot stand the light of day?

An even more pertinent question arises: How many of the whites in the black churches, who preach in black pulpits, who teach our children and young people and who have the numbers to outvote blacks in their own synod, belong to this organisation?

Can these very people who devise and plan and scheme against the liberation of black people now speak for them on national and international church platforms?

This is one of the reasons why white leadership is being challenged and white control of black churches in administration, ecumenical affairs and in theological institutions is being rejected.

Furthermore, blacks realise more and more that their dependency on white money is no accident. It is a direct result of the gross economic injustices maintained by the white Government—the very Government the white church (and whites within the black churches) aid and abet so faithfully.

CHANGE

Economic justice, we realise, does not mean that the whites should be willing to "give more for mission." Rather it should mean that the basic economic policies of their Government should be changed so that black people could earn what they deserve.

This critical attitude in the black churches causes a certain unhappiness in white church circles. Understandably so. But whites should not kid themselves and their leaders should not mislead their people in this respect.

Many tend to blame "outside agitators" (until lately this was the now-banned Christian Institute) who are "behind" all this. Recently even the Dutch churches were blamed for trying to "drive a wedge between mother and daughter churches."

But the reasons for the obstreperousness of the black churches are simple and the intelligent observer not blinded by emotion or ideology will recognise this.

The last ten years or so have seen profound and rapid changes in the black community. These changes are seen not so much in tangible political structures, but in a new political consciousness.

Christians in the black churches come to church with a highly-sensitised political consciousness, and they weigh the political value of all institutions, including the church.

While their white colleagues preach and go home, or vote in synod and go to their white areas to hear applause from other white people, blacks have to return to their black communities.

ACCOUNT

They have to give account of themselves and of the stand of their church vis-a-vis these crucial and inescapable problems. They have a sense of responsibility and accountability to the black community that white "missionaries" never have.

Also, blacks have become tired of being associated with an "apartheid church." Because of the close links with the white NGK they have lost credibility in the black community.

Although all churches in South Africa are infected with the cancer of racism, it is true that the white NGK does carry a special responsibility with regard to the political situation in this country.

Maybe the most important reason is the fact that black Dutch Reformed Church dominees recognise the situation of their people as a situation of oppression through white racism, and they realise that to acquiesce would constitute an act of unfaithfulness to the Gospel of Jesus Christ they seek to serve and are called to proclaim.

Contrary to the belief of their white brothers, they know that it is impossible to reconcile either Scripture or the Reformed tradition with the existence of apartheid.

These are the new realities in the Dutch Reformed Churches. The question must be asked: Is everything lost? Are there not people within the white NGK who recognise the situation for what it is?

Truly not all white dominees accept the status quo and there must be people who are gravely concerned about this rapidly deteriorating situation.

I daresay there are. But where are these people? Why are so many of them willing to speak about these things in private, while only a precious few have the courage to state publicly where they stand?

This gives rise to another pressing question: When the crunch comes, on whose side will they be?

Then there are those who have openly voiced concern, and yet it seems that they still are not fully acceptable to the black community in the churches.

A fundamental point should be made here: It is not merely a certain concern that we ask, it is the quality and the range (or depth) of this concern that is important.

QUESTION

Are these white dominees and professors prepared to identify themselves with the suffering and the oppression of black people and actively to resist the policies and institutions responsible for this suffering?

We don't ask them to be against apartheid. The question is whether they are willing to identify with what the oppressed are doing to secure their liberation.

For in making this choice, we believe, one does not choose ideologically for whites or black, but essentially for justice, peace and freedom for all the people of this tragic, beloved country.

There is an essential thing in Christian brotherhood that people who make this choice will do well to remember. Brotherhood involves at the very least an acceptance of the redistribution of the pain.

In saying this, one realises that one does not speak to NGK dominees alone. The scope has suddenly widened considerably. And fittingly so, for the sins of the white NGK, in a very real sense, are also the sins of white South Africa.

DOCUMENT 34. Minutes of a Black Sash meeting, Lower Houghton, Johannesburg, December 3, 1978

PRESENT: Mrs. J. Harris (in the chair)

Mrs. G. Dyzenhaus	Dr. N. Motlana
Mr. P. Soal	Mr. G. Budlender
Mr. C. Saloojee	Mrs. I. Menell
Miss M. Nell	Mr. M. Dangor
Mr. D. Rawliss	Mr. D. Mateman
Mrs. S. Duncan	Mr. M. Richards
Mr. B. Godsell	Bishop D. Tutu
Mrs. R. Ndzanga	

APOLOGIES: Mr. G. Waddell, Mr. P. Davidson

Mrs. Harris welcomed all to the meeting and briefly recapped on previous meetings. She regretted that Mr. du Preez was not present as he had agreed to present a paper on the National Party Constitutional proposals. It was agreed that the Agenda would be reserved and Mr. Godsell would report on the Constitutional proposals of the PFP [Progressive Federal Party]. Mr. Godsell then gave a brief outline of the PFP plan. He dealt in particular with the franchise and the protection of minority rights. Points raised during discussion were:

1. Worries about the nature of participation at the National Convention were voiced. People were very distressed at the decision to exclude people who had been convicted under South Africa's terrorism or sabotage laws.

2. It was felt that the PFP proposal was a significant document as a beginning point for negotiations but that it was not acceptable as an end point.

3. Many of the blacks found the minority veto unacceptable. It was felt that the minority veto was an attempt to woo an Afrikaner vote and it was pointed out that this was an unrealistic assessment of the South African situation. Bishop Tutu stressed that the only protection that whites could expect was an assurance by the blacks that their rights would be protected. He pointed out that blacks were still prepared to negotiate with whites.

4. The blacks also rejected the concept of cultural councils.

5. It was suggested that the whole concept of consensus government was unrealistic.

General discussion arose. There was a great deal of discussion about the role of the PFP in the parliamentary system. The blacks expressed the view that the Progressive Party had been much more effective when it had been represented by Helen Suzman alone than when they had more people in parliament. They said that the PFP should not concern itself unduly with trying to win major white support as it probably would never be elected as a government but that it should concern itself with stating its position clearly. Bishop Tutu said that the choice was between the Afrikaners and the interests of black South Africans. He said there was no middle road choice.

Dr. Motlana said that he resented the impression created that blacks who had met with the Progressive Party had approved their Constitution.

Mr. Dangor said that the PFP emphasis on creating a non-racial society was unrealistic. What was required was the creation of a liberated society.

Mr. Godsell said that the most important thing was to create a black/white alliance and to create meaningful interaction between blacks and whites in South Africa. He pointed out that the PFP Congress had been swayed by a number of conservative people simply because there had been no blacks present to counteract them.

It was generally agreed that too much emphasis had been placed on winning Afrikaner support at the PFP Congress.

People discussed the mechanics of a National Convention. It was generally agreed that the present government would never be persuaded to call a National Convention and the question arose as to whether some kind of freedom charter or "Tennis Court Oath" would not be a more suitable strategy. It was strongly suggested that the formation of a popular movement be investigated. Bishop Tutu said that the whites needed to be quite clear about the consequences of their action and they needed to commit themselves irrespective of sacrifice in the same way as the black community had.

It was agreed that it was important to have something positive to motivate people towards.

It was agreed that an important function of the group was to discuss ways and means of getting all opposition groups to act together—if necessary outside parliament—as an effective opposition.

The blacks strongly recommended that the Progressive Party leave the parliamentary structure and refuse to collaborate.

It was emphasised that no constitutional plan would be acceptable if it were drawn up by one group in isolation from the others.

Mrs. Duncan said that it was important to have some kind of vision of what South Africa would be like after liberation. Dr. Motlana said that the Black Consciousness Movement had a very clear vision of the future but were not prepared to discuss it in the present political climate.

Mr. Godsell said that he thought it was unwise for one group to devise a plan in isolation from other groups.

The point was made by Bishop Tutu that protest politics could be used to teach people to question authority. He also said that any movement needed to be able to count its successes. Therefore it might be advisable to set limited objectives which could be achieved.

It was pointed out that all black initiatives had been banned before they could get moving. Dr. Motlana spoke particularly about the BCP experience. He said that small initiatives had more chance of surviving than large ones.

Mr. Mateman raised the question of whether it was not possible to achieve more through government structures than by non-participation. Mrs. Duncan said that she was worried that participation also enabled the government to contain the opposition.

The meeting broke for lunch.

The meeting reconvened at 2.00 p.m.

Dr. Motlana was asked to explain why the Committee of Ten had refused to participate in the Community Council elections. He said that their decision had been based on the fact that the Community Councils were not seen by government as a City Council but rather as a consultative body joined to the homelands which would be manipulated by the government in the control of urban blacks. The Committee of Ten had prepared a blueprint which had been very moderate and mild and which had been worked out by the people themselves. This blueprint had been rejected. The primary provisions in the blueprint had been:

1. A City Council to control Soweto.

2. Based on freehold tenure. The City Council would have needed to raise money from property taxes.

3. They rejected any linkage with the homelands but were prepared to accept linkage with other City Councils in the metropolitan area.

The meeting then discussed future meetings. The next meeting would be held on Sunday, 14th January, 1978 at Mrs. Harris' house.

The meeting then discussed the Agenda for the following meeting. Suggestions included:

1. The establishment of a Kliptown Freedom Charter movement.

2. The drafting of principles on which there was consensus.

3. A discussion on the values of participating in government structures or non-participation. It was agreed that most people present were in favour of non-participation, but that all pros and cons needed to be examined in order to persuade the various parties.

It was agreed that the PFP representatives would give the reasons for participation (I am not sure whether Mr. Richards agreed to present a case for participation or not). The meeting would also develop a point by point argument on why they disagreed with participation. Strategies of non-participation would then be discussed.

Agreed that Mr. Soal would talk to Mr. Mayet. Mr. Godsell would talk to Mr. Khanyile and to Inkatha, and Dr. Motlana would talk to Dr. Asvat.

The meeting closed at 3.15 p.m.

Document 35. Statement critical of the South African Broadcasting Corporation by Bishop Mandlenkhosi Zwane of the Southern African Catholic Bishops' Conference, February 1, 1979

Yesterday morning the editorial comment of the South African Broadcasting Corporation "Current Affairs" commended Pope John Paul II for allegedly condemning liberation theology and its exponents. This declaration was apparently made at Puebla, Mexico, where nearly 400 Latin American bishops and theologians were meeting.

The so-called left-wing and political priests were singled out for a special tongue-lashing.

By implication, the Holy Father presumably chided the progressive Christians who believed the church should identify itself tangibly with the victims of structural violence, economic exploitation, fascist dictatorships and cultural alienation.

Nothing could be further from the truth. All the experts on the subject would dismiss the SABC's comment as an irresponsible and mischievous caricature of liberation theology.

"Current Affairs" has either completely misunderstood the Pope's statement on liberation theology or the SABC commentator has deliberately distorted it for reasons best known to himself and the media that employ him.

I need not even have read the Pope's address to realise the tendentiousness of the comment.

Theology is concerned with our life as men and as Christians. Since theology concerns itself with man's total life and his environment it cannot remain indifferent to the structures of economic exploitation, political domination of the majority by the few, and racial discrimination, etc.

Jesus is our saviour because he sought to restore the wholeness of mankind.

Personal and collective quest for authentic freedom is a characteristic of man. The struggle for full human liberation is central to Christianity and the Gospel.

Evangelisation is liberating because it is a message of total freedom which necessarily includes a demand for the transformation of the historical and political conditions in which men live.

The Catholic Church, through the Pope's encyclicals in recent times has openly identified itself with the plight of the workers, the marginal people and the victims of oppression and injustice.

In the face of brutal and flagrant violation of human rights in most of Latin America it is easy to see why theologians there should produce a theology which truly reflects their situation. To accuse progressive Latin American theologians of "dabbling in politics" is nonsense.

A statement such as yesterday morning's "Current Affairs" can only do untold harm to the image of the Catholic Church in South Africa. The election of Pope John Paul II was greeted with jubilation and hope in Africa, Asia and Latin America.

As recently as 1977 the Roman Catholic Bishops of Southern Africa, meeting in plenary session, committed themselves to:

> "Promote the awakening of social conscience and the awareness of injustice and social problems as central to evangelisation and an essential element of preaching, liturgy and catechetics and of priestly and religious and lay formation, of church work and witness."

> "Give practical expression to the conviction that the church's mission includes work for complete human liberation and to the teaching of "Evangelii Nuntiandi;" that evangelisation includes trans-forming the concrete structures that oppress people, and in the light of this, to strive that the church be seen in solidarity with all those who work for the promotion of human dignity and the legitimate aspirations of oppressed people."

It would be equally foolish to condemn other methods of doing theology, because theology is deeply influenced by the experience of people.

That is why liberation theology, correctly understood, continues to enjoy an extraordinary appeal to the so-called third world countries.

Document 36. Reply to government allegations against the South African Council of Churches by Bishop Desmond Tutu, Johannesburg, October 11, 1979

The Minister of Police and Prisons, the Hon. Mr Louis le Grange, is quoted in newspaper reports as having made serious allegations against the SACC. My response is based on these reports which we hope reflect accurately what the Minister said.

If that is the case, then I can only say I am now deeply shocked. I am shocked that someone holding such a responsible position could speak so irresponsibly and so tendentiously. It is distressing to find that Mr le Grange is picking up where his predecessor left off by making statements which cunningly link up the SACC and the Churches with, for instance, the Communist Party, so that there will be guilt by association and innuendo.

I want to declare categorically that I believe apartheid to be evil and immoral and, therefore, unChristian. No theologian I know of would be prepared to say the apartheid system is consistent with the Gospel of Jesus Christ. If Mr le Grange thinks that blacks do not have their human rights denied and that they are not suppressed and exploited and do not have their human dignity infringed, then I invite him to be black for just a day. He would know that [white mineworkers' leader] Mr. Arrie Paulus has said he is like a baboon and a high ranking police officer has said he is violent by nature.

What price black dignity then?

In the land of their birth, blacks who form 80% of the population, have 13% of the land, when the white minority of about 20% have 87% of the land; a white child of 18 years can vote in this country and a black person, be he a university professor or a bishop or whatever has no franchise; a black doctor with the same qualifications as his white counterpart is paid less for the same job.

One could go on with this sorry catalogue—do whites have to be subject to the humiliations of pass raids; have any whites had their homes demolished and then been asked to remove themselves to an inhospitable area where they must live in tents until they have built new houses as happened last week with the Batlokwa people?

Why have the Government suddenly decided to remove discriminatory signs if these were not unjust and oppressive? Why have they only now decided to extend trade union rights to black workers if it is not that they recognise they have been denying them basic human rights?

Can the Minister still stand up and say that this is not an unChristian and unjust system where human rights are denied etc?

I am sorry that he speaks of propaganda actions on the part of Churches. Fortunately, the Churches have not been guilty of using R64 million to sell an unsellable commodity and they have not engaged in any nefarious activity [as in the Information Department scandal].

The right to conscientious objection is one recognised in most non-totalitarian countries. There are persons who in conscience cannot partici-pate in war and the preparation for war. The Dutch Reformed Church acknowledged this right because during the Afrikaner rebellion in 1914 it declared "no one may revolt against lawful authority other than for carefully considered and well grounded reasons based on the word of God and a conscience enlightened by the Word of God." (Resolution of Afrikaans Council of Reformed Churches.)

The resolution on obeying God rather than man was taken by a responsible Conference made up not of fire-eating so-called leftists, but of responsible church leaders and duly elected representatives from the member churches and organisations of the SACC.

The SACC and the Churches reserve the right to condemn if need be, any legislation which is abhorrent to the Christian conscience and which represents an abrogation of the rule of law. Certainly, detention without trial and the arbitrary banning of people are in this category and we do not apologise for being ever vigilant in this regard.

The SACC has been critical of the role of the foreign investment but has nowhere yet advocated, cautiously or otherwise, an anti-investment policy.

Is the Minister aware of what he is saying when he accuses the SACC and the Churches of the crime of providing relief for political detainees and for providing legal defence for those involved in political trials? If these are crimes, then we openly and proudly plead guilty. We declare that everybody is entitled to the best defence possible. We should be praised rather than vilified for our part in ensuring that there is an equitable administration of justice.

It seems it is reprehensible to condemn an educational system that has been acknowledged to be inferior and advocate a more equitable distribution of resources for the greater good of an undivided South Africa. We plead guilty to the crime of condemning an unjust educational system and for proposing a better system.

We are accused of doing something quite evil in trying to alleviate the distress of unemployed people by helping them to produce income through self-help projects. The Minister says we are exploiting the unemployment situation. Instead of thanking us for helping defuse a highly explosive situation, he condemns us for acting so responsibly and patriotically.

We want to say as respectfully as possible, that the Minister is talking arrant nonsense and we would hope he would apologise for all these groundless attacks, especially this one.

If the demolition of squatter camps was not such a horrendous thing, then why did Dr. [Piet] Koornhof halt the demolition of Crossroads? Does Mr le Grange wish to say that these demolitions are in fact Christian acts? The opposition to these demolitions can certainly be justified on Christian grounds.

The Minister is guilty of gross untruths and he knows it when he says we have channelled funds to resistance movements. Why does he not use the wide powers he has to prosecute us if we have done what is obviously so illegal in South Africa.

We know the tactics of the Government. They plan to take action against the SACC and they wish to prepare the public for that action. We want to remind them of a few things. First of all, they must stop playing at being God. They are human beings who happen to be carrying out an unjust and oppressive policy with a whole range of draconian laws. But they are still only mere mortals. And we are tired of having threats levelled at us. Why don't they carry them out?

Secondly, we want to warn Mr le Grange and others who may be tempted to emulate him. The SACC is a Council of Churches, not a private organisation. The Church has been in existence for nearly 2000 years. Tyrants and others have acted against Christians during those years. They have arrested them, they have killed them, they have proscribed the faith. Those tyrants belong now to the flotsam and jetsam of forgotten history— and the Church of God remains, an agent of justice, of peace, of love and reconciliation. If they take the SACC and the Churches on, let them just know they are taking on the Church of Jesus Christ.

4. The Black Consciousness Movement: The Formative Years, 1967–1971

Document 37. "Black Power—Students Forced to Leave Meeting." Article in *Dome* (University of Natal), March 27, 1969

Four students of UND [University of Natal-Durban] walked out of a student body meeting at Alan Taylor residence last Thursday. The tension had been apparent from the moment they entered the Students' Common Room.

The students, Halton Cheadle (NUSAS Local Chairman), Dave Hemson, Jennifer Brown and Veronica Vorster were greeted at the door by a 'Hello Baas, Hello Missus!' Instead of standing at the back of the room, the students took a seat, but their presence evidently caused great suspicion.

The meeting began without further antagonism, but during the discussion of SASO (South African Students' Organization) queries were increasingly made about the 'foreigners', 'strangers' or 'intruders' at the meeting.

'This meeting is called to discuss the formation of SASO, which is a non-white body, and yet we have intruders here. Who invited them?', asked one student.

Mr. Mokono again repeated his ironical 'Baas' in reference to the white students and laughed. He was immediately called to order by the Chairman, SRC President, Ben Ngubane, who had arrived by this time.

Mr. Ngubane demanded that Mokono leave the meeting, which he refused to do. Mr. Ngubane then insisted he had no rights at the meeting, and that he could not participate further.

Many African students reacted vehemently to the ruling, and disruptions continued to rock the meeting.

'Mr. Chairman, Point of Order.'

'Yes.'

'You are out of order!' (General laughter and further objections).

After a lengthy discussion of the duty of the President to introduce the visitors, the white students were allowed to introduce themselves. "Will all Caucasians stand up?' asked Mr. Ngubane. This they did and introduced themselves and were listened to in silence. A tape-recorder was discovered at the back of the hall. Despite the fact that a woman student claimed the tape-recorder back, it was placed on the table, and the Chairman said he would confiscate any tape.

This still did not satisfy the African students who mainly stood at the back of the hall. One student linked the presence of the tape-recorder and the white students, and mentioned the Security Branch.

'Let's go; we have to go.' The whites left amongst sporadic clapping.

The students were invited to have tea at one student's room, and stayed as the tension lapsed.

CHEADLE: 'I felt we should have stayed and countered the objections raised by our presence, and confront their racialism. I think that the tension at the meeting is a result of the emergence of a new black consciousness.'

HEMSON: 'We had to leave the meeting, as it was obvious discussion could not continue if we stayed. It was a very frustrating experience to be discussed as a stranger and foreigner, and not to be able to reply. The atmosphere of nihilism and rage directed at us as symbols of white oppression, was explicable but misplaced.'

VERONICA VORSTER: 'As one of the UND students at the UND Student Body Meeting, I was shocked by the hostility of the students, many of whom I consider as friends. There were loud objections to the presence of members of the 'Special Branch' [security police].'

DOCUMENT 38. "Communique" by SASO, July 1969

For the first time after 1959, Non-White student leaders met at Stutterheim in July 1968. A need for contact, especially among the University Colleges, was strongly expressed. This meeting then requested UNNE to act as host to a conference which would investigate ways of establishing effective contact.

In response to this general feeling of dissatisfaction a meeting of student leaders was held at Mariannhill in December 1968. Much as they did not want to form any organisation, this was imperative as this was discovered to be the only way in which effective contact could be effected.

A draft Constitution was drawn and was sent to the different centres for consideration. A steering committee elected at this meeting contacted those centres which were not represented at this conference.

The next meeting was held at the University College of the North and here, a final Constitution was drafted. This then is how the South African Students' Organisation (SASO) came into existence.

One immediate problem therefore is to dream up a workable solution that will lead to a more meaningful, and more lasting yet an acceptable way of communication.

That there is a need for more effective contact is unquestionable, especially in view of the ever increasing enrolments at the non-white institutions of higher learning, particularly the University Colleges. For all intents and purposes, these students have remained isolated not only physically but also intellectually. There we find institutions which seek to breed or breed pseudo intellectuals with an absolute bogey for anything that associates them with the society in which they live, particularly if this is related to some kind of disagreement with any particular aspect of the general policy of the powers that be. There is no way of stopping this process except by interfering with the programme of indoctrination and intimidation so effectively applied at all South African Universities. What happened at Fort Hare is an indication of just how far the government is prepared to go in maintaining their policy of "divide and rule."

There are two ways in which we can effectively break the isolation of the Non-White centres, and bring them more into the orbit of interaction.

(i) We can intensify our correspondence with one another—not only exchanging minutes but also letters, publications and any other material on which we lay our hands. We could then supplement this with inter-visits amongst our SRCs.

(ii) We can form a loose structured alliance provided for by the SASO Constitution. Thereby we shall be engaging in a prescribed form of interaction which shall include all the provisions in the first suggestion.

These two forms of contact were very effectively discussed at a conference of student leaders from Non-White campuses held at Mariannhill last December. The feeling here was that an unstructured form of contact like the one envisaged in the first suggestion is too fluid and may very easily break down. There is no body to see to it that contact is maintained and no one feels any particular obligation in keeping contact with the others. In addition to this there is a difficulty in maintaining a loose contact. This form of contact is bound to fail merely because of the lack of functional ties amongst the people engaged in it.

The second contact pattern—that of forming an organisation—has also got its own faults and good points. Let us deal with the faults first:

(a) At the time when events are moving so fast in the country, it is not totally advisable to show any form of division amongst the student ranks—especially now that students appear to be a power to be reckoned with in this country.

(b) Any move that tends to divide the student population into separate laagers [camps] on the basis of colour is in a way a tacit submission to having been defeated and apparently seems an agreement with apartheid.

(c) In a racially sensitive country like ours provisions for racially exclusive bodies tends to build up resentment and widen the gap that exists between the races and the student community should resist all attempts to fall into this temptation.

(d) Any formation of a purely non-white body shall be subject to a lot of scrutiny. So the chances of the organisation lasting are very little.

All these points were taken into consideration by the conference that drew up the draft Constitution of SASO, but the participants there felt they should go ahead for the following reasons:

(1) Contact among non-white students is of paramount importance at this stage, and where this is possible we should exploit the situation as much as we can.

(2) The alternative to meeting on a segregated platform is not meeting at all, which will be more welcome to the perpetrators of evil and detrimental to our course. This is in fact the ultimate goal of the "divide et impera" policy.

(3) Meeting on a segregated platform because we cannot help it does not necessarily mean that we agree with segregation.

(4) In choosing to meet on a limited scale rather than not meeting at all, the non-white students shall be choosing the lesser evil, and striving to offset some of the evils that have accrued from the same system that made it impossible for them to meet freely with other students.

It has been argued that we should keep to our idea of collective policy, i.e. We should battle together with all the other centres in NUSAS by protesting alongside the students at the University Colleges. This unfortunately is not a positive policy. We know very well that at no stage will those students be allowed to take part in NUSAS. The only results of the protests is, therefore, a further curb on their freedom and a victimization of the few students' leaders who sprout out at these places. This serves to intimidate the students further and to frustrate those of them who have been victimized. NUSAS has been encouraging this sort of "protest after the fact." What we need now is a more positive way of approach that will reduce individual hazards and improve the lot of the students at these places.

The position of centres like UNNE is unique in that, since they have relatively more freedom than the University Colleges, their eagerness to participate in a seemingly racially exclusive body may be questionable. However, nobody who understands, seriously, the interrelated structure of souls in bondage should be surprised at this. Although they are in a more advantageous position they share the colour of skin that has led to the students at the University Colleges being in their present position. They have the same interests as these students. Since they have some room for better manoeuvre, they should provide not only firm support but also strength and direction in their long struggle towards the realisation of the aspirations of these students, which in the long run are the aspirations of any sane South African.

There is another light in which people tend to see the role of centres like UNNE. Because of expressed policy of non-racialism, they find it difficult to support anything that has a colour tinge attached to it. The same view is held by NUSAS and all its affiliated members. It would be tragic however, if they apply this rigidly even if it is to the detriment of our kith and kin, who through no fault of theirs have found themselves in this present position. As far as we know there is no truth in the claims made by the press that SASO is formed in opposition to NUSAS, or as a Black equivalent of NUSAS. According to the draft Constitution SASO makes no claims of being a 'National Union' but is simply an organisation formed to promote contact. The clause limiting membership to non-whites is a sine qua non to the very existence of this kind of limited contact mechanism. In other words, as the preamble shows, SASO is formed under protest and makes no claim of being a pure organisation. It upholds the universal principle that all students in a country should have a right to affiliate to the National Student organisation of that country. The malicious claims, therefore, cannot be reconciled with the draft Constitution, nor the Preamble thereto. Neither we, nor NUSAS nor any other body should seek to thwart the attempts of the student leaders who wish to try to effect this kind of contact, for it is the lifeline to intellectual salvation of not only the students at the University Colleges but of a non-white population as a whole since they shall draw their future leaders from these students.

Man has always been a storehouse for ideas and innovations to make the world he lives in a better place for himself. In the face of apparently insurmountable problems, man seeks to conquer by working out ingenious schemes designed to get him out of the doldrums. Where isolation seems perfect, and intellectual stifling apparently complete, let us allow the protagonists of SASO the chance to show how effective contact according to their new formula can be achieved. Only when they fail or when a gross voluntary deviation from accepted principles is seen, may we raise our voices and shout out our repugnance towards the proposed organisation. We apparently conform to the general pattern in South Africa—the tendency to be unreasonably afraid of "dangerous precedents." The theory of the "thin end of the wedge" would also apply equally to us. We refuse to do anything new simply because it will be "dangerous precedent." This attitude we must reject.

Document 39. "Regional Formation Schools." Report in *SASO News-letter*, September 1970

The regional formation schools for the Natal and Transvaal regions were held on the 5-7th and 19–20th September respectively. The attendance at each formation school was in the region of 25 or so people. A full report on the formation schools will be circulated to all centres. We want merely to deal briefly with the major points of both formation schools.

From our point of view, i.e. Exec. the formation schools were extremely successful. We sought to achieve 2 major objects, firstly, we wanted to create a core of people in each campus who not only understood in detail what

SASO is all about, but, also who are prepared to do SASO work on their respective campuses. Secondly, we sought to make all those who attended fully conversant with the approach we are adopting in an effort to make students aware of their responsibilities both as students and as members of society.

Questions set for us to answer, such as who are we? What are we talking about? Where are we today? Whither are we going?, helped to put us in a good frame of mind for the business we meant to deal with. We then went further to highlight the important aspects of "black consciousness" and our historical background with a view to creating good ground for discussion.

The study of the Afro-American approach to their problems offered interesting comparisons between their situation in the [United] States and ours in this country. To give a concrete example one group was asked to study the significance of the statement "before entering the open society, we must first close our ranks." This statement underlies the "Black Power" philosophy of people like [Charles] Hamilton and [Stokely] Carmichael. This particular group made the observation that an open society in this country can only be created by blacks and that for as long as whites are in power they shall seek to make it closed in one way or the other. We then defined what we meant by an open society. Does it entail the competitive type of approach to a country's economical problems, or does it open the ranks fully and allow joint participation by everybody in the country's economy. In other words does our concept of an open society imply a retention of the opportunities for exploitation that one finds in Western-based societies? This was rejected by the group in favour of a more inclusive approach. The group went on then to note that none of the present parties would dream of fully allowing people to participate equally as members of a society in the economy of the country.

Closing our ranks was seen as necessary in this country purely to establish a common starting point. The difference in starting points was seen as the major reason for the diversification of interests and aspirations. Hence the group ended up by stating that the original statement should read "before creating an open society we must first close our ranks." The difference of course is of paramount importance in that in the first one the Afro-Americans accept that they will never be in a position to change the system in America and adopt the approach that if you can't beat them, join them but join them from a position of strength, whereas implicit in the latter statement is a hope to establish a completely new system at some stage. The second point here also is that purely from a consideration of who we are we realise that it is we who must be allowing others to participate in our system. We must not be the ones to be invited to participate in somebody else's system in our own private yard.

Then came a consideration of practical ways of implementing what we saw as the only valid approach—creating a black consciousness. The ideas considered varied from simple community orientated projects to exploitation of the system i.e. making use of institutions created in black areas for blacks. One does not wish to go into detail in this topic. Let it suffice to say that we saw a major difference in approaches to be made to the urban areas and those to be made to the rural areas.

Considerable time was spent in discussing "Black Theology" and what it entails. SASO is aware that it is a secular body but acknowledges the functional importance of working closely with other groups in an effort to stress the importance of this topic.

A sense of nostalgia was instilled in the group by a historical consideration of the black man's struggle in this country. Although this was dealt with very superficially it served to illustrate just how complacent people are at this moment.

All in all people left the formation schools with new determination to do what can be done in the direction of making themselves and the student community at large useful in being members of the vanguard ranks in this stage of our involvement. The regional and local organisation of SASO in both the Transvaal and Natal regions was given a tremendous boosting by the formation schools. This makes it much more of a pity that the Eastern Cape Region has seen it necessary to postpone its regional formation school to early next year.

DOCUMENT 40. "Who Is Black?" Editorial by Steve Biko, SASO Newsletter, September 1970

There is something to be said about the question "who is black?"

In his talk at the SASO Symposium on "Black is beautiful" Mr. Mphahlele warned that people should resist the temptation of being preoccupied with defining "how black is black." To me it would seem that this is just what people are doing—not necessarily at student level, although to some extent this is true of students too, but more so with the public at large.

Some Coloured and Indian people are refusing to identify with African people in calling themselves black. They see this as a disadvantageous categorisation that will limit chances of assimilation into the more affluent group—the white world. Others do so because of a fear for the unknown—the rise of African nationalism and its possible effects. They point to what is happening to the North of us as the example of what lies in store for Indian people in this country. Needless to say, their source of information is ill-informed and deliberately distorted accounts of events there as reported in South African newspapers and other agencies of government propaganda.

On the other hand, the African community too—being at the bottom rung of the ladder—has become over-sensitive to anybody who has a slight advantage over them. They point at the large and "highly successful" Indian middle class as a strong obstacle in the way towards full emancipation of black people. Because of this, they tend to bundle together all those not like them by way of privilege.

In the midst of all this confusion, certain people are talking about "black consciousness" and are being understood differently by all these various schools of thinking (or should it be schools of non-thinking?) Some Africans claim the monopoly of being called black and some Indians and Coloureds refuse to be called black. Probably one here is talking of minorities in all these cases but then these are worth considering.

Where does the term "black" originate as applied to people of colour? One notices that it comes from various areas where dark-skinned people were regarded as inferior socially, intellectually and otherwise. It became popularised in the [United] States and in the Caribbean under the banner of "Black Power." It was adopted as a means of inculcating pride amongst black people in the French colonies under the slogan of Negritude *BUT* nowhere in Africa has the term assumed such emotional importance as in the non-African countries where black people still experience oppression. People to the North of us talk of Africans and not of blacks. Whenever they use the term black, it refers to the people of colour the world over and not just to themselves. Equally, one should realise that the Afro-Americans, or Negroes as they are called by others, are in fact Coloured people. Many of them have lost the likeness to the African of Africa not only socially and culturally but also physically. Hence the Coloured people of South Africa are much more African in outlook than the Negroes. But the Negroes are the people who are so sentimentally attached to the term "black."

The essence of what I am saying is that the term "black" must be seen in its right context. No new category is being created but a "re-Christening" is taking place. We are merely refusing to be regarded as non-persons and claim the right to be called positively. No one group is exclusively black. Instead, adopting a collective, positive outlook leads to the creation of a broader base which may be useful in time. It helps us to recognise the fact that we have one common enemy and defines our aspirations in fairly uniform terms. One should grant that the division of races in this country is so entrenched that the blacks will find it difficult to operate as a combined front. The black umbrella we are creating for ourselves at least helps us to make sure that if we are not working as a unit at least the various units should be working in the same direction, being complementary to each other wherever possible. By all means be proud of your Indian heritage or your African culture but make sure that in looking around for somebody to kick at, choose the fellow who is sitting on your neck. He may not be as easily accessible as your black brother but he is the source of your discomfort.

Placed in context therefore, the "black consciousness" attitude seeks to define one's enemy more clearly and to broaden the base from which we are operating. It is a deliberate attempt by all of us to counteract the "divide and rule" attitude of the evil-doers. If any of the groups fails to play its part this will be unfortunate but those who feel the pinch must march on with a sense or urgency, bearing in mind all the time that your enemy is not the one who refuses to co-operate but the fellow on your neck. The Judases of the struggle are to be found in all races, African as well as Indians,

Coloureds as well as Whites. While you may ignore these who shirk their duties, never ignore the Judases for they are an extension of the enemy into your ranks.

Document 41. "White Racism and Black Consciousness." Speech by Steve Biko, Abe Bailey Institute, Cape Town, January 1971

THE TOTALITY OF WHITE POWER IN SOUTH AFRICA

"No race possesses the monopoly of beauty, intelligence, force, and there is room for all of us at the rendezvous of victory." I do not think Aimé Césaire was thinking about South Africa when he said these words. The whites in this country have placed themselves on a path of no return. So blatantly exploitative in terms of the mind and body is the practice of white racism that one wonders if the interests of blacks and whites in this country have not become so mutually exclusive as to exclude the possibility of there being "room for all of us at the rendezvous of victory."

The White man's quest for power has led him to destroy with utter ruthlessness whatever has stood in his way. In an effort to divide the black world in terms of aspirations, the powers that be have evolved a philosophy that stratifies the black world and gives preferential treatment to certain groups. Further, they have built up several tribal cocoons, thereby hoping to increase inter-tribal ill-feelings and to divert the energies of the black people towards attaining false prescribed "freedoms." Moreover, it was hoped, the black people could be effectively contained in these various cocoons of repression, euphemistically referred to as 'homelands.' At some stage, however, the powers that be had to start defining the sphere of activity of these apartheid institutions. Most blacks suspected initially the barrenness of the promise and have now realised that they have been taken for a big ride. Just as the Native Representatives Council became a political flop that embarrassed its creators, I predict that a time will come when these stooge bodies will prove very costly not only in terms of money but also in terms of the credibility of the story the Nationalists are trying to sell. In the meantime the blacks are beginning to realise the need to rally around the cause of their suffering—their black skin—and to ignore the false promises that come from the white world.

Then again the progressively sterner legislation that has lately filled the South African statute books has had a great effect in convincing the people of the evil inherent in the system of apartheid. No amount of propaganda on Radio Bantu or promises of freedom being granted to some desert homeland will ever convince the blacks that the government means well, so long as they experience manifestations of the lack of respect for the dignity of man and for his property as shown during the mass removals of Africans from the urban areas. The unnecessary harassment of Africans by police, both in towns and inside townships, and the ruthless application of that scourge of the people, the pass laws, are constant reminders that the white man is on top and that the blacks are only tolerated—with the greatest restraints. Needless to say, anyone finding himself at the receiving end of such deliberate (though uncalled for) cruelty must ultimately ask himself the question: what do I have to lose? This is what the blacks are beginning to ask themselves.

To add to this, the opposition ranks have been thrown into chaos and confusion. All opposition parties have to satisfy the basic demands of politics. They want power and at the same time they want to be *fair*. It never occurs to them that the surest way of being unfair is to withhold power from the native population. Hence one ultimately comes to the conclusion that there is no real difference between the United Party and the Nationalist Party. If there is, a strong possibility exists that the United Party is on the right of the Nationalists. One needs only to look at their famous slogan, "White supremacy over the whole of South Africa," to realise the extent to which the quest for power can cloud even such supposedly immortal characteristics as the "English sense of fair play." Africans long ago dismissed the United Party as a great political fraud. The Coloured people have since followed suit. If the United Party is gaining any votes at all it is precisely because it is becoming more explicit in its racist policy. I would venture to say that the most overdue political step in South African White politics is a merger between the United and Nationalist Parties.

The flirtation between the Progressive Party and blacks was brought to a rude stop by legislation. Some blacks argue that at that moment the Progressives lost their only chance of attaining some semblance of respectability by not choosing to disband rather than lose their black constituents. Yet I cannot help feeling that the Progressives emerged more purified from the ordeal. The Progressives have never been a black man's real hope. They have always been a white party at heart, fighting for a more lasting way of preserving white values in this southern tip of Africa. It will not be long before the blacks relate their poverty to their blackness in concrete terms. Because of the tradition forced onto the country, the poor people shall always be black people. It is not surprising, therefore, that the blacks should wish to rid themselves of a system that locks up the wealth of the country in the hands of a few. No doubt Rick Turner was thinking of this when he declared that "any black government is likely to be socialist," in his article on "The Relevance of Contemporary Radical Thought."

We now come to the group that has longest enjoyed confidence from the black world—the liberal establishment, including radical and leftist groups. The biggest mistake the black world ever made was to assume that whoever opposed apartheid was an ally. For a long time the black world has been looking only at the governing party and not so much at the whole power structure as the object of their rage. In a sense the very political vocabulary that the blacks have used has been inherited from the liberals. Therefore it is not surprising that alliances were formed so easily with the liberals.

Who are the liberals in South Africa? It is that curious bunch of non-conformists who explain their participation in negative terms; that bunch of do-gooders that goes under all sorts of names—liberals, leftists, etc. These are the people who argue that they are not responsible for white racism and the country's "inhumanity to the black man;" these are the people who claim that they too feel the oppression just as acutely as the blacks and therefore should be jointly involved in the black man's struggle for a place under the sun; in short, these are the people who say that they have black souls wrapped up in white skins.

The liberals set about their business with the utmost efficiency. They made it a political dogma that all groups opposing the status quo must *necessarily* be non-racial in structure. They maintained that if you stood for a principle of non-racialism you could not in any way adopt what they described as racialist policies. They even defined to the black people what the latter should fight for.

With this sort of influence behind them, most black leaders tended to rely too much on the advice of liberals. For a long time, in fact, it became the occupation of the leadership to "calm the masses down," while they engaged in fruitless negotiation with the status quo. Their whole political action, in fact, was a programmed course in the art of gentle persuasion through protests and limited boycotts, and they hoped the rest could be safely left to the troubled conscience of the fair-minded English folk.

Of course this situation could not last. A new breed of black leaders was beginning to take a dim view of the involvement of liberals in a struggle that they regarded as essentially theirs, when the political movements of the blacks were either banned or harassed into non-existence. This left the stage open once more for the liberals to continue with their work of "fighting for the rights of the blacks."

It never occurred to the liberals that the integration they insisted upon as an effective way of opposing apartheid was impossible to achieve in South Africa. It had to be artificial because it was being foisted on two parties whose entire upbringing had been to support the lie that one race was superior and others inferior. One has to overhaul the whole system in South Africa before hoping to get black and white walking hand in hand to oppose a *common* enemy. As it is, both black and white walk into a hastily organised integrated circle carrying with them the seeds of destruction of that circle—their inferiority and superiority complexes.

The myth of integration as propounded under the banner of the liberal ideology must be cracked and killed because it makes people believe that something is being done when in reality the artificially integrated circles are a soporific to the blacks while salving the consciences of the guilt-stricken white. It works from the false premise that, because it is difficult to bring people from different races together in this country, achievement of this is in itself a step towards the total liberation of the blacks. Nothing could be more misleading.

How many white people fighting for their version of a change in South

Africa are really motivated by genuine concern and not by guilt? Obviously it is a cruel assumption to believe that all whites are not sincere, yet methods adopted by some groups often do suggest a lack of real commitment. The essence of politics is to direct oneself to the group which wields power. Most white dissident groups are aware of the power wielded by the white power structure. They are quick to quote statistics on how big the defence budget is. They know exactly how effectively the police and the army can control protesting black hordes—peaceful or otherwise. They know to what degree the black world is infiltrated by the security police. Hence they are completely convinced of the impotence of the black people. Why then do they persist in talking to the blacks? Since they are aware that the problem in this country is white racism, why do they not address themselves to the white world? Why do they insist on talking to blacks?

In an effort to answer these questions one has to come to the painful conclusion that the liberal is in fact appeasing his own conscience, or at best is eager to demonstrate his identification with the black people only so far as it does not sever all his ties with his relatives on the other side of the colour line. Being white, he possesses the natural passport to the exclusive pool of white privileges from which he does not hesitate to extract whatever suits him. Yet, since he identifies with the blacks, he moves around his white circles— white-only beaches, restaurants, and cinemas—with a lighter load, feeling that he is not like the rest. Yet at the back of his mind is a constant reminder that he is quite comfortable as things stand and therefore should not bother about change. Although he does not vote for the Nationalists (now that they are in the majority anyway), he feels secure under the protection offered by the Nationalists and subconsciously shuns the idea of change.

The limitations that have accompanied the involvement of liberals in the black man's struggle have been mostly responsible for the arrest of progress. Because of their inferiority complex, blacks have tended to listen seriously to what the liberals had to say. With their characteristic arrogance of assuming a 'monopoly on intelligence and moral judgement,' these self-appointed trustees of black interests have gone on to set the pattern and pace for the realisation of the black man's aspirations.

I am not sneering at the liberals and their involvement. Neither am I suggesting that they are the most to blame for the black man's plight. Rather I am illustrating the fundamental fact that total identification with an oppressed group in a system that forces one group to enjoy privilege and to live on the sweat of another, is impossible. White society collectively owes the blacks so huge a debt that no one member should automatically expect to escape from the blanket condemnation that needs must come from the black world. It is not as if whites are allowed to enjoy privilege only when they declare their solidarity with the ruling party. They are born into privilege and are nourished by and nurtured in the system of ruthless exploitation of black energy. For the 20-year-old white liberal to expect to be accepted with open arms is surely to overestimate the powers of forgiveness of the black people. No matter how genuine a liberal's motivations may be, he has to accept that, though he did not choose to be born into privilege, the blacks cannot but be suspicious of his motives.

The liberal must fight on his own and for himself. If they are true liberals they must realise that they themselves are oppressed, and that they must fight for their own freedom and not that of the nebulous 'they' with whom they can hardly claim identification.

What I have tried to show is that in South Africa political power has always rested with white society. Not only have the whites been guilty of being on the offensive but, by some skillful manoeuvres, they have managed to control the responses of the blacks to the provocation. Not only have they kicked the black but they have also told him how to react to the kick. For a long time the black has been listening with patience to the advice he has been receiving on how best to respond to the kick. With painful slowness he is now beginning to show signs that it is his right and duty to respond to the kick in the way he sees fit.

BLACK CONSCIOUSNESS

"We Coloured men, in this specific moment of historical evolution, have consciously grasped in its full breath, the notion of our peculiar uniqueness, the notion of just who we are and what, and that we are ready, on every plane and in every department, to assume the responsibilities which proceed from this coming into consciousness. The peculiarity of our place in the world is not to be confused with anyone else's. The peculiarity of our problems which aren't to be reduced to subordinate forms of any other problem. The peculiarity of our history, laced with terrible misfortunes which belong to no other history. The peculiarity of our culture, which we intend to live and to make live in an ever realer manner." (Aimé Césaire, 1956, in his letter of resignation from the French Communist Party.)

At about the same time that Césaire said this, there was emerging in South Africa a group of angry young black men who were beginning to "grasp the notion of (their) peculiar uniqueness" and who were eager to define who they were and what. These were the elements who were disgruntled with the direction imposed on the African National Congress by the "old guard" within its leadership. These young men were questioning a number of things, among which was the "go slow" attitude adopted by the leadership, and the ease with which the leadership accepted coalitions with organisations other than those run by blacks. The 'People's Charter' adopted in Kliptown in 1955 was evidence of this. In a sense one can say that these were the first real signs that blacks in South Africa were beginning to realise the need to go it alone and to evolve a philosophy based on, and directed by, blacks. In other words, Black Consciousness was slowly manifesting itself.

It may be said that, on the broader political front, blacks in South Africa have not shown any overt signs of new thinking since the banning of their political parties; nor were the signs of disgruntlement with the white world given a real chance to crystallise into a positive approach. Black students, on the other hand, began to rethink their position in black-white coalitions. The emergence of SASO and its tough policy of non-involvement with the white world set people's minds thinking along new lines. This was a challenge to the age-old tradition in South Africa that opposition to apartheid was enough to qualify whites for acceptance by the black world. Despite protest and charges of racialism from liberal-minded white students, the black students stood firm in their rejection of the principle of unholy alliances between blacks and whites. A spokesman of the new right-of-middle group, NAFSAS [National Federation of South African Students], was treated to a dose of the new thinking when a black student told him that 'we shall lead ourselves, be it to the sea, to the mountain or to the desert; we shall have nothing to do with white students.'

The importance of the SASO stand is not really to be found in SASO *per se*— for SASO has the natural limitations of being a student organisation with an ever-changing membership. Rather it is to be found in the fact that this new approach opened a huge crack in the traditional approach and made the blacks sit up and think again. It heralded a new era in which Blacks are beginning to take care of their own business and to see with greater clarity the immensity of their responsibility.

The call for Black Consciousness is the most positive call to come from any group in the black world for a long time. It is more than just a reactionary rejection of whites by blacks. The quintessence of it is the realisation by the blacks that, in order to feature well in this game of power politics, they have to use the concept of group power and to build a strong foundation for this. Being an historically, politically, socially and economically disinherited and dispossessed group, they have the strongest foundation from which to operate. The philosophy of Black Consciousness, therefore, expresses group pride and the determination by the blacks to rise and attain the envisaged self. At the heart of this kind of thinking is the realisation by the blacks that the most potent weapon in the hands of the oppressor is the mind of the oppressed. Once the latter has been so effectively manipulated and controlled by the oppressor as to make the oppressed believe that he is a liability to the white man, then there will be nothing the oppressed can do that will really scare the powerful masters. Hence thinking along lines of Black Consciousness makes the black man see himself as a being, entire in himself, and not as an extension of a broom or additional leverage to some machine. At the end of it all, he cannot tolerate attempts by anybody to dwarf the significance of his manhood. Once this happens, we shall know that the real man in the black person is beginning to shine through.

I have spoken of Black Consciousness as if it is something that can be readily detected. Granted this may be an over-statement at this stage, yet it is true that, gradually, the various black groups are becoming more and more conscious of the self. They are beginning to rid their minds of imprisoning notions which are the legacy of the control of their attitude by whites. Slowly, they have cast aside the 'morality argument' which prevented them from going it alone and are now learning that a lot of good can be derived from specific exclusion of whites from black institutions.

Of course it is not surprising to us that whites are not very much aware of these developing forces since such consciousness is essentially an inward-looking process. It has become common practice in this country for people to consult their papers to see what is said by black leaders—by which they understand the leaders of the various apartheid institutions. While these bodies are often exploited by individuals in them for candid talking, they certainly cannot be taken seriously as yardsticks by which to measure black feeling on any topic.

The growth of awareness among South African blacks has often been ascribed to influence from the American 'Negro' movement. Yet it seems to me that this is a sequel to the attainment of independence by so many African states within so short a time. In fact I remember that at the time I was at high school, Dr. Hastings Kamuzu Banda was still a militant and used to be a hero of a friend of mine. His often quoted statement was, 'This is a black man's country; any white man who does not like it must pack up and go.' Clearly at this stage the myth of the invincibility of the white man had been exposed. When fellow Africans were talking like that how could we still be harbouring ideas of continued servitude? We knew he had no right to be there; we wanted to remove him from our table, strip the table of all trappings put on it by him, decorate it in true African style, settle down and then ask him to join us on our own terms if he liked. This is what Banda was saying. The fact that American terminology has often been used to express our thoughts is merely because all new ideas seem to get extensive publicity in the United States.

National consciousness and its spread in South Africa has to work against a number of factors. First there are the traditional complexes, then the emptiness of the native's past and lastly the question of black-white dependency. The traditional inferior-superior black-white complexes are deliberate creations of the colonialist. Through the work of missionaries and the style of education adopted, the blacks were made to feel that the white man was some kind of god whose word could not be doubted. As Fanon puts it: "Colonialism is not satisfied merely with holding a people in its grip and emptying the Native's brain of all form and content; by a kind of perverted logic, it turns to the past of the oppressed people and distorts, disfigures, and destroys it." At the end of it all, the blacks have nothing to lean on, nothing to cheer them up at the present moment and very much to be afraid of in the future.

The attitude of some rural African folk who are against education is often misunderstood, not least by the African intellectual. Yet the reasons put forward by these people carry with them the realisation of their inherent dignity and worth. They see education as the quickest way of destroying the substance of the African culture. They complain bitterly of the disruption in the life pattern, non-observation of customs, and constant derision from the non-conformists whenever any of them go through school. Lack of respect for elders is, in the African tradition, an unforgivable and cardinal sin. Yet how can one prevent the loss of respect of child for father when the child is actively taught by his know-all white tutors to disregard his family's teachings? How can an African avoid losing respect for his tradition when in school his whole cultural background is summed up in one word: barbarism?

To add to the white-oriented education received, the whole history of the black people is presented as a long lamentation of repeated defeats. Strangely enough, everybody has come to accept that the history of South Africa starts in 1652. No doubt this is to support the often-told lie that blacks arrived in this country at about the same time as the whites. Thus, a lot of attention has to be paid to our history if we as blacks want to aid each other in our coming into consciousness. We have to rewrite our history and describe in it the heroes that formed the core resistance to the white invaders. More has to be revealed and stress has to be laid on the successful nation-building attempts by people like Chaka, Moshoeshoe and Hintsa.

Our culture must be defined in concrete terms. We must relate the past to the present and demonstrate an historical evolution of the modern African. We must reject the attempts by the powers that be to project an arrested image of our culture. This is not the sum total of our culture. They have deliberately arrested our culture at the tribal stage to perpetuate the myth that African people were near-cannibals, had no real ambitions in life, and were preoccupied with sex and drink. In fact the wide-spread vice often found in the African townships is a result of the interference of the White man in the natural evolution of the true native culture. 'Wherever colonisation is a fact, the indigenous culture begins to rot and among the ruins something begins to be born which is condemned to exist on the margin allowed it by the European culture.' It is through the evolution of our genuine culture that our identity can be fully rediscovered.

We must seek to restore to the black people a sense of the great stress we used to lay on the value of human relationships; to highlight the fact that in the pre-Van Riebeeck days we had a high regard for people, their property and for life in general; to reduce the hold of technology over man and to reduce the materialistic element that is slowly creeping into the African character.

"Is there any way that my people can have the blessings of technology without being eaten away by materialism and losing the spiritual dimension from their lives?" asks President Kaunda and then, talking of the typical tribal African community, he says:

Those people who are dependent upon and live in closest relationship with Nature are most conscious of the operation of these forces: the pulse of their lives beats in harmony with the pulse of the Universe; they may be simple and unlettered people and their horizons may be strictly limited, yet I believe that they inhabit a larger world than the sophisticated Westerner who has magnified his physical senses through invented gadgets at the price, all too often, of cutting out the dimension of the spiritual.

It goes without saying that the black people of South Africa, in order to make the necessary strides in the new direction they are thinking of, have to take a long look at how they can use their economic power to their advantage. As the situation stands today, money from the black world tends to take a unidirectional flow to the white society. Blacks buy from white supermarkets, white greengrocers, white bottle stores, white chemists, and, to crown it all, those who can, bank at white-owned banks. Needless to say, they travel to work in government-owned trains or white-owned buses. If then we wish to make use of the little we have to improve our lot, it can only lead to greater awareness of the power we wield as a group. The 'Buy Black' campaign that is being waged by some people in the Johannesburg area must not be scoffed at.

It is often claimed that the advocates of Black Consciousness are hemming themselves in into a closed world, choosing to weep on each other's shoulders and thereby cutting out useful dialogue with the rest of the world. Yet I feel that the black people of the world, in choosing to reject the legacy of colonialism and white domination and to build around themselves their own values, standards and outlook to life, have at last established a solid base for meaningful cooperation amongst themselves in the larger battle of the Third World against the rich nations. As Fanon puts it; "The consciousness of the self is not the closing of a door to communication. . . . National consciousness, which is not nationalism, is the only thing that will give us an international dimension." This is an encouraging sign, for there is no doubt that the black-white power struggle in South Africa is but a microcosm of the global confrontation between the Third World and the rich white nations of the world which is manifesting itself in an ever more real manner as the years go by.

Thus, in this age and day, one cannot but welcome the evolution of a positive outlook in the black world. The wounds that have been inflicted on the black world and the accumulated insults of oppression over the years were bound to provoke reaction from the black people. Now we can listen to the Barnett Potters concluding with apparent glee and with a sense of sadistic triumph that the fault with the black man is to be found in his genes, and we can watch the rest of the white society echoing 'amen,' and still not be moved to the reacting type of anger. We have in us the will to live through these trying times; over the years we have attained moral superiority over the white man; we shall watch as time destroys his paper castles and know that all these little pranks were but frantic attempts of frightened little people to convince each other that they can control the minds and bodies of indigenous people of Africa indefinitely.

DOCUMENT 42. Report by Stanley Ntwasa on the National Seminar on Black Theology, Roodepoort, March 8–12, 1971 (abridged)

A PERSONAL REPORT AND ASSESSMENT

Despite organisational difficulties and interference from outside bodies such as the police, the National Seminar on Black Theology was a great success. The tremendous interest of the participants in the subject was the major factor contributing to the success of the venture. This interest was shown both in the discussion in groups and plenary sessions, and the standard of the debate was generally very high.

The seminar was hampered not only by some interference with those who did attend, but also by interference with some of the speakers who had been invited to attend, had agreed to attend, but who had to withdraw at the last minute.

From the beginning one was very aware of the deep expectations of the participants. This was the very first time that black clergymen and black seminary and university students had come together to discuss their work from the perspective of Black Theology. One could not help feeling that here were a group of black theologians, ministers and theological students coming together to do their own thing.

At an early stage in the seminar the decision was taken that the seminar would be open to black participants only. There was also a long debate on whether or not the press should be allowed to be present. Despite fears about press reporting on discussions which were still of an exploratory nature, and press sensationalism, it was decided that it was important that black people should be aware of the sorts of issues they were discussing. Thus the press was admitted to the discussions with the proviso that black reporters only would be admitted.

The diversity of views expressed by the participants was stimulating. It was clear that there was no 'party line' being followed. People had come to explore the issues and to try to understand what "theologising around the Black Religious experience" meant.

At the same time I am convinced that on many occasions when participants disagreed most vigorously, their differences were over priorities and stress rather than fundamental principles. In some cases it was a matter of sheer semantics.

On the question of strategy there were strong and deep-rooted differences of opinion. The chief issue was whether or not Black churchmen should remain in the white-dominated churches. Some felt that the degree and extent of white domination in the major churches was too great for any real impact to be made which would bring about significant changes for the black members. If black competent and respected leaders withdrew to do their own thinking and planning there was a greater chance of white churchmen being prepared to take not only their grievances but also their creative contributions seriously. Only then would there be any chance of creating a truly non- (rather than multi-) racial church.

Those who opposed withdrawal as a strategy felt that it was still possible for them to make their presence felt in the white-dominated church structures, patterns and institutions. Even within this group there were differences. Some felt that they should remain in the present structures and attempt to change them by bringing moral and other pressure to bear on the white leaders and hierarchy. Others felt that this was pointless because it would be ineffective. They questioned why they as blacks should allow themselves to be squeezed out of their majority black churches by a white minority. They felt strongly that what was required was the development of a strong black pressure group who would work towards taking over the control from the whites until the churches were led by representatives of the majority of the members, i.e. blacks. When that happened it would be up to the whites to decide whether or not they would remain in black-led churches.

But all these groups agreed that it was urgently necessary that further discussions on this issue take place amongst black churchmen and that further seminars on "Black Theology" were very necessary if a sense of unity were to develop among black churchmen. Without this unity little change would take place in the church's structures, thinking and goals.

This particular discussion occurred frequently during the course of the seminar. There was unanimity on the goal of a non-racial church, but it was clear that the majority of the participants favoured not withdrawing at this stage.

An issue on priorities which aroused a great deal of debate was whether the 'blackness' of Black people should come before their humanity. There was complete agreement that all our energies should be concentrated on the Black masses to make them totally aware of their value as God-created human beings—not just "Black things" but "Black people." The issue was one of priority of focus. Some felt that prior stress should be laid on the 'blackness' of Black people, trying to enable people to rid themselves both intellectually and emotionally of the negative connotations of blackness (as sinful, inferior, gloomy, unattractive, etc.) and to build up a conscious sense of pride and dignity in their blackness (as good, beautiful, and positively creative). The argument was that people could never accept their humanity fully until they had thrown off their 'hang ups' about being Black and had accepted it as an unavoidable but positive experience of their humanity.

On the other hand others contended that this sort of emphasis might tend towards racism, or encourage a new racism. Biblically the prior affirmation must be that of humanity, 'God created man (all men) in His own image'. When this becomes the central affirmation of any and every man, then they are freed to accept any other man with his particular racial characteristics, and thus also free to accept joyfully and positively their own blackness.

Despite this disagreement, all were agreed that the fundamental experience of Black people in this society is the negative and debilitating effect of their blackness. They experience themselves as black, and this experience makes it hard for them at all times to experience themselves as men.

The Papers

1. *James Cone—The Black Christ*

The Seminar began with a taped address by Prof. James Cone, Associate Professor of Theology at Union Theological Seminary, New York. This was an extract from his latest book 'A Black Theology of Liberation.'

The first issue arising from the tape was whether or not a legitimate case could be made out for 'Theologising around the Black religious experience'. Here agreement was quickly reached. A man's religious experience cannot be isolated from his total human experience and treated as if it bore no relation to his total human condition. To attempt to do this would be a travesty of Christian theology. When a black man's religious experience is integrated into his whole experience of life, then it becomes integrated into his experience of suffering, poverty and oppression. It is the human experience which colours his religious experience, whether this be in worship or in his systematising of the biblical data and relating them to his condition.

Arising out of this there was considerable agreement that the term 'Black' was a legitimate theological concept, denoting not so much pigmentation as the condition of the oppressed and the poor. . . .

3. Dr. Anthony Mabona—"White Worship and Black People"

Dr. Mabona's paper dealt with the issue of Black people using the forms of worship set by Europeans.

He started by speaking very highly and meaningfully of prayer, which he considered to concern the total human condition, and made it clear that it seemed impossible to him that anyone whose faith does not include an eschatological and transcendent dimension could find any meaning and relevance in worship. He went on to say that 'the God of Christian worship is a personal and loving God, not a metaphysical or mathematical abstraction. He is the God who sent Jesus Christ to us and poured his Spirit upon us. His transcendence over us is that of superiority and not one of metaphysical or mathematical infinity. The peoples of the universe are His family and this is the inheritance of the Kingdom to which he calls us through Christ."

Most strikingly, perhaps, he said that worship was to be seen as a function of life, action and suffering. He made it quite clear that worship was not 'a stepping out of the world' and therefore that it is wise to stress those elements of worship which promote an authentic relation to reality, such as intercession, offertory and the experience of an actual fellowship. He recognised the need for symbols, but stressed that we needed symbols not of some vague religious mystery but symbols which were natural and encompassing expressions of reality. He called strongly for less cringing and scraping in the liturgy as if God were a white capitalist or aristocrat who thrives on seeing us belittle our humanity and bury our healthy pride in ourselves.

He also strongly criticised the type of spiritual training that is used particularly in the seminaries; the type of meditation in which one is supposed to get alone to stimulate memory, imagination and emotional responses, e.g. especially in trying to call up scenes from the life of Jesus, fixing them in the imagination and trying to express one's sentiments about this. This, he claimed, is designed to help one increase one's moral excellence, one's spiritual perfection. But this, he claimed, is foreign to our tradition. "I cannot remember in any of the traditional practices of Black people that persons were encouraged to cultivate high moral excellence or self-perfection by 'entering into themselves.' A sensible person in our society was supposed to be one who knew and performed his or her duties towards ancestors and members of the community. The faithful performance of these duties and the development of the correct attitudes also towards natural objects was not supposed to imbue such a person with any kind of halo of sanctity or holiness. It was supposed to make a person a sensible and well-adjusted member of society and the universe."

A point slightly touched on, and obviously worth a great deal more attention was the role of white Western styles of worship in keeping Blacks out of leadership roles in the church—especially those blacks who have not left the rural areas for the great cities where Western influences are felt strongly even by the blacks. Only those blacks who have themselves become thoroughly westernized felt sufficiently free in the cultural idioms to assume creative leadership roles. Thus control is kept in the hands of whites by using white culture to debilitate Blacks.

In the discussion that followed on this paper it was obvious that participants were unanimous in their agreement with the feelings and sentiments presented, and felt that the established churches had much to learn from the Black sects which many in the established churches tended to ridicule. The Black sects have a great deal to teach us concerning spirituality.

4. Mr. Stanley Ntwasa— "Some thoughts on the training of Black Ministers"

Mr. Ntwasa began his paper by outlining the general humdrum of day to day life in our seminaries—the packed lecture and assignment programme culminating in an examination which may make or break a young black theological student. The general lack of mutual staff/student confidence he blamed primarily on the fact that the vast majority of seminary lecturers were whites, and on the attitude of black students which was to pass the examinations set by the whites in order to be ordained.

The paper was followed by a fairly passionate discussion on whether or not blacks should replace the present white lecturers. While the majority felt that this ought to happen, this was balanced by a feeling that it would be unsound to replace qualified lecturers who were white with less qualified black lecturers. This raised the question of what constitutes being 'qualified' to teach young prospective black clergymen. Is it high academic achievements at Oxford or Cambridge? Or is a thorough familiarity with the situation and aspirations of Blacks in the country and an ability to do theological reflection on these fundamental issues? Unfortunately this question was not debated sufficiently. . . .

7. Mr. David Thebehali— "Has Christianity a future among and relevance for Blacks in South Africa"

Mr. Thebehali began by giving a detailed account of the approach of the early Christian missionaries. He argued that because Black converts were actively encouraged to leave their tribal environment to reside next to the home of the missionary, or on the mission station, which they did, the power and authority of the chief was undermined and introduced a strong dividing factor into the running of tribal affairs. Hence the missionaries had been prime dividing factors in African society. This divisiveness was further enhanced by the missionaries' adherence to the denominational divisions that they had transplanted onto African soil from Europe. Because of this "we black people ought to be a little less Anglican, a little less Roman Catholic, a little less Methodist," but "a little more black."

In the light of his indictments against the earlier missionaries and the present so-called 'multi-racial' churches, he could not see what blacks were still doing in these majority black but still white-oriented and dominated churches. He concluded by calling on the participants at the seminar to consider seriously withdrawing from these 'multi-racial' churches as they were of no relevance at all to the plight and suffering of the black community.

It has already been mentioned that this was one of the major points of discussion in the seminar but was regarded as unacceptable to the majority of the participants. Nevertheless, it is clear that this particular issue has assumed great importance, and discussion on it is by no means over.

Overall impressions of the seminar and its content are that it was a most valuable experience, and that a great deal was learned. During the course of the seminar conviction about the validity of and commitment to Black Theology increased, and plans were laid for further Regional seminars during the course of the year.

P.S. One need not mention all the police interference with the seminar; some of it has already been mentioned in this report; other aspects were given a good deal of coverage in the Press, including the arrest of Bishop Zulu on a pass offense, and the trial of Dr. Marcus Braun (the host of the seminar) for housing 'Bantu' persons without a permit in a 'white' area. Nevertheless, it is amazing that a Cabinet Minister could expect a Bishop, rudely aroused at 4:15 a.m., to be wearing his episcopal robes as a means of identification of his episcopal status—rather than his pajamas!

Document 43. Report of the Commission on Black Theology, SASO General Students' Council, Durban, July 1971

This commission did not present any fact papers but tabled its findings in the form of resolutions.

Stanley Ntwasa, delegate of the Reeso [Reef SASO] Branch, led the commission on Theology. All investigations on Theology were geared towards Black consciousness. The result of the commission's findings determined the role of theology in the Black man's struggle. Theology a taught in schools conducted by the various education departments wɛ aimed at brainwashing pupils. The commission also found that religious instruction was being used as a part of the propaganda machinery. The commission also agreed that teachers were not given any latitude to question the values of such religious instruction.

Realising these facts Council decided that the Executive look into possibilities of revising the religious instruction syllabus in collaboration with IDAMASA and make recommendations to the departments concerned.

But most important of all was the decision taken by Council concerning Black Theology. The analysis of Black Theology and its role as SASO saw it was clearly set out in a resolution tabled by Rubin Phillip, the present Vice-President, and seconded by David Modiba, delegate of the Fort Hare Branch. The motion on Black Theology was carried unanimously with acclaim. Below is reprinted the Resolution 57/71 on Black Theology:

THAT THIS GSC Believes that:
(1) Black Theology is not a theology of absolutes but grapples with existential situations. Black Theology is not a theology of theory but that of action and development. It is not a reaction against anything but is an authentic and positive articulation of the Black Christian's reflection on God in the light of their Black experience.
(2) Black Theology asserts its validity and sees its existence in the context of the words of Christ, who in declaring His mission said: "He has sent me to bring good news to the poor, to proclaim liberty to captives, and to the blind new sight, to set the down-trodden free, to proclaim the Lord's year of favour."
(3) Black Theology, therefore, understands Christ's liberation not only from circumstances of internal bondage but also a liberation from circumstances of external enslavement. Black Theology means taking resolute and decisive steps to free Black people not only from estrangement to God but also from slave mentality, inferiority complex, distrust of themselves and continued dependence on others culminating in self-hate.
AND NOTING THAT:
(a) Christianity as propagated by the White dominated churches has proved beyond doubt to be a support for the status quo, which to Black people means oppression. This is clearly demonstrated by their over-emphasis of interracial fraternization as a solution to the problems of this country, whereas they are fully aware that the basic problem is that of land distribution, economic deprivation and consequently the disinheritance of the Black people:
(b) we hereby support those Christians in this country who are making a new departure to make the Christian message for the people of God, and consequently welcomes the emergence of Black Theology;
INSTRUCTS:
(i) the Secretary-General to convey the following message to all Black seminaries and Faculties of Theology in Black universities that they take a serious look at the training of Black ministers and theologians whose roles

SASO sees as being intrinsically interwoven in the surge towards Black Consciousness and liberation;

(ii) AND FURTHER INSTRUCTS the Secretary-General to convey our belief that Black people are the best qualified to teach in these institutions, since they are the only ones who are able to focus theologically from the basis of their experience as Blacks in a racist South Africa;

(iii) that Black seminaries and Faculties of Theology take a serious look at the syllabuses with the intention of incorporating Black studies as a necessary discipline in the training of Black ministers and theologians since it is important that they be enabled at least to focus theologically on their blackness, which entails looking back and reassessing one's history, culture, traditions and beliefs, looking at the present and assessing the theological and secular realities of the Black experience, and looking to the future and their Christian goals.

DOCUMENT 44. "SASO Policy Manifesto," July 1971

1. SASO is a Black Student Organization working for the liberation of the Black man first from psychological oppression by themselves through inferiority complex and secondly from physical oppression accruing out of living in a White racist society.
2. We define Black People as those who are by law or tradition, politically, economically and socially discriminated against as a group in the South African society and identifying themselves as a unit in the struggle towards the realization of their aspirations.
3. SASO believes:
   a) South Africa is a country in which both Black and White live and shall continue to live together,
   b) That the Whiteman must be made aware that one is either part of the solution or part of the problem,
   c) That, in this context, because of the privileges accorded to them by legislation and because of their continual maintenance of an oppressive regime, Whites have defined themselves as part of the problem,
   d) That, therefore, we believe that in all matters relating to the struggle towards realizing our aspirations, Whites must be excluded,
   e) That this attitude must not be interpreted by Blacks to imply "anti-Whitism" but merely a more positive way of attaining a normal situation in South Africa,
   f) That in pursuit of this direction, therefore, personal contact with Whites, though it should not be legislated against, must be discouraged, especially where it tends to militate against the beliefs we hold dear.
4. (a) SASO upholds the concept of Black Consciousness and the drive towards black awareness as the most logical and significant means of ridding ourselves of the shackles that bind us to perpetual servitude.
   (b) SASO defines Black Consciousness as follows:

(i) BLACK CONSCIOUSNESS is an attitude of mind, a way of life

(ii) The basic tenet of Black Consciousness is that the Blackman must reject all value systems that seek to make him a foreigner in the country of his birth and reduce his basic human dignity.

(iii) The Blackman must build up his own value systems, see himself as self-defined and not as defined by others.

(iv) The concept of Black Consciousness implies the awareness by the Black people of the power they wield as a group, both economically and politically and hence group cohesion and solidarity are important facets of Black Consciousness.

(v) BLACK CONSCIOUSNESS will always be enhanced by the totality of involvement of the oppressed people, hence the message of Black Consciousness has to be spread to reach all sections of the Black community.

(c) SASO accepts the premise that before the Black people should join the open society, they should first close their ranks, to form themselves into a solid group to oppose the definite racism that is meted out by the White society, to work out their direction clearly and bargain from a position of strength. SASO believes that a truly open society can only be achieved by Blacks.

5. SASO believes that the concept of integration can never be realized in an atmosphere of suspicion and mistrust. Integration does not mean an assimilation of Blacks into an already established set of norms drawn up and motivated by White society. Integration implies free participation by individuals in a given society and proportionate contribution to the joint culture of the society by all constituent groups.

Following this definition, therefore, SASO believes that integration does not need to be enforced or worked for. Integration follows automatically when the doors to prejudice are closed through the attainment of a just and free society.

6. SASO believes that all groups allegedly working for "Integration" in South Africa—and here we note in particular the Progressive Party and other Liberal institutions—are not working for the kind of integration that would be acceptable to the Black man. Their attempts are directed merely at relaxing certain oppressive legislations and to allow Blacks into a White-type society.

7. That SASO while upholding these beliefs, wish to state that black consciousness should not be associated with any political party.

Document 45. "Understanding SASO." Discussion document by Steve Biko for SASO formation school, Pietermaritzburg, December 5–8, 1971

The formation school on which we are about to embark is directed at putting our efforts in the right context. It is no use for us to emulate existing student groups. It is in fact the first step in the wrong [path] to even accept and adopt their set of values, for indeed we have a different path to tread. Our goals, by their very nature demand of us a dedication unparalleled in the history of student organisations. Our methods and our approach, in order to achieve fruition, must radically depart from the impersonal, bureaucratic and bourgeois type of approach that we have inherited from western-based student organisations.

Thus we must start this formation school with some kind of mental preparation. We must ask ourselves a few basic questions—who are we? What are we talking about? Where are we today? Whither are we going? We have to answer these questions sincerely in order to even approximate the kind of mental preparation that is necessary for the work we want to engage in.

1. WHO ARE WE?

Basically we are a black student group springing from a Black community. People at the helm of a ship that constantly sails in troubled waters. People who themselves are not sure how to steer the ship to better waters; people at the vanguard of a new type of thinking that has become reduced to mere slogans without necessarily achieving depth and clearcut definitions. People whose proximity to economical sufficiency dulls their senses of perception to reality and makes them shirk their duties and responsibility to the community. People who constantly pass on the responsibility for the community's emancipation to others as if it were a soccer ball.

Yes, we are a community of cynics whose close identification with the Western world has made them adopt a scientific attitude to the problems of the black community and to declare them insoluble in the face of apparently [overwhelming] opposition. In trying to oppose a power-based and ma-chine-orientated society we have ourselves ceased to rely on our traditional leanings on a strong man-based society. We seek to assure our Western friends of our ability to play their own game while we, stripped of our true traditional selves are a mere shadow of the powerful forces we could easily be. Nowhere is this imbalance of personality better demonstrated than in the student community. Dazzled by the twilight of raised hopes of participation in the white man's world of technology and intoxicated by the flattering remunerations that can be derived from our white-collar jobs, we exist between two worlds. On the one hand there is our own community with whom we increasingly share very little sympathy, ill-defined "powers that be," and on the other there is the white community whose values we have learnt to respect through our days at school and whose heritage has a magnetic and tantalizing effect on us.

Who are we indeed? We are a mere shadow of what we claim to be. Besides engaging in mere philosophical and intellectual masturbation about problems that vitally affect our people, we do nothing, but stand at the touchlines and witness a game we should be playing. We console our guilt-stricken consciences with ill-considered claims—at best half-truths—to the effect that we also as students are oppressed but really we know full well that we live in a moated and heavily protected world of studenthood and that what occasionally hits us is nothing but the occasional rock that results from a ricochet of the actual hail of bullets continually falling on our people.

We must accept that it is not enough to sit and put complaints into words. Each one of us must take it as his personal responsibility to be of meaningful value in this long journey that we claim to be walking jointly with our people, only then shall we have discovered who we really are. This question has to be answered not tomorrow, not some other time but in this formation school.

2. WHAT ARE WE TALKING ABOUT?

Here we are primarily concerned with SASO and its work. We talk glibly of "black consciousness" and yet we hardly show that we understand what we are talking about. In this regard it is essential for us to realise a few basic facts about "black consciousness."

"Black consciousness" is essentially a slogan directing us away from the traditional political big talk to a new approach. This is an inward-looking movement calculated to make us look at ourselves and see ourselves, not in terms of what we have been taught through the absolute values of white society but with new eyes. It is a call upon us to see the innate value in us, in our institutions, in our traditional outlook to life and in our own worth as people. The call of "black consciousness" is by no means a slogan driving people to think in a certain way politically. Rather it is a social slogan directed at each member of the black community calling upon him to discard the false mantle that he has been forced to wear for so many years and to think in terms of himself as he should. In this regard therefore "black consciousness" is a way of life that must permeate through the society and be adopted by all. The logic behind it is that if you see yourself as a person in your own right there are certain basic questions that you must ask about the conditions under which you live. To get to this stage there are three basic steps that have to be followed.

(i) We have to thoroughly understand what we are talking about and to impart it in the right context. This becomes especially necessary in a country like ours where such an approach lends itself easily to misinterpretation. For this reason we have made provision for a historical study of the theory of "black power" in this formation school.

(ii) We have to create channels for the adoption of the same approach by the black community at large. Here again one has to be realistic. An approach of this nature, to be successful, has to be adopted by as large a fraction of the population as possible in order to be effective. Whilst the student community may be instrumental in carrying the idea across to the people and remaining the force behind it, the approach will remain ineffective unless it gains grass-roots support. This is why it is necessary to create easily acceptable slogans and follow these up with in-depth explanations. Secondary institutions built up from members of the community and operating amongst the community have to be encouraged and these must be run by people who themselves understand what is involved in these institutions and in the approach we are adopting. One can expand and give many examples of such institutions but we expect this to come out of discussions at this formation school. Let it suffice to say that such institutions must cover all fields of activity in the black community—educational, social, economical, religious, etc.

(iii) People have to be taught to see the advantages of group action. Here one wonders whether a second look should not be taken at the government-instituted bodies like UBCs and Bantustans. It is a universal fact that you cannot politicise people and hope to limit their natural and legitimate aspirations. If the people demand something and get it because they have an "UBC" or "Territorial Authority" to talk for them then they shall begin to realise the power they wield as a group. Political modernization of the black people may well find good expression in these institutions which at present are repugnant to us. In contrasting the approach adopted in the [United] States by the black people and our own approach here it will be interesting what this formation school thinks of the various "Territorial Authorities" at our various "own areas."

There are some dangers that we have to guard against as well as we make progress in the direction we are pursuing. The first and foremost is that we must not make the mistake of wishing to get into the white man's boots. Traditional indigenous values tell us of a society where poverty was foreign and extreme richness unknown except for the rulers of our society. Sharing was at the heart of our culture. A system that tends to exploit many and favour a few is as foreign to us as hair which is not kinky or a skin which is not dark. Where poverty reigned, it affected the whole community simply because of weather conditions beyond our control. Hence even in our aspirations basic truth will find expression. We must guard against the danger of creating a black middle class whose blackness will only be skin-deep literally. The paper on African socialism will provide us with enough grounds for discussion along these [lines].

Secondly we must not be limited in our outlook. There is miles of difference between preaching "black consciousness" and preaching "hatred of white." Telling people to hate whites is an outward and reactionary type of preaching which though understandable is undesirable and self-destructive. It makes one think in negative terms and preoccupies one with peripheral issues. In a society like ours it is a "positive feed-forward" approach that leads one into a vicious circle and ultimately to self-destruction through ill-advised and impetuous action. In fact it is usually an extreme form of inferiority complex where the sufferer has lost hope of "making it" because of conditions imposed upon him. His actual aspirations are to be like the white man and the hatred arises out of frustration. On the other hand black consciousness is an inward-looking process. It takes cognisance of one's dignity and leads to positive action. It makes you seek to assert yourself and to rise to majestic heights as determined by you. No doubt you resent all forces that seek to thwart your progress but you meet them with strength, resilience and determination because in your heart of hearts you are convinced you will get where you want to get to. In the end you are a much more worthy victor because you do not seek revenge but to implement the truth for which you have stood all along during your struggle. You were no less angry than the man who hates whites but your anger was channelled to positive action. Because you had a vision detached from the situation you worked hard regardless of immediate setbacks. White hatred leads to precipitate and shot-gun methods whereas we are involved in an essentially long-term struggle where cool-headedness must take precedence over everything else.

The third point is that we must not make the mistake of trying to categorise whites. Essentially all whites are the same and must be viewed with suspicion. This may apparently sound contradictory to what I have been saying but it is in actual fact not. A study of the history of South Africa shows that almost at all times whites have been involved in Black struggles and almost in all instances led to the death or confusion of what they were involved in. This may not have been calculated sometimes, but it arises out of genuine differences in approach and commitments. That blacks are deciding to go it alone is not an accident but a result of years of history behind black-white co-operation. Black-white co-operation in this country leads to limitations being imposed on the programme adopted. We must by all means encourage "sympathetic whites" to stand firm in their fight but this must be away from us. In many ways this is dealt with adequately in an article that appears in the SASO Newsletter—August issue, "Black Souls in White Skins." The fact that "sympathetic whites" have in the past made themselves the traditional pace-setters in the black man's struggle has led to the black man's taking a back seat in a struggle essentially his own. Hence excluding whites tends to activate black people and in the ultimate analysis gives proper direction to whatever is being done. This is a fact that overseas observers visiting the country find hard to accept but it remains very true. Racial prejudice in this country has gone beyond all proportions and has subconsciously affected the minds of some of the most well-known liberals.

3. WHERE ARE WE TODAY?

SASO stands today at a very important stage of her life. The establishment of the organisation has had a very great impact in three major directions.

Firstly we have created a mood at the black campuses which has set the stage for a complete revision of thinking. Our blacks-only attitude has infused a sense of pride and self-reliance on almost all black campuses. Where originally one met with stiff opposition to all exclusive talk, it is now generally accepted that blacks must go it alone. This attitude is welcome to us but has to be guided very carefully and steadily lest it falls prey to some of the dangers we have already mentioned. It is hoped that we shall translate all the intellectual talk about "black is beautiful" to some kind of meaningful practical language.

Secondly we have given impetus to meaningful thinking outside the campus. Suddenly black people are beginning to appreciate the value of their own efforts, unpolluted by half-hearted support from the white world. Though this kind of thinking is still limited to the "black intelligentsia" at present there are all the signs that it shall spread to the rest of the community.

Thirdly we have dealt almost a fatal blow to all black-white movements. One does not know whether to take pride in this or not but definitely it is obvious that we have wasted a lot of valuable time in the so-called non-racial organisations trying to cheat ourselves into believing we were making progress while in fact by the very nature of these bodies we liquidated ourselves into inactivity. The more radical whites have in fact rejoiced at the emergence of SASO and some of them have even come up with useful support in terms of valuable contacts etc., but radical whites are very rare creatures in this country.

Our strength has been difficult to assess because of the battle we were waging for members. With the latest affiliations by Fort Hare and Ngoye we now stand in a position to get down to practical stuff.

WHITHER ARE WE GOING?

Since we know what we are talking about it becomes a matter of commitment to go where we want to go. What we need now is dedicated people who are prepared to lose a lot to see an idea blossoming into fruition. That is why you are here at this formation school. You must prepare yourselves to be the vanguard group spearheading all our efforts in your individual campuses. You must count yourselves not amongst many who shall follow but among the few who shall lead. In an effort to bear witness to our determination to play our role as future leaders of the community we must inculcate in our minds the martyr mentality. We must cease to see ourselves as people affected by history but as people who will shape history. We must carve and shape the destiny of our people and defy all provisions that limit our aspirations. As you sit about to start deliberations at this formation school you must be aware that you are setting a programme that you yourselves will put into effect. In other words we must make a habit of thinking about SASO not as "they" but us, our efforts, our sweat, our struggle, our successes and our failures. Not unless one is in this frame of mind will we be able to be what should be.

We have noted that our struggle is essentially a long-term struggle. We have also seen the pitfalls that lie in our way. Hence we must embark on this long journey with the necessary caution and astuteness. We must take a vow jointly that we shall not turn back until we have reached our goals. Those of us who fall by the wayside must be aware of the reduction in total strength. Hence the need for that fine balance between staying up and going forward.

At all costs we must make sure that we are marching to the same tune as the rest of the community. At no stage must we view ourselves as a group endowed with special characteristics. While we may be playing the tune, it is the rhythmic beating of the community's boots that spurs us to march on and at no stage should that rhythm be disturbed. As the group grows larger and more boots join the rhythmic march let us not allow the beating of the boots to drown the pure tones of our tune for the tune is necessary and essential to the rhythm.

Somewhere far ahead lies the coveted glittering prize barely visible except for the radiating rays it casts over the hill top. Let us keep our eyes on those rays and march on with a sense of raised aspirations lest if we look at the dividing distance our hearts may be filled with despair.

DOCUMENT 46. Report by Strini Moodley on SASO leadership training seminar, Pietermaritzburg, December 5–8, 1971 (abridged)

INTRODUCTION

With the rapid development of SASO as an established student organisation, that was based on and stood by the philosophy of Black Consciousness and Black Solidarity, it became necessary to go into these concepts much more thoroughly. A clearer understanding of these concepts was essential so that students can expand the philosophies with a certain degree of clarity when speaking to people. It was also noticed that despite the clarity of many it was difficult to continue any self-reliance projects in the community because of a lack of training in that particular field.

Subsequently, the December Seminar was drawn up to combine Black Consciousness and Community Development and [to] conduct this seminar with a view to showing the interrelationship between these concepts and how necessary an understanding of Black Consciousness was in the implementation of Community Development projects.

STRUCTURE OF THE SEMINAR

The Seminar was divided into four phases.

Phase I dealt with the rationale behind Black Consciousness, the definition of Black Consciousness, and the Practical application of the ideology of Black Consciousness.

Phase II dealt with Community Development and the various approaches to a successful project.

Phase III examined student leadership and discussed the importance of and necessity for the student to develop strong and harmonious links with his community.

Phase IV stressed the importance of Planning. Here the students were given situations which related to all three phases and were asked to plan them.

The seminar ran for five days and was divided into three sessions— morning, afternoon and evening.

Steve Biko was the trainer for Phase One. Phase II was handled by Ben Khoapa and Steve Manyane. Ranwedzi Nengwekhulu and Maphiri Masekela conducted Phase III, and Temba Sono Phase IV.

Phase I. Black Consciousness—the Rationale, Definition, Practical Application

The first step in this phase was to test the degree of awareness among trainees as regards the rationale behind Black Consciousness. The trainees were divided into four groups and each group was given a situation to discuss and then report back. For example one group was told that a group of militant young blacks from the [United] States were interviewing them and they asked the group to give the rationale behind Black Consciousness in the South African political context. Another group was asked to explain to an old politician why SASO had chosen Black Consciousness and not any of the ideologies of the old political movements.

Each group comprising about 15 students then discussed and explored the situations they had been given.

At their report backs many new avenues of Black Consciousness were revealed. The in-depth group discussions were eye-openers to many students who were still carrying the "burn, baby, burn" tag in their own analysis and in fact, life-style in terms of black consciousness. In the evaluation questionnaires many students expressed their satisfaction with the group discussions. Following the rationale the trainers' input was logical. Various papers by people on the subject of Black Consciousness were read. The definition of Black Consciousness itself was explored in the light of Adam Small's "Blackness vs Nihilism." Steve Biko's "African Cultural Concepts" and Frank Talk's "Black Souls in White Skins."

It was during the definition of Black Consciousness that Black Solidarity as opposed to the system-created "tribal" platforms came under real in-depth discussions. A fiery and stimulating plenary discussion followed. However, students in their evaluation questionnaires noted the fact that plenary caused discussion to become somewhat restricting in that only a few individuals became involved. The main bone of contention with "Black Solidarity" as opposed to "Tribal Platforms" accrued out of the fact that students felt certain "well-oriented" people in the system were doing some good work.

From an assessment of the evaluation questionnaires students saw Black Solidarity as the only viable and acceptable corollary to Black Consciousness. "Tribal platforms" could not enhance or be part of Black Consciousness. In the definition of Black Consciousness the students agreed that this ideology was not an end in itself but was the only feasible means in the attainment of a free and just society where true integration would be the natural social order. However, the plenary agreed completely that "What Black Consciousness seeks to do is to produce at the output end of the process, real Black People who do not regard themselves as appendages to White Society." The definition went on to lay the basis for the re-examination [of] ourselves in terms of culture, education, Religion and economics. It was also agreed that Black Consciousness should attract real, committed Black people and it should not be our endeavour to see that there is an equal distribution of Indians, Coloureds and Africans; this is a stereotyped innovation of the liberals. The practical application of this ideology was divided into four parts. Directive politics, Infiltrative Politics, Orientation projects and Self-Reliance projects. Directive Politics implied direct involvement with the students and the community. Each and every platform that could be used was to be utilized. This conclusion was drawn because, in as much as Black Consciousness, as far as SASO was concerned, was the only "viable means" many black people still saw other answers to the White problem. The first step in Directive Politics was vocalization with "disciplined protagonists" leading the way. Starting at grass roots level was equally important where people spoke to five or six people at a time—making them thoroughly conversant with Black Consciousness and then sending them out into the community to speak to other people. Organisation of Black groups, by blacks and for blacks was seen as another step in Directive politics. Students felt it was important that Blacks built up a sense of self-confidence. This was seen as a necessity because blacks had been, for too long, led to believe that they could not organise on their own. Publicity stunts, slogans and emotional images were also part of the practical application. Slogans like "Blackman you are on your own" and images like SASO T-shirt were seen as vital in the propaganda of Black Consciousness.

When it came to the discussion of "Infiltrative Politics" the "tribal platform" issue was again discussed. Many students tried to probe the possibilities of infiltration and re-orienting these platforms to adopt the Black Consciousness approach. This problem kept re-appearing and became a major problem when dealing with Community Development. . . .

Phase II. Community Development Seminar
SESSION 1: Plenary—preparatory.

Background development projects from Europe and America, Israel, Pakistan and India compared to the developing nations of Africa.

An examination of the extent to which community can function on the academic level. Whether it happened on the level beyond the crisis situation. There were eleven (11) participants who have had a personal experience or took part in any community development project. Seven centres were represented of which four had engaged in a project.

Participants divided into groups according to the centres embarking on projects. Those who had no experience of projects joined groups of their choice. The groups were Fort Hare, Federal Seminary, UNB [University of Natal—Black] and UNIN [University of the North].
SESSION 2:

Fort Hare: Engaged in building a class room. Mud was used to make bricks which had to be dried. This was a very advantageous medium as all the surrounding houses were similarly constructed. The structures were meant to be of a temporary nature because of impending removals. The walls were falling and the pupils were suffering. Use of mud also kept the inspectors away. The invitation came from a local minister.

Five days spent in July by some fifty students. They laid the foundation and the walls were built up to window level. All this was subsequently destroyed by a deluge and most students got very discouraged. After vacation the students had to make and dry bricks first and also patch up the semi-destroyed building. When a new group of students subsequently came after the vacation they complained about the dirty nature of the job, they were very discouraged. They came from urban areas mainly. The project was postponed after the rain till November and because of lack of funds.

The money would be used to buy corrugated iron which will be used to cover the walls as soon as they were up. Attempts to raise funds unsuccessful but for some donations. It was felt that students were cooperating with the government yet the students wanted to demonstrate that there [are] things the people can do as a community e.g. to provide education for all children. Subsequent S. B. [Special Branch, i.e. security police] interest tended to intimidate the people hence the very minimal cooperation from them and even from the teachers themselves.

UNIN: Their project, a local clinic, was merely a humble beginning. They renovated and cleaned the yard and provided food from a feeding scheme. The major problem was to convince the authorities that they had no political association. The mission was sought for students to give part of their meals to the clinic. The doctor comes to the clinic once a fortnight. The idea was to get the students involved and concerned about the welfare of the people. Opposition to the scheme was hedged around the fact that [it] was a paternalistic hand-out. It was hoped however that the situation would improve. The clinic fell under the Lebowa Territorial Authority and no permission could be found for the renovations. Towards the end of the year the students renovated a school. Funds were raised and given to the social workers.

FEDSEM: The project at Dyamala was undertaken by the community. Money for renovating the school could not be found but after an appeal it was recommended to a firm to give roofing material to the school. The students offered help in the cutting of bricks to finish up the wall.

The major difficulties were that there was no transport to carry the students from college. The students helped in cutting bricks and drawing water. The students were very keen and were motivated by the sight of the deplorable living conditions. It was noticeable that the community appreciated the gesture and also helped. They were impressed by the attitude of the students. When the building was being completed the students were asked to be present and feasting was provided.

The *Melane* scheme was similar to the above. Again the initiative was that of the people but they later got stuck with financing. Fifty Rands raised from Compassion Week was offered as a donation.

UNB: The New Farm scheme is a preventative medicine one.

Phase I—was involved with collecting data about the living conditions there and the prevalent diseases.

This is an illegal squatter community that is living under very poor conditions. None of the essential amenities are available.

The people became very suspicious for they could not understand their interest, they [are] always harassed by police raids and feared that the student involvement will draw attention on the area. Later they understood our interest.

The area is poverty stricken, unemployment is high and thuggery is rife. These people cannot work because they cannot get work permits because of influx laws. There is no organised community society hence it was difficult to communicate with them. Use was made of their landlords whom they did not trust and are exploiting them. Because of their suspicion the true picture of their conditions was blurred and they had no confidence in anybody.

After the storms in May their tiny wattle and daub houses were destroyed or damaged. Students invited to help in emergency operations. The people saw a father Xmas image in the students. Timber was bought. But the people demanded more than was necessary to fix their damage. No concern was expressed for the next person. They were not cooperating because they thought the students were sent by the government to come and help them.

Phase II—involved health education and counselling. A simple diagramatic pamphlet was compiled and distributed on a family basis. They did not appreciate why they must learn. There was, however, beginning to develop a rap with the people, the students were also helping at the clinic over weekends. It was very difficult to find money to transport the students. Assistance was greatly appreciated because the one doctor at the clinic was not adequate.

Phase III—concerned the actual physical projects i.e. improving the lot of the people, i.e. providing a better water supply scheme. The people had to walk quite a distance to get to an irrigation scheme which has contaminated water. Their major diseases result from unhealthy water.

Several attempts were made to call a community conference to discuss ways of improving the water supply. The landlords seemed to see this involvement as a threat to them because the people would start making demands. However after an independent intermediary (Induna) was found, a meeting became successful [and] the people agreed to contribute towards the scheme. They would not give money until the taps and tanks were available because they feared that they would be robbed. Financing is again the problem.

Another scheme is trench digging for the marshy drain water to escape. The students were generally cooperating but the people did not turn up and the scheme was abandoned because it was felt that the people had to be involved. In the end students got discouraged about their projects. The community was beyond redemption and nothing could be done to help themselves; hence the situation there can never improve and the students could [not] afford the financial demand of the projects.

SESSION 3: Report back

Group 1: Fort Hare combined [with] Fedsem. Reports were given on Fort Beaufort and Dyamala. *Fort Beaufort*—The real spirit behind the project was not properly understood. The scheme was supported by students from the North who did not speak Xhosa. The project depended on the local minister. The schools were approached through the inspector of schools. The major drawback was that the students could not work with the mud. The people attended to church work. The minister attacked them for their apathy. People intimidated by SB visit which hampered the involvement and cooperation of the community. Fort Hare students who could speak Xhosa were ashamed because of the "up country" people's involvement. In a further effort volunteers comprised sympathisers with SASO, UCM, NUSAS.

PROBLEMS

1. The students' lack of knowledge about building skills—artisans employed by Fort Hare.
2. Lack of finance and poor planning—the cost of scheme was underestimated.
3. The community did not see the need for additional classes and some students did not see the need to go out and help.
4. SASO local stepped [in] and decided to build classes.
5. The scheme met with disapproval at Fort Hare; disapproval of mud buildings—no understanding of the use of mud for building purposes.

Dyamala: FedSem students approached by the community after many frustrations.

PROBLEMS

1. Lack of transport and money.
2. Failure to encourage groups around the area to join in project.
3. The community not really made to realise the need because if this could be achieved there would be a better response from the community. . . .

Phase III. The Dynamics of Student Leadership

To initiate phase III the trainees were sent on a "plunge" into the surrounding community of Edendale. Split into groups they were given different areas to cover. The idea behind the "plunge" was to get the students to acquaint themselves with the community; to get the feel of the community; to acquaint themselves with the problems of the community and finally to try without committing them or forcing comment to find out their political affiliations and how they saw themselves solving the problem.

The "plunge" served to lay the foundation for Phase III. Report backs from the "plunge" gave students an idea of the feeling of the people and how important it was the student maintained links—very close ones—with the community. From the "plunge" the basic principle of the dynamics of student leadership vis-a-vis the community and how the student can mobilize the latent "left" feelings that are typical of the oppressed community was established.

The in-put from the trainers dealt with the historical background of black student activism and how this activism was at all times diluted or frustrated because of white and/or multi-racial involvement. Much later black students began to realise that their aspirations and that of the white student differed vastly. They also saw how involvement with whites placed them out of reach of the Black community. Hence the emergence of SASO and Black Consciousness. The definition of leadership was investigated. It came out that leadership was born out of a particular situation and his relevancy was subject to his feel for the situation, the needs and problems of the situation; and how the leader applies his skills in his situation.

The trainers then set out to relate this analysis of leadership with the student and, in particular, with SASO—its policies and theoretical philosophy of Black Consciousness. Primarily the problem that faced SASO was that she had to "grapple" with the [question which] is whether its philosophy [is] applicable to the Black Community"—the trainers posed a dual question; SASO in a leadership role and the individual in a leadership role.

The trainers cautioned that people would espouse SASO ideals for personal glory. SASO could not afford to relapse into an end situation itself and deny the community it purports to serve the Full Fruit of its plant.

Thus the "Overall Ideals" of any student leader within SASO had to place the needs of the community above all else. Voluntary work within the community was an essential part of the "Overall Ideas". The individualistic approach of Western Culture must be done away with if Black students want to strive for cohesion with the Black community.

The paper then investigated the methods of achieving those goals. Identification with the Black Community by the Black student was of prime importance. Students would have to question their personal existence; evaluate their personal situation and then relate it with the situation of his fellow black sufferers. This kind of realization would place in perspective how he is more BLACK than he is a student. At the same time students should learn not to create a dependency on students by the community. In this respect students should do things *with* the community rather than *for* the community. Creating a sense of dependency in the community curbs and destroys the initiative and leadership potentiality of the community. Students who worked in the community would have to adopt the life-style of the community they are involved with. Patience and humility were prime factors in the laying of the foundation for sound and beneficial communication. Projects had to be simple in design, inexpensive and practical. Simple skills were to be taught to the community so that they can develop a sense of self-reliance. First aid, sewing, basic hygiene were some of the suggestions. This base—mentioned above—would prepare the way for more positive and independent action from the community.

The technical aspects of a project were then thoroughly dealt with. Follow-up—the process of a return to an original area of operation so that progress can be measured. Follow-up involved an analysis of and deduction from the initial Input, its conversion, the Output and the Feed-back was in fact the community reaction to the Input.

Follow-up could also be examined at two levels:

(a) Student to the community and

(b) Student to the student.

On level (a) the idea was to maintain contact and harmony with the community, besides evaluating progress. However, both evaluation and maintenance of relationships were to be done informally as possible.

On level (b) the motivating factor would be to compare notes and discuss problems and to plan for the future.

Actual techniques of involvement with the community were then investigated. The most important technique for the implementation of methods was "Effective Communication." The concept of communications was investigated and it was agreed that Effective Communication was the reciprocal involvement of the talker and the listener. Certain cautions were sounded to the trainees with regard to "imparting of meaningless words." Students had to at all times see to it that they do not speak over the heads of the people they work with.

This led to "Non-Judgemental Attitudes" where students tend to view situations subjectively instead of them analysing and evaluating the situation thoroughly.

Pre-Judging a situation can harm an entire project. Rapport had to be established with the community and especially its leaders [who] are in a position of making or breaking a project.

It was at this point that trainees brought up the issue of Bantustan chiefs—wanting to know whether SASO should work in cooperation with them. After much discussion it was agreed that students should use discretion where the name of the organisation is involved. It is not necessary to push the name of SASO when involved in a project. With regard to the "chiefs" it was agreed that when involved in a project with the community every possible means to make the project successful must be used. The fact that the "chief" was being used did not imply agreeing with the policy of "Bantustans."

This led to a discussion on "Force-Field Analysis" where the degree of involvement was analysed. "Pushing Forces" from the student side and its effectiveness would determine the level of involvement and how they overcame the "restraining forces." "Pushing forces" i.e. the students—had to examine the weakness of the "Restraining forces" and apply their strategies in such a manner as to overcome these "forces." Restraining Forces" were seen in the guise of tribal leaders and white liberals. Trainees also included "Security Branch" intimidation in the list of Restraining Forces. For effective leadership therefore trainees were urged to approach a community project with a great deal of flexibility. There can be no success in a project where there is a rigid application of one particular method or technique. The overall appraisal of the dynamics of student leadership concluded that the needs, aspirations, problems and expectations of the black community had to be carefully analysed. Against this analysis, the degree of involvement and the sincerity of identification with the community, was of prime importance if SASO and its members were to make any headway in achieving the goals and aspirations it sets out to do.

Phase IV. Planning

Planning involved the students in problem solving situations. Given certain situations e.g. as President of SASO; or Gen-Secretary; Permanent Organiser—the trainees were asked to find solutions for the problem. The idea behind planning was to try to judge whether students had benefited from the course. Situations that were created in the exercises also posed problems where they as the students body, would have to make vital decisions e.g. in the event of SASO going bankrupt, etc.

EVALUATION

Most of the trainees found the course very helpful. The thorough analysis of all SASO concepts impressed the students and they felt much more confident to propound the philosophy of Black Consciousness.

To most of the students "The Dynamics of Student Leadership" was a completely new dimension and [they] admitted that before this [they] had gone into community projects without really planning the development of the project.

Most of trainees in answering the questionnaire combined student leadership with Community Development.

The students found the input by trainers very adequate although some found it a bit too intellectual.

However the discussions helped to clear up their haziness on certain issues. Most trainees found that Plenary discussions were restricted to a few but were very pleased with the group discussions which were smaller and gave everyone a chance to speak.

On the whole students were extremely satisfied with the entire course. The organisers and trainers were equally satisfied and the seminar is being hailed as the "best SASO has ever had". . . .

5. The Black Consciousness Movement: Confronting the State, 1972-1976

DOCUMENT 47. Graduation Speech by O. R. Tiro at the University of the North, Turfloop, April 29, 1972

MR. CHANCELLOR, Mr. Vice Chancellor and gentlemen, allow me to start off by borrowing language from our Prime Minister, Mr. Vorster. Addressing A. S. B. [Afrikaanse Studentebond] Congress in June last year, Mr Vorster said, "No Black man has landed in trouble for fighting for what is legally his." Although I don't know how far true this is, I make this statement my launch pad.

R. D. Briensmead, an American lay preacher says, "He who withholds the truth or debars men from motives of its expediency, is either a coward, a criminal or both." Therefore Mr. Chancellor I will try as much as possible to say nothing else but the truth. And to me "truth" means "practical reality."

Addressing us on the occasion of the formal opening of this university Mr. [Cedric] Phatudi, a Lebowa territorial authority officer, said that in as much as there is American Education, there had to be Bantu Education. Ladies and gentlemen, I am conscientiously bound to differ with him. In America there is nothing like Negro Education, Red Indian Education, and White American Education. They have American Education common to all Americans. But in South Africa, we have Bantu education, Indian Education, Coloured Education and European education. We do not have a system of education common to all South Africans. What is there in European education which is not good for the African? We want a system of education which is common to all South Africans.

In theory Bantu Education gives our parents a say in our education but in practice the opposite is true. At this University, U. E. D. [University Education Diploma] students are forced to study Philosophy of Education through the medium of Afrikaans. When we want to know why, we are told that the Senate has decided so. Apparently this senate is our parents.

Time and again I ask myself: How do Black lecturers contribute to the administration of this university? For if you look at all the committees they are predominantly white if not completely white. Here and there one finds two or three Africans who, in the opinion of students are white Black men. We have a Students' Dean without duties. We feel that if it is in any way necessary to have a Students' Dean, we must elect our own Dean. We know people who can represent us.

The Advisory Council is said to be representing our parents. How can it represent them when they have not elected it? These people must of necessity please the man who appointed them. This Council consists of chiefs who have never been to University. How can they know the needs of students when they have not been subjected to the same conditions. Those who have been to University have never studied under Bantu Education. What authentic opinion can they express when they don't know how painful it is to study under a repugnant system of education?

I wonder if this Advisory Council knows that a Black man has been most unceremoniously kicked out of the bookshop. Apparently, this is reserved for Whites. According to the policy, Van Schaiks has no right to run a bookshop here. A White member of the Administration has been given the meat contract to supply the University—a Black University. Those who amorphously support the policy may say that there are no Black people to supply it. My answer to them is: Why are they not able to supply the University? What is the cause? Is it not conveniently done that they are not in a position to supply these commodities?

White students are given vacation jobs at this university when there are students who could not get their results due to outstanding fees. Why does the Administration not give these jobs to these students? These White students have 11 universities where they can get vacation jobs. Does the Administration expect me to get a vacation job at the University of Pretoria?

Right now, our parents have come all the way from their homes only to be locked outside. We are told that the hall is full. I do not accept the argument that there is no accommodation for them. In 1970, when the Administration wanted to accommodate everybody, a tent was put up and a close-circuit television was installed. Front seats are given to people who cannot even cheer us. My father is seated there at the back. My dear people, shall we ever get a fair deal in this land? The land of our fathers.

The system is failing. It is failing because even those who recommended it strongly, as the only solution to racial problems in South Africa, fail to adhere to the letter and the spirit of the policy. According to the policy we expected Dr. Eiselen to decline Chancellorship in favour of a Black Man. My dear parents, these are the injustices no normal student can tolerate—no matter who he is and where he comes from.

In the light of what has been said above, the challenge to every black graduate in this country lies in the fact that the guilt of all wrongful actions in South Africa, restriction without trial, repugnant legislation, expulsions from schools, rests on all those who do not actively dissociate themselves from and work for the eradication of the system breeding such evils. To those who wholeheartedly support the policy of apartheid I say: Do you think that the white minority can willingly commit political suicide by creating numerous states which might turn out to be hostile in future?

We black graduates, by virtue of our age and academic standing are being called upon to bear greater responsibilities in the liberation of our people.

Our so-called leaders have become the bolts of the same machine which is crushing us as a nation. We have to go back to them and educate them. Times are changing and we should change with them. The magic story of human achievement gives irrefutable proof that as soon as nationalism is awakened among the intelligentsia, it becomes the vanguard in the struggle against alien rule. Of what use will be your education if you can't help your country in her hour of need? If your education is not linked with the entire continent of Africa it is meaningless.

Remember that Mrs. Suzman said, "There is one thing which the Minister cannot do: He cannot ban ideas from men's minds."

In conclusion Mr. Chancellor I say: Let the Lord be praised, for the day shall come, when all shall be free to breathe the air of freedom which is theirs to breathe and when that day shall have come, no man, no matter how many tanks he has, will reverse the course of events.

God Bless you all.

DOCUMENT 48. "Alice Declaration." Statement by SASO on the boycott of black universities, May 14, 1972

That this Formation School noting:
1. the series of expulsions from various black Universities/Institutions;
2. the oppressive atmosphere in the black institutions of higher learning as demonstrated by the expulsion of the Turfloop student body;
3. that the "wait and see" attitude, if adopted by other black institutions, will be a betrayal to the black man's struggle in this country.
4. that the black community is anxiously and eagerly waiting to learn and hear of the stand taken by black students on other campuses who invariably are subjected to the same atrocities and injustices suffered by the Turfloop students; and believing:
    (a) that this cannot be viewed as an isolated incident;
    (b) that black students have long suffered under oppression;
    (c) that this can be escalated into a major confrontation with the authorities.
THEREFORE RESOLVES
that all black students force the institutions/universities to close down by boycotting lectures;
that the date when a simultaneous boycott of all classes be effected be on 1 June when it is expected that all Turfloop students will be returning to University.

DOCUMENT 49. Agenda and resolutions, SASO General Students' Council, Hammanskraal, July 2–9, 1972 (abridged)

AGENDA:

Sunday, 2nd July
1ST G. S. C. SITTING, 4,00 pm
(1) Opening remarks by President
(2) Adoption of minutes of 2nd G. S. C.
(3) Procedural Motions:
   —centre roundup re affiliation fees
   —admission of new centres accepted by Executive
   —presentation and adoption of Standing Rules

2ND G. S. C. SITTING 8,00 pm
Presidential Address
Consideration of Executive Report

Monday, 3rd July
3RD G. S. C. SITTING, 8,00 am
CENTRE REPORTS:
(1)   University of the North
(2)   Transvaal College of Education
(3)   Reef SASO Local Branch
(4)   Pretoria SASO Local Branch
(5)   Springs SASO Local Branch
(6)   Bloemfontein SASO Local Branch
(7)   Kimberley SASO Local Branch
(8)   Fort Hare SASO Local Branch
(9)   Federal Theological Seminary
(10) Western Cape Branch
(11) University of Natal-Black Section
(12) Durban-West Branch
(13) Lutheran Theological College Branch
(14) University of Zululand

EVENING SESSION: Art and Poetry
Speaker: Oswald Mtshali (to be confirmed)

Tuesday, 4th July
4TH G. S. C. SITTING, 8,00 am
Continuation of Centre Reports
1st Commission Sitting, 12,00 noon
   Internal Relations
   International Relations

Education
Community Development

5TH G. S. C. SITTING, 3,00 pm
Continuation of Centre Reports
Report Back: Internal Relations

Wednesday, 5th July
6TH G. S. C. SITTING, 8,00 am
Report Back: on International Relations
Report Back: on Education
2nd Commission Sittings, 12,00 noon
    Culture
    Community Development
    Publications

7TH G. S. C. SITTING, 3,00 pm
Report Back: Community Development
               Publications
               Culture

EVENING: 8TH G. S. C. SITTING, 8,00 pm
Continuation of Commission Reports

Thursday, 6th July
9TH G. S. C. SITTING, 8,00 am
Continued: Consideration of Commission Reports
3rd Commission Sitting, 12,00 noon
    Planning

10th G. S. C. SITTING, 3,00 pm
Consideration of Commission Reports

EVENING SESSION: Drama Festival

Friday, 7th July
11TH G. S. C. SITTING, 8,00 pm
Consideration of Commission Report:
    Planning

12th G. S. C. SITTING, 2,30 pm
Continued

EVENING SESSION:
Symposium: Creativity and Black Development
Speakers: Revd. T. S. N. Gqubule

Don Mattera
Mafika Pascal Gwala
Njabulo Ndebele
Day Joseph

Saturday, 8th July
13TH G. S. C. SITTING, 8,00 am
General

14TH G. S. C. SITTING, 2,00 pm
Continued

15th G. S. C. SITTING, 4,00pm
Elections

EVENING SESSION: Jazz and Music Festival

COUNCIL DELEGATES:
Executive:
T. J. Sono (President) (left on 2nd morning of proceedings)
R. Phillip (Vice President)
N. Pityana (Secretary General)
H. Nengwekhulu (Permanent Organiser)
S. Moodley (Publications Director)

University of Natal (Black Section)
B. S. Biko
F. Elias
P. A. L. Selele
J. Matsipa
D. Itsweng
K. Mokoape
V. Mafungo (alt. del.)
M. A. Ramphele (alt. del.)
J. M. Malebo (alt. del.)
P. Gulube (alt. del.)
I. Sardiwalla (alt. del.)
W. Palweni (alt. del.)

Reef SASO Local Branch
L. Mabandla
T. Kubheka
W. Nhlapo
B. S. Ngoma (Miss) (alt. del.)

Federal Theological Seminary
M. K. Boshomane

Lutheran Theological College
  V. M. Mayatula

University of the North: (7 votes)
  A. D. Mokoena
  M. D. Matsobane
  M. O. Makhale (alt. del.)
  M. P. Lekota
  I. P. Ntlhe (alt. del.)
  M. B. Mashugane (alt. del.)
  J. Rooi (alt. del.)
  O. Ngoma (Miss) (alt. del.)
  Y. Kraai (Miss) (alt. del).
  D. T. Mafole
  O. R. Tiro
  K. H. Mogapi
  M. Nguyuza

Transvaal College of Education
  S. Variava
  K. Pather

Western Cape
  J. Issel
  I. Smith (Miss)
  B. Louw
  R. Hare (alt. del.)
  H. Isaacs

Fort Hare
  J. Modisane
  B. Langa
  J. Baqwa
  S. Baqwa

Durban-West
  Alan Jeffrey
  Neville Rambritch
  Yugen Naidoo
  S. L. Reddi (alt. del.)

Zululand
  A. E. Mhlongo
  S. F. Duma (Miss)
  F. Mazibuko (Miss)
  M. D. Taka (Miss)

S. D. Mathebula
B. A. Ndaba
V. I. V. Made
M. Shezi

Pretoria
A. M. Mangena
E. S. Chauke
L. Khoza (Miss)
J. M. Paile (alt del)

Springs
M. T. Rapudile
E. Mampane

Kimberley
T. O. Ntsiko
Fikile Mtshatshani

Bloemfontein
A. Setai
C. Motlaung
J. Makofane
E. Phayane (alt. del.)

RESOLUTIONS:

1/72
THAT THIS G. S. C. adopts the minutes of the 2nd G. S. C.

PITYANA
MOODLEY   CARRIED UNAN

2/72
THAT THIS G. S. C. accepts applications for branch status from:
  (1) Durban West
  (2) Springs Students Organisation
  (3) Pretoria SASO Local Branch
  (4) Kimberley SASO Local Branch
AND grants them voting status in this 3rd G. S. C. on condition that they have
paid affiliation fees or promise to pay them before August 31, 1972.

BIKO
MATSIPA   CARRIED UNAN . . . .

3/72
THAT THIS G. S. C. NOTING

(1) that in this 3rd General Students' Council there are people who were enrolled as students at the beginning of the year;

(2) that such persons were either rusticated from such institutions or cancelled their registrations on their own accord;

THEREFORE RESOLVES THAT:

(1) for the purposes of this Council, such people be considered as students of the institutions in which they were registered at the beginning of the year.

(2) but that the question of their status as observers/delegates/alternate delegates be left to their centres or that the Council request such people to represent their centres as presented by the SASO Constitution.

MADE
MHLONGO   CARRIED UNAN . . .

6/72

That this G. S. C. WHILE UPHOLDING the fact that SASO upholds the right of free speech as inalienable:

NEVERTHELESS NOTING THAT:

(1) the speech that has just been delivered by the President, Mr. Sono is in parts contradictory to either SASO policy or the spirit of that policy;

(2) that great publicity is likely to be given to the speech;

(3) [that] only damage to SASO's name can result from such a move;

THEREFORE

wishes to completely dissociate itself from the President's address and only view it as his personal opinion which does not find any real favour with the council.

BIKO
SHEZI   CARRIED UNAN. . . .

7/72

That this G. S. C. NOTING THAT

(1) the President's "Opening Address" has been a matter of grave controversy in this house;

(2) the dangerous and horrifying references to 'security police' and 'bantustans' smack of 'sell out' tendencies;

(3) this is adequate proof of the President's being a security risk to our organisation and to the Black Community;

(4) the stand taken by the president in his opening address is completely rejected by the Executive Committee and this G. S. C. DO HEREBY CALL THE PRESIDENT

   (1) to recuse himself from the chair for the full duration of this G. S. C. after having publicly declared that his address was in no way meant to represent the goals and aspirations of SASO but was his personal "non-white" stand;

   (2) to resign as President of SASO and member of Executive forthwith;

(3) to leave this conference forthwith.
MOODLEY
PITYANA　　　　　　　　　　CARRIED UNAN . . .

12/72
That this G. S. C. noting with appreciation:
(1) the laudable and brave stand taken by PUTCO busdrivers in fighting for their rights;
(2) that this stand is further proof of the oppression and the injustice suffered by the black people in all spheres of life;
RESOLVES
i. to congratulate and express solidarity with them;
ii. to assure them that a man who saves himself commits no crime;
AND FURTHER instructs the Secretary General to communicate this resolution to them.

O. R. TIRO
J. MODISANE　　　　　　　CARRIED UNAN

MOTION:
THAT THIS G. S. C. NOTING the following problems:
a) the difficulty of dealing successfully with situations arising out of confrontation with the enemy;
b) the lack of clarity on the terms of Nationalism, Separatism and Discrimination which are used by anti-SASO organs;
c) the ignorance surrounding the type and character of community projects which SASO must and ought to undertake;
THEREFORE RESOLVES
(i) That SASO compile a dossier on the attitudes, the power resources and tactics which the white enemy can use against us. Such information would give us a thorough knowledge of the enemy and therefore equip us to react positively during a crisis situation;
(ii) clarify the terms Nationalism, Separatism and Discrimination to eradicate the fear which has been planted in the minds of students by anti-SASO people and hence counteract arguments against SASO;
(iii) that SASO examine and present a detailed information on the type and character of community projects that SASO can embark upon.

JEFFREY
NAIDOO　　　　　　　　　WITHDRAWN

13/72
That this G. S. C. Noting:
(1) the strides and progress achieved by the government in further destroying the black people's work for emancipation as represented by the creation of Bantustans, CRC, SAIC and UBC.
(2) Aware that these institutions are extensions of the oppressive system

which are meant to appear as if "FOR" us whilst working "AGAINST" our interests;

(3) Realising that black people are thereby beginning to be systematically divided in terms of aspirations;

(4) NOTING THAT constant usage of these false platforms by some dissident government-appointed leaders, with the cooperation of the press, has led some black people to believe that something can be achieved out of exploitation of the system;

THEREFORE RESOLVES

(a) to commit ourselves to the task of explaining to the black people the fraudulence and barrenness of the promise falsely suggested by these white racist institutions;

(b) to instruct the Executive to have nothing to do with the so called leadership of the white racist institutions;

MAFUNGO
ELIAS   CARRIED UNAN

MOTION:

THAT THIS G. S. C. NOTING THAT:

(1) attempts of SASO to win over such bodies as NIC, IDAMASA, AICA, to the philosophy of Black Consciousness, has had little success mainly because of their dubious leadership;

(2) there is a great urgency and need to unite black people under a common banner;

(3) there are non-white opportunists who are out to mislead black people;

THEREFORE RESOLVES

to explore and destroy non-white opportunists and bodies which obviously militate against black consciousness and black solidarity.

JEFFREY
MOKOAPE   WITHDRAWN

14/72

THAT THIS G. S. C. NOTING THAT there are Black organisations/clubs which voluntarily call themselves "Bantu," "Coloured" at the expense of their human dignity

RESOLVES

(1) to instruct the Permanent Organiser to have contact and communications with these bodies with the purpose of showing them that calling themselves "Bantu," "Coloured" they are only degrading and insulting themselves and adulterating their human dignity.

(2) that the Permanent Organiser put across the message of Black Consciousness and self-respect to them.

TIRO
BIKO   CARRIED UNAN

15/72

That this G. S. C. noting that the BPC Ad Hoc Committee will be tabling the draft constitution of BPC for adoption in the near future, and that there is a strong need to support the body and help direct its cause.

THEREFORE RESOLVES

(1) to note with appreciation that such a move has been brought about in the black world and calls to the BPC to strive to bring the black people together to the realisation of their goal;

(2) to call on BPC to note that for the past decade the Black world has been at a loss as far as the political direction is concerned AND FURTHER

(3) calls on BPC to toil and struggle to bring it to the notice of the Black community in all possible means;

(4) calls on SASO members to be among the first people to acclaim the formation of BPC in the press and the public.

SHEZI
BAQWA   CARRIED UNAN . . .

22/72

That this G. S. C. noting :

(1) the stand taken by our black brothers and sisters in Zimbabwe in overwhelmingly rejecting the paternalistic independence terms as set out [by] Great Britain and the illegal Smith regime;

(2) that about fourteen people died during the disturbances during the Pearce Commission visit;

(3) that if ever Britain wanted to 'grant' independence to Zimbabwe such independence would have to be on black terms;

(4) the solidarity and unity the black people expressed is a lesson to black people the world over;

THEREFORE RESOLVES

(i) to express our condolences with the bereaved;

(ii) to express solidarity with the black people of Zimbabwe;

(iii) and in particular congratulates Bishop Abel Muzorewa and his ANC for giving his people the right direction during this period of turmoil

(iv) FURTHER INSTRUCTS the Secretary-General to communicate the contents of this resolution to the African National Council.

TIRO
NENGWEKHULU   CARRIED UNAN

23/72

That this G. S. C. noting

(1) the positive stand taken recently by the Namibian workers in leaving their jobs in protest against economic, social and political injustices as manifested by the abominable contract system,

(2) that the unity and solidarity they expressed is full proof that Black people "owe each other allegiance in terms of their common oppression"

(3) and that their brave stand cannot be ignored;

THEREFORE RESOLVES

(i)   to express solidarity with them;

(ii) to encourage them to continue fighting for their rights

(iii) if possible to communicate the contents of this resolution to them.

TIRO

NENGWEKHULU   CARRIED UNAN . . .

24/72

That this G. S. C. noting

(1) the lack of programmes and opportunities that are designed to direct
     and orientate black youth towards a positive and creative contribution
     to self-development of the blackman;

(2) that this lack of progress and opportunities is to a large extent responsible
     for the lack of creativity that manifests itself among black youth;

(3) that the educational system for blacks is not geared towards this
     creativity and black development but is aimed at indoctrination and
     perpetual servitude;

(4) that the separation of the different black groups leads to intergroup
     estrangement and militates against black solidarity;

THEREFORE RESOLVES TO MANDATE THE PERMANENT ORGANISER TO:

(i)   contact and promote the establishment of youth clubs and/or
      organisations

(ii) contact with social workers and/or voluntary workers dealing with the
      youth with a view to making their contribution relevant;

(iii) organise leadership training sessions to promote intergroup interaction
      and leadership amongst youth;

(iv) in conjunction with teachers and relevant or interested parties give
      vocational guidance to youth to make education more relevant and
      valuable

NHLAPO

MADE   CARRIED UNAN

25/72

That this G. S. C. noting that

(1) Black workers are a massive force which is a great factor in the economic
     advancement of white South Africa;

(2) for a long time the repressive norms and legislations have militated
     against effective bargaining by black workers;

REALISING THAT

(i)   that black students have an obligation towards making available their
      skills and techniques for the development and conscientization of this
      force in the black community;

(ii) the history of sporadic action by workers against exploitation have met
      with limited success;

(iii) moves towards "trade unionism" as presently constituted are only in the nature of producing a contented worker;

THEREFORE RESOLVES

1. to mandate the Permanent Organiser to look into the effectiveness of establishing a BLACK WORKERS' COUNCIL whose aims and objects shall be:

a. to act as a co-ordinating body to serve the needs and aspirations of the black workers;

b. to unite and bring about solidarity of black workers;

c. to conscientise them about their role and obligation toward black development

d. to run clinics for leadership, in service training and imbue them with pride and self-confidence as people and about their potential as workers;

FURTHER APPOINTS a field-worker who will organise workers groups throughout the country and arrange a national workers seminar within six months where the council will be formally launched; to communicate the contents of this resolution to Black trade union leaders, relevant Black Community leaders and organisations.

PITYANA
MOODLEY   CARRIED UNAN

26/72

That this G. S. C. noting

(1) the disgusting attitude of the *Rand Daily Mail*—despite two G. S. C. Resolutions warning strongly against the use of labels such as "Non-White" and distortions of G. S. C. proceedings;

(2) that the *Rand Daily Mail* has deliberately commissioned white reporters in order to smear us and present the white viewpoint of these proceedings in their so called "liberal" publication which is widely read and respected in the black community;

(3) that the *Daily Mail* is deliberately engaged in an effort to alienate us from the black community by making irrelevant references which are so dangerous that they may make us appear as traitors of our people;

(4) that this further illustrates the urgent need for a Black Press in view of great calculated psychological damage which is part of the maneouvre of the white racist press;

THEREFORE RESOLVES TO EXPEL THE RAND DAILY MAIL FROM THE ENTIRE PROCEEDINGS OF THIS G. S. C.

MHLONGO
BAQWA   CARRIED UNAN

MOTION:

That this G. S. C. noting:

(1) the importance of a black culture to the movement of black consciousness;

(2) the utilitarian value of culture as a unifying force;

(3) the need for SASO to take the lead in promotion and dissemination of the black culture

AND FURTHER NOTING

(4) the office of the Permanent Organiser which has been so far in charge of cultural affairs, is pre-occupied with many projects such as community development projects, education, etc.

THEREFORE RESOLVES

a.   to mandate the executive to appoint a cultural committee—CULCOM—forthwith

b.   that CULCOM consist of our members with the Publications Director being ex-officio member,

c.   that CULCOM sees to the establishment of:
    1. Writer's Club
    2. Film, Music, and ART studies,
    3. Theatre Council to cater for poetry, music, drama, fine arts and film, and

d.   that together with SASO local committees stage and promote cultural activities.

PHILLIP GULUBE
L. NTLHE   CARRIED UNAN

27/72

That this G. S. C. aware:

(1) that the theme of this Conference is Creativity and Black development;

(2) the need for a National Black Dress;

FURTHER NOTING

(i)   the total absence of relevant liberation songs.

(ii) that these together namely Black dress and liberation songs are necessary for the consolidation of Black Consciousness, Black Pride and Solidarity

THEREFORE RESOLVES:

(1) To mandate CULCOM to provide a Black National Dress within 3 months from the end of Conference;

(2) That this be done by a firm of Black tailors;

FURTHER RESOLVES:

(1) to mandate CULCOM to approach a Black Artist, poet or songwriter to compose such liberation songs.

M. LEKOTA	Against:	27
B. J. LANGA	Abstaining:	7
	For:	19. . . .

30/72

That this G. S. C. noting with appreciation the courageous stand taken by one of our members Mr. Bokwe Mafuna, by resigning his post as a reporter of the so called liberal *Rand Daily Mail* in protest against their lack of proper perspective in editing and the continuous thwarting of his sincere and honest efforts at representing genuine black opinion by his white superiors;

THEREFORE RESOLVES

to congratulate him for his positive action not only as SASO but also as concerned members of the black community.

MASEMOLA (MISS)
BAQWA S. A. M.   CARRIED UNAN WITH ACCLAIM
                STANDING OVATION

31/72
That this G. S. C. noting:
(1) the amount of work resting on the shoulders of the executive staff;
(2) that the Permanent Organiser has to return to head office so that he can work in concert with the whole executive;(3) the idea of city branches is mushrooming and should be encouraged

THEREFORE RESOLVES THAT
(i) Regional Offices be opened in regions such as Cape Town (Western Cape), Johannesburg (Reef Area), Durban (Natal), and King William's Town (Eastern Cape)
(ii) that such offices be manned by non-executive staff appointed by and responsible to the Executive

FURTHER THAT
a.   in view of (ii) above a student be appointed by the in-coming Executive to run the Johannesburg office as an honorary regional officer until such time that a permanent staff is appointed;
b.   that an additional typist be appointed for the head office;

TIRO
BIKO   CARRIED UNAN

32/72
That this G. S. C. noting that:
(1) SASO is committed to self-reliance and liberation
(2) SASO acts as a trade union of black students;
(3) to date centres have been amorphous and inconsistent in their activities due to lack of detailed planning;

THEREFORE RESOLVES THAT
(i) fund raising by campus and branches be given priority
(ii) discount schemes, vacational employment and other student benefits [be] embarked upon at both the national and local levels;
(iii) head office in consultation with branches draw up papers on detailed programming on a three monthly basis;

(iv) that this should start immediately, catering for all SASO branches and centres,

(v) FURTHER all these projects be geared at conscientization

TIRO
BIKO   CARRIED UNAN

MOTION:

That this G. S. C. noting that:

(1) the resolution calling upon all leaders of the government created institutions viz. leaders of Bantustans, to forthwith withdraw, which resolution was unanimously accepted,

(2) [students] in the government created institutions of higher learning are in the same predicament as the above mentioned leaders;

(3) the declaration prohibiting as well as limiting the said leaders' movements [is] equivalent to the regulations operative in the government created institutions of higher learning,

(4) this [organisation?] passed a motion condemning non-white education,

FURTHER NOTING:

a. the resolving part of the Fort Hare Students Manifesto,

b. Resolution MR 13/72 of the Turfloop students,

c. the walk out of some students from these government-created institutions of higher learning,

d. the solidarity expressed by the Black students who are still in these institutions of higher learning,

THEREFORE RESOLVES

(i) that the students attending this G. S. C. withdraw from these non-white institutions of higher learning,

(ii) that this G. S. C. now draws up an Action Programme for the students.

K. MOKOAPE   Against: 29
M. LEKOTA   For: 15
                  Abstaining: 7

FORT HARE STUDENTS MANIFESTO:

THEREFORE WE THE FORT HARE STUDENTS RESOLVE:

(i) to leave this tribal university of Fort Hare;

(ii) to struggle all our lives until this corrupt Bantu Education is changed and Education is free for all;

(iii) to register our support to all those who are committed to this course;

(iv) to struggle for the pursuit of truth, justice and equality in order to fulfill our human worth;

(v) to put the Black Community in the correct perspective as regards the struggle;

THIS MOVE IS TAKEN AFTER A LONG PERIOD OF ENDURANCE, NEGO-

TIATIONS, DEEP THINKING AND A THOROUGH ANALYSIS OF THE
SITUATION ON THIS CAMPUS.

33/72
That this G. S. C. noting:
(1) that the Literacy Project as conducted by the U. C. M. has been the most
    relevant of all the agencies presently operating in the black world;
(2) that in anticipation of the dissolution of the U. C. M. the Executive held
    discussions with U. C. M. where guidelines on the possible transfer and
    merger of the project with SASO's were laid down;
(3) that subsequent discussions indicate overbearing confusions about the
    actual "transfer"
AND REALISING
a. that literacy is a very important programme which could rightfully be
    handled and administered by SASO;
b. that this would help give depth to our community development schemes
    and commit students to providing their skills for the betterment of their
    people;
HEREBY RESOLVES
(i) to establish a fully-fledged and semi-independent Literacy Project;
(ii) that further negotiations for the transfer of the Project be pursued by the
     in-coming Executive;
(iii) AND FURTHER SETS OUT THE FOLLOWING STRUCTURE FOR THE
     PROJECT
a. that a Director of Literacy be appointed by the G. S. C. on a three year
    basis ratifiable annually,
b. that he be responsible to G. S. C. and liaise with the Secretary-General:
c. his duties shall include programming, planning and directing the
    execution and implementation of the Project.
d. he shall, in conjunction with the Secretary-General, appoint regional
    staff officers who shall be trained literacy managers.
e. it shall be their duty to obtain volunteers and manage projects on a local
    and regional level;
f. the Permanent Organiser shall from time to time make himself available
    for visits to areas where projects are being undertaken and shall present
    his findings to the Director and the Secretary-General.

N. PITYANA
H. NENGWEKHULU   CARRIED UNAN

34/72
That this G. S. C. hereby submits the following as the :

BLACK STUDENTS' MANIFESTO
WE the Black Students of South Africa, believing that the Blackman can no
longer allow definitions that have been imposed upon him by an arrogant

White World concerning his Being and his Destiny; AND that the Black Student has a moral obligation to articulate the needs and aspirations of the Black Community;

HEREBY DECLARE THAT: We are

(1) an integral part of the oppressed community before we are Students coming out of and studying under the oppressive restrictions of a racist education,

(2) committed to a more disciplined involvement in the intellectual and physical process and to the consistent search for the BLACK TRUTH;

(3) committed to work toward the building of our people and to the winning of their struggle for liberation and guided by the central purpose of service to the Black Community on every technical and social level;

THEREFORE REJECT THE WHOLE SPHERE OF RACIST EDUCATION AND COMMIT OURSELVES TO:

(1) the intellectual and physical development of our community and to the realisation of liberation for the Black peoples of South Africa;

(2) the definition that education in South Africa is unashamedly political and therefore, believing that Black Education is tied to the liberation of the Black people of the world.

DO HEREBY COMMIT OURSELVES TO:

(1) the assertion, manifestation and development of a sense of awareness politically, socially, and economically among the Black Community;

(2) the belief that Black Students should maintain a spirit of fraternity amongst themselves, free from the prejudice of white fallacies by virtue of common oppression;

(3) striving to break away from the traditional order of subordination to whites in education and to refuse to be educated for them;

(4) encourage and promote Black Literature relevant to our struggle,

(5) ensure that our education will further the preservation and promotion of what is treasured in our culture and in our historical experience.

J. BAQWA

L. MABANDLA   CARRIED UNAN WITH ACCL. . . .

36/72

That this G. S. C. noting that:

(1) sectional politics in the black ranks serve nothing but to retard progress towards the realisation of our goals viz. solidarity;

(2) the Natal Indian Congress (NIC) more than just being exclusively Indian is also restricting its membership to Natal Indians;

(3) attempts have been made by SASO to bring the message of black consciousness and black solidarity to the NIC leadership;

AND FURTHER NOTING WITH REGRET THAT:

(4) the NIC has made public utterances in the press which might have prejudiced our organisation;

(5) the NIC seems to be committed towards destroying SASO and killing the philosophy of Black Consciousness and black solidarity;

THEREFORE RESOLVES:

(i) to instruct the Executive to shelve their plans to take legal action against NIC;

(ii) to sever relations with NIC

MOKOENA
SHEZI   CARRIED UNAN . . .

41/72

That this G. S. C. noting:

(1) that field projects are most important means of actively involving students in the physical developments of the black community;

(2) the involvement of the black community is necessary for black students so as to identify themselves with the plight of their people and to plough back their knowledge into the community;

(3) that this is geared at instilling a sense of self-reliance in the minds of both students and community at large which is a prerequisite for emancipation and liberation;

(4) that factors such as poor planning, lack of funds, insufficient teachers, transport problems, have hindered progress in our projects very greatly;

(5) that literacy is likely to be the basis of all projects,

THEREFORE RESOLVES THAT:

(i) all other projects suggested by the commissions eg. building youth programmes etc. should where possible be superimposed on literacy but handled by different groups of workers;

(ii) areas where such projects can be carried out be identified and that the Permanent Organiser obtain from all centres the names of volunteers three months in advance;

(iii) arrangements be made for training [participants] in the relevant fields;

(iv) arrangements be made with local authorities for sites for the camp and accommodation for participants;

(v) all financial arrangements related to the projects be fixed before the universities close;

(vi) the permanent organiser takes all the responsibilities for planning 1, 2, 3, 4, above and FURTHER that he arrange for these projects [to] be carried out during the Dec/Jan and July vacation;

S. A. M. BAQWA
P. KGWARE   CARRIED UNAN

42/72

That this G. S. C. noting with great concern:

(1) the lack of records of relevant vital statistics concerning Black people:
    a. records of achievement

b. average wages of area etc;

(2) the lack of records on tape and on paper of relevant speeches made by blacks

(3) the unavailability of cultural artifacts attributed to blacks

(4) the lack of records of writings by Black people,

(5) the unavailability of and inaccessibility to some of the things that black people ought to have and know about;

THEREFORE RESOLVES:

To mandate the the Executive to:

(i) Establish a central point in each region which shall act as a cultural resource centre for Black people in all fields, and

(ii) that these resource centres should be attached to the SASO regional offices and to the main office and be taken care of by the same regional staff,

(iii) and that the Executive shall present a report at the December National Meeting that these recommendations can be implemented in January 1973.

H. E. ISAACS
A. M. MHLONGO   CARRIED UNAN

43/72

That this G. S. C. noting:

(1) that JASC [Junior African Students Council] of Inanda Seminary, a girls' High School, has been banned by the principal, Mr. Ayllard;

(2) that SASO has subsequently been banned at that school;

(3) that this action is meant to break the initiative of the black students in their efforts to liberate the black community;

(4) that this Council in terms of Resolution 44/71 expressed interest in the body and instructed the Executive to keep in close contact with JASC;

THEREFORE RESOLVES:

(i) to express our concern at this high-handed action of the Inanda authorities;

(ii) to write to the Principal and the Black teachers of Inanda and tell them that this [is] viewed as a serious damage to the black student initiative;

(iii) to instruct the Executive to look into possibilities of reviving the apparently broken morale of Inanda students on this issue;

(iv) to instruct the Executive to report on its findings in the National Executive Council Meeting to be held in December

SHEZI
MADE   CARRIED UNAN . . .

44/72

That this G. S. C. recognising the possibility of the SASO Executive finding itself experiencing problems through resignations forced or voluntary, of one [or] some of the Executive members;

THEREFORE RESOLVES:
(i)   empowers the remainder of the Executive in such situation to call up a Council meeting and to elect office bearers to fill up such vacancies;
(ii) instructs the Council to conduct such elections according to the rules laid down by the Planning Commission;

BIKO
TIRO   CARRIED UNAN

45/72
That this G. S. C. noting:
(1) that the Black People's Convention is holding its inaugural conference in Maritzburg this weekend;
(2) aware of the full importance of this conference and of the duty SASO has towards BPC;
THEREFORE RESOLVES:
(i)   to elect a delegation of 3 members to represent SASO at BPC conference;
(ii) encourages all students to attend the conference
(iii) urges the delegates and students to put forward the SASO viewpoint at this conference and to offer themselves in their personal capacities for whatever service BPC may call them to:

BIKO
TIRO   CARRIED UNAN

46/72
That this G. S. C. noting:
(1) the fact that SASO Executive staff is appointed on a permanent basis;
(2) the need for SASO to take care of the people committed to her service;
(3) the inadequate salaries that SASO has been paying her staff;
THEREFORE RESOLVES:
(i)   to upgrade the salaries of the existing staff and to pay any new staff according to the new rates;
(ii) to fix the salary scales as follows:

Secretary General	R200
Permanent Organiser	R200
Director of Literacy	R200
Administrative assistant	R160
Secretary-Bookkeeper	R100 per month with top notch of R150
Typist	R70 per month

BIKO
TIRO   CARRIED UNAN . . .

56/72
That this G. S. C. noting that we are indebted to various people for the success of this conference who contributed in various ways;

THEREFORE RESOLVES: to express our gratitude to
(i)   Revd. Fr. D. Scholten for allowing us the use of this Conference Centre;
(ii) Mr. Vincent Maphai, the bursar of St. Peter's Seminary for making our
      stay here as comfortable as possible;
(iii) the sisters and the kitchen staff for the pleasant catering;
(iv) all the donors who contributed financially or offered stationery and
      other amenities;
AND INSTRUCTS the Secretary General to inform all these partners of the
gratitude of this Council for their help and assistance when it was needed
most.

SHEZI
MABANDLA   CARRIED UNAN

ELECTIONS

PRESIDENT
Jerry Modisane   (Fort Hare)   (24)   Mokoena
                                          Chauke
Jeff Baqwa   (Fort Hare)   (23)   Biko
                                          Mabandla
J. MODISANE—ELECTED

VICE PRESIDENT
H. E. Isaacs   (Western Cape) unopposed

SECRETARY-GENERAL
N. Pityana   appointment ratified

PERMANENT ORGANISER
R. H. Nengwekhulu   appointment ratified

PUBLICATIONS-DIRECTOR
Ben. J. Langa   (Fort Hare)   unopposed

Conference closes ! ! ! ! !

**Document 50. Speech by Reverend Mashwabada Mayatula, first
national congress of the Black People's Convention,
Hammanskraal, December 16, 1972**

Thank you, Lord, for your blessings. Amen.

Black brothers and sisters, I am grateful that today we begin to open the
first page of the history book of the newly resurrected Black nation in South
Africa. At long last, the LIBERATOR, namely, the promised Black Messiah,
"the very God of the very God" has come. He has freely given us what we

prayed for, for decades, that is, the HOLY SPIRIT—the "Spirit" of Black Consciousness, of Black Solidarity and Black unity. The spirit of Black Solidarity is the same Holy Spirit that once caused deliverance of Israelites from the house of Bondage, and the only difference being that we are not involved in an exodus but ours is to "'arise with Christ, the Son of God'—the Black Messiah, from the dead for the riches of our 'Beloved Country'". (Plate XXXIII—The version set forth a.d. 1611—Printed for the Universities of Oxford and Cambridge). "Nkosi Sikelel' i-Afrika" has become a reality.

We are gathered here as apostles responsible in building the Black nation, having only as our armament the "two-edged sword," the Word of God, that is, the Black Messiah, and our shield is justice. Let us therefore, seek and pray for more strength in order to win all battles we are faced with. First and foremost an American Black Theologian of note, James Cone says, "a man is free when he sees clearly the fulfillment of his being and is thus capable of making the envisioned self a reality." Since this is the first chapter of our historical achievement, may I be allowed to welcome you all, "Sons and daughters of the fertile soil," by exegiting the two main objectives of the Black People's Convention, which read thus:

"The object of the Convention is to unite the South African Blacks into a Black Political Organisation which would seek to realise their liberation and emancipation from both psychological and physical oppression.

The Convention shall operate outside the white government created systems, structures, and/or institutions and shall not seek elections into this."

BLACK MAN! STAND ON YOUR OWN

Unity means power. Black people must now know that we live in an epoch of struggle between two opposing monstrous social systems, namely, capitalism and communism, an epoch of national liberation revolutions, of total breakdown of imperialism, and the abolition of all colonial systems. It is an epoch of the transition of more Blacks to the Christian path and the triumph of Black communalism and Black theology on a national wide scale.

These vast changes in the Black world spell the doom of foreign concepts. A reawakening is taking place among the oppressed peoples of this country, a reawakening that will spell the doom of white oppression, of imperialism and all other misleading ideologies and values that are being imposed on black people. We as a people refuse to become products of western capitalism or of eastern communism. We shall chart our own course as determined by our black experience and our aspirations as a nation. Gone are the days when we looked at ourselves through the whiteman's mirror, the days when our endeavours and achievements were measured by white standards. Gone are the days when we used to view Christ, and indeed God, as white.

No man other than us has the right to find solutions to our problems. It is within the folds of the BPC that we shall endeavour to create new men— independent Black men. We have got to work very hard for the implementation of the principles of BPC which are:

To unite and solidify the Black people of South Africa with a view to liberating and emancipating them from both psychological and physical oppression;

To preach, popularise and implement the philosophy of Black Consciousness and Black solidarity;

To formulate and implement an educational policy of Blacks, by Blacks for Blacks;

To create and maintain an egalitarian society where justice is meted equally to all;

To formulate, apply and implement the principles and philosophy of Black Communalism—the philosophy of sharing;

To create and maintain an equitable economic system based on the principles and philosophy of Black Communalism. (This is purely Christian: "Acts 4:32 ff")

To co-operate with existing agencies to re-orientate the theological system with a view to making religion relevant to the needs, aspirations, ideals and goals of the Black People.

This means that all forces like capitalism and denominationalism that divide the Blacks have to be destroyed in Black circles.

THE CHURCH

What is this organisation known as the Church? Is it worth working for?

James Cone also asks a question and answers it himself. He asks, "What is the Church and its relationship to Christ and Black Power? The Church is that people called into being by the power and love of God to share in his revolutionary activity for the liberation of man. The history of Israel is a history of God's election of a special, oppressed people to share in his creative involvement in the world on behalf of man. The call of this people at Sinai into a covenant relationship for a special task may be said to be the beginning of the Church. The Church of Christ is not a building or an institution. It is not determined by bishops, priests or ministers as these terms are used in contemporary sense. Rather, the Church is God's suffering people.

It stands to reason that Blacks should be involved in the Church. Nevertheless, I warn Blacks not to be English, Dutch, Roman, German, etc. Plainly Blacks should be Blacks not white persons in Blacks skins.

All Blacks must organise themselves and break through the white dominated Church. It is high time that the Black man is on his own religiously. We should learn and understand that the first real freedom should be religious independence and other freedoms will automatically follow up.

AUTONOMY IN THE "STANS"

Some people want to know the reasons that cause BPC to operate outside the white government created systems and structures and NOT to seek election into these. The answer is simple. The miserable rule of all the

Bantustans, the CPRC and the SAIC which are in fact a bluff as they can never have any political and economic viability. The real power in these reservoirs of black cheap labour is in the hands of well trained and experienced officials of the Department of Bantu Administration and Development, Coloured and Indian Affairs Departments. These white Officials in the so-called "homelands" have been given permanent positions of being ministerial secretaries. The non-White Chief Ministers or Chief Executive Officers or so-called prime ministers and their henchmen are quislings and sell-outs. All bills passed by these so-called governments can be unquestionably vetoed by the single hand of one white cabinet minister of the BAD [Bantu Affairs Department] or Coloured and Indian Affairs Departments. Truly speaking, the white cabinet minister responsible for a particular "stan" is the "emperor" or the "Big Baas" of that "Stan." Who then hasn't eyes to see that the whole structure is the internationally hated "Baasskap Pill" sugar-coated? The non-White national leaders of the stans, some of them highly learned chiefs, have been turned into puppets of officialdom. They become employed—supporters of the old imperialist maxim of DIVIDE and RULE. They are champions of tribal division and yet there is no place for it in modern exchange economy based on a large scale industry and gold mining etc. Even people who reside in the reserves, especially the men-folk, the victims of Influx Control Laws, spent most of their lives on the reserves as migrant wage labourers on the mines, in agriculture and industry. THE MAIN OBJECTIVE OF BANSTUSTAN PHILOSOPHY is to trap all Blacks into this network of migratory labour oppressive pass laws. Approximately one-third of the Black people live on the reserves at present and there is a great manoeuvre to increase the number exceedingly as the preposterous Bantustan scheme aims at sending all Black people in industrial areas to the 13% of the worst of South Africa set aside for about 30,000,000 Blacks and 87% of the best remaining for less than 4,000,000 Whites. Hunger and special taxes drive this small number of Blacks to work in mines and farms through the imperialist migrant labour agency which operates in many forms. This monstrous system is responsible for the diabolical exploitation of Blacks in our country of plenty: gold, diamonds and internationally much needed uranium. The oppressive influx control laws are responsible for the wretched and lowest wages and high rate of crime in South Africa; "three-quarters of the world's hangings" and all white designed diseases such as pellagra and kwashiokor.

The "system" speaks of Reserves as the *homelands* of the Black people but the given 13% of the land is already grossly overcrowded and the soil exhausted. The small percentage of land is insufficient to make a living from. As Reserves are far away from gold and industrial centres, they lack communications and power resources. There will never be enough capital for improvements and mechanisation. Freedom loving Blacks rejects this balkanization of our country into mini-Bantu States within the provinces of a huge white state. We feel there are no grounds in history or in reality for the whites to claim any part of South Africa exclusively for the whites. Blacks as a matter of fact, live in every part of our country; their labour has gone to develop its farmlands and its cities, its mines and industries, its railways and harbours; and finally its highways; they claim every inch of South Africa as their homeland.

The Bantustan scheme is not only undemocratic, unchristian and opposed to every principle of self-determination and human rights, it is also fraudulent. Even those non-Whites who have accepted the scheme complain that the land is small as there is no additional land given to the "stans." Instead white spots are to be found in fertile parts of the so-called homelands and in valuable sites for sea-ports. There is no intention, whatsoever, of conferring any genuine independence on any group of Black people. Even if concessions would be made in this direction, the economy is so backward and completely lacking in capital that there can't be any possibility of any real independence for these areas.

All Black people are called to come forward and register as members of the Black People's Convention in the struggle against colonialism and imperialism, in the fight for psychological and physical liberation for all Blacks. Black workers have to be conscientized all over the Republic of South Africa, especially millions of Black mine and agricultural workers [employed on] gold and diamond, platinum, manganese and coal mines and white owned farms. These are the most exploited workers in the rich South Africa. They work without any protection from labour laws, from dawn to sunset for wretchedly low wages. The food they are given is too little, it is always the same and it is an unhealthy diet. On most farms the housing for them is the same as that provided for the farm horses and pigs. The use of convict and compound labour and other forms of forced labour, is common on farms in many parts of the Republic of South Africa. Farmers and their foremen frequently employ physical violence against Black farm labourers, beating them with sjamboks [whips], often to death. Agricultural labourers are not really free workers. They are tied, some for life, to a particular farmer because of the operation of the labour tenancy system and vagrancy laws.

The hundreds and thousands of labourers working on the gold mines have to do most dangerous and unhealthy work, for wages which are a scandal and a disgrace in an industry which distributes millions of rand annually to its shareholders. They are separated for long periods from their wives and families. This sort of life is very dangerous to society.

HOW COULD SMALL SCATTERED STATES ARISE?

On 1st May 1951, Verwoerd, the apostolic philosopher and father of Bantustanism and what have you, in the Senate said, "now a Senator wants to know whether the series of self-governing areas would be sovereign. The answer is obvious. There are Native areas all over the place in South Africa as in Pietersburg, for example. There is Zululand. There are other areas everywhere in the heart of South Africa. It stands to reason that white South Africa must remain their guardian. We are spending all the money for those developments. We are leaving the Natives to develop. How could small scattered states arise? The areas will be economically and otherwise dependent on the Union. It stands to reason that when we say the Protectorates [Basutoland, Swaziland and Bechuanaland] should be incorporated in South Africa and at the same time talk about the native's rights of self-government in those areas we cannot mean that we intend by that to cut large slices out of South Africa and turn them into independent states."

This music does not at all correspond to our own way of Black dancing. We know our own music well. We dance gracefully when songs of Black consciousness, Black solidarity, Black unity and Black power are sung.

In short, we have to work very hard for Black unity. United we shall economically, politically and religiously stand upright, and divided we experienced centuries of oppression and ignorance. The Black Messiah is all out to save all of us, to liberate us and to comfort us. One may ask, "Who is this Black Messiah?" Black Messiah is the new name of our Creator. He is the holy spirit of Black consciousness and Black solidarity. He is our power. We have won because we have justice on our side. We will win more approaching battles when we organise for and realise our economic power.

Even the present White Prime Minister cannot act against the truth he said, especially when we shall always stick to our constitution on the highway to total liberation, because it is John Balthazar Vorster himself who said in a statement on July 30th, 1964 that "every man had the undeniable right to endeavor to bring about a change of Government in his country, but no man had the right to force such a change with violence on their people."

Conclusively we have our constitution which I have successfully defended when I was called upon and nationally challenged to do so. The Black Messiah helped me through. He will help us through all the way. He is the Alpha and Omega. He is the deliverer who always delivered those in bondage and oppressed. WHY NOT US? History repeats itself.

POWER AND SOLIDARITY!!!

Document 51. Flyer by Black People's Convention supporting Durban strikers, January 9, 1973, in Zulu (with translation)

BAFOWETHU ABANSUNDU,

I-BLACK PEOPLE'S CONVENTION INISEKELA NGOKUPHELELE EZINYATHELWENI ENIZITHATHILE NAMUHLANJE.

ISIKHATHI SEZIKHALO ZENU NGOKWEMPELA KADE SADLULA KODWA NATHULA. LOKHU BEKUNGASHO UKUTHI NENELISIWE.

NAMUHLA NIBONILE UKUTHI KUFANELE NIZIMELE NGEZINYAWO ZENU.

NJENGOBA SENISITHATHILE LESI SINYATHELO BAKITHI, NINGABE NISAHLEHLELA EMUVA NOMA ISITHA SESINIKHANGA NGOKUNGEKONA. YIMANI NJENGAMAQHAWE. UMA NINGAYIBAMBA KANJE NIYOPHUMELELA.

QAPHELANI ISITHA SINGANEHLUKANISI PHAKATHI NJENGOBA SIHLALA SENZA.

NAMUHLA YISIKHATHI SOKUBA SIBAMBANE NGEZANDLA SIME NDAWONYE.
SIYAPHAMBILI SOFEL' ISIZWE KUF' OYAYO MADODA.
AMANDLA!

> MOTLALEPULA KGWARE
> UMONGAMELI
> 5 p.m. Tuesday, 9 January '73

[Translation: Our Black Brothers,
The Black People's Convention is in complete support of the stand you have taken today.

The time for your real complaints has long passed but you kept quiet. This did not mean that you were satisfied. Today you realize that you should stand on your own feet.

Since you have made this move, my comrades, do not retreat, even if the enemy tries to divide or bribe you. Stand like heroes. If you do this you will succeed. Look out that the enemy does not divide you as he often does.

Now it is time to stand together. We are marching forward to die for the nation. It is those who fight who will win.

Power!

> Motlalepula Kgware
> President
> 5 p.m. Tuesday, 9 January '73]

DOCUMENT 52. Statement of demands by students at the University of the Western Cape ("Die Geel Dokument"), June 5, 1973

PREAMBLE:
WHEREAS we the students of the University of the Western Cape hold the following to be a true conception of a University, namely;

THAT A UNIVERSITY IS A GATHERING OF PERSONS ENGAGED IN THE SEARCH FOR TRUTH

THE SEARCH FOR TRUTH IS A SEARCH FOR UNDERSTANDING AND KNOWLEDGE

A UNIVERSITY SHOULD NOT BE BOUND TO A CERTAIN RELIGION, POLITICAL POLICY OR SOCIAL CREED, FOR THESE DEMAND AN ADHERENCE THAT EXCLUDES OTHER RELIGIONS, POLICIES OR CREEDS.

We reject completely the idea of separate ethnic universities because it is contrary to the historic concept of a University—that of universality—but are forced by the laws of the land to study at the University of the W. Cape, a fact which must not be construed as conformity to or acceptance of the status quo. This does not however preclude our interest in events and developments at the University or our perturbance at these events. It is our contention that a student attends University not only to learn a profession but to learn how to think logically, to reason scientifically, to sift the true from the false. No university man would willingly fall prey to the creeping paralysis of indifference to the welfare of others, or he would fail to have a moral basis for thought and action.

The idea that a University could ever be neutral in issues of importance is repugnant. Neutrality can be another word for cowardice. It is because we feel that as students we are a vital part of [the] society in which we live, and because of our responsibility not only to society but to posterity, that we have compiled this memorandum; and we have submitted it to the authorities in the hope that they will act upon it to improve the situation.

POOR STUDENT-LECTURER RELATIONS

Relations between students and lecturers in all departments in all faculties are deplorable. One fact which cannot be argued away is that the University is a microcosm of South African society and that [the] student-lecturer relationship must be viewed within this context. The majority of the lecturers are white: our worlds and our experiences differ radically. Science lecturers still firmly believe that they are doing mission work among heathens. Thus, communication between ourselves and lecturers can never be meaningful.

We reject the paternalism, patronism and condescension of certain lecturers, the racism that could prompt a Professor in the Commerce Faculty to say to a student (a senior at that): "Julle Kleurlinge is daarin nader aan ons." [You Coloureds are really more like us].

As students and as part of the oppressed community we seek more than book-shop discussions about pencils, pens, ink and rubbers. There is a tendency on the part of lecturers to shy away from so-called "race-relations" topics, especially in the Behavioral Sciences. This is because of the lecturers' favourite pastime of 'steering clear of politics' which is a very naive escape mechanism when we bear in mind that this university was established for the so-called 'Coloured' people (without consultation of such people) and in pursuance of the Government's policy of racial segregation. Lecturers are thus doing a job, a political job, which is to maintain the status quo.

In an oppressive racist society like the S. African one there can never be identification by the privileged group with the deprived group, the Black group. We define Black people as those who are by law or tradition politically, socially and economically discriminated against; as a group in the S. African society who identify themselves as a unit in the struggle, towards the realisation of their aspirations. What we as students would like to see is the acceleration of the appointment of Black lecturers with whom we can identify and with whom we as students can communicate meaningfully and share our experiences and aspirations as members of an oppressed community.

PREPONDERANCE OF WHITE OVER BLACK LECTURERS

We do not think that this is an accident or because there [are] no Blacks available to occupy teaching posts at UWC. After 13 years of existence there are only 12 Blacks on the teaching staff and 79 whites. After 13 years, there is not a single black professor and only ONE black senior lecturer.

Nor do we think it merely incidental that only 4 of the 79 white lecturers received their academic training at English-language universities.

The position is not much better in the Administrative section, only 6 of the personnel of 16 are 'Coloured.' Of those on the Administrative staff that have academic qualifications, all acquired their training at Afrikaans-language universities. Another deplorable fact is that a senior Administrative staff member, occupying a very responsible position, has no academic or technical training at all.

The conclusion that can be drawn from this statistical analysis is that the UWC is an institution that is being run by Afrikaners for Afrikaners. This assertion can further be strengthened by the fact that there are virtually no blacks on the decision making bodies of the University. Only after 12 years has one senior Black lecturer been appointed to the University senate. Now two blacks have been appointed to the Council. If the UWC was created out of kindheartedness of the Afrikaner for the Coloured, then surely all the decision-making bodies should be controlled by Coloureds!

DISCREPANCIES IN SALARIES BETWEEN WHITE AND BLACK STAFF

We reject out of hand the Minister's statement that "the traditional policy of the country dictates differences in salaries" as between the staff of different racial groups.

(a)	Senior Lecturer:	White	R5400 x 300—6600
		Coloured	R4080 x 120—5040
(b)	Junior Lecturer:	White	R3000 x 150—3900
		Coloured	R1980 x 90—2880
(c)	Senior Lecturer:	White	R4200 x 150—4800 x 300—5400
		Coloured	R2880 x 120—4080

Equal qualifications should merit equal salaries.

POOR TEACHING METHODS

There is common practice among teachers to dictate or read-off notes to students. This is unbecoming of a university lecturer, and these notes are very often lecture guides from the University of S. Africa. University teaching is the only kind for which no professional training is required and obviously there are those who will fall below the minimum standards of good teaching, but how can a teacher who reads from notes—perhaps last year's notes—win the respect of his students?

RUDENESS OF MEMBERS OF THE ADMIN. STAFF

We have long and painfully been aware of the rudeness of a certain member of the Admin. Staff towards students, the rudeness and racist arrogance of this same member. How else can we describe such behavior when a senior student is told by this member: "GET OUT OF MY OFFICE, YOU PIG." Or when a member of the staff is chided in the same rude manner in the presence of an ex-student and other members of the Admin. Staff; or when an ex-student is threatened with physical eviction by this member personally? This ex-student was later banned from the campus by this same officer—an action later confirmed by the rector.

At the beginning of the year we requested, through our SRC, from the Registrar why several of our fellow students were not permitted to continue their academic careers—no reply was received to our communication. We seek an explanation why these students were forced to terminate their studies after their registrations had been accepted at the beginning of the year.

The students are:

Miss Jeanne Majoos	B. A. (SW 111)
Mr. Hadley Abrahams	B. Sc 11
Mr. Albert Beukes	B. Com 111
Mr. John Issel	B. A. Hons

PERSECUTION OF INDIAN STUDENTS

Knowledge and understanding are founded upon discussion. This can only take place where there is a variation of viewpoints and backgrounds. The colour of skin, social class or religion of participants should be irrelevant to the University. What matters above all is that the student should have the required ACADEMIC qualifications.

By law of the land so-called Indian students cannot study at UWC except by consent of the Minister. Those who ARE allowed to study at UWC are NOT allowed to participate in student activities. In terms of their permits such students should not engage in any political activities within or without the University, nor may they engage in any student activities.

This is in itself a reprehensible limitation upon the students' freedom of activity and association, but there has lately been an atrocious persecution of Indian students by the Administrative personnel who have hounded such students out of lecture halls demanding identity documents and the like.

THE HOSTEL

Last year the resident students submitted a memorandum-cum-petition to the authorities drawing to their attention the conditions prevailing in the hostel.

The concluding paragraph of the petition is quoted here: "That rules designed for the school situation [are] . . . repugnant to us." There was no response to this petition, [so] the students in desperation decided to boycott meals in an effort to have their grievances redressed.

The reaction was one of typical authoritarian dictatorship. Rather than investigate these grievances the authorities expelled all the students who then [were] forced to re-apply to the hostel. Eventually those who, in the opinion of the hostel superintendent and matron were "agitators" were excluded.

This year the situation in the hostel has not changed. In fact recently students from the Theological School hostel submitted a petition to the authorities in which they requested, among other things that their food be prepared at the Theological School hostel. This hostel has the facilities, and if food was prepared there it obviates students having to walk to other hostels for their meals, which in practice caused much discomfort during the rainy season.

8 students from the Theological School recently refused to eat at the other hostel and instead carried their food to their own hostel. For this they were charged with 'undermining authority' and were summoned to [the] rector's office, who informed them that they could be expelled. Intimidation—subtle—but intimidation yet.

SCIENCE STUDENTS BEING MADE TO BEGIN AT 1.30 P.M. WITH PRACTICAL WORK

Students in the faculty of science are forced to commence with practical work at 1–1.30 p.m. during the week and at 1 p.m. on Fridays. Students are thus being forced to work during the only official lunch break and are consequently barred from actively participating in student activities. The lunch breaks are the only times that clubs and societies can arrange meetings which can be attended by all students.

Student mass meetings are held on Fridays at 12.45 p.m. It is our contention that a student does not attend university only to learn and pass examinations, but should be able to participate fully in activities offered by the various clubs and societies. Consequently the lecturers should abide by the official time-table and allow students freedom of a daily lunch break. Rules and regulations are essential in order to maintain a certain amount of order, but such rules and regulations should be designed and implemented with due consideration for those who are subjected to them. The present rules and regulations are oppressively rigid and make of this institution "a glorified high school" to quote a white parliamentarian. The rules prevent the development of a sense of responsibility among the students in that liberty and responsibility should temper each other: now without any liberty how can we develop a sense of responsibility? As students there is nothing (except possibly executing elementary biological functions) which we can do without the permission of the rector. The rules and regulations leave absolutely no scope for effective self-determination. We reject completely this attitude that we must be closeted like Victorian daughters.

All our behavior is regulated from our associations to our manner of dress. It is a sad pity that the framers of norms, values, standards and customs in society are constantly changing. Rules and regulations which held good 12 years ago do not necessarily hold good today: the rules and regulations which were enacted in September of last year do not reflect the mood of the times.

LACK OF UNIVERSITY AUTONOMY

University autonomy has been defined as "the right of a University to decide for itself, on ACADEMIC GROUNDS, who shall teach, what shall be taught, and who shall be admitted to study. The Govt appoints not only the

University Council and staff, but also provides and decides the financial policy and controls the admittance of students. We believe that a university is best qualified to decide for itself who shall teach. A Minister is at best an administrator and at worst a politician, concerned with political necessities, and values. What does a non academic know of syllabi, teaching methods, the necessity for research or the merits of tutorials?

What we as students of UWC would like to see is the University authorities making a determined stand for greater autonomy, to try to convert UWC into a university rather than allow is to continue existing in its present nature as an instrument of apartheid.

WE REGARD IT AS RIGHT TO LISTEN TO THE VIEWS OF PERSONS WE CHOOSE TO LISTEN TO, and in the light thereof to analyse and evaluate critically. The authorities attempt to deny us this right. We submit that the SRC acting upon the instructions of the student body, should be allowed to invite speakers to address us. We reject the practice of speakers being invited by authorities to address us as it is a practice which is open to abuse since only persons who [are] "acceptable" to the authorities would be allowed to address us.

Document 53. Report of Fort Hare Local Committee to SASO annual General Students' Council, by Pumzile Majeke, July 1973

1. STUDENT ENROLMENT:
   The number of students enrolled at Fort Hare this year stands at 1026. A low increase of only about 100 students over last year's enrolment. This low growth on enrolment is the result of (i) the turning down of several hundred applications due to lack of accommodation, (ii) the exclusion of more than two hundred students for "poor academic progress," (iii) the exclusion of an unknown number of "old" students for "bad social and moral" conduct, which include unsubstantiated claims that some people are "bad elements," and use the university campus for their own political ends.

2. FACULTIES:
There are seven faculties in all, viz.

(a) Science	—about 30% of total enrolment.			
(b) Arts and Fine Arts	— "	35%	"	"
(c) Agriculture	— "	3%	"	"
(d) Commerce/Admin.	— "	10%	"	"
(e) Education	— "	8%	"	"
(f) Law	— "	12%	"	"
(g) Theology	— "	2%	"	"

3. STUDENT ADMINISTRATION AND REPRESENTATION:
   (a) Administration: The University Administration exercises complete and absolute control over all student matters, both academic and non-academic. The whole range of administrative bodies, including the Disciplinary

Committee and even the Bio Club, consist of members of the administrative as well as the academic staff. For instance a female convicted of being found in the Men's residence, is directly taken by the warden to the Rector who expels her personally even without the case being handled by the Disciplinary Committee.

(b) Representation: Fort Hare has become notorious for clinging to the tradition of refusing to elect an SRC. As a result, there is in existence an amorphous non-constitutional body called the Joint Inter House Committee, which sometimes casually makes representations to the administration on some bread and butter issues like requesting for an extension of visiting hours for Men students at the Women's Residence.

In this situation, SASO Local Committee has become the sole voice of the students, and the only living body which can boast of representing a cross-section of the student body opinion.

4. S. R. C.

(a) With Administration: Relations with the admin. have been strained for a long period now, and do not show any signs of improvement. Since late last year, the Rector is withholding the subsidies of SASO Local in order to "cripple" the organisation. He is generally keeping a Hawk's eye over the activities of SASO Local, and trying hard to intimidate us. For instance, when we responded to the bannings of our leaders by convening a general students meeting attended by over 900 students at the sportfield, the branch chairman and Mr Selby Baqwa were "charged" for holding an illegal meeting on the Fort Hare grounds. They subsequently appeared before the D. C. [Disciplinary Committee] where the hearing was bulldozed, and in a matter of some 40 minutes, the defenceless accused were found guilty of "resisting and undermining authority," and each given a 1 year's suspended sentence of expulsion. No "state witnesses" testified at this strange hearing, as the Rector declared that he was protecting them from the "workshops" [beatings] he had so often heard about.

Further to this SASO Local is refused permission for the use of the halls for the purposes of staging plays or showing films. This is a great handicap as far as our fundraising efforts are concerned, and often we have to go down on our knees and request the use of the Seminary Hall plus their film projector. As far as SASO local is concerned, perhaps this following quotation of the Rector sums up everything beautifully, "I want to kill SASO, because of the uncompromising attitude adopted by their national leaders, and now spreading to their rank and file".

(b) With the Lecturing Staff:

(i) White staff—these present no problem, as they have one clear stand viz. that of subtle intimidation and general white arrogance.

(ii) Black staff—these present a variety of species; there are those who vehemently object to being included in the category of 'non-whites' and choose be be called Black—which is an indication that they are at last reacting to the call. These are often ready to support us financially when requested to do so. Then there are those who either ignorantly or simply stubbornly resist conscientization, and these manifest extreme non-whitism, and are most unpopular and oppressive. The remainder comprises the apathetic and politically unaware lot, whose relationship with the students is simply that of non-involvement.

(c) With External Organisations:

(i) B. P. C. Branch King Williams Town: A viable contact has been established, and there is a healthy exchange of ideas, material, co-operation where feasible etc. e.g. when Jeff [Baqwa] came around for literacy training, joint sessions were organised to include both the Fed Sem [Federal Theological Seminary] and BPC, KWT [King William's Town].

(ii) [illegible] market on and around campus.

(iii) Nurses Association: Some very healthy relationship has developed between us and the nurses at the two neighbouring hospitals vis: Victoria Hosp., and Tower Mental Hosp. These nurses are always invited to our symposia, discussions and even introduced to some of our projects like literacy trainings. In fact a SASO branch was in the making, until the Hospital authorities at Victoria stepped in with an intimidation campaign that resulted in some withdrawal by some of the up and coming members. However, there is a hardcore group which is persisting and these have become instrumental in spreading the philosophy at the concerned hospital.

6. STUDENT ACTIVITIES

(a) Academic: There are a number of academic societies, which are just amorphous plastic bodies which are fast losing fame with the students. Their activities are so rigidly controlled by the University Admin. that they have deteriorated into structures having one meeting per year, viz, the AGM [Annual General Meeting], where election of office-bearers are conducted as a matter of formality. However, several of these societies are being dissolved one after the other. To date there are the ff.

(i) Science Society. (ii) Juridical Society—this was dissolved in April. (iii) English Dramatic Society—which died a natural death. (iv) Psychology Association (v) Comparative African Studies Society—which is practically defunct. (vi) Xhosa Dramatic Society—which is involved in some Archaic irrelevant task of enacting Xhosa books prescribed for high school students. (vii) Social Workers Society—this is the only society adopting a relevant attitude, and its members have been instrumental in advocating for the change of name for the National body "South African Bantu Social Workers Association" to "South African Black Social Workers Association."

(b) Extra Mural:

(i) Sport: The Athletics Union, which co-ordinates the activities of all sports clubs has been successfully infiltrated. The following sports clubs are in existence: Tennis, Rugby—which has just broken away from the South African Bantu Rugby Board, and affiliated to the essentially "non-racial" South African Rugby Union, Soft Ball, Chess and Cards-clubs.

(ii) Cultural and Entertainment: Under this heading comes the Music Society (which successfully staged a "Black music festival" in May), the

Entertainments committee, the Ballroom club (which is resisting destruction) and the Bio-club, which has been rendered impotent by the rector.

7. EXTERNAL RELATIONS:

[illegible] like Ntselamanzi and Gaga, where we are conducting surveys with the aim of establishing Literacy projects.

Neighbouring high schools like Lovedale and Healdtown, although their authorities are oppressive, continue to have students who continually invite us, and take keen interest in the struggle—thus from time to time, SASO Local members visit these institutions on an informal basis, as well as selling them black publications.

The Fed Sem has become our twin, with whom we work together in projects, organise joint celebrations etc. Together with the Fed Sem we are establishing a bursary scheme called the Fed-Fort Bursary Fund.

8. MATTERS OF GENERAL INTEREST:

(a) Visits from Head Office.

(1) Mr Jeff Baqwa was the guest speaker on Heroes' Day [March 21], when we held a successful evening of Drama, Poetry and Music befitting the day.

(2) Mr H. E. Isaacs, acting President also paid us a visit and delivered a paper.

(3) Jeff came around again to conduct literacy training.

(4) Just before the National Formation School in Alice Mr O. A. Tiro hit town and in addition to delivering a paper on campus, he was hijacked into being one of the panel speakers in a Symposium on Education for Self Reliance which drew crowds from Fort Hare, Seminary, Victoria Hospital and members of the neighbouring communities.

(6) In response to the Permanent Organiser's call, we are holding seminars every Sunday afternoon on topical issues.

(7) Fundraising Schemes—we are struggling to reach the target of R500, but it is of particular note to report that one member, Miss Mapitso Tabane, went on a one-man fundraising campaign in Pretoria and came back with a haul of over R100.

In conclusion, we can only submit that, while Fort Hare is relatively a rather difficult campus to handle, SASO Local Com. is successfully making an impact, and we hope that with time, SASO and the struggle in general will see a day when central affiliation will be resumed.

POWER AND SOLIDARITY!!!

Document 54. Report by Father Smangaliso Mkhatshwa on the Black Renaissance Convention, Hammanskraal, December 13–16, 1974

FRIDAY: 13TH DECEMBER

The registration office opened at 2.00 p.m. Many delegates started pouring into the Conference Centre, the majority in the early part of the evening.

In spite of the ruling by the Steering Committee that no White reporters would be allowed at the Convention, two White newsmen presented themselves early in the afternoon. They were dealt with without further ado. Fortunately, they cooperated very willingly. At 8.30 p.m. the house was called to order. Ds. Allan Boesak, presently a candidate for the Doctorate of Divinity in Holland, requested Bishop James of the A. M. E. Church to open the proceedings with a prayer. He welcomed the delegates to Hammanskraal. Only informal business was conducted that night. The rest of the night was taken up with a general "Let-us-know-each-other."

SATURDAY: 14TH DECEMBER

Speaking on behalf of the Steering Committee, Ds. Allan Boesak welcomed everybody. A few announcements were made:

1) Rev. John Thorne, President of the South African Council of Churches, was appointed to chair the day's meeting, followed by Rev. Stan Mogoba on the 15th December.

2) No electronic equipment would be allowed into the conference hall during the proceedings. Only one tape-recorder could be used by the Committee to record the speeches of the guest-speakers.

3) Photographs were not to be taken during the sessions, except outside and with the permission of the subject.

4) There were slight alterations in the Agenda, e.g. Mrs. Meer would replace Mr Collins Ramusi as first speaker.

Rev. J. Thorne took the chair. He thanked the Ad Hoc Steering Committee for bringing so many Black people under the same roof. "If you fail to plan you have planned to fail," he quipped.

He allowed a five-minutes-break for the delegates to know one another and to share some of their anxieties, fears and expectations about the Convention.

Fraternal greetings of solidarity were given by Rev. M. Ngakane (Mission and Evangelism—S. A. Council of Churches), Rev. E. Tema (N. G. Kerk in Afrika—Ministers' Fraternal), Mrs. J. Phakathi (Christian Institute of Southern Africa), Rev. Andy Makhene (IDAMASA—in the place of Rev. Sol Lediga). Ds. E. Tema, of the N. G. Kerk in Afrika, uttered some significant words: "We wish the Conference well and welcome the opportunity where Blacks come together. We find ourselves living in a fragmented Church structure. The Black section of the N. G. Kerk is aware of the oppression and is no longer prepared to put up with it."

Ds. Allan Boesak informed the Conference of a similar Convention which was taking place in Namibia, 3th–16th December. The Black Renaissance pledged its absolute solidarity with the Namibian people, and asked this to be recorded.

At 9.40 a.m. the chair allowed the delegates to shout their fears and expectations as these arose in their minds:

Expectations: Solidarity, Liberation, Commitment, Self-determination, Power, Fearlessness, Direction, Togetherness, Confrontation, Concrete Action, Honesty, Facing Reality.

Fears: Problems too many to cope with, misinterpretation and distortion of the facts, Isolationism, Glorified workshop, What after Convention?, Fear of ourselves and our shadows, Lack of single mindedness, Homelanders will be attacked, not sincere in talking about liberation, How can Christians accommodate Muslims in their theology?

Rev. Moeti Maurice Ngakane's Presidential Address:
In it he emphasised concepts like solidarity, the opportuneness of the Convention, its historic nature and the need for united practical action.

10.15 a.m. TEA BREAK—Meeting resumed at 10.40 a.m.

Before Mrs. Fatima Meer could present her address, a tirade of questions and "points of orders" were directed at the Chairman. Some of the questions concerned the composition and nature of the Steering Committee; others questioned the aims and objects of the Convention and felt that they should and had to be radicalised. The Steering Committee replied to all the queries. Other interjections were purely childish and showed a serious lack of understanding of democratic procedural rules at such conferences. The Chairman gently allowed the debates to drag on. The Steering Committee made it clear that its programme was flexible, because it did not wish to stifle proposals and wider discussions. One motion after another littered the chair's table.

As the session progressed, it became evident that some delegates (later identified as BPC) were terrified of a new rival political organisation. Their fears were allayed when they were reassured that this was never the original intention of the organisers. The Steering Committee readily endorsed the suggestions that the Convention should be seen as a reinforcement of other black organisations who had also struggled for the liberation of the Black people.

Another element came to the fore—i.e. the presence of some persons who are actively involved in the political institutions of Apartheid. It was becoming clear that "separate development and its institutions" would come under heavy fire from the Conference.

Before the lunch-break, the house agreed that two committees be formed in order to expedite matters:
1. Resolutions Committee
2. Committee to deal with "Aims and Objects"

1.35 p.m.—Third session
Telegrams, letters of congratulations and good wishes for the Black Renaissance Convention were read. They came from South Africa, United States of America and Western Europe. One or two of the telegrams were

queried, especially the one from the United States. One delegate expressed his fears of the C. I. A. [Central Intelligence Agency] and U. S. imperialism and that the Convention should watch against this menace.

The members of the Committee to revise the "Aims and Objections" were: Oscar Motsepe—E. Tema—Mike Rantho

Resolutions Committee: J. Phakathi—L. Rassool—D. Curry—Mrs. Qunta—D. Ntuli

Mrs. Fatima Meer's Speech: "Role of women in society"

She requested the Conference to rise in order to pay respect to:

Rev. Mayatula—who symbolises the detainees-without-trial.

Nelson Mandela—who symbolises those on Robben Island.

Oliver Tambo—who symbolises those in Exile.

Abraham Tiro—who symbolises those who died in the struggle.

After her brilliant speech and presentation, Mrs. Meer was subjected to a barrage of interesting questions.

When the Chairman called upon Mr. S. Motsuenyane—President of NAFCOC—to address the Conference on "Black Consciousness and the economic position of the Black man in South Africa," some "points of order" calls were made. It was at this stage that Rev. Ngakane threatened to "take very strong measures" against those who failed to conduct themselves in an orderly fashion. Mr. Motsuenyane then proceeded to deliver his address. He answered all the questions that were put to him, following his talk. At 4.10 p.m. the Conference adjourned for tea.

When business resumed at 4.55 p.m., Rev. Ngakane assured the Conference that the Committee responsible was still condensing the 21 suggested "Aims and Objects" into a digest form. In the meantime the Conference was to continue with the papers.

Speaking on behalf of the group that had come to be known as the SASO/BPC axis, a delegate publicly apologised for the irresponsible behaviour of his allies without withdrawing their sentiments, especially on the need for unity and solidarity. Rev. Ngakane accepted the apology. He assured everyone that all the delegates were free to express themselves and make whatever contribution they deemed fit. Only the unruly elements would not be tolerated.

Dr. Manas Buthelezi spoke on: "The relevance of Black Theology in the liberation of a people—the Christian challenge of Black Theology." Questions and a brief discussion ensued as usual. Ds. Allan Boesak announced that the papers of the guest-speakers would be made available in due course.

The Conference adjourned for supper and returned to the night session at 7.45 p.m. In order to push forward with the agenda, the house voted in favour of working till late into the night. It was announced that the "Dashikis"—a Black musical group—would render a performance soon after the evening session.

The Convenor of the Resolutions Committee reported their findings. Mrs. Phakathi pointed out that her committee had seen it fit to draw a clear distinction between what they saw to be AIMS from other proposals which sounded more like Resolutions. The discussion centred around the aims, postponing the Resolutions to a later stage, in order to allow amendments. Clarificatory questions about the "modus elegendi" were directed at the Steering Committee and were satisfactorily answered. The presence of the "Homelanders" was challenged. It was repeatedly stated that the leaders of the Black people were the Sobukwes, Sisulus and Mandelas, and certainly not the "Homeland Leaders" who are a Government imposition on the people. (N. B. all the original as well as subsequent "Aims and Objects" as well as Resolutions of the Convention can be found under appendix).

Finally, the aims of the Convention were reduced to five points:

1. Black solidarity for total Black liberation.
2. To articulate the Black people's aspirations.
3. Acknowledge the existing Black organisations and give moral and other Support for liberation of Black people.
4. To outline a programme of action for Black liberation.
5. To appoint a Steering Committee for organising and co-ordinating future meetings of Black organisations.

The Resolutions were cut down to six (cf. appendix). Following some lively debates on the implications of the aims, the night session ended.

SUNDAY: 15TH DECEMBER:

At 9.00 a.m. the first session of the day began under the chairmanship of Rev. Stan Mogoba. The Chairman warned the house that we were behind schedule. One speaker, subsequently supported by a tiny minority reminded the chairman that the house had been promised that the items on Resolutions would take precedence over other business. The majority felt that it was nonsense to try and discuss motions or resolutions in a cumbersome crowd of three hundred people. Instead it was suggested that the house had better divide itself into eight workshops for a thorough discussion on each of the suggested resolutions. Mrs Fatima Meer resolved the matter by tabling a motion which was unanimously accepted. It read: "We accept the objectives and resolutions submitted by the Resolutions Committee of this house. We now instruct the workshops to discuss these resolutions and objectives with a view to formulating a declaration of the Black Renaissance Convention."

The names of the eight groups were accordingly read. After calling out the names, the Secretary asked all those whose names had been omitted to come to the chair, so that they could be allocated to the eight groups. Because most of the SASO/BPC people had registered too late and because some of them had not been registered then, naturally, a number of their names did not appear on the official list which had been drawn up early in the Conference. Led by one or two dubious characters, the SASO/BPC axis decided to form themselves into the ninth group. The Steering Committee had no objections to this move and apologised to them. It is surprising then when these students accused the house of discriminating against them, dubbing them "foreign elements." Some precious time was wasted on arguments which went in circles and split hairs on stupid trifles.

Though not following a logical pattern of argumentation, some valuable statements were uttered. e.g.:

a) The regaining of our country and its wealth.

b) The type of social order after liberation.

c) The dangers of elitism.

d) Foreign investment in South Africa generally and homelands in particular.

e) The keen interest of the imperialist foreigners in our liberation struggle.

At 4.45 p.m. Fr. A. M. Zwane spoke on: "Social Communications media in developing countries." Questions followed his dynamic paper. The house concluded that there was at least only one way of controlling the news media—viz. the founding of a Black-owned newspaper or magazine. Otherwise, Black people in South Africa will never communicate the way they would like to.

Father Zwane's paper was followed by a joint presentation of their speech by Miss Foszia Fisher and Mr. Harold Nxasana. They spoke on: "The Labour situation in South Africa and Black awareness." Inevitably, this paper sparked off much discussion, revolving around the role of the proletariat in the struggle, Trade Unionism etc. After the Chairman had thanked all three speakers, the Conference adjourned for supper. The women were requested to carry their supper to the conference hall where they would have a private session.

At 7.15 p.m.: A speaker insisted that the Conference had to deal with the matter of the declaration as a matter of priority. Finally, it was agreed that Professor G. Nkondo's paper on "The Educational World of Blacks in South Africa" should precede a discussion on the proposed Declaration. Having answered a barrage of challenging questions, Professor G. Nkondo was given a spontaneous standing ovation by the Conference.

Then the most dramatic and crucial moment of the Convention started. After the Resolutions Committee had reported its findings, especially the section concerning the Declaration and Resolutions, a heated and lively debate ensued. Before a vote on the whole corpus of the Declaration was taken the Conference discussed every clause of the document plus the Resolutions, individually.

Once again, the matter on separate development caused tempers to flare up. In due course, the house made it clear that the Black people in South Africa rejected what was constantly referred to as "that iniquitous fascist system." At some stage one delegate condemned homelands as "fascist excretions. . ." As the Resolutions condemned "separate development and all its institutions. . . ," certain delegates sounded a note of warning about a possible ambiguity. What sort of institutions are we referring to? One speaker pointed out that the so-called Bantu, Coloured and Indian "universities" were also institutions of separate development. In fact, our whole life as Blacks was based on separate development. The delegates then made it clear, they meant primarily the "political institutions" and such like bodies.

At one moment, a delegate threatened to "scrap" the students from the Convention, because by studying at those "universities" they were collaborators of the system too! (Loud laughter).

Mrs. Fatima Meer sounded a word of warning about the dangers of black racism. South Africa had to be shared among all its people, irrespective of race, religion or colour. She was reacting to remarks which could easily have been interpreted as racist attitudes. Mandela, Sobukwe, Biko, Tiro and Pityana can never be accused of racism.

Another clause which caused a flare-up was the one dealing with detainees and exiles. Someone denounced SASO for condemning the Homeland leaders in public, whilst making secret approaches to them for help. It was disclosed, for instance, that SASO had appealed to two Homeland leaders—viz: Gatsha Buthelezi and Sonny Leon, for the release of detainees. This proved to be a damning revelation. Whereupon one SASO "leader" vehemently and very rudely denied the allegation. Mrs. Meer who was involved in the bitter exchange of words with the insulting SASO "leader," blamed the Chairman for failing to protect her against such shameless uncouthness and for stopping her (Mrs. Meer) from explaining the matter further. That was when she was falsely reported to have resigned from the Convention in protest. All this happened after the Declaration and Resolutions had been unanimously passed. By adopting the Declaration and Resolutions with such acclamation, the Convention felt that its most important work had been accomplished. However, such a statement should not detract from the marvellous work which followed the Declaration.

A sub-clause demanding the exclusion of the "protagonists of Apartheid" from Black Conferences was debated. Quite a number of the delegates felt that even if we totally disagree with the "Homelanders," we should still talk to them. Delegates cautioned against "expelling" the homeland officials, because such an action might antagonise them even further. From time to time the Honourable Collins Ramusi interjected and was given audience, although subsequently booed. He publicly condemned separate development and gave reasons why he operated within the frame-work of that system. It became evident that Collins Ramusi was an extraordinarily courageous leader. He was not too astonished by the hostile attitude of the audience, as the Steering Committee had forewarned him about the mood of the Convention. Collins Ramusi had assured the Organising Committee that the risk was worth taking. By a wide margin the house voted in favour of excluding homeland leaders and all "protagonists of Apartheid" from all meetings of Black people. Some people thought that a re-count of the votes was necessary. After the Chairman had clearly explained what the Conference was voting on, Mr Collins Ramusi and other "homeland leaders" remained seated until the Chairman adjourned the meeting for the night. The Homeland officials were not physically evicted.

Mrs. Jane Phakathi of the Christian Institute of Southern Africa, was elected Chairlady for the following day. That Sunday evening, 15th December, 1974, was indeed one of the most dramatic and most significant highlights of the whole Convention. The so-called "expulsion" of the Homeland leaders was of little importance, many delegates maintained. Its significance lies in the fact that symbolically separate development and its authors were unconditionally and utterly rejected by a representative group of the Black Community.

At the end of that session, some delegates spontaneously burst into songs of jubilation. Black Power fists flew into the air. As it had already been indicated, SASO/BPC axis formed not more than twenty persons altogether, the results of the voting clearly proved that the whole house had taken all the decisions of the Convention.

MONDAY: 16TH DECEMBER—LAST DAY OF THE CONVENTION:
Mrs. Jane Phakathi chaired. She confused the house by reintroducing previous motions which had already been dealt with and disposed of e.g.:
a) the constitution of the Steering Committee
b) reference to some complaints from the "rebel" group 9.
Although she tried her utmost to justify her questions and actions, the majority of the people strongly believed she was secretly working with a definite clique. Bitter complaints about her chairing were later submitted to the Organising Committee.

Mrs. Fatima Meer threatened to resign because of some of the developments of the previous afternoon. But she never carried out her threat.

The last of the guest-speakers proceeded to read his paper on "Towards the manifestation of Black Consciousness." Mr. Mafika Gwala from Durban, was his name. His paper, judging from the enthusiastic response of the Convention, turned out to be a fitting closing speech. He was very good in his answers. The underlying challenge of his talk was a call to action without further delay. After he had been thanked by the Chairlady the Conference debated the question of whether or not to establish a permanent Committee. The house decided to entrust the Ad Hoc Steering Committee with the task of completing whatever work was connected with the first Black Renaissance Convention, including the printing and publication of the book originally envisaged by the Committee. It was felt that to found another permanent structure might provide the "enemy" with another opportunity of cracking down on those concerned. The house was in favour of organising committees on an Ad Hoc basis and to intensify organisational work in the Black associations and movements. The present Steering Committee was asked to handle press reports, although any of the delegates could answer certain questions that arose out of the newspapers.

VOTE OF THANKS: This was given by Mr. P. Gumede, Vice-President of NAFCOC. He thanked all the delegates. But above all, he was very grateful to the Steering Committee who had had the vision to bring together a cross-section of the Black people of South Africa and provided them with a public platform to air their honest views. He said that he was certainly sure that he was expressing the sentiments of the house. He particularly stressed the amount of work which was involved in organising the Convention and the absolute dedication of the organisers to their work. He praised the cooperation of the younger delegates, although he was aware that the Whiteman's news media would distort the heated but constructive debates. Mr. Gumede thought that although Black organisations are very necessary to serve the Black Community, they could nonetheless be a source of bitter divisions. Hence the need for some loose machinery which could bring the Black organisations and other Blacks together from time to time and for joint planning and action.

Finally Mr. Gumede warned that the mass media would seize upon the "expulsion" of the Homelanders to divide us and attempt to annul our deliberations. WE SHOULD TAKE A FIRM STAND AGAINST THAT! he cautioned.

The Chairlady asked the Conference to rise for the National Anthem "Nkosi Sikelel' i-Afrika" (God bless Afrika our beloved country). Black Power fists jabbed the air and beautiful Black brothers and sisters hugged one another with feelings of joy, gratitude and SOLIDARITY.

SO ENDED THE FIRST BLACK RENAISSANCE CONVENTION—The time was 3:25 p.m. 16th December, 1974.

White South Africa was celebrating the "Day of the Covenant."

Prepared by: Smangaliso Mkhatshwa (Secretary of the Black Renaissance Convention). Assisted by three scribes.

Types of groups and persons who participated in the BLACK RENAISSANCE CONVENTION:

CATEGORIES: 1. Black Theologians 2. TECON—Artists/Dramatists 3. Teachers 4. Entrepreneurs 5. Black Labour Organisations 6. Industrial workers 7. Academics 8. Housewives 9. Medical Practitioners 10. Nurses and Para-medics 11. University Students' Organisations 12. Youth 13. Journalists and Radio men 14. Political activists and Politicians of standing 15. University lecturers 16. Musicians 17. Social workers 18. Sociologists 19. Urban and Country Representatives 20. Lawyers

DECLARATION
Section A

We, the Black People of South Africa, meeting at the Black Renaissance Convention in December 1974, declare that:
i. We condemn and so reject separate development policy and all its institutions.
ii. We reject all forms of racism and discrimination.

Section B

We dedicate ourselves towards striving for:
i. A totally united and democratic South Africa, free from all forms of oppression and exploitation.

ii. A society in which all people participate fully in the Government of the country through the medium of one man, one vote.

iii. A society in which there is an equitable distribution of wealth.

iv. An anti-racist society.

Section C (Draft proposal)

We call upon our people and all their organisations to organise their efforts towards securing the release of all political prisoners, detainees and banned people.

Section D

RESOLUTIONS

This Convention:

i) Declares that legalised racism in South Africa is a threat to world peace and therefore call upon all the countries of the world to withdraw all cultural, educational, economic, manpower and military support to the existing racist Government and all its racist institutions.

ii) Expresses its shock and dismay at the expropriation of the Federal Theological Seminary in Alice and calls upon the Black Community to fight for the continued survival of this institution.

iii) Acknowledges that it is not the first to convene a meeting of Black people and it states firmly that it wishes to continue on the efforts that have taken place in the past.

This Convention noting that:

1. The great majority of Black people are workers,

2. besides being discriminated against, the workers also suffer the most blatant forms of exploitation,

3. the wages that workers receive is far below the bread line and they are therefore frustrated in the attempt to use their bargaining power, therefore resolves that:

a) the Government immediately recognise African Trade Unions;

b) that the need for workers to organise themselves into trade unions free from Government interference.

This 3 day national conference of the Black Renaissance Convention held under the auspices of various religious, cultural and political bodies has ended in a massive vote of Black Solidarity.

Document 55. "The Movement in Relation to the Black Community." Article by "Black Student Leader," *SASO Newsletter,* May/June 1975

This paper sets out to review the position of any movement born in the Black community, with the objective of being relevant to the needs of the Black community. In terms of its role obligations. And, also, factors which are conducive to it being accepted and supported by the community, and thus its insured, continued, existence.

First, it is important for us to accept the fact that any meaningful change in this country's social, political and economic situation, shall be brought about by the proletariat—the people who really feel the pinch of white domination, exploitation and oppression. They possess the power to effect radical changes because they are at the base, and thus shoulder the whole weight of all social, economic and political pyramids of this country.

The Black people of this country are not only suffering from dominance by a foreign minority white race, whose advent in this country marked the beginning of an era of persecution for black people, but they suffer repression and exploitation from capitalism and the various forms of imperialism. All this militates against the communalistic basis of our society and our beliefs in the fundamental dignity, and equality of man. Thus our struggle is not only a struggle to get back our land; but it is also an ideological one—i.e. an attack and elimination of capitalism and imperialism and all social systems that promote exploitation and dehumanisation of Black people. Ours is a struggle to restore our stolen land and also a struggle to restore the dignity of man and our traditional attitude towards man. We quest for socialism and denounce capitalism.

Our main task is to organise the masses of our people into one cohesive force to confront oppression. This will mean total identification with the working-class. And in the process will instill self-reliance and national consciousness. A will to stand up to the enemy; to defend black values and dignity. It is this mental, physical and spiritual readiness, that shall decide the day of reckoning with the forces of the negative darkness.

For a long time now we have been expounding the philosophy of Black Consciousness, Black solidarity, etc.

The social, economic and political situation of this country has been analysed from various angles a great deal. This subject is dangerously bordering on being a pastime for Black liberals and intellectual exercise for the fast emerging Black cultural activists. This paper shall attempt at showing certain ways through which we can bring the struggle from the table to the people. This process of taking the message to the people is not possible unless we first rid ourselves of certain misconceptions and attitude towards ourselves and the Black Community at large.

The Black intellectual finds himself alienated from the rest of the Black community by his educational background, the attainment of certain "refined" manners. Which is why most educated people find it hard to communicate with fellow Black people in a train, who are uneducated. The educated person, to escape this persistent emptiness in his being, usually seeks refuge in a copy of the "Daily News," or a book. Thus the Black intellectual finds himself saddled with a "message" he can only pass on to another intellectual. The frustration here is that the Black intellectual is all the time aware that the "message" should be taken to the man in the street. The "HOW" is the problem.

To solve this problem of communication, the Black intellectual must first review all the factors which alienate him from the rest of the Black community; sincerely and realistically. He must radically adjust himself to the community and totally integrate his whole personality to the accepted value-norms, beliefs and prejudice of his community. He must get off from the high black pedestal from which he addresses the community and get to work with and among the people, rather than pull them or drag behind them.

Communication is a vital aspect of the revolutionary process. For communication to be meaningful and healthy, there should prevail throughout the process a spirit of sharing of ideas, rather than the condescending-ascending mood. The attitude of the Black leader is thus very crucial. He must always be aware that in "taking the message to the people," he is not telling them anything new—something they neither know nor understand. But he is merely articulating their everyday feelings and aspiration. He must allow, throughout the process of communication, for communication to be two-way. We have a lot to say to the masses as we have analysed the problem, but there is a world of things we have to learn from our people. For instance, our traditional culture, our history, our past and everyday experiences and perception of the situation. This would broaden our whole outlook and approach towards the problem at hand.

It is also very important in communication to take into account the level of consciousness of the people. The Black leader should guard [against] intimidating the people by ultra-radical ideas. This is not to mean that we should discard ideas on the basis that they are radical, but what is important here is how that idea is presented. To get an idea across one has to present it in such a way that the person he is communicating with shall be able to understand it and relate it to his situation and also to enable him to interpret that idea his own way in his situation, using his own models. He must see that idea as his own, so as to cherish and defend it.

One other important aspect of communication is the character of the person himself. As a proponent of Black liberation, Black dignity, pride and consciousness of self, the Black leader should totally integrate with the people and behave in accordance with the accepted value-norms and culture of the people. That is, "do what you preach, and preach what you do." The leader must always remember that the people expect the impossible from him—they expect that he be the symbol of their nation in its most progressive and highest stage of development. By one's personality one can win the acceptance and support by the people, one can even preach through one's character. An easy character is conducive to fruitful communication whilst a repugnant one can render the best of ideas ineffective. In rejecting the person, people tend to reject his ideas also and all that he stands for. Bad morals of one member of an organisation can seriously prejudice and, in fact, damage the organisation he supports.

We have stated earlier in this paper that change in this country shall be brought about by the oppressed masses. This means that the Black intelligentsia should get to the brass tacks and move with and among the people. And sections of our community have to be mobilised and this requires total commitment from all those working for radical change. Wherever one is, he must do what he preaches and organise all those around him. This is the only way the struggle can be a struggle of the people, for the people and by the people.

Document 56. "A Night of Blackness with 'Dashiki' and 'Black Jazz'." Article in *SASO Newsletter*, March/April 1976

Putting a cultural show together can be a drag, as those charged with the duty of organizing artists—people who have come to believe themselves a race apart—have discovered in a painful way indeed. But then, as someone wryly observed in a moment of high melancholy, the show must go on; especially in these halcyon days when people are inundated with banal plays, musical shows that end at dawn with the people feeling like a man trying to go cold turkey after a trip on an esoteric and benevolent hallucinogen. The difficulty is mainly at the choice of artists. One does not want, because a cultural thing for blacks has to have an unmistakeable black stamp, artists who have been so tainted with the white experience that they become gray in the dark; no, one wants people obsessed with the truth and who'll keep on ramming it down the throats of the populace so as to exorcise the evil spirits in our people's blood so that they go home seeing liberation not as a figment of the imagination of black consciousness ideologues and proponents but as something as tangible as a policemen's .45 or his rubber truncheon. It's got to be something real, not something dreamt up by people who want to be a feeble and reasonable facsimile of the great white dream. Not that white dreams are essentially bad or obscene, but in our existential life-situation they are non-functional and passe.

The number one thing that frustrates, nowadays, is that whenever you tell people that there is a show at the YMCA featuring 'Dashiki' and 'Black Jazz' and a bevy of ultra-funky beautiful girls displaying high African fashions from as far north as Gambia down to South Africa—pieces worn by Princess Elizabeth of Toro and definitely not by Margaux Hemingway and Elizabeth Taylor—people look at you as though you're out of your mind, and in tense and hushed tones the conversation goes as follows:

"Man, SASO organizing a 'Night of Blackness!' You sure the thing has no connection with the Frelimo Rally?"

"No man," you say tiredly. "This is just a night when black people read poetry, watch the traditional dress parade and listen to music by 'Dashiki' and 'Black Jazz'. It's got nothing to do with the rally whatsoever. Do you want to buy a ticket?"

"Don't think I'm prying, brother. It's just that I did too much running in Curries Fountain. And I don't want to see a police Alsatian dog for the rest of my life."

But he, being a black man, proud and determined to be free, will buy the ticket programme; in fact he'll buy two: one for a friend.

So on the evening of 28 February, 1976—a warm and sultry evening that promised rain—about two hundred people were already outside the brown stoned YMCA building in Durban. It being a Saturday and a month-end, many people were apprehensive that they would witness widespread bloodshed. In fact many were already visualizing themselves lying in their own pool of blood in the gutter or on the asphalt. Happily nothing happened.

The musical instruments—a curious mixture of monstrous African drums, bongo drums carved with motifs reminiscent of the Nigerian mgbedike masks, shekeres, maraccas, flutes, reed instruments whose origin and designation escape the writer, guitars, amplifiers and Rajah's sound equipment—must have filled the uninitiated casual observer with awe if not a sense of bewildered dread. 'Black Jazz' personnel, under the leadership of guitar maestro Sandile Shange, lugged their bass guitar, drums, tenor saxophone and a trumpet. Jabu Sithole who'd be doing the singing, was already caught up in a trance as he improvised on Rahsaan Roland Kirk's Clickety-clack, a poem.

> Clickety-clack!
> What's all this madness.
> Who'll bring our spirit back?

Bringing the black people's spirit back (collectively) seemed to be just the thing the 'Dashiki'/'Black Jazz' collaboration was all about. The 'Dashiki' combo, also known as 'The Poets', consisted of Lefifi Tladi—by far one of the most articulate and innovative artists of our time—Tebogo 'Gilly' Mabale on flute, Kanakana Matsena (who, one joker observed, must have been born with a silver microphone in his mouth—the way that guy talks a mile-a-minute!), on shekeres and a horn which, when blown, sounds like the bellow of an enraged bull, and Fikile, a consummate artist of great skill who helped in poetry, like in the poem 'New York'.

> 'New York'
> The Big Apple
> Sixteen million feet National Tom McCanns
> Florsheims, stepping on each other
> Rejoicing the death of one nigger toe . . .

There wouldn't be enough space to describe the effect of music and poetry upon the people who were at the YMCA that Saturday evening. Many sat glued to their seats while the show was going on waiting, as it were, like canaries waiting for a grain of wheat to fall. Others, especially those in the back who obviously couldn't hear much because of the faulty sound-system, showed impatience with poetry and pressed for more music. One thing the patrons agreed with though, was the traditional dress parade. The girls were beautiful. They walked and paraded with confidence that left the organizers out of breath. For this was so unexpected! Jabu sang—and, oh, how he sang!—and was accompanied by 'Black Jazz'. Guest artist Abbey Cindi, flautist and soprano saxophone extraordinary, was also there to augment 'Dashiki' whose guitarist, Lawrence Moloisi, couldn't be there with them for some reason. Abbey used to play with the legendary 'Malombo'. Lefifi, Gilly, Kanakana and Fikile recited The Last Poet's "When the Revolution Comes.'

When the revolution comes
Some of us'll probably catch it on T.V.
With chicken hanging down our mouths
and you'll know it's a revolution
For there won't be any commercials then
Preacher pimps are gonna split the scene
With communion wine stuck in their back pockets
Faggots won't be so funny then.

Faggots were really not so funny that night as a whole spectrum of black oppression was laid bare by the musicians and poets. Alien agents that aim at the destruction of blackness were exposed for all to see. At the end of the small hours 'Black Jazz' and 'Dashiki' had a jam session that left everybody asking for more, and there was no more to be given.

It was indeed, and, one suspects, will continue to be, a Night of Blackness!

On Tuesday 2 March, 1976, a repeat performance was staged at the University of Zululand. This night saw the artists at their best. Perhaps it was the influence of the students themselves that so electrified the atmosphere or maybe it was because many young and beautiful people were attired in African garb, one wouldn't know. One had that weird feeling of timelessness, as though one had been thrown back into space and time to a situation in history when Africa was proud of what was truly hers; when airplanes, tanks, machinery, judges, juries, guns and policemen as we know them are an unknown phenomenon. One was immersed in a two-hour cultural deja vu. One had an impression of explosive colours and war songs; a hurrying and fluid sensual movement of people basking in the reflected glory of an even more glorious past so that the poem 'Before the white man came' was so apt. One felt that it wasn't the guitar string Sandile was pulling but our own hearts-strings, the drums were the thumping of our hearts and the stomping of feet by dancers accompanied by a song of victory after the end of a long war.

POSTSCRIPT

Many things will lie buried and unknown in the uncertainty and darkness of the past. SASO, through the cultural committee (CULCOM), aims at reawakening the people to the beauty of their past kingdoms so that they will be able to deal with this turbulent present and an even more unpredictable future. It's not funny—in fact it's downright obscene—that black people have to read their "history" written by people who haven't the foggiest notion of how it feels to be be black. This also goes for those so-called black academics who spend days and nights on end with icepacks around their inflated domes and their spindly legs immersed in wash-basins full of cold water who write these about black people's behavioral patterns as though blacks were rats in B. F. Skinner's Box. History and thus Culture, of black folks has to be enspirited with the soul-force of black people. And whites and their plastic images—the nonwhites can never do that! Myths have been created about blacks and the unfortunate thing is that most blacks end up believing these falsities. Why, some actually endorse them! That is why we find a book (thoroughly profane, obscene and certainly devoid of any literary merit) passing uncensored and unbanned by the PCB [Publications Control Board]. This book which, among other things, says Africans stink like stale biltong and their sexual habits are "beastly," is called *Agter die Magalies* and was written by an HNP [Herstigte Nasionale Party] supporting Afrikaner. If one were to write a book based on the same format and say that whites stink even after a bath, that their society is decadent, that their sexual habits would nauseate the most seasoned pig, that they are the ones who brought disease and sexual deviations like homosexuality, lesbianism, incest-rape, syphilis, one wouldn't even be risking one's book getting banned. One would be laying one's life on the line. Instead of receiving congratulatory letters in one's mail, one would receive something else. These are some of the things that are said and done in this country in the sacred name of Christ, democracy, progress and allegiance to the flag.

There is a need in this country for academics, students, dramatists, poets, writers, musicians and just about everybody concerned with black truth triumphing over lies to come together and help in the formation of one cultural body that will take care of all artists' aspirations. In December SABTU (South African Black Theatre Union) was formed but due to bannings, detentions and deaths the whole project was discontinued. It's about time that such bodies were resuscitated because the black man is on his own and will continue to be on his own until the end of time.

Document 57. "The Mafikeng Manifesto." Statement on economic policy debated at a symposium of the Black People's Convention, May 31, 1976

BPC adopts black communalism as its economic policy, noting:

* that black communalism is a modified version of the traditional African economic life style which is geared to meet the demands of a highly industrialized and modern economy;

* that the sharing envisaged will not be necessarily monitored by the state for the benefit of the state itself, but many will be either between groups of individuals or specific communities within the state or all the communities comprising the state;

* that sharing shall imply sharing of property, wealth, services and labour.

Black Communalism implies that:

1. Land is a God-given gift to the people, therefore it shall be owned by all the people with the State being entrusted with its control.

2. All industry which involves direct exploitation of the land shall be owned by the state.

3. Family units shall be allocated land for dwelling.

4. Plots allocated to family units may neither be bequeathed, transferred

or otherwise disposed of without prior consultation with the state, provided that the state will however consistently protect the interest of the family units concerned and their future generations.

5. Land allocated for private agriculture, commerce and industry shall be rented by the people concerned from the state.

6. Organised societal and religious groups, e.g. churches, sports groups, shall be allocated land according to their reasonable needs and shall rent such land from the state.

7. Agricultural activity shall centre around the formation of co-operatives which shall be entrusted with the responsibility of spearheading agriculture in consultation with the department.

8. Rural life shall be recognised such that more economically manageable villages shall be established whereby basic essential services can be made available to the village and in turn the people's agricultural activity can be jointly organised.

9. It shall be the duty of the state to assist such villages and co-operatives in marketing their agricultural products for both internal and external consumption.

10. The state may play a leading role in the planning and development of industry and commerce.

11. Industries whose products are of strategic importance to the nation shall be owned by the state, e.g. manufacture of arms and armaments.

12. Also industries of vital importance to the economy of the nation, e.g. major corporations shall be owned by the state.

13. Community initiation and ownership of industry shall be encouraged where this can be easily productively organised.

14. Private owned industry and commercial undertakings shall be allowed to operate without state assistance and within the framework drawn up by the state department responsible for commerce, industry and trade.

15. The level of foreign participation in industry and commerce shall be kept to a minimum as defined by the department responsible for commerce, industry and trade.

16. Salaries paid by employers to their employees in private industries and commerce as well as in co-operative, community and state-owned enterprises shall be carefully supervised by the state to lay specific minimum for specific categories of undertakings.

17. In all cases the state shall specifically protect the interest of workers against exploitation and unsatisfactory working conditions.

18. Trade unions comprising the workers within certain crafts shall be encouraged and recognised and shall enjoy a particularly privileged relationship with the department controlling labour.

19. Wages and salaries assessments shall be periodically reviewed by a special tribunal consisting of representatives of trade unions and the department controlling labour.

20. Village stores shall be owned by the communities they are intended to serve.

21. Organisation of small time commerce, e.g. grocery stores, shall vest in the hands of district commercial councils operating on behalf of specific geographic communities in consultation with the department controlling commerce.

22. Such commercial councils shall seek to generate profits for the development of the communities they serve.

23. The state will on its own participate in finance institutions in competition with private enterprise through the formation of a National financial corporation which shall run a National Bank with branches and an insurance house with branches.

24. The state financial institutions shall operate a developmental loan policy for the assistance of co-operative, community and individual enterprise provided that there shall be a differential interest charge for private and community enterprise.

25. The state through its department controlling commerce and industry shall at all times restrict importation of goods only to those categories and levels that are essential for complete existence and shall encourage local production of goods which can be sustained from natural resources and industry within the country.

26. The state shall operate its own importation programme through a National corporation in competition with privately owned import houses so that imported goods can reach the people at minimal and acceptable prices.

27. The state shall control the marketing of local products and goods intended for both internal and external marketing so that such products and goods can be available for internal consumption at minimal prices, and external consumption at advantageous prices.

28. All public transport shall be controlled by the department responsible for transport such that the state through its various organs participates maximally in intra-inter-town, inter-provincial as well as national and international transport.

29. There shall be no provision for private ownership of public transportation except by special licence, provided that all railways, harbours, and airways transportation shall be owned completely by the state.

30. The state shall allow a fair competition between privately owned and state owned mass media enterprises except that all radio and television stations will be owned either wholly or jointly by either the state or the communities and provided that all postal and telegraphic services shall be in the hands of the state.

6. The 1976 Soweto Uprising

DOCUMENT 58. "To Be or Not to Be . . . ?" Article by Nthanyane Maaga, *SASM Newsletter,* April 1973

That is the question whether 'tis nobler for our teachers and principals to despise and ridicule the Black gospel in order to appear as "good-boys" to Whitey: or to face the truth and do justice to their scholars; to conscientise, to spearhead the Black Consciousness philosophy, and lose their posts and be restricted to Sibasa.

Of course one of the biggest stumbling-blocks facing SASM at present is the uncooperativeness of school authorities. Some principals are uncooperative, it is a fact but none has said it openly. A man who wields tremendous power such as a principal tells you for once that he is a servant, and he therefore cannot accept Black Consciousness in an official capacity. Yet the ridicule is that he does "attack" Black Consciousness in an official capacity. S.A.S.M. may constitute of hot-heads, depending on one's definition of the noun, Black Consciousness may be a philosophy mainly supported by those who did not fully comprehend the "hard times of the Sixties." Yet we know what we are saying. We say it with all honesty. We idolize Black Consciousness. It is our only defence against a corrosive system. A system that corrodes one's spirit. It kills the pride that you are naturally born with. This system, yes, makes Non-Whites curse their mothers for giving birth to them. It makes Koolies cry, Boesmans weep, and Kaffirs lament. But thanks God, it makes Blacks all the more Blacker at heart; because without it, a Black man could not be existing so would a White man; for we are Black because the White has made us aware of his abhorable Whiteness.

But the light of the nation, our teachers, have seldom if ever shown their support of this awakening. Perhaps it is because they have families to support or perhaps they would like to be principals and ultimately inspectors. If it be so, then the word "teacher" has lost meaning. A teacher is a teacher of morals, a teacher of religion and environment. Adaptation to your surroundings and that doesn't exclude politics. I think some of our teachers have been subjected, like some of our Non-White brothers, to much social bribery. Fat cheques. Because one earns a comfortable living does not make one an honorary White.

In fact, what is there to adore in whiteness; Pink skin? Oppressive hearts and regular nightmares about SWART GEVAAR [black danger]? Oh no, no, thanks, not for me. Some teachers act white in class. They teach students about etiquette—White etiquette of course, which involves accent of speech, the manner of walking, the manner of laughing—all reflecting Whiteness. But who can blame them? That has been their lesson from childhood—the superiority and infallibility of Whiteness.

Some Non-White "experts" on Black affairs say that things are changing slowly. This in fact implies that something is wrong with our rulers. The only snag is the time taken to right the wrongs. But if there be a wrong, why prolong it for another hour?

We have always cried about oppression by Whites. But looking at the attitude of some of our Black People—teachers and all; leads one to believe that there are also Black oppressors. Where do you stand? Waiting for a Messiah of Liberation? But the Miracle Age is past. We must reap the fruits of our efforts. If we are to attain liberation, we must work for it.

We have shown that to be or not to be is a question no more. We "MUST" be part of the struggle—or part of the oppressors. Over to you teachers!

SOLIDARITY!

Nthanyane Maaga

Document 59. "Strategies of Operation." Discussion paper by Malusi Mpumlwana for SASM conference, King William's Town, Easter 1975

This afternoon, brothers and sisters, I would have you consider with me the topic, "Strategies of operation." It is near nigh impossible to do this without a prior analysis of the political alternatives open to the Black man in the South African socio-political scene which I shall endeavour to do presently. There only two alternatives open to a Black political activist, namely, to work within the separate development policy and platforms which have been created by the self-imposed white director society without consultation, or to work within the law but outside the system and thereby incur the displeasure of the director society despite the fact that your activities may be perfectly legal—a clear indication that the white society is hell-bent to maintain its privileged position until eternity. It is for this reason that Black consciousness movements have elected to operate outside the system—a much more difficult route to liberation than the former but the shorter and the surest. You therefore, obviously have to go out of your way to formulate strategies adaptable to different situations that will arise from time to time en-route to the realisation of your objectives.

You are primarily students and that is to say, those whose main occupation is the acquisition of knowledge. The kind of knowledge you are acquiring has been designed for you by the director society such that you may be useful tools in the fulfillment of their main aim—to stay directing. It therefore goes without saying that it is necessary that whilst you remain studying at the only schools available—those provided by them, you have to set yourself a programme of self-education in order to acquire those skills which matter most en-route to freedom. Such skills as political knowledge, knowledge of economics, law, agriculture and other disciplines can be acquired easily by extensive reading of books, newspapers and independent research which can be carried out in libraries provided by the Institute of Race Relations and other bodies. The main purpose of all this is to develop knowledgeable, perceptive and analytical minds that are so invaluable to the realisation of our aims. I am sure you do not want to be engineers, doctors and builders for money and development of the homelands. The ideals you embrace point to goals much loftier than that. The ideals of SASM imply selflessness, sacrifice and service and you have at all times to exude these attributes at school, at home, at work and at play.

You as students come into contact with three main classes of people, namely, parents, teachers and students. Most parents will be opposed to your activities and this has resulted in some members backing out of Black organisations. But if you are a good child, you study hard at school and you are honest, respectful and working hard around the home, no parent will forsake you. The same applies at school as well. In this way you will be creating good public relations for your movement and making your parents and teachers your best friends. But be always vigilant that you never sacrifice principle in the process. The purpose of this goodwill is only to further your aims and not to do the bidding of the parent or teacher but of your movement. The question of fluid communication between student and teacher also arises here. Parents and teachers, unlike you, have lived under conditions of spiritual oppression for a long time and their independence of mind and self-respect have moreover been systematically crushed by a host of intimidatory laws and actions. Be patient with them but always take every opportunity to challenge any false notions on their part about what the director society's true intentions are. Challenge all false notions about our history, our liberation and our way of life.

But as far as possible, do it discreetly and respectfully to facilitate fluid communication.

In your relationship with students, who are the people whose support you want to enlist most, lead them. Help those who come from indigent homes, challenge any unreasonable action against a student member, initiate student cultural bodies like debating societies where none exist, always bearing your goals in mind. Take heed to try and avoid inconsequential strikes that may result in unnecessary casualties but always exercise discretion in such situations and avoid acting against strong student opinion and thereby creating hostilities against SASM. Discretion is the key word in all successful political activities. Be calm, cool and composed in all situations and avoid emotionalism in your actions and speeches. Live a clean disciplined life so as to enhance the image of SASM.

Your ultimate goal is the emancipation of the Black man from the tutelage of white society and in your activities you will deal with people. For strategical convenience, Blacks can be divided into three classes, namely, those who have completely surrendered to the white man, those who although not surrendered are hesitant to stand up against oppression because of economic considerations and fear of reprisals, and those who are working for liberation but are unwilling to do so within the Black consciousness fold. Black consciousness groups have evolved a formula called the "three C's" for dealing with all these classes. The C's stand for confrontation, conscientization and co-operation. The first group or class is to be found in homelands and other governments. They are leading simple blacks and others who lack the intellectual resources to weigh objectively the glib allurements dangled before them, astray. They are to be confronted urgently as some of them are already looking to an empty independence. The second group are to be conscientised. Some of them are even found in homeland opposition parties, the Labour party, and mostly among the passive, inactive people who feel listless and unable to do anything to free themselves. The third group is found mainly in churches, newspapers and social welfare organisations. Their remedy is co-operation as well as conscientisation. These suggestions are to be reviewed from time to time according to circumstances. They are mere suggestions and not "MAO's thoughts" on how to run your organisation.

I wish SASM a successful inauguration and a fruitful future. I know that by the selflessness which you have already shown and your dedication, you will enlist the support of a million and more other boys and girls who are young, dedicated and Black.

POWER AND SOLIDARITY

Document 60. Statement by Belinda Martin, aged 22, on her detention, July 17–August 28, 1975

I am resident at 129 Cumberland Avenue, Nancefield, Johannesburg.

I am employed as a computer programmer by Generex Computer Bureau, Fedmis Buildings, Marshall Street, Johannesburg.

I was detained by plain-clothes Security Police at my place of employment at 8:30 am on July 17.

I was handcuffed and taken by car to John Vorster Square, to the 9th floor.

There were eight White Security Police present and one Coloured lieutenant Sons, the policeman who arrested me. I was threatened with violence if I didn't answer their questions. I was told that if I didn't answer questions put to me I would not be released.

I was then taken to the 10th floor where a number of photographs were taken of me.

The police then handed me over to two White police women. They were middle-aged (more than 32); one was uniformed the other not.

The policemen told the two women to rough me up to give me a taste of the treatment I was to get from them. I was left alone with the women. They stripped all my clothes off me. I was handcuffed by my hands and feet. Then they beat me. They hit me with their hands and fists. I fell over and sprawled on the floor. The policemen stood outside the door during this beating.

The police had told me earlier they could beat me as much as they wanted to because I would have no proof against them.

They then took the handcuffs off, and they allowed me to dress. I was then handcuffed again, hands and feet. I was put at a chair in front of a desk. It was a front room of the building. They closed the blinds and stacked chairs against the door.

Now there were eight White policemen and Lieut. Sons. They all crowded around me, and all spoke and shouted at once.

I remember them asking which organisation did I belong to. Had I formed my own revolutionary group? I just looked and stared them. They pulled my hair, whole handfuls, and they used terrible language.

They said they would not let me leave the room. I would have to wet the floor if necessary.

This went on till about 4:30 pm. I didn't answer any questions. They then unhandcuffed me, and left me with a uniformed male and female policeman and woman who booked me in. They took me to a cell on the first floor. The cell was stinking and filthy. The toilet was full and couldn't be flushed.

Before reaching the cell, we passed through two steel doors. I was given two blankets, if you can call them blankets, they were more like rags. And I was told to sleep on the cement floor. There was no mat. There was nothing in the cell besides the toilet.

I was not given anything to eat or drink, nor was I allowed other clothes. I was to stay in the same clothes I was arrested in for the next 2-3 weeks.

Also I was not given any food or water for the next two weeks, and only survived by drinking water from the toilet pan in my cell the fourth day after my arrest—on Monday July 21.

The next day, Friday (July 18) I was fetched from my cell at about 8:30 am and taken to the 9th floor of the building again. This time there were more security police than the day before. They were all in plain clothes, and included my main interrogator, a Lieut. Cornelius, a White policeman.

I was again handcuffed hand and feet and sat in a chair in front of the same desk. I was asked many questions about my brother (Leonard) in exile in Botswana, and about his friends.

During this questioning, Lieut. Sons hit me in the face twice with his open hand—he always gave the first shots.

My nose started to bleed. Even today it still bleeds sometimes. I just sat there and said I could not answer their questions. They said that if I wanted to get out I should just agree with what they said. They questioned me about SASO, BPC, AFRO (South African Students Organisation, Black Peoples' Convention, Anti-Coloured Peoples Representative Council group) and about exiles, and if they were engaged in a revolutionary project.

They accused me of having gone to Botswana for revolutionary military training—I had gone there three times to take money and clothes to my brother.

I have never belonged to SASO, BPC, or AFRO.

I was questioned all day, and again given no food or water. Besides hitting me in the face, Lieut. Sons also kicked me in the stomach with his knee.

I don't think the White security police would have assaulted me if Sons had not been there.

They suggested at one stage that the women should rather beat me up. He said no. He said I was a revolutionary bitch and should be treated as such regardless of my sex.

I was taken back to my cell, and that night I was given no food or water. I was deprived of food and water for 14 days. The security policemen said that I should talk if I wanted a drop of water.

That day, Friday, they had fixed the toilet, but I didn't drink out of it until the Monday.

Also the cell light did not work, and I was left in the cell in the dark.

I was left in the cell the whole of the next two days, Saturday and Sunday, without food and water.

On Monday morning (July 21) I was fetched from my cell. I asked to be allowed to wash and was told "you're not in a hotel, remember you are in prison."

I was taken to the same interrogation room. This time there was only Lieut. Sons and Lieut. Cornelius present. I was again handcuffed hands and feet.

They removed my shoes, and in my socks, I was made to stand on a block of hot ice (dry ice). The ice was standing on a tray, and a row of iron spikes was put in front and behind the tray, so that if I fell or wanted to get off the spikes would stick into me.

I must have stood for about 8 hours in this way, without moving. I can tell it was about this long, because I remember the two policemen preparing to stop work, as they did each day from about 3:30 pm.

Throughout that day they just carried on with office work at desks in the office.

They told me that if I was prepared to tell them what they wanted to know, they would release me.

I was completely dazed after a while. They may have removed the spikes. I complained of feeling dizzy and said I could not see.

My feet swelled up and I felt a burning pain through my body. Then at some stage everything went black. I must have collapsed and lost consciousness.

I woke up in my cell. I had a terrible migraine. My whole body was swollen, as if it was full of water. I was very thirsty and drank from the toilet in the cell for the first time.

The following morning (Tuesday July 22) I was taken to the District Surgeon in town. I wasn't handcuffed, and was taken there by Lieut. Sons and a White policeman.

I didn't answer to any of the doctor's questions. I had difficulty walking, and he must have seen the swelling on my body. He checked me over. He gave me tablets for a migraine, although I didn't complain of one.

He was a very old doctor. He could hardly see. He had thick glasses.

He asked if I had been assaulted. I didn't say I had been—it wouldn't have served any purpose. I didn't tell him anything. I saw no reason to complain.

I was then taken back to my cell and left for the whole day.

The next day, Wednesday (July 23) my nose started bleeding, and I started retching and my bowels produced blood.

I didn't ask to see a doctor.

I retched all over the cell floor. Nobody cleaned up, and I used my pantyhose to clean up.

I felt I was dying, as I had a burning inside me.

The toilet was still filthy, and I used the same pantyhose to wash it out.

I was then left alone altogether. I was not brought any food or water for two to three weeks. I was told that if I wanted to talk, I should just press the red button on the cell wall.

I lost some sense of time, but could tell it was day by the light from the window high up on the wall of the cell. I was given no toilet paper or soap, and washed myself from the water in the toilet pan with my pantyhose.

I was terribly cold, especially at night. I had a cough, and my throat used to burn.

Then the Friday of the next week, I think, a magistrate came to see me. I couldn't tell him anything. I just couldn't communicate with him—I saw no purpose being served. He asked me a number of questions. I didn't reply. He must have seen I wasn't washed, that my clothes were dirty and that the cell was filthy and smelled.

After that weekend, on the Monday morning I was taken for a shower on the first floor. I was given a piece of Lifebuoy soap, but no towel. I was given toilet paper to dry myself with. After the shower I had to get back into the same filthy clothes.

The next day, Tuesday (August 5) I was given clean clothes which my family had sent.

That Monday (August 4) I was given food for the first time. I was brought a piece of fish with carrot or beetroot peels. There was no bread, but a cup of cold coffee. I only ate the fish. After eating it I had a terrible craving for more food. My head started swimming and I started shivering, going from hot to cold.

That night they brought me a sort of stew, with pieces of fat in it. I ate one spoonfull and felt great relief, but decided not to eat the rest—I thought it might be drugged.

The next day (Tuesday, August 5) besides the clean clothes, I was brought some sandwiches which I decided not to eat also because I thought they had been drugged.

Then a White matron in the cell block started smuggling sandwiches which she had made to me. Also fruit juices and milo and cocoa. I don't think I would have survived without those.

She could see what a state I was in and probably took pity on me.

From then on they brought food to me regularly. All I took was the water they brought.

I wasn't interrogated again.

Then in the 4th week of detention they brought me more clothes, and a packet of biscuits, two packets of crisps, a bar of chocolate, a bar of soap and a packet of washing powder sent by my family.

I was able to wash my clothes, and kept a spencer [jacket] and slacks back of the dirty clothes so as to keep one set clean. The matron who brought me her sandwiches told me she had been threatened that she could be jailed if seen speaking to me. She had been asked if I was sending notes through her.

On Wednesday (August 27) I was taken to the 9th floor to see my parents. I didn't want them to see me in such a terrible state. My feet were swollen.

There were two security police present, including Lieut. Sons, and they had a tape recorder on.

My mother started crying, and asked what had happened to my feet. She could hardly speak. We chatted for a while and I was taken back to my cell.

That day I was accused of sending letters out of my cell.

The next day (Thursday Aug 28) at about 2:30 p.m. Lieut. Sons came to my cell and told me to get ready to go home. I was again taken back to the 9th floor and told that my release was temporary. I was told that I would be put under house-arrest if I spoke to the Press or had any contact with people they still wanted to arrest. They didn't say who these people were.

They gave me a typed slip saying I would have to appear as a State witness against Joseph Molokeng [accused no. 1 in the NAYO trial]—whom I don't even know.

In all the time I was detained I never made any statements to the police, and never signed anything.

At one stage they asked me to copy from a book onto paper saying they had [a] hand-writing expert.

That day Lieut. Sons drove me home. The next day he returned and asked for my passport, which my father gave him.

I broke down for the first time when I got home. I just cried and cried.

I cannot sleep at night.

There are three other things I should mention.

The night I woke up in my cell after being made to stand all day on the hot ice, I found a burn mark on my neck. It was as though I had been burned with a cigarette. It was painful. I still have the mark.

Also, one night, I don't remember which night, the security police came to my cell in the middle of the night with a doctor, who was dressed in black.

They shone a bright torch in my face. They said they had arrested my brother and others. The doctor asked if I was unwell. I said I was well and feeling fine. I don't remember anything more.

During my detention there were times when I found myself talking and laughing to myself. When this happened I stopped myself and clenched my fists and tried to sleep. I found great difficulty in ever getting to sleep, and when I did, it was only half-sleep.

DOCUMENT 61. Letter from Stanley Gqajela to Monwabisi Yako, giving instructions for leaving South Africa, late 1975 (handwritten, in Xhosa with translation)

Dibanisa naleyo uyifumene kuqala ndipose mistakenly.

Comrade Nweyi andikugxeki ngondixelela into engekhoyo ngathi sonke kweli cala sifumana eleta ezinjalo ngenxa yabantu abeza apha ngokungaqondakaliyo. So nathi sibanika lo impression yokuba asizimiselanga ntweni to keep the enemy blind, ngoba xa unga lumkanga kuyo kidnaptwa. So neleta endiyibhalayo kumele ndibanike loo impression especially xa ndibhalela umntu o unrellevant. Wena ndingakubhalelanga msinya nje kungenxa ka Kupa no Makoko. Andiyazi into ebajikisileyo ndingazi bebesithi bayaphi, nenjongo zabo zokujika andinakuxelela. So mna ndizenzela my own opinion ngabo. As a result andakubhalela ndicingelai safety yakho nabanye. Yithi bakuncokolele uhambo ngokupheleleyo, undibuzele lo mbuzo wokuba sezingaphi iidolophu needolophana abase-bezazi ngemali ye struggle evela nje uyinikwe ukuba ukhwele ii train ujike apho uthe waziva ufuna ukujika. Kukho abajika sebelapha, that is sell-out's, kodwa okwangoku sekemnye. Omnye sambhaqa ukuba yi system naye wavuma ukuba wenza umsebenzi woo Searge so okwangoku use prison. Yi cherrie.

Nweyi, izinto ndizizamile, yonke into ilungile. Qha siselapha nje besisalindele inani ligcwale, that is libambeke (50 people), kuba i aeroplane azinakukhona ukuthatha umntu abamnye okanye ababini everyday. So u January akuzubetha siselapha kanti ne Christmas kuno kwenzeka ingasibetheli apha, qha asinako ukubeka e definite date for security reasons.

Mfondini, ndakubhalela some three weeks back or two, kodwa indlela andiyibhalanga yoku hamba kuba bendisamele ireply laubantu abathembekileyo ebesibabhalele kwelo cala e Mafekeng. Indlela e safe, nantsi: kuyiwa e Mafekeng, xa kufikwa khona kuthathwa iibhasi eziya e Pitsane-Molopo. Xa ubuzwa ukuba uyokwenzani u biza nokuba yeyiphi isurname efike entloko uthi uyakuloomntu, nokuba ubeke esiphi isizathu sokuya kuloo mntu. Xa ufika khona ucingo olwahlulayo luhamba phakathi elalini, that is lwakihlele le lali kubini, elinye icala lingapho elinye lingapha. Kodwa ube very much careful xa ufika khona, ungabuzi nokuba ngubani apho ucingo lukhoyo ukuba awukaluboni. Ukuba uphethe imali unga briber (bribery) nentwana kodwa wenze sure ukuba awuvusanga isuspicion. Xa

utsibileyo uye straight kumapolisa alapha (Botswana) okanye ubuze i immigration office apho ikhoyo ubaxelele ukuba you seek political asylum. Xa
bebuza into ekususileyo ekhaya okanye ubaleka ntoni, wenze i story
esinokubangela umuntu abaleke kwelo cala. Ubaxelele ukuba ufuna ukuba
apha e LOBATSE (LUBATSI for pronunciation purpose) kuba wazi mna no
CHRISTIAAN MATEBANE. Nixele ukuba kuza abantu aba ngaphi ukuze
sikwazi ukulungisa i-accomodation nezinto ezifana namatikiti o kugqithela
phambili. So kweli cala sizakulindela abantu from 5 to infinity at the same time.

Nweyi, wena sukuza kuba ndinomsebenzi for wena, kodwa xa uziva
ukuba awusena kuhlala apho ungeza. Qha le information uyishiye ezandleni
ezi safe nasemntwini ozakwaziyo uku-organizer amajita eza ngapha. Enye
into, organizer i transport up to Mafekeng or Pitsane-Molopo for that matter,
okwangoku singeka phendulwa ngumntu ebezakwamkela amajita
eMafekeng. So owenu umsebenzi kwelo cala kuku-organizer amajita, not
less than five a trip, ne moto ezakubasa e Mafekeng.

Andikucengi ndingakuceli kule nto endiyithethayo ndiyakuxelela.
Okanye ungayenzi xa ungafuniyo, kodwa cinga ngesizwe (23.5 million).
Mandikuhlebele aphokuyiwakhona UGANDA, EGYPT, TANZANIA,
LIBANON, finally to Peking (China) or Russia. So Nweyi

[*Translation:* Add the one you received first mistakenly posted.

Comrade Nweyi, I do not blame you for telling me something which does
not exist. It appears that all of us who are at this end receive similar letters
because of people who come here mysteriously. So we give them the
impression that we intend to do nothing, to keep the enemy blind, because
if you are not careful you are being kidnapped. So even in the letter I write,
I must give them that impression especially when writing to an irrelevant
person. Why I did not write soon to you is because of Kupa and Makoko. I
do not know what turned them back, and do not know where they thought
they were going to. And their reasons for turning back I cannot tell you. I
personally came to my own opinion about them. As a result I did not write
to you, thinking of your safety and others. Ask them to give you a full
account about their journey, and ask this question on my behalf as to how
many cities and towns they happen to know through the money furnished
by the struggle that one just received, to entrain and merely return whenever
you feel like returning. There are those who turn back even though they
have already arrived here, that is sell-out's; but at present there has only been
one we spotted. The other one turned out to be a "system" who admitted that
she was doing the work of [the government] but at present that one is in
prison. It is a woman.

Nweyi, I have managed things, everything is all right. The reason we are
still here is that we are waiting for the number to be complete. We are 50
people but the aeroplane travelling to that direction can only take one or two
people everyday. So by January some will still be here. It might be that we
may be away by Christmas, only we cannot give a definite date for security
reasons.

Man, I wrote to you some three or two weeks back, but I did not write about the route to be taken as I was waiting for a reply from trustworthy persons to whom we have written that side of Mafikeng. The safe route is this: you go to Mafikeng, on arrival there buses are boarded travelling to Pitsane-Molopo. When you are being asked what you intend doing, merely mention any surname that crosses your mind and say you are going to see that person, whether or not you furnish any reason why you are visiting that person. On arrival there the dividing fence runs through the location. That is, it divides this location in two; one portion is on that end, the other this end. But you must be very careful. On arriving there do not just ask anybody where the fence is if you have not seen it yet. If you have money you may bribe a youth, but make sure that you have raised no suspicion. After having jumped, go straight to the police here (Botswana) or inquire where the immigration office is and inform them you seek political asylum. When they ask what took you away from home, or what you are running away from, furnish a story which will sound reasonable for a person to run away from that end. Tell them that you want to come to Lobatse (Lubatsi for pronunciation purposes) because you know me and CHRISTIAAN MATEBANE. You must also inform us of the number of people coming so we can arrange accommodation and things like tickets, so as to enable them to proceed onwards. On this side we will expect people from 5 to infinity at the same time.

Nweyi, you must not come personally as I have work for you, but if you feel you can no longer stay there you may come. But the only thing is you must leave this information in safe hands, someone who will be in a position to organise young fellows coming here. Another thing, organize transport up to Mafikeng or Pitsane-Molopo for that matter, but we are at present waiting for a reply from the person who is to receive the young fellows at Mafikeng and take them to Pitsane-Molopo. So your job that end is to organise young fellows, not less than five a trip, and a car transporting them to Mafikeng.

I am not begging nor asking you in what I am saying, I am telling you. You may not even do it if you feel like it, but think of the nation (23.5 million). Let me disclose to you secretly where the destinations are: UGANDA, EGYPT, TANZANIA, LEBANON, finally to Peking (China) or Russia. So Nweyi]

Document 62. Account by unknown spectator of disturbance outside Johannesburg Magistrate's Court, March 18, 1976 (handwritten)

[The] court case of Sandile [Mfenyane], Malebelle [Molokeng], Amos [Masondo], Phumza [Dyanti], Kgoti [Molotsane], David [Nhlapo] and Bheki [Langa], is proving to be more dramatic than the Pretoria (SASO) trial. They are in fact popularising it through their inefficiency to handle crowds, especially [at] political trials.

After hearings, as usual, people moved out to the street to salute our accused Brothers and a sister but this day the police were supervising lifts so that people should not move out immediately, hence them quickly moving out our Brothers and Sister.

We used steps to move down and quickly went to the garage exit were we started singing, whilst waiting for the accused. Just like yesterday, passersby started to look and actually joining in the singing. It was lovely to see Black people joining in singing to boost the morale of those who would be left brotherless, fatherless, sisterless and also that of the accused Brothers and Sister.

Policemen (Black and White) came towards the people (from the garage to the street) waving batons only to be met by unshaken people who were not prepared to leave until the Brothers and Sister have left the court buildings. One Kolonel actually came to Phaks [and] said, "You people are making noise, we will arrest you for public disturbance, you must stop this singing and go home." Phaks told him we are waiting for the "accused" to leave and we are not going to leave before them.

People kept on singing until the van carrying our Brothers and Sister emerged from the exit. They were saluted by almost everyone around there, their fists emerging from the kwela-kwela [police van].

People started dispersing. Then a squad car with a police dog came and the Kolonel who was speaking to Phaks ordered the policeman to set this dog to the people, which he did. This attracted more people and the street was a mass of Black faces and a dog, [and a] few White police faces.

It was interesting to see Black policemen not committing themselves in this whole arrogancy against their people. This was clear white arrogancy with no black person involving himself on the side of Whites. They started the dog affair, they must finish it. (Dogs were the instruments of dispersing crowds in the countries occupied by Germany. Vorster's police and army like this method very much. It's used in every situation where blacks have grouped themselves against any injustice or in riots at the stad[ium?].)

Sandile's sister was chased by three policemen, (dressed in Gestapo kind of uniform.) She outran them but ultimately fell and was arrested. Then came Mefi [Murphy Morobe] who was also pointed at random and was chased, ultimately arrested after a two minute chase. Miki was also pointed at random and the police handling the dog was clearly heard when he said "Kill that bastard." He was arrested in a shop where he was hiding. They had a tough time in taking him to their car, they actually had to heave him into the car; as they drove off he gave a power salute through the window.

From there on I moved amongst the people listening to their comments which depicted the selflessness and frustrations of the Black masses as a whole but the most were inclined towards "Revolution is the only situation." Where people were just standing I politicised and stimulated discussions. Comments like *"Sies yizinja lezinto; after iRhodesia siyobathela, bayeza amaterroristi; qhubehang bana baka le bo ntate ba lona ne ba le tjena"* [These police are stinking dogs; after Rhodesia we will get them; the terrorists are coming; go on, children, even our fathers used to do just like you are doing] came out.

We started pamphleteering for the commemoration of the "Heroes Day" [March 21]. People actually demanded pamphlets, saying "*re yetla moho* [we are with you]." Jairus was picked up for pamphleteering [but] this did not intimidate us.

As people dispersed moving toward the [train] station they found the tax collecting truck and vented out their emotions and frustrations at it. Lynched the cops (I cannot tell what happened to the cash). Then all hell broke loose at the station. Black people stoning cops and police batoning and setting dogs at the people; one white civilian was beaten up [and] came out of those Black hands groaning and writhing in pains.

To further intimidate the people four young boys (soldiers) came clutching FN rifles. They were met with bricks, stones and cans. "Hot pursuit was really at Park Station." They were heckled, done all sorts of things so to expose their Black hatred, which they did very well.

All this "minor" spontaneous thing exposed the ill training of both their police and army and a revolutionary preparedness of the Black masses. They only need a powerful vanguard prepared to take up arms with the people for a showdown with the capitalistic Racists.

Never forget that the "duty of the Revolutionary is to seek revolution." People *must* have a strong revolutionary organ!

There is more drama anticipated tomorrow.

DOCUMENT 63. "The System and You." Article in *SASO Newsletter*, March/April 1976

Because of the rampant increase in the number of students and other concerned individuals being arrested or being taken in for questioning, it is about time students looked [at] the system's manner of operation. Someone may differ on my observations and assessments borrowed from other personal or literary sources. But this is how I figure it out.

Firstly let us concede to the fact that the System arrests people at random, so as to confuse the ranks and to serialize individuals, particularly the leadership.

(1) They'll make every attempt and try every effort to stir up anxiety, to instill guilt feeling through such statements as, "You are on the campus to study and not to let down your parents" or questions such as, "Why don't you work and stop being a parasite?"; or "Do you not feel for your parents/wife and children?"—so as to confuse you and let you not know what is going to happen to you next.

(2) The next step is to try and disrupt your normal behaviour patterns. That is why they'll call for you from your working place for interrogation or grab you in the street or wake you from sleep in the night. Several such questionings may take place before your eventual arrest.

(3) Tension may be increased in various other ways, like keying you up to trials which are constantly being adjourned or postponed.

(4) Arrest, should it take place, will be either in the wee hours of the night or in the street or at your place of work/study. In an effort to inject or increase fear.

(5) Even in custody they'll try to virtually cut you off from the outside world.

(6) Even when convinced of your righteousness, if you are weak or unstable, you may find yourself playing back (or signing) on your "old record," i.e. confessing "crimes" suggested by the system in earlier cross examinations.

(7) Where the system opts for a "sympathetic" approach they may suggest that you are too intelligent to have mixed with SASO, BPC, ANC, PAC, or any "Communist party inspired activities" without rhyme or reason but that perhaps you are frustrated and could still start afresh and "lead a normal life."

All the way the idea is to beat down your defences, to get you cornered, trapped (so they'll say, "here's a kaffir/coolie/bushy [insulting terms for African, Indian, Coloured] who thought he could be Castro/Mao/Guevara"). Sometimes sounds of a baby crying (in case of young fathers or mothers) or voices of people known to you may be heard from the cell. The idea being to create hysteria in your mind.

Counter Measures:

1. The old pointer that "a good pig is a dead pig for pork" should guide you. They want your soul either on pretended good or bad intentions. A wolf is a wolf, in sheepskin or out of it. Don't let them have your soul; so try to sharpen your mental balancing.
2. The struggle is life. Azania is our mother, our bread and soul. You are just a part of a greater mass of blacks in process of struggle. A mass that can be assured of final victory one day. So do not [flinch] in your convictions for eventual liberation.
3. Work for an intellectual, psychological and ethical upper hand against the System. The System is dirty. Let the System "feel" dirty at all levels or know what you think about it.
4. Do not allow emotions to get the better of you. Be cool, calculating and detached from your personal attachments wherever possible; but retain your black "soul."
5. There is no "poor adaptation to the social environment" in a repressive system. So don't let psychological terminology or vain insult fool you. It is not you who needs psychiatric treatment but your interrogator.
6. Have basic demands. You are human all the time. Hunger strikes, prison riots and other daring acts have come about because the individuals concerned refused to part with their humanness. There are times when a man has to refuse to be a mouse, simply because a man is never created a mouse. Only when he fails his social obligations does he join the world of mice.
7. The system is a brute. Be a better brute for your rights. This will give you a moral boost-up. Depending on your physical and moral preparedness,

set down your basic demands by gaining leverage above the system and keep a check on how you move step by step by not co-operating in any technique of conversion or psychiatric treatment.

8. Instead of giving any attention to the system concentrate mentally on some quite different problems and show contempt for everything systemish. You'll last longer.

9. Amuse yourself on scoring a point against attempts to corner you and be unpredictable in your responses.

10. Work on guerrilla strategies of attack and withdrawal according to your physical and mental condition, hitting hard against the system when the strength of body and mind is stronger and always moulding and polishing the will to resist. Make resistance an art. For the making of a revolution should by right be regarded as an art.

DOCUMENT 64. Letter from Bishop Desmond Tutu to Prime Minister John Vorster, May 8, 1976 (abridged)

The Hon. Prime Minister Mr John Vorster,
House of Assembly
CAPE TOWN   8000

Dear Mr Prime Minister,

This will be my second letter ever to you. In 1972 after I had been refused a passport to take up a post as Associate Director of the Theological Education Fund, I appealed to you to intervene on my behalf with the appropriate authorities. Your intervention was successful because soon thereafter, the then Minister of the Interior changed his mind and granted me and my family our passports. I am writing, therefore, optimistically in the hope that this letter will have similar happy results for all of us.

I am writing to you, Sir, in all deep humility and courtesy in my capacity as Anglican Dean of Johannesburg and, therefore, as leader of several thousand Christians of all races in the Diocese of Johannesburg. I am writing to you as one who has come to be accepted by some blacks (i.e. Africans, Indians and Coloureds) as one of their spokesmen articulating their deepest aspirations as one who shares them with equal steadfastness. I am writing to you, Sir, because I know you to be a loving and caring father, husband, a doting grandfather who has experienced the joys and anguish of family life, its laughter and gaiety, its sorrows and pangs. I am writing to you, Sir, as one who is passionately devoted to a happy and stable family life as the indispensable foundation of a sound and healthy society. . . .

I am writing to you, Sir, as one who is a member of a race that has known what is meant in frustrations and hurts, in agony and humiliation, to be a subject people. The history of your own race speaks eloquently of how utterly impossible it is when once the desire for freedom and self determination is awakened in a people for it to be quenched or to be satisfied with anything less than that freedom and that self determination. Your people against tremendous odds braved the unknown and faced up to daunting challenges and countless dangers rather than be held down as a subjugated people. And in the end they emerged victorious. Your people more than any other section of the white community must surely know in the very core of their beings, if they were unaware of the lessons of history both ancient and modern, that absolutely nothing will stop a people from attaining their freedom to be a people who can hold their heads high, whose dignity to be human persons has been respected, who can assume the responsibilities and obligations that are the necessary concomitants of the freedom they yearn for with all their being. For most blacks this can never be in the homelands because they believe they have contributed substantially to the prosperity of an undivided South Africa. Blacks find it hard to understand why the whites are said to form one nation when they are made of Greeks, Italians, Portuguese, Afrikaners, French, Germans, English, etc. etc; and by some tour de force Blacks are said to form several nations—Xhosas, Zulus, Tswanas etc. The Xhosas and the Zulus, for example, are much closer to one another ethnically than, say, the Italians and the Germans in the white community. We all, black and white together, belong to South Africa and blacks yield place to no one in their passionate love for this our beloved land. We belong together—we will survive or be destroyed together. Recently a multiracial soccer team represented South Africa against a visiting Argentinian side. The South African team won all hands down and perhaps for the first time in our sporting history South Africans of all races found themselves supporting vociferously the same side against a common adversary: The heavens did not fall down. Is it fanciful to see this as a parable of what will happen when all South Africans together are given a stake in their country so that they will be ready to defend it against a common foe and struggle for its prosperity vigorously and enthusiastically?. . .

I write to you, Sir, because like you I am deeply committed to real reconciliation with justice for all and to peaceful change to a more just and open South African society in which the wonderful riches and wealth of our country will be shared more equitably. I write to you, Sir, to say with all the eloquence I can command that the security of our country ultimately depends not on military strength and a Security Police being given more and more draconian power to do virtually as they please without being accountable to the courts of our land, courts which have a splendid reputation throughout the world for fairness and justice. That is why we have called and continue to call for the release of all detainees or that they be brought before the courts where they should be punished if they have been found guilty of indictable offences. There is much disquiet in our land that people can be held for such long periods in detention and often either be released without being charged or when charged are usually acquitted; but this does not free them from police harassment. Though often declared innocent by the courts, they are often punished by being banned or placed under house arrest or immediately re-detained. How long can a people, do you think, bear such blatant injustice and suffering? Much of the white community, by and large, with all its prosperity, its privilege, its beautiful homes, its servants, its leisure, is hagridden by a fear and a sense of insecurity. And this will continue to be the case until South Africans of all races are free. . . .

I am writing to you, Sir, because I have a growing nightmarish fear that unless something drastic is done very soon then bloodshed and violence are going to happen in South Africa almost inevitably. A people can take only so much and no more. The history of your own people which I referred to earlier has demonstrated this, Vietnam has shown this, the struggle against Portugal has shown this. I wish to God that I am wrong and that I have misread history and the situation in my beloved homeland, my mother country South Africa. A people made desperate by despair and injustice and oppression will use desperate means. I am frightened, dreadfully frightened, that we may soon reach a point of no return, when events will generate a momentum of their own, when nothing will stop their reaching a bloody denouement which is "too ghastly to contemplate" to quote your words, Sir. . . .

But we blacks are exceedingly patient and peace loving. We are aware that politics is the art of the possible. We cannot expect you to move so far in advance of your voters that you alienate their support. We are ready to accept some meaningful signs which will demonstrate that you and your government and all whites really mean business when you say you want peaceful change. First, accept the urban black as a permanent inhabitant of what is wrongly called white South Africa with consequent freehold white property rights. He will have a stake in the land and would not easily join those who wish to destroy his country. Indeed, he will be willing to die to defend his mother country and his birthright. Secondly, and also as a matter of urgency, to repeal the pass laws which demonstrate to blacks more clearly than anything else that they are 3rd rate citizens in their beloved country. Thirdly, it is imperative, Sir, that you call a National Convention made up of genuine leaders, (i.e. leaders recognised as such by their section of the community) of all sections of the community, to try and work out an orderly evolution of South Africa into a nonracial, open and just society. I believe firmly that your leadership is quite unassailable and that you have been given virtually a blank cheque by the white electorate and you have little to fear from a so-called right wing backlash. For if the things which I suggest are not done soon, and a rapidly deteriorating situation arrested, then there will be no right wing fear—there will be nothing. . . .

Please may God inspire you to hear us before it is too late and may he bless you and your Government now and always.

Should you think it might serve any useful purpose, I am more than willing to meet with you to discuss the issues I raise here as you say in Afrikaans "onder vier oe" [confidentially]. . . .

Yours respectfully

(Signed) Desmond M. B. Tutu

DOCUMENT 65. Minutes of the annual General Students' Council of SASM, Roodepoort, May 28–30, 1976

Venue: St. Ansgar's Conference Centre, Roodepoort
Date: 28th–30th May, 1976
Theme: Reconstruction towards Self-determination

AGENDA

Interim Executive
President: Vusi TSHABALALA
Vice President: Sipho Ciko MBATHA
Sec. General: Nkululeko XELITHOLE
Organising Sec.:   Zwelinzima SIZANI
Additional Members:
                    Themba MAJOKA
                    Kabelo MOFOKENG
                    Lesedi B. MASETLHA

Sittings:
28th May, 1976
   The President, Vusi TSHABALALA, opened the GSC formally and led the house in singing "Unzima lo mthwalo" ["This Burden is Heavy"].
   He then delivered his official Presidential Address (refer: Presidential address)
   Nadikoe T. [Tom] MANTHATA led GSC in a symposium on Campus Militancy.
   The Organising Secretary read the Executive Report and [it] was adopted. (refer: Executive Report)

GSC broke into three commissions:
   a. Education
   b. Policy
   c. Constitution

a. The Report on Education was adopted as presented.
b. The Commission on Policy presented the Black Students Manifesto of SASO as its report, which was adopted.
c. A new structure of the Executive Committee was proposed and accepted. A new portfolio that of Director of Publications was introduced and number five under "Powers and Duties of the National Executive Committee" was scraped off.

   In a symposium on Black Theology a paper was read by Puso K. KHUTSOANE [of SASO].

29th May, 1976
GSC sat to listen to a speech on Black Consciousness by Aubrey MOKOENA, thereafter the house broke into three commissions:
  a. Sport
  b. Culture
  c. Community Development

a. The report on Sport was adopted as presented
b. The report of this commission was in the form of a motion which was adopted.
c. [words missing] the house and the speaker on Black Consciousness' points on Community Development were acccepted as a guide for the Movement.

30th May, 1976
GSC broke into two commissions:
  i. Relations
  ii. Operation and Communication
Both these commissions' reports were adopted as presented.
The Commission on Planning sat, then a paper on the "History of the Struggle" written by Mr. [W. B.] Ngakane, was read by the Organising Secretary.

Elections:
Puso KHUTSOANE acted as the electoral officer.
The following were elected into the Executive Committee

President: Mzuvukile MAQETHUKA
Vice President: Gosebo MWALE (SHIFT)
Secretary General: Tebello MOTAPANYANE
Organising Sec.:   Zwelinzima SIZANI
Director of Publications: Similo MABHEKA (DESMOND)

GSC closed its deliberations by singing the National Anthem: "Nkosi Sikelel' i-Afrika."

MOTIONS
The following motions on current issues were tabled and were unanimously adopted by GSC

Afrikaans Strikes
That this GSC noting:
1. The recent strikes by schools against the use of Afrikaans as a medium of instruction is a sign of demonstration against schools' systematized producing of "good Industrial boys" for the powers that be,
2. The national implications of these strikes,

Therefore resolve:

1. To totally reject the use of Afrikaans as a medium of instruction.
2. To fully support the students who took a stand in the rejection of this dialect.
3. Also to condemn the racially Separated Educational system.

MOVER: MOTAPANYANE T.
SECONDER: HLATSHWAYO T.

Transkei:

That this GSC noting

1. the "independence" of the Transkei is "given" so as to "frustrate" and "divert" our struggle for national liberation,
2. the Transkei "independence" is a show case to the world by the Pretoria regime to serve its interest of catalyst ideology,

Therefore resolve:

To totally reject the independence of the Transkei and any other thing pertaining to it.

MOVER: MWALE G.
SECONDER: THEMBISA M.

Leslie SEHUME:

That this GSC noting,

1. the "famous flying object of Sport," Leslie SEHUME, will undertake his treacherous adventures in New Zealand [to publicize reforms in sports policy]
2. the warm "exposing" article in the *Vaderland,* "Ons stuur Swartman na N-Seeland" [We send Blackman to New Zealand] on the 30/5/76.

Therefore resolve,

1. to condemn intorte [in toto?] his mission as Anti-Black cause actions,
2. to inform him that his Judas Iscariot's actions won't in any way deter the struggle.

MOVER: SIZANI Z.
SECONDER: MATSHI S.

Culture:

That this GSC noting

1. our culture has been good to meet our needs all the times,
2. our culture has been polluted by Western Culture,

Therefore resolves,

1. to organise rural camps wherein urban students will have to live with rural families,
2. to encourage people to wear African garbs.

MOVER: NGEMA V.
SECONDER: HLATSHWAYO T.

Internal Security Bill:

That this GSC noting,

1. the provision of the I. S. [Internal Security] Bill and the likes are mere intimidatory laws planned by the powers that be to maintain the status quo,
2. Black people of Azania have been victims of these draconian laws from time immemorial,

Therefore resolve

1. to totally reject all such draconian laws,
2. to maintain blacks dignity and convictions irrespective of what the Pretoria regime legislates.

MOVER: MOTAPANYANE T.
SECONDER: MAQETHUKA M.

Presidential Speech

Black Brothers and sisters of Azania. Rightful owners of the fertile soil. Our issue at hand is one of the greatest of its nature, if not the greatest in the whole world. This means that we are the people mostly directed to the issue as opposed to other people. We are second to none towards changing South Africa into Azania. If we are second to none change won't come unless brought by us.

Again, Brothers and Sisters; though we are directly involved in this cause as Black people: We are much more involved as students. By so saying I am trying to pinpoint the slight difference of the level of engineering change as students and as laymen. The student has all the capacity to build and after to lead our cause with all the necessary diplomatic strategies at hand.

So, we are here today as a student, not to come and question or to come and ask the Executive of SASM about what is to be done; but to fulfill the obligation of Azanian students by jointly contributing in our struggle towards bringing the necessary change. Let us not take this conference as [a] most talked about social gathering where people meet one another for mere furthering of introductions or "popularity." Let us direct our thinking towards our cause as one organisation. By so saying I merely appeal to you to contribute as far as our brains can carry us.

Let us remove all the fear which might act as a stumbling block towards our obligatory task. I want to assure you that one must really fear nothing in doing the right thing. For the truth we shall stand irrespective of any bitterness encountered. For justice we shall stand irrespective of any evil spirits prevailing. For freedom we shall stand irrespective of any amount of torture involved. We shall not allow ourselves to be turned from our God who is not armed with a gun; our God who is armed with justice, truth and love; only to be incorporated to evil. We shall not allow ourselves to be separated from Him irrespective of the amount of money or partial freedom promised us by our oppressors. We shall rather die in His hands if death becomes the only alternative from sticking to the truth. Any way, death is the necessary end for human life. That is why our leaders decided to stay in Robben Island rather than coming to perform duties for Satan operating his hell at the Transkei, KwaZulu, and you name them. We shall not ignore them (leaders) in our daily struggle because they pioneered a great way for us. Leading us to freedom.

Should they have decided to do nothing; they should have landed on the "safe" side; getting Honorary doctoral degrees coupled with daily trips to America, like our pseudo-leaders, Gatsha Buthelezi, Matanzima and all who try to show us that the Bantu Homelands are here to stay.

Sons and Daughters of the soil; we are not here because we volunteered for the struggle to freedom; but because we are obliged by the thirst or need to struggle. The word itself (struggle) shows that no one must expect tortureless nursing or luxury like our pseudo-leaders. We have seen people getting paid for their traitorship, we have seen people being turned into dogs to bark and bite their own nations. That is why we (students) are daily barked at or threatened that we shall lose our Bantu education and rot in prisons if we involve ourselves in the task for liberation. Most unfortunate, some little number of students, who do not have objective and/or independent thinking minds have accepted this venom. They will thus tell you that they suspend the struggle for a while; until they complete their studies. This view is out. Every step of a Blackman is suffering. I wonder whether this student who suspends the struggle changes to the phase of freedom during the period of suspension; or he still suffers, but he does not want to respond because he is in the phase of suspension; non-involvement. Our struggle is not a part-time hobby.

Let our intellectual strongholds be the building pillars of the inevitable hotting of the struggle; without any cheating. It is undeniable that change is coming. Everyone hears the strong winds of change unless when he lacks sensory receptivity. The bells of history toll louder and louder everyday. They tell us that history will never at one stage come to a standstill. This is another emphasis of the coming of change. The Great Roman Empire fell. She thought she [was] too strong to an extent of not being shaken by anything. America was recently shown by Vietnam that pride comes before a fall. All these show that the advantages of change are on our side. We are fighting [a] winning battle, with our God on the other unused hand.

To our long detained brothers, I would like to say stick on. To our recently detained brothers and sisters, I would like to say hold tough. To our "just to be detained brothers," I would like to say change not. We want freedom. We shall rather be "free" in prison rather than serving evil spirits outside. To all the black students; let us flow with the current of liberation. We are all called. Those who shall come, or who shall take an opposite direction, shall be known. What shall happen to them, is not yet revealable. POWER!

Vusi Tshabalala

National Report
Interim Committee:

President	Vusi Tshabalala
Vice President	Ciko Sipho Mbatha
Secretary General	Nkululeko Xelithole
Organising Sec.	Zweli Sizani
Comm. Members	Billy Masetlha
	Kabelo Mofokeng

Not much has to be expected from this committee in that they only started working together from the beginning of this year after the movement's elected executive had been disturbed by the interference by special branch members [security police] through detentions, etc.

From the 1975 conference of SASM everything seemed to be working up fine, there was really co-ordination of work within the movement. The then National Executive was:

President	Vusi Tshabalala (Vaal Complex)
Vice President	Zuzile Cindi (E. Cape)
Organising Sec.	Nkosiyakhe [Amos] Masondo (Jhb.)
Sec. General	Billy Masetlha (Jhb.)

Through the everyday harassments from the Security Police in the eastern Cape especially on our Vice President we found ourselves having to do without one for they had forced him into exile. All this did not deter our Executives' courageous leadership.

The remaining three seemed to be working fine in that no one was co-opted into the Vice Presidency but this indirectly broke the communication between the Executive and the Eastern Cape Branch for quite some time.

In September, our Organising Secretary was detained and some of the Jo'burg branch members were either detained or forced into exile. The detention of Nkosiyakhe completely broke down the executive in that only two executive members remained and by then most students were preparing for their examinations so then not much could have been done. And we are here today without our Organising Secretary for he is serving a five year sentence.

The two remaining executive members co-opted four members whose names and portfolios are stated in the beginning of this year. So far we have been together.

Our top most duty was to work towards a GSC which it was agreed the Transvaal will have to host.

In the Vaal complex, after the President had left for Varsity together with other members, there was absolutely nothing doing in that area.

Johannesburg branch—we found no student wanted to meddle with it in view of the arrests and exiles experienced there. Students turned to sympathize with SASM and though everything was done to co-ordinate them but in vain.

In Natal everything had to be started from the beginning for little or none was known of SASM and it was only in the last few months that encouraging contact was made with students in the Pietermaritzburg area.

In the Eastern Cape SASM is met with enthusiasm by students though some tend to avoid it because of the 31 members who were detained and five of them have been charged under the famous Terrorism Act.

In this region we witness the speedy growth of branches established recently, namely, Tembalabantu [High School] (Zwelitsha), Nompendulo, Gold, Forbes, Kuyasa and Sehushe (Transkei). One of the most promising branches in the Eastern Cape is Healdtown [High School], [where] membership is growing at a fast rate.

This region has undertaken projects jointly with the local branch of Saso, due to lack of funds. At the moment this branch is involved in developing the [line illegible].

DOCUMENT 66. Speech by Winnie Mandela at launch of the Soweto Parents Association, early June 1976 (abridged)

On this occasion it is necessary from the onset to state that we are gathered here as fellow blacks in a black atmosphere in the black community, which has been designed for us without consulting us and against our wishes. We are not conforming to anybody's concept. In the same way we have to carry passes which we abhor because we cannot have houses without them, we cannot work without them, we are endorsed out of towns without them, we cannot register births without them, we are not even expected to die without them; so do we find ourselves in a situation where we have been made to accept the fact that only blacks have a right to speak for blacks and white for white. This is why we are gathered here not only to discuss common problems but also to rediscover ourselves, our dignity, and to instill in ourselves self-reliance and self-respect. . . .

We shall not delve into the finer aspects of our history at this stage. All we need remember is that not one city, one building, road, railway line was ever built without us. We have made our country what it is, we have dug up, and we are still digging, the wealth of our land—the gold, diamonds, coal, etc.— and surrendered these to the whites who own them by virtue of being white. As soon as we finished building up the cities the white man threw us out of them and designed the matchbox houses for us, these monotonous, depressing grey structures whose very appearance kills your soul. As we were housed in these we were simultaneously and systematically stripped of one right after another. . . .

Today we are meeting once more to re-examine ourselves, our role as parents, residents and citizens of our country. We are meeting at a crucial period in our history when race relations have deteriorated to the doldrums. Legislation for our separation from the whites has done a lot to unite us and drive us further and further apart from them. This has conscientised us and we have developed more than ever before black pride and black honour and we are recovering our black dignity. We are in the process of liberating our masses from white paternalism.

Our duty at this stage is to establish a black parents' organisation which will be truly representative of the urban residents without any ethnic or tribal affiliations, an organisation which will stand for us as we are, as parents in this meeting.

Events in our own locality have reduced us as parents to shame. . . . It is an absolute disgrace that our children fight battles for us whilst we run around looking for the actual tribal origin of these children before grave matters are attended to. There could not be a worse insult to our national home. . . .

Our duty is to fight for black solidarity, black unity and black respect. . . .

I now wish to call upon this house to resolve to form a residents association. . . , a body which will represent us as we are. Such an association's aim will be:

(1) To represent the Soweto residents at all levels;

(2) To bring about contact with other residents associations in other areas or assist in the formation of same where they do not exist, for the purpose of discussing common black problems and seeking a common solution;

(3) To promote contact with other organisations that may assist us in our problems common to us in view of the social structure imposed upon us;

(4) To draw up a Constitution through a Constitution Committee which this house should elect. Such a committee should, if need be, consult our legal adviser about the draft Constitution;

(5) To handle all matters affecting the Soweto residents as residents, and those in other areas in future, thereby catering for the interests of all the residents or blacks as a whole.

When such a body has been established it might be an idea to form a "Soweto Mothers' League" which would be part of the parent body. The role of women in such a body would be vital. There are problems that require women as women . . .

It is only when all black groups join hands and speak with one voice that we shall be a bargaining force which will decide its own destiny. This is the only way in which we shall manifest our oneness. We know what we want, our aspirations are dear to us. We are not asking for majority rule; it is our right, we shall have it at any cost. We are aware that the road before us is uphill, but we shall fight to the bitter end for justice. . . .

Let us leave this meeting with the spirit of rebirth, of purification from the humiliation of domination. If you are to free yourselves you must break the chains of oppression yourselves. Only then can we express our dignity, only when we have liberated ourselves can we co-operate with other groups. Any acceptance of humiliation, indignity or insult is acceptance of inferiority. We have to think of ourselves as men and women. As one quotation goes, "Once the mind is free, the body will soon be free."

In the name of those who have sacrificed their lives for the cause of the black man, let us launch the Soweto Residents Association [another proposed name was the Soweto Parents Association].

Amandla ngawetu.

Power to the people.

Document 67. Report by anonymous African on a public meeting, Jabulani Amphitheatre, Soweto, August 1, 1976

This meeting was the first after the Minister [of Justice] Jimmy Kruger had lifted the ban on open air meetings following the riots in Soweto by students, and it was a report back by the delegation of the Urban Bantu Councils (UBC), teachers and school board.

The meeting started by clapping of hands from the crowd estimated at 3000 parents, students and other members of the community. This clapping was not the formal opening of the meeting, but a sign of impatience from the people. For the meeting was scheduled to start at 10hrs00 and it was already 11hrs00.

There was some kind of indecision from the speakers as how they sit themselves, because they did not have any proper table or chairs set for the meeting, apparently they were not certain about this meeting so proper arrangements were not taken. Hence only two benches were available for about 20 delegates and megaphones were used.

From the set-up I predicted the meeting ending up with an indecision. Because it was the first UBC meeting I had attended, I was curious to see how would they meet not only the challenge but this "golden opportunity" that Jimmy Kruger had accorded them. To report back to people from all sides of Soweto. To prove their worthwhile—make resolution and be mandated by the people and to report back to (Jimmy), it was a chance in a life-time. I'm sorry to state here that it was a dismal failure.

The amphitheatre is an arc shape structure with the stage just at the pointers of this arc. The set up of the crowd—students occupied mostly the pointers that is near the stage and others were amongst the people (parents) in the center of the arc.

Mr. [T. J.] Makhaya the mayor of Soweto broke the ice with a brief report of the events prior to the riots, and told how some of the officials in the Bantu Education Department (BED) were intransigent as to the use of Afrikaans in school (viz) Mr. [W. C.] Ackermann regional director of Bantu Education who said he was merely implementing government policy of 50–50 medium of Afrikaans and English and who arrogantly told them that they were not academicians and therefore knew nothing about education. And during these talks the inspectorate went ahead enforcing the language issue in schools.

The supposed master of ceremony Mr. M. T. Moerane was booed through the whole meeting.

The second speaker Mr. Tshabangu took the megaphone and despite the promise made by Makhaya that questions will be asked somewhere between the proceeding, said he would like to answer straight away questions posed by the crowd of the detained students and he said Jimmy Kruger had told them that all students detained were released. He was told by angry voices that it was a lie and shame. They then demanded to see Kruger so he can tell them about these students, but the speaker told them that Kruger won't come to Soweto, the only place to see him is in the Cape or in Pretoria. The speaker was then told to sit down as there was nothing from him to report.

The third speaker Mr. [Lennox] Mlonzi almost made it, he opened by saying that we shall not rest or sleep until every student had been released. There were shouts of approval from the crowd. Mr. Mlonzi went further by saying they told Jimmy that the struggle is not today's, it was started in 1912 by the now banned ANC and PAC and that the grievances that reached their apex on the 16th of June started then (1912) even during the absence of the

Mandelas and Sobukwes who were tagged "agitators". All these were applauded by the crowd, until the speaker came to the thorny issue of the day. The appeal to students to go to school and the parents to help them do so. Despite a great deal of diplomacy used in the appeal such as "The schools are ours"—"we can't afford uneducated leaders such as Idi [Amin]"—"why whites don't burn their schools, they are learning whilst we are not"—"Go back to school whilst we parents are continuing to struggle," all these were rejected by the students. And I must say it killed the best speaker of the UBC, and of the day.

Then followed the teachers delegation which gave its account of their meeting with the Department and their urge to Students to go back to school. More speakers from the UBC, that they amongst other things asked for:

Police and their Hippos [armored vehicles] to be kept away from schools,
Equal pay for equal jobs irrespective of colour.
Recognition for Black trade unions.
Homeland citizenship to be scrapped.

By then people were restless and impatiently waiting to ask questions, make resolutions and mandate these representatives which things were promised by the representatives. But seeing that this time seemed to delay, one lady from the crowd asked to be permitted to address the people. She said in her speech when next the delegation meet Kruger, they should tell [him] that they as parents are not prepared to pay the sum of R50.00 which was said to be the pre-condition for the re-admission for the Fort Hare University students, and also that it is going to be used for the repairs of damages done. This was unanimously adopted by crowd.

Then the students were called to give their views about the situation. There was a spontaneous jump at the opportunity, and three Students gave their accounts, and they brought it to the parents that Afrikaans is just one aspect of the whole issue, therefore the starting point. And that the ultimate aim is to remove the tag "Bantu" from their education, further to draw the parents' attention to the fact that as long as the term "Bantu" prefixed their education they will continue to struggle to scrap it off even if it means more bloodshed. They told parents that their teachers were Bantu education orientated hence their urge for Students to go back to school. And that they (Students) have their future to consider and they envisaged a future minus oppression, and this cannot be achieved by the present kind of education and examples were cited such as job inopportunity and pay disparity despite the same educational qualifications between Blacks and Whites.

Lastly they drew both representatives' and parents' awareness to the fact that their failure prompted the Students to leave the desk and wage the bloody struggle of the 16th of June and subsequent days and dates, and that they are prepared to go on—uncompromisingly. Therefore the parents should go on with their yesteryear attitude of accepting the "status quo" and leave Students to do their thing.

And as I initially said that I expected the meeting to end with an indecision, truelly it were so. After the students had stated their case it was apparent to both UBC and parents that the new breed of African was a force to reckon with. Thus Mr. Makhaya tried to bulldozed people by asking them to sing the National Anthem to end the meeting. The meeting ended on a disorderly note, though there were no incidents, but people moreso Students were dissatisfied, because no definite conclusions were discussed.

When UBC and parents had left, Students remained and these are some of the things they said:

They doubted if the UBC really saw Kruger.

The report back was a lie.

That the UBC was sent by their *Baas* [boss] as detectors of the people's moods.

That they were used as "Human Barometers" and therefore sell-outs.

That they were a Useless Boys Club (UBC) which name Mr. Makhaya tried to refute on the Friday's newspaper (*World*). He claimed there were some organisations which were turning people against them by terming them these negative names, and he thought these organisations were doing it all for their political gains. But the Sunday's failure to contain and convince the masses confirm the uselessness of this boys club.

The question that came to me when I left the meeting was "to be or not to be" and I knew the answer was to be. That since the Students belled the cat and now I can hear him coming from afar and be ready, not for a scuttle, but for a blow.

DOCUMENT 68. Press statement by Tsietsi Mashinini, chairman of the Soweto Students' Representative Council, August 18?, 1976 (handwritten)

We, the SSRC condemn

1. Police action in Soweto by irresponsibly shooting at students on their way to school or black children playing in the location as it has been reported in the newspapers. We see it as an unofficial declaration of war on black students by our "peace-officers."

2. The statement by [Police Commissioner, General] Mr Gert Prinsloo that the racist regime will not succumb to the demands of a "handful [of] students." Instead we are the voice of the people and our demands shall be met.

3. The response by [Minister of Justice] Jimmy Kruger that he will not accept the B. P. A. [Black Parents Association] as the authentic body representing us. We see no peace and order if our demands are not met.

4. The statement by the Prime Minister that the racist regime "will not panic." We do not anticipate panic but expect responsible ACTION from the leaders of this country.

5. The action of elements burning schools. We believe that is no black man's action.

6. The brutality experienced by students in police hands especially those who have been recently arrested and released.

7. The abuse of power by security officers to refuse relatives to see detainees and demand a just investigation in the suspicious conditions in

which Mr Mapetla Mohapi died and we are afraid the same may befall our people detained in connection with the so called "riots."

I, Tsietsi Mashinini appeal on students to report back to school and notify the authorities of any injured, dead or missing students. We still have our end exams to write and we must have our priorities sorted.

8. We lastly condemn the detention of B. P. A. members and see it as an unwarranted move by the system. We never meant them to meet Mr Kruger in detention.

Ours is a peaceful struggle which only the racist regime can curb by a dialogue with our leaders.

DOCUMENT 69. "To All Residents of Soweto, Hostels, Reef and Pretoria." Flyer in English and Zulu by Soweto Students' Representative Council, September 7, 1976

WE SAY:
1. *REMEMBER YOU ARE ALL BLACKS:* Whether you are Zulu, Mosotho, Mopedi, Xosa, Shangaan, Motswana, Venda, etc. YOU ARE ONE: sons and daughters of the BLACK CRADLE.
2. YOU WILL NOT KILL YOUR BLACK BROTHERS, FATHER, MOTHER, SON OR DAUGHTER: stop fighting among yourselves. Stop killing each other while the enemy is going strong.
3. *DO NOT ALLOW YOURSELVES TO BE DIVIDED:* Be united to face the common enemy: APARTHEID, EXPLOITATION AND OPPRESSION.
UNITY IS STRENGTH !
SOLIDARITY IS POWER !
4. *BEWARE OF FALSE LEADERS:*
   They will always run in the dark to [Minister of Justice] Jimmy Kruger to sell out the true sons and daughters of the Black nations. They are tools and stooges of the oppressive system.
5. *BEWARE OF POLITICAL OPPORTUNISTS:*
   Who will always agitate Black people for their own ends.
   They are cowards who cannot face the enemy by themselves.
   They want to use us.
   They will always spread false rumours in the name of students.
6. WE SAY TO ALL BLACK STUDENTS, RESIDENTS AND HOSTEL INMATES:
   You know your true leaders.
   Listen to your leaders.
   Support your leaders.
   Follow your leaders.
7. TO VORSTER AND KRUGER: WE REPEAT OUR DEMAND:
   (a)   RELEASE ALL STUDENTS AND BLACK LEADERS IN DETENTION;
   (b)   Scrape off BANTU EDUCATION. It is poison to our minds.
   (c)   Away with the oppressive system of APARTHEID;
   Separate development means DEATH to Black peoples' economy and political life.

(d) Consult with our parents and Black leaders to settle the present school and political crisis.

8. ALL STUDENTS IN THE LOWER, HIGHER, SECONDARY AND HIGH SCHOOLS

—MUST GO BACK TO SCHOOL.

—Teachers must start teaching and stop wasting time discussing about us and not with us.

—Our struggle is NON-VIOLENT.

—You are neither duplicate nor carbon copy of your father or mother.

—Where our fathers failed, we shall succeed.

—Our future is in our hands!

"UNITED WE STAND
DIVIDED WE FALL"

[Reverse side:]

Kwizakhamuzi zase Soweto nase mahostela
ASIKHUMBULENI UKUTHI SIMNYAMA SONKE.

1. Noma ungaba ngumZulu, ngumSuthu, ngumPedi, ngumXhosa, njalonjalo.

2. Asingabulalani sodwa ngoba sizobe sijabulisa uKruger namaphoyisa akhe.

SONQOBA SIMUNYE!
AMANDLA NGAWETHU!

3. QAPHELANI ABAHOLI BAMANGA:

Balokhu begijima ebumnyameni bethengisa ngathi ku Jimmy Kruger.

Basetshenziswa ngabelungu ekubeni basicindezele ngokweqile.

4. QAPHELANI ABAKHOHLISI:

Badla ngathi ngokusithengisa emaphoyiseni.

Bangamagwala asaba ukubhekana nesitha sethu:

Baqamba amanga ngegama lezingane zesikolo.

5. KININA NONKE SITHI:

   i   Niyabazi abaholi benu bempela.

   ii Lalelani abakushoyo.

   iii Yazini nendlela abazidele ngayo, bengasabi 'kufa nakuvalelwa ejele.

   iv Isikhalo sabaholi bethu ngesethu nathi.

   v Lokhu abakulwelayo sokujabulela sonke uma sebekuzuzile.

   vi Asibakhuthazeni, sibalandeleni sibe moya munye khona sizohlula.

6. KU KRUGER NO VORSTER SITHI:

Khiphani abaholi bethu ejele kanye nezingane zesikole.

Imfundo ye Bantu Education ngushevu ezingqondweni zethu, asiyifuni.

Umthetho oyincindezelo we Apartheid awususwe.

Yekani abaholi bethu nikhulume nabo.

ZITSHUDENI BUYELANI EZIKOLWENI!
BOTHISHA FUNDISANI BO!

ASIHLANGANENI MA-AFRIKA SINGALWI SODWA KHONA SIZONQOBA

DOCUMENT 70. "Azikhwelwa on Monday." Flyer by Soweto Students' Representative Council calling for a stay-away from September 13, 1976

The people of South Africa are going into the third phase of their struggle against the oppressors, namely: Operation Azikhwelwa!!

The racists in our last demonstration—called by the cynics a riot—lost millions of rands as a result of the people not going to work. Thus they thought of immediately breaking the student-worker alliance. They immediately called on workers to carry knob-kieries and swords to murder their own children—who are protesting for a right cause.

Parent workers you should take note of the fact that if you go to work, you will be inviting Vorster to slaughter us your children as he has done already. Vorster and his gangsters have already claimed that last week's shootings were made to protect you, our own parents, from us, your own children. You are giving Vorster a pretext for murdering us. Please do not allow Vorster to instigate you to murder your own children—let him do his dirty and murderous job without making you a scape-goat. We want to avoid further shootings—and this can be done by you keeping at home without being stopped.

We want to write Exams, but we are not so selfish as to write even if our brothers are being killed at John Vorster [John Vorster Square police headquarters]. Parents, you should rejoice for having given birth to this type of a child. A child who prefers to fight it out with the oppressors rather than to be submerged in drunkeness, frustration and thuggery. A child who prefers to die from a bullet rather than to allow a poisonous education which relegates him and his parents to a position of perpetual subordination. Aren't you proud of the soldiers of liberation you have given birth to? If you are proud, support them! Do not go to work on Monday.

Do not shiver and think that we have wasted a year. This year will go down in history as the beginning of the end of the oppressive systems, the beginning of the end of the oppressive conditions of work in South Africa.

Vorster is already talking of home-ownership for Blacks in SOWETO. This is a victory achieved because we, the students, your children, decided to shed their blood. Now for greater victories: the scrapping of BANTU EDUCATION, the RELEASE of Prisoners detained during the demos [demonstrations], and the overthrowal of oppression, we the students call on our parents to stay at home and not go to work from Monday.

Parent-workers, heed our call, and stay away from work. We the Black society have nothing to lose from Operation Azikhwelwa, but our chains. Let our oppressors tremble! The people of South Africa are resolved—in one word they will be crying: "KRUGER, RELEASE OUR CHILDREN"

"Racists We Won't Abort OUR CHILDREN by Going to Work!"

"We won't MURDER Our CHILDREN With Knob-Kieries!"

Our slogan is: AWAY WITH VORSTER!!! DOWN WITH OPPRESSION!!! POWER TO THE PEOPLE!!!

When have this criminal Vorster cared for you? Didn't he order for killing of twelve [mine] workers in Carletonville? Were not dogs called when in Croesus people went in Strike? Were not pregnant women strangled and battered to near death by Vorster's police thugs at the "HEINEMANN FACTORY"?

AZIKHWELWA MADODA!!!! Kufayayo Bazali Yinile! [Don't ride, people!!!! He who goes dies, parents!]

Document 71. "To Town!!! To Eloff!!! To That Exclusive White Paradise!!! From Monday!!!" Flyer by Soweto Students' Representative Council announcing demonstration on September 23, 1976

This will be the new step—the fourth in series—by the revolutionary people of South Africa. Countrymen, the liberatory struggle has brought a new phase, namely the shattering of the myth that the Coloureds are more white than black. The killing of many of them in Cape Town and their stand, together with their African brethren to rock the centre of the oldest city, that symbol of white occupation of our country—Cape Town—is the greatest victory and marks another step in the development of a people, namely, to each one of them, the consciousness of oppression irrespective of degree. Divide and Rule was dealt its death blow in Cape Town.

Johannesburg or Soweto, the capital and the supposed centre of this National Drive, has already lagged behind the country-side. The heart of Cape Town city—Adderley Street—was rocked by revolutionary demonstrators. Are we made of a different metal from them? Surely Not! they are mortals like ourselves. But their discontent about the present oppressive structure has made them bold. They burnt buildings, they took possession of what was forcefully raped from them a number of years ago. They did not plead for wealth any more. They brought so much panic to the already frightened whites that all guns obtained in public market were sold out.

Police re-inforcements were called as far afield as Johannesburg. Therefore we are in the process of selling out the country-side, which we have stirred to revolt, only two months ago, for we failed to keep busy our local police to such an extent that they are free to murder elsewhere.

Countrymen, this is not yet the time to retreat. Surely not at a time when two universities have reduced their institutions to ashes to support the revolution. Surely not when everybody conscious has been arrested, surely retreat is impossible when our fellow brothers studying in the country-side have razed their schools to the ground and closed them for the rest of the year. These people also value their education but have abandoned it for a better cause—namely the elimination of oppression. We cannot retreat to the classrooms unless we can reverse the whole course of events this year. And Reversing The Tide Is Tantamount To TREACHERY.

We cannot succumb to the threats of this wounded and vicious bull Vorster. Already his police thugs are demanding passes at gun point. Already rents have gone higher. Are these concessions. No! Surely lets move forward, Vorster must not delude himself and think that we will stop anywhere short of freedom. Let us not betray the nation by pursuing selfish ends like writing Exams. If we profess to be leaders, the first and indispensable character is: Independent Thought and Moral Courage. If we are still looking for favours from [Minister of Bantu Education] M. C. Botha to recognise us as matriculants it simply means that we are not independent—but like Gatsha Buthelezi who is paid by Vorster we also want Vorster Matriculation Certificates. To Hell with Paper! a Certificate! the Certificate we want now is our land and for that we shall fight till the bitter end. CRIMINAL VORSTER Keep your Certificates and give us back our land. Give us back our birth rights—we won't exchange them for a paper of enslavement. Education is itself good, but the first school for an oppressed people is a revolution.

TO TOWN!! To Johannesburg!! that pride of the white racists will be rocked by the revolutionary people. From MONDAY Eloff [Street] and the surroundings will be the operational area for the people are resolved and have taken the fate with their leaders, to their own hands. The counter-revolutionaries and traitors and all those who are tired will call us the Tsotsi element but we call ourselves the Revolutionary Force in Society.

TO TOWN! Town will be centre of the demos [demonstrations]. We did it early this year and the SASO trial was transferred by the Racists to Pretoria. They have done it in Cape Town! What will Stop Us Now? TO TOWN is the slogan of the people in revolt. It is the very cry of an oppressed but determined people. It is a slogan of the most deprived part of humanity.

Trains will [be] boarded not for work—but for a violent Demonstration of our bitterness. TO TOWN FELLOW COUNTRYMEN.

POWER TO THE PEOPLE . . !!

Document 72. "To All Fathers and Mothers, Brothers and Sisters, Friends and Workers, in All Cities, Towns and Villages in the Republic of South Africa." Flyer in English and Sesotho by the Soweto Students' Representative Council, October 15, 1976

We appeal to you to align yourselves with the struggle for your own liberation. Be involved and be united with us as it is your own son and daughter that we bury every week-end. Death has become a common thing to us all in the townships. There is no peace, there shall be none until we are all free.

1. Soweto and all Black townships are now going into a period of MOURNING for the dead. We are to pay respect to all students and adults murdered by the police.
2. We are to pledge our solidarity with those detained in police cells and are suffering torture on our behalf.

3. We should show our sympathy and support to all those workers who suffered reduction of wages and loss of jobs because they obeyed our call to stay away from work for three days.
4. We should stand together and be united in the demand:
   CHARGE OR RELEASE ALL POLITICAL PRISONERS!
5. WE MUST BE FREE!

OUR CALL IS: ALL THINGS THAT WE ENJOY MUST BE SUSPENDED FOR THE SAKE OF OUR KIDS WHO DIED FROM POLICE BULLETS.
- NO CHRISTMAS SHOPPING.
- NO CHRISTMAS CARDS.
- NO CHRISTMAS PRESENTS.
- NO CHRISTMAS PARTIES.
- NO SHEBEEN [speak-easy] DRINKING.

Let us, your kids, for the first time, neither buy nor put on any new clothes for Christmas or New Year.

The year 1976 shall go down into our history as the YEAR OF MOURNING, the year that flowed with sweat, blood and tears for our liberation.

We shall demonstrate this solidarity and sympathy with those who lost their lives and their wages and jobs by:

NO MORE GOING TO DO SHOPPING IN THE FOLLOWING:
ALL CLOTHING SHOPS
ALL FURNITURE SHOPS
ALL BOTTLE STORES
ALL TOY SHOPS
ALL RECORD SHOPS, etc.

We appeal to all Parents, Workers and Students, and all Shebeen dealers to obey this call. We cannot find happiness in death.

We cannot CELEBRATE!

N.B. Your sons and daughters and all Black leaders shall be on the watch-out for sell-outs and traitors of the Black struggle!
"UNITED WE STAND"

[Reverse side:]

HO BOHLE BO NTATE, BO MME, BARENA LE DIKHAETSEDI, METSWALLE LE BASEBETSI KAOFELA METSENG, DITOROPONG LE HOHLE HOHLE REPUBLIKING:

Re sa boela re le kopa hoba le rona ntweng ena ya tokoloho, bitsong la bana ba lona ba bolokwang beke le beke, ba bolaiwa ke maponesa metseng le ditoropong. Khotso ha eyo, ebile ha eno ba teng ha feela re sa fumane tokoloho lefatsheng la bo rona.

1. Re tshwanela ho llela batho bohle ba ileng ba bolawa ke maponesa ka sehloho teronkong, bana ba dikolo le batho ba baholo.
2. Re hopoleng ba phediswang ha bohloko ka chapo tshankaneng ke maponesa.

3. Re bontsheng kutlelo-bohloko ho bohle ba senyehetsweng ke mesebetsi le meputso ya bona ka ho mamella khoeletso ya setshaba hore ba se ye mesebetsing matsatsi a mararo.

4. Re be Ntswe-leng rere: "LOKOLLANG KAPA AHLOLANG BATSWARIWA BOHLE!"

KOPO YA RONA KE ENA:
- Ho se rekelwe bana Keresemese.
- Ho se rekwe dikarete tsa Keresemese.
- Ho se khabiswe matlo a rona ka Keresemese.
- Ho se rekwe diporosente tse ntsha ka matsatsi a Keresemese.
- Ho seke ha iwa diSHEBEENING le botahweng.
- Selemong sena hareno ithabisa ka Keresemese.

Selemo sena ho rona ebe sa ho ila bitsong la madi a tsholotsweng ka bongata bathong ba batsho. Re lla dikeledi tse keleketlang marameng a rona; mefufutso e tsholohile tshabeng sa rona ho lwanela tokoloho ya tshaba se setsho, ya bana ba AZANIA.

Re tla bontsha boitelo le tiisetso ntweng ena ka ho itima ntho tse monate le menyakallo ka ho se reke phahlo tsa Keresemese mabenkeleng:
- OHLE A DIAPARO
- OHLE A DIFENISHARA
- OHLE A DINO (BOTTLE STORES)
- OHLE A DITOY TSA BANA

BATSWADI LE BASEBETSI BOLOKANG TSHELETE TSA LONA.

Tsebang hore re tla be re le shebile ka mahlo a ntshontsho lona Batswadi le bana ba sekolo, le lona beng ba di-Shebeen bohle ho phethisa kopo ena ya rona. Mahlaba-phiyo a tla ipontsha.

RE KA KETEKA JWANG RELE BOFIFING.
RE KA THABA JWANG RE LE DILLONG TSA BANA BA RONA!
"KOPANO KE MATLA!"

DOCUMENT 73. Press release by Khotso Seatlholo, chairman of the Soweto Students' Representative Council, October 29, 1976

There are a few points which, on behalf of the Black youth and students of South Africa, I wish to make clear—what we think about them, and what our stand is.

It is a pity that I speak at a time when there is no happiness in the Black community; at the crucial moment when the whole country is plunged into a period of unrest and bloodshed. This is the time when the whole of Black Azania has gone into mourning for their dead sons and daughters who have been killed by White police gangsters. Yet, at this serious moment when Rome has gone up in flames, the Hon. Chief Kaiser Matanzima and other stooges of the South African Government, have decided to go feasting with meat and wine while their Black brothers are being shot and killed at their grave yard.

I wish to start with the most recent event, which is:

TRANSKEI INDEPENDENCE: 26th Oct, 1976

The Black youth of Azania totally reject the whole idea of the independence of the Transkei; and that of any Homeland. We see this as the final product of the policy of Separate Development, and the culmination of a political fraud. We see Chief Matanzima as being seduced by the White racist Government to fall for the political joke of the year. We regard him as a betrayer of Black peoples political aspirations by selling out our birthright to the White minority Government.

We reject the policy of Separate Development in toto. We are opposed to the fragmentation of our Mother-land into some ethnic political entities that are neither politically nor economically viable. We see this policy as the basis for the creation of tribal colonies that would still remain in all aspects dependent on the main colonial power, the so-called White South Africa. Our fear is that this might be the creation of rivalries that might end up in the creation of another "Biafra" tribal conflict in South Africa.

Besides, we are simply opposed to the division of the Black nation into some ethnic sovereign states. We see this as the breaking of Black solidarity and power. We see it as the "divide and rule" method designed to subjugate Black people politically and otherwise. Blacks in the Homelands shall, forever, remain subservient to the White Government; and they will be used as tools for cheap labour in order to maintain the White man's economic power and political domination.

We take the acceptance of the policy of Separate Development by the so-called Homeland leaders as shameful give-in and a betrayal of the Black struggle for the achievement of political freedom and economic independence. We see the step that Matanzima has taken as a grave act of political blunder that we, the youth of today and even those of the coming generation shall never forgive him.

We thus do not recognize the Transkei Independence as meaning anything to us and the Black people as a whole. To us, Azania belongs to us in whole. It is our land. It is our birthright. All the wealth of Azania belongs to all its citizens irrespective of ethnic group, race or colour of the skin. We have an inalienable right to live and die on this land. We shall not accept any policy that is designed to rob us of our birthright.

Therefore, we see the Hon. Chief Matanzima, the so-called Prime Minister of the Transkei, and the rest of the Homeland leaders as political cowards, stooges and puppets who could not hold their own in the fight and defence of their birthright.

They are sell-outs who were just too ready to capitulate to the oppressor and collaborate with the exploitative, oppressive and suppressive system.

They shall go down into annals of Black history as Judas Iscariots who sold the Black nation down a political drain.

The blood of our brothers and sisters who died in the struggle for the liberation of Blacks shall be on their heads until eternity. We shall carry on with the fight for our freedom and ultimate peace in this country.

PRESENT UNRESTS

Many people, including the Vorster Government, [Minister of Justice] Jimmy Kruger's police and some fascist Government's secret agents, have attributed the present unrests in Soweto and all over the country, to the ANC, PAC or some subversive Communist organisations. Some Government officials have even had the guts to point a finger at the Black Consciousness movements who have to date operated overboard in broad day light. If this be true that the above organisations are the cause of upheavals, then we take off our hats for the South African Security force. They seem to be efficiently inefficient in their detective work. They deserve a Noble Price for being too fast to accuse, and faster to find a scapegoat.

We tried to locate symptoms of the above revolutionary organisations, we failed. We worked hard to unearth the communist agitators who caused so much loss of life and bloodshed in our peaceful Black community, we found none. Then our main task was to find the real cause of the unrest and riots all over the country. We found it. It was glaring right into our face—it was the *WHITE FASCIST MINORITY GOVERNMENT OF JOHN VORSTER* and his gang of pro-nazi Ministers.

It is a pity that Mr Kruger and his security police could not see this monstrous beam in his regime's eye and racial policies. When we were born, we found our fathers struggling under the yoke of oppression. We found ourselves ushered into a socio-economic and political situation which was neither of our father's nor of our making. Black people have never been consulted in the making of laws that are today oppressing us; and have made South Africa the stink-cat (meerkat) of the world. We cannot afford to be ostracised from the world community because of no fault of our own. We strongly reject the subservient heritage that our fathers have handed down to us. Our fathers stood up to speak and fight for their rights, they were given Robben Island as eternal place of residence. Their peaceful pleas were answered with ruthless violent acts of suppression, and they lived on as a politically crippled nation.

We came. We saw. We judged and ACTED or REACTED to the whole system of oppression discriminatory racist laws. We refuse to bend down that the White man can ride on our back. We have the full right to stand up erect and reject the whole system of apartheid. We cannot accept it, as our fathers did. We are neither carbon nor duplicate copies of our fathers. Where they failed, we shall succeed. The mistakes they made shall never be repeated. They carried the struggle up to where they could. We are very grateful to them. But now, the struggle is ours. The ball of liberation is in our hands. The Black student shall, fearlessly, stand up and take arms against a political system which is stinking with immoral policies that we have found distasteful and unacceptable to us. We shall rise up and destroy a political ideology that is designed to keep us in a perpetual state of oppression and subserviency. We shall oppose the economic system that is keeping us in non-ending state of poverty. We shall not stand a social system of discrimination that has become an insult to our human dignity. We shall reject the whole system of Bantu Education whose aim is to reduce us, mentally and physically, into "hewers of wood and drawers of water" for the White racist Masters. Our whole "being" rebels against the whole South African system of existence, the system of apartheid that is killing us psychologically and physically. The type of education we receive is like poison that is destroying our minds.

It is reducing us into intellectual cripples that cannot take seat within the World community of academics. It is killing inherent sense of creation in us and thus, it is frustrating us.

Twenty years ago, when Bantu Education was introduced, our fathers said: "half a loaf is better than no loaf." But we say:" half a Gram of poison, is just as killing as the whole gram." Thus we strongly refuse to swallow this type of Education that is designed to make us slaves in the country of our birth.

The Afrikaans question that made us to stand together, as students, in one Solidarity to voice our grievances, was just but "Achilles heel" in the whole system of Bantu Education. The enforcement of Afrikaans as a medium of instruction was the last straw on the camel's back.

We wish to remind the government that it was the extra charge of a tickey (3d) that broke the British Empire (Boston Tea Party). In the same manner, through the rejection of Afrikaans we are prepared to break the spine of the whole immoral White Apartheid Empire. Morality and the World is on our side. Black Students are determined to die for the Fatherland, the land of AZANIA. The White fascist regime shall be blamed for all the blood shed and misery that shall take place in this country.

The main causes of the present unrests are:

(1) The White racist government's discriminatory racial policies. They have caused unbearable suffering to many Blacks socially, economically and politically.

(2) The White man's arrogance in their refusal to listen to Black man's grievances; and their unpreparedness to consult with Blacks in the making of laws that govern the country.

(3) Lack of contact and communication between Black and White at local and National levels because of the Apartheid policy.

(4) The White man's avarice and readiness to amass all the economic wealth in the country and keep Black races in a perpetual state of destitute and poverty. We cannot live on charity and patronisation by Whites.

(5) The undermining of the Students' Power and their determination to free themselves from the oppressive system of education and Government.

If Mr Vorster, Jimmy Kruger, [Bantu Education Department official, W. C.] Ackermann and all their gangsters had paid attention to our cry and warnings by our parents and Black leaders, there would never have been any riots in the country. Instead, they became stubborn. They used ruthless methods of oppression. They arrested, detained, imprisoned or banned nearly all our political and even Cultural leaders. They drove us like dumb cattle to jails. They thought they had solved the problem. What a mistake! Anyway, those whom the gods wish to destroy, they first make them mad. The White government is on the brink of insanity. Our task is how to save them, and thus save the whole of South Africa—the land of AZANIA.

RIOTS, STRIKERS AND SHOOTINGS

(1) When Adolf Hitler's Nazi Government liquidated the Jews in the "Final Solution," the whole world rose up in arms to crush the Nazis because lives of a White race were in jeopardy.

(2) When Idi Amin threatened to take the life of Mr [Denis] Hills in Uganda, the whole World raised a furious cry because a White skin was in danger.

(3) When a White Doctor was killed during the Soweto riots on June 16th 1976 the White press, local and overseas, played the murder for weeks on end because White blood had been shed.

(4) The destruction of West Rand Board's and government property: Beerhalls, Bottle Stores and the bombing of the Jabulani Police Station, received more publicity and emphasis because the White man's property had been destroyed.

The World abhored Hitler's atrocities, the cruelty of Idi Amin and the heartlessness of students in the killing of just one White doctor and the wanton destruction of symbols of White oppression.

But, when Jimmy Kruger's White terrorists shot down the innocent, defenceless school children in a peaceful demonstration when they killed our colleagues in the streets, on the football grounds in the school yards, classrooms and even in the grave yards, the whole World goes silent because the 10 year old child was throwing stones at the well-armed white police; and the police had no altenative but to shoot in self-defence(?).

The police who were attacked by the Black mob with some stones and brick missiles, have such strong hippo skins that these stones had to bounce back like rubber balls without leaving any wounds.

Still, it was the Black child that was shot down. It was the Black skin that was destroyed. It was the Black life that was taken in defence and protection of the burning car, the beer hall or bottle store that went up in flames. It is nothing!

It was all done in self-defence—In defence of a system that does not value human life, especially if that life is Black.

It was in the defence of the White racist system and policies that have turned the land of AZANIA into a blood bath. These incidents show a clash of sense of values between the Black and White races of South Africa.

For the last four months of unrests in Soweto and other areas, apart from the destruction of the White man's property in the Black man's ghetto, Blacks have neither killed nor harmed any Whites. We took our demonstration right into the heart of Johannesburg City, we shed no White blood. We proved our degree of discipline, dignity and value of human life whether it be Black or White.

If there were any casualties, they were very minor. But, the White South African Police have shot and killed hundreds of my Black brothers and sisters; they shot, wounded and maimed thousands of Black school children and adults; their prison cells are teeming with hundred thousands of Black students and leaders detained or imprisoned for having dared to oppose the Monster-Policy of Apartheid.

Black students have never taken any human life; but White police have triumphed in assault and murder of harmless kids. This is a proof to us Blacks that Whites value material property more than human life. They are materialists—a godless race that find pleasure in the violation of human or christian values. They are sadists who derive satisfaction in the shedding of human blood. They are worse than Communists.

We organise a peaceful march protest against the use of Afrikaans in our schools, they levelled guns at us and shot us down. We called upon a non-violent peaceful stay-at-home strike, they mobilised Black hostel inmates to club us to death and smash our houses and furniture. They set Black to kill Black. We neither begrudge nor feel any bitterness against our poor Black brothers in the hostels. We know it that they have been mentally raped, seduced and corrupted by the Police agitators of Jimmy Kruger. We forgive them.

We held the within-campus protest against the visit of [American Secretary of State] Dr Henry Kissinger to South Africa, then [they] shot and killed our brothers in the school yards. They slaughtered six students plus a Black housewife who was hanging washing in her yard for the reception of Dr Kissinger. And, the so-called American peace-maker never uttered a word of protest at this atrocity and bloodshed.

We carried our dead, whom they killed in the streets or prison cells, to bury, they opened fire at us at the grave-yard—killing further more seven including one of our most respectable Funeral undertakers, Mr Sydney Kgaye. They desacreded the dead without even a sense of shame or remorse. We cannot even bury our dead brothers without fear of arrest or death. Shall we leave them to rot in the streets like dogs, cats or rats?

Our fathers know what the White man has done for them. They know the good things that Whites did for them. The White man gave them jobs, *banzela* money [small bonuses], second hand clothes—and he did them many other favours. Our fathers may forgive Whites. But, there is only one thing that I, as a Black student and Youth of this country, know. That is: the White police shot and drove a bullet through the head and brain of my 10 year old brother. That the White police shot and killed hundreds of my colleagues; that they shot, wounded and maimed my father, mother, brother and sister at the graveyard; that they terrorise the streets of my ghetto and I can find no peace to rest my head.

This is what I know of the White man; and I cannot forgive him. I smelled the smoke of a gun. I felt the sting of a bullet. I tasted blood. I suffered wounds. I saw death snarling into my face. I became a fugitive in the country of my birth. I cannot forget. I can't forgive the White man.

The struggle for my freedom shall go on until each and every one of us drops dead. This is a vow, the vow that the Black youth have taken over the dead bodies, and written with the blood of our wounded brothers.

Thus, from Nov. 1st–5th 1976, we are calling upon all Blacks of Azania: coloured, Indians and Africans to go on a 5 day National Stay-at-home Strike. This call must be obeyed by all parents, students and workers. We also call upon all police to join us, to park their hippos [armored vehicles] and remain peacefully in their barracks. Businessmen should not interfere with Workers and thus cause confrontation between us and them.

In this national strike, we call upon Mr John Vorster, Jimmy Kruger and their White fascist, racist, oppressive regime to:

(a) Resign en bloc

- They have mismanaged the rule of Azania. They have plunged the country into violence, blood bath, loss of human life.

- They killed thousands of Black children and thus causing racial hostility in our peaceful country.

(b) Release all political detainees—Students and Black leaders rotting in your jails all over the country.

(c) Open detente with our Black parents in order to plan a future South Africa where there shall be justice, happiness and peace for all.

(d) Stop killing our brothers in the ghetto. We are prepared to stop unrest as soon as you take a move towards consultation, settlements and peace.

To all black people of Azania we say:
Take heart, have courage.
Victory is ours!
SOLIDARITY AND POWER!
AMANDLA!

Document 74. "Message for 1977—To Those in Authority and to White South Africa." Leaflet by the Ministers' Fraternal of Langa, Guguletu and Nyanga, Cape Town, January 1977

At the beginning of this new year we, the Ministers of various denominations in Langa, Guguletu and Nyanga, feel called to address ourselves to those in authority and to White South Africans generally. We do so in the name of Christ, who came to save mankind and set us free. (Gal. 5.1)

"And when Jesus saw the city he wept over it saying: 'Would that even today you knew the things that make for peace.'" (Lk. 19.41 f.)

It is tragically apparent that the Government presently in power still refuses to heed the things that make for peace. Too many of our people have been killed. We will continue to remember them and their families. Too many innocent people have been detained, and we have heard too many reports of young people being beaten up.

> "They crush thy people O lord and afflict thy heritage . . . and they say The Lord does not see! . . . " (Ps. 94)

Instead of hearing the cry for justice—a cry which God has spoken since his Prophets of old—instead of listening and heeding and obeying God's demands voiced in the Bible and in his people today—this Government has responded with Pharoah-like hardness of heart. In spite of all the upheavals, no significant changes have been made. The following are some of the issues requiring immediate attention and action:

1. *Students and Bantu Education: Scrap differentiated education.* Except for a few concessions, e.g. on the use of Afrikaans, the supply of free books to some forms [grades], and provision for a greater number of elected members on school boards, the detested Bantu Education system continues with inadequate adaptations. We wish to reaffirm our support of those students who have called for the scrapping of differentiated education. How can the students and the Black community in general, be expected to rest content until this is done? In demanding a free and equal education, the students are voicing the just and reasonable demands of the whole Black community.

2. *Workers should be allowed to live with families.* The right of any person to live with their family near their place of work is absolutely basic. It is central to Christian teaching concerning family life. At present thousands of Africans in Cape Town are denied this right. This is not only a blatant example of racial discrimination, it is appallingly destructive to our community, and constitutes an ongoing cause of unrest and instability.

3. *Pass Laws and endless arrests.* No government can claim to be upholding civilised and Christian standards when they allow, for example thousands of women to be arrested for visiting their husbands. It is no answer to say that they should get the necessary permission. It is shocking that a wife should require government permission to visit her husband. Furthermore, in practice women find it well nigh impossible to get permission to stay with their husbands where they work. The system of pass laws therefore remains one of the root causes of the unrest, and perpetuates a deep feeling of bitterness in the Black community.

4. *Liquor Outlets undermine our Community.* The Black community as a whole never wanted the liquor outlets—they were forced upon us. They have had the effect of undermining our family life and social structure. The re-opening of fortress-like beerhalls in the Port Elizabeth townships has not gone unnoticed. This only serves to confirm the widespread conviction in the Black community that the Government is determined to finance the administration of urban Africans as cheaply as possible, to the extent of undermining our whole social structure. The only way the Government can show its good intentions in this respect is by making immediate promises not

to open liquor outlets in the townships and by closing the one presently in operation in Langa.

5. *Total re-structure of Urban African administration required.* In the light of previous paragraphs it is clear that the present policy of financing the administration of urban Africans through, inter alia, profits from the sale of liquor, and fines for infringing pass laws, only serves to aggravate the spiral of instability in the African community.

As one of the necessary changes towards having a full say in running our country, we Blacks should run our own townships. They should not be run by the all-White Bantu Affairs Administration Boards. We should also sit as equals on public bodies administering the Metropolitan area.

6. *Home Ownership and Social Stability.* Home ownership rights have recently been extended to Africans in urban areas like Soweto, but we Africans in Cape Town have thus far been excluded. We regard this as a grave injustice. It is also very shortsighted and unwise. Home ownership and security of tenure are an essential foundation to longterm social stability. These elementary rights should be extended to the African community in Cape Town immediately.

Concerning the houses recently destroyed in Nyanga, if the Government is not prepared to pay for the repairs, then we are hopeful that commerce and industry will donate generously and help people at this time of crisis to restore the damage.

7. *Wages and Trade Unions.* Far too many of our people are receiving wages below the Poverty Datum Line let alone the Effective Minimum Level. There is a manifest need for a fairer distribution of the wealth of our country. The present huge gap between rich and poor is totally unjust and a major source of deep dissatisfaction.

Workers should not only be allowed, but should be encouraged to organise themselves into Trade Unions. This is one of the essential ways to achieve a more just distribution of the wealth of our country by peaceful and legal means.

8. *The Cause of Unrest is the sin of Racial Discrimination.* The cause of all the upheavals in our land and in our cities in particular, is not "the students," or "the tsotsis," or "Black consciousness" or "Communists" or "Christian agitators." The primary cause of unrest and of all the violence in our land is the sin of racial discrimination. It is this sinful White racialism which is the source of worsening relations between Black and White in our country. There can be no lasting peace, no meaningful reconciliation, until the issues listed in the above paragraphs are speedily put right.

White people claim a Christian allegiance, but they are guilty of gross failure to practise their faith and "do unto others as you would have them do to you." We do not claim to be righteous ourselves, but we feel bound to say that White people would not stand being treated as they treat us. When will they heed the Word of God? They affront our humanity and in this they sin against our one Maker (1 John 4.20). Time has run out. Unless the structures of discriminations are rapidly dismantled, and unless Blacks are allowed to have a full and equal say in the running of this country, our future, White and Black, will be one of escalating violence and conflict—a tragic and appalling race war.

CONCLUSION

Prayer and Doing the Word of God.

We call upon all Christians who sincerely seek to obey God's word, to be ready to make greater sacrifices than before. It is clear that too many laws of our land are contrary to the Spirit of the Gospel: we are guilty for doing far too little to witness to this truth. The time has come to ponder more deeply the words of Peter: "We must obey God rather than men" (Acts 5.29). We invite fellow Christians to work and pray with us, that we may all be truer disciples of Christ—our one Lord—that his will be done on earth as in heaven.

In the service of our Lord,
Members of the Ministers' Fraternal of Langa, Guguletu and Nyanga, Cape Town

DOCUMENT 75. Testimony of Nelson Ndwenwa about imagined political negotiations, *State v. Twala* (The "Soweto 11"), November 1978

Case No. 281/78
Date: 1st November 1978

ON RESUMING:

NELSON T. NDWENWA: sworn states:

MR. VON LIERES [State Prosecutor]: (Cont.) Now, Mr. Ndwenwa, at the beginning of your evidence you told his lordship that the topics that were discussed by the SSRC were the scrapping of Bantu Education, the burning of school books, commemoration of Sharpeville and the peace plan with the UBC? ——— That is so.

I want you this morning to tell his lordship about the peace plan, what was that all about? ——— At this stage, I beg leave to explain it in English.

BY THE COURT: Very well, you can explain.

MR. VON LIERES: (cont.) Ask the witness to speak slowly please and distinctly because of the machine? ——— The peace plan was based on a conventional meeting or summit where the Prime Minister, Mr. J. Vorster, would be the chairman of that summit, at his left and right hand at the table were to be all political parties in the government, on the far right the United Nations observers and, on the far left, the press, *The World, The [Rand] Daily Mail,* all of them included there. And on the right were to be all black political organisations and social parties, surrounding the whole scene in the Republic of South Africa, [the] Army.

BY THE COURT: I must say I don't follow a word of what you've said. Who conceived this plan, where did it start, perhaps you can tell me that?

―― The plan was brought to a SSRC meeting just on paper, foolscap paper.

By whom? ―― By our chairman, Daniel Montsitsi. And he wanted us to give our opinion about the plan. What I'm explaining now is what was on that paper because he was explaining it, sketching it on the board, looking at it from the paper.

So what he proposed was a sort of round table conference involving all parties in South Africa, all parties concerned? ―― Yes, M'lord, certainly involving all sectors in the Republic of South Africa.

Right. Well it's a very idealistic plan, and he explained that to you? ―― He explained that to us.

And the ever-present press would also be there although they would sit a little bit far from the chairman? ―― Yes, M'lord.

Is that the idea? ―― Yes sir.

MR. VON LIERES: (cont.) Now what was the purpose of this, was it explained to you what the purpose of this peace conference was? ―― The purpose of this peace conference was to end all our grievances in the Republic of South Africa, all of us, white or black.

BY THE COURT: In other words to discuss the grievances of all parties concerned, to see whether they could thrash it out and come to a satisfactory arrangement amongst all people present? ―― Yes, M'lord.

MR. VON LIERES: (cont.) Now at how many meetings was this plan discussed? ―― Only at one meeting.

Was anything discussed at this particular meeting in connection with political power? ―― I would ask that my interpreter come back now please, M'lord.

Apart from setting the scene now or drawing a sketch on the blackboard, I presume it was a blackboard on which the sketch was drawn? ―― That is so, it was a blackboard.

Now apart from sketching the set-out or the round table conference and where the parties where supposed to sit, apart from that, the question of political power, was that discussed, political power in each division or don't you know that? ―― No.

7. Black Workers and Trade Unions

DOCUMENT 76. Report by L. Kasi, general secretary, African Food and Canning Workers' Union, September 5, 1963 (abridged)

Dear Comrade President and Members of our Union,

Our 16th National Conference has to report due to many obstacles our Union has been unable to maintain a steady rate of progress in the face of great difficulties.

Our members *are* the Union. It cannot exist without them. Whatever success it has, the Union owes to them. We can claim without fear of contradiction, that the Union has taken firm root in the lives and hopes, not only of the members themselves, but also of the communities to which they belong.

Our main aim during the past year has been to consolidate our organisation, bring in new members, and carry on the fight for higher wages, better working and living conditions, protection against ill-treatment, whether from foremen, employers or the public authorities, and recognition of the right to organise.

The General Secretary and members of the Management Committee have kept in close touch with branches and members throughout the vast area over which your Union operates.

We had 5 Management Committee meetings, 2 adjourned Management Committee meetings and 2 NEC [National Executive Committee] meetings during the past year. We issued 13 circular letters to Branches. [Visits to branches by organisers:] . . . .

WHAT WE HAVE ACHIEVED

During the past year our Union made representation to the Wage Board on behalf of the workers employed in: . . . .

The FCWU negotiated a new Agreement on our behalf as well for Messrs. Jax Canning Co., Grabouw which granted workers higher wages, improved conditions of work and they became a party to our Medical Benefit Fund. The Agreement expired on the 31st March. . . .

We have recovered sums of money for underpayment of wages, workmen's compensation benefits and after taking up a complaint at United Macaroni factories, Bellville.

Fruit and Vegetable Canning Workers' Medical Benefit Fund:
We take great pride in the fact that our fund which covers the Fruit and Vegetable Canning Factories of Paarl, Wellington, Worcester, Wolseley and Grabouw is entering into its 13th year of existence, and continues to make satisfactory progress. . . .

Dispute at L. K. B. Daljosaphat
The workers at Langeberg Ko-operasie Daljosaphat factory were dissatisfied with the behaviour of the working Manager Mr. Laubscher and his use of abusive language to the workers, and the dismissal of two workers which the workers regarded as unjust.

Negotiations to adjust this dispute started on the 10th March 1963. . . . L. Kasi together with Mrs. L. Abrahams (General Secretary) of the FCWU and D. Hartogh (Paarl Branch Secretary of the FCWU) and 8 workers went to Mr. Richards office to discuss this matter. . . . He then agreed to come to the cloakroom to address the Workers. Before doing so he wanted to discuss the matter with the Department of Labour. He did not come and address the workers.

Officials of the Department of Labour arrived at the factory from Cape Town and warned the workers that their action was illegal.

After four hours of negotiation, the management of the Langeberg Co-operative agreed to take back the dismissed man. The workers who received the news with much cheering, agreed to return to work Tuesday.

The workers of L. K. B. Daljosaphat all received a summons to appear in court at the Outspanning Saal, Dutoit Street, Paarl, on the 13th June, 1963. . . . The workers wanted advocate [Albie] Sachs to represent them. Adv. Sachs made application on the 27th May to the Chief Magistrate to go to Paarl to defend these workers, but was notified on the 5th June, that permission has been refused. The FCWU then asked their attorneys to engage another advocate . . . .

The case was heard in the Paarl Recreation Club Hall [which] was converted into a vast courtroom with the relieving magistrate, Mr. V. Falck, presiding. The big crowd of non-whites who included 43 of our members, appeared before Mr. Falck on a charge of taking part in an illegal strike on March 11th and refusing to continue their work at the fruit canning factory of Langeberg Co-operative Limited at Daljosaphat. . . .

Originally 320 persons were charged but a number could not be traced. The accused came from Wellington, New Town, Paarl, Huguenot, Drakenstein, and Kuils River. The prosecutor Mr. A. J. Fourie withdrew the charge against 55 persons. He issued warrants of arrest in respect of seven accused who were not present. The exact number charged was 273. 34 were Africans and the rest Coloured. Most were Coloured women. . . .

After hearing the evidence, Mr. Falck, the Magistrate, found the workers guilty of taking part in an illegal strike on the 11th March, 1963. All were cautioned and discharged.

The FCWU paid Messrs. Frank, Bernadt and Joffe the sum of R100 to cover the cost of the case.

The workers felt happy at being discharged.

Following the strike at Messrs. Langeberg Ko-operasie Beperk, Daljosaphat, on the 11.3.63, Messrs. H. Jones and Co., Zuider Paarl, gave their peach-pitting machine workers an all round bonus of 50c per week.

Wellington Branch reported that they too had a dispute at Oakglen Canning Co. when a worker was assaulted and dismissed. The workers all decided to stop work whilst the committee interviewed the Manager. After heated argument with the employer the dismissed worker was reinstated.

Refusal of Permission to hold meetings on the premises . . . .

It was reported to us by the FCWU that the employers of the above mentioned factories will not allow joint meetings with members of our Union and members of the FCWU to take place on their premises. It was further reported that the FCWU were told that the employers will not meet officials of the two unions together to discuss conditions and complaints. It is understood that the employers have taken these decisions in accordance with the wishes or instructions of the Department of Labour. . . .

OUR RIGHT TO ORGANISE

Our achievements would be greater, our record of activities would show even bigger advances, if we were not hampered by interference on the part of the police and other public authorities. . . .

On Monday, 27th May, 1963, three members of the Special Branch [security police] namely J. F. F. van Wyk, D. J. Greef and P. Laubser, came with a warrant and searched our Union's office from 10 a.m. to 11 a.m. . . .

We warned our Management Committee members and branch officials not to be frightened by the police who would like to see our Union to be broken up. Remember to stand by your Union and by your fellow workers! . . .

It is a shame, and a blot on the government, that it refuses to give us the elementary right to organise for legitimate ends without interference. We have protested to the Ministers concerned and, since we obtained no satisfaction, the FCWU on our behalf brought complaints to the notice of the international labour movement. . . .

7. Expulsion of or restrictions on Officials: These petty but vexatious harassments of the Union's officials acquire a far more serious significance than they might appear to possess, when viewed against the background of persistent victimisation of the Union officials over a number of years. The latest of these is the serving of three orders, on Mrs. Francis Baard, the secretary of the Port Elizabeth branch of the African Food and Canning Workers' Union. The effect of these orders is to exclude Mrs. Baard from factories, to prevent her from addressing meetings of trade union members, or meeting individual members of the Union who do not reside in the New Brighton Location at Port Elizabeth where Mrs. Baard herself lives. She will not find it possible to conduct her trade union work under the severe restrictions imposed under these orders.

Although these orders have been issued by the Minister of Justice under the Suppression of Communism Act, Mrs. Baard is not listed as a Communist or supporter of Communism under the Act, and has never been convicted of an offence under the Act. No explanation has been given to Mrs. Baard as to why these restrictions have been imposed upon her.

The following are the names of the other members of the Union who have suffered a similar fate—

(1) Betty du Toit, Secretary of the Johannesburg Branch, removed from office in January, 1953.
(2) Ray Alexander, National General Secretary, removed from office in September, 1953.
(3) Mr. S. V. Reddy, Secretary of Durban Branch, removed from office in October, 1953.
(4) Mr. Frank Edward Marquard, National President, removed from office in September, 1954.
(5) Miss A. M. Coe, Secretary of Port Elizabeth Branch, removed from office in September, 1954.
(6) Miss Sarah Wentzel, Secretary of Worcester Branch, removed from office in November, 1954.
(7) Miss R. Lan, National General Secretary, banned from meetings in November, 1954 and removed from office in 1956.
(8) Mr. Oscar Mpetha, General Secretary of the African Food and Canning Workers' Union, banned from meetings in November 1954 and restricted to Cape Town Magisterial Districts in July, 1958.
(9) Mr. Leon Levy, Branch Secretary of Johannesburg Branch, banned from gatherings and confined to Johannesburg Magisterial District in January, 1957.
(10) Mrs. Elizabeth Mafeking exiled to Southy (72 miles from Vryburg in the Cape), but she fled to Basutoland.

Conclusions

No charges whatsoever were formulated within the framework of the Industrial legislation or any other law against the Union officials whose freedom of exercise of trade union rights was impeded by the police. Also on no occasion have the police alleged that the officials had committed an offence. However, by following the trade unionists while they were visiting factories to discuss trade union matters with workers or employers, by interrogating them and on occasions by illegally keeping them under arrest at the charge-office, they made the conditions of exercise of their functions almost intolerable. . . .

The attacks on our Union and officials continue in spite of the protests. Our office was again raided on the 25th July, 1963. The General Secretary and Leon Levy were detained. The General Secretary after being detained for sixty days was released. Leon Levy after being detained for two months was also released. He left South Africa and is now in London. We very much regret his departure. . . .

OUR PART IN THE UNION MOVEMENT

Your Committee knows that it has a duty to all workers, and has a right to expect assistance from all workers, in our struggle for the right to organise.

It is for this reason that we are affiliated to SACTU, which is the one national trade union body that is open to organised workers without distinction of race or colour.

We view with great alarm the attacks made on SACTU by the authorities. The following SACTU leaders have been banned and detained:- . . . .

CONCLUSION

We must ask ourselves why have so many people been arrested and detained; people of all races (mainly Africans), from all walks of life, unskilled workers, farm workers, professionals and scholars. These men and women, young and old, represent much of South Africa's opposition to the Government's apartheid system. Our people are not prepared to accept it lying down and are driven out of their homes, deprived of jobs and means of livelihood, and relegated to a state of subservience, because of the Government's apartheid policy as expressed in the Group Areas Act, Job Reservation and the Bantu Laws Amendment Act. We must ask ourselves why in the midst of great wealth are our people poor? . . .

Our workers are poor because they have no democracy and because they have no rights for collective bargaining. They are denied the right to have free trade unions and leaders. Their leaders are imprisoned and detained.

In our opposition to the Government's apartheid we are not alone—the world is with us, particularly the African countries that have liberated themselves, are determined that we free ourselves. We are particularly encouraged by the struggle for civil rights that the American Negroes are waging.

In the coming year we have many tasks before us. The Conciliation Board for the Fish Canning Industry is expiring on 31.10.63. We are now in the midst of negotiating a new [deal?] for the fruit and and vegetable canning industry, as [well as for the?] meat canning industry in Upington.

I am confident that in spite of all the Government interference with us we shall be strong enough to carry out and to play an even greater role in the people's struggle.

DOCUMENT 77. Speech by J. Phendlani, president, to the annual congress of the African Food and Canning Workers' Union, September 23–24, 1967

Dear Members,

The first African Trade Unions on our great continent were formed in South Africa nearly 50 years ago—1918. Six years later the great I. C. U.—the Industrial and Commercial Workers Union under Clements Kadalie had 40,000 members.

It was in the year 1924 that the Industrial Conciliation Act was introduced and laid down its definition of "employee" that we Africans were not included or covered by the Act. What does it mean? Simple—it means that we are a lower group, we are not worthy of labourers' rights. This was done to make us feel inferior; to make the white, Coloured and Indian workers feel superior; to divide the working people—divide and rule policy and to hamper the African desire to be organised and win a higher standard of living, benefit like other workers from our country's growth.

In 1930 even an African Miners Union was formed, which put terror in the hearts of our rulers. It is the African miner who produces the great wealth of our society at miserable wages, and organisers and leaders of African workers—miners, clothing, laundry—were arrested, imprisoned. Nevertheless by 1946, 70,000 African miners came out on strike for 10/—a day, for trade union recognition and for workers' right to be organised. The strikers were forced by police and government back to work but not before seven African miners were killed in cold blood. These are our heroes and we must now, 21 years later, remember them and tell our children about them. Their struggle is not told in School history books. Their story is similar to the story of the other African workers. In all these years since 1918 African dockers, railway, clothing, laundry, iron and steel, cement and quarry and municipal workers organised and struggled. Not all of these unions remained alive— they were choked to death by the hands of those that want to keep us in poverty—so that they can become richer, those that want to keep us as slaves so that they can live like lords.

Our African unions were choked—undermined by means of all the oppressive laws—pass laws, Master and Servants Act, Riotous Assemblies Act, Native Administration Act and all the other laws that are used to force Africans to work for little wages and threaten to put them in gaol if they refuse. We too have a story to tell and retell our children.

We were organised like our other fellow workers in 1941 in one Union, the Food and Canning Workers' Union by Ray Alexander. She believed and practised her belief that we are the same human beings as all others with the same desires, hopes and aspirations to progress. She fought this separation and apartheid policy of the Government and the Industrial Conciliation Act. We won great improvements for ourselves and our children. She and our Frank Marquard were harassed by the Government until in July, 1947—20 years ago—we were forced to set up our African Food and Canning Workers' Union. She remained our General Secretary, trained our leaders, Oscar Mpetha, Elizabeth Mafeking, Francis Baard and others. The Government introduced the Suppression of Communism Act and robbed her from us. After her they removed by banning orders and banishment order, both Oscar and Elizabeth. Today we miss our great friends, Elizabeth and Ray who have been forced to leave our country. We know that they are with us—their ideas are with us. Why was this done? Some bosses and the Government wanted to destroy our Union and they believed they will succeed by removing our leaders. We still live and we resolve here and now to grow stronger and stronger. Our good friend Mpungwana, Church of the P. E. A. said in October, 1953 when Ray was banned, "Ray has manured our land. We must keep up her work and our land with our labour, will give us food." Our Union lives because it is sheltered in the hearts of our people. Our Union has always cared for the interests of its members not only in the factory but for good homes, for their families, for creches [day care centers] and schools and we must now unite and resist the attempts to drive us out of the Western Cape.

Let us make it known here and now to all people that we African men and women are the original owners of this country. We shall never give up our right to live in any part of this whole country including the Western Cape. Our forefathers lived here more than a 100 years ago. Our people have travelled from many parts—from the mountains of Basutoland, the valleys of Zululand, from the hills of Transkei and Pondoland, and the rivers of the Eastern Cape, to work in Cape Town, Paarl, Worcester. Our forefathers built the breakwater, the docks, laid the tracks for the railway, dug out the rocks so that the roads could pass over Sir Lowry's Pass, Montagu Pass, Bains Kloof, Du Toits Kloof—our hands have ploughed the ground and milked the cows on farms throughout the Western Cape. It is we who worked on buildings, factories. We who have unloaded and loaded the ships in Cape Town Docks. Many of us were born here and have no other home. We shall defend it until we have won the right to move, work and live as free men and women. We appeal to our Coloured fellow workers to stand with us—today and tomorrow.

DOCUMENT 78. Speech by J. Altman, general secretary of the National Union of Distributive Workers, to conference of the Trade Union Council of South Africa, December 11–12, 1967 (abridged)

Mr Chairman, I am pleased to learn from yourself and the General Secretary, Brother [Arthur] Grobbelaar, that the Minister of Labour has acknowledged our right to disagree with him. I want to exercise that right here and now.

Despite the bombshell which Mrs [Lucy] Mvubelo has sprung upon us in making known the decision of the African trade unions to withdraw from

TUCSA, I feel that the policy which the co-ordinating body has followed has been the correct one. I hope that TUCSA will continue to follow that policy.

Miss [Anna] Scheepers has given us a very clear summary of the figures contained in the TUCSA analysis (of the labour force). These show the inexorable trend in the racial pattern in industry. The tide of African workers in industry cannot be turned. I make that statement categorically. The tide cannot be turned, except at the cost of cutting off all future development. Although Canute may have been successful in turning back the tide, I cannot see any of our Ministers turning back these tides.

We must recognise that the percentage of Whites in industry is going to decrease every year. This has been shown in the TUCSA summary which is now before you. . . . We have to face facts. All of us know only too clearly today that they, the Africans, are the bulk of the working population of this country, and they are going to continue to be the bulk of the working population. Unless African trade unions are recognised, or we accept the alternative which Brother Crompton has put forward, that is that the definition of "employee" in the Act be amended so that Africans can enter into registered unions, there won't be any workers left to organise into trade unions at all in 15 or 20 years' time.

The White and Coloured workers are all moving up in the hierarchy of industry and commerce, into skilled and supervisory positions. . . . Unless we are going to organise the white-collar workers soon, we are not going to have any production workers left to organise.

TUCSA has done a wonderful job to date, and in the past five years particularly I think TUCSA has reached its greatest prestige, influence and authority. It is during these five years that we have had the African unions with us. That may be a paradox, but it is a fact—we have achieved our greatest development in this trade union council of ours during the years that we have had our African unions associated with us. We have enjoyed enormous international prestige because of that fact. . . .

I feel that this special conference was called in haste. I was not present at the NEC [National Executive Committee] meeting last month when it was decided that this conference be called. We have heard the reasons given to NEC members, and those are that it was not only because the Minister had attacked TUCSA, but because there was a very real threat of certain unions withdrawing from TUCSA unless it was prepared to change its policy.

I feel, Mr. Chairman and fellow delegates, that it was not necessary to call a special conference at this stage, because unions which are here today have all come at short notice—they have not had time to discuss these great issues in the relevant councils of their own unions, and as a result we have all come here today with pretty clear-out ideas based on existing decisions in our unions.

I want to refer to the position of my own union. We have always, ever since we became affiliated to TUCSA, made it clear that we support the inclusion of African trade unions. As far as I am concerned we will continue to support that policy.

My union at the moment has, and for the past 18 months has had, quite a difficult struggle on its own hands with an opposition group called the Blanke Distribusie Werkers [White Distributive Workers]. They have been attacking us very solidly on this very point of our affiliation to TUCSA and the attendant fact that TUCSA has African unions within its ranks. It would have been a very easy way out for my union to say at this special conference: Yes, we will agree to exclude the African unions, because that will solve a lot of problems for the National Union of Distributive Workers in its fight against the Blankewerkers.

Mr. President, we are not going to do that. We are carrying on that fight against the Blankewerkers. We are adopting the same policy which TUCSA has adopted in trying to educate the membership and to get them to see why it is necessary for the Africans to be brought into the fold of the trade union movement. . . . We must lead and guide Africans who have not yet gained trade union experience, and there are hundreds and thousands of them.

My union will oppose any change in the present set-up, Mr. President, and we hope that the magnificent example that has been set by your own union (the Boilermakers) in educating its membership will be followed by other affiliated unions. I would like to pay very special tribute here to the S. A. Boilermakers' Society, which has done such a wonderful job of trade union education within its own ranks, to such good effect that the membership is almost unanimous in supporting the principle of organising African workers.

Education of our membership is a matter of patience. It is a long, uphill struggle. We know that there are plenty of racial prejudices amongst our membership. We know also that they have to be overcome. With patience and perseverance we will overcome them.

Document 79. Report by John Frankish, chairman, NUSAS Wages Commission, University of Cape Town, June 29, 1973 (abridged)

1) INTRODUCTION

The Wages Commission continues to suffer from a lack of manpower, many students being under the impression that only specialised persons can be involved. The result has been a thinly-spread work-force trying to cope with a very broad field of operations—in some cases one person has been shouldered with a full research project.

This must be rectified by drawing in more students—not only trained senior students, but new students who can be trained by the commission. Regular labour education seminars must be held. In addition to centralised recruiting, we shall have to continue making one person responsible for specific projects and for drawing in new people to help him on that project.

2) FINANCE

The Commission has been financially fairly well-off. But we have still managed to spend most of that money.

The Commission received an administration grant of R400 from the SRC [Students' Representative Council], as well as substantial donations from SAIRR [the South African Institute of Race Relations] and private individuals for research purposes. We have also had grants from NUSWEL [welfare projects division of NUSAS] national for specific projects. The Labour Campaign was financed by the SRC. . . .

3) LABOUR CAMPAIGN

Much of the time of the Wages Commission during the first half of the year was spent on the Labour Campaign. The Campaign was probably one of the best organised yet in terms of advance planning. Certain unforeseen situations cropped up to cause a few complications, but generally the Campaign went off very well.

At no time did it attract mass student participation, probably due to the "specialisation" of the topics discussed. The criticism was also levelled that too many functions were arranged, leaving the ordinary student completely bewildered. This might well be a point to consider in future.

We did, however, succeed in getting fairly wide press coverage virtually every day of the campaign and raised a number of questions in the minds of the white public. The domestic servant campaign was particularly successful in this regard. . . .

4) RESEARCH

A number of research papers were prepared and distributed by the commission during the Labour Campaign. . . .

5) FOREIGN INVESTMENTS

A well-thought-out strategy has still to be found—hopefully this will be achieved next term when the project can get underway with clearly defined aims and direction. . . .

6) WAGE BOARDS

The commission gave evidence to two Wage Boards: Unskilled labour and Liquor Manufacturing.

In both cases workers were pamphleteered before the sitting. About 50 workers came to the Unskilled sitting, while none turned up at the second. . . .

It would not appear that the Wage Board will ever offer any substantial improvement of worker conditions—all it is doing at present is keeping the low wages in line with increases in COL [cost of living] and with inflation. Its one beneficial aspect is that it brings home to workers the total inadequacies of the present system.

7) DOMESTIC SERVANTS PROJECT

A detailed report on the wages, working conditions and hours affecting domestic servants was published by the Commission in April. At the same time a public meeting attended by both employers and domestics was held. Both obtained wide press coverage (which is still continuing).

It seems that the project has had considerable impact on the white public. More importantly the project served to publicise the embryo Domestic Workers Union which has now started operating on a more regular basis. NUSWEL is now working with the Union in providing literacy classes.

8) WORKER EDUCATION PROJECT
    i) WESTERN PROVINCE WORKERS ADVICE OFFICE
    The Commission was approached at the beginning of the year to assist in the establishment of a workers advice bureau. The bureau is now operating in a virtually full-time capacity although its operations have been kept fairly independent of Wages Commission. . . .

    ii) BENEFIT SOCIETY
    This remains a priority of the worker education project. Background work has started and the society should be functioning by the end of the year.

    iii) SEMINARS/LECTURES
    A worker-training seminar was organised earlier this year—run by Eric Tyacke of the Urban Training Project. The seminar was poorly attended but very well received. . . .

    iv) PUBLICATION
    Abasebenzi [The Worker] has been produced at regular two-monthly intervals (3 have so far appeared). It had been proposed that they appear monthly but this has been impossible both organisationally and financially. *Abasebenzi* has been very well received by workers. . . .

    v) GENERAL
    The commission is still largely finding its way with regard to the worker education project and the project remains very flexible particularly with regard to the best methods of working with other organisations and interests. . . .

9. CAMPUS WAGES
    The SRC and Wages Commission have had representation on the Council Sub-Committee appointed to investigate campus wages. . . .

10. RELATIONS WITH
    a) THE PRESS have been good, particularly with the English-language newspapers. More attention must, however, be paid to press publicity as the press remains one of our more powerful allies.
    b) OTHER WAGES COMMISSIONS
    All our publications have been sent to other Wages Commissions, although the reciprocity (with the exception of UNP [University of Natal-Pietermaritzburg]) has not been very good. . . .

c) OTHER ORGANISATIONS

Contacts with the SAIRR, Labour Party, and Church groups remain good. Contact with trade unions has improved somewhat but still needs working on. Contact with workers has improved tremendously.

d) BUSINESSMEN

Relations reached an all-time low over the stickers and *Abasebenzi* distributed to workers during the Labour campaign. Meetings were held with leading businessmen at which an understanding was reached to co-operate more closely in future. The co-operation did not go very far, however, as the businessmen went back on undertakings made at the meetings. . . .

e) SRC AND ADMINISTRATION

The SRC has proved very helpful in many ways and has not tended towards obstructing our activities as many feared. The SRC has, in fact, served largely to protect the Commission. Difficulties arose with the Administration over the "businessmen issue" but again, Admin did protect the commission to some extent. . . .

11. ORGANISATION OF THE COMMISSION

The commission has been decentralised as much as possible in an attempt to spread the work load and give responsibility to every member of the commission. . . .

The Commission has been divided into two sections—Research and Worker Education. Each section has in turn been subdivided into a number of different projects (covered in the report above) with individual responsibility being conferred in each case. . . .

13. THANKS.

Appreciation must be expressed to all members of the Commission for hours of hard and often boring work which they have put into the Commission. Special thanks to Gordon and to Steven who has often rescued the commission from the bureaucratic quagmire.

Document 80. "Call to Organise and Form Black Trade Unions in South Africa." Statement by the Black Allied Workers' Union, Johannesburg, 1973? (abridged)

The Black Allied Workers' Union regard the insistent call to Black Workers (Africans) to join registered (white) trade Unions, fraudulent. We take it [as] deceitful—a big lie propagated by the Trade Union Council of South Africa (TUCSA) at their 1972 Annual Conference in Cape Town.

We see this call, being made by the 90% white trade Union Council, as an attempt to:

(1) Create false hopes among Blacks that they can form or join multiracial trade Unions;

(2) Make Blacks believe and hope that they can only enjoy the Workers'

rights, privileges, job opportunities and socio-economic fringe benefits through the patronage, goodwill and generosity of white (*BAAS*) [boss] workers;

(3) Make the World believe that white workers in South Africa are doing something for or about Black Workers, this being a special menu for overseas consumption so that South Africa can be re-admitted into the international labour arena;

(4) Perpetuate white patronage and leadership over Blacks in the labour field;

(5) Nib off and suppress Black initiative and creativity and thus kill Black leadership in the economic life of South Africa. The idea being to make sure that Blacks and Whites should never be equals in a work situation in the country.

(6) Deprive Black workers economic power and thus entrench status quo, racial discrimination and prejudice—and reduce Blacks to voiceless tools of labour that should depend and live on charity and kindness of the White worker in matters of collective bargaining for better working conditions and decent wages.

In their last (1973) conference, TUCSA, realising that they would run into a legal cul-de-sac in their loud call for Blacks to join existing registered trade Unions, quickly turned tail and passed a resolution with a hollow call; *to form PARALLEL trade Unions*. . . .

A refusal by TUCSA to admit the fact that the time has come *when Blacks must take the initiative* in organising themselves and *whites can only enable that initiativeness*. TUCSA is tenaciously clinging to the idea that it is their moral obligation and God-given responsibility to organise and look after the under-trodden Black workers. It is their relentless effort to ward off being ostracised from the world labour table because of the racial and racist labour system and laws of the country.

BLACK TRADE UNIONS: ORGANISATION

The Black Allied Workers' Union accepts and welcomes the call for the organisation of Black Workers and the formation of Black trade unions. We go further to say: Black workers must be allowed to form their own trade unions and be accorded the legal recognition that is enjoyed by the rest of the racial groups in South Africa. . . .

The Whites role should be that of *ENABLING*. Whites, with their skill and material power should enable Black initiative to achieve its final goal. Whites could offer skilled or qualified personnel to assist in the training of Black Workers—only when Blacks ask them to do so. Whites could play an effective role by offering, also, financial assistance with no dictates on how and on what these money [*sic*] should be spent. Whites should also go and evangelise their lot into accepting a Black worker as a human being deserving all respect due to him.

Let it be emphasised that: the Black man's task in the Black trade Union movement is not limited to the achieving of physical and material benefits such as good working conditions, increased wages, social fringe benefits etc.

Our concern and priority is the *formation of a people and the development of [a] sense of responsibility in them.*

Our task is to make up men and women who, being conscious of themselves as human beings, and being aware of their significance in a work situation, shall proudly take their seat side by side with other national groups and decide a future that shall spell security and prosperity for all peoples alike.

Black Allied Workers' Union, although not totally disregarding "the classical Western elements of trade unionism," and not being blind to the principle of "Workers interdependence" irrespective of race and colour of the skin, however, recognise the fact that: *"black Worker interests extend beyond the factory: they extend to the ghetto where black workers stay together in hostels under squalid conditions; to the crowded trains and buses—to the absence of amenities—to the stringent irksome and humiliating application of influx control laws—to the lack of proper channels whereby people could equip themselves with basic skills."*

"Taste of Power"

The problem of the changing of the labour system is ours. It rests squarely on our shoulders. Thus, [the] Black trade Union movement as a vehicle to bringing about a change, can never be initiated or directed by white trade union leaders.

HOW DO WE GO ABOUT IT?

Black Allied Workers Union hopes to achieve the above-expressed sentiments and aspirations through the following methods:

(a) *ORGANISATION:*

To embark on an intensive organisation of the 5 1/2 million unorganised Black workers in industry, commerce and other private sectors. For this, we need trained field organisers who will be able to reach ordinary workers and bring light to them.

(b) *EDUCATION*

The Union is preparing a crash Workers education programme. The idea is to (i) dispel ignorance from the minds of workers; (ii) improve skills and know-how; (iii) make workers be aware of themselves and their dignity as human beings (iv) inculcate a sense of responsibility in them (v) Assist them in the process of creativity so that they can become an asset to the economy and to themselves in the community.

Labour seminars and lectures on various subjects given by specialists; Newspaper articles—or the issuing of the "Workers' Newsletter."

(c) *COLLECTIVE BARGAINING*

The Union, when organised shall, from a position of power and strength,

(i)   Negotiate with employers in various industrial job categories on behalf of its members for better wages, acceptable working conditions, job opportunities etc.

(ii) Represent workers at Wage Board meetings when Wage Agreements are drawn. Although we shall not have any legal recognition, the Board will be forced by virtue of our existence and strength to accord us de facto recognition.

(iii) Make repeated appeals and demand to the Government that Black Unions be given legal recognition. The idea is to legalise "Collective bargaining" right of the Black Worker which is an inalienable right to all workers all over the world.

(iv) Consult with existing Black Unions to form a United body that can tackle their common problems together.

In conclusion, we still reiterate the Black workers' demand:

1. Freedom to organise and form Black trade Unions without fear [of] victimisation by employers or banning by the Government.
2. Legal recognition of Black trade Unions—a right which is enjoyed by Unions of other racial groups in the country.
3. The right for Collective bargaining—which is the only vital weapon that trade Unions can use to improve their lot.
4. A living Wage for all Black Workers in all job categories.
5. The removal of Job Reservation and the opening of Job opportunities to all workers irrespective of race and colour of the skin.
6. Training facilities for Black Workers in industry and commerce.

Document 81. Memorandum for the 21st annual general conference of the Trade Union Council of South Africa by the affiliates of the Trade Union Advisory and Co-ordinating Council, September 23, 1975

BROTHERS AND SISTERS,

It is a sad day for us as trade unionists that we are unable to attend your 21st Annual conference as delegates nor even as observers. You might well ask why the affiliates of TUACC who together represent over 45,000 workers in Natal at their 4th Council meeting felt it premature to consider affiliating to your institution.

Last year at your annual conference held in Port Elizabeth we the representatives of five unions affiliated to TUACC called on your organization to convene a conference where the problem facing unregistered unions could be examined. At that conference in Port Elizabeth none of your office bearers commented on the issues raised by us, in fact so little importance was attributed to our proposals that they have not even been recorded in the minutes of that meeting. While the general secretary read out a policy statement of TUCSA at the end of the debate on opening TUCSA's ranks to all workers in which it was stated TUCSA would consult unions concerned, we regret to say that no such consultation has taken place with our unions despite many possible opportunities in an entire year.

We thus take this opportunity through this memorandum to draw the conference's attention once more to what we believe are the crucial areas affecting workers in this country.

IS TUCSA'S POLICY OF 'PARALLEL' UNIONS APPROPRIATE TO THE NEEDS OF A UNITED TRADE UNION MOVEMENT?

Our stated common objective is to organize all workers into independent non-racial worker institutions dedicated to the protection of the rights of all workers and to the advancement of worker interests in industry and society as a whole.

TUCSA has argued for the organization of African workers into unions 'parallel' in scope to existing registered unions as the base for this struggle. While to its credit such organization shows a concern to build a united worker struggle, it is our deep-rooted fear that this concept has not yet been adequately thought out by leadership in the labour movement. Breaking up the working class into scores of minor sections of industries must surely weaken rather than strengthen the bargaining position of workers.

To take the point further it must be asked why unregistered unions should restrict themselves to provincial limits just because registered unions in the same industry have been unable to unify worker organisation in such industries. Surely we cannot want to divide unregistered unions along these lines.

The primary direction that the unregistered union movement is taking is to organise workers into broadly based industrial unions. We believe that TUCSA should take cognisance of this fact and endeavour to encourage many of its affiliates to become broad based and national in character. Were this to be done it would be possible to lay a far firmer foundation for a common future.

WE MUST KEEP PACE WITH HISTORY

We are all aware that events both within and outside our borders are moving at a tremendous pace. We have witnessed angry and frustrated workers taking to the streets for redress. We have witnessed government reaction consistently binding, gagging and avoiding the issue of democratic rights of workers to associate through trade unions.

In this crucial stage of the development of the labour movement we are as far from witnessing the granting of union rights to the mass of workers in this country as we ever were.

The question we wish to pose to conference is this. Is TUCSA's response adequate? Can it afford to simply go on passing resolutions calling on the government to extend the Industrial Conciliation Act to all workers?

We believe that TUCSA affiliates have a duty to the workers of this country to go far beyond conference pleadings and to embark on a systematic campaign to rally members to press for the extension of basic democratic rights on the factory floor.

Our strength lies in the factory not in the debating halls.

WHERE TO NOW?

It has been our call to TUCSA for more than a year now to evaluate the implications of the direction it is attempting to set TOGETHER WITH the unregistered union movement so that we can thrash out the crucial issues of our time. We hope this memorandum will be taken by delegates as an urgent plea for open and self-critical debate on the direction the labour movement needs to take in the coming future.

ISSUED BY:

1. National Union of Textile Workers
2. Metal and Allied Workers' Union
3. Transport and General Workers' Union
4. Chemical Workers Industrial Union
5. Furniture and Timber Workers' Union

DOCUMENT 82. "The 1976 Heinemann Strike." Interview with Gavin Andersson, general secretary of the Metal and Allied Workers' Union, by Johann Maree, December 3, 1979 (abridged)

What led up to the strike?

The first workers from Heinemann started joining the union in about October 1975. By about beginning of November there was a group of about 6 people who knew each other well and trusted each other very well.

We proceeded very, very cautiously, breaking down the factory into departments and then those people discussed who they would recruit into the union. Only if [there was] unanimity would they recruit that person. . . . We'd also learned at that stage that you can't just organise in the factories; you must also organise in the townships. By the time work started in the New Year there was a large number of very strongly pro-union members. By this stage there was a group of about 180 members.

They had elected a committee to represent them. . . . we called them a shop steward committee. They looked like a shop steward committee with elected representatives from each department. On the Friday the shop stewards would bring along new members and there'd be an explanation what the union was about, discussion generally, and so on. On the Saturday there would be a full factory meeting in the township. Just all the union members and groups from other factories would come as well.

By about mid-February we were approaching 75% of the workforce. At that stage we requested a meeting with the management. . . . We took along what was called a petition, it was like a memorandum. "We the workers of Heinemann reject works and liaison committees and want to work through our union, the MAWU, and its structures. We want you to meet our shop stewards and the union officials. That was signed by, I think, 470 workers out of 600; [then we] had this meeting with the MD [managing director], [W. E.] Wilckens.

At that stage began the real battle between management and the union. . . .

At one stage they tried to force an election [for a liaison committee] where they built special booths. One was a Yes booth, the other was a No booth. Each worker was called off one by one. I mean the departments were called off one by one. They were told they had to go into one booth or the other. Every one was given a disk. At the No booth were standing all the Security Policemen and even South African Police were called in for this thing. At the Yes booth it was all smiles. At that thing from the first department they got three yes votes. The department had 120 people in it. . . .

About the same time or immediately after this, management broke off dealings with the union. Up to then we'd been able to phone them, speak to them, to maintain some kind of contact. They refused to have any more dealings.

The workers then elected a committee of about 16 people to speak to the management. . . . Oh yes, they [management] tried to divide Coloureds and Africans. . . . So to some extent they might have kept some Coloureds with them through the strike. Certainly in the union there were many, many Coloureds, and there were Coloured shop stewards as well who'd been elected by Africans, and Coloureds voting for African shop stewards. . . . .

Then management started taking quite an aggressive stance. Management people started coming round asking the foremen who were the trouble-makers, and people were pointed out in the middle of work. Everyone became aware there was going to be some kind of victimisation happening.

One particular [day] there was a lot of tension in the factory because when they arrived at work there were some police outside the gates. Then on the Thursday of that week 20 people were fired. They were called to the office about 10 [minutes] to 5:00 and told that they were dismissed because there was a reduction in staff. And of those 20 there were about 3 shop stewards and 2 pregnant women. . . . People wanted to know why those people had been dismissed, particularly since during that week some new people had been taken on.

The next morning workers went there and gathered outside the gates. They asked to see [the managing director], but that was refused. The union officials were working on a potential court interdict when, at about 8 (a. m.), there was a phone call from one shop steward saying "you had better come quickly, everybody has just been fired." The whole factory had in fact been fired. There were police there, there was a Department of Labour official, so it seemed as if it had been a planned thing.

Was there something before the firing? What led to that?

They arrived at work and it was unusual. Normally the gates were all open and everyone would go to work. This time three of the gates were completely closed and one was half-open. In front of it were some police and management and so on. Workers arrived and wanted to speak to [the] MD [managing director] . . . . Von Lieres [the factory manager] said to them no, you can't speak to him and that's that. About 10 minutes later he said you are all dismissed. So that's that. Your wages will be ready in 2 hours or so.

That was the situation that we arrived at when we came from the union offices. We went to von Lieres and offered to help him resolve the bad situation. It seemed the best way to handle it would be to talk about it to everybody. He refused completely. . . . We appealed to everyone to remain calm. Management and the people watching such as the press must see that the workers are here to talk. They want recognition of the union and that is what the issue is about. So we suggested that we wait there until Wilckens came.

Then they started paying people out and there was a decision taken to leave that place after that and go to Alexandra [township near Johannesburg]. . . . The decision taken was that people should go back again on Monday morning and again ask for a meeting. At that meeting they should set out that they weren't prepared to have a liaison committee. They wanted union recognition, and they wanted those 20 people taken back. That was quite a unanimous decision. . . .

On the Sunday there were extensive township meetings. At that stage we divided each township into about 10 area committees and then one large central area committee for each of the main townships around there. This had existed before and it just swung into operation very smoothly. On that Sunday every single worker met in a group of minimum of 10 and discussed all the issues and affirmed the position taken on Friday, looked at what might happen the next day, and so on. So workers came there on Monday very strongly together.

On the Monday morning it was the same thing, except there was more police there this time, about 25–30 policemen and some police dogs. . . .

At about 10 o'clock the police colonel who was in charge made an announcement saying that people must leave by half an hour. Otherwise he was forced to disperse them. At that stage big trucks started coming, black marias or whatever they were called, and police-dogs coming out and policemen swinging around these pick-handles that they had. The atmosphere got quite tense. It became apparent that workers hadn't realised he had told them to move away. . . . workers started singing. . . . Anyway at 20 past, Sipho [Kubheka] was able to get through this police cordon and said to people look, what these guys are going to do if we are not out by 10 minutes, they are going to use these pick handles to beat people up and they are going to set the dogs on us. There is no point in doing that. I think we should just go away and have another meeting at Alexandra, decide what to do from here. Let's go away with dignity, not give them the chance to fight us. Show what we are standing for.

Everyone just agreed with that immediately and started moving off. It was about 22 minutes past 10. There wasn't any dissension. So people started moving off and went round the corner into Tunny(?) road, waved at the police, and went off singing *Nkosi Sikeleli,* and went off towards the buses.

That sort of wrapped it up as far as we were concerned. We moved around the corner about to get into the kombi [van] when suddenly there were just policemen everywhere with their pick-handles and dogs and things. Really laying into the workers who had kind of dispersed and were moving off. It became clear it was more than a dispersal exercise because some of them went round the front and cornered workers so they couldn't get away from them. And then came back two waves of policemen moving towards each other and beating down everything in their path.

It was very ugly. There was a pregnant woman whom they beat fairly deliberately on the stomach. Having knocked her to the ground then proceeded to hit her stomach. There was no possible justification for it. Workers just scattered everywhere. Some jumped over the fence into the veld next to 3M, some managed to get through down to the buses, some just milled around and got hit more and more. It was a very ugly scene altogether. Afterwards there were just shoes lying around and handbags and umbrellas and people lying bleeding and crying and so on.

Is this when you got hit too? And what happened there?
. . . he saw me and came for me and started coming down towards my head with this pick-handle. I put up my arm to stop that and that's when I broke the elbow and hurt this one a bit, but just bruises mainly. I think I was really furious at the whole thing and got up and started shouting at this colonel, look it's not even half past, they've dispersed already. He said, well we've got different watches, and then I was arrested at that stage. . . .

Arising out of that, immediately after that we started a court action against the police, the Minister of Police particularly. It took three and a half years before it got put on the roll, which was October 1979. And then they settled out of court at the last minute. . . .

And then the consequences for organisation?
Organisation at Heinemann was largely smashed by that. . . . Heinemann just couldn't meet their production deadlines. . . . Eventually it got to the position where Heinemann management were sending emissaries round to old workers saying please come back and work, we'll take you back. These guys were refusing. I think that was a mistake. At the time everyone just said that's fantastic because this guy who was asked was sticking with the rest of us who weren't asked and isn't going back there. But if those good strong people went back there we would have started organisation there much sooner.

When people went back there they had to make this sworn statement that they wouldn't have anything to do with the union, support the liaison committee, and then [they were] asking them who were the main trouble makers in their opinion. That was dropped very soon in the first week because we were using that as part of the legal battle. They realised that they were showing it was a lock-out. . . .

There was no real organisation at that factory for about 6–7 months thereafter. . . . A lot of those Heinemann workers went on to become strong organisers in other factories where they got jobs. The strongest organisers in the union today are ex-Heinemann people. . . . certainly [there] was a loss in the fact that up to then there was a very strong vibrant healthy factory committee with three meetings each week and subscriptions of 600 rand a month coming in from that one factory. . . . So that was lost and certainly that was a big blow for all of us. And it must be viewed as a defeat at that stage.

In the long term the positive thing that happened at Heinemann [was] the way of organising that happened in that factory. I don't think that people have forgotten that, so it's not a totally negative thing.

DOCUMENT 83. "'Stop Eating It Right Now!' Support the Fatti's and Moni's Boycott." Pamphlet by Fatti's and Moni's Workers' Support Committee, Durban, September 1979 (abridged)

MONDAY: April 23

5 workers fired at the Fatti's and Moni's factory in Bellville South, Cape Town. No reasons were given. All 5 workers were members of the Food and Canning Workers' Union.

TUESDAY: April 24th

78 workers in the milling section refused to go to work asking management to explain why the workers had been fired. Management called in the Labour Department. The officials from the Labour Department told the workers that if they did not go back to work they would have to pay a R200 fine or face imprisonment and that the police would be called in. The workers stood firm and the strike continued. Attempts to divide the strikers by race also failed. That day 5 more workers were fired.

WEDNESDAY: April 25

The strike continued. African and 'coloured' workers striking in solidarity with the 10 workers who had been fired. Officials from the Labour Department were called in again by management. They tried to divide the workers by trying to talk with the 'coloured' workers only. The African workers were told that they had broken their contracts and must now 'go home'. Both African and 'coloured' workers stood firm and said that only if the 10 were reinstated would they go back to work. The African and 'coloured' strikers left the factory together.

Since the strike, the workers have met everyday in the Lyric Theatre in Bellville South, near the factory. The workers have made a call to the community for support.

The strike started in April, it is now September and the strike goes on. Organisations throughout the country have responded to the striking workers' call for support.

WHAT IS THE BACKGROUND TO THE STRIKE?

Fatti's and Moni's is part of the food industry. The Food and Canning Workers' Union (10,000 members) is organising workers in this industry in the Cape. The workers are the very exploited food workers of the Western Cape. The Food and Canning Union consists of 2 unions which exist side by side, these are called parallel unions—a registered one for 'coloureds' and an unregistered one for Africans. Unlike almost all other parallel unions, this union acts as one, and not as two.

At Fatti's and Moni's, the union had been trying to win recognition and negotiating rights on behalf of all the workers for over a year. . . . The union represents over half of the 250 workers at the factory.

Although there was already a union which represented the workers, the management of Fatti's and Moni's of Bellville South decided to impose a liaison committee a month before the strike, at their mill. Workers were told to choose between the liaison committee and their union.

While management were in the process of informing workers of this 'choice', union members were busy organising a petition calling for a minimum wage of R40 a week (at present some workers receive only R23 a week).

THE WORKERS SIGNED A PETITION

The workers refused to accept a liaison committee. Instead, they signed a petition—which apart from calling for a minimum wage of R40 per week, demanded that a Conciliation Board be set up. . . .

A NUMBER OF WORKERS FIRED

2 weeks after the petition, on 23rd April 1979, 5 workers were fired. 15 workers had signed the petition. Other workers demanded to know the reasons why the 5 had been fired. Management fired 5 of the workers who now demanded reasons. . . .

88 WORKERS HAVE LOST THEIR JOBS

78 workers showed their solidarity with the 10 workers by going on strike. Now a total of 88 workers were on strike. The 78 workers joined their 10 fellow workers outside the factory gate in protest against the actions of the *Fatti's and Moni's* management.

Management called in the Labour Department, who threatened the strikers. They said that if the striking workers did not return to work, they would face fines and imprisonment. The workers refused to be separated, saying that they were one group because they all worked together. Management tried to buy off the 23 'coloured' workers by offering them jobs, but the 'coloureds' refused to be separated from the Africans. Once again the workers showed their solidarity. . . .

In the days and months that have followed the workers have had regular meetings at the Lyric Theatre at Bellville South and it was from one of the earliest meetings after the strike that a call of support went out to the community.

THE BOYCOTT

The boycott of Fatti's and Moni's products and support for the workers first began in the Cape. From there it has spread to Natal and the Transvaal. The Western Cape Traders Association was one of the first organisations to support the boycott. It called on its 2300 shopkeeper members to stop stocking Fatti's and Moni's products.

From there the call for support was taken up by the schools, training colleges and universities. Students supported the boycott but went further than this and immediately went into fund raising projects to sustain the workers in their strike.

A complete list of the organisations supporting the boycott is on the last page of this pamphlet.

WHAT HAS BEEN HAPPENING SINCE?

Management has consistently refused to negotiate with the union. Towards the end of August the South African Council of Churches (SACC) approached the management of Fatti's and Moni's to act as mediators. The management has accepted two of the representatives of the SACC to act as mediators between them and the union. The union has not as yet accepted or refused the two representatives of SACC as mediators.

After 3 months the Fatti's and Moni's management made a final offer and gave the workers an ultimatum to apply for jobs on the condition that they would lose all previously earned benefits and start at the bottom rung of the payscale. Management would thereby be able to choose which of the workers they would re-employ. The 25 workers did not go back to the factory at Bellville South, but to one of Fatti's and Moni's bakeries where the conditions are even worse than the factory. These workers are complaining bitterly about it.

The 63 workers, who are still on strike, see themselves as employees of Fatti's and Moni's and have refused to collect their pay since April. . . .

THE UNION ASSISTS THE WORKERS

The strikers are receiving R15 per week to live off which is supplied by the union and from donations to the union. They are also getting a daily meal. Union funds are low, and they need over R1,000 a week to assist the workers. Financial help is essential.

AND BOYCOTT THE FOLLOWING PRODUCTS.

All goods manufactured by the UNITED MACARONI FACTORIES LTD. are products of Fatti's and Moni's.

All flour sold under the brand name of RECORD FLOUR is produced by Fatti's and Moni's. This includes self-raising flour, cake flour, bread flour, sifted flour and Wheatie Treat flour.

Fatti's and Moni's markets a number of products under its own name. These include ice-cream cones, cake cups, wafers, macaroni, spaghetti, large and small noodles, and broad, narrow, plain and green ribbon pasta.

Fatti's and Moni's also packs pasta products for specific supermarket outlets. These are marketed under the following brand names—PRINCESS; POT O' GOLD; CHECKERS and ROMA. . . .

The right to strike over wages and working conditions is an essential element of collective bargaining between workers and management. Without this power workers have no ultimate leverage in the bargaining process. But workers do not welcome strikes. It means loss of vital earnings and possible unemployment. So it is only as a last resort that workers do go on strike.

In South Africa the right to strike is no "right" at all. . . .

THESE ORGANISATIONS SUPPORT THE WORKERS:

University of the Western Cape, Hewat College, Peninsula Training College, Bellville Technical Training College, Western Cape Traders Association, SACOS (South African Council of Sport), NAFCOC (Cape Town), 14 000 strong Union of Teachers Associations of South Africa, Cape Teachers Professional Association, Harold Cressy High School, Livingstone High School, Heathfield High School, Grassy Park High School, Spes Bona High School, Labour Party, A large Cape Town bakery, Silverleaf Bakery, has also suspended all purchases of flour from Fatti's and Moni's; UCT SRC, and over 15 clubs and societies, including the Medical, Law, Arts, Social Science, Fine Art, Science Faculty Student Councils; Anglican, Catholics and Evangelical Mission religious groups, Wages Commission, Women's Movement, Envirac, Projects Committee and Communities Commission; Muslim Students Association of South Africa; Inkatha; Merebank Ex-Students Association; NACOS (Natal Council of Sport); Bakers Union; Wits SRC; Durban SRC; Pietermaritzburg SRC; Black Sash and Diakonia Council; University of Natal Medical School SRC.

THE WORKERS OF FATTI'S AND MONI'S NEED YOUR SUPPORT
ABASEBENZI BAKWA FATTI'S and MONI'S
BAYALUDINGA USIZO LWAKHO!

DOCUMENT 84. "Summary of Grievances Raised by Black Employees at the Engine Plant." Statement by workers at the Ford Motor Company, Port Elizabeth, November 1979

1. Whites must apologise for comments that they were quoted in the newspaper as having been made.
2. Ford must take disciplinary action against the person whose photograph appeared on the front page of the newspaper.
3. The foremen have no respect for the Black workers:

(a) Workers are not allowed to go to the toilet 20 minutes before the end of the shift.

(b) If the foreman is not on the line when a worker wants to go to the toilet the worker must wait for him to return to ask permission to go.

4. Bonus be calculated from January to December and also accrued bonus should be paid out whenever an employee resigns or is dismissed.

5. Sometimes the Blacks work short time, but the Whites do not. The poorer people work short time, fall behind in their rent and then cannot get loans.

6. Blacks are compelled to work overtime when overtime is worked while Whites are sometimes let off.

7. (a) White foremen are recruited from outside the Company, while there are many Blacks who can do the job.

(b) The position of toolsetters is in doubt after Mr Skilton said to one of them—that he can be a labour grade 7 for many years.

8. Do foremen all possess N. T. C. III? [National Trade Certificate, grade 3] Foremen do not know how to deal with people.

9. One worker complained that he is doing the work of two people and said he will not do this work until he is given a helper.

10. (a) Workers want to know the production target for the day.

(b) When the assembly line stops engines have to be pulled aside causing a lack of working space.

11. Some machine operators are undergraded for the machines they are operating.

12. The medical Aid Plan should be changed to do away with the 20 percent additional payment.

13. R. Cooper, a superintendent, approached the operators directly. This caused a disturbance. He also shouts at people.

14. School books be made available to children along the lines of the system in effect at General Motors.

15. No department should work short time while others work overtime.

16. Minimum wage of R2,50.

17. Don't want the trade union [the National Automobile and Allied Workers Union] to be the spokesman of the workers. A referendum must be taken.

18. Employees who wish to, should be allowed to revert to the weekly pay system.

19. List of the workers wanting scrap wood should be completed at each plant and daily.

20. There should not be a three-year waiting period for workers to qualify for loans to buy or improve homes.

21. When security guards at the gate ask for identification badges they show leniency towards the Whites who can merely sign a book in the office. Also, Blacks have to wait at the gate for their foreman to come identify them; hence they arrive at their work station late and lose pay.

22. R2,50 charge to replace badges is too high.

23. Foremen should be rotated between departments so that they do not get into the habit of doing things their own way.

24. If two Black workers fight, they both get fired. If one White and one is Black, they get disciplined differently.
25. Safety shoes are too pricey.
26. When Black and White workers are taken to the Labour Relations Representative's office together, the Black is told to wait outside while the White puts his case forward.
27. Ford must make a press statement that Blacks do not get a special discount on cars purchased from Ford.
28. When short time is being worked, the line speed is increased.
29. Loans should be made available to buy houses in the homelands.
30. The following should not be terminable offences: continual absence through sickness; poor workmanship; old age causing inability to do the job.
31. When Black workers are caught stealing, their services are terminated and they are handed over to the police while Whites are merely asked to resign.
32. No reply was received to forms filled in applying for houses at KwaFord.

Ford Workers Committee Press Release
    To: Mr Allan Lukens—U. S. General Consul
        Ford (SA) Management
        Dismissed Ford (SA) Workers Representatives

Re: Reinstatement
    In a meeting held between the above mentioned parties on the 9th January 1980 with the main aim of reducing human suffering and to contribute to the prosperity and well-being of the area an agreement was reached that Ford (SA) would reinstate all former employees who wished to return to work.
    However, Ford (SA) appears to be violating the agreement according to the following report-back by workers.

1. Workers have to fill forms with a "REHIRE" endorsement instead of "REINSTATE."
2. Workers clock cards are written "REHIRE."
3. Plant Manager (Mr G L Berger) commands that inside the Ford (SA) plants the Black workers must speak only AFRIKAANS and ENGLISH, not their mother tongue, which is XHOSA: Furthermore they were even told not to wear the necklace with the map of AFRICA.
4. There were Security Police at the Personnel Office of FORD (SA) during the reinstatement process and some have even been allocated to the Cortina Plant.
5. The management of the Neave Plant (Mr G L Berger) bluntly tells the reporting workers that there will be no payment of 1979 bonuses because the workers are responsible for causing the company financial embarrassment.
NOTE: At the meeting it was decided to leave the bonus issue to the United

Automobile Rubber and Allied Workers of South Africa to negotiate it with the Company. The Union has since regained sound relations with the workers.

6. Ford (S. A) requires workers to submit their reference books for new endorsement because they were now being REHIRED and not REIN-STATED. Now it must please be appreciated that the workers have and in fact, intend to keep to the agreement as it is a civilised one.

But, from the above information FORD (SA) seems to be bent on violating the agreement and for this reason the workers are requesting that the US General Consul, the workers' representatives and the American Ambassador investigate satisfactorily in this matter, urgently.

All this attitude from FORD (SA) management is designed to intimidate the workers so that they may resign under duress. Because FORD (SA) is an American investment, then the Americans have an obligation and a responsibility in seeing that this inhumanity to mankind must stop at once and now.

Also, the fact that the detention of our fellow worker Mr Thozamile Botha comes sudden in the wake of the FORD management-Worker representatives reinstate agreement, that has smeared enormously the image of FORD (SA) not only in the Black Community, in South Africa but in the whole world. The Black community of South Africa believes that FORD (SA) is an extension of the South African government because of her confidence in the Security Police to resolve company labour disputes that are caused by FORD (SA) reluctance to fairly implement the Rev. Leon Sullivan Code of fair employment practice. At FORD (SA) a White high school dropout has greater job opportunities than a Black high school graduate.

Document 85. Draft resolutions on the formation of the Federation of South African Trade Unions, 1979

Draft Resolutions Based on the Policy Proposals Decided on at the Interim Central Committee Meetings on 18th and 19th October 1978 and on 10th and 11th March 1979

RESOLUTION 1

This Federation will adopt certain basic policy resolutions at its National Congresses and such resolutions will be appended to the Constitution and be considered as fundamental policy positions.

RESOLUTION 2

This Federation will be open to persons of all races, creeds and sexes. This fundamental non-racial position will have be to achieved by the willingness of all groups to cooperate, especially on the shop-floor, within the close working relationship envisaged within the Federation. Such a commitment will be our yardstick for deciding on the degree of cooperation between the Federation and its affiliates and other bodies.

This position is adopted because we believe that only by achieving the maximum unity of workers at the workplace can worker interests be adequately protected and advanced.

RESOLUTION 3

This Federation sees Industrial Unions as a major means of achieving many of our aims and objects since they allow organisations across job categories and where advantageous they facilitate use of existing industrial legislation and collective bargaining structures.

Being, however, aware of the possible differential development of industrial unions the role of the Federation is through maximum possible cooperation and coordination to prevent any divisive tendencies in the labour movement that could arise from Industrial Unions.

RESOLUTION 4. *RELATIONS WITH OTHER SOUTH AFRICAN ORGANISA-TIONS*

4.1. In starting FOSATU it is not our concern to begin our organisation by attacking others. Whilst we may disagree with other organisations it is more important to prove ourselves as able to meet our aims and objects rather than attack others.

4.2. That the following procedure be adopted. Any invitation to meet or participate in events organised by other organisations at a national level should be referred to the Executive Committee. Regional contacts should be referred to the Regional Executive Committees in consultation with the Executive Committee. However, any major initiative or commitment would have to be referred to the Central Committee.

RESOLUTION 5. *RELATIONS WITH OVERSEAS ORGANISATIONS*

5.1. FOSATU's main concern is with workers and their interests in South Africa. FOSATU will, therefore, independently decide what is in its best interests without being influenced or dominated by foreign organisations or Governments.

5.2. In dealing with international organisations FOSATU will be guided by the interests of South African workers, its own aims and objects as stated in its Constitution and the activities of those international organisations.

5.3. The procedures as regards overseas invitations should be as follows:

5.3.1. All overseas invitations should be directed to appropriate organisations. They should not be directed to individuals, nor can they be accepted by individuals within FOSATU.

5.3.2. All invitations of a general nature which would be of interest to all affiliates of FOSATU and which are from coordinating bodies or Governments should go through the Federation.

5.3.3. Invitations of a specific nature from International Trade Secretariats of sister industrial unions should go to the affiliate concerned. Such invitations should be accepted in consultation with the Federation.

RESOLUTION 6

FOSATU does not subscribe to, support or align itself with any party political organisation and would actively oppose any attempts by such party political organisation to control FOSATU or its affiliates.

RESOLUTION 7

That in order to prevent divisions that may arise through differential access to donation funds, all requests for donation funds will be directed through FOSATU and will be remitted to FOSATU for allocation on the basis of agreed upon budgetary estimates.

1. WHAT IS FOSATU TRYING TO ACHIEVE WITH ITS PARTICULAR STRUCTURE?

There are three key things that the FOSATU structure tries to achieve.

1. Worker Control
2. Worker Cooperation
3. National Coordination

However, in trying to achieve all three we must realise that in fact they have to be balanced against each other because they are somewhat contradictory.

WORKER CONTROL—this cannot be achieved by a Constitution. It is achieved by democratic organising practices. However it can be supported by constitutional structures. So in all FOSATU Committees that have any executive authority workers from the factories are in a majority. This gives workers rather than officials formal power. The rest of our policies and practices must make that real worker power and control.

WORKER COOPERATION—Our aim is to bring workers into contact so that they can cooperate on platforms wider than their own factories and unions. The best place to do this is at the Regional level or even better at the local level. So the Regions and beneath them the Locals are the key areas of cooperation.

NATIONAL COORDINATION—having said that the key area of cooperation is the Region which it must be since worker cooperation at a national level is practically more difficult and expensive we begin to see a conflict between national coordination and worker cooperation.

The danger is that Regions will begin to go their own way and we'll end up with a weak divided federation.

To correct this we have given the National bodies, that is the Congress and the Central Committee final powers to determine policy and to discipline. Furthermore, certain key policies will be binding on affiliates.

The balance then is between the Regions where most worker cooperation takes place and worker leaders develop and the National level that determines overall policy and direction.

2. WHO DECIDED ON THE STRUCTURE OF FOSATU?

The structure of FOSATU was decided on by a worker majority at the

Inaugural Congress of FOSATU on the 13–15th April, 1979. It is now part of the FOSATU Constitution.

3. THE WORKING OF THIS STRUCTURE

All structures in Constitutions look good on paper. But the important thing is to see whether these work in practice.

In order for FOSATU structures to work there must be *democratic structures* at the very first level i.e. in the factory. Democratically elected worker representatives then make sure that the workers voice is heard at every level and that the decisions that are made are the decisions of their members. There must also be efficient *report backs* at every level of the structures.

It is important to ensure that democratic structures create stable policies as a result of continuity and *experience*. It is only through some kind of structure which records and preserves its experience and its leadership, that the experience can be of use at a later date.

4. DANGERS OF STRUCTURE

Structures can be a dangerous thing. They can be powerful and be used in such a way as to confuse workers and hide things from them. Officials and committee members can hide behind a constitution and say things are unconstitutional or that some committee has to decide on things. This has happened to many unions and federations in the past. It is very important that structures are built up which do not entrench the position of people either as committee members or officials.

DOCUMENT 86. "National Union of Textile Workers: A Short History 1973–1980." Pamphlet, July 1980

INTRODUCTION

This pamphlet is a short history of the NUTW covering the period 1973 to 1980 during which the union established its basic direction and policies. The mistakes of the first few years of organising must never be forgotten, for only through understanding of those mistakes are we better able to plan the direction of our future unity.

1973 THE GREAT AWAKENING

The Textile industry was a great sleeping giant during the 1960's. Very little worker activity came to the fore. Employers had it too easy, and not surprisingly they turned the industry into a cheap labour industry. At the most notorious mills wages were as low as R5 per week and a great many textile workers were barely living on R10 per week.

In January 1973, however, Durban and Pinetown workers took to the streets in massive and spontaneous outbursts of solidarity against their employers. The prominent Frame Group overnight had its labour policies exposed to public scrutiny as workers refused to go on working without an increase.

THE UNION IS BORN

From that movement the National Union of Textile Workers was formed. It started with a Caretaker Committee of Pinetown textile workers who led the 1973 strikes. They tried to build the spirit of worker unity inside their mills and to raise the consciousness of their fellow workers on the need for a union for solidarity all year round.

By September 1973 the union movement had reached such proportions that no matter, everybody said "unions for African workers are illegal," workers had to be unionized. The union was inaugurated on the 23rd September 1973 at a mass meeting of some 1800 workers at the Clermont stadium Pinetown.

A SECOND BRANCH IS STARTED IN JOHANNESBURG

In the early period of enthusiasm for the new unionism many opportunists raised their heads. In Johannesburg the Clothing Union of Lucy Mvubelo crawled out from the skirt of the registered Garment Union and bravely announced it would help NUTW form a textile branch in Johannesburg. NUTW cards were printed, workers were enrolled there, and monies collected, all under the control of the National Union of Clothing Workers.

THE UNION LINKED UP WITH KWAZULU

The new union had very few friends if any when it was formed. All the old unions insisted it could not last—(they had to explain their own inactivity somehow); employers said it was just a political intrigue of White students and they would never recognise it; the state was ominously anti-union and insisted liaison committees were the only answers workers should think about.

With no friends the union linked up with Chief [Gatsha] Buthelezi and his Minister of Community Development, Mr. B. I. Dladla. Mr Dladla was invited to address workers and his assistance was often sought as workers took to the streets again in January 1974 to demonstrate their continued indignation at their bad wages and conditions.

THE BACKLASH HIT NUTW

In February 1974 the state smashed our union organisers—Halton Cheadle, Jeanette Cunningham Brown (Murphy) and David Hemson were banned together with David Davis, a Metal Union organizer.

The pressure was on and the new friends of the union were quick to be on their way. Lucy Mvubelo and company by pretending they had nothing to do with NUTW at all, changed the name of the branch of NUTW in Johannesburg to the Transvaal Textile Union (still run by the National Union of Clothing at that stage); Chief Buthelezi accused the union of undermining his standing in the community; Mr B. I. Dladla was dismissed and his successors much more careful about being seen with union officials or members.

A NEW LINE IS BORN

Out of every crushing defeat the union endured, a new positive direction began to emerge. Far from outside expectations (or hopes) the union did not crumble. It generated its own leaderships and survived—without friends and much the wiser.

NUTW accepted the loss of its Johannesburg branch and reverted to operating only in Natal.

It accepted its interests could not go far along the Zulu path—for the union was firstly a non-racial body. Its membership was open not only to Blacks but to all textile workers who were prepared to struggle in unity. Secondly the union was a worker movement—it was not open to leaders or members who came from other classes; it needed no doctors, teachers, lawyers and traders to fill up its leadership ranks—on the contrary it had to safeguard itself against being hijacked by such elements.

The new line consolidated itself in the slogan we are a non-racial worker union movement.

The union leadership kept struggling on their own in the factories and in July 1974 won a major victory at Smith and Nephew when the first agreement with an unregistered trade union was signed in Pinetown.

NEW LINKS ARE FORGED

The union quickly developed in its appreciation of real friends. It formed TUACC (The Trade Union Advisory and Coordinating Council) and resisted moves by TUCSA to incorporate it. Gradually the union tested the true strength of other unions—the tests were (1) are you a worker-controlled body and (2) are you committed to non-racial unionism.

From those contacts a new trade union federation was formed—FOSATU and NUTW finally made a home for itself.

NUTW FORMS A NEW BRANCH

Thus it is for the second time that NUTW links up with a second branch. This time however its movements are slower and more careful.

Has the union learnt from its past mistakes? Now is the time to reflect.

8. The Politics of the System

DOCUMENT 87. "Forward to Freedom!" Flyer by the South African Coloured People's Congress, in Afrikaans and English, 1968

VOORWAARTS tot die VRYHEID!

ONS ROEP OP DIE KLEURLING GEMEENTSKAP

Tom Swartz, voorsitter van die Kleurlingraad het onslangs verklaar dat as die Goewerment die "Bruinmense" vra om wapens op te neem teen "terroriste," dit sy geloof is dat ons mense weer vir Suid Afrika sal veg soos hulle in die verlede in twee wereld oorloë geveg het. Maar Swartz praat vir homself en sy klein groepie ja-broers and ja-base.

Wie is die dapper mans wat die goewerment en sy aanhangers en die pers beskryf as "terroriste"?

Vanaf Augustus 1967 het groepe guerillas bestaande uit Suid Afrikaners en Zimbabweans (Rhodesia) gebots met Ian Smith se leër. In sy angs het Smith haastig Vorster gevra om te kom help. Ten spyte van wat die koerante gesê het en wat hulle nog steeds sê (en ons almal weet dat hulle nie aan ons kant staan nie) het ons Vryheidsvegters die verdedigers van rassehaat van Rhodesia en Suid Afrika ernstig laat skrik. Hulle het dit nodig gevind om twee hospitale bekikbaar te maak om met die gewondes te handel. Die geveg gaan voort. Die van ons manskappe wat gesneuwel het, het soos helde geveg. ONS EER HULLE. Ons is trots van hulle. Hulle is ons seuns en broers, lede van UMKONTO WE SIZWE (Spear of the Nation). Dit was dieselfde organisasie wat in 1961 vir die eerste keer sabotage veroorsaak het. DIT IS ONS MENSE SE PLIG OM HULLE TE VERWELKOM. Hulle is ons eie mense. Hulle veg vir ons vryheid.

Laat Tom Swartz die baas se skoene lek, maar laat hy en sy ja-baas Raad dit allen doen.

ONS SAL WEIER OM VIR APARTHEID TE VEG!

Die is waar dat baie van ons jong mans geval het op die slagvelde van Europe en Afrika in die twee wereld oorloë. Die Cape Corps het 'n trotse geskiedenis van dapperheid en diens. Maar wat het die soldate afgewag toe hulle van die oorlog af terugkom? Dit is ons bitter ondervinding dat in plaas dat ons toegelaat word om 'n nuwe en beter Suid Afrika vir almal te bou, het ons posisie steed slegter geword. Daar was 'n tyd toe ons lot 'n bietjie beter was as die van die verslaafde Afrikaan (sogenoemde Bantoe). Vandag is dit nie meer so nie. Ons kan nie ons eie verteenwoordigers na Parlement kies nie en binnekort sal dit verwag wees dat ons 'n Kleurling-stamraad moet kies.

Die vernedering van aparte sitplekke in die bus, aparte ingange by ie poskantore en stasies, trein apartheid, apartheid op die strand en in die parke, DIT KAN NIE WEER VERDRA WORD NIE.

Die minderwaardige onderwys van ons kinders, slegter werk, laer beloning, die diefstal van ons huise onder die skuil van die Groepsgebiede Wet, DIT MOET NIE VERDER VERDRA WORD NIE.

Ons vakunies word beperk, ons politieke organisasies word van kant gemaak, ons leiers word beperk, verban of gehang. Nou is ons die slagoffer van die Coloured Cadet regulasies. Hierdie is die begin van die pas wet waaronder die Afrikaan ly, want netnou moet ons ook 'n pas dra wat die polisie kan vereis, en as ons nie registreerd is nie, kan ons opgesluit word. ONS MOET DIE ONREG TEENSTAAN. Met mans soos Nelson Mandela, Walter Sisulu, Bram Fischer en Yusuf Dadoo vereis ons die demokratiese reg om in Parlement te sit.

DIT IS WAARVOOR ONS SAL VEG! ONS MOET ORGANISEER! Vir jare was ons besig, wettig besig om op demokratiese wyse teenstaand te bied teen apartheid. Die EENDRAG van al ons mense onder die leierskap van die African National Congress, South African Congress of Trade Unions, South African Indian Congress, Congress of Democrats, Communist Party en die South African Coloured People's Congress was ons mikpunt. Maar die Nasionaliste en hulle volgelinge met hulle beleid van wit baaskap wou dit nie toelaat nie en het alles in hulle vermoë gedoen om ons pogings te verydel. Hulle word mos skatryk op ons sweet. Hulle het daarin geslaag om ons beweging tydelik ondergrond te dryf.

Alhoewel ons welbekende leiers nie meer deelneem in ons organisasies nie, is ons mense weer orals in ons land besig om te organiseer in groepies van twee of drie of vier, net soos die mense van Europa hulself georganiseer het teen Hitler.

DIE GOEWERMENT IS DIE TERRORISTE!

Die goewerment het keer op keer gewys dat hulle weier om te praat. Hulle is gereed om die geweer, die tronk of die galg te gebruik. Vandag is daar ongevaar 10,000 van ons seuns en dogters in tronke soos Robben Eiland, baie is verban, anders is op een of ander manier beperk en somige was gedwing om die land te verlaat. Terwyl Tom Swartz en anders betaal word om ten gunste van Apartheid te praat, regeer wreedheid en onreg in ons land. Suid Afrika word by die dag een groot konsentrasie kamp.

Maar ons sal aanhou veg tot dat al Suid Afrika se onderdruktes vry is. Daarom maak ons nou'n beroep vir nuwe moed en vasberadenheid. Ons moet die geweld van die owerheid met geweld uit die weg ruim om 'n nuwe vrye Suid Afrika te stig.

LAAT ONS GEREED STAAN OM TE VEG VIR ONS VRYHEID.

FORWARD TO FREEDOM!

WE CALL THE COLOURED COMMUNITY

Tom Swartz, Chairman of the Council for Coloured Affairs has said that if the Coloured People were called upon to fight "terrorists" he believed they would respond in the same way that our people responded to the call to join and fight as part of the Cape Corps in the two world wars. But Swartz speaks only for himself and his small clique of collaborators!

Who are these brave men called "terrorists" by the government, its lackeys and the press?

From August of last year a unit of freedom fighters of South Africa and Zimbabwe (Rhodesia) engaged the soldiers of Ian Smith's white racist regime. Smith was forced to call on the help of Vorster. In spite of what the newspapers said, and continue to say (and we all know that they are not on our side), our guerilla Freedom Fighters are causing wholesale panic among the racialists of Rhodesia and South Africa. To cope with government casualties, two hospitals had to be cleared. Today the fighting still goes on. Those of our men who died, died bravely, WE SALUTE THEM. They are your sons and brothers, members of Umkonto We Sizwe (Spear of the Nation). Members of the same organisation which carried out its first acts of sabotage in South Africa on 16th December, 1961. OUR COMMUNITY MUST WELCOME THESE MEN. THEY ARE OUR OWN. THEY ARE FIGHTING FOR FREEDOM.

Let Tom Swartz lick the white man's boots, but let him and his council do it alone.

WE WILL NOT FIGHT FOR APARTHEID!

It is true as many a mother will tell you, that we have lost many brave young men in the two world wars. Our people have a very proud record in the field of battle.

BUT WHAT DID OUR MEN COME BACK TO? Our experience is, that instead of our people being allowed to take part in building a new and better South Africa for all, our position became worse and worse. There was a time when we were treated a little better than the enslaved African. TODAY THIS IS HARDLY SO. *We cannot elect our own representatives to Parliament. Instead, we have four white representatives and the Council for Coloured Affairs.*

The insults and humiliation of separate bus seats, post office queues, train carriages, station entrances, separate parks and beaches CAN NEVER BE ACCEPTED. The inferior education being given to our children today, the inferior jobs, the lower wages, the stealing of our homes under the protection of the Group Areas Act CAN NEVER BE ACCEPTED. The crippling of our Trade Unions, and our militant political organisations; the banning, banishment, imprisonment and hanging of people's leaders MUST BE CHALLENGED.

Now we are the victims of the Coloured Cadets regulations. This is the beginning of the pass laws under which the Africans suffer. Soon our men will have to carry documents which can be demanded by the police and can be imprisoned if they are not registered.

We demand unconditional democratic rights and our right to sit in Parliament together with men like Nelson Mandela, Walter Sisulu, Bram Fischer or Dr. Dadoo. THIS WE WILL FIGHT FOR! WE WILL CONTINUE TO ORGANISE!

For many years we have been building massive opposition to the policies of Apartheid. Unity among the people was being built LEGALLY under the leadership of the African National Congress, the S.A. Congress of Trade Unions, the S.A. Indian Congress, the Congress of Democrats, the Communist Party and the S.A. Coloured People's Congress. The Nationalist government and the rest of the white supremists, anxious to divide our people, determined to continue to make huge profits out of us all; became frightened, banned certain organisations and individuals and FORCED THE MOVEMENT UNDERGROUND.

Today, known and respected leaders of our community can no longer participate in our organisation. But a new force is organising all over in small groups of two, three or four, just as the people of Europe under Nazi occupation had to organise.

THE GOVERNMENT ARE THE TERRORISTS!

The government showed that it had no intention of talking, it is only prepared to use the baton, the gun, the hangman, and the jail. Today, 10,000 of our best sons and daughters rot in South Africa's jails like Robben Island. Hundreds have been banished, forced into exile, house-arrested, banned and restricted, while Tom Swartz is paid to sing the Apartheid praises.

But we will not be turned from the road to the liberation of all South Africa's oppressed. That is why we now call for greater determination, and the use of force to meet force and win our rights.

WE WILL FIGHT!
TOGETHER WITH THE FREEDOM FIGHTERS LET US PREPARE TO FIGHT FOR A FREE SOUTH AFRICA.

No doubt there may be many hard battles ahead. The Freedom Charter, which is our policy for a democratic People's Republic states:
"SOUTH AFRICA BELONGS TO ALL WHO LIVE IN IT."
THIS IS WHAT WE CALL UPON OUR PEOPLE TO FIGHT FOR!
THIS IS WHAT WE SHALL WIN IN SOUTH AFRICA!
LONG LIVE THE STRUGGLE FOR LIBERATION!
FORWARD TO FREEDOM!

DOCUMENT 88. Speech by Chief Lucas Mangope at opening of furniture factory, Babalegi, March 20, 1973

Mr. Chairman, guests of honour, businessmen and industrialists. Ladies and gentlemen.

Seldom have I accepted an invitation to speak with a deeper sense of gratitude and privilege. Yet seldom have I accepted it with such a keen awareness of the tremendous burden of responsibility on my shoulders, a burden which often makes my heart heavy.

Though it is an occasion of joyful encouragement, of yet another landmark of development achieved, which brings us together here today, there is no doubt in my mind that in years to come we will remember the early months of 1973 as an important historical watershed.

It seems that there are still too few among us who can see to the full extent the significant historical implications of recent events in the field of Black industrial labour. One fact, however, has dawned on all of us: Since Durban, things can never be the same. But in which direction our destinies will move, nobody can as yet say. But we do know that it will depend on the wisdom and statesmanship with which our boat of destiny is steered through the troubled waters ahead of us.

I am said to be a politician. But it is in times like these that I am humbly praying that a Higher Hand may guide me to speak and act like a statesman rather than like a politician. And I am appealing with equal humbleness to all politicians, both Black and White, of this our beloved country, to try, in this hour of need, to be statesmen rather than politicians.

It is my wish to go on record that I am fully aware and deeply appreciative of the significant example of statesmanship which our Honourable Prime Minister has set in these critical days. When the labour unrest in Durban reached its climax and nobody knew which turn the events would take, our uneasy spirits inevitably turned to Cape Town. It was at that fateful moment, when the destiny of the country lay in his hands, that Mr. Vorster, in what historians may proclaim as one of his greatest moments, simply reminded Parliament that each one of the Black labourers on strike *was a human being with a soul.* I believe that the spirit of that utterance was the turning point in an otherwise unpredictable crisis. It created new hope, and bought precious time, to intensify an honest and bold search for a peaceful solution to our very real and urgent problems. How much that statement means to me, and probably to millions of my fellow-Blacks, very few White people have enough insight to realise. I am more than happy that my colleague, Chief Buthelezi, has made a positive public reference about this significant statement.

Looking back over the events of the last few months in perspective, I am prompted to say that we have cause for profound gratitude that Providence restrained the hearts and hands of men, and on both sides, in an almost miraculous way. The pages of history relate numerous instances of tragic deadlocks, where the bottled-up frustrations and grievances of underprivileged people exploded without much warning into uncontrolled violence, which swept all parties concerned along into unspeakable disaster.

Must we then not consider it a blessing that Providence has put the writing on the wall for everybody to see, that Providence has thereby given us the privilege of a breathing space, of a time of grace, to work out our salvation?

It is not for me to predict how long the time of grace will last. I cannot force the hand of Providence. But it is as clear to you as it is to me that we cannot afford to waste the precious time of grace. It will not come again.

It strengthens my hope and my faith to behold the signs of wholesome ferment and self-searching among employers, industrialists and authorities all over the country. But if this stream is allowed to lose itself in the sands of sectional self-interest, if it does not flow on to bring more meaningful and palpable opportunities for progress and advancement to the parched spirit of my people, then history will record that Providence bestowed this period of grace on us in vain.

To me, in my humble yet responsible position, this means that I am under a sacred obligation, as spokesman for my people, to try to indicate as honestly, courageously and wisely as I can, the direction in which the stream may be kept flowing towards peace and progress for us all.

In this spirit I will, therefore, make some recommendations and statements, which, if understood and implemented in the same spirit, will put us, I believe, on the road towards a mutually beneficial solution.

1. As things are at present, I am pleading for the most positive and creative use to be made of the *Works Committees,* as provided for in the Industrial Conciliation Act. If these are to be of any value, they must be established and function in a spirit which introduced genuine principles of democracy on the factory floor. This means that they must be truly and genuinely elected by the people they represent, and that there must be real and regular communication with management. Otherwise they won't buy us additional time.

2. Secondly, it is the intention of my government to appoint an official who shall function as a *Labour Liaison Officer.* His task shall be to keep my government in continuous touch, both with the Works Committees, and with industrial management. It is of utmost importance to me that he shall function in a spirit which will be beneficial to both labour and management.

3. Thirdly, I must, lest I take leave of my senses, dwell on the delicate subject of *wages.* But what I am asking here, I am sure you will acknowledge as being reasonable. To me the most important principle is not the starting wage of an unskilled labourer. Of course, I must appeal to you to pay a "living wage," and surely in industry anything less than R14 [$20] a week cannot be claimed to constitute a "living wage."

The real crux of the pay issue lies, however, in the fields of *training, promotion and advancement.* Unless industrialists create opportunities and facilities for, and give active and sincere encouragement to training and advancement of their Black labour force, how can I be expected not to take issue with them?

4. A fourth point, which should be as obvious as it needs to be emphasised, is that *job reservation* is definitely out in the homelands. On this point there must be complete clarity and finality. It goes without saying that White workers with skills not yet acquired by my people will always be more than welcome in Bophuthatswana. But they must have a genuine willingness to teach and convey their skills to my people. Depending on their skills, but even more on their spirit, I can see White workers and managerial staff staying in my country securely, happily and permanently. But no semblance of job reservation can be tolerated. Surely you will appreciate that its underlying principle is totally in conflict with our basic human dignity and self-respect.

5. My last point is indivisibly tied up with the vital fields of productivity, reliability and loyalty. I am pleading with all White industrialists and businessmen that they give their Black workers the *feeling of belonging*. At present too many of my people have reason to feel that they are hired and fired in an arbitrary fashion. Since such a company shows no interest, care or concern for them as individuals, why should they care for the company?

If, on the other hand, a company builds the sort of spirit where each employee feels that he is part of the big "family," that he has the security of really belonging, only then will he be encouraged to identify himself with the company and to take personal pride and interest in its progress and in his own productivity and reliability. What investment could pay better dividends? We all know that this is one of the major success formulas in the Japanese industrial miracle, and I know that it is working successfully in numbers of industries in South Africa.

I have made these points, ladies and gentlemen, with the sincere intention of promoting mutual confidence and progress, of finding a peaceful road into a more happy and prosperous future for all of us in this country. The destination may still be far, but perhaps not as far as we think, but it is better to know that one is at least moving in the right direction, than to drift into a bitter and cynical deadlock without meaningful communication. The latter road leads in a straight line to inevitable disaster.

Let us always remind ourselves of the simple truth, that life does not make provision for a standstill. We always move, and if it is not in the right direction, then we are most certainly moving in the direction of disaster. We are, lets face the facts, at this moment at the cross-roads.

DOCUMENT 89. Press release on Buthelezi and the Natal Indian Congress by A. M. Rajab, executive chairman, South African Indian Council, Durban, July 3, 1973

The warning given by Chief Buthelezi to the Natal Indian Congress that they were creating an explosive situation between Africans and Indians by their support of the critics of the Chief overseas has been given headline treatment in the Press. Press headlines, regrettably, summed up the Chief's admonition of the NIC [Natal Indian Congress] as a warning to the Indian community in general. This was unfortunate. The Chief had apparently not intended this, but it has created considerable unnecessary speculation in certain quarters as to the Chief's knowledge of Indian affairs generally as well as his attitude to Indian South Africans vis-a-vis his plans for the future.

To correct some of these misconceptions but more to clear the air than anything else, I consider it necessary to make it known not only to the Chief but to the public in general certain facts in regard to the matters that have been raised.

Firstly, I am surprised that Chief Buthelezi has placed such importance on the utterances of the NIC. He ought to know, living cheek-by-jowl as he does with Indians in Natal where more than 80% of them reside and with whom he has much contact, that the NIC has little or no support from the Indians whatsoever. This body represents an infinitesimal—but vocal—minority who will soon disappear from the political scene altogether because of their consistent failure to achieve anything constructive for the Indian people. From the time of their revival a few years ago they have made no headway whatsoever in gaining the support of the people. In fact, their policy has been rejected out of hand since it is so much out of touch with the present-day realities of the South African Situation.

In view of this, why Chief Buthelezi should be so incensed by the mouthings of these people is beyond my comprehension. A Lion should not so over-react to the squeakings of a mouse!

Secondly, I want to make it as clear as possible to Chief Buthelezi that the Indian community stand four square with him in regard to the retention of overseas investment and development capital in South Africa. Repeatedly and consistently the Indian Council has argued this question with hundreds of visiting industrialists, pressmen and moulders of public opinion overseas pressing home the point that any disengagement will inevitably result in a slowing down of the growing economic force that is providing ever-increasing job opportunities for non-whites in fields hitherto closed to them. As the Chief has pleaded overseas, so have we, that the solution to our problems lay not in withdrawal but in a greater involvement in the South African economic structure to speed up the tempo of development from which all would benefit by the raising of their living and social standards.

Finally, may I conclude by saying that as an integral part of the South African Nation, Indians believe in peaceful coexistence. They are here to stay and sincerely offer their many talents towards the growth and development of not only their own areas, which they are building up splendidly, but also that of the African people, if this should be considered acceptable by Chief Buthelezi.

DOCUMENT 90. Transcript of "all-race assembly" at Bulugha, near East London, November 9–11, 1973 (abridged)

MR. [Donald] WOODS: Seeing you all here fills me with a sudden sense of my own presumption in approaching so many distinguished people to give up time to be here and to travel here—but that is outweighed by the importance of the event and the need for it. . . . I thank you for attending and applaud your reasons for attending—concern for the future of our country and recognition of the need to find a formula and a spirit of consensus for the future. . . . [Greetings in Afrikaans]

And now I'd like to say a special word of welcome to our homelands chief ministers, and particularly our local Xhosa-speaking leaders: Kuni nina bahlobo bam, manditi-ndinovuyo olukhulu kuba ababantu bonke bahlangene apha elizweni lethu. Which means, for the benefit of you "maranuga" [newcomers] from elsewhere, that we in this area can be proud that this historic all-race summit meeting takes place here in this region, as indeed did the other historic summit meeting yesterday. Now who, Helen Suzman, says the Eastern Cape is conservative!

You are all here as individuals, but highly important individuals, because if you look around you will see that you are now part of the most representative gathering of South Africans ever to assemble in one room— more representative of all our people than any parliament that has ever assembled in Southern Africa. . . .

Imagine for a moment the sheer influence that is represented here. Here with us are the leaders of millions of people who will determine South Africa's future. Here with us are the authentic voices of the voteless multitudes. Among us are persons who have become living symbols of the aspirations of masses still inarticulate because of legislation or circum-stance—for example, Helen Suzman in her white parliament and Kaiser Matanzima and Knowledge Guzana in their black parliament. . . . And when, earlier this year, Sonny Leon and Tom Swartz stood united on one issue of principle, the hearts of two million Coloured South Africans beat with a new unity of purpose. . . .

Now it gives me very great pleasure to ask the Chief Minister of the Ciskei, Mr. Lennox Sebe, to open this conference. . . .

The conference adjourned for dinner and after dinner elected as chairman for the evening session Mr. K[nowledge] Guzana, proposed by Mr. R[ay] Swart and seconded by Mr. C[urnick] Ndamse.

MR. GUZANA: Ladies and gentlemen, I'm pretty overwhelmed by the honour . . . . now I have pleasure in calling on Mr. Leo Marquard to address us.

MR. MARQUARD: Mr. Chairman, ladies and gentlemen, in the first place I want to congratulate and to thank those who have organised this conference [regarding federation] . . . . to quote another great South African, Albert Lutuli, who once said to me: "It doesn't matter how fast the car goes as long as it's going in the right direction." If we can get things moving in the right direction, we will have achieved a great deal. . . .

(Chief Kaiser Matanzima indicated that he would speak through an interpreter.)

MR. GUZANA: Hy sal nou Xhosa praat. [He will now speak Xhosa]

MR. MATANZIMA: Xhosa is my home language. I have decided to address this conference tonight in my own language. I am glad to notice that most people will understand me because I can see there are so many white Tembus here! . . . Mr. Chairman, the aims of this conference are to show how the races of South Africa should sit together and discuss. . . . .

MR. GUZANA: Ladies and gentlemen, I don't think I can forget altogether that I am the Leader of the Opposition in the Transkei and once the Chief Minister has spoken I ought to reply. However, we'll leave that for the time being. Now I have great pleasure in calling upon Mr. Tom Swartz to address us. As we all know, he is the Chairman of the Coloured Representative Council. . . .

MR. SWARTZ: . . . . we are all bound by the bond of loyalty to South Africa, our country, and by our faith which is based on the fatherhood of God and the brotherhood of man. . . .

Why has this question of federation become so important, I ask myself? I think it is because there is a strong and growing feeling shared by many citizens of the Republic, and especially by the youth of the country, that what is being done for the non-whites or blacks, whichever term you prefer, is inadequate to meet the moral standards demanded in the modern world of today. South Africa, through its government in recent years, has made a tremendous contribution to the general upliftment and development of the underprivileged of this country—call them non-whites, call them blacks, I don't mind. But this is a fact I think which we must recognise. . . .

The Government's policy of separate development in my opinion up to this stage has still been the best. It has brought us all somewhere. True, it has its negative aspects, which have brought the country into disfavour and bad publicity. . . . The continued discrimination on the basis of colour is entirely unacceptable to the black people of South Africa and to the Coloureds as well. . . .

The conference reconvened the following morning, electing Dr. Alex Boraine as chairman of the new session. Dr. Boraine called on Chief Buthelezi as the first speaker.

MR. BUTHELEZI: . . . . As a black man I have personally been supporting the idea of a federation as announced by the Honourable the Chief Minister of the Transkei. This envisages a federation of black states of Southern Africa with a door open for non-black states to enter the federation if they want to. . . . it is imperative to make realistic entities of the homelands by redefining their boundaries without moving out so many people. This done one can easily envisage the homelands becoming autonomous states. . . .

MR. [Elias] OLIVIER: The views I'm going to express here this morning are my personal views and not necessarily the view of the organisation I am representing [Verligte Aksie, led by Theo Gerdener]. . . . Federation at its best is a difficult matter. In fact, it reminds me of a story I once heard which goes more or less like this—there was a wedding ceremony taking place. There were two old ladies in the back of the church listening to the ceremony. Towards the end of the ceremony when the minister proclaimed the couple to be man and wife, the one lady exclaimed: "Yes, now they are one," then the other quietly said: "Yes, they are one, but which one?". . . .[F]ederation in itself, if you go to the definition of federation, carries within itself the ingredient of domination of one group over another within the same unity. . . .

We should make haste slowly, we shouldn't rush into this thing. . . . [T]he various people of the Republic of South Africa should be given the opportunity to develop each on its own to the extent where they are merely autonomous entities so that when the time comes when these people are thinking of federation they should come into this organisation as equal partners because coming in, not being equal partners, would be already the beginning of, perhaps, the end. . . .

MR. EGLIN: Staff is handing out some papers which will contain four documents. One is a brochure on the Progressive Party's federal policy, we hope set out in simplistic form for the average voter to understand. Another one is a copy of the United Nations Fundamental Declaration of Universal Human Rights, to which I will refer briefly. The next one is a major part of the Lusaka Manifesto issued in Lusaka in 1969, to which I will also refer, and finally, to save me having to make the whole of my speech that I made a few months ago at our congress, there is a copy of the speech made in Johannesburg by myself in which I outlined the Progressive Party's federal policy. . . .

MR. [Pat] POOVALINGAM: Chief Gatsha never ceases to amaze me. He presented to us this morning a very erudite, a very scholarly paper . . . .

[If] there were any honesty in this concept of the homelands, Richards Bay would not be excluded from KwaZulu, so the entire homelands policy is based on complete dishonesty, and one cannot build something good on something which is bad. You have to scrap your present homeland boundaries. . . .

I want to make one final point, and this is developing the point I made yesterday and that is if we accept the ideal of a common society in which race plays no part, that ideal must be the goal . . . .

DR. BORAINE: Thank you Mr. Poovalingam. I would like to ask Donald Woods to lead comment or discussion from the floor and would ask you to keep these as brief as possible seeing there are a great number of people present.

MR. WOODS: It seems to me that from what everyone has said this morning it is agreed there is a need for this sort of change. . . . what do all our black delegates feel about this question. Is it not too late for anything of this sort? . . . what do you think of the feeling in Soweto, Mdantsane, Duncan Village, places like that? . . . Chief Buthelezi might want to look after us, Chief Matanzima might want to look after us, but what about the people, the workers, the people who have lived with resentment for 25 years, what about this vast majority? . . .

MR. [Curnick] NDAMSE: May I answer with all humility that it is not too late. . . . the black man, Mr. Woods, has got a very forgiving heart. We are always prepared to forgive and forget and any man entertaining the fear that the black man will never forget what was done to him may rest assured that in fact it is not so. . . . The days when it was customary that we were referred to as just the property of South Africa are over. At the same time we would like to tell all the people in South Africa that the days when we thought we could drive the white men into the sea, catch the snow-white maidens and make good cushions with their hair are over. . . .

After all, we believed that we were being driven out and every time when there were wars in South Africa, we killed as many whites as they killed the blacks, and for that matter we always want to make it clear that in fact we were not defeated, we were told by the Church to lay our arms down, that is why I always refer to the part played by the churches in South Africa as something of tremendous significance. And that is why I hope after Alex has done his work, one thing he must do this evening is to pray for the churches in South Africa, and I include this time the Dutch Reformed Church, because without our moving forward with the Dutch Reformed Church, even if it means we must drag them with their ears, we must move together in order to make our hopes come to realisation. In short, I wanted to say to Donald— it is not too late.

MR. GUZANA: I want to endorse what Mr. Ndamse has said as to the readiness of the African to share South Africa with everybody else who is in South Africa. As leader of the opposition party in the Transkei, I kept away from the urban cities of South Africa for eight years and it was only last year that I went into the urban areas to address Africans on the policy of multiracialism. . . .

One experience was in Soweto, where after I had addressed a political meeting, four young folk of about 22–23 years of age came out to me and this is their comment: "We have had enough of separate development, and homelands leaders have come here to pump us with separate development and we have been filled with frustration because we have been given the impression that our leaders are moving in this direction to our detriment. We have today found direction and we feel that the policy of multiracialism holds a future and a prospect, promises good race relationships in South Africa. We have been given direction." And this is indicative of the African's reaction in spite of what I might call very cruel treatment which they have received to date, and I want to assure Mr. Woods that the time is ripe, it's just not too late.

PROF. [Hudson] NTSANWISI: In answer to the question that was asked by Mr. Woods I would like to say categorically in endorsement of what has been said that as far as the black people are concerned it is not yet too late. . . . I'm not here this morning like the leader of the opposition in the Transkei to defend any political ideology or philosophy. I leave it to the National Party to sing praises of the policy of separate development so that as far as I am concerned, we, the homelands leaders, have stated categorically that we are aware of the fact that in separate development there are many things we do not agree with. . . .

I didn't think that we were here today to try and attack the homelands leaders because of their presence here. I thought we were here to discuss the role that federalism can play in improving our way of life here in South Africa and that to me is the important point, and I would be grateful if we would stick to the problem that we have come here to discuss today instead of trying to get a platform to speak about multiracialism and the like. . . .

MR. [D.] LUKHELE [Swazi National Council of South Africa]: . . . . The only thing we ask the whites to do is to accept us as human beings, to share the power with us, that is only what the black man is after. The idea of federalism according to my own opinion as it has been expressed here I think will be a solution to our problem.

MR. [P.] VERMEULEN [Transvaal Progressive Party]: First of all, as a white South African I feel quite humble today but tremendously impressed to hear of the goodwill that still exists among our black fellow South Africans, in spite of what we have done to them. . . . We hear so much about the frightening dangers of multiracial politics, what have we here today but a multiracial South African parliament, virtually? Is this what we're frightened of—what we see here today? I'd say this is what we want in South Africa. . . .

DR. BORAINE: . . . . May I say that . . . those of us who work fairly closely with young black people would like to underline just one thing surely and that is while one is tremendously encouraged by learning that it's not too late, one should not take too much solace from that, in that if it's not too late, it's almost too late.

The next speaker, Dr. L. van Oudenhove, is closely connected with Mr. Theo Gerdener in his own thinking and plans and so it is with particular interest that we welcome to the microphone Dr. Van Oudenhove.

DR. [L.] VAN OUDENHOVE [National Party]: Let me start by making an apparently contradictory statement—that I believe in a democratic common society in a unitarian South Africa and I firmly expect this to become a reality within a foreseeable number of years; but I equally strongly believe that this logical coexistence in one country and one nation, can only be reached through initial partition. . . .

There is no precedent in history for a situation in which an oligarchy has agreed to share its complete share of power with a so-called hostile majority and there South Africa will certainly not be an historical exception. There is on the other side practically no chance of a violent dismantling of the present oligarchic structure, and therefore multiracialism can be forgotten for all practical purposes, I'm sorry Mr. Guzana, in the South Africa of today. . . .

The final response to diversity in South Africa lies therefore not in federation but in confederation, or in a commonwealth of South African nations, such as vaguely predicted by the late Dr. Verwoerd, when he launched his policy of separate development more than ten years ago, and said today in much the same accent by Chief Buthelezi. . . .

DR. BORAINE: Thanks to Dr. Van Oudenhove. . . . you have stimulated thought and that's very important in a conference like this. . . .

MR. GUZANA: I find myself in a very difficult position because I was shot down in flames by the last speaker and it is impossible to gather myself all into one piece again and address you. . . . In any contemplation of federalism you must begin where you live. What is your relationship with your employee? What is the relationship between the master and the servant? What is the relationship between the man who has the money and the man who hasn't got the money? . . . Over the radio on Sunday morning—I'm speaking of Radio Bantu—you get a service broadcast in Xhosa. How many of you have allowed your servants to come into your lounge to listen to that service? How many of you have installed a speaker device extending the broadcast into the kitchen so that as the dishes are washed the word of God is preached to her? Because I believe that this is the sort of thing that will require to be done, every day in our own area of influence in order to develop goodwill so that we go into federalism with the right attitude and with the right mind. . . .

MRS. [Helen] SUZMAN: . . . . I think in the end the key is probably going to lie with the black homeland leaders. And what they do with this key, how they turn it in the lock or jam it in the lock is largely going to depend on their own ingenuity. I often sit and wonder, when I have time to sit and wonder, what would happen if one of the black homeland leaders or all of the homeland leaders, in fact, called the Government's bluff and demanded independence or autonomy.

CHIEF BUTHELEZI: You're corrupting me!

MRS. SUZMAN: Well, this is probably incitement! But I wonder what would happen if they did? Imagine six or seven or even eight black autonomous homelands forming a black federation within South Africa's geographic borders and bargaining away for all they're worth—for customs duties, for workers' rights, for workers who are working in South Africa, making their own arrangements with foreign countries, raising loans abroad, getting technical and other assistance from abroad, and I think this situation would probably eventually lead to constitutional change.

So maybe it's going to be necessary first to have a federation of the black autonomous states. . . .

DR. BORAINE: Thank you—well, Helen Suzman has done it again with characteristic vigor, has made a number of very provocative statements and we should enjoy quite a free-for-all for the next ten minutes. . . .

DR. BORAINE: Dr. David Welsh is the next speaker, from the University of Cape Town, and I have pleasure in asking him to speak now.

DR. WELSH: . . . . My own commitment to South African politics is to a completely open society. My personal preference would be to make Chief Gatsha Prime Minister immediately—set him up in business as a kind of philosopher king and let him sort out our melancholy situation, which I'm sure he'd do very swiftly. . . .

We've been talking about federalism, we haven't talked much about how you actually persuade the ruling group to share power. . . [one way is] the extraction of concessions by a subordinated group by the use of their labour power and by revolt . . . . Blacks and dissident whites have so far been unable to mobilise sufficient power to force the Government to come round a bargaining table. Now this is the basis of the logjam and why we can't move. And all I can say is it's going to require a great deal of courage from homeland leaders, and I'm sure they will not be found wanting in that regard, and from all of us who want change.

I think we South Africans face a very real danger of a descent into a local variant of fascism and the press, students, universities, churches are going to find themselves under increasing fire within the next year. A second task which I would urge upon you, is to do all in our power, I'm speaking to whites largely, to keep inter-racial contacts alive. If a new society is to be born it can do so only if the social tissue that can sustain it has not been irreparable. damaged. . . .

PROFESSOR [John] DUGARD [of the University of the Witwatersrand]: . . . . If the whites are not given adequate assurances that their safety will be assured, they will stand idly by while the black homelands leaders become independent and enter into a black federation. . . . How can we give the whites assurances that there will be adequate protection of their rights under a federal system? . . .

I think particularly of Proclamation 400 which applies in the Transkei. You will recall that this proclamation was introduced by the white central government in 1960 as an emergency measure and it is still with us. This is a white institution. I'm sure that the Transkei Government could manage quite well without it. I'm also aware that the central government may not be willing to withdraw it, but I do at least think this is an area in which the Transkei Government could impress South Africa with its sincerity if it were to request the central government to withdraw this white institution. . . .

MR. [M.J.] NAIDOO: . . . . At the outset I must point out that I am only here because my president [of the Natal Indian Congress] is not here, he was served with a banning order only last week. Our president before that was banned and the one even before that as well, and many others besides them have been banned, all of them for no reason and with no charges being preferred against them. . . . We are not a terrorist organisation under any measure. We have no intention of going underground, and in spite of the banning orders we will not break and we will not accept what is unacceptable to us. . . .

But despite the fear that anything we say may result in serious consequences being visited upon us, we in the Congress decided that we should attend this congress if only to listen. The reason is obvious: a political solution must urgently be found. Already I believe like so many here, that it may be too late to leave it for tomorrow. . . .

This conference has leaders from all sections of the community to discuss and consider an acceptable solution to the present stalemate. I would not dare to suggest that Mr. Eglin or Chief Buthelezi is not a leader but what about that considerable and significant section whose leaders are not here? Those who are banned or in exile or on Robben Island? Can any solution really be acceptable without the participation of these silent leaders? It is my view that if an honest solution is to be found in which there can be lasting peace, then a condition precedent is amnesty for these silent leaders so that they may take their rightful place around this conference. Surely it must be recognised that the blacks must be properly represented by leaders of their choice. This is not asking for too much. It is the only way as I see it in which the suspicions of the black man can be allayed and the bona fides of the solution tested. Nelson Mandela, Oliver Tambo and all the others must be present around this conference table to make the resulting solution palatable to all the black people of this country. In conclusion, I ask, with all the fervour that I can command, that this conference in its statement tomorrow sets out as one of its dedicated aims a call for the immediate release of these leaders. If this is done, I promise that the immediate reaction of the black man will be to trust the white man and his bona fides, a trusting without which I consider no solution can be lasting.

DR. BORAINE: Mr. Naidoo, you have introduced a note of soberness as you have referred to your colleagues who have been banned and are not able to be present, and we salute very especially your own personal courage in being here notwithstanding the risks of associating with a crowd of people like this. We wish you well in your work and take note of your comments. You are to be followed by Mr. Collins Ramusi, Lebowa Minister of the Interior. He is a man of peace who speaks without compromise, and we are very glad to hear him now.

MR. [Collins] RAMUSI: . . . . the pleasure we had at Umtata, this I can disclose, behind the closed doors, men dedicated with love to help their people. Chief Matanzima was one of them, George Matanzima was one of them. Chief Buthelezi rose like an angel and he led us with the Matanzima brothers and Professor Ntsanwisi. . . . if they do approach those who have locked up our people on Robben Island, in a proper spirit, I am sure they will persuade them to release Mandela and the others because all they are suffering for is because they ever said to the world and to the leaders of the white people in this country that our people should go free.

DR. BORAINE: Thank you Mr. Ramusi, for giving us a bird's eye picture—even a glimpse at least of the meeting which took place quite recently, and I say bird's eye because it's very difficult to get near an angel—perhaps an eagle would be more appropriate! . . .

MR. WOODS: . . . . I would like to suggest if it meets with your approval, a small committee consisting of the top table up there to meet right after tea, while all these other people are relaxing, with the addition, possibly of Professor Van Niekerk to consider all these suggestions that have been handed to me for the purpose of a draft of consensus up to this point. . . .

CHIEF BUTHELEZI: I must first apologise because to some people I might appear to be petty, but I think it would be morally wrong towards Paramount Chief Matanzima, Mr. Ramusi, Professor Ntsanwisi and others who are here from the homelands governments for me not to take issue with Mr. Naidoo. I would like first of all to explain that Paramount Chief Matanzima is a nephew of Nelson Mandela and a few months ago Paramount Chief Matanzima's brother, Chief George Matanzima, went to Robben Island to see Mandela. I am a personal friend of Mandela myself, and on certain occasions we have exchanged correspondence. . . .

I think that for those of us who travel abroad, who are constantly under fire because people make this point that we have no credentials to speak for our people, I think this was the implication made by Mr. Naidoo this afternoon when he says that he doesn't say that I'm not a leader or Mr. Eglin but that people must be represented around this table by people of their choice. I think personally it was quite petty to do it, but I think in view of the fact that the press is here and that one has been under tremendous pressure abroad because people try to paint us in this way as just stooges of Mr. Vorster. I think it is just right and fair for us to get this point very clear. In March this year I discussed the release of political prisoners and also allowing our refugees to return to this country with Mr. Vorster himself, which thing he said he would not do as long as he was Prime Minister of this country, he wouldn't do that. Now when we were overseas, Paramount Chief Matanzima and Chief Mangope and I, we made it a point through Chief Matanzima to invite Mr. Oliver Tambo, who is the president of the exiled African National Congress, and other refugees with whom we had a social gathering openly, because we didn't want people to think that there was anything hanky-pankyish that we did with these exiles because by way of necessity we are not committed to their way of bringing about change in this country . . . .

He [Naidoo] must remember that the African National Congress was banned, and I daresay that most of us if it was still existing would be members, but even if we wanted to be members of the ANC it doesn't exist today. . . .

Now I wish Mr. Naidoo or those who think like him in this country or abroad could travel with us in Langa or Guguletu where Paramount Chief Matanzima and myself have addressed meetings of black people. I wish you could be with me in some of my rallies in Soweto or travel with me to Kroonstad, to Bloemfontein and to other parts where there are no Zulus, where they are just black people and then perhaps you could judge whether we are, we have no right or mandate to speak as we do. For the sake of the record and in view of the fact that the world press is here I thought I should put the record straight because quite often when we are abroad we are under tremendous pressure even on this question of investments because it is said we defend investments because we are the stooges of Mr. Vorster. Thank you.

DR. BORAINE: Thank you. I know Mr. Naidoo would like a chance to reply but I really can't give that chance now—perhaps you could meet outside this conference. I really don't think it was Mr. Naidoo's intention to discredit anyone, and I know we have tremendous faith and regard in the people who are here who have responded to invitations to speak about the needs, the aspirations, the hopes, the fears of so many millions of people in South Africa. Could we please meet here at 5.00. The meeting is adjourned.

The conference reconvened an hour later to consider the following proposed declaration of consensus by the drafting committee, which consisted of Chief Buthelezi, Mr. Swartz, Professor Ntsanwisi, Dr. Boraine, Mr. Guzana and Mr. Eglin, with Mr. Woods as secretary.

"This conference of South Africans of all races: (1) Affirms the need for urgent change in South Africa; (2) Declares its belief in the fundamental right of each citizen irrespective of race, creed or colour, to live a full life with dignity, opportunity and justice under the rule of law; (3) Agrees, against the background of the realities of South Africa, that a federal form of government embodying autonomous states free of racial exclusiveness is most likely to create the conditions under which these rights will be achieved; (4) That in view of fears of group domination and discrimination the rights of each individual be protected by a Bill of Rights entrenched in the federal constitution; (5) Declares its commitment to these goals, each of us using areas of influence and power available to us, and commends these goals to all South Africans who share our concern for the future of our people."

There were several objections to point 5, Professor Bozzoli and other observers, including newspaper editors, pointing out that both as observers and in their professional capacities they could not properly be included in such a consensus. Paramount Chief Matanzima also mentioned that point 5 was one he would have to consult his cabinet on before ratification. After general discussion the conference decided unanimously to drop point 5 and issue the first four points as the unanimous Declaration of Consensus by all delegates to the conference.

The final session of the conference consisted of general discussion on how best to promote the terms of the Declaration. Mr. Olivier made the point that the ruling Afrikaans group should be represented at such conferences, and spoke in Afrikaans to underline his point. Dr. Boraine pointed out that such representatives had been invited and their absence was by their own choice.

The conference then elected a committee to plan further steps in promoting the Declaration of Consensus dubbed by one delegate the "Bulugha Declaration." The committee chosen was Professor Van Niekerk (convener), Professor Dugard, Dr. Welsh, Dr. Boraine, Mr. Poovalingam and Mr. Woods.

Document 91. Transcript of meeting between Prime Minister John Vorster and homeland chief ministers, Cape Town, January 22, 1975 (abridged)

The meeting took place under the Chairmanship of the Prime Minister in the Cabinet Room, H. F. Verwoerd Building, Cape Town, and commenced at about 10.30 a.m.

The following attended: The Hon. B. J. Vorster, M.P. Prime Minister; The Hon. M. C. Botha, M.P. Minister of Bantu Administration and Development and of Bantu Education; The Hon. A. J. Raubenheimer, M.P. Deputy-Minister of Bantu Development; The Hon. T. N. H. Janson, M.P. Deputy-Minister of Bantu Administration and Bantu Education; The Hon. Paramount-Chief K. D. Matanzima, M.L.A. [Member of the Legislative Assembly]; Chief Minister of the Transkei; The Hon. Chief L. M. Mangope, M.L.A., Chief Minister of

Bophuthatswana; The Hon. L. L. Sebe, M.L.A., Chief Minister of the Ciskei; The Hon. Dr. C. N. Phatudi, M.L.A., Chief Minister of Lebowa; The Hon. Chief P. R. Mphephu, M.L.A., Chief Minister of Venda; The Hon. Professor H. W. Ntsanwisi, M.L.A., Chief Minister of Gazankulu; The Hon. Chief W. Mota, M.L.A., Chief Minister of Qwaqwa; and The Hon. M. G. Buthelezi, Chief Executive Councillor of KwaZulu.

The meeting was also attended by the Secretaries for Bantu Administration and Development (Mr. I. P. van Onselen), Information (Dr. E. M. Rhoodie) and Bantu Education (Mr. J. Rosseau). Also present were the Under-Secretaries for Information, Mr. M. N. Zimmermann, and Mr. J. C. B. Eyssen, the Public Relations Officer, Department of Bantu Administration and Development.

THE HON. B. J. VORSTER: The Prime Minister said that he welcomed leaders in the New Year not only in their official capacities, but also in their personal capacities. He referred in particular to Dr. Phatudi, who had been sick. He then suggested that business commences as time was short.

THE HON. K. D. MATANZIMA: The Chief Minister of the Transkei thanked the Prime Minister on behalf of his Colleagues for words of welcome. He expressed gratitude that the Prime Minister had "summoned" him and his Colleagues, to have a discussion. He expressed a hope that the agenda would be disposed of within a reasonable time.

THE HON. M. C. BOTHA: The Minister of Bantu Administration extended an invitation to the black leaders to go with him to the Mount Nelson Hotel, for lunch at lunchtime.

The Prime Minister then called upon the Chief Minister to open the discussion. . . .

THE HON. K. D. MATANZIMA: The Chief Minister of the Transkei opened discussions in the following way: on the Security of Tenure and Home Ownership: . . . . Sir, it is now about 52 years since the principal act was passed and by now South Africans of all races should be able to give judgement as to whether Blacks are mere sojourners or are a permanent population of the cities in which they live without allegiance to any Homeland.

I submit that all reasonable men agree that blacks who occupy residential and business premises in the townships on a rental basis should now be regarded as a permanent part of the urban population until the contrary is proved. . . . What we ask is for freehold rights to property in townships occupied by blacks. . . .

THE HON. B. J. VORSTER: The Prime Minister made an observation to the effect that no white man can acquire land in freehold in the "Homelands." . . . He said the whole object of that provision was to prevent whites buying up all black land. There can therefore be no change of policy on freehold. . . .

On the question of land ownership, it seems clear that there can be no change of policy, but some system of leasehold will be considered and the government would go into the matter and inform the Homelands Governments of the outcome of investigations in due course. . . .

Item (c) Influx Control Regulations:

THE HON H. W. NTSANWISI: The Chief Minister pointed out that the leaders had presented a detailed memorandum at the March 1974 conference. . . . He said that influx control regulations should be abolished, as they were a denial of fundamental human rights. They caused a disruption to African family life.

THE HON. B. J. VORSTER: The Prime Minister said that he hoped that "homeland" leaders will appreciate that influx control regulations cannot be abolished altogether. This was a question of housing, of health and jobs. . . .

THE HON. K. D. MATANZIMA: The Chief Minister stated: "I think, sir, that our people should be free to sell their labour to any part of the country."

THE HON. B. J. VORSTER: The Prime Minister posed a question that if there was no influx control and 50,000 blacks came to Cape Town, who would take charge of their housing and amenities.

THE HON. K. D. MATANZIMA: The Chief Minister posed the following question: "What about the case of a man from the Transkei whose wife is not allowed to visit her husband, who is employed?"

THE HON. T. N. H. JANSON: The Deputy Minister said that certain rules were made, but they had to find out how they are applied to remove these pinpricks. . . .

THE HON. B. J. VORSTER: The Prime Minister said that this matter goes into the root of most of our problems. It was a practical matter. It was also a political problem, and he stated that we are all politicians. . . . a senior official, a certain Mr. Meyer, was making a report. He said that the black leaders had said that they, as politicians, were at the receiving end. The Prime Minister suggested that the black leaders should appoint three from their number to go with that matter with that official, to work out the hardships and see what we can cook out of it.

THE HON. M. G. BUTHELEZI: The Chief Executive Councillor said that this is a sensitive political matter as the Prime Minister has said. These regulations apply only to Africans and to no other racial group. If he had his way as an African, these regulations should rather be scrapped. . . .

THE HON. K. D. MATANZIMA: The Chief Minister said that he thought that the Prime Minister's suggestion was quite reasonable. He also had another suggestion, that people should not be prosecuted, and this should stop immediately. . . . The Chief Minister stated that members of the committee, from amongst black leaders, would not be elected at the meeting, but at another meeting of black leaders.

DR. E. M. RHOODIE: The Secretary asks for the record: "Will Chief Buthelezi join the others?"

THE HON. M. G. BUTHELEZI: "No.". . .

Item (e) Civil Rights for Blacks in Urban Areas:

The Prime Minister called upon the Chief Minister of Lebowa to lead discussions as set out in the agenda.

THE HON. C. N. PHATUDI: . . . . it was indefensible to imagine that the people who live in these urban areas, should have a vote miles and miles away. After living in a place for three generations in the city, you cannot be interested in the country.

THE HON. B. J. VORSTER: "I want you to define what you mean by civic rights."

THE HON. C. N. PHATUDI: "This was a question of a man who lives in a particular community, he wants to have a right to own property."

THE HON. B. J. VORSTER: "We have already dealt with that."

THE HON. C. H. PHATUDI: The Chief Minister said that a way should be found whereby the urban African can participate in local government.

THE HON. K. D. MATANZIMA: The Chief Minister pointed out that the leaders wanted them to have local government.

THE HON. M. G. BUTHELEZI: "They must have a budget of their own."

THE HON. B. J. VORSTER: "Local Government?"

THE HON. K. D. MATANZIMA: "Local Government."

THE HON. B. J. VORSTER: "What is the position, Mr. Botha?"

THE HON. M. C. BOTHA: The Minister stated that there was no provision for separate financial administration. . . . The City Councils did not want to delegate powers to these Urban Black Councils. . . .

THE HON. C. H. PHATUDI: The Chief Minister remarked to the effect that the Urban Councils had no power at all.

THE HON. B. J. VORSTER: The Prime Minister wanted to know whether the leaders wanted the Urban Councils to be clothed with more responsibility. . . .

THE HON. M. G. BUTHELEZI: The Chief Executive Councillor of KwaZulu then proposed that the question of Soweto, as a Homeland, be looked into. He said there was no consensus amongst the leaders, and yet he felt it should be presented to the Prime Minister for what it was worth. . . .

THE HON. B. J. VORSTER: "As far as the proclamation of Soweto as a Homeland is concerned, it is out of the question."

THE HON. M. C. BOTHA: (interjecting) "That is too easy a solution!"

THE HON. B. J. VORSTER: (continuing) "But if you asked me whether I am prepared to concede this matter, I must say 'no'."

At this point a suggestion to move to the next item was made, and the Prime Minister called upon the Chief Minister of Lebowa to lead discussions on item (g):

The Mass Removals of Blacks from Urban Areas:

THE HON. C. N. PHATUDI: The Chief Minister pointed out that these removals cause bitterness. He suggested that facilities should be provided. These people should not just be dumped. . . .

THE HON. M. C. BOTHA: The Minister objected to the use of the word "dumped" by Dr. Phatudi and said that the government took exception to the use of that word. He said that with due respect to Dr. Phatudi, he wanted to point out that compensation is provided to all. . . .

The Prime Minister suggested that Conference move to the next item, after the Chief Minister of Lebowa had indicated that he had nothing further to say.

The Chief Minister of Lebowa led discussion on item (h): *Ethnic Grouping in Urban Townships:* . . . . Our people intermarry, the Chief Minister said, so much, that almost on every Saturday and Sunday we have celebrations of marriages across ethnic groups. He appealed for some sort of modification in the application of ethnic grouping regulations.

THE HON. B. J. VORSTER: The Prime Minister stated that the people are free to associate with whom they want and pointed out that there were no regulations forbidding that free association. . . .

The next item was announced by the Prime Minister. The Chief Minister of the Transkei led discussions on item (f): *Public Transport Facilities:* . . .

The Prime Minister then called upon Chief Buthelezi to lead the next item on the agenda item (k): *The Detente in Southern Africa:*

After distributing copies of the text of what he wanted to say to the Prime Minister on the detente in Southern Africa, Chief Buthelezi read out the memorandum he had prepared, which reads as follows: *DETENTE IN SOUTHERN AFRICA* by M. G. Buthelezi:

We wish to repeat the felicitations we conveyed to the Honourable the Prime Minister, by telegram, on the 15th of November 1974, concerning his initiatives in the present detente in Southern Africa. . . .

We were encouraged by the Prime Minister's assurances to us at our March Conference, when he said that he also does not believe in racial discrimination. Although the Prime Minister added that he believed only in differentiation, it was not, as it is not even now, clear to us what the difference is between discrimination and differentiation.

After "the give us six-months" speech by the Hon. the Prime Minister our and our people's hopes had been raised. This has made us hopeful that it was worth our while after all, to cooperate with the government in the implementation of its policies. . . .

At our March 1974 meeting, the Prime Minister told us that he would not go beyond the 1936 Native Land Trust Act. After the Prime Minister's Senate and Nigel Speech we have now hopes that this might mean a change in that attitude and a more meaningful consolidation of those "Homeland areas." On the basis of the government's policy, some of us have proposed a federal formula based on properly consolidated homeland areas. . . .

THE HON. L. M. MANGOPE: "We would like to know the real import of these speeches, because there is an air of expectancy."

THE HON. B. J. VORSTER: "Carry on."

THE HON. L. M. MANGOPE: "I have already finished."

THE HON. C. N. PHATUDI: "We can all say that there is an air of expectancy. There is a lot of expectancy as a result of the speech the Prime Minister has delivered. . . .

THE HON. L. L. SEBE: The Chief Minister of the Ciskei said that when the Prime Minister made his speech, he was in Germany and he got a full report of the Prime Minister's speech at the Embassy. The Chief Minister said that throughout his visit to Germany the image of Homelands leaders was not so good, and it was difficult to cope. The Prime Minister's speech was received with great expectations. The Chief Minister said that his colleagues would know how one is snubbed. . . .

Everywhere he went, they were discussing this speech, as a result he was with his colleagues afforded the status of people who are Heads of State. He wished that what his colleagues say must be followed up. South Africa was in a position to teach the whole world, as the world was in confusion. He wishes that everyone around the Prime Minister and everyone in the streets should rally around the Prime Minister. . . .

THE HON. B. J. VORSTER: The Prime Minister said that in a way it was a pity that this important matter is raised so late, and that on account of the time factor, one cannot devote as much time as we should on this important matter. . . .

In the Senate he made one point only, on whether we were going to have peace in Southern Africa, it was not South Africa he was discussing. He had called on the governments of African States to consider the options very carefully now, as we were at the cross-roads. We had to decide whether we were going to have an escalation of violence. . . .

He had said that if we can have an escalation of violence, you will be surprised where South Africa will be in six-months, with deaths of millions of people. . . .

He did not create the black leaders. There were black leaders all along according to the black people's customs and traditions. But these leaders were not recognised by the political parties that now have Conferences with black leaders ("with you"). . . .

"As far as the political future is concerned, our policy is well-known. Each one of you stands on a platform created by this policy. A policy which does not give you entree only in South Africa, but a policy which also gives you entree in the world."

"It is my policy to make each and everyone of you independent to take your place at the United Nations, if you so wish." . . .

"With reference to what Chief Buthelezi has said: 'whether we can go back to our people and tell them that blacks are now going to share power and decision-making with their white countrymen in a new meaningful way.'" The Prime Minister asked what also had they done first around this table that morning. He found it strange that Chief Buthelezi now wants to share power and decision-making, as he had refused it, when this was offered to him that morning. . . . The Prime Minister went on to say that when it comes to political power, "you gentlemen will have all decision-making in your Countries. But when you are in my area, I will not share decision-making with you. You cannot have your cake and eat it.". . .

The Prime Minister then referred to Chief Buthelezi's memorandum on detente in Southern Africa, and the Prime Minister read out:

"I would like to make it crystal-clear that I am not saying these things in any spirit of ill-will or threats, but I feel that it is my moral duty, at this point in time, to point out, the only logical alternatives we have, if we do not want our people to resort to civil disobedience and disruption of services in this land. Not that I intend leading my people in this direction *at the moment,"* (at this point the Prime Minister reiterated, "at the moment?" and remarked "that is note-worthy"). The Prime Minister went on to read: "—but I feel judging by the mood of my people, that it is timely, that I should point out that if no meaningful change is forthcoming for them through the government's policies, this will come as a logical alternative."

After reading that portion of that paragraph, the Prime Minister said:

"I don't want to consider this as a threat. I want to say that I have been threatened before, but I have never run away. There will be law and order and people will not be allowed to take the law into their hands. I thank you for this discussion.". . .

The Prime Minister said that he was not prepared to accept federation as a solution in these words: "I am not prepared to accept federation as a solution, I accept independent states. This is my frank opinion, if you do not accept it, then I am afraid there is nothing I can do."

The Prime Minister then suggested that we move to the next item, item (i): *The Question of Amnesty for South African Political Exiles and Prisoners:* The Prime Minister called on Chief Buthelezi to lead the discussion, as set out, on the agenda.

THE HON. M. G. BUTHELEZI: . . . . He felt that this was the psychological moment in history, when it would be in the interest of both black and white, if our own political prisoners were given an amnesty. Chief Buthelezi said that, as he had said when he raised this matter with the Prime Minister a few years ago, such release of political prisoners would have the effect of taking the winds out of the sails of South Africa's critics. He felt also that on humanitarian grounds that an amnesty for these people should now be seriously considered.

THE HON. B. J. VORSTER: The Prime Minister asked Chief Buthelezi: "What people do you have in mind."

THE HON. M. G. BUTHELEZI: The Chief Executive Councillor said people like Mr. Mandela, for example.

THE HON. K. D. MATANZIMA: The Chief Minister of the Transkei said that he wished to second Chief Buthelezi. When they visited England with Chief Mangope and Chief Buthelezi, the political exiles came to see them. They did not meet them with demonstrations contrary to the expectations of many people. He felt that their cases should be considered, so that they can be allowed to return to the country.

THE HON. B. J. VORSTER: The Prime Minister said that the speakers had discussed these matters with him before. The Prime Minister said that if people left the country without a passport, and if they were not Communists, he would consider their return without any conditions. But if they were Communists, the Prime Minister would have no truck with them.

THE HON. K. D. MATANZIMA: The Chief Minister said that there were also other cases, such as that of people like Mbeki, Sisulu and Mandela. Their cases should be treated in the same way as that of murderers with extenuating circumstances. They should be allowed to return on that basis.

THE HON. B. J. VORSTER: The Prime Minister said that he had warned these people before time [*sic*], he had asked them to realise what they were doing. He had warned Fischer, and he had warned Bloomberg [*sic*], and he had also warned the non-whites amongst them. He had told them that they would get into trouble.

Mandela was a Communist, and he admitted it in Court that he was a Communist. Not that he was saying it, he said this himself in Court. Under these circumstances he was not prepared to let him out, as he had not changed his views. He was not taking this attitude only for the sake of his own people, but also for the sake of our own people. . . .

Therefore to sum up, I am not the Minister of Justice. The Minister will consider all those who left the country if they want to come back and if they abide by the law. They must keep within the law and God help them if they don't. But if you ask me about Communists, Govan Mbeki, Sisulu, then I am very sorry.

"Do you know Duma Nokwe?" When he was in legal practice, the Prime Minister stated that he had called him into his office and asked him why he had become an Advocate. He said that before Duma Nokwe replied he wanted to tell him that he (the Prime Minister) had become an Advocate first to make a good living and also because he wanted to help his people. He asked Duma Nokwe to tell him why he became an Advocate. Duma Nokwe had replied to the effect that he became an Advocate in order to help the Communist Party to govern his country.

When Duma Nokwe's home was raided, a letter was brought to the Prime Minister, which his wife had written to another woman. In this letter she spoke about the take-over of the country by Communists. She said that when we take over the country, my husband will take over Vorster's position. What was a coincidence is that his wife's name is Tiny and my wife's name is TINI (laughter).

THE HON. C. N. PHATUDI: The Chief Minister mentioned the case of those who had left on exit permits. He also wanted to know about Robert Sobukwe and whether he was also a Communist.

THE HON. B. J. VORSTER: "In all fairness I cannot say Sobukwe is a Communist. He had other troubles, but Communism was not one of them."

THE HON. C. N. PHATUDI: The Chief Minister said that he took it that Sobukwe's case was one of those which are reviewed from time to time.

THE HON. B. J. VORSTER: The Prime Minister responded by saying that all these cases were reviewed from time to time.

THE HON. M. G. BUTHELEZI: The Chief Executive Councillor asked directly from the Prime Minister whether Robert Sobukwe's case cannot be reviewed since he is not, according to the Prime Minister, a Communist.

THE HON. B. J. VORSTER: The Prime Minister said that the Minister of Justice will review his case.

THE HON. M G. BUTHELEZI: The Chief Executive Councillor asked whether Robert Sobukwe's case cannot be reviewed at the Prime Minister's special instance.

THE HON. B. J. VORSTER: The Prime Minister said that he will ask the Minister of Justice to do so, but he cannot bind him nor can the Minister of Justice bind him. His case will be reviewed.

THE HON. M. G. BUTHELEZI: The Chief Executive Councillor spoke about the banning of people, even students' leaders. To ban them did more harm than good in so far as it was like making them martyrs. . . . [He] asked whether the Pro-Frelimo Rally detainees cannot be brought to trial soon, than remain in continuous detention.

THE HON. B. J. VORSTER: The Prime Minister told the Conference that he had instructed the Attorney-General to expedite the matter.

DOCUMENT 92. Minutes of meeting between officials, West Rand Urban Bantu Councillors and other representatives, Johannesburg, June 29, 1976 (abridged)

[The meeting began at 9:00 a.m. and ended at 5:30 p.m.]

Mr. [H. P. P.] Mulder [West Rand Bantu Affairs Administration Board] extended a word of welcome to Mr. [I. P.] Van Onselen [Department of Bantu Administration and Development] and to all the representatives at the meeting, and Rev. Matloporo opened the meeting with prayer.

The Chairman said that he was glad that the leaders from the various areas could attend the meeting and explained that the meeting had been convened under his Chairmanship following talks in Pretoria on Saturday 19 June 1976 between the Hon. the Minister of Bantu Administration and Development and Bantu Education, Mr. M. C. Botha, Urban Bantu Council members, and other leaders from Soweto. The object of the meeting was to obtain the views and recommendations of the representatives on matters giving rise to friction between Black and White. He stressed the importance of the meeting and requested that discussions be held in a calm and responsible manner.

A memorandum, attached as Annexure B [Document 93], was presented by Mr. M. T. Moerane with the request that it be submitted to the Minister as the official representations of the Black representatives with a view to solving some of the matters giving rise to friction and thus adversely affecting racial harmony. . . .

The following items were then submitted for discussion by the meeting with a view to submitting representations to the Hon. the Minister of Bantu Administration and Development. . . . [The minutes of the meeting included resolutions following the discussion of each item on the agenda.]

2. *WAGES AND TRADE UNIONS*

A plea was made that trade unions be permitted for Blacks in South Africa in order to have a channel through which salary and wage demands may be submitted. . . .

3. *TRANSPORT*

Existing transport facilities were considered to be hopelessly inadequate. . . .

4. *HOUSING*

The meeting was unanimous in its view that there was an acute shortage of housing for Blacks and that the position had become critical. . . .

As far as hostels were concerned, it was stressed that they were considered to be a burden on the Black people as the men accommodated there on a single basis break up families in their quest for female company and thus cause serious sociological problems in the community. The plea was for the Department to discontinue the erection of hostels in all future development. . . .

The meeting also emphasised that the division of Black residential areas on an ethnic basis was totally unacceptable and should not be applied in future housing schemes. . . .

5. *HOMELAND CITIZENSHIP*

It was stressed that Blacks in White areas were obviously there to stay. . . . The Department's requirement of homeland citizenship in respect of home ownership and leasehold, and also for the renewal of the urban Bantu residential areas trading licenses, was strongly opposed by Blacks and gave rise to friction. It was deemed preferable for the people themselves to be able to make their own decision as individuals regarding homeland citizenship. . . .

6. *INFLUX CONTROL*

The point was stressed that influx control regulations are resented because they are being considered inhuman, often causing the separation of husbands from their wives who happen to come from different areas. This understandably causes hatred against Whites, which manifested itself, for example, during the recent riots when the Jabavu Influx Control offices were the first to be burned down by rioters. . . .

7. *TRADING*

Traders were said to be highly dissatisfied with the Department's requirement of proof of homeland citizenship as the condition of the renewal of trading licenses. Serious consideration should be given to withdrawing this requirement. Traders had looked forward with expectation to a new era in trading for Blacks in South Africa, such as supermarkets, night clubs, drive-in theaters, etc., but the Department's recently announced new policy had proved to be a big disappointment. . . .

8. *EDUCATIONAL FACILITIES*

. . . The standard of schools built, as well as the standard of maintenance, was considered to be poor and should be investigated. . . .

9. *JOB RESERVATION*

It was pointed out that it cost South Africa millions of Rands to recruit immigrants for the country's labour force, whereas this money could be better used to train Blacks to do the job.

The blame was placed at the door of Whites for neglecting to create training facilities for Black people and thus preventing them from performing skilled work. . . . Training also had the added advantage of keeping idle youngsters occupied and out of mischief. . . .

10. *STATUS OF URBAN BANTU COUNCIL*

Although the enabling act made provision for the granting of certain powers to Urban Bantu Councils when the Act was passed many years ago, and certain promises had been made in this regard over the years, to date there has been absolutely no progress in this regard. An urgent appeal was made for the permanency of Blacks in urban areas. As they are here to stay, it was felt that they should be granted meaningful representation at all levels of government, from local authority to central government level. . . .

The election of Urban Bantu Council members on an ethnic group basis was mentioned, and here again it was stressed that ethnic grouping should not be used as a factor as it was entirely irrelevant and merely served as an irritation giving rise to friction and discontent. . . .

11. *POLITICAL IMPLICATIONS*

. . . It was again pointed out that the absence of Black leadership and representation of Blacks in the various decision-making organisations was the main grievance amongst Blacks and was contributing to the hatred and ill-feeling towards the White people. If Black leaders had more executive powers and were represented on the various Government bodies, blacks could come to them with their grievances and thus avoid riots and violence.

It was recommended that Blacks should share in all the various Government organisations. A multi-racial board should be created in order to consider common problems, and from there matters could proceed to a provincial and finally to a national authority. . . .

A warning was issued to the effect that there were rumours in the townships that there was to be a second phase to the riots and any of the issues raised at this meeting could spark off further violence, which could conceivably spread to White Johannesburg. . . .

The Chairman thanked the representatives for the frank and fruitful talks and praised the spirit in which the discussions took place.

The meeting was unanimous in the view that the representatives have an obligation towards the Black people to inform them of the outcome of the meeting, and it was unanimously decided that a joint press statement be issued at the conclusion of the meeting. The joint statement . . . was compiled by Mr. Eyssen and read aloud to the meeting, which agreed to the contents of the statement.

A vote of thanks was proposed by Mr. H. P. P. Mulder on behalf of the West

Rand Administration Board and by Mrs. D[eborah] Mabiletsa on behalf of the representatives. Rev. Matloporo closed the meeting with prayer.

DOCUMENT 93. "Memorandum to the Minister of Bantu Administration and Development and Bantu Education by Soweto Black Community Leaders," written by M. T. Moerane, June 29, 1976 (abridged)

. . . . In actual fact this policy [of separate development], with its so-called "homeland" governments, in practice raises more questions than it answers; more problems than it solves and is at best a passing phase; a diversionary exercise; while the realities of the country cry out for real policies that guarantee the rights and welfare of all.

If such policies are not evolved and enacted, this country is drifting to situations of confrontation of such a dimension that the current unrest will be like a Sunday school picnic in comparison.

The policy of separate development is built on false historical premises. It is generally claimed that it has a moral purpose, i.e. to guarantee equal freedoms to the different sections of the country. In actual fact its purpose is the entrenchment and maintenance of white privilege and white sectional interests and welfare, at the expense of the Black man.

And that kind of order cannot last but will bring strife and disaster to this land. There is a school of thought prevalent among particularly the younger people, that the Black man is in the situation he is in, by sheer reason of conquest.

That if the white man arrogates to himself arbitrarily and unilaterally 87 per cent of the country, leaving the majority Africans 13 per cent, it is by reason of conquest.

That if the white man decides to sit alone in the only real parliament of this country in Cape Town, where the Black man is unrepresented, and he makes the laws that govern all of us, it is by reason of the right of conquest.

According to this school of thought, the only answer to this situation is to fight it out again; and lessons of events in such countries as Mozambique have not been lost on some of our people.

We here admit that many of the disabilities that frustrate the people of Soweto stem from the fact that they are not represented in the parliament and other councils of state that govern and administer this land.

If our workers had the franchise, their votes would count and such rights as Trade Union Rights and decent wages and employment conditions would be guaranteed.

If our people were enfranchised and represented in parliament, they would be assured adequate votes in the budget assuring them free and compulsory education and adequate provision of other public facilities and amenities needed; and if it must come, we would be assured a proportionately reasonable share of the land of this country and its resources unlike in the present setting where we Blacks are like foster children of the South African state, poor and without rights or privileges.

We here adopt the view that fighting it out is not the only nor the best way to resolve the basic political problems of this country of which many economic and social disabilities are a result.

We believe that through sincere dialogue and serious mutual consultation and discussion a way can be found that will assure that our people can have the opportunity to make their contribution in participation in decision making and administering this country, with whites.

Of one thing we are sure; that the status quo, whereby the Black man has no say in these matters even in his own areas like Soweto but is an object of instruction by whites, is outmoded and untenable and must change.

Accordingly we request the Government, in consultation with us, to seek ways and means of giving effect to this desire of providing a meaningful role to our leaders and participation in decision making and administration of national and local affairs, not in purely advisory roles such as in the Urban Bantu Councils.

Meantime, we submit some matters here, which can be attended to immediately with advantage and promotion of racial harmony, peace and an atmosphere of goodwill.

Document 94. Statement by Dr. M. B. Naidoo to fellow members of the South African Indian Council, Durban, late 1978 (abridged)

Five decades of this century had witnessed persistent demands for the elimination of discrimination, for social equality, for the removal of irritating restrictions such as the provincial barriers and the hope for an egalitarian society. These decades have also witnessed a steadfast opposition to the social inequalities by the Natal Indian Congress, that supreme political body which rebelled against the effrontery and arrogance of white citizens and policymakers. The outspokenness of the Congress, the dedication of the men who clamoured for social and political reforms, form heroic chapters in the history of the Indian people. . . .

The mid-forties were years when Indian political leaders were intransigent and rebelled against the expectations of obsequiousness by some extreme racialists. The many acts of defiance based on Gandhian principles were summarily dealt with and a near-decade of martyrdom for a cause had an abrupt ending. The leaders dispersed, some into exile and others under banning orders, who ceased to be vocal. Such was the turmoil when the Nationalist Government came into power with a vengeance and asserted a regime that was stern, inviolable and imperious. Effective political opposition by the Indians was suppressed and except for sporadic efforts to vindicate their grievances, the general body of the opponents of Government policy desisted from open confrontations. . . .

The uncertainty of the political future of the Indian community was a de facto situation until 1961 when the late Dr. Verwoerd pronounced that henceforth the Indians shall be a permanent part of the Republic's population. . . .

The bone of contention in the Indian community is that the South African Indian Council is without legislative powers and is therefore useless as a body without the power to legislate. A wide section of the Indian people view the limitation as a reflection on its calibre and its inability to assume responsibilities despite the high degree of sophistication of its members and their intellectual standing. . . .

It is understood that a fully elected council which is the goal of the present council is unlikely at this stage, for reasons best known to the Government. . . . The Indian community . . . disclaim the South African Indian Council (SAIC) as the mouthpiece of the Indian people and insist on a council composed of fully elected members. Again there are others who will not accept anything else but direct representation in Parliament. This is understandable but there is still a vocal element which repudiates the council and accuses it of collaborating with the Government and in doing so is nullifying the aspirations of the black people.

The general mass of the Indians however appear confused. . . . There is in evidence a surprising dichotomy in the attitude of the average Indian, more so among those who belong to the sophisticated class. There is the overt rejection of the SAIC and all locally constituted statutory bodies on the one hand and on the other an eagerness to enjoy the benefits of apartheid. There are clandestine requests for favours from members of the SAIC, whereas outwardly the opposition is vociferous and acrimonious. . . .

Then there are many individuals and organizations that censure the SAIC for not being an elected body and yet they would not hesitate to accept employment and privileges from a Government they had not elected into office. Such then are the contradictions that loom conspicuously in this painful exposure of double standards.

The SAIC is a statutory body involved in Group Areas, land and housing, religion and culture, education and local government administration. At no stage was it understood that the SAIC had legislative powers or that it could pressurise the Government to repeal discriminatory laws. It did not imply that in approaching the Government on issues affecting the Indian people the Exco [executive council] did so with hat in hand. It is to the enduring credit of the Exco that they discussed their problems with tact, resoluteness and propriety, in recognition of the limitations to which they are inextricably bound. In an atmosphere of cordiality many concessions were offered while many more were subject to a reappraisal or totally rejected. . . .

Indian politics just now calls for pragmatism, for involvement in new deals and an eagerness to accept every concession aimed at upgrading the Indian community by raising their standards of living and advancing and fulfilling their educational aspirations. When the time arrives for a common society in South Africa, the Indian will have equipped himself for his rightful role. It is important that we do not put the clock back for ideological reasons. In the framework of the present political limitations, it becomes imperative to pay heed to the advice, "stoop to conquer." In the history of mankind races have survived not by confronting superior forces, which could have led to annihilation, but by wise and patient compromise that assured their survival. . . .

The Government is committed to a policy. It stands for the preservation of the white group and let there be no mistake about this. It is in no mood to be intimidated by outsiders whether they be blacks or whites. It is pledged to uphold the South African way of life come what may, and its stupendous arsenal is an assurance of the survival of the white man in South Africa. . . . The extremist politician may gain the confidence of the public and may experience a feeling of euphoria in the pursuit of his crusade. But in all his efforts to bring about social and political reforms there will be but one pathetic outcome: the mesmerisation of his people. Whether nominated or elected, one cannot go beyond that which is prescribed in the policy of separate development. To pretend that an aggressive approach would bring results is to deceive oneself and awaken deception in the electorate. . . .

It can be argued that the absence of the SAIC would have strengthened political bodies to hasten change in this country and that the SAIC has only served to legitimise apartheid. Perhaps there is some merit in this argument, but seen in the context of the many benefits the SAIC has brought to the Indian community through peaceful negotiations, the efforts of previous political bodies, inspired by idealism and a burning sense of righteousness, has nothing material to offer to the community.

DOCUMENT 95. Editorial attacking collaborators, *The Educational Journal*, April–May 1979

"Coloureds" and "Indians": And Now?

Those sections of the unfranchised majority in this country officially classified and oppressed as "Coloured" and "Indian" are at present being called upon to make a declaration whose significance should not be underestimated. They have to make it plain, at a critical phase in the history of this country, where they line up in the continuing struggle to make South Africa a democracy, a land peopled and run and equally enjoyed by the citizens of one South African nation.

It is as plain as that. Stripped of all racist sludge about "ethnicity," shorn of myths and legends concerning the unique nature of their blood or religion or culture or language, and purged of historical lapse and error, the questions to be answered may be very simply stated: In the year 1979, do those called "Coloured" and "Indian" really understand what and who they are? Do they still harbour historically induced tribal hangovers or do they understand that the only identity common within each group is the only identity common to all of them: their membership of a non-citizen majority? Do they understand that the most meaningful aspect of that identity for the majority of them is the fact that at the same time as being non-citizens they are poor and economically exploited? And do they grasp the significance of the fact that, at this particular stage in their history and in the history of oppressed people up and down the African continent and beyond, a major attempt is being made to enlist, involve and embroil them against their own true social interests?

We refer, in the broader sense, to the politically orchestrated campaign which is being increasingly mounted in all parts of the Republic and at many, often barely tangible, levels to line up the "Coloured" and "Indian" non-citizens against the major section of the unfranchised and poor in this country, the so-called African section, who—except for their collaborators—are variously regarded as foreign, brutal, savage, tribalistic, uncultured and innately bloodthirsty. For purposes of this ultimately para-military campaign, those being wooed and referred to by the rulers as the "Coloureds" are not the wretched starvelings from the grim confines of Manenberg and Blikkiesdorp; and, as the "Indians," are not the denizens of the dormitories of Chatsworth. They come in the first instance from the quislings on the Coloured Representative Council and the S.A. Indian Council. But also from the collaborationist semi-establishment around them, and from the ghetto businessmen and liquor-outlet tycoons, the location business 'scientists,' the professional elements, the clergy (including many of those whom it has suited to give their Maker an identity card or pass), the Dove and Sable and allied antiseptic clubs, the whole of the *nouveaux riches* jet-setters on parole from 'petty-apartheid,' and their poor relations in the ranks of assistant schoolteachers. This group all foster the illusion that "it won't be long now," for them at any rate. However, while we look forward to seeing all of them in due course being sorted out in accordance with their deserts, at the present time they represent the broader aspects and not the main thrust of the major attempt to which we have referred and which is here our chief concern.

More immediately and more pertinently there is the current attempt to ensnare the "Coloured" and "Indian" unfranchised in and through the so-called Draft Bill to set up a "new Constitution" for the Republic of South Africa, with a law-making Assembly and "White Prime Minister" who will rule the country, a dummy House of Representatives complete with mascot "Prime Minister" for "Coloureds," and a dummy "Chamber of Deputies" complete with mascot "Prime Minister" for "Indians." For some of the details of this bizarre and desperate scheme, which can never be less of a failure than the present dummy council farce, we refer to an article elsewhere in this issue. The main point we are making here is that, apart from their answer to the broad overtures and *tutti* of the campaign we have described above, it is to this gazetted invitation that the "Coloureds" and "Indians" have to give an unequivocal answer. It is an invitation to them to betray themselves, to sell out politically the cause of all non-citizens and to set themselves apart from and against all those of any 'race,' colour, creed or sex who want to see and who strive for democracy in this country.

As everyone knows, in priestly garb, business suits, tailored costumes and jeans, the quislings and other agents of the rulers are very, very busy. With blandishments, promises, bribes, racism. And, above all, with threats of many kinds—from threats of the kind we have long known to those of the calibre currently being employed in Namibia and Rhodesia. All this was predictable. It is inseparable from this stage of the struggle. People just have to learn how to deal with it, despite the massive direct and indirect support the rulers are giving and will continue to give their agents and despite their liaison with law-enforcement agencies, from policemen, S.B.'s [special branch, i.e. security police] and magistrates to judges and army officers. Because it has never been so important in our history, the history of all of us, that the "Coloured" and "Indian" subsections of the unfranchised should demonstrate that on a principled basis they stand four-square with *all* the unfranchised, including those who have been forcibly kraaled off into bantustans and alleged homelands of varying kinds.

Those who have studied the history of the emancipatory struggles of the oppressed and exploited in this country will know. Readers of the series on 'Majority Rule' we have been running in this *Journal* since 1977 will know. Up to the funding of the Anti-CAD [Coloured Affairs Department] Movement in 1943 and thereafter of the Non-European Unity Movement on the basis of a minimum 10-point programme, the "Coloured" and "Indian" sections had a wretched history of opportunism, electioneering tactics, marriages of convenience and betrayal on the question of the unity of all the unfranchised in the struggle for full citizenship rights. The track-record of the political organisations of the major or "African" section was hardly less riddled with opportunism, compromise and double-dealing. In the 1940s there began the change to which all of us today, in varying degrees, are the political heirs. As is notorious, puppets from Hendrickse to Matanzima and Buthelezi have tried to misrepresent themselves as being in the tradition which was founded in the 1940s. But, for the purpose of the special point we wish to make here, we shall leave them aside, because—in the tradition of the pre-1940 carpet-baggers—they are all in the market for the present type of scheme and any other that might come into the fishermen's net of the Parliamentary Select Committee.

What we have to concentrate on, and by *we* is meant *all* sections of the non-citizens irrespective of the rulers' classifications and sub-divisions, is not merely where "Coloureds" and "Indians" stand on the question, but where *we* stand. It is *we,* including those for whom the trap has been specifically set, who have to make plain that we stand for the complete rejection of this Bill and all such anti-democratic and racist schemes. That we stand for nothing less than full citizenship rights for all in a single, democratic South African parliament.

The *Herrenvolk,* on their radio and TV and in their press and their Foundations, Groups, Institutes and "universities" can talk until they drop about how this idea of one nation and one parliament has failed here, there and elsewhere in selected parts of the world where 'identity' and 'ethnicity' have allegedly enshrined themselves. And they can bray about how we are crying for the moon when we talk about a single South African nation. We have heard that sort of self-serving racist cant and sophistry for a long time now. But, to go no further, the very fact that the rulers are now frenetically putting up the fraudulent scheme contained in the current Draft Bill, with its vast increase in the numbers of well-paid political collaborators, is proof enough of the irresistible political groundswell they have to contend with on the demand for full and equal citizenship in a democracy governed by one parliament in which all are directly and equally represented. It cannot be too plainly shown or too bluntly declared that basic citizenship rights are not negotiable. And that in the latest insulting and contemptuous attempt at diversion there is no basis for discussion.

Document 96. Transcript of meeting between Prime Minister P. W. Botha and the executive of the Coloured Persons' Representative Council, Cape Town, November 9, 1979 (abridged)

PRIME MINISTER: I see to it that the Cabinet Ministers go to their offices and I'm asking you under the law of this land, as Prime Minister of this country, are you carrying out your commitments?

MR. HENDRICKSE: Of course we do.

PRIME MINISTER: How many hours—how many days per week are you doing?

MR. HENDRICKSE: We are always—

PRIME MINISTER: No, it is not so and you know it is not so. You refuse to carry out your responsibilities.

MR. HENDRICKSE: I take exception to that.

PRIME MINISTER: You can take exception. I take exception to many things you do say. . . .

MR. HENDRICKSE: I must take exception to the threat, Mr. Prime Minister. I am the—and we as a party will not look for an extra parliamentary—

PRIME MINISTER: All right, I accept it. I now take you on your word that you are not in favour of violence. You reject violence?

MR. HENDRICKSE: Of course.

PRIME MINISTER: Fine. Then we are on the same basis. Now you say there is only one way in which the law of the country prescribes how I can find out what the people want to tell the State. And this is to create the broadest form of consultation, namely a Joint Select Committee [the Schlebusch Commission]. Now you say you are not prepared to use it.

In other words, you do not want violence, and I accept your word. And now I also accept your word, but you are not prepared to appear before this Select Committee. In other words you are not prepared to do something.

MR. HENDRICKSE: I am prepared to talk, Sir.

PRIME MINISTER: But we are talking this morning. I am asking you to use the instrument I am creating for you, but you don't do this.

MR. HENDRICKSE: This is where you are prescribing for us.

PRIME MINISTER: No, I'm not going to stand [sic] instead of this select committee. I'm the Prime Minister of this country. I have other work to do as well. I can't sit here for hours having my own investigation while Parliament has certain prescriptions. I am sorry. I can't do it.

Now, in this respect I want us to have absolute clarity with each other— I again I friendly invite you as a party to take part in the consultations as prescribed by parliament. That committee has not yet finished its work. It is still available to you—we are not bound by the reports, under no circumstances.

You asked me a second question. You asked me to refer to the fact that I have said that I get co-operation from other people but not the coloureds. No, I did not say that. I said I get much co-operation from the coloured people, groups, individuals for whom I have much appreciation. But I said I am not surprised that I do not get the same co-operation from a section of the Labour Party leaders.

While I am creating the opportunities for them—you refuse to partake in the budget process, from which pensions and salaries and welfare services have to be paid to a large section of the population. You reject it in toto. I want to ask you—how many days of the week do you spend full time doing the work for your own people the whites expect from you. You have to answer only these two questions for me.

MR. HENDRICKSE: Mr. Prime Minister, I think your attitude is an insulting one. I don't think any of us would ask any Cabinet Minister at any time how much time he—

PRIME MINISTER: You are not prepared to give evidence. Then good. Now what right do you have to take exception against me when I say in public that you do not give me your co-operation? I was correct then, was I not?

MR. HENDRICKSE: Mr. Prime Minister—the times in which we are living—

PRIME MINISTER: No, leave alone the times in which we are living—I don't think you are speaking for all the people in the party, and I don't think you speak as the responsible part of South Africans in the Coloured community and I shall carry on to look, on my road to consultation, for people who want to take the same road as I do, to defend the destiny of all South Africans—

As far as the Representative Council is concerned, the Government will have to consider to make an end to it and to suspend the services of the Executive Committee.

I thank you for your attendance. If you make any statements to the Press, I will release a tape recording to the Press. So, my advice to you is not to make your own statements before the time has come. I offer you the opportunity to check the tape together with your secretary and Mr. Neville Krige to release it jointly. But if you make a unilateral statement, I shall release the tape as soon as I have it. It is for you to decide what you want to do.

MR. HENDRICKSE: Mr. Prime Minister, what we want—before we go—

with reference to your summing-up remark. I want to say again, Sir, as we've said before that we are prepared to go the road of consultation; we have an interest in peace and security and the welfare of all South Africans. I also want to say, Sir, that it is evident that you expect by co-operation to mean for us to do that which you want us to do.

PRIME MINISTER: You know for a fact that we would have appointed the chairman as the practice was if you were prepared to co-operate and do the job, but you know for a fact that you are not prepared to see that the people get their pensions and salaries. You know it, don't try and bluff me, but I am going to ask you—

The party's national chairman, Mr. David Curry, said: Mr. Botha, while talking of new policies, did not know where he was going. That is the spirit in which you came here this morning. Mr. Curry said the white man wants us to give him a blank cheque and he calls us irresponsible because we won't talk with him. I would not walk with a blind man if he doesn't know where he is going. That is the spirit in which you came here this morning—

No, but nobody can understand you, naturally. But you won't accept responsibility. You want to stay in your positions and now I finally want to warn you. I say this now, again, one man one vote in this country is out. That is, never. And now I further want to say this: Don't try and do something unconstitutional—you will be sorry for yourself.

MR. HENDRICKSE: We don't need that warning, Sir—

PRIME MINISTER: And each man who tries it will be sorry for himself.

MR. HENDRICKSE: We don't need that warning, we are not interested in that type of thing—

PRIME MINISTER: Thank you, gentlemen. Thank you. The interview is over.

MRS. A. JANSEN (appointed chairman of the CRC): I would like to appeal to my colleagues to talk to the Schlebusch Commission, give that background. I feel that South Africa needs every South African and I am sure, Mr. Prime Minister, you agree with me. We need the ability of every South African, be it in a leadership capacity—or serving in a menial way—

PRIME MINISTER: Thank you, Mrs. Jansen. I appreciate your contribution. I think I owe you an answer regarding the position of Mrs. Jansen—she has shown herself very able—she only did what the law of the land expected from her. If it wasn't for her contribution, the teachers today would not have been paid.

Document 97. "A Brief History of the Party and Nationalist Rule since 1948." Labour Party pamphlet, 1982 (abridged)

Dear Reader

The Labour Party asks you to seriously consider the following facts about the political history of our community, the so-called coloured people. . . .

In 1948, there were approximately 47,000 "coloured" voters on the common parliamentary roll. In 11 parliamentary constituencies the "coloured" voter held the balance of power between the old United Party and the Nationalist Party. . . . The Non-European Unity Movement, the leading political organisation among our people at that time, called upon our voters to boycott the 1948 parliamentary elections on the following grounds:

a. The "coloured" vote was not the full franchise.

b. Parliament was for Whites only.

c. Both the UP and NP stood for White domination.

d. If the NP came to power with its extreme policy of baasskap [boss-ship], change would come sooner.

In response to the boycott call, thousands of our voters did not vote. To the surprise of the Nationalists themselves, their party won the 1948 elections by a tiny majority of 6 seats.

Since then, the Nationalist Party has entrenched itself in power by removing the "coloured" voters from the common roll in 1956. This was followed by our removal from all local government rolls as well. After having won every parliamentary election with increased majorities since 1948, the NP today, in 1982, sits in parliament with a 107 seat majority compared with 6 in 1948.

LOOKING BACK

Looking back over 34 years of NP rule, one is forced to judge our leaders of 1948 very harshly indeed. The parliamentary opposition has been reduced to a small minority with no hope of ever replacing the NP in power. Our people have been stripped of all political rights. We are afflicted by ill health, by poverty, unemployment, lack of housing, poor education and crime. *Can anyone deny that the boycott of the parliamentary elections of 1948 by the "coloured" voter was a disastrous mistake?* . . .

The correct strategy then should have been for our voters to have voted United Party and, thereafter, for our political organisations to have struggled for the extension of the vote to our women and eighteen-year olds; for direct representation in parliament by our own people, and for a political system acceptable to all South Africa's people. This would have been far easier to achieve had the United Party been in power, than it has been for more that thirty years *after we allowed the Nationalists to win the 1948 elections.* . . .

The Non-European Unity Movement, which called for the boycott of the 1948 elections by our voters, was crushed out of existence by the Nationalist government. The same thing happened to all other organizations who tried to resist the policy of baasskap *from outside the political system.* . . .

LABOUR'S POWER BASE

For these reasons, the Labour Party was established in 1965. It had learnt from the past that the only strategy that made sense was to operate from a power base inside the political system. From such a base (as the "coloured" vote was in 1948) our political goals could be achieved much easier and, especially, without violence.

But where was such a power base to be found, now that we were no longer on the common roll? In 1964 the government passed a law, the Coloured Persons Representative Council Act. . . . [It] also made provision for a "coloured" voters roll. By 1969, when the first elections were held for this Council, there were 637,587 voters on this roll. (Compare this with 47,000 on the common roll in 1948). *Here was the political power base we were looking for. You the voter!*

The Labour Party fully realised that the Coloured Representative Council, offered to us in 1964 by the government, was overwhelmingly rejected by our people. It was no substitute for representation in parliament. The CRC had to be done away with. How was this goal to be achieved?

Once again our so-called intellectuals called for a boycott! Once again they told the people that the vote they had was only "half" a vote, and that if they refused to vote, the CRC would disappear off the scene! It could be boycotted out of existence!

Had we listened to the boycotters, there is no doubt that we would have repeated the disaster of 1948—and worse! What the boycotters did not tell our people was that even if every single voter stayed away from the polling booths, the law made provision for 20 members to be nominated to the CRC by the State President. Those 20 members constituted a quorum. This meant that the CRC could carry on with the business the government expected of it, even if none of the elected seats were filled. But the 40 elected seats would have been filled! They would have been filled by 40 *UNOPPOSED* members of the late Tom Swartz's (pro-apartheid) Federal Party! . . .

Fortunately, the Labour Party recognised the folly of the boycott call. In the face of violent attacks and abuse from the "intellectual" boycotters, the Party contested the first elections for the CRC in 1969. It did so in the belief that given a chance to choose for or against apartheid by voting, the voters would state in no uncertain terms what they wanted. In this the Party was to be proved right, as the elections results later showed.

The Party's election slogan was *"A VOTE FOR LABOUR IS A VOTE AGAINST APARTHEID."* Of the 40 elected seats, Labour could only manage to contest 37 seats. However, the Party won 26 seats with 136,845 votes cast in its favour. The apartheid supporting Federal Party contested all 40 elected seats and only won 11, with 92,705 votes cast in its favour. Other parties received a total of 3 seats. Despite tremendous opposition and limited funds, the Labour Party won a resounding election victory over the Federal Party, which received massive financial support from apartheid sources. *But the Party's victory was in fact the victory of the "coloured" voter.* In their thousands our voters let their voice be heard in a way that nobody could contradict. The "coloured" people voted a clear rejection of separate development.

A SETBACK AND EXPOSURE

Despite Labor's elected majority of 12 seats over the combined total of 14 seats of the Federal Party and others, the Government nominated 20 Federal Party members, many, defeated election candidates, including Tom Swartz, thus giving his party 31 seats and a clear majority in the 60-seat Council. That election clearly exposed to South Africa and the world two things:

1. The total immorality of the CRC Act whereby the winners of an election become the losers because of 20 nominated seats.

2. That our people, by using the vote, which had to be counted, demonstrated by an overwhelming majority that they rejected the apartheid CRC and the apartheid supporting Federal and other parties.

Our critics now adopted a new line against us. They said, now that we had proved beyond doubt by majority vote that our people did not want the CRC, and that we promised that we would put an end to that body, we should resign from it.

If we had listened to our critics, would that have put an end to the CRC? Obviously not. Together with the boycotters, both the Federal Party and the Government would have rejoiced if we had marched out of the Council. Because surely, we would have given them a free hand to implement the apartheid policy without opposition. Our people would certainly have been the losers as a result.

From 1969 to 1975 the Labour Party made life in the CRC intolerable for the Federal Party by constantly exposing the real nature of the CRC and the stooge role the Federal Party was playing. The Party showed how worthless the CRC was when it came to satisfying the demands of the people, but how potentially effective it could be in chaining our people to apartheid. More and more it became clear that in order to end the CRC, Labour had to remain inside until we were in a dominant position.

VICTORY IN 1980

Our chance came in 1975 when the next elections were held. Once again we placed our trust in the voter. We firmly believed that the electorate would endorse, with a greater majority, the mandate it gave us in 1969. And so it turned out to be. This time 151,410 voters cast their votes for Labour, almost 30,000 more than in 1969. This time we took 31 of the 40 elected seats. The Federals were reduced to 8 and the others gained 1. We now had a clear majority out of the total of sixty seats in the CRC. Even if the Government now gave all the 20 nominated seats to the Federal Party, they would only have had 28 against our 31.

In the hope, no doubt, that the Labour Party would be co-operative, the Government gave us 4 of the nominated seats. But this did nothing to divert us from our goal—the closure of the CRC. This was the mandate from our voters to which we were committed. It took another five years before the Government decided to close the CRC in 1980. By then it had become quite clear to the government that the CRC, in the hands of the Labour Party, had become an instrument of obstruction instead of co-operation in carrying out the policy of separate development. This is what we wanted. *Only the Government could close the CRC. It could never had been done by boycotts or walkouts.*

The Labour Party had carried out its election promise to the people. It also proved that boycott was disastrous in the wrong circumstances. *It also proved that political goals could be achieved by working inside the political system, provided the Party enjoyed the support of the people. What is more, political goals can be achieved without violence.* . .

What is needed now is for the Party to be more firmly welded together with the voter, our political base. In this way we can together become a greater negotiating and bargaining force, right inside the political system. Once this is achieved, our hopes and aspirations *will* be realised and the bitter lesson of 1948 well learned.

9. Buthelezi
and Inkatha

DOCUMENT 98. Speech by Chief M. G. Buthelezi, at the inauguration of the Zulu Territorial Authority, Nongoma, June 11, 1970 (abridged)

The Honourable the Minister of Bantu Administration and Development, the Honourable the Commissioner General, His Royal Highness the Regent of Zululand, Members of the Zulu Royal Family, Chiefs and members of the Zulu Territorial Authority, other Distinguished Guests, Ladies and Gentlemen.

It is my privilege to address you on this historic occasion in the History of the Zulu people. The Zulu nation has been the last, but certainly not the least, to reach this milestone which the other six ethnic groups have already reached. The Zulu nation is for that matter the very last non-white homogeneous group to enter this era of self-government within the framework of Separate Development. All sorts of opprobrious terms have been used to condemn the slow pace at which this has come about. I think it would be well for us to remember the words of the British Premier Disraeli, at the time of the Great Zulu War. I refer here to the now famous line quoted quite often, "A remarkable people the Zulu. They defeat our Generals, convert our Bishops, and put an end to a great European dynasty." The Zulu people are no less remarkable today than they were when this memorable remark was made during the last century, despite the vicissitudes they have gone through, throughout the years.

This necessitates a brief historical survey which will put today's event in its correct and proper perspective. Initially the Zulu people were made to understand by officials of Your Department, Sir, that the Bantu Authority Act of 1951 was optional. It was for this reason that at a Conference of Chiefs convened by our late INGONYAMA H. M. Cyprian Bhekuzulu ka Solomon, to consider the Act, we decided that the matter be decided by the Zulu nation, who had to make the choice we were made to understand we had. As no steps were taken to implement our resolution, the matter rested just there for a few years. Some tribes in Natal "accepted" the Act.

About 1967, officials of the Department of Bantu Administration told some of us that the Bantu Affairs Commissioners who gave us the impression that we had a choice in the matter "were wrongly instructed," that we were merely being consulted and that consultation did not mean we had to give consent. Those of us who had been waiting for our people to decide, had after this explanation no option but to comply with the law, as the question of "accepting" or rejecting the Act, fell away.

In spite of this directive from Pretoria, some tribes were still without tribal authorities, some had tribal authorities and some districts had Regional authorities and others still had no Regional Authorities. It was at this stage that our late Ingonyama saved the situation by having that important and historic interview with you, Sir, in August 1968. On that occasion he presented to you, Sir, a certain letter, the relevant extract from which is as follows: "Sir, Your Excellency, I believe that with the establishment of a Territorial Authority, a new and historic day will dawn for the Zulu people. I believe this will be a step in the direction of giving my people the self-determination, self-government and eventual independence and freedom which is the natural ambition of every nation. . . . "

It is indeed very sad that our King was not spared to see with us today his dream for his people coming true. It was this historic visit of Ingonyama to Pretoria which has united his people, that is those who had "accepted" the Act and those who after they were told they have no option, complied with the law. I remember him saying to me on the eve of his visit to Pretoria that whatever the merits or demerits of this law were, it was essential for us to have such a body as you have inaugurated so that we can speak with one voice.

It is interesting to compare what the Ingonyama said in the above letter with the preamble to "The Promotion of Self-government Act, 1959.". . .

If what the Ingonyama asked for and what I have just quoted materializes, as we hope it will, it will be something quite unique in the history of the human race. It will be the first time [for] a Metropolitan power such as South Africa, to relinquish power voluntarily for a subject nation such as we are. South Africa itself struggled very hard to shake off the shackles of Colonialism. Other African countries have also struggled hard for their freedom. White South Africa, particularly the Afrikaners, value their freedom and independence so much, because they got these things through blood, sweat and tears. If this can happen to us peacefully, then our late Ingonyama will rank as one of our greatest Zulu Kings.

Having reached this stage, therefore, we would like to assure the Hon. the Minister of our full cooperation. Sir, we would also like to make it clear that there may be Zulus who have reservations about certain aspects of Your policy, but all of us are united in assuring you of our co-operation. The divergence of views on any aspect of your policy does not necessarily mean any disloyalty to you, Sir, or your government. Nor can reservations about just some aspects of such a wide policy mean that those who have reservations are Communists or Saboteurs. To make the point I am trying to make here clear, may I again be excused if I ask all of you to have a very quick look with me at our history in the last 60 years.

Ever since the establishment of the Union of South Africa, in 1910, we Zulus have been loyal and have always co-operated in the implementation of the policy of whatever Government was in Power. This did not necessarily mean that we agreed with every facet of the Government policy of the day. We have nonetheless always been loyal. In 1914 and 1939 when the World Wars took place, our people freely cooperated in the war efforts of South Africa. During the last World War, I recall that the late-Ex-Regent of the Zulu nation UMntwana uMshiyeni ka Dinuzulu, the late UMntwana nMnyaiza ka Ndabuko, the late Chief Langalakhe Ngcobo and my late father Chief Matele Buthelezi, left their homes and camped with what were called the Native Military Corps. I mention these things as they are a demonstration of loyalty not only to the government of the day, but to White South Africa. . . .

The Present Government was then elected in 1948 on this policy of Separate Development. The 1936 Native Representation Act was then superseded by the Bantu Authorities Act of 1951 and the Promotion of Self-Government Act of 1959. . . . The duty that falls on our shoulders now as a Territorial authority is not to spare ourselves in working with your Department and your government to implement this scheme and to do all to make it work. This raises quite a number of issues. The first of these, which I consider a priority, is for the government to give the Zulu nation more territory for without more territory our scheme will not make sense. According to a publication issued by the Department of Information published in 1965, there are 3,340,000 Zulus scattered all over South Africa. That is almost as many people as there are Whites in South Africa who number 3,536,000! This, Sir, makes me shudder when I think of the responsibility you have today placed on our shoulders.

It is in the interest of South Africa that this policy must be made to work as soon as possible. . . . What also makes it urgent is the position of our people from farmlands. Not one day passes without some of our people from farmlands approaching us (chiefs) for sites and arable lands, and yet we are already forbidden by the officials of your department from granting these people land as our areas are already occupied to their full capacity.

We further request the Hon. the Minister and his Department to assist us in devising a constitution which will include representations of Zulus, scattered throughout the metropolitan areas of South Africa and from these farmlands. This is urgent Sir, because we cannot hope to move as quickly as we would like to if we exclude such a substantial and sophisticated number of Zulus from this Authority. Our present Acting Paramount Chief is deeply concerned that this should be done as soon as possible. The whole Zulu nation is behind him in wishing this to happen so that we can develop as a united nation.

We thank the Hon. the Minister for all the assistance and guidance he has promised us in his speech and thank him in particular for the cheque he has just presented to set us going. We admire the work done by your officials in improving agricultural methods in our areas. Only a few weeks ago some of us heard another encouraging speech from your Deputy, the Hon. Dr. P. G. J. Koornhof. He quoted to us figures showing us the number of our people who are today acquiring technical skills under your department of education. The Hon. the Minster summed up his speech by saying that we are now entering a new era, the era of homeland development.

We were also extremely heartened by a recent announcement by the Manager of the Bantu Investment Corporation, of an industrial growth point to be located at Sitebe. . . . With all these growth points you are creating, Sir, we have every hope that our people will for the first time get rates for the jobs they perform.

We also applaud the creation of these growth points as a solution to the migratory labour problem. This problem has not only destroyed the fabric of our society, but it has destroyed the very moral fibre of our people. The spiritual development of our people, also envisaged under your policy, cannot take place so long as this is the position.

We wish also to plead with you, Sir, to see to it that your officials exercise more tolerance in applying influx control regulations for as long as the Zulu state is not yet a fait accompli, and as long as most of it is underdeveloped as it is today.

We also feel that this development must take place as soon as possible. We have to plead with you, Sir, and your government to assist us financially and in other ways to establish a free and compulsory education. . . . we wonder whether you would not consider allowing our children to be taught through the medium of Afrikaans or English from Standard 5 as was the case in the past. The standard of these languages is getting poorer and poorer, and as long as this is happening we are not going to get the personnel we require to take part in the rapid development you have planned for us in our homelands. This to me seems to be the key to our whole development.

We admire your Government's outward policy in relation to African States of Southern Africa and the North. We think that Dr. Banda knocked the nail on the head when he said to the Hon. the Prime Minister, "If we are going to solve the problems of Black and White, we have to start talking to each other.". . . If we make a sincere attempt to have proper dialogue between your government and us, now that we have been recognised today as leaders of our people, then there is every reason to hope for a peaceful solution of our problems. We would like to say emphatically, Sir, that it is our fervent prayer that this should happen peacefully. . . .

To the Zulu people I wish to say that we cannot hope to touch even the fringe of our problems, as long as we do not unite and tackle these problems as a united people. We know that our people are now too conditioned to work for White people diligently and it seems to me that we must now learn to work just as diligently for ourselves and under the supervision of our own people. . . .

We do hope that it will not be long before our Territorial Authority is granted more power and before we get full self-government. It is often said that we are not yet ready for such a step. We challenge such assertions as we Black people of South Africa have had three generations of contact with your people. . . . When I visited England in 1963, I met President Jomo Kenyatta and his Cabinet who were attending the final constitutional talks with the Representatives of the British Government, and to my surprise I discovered that quite a number of his Cabinet Ministers were men who were educated here in South Africa and they included his Minister of Defence, a gentlemen who was with me at Fort Hare. Quite often we enjoy boasting about the fact that we in South Africa have more African graduates than the rest of Africa, how can we therefore dare to think that our own Black people are not good enough to govern themselves.

I feel certain, therefore, Sir, that with your guidance and assistance, we will soon prove ourselves in this new role.

We shall all rejoice if, when we eventually get our freedom, that this shall be freedom in the truest sense of that word. That is, freedom embodying all the four freedoms which were so well set out by President Roosevelt of America in 1941 when he said: "The first is freedom of speech and expression, the second is freedom of every person to worship God in his own way, the third, the freedom from want and fourth is the freedom from fear." A South African Afrikaner leader added a fifth one, which is freedom from prejudice.

Thank you, Sir.

DOCUMENT 99. "Famous Gatsha Buthelezi." Editorial in *SASM Newsletter,* April 1973

Some of the old timers believe that Chief Gatsha Buthelezi will free the Black People. This famous "daddy" of the "Zulus" with his "tricks" manages to confuse so many black people. Content, they relax, since their "leader" champions their liberation.

We can sanely advise Mr. Buthelezi that he pauses and examines the amount of responsibility he has assumed. He must try, with sincerity, to assess whether he has the super-ability to liberate the "Bantus."

Some of the masses have pinned their hopes on him and him alone. When Gatsha speaks, they clap hands and say: 'he is giving it to them (Whites) and is sure going to liberate us! We doubt if Chief Buthelezi is that much super.

When Chief Buthelezi was invited to Holland by four World Organisations, he accepted the invitation. Alas! when Baas [Minister of Bantu Administration and Development] M. C. Botha *"asked"* him not to undertake this trip, he was game. Again he is invited by the Black people in Namibia but he turns down the invitation. Mind you, he is supposed to liberate these very people one day. This time Baas M. C. Botha has *"requested"* him not to go.

We see this as the same paternalistic attitude over the black people by Whitey. He (Whitey) always has instructed and we always have obeyed. In the same way do we view the M. C. Botha-G. Buthelezi relationship. We regret that this "super-man" is known to be our leader by some sects overseas.

DOCUMENT 100. Column by Chief M. G. Buthelezi, *Rand Daily Mail,* October 1, 1973

In my first article I mentioned the National Convention in 1908 to which Blacks were not invited.

It is significant that in spite of this cold shoulder, Blacks have attempted to keep in touch with White South Africa through bodies like the African National Congress.

One needs only to remember the delegations Congress sent to meet the then Minister of Native Affairs and Prime Minister General Louis Botha, which were all ignored. This is worth noting, particularly after the passing of the Native Land Act of 1913, which entrenched "possessory segregation" in South Africa.

When the First World War broke out, Africans decided to forget their grievances and joined in the White war effort.

Even when General Smuts told them that he could not arm them in a war between White people, African leaders still organised some of their people who became the labour force, and hundreds of Africans died when the Mendi was sunk.

To show their goodwill, Africans made representations through delegations and petitions, but true to form, White South Africa ignored all these.

Africans were not consulted, even before the passing of the Statute of Westminster in 1931, but they always hoped there would be a change of heart among Whites.

The Hertzog Bills of 1936 further entrenched segregation, an openly avowed policy of the Government of the day. The African National Congress and other African organizations protested against the passing of these Bills, but they were passed with complete disregard for African objections.

To show their goodwill, Africans continued to co-operate in the implementation of these laws.

The leaders of the day became members of the Native Representative Council from 1936 until 1946, when they passed a resolution refusing to operate the council until all discriminatory laws were repealed.

General Smuts and Mr. Hofmeyr, while the former was absent, did not attempt to meet African demands. This is typical White conduct. White South Africa thinks it is a sign of weakness and a dent in "kragdadigheid" [power] to try to meet Blacks even halfway.

In spite of shoddy treatment at every turn, Africans still supported the war effort when the second World War broke out, but this brought no change for Blacks, even in the post-war period when human rights was a fever around the world. The African National Congress, the Pan-African [Pan Africanist] Congress and the South African Indian Congress all dealt with South Africa as if it was a society based on democratic principles. All their efforts were defeated by the granite-wall response from Whites.

Even when the 1960 demonstrations against passes were organised, all these things were done on the assumption that this would appeal to White South Africa's conscience.

Thus, while separate development is based on the apartheid philosophy, which is abhorrent to most Blacks, we have cooperated with Whites in the implementation of it, mainly because we had no option.

I am one of those who have strong reservations about the policy of apartheid, but I am participating in it since we are not yet committed to violent change, in spite of the violence against Blacks inherent in the policies pursued against them.

I mention these attempts because very often White people look at people like me—those of us who must articulate Black aspirations—as extremists.

I leave it to readers to judge for themselves whether we are in fact extremists in the light of the good faith and goodwill we have shown over generations to White South Africans.

These attempts at dialogue, even on the basis of the segregationist policies of the past and the separate development of our day, stand out as irrefutable evidence of the Black man's goodwill in an impossible situation.

I have tried to show how far Africans have gone to display goodwill to Whites. They have not received any significant goodwill in return.

In other words, the disillusionment now so evident among young Blacks should be understood to be a natural result of White intransigence. The question now is whether there can be any meaningful dialogue between White and Black South Africa, in the light of history.

I am one of those who have not completely given up hope that such a dialogue can still take place.

I think that under certain conditions there may still be dialogue, which might yet avert violent confrontation.

First, I wish most Whites would place themselves in our shoes. They should imagine themselves as Black and ask themselves how they would react to the situation if they had darker skins.

If they did so, it would be easy for them to see that certain actions are needed to convince Blacks of the White man's bona fides.

Second, I think it must be appreciated that Black political leaders of the past, while they might appear to be so-called "subversive elements" to whites, are in fact heroes to Blacks.

It follows then that the release of Nelson Mandela and other Black leaders on Robben Island would create a wholesome climate for meaningful dialogue.

It would also convince Black African and the international community that White South Africa was beginning to have real dialogue with Black South Africa.

This is not such an unreal expectation since Japie Fourie and others like him who rebelled during the First World War are heroes to many Afrikaners, even today.

Some of us have seen during our lifetime the release of Robey Leibbrandt by the present regime and this strengthens my argument that the release of Nelson Mandela would not be without precedent.

There are many precedents in Africa, including South Africa, of many politically-motivated, apparently treasonable actions which landed leaders in detention, but for which they were forgiven. Many of them are heads of governments today.

It must be remembered that Mandela and his contemporaries wanted dialogue which they were denied and they indulged in extra-parliamentary actions in utter desperation. They would still be prepared to be involved in any dialogue today with the leaders of White South Africa.

I also consider the lifting of the banning order on a leader of Robert Sobukwe's stature in the same category. I am convinced that he would also be willing to be involved in such a dialogue.

White South Africa must remember that we know what led to Paul Kruger's flight to Europe.

In this spirit, if some kind of immunity could be given to some of our refugees, such as Oliver Tambo, this would ensure some peaceful settlement of Black-White differences.

This would lessen tensions on the country's borders and would help to end that Black-White tension which is bound to grow as more pressure is felt on those borders.

If the present leadership were to be joined by the Black leadership I have mentioned, I would bet my last rand that this would guarantee a peaceful solution of the South African situation.

The ball is in White South Africa's court and it is up to White leadership to save us all from a confrontation that is bound to destroy all of us, and whose aftermath is too terrible to imagine.

DOCUMENT 101. "In This Approaching Hour of Crisis." Speech by Chief M. G. Buthelezi, Soweto, March 14, 1976 (abridged)

My dear sons and daughters of Africa, I greet you in the name of mother Africa, and in the name of freedom. I dare say that this is perhaps the most important of my yearly pilgrimages to Soweto, if we look at it in the context of the present political climate in Southern Africa.

Last year, on the 22nd of January, I issued a friendly warning to the Prime Minister, Mr Vorster, that if we as Blacks did not reach fulfillment through his policies as appeared to me to be the case, that we would have no option but to resort to unrest and possible civil disobedience. I did so with all the responsibility in the world, as I sensed the euphoria that pervaded the whole of white South Africa, as a result of the Prime Minister's so-called detente policy.

I made it quite clear that when I spoke as I did, it was because I was hoping that violence could be warded off, as a result of my warnings, but there is not even a ripple in the pen as far as the sharing of power and decision-making by all South Africans, is concerned.

My brothers and sisters, today we meet in what is no doubt one of the most dramatic moments of South African history. We have been through 150 years of white domination, and have been subjected to 66 years of oppression. This has been perpetrated against us in the name of western democracy, and Christian civilization, by white manipulation of the Houses of Parliament.

Despite all this length of time today the very foundations of apartheid society have been shaken. 10 years after Prime Minister Macmillan's 'Wind of change' warning, who can deny today that these winds of change are blowing not north or west of us, but right on our borders?

Prime Minister Vorster's detente policy has not succeeded. Not only has it not succeeded but white South Africa has burnt her fingers in Angola. . . . Every hour of the day, the time is drawing nearer, when we will see white South Africa's enemies encamped on South Africa's borders.

I know that the Prime Minister, if I am to judge by his past attitudes, is going to think—with many white South Africans—that I am speaking as I do because I am a kaffir who has forgotten his place. This thought makes many white South Africans mad, as there is nothing they loathe as much as a kaffir who has not been successfully kept in his place. A place not assigned for us by the Almighty, but which our white countrymen have assigned for us for generations through the only power they have used to maintain the status quo, which is through the barrel of the gun. Many white elections have been fought on the basis of who can best keep the kaffir in his place.

What precluded the Prime Minister from consulting me about his so-called detente policy, in the light of my contacts in black Africa? . . .

It is still not too late to call for a white change of heart. I believe this not because I think that whites are going to have a sudden spasm of benevolence towards blacks. I believe that now the whites can see the writing on the wall and can realise that the country must move towards majority rule.

It is this single principle that is central to any question to do with Southern Africa's politics. This is the burning question in Namibia, Zimbabwe, Mocambique, and Angola. It was the burning question in every other African State.

I realise what I am doing here today, by saying these things as I do, but they have to be said. If they were not said, I would not be responsible. I am offering a black hand of friendship to the whites of South Africa, probably for the last time. Yes, it is a black hand, but it is still a hand of friendship. . . .

I sympathise with you my brothers and sisters because just like you, I am not free. Like you, I do what I can. Together we suffer oppression. Together we must throw off the yoke of oppression.

The whole world must be told that we despise what some people euphemistically call 'separate development' or 'separate freedoms,' which we know to be nothing more or less than white baasskap [boss-ship]. South Africa is one country; it has one destiny and one economy. . . .

I believe it is essential that we hold a series of representative National Conventions representing all shades of black opinion.

I have called for a black National Convention on economic matters, to take place in August, if all goes as planned.

It is warranted to call for a National Convention on the so-called homeland independence issue.

I also call for a National Convention on South Africa's foreign policy. . . .

I am hoping that we will invite international speakers to these Conventions. We will hear their wisdom. We will then close our doors and go into a black caucus where we will deliberate among ourselves.

It is high time the privileged in this country heard the voice of the underprivileged. They have failed to do this so far. It is this willful persistence in social and political stupidity which produces despair and anger, which in turn create racial tension.

I see very serious problems arising in the very near future if the government's policies result in a black majority rejecting the contributions from the white minority. It is good that black nationalism born in 1912 in Bloemfontein, with the founding of the African National Congress, has had a fillip with the emergence of black consciousness. This dignity must receive the dignity it deserves. It is my hope that the operative majority in this country will be a multi-racial majority. . . .

I implore the white government to release black political leaders who are now withering in jail. My brothers and sisters, when I lie awake, thinking about you and your suffering, I know that thousands of you get up in the dark to get on crowded buses and trains to go to a menial job for a pittance. Most of you work without security and social benefits, and are denied real trade unions. I know you are exploited. I know you feel anger because there seems to be no hope of improving your circumstances. . . .

We cannot wait until the Parliament in Cape Town falls before we achieve that dignity which comes from self-help and from making the best of the miserable mess we find ourselves in. Blacks in every corner of the country are shrugging off the dependency mentality, and this philosophy has been expressed in the formation of Inkatha YeNkululeko YeSizwe.

In Inkatha people are getting together. It is a movement of ordinary men and women in ordinary walks of life; such as you see here today. As this movement gains momentum we will produce a ground swell which will bring about change in South Africa. . . . Inkatha has grown phenomenally during the past year. It is continuing to grow and will continue to grow steadily.

Some people might think that when I talk of freedom and liberation I am thinking of the Zulus as distinct from my other African brothers in South Africa. This is far from being the case. There is no Zulu freedom that is distinct from the black man's freedom in South Africa. Black oppression has no ethnic boundaries. We have a common destiny as black people. We have indeed a common destiny even with our white countrymen who have rejected this idea for several generations. These are the implications of a just and non-racial society.

In KwaZulu we have founded Inkatha, a National Cultural Liberation

Movement, because we have learnt that it is no use to wait for others to come and help us in our predicament. In helping ourselves we are taking an important step on the road to liberation. We hope that our brothers throughout the length and breadth of this land will set out from the apartheid strait-jacket and set up Inkatha. We are quite prepared to assist if there are problems about this, because we believe that black brotherhood will in due course become a reality in an all-embracing South African Inkatha. . . .

Africa needs you my brothers, Africa needs you my sisters. Yes. Africa needs you and me. This may be Africa's finest hour. The time has come for you to organise and act.

It seems to me most unfortunate that as we face this greatest challenge, we have also to lose some of our brothers and sisters through a balkanisation which can only give white domination a breathing space and further prolong our people's suffering. I say these words not in a spirit of castigation. I respect my brothers in the Transkei and BophuthaTswana far too much to attempt to do this. . . . Mr. Vorster's stand seems to spell a life of perpetual destitution and step-children status for black people within their so-called "independence," confined to 13 per cent of South Africa's surface area. I hope it will never be too late for us as brothers to save one another from the political wilderness where there can only be want, insecurity and desperation.

God Bless Africa
God Bless all her children
Strength in the struggle
Hope for the future
Power is Ours
AMANDLA! NGAWETHU!
MATLA! ARONA!

Document 102. Transcript of meeting between Chief M. G. Buthelezi, Minister J. T. Kruger and others, Pretoria, September 19, 1977 (abridged)

Note: "Meeting between Chief Gatsha Buthelezi, President of Inkatha, and Mr. J. T. Kruger, Minister of Justice, Police and Prisons, at Union Buildings—Pretoria, 19 September 1977. Also present: Mr. C. J. Mtetwa, Mr. G. Thula, General Gert Prinsloo, Mr. Coetzer"

CHIEF BUTHELEZI: . . . . Sir, I want to assure you that the process of radicalisation which has embraced me and which in return I embrace is far more than just political stancing. I think it is a serious stage I have reached willy nilly in my long political career. . . . I really do believe that we should be talking today about an impending race war in South Africa. South Africa is rapidly polarising along racial grounds. . . . I am speaking as somebody who has a real anticipation that your department will act against me sometime in the future. . . .

MR. KRUGER: . . . . we should first discuss, Chief, whether we should have this as a confidential discussion, or whether you want to make a public statement later on or not.

CHIEF BUTHELEZI: Well personally, Mr. Minister, I always believe in operating openly, even in dealing with the Prime Minister because I think it's the best way, to be open because there is nothing hanky panky or anything that we discuss in this room which we are ashamed of discussing outside. . . .

I try to meet many people, even those with whom I do not agree, because it seems from what the Honourable Minister, Mr. Mtetwa [KwaZulu Minister of Justice], told me, he said that the Minister was perturbed that I do meet people on my travels abroad.

MR. KRUGER: Yes, that's right. I understand you had met somebody in Dar-es-Salaam on this point, is that so?

CHIEF BUTHELEZI: In fact, Yes, I met Mr. Leballo in Dar-es-Salaam. . . . in fact, two members of the Pan Africanist Congress came to see me because they had seen a statement I had made in the Assembly . . . that certain people of that Movement were giving instructions to the younger people that when they got back I should be the target, that they should kill me.

GENERAL PRINSLOO: This is the African National Congress or PAC?

CHIEF BUTHELEZI: The PAC.

GENERAL PRINSLOO: The PAC.

CHIEF BUTHELEZI: So then, when I was in Dar then they decided to come and say it wasn't true and so on and also to apologize for the statement that was made by Mr. Sibeko in Maseru when he said that I was a pedlar of apartheid. . . .

MR. KRUGER: May I ask you, and if you don't want to answer it, you mustn't, you don't have to answer it, Chief, did he discuss the possibility of a link up between PAC and the Inkatha movement at all?

CHIEF BUTHELEZI: Not at all, No, No, I will be truthful about that because, I mean they have a constitution, we have a constitution, and they are committed now to a violent change and we are not committed to a violent change.

MR. KRUGER: I see, I see. So in actual fact, there is no, there is no truth in the allegation that there is a link-up or an alignment with the African National Congress or the PAC?

CHIEF BUTHELEZI: No, there is none, because I am sure the Minister is aware more than anyone in South Africa that some actually, there are some of them who attack me from time to time . . . . I want the liberation of South Africa in which all the people have a common destiny. They believe in that too.

GENERAL PRINSLOO: But you associate yourself with the ANC and PAC by this statement as far as I can get it.

CHIEF BUTHELEZI: Do you know that the founder of the ANC was actually, is a man I knew very well, Dr. Seme. He was actually married to my mother's sister.

GENERAL PRINSLOO: Dr.?

CHIEF BUTHELEZI: Dr. Seme, Dr. Pixley Seme.

GENERAL PRINSLOO: Seme.

CHIEF BUTHELEZI: He was my uncle, actually and I knew him as a boy when I was in matric. In fact, I remember that he had an operation on his eye and I had to write letters for him and so on.

GENERAL PRINSLOO: Since those days the communists have taken over the ANC to a certain extent or they have amalgamated.

CHIEF BUTHELEZI: No, you see, that's why I talk about ideals as set out by the founding fathers of the movement.

GENERAL PRINSLOO: Well, you are not very clear on that. I mean, you say you are furthering those ideals now.

MR. KRUGER: Those ideals at the moment are purely communistic ideals in actual fact. They are Marxist based as far as the ANC is concerned.

MR. MTETWA: I am sorry, this can be interpreted like that—

Mr. KRUGER: Ya, on the face value of it, that's why we are asking that because we don't want to interpret it incorrectly. I would like the chief to explain to us exactly how we should interpret it.

CHIEF BUTHELEZI: In fact, as I have stated, Mr. Minister, that as far as I am concerned, you know, I find nothing wrong; from what my colleague told me this issue came up during the last discussion and in fact initially I think even the Minister admitted that there was nothing wrong with the ANC as such at the beginning and so on as far as the other things that have taken place are concerned, that the ideals as set out by the ANC founding fathers, I believe that those ideals are ideals I would support, because I think they do create, as I say, the only common ground where all South Africans of all shades can find each other. . . .

MR. KRUGER: We must find out whether you people are lumping yourselves with all the other black people in a black polarization against white people or not, because this I think is physically firstly and spiritually impossible. I don't think this can happen because it's against nature. . . .

CHIEF BUTHELEZI: With due respect to the Minister, I don't accept it's against nature insofar as whites, Greeks and Jews and what have you have merged together into one South African nation, and I don't, I think then of course it's a very terrible admission if the Minister says that there is this— white ethnic groups got together because they want to, they were polarizing against us blacks.

MR. KRUGER: . . . . I am asking you . . . whether you want to start anew as a black man instead of as a Zulu. This is the point. This is the whole point. . . . PAC—let's make no bones about it, PAC believe in Pan Africanism. It's a racialistic thing. It's the black man against the white man. . . . The African National Congress goes one better. They want to have a communistic regime. They want to have, they simply want to have a dictatorship which you and I certainly cannot ever serve. This is our tragedy. This is our dilemma. That's what we are talking about. . . .

If Inkatha wants to become a nationalist organisation like my people have had nationalist organisations, then I am not going to do anything against Inkatha. . . . but I get the impression that Chief Gatsha Buthelezi wants to broaden the base on to a black polarisation, then of course it's going to, there's going to be trouble. No doubt about it. Because you can understand, we've got to react. We cannot sit quiet while the blackman polarises against the white man. It will become a life and death struggle then. . . .

I am very worried that the white man will put his back against the wall and say, No, go to hell, we do nothing for them. They want to fight, let them fight. My people did that at Blood River. They will do it again, and I don't want that. . . . The only possible way for you to live in peace, and let me tell it to you today, the only possible way for you to live in peace with the Xhosas is to say, look, I remain a Zulu, I am not going to take the whole of Xhosaland, I am not going to take the whole of Mangope's people, I don't want to be the leader of South Africa. . . .

I accept the black man of Africa as my black brother. I have always accepted him. He is part and parcel of Southern Africa. But he's a different nation and this is the whole point and that nobody can go against history, you now, not the PAC, not ANC, not Leballo, not Sobukwe, not anyone. This is what this argument is about. . . .

Well, what formula, what formula do you want?

CHIEF BUTHELEZI: I want the formula where I participate with you in decision-making, where you don't decide that this is good for me, that in your wisdom that this is good for me without me participating in finding the formula.

MR. KRUGER: Our government doesn't want to decide for you, Chief. We are asking you to go independent and decide for yourself.

CHIEF BUTHELEZI: Well, the point is that the independence as defined and as taking place is empty. . . .

MR. KRUGER: The framework of government policy is to give independence. I mean, what more can you really expect from any governmen in the world to divest itself of its authority over other people? It's a tremendous thing to do.

CHIEF BUTHELEZI: And also as far as majority rule is concerned, Mr. Minister, personally I challenge anyone to say that I have ever spoken about black majority rule. . . . But I stand for majority rule—

GENERAL PRINSLOO: . . . one man one vote—

CHIEF BUTHELEZI: I stand for majority rule.

GENERAL PRINSLOO: For one man one vote.

CHIEF BUTHELEZI: Well, I stand for majority rule which would be a multi-racial majority rule, not what you call black majority rule because this country has different ethnic groups, so I have never really ever spoken about black majority rule because I don't think that is possible.

MR. KRUGER: If you don't think that is feasible, then the only other possibility is to accept separate development, my dear fellow. . . . If you talk about majority rule then you must by necessity mean that the black man polarizes as a black man against the white man which is racialistic.

CHIEF BUTHELEZI: It's not polarizing—

MR. KRUGER: But of course it is. What else would it be?

CHIEF BUTHELEZI: But it's the whites who do the polarizing by excluding us from the table.

MR. KRUGER: No, but we are not excluding you. We want to give you total freedom, what more do you want? . . .

The main thing of politics is to get yourself into the line of God's will and what was made by God. I don't make you a Zulu, God made you a Zulu. You didn't make me an Afrikaner, God made me an Afrikaner. I can't deny these facts. And I must get into the Will of God as quickly as possible and this is the truth. And you will be a very very great statesman, a great statesman, like General Hertzog was a great statesman when you realise this fact, when you say, look, I am not going to Europe again, I am not going to listen to the American story and the American experience of the black people and the black consciousness movement, and the black power movement in America. I'm a Zulu and I want to develop my own people. Then you will become a statesman. You won't be an international politician that everybody says that you are sitting on the fence. This is the big difference.

CHIEF BUTHELEZI: Who is saying I am sitting on the fence?

MR. KRUGER: Well you tell me that the PAC and those people say that you are a stooge. I didn't say that. . . . If you want to be a statesman, a Zulu statesman, to lead your people to freedom, to prosperity, my people are more than willing to try and help when we can. That's all I can tell you this morning. . . .

You don't like the smallness of the cake, this is your trouble.

CHIEF BUTHELEZI: Why should we like—

MR. KRUGER: You want the whole cake, Chief.

CHIEF BUTHELEZI: Not for me alone. I want to share the whole cake, Mr. Minister, all of us.

MR. KRUGER: But I am sharing it out. I am cutting the pieces out. I am giving you your share.

CHIEF BUTHELEZI: It's hardly an icing that you are trying to give me, and I can't accept it. . . .

MR. KRUGER: Tell me what you people want to arrive at? You say that we leave you with nothing but violence. What do you want to get with violence?

CHIEF BUTHELEZI: We will all be destroyed. You will be destroyed too. . . .

MR. KRUGER: . . . you must never forget one thing, we people will not run away if other people want to cause trouble for our identity, we won't run away.

CHIEF BUTHELEZI: You mean that you'd die.

MR. KRUGER: We won't die, we will win.

CHIEF BUTHELEZI: Against—

MR. KRUGER: We will win, Chief Gatsha.

CHIEF BUTHELEZI: Against the whole of Africa?

MR. KRUGER: The whole of Africa. Why do you want to polarise Africa against us? . . .

I want to give you a formula for a solution to these problems and the formula is really laid in the word development. Let's each culturally develop his own. I don't want you to go and have a fight with Matanzima. You know that that's coming—

CHIEF BUTHELEZI: What fight?

MR. KRUGER: Yes, you know exactly how you feel towards the bottom portion down there. And I don't want you to fight with anyone else.

CHIEF BUTHELEZI: No. [later in the discussion:] the Minister doesn't quite understand black consciousness because I don't think there is anything wrong with black consciousness myself. I know that some of the exponents of black consciousness disagree with me and some have been very vitriolic in their attacks on me, but nevertheless I do believe that it's a very healthy thing.

MR. KRUGER: Black consciousness has taken a wrong step and that's what I'm trying to save Inkatha from. I am trying to save you from the black consciousness movement because the black consciousness movement polarises all black people and this is a fact, Chief, let's not run away from it. They took their analogy from the American negro, which was wrong, fundamentally, historically, culturally wrong and black consciousness came over from America and have started polarising black people against white people. That's why the black consciousness movement cannot last. . . . this is the big difference between us. You are not seeing this thing historically correctly, Chief, although you are a great man, I know that, and that's why I have taken the trouble to talk to you because I believe you still can be spoken to. . . .

CHIEF BUTHELEZI: My horizons are the great South Africa and my horizons are South Africa and Southern Africa. I am a South African of Zulu-extraction within the South Africa context.

MR. KRUGER: Ya, well, I don't know. Where do my people fit in then?

CHIEF BUTHELEZI: You are also a son of the soil, of the South African soil. You are an indigenous son of the soil, just as I am. You are an indigenous son of the soil just like myself. You are not a settler.

MR. KRUGER: But you may want to give your identity up but we are not prepared to give up our identity. . . . Remember what I'm telling you today, you will be very very sorry the day that John Vorster is not there. . . . you make a friend of him, my dear Gatsha Buthelezi, if you made a friend of John Vorster, you will be surprised [with regard to] all these little advisers and all these little church people that are telling you all sorts of things, and what the Americans are telling you overseas and everybody holding you up, trying to make as if you are such a marvellous chap, you know. Don't believe everything that people tell you. Everyone's got something in his head that he wants to get out of Gatsha Buthelezi, and I tell you that John Vorster is the only man that's not trying to get something out of you, is trying to give you something. The only man in the world that really is only interested in the goodwill of this country. He's got more goodwill towards black people than any man in history in this country.

CHIEF BUTHELEZI: Now I don't know what the Minister is referring to by the small church people. I don't know, which church people?

MR. KRUGER: I know how people advise you, I know these things. Man, because they do that all over the place. They have all sorts of symposiums and this and that and they bring you to the university to deliver speeches on their great days, and what have you. All I'm telling you, my friend, keep a level head and get to know your true friends. . . .

MR. MTETWA: . . . If the Zulus got the whole of Natal, it will be no problem—

MR. KRUGER: Oh, Mr. Mtetwa. First take that which you've got before you start asking about something more. I mean, you can't—

CHIEF BUTHELEZI: I don't think that even if we were given the whole of Natal that we would accept independence. I don't think that's our problem.

MR. KRUGER: You don't have to take independence, Chief. My Prime Minister told you that. You want to take up this attitude, that's all right, we understand, we understand.

CHIEF BUTHELEZI: No, Minister, I came really because the Minister was unhappy—he has expressed—

MR. KRUGER: I was unhappy about Inkatha as a security risk and that's what I—

CHIEF BUTHELEZI: But how can it be a security risk? It doesn't—Colonel Steenkamp and Colonel Dryer give you any reports about us?

MR. KRUGER: They give me reports.

CHIEF BUTHELEZI: What do they say we are doing?

MR. KRUGER: The things that worried me, I told you, Chief, that you were trying to broaden the base for the whole of the black people instead of just the Zulu people and secondly you were allowing an infiltration by ANC members. . . . You told me once before, you said to me, Mr. Minister, if Inkatha takes a turn that you think would be wrong, I want you to tell me about it. Didn't you tell me that?

CHIEF BUTHELEZI: Yes, I have said so. . . .

MR. KRUGER: You give me the assurance that you will not use Inkatha to have a black power movement, you give me that assurance . . . . and you give me the assurance you won't allow the subversive elements against my country to infiltrate into Inkatha—

CHIEF BUTHELEZI: But who are they, Mr. Minister?

MR. KRUGER: If you do that, then I'll be no trouble with Inkatha.

—Cross talk—

CHIEF BUTHELEZI: Because you see, I mean Inkatha today has over 100,000 members. Now I cannot guarantee that some people will not try to infiltrate Inkatha from—. . . .

MR. KRUGER: I think up to now Inkatha has been a force for good, up to now.

CHIEF BUTHELEZI: It [violence] is against our policy.

MR. MTETWA: We have been attacked by all organisations just because of that.

MR. KRUGER: I know, I appreciate that very much and that's all I'm saying—

MR. MTETWA: We have been attacked by the government again, we don't know now which way to go.

MR. KRUGER: . . . . Is there anything more we should discuss, that you would like to discuss? . . .

CHIEF BUTHELEZI: I would also, I think Mr. Minister, like to express my deep sorrow at the death of Steve Biko because although philosophically maybe there were differences in our politics, but I knew him when he was in Natal, when he was studying there and I thought he was a very bright and possibly very brilliant leader of the future, and I am very, very distressed about it, his death.

MR. KRUGER: No, well I have said there will be an inquiry when once I get the full reports, either an inquest or whatever the case may be from the reports that I will then make a decision. Do you want us to issue a press statement now of our meeting?

CHIEF BUTHELEZI: I don't see why we shouldn't.

MR. KRUGER: Do you want to make a press statement or shall we leave it?

CHIEF BUTHELEZI: I don't think it's private our coming here. I think people know that we are—

MR. KRUGER: What would you like us to say? We should issue a joint statement because I'm allergic to the press at the moment. Whatever I say, they don't seem to report quite correctly, so I would prefer to put it in writing what we are going to say.

Discussion of the press statement.

JOINT PRESS STATEMENT

The discussions were open and frank.

Mr. Kruger raised the direction of the Inkatha Movement and this was discussed.

An alleged alignment of Inkatha with the ANC and the PAC was discussed. Chief Buthelezi assured Mr. Kruger that although he is prepared to speak to anybody, the Inkatha Movement is not aligned with the ANC and the PAC in their activities.

The discussions ranged across the full spectrum of black aspirations and Mr. Kruger explained the position of the Government to Chief Buthelezi.

Chief Buthelezi also expressed his distress in the death of Mr. Steve Biko.

Mr. Kruger assured Chief Buthelezi that once the result of the Post Mortem is available, the Attorney General will be in the position to decide what further legal action should be taken in consultation with the Minister of Justice.

DOCUMENT 103. Speech by Chief M. G. Buthelezi at Third International Christian Political Conference, Sioux Center, Iowa, August 25, 1979 (abridged)

I thank the Research Director and Conference Organiser of this Third International Christian Conference, Mr. James W. Skillen for inviting me to participate in this Conference, as a Christian who is seeking to find political solutions for the very complex problems of political participation in government by all the population groups of my Country.

We who are in South Africa wrestling from within with these problems, do not often get a chance to have our viewpoint heard outside the borders of South Africa. If we are ever heard at all, it is not quite our voice that is heard but a distortion of our voice by various elements who often have an axe to grind in making the distortions that filter out of South Africa. . . .

I have chosen the question of black unity as my starting point because my Country is passing through a phase in which the ordinary people are finding each other—and they are doing so despite the fact that the international community and our brothers and sisters in exile remain too preoccupied with protest and ephemeral politics. It seems to me as though far too many people, organisations and groups live on a diet of protest and dabbling in violent programmes which give respectability to their impotence. . . .

I have openly identified with the ANC's traditions and I have publicly called upon the ANC to recognise Inkatha and thereby reciprocate the recognition my stand has afforded them both in South Africa and abroad. . . . There is nothing whatsoever in that which the ANC has ever stood for, which says that liberation will come by violence alone. Any statement to this effect will result in the alienation of ANC's rank and file support inside South Africa. In saying this, I am simply putting the record straight. All of us are deeply aware that if the ANC spurned those who worked for non-violent change in South Africa, any violence they could employ would be no more than barbarism, and banditry. . . .

It is of vital importance for us all to realise that that which Bishop Muzorewa is doing in Zimbabwe could have been part of a joint strategy shared by him and Joshua Nkomo and Robert Mugabe. . . .

When I stepped into this position of continuing with the struggle, I had abuse hurled at me from many ANC quarters and virtually all their fellow travellers. When in the position I occupy I have perforce to reflect the ordinary peasant and workers' rejection of disinvestment as a strategy, I am again made to look despicable. . . . I cannot continue to seek alliances from quarters hurling abuse at me. . . .

The black people of South Africa want to get on with the struggle for liberation. They know that disinvestment is fiction politics in the first place, and in the second place they know that those who argue disinvestment are careless of the agony of men who have cold and hungry families. . . .

The fundamental constitutional question we have to face in South Africa is the question of whether politics can afford to aim at the full inclusion of blacks in the existing constitution. Our early cries for one man one vote ignored the reality of racial hatred, racial fear and entrenched power groups. . . . I face the agony of debating this question with myself. There is firstly the aspect of the present constitution's desirability. Secondly, there is the question of the feasibility of getting whites to share power within the existing constitution. A question here is—is the democratic procedure involved in the multi-party system we have such that the impoverished peasant and the semi-literate black will be able to influence political decision-making? Another aspect of the constitutional question is that of providing the various organisations (both internal and exiled) with the ways and means which are fair to them of participating in the reconstruction of South African society, which may have to precede true political equality. Then, there is the relationship between a political system and an economic system. Here the question is—can our present type constitution survive the political unrest which will inevitably flow from continued unemployment? How is continued industrial productivity to be ensured? . . .

As we move from the present political dispensation into a future dispensation where one man one vote will ensure the perpetuation of justice, we may have to pass through phases which on the one hand accommodate white fears, and other minority interests, and on the other hand make manageable the formidable task of salvaging the human jetsam and flotsam created by apartheid. . . .

The amount of blood which will flow, the vagrant influences of foreign vested interests, the whites' preparedness to commit mass suicide, the degree to which blacks are mobilised and disciplined, the dominance of racism over rationality and many other things could well emerge as the determinants of South Africa's constitutional future. . . . While, however, there is any chance of negotiation succeeding, we must attend to negotiation. . . .

We [in Inkatha] have established with other black organisations the South African Black Alliance of which I am the current Chairman. We carry on the job of mobilising the politically deprived black population of South Africa. We value the strength which comes out of speaking to Pretoria with one strong voice, which represents the majority of the politically deprived black population.

On the other hand, the Inkatha think-tank has started creating bridges for the whites who are in power. The Inkatha Central Committee think-tank is already holding conversations with members of the ruling Nationalist Party, including members of Parliament. . . .

We will move into the next phase of the constitutional struggle when we decide to take over the Community Councils recently introduced by the government. We will take another step as we bring about an alliance between Inkatha and the trade unions as we mobilise consumer power, and in everything we do, we will keep open the channels of dialogue with whites. Those are viable alternatives to violence which Inkatha has espoused. If they cease to be viable, it will be because we have failed in our own resolution, and not because they cannot succeed.

It is in these ways that I and Inkatha are seeking new ways of reaching an equitable political dispensation for all the people of South Africa.

DOCUMENT 104. "Who Collaborates with Whom?" Press release by the Pan Africanist Congress, Dar es Salaam, November 6, 1979

The meeting of the Chief Minister of Kwazulu, Bantustan Chief Gatsha Buthelezi, with the leadership of the ANC in London did not come as a surprise to P. A. C.

Chief Buthelezi and his entourage went to London to meet the ANC not only with the knowledge of the racist regime but with its full approval as Inkatha Movement is favourably associated with Botha's constellation of states of Southern Africa, which is a conspiracy against the interests of the people of this region, particularly those of Azania who continue to be denied principles of human equality and the right to national self-determination. The meeting of the Chief of Kwazulu Bantustan is the logical outcome of the past efforts by a number of dialogue peddlers and apologists of apartheid. It is no secret that white diplomats with faded jacaranda droppings on their patent leather shoes have been calling on African Capitals in the past, sounding the opinions of Africa on how to discourage or stop the march of freedom in Southern Africa.

The racist Minister Dr. Koornhof and Gatsha Buthelezi who specialise in hyena howls attitude continue to mumble friendly noises in the direction of Pretoria and completely behave like buddies for all to see. In the meantime, other puppets in the newly racist created Urban Councils want palaver between oppressor and the oppressed.

While efforts are exerted internationally by all the peace-loving peoples and nations to isolate South Africa because of her evil and oppressive apartheid policy, Gatsha Buthelezi goes around the Western World pleading for investments in the apartheid land to boost its economy and undermine the interests of those oppressed and exploited by such collaboration.

The Zulu chief must be recklessly naive to think that the racist regime, the oppressor, can willingly solve the national relations and social question in Azania in favour of the Black people and cut its own throat.

The P. A. C. stand is that if the racists feel concerned about human relationships and realising that their bag of oppressive intrigues is getting empty, they should go to Robben Island where the leadership of the national liberation movement of Azania is, men like Messrs. Zeph Mothopeng, John Pokela, Nelson Mandela and Walter Sisulu,—rather than sending its agents like Gatsha Buthelezi to go and attempt to seduce the fighters and leadership in exile.

P. A. C. stands by the OAU resolutions and condemns collaborations of any kind with the racist policy of Separate Development, which promotes the balkanization of our Country into tribal ethnic groups.

10. The Liberation Movements 1975–1979

DOCUMENT 105. "People of South Africa—Sons and Daughters of the Soil." ANC flyer on anniversary of 1960 Sharpeville massacre, March 21, 1976

PEOPLE OF SOUTH AFRICA—SONS AND DAUGHTERS OF THE SOIL—
THE AFRICAN NATIONAL CONGRESS BRINGS YOU THIS MESSAGE

The conditions for developing our liberation struggle, smashing the Apartheid monster and winning our freedom, are greater than ever before. Nothing can hide the fact that White South Africa is in irreversible crisis from which it cannot escape. The opportunities for developing the armed struggle right inside South Africa are becoming more possible. Through armed force, with Umkhonto We Sizwe—the ANC's military wing—as the armed spearhead, we will smash the brute force of the oppressors. But do not wait for that day. It cannot come unless the masses are involved in all forms of struggle. The time to act—to hit back—is NOW!! Rally to the ANC—the tried and trusted organisation of all our people that Vorster and his police can never crush!

EVERYONE MUST BE A FREEDOM FIGHTER! Our men, our women, our youth—the toilers in the town and countryside—the scholars and the professional groups. The MPLA and FRELIMO are victorious because the entire people supported them.

OUR ORGANISED STRENGTH, UNITY AND MILITANT ACTIONS ARE THE KEY TO FREEDOM! Organise wherever you are. In the factories, townships, mines, farms, schools, countryside—mobilise the power of our people and of all genuine democrats. Intensify the freedom struggle in every possible way. We, African, Indian and Coloured people must resist Vorster's policy of divide and rule. Reject tribal politics, Bantustans, Indian Councils and all dummy institutions! Smash the stooges and traitors! Fight the unjust laws and fight for a new life!

PEOPLE OF SOUTH AFRICA—DEMONSTRATE OUR SUPPORT FOR THOSE VORSTER SEEKS TO CRUSH! It is within our power to prevent his aggression against our brothers and sisters in Angola, Namibia or anywhere else. We must not permit subversive activities against the people and state of Angola! By intensifying our struggle we will tie Vorster's army down and make it impossible for him to launch his war machine across the borders. The struggle in Angola, Zimbabwe, Namibia is our struggle—a struggle against a common enemy—racism and imperialism. Together we will win!

THE ANC SAYS: AMANDLA NGAWETHU! MAATLA KE ARONA! POWER TO THE PEOPLE!

THE ANC SAYS TO VORSTER AND HIS RACIST REGIME:
ALL POWER TO THE MPLA—LIBERATORS OF ANGOLA!
ALL POWER TO THE PEOPLE!
VORSTER—GET OUT OF ANGOLA! GET OUT OF NAMIBIA!
NO INTERFERENCE IN ZIMBABWE! HANDS OFF AFRICA!

PEOPLE OF SOUTH AFRICA! The MPLA have scored an outstanding victory over the forces of racism and imperialism. Vorster's defeat in Angola is of outstanding significance to our struggle.

VORSTER TRIED TO SWALLOW ANGOLA BUT NOW HE IS CHOKING TO DEATH! THE MPLA have taught him the lesson of his life. He thought he could send his army into Angola and place his stooges in power, but the MPLA thrashed him in battle and sent his White soldiers and stooges fleeing in terror. The MPLA proved that his racist arrogance is hollow, that White South Africa is not invincible, that the forces of freedom are growing in strength and will soon be powerful enough to completely destroy him.

DOCUMENT 106. "People of South Africa—The African National Congress Calls on You. Amandla Soweto!" Flyer, July 1976

PEOPLE OF SOUTH AFRICA—
THE AFRICAN NATIONAL CONGRESS
CALLS ON YOU. AMANDLA SOWETO!

BROTHERS AND SISTERS: Vorster and his assassins have learnt nothing since Sharpeville. Once again he has called out his murderers to shoot down in cold blood innocent people in the name of preserving 'law and order.' Once again the racists have blamed agitators, inciters, communists and black power militants for the disturbances instead of their hated Apartheid system. They will never admit that it is their system of racial oppression that has aroused the collective fury of our people, for to do so they would have to admit that it has been a complete failure. They have shown us again that they are not prepared to listen to our grievances and would rather shoot anyone who dares to stand up to register them. The massacre of our people must end. We have had enough!

THE AFRICAN NATIONAL CONGRESS calls on our people in every walk of life—in the factories, townships, mines, schools, farms, to embark on massive protests, actions and demonstrations against white supremacy, against the murder of our children, against Bantu Education, Bantustans, the pass laws and all the hated policies of Apartheid. NOW IS THE TIME TO ACT !!

SONS AND DAUGHTERS OF AFRICA: stand together firm and united and show the oppressor that we will not be intimidated. We have the strength to hit back. Our organised strength, unity and militant actions will give us more power than Vorster and all his guns. Rally to the call of the ANC—the tried and trusted organisation of all our people that Vorster and his police can never crush! United in this task we will smash the brute force of the oppressor!

DEMONSTRATE AGAINST THE BRUTAL MURDER OF OUR CHILDREN, OF OUR BROTHERS AND SISTERS IN SOWETO AND OTHER TOWNSHIPS. DEMONSTRATE YOUR RESOLUTE OPPOSITION TO THE APARTHEID STATE, TO RACIAL OPPRESSION AND THE MASSACRE OF OUR PEOPLE.

VORSTER YOUR DAYS ARE NUMBERED! IZAKUNYATHELI AFRIKA! [Africa will trample you!]

AMANDLA SOWETO!! FORWARD TO THE LIBERATION OF OUR SOUTH AFRICA! AMANDLA NGAWETHU! MAATLA KE ARONA! AFRIKA MAYIBUYE! FORWARD TO PEOPLES POWER!!

DOCUMENT 107. Statement made to the police by Mosima "Tokyo" Sexwale, ANC guerrilla, December 31, 1976 (abridged)

Mosima Gabriel Sexwale—I.D.—N/A
Pedi male—born 3/3/1953 (23 years)
1995 Dube Village, Soweto

SWORN STATES:—
    1. I am also known by the following names:

(a) Galaza   (b) Tokyo
(c) Ezekiel   (d) China LEBURU
(e) Solly KHUMALO   (f) KALASHNIKOV

2. My father FRANK SEXWALE age about 59 years employed at Johannesburg Non-European Hospital as a clerk and residing at 1995 Dube Village, Soweto.

3. My mother is GODELIVE SEXWALE about 51 years of age employed as a domestic servant. Six children were born out of this union:

1. Peter SEXWALE born 1946—Television technician in Lesotho.
2. Joseph SEXWALE born 1950—student—left the country for military training during 1975. He was trained with me in Russia. He is also known by the name of Reggie VILAKAZI and LESETSA @ JOSEPH.
3. Mosima Gabriel SEXWALE (myself).
4. Rebecca SEXWALE born 1956—student Orlando West High School.
5. Johny SEXWALE born 1958—student—left the country 1976 for military training.
6. Ester SEXWALE born 1960 student Orlando North Secondary School.

4. I was born and bred in Johannesburg and started my schooling there. . . . The financial situation at my home could not meet my wishes to go to a boarding school. I therefore received admission at Orlando West High School. . . .

11. All along in Form I and Form II I would not really say there was any political philosophy that I knew. By that time I just hated white people like most youngsters did. I hated them because I knew they came and robbed us of our land. However, all this was childish stuff, at least I realised that later in my life.

I hated the white missionaries who used to come and teach us biblical studies. It was in the midst of this hatred that I liked Communism simply because it was what the Government was against. (The law which applied here was that of "The enemy of my enemy is my friend"). But, however, this was still a very immature way of thinking. Typical of a form I or II student in this country.

12. What used to sicken me most were history lessons. I hated the South African history as a whiteman's creation and a complete distortion of the real concrete facts. . . .

13. . . . I was in Form II in 1969 and passed on to Form III in 1970. The real political tune was as a result of the following: (1) Literature: into my library one could notice certain changes. I had friends of all sorts, criminals, politically inclined people and Christians. From all these associates I received books and also exchanged some of mine. Within a short space of time I stopped reading any book which dealt with criminal matters whether factual or fictitious. Christian books also, ranging from the Bible to pamphlets. These I terminated and forgot completely.

14. I began a thorough study of all sorts of political material. Books, newspapers, magazines, journals, all these I began reading thoroughly. The

authors of the books ranged from COSMAS DESMOND, TREVOR HOWARD, MALCOLM X, NELSON MANDELA, EDUARDO MONDLANE and many others.

15. ARGUMENTS: These too contributed a great deal in my shaping. I would find myself engaged in hot battles of words with Christians from the Christian Students Movement, with teachers, friends or even with my father. I had no time for compromises. If we differ we differ, there was no coming together.

16. DISCUSSIONS: These we had with friends whenever we analysed information from the radio, in fact the mass media and even ideas of our own. The subjects ranged from history, science, sociology, films, school life and the day-to-day events in the country.

17. BLACK CONSCIOUSNESS: . . . . [I]t was during 1969–1970 that we were hearing for the first time about the theme of Black Consciousness, Black Power and the whole Black philosophy. . . .

18. I enrolled with SASO and attended most of their meetings around the Reef. Also meetings were organised at our school and seminars, where vehement anti-white speeches were made by different student speakers. SASO leaders like HARRY NENGWEKHULU, THEMBA SONO, DRAKE KOKA and most others addressed us. . . .

21. Because of attending lots of meetings, looking for action, reading many non-school books, newspapers and pamphlets, I had very little time for studying my proper books, hence I failed my matric exams. However the following year I promised my dad and mom that I would do better. I repeated matric and although I did not stop my activities in SASO and SASM, I was also taking good care of the school material and I studied very hard every evening.

22. It was during this time that I met a friend by the name of NZIMA. . . . who was staying at NELSON MANDELA's house helping WINNIE MANDELA with gardening, cleaning and sometimes driving. It was through NZIMA that I met WINNIE personally and she even allowed us to use her storeroom for studying. We studied together and discussed lots of ideas about SASM, SASO and BPC.

23. We realised that there was a lot of talking in these organisations and no action. We became radicals, extremists, we admired the actions of organisations such as: POPULAR LIBERATION ORGANISATION OF PALES-TINE (PLO) [and African liberation organizations] . . . . Especially we favoured the P. L. O., its hijackings, kidnappings etc. With NZIMA we were typical examples of the youth gripped by films (military films) and radical actions. We desired to become "Freedom Fighters." We wanted to join the struggle of the AFRICAN NATIONAL CONGRESS (ANC) and its military wing (UMKONTO WE SIZWE). Although our aspirations as far as armed struggle were positive, we did not understand much.

24. WINNIE MANDELA could only tell us the history of the ANC but could not give us a lead as to how to join the UMKONTO WE SIZWE. Moreover she was a banned person, hence we could not see her as we pleased. At

MANDELA's house we read a variety of books which belonged to NELSON MANDELA including political philosophy, law and history. However, I did not very much agree with the ANC Freedom Charter that our country belongs both to the black and white. I became very much doubtful about its stand. I believed in Black Power! I was sure that the white state must be replaced with a Black one categorically, i.e. Black majority rule. Our friendship with WINNIE broke down when she one day discovered that we had brought girls into the storeroom. She was mad at us. . . .

25. Back at school we wrote exams and then the schools closed. I had to start looking for a place in a university. First of all I was adamant and did not want to go to any of the black South African universities. I preferred to work and simultaneously study with UNISA [correspondence study with the University of South Africa]. I had also heard lots of stories about the quality of the degrees of these universities. . . . I told myself: "If you want a degree, go somewhere but not in South Africa. If you want expulsions, strikes, bannings, go to Turfloop or anyone of those."

26. I decided to choose the former, to go outside the RSA to study. I knew that if I went to Turfloop I would not sit back when others went on strike or going home or any militant actions. Therefore, I concluded, going to any of the black varsities would be going to look for a "banning order," for nothing. I therefore applied to the following universities: [in Dar es Salaam, Zambia, Egypt, Moscow, Kenya, and Uganda] . The letters of applications were posted in Lesotho under a friend's address. . . .

[Sexwale received a United Nations scholarship and was admitted to the University at Roma, Lesotho for an LL.B. degree. Meanwhile a friend gave him the following books:]

(1) SPEECHES AND WRITINGS OF CHE GUEVARA the Argentinian Revolutionary who fought with Fidel Castro as a guerilla.
(2) MAO TSE-TUNG—ON MILITARY—VOL. 4. This book is about MAO's theories of guerilla warfare.
(3) WHAT'S TO BE DONE—by LENIN. This is about the struggle of the Bolshevik party before the Russian revolution.
(4) DAS CAPITAL by Karl Marx. About the system of the capitalistic economy.
(5) I.R.A. (Irish Republican Army). About the struggle of the Irish people against Britain.
(6) Several books on guerilla warfare.

For the five months left before the schools re-opened I made a thorough research into this new literature. I was heavily impressed by CHE GUEVARA's book. However, Lenin's book "WHAT IS TO BE DONE" was a decisive factor. The prominent book was Marx's CAPITAL. This was the beginning of my first direct venture into the Socialist and Communist Philosophy.

30. . . . [At Roma] Two months passed and I noticed that [the University] did not have South African Criminal and Native Law, served properly. I was afraid that also Afrikaans was not studied, [and] this would limit my scope greatly. [For this and other reasons, he transferred to the University in Swaziland to study economics.] . . .

34. During this period I had in the meanwhile begun to conduct a research into the archives of the university library. Here I discovered Marxist books which I studied. I got hold of Economics books which dealt more with the socialistic economic theories. We had arguments with lecturers and students concerning ADAM SMITH, RICARDO and especially the KEYNESIAN theories of capitalism. . . .

36. Using Lenin's other books I ventured and understood the concept of the philosophy and the theory of dialectical and historical materialism. The materialist conception of history, nature, science and all aspects of the social sciences dealing directly with the history of society as it stands today. I later read the selected volumes of Marx and Lenin which were in the library.

37. The following year marks a drastic revolutionary step in my life with the arrival in Swaziland of the A. N. C. officials. By then I was the chief prosecutor in the S. R. C. for the whole student body.

I was a very outspoken student (I think) and also I had bought a car from a man in Soweto called Matebese. The money with which I bought the car was accumulated from my R300 pocket money I received yearly from the UNITED NATIONS, and the left over of my R200 book fees yearly. I also received R150 yearly for travelling expenses. Naturally I used my car for a lot of students' work and was well paid for the use of my car by the SRC. . . .

38. One day in my life a girl friend—in fact a classmate of mine, KGOTOKI, told me of the presence of the two ANC officials viz. THABO MBEKI and ALFRED DLOMO. Later to be joined by a younger man KEITH MOKOAPE, the younger brother of Dr AUBREY MOKOAPE. [And later, Stanley Mabizela.]

Naturally I had a discussion privately with THABO and raised a few points about the Freedom Charter. THABO explained these points to me—however, I was already aware that the Freedom Charter is also my freedom document before meeting THABO. This was through my own efforts in making researches and reading lots of political material.

39. [Many discussions followed, including discussions with students visiting from South Africa.] . . . .

Here I therefore became convinced that the ANC is on the same stand with what I had in mind. Hence I voluntarily and wholeheartedly went and joined the UMKHONTO WE SIZWE. Thus I went for more experience abroad.

I left Swaziland for Mozambique [en route to Moscow]. I do not remember the exact date, but it was a few days before Christmas 1975. . . .

DOCUMENT 108. Report on meeting of the ANC National Executive Committee, Morogoro?, July 15–24, 1977 (abridged)

The recent ten-day session of the National Executive Committeee considered many vital questions which face the entire revolutionary movement in our country at this historic turning point of the struggle of our people.

A few leading members of our organisation, who have recently left South Africa where they were actively involved with the work of our underground organisation, were invited to attend the session.

The main issue before the National Executive Committee was the consideration of the internal situation in the light of developments that are currently taking place. What are the main features of the situation?

The economic crisis currently hitting South Africa and which has been aggravated by the intensified struggle for National Liberation has sharpened the economic plight facing our people. . . . economic booms which enabled the capitalist class to buy off and bribe the white working class are over, and gradually this section of the working class will realise that its best interests are intricately bound up with those of their Black counterpart.

The National Executive Committee underlined the fact that the people have continued to maintain a high state of militancy and organisation and are hitting back at the enemy despite the mounting brutality of the fascist regime. Anti-rent increase movements have sprung up in Soweto and the Southern Transvaal. As a result of militant opposition, the enemy was forced to back down on the issue of rent increases in Soweto. People's resistance has also brought about the disruption of the Urban Bantu Councils in Soweto and there can be no doubt that other areas are bound to follow.

Before and during the 1st Anniversary of JUNE 16, a wide movement of resistance sprung up in many areas such as Uitenhage thereby drawing into the arena of struggle wider sections of the oppressed population. Thousands of Blacks took part in strikes that were widely successful in many parts of our country following a call made by the African National Congress and the militant student movement. It was further noted that the solidarity of genuinely patriotic forces of the oppressed people is growing also as a counter measure to the intensifying repression directed against the people. A vivid demonstration of this important trend was the resolution adopted by a recent students' conference expressing solidarity with our 12 comrades who are presently appearing in a trial at the Pretoria Synagogue [the Gqabi/Sexwale trial]. Some of the comrades involved in the trial are known leaders of the African National Congress. . .

UNDERGROUND ACTIVITIES OF THE AFRICAN NATIONAL CONGRESS

From reports received from the various sub-committees of our Revolutionary Council, the National Executive Committee noted that the work of the underground African National Congress is spreading inside the country. This was clearly evident from the increased activities of the underground combat groups of UMKHONTO we SIZWE during the period of the 1st Anniversary of *June 16*. It is known that successful sabotage actions were undertaken on railway lines in Johannesburg, Durban and other areas. The armed teeth of Umkhonto we Sizwe were felt in other actions during this period.

The National Executive Committee paid a warm tribute to all the brave combatants of Umkhonto we Sizwe and other revolutionary fighters whose heroic actions lent strength and teeth to the militant mass political movement involving large sections of the oppressed population. It further underlined the conviction that an important pre-requisite for the rapid development of our revolutionary struggle is to strengthen the combination of the illegal with the legal forms of confrontation. This was demonstrated in practice during the events surrounding the 1st Anniversary of JUNE 16.

The National Executive Committee learned of further efforts to increase the combat strength of our underground organisation, including efforts to arm the people against the ferocious enemy. It is natural that the growing revolutionary activities of our organisation have had a great psychological and political impact on the masses of the oppressed population. This is a development of tremendous significance.

The National Executive Committee also examined organisational weaknesses which were very graphically pointed out by comrades working underground, some of whom are appearing in the current political trials. It was admitted that some of these weaknesses have directly contributed to the serious setbacks suffered by our underground machineries and the revolutionary organisation as a whole. . . .

It was resolved to strengthen and tighten our organisational machinery both inside and outside the country. In this respect, the membership of the National Executive Committee itself has been increased by an additional 5 (five) comrades, all of whom have recently completed their terms of imprisonment on Robben Island. These comrades are: Steve Dlamini, John Nkadimeng, Henry Gordon Makgoti, Jacob Zuma and Robert Manci. Comrade Andrew Masondo had been co-opted to the National Executive Committee during its March 1977 session. . . .

Special attention was directed towards the need to raise the level of political understanding and consciousness of the membership of the African National Congress. Towards this end it has been directed that all units of our movement must rejuvenate their political life through constant discussions of topical issues both in relation to the situation in our country and on the international scene.

A group of suitably qualified and experienced comrades has been appointed to conduct political lectures to assist the political developments of the young comrades who have recently joined our movement since the beginning of the current political upsurge in our country. This should benefit both those who have recently joined MK and those who are waiting to proceed to centres of learning abroad.

THE ENEMY COUNTER-OFFENSIVE

The fascist regime of Johannes Vorster, despite its loud claims of invincible strength, has been unable either to smother or control the revolutionary upsurge of the masses of our people. Faced with this situation, it has intensified its two-pronged attack against the revolutionary movement aimed at winning the minds of the people and at the same time intimidating them away from the course of revolutionary struggle.

In the past year, thousands of patriots of all age groups have been detained and subjected to indiscriminate methods of torture. Many of our comrades have perished in torture chambers of the fascist regime, including well known leaders of the African National Congress who had previously fought tirelessly to re-build the fighting capacity of our organisation and its revolutionary ally, the South African Congress of Trade Unions (SACTU). Scores of our comrades are today appearing in Court trials in some of which, we have reason to believe, death sentences will be passed by the regime's judiciary. Those who were appearing in the Pietermaritzburg Trial until recently have received long terms of imprisonment. A few of them have been imprisoned for life and these are Comrades: THEMBA HARRY GWALA, ANTON FANO XABA, JOHN VUSUMUZI NENE, ZAKHELE ELPHAS MDLALOSE, MATHEWS MEYIWA. Four other comrades received prison sentences ranging from seven to fifteen years. They are: VUSUMUZI TRUMAN MAGUBANE (15 years); AZARIA NDEBELE (7 years); JOSEPH NTULISWE NDULI (18 years); and CLEOPAS MELAYIBONE NDLOVU (15 years).

The killings of young patriots participating in the current uprising still go on, adding to the hundreds who have already been murdered by the regime from *JUNE 16* last year. On the other hand, the regime is vigorously pursuing its counter-revolutionary Bantustan programme. . . .

THE INTERNATIONAL SITUATION

The National Executive Committee noted that in the wake of the favourable situation brought about by the collapse of Portuguese colonialism and also as a direct consequence of the intensified onslaught of our people and elsewhere in Southern Africa against reactionary regimes of oppression, favourable conditions have arisen for the further all-round development of the international solidarity movement.

The international prestige of the African National Congress has grown tremendously. More and more African states now accept the African National Congress as the only authentic revolutionary vanguard of our struggle. Our organisation is now actively participating in the periodic meetings of the 5 "Front Line" African states which have been charged with the task of assisting the revolutionary movements in Southern Africa to successfully and rapidly develop the oppressed peoples struggles against the remaining vestiges of colonial and racial oppression.

A position has been reached where the African National Congress viewpoint cannot be ignored even by the Security Council of the United Nations. This is consistent with the tremendous authority and respect which the President of our organisation, Comrade O. R. Tambo, generated at the United Nations General Assembly when he addressed that august body on the 26th October 1976. The international progressive movement, represented by numerous national and international organisations from practically all the five continents of our globe at the Lisbon International Conference in Support of the Peoples of Southern Africa held on the 16th to 19th June, 1977, expressed its determination to intensify support for the revolutionary struggles under the leadership of the African National Congress, the Patriotic Front of Zimbabwe and SWAPO. . . .

The international imperialist supporters of the racist-colonial regimes of terror in Southern Africa have been actively engaged in counter-revolutionary maneuvers of seeking to blur the revolutionary goals of the fighting peoples in the whole unliberated region. Evidence of this has come out clearly in their attempts to canvas for their own brand of African majority rule which would, however, entrench the vast economic and political and ideological interests of international imperialism. . . .

How then does the National Executive Committee summarise the main and in fact [sic] tasks facing our revolutionary movement today? We must:

1) raise the level of political understanding throughout the movement and consolidate the political unity among all its members, inside and outside the country, inside and outside Umkhonto we Sizwe (MK).

2) increase our internal underground organisational strength.

3) increase our contact with the broad masses of our people through such an organisational machinery, through legal organisations and through propaganda.

4) pay particular attention to the strengthening and consolidation of our contact and dialogue with all the genuine people's movements that have sprung up so as to make the broad front against the fascist regime of terror more effective.

5) consolidate the trend of rejection of the fascist regime by a growing number of white radical youth within the country who are clearly looking for a way out of the deepening crisis. To this end, urgent steps must be taken to work for the enhancement of the trend in the interests of our revolutionary struggle.

6) increase our combat capacity through the accumulation of war material inside the country and also by increasing the number of underground combat groups.

7) take further steps to protect the movement from disruption by the enemy against whatever means and methods the enemy decides to use from one day to the next. This includes taking appropriate measures against the expelled "group of 8" renegades.

8) raise the level of our international solidarity work to new heights. The African National Congress must be accepted by all as the only authentic leader of the revolutionary struggle of our people. This will further enhance support for our heroic struggle for national liberation.

The National Executive is confident that our organisation which enjoys unprecedented popularity amongst the broad masses of our people inside the country and has won the acclaim and respect of the international

democratic community will gear itself to the tasks that have been set out by
its recent session.

AMANDLA NGAWETHU !

MAATLE KE ARONA !

POWER TO THE PEOPLE !

ALFRED NZO

SECRETARY GENERAL (AFRICAN NATIONAL CONGRESS)

DOCUMENT 109. "The Crisis in the PAC." Statement by T. M. Ntantala, deputy chairman of the Central Committee of the PAC, April 4, 1978 (abridged)

Introduction

A crisis of the greatest dimensions has taken place within the ranks of the Pan Africanist Congress of Azania. The leadership and the membership have split right down the middle: in the Central Committee, High Command, the whole army, the entire Party and its Office administration. In a word, the entire Party has been divided in a manner that has had far-reaching effects on our complex struggle, at home and abroad.

The November 1977 Coup d'Etat:

The long-smouldering contradictions within the PAC leadership finally exploded in an incident that occurred at our External Mission Headquarters in Dar es Salaam last November. Unlike previous crises in the PAC, this one was marked by a determined use of violence and the utilisation of completely new recruits from the home front who knew absolutely nothing about the PAC's history, policies, struggles and procedures for handling internal differences. . . . [T]he whole ugly, disruptive and retrogressive episode was deliberately engineered from the topmost position in the PAC leadership, with clear and unyielding political objectives to be accomplished.

What happened last November can be simply recounted with precision. First, Leballo (our Acting President), acting without consultation with other Central Committee members and our army commanders resident in Dar, and, instead, wrongly going over their heads in army and military matters, started frequenting our camp, made inciting speeches there, told our armymen there that he was giving them the right to go to Dar or Mbeya without bothering to get appropriate authority, and that nobody had the power or right to stop them or refuse them permission to leave the camp, and then in subsequent weeks, he began drawing a few army cadres to Dar. . . .

They did not return to the camp; instead, they encouraged a steady flow that increased their initially small number in the city. Thus a new situation where Leballo and the commanders were clearly working at cross purposes had been deliberately brought about, despite the commanders' efforts to stop it in several consultations with him. . . .

As a direct result of his bad personal influence over them [the new PAC recruits], which has poisoned the young, untrained minds, many began hating whosoever happened to be pointed out to them by him as "plotters that conspired against the leadership" or those whom he painted as "anti-Party" or "counter-revolutionary" elements, etc., etc. Yet the simple fact is that all such people were Party members, old and new, who, having been officially assigned the task of giving the young new recruits initial political education, to prepare them for the rigours of their forthcoming training abroad, as well as for the greater hazards in the Azanian struggle than they had witnessed in the June 1976 Uprising, would naturally go straight into the fundamentals of their assignment, and not dwell on eulogizing Leballo. . . . [T]hey saw no need for leader-hero-worshipping, empty sloganeering, and the like.

But this is precisely the kind of disregard that Leballo hates most vehemently; so they fell out of favour with him. Consequently, he repeatedly agitated for their removal from the assignment and the residencies of the young recruits, upon failure of which he ordered the young recruits to throw them out by force. As a result, one of the stalwart cadres of the PAC was subsequently attacked and stabbed early one morning, right on the premises of our offices, by the more psycophantic [sic] of Leballo's "new blood. . . . "

A little while afterwards, the new recruits themselves, some of whom had begun having doubts and misgivings about all these goings-on, held some general meeting on a Wednesday in which they attempted to review the situation and mend their relationships. One of their decisions was to call all Central Committee and High Command leaders into a Sunday meeting, where they would air their views and ask for explanations from all the leaders, and not just listen to one man (Leballo) always vilify his colleagues in their absence. . . .

On the appointed Sunday afternoon, everybody went to the meeting and the recruits, as well as some Party members, spoke their grievances, criticisms and views with great clarity. In the process, however, it became clear that not only was the house divided between "pro-Leballo" recruits and "anti-Leballo" critics, but also that Leballo had earlier on mobilized "his forces" (as he is fond of calling them) to heckle, threaten or actually assault any of his critics physically. Thus the tension that had obviously built up long before this meeting exploded when "his forces" took out their long knives, attacked some predetermined targets (Party members and non-members critical of Leballo's "methods" in handling PAC affairs and internal relations), beat and stabbed them in a general pandemonium that ensued, and broke up the meeting in an unprecedented manner.

Victims were rushed to hospitals, all other people were advised to go home, and to remain calm. . . . All seemed to have subsided. Yet at about 2 a.m. in the night, a whole gang of new recruits, clearly under the leadership of those army cadres that Leballo had been drawing out of the camp, as well as some members of the Basutoland Congress Party, attacked the residence of all the other Central Committee and High Command members, as well as some PAC and BCP [Basutoland Congress Party] members and new recruits (Mwananchi Flats on Nkrumah Road). The attackers woke everybody up in the rudest manner, manhandled everyone on sight, wielded their long knives in a clear menace to their lives, demanded briefcases, working documents of the leading persons, and the keys to the High Command's cabinets and office. In the process, they were turning everything upside down in search of some mysterious revolver allegedly kept in that house of the imagined "purpose" of assassinating Leballo. Not finding any gun, they left, taking all the other things with them.

But at 6 a.m. they returned looking for one Central Committee member whom they had not found in the night raid, the mysterious revolver, and some other unspecified things. In the course of their noisy search, they once again stabbed, manhandled and then captured one Party functionary of the High Command office. Finally, they took him and other captives as hostages to another PAC house (Upanga West), allegedly for some "interrogation." But since some had escaped seizure in the morning uproar, it became possible to alert the police, the Prime Minister's Office [PMO], and the OAU Liberation Committee; and that was done speedily. Thus towards midday, an official of the OAU/ALC, in the company of Leballo, went to the rescue of the hostages. They were all released then.

The following day, Tuesday afternoon, a "joint" meeting of all the victims of stabbing and terror, kidnapping and confiscation, and "a representative few" of the culprits, as well as Leballo, Central Committee and High Command members in Dar es Salaam and the office staff, was held. . . .

As things turned out the following day, nothing was returned that morning, instead, the culprit armymen demanded access to the High Command's bank account and safety deposit box where cash was kept for the High Command's emergency operations. More than that they, together with many of the culprit new recruits, behaved in a threatening manner that once more raised tensions in the office. All this was happening right before Leballo's eyes, but instead of calling it off, he allowed it to go on, obviously since he was not being personally menaced.

At any rate that afternoon the meeting took place as scheduled, all parties concerned participating. But what emerged was a rancorous argument between all the victims, on the one hand, and Leballo and the culprit armymen, on the other. They (Leballo & Co..) had obviously decided in the intervening period that (1) nothing would be returned to normal, and that the overthrown commanders (Chief of Staff, his Deputy Political Commissar and Secretary for Logistics) remained "suspended," and (2) the proposed Commission of Inquiry should be headed by one of the chief culprit armymen, and should consist largely of the other culprits (armymen and recruits involved in the raids, etc.). . . .

Several days later, news of these events reached the camp, and the old Party members there decided to intervene in an attempt to help restore law and order. They came to Dar es Salaam, and then tried. But they failed because they found that Leballo and his henchmen had already consolidated their positions. They reported their presence to the police and other government and CCM [Chama cha Mapinduzi, Tanzania's ruling party] officials, where they also made their own recommendations for the resolution of the crisis. Subsequently, the Central Committee and High Command in question drew up a memorandum requesting the government and the OAU/ALC to jointly intervene, and then presented this to both the ALC and the PMO. . . .

[At a meeting of the Central Committee in December] some decisions were reached solely because the four [anti-Leballo] CC members had sufficient good sense and courage to compromise on certain issues in a sincere bid for unity and a return of things to normalcy. . . . [At a meeting in January, Leballo] . . . called for the final and total overthrow of the whole High Command, that is, commanders both in Tanzania and out on the Home Front or in our Forward Posts [Botswana and Swaziland]. This was nothing less than asking the Central Committee to do what he and some thirty-five young ones had agitated for a little before the November '77 coup d'etat and the resultant crisis, and to ask the Central Committee to throw away its December decisions and instead endorse his military take-over through the instrumentality of the few armymen, some mentally poisoned recruits and some members of the Basutoland Congress Party of Ntsu Mokhehle. Thus the enraged members of the Central Committee who had all along witnessed and combatted Leballo's politics of tricks, and were now seeing the final collapse of the PAC, made their feelings known to everyone present and then *walked out.* As it is right now, they have despaired of every getting proper leadership from Leballo.

DOCUMENT 110. "Programme of Action." Statement signed by Potlako K. Leballo, acting president, PAC Consultative Conference, Arusha, June 27–July 2, 1978 (abridged)

In order to play its rightful role in the liberation struggle, the PAC must resolve the organisational problems of the revolution in a positive way. It therefore needs large numbers of cadres who are trained in revolutionary activity ideologically and militarily to operate in the countryside as well as in the cities in accordance with the revolutionary situation prevailing in the country at all times.

There are five organisational tasks which, in the main, constitute the immediate programme of the National Democratic revolution in our country today. These are:

1. Building the Party throughout the country;
2. Creation and expansion of a people's army inside the country;
3. Development of the armed struggle in the countryside;
4. Organising political and industrial strife in the towns and cities;

5. Setting up the political power of the people at local level at strategic points around the country.

I

The building of a permanent foundation for the Party involves setting up cells in factories, mines, farms, schools and all other types of settlements among youth, workers, peasants, businessmen, women, cultural groups, sporting groups, professional people, thereby exercising leadership over the whole National Movement.

II

The execution of the armed struggle means, first of all, finding the weakest link in the chain of oppression and working out a strategy and tactics of struggle based upon the concrete situation in the country. There must be long-term as well as short-term plans for the execution of the strategy.

Strategy is

(i)   the determination of the targets of the revolution at a given period,

(ii) elaboration of a suitable plan for the gathering, training and deployment of the forces of the revolution and

(iii) the actual fight to carry out the plan of struggle during the given stage of the revolution.

MANDATE

In order to get the armed struggle going, our mandate is to return to our country to lead the revolution. We are called upon to send our trained leaders and cadres back over a certain period of time taking into account the objective situation in which this must take place. The first point is how to deal with the armed enemy and the heavily guarded borders of our country. The second is that of co-ordinating the party work at home and abroad. This requires a revolutionary network with the aptitude and ability for this kind of work. The third is the programme that follows the successful infiltration of the trained cadres and the mobilisation of the people for armed activity. The fourth is the political line of the revolution to ensure that the directives of the Party are carried out. We must find the correct way of doing things and in doing so we must base ourselves on concrete reality and this needs down-to-earth preparatory work.

There are four ways of ensuring that those tasks are performed positively. The first is to strengthen the decentralized organs of the movement. The second is to unite solidly the cadres of the movement as seeds of the revolution. The third is to lead the actual struggle of the masses. The fourth is to rally everyone around the political line of the revolution which in essence is the sum total of the historical tasks the Party has set itself in order to advance its strategic and tactical work. It is only when we co-operate to execute the particular tasks of the given time and place that we can achieve success in our work. That unity is carried forward to a higher level as more advanced tasks are planned and carried out successfully.

The Unity of the Party is the key factor in leading the revolution. The Party can only be united around a disciplined Nucleus which is itself built around the decisive tasks of the revolution as defined above.

STAGES OF EXECUTION

The tasks we have set ourselves and the programme of action for their execution can only be carried out in stages, the stages must be defined, strengthened in practice and consolidated in depth and volume. The main task of our stage of preparation is to achieve the Unity and Mass technical abilities of the cadres of the revolution and the oppressed section of the population to enable them to crush the resistance of the oppressing classes. This is crucial because once we place ourselves in the position of being crushed or liquidated by the enemy, to whom will our people turn for land and liberty? From whom will they seek support against the power and the tyranny of the present rulers and their running dogs?

The decisive factor of the revolution, however, is that of strategic leadership. The ability to set the tasks of the struggle and mobilise the main forces of the revolution to strike the main blow at the weakest link in the enemy fortress is a matter of strategic leadership. It presupposes understanding the conditions necessary for the revolution to take off and to know how to create the point of departure when the conditions are not yet ripe, and to determine the general direction along which all the work must be done. It must have the necessary experience to see adequately the twists and turns in the road, to remove the stumbling-blocks and other obstacles that are found almost everywhere and that it can deploy its forces so that they are concentrated at the enemy's most vulnerable spot at the decisive moment when insurrection is knocking at the door. Strategic leadership must therefore do two main things:

Put in the forefront those forms of struggle and organisation that are best suited to the objective conditions of a given period or stage of the revolution in order to facilitate the mobilisation and deployment of the revolutionary forces at the revolutionary front and thus enable the masses of the people to realise the moment of decision from their own experience.

Single out from all its tasks the particular one that constitutes the central point of the main objective, that is, the one whose immediate achievement will open the way to the achievement of the other equally important tasks. How can we, for example, in our effort to resolve our internal contradictions in order to unite our Party, create a solid core to prepare the conditions for ideological and tactical unity and thereby build the foundations for a really revolutionary Party?

SUMMARY. . . .

LONG LIVE THE STRUGGLE OF THE PEOPLE OF AZANIA FOR NATIONAL LIBERATION AND SOCIAL EMANCIPATION!!!!!!!!
LONG LIVE THE ORGANISATION OF AFRICAN UNITY!!!!!!!!!
LONG LIVE THE PAN AFRICANIST CONGRESS OF AZANIA!!!!!!!!!!!

LONG LIVE THE AZANIA PEOPLE'S LIBERATION ARMY!!!!!!!!!!
LONG LIVE THE AFRICAN REVOLUTION!!!!!!!!!!!!!!

Document 111. Diary of Jack Simons at Novo Catengue camp, Angola, January–March 1979 (abridged)

Jan. 5, Friday: Start work. Arrived at Novo last night at 8:30. Moved into quarters—room formerly occupied by Ronnie [Kasrils]. Moved about—spoke to the batch of students with whom I'll be working. Gave them a short talk on Vietnam and sorted out some problems of classes with Raymond Nkuko [head of political department] and Arthur [Sidweshu] (Commissar). See Larry Isaacs (here called Castro Morris) who seems to be running *Dawn* [Umkhonto we Sizwe publication]. Also Khumalo—veteran trade unionist who came from Island and insisted on receiving MK training (though he is much older than other students). . . .

Jan. 6, Saturday: Work schedules taking shape. I foresee 3 classes, each 2 months: 1) Returned group ["special group" from Moscow] to be given advanced course on SA. 2) Instructors class—about 12 selected to take place of present instructors who will go abroad (G. D. R.) [German Democratic Republic] 3) Preparatory class—for about 29 students chosen to study in S.U. [Soviet Union]. Departure unknown—might be in a month or two.

Parade this morning in preparation for oath taking ceremony on 8th with President presiding . . . to swear loyalty with the Spear of the Nation till Victory or Death? . . . Delay has taken much of the zest out of the proceedings. Students had to cancel their usual weekend football games, fruitlessly, as it turned out. . . . At yesterday's "rehearsal," camp commander (Julius) [Mokoena] admonished the students on the need to maintain high standards of conduct in keeping with the oath. Referred to misconduct of one person at Benguela who sold a pistol for money. Warned against dagga and liquor. Had much to say about the penalty for rape.

Mzwayi [Piliso] followed in similar vein, stressing that oath-taking subjected soldiers to the code laid down, breach of which could be punished even by death. More was said about students who cross the mountains (carrying blankets) to visit villages for liquor, dagga—perhaps women. I heard similar complaints more than a year ago. Yet am told that standard of discipline is high. . . .

Jan. 8, Monday: The great anniversary of ANC, plus swearing of allegiance to MK. But Presidential party does not arrive until after nightfall. Delayed by closing of airport at Benguela for repairs to tarmac. . . .

Jan. 9, Tuesday: Taking of oath. Proceeds slowly. Only 150 out of 250 sworn in by midday when President adjourns proceedings. Says he has tummy upset—probably due, he suggested, to rich food provided by Cubs [Cubans] (hardly diplomatic).

We resume at 4 p.m. after heavy rain—and complete another 40—leaving

60-70 to do (I count 53). President is hardly fit but finds stamina to talk to Political Department, on Isandhlwana Centenary Celebration [on January 21, 1879, Zulus defeated British infantry at Isandhlwana Hill in Natal]—and to sit through 2 hours of singing by camp choir. He conducts two songs with great verve and energy. That is evidently close to his heart. . . .

Jan. 10, Wednesday: Oath taking ceremony is hurried through by 8:00. President and party take off after a short speech—to Lobito where a plane is waiting. . . .

Jan. 11, Thursday: Work in earnest began today. Met political instructors a.m., the "special group" (ex-Moscow) p.m., and an audience mainly of instructors and heads of departments at night for a talk on Zambia and the Southern African situation. . . .

My main responsibility is "special group." I quizzed them for two hours on their Soviet experience in the sense of academic work only. My opinion is that they do not obtain new knowledge or insight into SA struggle. But this is a premature conclusion. I need to work more closely with the group and also I'm probably biased!

Note comment by Chico [Lukas, printer] that members of the group returned with expensive goods—watches, radios, clothing. Is this advisable?

Jan. 12, Friday: . . . . Commander speaks to detachment on discipline and morale, citing cases of delinquency; a guard sleeping at his post; a combatant trainee who "loses" his pistol; another (or the same) in possession of 1000 kwanza, and another 200 given to fellow student to buy liquor (at B?) [Benguela camp] . . . .

Jan. 13, Saturday: Heavy and continuous rain—far more than at same time last year. Many roofs are leaking badly. . . . Two long walks today. Rains have brought vegetation to life. Much green and many flowers, purple and yellow predominate. . . .

Jan. 16, Tuesday: Big upheaval—last minute as usual. All political instructors withdrawn, plus choir (temporarily), which disrupts my classes. Have to find replacements for instructors immediately—from among "special group". . . .

N.C. [Novo Catengue] is now virtually a "transit" camp (perhaps because Vorster disclosed his knowledge of its whereabouts). Guard duties and essential services are maintained, with temporary units (such as "special group"). But we must maintain classes for detachment—two weeks on Isandhlwana.

My workload is all the greater because instructors have to be trained and to teach at the same time. . . .

Jan. 19, Friday: Heavy rains which bring to surface multitude of flying objects! Mosquitoes (how they bite me in bed!), flying ants, moths, hornets—plus crawlers—the lizards, cockroaches, beetles that invade the room in a flash if the door or window is ajar. I therefore sleep with door and window tightly shut. No airbricks. Foul hot air. Wake up early (as today 4:30) soaked in sweat. . . .

Long staff meeting. Minutes read and recorded. Outline number of activities—teaching course for next month; ANC meeting; conference; briefing sessions; work on course for new detachment. Some of my 1977 innovations have fallen away—like evening classes for platoon leaders. Should be revived, but only when lectures have been written. . . .

Chief of staff asks me to give the talk on Isandhlwana on Monday 22. I suggest a student—but he explains that occasion demands a "senior" representative to match the Cuban speaker. . . .

Jan. 23, Tuesday: Isandhlwana centenary last night. . . . Vusi [administration secretary] added comments on heroes of today (very appropriate and neglected by me). . . .

[Diary discusses deterioration in fraternal relations with the Cubans, their isolation, separate kitchen and eating arrangements, use of Lobito seaside cottage, etc.]

I doubt estrangement is due to personality clashes. Our people blame the major—think a new man in his place would change things for the better. I doubt this. The isolation is being institutionalised and in my view is political in origin. The Cub trainers and administration are under impression that MK is not being seriously prepared for combat—but is more a political organisation. They feel we lack drive—allow long periods to elapse between transfer of detachment after completion of training and arrival of new batch. . . .

Isandhlwana series is drawing to close. Next step is to write up material in form of lectures, available for reproduction, booklet perhaps? "Old" instructors have been assigned this task and should be working on it now. The Special Group to embark on series "National and Class Struggles in SA"—to run as seminars.

New instructors to work on ANC constitutions and FC [Freedom Charter]—theme of next week's classes. . . .

Cubans obtain clear water for themselves from spring on mountainside—making 2 or 3 trips a day. Clear that they can't supply whole camp, but they should have talked things over with our people who put up with muddy water, but lack sensitivity—or regard for our own sentiments. As in treatment of patients in the detachment. . . .

Jan. 26, Friday: . . . . This evening was visited by Company 1 Commander (excellent officer who was in charge of party going to Luanda). He came to talk about his notion of how the war would develop—intensified military activity leading to general uprising—like in Russia Oct. 1917. Altogether wrong (though I did not say so). Bolsheviks had developed a small but tight, influential party organisation, skilled in agitation and propaganda inside and capable of giving leadership. We have to build such an organisation as the NEC meeting revealed. . . .

Jan. 28, Sunday: Mzwayi [Piliso] came last night. Paper by Sizakele [Sigxashe] (June 1977) on sources of study to equip our people for governing the country after the Revolution. . . .

Jan. 29, Monday: . . . . Mzwayi's address to Detachment—8:15 to 10:45 in broiling sun—was about Vietnam, united front at home, Bantustans . . . .

Spoke of Joe Gqabi's address in camp and reminded us that detachment was to have discussed Joe's insistence on working with organisations opposed to Apartheid. Bishop Tutu, who testified in trial of 12, Inkatha (200,000 strong) with question mark about Gatsha. . . .

As regards operations, he dwelt on clash 3 weeks ago when 7 combatants were attacked. One of the 7 deserted to the enemy, alerted a farmer, who called in police. The renegade (who slipped away on pretext of toilet needs) accompanied police when they attacked, and revealed pre-arranged signal and positions. Commander was shot dead. The remaining five detached themselves and are now in safety.

He warned against agent provocateurs and infiltrators. All of us had to flush them out and report. Our safety and success demanded this vigilance. . . .

Feb. 3, Saturday: 9 a.m. Have been laid up in bed since Tuesday morning—malaria—horrible. . . .

Feb. 6, Tuesday: Attend 1st class since Monday week ago. Very good performance, both the paper and discussion. Sound Marxists are coming up—not concerned with hair-splitting or abstractions—and able to apply concepts—also to SA. . . .

Feb. 7, Wednesday: Back from class—Andrew's Platoon, good discussion—as yesterday. Much interest in "nationalism," as dealt with in classics, and in relation to our situation. Most of members participate and we do manage to resolve problems, reconcile differences and arrive at conclusions. . . . .

Feb. 8, Thursday: . . . . Am told that +/– 120 cases of malaria—nearly half our population. But not a single case among Cubans. According to table gossip, they allege malaria is an African disease—very vulgar and ignorant comment. Cub doctor, I'm told, shows no interest in what amounts to an epidemic—surely concern to medical science, and inclines to view that many of us are malingering. If true, this attitude reflects the width of chasm between "them" and "us."

My "special platoon" is progressing. Members do most of the talking—I join in to give factual information or ask questions or dispute points of view. But some members of the group hardly participate and seem to be below average. . . .

Feb. 11, Sunday: . . . Lying awake last night and pondering next move. I recognised that I'm not a free agent, but duty bound and must carry out orders. Organisation must decide where to place me. If it considers that my contribution is best made in military camp, I must and shall abide by decision without protest—as in the past.

Feb. 12, Monday. 12:10. Precisely 8 weeks since leaving Lusaka. Hard to realise this. On other hand, Lusaka seems far away in space and time. But I'm still below par. Much backache, poor appetite, sluggish bowels, dryness in mouth and back of throat, husky voice. I suppose these are after effects of malaria and hope they will disappear. Very debilitating. . . .

My mandate was to "reorientate" the "Moscow" platoon to SA. This is

being done effectively, first by the Isandhlwana series, secondly by participation in the instruction of platoons, and thirdly by the course on National
and Class Struggle.

This last, based on propositions from the Marxist text, is more successful
than I had thought likely. Only half a dozen take part—but those who
discuss are obtaining a grasp on our situation, not only the theoretical
concepts, but more important their actual application in our conditions, as
strategy and tactics.

The programmatic aspect tends to be overlooked. Never by Lenin,
however, the supreme tactician. No principle is "absolute"—except the
revolution itself. That is the key to his approach.

Feb. 13, Tuesday: . . . Commander pressing for special classes for staff. I
have in mind various themes. Problem is suitable literature for class to read.
Will they wade through big tomes as instructors are expected to do? On other
hand, one can't present elementary stuff—they must be credited with some
basic knowledge of Marxism—if not of SA.

1:45 Excellent lunch—vegs, mashed potatoes, bananas (sweet, large).
This sparked off conversation about Angola's natural advantages. People
talked about apples, grapes, pears, as well as bananas and pineapples,
grown around Benguela. They then related experiences in USSR—kilometres
of apples, vines and other fruits. USSR is a constant term of reference and
index for comparison.

Feb. 14, Wednesday. . . . Waiting anxiously for letters from Ray [his wife]—
more so than ever. I think malaria has shaken me badly—morale, drive,
interest in work, the lot. Certainly took the glamour (such as there was) out
of Novo. It's a harsh, forbidding place, exposed to elements, untamed, a
pioneer camp, with few comforts. Running water (twice a day—1 hr at a
time) is dark brown and unpleasant to taste; rooms are stifling at night
(sealed to keep out mosquitoes), food is often unpalatable and always
monotonous, and so on. I dislike crawling under mosquito net, and dislike
even more being bitten!

Feb. 15, Thursday. New series with special platoon: "How to combat
enemy propaganda." Argument that political struggle, no less than military,
requires us to "know the enemy." Political leader, instructor, organiser,
agitator must know and explain our policy. First and most important
requisite for political mobilization. . . .

Worked with class (doing all talking) from 8–11:15. Exhausting. . . . Doubt
if I could repeat 1977 effort—conducting classes 8–12, 3–5, and often 8–10
p.m. What stamina! and doing much the same in weekends. . . .

I arranged a program of "seminars" for staff (i.e. Commander, Chief, Dr.
Peter [Mfeleng])—2 sessions a week of 2 hours each. Topics cover 20
sessions, i.e. 10 weeks. . . .

Feb. 16, Friday. Last morning class this week. Great relief. "Special
platoon" is uneven—a few alert members, who can follow and participate.
2/3 are dull, seldom speak and might not keep in touch. The group spent 9

months in a Moscow "school" receiving lectures from Soviet academics (professors) who no doubt set a high standard. But the students (with exceptions) were not up to the mark. . . .

'Feb. 17, Saturday: Two hour "seminar" with staff (Commander, Commissar) last night. Silent audience for most part—only Commander and Dr. Peter attempted to contribute. Heavy going. I spoke on"colonialism" with a dash of Marx—but lack of response indicates that topic is strange to them— though all have had training in USSR or GDR. . . .

Feb. 18, Sunday: . . . . Prepared 14 topics for staff seminars—ranging from colonialism to SA history (wars of resistance and rise of ANC-MK). Question: will the personnel do the "research" (reading) necessary? They might prefer to listen to me—but that practice is relatively unrewarding. . . .

Feb. 19, Monday: Special Group is responding poorly to series on Afrikaans propaganda. Half a dozen participate, usually the same persons in each discussion session. Rest are indifferent or unable to comprehend. . . . only a minority benefited from the 9 months in USSR (i.e. in terms of concepts and intellectual growth. They probably gained much as "tourists" of a very privileged class.)

There ought to be more care in selection. If a socialist country offers 20 places and we have only 10 suitable candidates, let us not "make up" the remaining 10 by random selection or including "rejects." Not fair to them or to the hosts!

Feb. 20, Tuesday: Special group discussed my criticism amongst themselves (in my absence) and agreed to continue series on condition that each member prepares outline (i.e. does research) on every topic, that chairman inspects outlines and if necessary calls on individuals to take part in discussion.

Livelier response today. Perhaps we are getting somewhere positive with group. . . .

Tonight (8–10) seminar with administration. Topic introduced by Commander. Brief, to the point, systematic, but limited in scope. Insufficient background information and theoretical insight.   Discussion generally mediocre—for same reasons.

Feb. 22, Thursday: Am not sure whether my presence here is rewarding— whether there is need for my services. Training of instructors, preparation of material for classes, organisation of meetings, conferences, seminars—all could be handled by existing staff. I came here under impression that "old" instructors would be moved (to GDR) long before end of January (when course begins) and that training of new instructors should begin at once— as a matter of urgency. But the group is still here—only half employed and "running down."

As for the "special group"—I suspect that the administration (Mzwayi) does not know what to do with them, or how useful the "Moscow" training was. Actually, the best among them have been drafted into the instructors "class," will be employed in Political Department. The class will have to be absorbed in the general student body—elsewhere?

Feb. 23, Friday: "holiday" in honour of Red Army Day, Anniversary of Soviet Army. Rather sweet—tribute to our ally and host (who is not represented in NC [Novo Catengue]. Good thing to imprint on students the concept of int[ernational] solidarity with socialist Africa (also USSR and Cuba which help to identify us as a "Party" of socialism). . . .

Feb. 24, Saturday: Yesterday's commemoration of Red Army Day went off well, with a display of relevant Soviet literature, introduced effectively by members of ex-Moscow "special" platoon—a baseball match (in which Cub predominated) and a football match between the "champion" Dynamoes and a "picked team." At night a culture evening—speeches by Cuban Commissar and Camp Commander (very good), followed by concert (highlight a drama, centred as usual around a shebeen, the most vividly remembered social aspect of Soweto life—coupled with crime). B/stan removals and resistance (the political element a relatively new note in "Shebeen" acts). . . .

This afternoon "briefing session" in Development of capitalism. Pauline (Olga) "presents" one of the two parts. Good fluent speaker—but poor researcher, who depends on memory and makes awful factual blunders. . . .

Feb. 26, Monday: . . . Camp life isolates one—and creates a deplorable lack of concern with family-domestic affairs. Is this why many people (also women?) like the army? A world of its own . . . . in a firm structure of organisation and command. . . .

State of alert following raid on Luso [Zapu camp?] by [Ian] Smith's mercenary thugs. A mini alarm last night and a bigger more protracted one this morning starting at 4 a.m. Operation entailed evacuation of camp and taking cover some 100s of metres away. My Party (HQ) and Cubans moved into a viaduct under Railway bridge. From 6 to 10 we were told alarm is over and went back to camp. I'm told that exercise will be repeated till further notice, but don't see what purpose it serves except as an exercise in preparation for an actual assault—the motive for which (on part of Boers) is obscure to me. Are we such a threat that they must risk an international storm? . . .

Feb. 28, Wednesday: Another "alert"—breakfast at 5:30, long trek along river bed, scrambling up ravine to reach culvert from the back. Return at 10 a.m. Rest of morning recuperation! No classes. I'm told this is likely to be repeated until end of week (but will Cubans give up this weekend in Lobito [seaside cottage] to participate?).

March 1, Thursday: . . . . Another "alert" action this morning—dressing in dark and leaving camp at 5:30 for "stations." Disrupts normal work—but we managed to resume classes in the afternoon. Students are exhausted, but I manage to keep my end up—even to extent of preparing another round of themes for seminar on apartheid and nationalism in SA. The target is pitched high, probably above the head of some students, but they are being "exposed" to fairly basic issues in our political situation.

March 2, Friday: "Alert" extended from 4:30 a.m. to 1 p.m.—apparently because Cubans expected arrival of helicopters with a "commission" on board—to check security. . . . [B]rought 3 anti-aircraft guns to reinforce our battery. . . .

March 3, Saturday: 3:45 pm. Up at 4 this morning—breakfasted on tea and marched off about 5, while dark enough to make walking a problem. Long uncomfortable morning until past 2 p.m. Purpose was to demonstrate defensive position to the visiting Commission, headed by Cuban General in charge in Angola. . . .

8:20 p.m. Cuban "High Command" is perturbed at failure of Frontline states to offer (put up) resistance to the "strikes" by Rhodesian planes. This weakness, they say, throws doubt on the credibility of the governments and the liberation forces, lowers their standing internationally, and encourages more assaults. Hence the serious view taken of Novo's position—very vulnerable to attack from SA. . . .

March 4, Sunday: 8.10 pm. Exhausting, big inactivity, sitting around from 4:30 am to 6:45 p.m, waiting for "next" order. . . . Meanwhile political education is "scrapped"—no effort is being made to continue classes "in the bush." (probably rightly so). With this prospect I suggested (to Commissar) that I be posted back to Lusaka. He tells me that this possibility was raised today. . . . Not "sorry." This tour was poorly planned, ill conceived. Administration was stuck with the ex-Moscow group and called me in as stop gap. . . .

Two helicopters arrived today. Evident that top brass take the position seriously—a matter of urgency. . . .

March 8, Thursday: Benguela. I arrived here Tuesday at 6:45 a.m, having left Novo at 5:30 or earlier in Cuban landrover. . . . I'm pleased to have been around when the state of "alertness" was proclaimed. It gave me an insight into the problems involved in preparing a camp for defense against an attack—and also better understanding of Cuban's role. They took immediate, decisive action, planned the entire operation and brought in massive equipment. . . .

March 9, Friday: . . . Pleasant experience at function of Angola Women's Section celebration of Women's Day. . . . I walked there with Gertrude Shope and Oria [member of June 16th Detachment and wife of Julius Mokoena]—both in MK uniform. We were admitted without question when I explained we were from ANC (SA). Received warm welcome, seated at table and served with Coca-Cola and (for me) beer from a long jug. . . .

Celebrations (dancing and slogan shouting). . . . While watching the dancing I was grabbed by a middle aged woman—shanty town type—who insisted on dancing. I did my best, but her pace was too fast—prancing and kicking of feet, which I had to emulate to maintain the rhythm. I pleaded exhaustion after 10 minutes and literally tore myself away—hopefully having contributed my bit. . . .

March 11, Sunday: Luanda. Arrived yesterday—after tedious wait of 4 and half hours at Benguela airport—no food (other than rolls and tea at the Residence for breakfast). No money for a meal ticket in airport restaurant. . . .

March 13, Tuesday. Back in Lusaka—by Aeroflot. . . .

[On the next day, South African planes bombed and strafed Novo Catengue, razing all the buildings to the ground, killing two South Africans and one Cuban, wounding about fourteen, and, reportedly, losing one or two planes and crew. Evacuation saved most lives. The camp was abandoned.]

DOCUMENT 112. Testimony of Zephania Mothopeng, PAC trial, Bethal, April 3, 6, and 9, 1979 (abridged)

[Joe Thloloe] told me that he had been to Kimberley on his assignment and there he met Mr. Robert Mangaliso Sobukwe, and then Mr. Sobukwe asked him to pass his regards to me and then he further told me that Mr. Sobukwe would like to see me. I mean he was keen. I mean he longed to see me.

I expressed the desire to see Mr. Robert Sobukwe. . . . They fetched me and then we drove to Kimberley. . . .

Did you discuss PAC affairs with Mr. Sobukwe at all? ——— Not at all. . . .

Since your release from Robben Island, have you taken any active part in PAC activities? ——— No. . . .

Do you approve of the use of violence? ——— No, I do not approve of the use of violence. I believe in non-violence, positive non-violence.

Do you still believe in Pan-Africanism? ——— Yes, as a philosophy, I do. . . .

As a member of the national executive of the PAC did you not at that stage make any plans for the future of the PAC? ——— No, I would not make the plans of a banned organization. . . .

While you were there in the separate cells or isolation cells, did you have conversations with your fellow prisoners? ——— . . . . well I did manage, you know, with the man who was next to me to have some talks.

Who was he? ——— Mandela was next to me.

Mandela was right next to you? ——— Yes. . . .

Naturally you had conversation about the PAC. ——— Mandela and I are old friends. We were in the Youth League together.

The Youth League of the ANC? ——— Of the ANC and we parted when PAC took its own way. We did talk about past history and what happened.

And about the future? ——— We hardly talked about the future. . . .

And [this morning, after hearing of the hanging of Solomon Mahlangu] you sang together with the other accused in a chorus. ——— Quite correct.

And you sang certain unsavoury songs. Is that correct? ——— I do not know. It depends on your outlook on life, you know, how you look at it.

Well, it appears that you sang certain things against the White population of this country. Is that correct? ——— Yes.

You sang: The Boers are Dogs, that is one of the songs you sang. ——— Yes, we did.

Why did you sing that? ——— I have been singing such songs from childhood. As a child, when I was a young man, I used even to conduct, you know, what we call weddings. . . . [singing songs] meaning that now we are braver, then we will burn you fellows now who are opposing us. . . . now we will, you know, pierce you with a spear. All those were in the spirit of the occasion.

So according to you, those songs were actually fairly innocent. ——— Well, these songs besides anything else, when you sing it is also for boosting your morale. . . .

Yes, and especially this morning, there was another song this morning. — ——— Yes.

Do you know about it? ——— Yes, I know.

This morning the following was more or less sung: They killed Mahlangu. ——— Yes, we sang that.

The Boers are Dogs, the dogs will also die. ——— Yes.

And they will also die like dogs. ——— Yes.

Is that correct? That was sung this morning. ——— We sang it.

What was the reason for that sort of thing, which was sung this morning? ——— Yes, unfortunately we heard this morning that Mahlangu was hanged, and that is a tragic incident in the history of our country.

Why is that a tragic incident? ——— I will say so because as far as I am aware of it, these children were the victims of the circumstances, the victims of the things of their fathers, the laws which are made by the society. If you saw what happened in 1976, you would sympathize with the youngsters who are. . . (inaudible)

He was involved in the death of two people. ——— I say he has been the victim of history, history which has been brought by his parents and the whites and all. That young man is suffering because of my sin as an older generation, of your sin as the older generation, of everybody [in] the older generation. We are responsible for that.

Yes, and what about the two people who died? Are they not victims? Have you no sympathy for them? ——— You are looking at the result, you do not look at the cause. What is important is the cause, not the result. . . .

He [Sobukwe] was then still considered to be the leader of the PAC inside South Africa. ——— Well, according to the newspapers, I mean the reporters, I mean to say, but we were no longer, I mean, regarding him as the leader of PAC because there was no PAC then. . . .

But isn't it that you were actually going to him in secret? ——— No.

To go and discuss certain important matters relating to the PAC? ——— No.

You deny that? ——— I am denying that.

You must have been very great friends with Sobukwe? ——— We were, we were. . . .

The only thing you did was to ask him about his health and to congratulate him on his admission as an attorney. ——— Yes, I asked him about his health, and we would talk about his admission and further, of course, he also contributed. He told me that in the first instance about his health, he revealed something to me that he was towards the end of his term on Robben Island poisoned by the police.

Poisoned by the police? —— Yes, and he said, now Zeph, you are the only man, one day you will be able to tell the world. Then, in fact, when he did that, he gently, I mean his outlook really, I mean his face and all you know, it was the first time I had seen Sobukwe in that mood, but after he told me that, he now relaxed again. . . .

And then on the island was also a lecturing team, a team giving lectures. Do you know anything about that? —— In my cell there were no lecturing teams.. . . .

Now according to Ngomezulu, the lecturing team had to visit the cells for these lectures and every member of the PAC was thoroughly schooled on PAC history. —— In my time or in my cell, I did not experience that.. . . .

And according to Ngomezulu, all the lectures on Robben Island were to indoctrinate the prisoners there, the members of the PAC in the aims and objects of the PAC and also to prepare them for the revival of the PAC after their release. —— It is not correct. . . .

Did you continue recognizing Sobukwe as the leader of the PAC until his death? —— Sobukwe was my friend, but he was no longer PAC, so that I could not recognize him as the leader of PAC. He was my friend. I knew he was once, he was the leader of the PAC when it was still active. . . .

You deny that you are a senior member, you are just Zeph Mothopeng? —— —— Yes, that is all. . . .

Did the leaders ever call the struggle off? —— The leaders, they were no longer there, they were banned unfortunately before they could even think of it. . . .

So according to you the organization just disappeared into mid-air, it just vanished. —— Yes, I mean it was banned but certain people who belonged to the organization did certain things. . . .

Have you at any time had any contact with what is sometimes referred to as the external wing of the PAC? —— No.

DOCUMENT 113. Meeting of the Administrative Committee of the PAC Central Committee ("Confidential"), Dar es Salaam, April 30–May 1, 1979 (abridged)

Present:

Comrade P. K. Leballo	- Chairman
Comrade Vusumzi L. Make	- Administrative Secretary
Comrade David Sibeko	- Director of Foreign Affairs
Comrade E. L. Makoti	- Secretary for Defence
Comrade E. L. Ntloedibe	- Director of Publicity and Information
Comrade Ernest Radebe	- Director of Finance
Comrade Henry E. Isaacs	- Director of Education and Manpower Development
Comrade Reginald Xokelelo	- Special Assistant in the Office of the Chairman. . . .

Comrade SIBEKO: . . . . It is clear that there is a parallel leadership. The accreditation of representatives, disbursement of funds, choice of delegations have been made in utter violation of CC [Central Committee] decisions. There is the need for a clear soul-searching and the taking of drastic decisions as the leadership has been completely undermined.

Comrade MAKE: . . . the Party is poised on the eve of open gang warfare. There has been a systematic corrosion of leadership: the disruptions that took place at the commemoration of the 20th Anniversary of the Party were a rejection of the leadership. Comrade Make referred to the lack of consultation demonstrated by the Chairman. . . . It is clear that the members of the CC are just there as stool pigeons.

Comrade MAKOTI: . . . The Department of Finance has been completely emasculated as the Chairman has arrogated functions to himself. . . . Parallel appointments have been made even to positions within the CC and are simply awaiting complete take-over. . . . The Chairman has to be persuaded to change if the Party is to be saved from ignominy.

Comrade NTLOEDIBE: At the Plenary he had warned of a take-over of the Party by the Military. The Central Committee has been rendered irrelevant. . . . The Chairman has implanted it into the cadres that only he cares for them. . . . Considering that the decisions of the Plenary have been flouted and unless this is corrected, the Party is heading for disaster. Unless there is assurance from the Chairman that he will change, then we cannot continue. The Central Committee is reduced to ridicule. The Comrade states that he has reached the end of his role.

Comrade RADEBE: . . . there is perpetual confusion at Headquarters due to Chairman's duplicity and divisive activities. . . . Comrades have been terrorised and yet the Chairman will cover up. As of today Comrade Radebe is not willing to continue to work under the prevailing circumstances.

CHAIRMAN: The Administrative Report [by Isaacs] is merely an attack on the Chairman and APLA. . . . no provision was made for the financing of the Programme of Action. At great sacrifice, APLA has made attempts without the necessary funds. He will continue to work for the success of the Programme, and by June there will be activity in the country. . . . He has taken no unilateral initiatives without justification. . . . The Secretary of Defence has abandoned his duties to APLA.

Comrade SIBEKO: . . . There is no team work with the Chairman acting as a law unto himself. The credibility of the PAC is at rock bottom and is not as rosy as we think.

Comrade MAKE: Responded to Chairman's reaction to the administrative report. There is a belief by the Chairman of a vendetta against himself and APLA. . . . In the final analysis, the programme of PAC is entrusted to the entire Central Committee. . . . Comrade Make said he will not stand up and continue to work in the prevailing conditions. . . . He concluded by repeating that if anything happens to the Party here in Tanzania, we will be out on a limb. . . .

Comrade NTLOEDIBE: All the Comrades have made a plea to the Chairman to recognise his own shortcomings.

CHAIRMAN: He does not love the PAC more than all others and has had no intention to project himself. He has always been a controversial figure, but during his work with President SOBUKWE he always accepted his guidance. If we were to part, this would eat all of us to the grave. His colleagues would be clubbed together with him for his mistakes. For the sake of the revolution, is it not possible to create the necessary climate to facilitate the revolution? . . .

Comrade SIBEKO: Admires the Chairman's recognition of the commitment of all other colleagues. . . . Suggests that there must be a Political Directorate of three to run the affairs of the PAC and that the Chairman take a respite so that the Central Committee can rebuild APLA and implement the Programme of Action. . . .

Comrade MAKOTI: Supports proposal made by Comrade Sibeko that Chairman take a respite, and when Comrade POKELA is released, he might come and reinforce us.

CHAIRMAN: Remembers that he has in the past agreed to take a respite. He has thought of the need to create a Presidential Council.

Comrade MAKE: . . . [A new] structure must accommodate (a) Comrade Leballo's continued role in the struggle and (b) put the Party in order. . . .

CHAIRMAN: There must be great secrecy so that the formula must not be scuttled.

Comrade SIBEKO: There should be a Press Release, and Comrade Isaacs should act as spokesman. . . .

MEETING ON MAY 1, 1979

. . . Central Committee decides to appoint Presidential Council comprising three members of Central Committee. . . .

Comrade SIBEKO: The Press Release [should] be delayed until consultations are completed. It should also be after the departure of the Chairman when modalities of place of stay would have been corrected.

Comrade ISAACS: Concurs with Comrade Sibeko and requests Chairman to record his memoirs for publication. . . .

CHAIRMAN: Suggests making nominations which can be discussed on membership of Presidential Council. Should be composed of Comrades Sibeko, Ntloedibe and Make due to their integrity and dedication. They would also be the most acceptable in the Party as they have not been involved in the happenings here at HQ. . . .

Comrade RADEBE: Supports Chairman's proposal.

CHAIRMAN: Notes adoption of his proposal. . . .

Comrade SIBEKO: Thanks for the Chairman and colleagues for confidence reposed. In particular for the magnanimity of the Chairman.

CHAIRMAN: It is a great honour for our Party and our revolution to have arrived at the conclusions we have reached. It is a vindication of our heroes, Lembede, Mda, and Sobukwe's principles. . . .

Comrade MAKOTI: . . . . Pays tribute to the Chairman for his acceptance of CC proposal so that he can rest and return to play a decisive role when the situation demands it. . . .

DOCUMENT 114. Report of the Politico-Military Strategy Commission (the "Green Book") to the ANC National Executive Committee, Parts One and Two with two annexures, August 1979

PART ONE—Introduction

1. A joint meeting of the full NEC [National Executive Committee] and RC [Revolutionary Council] was held in Luanda between 27th December 1978, and 1st January 1979, to hear a report from the NEC delegation which visited the Socialist Republic of Vietnam in October 1978. After discussing the report of the delegation, the meeting proceeded to consider its relevance for our own struggle and concluded that "the Vietnam experience reveals certain shortcomings on our part and draws attention to areas of crucial importance which we have tended to neglect."

2. The meeting then discussed and adopted a statement containing a summary of its views, which is annexed, marked "A". [Annexure A, not included here, is "Statement of a Joint Meeting of the NEC and the RC"]

3. Thereafter the meeting elected a Commission of 6 comrades to be headed by the President and including Thabo Mbeki, Joe Slovo, Moses Mabhida, Joe Gqabi and Joe Modise.

The Commission was instructed to begin its work immediately and to make recommendations to the NEC on the items contained in Paragraph 5 of Annexure "A". [This annexure is the statement of the joint meeting of the National Executive Committee and the Revolutionary Council, which set up the Commission. Four of its recommendations are quoted in Part Two below.]

At a subsequent meeting of the NEC immediately after the joint meeting, it was resolved that the Commission, to be known as the *Politico-Military Strategy Commission,* should complete its work in time for the projected meeting of the NEC in February 1979.

4. Immediately after the joint meeting, the Commission proceeded to carry out its mandate. Three sessions were held in Luanda for the purpose of mapping out a programme of work. Thereafter, the Commission adjourned and completed its task in Maputo, where 15 sessions were held between February 1–20 1979. A final session was then arranged for Lusaka for 9 March to finalise the Report.

5. In order to facilitate its work, the Commission immediately took the following steps:

a. Comrades Yusuf Dadoo and Reg September were invited to meet the Commission to discuss the question of the institutions which are being imposed on the Coloured and Indian people and to examine the general question of organisation and mobilisation of these communities as part of the revolutionary alliance of oppressed peoples. After this discussion, it was agreed that the two comrades urgently convene meetings of cadres engaged in work among these communities in order to make recommendations on this question. This decision was carried out and the Commission subsequently received extremely helpful reports which will be referred to later under the relevant section.

b. Annexure "A" was taken to the Island [Lesotho] by special emissaries with a request to the comrades there to submit their thinking and recommendations to the Commission. This was done, and we will refer to their memorandum under the relevant section.

c. Annexure "A was submitted to the meeting of the SACTU executive with a request to make proposals on how best the ANC and its allies can help to implement item 5(g). The Commission received a written report from SACTU which will be referred to under the relevant section.

d. The London Research Unit was requested to supply available documentary information on the existing mass organisations. Some of the information supplied will be referred to later under the relevant section.

e. Comrade Jack Simons was asked to pay special attention to item 5(j) in the camps. He has replied that he is beginning the process in consultation with the camp administration and will report results later.

f. The SACP was requested to table its recent discussion document on the Bantustans together with the comments which it had received from its units. This was done. A copy of the document has already been circulated to NEC members, and the comments will also be made available to the forthcoming NEC meeting. Those documents assisted the Commission in its discussions and formulation of recommendations on the question, which will appear later in the report. The minutes of an earlier discussion by the NEC on the Bantustan question were also tabled.

g. Annexure "A" was also sent to the Women's Section and the Youth and Students section with a request that they discuss and submit a report on plans for relating their work to the internal struggle. Both sections have submitted reports which will be referred to later.

6. Comrade Mac Maharaj was invited to attend a number of sessions of the Commission in Maputo and participated fully in our discussions on the Bantustans and the institutions being imposed on the Indian and Coloured people.

7. The Commission assumed that items 5(k) and (l) of Annexure "A" dealing with the question of membership of the ANC and the capacity of the NEC to discharge its responsibilities was not within the scope of its terms of reference, and should be handled directly by the NEC.

8. The Commission's discussion on certain items and its recommendations will appear separately under the main subject sections which now follow. Certain of the documents which were received by the Commission and which are not annexed to this report will be made available to the NEC when the Commission's report is discussed.

9. Finally, it should be emphasised that the paucity of information on a number of important questions stood in the way of the Commission being able to develop its proposals more fully. This is, in itself, a reflection of the movement's poor style of work in many important areas. We therefore regard our recommendations as merely providing the launching-pad from which

the whole spectrum of mass mobilisation and organisation can be approached with a new urgency and vigour.

PART TWO—Our Strategic Line

The Commission started its main deliberations by considering the first four terms of reference [among the 12 listed by the joint meeting of the ANC/RC] which required us to make recommendations on the:

(a) *elaboration of an overall strategy based on mass mobilisation.*

(b) *creation of the broadest possible national front for liberation.*

(c) *strengthening the underground machinery by drawing into it activists thrown up in mass struggle.*

(d) *development of operations out of political activity, guided by the needs and level of political mobilisation and organisation.*

Because these items are so closely connected with one another, we decided to consider them together. After lengthy discussion, we adopted the Document *(Summarised Theses on our Strategic Line—Annexure "B")* which we submit for the NEC's consideration. [Reproduced below.]

The Document is an attempt to set out in succinct and concentrated form a bald statement of our main strategic line. We did this in the knowledge that the broad approach to our revolutionary strategy and tactics is reflected in many of our basic documents such as the Freedom Charter, Strategy and Tactics, etc. In addition there are numerous documents, memoranda and writings which have developed our basic ideas in relation to the changing situation. Some of these (e.g. the Memorandum submitted during 1978 to FRELIMO) were referred to in our discussion.

The Document we are submitting does not therefore claim to be a new departure in all respects from previous analytical perspectives. On certain questions it contains a re-statement of basic propositions. In regard to others, it attempts to sharpen, clarify, or emphasise some basic propositions. But in some important areas, the Document attempts to incorporate the new thinking which emerged at the Luanda meeting, in particular on the vital question of mass political mobilisation and the relationship between the political and military struggle.

We deliberately attempted to present the basic propositions contained in the Document in concentrated form, avoiding argumentation, and without including references to past errors. As was the case at the Luanda meeting, the Commission was, however, conscious of the fact that *our revolutionary practice* has, in the recent past, not always conformed to the strategic approaches contained in some of our basic documents, and has ignored key experiences of earlier phases of struggle. This is so particularly in the vital areas of our approach to mass mobilisation, the character of our armed struggle, and the way we see it taking root and growing. If there has been such departures or uncertainties in our practice, this implies that in some important areas our line has not been commonly understood and interpreted at all levels of our movement and that it perhaps needs sharpening in order to eliminate vague and ambiguous formulations. Even at the level of the

Commission, different interpretations emerged and we found it necessary to debate some very fundamental propositions (referred to below) which go to the root of our strategic line.

We also noted that very often a basic issue is debated at length and leads to what appears to be a consensus, only to find later that even the participants express diametrically opposing views on its true meaning. We therefore considered that, as a starting point for carrying out the Luanda directive, it would be necessary to place before the NEC a document containing a definition of, and an answer to, the main questions facing our revolution. Such a document would not only be a useful tool for consolidating previous thinking and hammering out a united consensus at top levels, but could also become the guidelines for further discussion, elaboration and education throughout our movement, bearing in mind *item 6* of the Luanda decision [by the joint meeting of the ANC and the RC] that: *"all discussions around these proposals should continue beyond the limits of the NEC and the RC, ideally to encompass the entire membership, and to culminate in an authoritative and representative conference convened to review and formulate policies."*

We draw attention to some of the main issues which came up for debate and discussion in the Commission:

1. In the original draft considered by the Commission an attempt was made to set out a *minimum programme of aims* which would be designed to attract the broadest possible spectrum of organisations, groups and individuals who are, or can be, engaged in the struggle against the regime. After debate, the Commission felt that it would be premature to attempt such a definition.

We were influenced by the argument that the process of creating a single broad platform of *common aims* would be the culmination rather than the starting point of *united action* at different levels of the mass struggle. Such a minimum programme would also be more appropriate at the time when it becomes possible and necessary to create a *structured* nationwide liberation front.

As indicated in paragraph 9 of the Document, the more precise content and shape will only emerge in the course of the actual unfolding of our struggle. At this stage the vital tasks of mass mobilisation demand that we work for the maximum *unity in action* between organisations, groups and individuals at the various levels of confrontation with the regime. For this purpose we considered it far more urgent that a *programme of action* should be elaborated round which mass activity can be generated at all levels of our society. We did not ourselves attempt to elaborate such a programme of action because this would have to be proceeded by a more detailed study of national, regional and local issues and organisations than was allowed by the time at the disposal of the Commission. *We therefore recommend further that one of the priority tasks to be undertaken by the control organ (referred to in Part Three) is to work out such a programme of action for consideration by the NEC.*

2. We debated the more long-term aims of our national democratic

revolution, and the extent to which the ANC, as a national movement, should tie itself to the ideology of Marxism-Leninism and publicly commit itself to the socialist option. The issue was posed as follows:

In the light of the need to attract the broadest range of social forces amongst the oppressed to the national democratic liberation, a direct or indirect commitment at this stage to a continuing revolution which would lead to a socialist order may unduly narrow this line-up of social forces. It was also argued that the ANC is not a party, and its direct or open commitment to socialist ideology may undermine its basic character as a broad national movement.

It should be emphasised that no member of the Commission had any doubts about the ultimate need to continue our revolution towards a socialist order; the issue was posed only in relation to the tactical considerations of the present stage of our struggle.

The Commission finally resolved its thinking on the question in the formulations contained in Paragraph 1 of the Document read with Paragraphs 4 and 5. We all agreed that the way in which we publicly expand on the contents of these paragraphs requires a degree of tactical caution. At the same time it is necessary:

a. for our movement itself to entertain no ambiguities about the aims of people's power and the role of the primary social forces, both inside and outside our movement, which will underwrite these aims, and

b. to gain increasing mass understanding for the idea that, in contrast to many old-style nationalist movements in Africa, we believe that there can be no true national liberation without social emancipation.

The seizure of power by the people must be understood not only by us but also by the masses as the beginning of the process in which the instruments of state will be used to progressively destroy the heritage of *all forms of national and social inequality*. To postpone advocacy of this perspective until the first stage of democratic power has been achieved is to risk dominance within our revolution by purely nationalist forces which may see themselves as replacing the white exploiters at the time of the people's victory. We emphasise again, however, that, as was the case with organisations such as FRELIMO and MPLA (both of which committed themselves to the aim of abolishing the exploitation of man by man early on in their struggle), care must be exercised in the way we project ourselves publicly on this question.

3. Another issue which gave rise to considerable debate relates to the basic perspectives of the armed struggle itself. The following question was posed: Do we see the seizure of power as the result of a general all-round *nation-wide insurrection* which a period of armed struggle will have helped to stimulate; or are we embarked on a *protracted people's war* in which partial and general uprisings will play a vital role? The Commission opted for the latter approach (see Paragraph 8 of the Document), and this choice has an important bearing on strategic planning. This approach is broadly consistent with the thinking of the movement up to now as expressed in the

bulk of our basic documents (see Strategy and Tactics), with an added emphasis on the possible role of partial and general uprisings. Therefore, without excluding the possibility that conditions may emerge in the future in which a successful general insurrection becomes a realistic slogan, this cannot be an exclusive perspective in relation to conditions as we know them today.

4. We draw attention to the fact that in the Document there is no specific reference to the peasantry. We have restricted ourselves to the expression "landless mass in the countryside" to describe the rural stratum. We concluded that not enough research and analysis have so far been undertaken to enable us to characterise both the size and social significance of what could classically be regarded as the peasant class and the process of differentiation within it. We consider it of vital importance that such a study should be undertaken. It should also cover those who, as migrant workers, live and work both in the industrial and the rural sectors, and the extent to which these workers continue to rely in part for their survival on "subsistence" farming undertaken by their immediate and extended families. Such a study would better equip us to assess not only the nature of the existing class relations in the countryside and the full extent of the land hunger, but also to evolve a more detailed and specific programme for the mobilisation of the masses in the countryside.

5. Although the Bantustans are referred to in the Document, because of the importance and immediacy of the problem, we considered it necessary to incorporate our fuller policy recommendations in a separate document which will be referred to later in this Report. This applies also to the other government-created institutions which affect the Coloured and Indian people. But it may be said in passing that in this area too, the need for a collective and common understanding of our strategy and tactics is underlined by a number of differing approaches which emerged in the initial stages of the discussion in the Commission.

6. We are of the view that our fundamental strategic objectives must be thoroughly understood not only at all levels of our movement, but that we should also do more than in the past to convey their content amongst the people in a form which will be understood. We therefore regard our proposed Document as primarily serving the purpose of defining the issues more sharply for ourselves as a movement. The elaboration of the main contents for mass circulation and education will require additional popular elaboration and presentation.

7. We attach marked Annexure "C" the information received from the London Research Unit on internal mass organisations.

Annexure "B"—Summarized Themes on Our Strategic Line
1. *What is the main content and aim of the present phase of our revolution?*
   The main content of the present phase of our struggle is to achieve the aims of our national-democratic revolution whose essence is the national liberation of the black oppressed. Among the black oppressed it is the

African majority which, as a community, suffers the most intense forms of racist domination. The colonial conquest, by force of arms, robbed them of their sovereignty and of their land and transformed them into the main object of economic exploitation. The maximum mobilisation of the African people, as a community robbed of its land and sovereignty, is a fundamental pivot of the alignment of national revolutionary forces.

The aim of national liberation guides our assessment of who the principal enemy is, which are the primary revolutionary forces, and what strategic and tactical methods of struggle are called for. The victorious outcome of the present phase of our struggle will create a people's power whose main immediate task will be to put an end to the special form of colonial-type oppression, guarantee democratic rights for all South Africans and place the main means of production into the hands of a people's state.

The aims of our national-democratic revolution will only be fully realized with the construction of a social order in which all the historic consequences of national oppression and its foundation, economic exploitation, will be liquidated, ensuring the achievement of real national liberation and social emancipation. An uninterrupted advance towards this ultimate goal will only be assured if within the alignment of revolutionary forces struggling to win the aims of our national-democratic revolution, the dominant role is played by the oppressed working people.

2. Who is the principal enemy?

The principal enemy of our revolution is the South African ruling class, which is distinguished by a *combination* of several key characteristics. Like its counterparts in other capitalist countries, its power is rooted, in the first instance, in its ownership and control of the basic means of production. But in South Africa, the system of economic exploitation is reinforced and deepened by the *national oppression* of the black majority. Thus, capitalist exploitation and racial oppression operate together and reinforce one another. This combination of class exploitation and colour oppression imposes a double burden on the black majority, who are exploited as working people and also as members of a nationally oppressed group.

To maintain this system and safeguard its control, the ruling class operates through a state apparatus whose political institutions and instruments of repression—the army, police force, civil service, judiciary etc.—protect the existing relations of production and, at the same time, the race rule which excludes all who are not within the white minority group from political rights and civil liberties in the land of their birth. Real liberation is inconceivable without the overthrow of the economic and political power of this class and the total destruction of its state apparatus.

3. Who are the enemy's principal allies?

Externally, the enemy is closely linked to imperialism whose economic and political interests are served by the perpetuation of the existing relations of production and the preservation of the main features of the political and social institutions which reinforce these relations. At the same time, open imperialist collusion with the South African state faces a number of tactical obstacles. The global spread of imperialist investment covers important newly-independent regions which, in varying degrees and for special historical reasons, form part of the anti-racist groupings and nations. Anti-imperialist rivalries, played out at both the national and multi-national level, give rise to secondary contradictions within imperialism and partly explain the existence of conflicting political lobbies on the South African question within the ruling circles. In addition, the contradictions are deepened by the popular revulsion which the racial oppression excites, leading to pro-liberation pressures within the imperialist countries, particularly from the working class and other democratic social forces. This aspect of our external diplomatic front thus constitutes a vital area of our struggle and calls for tactics designed to exploit these secondary contradictions so as to divide and weaken the regime's external support base.

Internally, the South African ruling class draws its political support from all the classes and groups amongst the white community, including the white working class, which in return for such support enjoys economic and political privileges vis a vis the black majority. All factions of capital and the white middle and working classes benefit, in varying degrees, from the system of race oppression and exploitation. But the fact that they do not benefit equally or in the same way gives rise to secondary contradictions. It is our duty to take full advantage of such secondary contradictions within the enemy camp in order to win over sections of the white community to our cause.

4. *Which is the principal social force of our revolution?*

The principal and most consistent social force for the achievement of the aims of our national-democratic revolution is the exploited and nationally-oppressed working people in the towns and the landless mass in the country-side. This social force has no stake in the existing relations of production and suffers the worst excesses of oppression and economic exploitation. Its dominant role in the struggle for people's power will ensure uninterrupted advance towards a social order which will eliminate both the forms and substance of national oppression and lead to complete social emancipation.

5. *Who are the main allies of the working people?*

The place which the other classes and strata of the black communities occupy in the social and economic structures does not give them an *equal* interest with the working classes in the achievement of all the aims of our revolution. Nor are all those classes and strata *equally* consistent, reliable and unvacillating in their resistance to racist domination. Nevertheless there is no single class or strata within the black communities which is untouched by the political, economic, social, cultural or religious consequences of racial discrimination. This provides the basis for contradictions and conflict between the regime, on the one hand, and every class and stratum within the black communities, on the other hand. It is our duty to exploit these contradictions and to ensure the maximum participation in immediate struggle of all these groups and strata, even if they do not support every plank in our immediate or long-term platform.

6. *Who are the main external allies of our struggle?*

Externally, the main allies of our national liberation struggle are: the Socialist world, those newly-independent states (particularly on our continent) who have already won the first stage of their struggle against colonialism, especially those consolidating their political independence by the demolition of the vestiges of colonialism and total economic reconstruction of their societies, those states in the western world which have given consistent political and material support for our liberation movement, the people still engaged in the struggle against colonial rule, and the working class and other democratic forces in the imperialist countries.

7. *What are the key elements of the enemy's political strategy?*

The key elements of the enemy's political strategy to maintain and perpetuate its system of economic and social domination are as follows:

(a) It seeks to maintain and strengthen the political unity of all class and social forces within the white community against black liberation. To achieve this aim it entrenched the basic economic, political, and social privileges of all strata amongst the white community. It uses its ideological weapons, relying particularly on anti-communism, in an attempt to confuse the people and to rally all reactionary forces within the country and internationally in defence of its system.

(b) The regime is founded and survives on violence and terror. Externally, it uses its economic resources and strengthens its conventional armed force in order to advance its regional imperialistic aims and to weaken the capacity of the newly-liberated states to support our struggle. It seeks to strengthen its international support by exploiting its role as one of the main suppliers of vital strategic raw materials to imperialism and as its chief gendarme on the African continent.

(c) Through the political fragmentation of our country into so-called Bantustans, the regime seeks to reverse the historic process of African national consciousness and to revive and entrench tribalism. The plan to institutionalise the division of the African people along tribal lines is calculated to defraud their right to full economic, political and social equality within one united South Africa and to create a more manageable reserve of cheap black labour, with an only transitory presence in the country's industrial strongholds and no rights of labour or political organisation,

(d) In furtherance of its policy of divide and rule, the regime attempts to play off the main black groups against one another by a system of differential levels of oppression and the imposition of separate sham constitutional "solutions." Within the black groups it tries to win over collaborators and agents so as to separate them from the mainstream of the revolution.

(e) Using all the techniques of fascist state terror, the regime seeks to prevent the political organisation of the oppressed and their struggles for their rights. It blocks the emergence of a trade union movement which would genuinely represent the interests of the working class. It persecutes all attempts by the masses to associate together in order to confront the system on even minimal demands. Above all, it acts to weaken and try to destroy the ANC and its allies and to isolate the people from the revolutionary vanguard. Although the repressive measures of the regime are directed mainly against the black oppressed generally and our revolutionary movement in particular, they also infest inter-white politics and, from time to time, trigger off secondary political contradictions within the privileged group.

(f) The regime is doing all in its power to prevent our armed struggle from taking root. It is continuously sharpening its counter-insurgency strike forces and undertaking intensive propaganda campaigns amongst the people in order to win their "hearts and minds" for the counter-revolution.

8. *What is our principal immediate strategic line of struggle?*

The strategic objective of our struggle is the seizure of power by the people as the first step in the struggle for the victory of our national democratic revolution. Seizure of power by the people means and presupposes the all-round defeat of the fascist regime by the revolutionary forces of our country. It means the dismantling by the popular power of all the political, economic, cultural and other formations of racist rule and also necessitates the smashing of the state machinery of fascism and racism and the construction of a new one committed to the defence and advancement of the people's cause.

The character of the South African ruling class and the nature of its state apparatus dictates that national liberation and people's power can only be won by revolutionary violence in a protracted armed struggle which must involve the whole people and in which partial and general mass uprisings will play a vital role. Such a people's war can only take root and develop if its grows out of, and is based on, political revolutionary bases amongst the people.

The leadership core of our struggle is the ANC and its revolutionary allies. It is this core which must provide guidance to the whole revolutionary process. To carry out this task:

(i) we must work unceasingly to reinforce and extend our underground presence in every part of our land. In this connection, it is vital to attract to our ranks the most committed and advanced militants who are engaged in struggle and confrontation with the racist regime at various levels of the mass movement. It is particularly vital to ensure that the best elements from the principal social force of the revolution—the workers and landless mass—are recruited and involved at every level of our movement.

(ii) we must work for the political mobilisation and organisation of the masses of our people into active struggle as a matter of priority. We must aim to attract all forces—at national, regional and local levels—who have potential to confront the regime in the struggle against racism and for one united non-racial South Africa. We must bring about the broadest possible unity of all national groups, classes and strata, organisations, groups and prominent personalities around local and national issues. This means we must combine illegal with legal and semi-legal activity to ensure such mass mobilisation and to establish our presence and influence wherever the people are. We must not mechanically reject all participation in government-created bodies, if such participation will advance our revolutionary aims, contribute towards the undermining of such bodies and towards the exposure and isolation of the out-and-out collaborators

(iii) we must help organise genuine mass organisations among all sections of our people and establish contact with and provide guidance to those which have been formed through the initiative of others. In carrying out this task we must avoid exposing the legal and semi-legal mass organisations to more intense police harassment. This means that the guiding hand of our liberation movement does not always have to be seen or publicly acknowledged.

(iv) we must be on a constant alert to provide, either directly or indirectly, the main campaign slogans and issues around which the people can be mobilised to organise and act at national and regional levels. This can only be done if we are closely in touch with the masses of the people and are so organisationally structured that the bulk of our talents and the bulk of our resources give *day-to-day* attention to the internal situation and to the effective co-ordination of internal political and military activity.

(v) together with our ally, the S. A. Congress of Trade Unions, we must work for the strengthening of a Trade Union movement which will genuinely represent the interest of the working class and ensure their organised participation in the struggle for national liberation.

(vi) we must work for the creation of a widespread network of nuclei among the people which can undertake military and para-military activities, guided and determined by the need to generate political mobilisation, organisation and resistance, which nuclei will become the basis for creating an armed people as the foundation of the struggle for power.

(vii) we must maintain our independence as the vanguard of our revolution and win growing acceptance for our long-term programme, strategy and tactics. At the same time we must encourage, provide guidance to *all* opposition to tyranny and racism and to every struggle for democratic rights and better conditions of life. In this connection we must regard every act of opposition as furthering the cause of our revolution even when the participants do not yet fully understand or accept our immediate or long-term policy.

9. *What is the character and shape of our broad front of struggle?*

In general, it is our duty to counter the enemy's strategy to divide and narrow the base of the liberation opposition, by our strategy of creating a nation-wide popular liberation front. In the first place, we must recognise all expressions of opposition to the racist regime as part of such a front. We must aim to progressively harness such opposition toward a common content and purpose.

This does not imply the immediate creation of a single, formal and publicly-defined structure. At this stage such a front will operate at a number of levels simultaneously and in different ways. It will express itself in independent as well as supportive actions between the various mass organisations and will include varied forms of direct and indirect collaboration between our liberation movement and the mass organisations. Such collaboration must be in a form which will safeguard the division between legal and illegal work and must respect the independence of the participants. It is not conditional on the acceptance of all aspects of our revolutionary strategy.

In the long-term, conditions may mature demanding the creation of a broad *structured* organisational front in which our movement will have won a guiding position by virtue of the calibre of its leadership of the revolutionary process as a whole. The more precise content and shape of such a *structured front* will only emerge in the course of the unfolding of our struggle in the immediate future.

10. *What is our approach to the relationship between the political and military struggle?*

(a) The preparation for People's Armed Struggle and its victorious conclusion is not solely a military question. This means that the armed struggle must be based on, and grow out of, mass political support and it must eventually involve our whole people. All military activities must, at every stage, be guided and determined by the need to generate political mobilisation, organisation and resistance, with the aim of progressively weakening the enemy's grip on his reins of political, economic, social and military power, by a combination of political and military action.

(b) The forms of political and military activities, and the way these activities relate to one another, go through different phases as the situation changes. It is therefore vital to have under continuous survey the changing tactical relationships between these two inter-dependent factors in our struggle and the place which political and military actions (in the narrow sense) occupy in each phase, both nationally and within each of our main regions. The concrete political realities must determine whether, at any given stage and in any given region, the main emphasis should be on political or on military action.

(c) The creation of a national liberation army, with popularly-rooted internal rear bases, is a key perspective of our planning in the military field. Such an army unit must, at all times, remain under the direction and control of our political revolutionary vanguard.

11. *What is the main emphasis at the moment?*

At the present moment we are at the stage when the *main task* is to concentrate on political mobilisation and organisation so as to build up political revolutionary bases throughout the country. In as much as the growth of the armed struggle depends on the rate of advance of the political struggle, the armed struggle is *secondary* at this time. This assessment of the balance between political and military activity in the present phase must reflect itself at all levels of our planning and in the way we use our energies and resources.

12. *What is the role of armed activity at this stage?*

Organised armed activity continues to be one of the vital elements in helping to prepare the ground for political activity and organisation leading to the creation of a network of political revolutionary bases which will become the foundation of our People's War. More particularly, the purpose of such organised armed activity at the present stage is:

(a) to keep alive the perspective of People's revolutionary violence as the ultimate weapon for the seizure of power.

(b) to concentrate on armed propaganda actions, that is, armed action whose immediate purpose is to support and stimulate political activity and organisation rather than to hit at the enemy.

13. *How do we answer the enemy's counter-insurgency tactics?*

In general, the answer to the enemy's counter-insurgency tactics lies in the field of all-round political mobilisation and organisation of the masses. More particularly:

(a) We must spread an understanding amongst the people of the place of revolutionary violence in the struggle for power, the relationship between armed and non-armed forms of struggle and the meaning and content of Peoples War in our conditions.

(b) We must be on the alert to answer the enemy's continuous campaign of slander against our liberation movement and its armed wing—MK, especially his attempts to distort the aim and purpose of armed combat actions.

(c) We must undertake a detailed and on-going study of the enemy's counter-insurgency tactics amongst the people and continuously find ways of defeating them.

(d) We must imbue the people, and especially the working and student youth, with a deep pride in and respect for the fighting traditions of our people whose outstanding military prowess showed itself during the wars of resistance to foreign conquest.

(e) We must work systematically to undermine the morale and cohesion of the enemy's forces and their social support base within the country. We must in the first place work to win over or neutralise those amongst the black oppressed who have been recruited into the regime's puppet armed force.

(f) We must ensure that our armed actions are, by their nature, always seen to reflect the people's interests. They must always be directed against the main enemy and must be consistent with the ideological perspectives of our revolution.

Annexure "D"—Memorandum to the Politico-Military and Strategy Commission [from Chris Hani in Lesotho]

1. We have always felt that political work is primary and that everything else flows from it.

2. In all the areas we have tackled, we have made it a point to begin by establishing an underground presence of the ANC. We have thus made it compulsory for all MK members to start with political organisation before carrying out any military tasks.

3. We have adopted the above-mentioned methods out of a realisation that political work provides the following advantages for our cadres:

(a) Protection and shelter from enemy attacks and surveillance.

(b) Increase the survival period as the political organisation serves as eyes and ears of the MK cadres.

(c) Collection of intelligence data facilitating armed actions.

(d) Advice on proper and suitable hiding places.

4. In order to make our local MK cadres suitable for this type of work we have embarked on regular political classes making each and everyone of them self-sufficient in the task of political mobilisation.

5. Internally we carve the areas into sectors appointing comrades to be in charge of these sectors. The comrades in charge are responsible and accountable individually to the collective here. There is no link and communication between the comrades in charge of the different sectors. The sector leader is in charge of the various units in the sector but meets the leaders of each unit separately. Some of the sector leaders are based in our area but undertake visits into their sectors for discussions and exchange of views and implementations of decisions. Others are based in the Transkei and come now and again to discuss with the collective. At other times the collective delegates some of its members to get inside to consult and satisfy themselves that the work is being carried out.

6. The collective has established political and military training facilities for short training for comrades sent by the different sectors. The training course lays special emphasis on trade unionism, underground political organisation, conspiracy and security.

7. The collective has also begun to set up intelligence groups inside the country and locally to collect information on various aspects of our work and advise the movement on dangers facing it, liquidation of those posing a threat to our survival. These intelligence units function independently of the internal units and are responsible to the collective.

8. We have also established a production and propaganda unit in our area. It produces a sheet as regular as resources allow. The propaganda is then fed into our internal machinery for distribution. We decided that the contents should be in our own languages to ensure that our messages are understood by the working people and peasants. We also encourage the units to prepare their own material and send them to us for production until such time that they are in a position to produce these themselves. The advantage is that this enables them to tackle the burning issues themselves.

MASS POLITICAL MOBILISATION

We believe that serious efforts should be made to involve as many of our people as possible in our struggle. In order to realise this, our collective feels that we should explore the potential of existing legal and semi-legal organisations. It is of the view that our organisation as the vanguard of the National Liberation Revolution must seek a common denominator with legal and semi-legal organisations. This common denominator must among other things embrace an uncompromising opposition to racism and White domination as well as the upholding of the principle of the oneness of our country. Our collective has thus made discreet approaches to the Democratic Party in the Transkei. Useful talks have been held and important decisions taken. We are hopeful that we shall be in a position to make progress in this field.

Our collective has seriously discussed the need to contact the Labour Party to explore possibilities of establishing some links, especially with those elements recognising our leading role. These approaches are to be secret and underground. But we think serious efforts should be made to establish ANC cells among the Coloured people. The aim is to take politics and activity outside the Coloured Representative Council. We want to make the Labour Party a vehicle for mass political mobilisation among the people. At the same time we think that attempts should be made to strengthen the influence of SACTU among the Coloured workers, thus destroying or reducing the reactionary role of TUCSA.

Non-racial sporting bodies are playing a good role in fighting Apartheid. These bodies are beginning to tackle political issues as well, thus correctly arguing that "there can be no normal sport in an abnormal society." Bodies like SARU [SA Rugby Union], SACOS [SA Council on Sport], the Soccer Foundation, etc. must be contacted to explore areas of co-operation as well as trying to involve them in the task of mass political work.

Document 115. Editorial on the PAC and Marxism-Leninism, *Ikwezi* (Nottingham), March 1980

In successive issues of IKWEZI we have called for the building of a Marxist-Leninist Party and the building of the PAC as the mass national movement in the country. These two tasks are not opposed to one another.

At the stage of the national democratic revolution, the struggle can only be fought through the instrumentality of a national movement. This national movement might take the form of one great movement or a United Front, depending upon the conditions in a country. The national movement unites all the classes and strata in society around a minimum political program based on common democratic and national demands. Only in this way can the national liberation struggle be conducted effectively. Without a national movement of this kind we cannot defeat the class enemy. The key question is who leads the national movement. Must it be led by the petit bourgeoisie or by the proletariat through its vanguard Marxist-Leninist Party? Our position is that if the national struggle is to be fought on the highest level it must be led by the proletariat. The proletariat is the most revolutionary class in Azania. It must draw around it all the other oppressed sections in Azanian society—and mainly the peasantry—and lead the national struggle.

If the Marxist-Leninists do not lead the national movement, then it will degenerate into a small sect engaged in revolutionary rhetoric. Azanian Marxist-Leninists will only achieve this if they are the best exponents of the national struggle and do not in any way undermine the legitimacy of the national struggle. Too many Azanian M-Ls regard the national struggle as of some passing interest and see the struggle mainly as one for socialism. In this way they tend to liquidate the importance of the national struggle and to degenerate into a Trotskyite position.

The main demands of the Azanian masses at the moment are democratic and national demands. Azanian Marxist-Leninists must be in the forefront of these demands in the various mass organisations around which these demands are made—like the youth, student, women's and workers movements.

We have opted for the PAC as the principal national movement to build because of its correct position on the national question (i.e., the principal national demand as the repossession of the country and the land as an African country, and the ending of the foreign domination of white settler colonialism) and also because of its militancy and potential mass character. The PAC is far from being the dynamic mass organisation that it can be. But it has the very definite potential of becoming so. With correct positions toward the national minorities (the Indians and the Coloureds) and drawing them toward Africanist positions, the PAC can be built as the mass national movement in the country. The task of Azanian Marxist-Leninists is to assist in achieving this. With correct M-L leadership too the factionalism and clichism [clique-ism] that characterizes the PAC can be brought to an end. But for a M-L Party to achieve this, it must be based on correct policies and not on opportunism.

For this reason IKWEZI does not see the building up of the PAC as the principal mass national movement as being antagonistic to the building of a Marxist-Leninist Party. The Marxist-Leninist Party must be built separate and apart from the national movement, based on its own independent strength. But it must be wholly involved in the national struggle and lead the united front or the principal national movement leading the struggle.

The skill of a mature Marxist-Leninist Party at the phase of the national struggle is to do united front work and to lead the non-proletarian elements, to unite the different strata and sectors of society fighting for common demands under proletarian leadership. If this cannot be attained, then the national struggle cannot lead to the smashing of the South African bourgeois state and pass uninterruptedly over to the phase of socialism.

11. Crackdown and Resistance After Soweto

DOCUMENT 116. Constitution of the Pimville/Klipspruit Residents' Committee, Johannesburg, 1975

1. NAME:

The name of the body shall be known as: The Pimville/Klipspruit Residents' Committee, herein referred to as the Committee.

2. AIMS AND OBJECTIVES:

Aims and objects of the Committee shall be:

(i) To pursue on behalf of the residents of Pimville/Klipspruit their legal rights to all the facilities, amenities and relevant matters for the well being of an orderly society.

(ii) To bring to the attention of the authorities the requirements, demands and/or requests of the residents for the common good of both residents and the authorities.

(iii) To appeal and demand the electrification of the Township as a matter of urgency.

(iv) To demand for the electrification of the residents houses.

(v) The improvement of medical, dental, ante-natal and post-natal clinics for the residents.

(vi) The erection and establishment of educational institutions—from creches [day care centers] to high schools.

(vii) To demand and appeal for improvement to roads in the Township.

(viii) To demand the erection of libraries and the supply of books therein.

(ix) To establish, encourage and develop social, cultural and sporting clubs and/or organisations.

(x)   To demand for the erection of swimming pools, tennis courts, bowling greens and the completion of the Pimville Stadium to international standards.

(xi)   To encourage residents to buy the houses they occupy.

(xii) To provide a means whereby the West Rand Administration may explain its policy to residents.

(xiii) No unmarried child of a registered tenant should be removed from the [house] permit.

3. CO-OPERATION:

(i)   The Committee will co-operate with any committee, society or body with similar aims and objects.

(ii)   Will not encourage its members to use the Committee as a platform for Urban Bantu Council elections.

(iii) Will not allow any of its members to use the Committee's constitution as a manifesto for the Urban Bantu Council elections.

4. MEMBERSHIP:

Membership of the Committee shall be open to ALL registered tenants of the Pimville/Klipspruit complex.

5. ELECTIONS:

(i)   Members of the executive Committee shall be elected by show of hands.

(ii)   The executive Committee shall consist of a Chairman and Vice-Chairman, the Secretary and Assistant Secretary and five members.

(iii) The executive Committee shall be in office for a period of one year.

(iv)   Should a member of the executive Committee resign, die or absent himself on three consecutive executive meetings without an acceptable reason, such member shall be deemed to have resigned.

(v)   Should there be a vacancy in the executive Committee there shall be a bye-election.

6. DUTIES AND FUNCTIONS OF THE EXECUTIVE COMMITTEE:

(i)   a) The executive Committee shall handle the day to day affairs of the Committee.

b) Be vigilant by collecting any information that may affect the residents.

c) Keep the residents informed of the latest developments.

d) To make representations where necessary and also authorised by the members for the residents.

e) Enquire from the right channels any matter within the constitution for the benefit of the residents.

(ii)   a) The executive Committee shall meet at least once a quarter, i.e. once in every three months, unless it decides to meet more frequently due to its business.

b) The executive Committee shall decide at its meeting when to call a general members meeting and the agenda for that meeting.

c) The executive Committee shall invite members of the Urban Bantu Council to its general members meetings as speakers.

d) The general meeting shall be called by the executive at least once a year or at any time the executive may decide.

7. AMENDMENTS:

Amendments to the Constitution shall be decided by a majority vote of residents at a meeting—after the residents have discussed the requisition for an amendment.

Document 117. Speech by Diliza Mji, president, to General Students' Council of SASO, Hammanskraal, July 1976

The theme for this year's conference is appropriate for the following reasons: (a) the map of Africa has changed so much since last we were here and quite fast at that, (b) because white racism and oppression and the end of exploitation of man by man be he black or white, is no longer a myth or Utopia but is more of a reality now to all who strive for peace and justice in Azania.

Change (and therefore liberation) as a product of an effort by progressive forces against the resistance of the oppressor, is quite heavily dependent on the contribution of all our people; the youth and students have a special role to play. This is true, not for this country alone but has been seen to be the case in all the struggles of the world. It is however, also true that students can be the oppressors of the people if not armed with a clear analysis and strategies and an accurate perception of who the enemy is and in what different forms he is capable of presenting himself. It is my belief that we are not committed to the struggle because we would have liked to have been at Wits [University of the Witwatersrand] or UCT for our university careers but could not and therefore begrudged the system. If it is so we have missed the point.

Nor do I hope that we associate with the movement because it precludes white membership or maybe it is fashionable to be in SASO. Black Consciousness as a philosophy we adhere to, is still being misrepresented by those who refuse to understand it and more important it needs to be better understood by those who are like all of us here, who identify themselves with the movement.

The White South African Government is today carving and promoting an aspiring middle class amongst Blacks that is going to do their dirty jobs for them in maintaining the status quo. The call today from liberal and "verligte" [enlightened] quarters to the Nationalist Government is that Blacks should be given more opportunity to participate in the so-called "free-enterprise" system so that they should identify with it and be able to defend it against "advancing communist aggression that is now at the door-step of South Africa." This aspiring Black middle class is at the top of the Bantustan programmes with its appendages, the Black Bank, BIC [Bantu Investment Corporation], XDC [Xhosa Development Corporation], Nafcoc [National African Federated Chamber of Commerce], and others. These are trying to compete with capitalistic concerns like the OK Bazaars on the basis that Black markets should be left to the Black entrepreneurs. All they are saying is that Black should be exploited by Blacks and this sounds better to the Black community. We are therefore faced with a monster that has a big White trunk and with black appendages. Furthermore, this black middle class aligns itself with imperialism, the highest form of capitalism, for they have to make trips to Europe and America to seek foreign investment. This black middle class is the victim of a strategy to render them comfortable so that they may [not] worry about communal commitments. The need is therefore to look at our struggle not only in terms of colour interests but also in terms of class interest, skin colour in fact has become a class criterion in South Africa. Just as the Roman Catholic Church in Mozambique was pro-imperialist and counter-revolutionary, there are a lot of institutions and practices even amongst ourselves that are part of the general strategy of oppression.

In order to proceed in our struggle for change and true humanity, we ought to know the position of our enemy inside and outside the country. Apartheid as an exploitative system is part of the bigger whole, capitalism. Foreign investment (imperialism) has committed overseas economies in South Africa's domestic politics against social change in the same way that Western powers that were backing the FNLA-UNITA [Frente Nacional de Libertação de Angola—União Nacional para a Independência Total de Angola] axis against the progressive MPLA [Movimento Popular de Libertação de Angola] in Angola. We should learn the lesson that forces of reaction were put against the progressive forces (both were black) and hence try and look around in South Africa even amongst ourselves whether we are progressive or reactionary. In most independent African countries today colonialism was replaced by neo-colonialism which means that the countries today concerned are politically independent but still economically servile. If Black Consciousness must survive as a viable philosophy and continue to articulate the aspirations of the masses of the people, it must start interpreting our situation from an economic class point of view. The [Kaiser] Matanzimas and the [Lucas] Mangopes should be seen in the light of bourgeois counter-revolutionaries alongside the [Richard] Maponyas [black businessman]. When we talk of the "system" we should understand not only the upholders of racial-discrimination and apartheid but also the exploitative machinery of capitalism that in this country is run along the basis of a man's colour, where black is the passport to naked economic exploitation and political deprivation. This will lead us to the point where we ask ourselves the question whether our struggle is an isolated struggle or part of a bigger struggle of the Third World that wants to shake [off] the yoke of imperialism and replace it with socialistic governments in which the power is wielded not by a few wealthy families but by the people.

The system as we have talked about above is kept going by a numerically weak group of persons who are materially strong. This means that amongst Blacks in this country, Vorster's strategy is to corrupt each and every Black student by exposing them to the luxuries and comforts of a "free-life" by making education a means towards a better living. This is the strategy of Vorster. This means that the student group is fertile ground for the temptation to forget about the next man and to prepare his future for himself. This is why Blacks in this country can never boast even about the few professional people that they have because they are not theirs, they live for themselves. All tragedy is based on the individualistic nature of the education meted to us. It needs a conscientized mind not to be receptive to this corruption.

It is against this background that in a capitalistic set-up like it is in South Africa we have to align ourselves with the majority of working people and be with them. Personal desires can only make us drift further and further away from the people. You cannot lead people when you are staying in a R110,000 house, because you will not want to change the system because of your own class interests which shall always clash with those of the people. When houses are being burnt, like it was happening in Soweto, the people will be saying "we have nothing to lose," and you will be saying "this is madness, what? my beautiful house!" Class interest will always affect the political outlook of people, as you have seen. This is why we have people who say that they want to study first and then think of doing something about the political situation later. They are having in mind the social status and economic advantage, which are the criteria of middle class interests.

Having taken into account the socio-economic factors affecting any person involved in a struggle for change, then it is logical to expect that group action is more effective than individual action. Group action means organisation of the people having common values and aspirations. We are aware that times have changed, therefore [we] have a greater need to be more organised than before. SASO as a meeting point can never die before the ultimate liberation of the Black people. We affirm our belief in the saying that "BLACK MAN YOU ARE ON YOUR OWN" and further we maintain that Black is an attitude of the mind and not the colour of the skin. We will not be fooled by little concessions like the appointment of Black Rectors in the tribal colleges because this does not alter their separatist or their tribal nature. Generally, Black Consciousness as a way of life amongst blacks in South Africa has been entrenched in the community. The eras of "Yes, sir" are over. In churches, black priests are waging an internal battle and are demanding more control and representation in the decision making.

In the continent of Africa today, radical changes have occured and are still taking place. When Frelimo took over Mozambique, we evidenced the setting up of a Government of the people for the people's interests in the true sense of the word "democracy." Not a misconstrued democracy, and this being so near South Africa.

The Angolan issue reinforced the reactionary fears even more to the Vorster regime: hence we witnessed the invasion of Angola by the South

African troops which were terribly humiliated. Angola is now a stable state under the people's leadership of MPLA.

In Zimbabwe, the bourgeois nationalist leaders have been barred from visiting the bases because they are "land-owners." The leadership is now in the hands of the guerillas. This demonstrates that at crucial stages of struggle people who have middle class aspirations have no future in the solving of issues affecting the people. These are the realities of our times. Moreover this is the background against which:

(i) South Africa's dead detente exercise was to create economic dependency of Black Africa on South Africa,

(ii) the African tour by [American Secretary of State Henry] Kissinger and his subsequent meeting with Vorster in West Germany has taken place.

America, the big brother of capitalism, can no longer ignore the threat of a takeover of the "last bastion of the so-called free enterprise system."

In effect South Africa is becoming more obviously a partner of the West because the struggle in Africa is no longer a matter of national independence only, but also of progressive forces against imperialism and neo-colonialism. Now, the imperialist forces are threatened because they have economic interests in South Africa. It is expected that we will see a greater co-operation between South Africa and the West. Israel, also a fascist country that has an identical ideology with apartheid in Zionism, [is] in cahoots with South Africa. We are still aware of the West German scandal coming out of the co-operation of the West Germany government with South Africa towards the setting up of a nuclear power station in South Africa.

From this analysis, it is becoming more clear that our oppressors [are] in Pretoria, Bonn, Tel Aviv, London, New York, etc. This is the picture as I see it.

Therefore, it stands out clearly from the above analysis that we as students can never effectively contribute positively to this changing South African scene if we pursue middle class interests. Neither can we hope to effectively solve problems affecting us as students in different campuses in particular or national in general.

The rationale of this year's conference is to come and assess the role we have played in our society and the role we can still play towards change.

Power and Solidarity.

DOCUMENT 118. "The Future Society as Seen by Black People's Convention." Statement signed by Thami Zani, June 1977

At the heart of the BPC policy outlook is the constant reminder that we are striving for the attainment of an open society.

This is an important point of departure because the implicit claim by the Black Consciousness movement is that none of the white political parties and organisations can by themselves and on their own manage to bring about the envisaged open society. So tied are they to the consideration of colour, ethnic grouping and other manifestations of irrational prejudice that they see the future either in terms of a false multi-nationalism or a pretense of geographic or ethnic federations, all of which have in common the preservation of power in the hands of those who are white and those who have money.

The best of the white formulas, emanating from the Progressive Reformists, has at its heart the creation of a dangerous coalition between the white "haves" and an upper crust of black "haves", against the interests and aspirations of a multitude of black "have nots" who form 95% of the black majority.

This is what makes it impossible to move away from the present closed, balkanised and segmented community that constitutes the present South African plural society to a truly open society belonging to all citizens of the country.

The Black Consciousness movement has often stated that it is fighting for an egalitarian society. This term is defined in the Oxford Dictionary as "asserting the equality of mankind." This is a value-laden expression which feeds one with hope for the future. It is new to us in this country used as we are to a completely amoral political system based on the exploitation of man by man on the basis of skin colour.

The term egalitarian when used to describe a political system implies:
• all sane persons shall be eligible to participate in the making of the laws under which they shall live, through the people's National Assembly which shall be a body constituted of elected representatives of all people.
• all people shall be equal in the eyes of the law irrespective of colour, religion, status in life, or other considerations.
• all citizens shall be protected from exploitation of one by the other, and some by the others.

Used in this context therefore the term "egalitarian society" implies a radical departure from what we are used to in this country. It means total blindness by the State and its organs to colour as a factor in deciding a man's fate and judging a man's ability. In such a society there cannot be recognition of minorities because this is symptomatic of the sickness of using skin colour to place a man in a specific social box. Neither will the State tolerate anybody who tries to turn the clock back by fighting for narrow "nationalism" in a way that defeats the pursuit of an egalitarian society.

In the new society to be created, a guarantee of *the rights of man will form an integral part of our legal system.* The Universal Declaration of Human Rights of the United Nations will be observed and respected. Born, as we have been, out of centuries of denigration, dispossession, oppression and exploitation, we shall constantly demonstrate our abhorrence in any form of oppressive and exploitative measures, through rigorous attachment to a system that enshrines basic human rights.

Following from this it becomes obvious that the economic system to be followed will not countenance exploitation of any segment of the masses for the benefit of greedy and capricious individuals. We have declared ourselves in favour of the promotion of communalism which has at its heart a profound spirit of sharing. The practice whereby the wealth of the country is locked in the hands of a very small greedy minority, will receive attention. Unbridled capitalism has its days numbered throughout the world and there will be no exception in the future of Azania.

A proper *redistribution of the wealth* of the country also implies that those who have been living on an artificially high standard because of exclusive privileges and opportunities, must be prepared to suffer setbacks in the interests of national good. We believe that it is much better for many to make definite progress, though at a slow pace, than for a few to advance by leaps and bounds, at the expense of all. This will be the guiding light in economic planning for the country in years to come.

We do not see our country entering into alliances with either the East or the West. We regard *non-alignment* as an essential part of our overall freedom and sovereignty. We shall carefully shy away from imperialist forces either of the old stock or new. Nonetheless, we shall join forces with the rest of the Third World in their struggle to break away from imperialist control by the big powers.

As people building a new society, we cannot but be aware of the important role played by *education* in creating proper values and a new outlook. The essence of our educational system will be the promotion of self-reliance, a high level of critical awareness, proper understanding of the community and its problems and a sense of positive identity amongst as many of our people as possible. To get ourselves out of the present quagmire, such an educational system will also need to be pruned to work for the destruction of racist, tribalist, sectionalist, imperialist and exploit-ationist notions. This is especially necessary because of the long standing prejudices that have been entrenched in the minds of our people in this country. The duplication of languages at all levels of general education will need to be replaced by a concentration on one international and one vernacular language selected after careful research.

For the creation of a broadly based mental development, comparative *environmental studies* covering economics, geography, history, political and constitutional structures will form the major content of instruction at an early stage. Humanities, including social anthropology, sociology and elementary community development, and basic sciences including maths and natural sciences will also form part of the early syllabuses.

An *elementary education will be free and compulsory for all citizens and will be followed by specialization introduced at the minimum effective level.* Learning facilities and teacher training will receive priority consideration in order to create the best atmosphere for the learning process. A programme of *rapid elimination of illiteracy* will be designed and implemented for the adult population. Education will take up the greatest percentage of the national budget, and not defence of an immoral system as is currently the case.

There will be no "national church" in our country though there will be *complete religious tolerance.* We cannot countenance a system whereby everybody is free to establish his own personal church, hence churches will be encouraged to establish a permanent Council which shall regulate the recognition of churches and the day to day work of churches.

The State will contribute largely to the training of ministers and will work with the envisaged Council and ensure that ministers receive adequate training in social work to be able to contribute to the social welfare and community development programmes of the nation.

In the field of defence it will be expected of every sane and adult person to form part of the *National Defence Force*. There will be no use of national territory by foreign forces. Our guiding defence policy will be one of *peaceful collaboration* with all nations of the world on the basis of the principles of mutual respect, national sovereignty, territorial integrity, non-aggression and non-interference in domestic affairs, and peaceful co-existence.

In all its forms therefore the future State envisaged by the BPC will seek to derive prosperity from the acceptability of its maintenance by the greatest number in the population. Coercive measures and dictatorships thrive in situations where those in power are aware of the non-acceptability of their authority and what it stands for to the majority of the people they govern. Inflated defence budgets are a measure of the lack of popularity of a government both internally and externally.

Our greatest asset will be a basic morality in our everyday operations, and flowing from that a persuasive influence on the minds of the people to support what we stand for. This we believe is the greatest insurance policy that any government may have in order to insure its continued acceptability to the people.

Document 119. "Steve Biko." Editorial, *Pro Veritate*, September 1977

Steve Biko lived the liberated humanity which he sought for others. Through the sheer strength of his personality, he became a leader of men recognised far and wide. Courageous and compassionate, tough and quiet, he had a piercing insight and vast resources of confidence, hope and laughter.

His martyrdom cuts through the fog of confused thinking and muddled motives and illumines the true circumstances of our life with the clarity of death.

It reveals Government policy which for all of Steve's life has sought to impose white domination on South Africa, with power and violence. To this end the country has been put on a war footing, and a military presence rules the townships, terrorises the population, and burdens the economy. Youths are trained to hate and kill, or assaulted by bullets, gas and dogs. The Minister of Justice, disclaiming responsibility for such atrocities, fails to explain why his methods cannot prevent people jumping from windows, hanging themselves, or starving themselves to death. Government policy and practice is seen to be abhorrent to those concerned for the Kingdom of God.

It reveals the position of those who support the status quo. By their votes, their acquiescence, their investments, their excuses, or the nauseating fascist-type enthusiasm of their political rallies, they support this oppressive regime, and share responsibility for the deaths it causes. There is no way forward except through repentance.

It reveals the blindness of the authorities: Far from intimidating the population, repression has stiffened people's resolve, immeasurably. Under the anguish of Steve Biko's death is a total commitment to remove the heretical horror of apartheid, once and for all.

It reveals the weak folly of those who think in terms of trying to reform the Government. A false Gospel, an evil blinding ideology, cannot be reformed; it must be rejected. The only acceptable form is total and fundamental change.

It reveals that Black Consciousness, in direct rejection of charges of racism and communism, is accepted by many of all races as a valid and vital part of man's quest for that fullness of humanity and liberation which Christ proclaimed.

One of the moments of truth in the life of Jesus is recounted in Luke 19:41–44, when Jesus saw that his society was bent on a course that led inevitably to its destruction. 'If you only knew today what is needed for peace! But now you cannot see it! The days will come when your enemies will surround you with barricades, blockade you, and close in on you from every side. They will completely destroy you and the people within you walls; not a single stone will they leave in its place, because you did not recognise the time when God came to save you.'

Yet into the heart of this troublesome period he sent his disciples to spread the Gospel of the Kingdom throughout the Earth.

A similar awareness has come to many with the death of Steve Biko. It is a portentous event. From the ghettos of Ginsberg to the chancelleries of the West his death leads to a clear awareness that this ungodly and revolting society will be destroyed. Judgement and the destruction of evil are inescapable facets of history and scripture.

In this turmoil of a collapsing society Christ calls for people with vision, conviction and courage to reach out together for the real power of brotherhood and a whole community. Bodies will die, hearts will break, but nothing will detain our spirits or deter God's purpose.

Document 120. Editorial on the funeral of Steve Biko by M. V. Mrwetyana, *Isaziso* (Umtata), late 1977

As one of the most responsible and moderate true Black newspapers in South Africa, we want to give a serious warning to South Africa to either change discrimination against Blacks today or face a bloody revolution very soon. We say this without any madness or Black power in our heads but as a result of careful and objective analysis of the intense atmosphere at Steve Biko's funeral service in King Williamstown last Sunday. One speaker made it loud and clear that the late Steve Biko was peaceful and non-violent yet was victim of this system; however, he leaves behind Black men and women who have an alternative if non-violent protests are not met. "But we are not helpless," Mr Fikile Bam of Zimele Trust said it most sincerely and this statement fetched a thunderous applause from the 25,000 mourners. There was visible anger whenever speaker after speaker mentioned the torture and brutality meted out to Black people in South Africa by the Government officials such that angry interjections like "Biko is the very last to die under South Africa's security laws," were shouted repeatedly. The Black conscious-ness movement as an organisation is basically against violence. To under-stand that, one has to read from the speeches by speakers who paid tribute, but the Police, we repeat, the Police, some of them are provocative. Sometimes either out of ignorance or ineptitude, they will go out of their way, brag about their power of the barrel, handcuffs and dogs even to highly charged situations. For instance Biko died in the hands of the Police.

Though we hold Oom Kruger [Minister of Justice Jimmy Kruger] and his government responsible for his death, the point is that the Police are directly responsible. With due respect to the Police force as a career, we feel that some of them [should] be taught to differentiate between criminal and political acts. Like for instance, a Policeman could get away with shooting a burglar but torturing and killing [Mapetla] Mohapi, Biko, [O. R.] Tiro and Soweto students made the blood of all Blacks in Africa boil because the reason here is based on the colour and leaders who fight to end injustices perpetrated by South Africa to Blacks. It is only a fool who maintains that Blacks are disunited and Vorster's belief that Biko was not known is nonsense. His police will tell him that 25,000 people attended Steve's funeral and twelve buses were turned back by Police in Transvaal. Vorster's and Kruger's funeral combined would be so cold and insignificant that they will never match up to Biko's in the number of mourners and sympathisers let alone telegrams and messages from all over the world. For that matter no Black faces would be seen at their funerals because of their policies.

Black people in South Africa have lost one of their greatest leaders but Biko's death has not been in vain. His spirit is very much alive. After his death thousands of people began to be aware of his organisation and are with it in spirit. His death, make no mistake, has united the Black people who rededicated themselves to his cause on September 25. Cries like "Kruger, the murderer" from the audience are eloquent signs to indicate to an average person where the wind is blowing.

We shudder to see the day when all what we together built over centuries, disappearing overnight as though Afrikaner leaders and individual leaders in Southern Africa were a jumble of unschooled idiots. Like any people, the Blacks in South Africa, for God's sake demand an equal treatment or at least [to] be seen as human beings and not objects. The same thing the Boers wanted under the British yoke. Nothing and no power of man will ever stop this desire on the part of Black people. South Africa knows this clearly but she is trading on time—something if overdone would bring this country to ruins. No guns, no jails and no detention laws will ever stop this will. Again we repeat our advice to South Africa to change today or face a bloody revolution "too ghastly to contemplate" [quotation from speech by Vorster].

DOCUMENT 121. "The Banning of 18 Black Consciousness Organisations." Unsigned flyer, October 1977

It is a very pathetic situation for the WHOLE GOVERNMENT of South Africa to apply naked conspicuous tactics by attempting to cripple Black Assertiveness. By these bannings it has been proved beyond any reasonable doubt that the White Government has reached a point where its sources of tricks have been exhausted. They have untactfully banned the verbal black consciousness, and left the whole spiritual black consciousness with the people.

The Government has proved itself to be 100% unchristian. They have proved beyond any reasonable doubt that theirs is to legalise injustices on this earth and illegitimise justice in this once Peaceful land of BLACKS. The proofs to this effect are:

1. They brutally murdered black people in Sharpeville, for conducting peaceful demonstration against DOM PASSES [pass books]. This we will never forget until final victory.

2. They underpaid our parents, who in turn decided to sacrifice from their meagre remuneration to see to the education of their children. They proved to be assertive by building schools of their own, but still the unchristian government decided to ill-display their uncouthness.

3. On the 16th June 1976 Black Students demonstrated against the use of AFRIKAANS as a medium of instruction. Instead the illegitimate South African Regime which boasts of democracy, mercilessly massacred helpless, innocent armless [unarmed] young black students. Imagine a 13 year old Hector Pieterson dropping dead at the hands of a legalised-gangster element i.e. White Policemen.

4. They indignantly murdered one of the most democratic assertive, prospective and humble national black leaders, The Honourable STEVE BANTU BIKO.

5. They again decided stupidly to ban the cream of black leaders and legalised their theft by taking the BCP properties and monies to go and give to the defence force which in turn shoots black armless children. They closed down clinics [i.e. the BCP's Zanempilo Clinic in King William's Town], through which blacks proved their ability to be independent of whites which indirectly pricked them.

It is very unfortunate for the Government that we know that those bannings and detentions without trial were paving [the] way for the following:

a. To promote the Community Councils which are still UBC's at their best levels.
b. To bulldoze us by increasing rents, smoothly since we appeared to be leaderless.
c. To seduce opposition to the implementation of apartheid.
d. To destroy any form of recognised leadership relevant to the black community.

It was a most naked stupidity for the government to decide to ban a student body which it never legalised nor approved of their existence. We want to make it clear to our brothers and sisters that we shall not despair, nor shall we retreat, instead we shall go on through your faithful support until final victory.

To you Kruger, we are giving you up to the 31/11/77 to uplift the bannings and the detentions of our leaders unconditionally. OR ELSE!!! Only through unity shall we stand. *MA AFRICA* [Mother Africa] VICTORY IS CERTAIN.
POWER!!!

DOCUMENT 122. Statement of a Crossroads resident, Mrs. N., 1978

Having been directed by the inspectors to come and build here we came by car. Then we went to look for some zincs [corrugated iron sheets] in the scrapyard and then we were able to put up this pondok [shack]. It was on a clear day in February. There were a few Coloured houses in the area. I would imagine there were about six. But to a great extent the area was bush. I am one of the first residents here at Crossroads. The BAAB [Bantu Affairs Administration Board] inspectors actually pointed out to us that this was an area allocated for Africans. One white inspector especially came to us and told us that.

We worked very hard to build this home. We cleared the bush, then we laid down mats. We initially built up a shelter to prevent the wind from blowing at the primus stoves. On the first night we were not able to put on the roof (the zincs) and we were told to build some toilets ourselves. Then we were only able to get water pipes installed after three months, as a result of some nurses, I would think. We had to fetch water from the Coloured families on the other side of the road.

The first people who came with us were the people who were staying there with us at Brown's Farm. Then people came from the airport area. And then more and more people came from various areas as individual families but we came as a village/settlement from Brown's Farm. I still have the same neighbours with whom I came. Some people came from the townships, some were women who were staying with their men in the 'single' quarters. They came with their husbands here and built their homes. There were some people whose houses were demolished by the Board Inspectors.

One of the important events which happened upon our coming here was the harassment and arrests. People were continually arrested and their houses demolished and that troubled our lives for some time. We were maltreated for some time and I was also arrested. They used to send people who were speaking on our behalf. We spent sleepless nights, would see some torches in the early hours of the morning and we knew that they were arrested: kubomvu (to raid). They used to come as early as 2 a.m. We would see about 16 or 17 vans surrounding the area. And the whole area would be lit up as if there was electricity at Crossroads, whereas there is none here at Crossroads! They would light up with the vans, and then use the torches, so that it was as if it was daylight.

I like staying here at Crossroads very much. I like it because now we pay rent, water has been installed and they are servicing the toilets. I have a certain measure of security, and I'm not thinking of moving anywhere. Though at this moment in time I have been informed that I must move from here, and this is a problem for me because life here at Crossroads is quiet. Life is not the same as it is in the townships because, you, see, here I am breeding chickens and even these dogs. They help us. They keep away troublemakers and in the townships, this you cannot do. In the township you cannot do what you like.

The question of me moving over to another area is still a problem for me and I do not know how it will resolve itself. There is definitely a difference between Crossroads and KTC [another squatter area]. One noticeable thing is the smallness of the plots allocated to people at KTC. Here we more or less allocated areas to ourselves but there they are allocated for them. As a result we have somewhat bigger houses than they have at KTC. I have been informed that I'm going to be moved. I feel powerless to resist though I am renting here as a resident. If I could resist I would but I know they are going to use the pass issue as a leverage to force me to go especially when I have to go and change it. In that way then they may be able to force me because they may refuse to renew my pass when it is due. It goes absolutely against the grain to leave this place. I have no intention. It hurts me to know I must leave.

With women who have come here to join their husbands I think it is right and just that they should stay together. Quite some time ago it was said that it is permissible for a person who quaifies to marry anyone from any area and come and stay here in Cape Town. Nowadays I observe that married women are harassed and arrested. I would imagine this is because we are the oppressed race. But according to the law of truth the wife is supposed to be where the husband qualifies to be. Wives are supposed to be alone with their husbands.

At the time that I was arrested we were sixteen people. And then I had to stand for the case and the magistrate said that he found me guilty but there was no basis for sentencing me, because he is supposed to sentence and he said that he himself was not clear. According to the questions of the lawyer I was said to have rights to be here but I was charged for trespass. The question is how could a person who has rights be accused of trespass? But it was clear that the magistrate had to sentence me, find me guilty, and he did. I was fined R10 or 14 days, and paid R10. It was quite a painful experience to go through because I felt powerless. They could do whatever they wanted to do, and I couldn't stop them. And I was thinking they could also demolish my house and make me stay in the open without a house.

My belief is this: that when you are married to your husband, whether he be working in Cape Town or whatever, according to standards of refinement or culture, you should stay together where he is working. Stay together. Because you are depending on this husband for food, for clothing, for shelter and in case of illness. Because it is difficult for a male person to be away from his wife. It does happen that men will have a girlfriend, they'll have children during the time that you as a wife are in the country. By the time you wake up you discover that you are incompatible with your husband and that he has problems of maintaining other children. Even though he may not marry the other girl he is legally supposed to support those children because he found himself in a situation of temptation during the time that you were not together. It is the law that separates that is to blame here. Because husband and wife are supposed to be together at all times.

Before I came here to Crossroads I spent many years as a subtenant in Guguletu. I stayed in NY 55 and also Section 64, and at Section 2 in NY 50. And in the end I resorted to staying in the bush. The reason why I went to the bush is because there are all sorts of problems staying as a subtenant. It is that there is you, your husband and your children. If there are no problems between the two families in that way, it might be about cooking, problems around organising and paying for groceries because you may not have equal means and in most instances the owner of the house, even if he doesn't have money, expects to eat, and quite often he is not to blame for not having money. But the tenant is.

I once had the experience of the house I lived in being demolished. It was in Guguletu, the pondok in the backyard. Also on Brown's farm, when we had to move over here, the house was demolished. At Guguletu they told me when I went to renew my pass that I must remove the house and they warned me again and again, using the rights of my pass as a way to making me do it. They demolished it whilst I was at work. Also at Brown's farm we were informed to move away. And whilst I came over here to build this house here, they were busy removing the houses there. When I came back I found my belongings in the open.

Fortunately I had my children with me because they removed all the building materials, the zincs, leaving my furniture and my suitcases in the open. In this instance they did not specify when they would demolish but when I came back there was no house. Though my spirit was troubled there was nobody there that I could ask but I knew that it was the act of the inspectors. I felt very bad and I heard from my Coloured neighbours that the inspectors came and demolished.

It does seem that the black nation is always regarded as a child. History has been this: that those who regard themselves as adults have been making laws whatever their nature, just or unjust, and we have always been receiving them because we cannot say 'no'. We have no choice to speak. You are not asked whether you like this. You are told 'do this' (*Yehza nje John! T.*) We are forced to do things like that.

Crossroads is supposed to stand. It is proper for it to stand. Crossroads is in the area of the XHOSAS. I do not see why it should be demolished because even the office where Guguletu people pay rent is in the area here. It cannot be said to be a Coloured area. The area is absolutely definitely Xhosa. Mostly because nothing was done in this area. That is why the Divisional Council placed us here. I think then that since we have been paying rent, allowed to rent, that we should be allowed to continue to do so, instead of being tossed about, pushed around. This is still part of Nyanga East in as much as KTC is part of Nyanga. Life will definitely be different at KTC from what it is here and I won't be able to breed my chickens. Here we had enough space and I fenced around, though KTC does not have the same facilities as the townships, life seems to be the same in these two areas. I am particularly concerned about the size of the plots and the houses are too close to each other. Here we were told to allow space in between the houses to prevent fire from spreading easily.

Document 123. Speech by Reverend Sam Buti at Day of Solidarity with Crossroads, July 30, 1978

Scripture Reading: Matthew 25: 31–46
Text: Matthew 25: 40 and 45

"I tell you, whenever you did this for one of the least important of these brothers of mine, you did it for me!" It brings us to the theological question of Anselm "Cur Deus Homo." He came to liberate man to be true man for and of man.

My dear brothers and sisters in Christ Jesus, I would like to thank the Ministers' Fraternal of Langa, Guguletu and Nyanga for having invited me to conduct this Ecumenical service here at Crossroads this afternoon.

How pleased I would be if I could say something joyful to the people of the Crossroads, and the people of the entire South Africa. If I could say something you could afterwards carry back to your homes and community to comfort and encourage you. Unfortunately, I haven't got the words myself, but this afternoon I will ask God to speak to us through the message of Jesus Christ in the parable which we have just read. Christ's message in this parable is very clear. This message is the acid test. It is the acid test placed before the church of Christ. It is the acid test placed before the rulers. The conclusive proof of one's LOVE for Christ is found in the concrete expression of one's compassion to one's fellow-man in need. To neglect this, or to refuse to identify oneself with the need and suffering of the oppressed, the poor, the hungry, the naked, the stranger and the imprisoned is the conclusive proof of one's total lack of love.

Cape Town and Cape Peninsula is in need of the labour of the people of

Crossroads. Without them the wheels of industry which churn out the riches, the dividends and wealth for those who possess the money, would not be possible. The sweat of the black labour is indispensable to the sweet life of the white management. But Christ wishes to point out in this parable and elsewhere in the scripture: that you dare not accept a man's sweat and labour and at the same time reject him as a person; you dare not view him purely as a labour unit and dismiss or ignore him as a human being. If you accept him as a human being, then you must accept his normal basic needs, and make provision for such needs as: family life, housing, transportation, medical care, recreation and education. Anything less than this is exploitation—in fact it could even become another form of slavery.

In the history of our country we have a number of such acts of removing and resettling people which have cast a stigma on the name of our land; I name the following, there are so many of them, where is Sophiatown? Where is Lady Selborne? Pageview and Alexandra, the area in which I live. And today we stand before Crossroads: the name which is symbolic of the road which can lead to the Cross, the cross of suffering and pain for the inmates of the squatter camp if they are again driven out into the wilderness, or should I say into the sea of frustration which our rulers themselves are afraid of. But it could also become a Cross for the rulers who would be responsible for driving the community out of their living area. My fellow Christians how much more must happen in this way of suffering, this via dolorosa, before the consciences of the white community and rulers of this country cry out loud and clear: "Stop! It is enough!" or—if this does not happen—how much longer will it be until the wrath of God calls down judgement on the white rulers of this land by saying: *Mene, mene tekel upharsin*—numbered, numbered, weighed, found wanting and removed (Daniel, 5:24).

The writing is on the wall, and the message is clear for everyone to read, the criteria of Christ's test has been spelled out; Love your neighbour as yourself. "I tell you whenever you did this for one of the least important of these brothers of mine, you did it for me!" (Matthew 25:40).

My brothers and sisters, I agree and I am sure you agree with Saint Aquinas, that: An unjust law is a human law that is not rooted in the eternal law of God and the natural law. Any law that uplifts human personalities is just and any law that degrades human personality is unjust. And in Saint Augustine's words: "An unjust law is no law at all!" It must be stated clear here and now to our rulers that a law that persecutes people for living as husband, wife and children together is no law at all, it is sin. There are some instances when a law is just on its face but unjust in its application. There are a lot of instances which can prove this. The law is unjust when people as these at the Crossroads are being persecuted for living a normal family life here in Cape Town near their place of work.

I appeal to the white churches, I appeal to all Christians, more especially the Dutch Reformed Churches, to make a plea to the government on behalf of the people of Crossroads. Remember the judgment is upon the Church as never before. If the Church of today does not recapture the sacrificial spirit of the early Church it will lose its authentic ring, forfeit the loyalty of thousands of its adherents, and be dismissed as an irrelevant social club with no meaning.

I call upon the government of the Republic of South Africa, let Justice roll like waters, and Righteousness like a mighty stream. Will the people in authority and power hear and heed the writing is on the wall, the wording which is vivid: "I tell you, whenever you did this for one of the least important of these brothers of mine, you did it for me."

My brothers and sisters, this is the deep theological meaning of the text we have read. Christ became Man, Man for God. He became Man, Man for men. He has come to liberate us from the bondage of selfishness. I appeal to all Christians, Come let us identify ourselves with the people of the Crossroads. In conclusion, I address myself to the people of the Crossroads. God showers upon you words of hope. You should not despair. Keep courage." Comfort my people" says our God. "Comfort my people." Amen.

DOCUMENT 124. Minutes of the annual congress of the Writers' Association of South Africa, Roodepoort, August 31–September 3, 1979

PRESENT:

National Executive Committee: Zwelakhe Sisulu, Phil Mtimkulu, Thami Mazwai and Willie Bokala.

REGIONS:

Southern Transvaal: Enoch Duma, Joe Thloloe, Goba Ndlovu, Jon Qwelane, Mike Norton, Derrick Thema, Zandi Sikwebu, Solly Liefman, Matthew Makobane, Ernest Shuenyane, George Luse, Willie Nkosi, Gabu Tugwana, Sinnah Kunene, Zodwa Mshibe, Ameen Akhalwaya, Mandla Nklazi, Dan Radinku, Nathan Molope, Sekola Sello, Bessie Banda, Mashadi Mashabela, Nkopane Makobane, Vusi Radebe, Chris More.

Western Cape: Rashid Seria, Aneez Salie, Enrico Kemp, Sakiem Samodien.

Natal: M Subramoney.

Port Elizabeth: Mono Badela, Tessa Sehume.

Witbank: John Simelane, Petros Mthimunye, Matthews Ncongwane.

Pretoria: Maluse Matsemela.

Pietersburg: D Langa, Mathata Tsedu, K Makhado.

Border: Thulashe Damane, Charles Nqakula, Matthew Moonieya, Barbara Geza, Lifa Gqasana.

Orange Free State: Seruthu Seruthu, AS Selekisho, M Mosimane, L Tsenoli.

Kimberley: Ronnie Joel.

Umtata: Sydney Moses.

REPRESENTATION:

Diplomats: Britain—Bill Vose, John Taylor: Canada—Janet Graham;

France—Jean Michel: Sweden—Cecilia Hogland; Switzerland—Dr Rolf Bodenmuller; Norway—John Ramberg; Netherlands; United States—Richard Roth; Sigrid Maitrejean.

Press: International Federation of Journalists (IFJ)—Mike Pitso; Lesotho Union of Journalist—Mike Pitso, National Public Radio (USA)—Julie Frederickse, observer from California—Pearl Marsh.

Local Bodies: Tom Manthata, George Wauchope and Kehla Mthembu (Committee of 10), N J K Molope (Teachers Action Committee).

Speakers: Father [Lebamang] Sebidi (guest speaker), Mr. Ratha Mokgoathleng, Dr Allan Boesak, and Mrs [Winifred] Kgware,

SEPTEMBER 1

The third congress of WASA was opened by the president, Mr Zwelakhe Sisulu. The vice-president Mr Phil Mtimkulu, welcomed the guests and introduced all the observers who included foreign diplomats and people from local organisations. The WASA delegates introduced themselves.

The house paid tribute to detained colleague, Thami Mkhwanazi, banned lawyer, Mrs Priscilla Jana, and all other victims of security legislation. Hereafter the president and the guest speaker, Father Lebamang Sebidi read their addresses to congress.

Minutes of Last Congress

The secretary, Mr Thami Mazwai, read the minutes of the last congress and they were adopted.

MATTERS ARISING:

There was general unhappiness about the failure of NEC [National Executive Committee] to write to the editor of POST, Mr Percy Qoboza and news-editor, Mr Aggrey Klaaste, objecting to their acceptance of the Pringle Award from the Southern Africa Society of Journalists (SASJ).

NEC clarified query on "action to be taken against journalists who bring WASA into disrepute" to mean journalists who raise money or make representation on behalf of WASA for their own ends.

It was suggested that NEC should scrutinise journalists who want to join WASA. Since there was no unanimity on this point it was decided to defer it to the Constitutional Committee.

The house also urged NEC to make a positive protest about the usage of the word "Black" because certain newspapers were using it for only one section (Africans) of the People who constitute this group.

Secretarial Report

The secretary read the secretarial report. It was adopted.

MATTERS ARISING:

The Prisoners Education Committee which is attempting to have the South African authorities to allow security prisoners to study beyond matric came under discussions. It was not clear whether it was a Black or White organisation. It emerged however that it was originally started by Blacks but later Whites joined and they were playing a superior role. It was suggested that WASA together with other organisations should look into PEC.

NEC explained to the house the absence of the Federated Union of Black Artists. FUBA is not a Black organisation per se. It has White members in their Board of Trustees.

CORRESPONDENCE:
Correspondence was read by the secretary.

Vice-Presidential Report
The vice-president-organiser's report was read by Mr Mtimkulu.

MATTERS ARISING:
It was suggested that KWASA which [is] WASA's bulletin should be produced quarterly and cheaper paper should be used. Mr Mtimkulu had explained that expensive paper was used as KWASA was the organisation's prestige publication and durable paper should be used because newsprint fades with time.

Mr Mtimkulu then gave [a] rundown of the Lord Thomson Foundation muddle. A journalism course to be run by the Lord Thomson Foundation is planned for October. Mr Mtimkulu had been liaising with a representative of the British Embassy, Mr Taylor, who are partly sponsoring the course. Mr Taylor had secured a class at the South African Associated Newspapers, despite assurances that the course will not be held on SAAN [South African Associated Newspapers] premises as WASA was unhappy about this venue.

After a lengthy debate on this issue it was decided that a letter be written to the British Embassy voicing our displeasure. However Mr Bill Vose who represented the Embassy intervened and suggested that the matter be left in abeyance and he will get Mr Taylor to attend the congress on Monday to give his explanation on the "muddle."

TRADE UNIONISM:
Mr Joe Thloloe read a paper on trade unionism. The house was divided into commissions. The commissions returned and tabled their reports. From their reports the following motions were adopted:

1. WASA agrees that it will broaden its base to involve all Black workers in the newspapers industry.

Now therefore, this Congress resolves to appoint a committee to meet with other Black workers in the different categories of the newspaper industry to discuss and effect the implementation of this principle.

And, furthermore, whereas this Congress appreciates the necessity for a united Black worker force in this country; now, therefore, this Congress also resolves to forge links with other Black workers and unions with similar ideals.

And wheras this Congress accepts the importance for WASA to involve itself in community issue;

Now, therefore, this Congress resolves that WASA shall in future relate itself more closely to the community and its aspirations for liberation.

This ended the day's congress deliberations. In the evening there was a drama presentation, "Isandhlwana."

Council members however held a Council meeting.

SEPTEMBER 2

Regional reports opened the congress on Sunday.

Western Cape: They have had tremendous success in membership drive. Membership is now 24 with hopes for more members.

Planning to appoint permanent organiser and to initiate community newsletter called *Grassroots*.

A training scheme has been started on an informal basis.

The following Blacks have addressed the region, Professor Mphahlehle, Dr Allan Boesak, Mr Buntu Mfunyana and Mr Richard Stevens.

Natal: Progress and activity in WASA Natal over the past year has been fluctuating according to their report. The problem is that there is no follow-up of enthusiastic support for projects and ideas from meetings.

Irregular attendances at meetings has also been a problem.

On the credit side they now have representatives from eight Natal newspapers bringing their membership to 14.

Border: The region was complimented for their good report. They had a single copy of their report. They however promised to avail it to other regions. They had made headway in their area and were recruiting more members.

Port Elizabeth: They also did not have sufficient copies of their report. They also promised to send it to other regions later.

Points: (1) Banning of congress last year had adverse effect on potential members (2) Members who joined them from other newspapers are now full members (3) Region observed October 19, and June 16 commemorations (4) Security Police keeping close watch on their chairman (5) They are keeping in close contact with other Black organisations (6) They have two freelancers—a student and a fulltime industrial worker.

Witbank: They apologised for not having made sufficient copies of their report. They also promised to circulate their report to other regions. They have 34 members but only 18 are active.

They cannot raise funds because most of their members are still students.

They have not implemented any projects yet. They are however thinking of starting a mobile library, poetry reading sessions and a Miss WASA contest. The house discouraged them from holding a beauty contest.

It was suggested that they should put more effort in recruiting adults.

It was also agreed that a projects committee which will advise the regions on what kinds of projects to implement should be formed.

Pietersburg: The chairman read their report. The report was not accepted and the region was told to go and prepare a coherent report.

Orange Free State: This region was making its first appearance at congress. It was operating on an interim basis. They were however commended for the efforts they have made. They are planning a symposium to honour the International Year of the Child.

Kimberley and *Umtata* who will soon be fully fledged branches gave brief reports on their impressions and problems. Mr Ronnie Joel who was the Kimberley delegate said he would convey his impressions to his colleagues.

Southern Transvaal: Theirs was a comprehensive report. Their membership stands at 101. They have eight units. Two ad hoc committees—finance and projects—and welfare officer were appointed. They reported on their projects:

   (i)   A Black Press Agency
  (ii)   A Seminar on Modern Journalistic Techniques.
 (iii)   A communication week-end.

Pace [a magazine secretly sponsored by the government] issue was raised by delegates. Mr Mtimkulu explained that the matter was under investigation since they now have new owners.

Western Cape: The Fatti's and Moni's boycott was raised. Western Cape was asked to give guidance on the matter. The house wanted to know if there was any contact between Western Cape region and the sacked workers of Fatti's and Moni's.

Aneez Salie said they were supporting the workers. WASA members were given preference by the Fatti's and Moni's workers when they wanted to release a statement.

Quraish Patel read his paper followed by Ratha Mokgoathleng. House divided into commissions—2 for each paper. Following motions were adopted:

(a) That this 3rd Annual Congress of WASA hereby resolves that Black Consciousness be the necessary base on which workers can become conscious of themselves as a class and that all means should be used to conscientise black people along these broader principles.

Therefore, this congress calls on NEC to convene a symposium on this broader consciousness with a view to giving further political direction.

(b) This Congress, convinced:

(i) that so-called multi-racial or non-racial organisations in this country only help to denude blacks of their self-respect and dignity;

(ii) that dummy institutions like the community councils—that merely echo their master's voice when they increase rents, claiming to be independent budget-makers—the Coloured Representative Council, the South African Indian Council, the so-called homeland governments and their politics, Dr. Piet Koornhof's regional committees, are red herrings designed to get us at each others' throats and divert us from the goal of liberaton; and

(iii) that only blacks, who are at the bottom of the South African social structure know the meaning of oppression, are capable of bringing about meaningful change;

Calls on all blacks to stop collaborating in any manner with the oppressor by voluntarily participating in their own oppression.

Evening Session consisted of address by Mrs Kgware.

MONDAY—SEPTEMBER 3:

The resolutions committee which was appointed the previous day presented the resolutions.

Except for one resolution most of the resolutions were adopted with little or no motivation as they were common cause.

Dr Allan Boesak was congress's last speaker.

The constitutional committee presented amendments to the constitution

ELECTIONS:

The following people were elected into the expanded NEC.
Zwelakhe Sisulu—President
Phil Mtimkulu—National Secretary
Willie Bokala—Treasurer

Vice-Presidents:
Charles Nqakula—Senior Vice-president
Thami Mazwai, Rashid Seria and Marimutu Subramoney.

DOCUMENT 125. Speech by Zwelakhe Sisulu, president, to the annual congress of the Writers' Association of South Africa, Roodepoort, August 31–September 3, 1979

Today we pay tribute to the spirit of our time—the spirit of Black solidarity. It is a spirit born and nurtured in bondage but that will culminate in the freedom of all our people. Today we recall our heroes, compatriots and colleagues languishing in jail for their beliefs, forced out of the fatherland for their commitment, to become wanderers of the world. This is an occasion for us to renew the belief in ourselves and what we stand for, to renew our belief in the rightness of our cause. The message we bring to you is the message of Black solidarity that is based on the firm understanding that we will achieve the Black ideal and all that we set out to do, and be free from the impediments of political creation that have for so long trammelled Black aspirations, that have removed from us leaders of great vision and children of courage. Remember today the names of Biko, Mandela, Sobukwe. Remember colleagues Juby Mayet, Thenjie Mtintso, Isaac Moroe.

The frontier wars of centuries ago are still being fought in the dark dungeons of this country's prisons. We have witnessed, for decades on end, the systematic strangulation of Black culture, of the Black way of life, of the very being of Black people. A people's culture is the cornerstone of their freedom, and in times of oppression it becomes the cornerstone of their resistance. This brutal onslaught by a marauding white invading force has not ceased, it has spiralled, gaining momentum as it confronts more resistance.

If you are a lover of freedom, as we are, you will recall the events of October 1977, when Black people awoke to a grey dawn of blatant repression—robbed of even a whisper of protest. If you are a lover of freedom you will know that these acts were arbitrary, callous, despotic and shameless, and if you are a lover of freedom you will know that repression breeds resistance. That is why today we call on all lovers of freedom to stand together and fight until there is no life left in us or until our land is free. Grave inroads have been made into the freedom of the press—the banning and detention of journalists continues, propaganda monstrosities in the media have been elaborately set up. These attacks are not aimed at the press as an institution. We must realise that they are aimed at the press as the conscience of a land ridden by its own guilt, a land entrapped in its own racial ideologies. Having silenced the press this racist regime devised a scheme to bring into being propaganda monsters that would manipulate Black thinking, to temper Black impatience and to arouse a false sense of security in our communities—while on the borders sons of this land die from their bullets. We say there can't be press freedom while the majority of the people in our land do not control their destiny, when the worker cannot bargain for his labour. As long as all these basic freedoms of our people do not exist, no other form of freedom can exist. Freedom either exists completely or does not exist at all. It is in this spirit that we assert today that we are part of the social and political dynamic of the Black people—we are part of the situation before we can be assessors of that situation. We no longer fear, for once confronted by fear, you begin to understand that fear feeds on itself, it becomes an entity in itself—no longer needing a perpetrator.

We know that this government is making strained efforts to drive Black people into the laager [circle of pioneer wagons] with them, not as part of the laager but as part of the buffer—this is their total strategy. We have seen how this strategy tries to delay the inevitable by claiming to move away from discrimination. We have seen how as part of this strategy this government seeks to use the trade union movement as an active agent of its racist, diabolical policies. These attempts are all aimed at gaining more control of trade unions, the church, schools, the press, and all other remaining bastions of protest and resistance. This is the strategy against the Black man—and no Black man can escape the truth of his situation—no Black man can ignore the historical imperative that awaits him—a clear directive that you do not call for change—you make change.

Under the pretext of a more liberal dispensation, through various commissions on the trade union movement, the white Government tries to use the workers to police its racist thinking, and consolidate its policies. This is geared to stop the Black worker from responding to the universal cry: "Workers of the world unite." This government seeks to place Black people in carefully selected pockets where their movements can be monitored and kept in check. Why should this government suddenly show interest in the Black worker when it has:

Brutally destroyed his leadership, systematically driven him off the land, when it continuously insults his dignity, banishes his children to some desolate place in the country and kills his children in cold blood. Remember the fallen children of Soweto and all other areas of conscience in our country.

We are engaged in a protracted struggle that knows no bounds and no laws. It is in the spirit of our time that we say that no political or military force, however vicious, callous and mighty will stop our fervour for freedom. What the Black man wants is what every rational man wants.

We believe in the inherent nobility of Black Consciousness as a vehicle for the worker's aspirations. We believe that black consciousness and its message of black self-reliance are an imperative phase in our struggle, an indispensable part of the chain. We say that Black Consciousness is an idea whose time has come. It is a progressive force that reflects the mood and needs of the people.

WASA says the interests of the worker are paramount in this struggle. We say they are the very essence of our struggle. As I speak to you countless honourable sons and daughters of this land have been forced out of the fatherland, more lie still in the silence of their graves, others have become wanderers of the continent—but it shall not always be so. We were a free people once, and again we shall be a free people. You and I do not know what tomorrow brings, we do not know our fate, that is why it is important to speak up while we can, because they will come for you too as they have come for the church, for the students and our leaders. We reject peripheral changes, we reject gradual change, we say that change in this country shall be determined by the majority of the people in this country. Change is something that Black people will achieve, it is not something that they will be given.

There are certain things that we live for and are prepared to die for, things that we love, honour and cherish, there are things without which man cannot live in peace, and that thing is freedom.

Without freedom there can be no peace, without peace there can be no development, in industry and human relations, without this development the whole country crumbles. Remember the visions of Biko and Sobukwe—unfulfilled and violently ended.

The humanism and strength that God gave us will sustain us into another glorious day.

The detention and harassment of Black journalists and writers continues unrestrained, but we want to pledge that we shall not be intimidated, we shall not cower at these methods, the scourge of [words missing] but we shall continue to fight, we shall fight wherever racism rears its head, we shall fight whenever the life of our people is threatened, we shall fight whenever the dignity of man is at stake. Today there is turmoil in our land, there is the decimation of whole communities by hunger, there is an abrogation of human rights, of basic rights to life. In the Road Ahead we will encounter blood, there will be death in this great struggle, there will be pain, there will be sorrow and fear, but we shall continue to strive for truth until victory is won. We must go on participating in this struggle with abounding energy, dedication and resourcefulness.

We hold that nonparticipation is as much a moral evil as is collaboration. We hold that silence is as much a moral evil as is participation without conviction. It had to take an oppressed people to value and cherish the concept of freedom, that where it does not exist men who love it shall guard it with their lives. We shall continue to sing and chant and fight until freedom is attained.

We shall be steadfast, unyielding and immovable until final victory. We shall die in this struggle, but it shall not be in vain.

We shall not stand idly by while children are being robbed of a normal life. We believe in the Black ideal, we believe in the rule of law.

We shall not be intimidated by diabolical, unjustifiable and unpardonable acts perpetrated by agents of this State.

We believe in human dignity.

When we achieve our ideal, there will be peace in our land and there will be freedom. And the people shall govern.

Document 126. Resolutions adopted at the inaugural conference of the Azanian People's Organisation, Roodepoort, September 29–30, 1979

1. This congress noting that religion has been used by the oppressor to keep blacks in perpetual bondage with dogmas preached that they strive for a life beyond death.

   That it is used to justify the continued tutelage of the black man, and that blacks are subjected to this indoctrination from infancy, hereby resolve:

(a) To initiate religious training programmes for all children through religious classes that will teach the black child the message of religion as it relates to the child's human dignity.

(b) Assist the Black Priests Solidarity Group to embark on a membership and conscientising drive of all black priests with the message of liberation as a driving force.

(c) Involve ourselves in our respective churches where we will play a significant role in giving direction to the church, the minister and his council.

(d) Involve or embark on projects with religious youth clubs and societies that will make them play a more direct role in community and religious work with the emphasis on black self help.

Mover: Joe Thloloe
Seconder: Zwelakhe Sisulu

2.   (a) That this Congress rejects the forthcoming ethnic elections for the South African Indian Council and such related bodies and Azapo therefore pledges active support for the Solidarity Front and all other bodies campaigning against these elections.

(b) That in the event of any Press statement being released by AZAPO, it be given to WASA only.

(c) That AZAPO recognizing that all black people are one wishes to remind blacks within the reserves of Venda, Bophuthatswana, Transkei that the struggle continues with them.

Mover: Curtis Nkondo
Seconder: Letsatsi Mosala

3. Noting that as blacks we are in a weakened position to fight for our rights on a political platform, and further noting that whatever resistance we have given in the past to the inhuman laws of the country was met with brute force with hundreds of our people killed, and realising that the oppressor has now extended his ideological war to the labour front.

This congress hereby resolves to play a positive role in this new dimension of the struggle by:

(1) embarking on an awareness and aid program regarding labour issues with clinics and seminars;

(2) training a corps of at least 10 members to act as researchers into trade unionism and labour issues;

(3) making approaches to present trade union leaders for joint strategy talks;

(4) organising a summit involving all trade union leaders;

(5) preparing documentation on trade unionism and labour issues with some documents in our language.

Mover: Thami Mazwai
Seconder: Derrick Thema

4. That a commission be appointed to investigate organisations and other local bodies purporting to be relevant to the black struggle and give a full report on each organisation to the National Council [which] will in turn decide whether such organisations are relevant or hostile to the aims, principles and interests of Azapo and give some direction on their activities in order to avoid confusion and misunderstanding.

Mover: Gabriel Malaka
Seconder: Zakes Mofokeng.

Document 127. Statement by families of the Makgatho tribe on their forced removal, northern Transvaal, September 1979

500 FAMILIES RENDERED HOMELESS BY THESE REMOVALS

On 25 September 1979 Government officials started removing willing families to Kromhoek. Things ran smoothly up to 28–09–79 as only those who wished to be resettled were removed and unwilling families were made to believe that they would remain untampered with.

On 01–10–79, however, the removals took a new turn. Families were forced to move. It was on this day that families who were opposed to removals sought shelter at the neighbouring villages. In the meantime those Government officials started breaking down houses and carrying the contents and roofing materials to Kromhoek. Even when the owner of the house was absent, they would carry a 12 year old child with his/her family's belongings. In the case where a woman was present she was carried away in the absence of her husband to Kromhoek. When the head of the family resisted the removals he was abused by a police van and police dogs, and if he was caught he was thrown into the removing truck and taken away together with his belongings. In such cases doors were broken down and in other cases they entered locked houses by removing the iron sheet from the roof, and would from within force the door to open.

From thatched roofed houses they took doors and windows away, together with what they found in the house. In many cases walls of rondavels were broken down and the thatched roof would eventually fall in and break. Where a teenage boy resisted the removals he was bitten by police dogs and when he surrendered he was removed with whatever belonged to his family. There are families whose properties were removed to Kromhoek in their absence.

Houses were carelessly broken down in these removals. Herds of cattle, sheep and goats were carried away whilst their owners remained behind. Amongst other things there are two tractors and a trailor that were taken away leaving the owner behind. We who remained behind received no compensation for all these losses.

TRIBAL PROPERTIES TAKEN AWAY

SCHOOLS:

a. Roofing materials.

b. Door frames and window frames and doors.
c. Benches and desks.
d. Schools record books, viz
    (i) Scheme books
    (ii) Registers
    (iii) Financial books etc.

CLINIC:
a. Roofing materials
b. Door frames and window frames and doors.

TRIBAL AUTHORITY:
a. All equipment viz
    (i) Roofing materials
    (ii) Door frame and window frames and doors.
    (iii) Benches, tables, chairs, water tanks and fencing materials.
b. The Tribal car.
c. 6 Afrikander bulls belonging to the tribe.

The families who were willingly removed are less than one hundred, that is why we mention these tribal properties as the bulk of the tribe has remained behind.

Document 128. "Why We Went on Strike." Article by Thozamile Botha about the founding of PEBCO, *The Voice,* December 4, 1979

I decided to form the Port Elizabeth Black Civic Organisation (PEBCO) because there was no organisation in the area that was prepared to articulate the aspirations of the black people.

I felt the Community Council was not representative of the people as it had never been accepted by the Port Elizabeth Black community. It was worthwhile to note that [only] four per cent of the more than 250,000 people residing in PE voted when the members of the Council were elected last year.

It is also worthwhile to note that after a year in existence there has been no improvement in the lot of the people in the area.

Instead, things are getting worse. And the Community Council itself was proving more of a liability to the people, than an asset.

People were asked to pay for the services of the Council members. This was in addition to the huge salaries paid to the White staff employed by the Eastern Cape Administration Board.

In other words, the Council was becoming more of a burden. The Community Council as an institution is an extension of a homelands system which no same Black man can embrace. The people who have accepted Community Councils were those who have thrown their lot behind the homeland leaders.

The same Councils are asking for the autonomy of our townships in an effort to further link Blacks living in urban areas with the homeland leaders. People have been rejecting this but lacked an organisation or a mouthpiece which they could use to show their rejection of the homeland system.

They have always been regarding the homeland leaders like Chief Sebe, Chief [Kaiser] Matanzima and Chief [Lucas] Mangope as nothing but "stooges." Because of these things I felt that there was a need for an all-embracing body that would deal with the civic matters pertaining to Blacks in urban areas.

PEBCO emerged at the time when the Black community of Zwide [township] was saddled with huge water accounts, something that has never been experienced by Blacks living in townships.

This was one of the grievances that resulted in a deputation led by me, to face the Chief Director of the ECAB [Eastern Cape Administration Board], Mr L Koch, and demand the withdrawal of the account or face refusal to pay. The people had taken a firm resolution not to pay water accounts and the situation has remained as such.

PEBCO therefore started [as] a small Zwide Residents Association that held open-air meetings, fighting water accounts, huge rentals, lack of craftsmanship of houses built for residents. Including electric sub-stations.

At a report-back meeting where tenants were dissatisfied with Mr Koch's response that the (water issue was an in-thing). People felt that there was a need for a body that would operate outside the Bantu Administration Affairs Board and Community in championing their view.

Hence on the night of October 10 PEBCO was formed.

Document 129. "Policy of the Congress of South African Students." Statement, 1979

Our policy will be towards a philosophy that:
-will determine the interest of all in the education of the country.
-will disseminate ideas that will lead the people towards an education which will leave every one free to think, Act and live.
-will in the final analysis lead to total liberation in South Africa.

ON EDUCATION:
We strongly condemn the present system of Education which is aimed at;
-White superiority in the country of our birth;
-The homeland policy by structuring our education along tribal lines.

WE ENVISAGE:
A society where free and compulsory education will cease to be a privilege but a right and one that is democratically determined to teach the people to love one another, maintain their culture and dignity and, honour human brotherhood.

ON SPORT:

We view the present system of multiracial [sport] as an attempt by the government to create an impression of a genuine change so as to gain international recognition. As an anti-racial organisation we will recognise non-racial sport from grassroots.

ON RELIGION:

We do not recognise the kind of religion introduced by the colonialists with the aim of keeping the oppressed inferior and subservient to the oppresser. We recognise religion as a living reality and identify it with the social problems of the oppressed.

DIALOGUE:

We maintain that a genuine and meaningful change will be brought about by the will and power of the people. We reject any direct or indirect dialogue with government created bodies or institutions.

RELATIONS:

Our organisation will work and identify itself with any progressive group whose policy and principles are similar to those of ours.

CLASS:

We outrightly reject the government's strategy of granting concessions to a sector of our society as an attempt to create a middle class in order to render our struggle ineffective.

ON EDUCATION:

We condemn the present system of education which is aimed at rendering the society the perpetual slaves in the country of our birth, maintaining white superiority and dividing the people into ethnic races/classes that are going to render the struggle ineffective.

CLASS:

We feel the government and so-called concessions of improving the standard of the "black" people is aimed at creating a middle class in a bid to make our struggle ineffective.

We do not recognise concessions and grouping of people into classes. We will fight as a single group and close this gap in the society.

1960

Sharpeville massacre leaves 69 Africans dead, 186 wounded (March 21)

Government declares a state of emergency (March 30)—detains nearly 2,000 political activists of all races

ANC and PAC banned (April 8)

End of emergency (August 31)—emergency proclamation in the Transkei (November) remains in effect into the 1980s

1961

South Africa becomes a republic (May 31)

ANC leaders abandon policy of nonviolence (June)

Sabotage by the National Committee for Liberation (October)—later renamed the African Resistance Movement

National Party wins general election (October 18)

Umkhonto we Sizwe begins sabotage (December 16)

1962

Verwoerd announces that the Transkei will move toward "self-government" (January)

South African Congress of Democrats banned (September 14)

ANC conference in Lobatse, Bechuanaland, the first since 1959 (October)

Nelson Mandela sentenced to five years in prison for leaving South Africa without a passport (November 7)

Poqo attacks whites in Paarl (November 21–22)

Sabotage Act

1963

Potlako Leballo, PAC acting president, announces in Maseru that violence is imminent in South Africa (March 24)—PAC messengers apprehended—mass arrests in South Africa

"90-day Act" abrogates right of habeas corpus (May 1)

Police raid underground headquarters of Umkhonto in Rivonia (July 11)

Independent African states form Organization of African Unity, which later creates African Liberation Committee to recognize and assist liberation movements

1964

Mandela and 7 others sentenced to life imprisonment in the Rivonia trial (June 12)

Johannesburg station bombing (July 24)—police crush African Resistance Movement

Zambia becomes independent (October 24)

1965

Southern Rhodesia unilaterally declares independence (November 11)

180-day detention act succeeds the 90-day act

Coloureds found Labour Party

1966

Defence and Aid Fund banned (March)

South African Coloured People's Congress dissolves to join PAC (March)

National Party wins general election (March 30)

Bram Fischer sentenced to life imprisonment (May 9)

Robert F. Kennedy attracts huge crowds on English-speaking campuses (June)

World Court dismisses challenge to South Africa's rule in South West Africa (July 18)

Vorster becomes prime minister after assassination of Verwoerd (September)

Botswana becomes independent (September 30)

Lesotho becomes independent (October 4)

1967

University Christian Movement formed (July)

Death of Albert Lutuli, ANC president (July 21)—Oliver Tambo becomes acting president

ANC fighters in Wankie campaign in Rhodesia (July–August and later incursions)

Terrorism Act

1968

Steve Biko canvasses support for blacks-only student organization at conferences of NUSAS and University Christian Movement (July)

Zambia bans PAC and expels its leaders (August)

Swaziland becomes independent (September 6)

Urban Bantu Council replaces Soweto Advisory Board

Multiracial political parties outlawed—Liberal Party disbands—Parliamentary representation of Coloureds by whites ended—Coloured Persons' Representative Council and South African Indian Council established

1969

Lusaka Manifesto signed by 13 heads of independent African states (April 16)

ANC conference in Morogoro, Tanzania, opens membership to exiled non-Africans (April 25–May 1)

Robert Sobukwe released from prison to restriction in Kimberley (May)

South African Students' Organisation holds inaugural conference (July)

First election for Coloured Persons' Representative Council (September)

1970

Winnie Mandela and 21 other trial defendants acquitted but redetained and recharged (February)

National Party wins general election (April 22)

South Africa expelled by International Olympic Committee (May 15)

Gatsha Buthelezi becomes Chief Executive Officer of the Zululand Territorial Authority (June 9)

World Council of Churches announces humanitarian grants to African liberation movements (September)

South African team cancels cricket tour of Britain after campaign of protest by critics

1971

Hastings Banda of Malawi visits South Africa (August)

Natal Indian Congress is formally revived (October 2)

Ovambo migrant workers go on strike in South West Africa (December–February)

Government introduces "multinational sport"

1972

South African Students' Movement is formed (January)

Secret decision of Kissinger/Nixon (January 1970) to tilt toward white southern African regimes becomes public (April)

13 sentenced in APDUSA trial (April)

O. R. Tiro expelled for critical graduation speech at Turfloop—campus protests ensue (April–June)

Black People's Convention founded (July)

University Christian Movement disbands (July)

Government appoints Schlebusch Commission to investigate multiracial organizations

1973

Spontaneous strike wave in Durban area (January–February)

Government bans top NUSAS and black consciousness activists (February)

NAYO formed (May)

Summit meeting of homeland leaders in Umtata, followed by "all-race" Bulugha conference near East London (November 8–11)

Beyers Naude of Christian Institute and others found guilty of refusing to testify to Schlebusch Commission

1974

Johannesburg municipality opens parks, libraries, museums to all races and ends separate queues in post offices (January)

O. R. Tiro assassinated in Botswana (February)

Kaiser Matanzima's party votes to negotiate for Transkeian independence (March)

National Party wins general election (April 24)

Military coup topples Portuguese government (April 25)

South African Council of Churches endorses conscientious objection (August)

Vorster makes secret visit to Ivory Coast to press for detente (September)

SASO and BPC hold pro-Frelimo rallies—many arrested (September 25)

Vorster speech: "Give South Africa six months" (November 5)

First vote for elected members of the South African Indian Council (November)

Black Renaissance Convention (December 13–16)

Masters and Servants Act repealed

UN General Assembly suspends credentials of South African delegation—ANC and PAC invited to participate as observers

Affected Organisations Act enables government to bar NUSAS and the Christian Institute from receiving foreign funds

1975

SASO/BPC trial begins (January)—ends in December 1976

Vorster meets with eight homeland leaders (January 22)

Vorster secretly visits Liberia (February)

Labour Party wins election for the second Coloured Persons' Representative Council (March)

Buthelezi launches Inkatha as a "national cultural liberation movement" (June 14)

Mozambique becomes independent (June 25)

Ambrose Makiwane attacks South African Communist Party in London speech (July 19)

Desmond Tutu installed as first black dean of Johannesburg's Anglican cathedral (August 31)

South African army invades Angola in unsuccessful effort to prevent MPLA from coming to power (October–December)—Angola becomes independent (November 11)

Banning orders of Winnie Mandela lapse after 13 years (October)

Lucas Mangope's party votes to negotiate for independence of Bophuthatswana (November)

Breyten Breytenbach sentenced to nine years for Okhela activities (November)

Labour Party refuses to pass Coloured Persons' Representative Council budget—government fires Sonny Leon as chairman (November)

ANC expels the "Makiwane 8" (December 11)

Formation of Black Women's Federation

Television is introduced

1976

Internal Security Act (May)

Biko testifies for the defense in SASO/BPC trial (May 3–7)

Desmond Tutu writes to Vorster warning of violence (May 8)

Soweto uprising begins after police shoot at student demonstrators (June 16)—revolt spreads leaving hundreds dead nationwide—students flee into exile

Government rejects main recommendations of Theron Commission on Coloureds (June)

Violence, arson, protests, absenteeism plague black schools nationwide—black universities disrupted (July–December)

Soweto Students' Representative Council stages first three-day stay-away in Soweto (August 4–6)—second and third stay-aways later in August and in September—work stoppages spread to Cape Town and elsewhere

Mapetla Mohapi dies in police custody near King William's Town (August 5)

Violence plagues eastern Cape and Cape Town (August–September)

Incited by police, Zulu hostel dwellers attack Soweto residents (August 24–25)

Blacks demonstrate against Kissinger visit to Pretoria (September 17–19)

Hundreds of arrests as students "invade" downtown Johannesburg (September 23)

First attack since the early 1960s by an ANC guerrilla unit, headed by Naledi Tsiki (October)

Transkei becomes independent (October 26)—within hours, the UN General Assembly votes against recognition

SASO/BPC trial ends—all nine defendants convicted (December)

Minister of Prisons James Kruger visits Mandela on Robben Island—Mandela rejects offer to move to Transkei

1977

Some Catholic schools begin admitting black pupils despite government prohibition (January)

Winnie Mandela banished to Brandfort in Orange Free State (May)

U.S. Vice President Walter Mondale meets Vorster in Vienna—expresses support for principle of one person/one vote (May 19–20)

Soweto Urban Bantu Council collapses as last councillors resign—SSRC leaders detained (June)

Goch Street murders stoke white fears of urban guerrilla warfare (June 13)

Committee of Ten formed in Soweto (June 27)

United Party dissolves, leaving Progressive Federal Party as parliamentary opposition (June)

Harry Gwala and others sentenced to life for ANC activities (July)

Police destroy Modderdam squatter camp outside Cape Town—20,000 left homeless (August)

Government proposes tricameral parliament—Labour Party rejects plan (August)

Biko dies in police custody—outcry around world (September 12)

Government crackdown bans 18 organizations, closes *The World,* detains dozens of black leaders including the Committee of Ten, and bans many (October 19)

Soweto Action Committee formed (October 23)

UN Security Council mandatory arms embargo on South Africa (November 4)

Snap general election—National Party enlarges its majority (November 30)

Biko inquest absolves police of responsibility (December 2)

Bophuthatswana becomes independent (December 6)

European Economic Community formulates code of labor and workplace standards for European investors

Arrival of ANC's "June 16th Detachment" for training in Angola

1978

Richard Turner assassinated in Durban (January 8)

Government razes Unibel squatter camp in Cape Town (January)

Soweto Community Council elections a fiasco (February and April)—David Thebehali becomes "mayor" with 97 votes

Sobukwe dies (February 27)—Buthelezi forced by militant youths to leave his funeral (March 11)

Trial of "Pretoria 12" ends—six get severe sentences, six acquitted—Joe Gqabi leaves the country (April)

AZAPO founded—leaders detained (April 30)

PAC consultative conference in Arusha, Tanzania, leads to expulsion of seven members of the Central Committee (June 27–July 2)

Information Department scandal forces Vorster to resign as prime minister— P. W. Botha replaces him (September)

Labour Party continues to reject proposal for a tricameral parliament—Sonny Leon disagrees and resigns as leader (September)

Tambo and five colleagues make study-visit to Vietnam (October)

ANC's NEC and Revolutionary Council meet in Luanda, receive report of study-visit, and set up a Politico-Military Strategy Commission (December 27–January 1)

Sullivan Code promoted as standard of labor and workplace conduct for American companies

Verligte-verkrampte split in National Party widens

Buthelezi brings together South African Black Alliance

1979

FOSATU holds first national conference (April)

Soweto Committee of Ten revives (April)

Solomon Mahlangu, Umkhonto's first guerrilla to be executed, hanged for Goch Street murders (April 4)

Following recommendations of Wiehahn Commission (May), Industrial Relations Act officially recognizes African trade unions

First frontal assault by ANC guerrillas, who attack Moroka police station in Soweto (May)

PAC Presidential Council of three takes over from Leballo, who leaves for "medical treatment" (May 2)

Riekert Commission recommends improved conditions for permanently urbanized Africans (May 8)

Consumer boycott of Fatti's and Moni's products (May–November)

David Sibeko murdered by PAC dissidents in Dar es Salaam (June 11)

Zephania Mothopeng and 17 other PAC defendants convicted in Bethal trial (June 21)

Formation of Congress of South African Students (high school students, June) and Azanian Students' Organisation (university students, November)

ANC's National Executive Committee approves report of the Politico-Military Strategy Commission [the "Green Book"] (August)

Venda becomes independent (September 13)

Soweto Civic Association formed (September 23)

AZAPO relaunched (September 30)

PEBCO formed (October)

PAC plenary meeting expels Leballo (October 1–6)

Inkatha delegation meets ANC in London (October 30–31)

P. W. Botha has confrontation with Labour Party leaders—Coloured Persons' Representative Council collapses (November 9)

Botha meets top business leaders to promote "total strategy" (November 22)

Three ANC/SACP white prisoners escape from prison in Pretoria (December 11)

SOURCES

This is a guide to sources on South African political history in the period 1964–1979. In addition to the primary and secondary materials listed below or cited in the notes, the major source used in producing this book has been the Karis-Gerhart Collection, an archive of interviews and approximately 10,000 documents, which is available on microfilm and can be borrowed through research libraries or acquired from the Cooperative Africana Microform Project (CAMP) of the Center for Research Libraries, 5721 Cottage Grove Avenue, Chicago, Illinois 60637.

Archival Collections

The following universities and institutions have library collections containing records of black and other resistance organizations and papers of individual activists. The listing below also notes collections of special interest to researchers concerned with the period covered in this volume.

Cooperative Africana Microform Project (CAMP), Center for Research Libraries, Chicago: newspapers and periodicals, trial and trade union records
Inkatha Institute, Durban: publications of Inkatha, speeches
Institute of Black Studies, Durban: collections of Professor Fatima Meer and others
Northwestern University Library: hard copies of the Carter-Karis Collection (1882–1964)
Rhodes University, Cory Library
SACHED (South African Committee on Higher Education), Cape Town
Stanford University, Hoover Institution Library: trial records
United Nations Centre Against Apartheid
University of Cape Town: archives of NUSAS, Cillie Commission testimony, trade union records, oral history collection
University of Fort Hare: archives of ANC, PAC, AZAPO, and the Unity Movement
University of London, Institute of Commonwealth Studies
University of South Africa, Pretoria
University of the Western Cape, Mayibuye Centre: Robben Island archives, oral history collection

University of the Witwatersrand, Cullen Library, Historical Papers: trial records,
archives of UCM, FOSATU and other trade unions
University of York, England
Yale University, Sterling Memorial Library: trial records, hard copies of Karis-Gerhart
Collection (1964–1990)

Trial Records

1969–1970 *State v. Ramotse and 19 others* (the Winnie Mandela trial)
1971–1972 *State v. Hassim and others* (the APDUSA trial)
1971   *State v. ffrench-Beytagh*
1975–1976 *State v. Cooper* (the SASO Nine trial)
1975–1976 *State v. Molokeng* (the NAYO tria)
1975   *State v. Molobi*
1976   *State v. Moss and others* (the NUSAS trial)
1976   *State v. Ndukwana and 4 others* (the Healdtown trial)
1977   *State v. Sexwale and others* (the Joe Gqabi trial)
1978–1979 *State v. Twala* (the Soweto 11 trial/the Kempton Park trial)
1978   *State v. Mothopeng* (the Bethal trial)

Interviews

The following is a list of conversations and interviews cited in this volume. The
microfilmed archive of the Karis-Gerhart Collection includes approximately 900
records of formal interviews, many of them tape-recorded, and informal conversations conducted by the authors and other researchers. In the notes, "conversation"
has been used as a catch-all term for interviews and conversations conducted by
Karis and/or Gerhart, and the term "interview" has been used for transcripts and
notes contributed to the collection by other researchers.

Akhalwaya, Ameen	Johannesburg, July 1, 1980 (K/G)
Anderson, Bill	London, April 8, 1991 (Howard Barrell)
Bam, Fikile	Johannesburg, July 13, 1994 (G)
Biko, Steve	Durban, June 5, 1971 (Greg Lanning)
Biko, Steve	Durban, October 24, 1972 (G)
Bizos, George	New York, October 30, 1989 (K/G)
Boraine, Alex	New York, June 12, 1991 (K)
Buthelezi, Mangosuthu Gatsha	Johannesburg, August 15, 1979 (K)
Buthelezi, Mangosuthu Gatsha	New York, May 1971 (K)
Buthelezi, Mangosuthu Gatsha	Ulundi, January 23, 1983 (K/Gwen Carter)
Buthelezi, Sipho	Gaborone, October 9, 1977 (K)
Chikane, Frank	Boston, June 1995 (K)
Chinsamy, Yellan	New York, May 18, 1978 (K)
Choabi, Seretse,	Lusaka, April 5, 1989 (K)
Cindi, Zithulele	Johannesburg, July 5, 1989 (G)
Cooper, Saths	Durban, October 24, 1972 (G)
Cooper, Saths	New York, October 4, 1987 (G)
Curtis, Neville	Harare, June 19, 1990 (G)
Dhlomo, Oscar	Durban, December 18, 1989 (K)
Duncan, Patrick	Dar es Salaam, February 4, 1964 (K)
Fadana, P. S.	Engcobo, Transkei, October 2, 1977 (K)
Feta, Lerumo	Lusaka, February 1988 (Victoria Butler)
Fihla, Ben	Port Elizabeth, October 8, 1993 (K)
Gerwel, Jakes	New York, April 1990 (K/G)

Gqobose, P. L. M.	New York, April 1990 (K)
Gwala, Harry	Pietermaritzburg, December 15, 1989 (K)
Hassim, Kader	Pietermaritzburg, December 16, 1989 (K)
Hendrickse, Allan	New York, May 17, 1977 (K)
Hodgson, Rica	Mazimbu, Tanzania, November 1985 (K)
Holmes, Edward	Washington, March 23, 1977 (K)
Inkatha leaders group	Johannesburg, July 1, 1980 (K/G)
Isaacs, Henry	New York, April 1981 (K)
Issel, Johnny	Cape Town, December 1989 (K)
Jack, Mkhuseli and Stone Sizani	Port Elizabeth, July 14, 1989 (G)
Jones, Peter	Cape Town, July 21, 1989 (G)
Kasrils, Ronnie	Johannesburg, October 28, 1990 (Howard Barrell)
Kathrada, Ahmed	Johannesburg, September 24, 1993 (K)
Keke, Zolile	New York, October 1981 (K)
Khoapa, Bennie	New York, June 16, 1989 (K/G)
Koornhof, Piet	Johannesburg, September 1979 (K)
Kuzwayo, Ellen	Johannesburg, August 1979 (K)
Langa, Bheki	Lusaka, February 1988 (Victoria Butler)
Lekota, Patrick	Pinetown, December 1989 (K)
Mabandla, Oyama	San Diego, July 15, 1992 (K)
Mabasa, Lybon	New York, April 9, 1991 (G)
Mabiletsa, Deborah	Johannesburg, July 4, 1980 (K/G)
Mafole, Tebego	New York, March 24, 1992 (K/G)
Mafuna, Bokwe	Harare, June 21, 1990 (G)
Maharaj, Mac	Johannesburg, November 30, 1990 (Howard Barrell)
Maharaj, Mac	Lusaka, February 1988 (Victoria Butler)
Manthata, Tom	Harare, June 20, 1990 (G)
Manthata, Tom	Johannesburg, August 1979 (K)
Manuel, Trevor	Cape Town, 1985 (Julie Frederikse)
Masetlha, Billy	Lusaka, February 1988 (Victoria Butler)
Masondo, Amos	Johannesburg, July 5, 1989 (G)
Matiso, Khaya	Port Elizabeth, July 18, 1989 (G)
Mayson, Cedric	London, March 5, 1991 (K/G)
Mhlaba, Raymond	Port Elizabeth, December 7, 1989 (K)
Mhlongo, Sam	London, January 18, 1980 (K)
Mji, Diliza	New York, June 2, 1987 (G)
Mkhabela, Ishmael	Johannesburg, January 27, 1983 (K)
Mkhabela, Ishmael	Johannesburg, July 23, 1989 (G)
Mkhatshwa, Smangaliso	Johannesburg, July 4, 1989 (G)
Mlonzi, Lennox	New York, June 29, 1977 (K)
Mlonzi, Lennox	Umtata, October 6, 1977 (K)
Modisane, Jerome	Durban, October 23, 1972 (G)
Moerane, M. T., Drake Koka, William Nkomo, D. Thebehali	Johannesburg, February 11, 1972 (Gwen Carter)
Mogale, Pioneer	Mazimbu, Tanzania, November 1985 (K)
Moloto, Justice	Durban?, November 30, 1977 (David Mesenbring)
Moloto, Justice	Johannesburg, June 30, 1989 (G)
Molotsi, Peter	New York, 1977 (K)
Mompati, Ruth	Lusaka, March 1989 (K)
Montsitsi, Daniel	Johannesburg, July 9, 1989 (G)
Moosa, Imrann	Durban, July 11, 1989 (G)
Morobe, Murphy	Boston, May 4, 1991 (G)
Mosala, Leonard	Johannesburg, June and August 1979 (K)
Moseneke, Dikgang	Pretoria, July 2, 1980 (K/G)
Mothopeng, Zephania	Johannesburg, December 12, 1989 (K)

Motlana, Nthato	New York, June 1979 (K)
Motlana, Nthato	New York, June 26, 1987 (K/G)
Motlana, Nthato	Johannesburg, March 1, 1979 (Ina Perlman)
Mpumlwana, Malusi and Thoko	New York, June 7, 1987 (G)
Mpumlwana, Malusi	Johannesburg, July 18, 1994 (G)
Mpumlwana, Malusi	New York, November 30, 1987 (G)
Mpumlwana, Malusi	Uitenhage, August 7, 1989 (G)
Mpumlwana, Malusi	Uitenhage, December 5, 1989 (K)
Mthembu, Kehla	New York, February 24, 1989 (K/G)
Mueller, Marti	Nairobi, November 30, 1971 (G)
Muthien, Yvonne	Evanston, IL, May 1980 (George Fredrickson)
Mxenge, Griffiths	Durban, November 30, 1977 (David Mesenbring)
Naidoo, Indres	Lusaka, February 1988 (Victoria Butler)
Naidoo, M. J. and Ramlall Ramesar	New York, May 27 and 30, 1977 (K)
Naidoo, M. J.	Durban, December 19, 1989 (K)
Naude, Beyers	Johannesburg, July 7, 1980 (G)
Ndamse, Curnick	Umtata, October 26, 1972 (G)
Ndebele, Sibusiso	Durban, December 15, 1989 (K)
Nengwekhulu, Harry	Gaborone, September 17, 1975 (G)
Nengwekhulu, Harry	Johannesburg, October 17, 1972 (G)
Ngakane, Pascal	Maseru, October 1977 and March 1989 (K)
Nkondo, Curtis	Johannesburg, December 13, 1989 (K)
Nkondo, Curtis	New York, May 1989 (K/G)
Nkwinti, Gugile	Grahamstown, July 18, 1989 (G)
Patel, Quraish	Durban, December 19, 1989 (K)
Patel, Quraish	Durban, July 11, 1989 (G)
Paton, Alan	Botha's Hill, Natal, August 26, 1979 (K)
Phatudi, Cedric	Pietersburg, August 1979 (K)
Pityana, Barney	Durban, October 25, 1972 (G)
Pityana, Barney	New York, January 12, 1988 (K/G)
Qoboza, Percy	Johannesburg, August 22, 1979 (K)
Ramgobin, Mewa	Durban, July 12, 1989 (G)
Saloojee, Cassim	New York, October 2, 1987 (G)
Selebi, Jackie	Lusaka, March 21, 1989 (K)
Shubane, Kehla	New York, March 1989 (K)
Sibeko, David	New York, January 12, 1979 (K)
Sibeko, David	New York, May 1979 (K)
Sifora, Victor	Pretoria, October 19, 1972 (G)
Sikakane, Reverend E. Z.	Pietermaritzburg, August 27, 1979 (K)
Simons, Ray Alexander	Cape Town, October 5, 1993 (K)
Sizani, Stone	New York, May 4, 1990 (K/G)
Slovo, Joe	Lusaka, August 12–16, 1989 (Howard Barrell)
Slovo, Joe	New York, October 15, 1990 (K/G)
Slovo, Joe	Johannesburg, October 23, 1993
Smith, Timothy	New York, August 29, 1972 (G)
Sobukwe, Bishop Ernest	Umtata, September 29, 1977 (K)
Sonn, Franklin	Cape Town, January 1978 (K)
Sono, Temba	New York, November 8, 1973 (G)
Stofile, Mongezi	Harare, June 22, 1990 (G)
Tambo, Oliver	London, March 3–6, 1991 (K/G)
Tambo, Oliver	Lusaka, August 1968 (K)
Thebehali, David	Johannesburg, October 20, 1972 (G)
Thebehali, David	New York, August 9, 1972 (G)
Thebehali, David	New York, June 24, 1977 (K)

Tladi, Lefifi	Gaborone, November 29, 1976 (G)
Van der Merwe, Stoffel	Johannesburg, August 16, 1979 (K)
Van Harte, Edna	New York, April 25, 1992 (G)
Variava, Dr. Joe	Johannesburg, October 25, 1985 (G)
Venkatrathnam, Sonny	Durban, October, 1993 (K)
Wauchope, George	Johannesburg, July 7, 1980 (K/G)
Wentzel, Ernest	Johannesburg, July 1980 (K)
Xego, Michael	Port Elizabeth, October 8, 1993 (K)
Xundu, Mcebisi	New York, October 2, 1977 (K)
Xundu, Mcebisi	New York, March 14, 1989 (G)
Zuma, Nkosazana Dlamini	London, July 3, 1988 (G)
Zungu, Cap	New York, April 25, 1991 (K)

Published Collections of Documents

Benson, Mary, ed., *The Sun Will Rise: Statements from the Dock by Southern African Political Prisoners* (London: International Defence and Aid Fund, second edition, 1981).

Bhana, Surendra and Bridglal Pachai, eds., *A Documentary History of Indian South Africans* (Cape Town: David Philip; Stanford: Hoover Institution Press, 1984).

De Braganca, Aquino and Immanuel Wallerstein, eds., *The African Liberation Reader:* 3 volumes (London: Zed Books, 1982).

Hugo, Pierre, ed., *Quislings or Realists: A Documentary Study of Coloured Politics in South Africa* (Johannesburg: Ravan Press, 1978).

Johns, Sheridan and Hunt Davis, eds., *Mandela, Tambo and the African National Congress: The Struggle Against Apartheid 1928–1990* (New York: Oxford University Press, 1991).

La Guma, Alex, *Apartheid: A Collection of Writings on South African Racism by South Africans* (London: Lawrence and Wishart, 1972).

Mandela, Nelson, *The Struggle Is My Life* (London: International Defence and Aid Fund, 1978).

Mutloatse, Mothobi, ed., *Umhlaba Wethu: A Historical Indictment* (Johannesburg: Skotaville, 1987).

———, *Reconstruction* (Johannesburg: Ravan Press, 1981).

Reddy, E. S., *Oliver Tambo and the Struggle against Apartheid* (New Delhi: Sterling Publishers, 1987).

South African Communist Party, *South African Communists Speak: Documents from the History of the South African Communist Party, 1915–1980* (London: Inkululeko Publications, 1981).

Tambo, Oliver, *Preparing for Power: Oliver Tambo Speaks* (London: Heinemann, 1987).

Van der Merwe, H. W., Nancy Charton, D. A. Kotze, and Ake Magnusson, eds., *African Perspectives on South Africa: a Collection of Speeches, Articles and Documents* (Stanford: Hoover Institution Press; Cape Town: David Philip; London: Rex Collings, 1978).

General Bibliography on South Africa, 1964–1979: Selected Books and Articles

Adam, Heribert, *Modernizing Racial Domination: South Africa's Political Dynamics* (Berkeley: University of California Press, 1971).

Adam, Heribert, ed., *South Africa: Sociological Perspectives* (London: Oxford University Press, 1971).

Bernstein, Hilda, *The Rift: The Exile Experience of South Africans* (London: Jonathan Cape, 1994).

Brandel-Syrier, Mia, *"Coming Through": The Search for a New Cultural Identity* (Johannesburg: McGraw Hill, 1978).

Braithwaite, E. R., *"Honorary White": A Visit to South Africa* (London: Bodley Head, 1975).

Brewer, John D., *After Soweto: An Unfinished Journey* (New York: Oxford University Press, 1987).

Brickhill, Joan, *Race against Race: South Africa's "Multinational" Sport Fraud* (London: International Defence and Aid Fund, 1976).

de St. Jorre, John, *A House Divided: South Africa's Uncertain Future* (New York: Carnegie Endowment for International Peace, 1977).

Dugard, John, *Human Rights and the South African Legal Order* (Princeton: Princeton University Press, 1978).

Gastrow, Shelagh, *Who's Who in South African Politics,* 4 editions (Johannesburg: Ravan Press, 1985, 1987, 1990, and 1992).

Grundy, Kenneth, *Confrontation and Accommodation in Southern Africa: The Limits of Independence* (Berkeley: University of California Press, 1973).

Hain, Peter, *Don't Play with Apartheid: The Background to the Stop the Seventy Tour Campaign* (London: George Allen and Unwin, 1971).

Hanf, Theodor, Heribert Weiland, and Gerda Vierdag, *South Africa: The Prospects of Peaceful Change* (London: Rex Collings, 1981).

Hare, A. Paul, ed., *The Struggle for Democracy in South Africa: Conflict and Conflict Resolution* (Cape Town: Centre for Intergroup Studies, 1983).

Hellmann, Ellen and Henry Lever, eds., *Conflict and Progress: Fifty Years of Race Relations in South Africa* (Johannesburg: Macmillan, 1979).

Hill, Christopher, *Change in South Africa: Blind Alleys or New Directions?* (Totowa, NJ: Barnes and Noble, 1983).

Horrell, Muriel, *Action, Reaction and Counteraction: A Brief Review of Non-White Political Movements in South Africa* (Johannesburg: South African Institute of Race Relations, 1971).

Johnson, Jill and Peter Magubane, *Soweto Speaks* (Johannesburg: Ad Donker, 1979).

Kallaway, Peter, ed., *Apartheid and Education: The Education of Black South Africans* (Johannesburg: Ravan Press, 1984).

Kuper, Leo, *An African Bourgeoisie: Race, Class and Politics in South Africa* (New Haven: Yale University Press, 1965).

Lapchick, Richard E., *The Politics of Race in International Sport: The Case of South Africa* (Denver: Center on International Race Relations; Westport, Connecticut: Greenwood Press, 1975).

Magubane, Bernard M., *The Political Economy of Race and Class in South Africa* (New York: Monthly Review Press, 1979).

Marks, Shula, and Stanley Trapido, eds., *The Politics of Race, Class and Nationalism in Twentieth-Century South Africa* (London and New York: Longman, 1987).

Mathews, Anthony, *Freedom and State Security in the South African Plural Society* (Johannesburg: South African Institute of Race Relations, 1971).

Meer, Fatima, *Portrait of Indian South Africans* (Durban: Avon House, 1969).

Muller, A. L., *Minority Interests: The Political Economy of the Coloured and Indian Communities in South Africa* (Johannesburg: South African Institute of Race Relations, 1968).

Price, Robert M., *The Apartheid State in Crisis: Political Transformation in South Africa, 1975–1990* (New York: Oxford University Press, 1991).

Price, Robert M. and Carl Rosberg, eds., *The Apartheid Regime: Political Power and Racial Domination* (Berkeley: Institute of International Studies, University of California, 1980).

Ramsamy, Sam, *Apartheid: The Real Hurdle: Sport in South Africa and the International Boycott* (London: International Defence and Aid Fund, 1982).

Reader's Digest, *Illustrated History of South Africa: the Real Story* (Pleasantville, NY: Reader's Digest Association, second edition, 1995).

Sachs, Albie, *Justice in South Africa* (Berkeley: University of California Press, l973).

South Africa: Time Running Out—The Report of the Study Commission on U.S. Policy Toward Southern Africa (Berkeley: University of California Press, 1981).

South African Institute of Race Relations, *Survey of Race Relations* (Johannesburg: South African Institute of Race Relations, annual).

Stadler, Alf, *The Political Economy of Modern South Africa* (Cape Town: David Philip, 1987).

Starke, Anna, *Survival: Taped Interviews with South Africa's Power Elite* (Cape Town: Tafelberg, 1978).

Stokke, Olav and Carl Widstrand, eds., *Southern Africa* (Uppsala: Scandinavian Institute of African Studies, 1973).

Thompson, Leonard, *A History of South Africa* (New Haven: Yale University Press, 1990).

Thompson, Leonard and Jeffrey Butler, eds., *Change in Contemporary South Africa* (Berkeley: University of California Press, 1975).

United Nations Department of Information, *The United Nations and Apartheid, 1948–1994* (New York: United Nations, 1994).

van der Horst, Sheila T., ed., *Race Discrimination in South Africa: A Review* (Cape Town: David Philip, 1981).

van der Merwe, Nikolaas J., et al., eds., *Perspectives on South Africa's Future* (Cape Town, Centre for African Studies, 1979).

Walker, Cheryl, *Women and Resistance in South Africa* (London: Onyx Press, 1982).

Winter, Gordon, *Inside Boss: South Africa's Secret Police* (Harmondsworth, Middlesex: Penguin, 1981).

The Liberation Movements, 1964–1979

Alexander, Neville, *Robben Island Dossier 1964–1974* (Cape Town: University of Cape Town Press, 1994).

Amnesty International, *Political Imprisonment in South Africa: An Update to an Amnesty International Report* (London: Amnesty International, 1979).

Barrell, Howard, "Conscripts to Their Age: African National Congress Operational Strategy, 1976–1986," Ph.D. thesis, Oxford University, 1993.

———, *MK: The ANC's Armed Struggle* (London: Penguin, 1990).

———, "The Outlawed South African Liberation Movements," in Shaun Johnson, ed., *South Africa: No Turning Back* (London: Macmillan Press, 1988).

———, "The Turn to the Masses: the African National Congress' Strategic Review of 1978–79," *Journal of Southern African Studies,* vol. 18, no. 1, March 1991, pp. 64–92.

Benson, Mary, *The African Patriots* (London: Faber and Faber, 1963), reissued in a revised edition, *South Africa: The Struggle for a Birthright* (Harmondsworth, Middlesex: Penguin Books, 1966).

———, *Nelson Mandela: The Man and the Movement* (New York and London: W. W. Norton, 1986).

Bernstein, Hilda, *The Terrorism of Torture* (London: Christian Action Publications, 1972).

———, *The World That Was Ours: The Story of the Rivonia Trial* (London: SAWriters, 1989).

Breytenbach, Breyten, *The True Confessions of an Albino Terrorist* (New York: Farrar Straus Giroux, 1983).

Brokensha, Miles, and Robert Knowles, *The Fourth of July Raids* (Cape Town, Simondium Publishers, 1965).

Bunting, Brian, *Moses Kotane: South African Revolutionary, A Political Biography* (London: Inkululeko Publications, 1975).

Carlson, Joel, *No Neutral Ground* (New York: Thomas Y. Crowell, 1973).

Cook, Allen, *South Africa: The Imprisoned Society* (London, International Defence and Aid Fund, 1974).

Davis, Stephen M., *Apartheid's Rebels: Inside South Africa's Hidden War* (New Haven: Yale University Press, 1987).

Desai, Barney and Cardiff Marney, *The Killing of the Imam* (London: Quartet Books, 1978).

Dingake, Michael, *My Fight Against Apartheid* (London: Kliptown Books, 1987).

Dlamini, Moses, *Robben Island Hell-Hole: Reminiscences of a Political Prisoner in South Africa* (Trenton, NJ: Africa World Press, 1986).

Du Toit, Andries, "The National Committee for Liberation ('ARM'), 1960–1964: Sabotage and the Question of the Ideological Subject," M.A. thesis, University of Cape Town, 1990.

Ellis, Stephen, "Mbokodo: Security in ANC Camps, 1961–1990," *African Affairs*, vol. 93, 1994, pp. 279–298.

Ellis, Stephen and Tsepo Sechaba, *Comrades against Apartheid: The ANC and the South African Communist Party in Exile* (London: James Currey; Bloomington: Indiana University Press, 1992).

Ensor, Linda, *Security Trials 1978* (Johannesburg: South African Institute of Race Relations, 1979).

Feit, Edward, *Urban Revolt in South Africa 1960–1964: A Case Study* (Evanston: Northwestern University Press, 1971).

ffrench-Beytagh, Gonville, *Encountering Darkness* (London: Collins, 1973).

Frederikse, Julie, *The Unbreakable Thread: Nonracialism in South Africa* (Bloomington: Indiana University Press; London: Zed Books, 1990).

From Shantytown to Forest: The Story of Norman Duka (Richmond, BC, Canada: LSM Press, 1974).

Gerhart, Gail, *Black Power in South Africa: The Evolution of an Ideology* (Berkeley: University of California Press, 1978).

Gibson, Richard, *African Liberation Movements: Contemporary Struggles against White Minority Rule* (London: Oxford University Press, 1972).

Gilbey, Emma, *The Lady: The Life and Times of Winnie Mandela* (London: Jonathan Cape, 1993).

Holland, Heidi, *The Struggle: A History of the African National Congress* (London: Grafton Books, 1989).

Houser, George M., *No One Can Stop the Rain: Glimpses of Africa's Liberation Struggle* (New York: Pilgrim Press, 1989).

International Defence and Aid Fund, *You Have Struck a Rock: Women and Political Repression in Southern Africa* (London: International Defence and Aid Fund, 1980).

Jenkin, Tim, *Escape from Pretoria* (London: Kliptown Books, 1987).

Johns, Sheridan, "Obstacles to Guerrilla Warfare—a South African Case Study," *The Journal of Modern African Studies*, vol. 11, no. 2, 1973, pp. 267–303.

Jordan, Bojana Vuyisile, *We Will Be Heard: A South African Exile Remembers* (Boston: Quinlan Press, 1986).

Joseph, Helen, *Side by Side: The Autobiography of Helen Joseph* (London, Zed Books, 1986).

Karis, Thomas G., "The Resurgent African National Congress: Competing for Hearts and Minds in South Africa," in Thomas M. Callaghey, ed., *South Africa in Southern Africa: The Intensifying Vortex of Violence* (New York: Praeger, 1983), pp. 191–236.

————, "Revolution in the Making: Black Politics in South Africa," *Foreign Affairs,* Winter 1983/84, pp. 378–406.

————, "South African Liberation: the Communist Factor," *Foreign Affairs,* Winter 1986/87, pp. 267–288.

Kasrils, Ronnie, *"Armed and Dangerous": My Undercover Struggle against Apartheid* (Oxford: Heinemann, 1993).

Legassick, Martin, "Guerrilla Warfare in South Africa," in Wilfred Cartey and Martin Kilson, eds., *Independent Africa* (New York: Vintage Books, 1970), pp. 381–400.

Lerumo, A. [Michael Harmel], *Fifty Fighting Years: The Communist Party of South Africa, 1920–1971* (London: Inkululeko Publications, 1971).

Lewin, Hugh, *Bandiet: Seven Years in a South African Prison* (London, Barrie and Jenkins, 1974; Oxford: Heinemann, 1981).

Lodge, Tom, *Black Politics in South Africa since 1945* (London and New York: Longman, 1983).

————, "The politics of exile," *Third World Quarterly,* vol. 9, no. 1, January 1987, pp. 1–27.

————, and Bill Nasson, *All, Here, and Now: Black Politics in South Africa in the 1980s* (New York: Ford Foundation and Foreign Policy Association, 1991).

Mandela, Nelson, *Long Walk to Freedom* (New York: Little, Brown and Co., 1994).

Marcum, John A., "The Exile Condition and Revolutionary Effectiveness: Southern African Liberation Movements," in Christian P. Potholm and Richard Dale, eds., *Southern Africa in Perspective* (New York and London: The Free Press, 1972), 262–275.

Marx, Anthony, *Lessons of Struggle: South African Internal Opposition, 1960–1990* (New York: Oxford University Press, 1992).

Mbeki, Govan, *Learning From Robben Island: The Prison Writings of Govan Mbeki* (London: James Currey; Cape Town: David Philip; Athens, Ohio: Ohio University Press, 1991).

Meer, Fatima, *Higher than Hope: The Authorized Biography of Nelson Mandela* (Johannesburg: Skotaville Publishers, 1989; London: Hamish Hamilton, 1990; New York: Harper & Row, 1988).

Meli, Francis, *A History of the ANC: South Africa Belongs to Us* (Harare: Zimbabwe Publishing House, 1988; Bloomington: Indiana University Press; London: James Currey, 1989).

Moss, Glenn, *Political Trials: South Africa: 1976–1979* (Johannesburg: Development Studies Group, University of the Witwatersrand, n.d.).

Motlhabi, Mokgethi, *The Theory and Practice of Black Resistance to Apartheid: A Social-Ethical Analysis* (Johannesburg: Skotaville Publishers, 1984).

Mtolo, Bruno, *Umkhonto we Sizwe: the Road to the Left* (Durban: Drakensberg Press, 1966).

Naidoo, Indres, *"Prisoner 885/63," Island in Chains: Ten Years on Robben Island as told by Indres Naidoo to Albie Sachs* (Harmondsworth, Middlesex: Penguin Books, 1982).

No Sizwe [Neville Alexander], *One Azania, One Nation: The National Question in South Africa* (London: Zed Books, 1979).

Nolutshungu, Sam C., *Changing South Africa: Political Considerations* (New York: Africana Publishing Co., 1982).

Pampallis, John, *Foundations of the New South Africa* (London: Zed Books, 1991; Cape Town: Maskew Miller, 1991).

Paton, Alan, *Journey Continued: An Autobiography* (Cape Town: David Philip, 1988).

Pheko, Motsoko, *Apartheid: The Story of a Dispossessed People* (London: Marram Books, 1972).

Pike, Henry R., *A History of Communism in South Africa* (Germiston, South Africa: Christian Mission International of South Africa, 1985).

Pogrund, Benjamin, *How Can Man Die Better: Sobukwe and Apartheid* (New Brunswick, NJ: Rutgers University Press; London: Peter Halban, 1991).

Russell, Diana E. H., *Lives of Courage: Women for a New South Africa* (New York: Basic Books, 1989).

Schadeberg, Jurgen, comp., *Voices from Robben Island* (Randburg: Ravan Press, 1994).

Sikakane, Joyce, *A Window on Soweto* (London: International Defence and Aid Fund, 1977).

Slovo, Joe, "South Africa—No Middle Road," in Basil Davidson, Joe, Slovo, and Anthony R. Wilkinson, *Southern Africa: The New Politics of Revolution* (Harmondsworth, Middlesex: Penguin Books, 1976).

South African Institute of Race Relations, *Administration of Security Legislation in South Africa January 1976–March 1977* (Johannesburg: South African Institute of Race Relations, 1977).

———, *Security and Related Trials in South Africa July 1976–May 1977* (Johannesburg: South African Institute of Race Relations, 1977).

Tandon, Yashpal, "The Organization of African Unity and the Liberation of Southern Africa," in Christian P. Potholm and Richard Dale, eds., *Southern Africa in Perspective* (New York and London: The Free Press, 1972), pp. 245–261.

Thomas, Scott, "The Diplomacy of Liberation: the International Relations of the African National Congress, 1960–1985," Ph.D. thesis, University of London, 1989.

Turok, Ben, *Strategic Problems in South Africa's Liberation Struggle: A Critical Analysis* (Richmond BC, Canada: LSM Press, 1974).

Zwelonke, D. M., *Robben Island* (London: Heinemann, 1987).

Above-Ground Multiracial Opposition

Chikane, Frank, "A Critical Examination of the Theology and Praxis of the SACC, 1968–1988," M.A. thesis, University of Natal, 1992.

de Gruchy, John, *The Church Struggle in South Africa* (Cape Town: David Philip; Grand Rapids: Eerdmans, 1979).

Hope, Marjorie and James Young, *The South African Churches in a Revolutionary Situation* (Maryknoll, NY: Orbis Books, 1983).

Kleinschmidt, Horst, ed., *White Liberation: A Collection of Essays* (Johannesburg: Spro-cas 2, 1972).

Legassick, Martin, *The National Union of South African Students: Ethnic Cleavage and Ethnic Integration in the Universities,* Occasional Paper no. 4 (Los Angeles: African Studies Center, University of California, 1967).

Legassick, Martin and John Shingler, "South Africa," in Donald K. Emmerson, ed., *Students and Politics in Developing Countries* (New York: Praeger, 1968), pp. 103–145.

Mayson, Cedric, *A Certain Sound: the Struggle for Liberation in South Africa* (Maryknoll, New York: Orbis Books, 1985).

Michelman, Cherry, *The Black Sash of South Africa: A Case Study in Liberalism* (London: Oxford University Press, 1975).

Orkin, Martin, *Drama and the South African State* (Johannesburg: University of the Witwatersrand Press, 1991).

Prior, Andrew, ed., *Catholics in Apartheid Society* (Cape Town: David Philip, 1982).

Randall, Peter, ed., *Apartheid and the Church: Report of the Spro-Cas Church Commission* (Johannesburg: Christian Institute, 1972).

Randall, Peter, *A Taste of Power* (Johannesburg: Ravan Press, 1973).

Regehr, Ernie, *Perceptions of Apartheid: the Churches and Political Change in South Africa,* (Scottsdale, Pennsylvania: Herald Press, 1979).

Republic of South Africa, *South African Commission of Inquiry Into Certain Organisations* (Schlebusch Commission), Pretoria, 1974–75 (interim reports)

Ryan, Colleen, *Beyers Naude: Pilgrimage of Faith* (Trenton, NJ: Africa World Press, 1990).

Sundermeier, Theo, ed., *Church and Nationalism in South Africa* (Johannesburg: Ravan, 1975).

Suzman, Helen, *In No Uncertain Terms: A South African Memoir* (New York: Alfred A. Knopf, 1993).

Turner, Richard *The Eye of the Needle* (Johannesburg: Spro-cas, 1972).

van der Merwe, H. W. and David Welsh, eds., *Student Perspectives on South Africa* (Cape Town: David Philip, 1972).

van der Merwe, Hendrik, M. Nell, Kim Weichel and Jane Reid, eds., *Towards an Open Society: The Role of Voluntary Organisations* (Cape Town: David Philip, 1980).

Villa-Vicencio, Charles and John de Gruchy, eds., *Resistance and Hope: South African Essays in Honour of Beyers Naude* (Cape Town: David Philip, 1985).

Walshe, Peter, *Church versus State in South Africa: the Case of the Christian Institute,* (London: C. Hurst, 1983; Maryknoll, New York: Orbis Books, 1983).

The Black Consciousness Movement

Adam, Heribert, "The Rise of Black Consciousness in South Africa," *Race,* vol. 15, no. 2, October 1973, pp. 149–165.

Arnold, Millard, ed., *Steve Biko: Black Consciousness in South Africa* (New York: Random House, 1978).

Bernstein, Hilda, *Number 46—Steve Biko* (London: International Defence and Aid Fund, 1978).

Biko, Steve, *I Write What I Like: A Selection of His Writings edited by Aelred Stubbs* (London: Bowerdean Press; Oxford: Heinemann, 1978; San Francisco: Harper and Row, 1986).

Fatton, Robert, *Black Consciousness in South Africa: The Dialectics of Ideological Resistance to White Supremacy* (Albany: SUNY Press, 1986).

Grohs, Gerhard, "Difficulties of Cultural Emancipation in Africa," *Journal of Modern African Studies,* vol. 14, no. 1, 1976, pp. 65–78.

Gwala, Mafika Pascal, ed., *Black Review 1973* (Durban: Black Community Programmes, 1974).

Haigh, Bruce, "The Black Consciousness Movement in South Africa," *Australian Outlook,* vol. 35, no. 2, August 1981, pp. 169–80.

Hopkins, Dwight, *Black Theology USA and South Africa: Politics, Culture and Consciousness* (Maryknoll, NY: Orbis Books, 1989).

Kavanagh, Robert, *Theatre and Cultural Struggle in South Africa* (London: Zed Books, 1985).

Kgokong, Alfred [Themba Mqota], "The Black Peoples' Convention," *Africa Today,* vol. 19, no. 3, Summer 1972, pp. 31–38.

Khoapa, B. A., ed., *Black Review 1972* (Durban: Black Community Programmes, 1973).

Kretzschmar, Louise, *The Voice of Black Theology in South Africa* (Johannesburg: Ravan Press, 1986).

Kuper, Leo, "On the theme 'black is beautiful'," in Leo Kuper, *Race, Class and Power* (London: Duckworth, 1974), pp. 83–112.

Manganyi, N. C., *Being-Black-in-the-World* (Johannesburg: Spro-Cas/Ravan, 1973).

Mangena, Mosibudi, *On Your Own: Evolution of Black Consciousness in South Africa/Azania* (Johannesburg: Skotaville, 1989).

Mbanjwa, Thoko, ed., *Black Review 1974/5* (Durban: Black Community Programmes, 1975).

Moore, Basil, ed., *Black Theology: the South African Voice,* (London: C. Hurst and Co., 1973), also published as *The Challenge of Black Theology in South Africa* (Atlanta: John Knox Press, 1974).

Mosala, Itumeleng J. and Buti Tlhagale, eds., *The Unquestionable Right To Be Free: Black Theology from South Africa* (Maryknoll, New York: Orbis Books; Johannesburg: Skotaville, 1986).

Nkomo, Mokubung O., *Student Culture and Activism in Black South African Universities: the Roots of Resistance* (Westport, Connecticut: Greenwood Press, 1984)

Pheto, Molefe, *And Night Fell: Memoirs of a Political Prisoner in South Africa* (London: Heinemann, 1983).

Pityana, N. Barney, Malusi Mpumlwana, Mamphela Ramphele, and Lindy Wilson, eds., *Bounds of Possibility: The Legacy of Steve Biko and Black Consciousness* (Cape Town: David Philip; London: Zed Books, 1991).

Rambally, Asha, ed., *Black Review 1975–6* (Lovedale: Black Community Programmes, 1977).

Sono, Themba, *Reflections on the Origins of Black Consciousness in South Africa* (Pretoria: Human Sciences Research Council, 1993).

Thoahlane, Thoahlane, ed., *Black Renaissance: Papers from the Black Renaissance Convention* (Johannesburg: Ravan Press, 1975).

Woods, Donald, *Biko* (New York: Atheneum, 1981; London: Paddington Press Ltd., 1978).

The 1976 Soweto Uprising

Brooks, Alan and Jeremy Brickhill, *Whirlwind before the Storm: The Origins and Development of the Uprising in Soweto and the Rest of South Africa from June to December 1976* (London: International Defence and Aid Fund, 1980).

Counter Information Services, *Black South Africa Explodes* (Washington, DC: February 1977).

Diseko, Nozipho J., "The origins and development of the South African Students' Movement (SASM): 1968–1976," *Journal of Southern African Studies,* vol. 18, no. 1, March 1992.

Frankel, Philip H., "The dynamics of a political renaissance: the Soweto Students' Representative Council," *Journal of African Studies,* vol. 7, no. 3, Fall 1980, pp. 167–179.

Geber, Beryl A. and S. P. Newman, *Soweto's Children: the Development of Attitudes* (New York: Academic Press, 1980).

Herbstein, Denis, *White Man, We Want to Talk to You* (Harmondsworth, Middlesex: Penguin, 1978).

Hermer, Carol, *The Diary of Maria Tholo* (Johannesburg: Ravan, 1980).

Hirson, Baruch, *Year of Fire, Year of Ash, the Soweto Revolt: Roots of a Revolution?* (London: Zed Books, 1979).

———, "Language in control and resistance in South Africa," *African Affairs,* vol. 80, no. 319, April 1981, pp. 219–237.

Kane-Berman, John, *Soweto: Black Revolt, White Reaction* (Johannesburg: Ravan Press, 1978).

Molteno, Frank, "The uprisings of the 16th June: a review of the literature," *Social Dynamics,* vol. 5, no. 1, 1979, pp. 54–76.

Republic of South Africa, *Report of the Commission of Inquiry Into the Riots at Soweto and Elsewhere from the 16th of June to the 28th February 1977,* (Cillie Commission), Pretoria: Government Printer, 2 volumes, 1980.

———, *Commission of Inquiry Into the Riots at Soweto and Other Places in South Africa* (Cillie Commission), testimony, 1976–1977.

South African Institute of Race Relations, *South Africa in Travail: The Disturbances of 1976/77* (Johannesburg: South African Institute of Race Relations, 1978).

Black Workers and Trade Unions

Baskin, Jeremy, *Striking Back: A History of COSATU* (Johannesburg: Ravan Press, 1991).

Berger, Iris, *Threads of Solidarity: Women in South African Industry, 1900–1980* (London: James Currey; Bloomington: Indiana University Press, 1992).

Bonner, Philip, "Black Trade Unions in South Africa since World War II," in Robert M. Price and Carl Rosberg, eds., *The Apartheid Regime: Political Power and Racial Domination* (Berkeley: Institute of International Studies, University of California, 1980).

————, "Focus on FOSATU," *South African Labour Bulletin*, vol. 5, no. 1, May 1979, pp. 5–24.

Feit, Edward, *Workers Without Weapons: the South African Congress of Trade Unions and Organization of the African Workers* (Hamden, Connecticut: Archon Books, 1975).

Friedman, Steven, *Building Tomorrow Today: African Workers in Trade Unions, 1970–1984* (Johannesburg: Ravan Press, 1987).

Institute for Industrial Education, *The Durban Strikes, 1973* (Johannesburg: Ravan Press, 1974).

Luckhardt, Ken and Brenda Wall, *Organize or Starve! The History of the South African Congress of Trade Unions* (London: Lawrence and Wishart, 1980).

MacShane, Denis, Martin Plaut, and David Ward, *Power! Black Workers, Their Unions, and the Struggle for Freedom in South Africa* (Boston: South End Press, 1984).

Maree, Johann, ed., *The Independent Trade Unions, 1974–1984: Ten Years of the South African Labour Bulletin* (Johannesburg: Ravan Press, 1987).

Ncube, Don, *The Influence of Apartheid and Capitalism on the Development of Black Trade Unions in South Africa* (Johannesburg: Skotaville, 1985).

Southall, Roger, *Imperialism or Solidarity? International Labour and South African Trade Unions* (Cape Town: University of Cape Town Press, 1995)

Thomas, Wolfgang H., ed., *Labour Perspectives on South Africa* (Cape Town: David Philip, 1974).

Webster, Eddie, *Cast in a Racial Mould: Labour Process and Trade Unionism in the Foundries* (Johannesburg: Ravan Press, 1985).

The Politics of the System—Buthelezi and Inkatha

Bekker, Simon and Richard Humphries, *From Control to Confusion: The Changing Role of Administration Boards in South Africa: 1971–1983* (Pietermaritzburg: Shuter & Shooter, 1985).

Buthelezi, M. Gatsha, *Power Is Ours* (New York: Books in Focus, 1979).

————, *South Africa: My Vision of the Future* (London: Weidenfeld and Nicolson, 1990).

Butler, Jeffrey, Robert I. Rotberg, and John Adams, *The Bantu Homelands of South Africa: The Political and Economic Development of Bophuthatswana and KwaZulu* (Berkeley: University of California Press, 1977).

Carter, Gwendolen M., Thomas Karis, and Newell M. Stultz, *South Africa's Transkei: The Politics of Domestic Colonialism* (Evanston: Northwestern University Press, 1967).

Coetzer, Piet, *Awaiting Trial: Allan Hendrickse* (Alberton: Librarius Felicitas, 1984).

de Kock, Wessel, *"Usuthu! Cry Peace!": The Black Liberation Movement Inkatha and the Fight for a Just South Africa* (Cape Town: Open Hand, 1968).

Frankel, Philip, "The Politics of Poverty: Political Competition in Soweto," *Canadian Journal of African Studies*, vol. 14, no. 2, 1980, pp. 201–220.

Gerwel, G. J., "Coloured Nationalism?," in Theo Sundermeier, ed., *Church and Nationalism in South Africa* (Johannesburg: Ravan Press, 1975), pp. 67–72.

Ginwala, Frene, *Indian South Africans* (London: Minority Rights Group, 1977).

Hommel, Maurice W., *Capricorn Blues: The Struggle for Human Rights in South Africa* (Toronto: Culturama, 1981).

Horrell, Muriel, *The African Homelands of South Africa* (Johannesburg: South African Institute of Race Relations, 1973).

Kotze, D. A., *African Politics in South Africa, 1964–1974: Parties and Issues* (London: C. Hurst and Co.; Pretoria: J. L Van Schaik, 1975).

Laurence, Patrick, *The Transkei: South Africa's Politics of Partition* (Johannesburg: Ravan Press, 1976).

Mangope, Lucas M., *A Place for All* (Bloemfontein: Via Afrika, 1978).

Maré, Gerhard, *Brothers Born of Warrior Blood: Politics and Ethnicity in South Africa* (Johannesburg: Ravan Press, 1992). Also published as *Ethnicity and Politics in South Africa* (Totowa, NJ: Zed Books, 1993).

Maré, Gerhard, and Georgina Hamilton, *An Appetite for Power: Buthelezi's Inkatha and South Africa* (Johannesburg: Ravan Press; Bloomington: Indiana University Press, 1987).

Matanzima, Kaizer D., *Independence My Way* (Pretoria: Foreign Affairs Association, 1976).

Molteno, Frank, "The Coloured Persons' Representative Council: Its Place in the Evolving Strategy of South Africa's Rulers: an Historical Perspective," *Africa Perspective,* no. 10, April 1979, pp. 1–18.

Mzala [Jabulani Nxumalo], *Gatsha Buthelezi: Chief with a Double Agenda* (London: Zed Books, 1988).

Randall, Peter, ed., *South Africa's Minorities* (Johannesburg: Spro-cas, 1971).

Rogers, Barbara, *Divide and Rule: South Africa's Bantustans* (London: International Defence and Aid Fund, 1980).

Simons, Mary, "Organised Coloured Political Movements," in Hendrik van der Merwe and C. J. Groenwald, eds., *Occupational and Social Change among Coloured People in South Africa* (Cape Town: Juta, 1976).

Smith, Jack S., *Buthelezi: The Biography* (Johannesburg: Hans Strydom, 1988).

Southall, Roger J., *South Africa's Transkei: The Political Economy of an 'Independent' Bantustan* (New York: Monthly Review Press, 1983).

Streek, Barry and Richard Wicksteed, *Render unto Kaiser: A Transkei Dossier* (Johannesburg: Ravan Press, 1981).

Stultz, Newell M., *South Africa's Half Loaf: Race Separatism in South Africa* (New Haven: Yale University Press, 1979).

Temkin, Ben, *Gatsha Buthelezi: Zulu Statesman* (Cape Town: Purnell, 1976).

Vail, Leroy, ed., *The Creation of Tribalism in Southern Africa* (London: James Currey, 1989).

Van der Horst, S. T., ed., *The Theron Commission Report: A Summary of the Findings and Recommendations of the Commision of Enquiry into Matters Relating to the Coloured Population Group* (Johannesburg: South African Institute of Race Relations, 1976).

Van der Ross, R. E., *Myths and Attitudes: An Inside Look at the Coloured People* (Cape Town: Tafelberg, 1979).

———, R. E., *The Rise and Decline of Apartheid: A Study of Political Movements among the Coloured People of South Africa, 1880–1985* (Cape Town: Tafelberg, 1986).

Wollheim, O. D., ed., *The Theron Commission Report: An Evaluation and Early Reactions to the Report and Its Recommendations* (Johannesburg: South African Institute of Race Relations, 1977).

Crackdown and Resistance after Soweto

Cole, Josette, *Crossroads: The Politics of Reform and Repression 1976–1986* (Johannesburg: Ravan Press, 1987).

Cooper, Carole and Linda Ensor, *PEBCO: A Black Mass Movement* (Johannesburg: South African Institute of Race Relations, 1981).

Desmond, Cosmas, *The Discarded People: an Account of African Resettlement in South Africa* (Harmondsworth, Middlesex: Penguin Books, 1971).

Evans, Michael, "The Emergence and Decline of a Community Organisation: an Assessment of PEBCO," *South African Labour Bulletin,* vol. 6, nos. 2/3, September 1980, pp. 46–52.

Farisani, Tshenuwani Simon, *Diary from a South African Prison* (Philadelphia: Fortress Press, 1987).

James, Deborah, *The Road from Doornkop: a Case Study of Removals and Resistance* (Johannesburg: South African Institute of Race Relations, 1983).

Maclennan, Ben, *Glenmore: the Story of a Forced Removal* (Johannesburg: South African Institute of Race Relations, 1987).

Mare, Gerry, *African Population Relocation in South Africa* (Johannesburg: South African Institute of Race Relations, 1980).

Matiwana, Mizana and Shirley Walters, *The Struggle for Democracy: A Study of Community Organisations in Greater Cape Town From the 1960's to 1985* (Cape Town: Centre for Adult and Continuing Education, University of the Western Cape, 1986).

Murray, Christina and Catherine O'Regan, eds., *No Place to Rest: Forced Removals and the Law in South Africa* (Cape Town: Oxford University Press, 1990).

Platzky, Laurine and Cherryl Walker, *The Surplus People: Forced Removals in South Africa* (Johannesburg: Ravan Press, 1985).

Seidman, Judy, *Facelift Apartheid: South Africa After Soweto* (London: International Defence and Aid Fund, 1980).

Silk, Andrew, *A Shanty Town in South Africa: The Story of Modderdam* (Johannesburg: Ravan Press, 1981).

Unterhalter, Elaine, *Forced Removal* (London: International Defence and Aid Fund, 1987).

Periodicals

Africa Perspective
African Communist
Azania News
Dawn: Journal of Umkhonto we Sizwe
Drum
EcuNews Bulletin
Financial Mail
Frontline
IDAF Focus
Ikwezi
Pro Veritate
Reality
Sash
SASO Newsletter
Sechaba
Social Dynamics
South African Labour Bulletin

South African Outlook
Spotlight on South Africa
To the Point
Work in Progress

Published sources of documents in this book

Document 7: a pamphlet issued by Mayibuye Publications, 1966; Document 15: *Sash,* May 1970; Document 22: *The African Communist,* second quarter, 1976, pp. 16–40; Document 27: *Reality,* July 1972; Document 31: *Pro Veritate,* August 1974; Document 33: the *Sunday Times,* April 23, 1978; Document 35: *EcuNews Bulletin,* February 9, 1979; Document 36: *EcuNews Bulletin,* October 19, 1979; documents 39 and 40: *SASO Newsletter,* September 1970; Document 43: *SASO Newsletter,* August 1971; Document 55: *SASO Newsletter,* May/June 1975; documents 56 and 63: *SASO Newsletter,* March/April 1976; Document 57: *Black Review,* 1975/76; Document 64: *EcuNews Bulletin,* May 26, 1976; Document 66: "Mrs. Winnie Mandela: Profile in Courage and Defiance," UN Center Against Apartheid, February 1978; Document 84: *South African Labour Bulletin,* September 1980; Document 95: *The Educational Journal: Official Organ of the Teachers' League of South Africa,* April–May, 1979; Document 96: the *Rand Daily Mail,* November 12, 1979; Document 100: the *Rand Daily Mail,* October 1, 1973; Document 115: *Ikwezi,* March 1980; Document 118: *Pro Veritate,* June 1977; Document 119: *Pro Veritate,* September 1977; Document 120: M. V. Mrwetyana, *On My Life,* Umtata, n.d.; documents 122 and 123: *"We Will Not Move"; The Struggle for Crossroads,* compiled by the National Union of South African Students, September 1978; Document 127: *Work in Progress,* 12, April 1980.

INDEX OF PERSONS

INDEX OF ORGANIZATIONS

THOMAS G. KARIS is Professor Emeritus of Political Science at the City College, City University of New York, and a Senior Research Fellow in the Ralph Bunche Institute of the CUNY Graduate School. He visited South Africa in 1955 as a State Department researcher and was later a foreign service officer in Pretoria. He was Ford Visiting Professor of Political Science at the University of Zambia in 1968–69 and later a Rockefeller Foundation Fellow, and a Fellow at Yale University's Southern African Research Program. For many years he was a close colleague of Gwendolen Carter.

GAIL M. GERHART holds degrees from Harvard and Columbia universities. She has lived and worked in Africa for over twenty years and taught political science at the University of Nairobi, the University of Botswana, the American University in Cairo, Columbia, and the University of the Witwatersrand, where she was a Fulbright Visiting Professor in 1994. She is the author of *Black Power in South Africa: The Evolution of an Ideology* and co-author of volumes 3 and 4 of *From Protest to Challenge*. She is currently engaged in the preparation of volumes 6 and 7 of *From Protest to Challenge*.

DAVID LEWIS is a South African who worked in the trade union movement from 1976 to 1990. He was general secretary of the General Workers Union and, later, national organizer of the Transport and General Workers Union. He has written extensively on labor history and strategy. Since 1990 he has been based at the University of Cape Town where he directs the Industrial Strategy Project, which is a significant contributor to South Africa's emerging industrial policy. He is Special Advisor to the Minister of Labour and Co-chairperson of the Presidential Commission of Enquiry on Labour Market Policy.